THE DAM CODE
THE DAMN BOOK

LISE ROCHON

authorHOUSE

AuthorHouse™
1663 Liberty Drive
Bloomington, IN 47403
www.authorhouse.com
Phone: 833-262-8899

© 2023 Lise Rochon. All rights reserved.

No part of this book may be reproduced, stored in a retrieval system, or transmitted by any means without the written permission of the author.

Published by AuthorHouse 04/25/2023

ISBN: 978-1-7283-7897-8 (sc)
ISBN: 978-1-7283-7895-4 (hc)
ISBN: 978-1-7283-7896-1 (e)

Library of Congress Control Number: 2023901696

Print information available on the last page.

Any people depicted in stock imagery provided by Getty Images are models, and such images are being used for illustrative purposes only.
Certain stock imagery © Getty Images.

This book is printed on acid-free paper.

Because of the dynamic nature of the Internet, any web addresses or links contained in this book may have changed since publication and may no longer be valid. The views expressed in this work are solely those of the author and do not necessarily reflect the views of the publisher, and the publisher hereby disclaims any responsibility for them.

TABLE OF CONTENTS

SYMBOLOGY OF WORDS INTRO 1
THE FEMS IN HELL 2
A STORY FROM THE GREEK MYTHOLOGY 4
RULES TO FOLLOW TO UNDERSTAND THE CODE 6
THE CODE SQUARE PILLARS LETTERS 7
LETTERS THAT SUPPORT THE CODE PILLARS LETTERS 8
FEMS REPRESENTATIONS FROM THAT CODE 9
ANOTHER WAY OF LOOKING AT IT 9
LETTER A 10
LETTER B 70
LETTER C 124
LETTER D 221
LETTER E 275
LETTER F 316
LETTER G 358
LETTER H 378
LETTER I 417
LETTER J 435
LETTER K 438
LETTER L 444
LETTER M 463
LETTER N 496
LETTER O 509
LETTER P 525
LETTER Q 557
LETTER R 560
LETTER S 588
LETTER T 654
LETTER U 704
LETTER V 713
LETTER W 733
LETTER X 773
LETTER Y 775
LETTER Z 780
WORDS WITH ONLY FEM LETTERS 781
PROPER NAMES FAMILY NAMES PRONOUNS 782

THE ROMAN NUMBERS	787
THE NUMBERS	794
PUNCTUATION AND OTHER SYMBOLS	803
THE PLANETS	804
THE YEAR	820
THE ZODIAC	821
SOME BIG NAMES IN OUR CULTURE	829
THE CLOCK	834
THE 23 CARDS OF THE TAROT	840

SYMBOLOGY OF WORDS
INTRO

This Book is Not About True Religion
True Religion Lives in the Heart of Its Own Blessings
Carl Jung Said "Religion is a defense against a religious experience"

This Knowledge is Dedicated to All Fems
Who Will have Enough Courage and Wisdom to Cope
With Meeting with that Nightmare
And to The Good Men Who Wants to Advance with More   Awareness on their Own Evolutionary Spiritual Human Path

The Damn Book as I Called It   Is Extremely Difficult to
Read   Understood   it Will Bring a New Conceptual Frame of Mind for Most of Us Especially The Fems

Its Corrupted Sexual Code is Enormous   This Book is a Scatological Sacrilege   I am Warning All
That is Why it has been Kept Secret Right in Front of Our Eyes

It Took ½ My Lifetime to Research and Write
And My Discoveries About it   Put Me Through   Often to Severe Dark Emotions   And So Sad it is
This Book is an Empirical Study
I Wrote it Long and Diversified
It is as Complete as I could Do to the Best of My Knowledge   It is Unfinished

I Do Not Suggest Reading This Book to   a Pregnant Fem   or
to a Person   that is   Physically Weak   Mentally Weak   and/or   Emotionally Weak   This Book is Not for Children
Religious Zealots or Fanatics of Any Kind   Please   Refrain Immediately from Reading This Book   and Turn Away

Many People are Investing Time   on their Own   Researching the Secrets of these   Secret Societies

Lise Rochon

Because   People in General   Feel   They are Missing on Something   in their Lives
This Book Tells   How those Secret Societies Codes Kept Us   In this Violent Misery
The Coded Language has been Performing   as a   Sound Transformative Barrier to All Fems and Most Mascs
The Power of that Code Language and Sounds   is   Embedded Deep in   Our Psyche
That Code has Been Programming   All of Us   In the Same Patterns of Mind
Few (Mostly Initiates) are Sensitive to their Deep   and   So   Subtle Meanings   Those Narrows Us Down for Too Long
Linguists   Heads of State   Religious   Leaders   would have Permitted Certain Words to Become Immortalized in Dictionaries   While Others would have been   Thrown Out   Disappeared in   Anonymity   as they   Never Existed
In Our Long Past   Our Language is a Mix of   Hebrew   Latin   Roman   Greek   Norse   and More
The British have Not Invented The Letters Shapes and Sounds   But they have Created Many New Words Along with the   French   Spanish   Nordic etc
And Others Influences   Such as   The Roads to Slavery Transformed Languages Along Their Way   Fast   Many Languages Enlarged Massively   Every Year   Every Century   People Learning Forcefully Often
Both The Fems and the Mascs are Prisoners of That Code   Which was a Language Created   as a Step Above The Daily One Every One Uses
That Glass Ceiling has   Not   Permitted Us Humans to Understand/Hear   Because   We Could Not Hear   Through That   Glass Wall/Roof/Ceiling (Everyone Lives Under One)   Keeping Us Far Away from Loving Each Other Naturally
SYMBOLOGY   OF   WORDS   INTRO

THE   FEMS   IN   HELL

The Code has   Used   Weakened   Diminished   Humans
Freedom of Speech in General was Not Allowed   Especially for The Fems   (The She/Shh)

The Dam Code The Damn Book

Through the   T/Fems Cross/Great Curse   The Code   Advanced their   Personal   Political   Religious   Powers   to   Keep that   Curse/Spell   Strong and Evolving through Time   And Indeed   Succeed in That for More Than   2 Thousand Years

The Fems are Never Left Alone   and are   Not Considered   Independent Persons   Just an Object for Something

The Code Works that Way with The Fems Aspects

There are No Positive Words for The Fems in that Code   It is All Sorrows   Be Ready   It is All Hell Elle Ill Hail Ail   for Her   The Letter L/ Sweet Fem Love Light

The Fems are Viewed as The Code Objects

for   Disgrace   Pleasure   Maternity   Slaving   or   She is   Non Existent   or   Only   Existing Behind a Veil Covering Her Entire Body (Always a One Busy Hand on that Sheet (She/Shh   It)   Figuratively Also The Fems Were   So   Weakened

The Fems Intelligence and Identity have been Blocked

Instead of Being Supported by a Good Natural Life

The Fems were Thrown a Life of Being Cursed from Start   Since Eve (See Eve in The Words Chapter)

In That Code   The Fems Gender is the One that Carries that Curse

That Code   Keeps Us   Humans Asleep   Unconsciously in Those Regards

That was Not on The Fems Wish List

Instead of being Ruled Over   by The Code   The Fems could have been Permitted to Help Build   Our World Together   and There are Always Children   Ready to Build it Anew   With Hope

Except in Time of Wars   She was then Allowed to Work in War Factories   When that War was Over   Only to be Slammed Out   Was Sent Back Home   Have Children   and   Work Chores   All Day with   No   or   Little   Education   No Information to Her   Therefore Most Fems Remained Empty   Poor and Pregnant   Barefoot and Pregnant   Sounds Almost   Poetic

But No Says   The Code   That Black Veil is Always Around   for Her   It Prevails (Pre/Veil in S/Plural)

Communion Veils and its Confirmation and Wedding is The Endless Reminder of That Real Thick Black Veil   Which This Book is About

During that Time   Men would Slave on their Poor Jobs

Poverty was/is Everywhere

Lise Rochon

And on Top of All That   That   The Code Promotes
Homosexuality   Infidelity   Polygamy   Corruption
We could have had a Gentler Life bringing Benefits If The Fems and Their Adored Children could have Been Part of It as Partners
DONE INTRO FEM IN HELL

THE   FEMS   IN HELL
A Story from The Greek Mythology

Hades (Hide   His/Is/S Penis) is The Death God   He Lives and Rules in The Underworld   There is Where We Find Persephone (Pierce the Phone   The Code) Which He has Lured and Kidnapped in His Underworld   Her Mom Demeter   Tells the Story   She came back from there   and Her Daughter   Did Not
She is Known to be The Greek Goddess that Carries the Sins of All Men   (That is a Strange Resemblance with the Jesus   Sayings)
Hades Took Away One Piece   at the Time   of All Persephone   Magical Jewelry   that was Covering Her   and   When She was Naked and Powerless   He Pushed Her for Ever in an Endless Night Pit
Her Mother   Demeter   The Mother   Meet/Her   Mate/Her   The Meter   Mètre (Measured Length) (Measure   Her Maternity   as in being   Able to Control it)   Maître (Master in French
We Sometimes Hear   The Catholic Religion   Mentioning that the English Language was Entirely Corrupted
Demeter went to Look for Her Missing Daughter and Could Only Bring Back Seeds of Corn
Demeter had Extraordinary Daughters
Worth to Read for a Fem Self Worth Dose
The Secret Code is in Plain Sight and Hidden at the Same Time   Men of Power Used it at Length
It is All Hell for The Fems   and a   Collateral Hell for The Mascs of Good Conscience
We are Kept Prisoners and Hypnotized   from All   Symbols Including the Numbers   Letters   Sentences Astrology   Numerology   Tarot   etc
That Code is Sacrilegious to the Ears of The Fems   and   Good Mascs So   No One Listens to it   No One Comes to it   and   They Stay Away from It   The Code   is Safe Then   As Usual   Since Last 2000 Years
For The Fems   It is Always   Another   Code to Learn

The Dam Code The Damn Book

Now Learn That   The Women   in That Code   are Personified by   Different Animals   And That For a Very Long Time

Every Generation   The Secret Code Becomes More   Cryptic   It is Engulfed in the Constant Birth of   New Symbols   Often   Making them Attractive   Easier and Faster   to be Assimilated by the General Population and Their Children   Disney is a an Nice Example   Which We All Love   Tall and Small   Because it Lends an Emotional Relief   to Us All   Although   it Still Gives its Heroine Star Girls a Waist of 15 Inches Round   Creating a Terrible Thing to do   Pressuring the Girls to Imitate   and Now   The Boys too   To Self Mutilate   That Way   People Do it to Themselves   by Themselves   No External Force Needed   And it Starts So   Young too   with Extra Tight Diapers   And Little Girls Tight Corsets and Dressed Up Barbie Girl Type of Waist Which is Not Viable   but a Direct Connection with Our Unconscious (See BB in The Words Chapter)   Because The Pain is Calling on it   That Stomach Pain   That Back Bain
Along with That   Other Discomforts   Diseases/Illnesses Emerge from That   and   We Do Not See Connections
The   BB   Shape is Very Important (See BB in the Words Chapter)
The Code   does Bottom Fishing   as a   Lurking   and   Creating Subliminal Messages from the Deepest Abyss of Our Oceans of Consciousness (See Ocean and Fishes in The Words Chapter)   Our Deepest Inner Functioning
Most People in The Past   did Not Know about   Evolution   and   Future Knowledge
But We Are   Now   More Intelligent and More Subtle   Than Since   Now We Read the Finer Print
The Aleister Crowley Book "The Book of Thoth" and the Rider Tarot Deck   Created a Breach in That Code   by Interpreting it in Different Smaller Codes
These being Simplified   therefore   More Accessible and in   The Future   To Brains that Can Hopefully Diffract it Completely   And *Get* Rid of it   As I am Trying Now With This Book
That Veil of Ignorance   will Fall Down   as an   Unconscious Liberation   from   That Code
We Will Enter   The End of Times (See Time in The Words Chapter)   As We Know it   and   Enter a New World of Consciousness with a Different

Lise Rochon

Notion of Time   Where Time Will be Ours   Where Saturn   The God of Time and Sorrows   will have Lost its Influence   Over Us
FEMS   IN   HELL   END

RULES TO FOLLOW
TO UNDERSTAND THE CODE

INTRO

To Understand Better   Here are The Code Rules
How It Works in its Conceptual Constructions
Learning a Few New Rules Makes it Easier
To Interpret it Faster
Best is Learning First   All The Sounds Letters
Their Conceptual Meanings   It is Easy

When That World of Symbology Opens its Doors to You
It will Show its Ugliness in Full Force   So
Be Ready to be Insulted to the Core
Especially   The Fems
The Code Is Created from Millions
of Those Associations
This Book is About Some Of Them

RULES

In That Code
We Live in Sounds Words
Which do Not Match the Mental Picture
Of Our Understanding of those Words
According to Our Dictionaries
Letters Moves Together Writing a Word
As Riddles
That Code is an Immense Live Puzzle

The Letters of a Word   Tells a Different Picture   which will Hide   the Real   But Hidden Meaning of that Word

Every Code Letter has its Own Meaning (s)

The Older the Word   The Easier to Intercept What its Code Meaning is

The Longer   and   The Newer   the Word   the More Difficult it is to Interpret

The Shorter the Word   The More Strict to The Point it is

The Dam Code The Damn Book

- The Code Uses All Short Words   That are Commonly Used   Such as   Of   It   The   In   A   At   Etc   in The Code Connection   Those are Important

   Most of the Time   The First Letter of a Word   Defines its General Meaning   It Gives it its Tone

   The End Letter is Important   It is Related to The Outcome

   The Middle Letters Indicates   the How   or   Details

   The Masc Letters/Symbols Explains the Different Forms and Actions The Code Takes to Get there

   Some Letters will Hide their Sound into Another Letter (C/Young Girl/ See   For   S/Penis) Blending   Symbolically those 2 Letters Concepts Together in a Different Result   The Code Way

   Some Letters are Silent   E/He   is Often Entirely Silent (See Words With   E   as First Letter)   H/Silent Secret   Code Letter is Often Silent   and   Hides in Words   E/He   Also Hides in Words   Just Watch it

   Looking at Other Words with Similar   or   Almost the Same Sounds   Will Help Developing a Larger Picture of that Same World of Sounds   Relationships

I Must Say Now   In The Code Dimensions   Words Starting with Con (Cunt) are a Must to Look for   And   When Arriving at the Word Constitution or Other Precious Words   Start to Cry   Again   or   Fight it   Move On   into Knowing More About That Which Will Free Us

           THE   CODE   SQUARE   PILLARS   LETTERS
Those Are
E/He   T/Fem Cross   il/(Pronounce High) Sex Act (In Both Small and Large Caps)   H/Secret Code Letter (Pronounce Age)   l/Pronounce Hell   and   L/Hell   it is Again
Letter i/I is Both Sexes as in   i/Marriage Act (The Dot is Her   The Stick is Him) Then I in Large Caps and Is Now Only a l/Stick

   There are 2 Masc Pillars Letters
E/He   H/Secret Code

   There are 2 Fem Letters Pillars and One Repeat From Small Cap to Large Cap
T/Fem Cross   IL/Sweet Fem Love Life Light/Hell   and   Hell Again (In Small Cap and in Large Cap)

Lise Rochon

    Her Fems Grid Pillars Letters   Say to Her   She Is   T/
Cursed   and   L/Ill/Ail/Hell/Elle (L is Also Called Sweet Fem Love
Light)   i/Marriage Act
Because   i (I   Pronounce High)   in Large Cap is Almost The Same as
with Small Cap l(L/Pronounce Hell)   It is As Twin Sisters   A Seamless
Transfer   Adding Another Bar in The Making   to Her
All The Same   All/Ill/Ail/Hell/Elle   Says The Code   to Her
    His Masc Grid Pillars Letters   Say To Him   Superpose E and H and Get
a Finer Grid   It Makes a Full Grid Segment Pattern   Closed Square (4
Corners) Twice   Tighter Too
Back to the Pyramid Number   4 Corners   The Square   The Foundation
It Went to Doubling itself   Just By Positioning   Two Perfect Squares on
Top of Each Other
    Compare   The Grid/Box   to a   Giant Screen
Door   Much   Much   Bigger   The H/Code Grid   Weaves Endlessly Its
Grid of Crosses
The Letter   T/Fem Cross   Is its Top Box/Grid   Structure   And   Its
Roof   and   the   Center Pillar of The House   Along with I (i High   Fem
Dot)   and   l/(Hell   Fem)
Letter Z is   The Only Other Letter   that has a Roof too Besides
Letter   T   It Reminds Us to Forget about it   Sleep on it   ZZZ   The Z
Blocks it from the Floor (Foundation)   Also

                        Letters That Support   The Code Pillars Letters
    Circles are Fem   Bars are Masc
    Letters that Are Made Entirely of Curves   or   Circles
Those are Called   Entirely Fem Letters   They Lives   Inside   The Grid
O   C   U   Q
Exception for   S   a Masc Letter   S   is Also in inside The   Box/
Grid   Too   Because it   Sneaked In   S is His/Is/Serpent/Penis (Which
Could be a Natural and Nice Thing   Sex is Normal in Real Life Too   But
No Says The Code)
    Other Fem Round Symbols   Formed with a   Bar or a Stick in
it   Means   It Includes a Masc
R   P   D   G   J   B
The Others   All Sticks   Letters
W   Y   K   X   V

The Dam Code The Damn Book

Happened to be Fems   Those Are All The Programmed Coded Fems Letters   They Strengthen   The Grid/Box   By being Other Code Shapes Characters Identities
Letter   Z   is a Masc Letter   Because it Represents   The Code   Z (Not The Code X) is The End   and   The Completion of   That Code   Message   Which is to Keep Repeating   The Same Message   Endlessly   Z/As Above as Below/Sleep on It (Or Get a Hit)
END OF PILARS

      FEMS   REPRESENTATIONS   FROM   THAT   CODE
O/is The Fem Hole/Loins   R/is Her (The Heir or The Whore)   M/ Motherhood   N/is The Virgin Growing into Motherhood   D/is Pregnant   B/Boy Holding All Fem Breasts   or   Man/Stick   Holding All Fems 2 OOs/Fems Holes and All Circles   A Circle is Essentially a Fem Symbol   So   is Water)   Q/is Her Loss of Blood (Letter O with a Leak)   U/is Her Natural Ovulation   V/and W/are Fem (s) Sex Active on a False Ovulation Cycle   Y/is the Wounded Fem   C/is the Young Girl/ See   F/is Feminine/Gender/Fuck   T/is The Great Curse/Fem Cross   X/is the Fallen Fem Cross/The Axe
Letter F/Fem   and   Others too   Cannot Stand by Themselves   Giving it a Severe Handicap
M and N are Solid Standing Letters   because   Motherhood is One of The Most Important Rule in That Code
Some Masc Letters   A/All Men   E/He   H/The Secret Code Grid   I/ High   Stay   Strong Standing   Being All Mascs Too
Find in   The Letters Chapters   a Detailed Definition of All   American English Alphabetical Letters
   When a Word Starts with These Fems Letters   F   W   V   T   C   They Can Deliver Surprising Delusional Concepts to Readers

      ANOTHER WAY OF LOOKING AT IT
Every Letter Empowers The Code Symbols
X   is a Hex   Is a Curse   is The Axe   is the   X/is The Fem Fallen Cross   She has been Under   The Axe   and   Cursed
   The Letter   U/You/Ovulating   as   She is Hew   You hew: to strike with an axe

Lise Rochon

The Code is Not Kidding   She Must Die to be Rebirthed as the   Dot   Again (See Letter i)   ZZZ
   A   In Reverse   Become   Some Fems Letters   V/Fem Sex Active   W/All Fems Sex Active   Y/Wounded Fem
V   W   and   Y   have Very Little Balance   Only W   Stands because it has Attained   A Code Goal (W/All Fems are Sex Active from   V (Her Opened Legs   Sex)   V   will become   W   and Tilting   Y   will Split in   L/Hell   and Form   K/Broken Fem Warrior (See Letter K in the Letter Chapter)   to End in   R/Whore/Heir/Sex
Other Fems Letters Symbols   M/Motherhood   and   N/In/Hen/Virgin   are Different   M and N are Not Receiving Sex as Much   Both Letters Stands Up and have Balance   Because   M has Attained a Code Goal (Motherhood)   and   N/In/Hen/Ann/Virgin   Because She is Already in the   Mother Role
The Transition from   N/In/Hen/Virgin   into   M/Motherhood   is Easy   Add Another Bar to   N (Another Bar is   Another   Lost   hope)
   Same Kind of Transition for   V/One Fem Sex Active   into   W/All Fems Sex Active   It is Easy   Add Another Bar   Too (Too/Two as in Bigamy)
The Bar is the Ban   or   The Code   in Action   The Code   Stands on Bars (The Grid/Box)
From the Word Bar   Switch   R/Whore/Her/Heir   to   N/In/Hen/Virgin   and She Gets Ban
The Virgin is Always Banned   The Men Go to the Bar   or   Study The Bar   or are   Part of the Bar   There is Such a thing as being Behind Bars   That Will Keeps the Curious Out

A a
INTRO
In General   In The Code Alphabet   Letter A is Considered a Strong Positive Letter   and   Words   with   A   are Often Positive Good Strong Words   as an   A + Student   an   A + Job   Etc
Letter A is One of the Most Important Symbol in the Alphabet   Along with   H   and   I (Hi   His Stick)
A   and   H   have Similar Sounds and Shapes
A (Pronounce Hey)   is The Precursor of Letter   H (Pronounce Age) Being a Shorter Sound   A   is Probably One of the Oldest Human Sounds
Letter A Represents All Men   as One   And God

The Dam Code The Damn Book

Letter A/All Men   is Part of the Sign of the Pyramid with its 4 Angles/Angels   as Seen from Above It
The Pyramid Symbol   Holds the   Secret of the Ancients
Letter A   Empowers   a   Father God   and   A/All Men   Only   No Fem here
The First Letter   A   and   The First Number # 1   are Related   As One   (See Number 1 in Numbers)
A   is The   Basic Symbol   of the   Secret Code   Great Seal   Shown on the Dollar Bill   A is The First Letter   A is The Boss   The Eye (of   God   or   The Code) is in that Pyramid   On   Our Money   It Must be Important   It Stands Above the Top Portion of a 2nd Pyramid   The First One Under it   Is Not Finished   They Do Not Touch
A Pyramid Shape can be Seen from   1 Side Seen from The Front   2 Sides Seen from One Side   4 Sides as in Looking from Above   Every Side has a Triangular Shape   #3 indicates The Number of Corners (Triangle)
One of The Meaning of the Pyramid is
1 Man at the Top   2 Fems Down (Letter V/All Fem Sex Active) to Support   The Code   Structure   as Polygamists   Also
The Pyramid has 4 Sides   Not 3 or 2 or 1
Another Illusion Created by   The Code   4 Wives for a Man was an Good Number in the Old Muslim World
The Pyramid Sign/Letter is Letter Delta   The Fourth Letter of the Greek Alphabet   It has the Value of 4   (See # 4 in the Number Chapter)
delta: the fourth letter of the Greek alphabet   the consonant represented by this Letter   the fourth of a series of items   anything triangular as the Greek Capital delta
In This Code   The Secret Code Letter   D/Delta   D is Her Pregnant (See D in The Letter Chapter)   A Delta is Where High Nutrients Food Accumulates   from Water and Land   And Mix Together Naturally   Where Animals go to Feed   A Perfect Hunting Place for the Hunters
That Code   Barrier Starts with Letter   A
Many Pyramids Together Form a Fence   AAAAAA
A Pyramid is Almost a Sealed Place   It is Also a Tomb   The Secret of   The Code   is That Too
Letter A   is 2 Sticks Meeting at the Top   with a Lien   in The Middle   Called a Bar in Between   Which Reinforces Its Structure The

2 Upward Sticks that Meet at the Top   Is   The Men Code   Bonding (Knowing its Secrets or Not)
Letter A is That Pyramid on 2 Legs   It Stands Strong and Can Move   It has Balance
Letter   A   Is the Only Letter that has the Shape of a Tent or Pyramid   A   is the Symbol for a House   △   A   is the Roof too
Just As in Young Children Drawings   Usually a House Drawing by a Child has an X/Axe in the Windows   The Secret Code Brainwash Starts at Birth
The 2 Genders Sex Symbols Code IDs are
   The Masc is an Arrow (Letter A   Stick   a Sound Letter   A/All Men) Attached to a Circle (Fem)   Pointing Anywhere Around it (Giving it a Direction   and   Gravity)
   A Circle is Essentially Fem   It Represents in   The Code   Endless Pregnancies   It Is   O/Fem Hole   Her Circle is Attached to a Cross (Fem Cross/T)   Gender   The Code   Fems Sex Gender Symbol is   T/Fem Cross/Great Curse   That Cross is Attached to Her Circle   It Moves Around That Bubble Also (a Circle is Essentially a Fem Symbol/Pregnancy) (See T as Cross and Nail in The Words Letters)
The Code Letter   A   Points to the Whole Movement of the Other Symbols/Letters in   The Code Alphabet
Directing Us in Life From those   Code   Experiences
Us Not Knowing How it Ends for Us
When a Circle is Around a Cross   It Creates a Wheel (Ring) Pattern   (See Wheel of Time In The Words Chapter)
Letter A is Can be Silent and Almost Invisible in   Words Starting with   Af   Ai   Al   Am   An   Ar   As   Au   Ax
Letter Aa Words with Letter A are Hey (Horse/Whores Command)   Hay (Whores/Horses Food) YA   Amplifies it   as in being Nice   Hey is to Say Hello (Hell/O)   (See Hello in The Words Chapter)
END   OF   Aa   INTRO

A   a
Able: A/Ball   Hey/Ball   Hay/B/All   Hey/Belle (Ring that Bell)   Hay/Be/Hell   Abel

About: A/Butt   A/Bout   A/Boot
about: of concern

The Dam Code The Damn Book

The Concern or the Objective here is   The Butt   or   The Boot (Slang for Sex) in a Bout   But
A/All Men   B/Boy Holding All Fem Breasts   Out
All Men Own The Fems   but Are Out   When Done with Sex
In The Code   It is about Sex or Related to it
about: a contest or trial of strength   as boxing   period   session   spell   a turn at work or any action
The Roman Church (See Church) Restricts Sex with Heavy Fears of Hell (See   Hell/Ill in The Words Chapter)
Switch B for G/Penis Penetration and He Gets Gout (Boys are Too Young for The Code)   Another Reason to get Out

Above: A/All Men   B/Boy Holding All Fems Breasts   Ov/Fem Egg (OV Means   Available Hole)
Above The Fems is the Masc   The Boy and Her Ovulation
The Endless Cycle Starting in Youth
Because It is Above Her She Cannot See it   Says The Code

Accolade: Hack/All/Aid
hack: to cut   notch slice   or sever something with or as with heavy irregular blows   to break up the surface of (the ground)   to damage or injure by crude harsh or insensitive treatment   mutilate   mangle
So Accolade is a Serious Blow for Her if She Tries this Gentle Gesture Accolade that just Wants to Help
Add the Letter M/Motherhood and Get   Hack All Maids

Ace: S/Serpent/Penis   Hiss/His/Is   Ass   SSS
Close to 666
Too Bad for an Ace to be Affiliated to Such a Bad Logo   666
A/All Men   C/See/Young Girl/Young Girl   E/He (He/E is Silent here)
A Silent Letter Means Hiding/Spying/a Hidden Agenda
The S/Ass/Serpent/Penis is The Subject of Spying in Ace   Implying on a Sound Level a Change of Gender (From C to S) Homosexuality   The Ace is His/Ass (Having His Ass   Bad Ass   Bad Language
   Add B/Boy Holding All Fems Breasts and   He Gets the Word   Base
She Cannot have the Power of having a Base   She can Only be Moved   into a Masc Base   Call it a House an Office etc

Letter B/Boy Holding All Breasts   is OK here   He Cannot See the C/See/ Young Girl/Young Girl
He is Focused on His Own Base   His Own Hurting S/Is/His/Us/Ass/Hiss/ Serpent/Penis
Add   C/See/Young Girl/Young Girl   and She Gets a   Case (Confinement of Some Sort   Close to   Cage   When G/Penis Penetration Happens to Her)
Add F/Fem/Fuck and She Gets a Face
Add P/Man Power and He Gets a P/Ass   A Pass for Him   The Code Says   is To get to the   Ass/S/Serpent/Is/His/Us/US
    US   Is to Me the Most Powerful and Most Loving as can be a Word   In That Code   As it can be   Because   Of   Its   Configuration of Letters   that was chosen to be the Name of This Great Country
Ace is Close to US (Os is a Bone in French   A Bone is an Erection)
U/Natural Fem Ovulation   and   S/Serpent/Us/Ass/His/Is   Nice   (Letter U is The One We want to Protect the Most   She is Kind By Nature)
    That Is The Name of This Great Country   The United States of America   I Lived there 30 years   I am a Little American
Add M/Motherhood and She Gets Mace
mace: a club usually having a spiked metal head used esp in the Middle Ages
Mace is an Old Word it Originates in 1250 French with Masse   There are No Happy Motherhood in The Code
Add   R/Her/Are/Our/Hair/Ear/Hear/Whore/Or/Heir/Err/Sex and She Gets a Race   (Letter R has 11 Different Definitions   When it Comes to Letter R   They All Coincides Bringing Different ID Elements
Add V/Fem Sex Active and She Gets a Vase (Uterus/Cup/Chalice)

Accept: X/Cept   Act/Cept   Axe/Set   Asset
The Acceptation of the   Axe/X/Fallen Fem Cross   for   The Fems Virgins   and The T/Fem Cross   as a Set Thing

And that   S/is/His/Us/Ass/Hiss/Serpent/Penis   is   and has   The Scepter Which Rules Her Entirely
Cept Means Except
    Picture it   That is Protocol
scepter: a rod that shows royal power and authority
A Rod is an Entirely Masc Symbol

The Dam Code The Damn Book

Scepter   Scept/Her   Except/Her
Here The Code Rejects The Fems   in a Subtle Way
Except   X/Fallen Fem Cross   cept
X/Fallen Fem Cross   Under the   X/Axe/Eggs
She Being the Exception to be Accepted in that Word Accept   Hack/Cept
Accept is a Big Word Because
The Fems goes Forward as in Accepting the Axe/Hex
There No Fem Power Here   She is the Object of Sacrifice Under
The   Axe/X Power (Pow/Her) as in to Terminate Her
The Eggs also Bring Another Termination   as   She has Her
Eggs   Ready   to be Impregnated
Ass/Cept   is Also Sex in the Ass   Ass/Set

Access: Axe/His   X/Fallen Fem Cross   His/Is   Hack/S
More of the Same Here   So   is the Accept Word Above

Accident: X/Fallen Fem Cross   E/He   Dent
X/He Dent   Axe/He/Dent
dent: hollow on a surface from a blow
The   X/Fallen Fem Cross   is an Entirely Fem Letter
X is the Letter of Her Death
An   X Rated Movie   or an   X Spouse   It is in the Past   It is
Gone   Or   Limited
X/Axe   Follows   T/Fem Cross/Great Curse   in The Code
The Word Accident is an Axe or a Dent for Her

Account: A/All Men   Cunt
Accounting: A/All Men   Cunt   N/In/Hen/Virgin
Count the Cunts as Things to Count
In The Code there are No Coincidences   All Virgins are Cunts   They are
Accountable
cunt: the vulva or vagina   *Extremely Disparaging and offensive   a contemptuous term used to refer to a woman   sexual intercourse with a woman*
Counting Numbers   (Cunt/In   Numb/Her)
Numbers are an Important Hypnotic Tool for The Code (See the Numbers Chapter)

15

A Count is an Honorable Title for a Man   And that is the Way Out of The Code for Him

Accountable: A/Cunt/Able
Cunt is a Powerful Insulting Old Word (Cunt Origin is 1275) for The Fems Genitalia
Cunt: "all senses are vulgar and are strongly tabooed and censored slang   the meaning is highly insulting and demeaning"
Note that Cunt also Denotes the Actual Act of Sex itself
That is How Contempt Makes its Way in the Word Accountable
The Word Cunt Irritates the Ears and is Rarely Used Now
Accountable: subject to the obligation to report explain   answerable
That is what A/Cunt does   it is Accountable to the Masc

Achieve: A/She/Eve   A/She/He/V
Eve (See Eve) and the Letter V is Identical in Meaning
It is Where The Fems as Letter V is Sex Active at Any Time Since the Adam and Eve Age   Which We are Still In
Before Our Age   The Fems   Sexuality was   Different
The Fems were Not Bleeding and there was No Curse on Her
To Achieve is a Strong Word   it Means to Succeed
Here in That Code She Cannot Achieve (A/She/V) Except as a Semen Receptacle
Our Own Code History Shows that Very Few Fem Achieved Power in Our Known History   Fem Power was Mostly Inherited then
The Fems Religious Power is Practically Inexistent
Except for Extreme Sacrifices Cases As   Sister Theresa or Princess of Whales Diana Story
The Fems is Meant by The Code to Remain in the Shadow and be Ignored
That is Why they did Not Honored Princess Diana   Even in Her Death to Have Law Mines Abolished by the Law   She went All the Way to President Clinton
So what The Fems has to Achieve is the
A   She/Shh   Eve/V/Fem Sex Active
It is   A/All Men   and She is Silenced as the   V/Vase/Uterus   to Receive Him   That is The Achievement

Achievement   A/She/Eve/Meant

The Dam Code The Damn Book

According to The Code   A/All Men Transforms The Fem Natural Ovulating Time into an All Year Long Permanent Ovulation Time   She is Meant for it   Or   Is it a Hit

Acne: Hack/Neigh
hack: to cut   sever
Neigh is the Cry of Horses/Whores/Ours
The Code Want us to Ignore the Cries of the Whores/Horse
So   it gave it a Real Bad Name   Acne
Neigh is also the Donkey Sound
The Âne In French is Letter N/In/Hen/Ann/An/Virgin
N and M are Interchangeable in The Code
It is Where   N/In/Hen/Ann/Virgin   Expands into   M/Motherhood
Act/Me is Not a Word because M would Include a Fem/Mother with a Power to Act   A Big No from The Code
Acne is a Cover Word
The Only Thing in Common here is their Pain from being Hacked into Crying   As Acne is So Hard Especially on The Fems   Because She is Taught to Rely on Her Natural Beauty for Self Esteem

Acknowledge: Hack/No/Lay/Egg
hack: to cut   notch   slice   sever
Clear Enough by Repetition
Egg/Null/Egg
null: without value or significance
Null is Made Entirely of Fem Letters
The Code Says here that the Egg does Not Lay the Egg (?)   and The Fems have to Say   Yes   to that Concept
The Code Also Says that the Egg has No Value from Before and After acknowledge: to admit to be real or true
Here is The Code in a Full Hypnotic Dimension
Hack that Egg   It is Acknowledgeable

Across: A/Cross   Hack/Ross (Ross is the Color of Dry Blood)
To Go Across is to go from One End to the Other
The Code is Thorough
The Word Cross is Heard here but there are No   T/Fem Cross Letter in It   No Need Says The Code   It is There/Heard

Lise Rochon

Action: Hack/She/On   Axe/He/On   Act   Eon/He/On
The Code Action is to X Her (as in being 89 in a Bar) Axe (X/Fallen Fem Cross) Her   for An Eon (An Eon is a Billion Years)
Act/Axe/On

Actual: Act/Hack/Axe   You/U/Ovulating/Cup   All/Ill
Axe   You   All
Actually   Act/Hack/Axe   You/All/He
He/E   Act/Hack/Axe   You/Letter U/Ovulating   All
Actuality   Act/Hack/Axe   You/U   All/Ill/Letter L   He/E   T/Fem Cross   Today
Hat/You/All/He/T   The Hat is Where The Code Hides
Add W/All Fems Sex Active as Starting the Word and She Gets a Whack   No Fems in that Front

Acute: A/All Men   Cut
The Cut is the First Time Sexual Intercourse for the Girl
Or   The Clitorectomy which was a Common Practice in the East
That is Acute Pain for Her as a Child
A Cute Little Girl   Is an Uncut One

Adage: Add   Age/Egg   Add/H
Add the H/Secret Code Letter Sound
adage: traditional way expressing common experience
How Convenient
To Add is to Reinforce   So The Code Says it can Hit a Fem and Make Her go Down More by Just Mentioning that She is getting Old
The Message here is to Include   The Code   in Our General Knowledge as a Soft Word Adage

Adam: A/All Men   D/Pregnant   A/All Men   M/Motherhood
When All Men are Surrounding D/Pregnant into Motherhood   It is   A/Damn/Dam   and   The Dam   is The Fems   as in Madame   Mad/Ame   Âme is Soul in French   Mad/Aim   Maid/M)
A Dam is a High Barrier (Bar/He/Her) that Keeps Water (Emotions) from going to the Other Side
Adam and Eve: A/Damn   End   He   V/Fem Sex Active
Add/Ham/End/Eve

The Dam Code The Damn Book

Ham is HM   H/Secret Code Letter   and   M/Motherhood   ham is Also M
Adam Means Literally Man Made of Blood
Dam is Mad in Reverse
adamant: inflexible
The Code does Not Allow Changes

Admire: Add/Mire
mire: an area of swampy ground bog marsh
Had/Mare
mare: a fully mature female horse
Admire is a Special Word for Her   Says The Code
The Word Admire Starts by Adding Her as a Mare Looking at Herself in the Mirror
From a Swamp Anything Looks Good
Mirror has Reflection
That would be a Big No from The Code to Add Anything to The Fems
Especially with Letter R/Her/Hair/Are/Here/Hear/Ear/Whore/Or/Heir/Err/Air/Our/Sex   Even if it is Motherhood   She is Still Admiring Herself as a Mare in the Mire   The Code Acts That Way

Adopt: Add/Hop
To Hop is Slang for Sex
For Her is to Adopt to have More Sex   The Code Says
Add Hope to That
A/All Men   2 DD s/Pregnants   Opt
All Men Opt to Make All Fems Pregnant   And Adopt Too

Adore: A/All Men   Door
The Code Uses Religions to Corrupt Us
Add/Whore
Adorable   A/Door/Able   Add/Whore/Able
A/Door/Bell   is   a Door   to   Able the Whore
Belle and Bell (Belle in French is a Great Fem Name)
Ring the Bell   Ring that Belle (Wedding Ring)
The Bell is Her Clitoris (Look Bell in the Words Chapter)
Adored   Add/Whore   is Now   D/Pregnant
Saying   Going   To/This/Door   Going To/The/Store

Lise Rochon

Whores Sell at Certain Stores

Adornment: A/Door/Meant   Add/Whore/Meant
Add/Horn/Meant   The Horn would be the Penis here
adornment: ornament
Her Door Opens to the Penis   as a   Whore/Her/Are/Or/Heir

Adult: A/Dull   T/Fem Cross
When The Fem is Older and Wiser   She is Dull   Because Her   T/Fem Cross   Is Weighting on Her Reality   A/Doll/T
Dull and Doll are Meant to be Together in The Code to Represents Her   2 Facets   at   2 Different Ages
Make a Doll   of all Those Little Girls so they can be   Dull and be Manipulated Straight into   T/Fems Cross/Great Curse

Advice: Add/Vice   is the Advice from   The Code
A Vice President Title   The Code goes All the Way to the Top   Especially into making Us Fools if We Try to Understand How That Code Works   It is Not True   Vice President are Very Good People and the Pope is Not Made of Poop   So The Code Remain

Affair: F/R   F/Fem/Fuck   Whore/R/Her/Are/Heir/Sex
Affair Means Business in French
affair: anything done or to be done   an event a performance   a sexual relationship between 2 people who are not married to each other
The Code Picture Here is   Being Unfaithful to Your Spouse   It Is a Thing to be Done   Even as or at a Special Event
Affair has the Word Fair in it
It Reminds Us of a Fair or a Fairy or a Ferry (Fair/He)
It Puts you to Sleep
FR   is   The Fem/Whore
Affair   as   FR   with   2 Silent Letters   Accompanying it   A/All Men (Twice) and i/Marriage Act
Add E/He and it is a Fairy (Free)
Fairies are Delicate Fem Entities that can have a Temper   They have Pixie/Dust (Pig/See)
Because Fairy End with a He/E Sound   It Compliment the Male   Fair/He   By Making Him Fair   and   Carried Safely by a Ferry

The Dam Code The Damn Book

fair: free from bias
fare: something offered to the public for entertainment   a price for a passage
Take Away i/Marriage Act   and it is the Word Afar
Note that   A   in Affair is Silent   So Men are having Affairs   But are Not Visible/Present on That level
Affair is   F/Fem/Fuck   and Her/Whore/Are/R/Her/Hair/Are/Here/Hear/Ear/Whore/Or/Err/Air/Our/Sex   Sex is here Twice

Afar: Off/R
If   R/Her/Hear/Ear/Are/Whore/Or/Heir/Err/Air/Our/Sex would be   Off   That would be Against The Code Goals   So it is a Big   No
afar: far away   from a long way off
A/All Men   Far
And All Men Stay Away from That   Says The Code

Affirmation: A/Firm/Ass/He/On   A/Firm/Ass/Eon
A/Formation (See the Word Row)
A   Farm   A   She   On
How Convenient for The Code   Keep on Telling The Fems that She is a Farm Animal   And Keep Them in Formation   For an Eon
The Fems According to The Code are   the Fishes   the Cows   the Chickens   the Ants   the Horses (Whores)   and Others

Affliction: F/Lick/She/Shh/On
The Code Says here   When a Fem Gives a Blow Job   it is an Affliction for Her   Her Affliction is to Keep on Licking   and Shh about it
Flick/She/On
flick: a sudden blow or tap   as with a whip or the finger   something thrown off with or as if with a jerk
There are No Rewards in The Code for Her   Even   When She Gives Loving Pleasure to   A/All/Her/Man
Affliction Includes Corporal Punishment for The Fems   And When the Word Whip is Mentioned   Be Even More Careful
affliction: a state of pain   distress   or grief   misery

Afford: F/R/D   F/Her/D   F/Horde   F/Herd   F/Heard
All Connected

Lise Rochon

F/Fem/Fuck   R/Her/Hair/Are/Here/Hear/Ear/Whore/Or/Heir/Err/Air/Our/Sex   D/Pregnant
The Fem as a Whore Get Pregnant
She Can Afford that   She is Part of the Herd   She Heard it Before   Says The Code

Afraid: F/Fem/Fuck   Raid   F/Ride
The Code Says   She is Afraid   Being Under a Raid
She is on a Ride   The Code Raid Her All the Time

After: FTR
The Code Sends in the Future   a Concept   F/Fem/Fuck   as   T/Fem Cross/Great Curse   and   R/Her/Hair/Are/Here/Hear/Ear/Whore/Or/Heir/Err/Air/Our/Sex
Letter F is Kind of Asexual by Herself   So   R/Whore/Heir   is here to Join Off/To/Her   Ov/To/Her   Ov/T/Her   is the   T/Fem Cross with the   OV/Egg/Ovulation
Everything Else is Off
Heft/Her
heft: weight   heaviness   significance or importance
The Heaviness will Weight on Her and Make Her Weaker   Says The Code

Afternoon: Heft/Her/Noon
With 2 OOs/Fem Holes   Which Implies Polygamy with All Fems   She is Going for it   Off/T/Her/Noon
Noon because of its 2 OOs/Fem Holes makes it is a Rare Word   Especially Between 2 NNs/Virgins
N/In/Hen/Virgin   Is Noon (Day Time)   Moon is the Other M/Motherhood (Night Time)
(M and N are Interchangeable in The Code   Because   M/Motherhood   is in the Waiting for that   N/In/Hen/Virgin)
Son and Sun   Noon and Moon   Except that The Fems Goes Down 9moon) and the Masc (Sun) goes Up
The Moon is the Card # 18 in the Tarot   The Moon Rules in the Astrological Sign Cancer   A Sad Fem Sign

Again: A/Gain   A/All Men   Gain
All Men Gain   To All Men/Again

The Dam Code The Damn Book

i/Marriage Act   N/In/Hen/Virgin
The Repeating Gain for Him   Says The Code   is   The   N/Virgin Having   i/Marriage Act   with   A/All Men   and End on And A/Gun   is Close
Every Man Penis is a Gun   Say that Again
Again is Also   Egg   N/In   The Gain is in for The Code As Another Fem has Her Eggs Ready and Going   Again
Then   A/Gay/In
Again Sexually Goes Both Genders here
Une Gaine is a Corset in French   Another Curse this Thing   It is A Very Bad Thing for a Fem to have a Small Waist   It is A True Waste   It Incapacities Her   At The Amount of Guts We have Inside Us   and Squish All   Until All Squished (See BB in The Words Chapter)

Against: A/All Men   Gain   S/is/His/Us/Ass/Hiss/Us/Serpent/Penis   T/Fem Cross
Against has   a Gain   in It
A/All Men   S/Penises   are there with   G/Fem Penetration   and in   i/Marriage Act   to the   N/Virgin   Which Ends in   T/Fem Cross   Because Now there is an Opposition   Against is there to Say No   to The Fem Cross   to have Benefits

Agenda: Age/End/A
Age   Hand   D/Pregnant   A/All Men   Agent/A
The Code Message from Agenda is   A/All Men   are Agents to Have All Fems Pregnant at the Right Age   or   at Hand When   Ready
The Agent   and the Word   Gene   Reinforces The Code Agenda

Agnes: A Fem Name   A Holy Name for Christ
In Ancient Paintings Agnes is Painted as a Sacrificial Lamb that Carries a Flag with a Red Cross on it Which is Bleeding in a Chalice
Those are Great Mystical Paintings of the Great Curse
There is Also a Shepherd with His Stick (See Shepherd in The Words Chapter))
Note that the Lamb of God is Not Called Jesus   It is Called a   Real Lamb
The Lamb and the Dove are Fem Symbols
Agnes Means Fire in Latin   One of the 4 Basics Elements
But She is Still Called in The Code as a   Hag/N/S

Lise Rochon

hag: a nasty old vicious woman   a sorceress
Nag   Bag   Rag Wag   Weakening Words for Her
Agnes is Agneau in French (Egg/New)
Ann/N/Knew Would be for Her to Know Things from   The Code So   A
Big No   So   They Slaughter   Agnes/Lamb   for That

Ago: A/All Men   G/Penis Penetration   O/Fem Hole
When A/All Men   Penetrates The O/Fems Loins   it is A/Go   In The Past Too
Egg/O   Egg/Go   Ovulation is On for the O/Fem Hole
It is A/Go (Ago) from the Past and A/Go into the Future
Replace A/All Men with an E/He and He Gets Ego (He/Go)
The Word Go is   G/Penis Penetration   of The   O/Fem Hole   A   Go

Agony: Hag/On/He
hag: ugly old woman   especially a vicious or malicious one   a witch or sorceress   a hagfish
A hag/fish   So to Mention   is the Most Ugly Fish you can Imagine   So Fems Are Associated with Fishes   In The Code
Agony Here is   the Man   with and Old Ugly   Fem
Is Gone   A/Gone/He   A/Gun/He
It is Difficult to Love Someone   Ugly   Especially for a Man   Why do People Get Ugly   Lack of Love   Food   Care   Beauty Essentially Accompanies Love   Love Carries You   Happy   Even if Anxious   Love Creates a Special Harmony
From Our Partners Especially   if they have been with Us a Lot in Our Lives   Love has a Lot of Influence   But No Says The Code   Love Cannot Exist   So
Nag About it   It is a Hag   It is in The Bag   You Rag   It is a Gag   Wag it On the Rag   Again
Where there is Agony
A   Gone   He

Agreed: A/Greed
The Greed/Grid is The Code
That Greed is the Source of Hell and Poverty   Letter L/Elle/Ail/Hail/Elle/Hell/Sweet Fem Love Light
The Code   Makes Us Agree on   Greed   with the Word   Agreed

The Dam Code The Damn Book

Agreement: Hag/Egg   R/Her/Hair/Are/Here/Hear/Ear/Whore/Or/Heir/Err/Air/Our/Sex   E/He   Meant
Words with Sound Similarities Attract Each Other in That Code
Here the Egg is Transformed into a Hag   And   it is an Agreement

Ahead: A/All Men   Head/Had
All Men Heads are Together   Going Ahead   In the Past   Also
No Fem here   Except for D/Pregnant

Ahem: AM   A/All Men   and   Ham/M/Motherhood/Him
When   A/All Men   is with   M/Motherhood   It is Uncomfortable to The Code   So
ahem: clearing throats to express doubt   mild warning
A Hem is a Circular Decorative Part of a Column (Call/Him) Since Antiquity   The Column is the Penis Symbol

Aid: A/All Men   i/Marriage Act   D/Pregnant
it is Called Aid When   A/All Men   have a   i/Marriage Act   to Make a Fem   D/Pregnant
Add L/Sweet Fem Love Light/Ill/Hail/Ail/Hell/Elle/Ill/Ail/Hell/Elle and She Gets Laid
Add M/Motherhood and She Gets Made as a Maid
Add P/Man Power and He Gets Paid
Add R/Her/Hair/Are/Here/Hear/Ear/Whore/Or/Heir/Err/Air/Our/Sex   and She Gets   Raid
Switch D for M/Motherhood and She Gets Aim/M/Motherhood (Aim at Motherhood for Her)
Switch D for R and She Gets Air/Letter R/Her/Are/Heir/Whore   Air/Hair/Heir/Here/Err
Take Away Letter i and She Gets Ad (More Children to Add)
Switch D for T/Fem Cross/Great Curse and She Gets Hate
The Code Moves in Flawless Moves in an Enclosed Circle of Concepts/Symbols that Keep on Pointing and Repeating the Same Weaknesses or Strengths on the Same Spots in Different Angles and Ages

Aim: Letter M/Motherhood
I/Am   I/M   A/M

The Code Gives its Direction to   The Fems as Mothers   What to Aim For   Am   Him   Ham   Ame   Ahem
That Letter I is that Stick that Direct the Mothers   As Ham   With an Ahem (Rejection)
Letter M is Him   Says The Code   Because The Fems Should Never be Left Alone   Or Have Any identity (Even as a Mom)   Aim for That   You Ham
aim: to position   to direct
There is More   All The Way to the   Soul   Âme (M) in French   and last
Aime (M) is Love in French
Aimer   One of The Most Beautiful Word in the World
Ahem to That   and Aim at All The Above
The Whole   Letter M   Word Meanings are Cover Words here

Air: Letter R   is Heavy of Important Code Meanings
Air is Vital to Life   So   The Code Says   Is   Letter R
Letter R will be Explained in The Numbers Chapter
Letter R   as   Heir/Or/Whore   and Follows All the Other Secondary Ones Definitions that Incites to that   or   Remind Her in a Nice Way of that Message which is Essentially the   Whore   Or   Heir   And Not so Nice too When Err is Mentioned   because Back Then   They Abandoned People/Fems in the Desert Alone to Die
Err is a Very Serious Word   So   When The Code Says
Heir   or   Whore   or   Err   It Mean it

Heiress: R   Ass   or   R   Is/His/Hiss/S
The Heir   and   S/Penis
No Fem Letters or Fem Concepts in Heiress
She is Represented as the   Ass   on the Many Masc Words As
Actress   Mayoress   etc   Those 2 Words have Almost Disappeared from Our Vocabulary

Aladdin: A/Lad/In
A/All Men   Lad/Laid   In/N/Hen/Virgin
All Men   Are Laid/Lads   Around   Virgins
lad: a boy   a chap   a staple boy   affectionate
That Boy Comes with a Magic Lamp   (See Lamb in the Words Chapter)

The Dam Code The Damn Book

Albumen: All   Be   Men
albumen: the white of an egg
The Inside of an Egg is Meant to Feed the Chick
But No   Men Only Own the Word here   And the Inside of that Egg should be for the Masc Only   Says That Mad Code

Alchemy: All/K/Me   In English   Alchemy is about K/Broken Fem Warrior (See Letter K)
All/She/Me   In French   Alchemy is About Her
alchemy: the science of transmuting a common substance of little value into a substance of greater value
In The Code it is the Road to Change Metal (Mate/All) into Gold (G/Hymen Perforation   Hold/Old)
The Alchemists were Working with a Dark Burgundy Powder   that is the Color of Dry Powdered Blood
All Fems Know That One
Alchemist would be   All/She/Miss   with the   T/Fem Cross
It was the Trying of the Transubstantiation of Her Blood into Gold here
It is The Catholic Church Communion Sacrament
Wine/Whine/Win is Transformed into Jesus Sacrificial Blood
It is the Blood Loss of All Fems that is Symbolized here
And that is What the Great Curse Does   to The   Fems
It Puts in Her Way   So Many Obstacles
(Physical   Emotional   Mental   and   Spiritual) that it Transforms Her into a Different Stronger Person   Therefore the Alchemy Succeeded   Which Includes as Priority   Her Endless Loss of Blood which Curses Her   Among   All Men
The Alchemical Lead Represents Saturn (See The God Saturn in Astrology   A Bad Guy)   Poisonous Mercury is Also Part of the Alchemy and it is Represented in the Tarot Deck in Card # 1 the Magician (the One that Lures Her into The Code World   By making it Look Really Good   Almost magic)

Alcohol: All/Cool   The Fems was Not Allowed to Drink Alcohol   or go to   Bars   Where Men Play   It was Barred to Her

Alien: Ill/He/N   A/Lien
Hell/He/N   All/N   Helen (Hell/In)   L/Hail   He/E   N/In/Hen/Virgin

Lise Rochon

The Lien   here is that   N/In/Hen/Virgin   is Under   L/Hail/Hell/All/
Ill   And Do Not Know it   It is Foreign/Alien to   Her
alien: a foreigner   a person that has been estranged or excluded
lien: the legal claim of one person upon the property of another person to secure the payment of a debt or the satisfaction of an obligation
All/He/N   All Men as One   and the   N/In/Hen/Virgin   Alien to Each Other
It has been Always As that in the History of Our Age   The Fems Owed Nothing   Were Worth Nothing   That Shows How Powerful that Code is   Slavery   Everywhere
    Un Lien in French has Another Connotation   it is Much More Soft   Emotional   and   Human   Which The Code Hates
    Les Liens de la Famille   Les Liens de l'Amour   Love is on a Chain   According to the Official Definition
In This Code Everything is Registered According to The Laws of That Code
Aliens as in UFO People Brings Us Even Further Away from Each Other
Concept of that Lovely Sound LN   Which is So Nice
Alien is a Cover Word Here   especially Because it Covers LN with a Jurisdiction   Could Not They Choose Another Word

Alive: All/Hive   All/Eve
Eve as in the   V/Fem Sex Active   is Alive   says   The Code
The Word All is   A/All Men   with 2 LLs/Sweet Fem Light/Ill/Hell/Elle
Letter L is in Plural   or   is All of Them   Implying Polygamy   here
Alive is   All Men Hold Power Over   V/Eve   to Maintain Her Alive as in   Active Sexually   Alive
Letter L being the Right Angle of the Masons   or   the Fifth Angle in the Jewish Kabala   The One that Never Fitted
Alive as in   All/Hive   All The Fems   Part of the Hive as Bees(A Fem Symbol as Old as Egyptians Antiquity)   Bees Work Hard All The Time
A Hive is Made of Honey (Horn/He) Bees
B in The Code is the Boy Holding All Fem Breasts   Double 2 EEs/He   The Hive Bring Food for Men Only here
The Fem is a Worker with Breasts   in The Code
Hives is a Rash   It Hurts
Nothing Fem is Entirely Positive in The Code
There is Always a Tarnish   a Reverse

The Dam Code The Damn Book

All: A/All Men   2 LLs/Sweet Fem Light/Ill/Hell/Hail/Elle
All Men   Get All the   Love/Light
The Fems Gets   L/Ill/Hell/Heel/Oil/Ail/Hail
Oil is Close to Her Ill
Add Eve or V to Ill/Hell   and   Hear and See the Word Evil as in Eve that is Ill   Evil

Ally: All   I/High   The I   as the   I/Stick
Hell/I   Heel/Hi   All/High
ally: to unite formally as by treaty league marriage or the As (usually followed by or to)
Ally is Made Entirely of Bars Letters   It is The Bonding of All Men
Ally is a Tricky Word   It is a Transformative Word
Because   There are No Fem Letter   in the Word Ally
And Ally   Sounds As   All/i   That is a Lot of   i/Marriage Act
Ally is   Y/Wounded Fem   with the   2 LLs/Sweet Fem Light/Ill/Hell/Ail (Making it Plural   or   All of Them)   With   A/All Men
The Code is Fully Occupying the Word here
It is Not All/I   It is Really   All   A/All Men   that makes the Word   All Men   Together   Eliminating the Fem Completely Except for the Sex Act as The Dot Above the   i   in Small Cap (Large Caps are More Important)
The Code Says   All   Are with the A/All Men in Ally
Letter I is the High   The Eye   The God Code   A Friendly Hi   Letter I(i)   The Voice from the High has been Transformed here into a Y/Fem Wounded
A God Emerges from Any Man Stick here
A Lie is Also an Ally
He/Lay/High
Allies   All/Lies
Allies is a Strong Cover Word in The Code   He/Lie
All I/Sticks (Masc) are with   i/Marriage Act   Only When in Small Cap or Young After that   the Daughter (Dot/Her) is Integrated in the Big Cap I/ The Stick and Disappears
A Small Example here is When She Adopts the Man Name in Marriage   She is Assimilated into That
Add   R/Her/Hair/Are/Here/Hear/Ear/Whore/Or/Heir/Err/Air/Our/Sex   to Ally and   The Sound has Changed   She Gets a Rally   He Gets   Rail/

Lise Rochon

He   As in being Transported there   and   Easy Way for Him to get to The Heir   or   R/Whore/Her/Heir/Sex
rally: to draw people for a common action

Alma Mater: a graduate from college
Only Men have been Graduating from College in Our History   Since Lately
Imagine The Choc   The Name of That Diploma is Alma   Mater   All/Ma   Matter/Mother   All/Mother   All/Mate/R/Her   All/Meet/R/Her
The Code Created Her Graduation a Long Time Ago   All Mothers For All Fems

Almost: All/Must   LMST   All   Mast/Must/Most
L/Sweet Fem Light/Ill/Hell/Elle/Hail/Elle   M/Motherhood   S/Is/His/Us/Ass/Hiss/Serpent/Penis   T/Fem Cross
All Fems Including Mothers   All Must/Most   Go to Be   T/Fem Cross
All/Hell/Ill/Letter L   Most
All/Hell/Ill   M/Motherhood   Host   Motherhood the Host of Hell/Ill/Hail   Says The Code
Here the Word Sound Meaning   Destroys its Word Definition   Hell/Most   Hell/Must   Hell/Mast
Mast is Penis   in Slang
Switch O for i/Marriage Act and Get All Mist
That Hell is As a Mist   Says The Code

Alone: LN   2 Fem Sounds Letters
All/On
L/Sweet Fem Love Light/Ill/Hail/Ail/Hell/Elle/Ill/Elle/Hail/Hell   and   N/In/Hen/Virgin   Alone   On Their Own   In Her Hell and Ills
L/All/Ill/Hell/Hail/Elle   Own   The Fem as   I   Owns All This Hell   Etc
Helen   All/N   A/Loan
In History The Code has Isolated The Fems   So much
She Could Not Exchange Information or Friendship with Other Fems   As Men did with Their Clubs   Brotherhoods   Bars   and   Businesses
There is Not such a thing about being   Alone for Her in The Code   Even If She is Isolated
Add i/Marriage Act and Get a   A/Lion   A/Lay/On
Alone   All Along   A/long

The Dam Code The Damn Book

All/On   On a   A/Loan

Alphabet: All/For/Bet   All/For/Beat   All/For/Bat   Alpha/Bet is an Important Word in The Code
alpha: the first Letter of the Greek alphabet   the first   the beginning

Already: All/Ride/He   All/Ready   All/Red/He   Elle/Read/He   L/Read/He   L/Red/E
That is What She Read   and Learn as   L/Fem Sweet Love Light/Ill/Hail/Hell/Elle
Already   Happens in the Past
She will be Ready to Ride Him

Also: LCO   3 Fem Sounds Letters
L/See/O   All/See/O   All/Slow   Hell/So
(See   So   and   Sow in the Words Chapter)
All What Sees   L/Sweet Fem Light   as the   C/See/Young Girl/Young Girl   is Her   O/Fem Hole

Allow: LO   2 Fem Sound Letters
All/O   All Fems are   Holes
And All   Owe   or are   Owned   by   A/All Men
When   L/Sweet Fem Light/Ill/Hail/Hell/Ail/Elle is a   O/Fem Hole   It is Allowed
A Friendly Hello is   Hell/Elle   and Her   O/Fem Hole Together
Note Letter   A/All Men   is Silent here   Leaving Only The Fems Letter Sounds   LO   or   All/Ill/Hell   O
A/Low   as in Another Low Point for Her in The Code
A Lou (Toilet) is Close

Altar: LTR   3 Fem Sound Letters   Alter   Halt/R   All/T/R
When   L/Sweet Fem Love Light/Ill/Ail/Hail/Hell/Elle   is with   T/Fem Cross   as   Whore/R/Her/Are/Heir/Sex
The Code Brings Her to the Altar
It   Halts/Her   It   Alters/Her   The Code Says   Yes to That   all The Way to The Altar
Do Not Litter That

Lise Rochon

Altitude: All   T/Fem Cross   You/U/Ovulating   D/Pregnant
High Up there   All Fems are   Open   and Carry that   Cross   All The way to The Altar

Always: L/Sweet Fem Light/Ill/Ail/Hail/Hell/Elle   All/Ways   Ill/Ways   Hell/Ways
Hell   Way   S/Is/His/Us/Ass/Hiss/Serpent/Penis
Always is   When The Fems is Lured   by the Penis
The Way it Always was
L/Ways   The   L/Sweet Fem Love Life (Before She was Ill   Ailing   Under the   Hail   Elle   in   Hell   etc   Ways
Love as Whey   Whey is Coagulated Milk
Whey in French is Called Petit Lait or Breast Milk
Always   All/Ways   All Ways are Used by The Code
Anyways and All Ways are Good to Get to Her Each Time
The Language Code is All About Her Being Available and Sexually Confusing The Fems
Always is an Ugly Name for Sanitary Napkins

Amateur: A/Mate/Her
amateur: a fan   a person inexperienced in a certain activity
Here The Code is in Force   Mating Her   With A/All Men   on a Sound Level   while Keeping Her   Ignorant or Amateur   in the Same Time

Amaze: A/Maize   A/Maze   A/Ma/Z
In Becoming a Mother   She Sleeps with it   Letter Z/as Above as Below/Sleep on it
Snoozing in the Yellow Maize Dreaming of Maze Amazes Her
Switch Z for D/Pregnant and She Gets Made a Maid

Amazing: A/Maize/In   A/Maze/N
M/Motherhood   Z/as Above as Below/ZZZ Sleep on It
Amazing is As Eating Something Yellow and So Good As Corn (K/C/Q   Horn)
Z is the End Letter of the Secret Alphabet Code Systematology
systematology: the science of formation of systems
Mothers and Virgins can Never Know about that Very Important Secret Code Language System

The Dam Code The Damn Book

It is a Maze to The Fems and a   Maize   To Look at   N/In/Hen/Virgin   it Sounds All Good
maze: a complex system that causes confusion
It Loses Her in Complexities   Such as
M/Z/N   A/Maize/In
M/Ham/Am   A/All Men   Zing
Maids/In   M/Ace/N
maize: yellow corn
(Yell   O/Fem Hole   C/See/Young Girl   Horn/Penis)
A/Mess/In   A/Mass/In   Motherhood/Ass/In
M/Ass/Is/In
Ancient Fem Deities had Maize for their Symbol of Prosperity
The Word Corn Without   C/See/Young Girl   is Horn (Horny)   H/The Code Letter
The Corn is in the Horn (Penis) of Abundance
Amazing is a Big Cover Code Word here

Ambitious: M/Motherhood   B/Boy Holding All Fems Breasts   T/Fem Cross/Great Curse   S/Is/His/Us/Ass/Hiss/Serpent/Penis   or   Plural
Ambitious is When   The Code Goal Says   Mothers as Fem Cross are Mothers of Boys
Words As that in   AM/M   Are Sounds Words   Starting With an M   Not an A   A is Silent here
M/Ham   Bush/Us   M/Bitches
When   M/Motherhood   is   M/Ham   Ham/Bitch/She/Us
It Can be Very Tricky   Thread Carefully

Ambush: M/Motherhood   Bush
The Bush is the Outside of the Genitalia Area   or   the Fanny (Fan/Fun   He)
Am/Bush   M/Bush
The Code Keeps   M/Motherhood   Next to it
The Burning Bush   to This Day Families are Called Bush

American: A/All Men   Mere   He/Can (Mère is Mother in French)
The Fem are there with Honor   Represented as Mothers
M/Am/Motherhood/Him   A/All Men   R/Her/Hair/Are/Here/Hear/Ear/Whore/Or/Heir/Err/Air/Our/Sex   E/He   Can

Lise Rochon

Sorry   All Men with Fems as Whores and Mothers   The Code Says
M/Motherhood   R/Her/Heir/Whore/Are/Here   He   Can

Amour: Am/M/Motherhood   Whore
Amour is a the Word for   Love   in French
In The Code   it is Integrated Differently   it is Degraded
Am/Whore   M/Whore   A/More   Am/Or
The Connection with the Mother   as Whore   is Loud
The Word   More   is in it Too
Or (Whore) Means Gold in French
In French L'Amour   La/Mort Means Death   Law/More
Now it is a Law
Those Words Symbols Create the Mother   as   Whore and it is
in   The Law
That Code Hates   True Love   It Takes Its Power Away
Amor Is the Universal Term for Love
In The Code   A/More   is   A/All Men   More
There is Always the   Go Down   Next to The Fem
Amour is Ame/Our   Âme is Soul in French
There Can be No Soul without Love   Aim
The Code Urges Us to Destroy   All of it   for What it
Wants   Amour   is   Am/Whore (It Includes M/Motherhood)
That is Why The American English is Considered a Corrupted Language

Amphora: M   For   A
Mothers   to   A/All Men
M/F/R/A
M/Motherhood   F/Fem/Fuck   R/Her/Hair/Are/Here/Hear/Ear/Whore/Or/
Heir/Err/Air/Our/Sex   A/All Men
The Fems as Mothers   F/Fuck/Fem   and   Whores   Serve as
Receptacles to All Men
An Amphora is a Jar with an Oval Body (Ov/Egg/Shape) with 2 Handles on the Shoulder and One Under the Lip
and was Used to Contain Wine (Fem) Oil (Fem) and Ashes(Death)
As in Many Other Code Words   She has No Identity (Therefore No History) She is Sex itself being   a Jar (Ajar)   or   Any Receptacle

Amulet: M/U/Let   (Lait is Mother Milk in French)

The Dam Code The Damn Book

If   M/Motherhood   and   U/You/Ovulating   would be Let To be Free
(from Forced Pregnancies) With Special Magic
A Big No   Says The Code   So
amulet: a small trinket worn to protect against evil
As this could Work Against the Great Curse
It is the Great Curse that Created The Fems as Evil
(See Evil in the Words Chapter   Eve that is Ill)
A/Mule/Let   The Mule is Another Term for Her   MUL is All Fem Sounds
Letters
It is the Ann/Âne/N (See N/In/Hen/Virgin Letter)
Mule   and   Âne   are   Donkeys   in French

An: A/All/Men   N/Virgin   An is Pronounced as N)
an: an indefinite   article   a suffix
The Code Ass to Appropriate Vague Definitions   as   Her
Not to Attract Questions or Doubts
Ann/Anne   is a Fem Name in   French
The Code Closes its Ends   that Way
Having Sex with Animals was Forbidden by All Religions
It was Mal (Male)
But   So Many Men did it   And Still Do
The Fems could Never have Sex without Marriage
Under Death   Her Choice   NO

Anal: NL   2 Fem Sounds Letters
Anal   Ann   L/Sweet Fem Love Light/All/Ill/Hell/Ail/Hail/Elle
The Donkey/The âne for   N/In/Hen/An/Ann/Virgin
A   Nigh/Neigh   L/Sweet Fem Love Light
neigh: to utter the cry of a horse   whinny
Anal as in   A/Nail (See Cross in The Words Chapter)
N/Ail/Hail   A/Nail/All/Ill   Nail   Nell   Nail Someone Says The Code
Again here   Without being Part of that Word Implications   A is
Silent   Implying Only Witnessing   There are 2 of Them in Anal
anal: a record of events of a particular year   of pertaining to involving
or near the anus
Back to Feces for Her Again in the Anus   And Retention Also
FC is 2 Fem Letters with an S as in Plural   or   The Ass/S/is/His/Us/
Ass/Hiss/Serpent/Penis is Involved   Because there is No Singular to

35

Lise Rochon

Feces   FCC is Feces too   C/Young F/Fem   Girls   Be Treated as Feces   I Have seen in Far Away Countries Examples of That   Total Disrespect for Her Humanity   So Much Suffering
The Code Says   The Anus (Ann/Us)   are the   N/Virgins   (in Plural or All of Them)
Ann/N   Us/S/is/His/Us/Ass/Hiss/Serpent/Penis   Or   N/In/Hen/Virgin   S   The Anus is Where   NS   are Together with S/Is/His/Us/Ass/Hiss/Serpent/Penis   Says The Code   Under the Eyes of   A/All Men
The Code Says   Sex in The Butt for The Virgins   Because They are All Donkeys
Sex with Donkeys was Common in The East   in The Past   When There was Only that Accessible   for Horny Men   No One Talks About that

Ancestor: Incest/Her   Ann/Zest/Her
Much Child Sexual Abuse   in Our Human   History   No Animal Specie do that   But they do Not have a Code above/in Their Heads that Tells them those Atrocities
That is Why The English Language is Disgraced as being a Corrupt Language
Sex Between Animals is Much Simpler   Because of the Ovulation Limited Time
N/In/Hen/Virgin   Sis/Sister   or   C/Young Girl   T/Fem Cross   R/Her/Whore/Are/Heir/Err/Sex
Many Types of Fems are Named here   You Can Incest   Her   N/Virgin   C/See/Young Girl   The Fem Cross   as in All Fems   the R/Whore   or   the One with the   Heir
All Syllables Above are Fem   Except for S/Penis That Sneaked In   Here It Disguised itself as a   Sis (Which is the Abbreviation for Sister)   A double S   or in Sys
Sys is a System   The Code is Systemized   Especially for Ancestry   And it Knows how Sisters are Systemized and Organized
In   Incest/Her   Ancestor   All Sisters Get to Know Sex   and the Great Curse   with Fear and Panic
Ann/Sex/Her

Anchor: Ankh/Her
The Ankh is a   Circle   and a   Cross   Together
ankh: Egyptian symbol of regeneration or enduring life

The Dam Code The Damn Book

(See Ankh in The Words Chapter)
The Ankh is a Cross Opened at the Top in a Shape of a Reversed Drop of Water or a Tear
A Cross With a Tear/Tears
A Cross to Bear will Make you Cry
Nail and Cross
Other Form of Crosses have Flowers (Fem Symbol) at their Ends (Hands)
Any Cross Symbol   is a Fem Symbol   or   the Great Curse   and   Her Death in   X/Fallen Fem Cross
It is the Egyptian Tau Cross with the Egg Shape   as Top   which is Used as a Handle   and is   Carried as a   Key   or a   Tool
To Ankh/Her would be to Give Her a Cross
The Fems Curse Cross Existed in the Time of the Antique Egypt
   A Ship (See Ship and Fishes in The Words Chapter) Anchor   Keeps a Ship on a Same Spot on Water (Water is an Entirely Fem Symbol)
Few Words Rhyme with Ankh   but Bank   Rhymes with Ankh   The Code is Where Big Money and Power Are

Ancient: N/In/Hen/Virgin   She/Aint   Ann/She/Hint
An and Ann are Interchangeable in   The Code   as Mentioned in the Word   An
Here One Stone Hits Two Targets
The Word Ancient is   Ann/She/Ant   and   Ann/She/Aint
Ancient is Far in the Past   But Ann is still being an Ant or Nothing at All   Says The Code
Which is a Lie   She IS that Cross of Life   See Ankh Above

Anemia: N/In/Hen/Virgin   M/Motherhood   He/E   A/All Men
Weak   or   Uncomfortable   or   Sickly   Words Will Often Start with   Fem Sounds Letters
Putting M/Motherhood   and   N/Virgin   in Front of   He/E   and/or   All Men   That Would be a   Big No from The Code   So   No   She Will be   Too Weak   to do that with Anemia
Her Immense Lost of Blood Often Conducts (Con   Duct/Duck) to Anemia

Anger: Hang/Her
The Code Works The Fems Down in Every Way

Lise Rochon

Angry: N/In/Hen/Ann/Virgin   Grey
When Ann Turns Grey   She is Not Healthy   Grey is the Color of Death   The Fem is Not Allowed to be Angry

Animal: NML   3 Fem Letter Sounds
N/In/Hen/Virgin   M/Motherhood   L/Sweet Fem Light/Ill/Ail/Hell/Hail/Elle
The Virgin   Transcends into a Mother   She is Animal   Says The Code   And it is All   Mal
Hen/He/Mal   Ann/He/Mal   Ann/Him/All   Anime/All   N/He/Mal
Here are More Animals Examples as   Her
The Donkey (Âne/Anne/N/In/Hen/Virgin) Horses (Whores) Sheeps (She/P) and the Fishes
Annie/Mal (Mal is   M/Motherhood   All)
The Word Male is So Close to Mal   but it is All Carried for Him by   Mail
An is a Connection Between One Word to Another
An   as N/In/Hen/Virgin   Has No Value/Meaning   By itself
Ann is an Old Popular Fem Name Since   Bible   Time
Ann Translates in French as   âne   or   the Donkey
Men Always Told The Fems   She Could Not Learn Anything   Or   Focus (Fuck/Us)   So
Focus   on the   Breeding
Uranus (Your   Anus   Ann/Us) is the Planet for Evolution and Creativity Those 2 Subjects Were Forbidden to The Fems   By The Code   Remember The Forbidden Tree of Knowledge   That We All Transgressed
Emma (He/Ma   A/Ma)   Aimée in French is a Fem Name   To be Loved is   être Aimée in French (A Big No from That Code)
From Ann/Anna   the Donkey   to   Emma (EMA) the Mother of   E/He   and   A/All Men   In Singular (He) and Plural (All/Men)
Those are Masc Sounds   M is Him   Too   So   Motherhood is   Entirely Masc   According to   The Code
Anne: Letter N/In/Hen/Virgin
Anne/Âne is Donkey   or   an   Ass (3 Masc Letters)
3 SSSs/Is/His/Us/Ass/Hiss/Serpent/Penisses in English
Ass is Also Butt in French

Annoy: Ann/Oy
oy: used to express dismay pain annoyance grief etc

The Dam Code The Damn Book

Annoying   N/Oy/N
When   N/In/Hen/Virgin   Surrounds Fems   Pain/Grief   with
Another   N/In/Hen/Virgin   They Could Question it   That is too Much
Information for Her   Says The Code   So
annoy: to disturb or bother (a person) in a way that displeases troubles or slightly irritates   to molest   harm
Molestation and Harm are Parts of Annoying Definition
So   it is a Dangerous Path of Questioning to Enter for Her   As She Becomes Annoying   Discussing Her Pain/Grief
A/All Men   No/Know   N/In/Hen/Virgin   A/All Men Say No   to That Chicken/Hen Clucking (See Clock in The Words Chapter)
A/No/N
A Virgin do Not Give Sex   It is Annoying
To Remain a   N/In/Hen/Virgin   is a   Big No from The
Code   So   Annoying   She is
The Fems at Any Age is   Rejected in Every Way   in That   Language Code

Annual   N/Ann/Hen/Ane/In/Virgin   You/U/Ovulating   All
Take Away One   A/All Men   and Get   Annul   or   Ann in Hell   Annul
That   Says The Code
N/Null   Which Means N is Annulled by Herself Here
Null is Made of All 4 Fems Sounds Letters
A/Nil
NL   2 Fems Sounds Letters
annul: to make void or null   abolish   cancel
Take Away   U/You/Ovulating   from Annual   and Get   Anal (Anal has No Fem Vowel   So   It would be a Man with Another Man with   N/In/Hen/Virgin   Anus is the Object of the Word Anal   Annul that   Says The Code   That Happens Only Annually   Says The Code
Also Taking about Artificial Impregnation
Switch N for P/Man Power and He Gets Pal

Anoint: Ann   Oint
anoint: to dedicate to the service of God   to rub with oil
Anointed is an Initiate Word

Anomaly: N/In/Hen/Virgin   O/Fem Hole   M/Motherhood   Mal   He/E

39

It is a Big No from The Code   to Have   Moms and Virgins   Close to their Sexuality   So No   it is an Anomaly
Ann/O/Mal/He
Mal Cannot be done by a M or N to a Man   Says The Code   So   it is an anomaly: a deviation from the common rule type arrangement or form
The Starting A is Silent here   and the Second is Hiding in Mal

Anonymous: Ann/N   On   Him   Us/Letter S/Is/His/Us/Ass/Hiss/Serpent/Penis
Ann   Own   M/Motherhood   Us
The Sound Word Start with   N/In/Hen/Virgin
Letter A/All Men   Which Open and Guide the Word is Silent here as in   Not being Seen   or   Not being there

Another: A/Nut/Her   Ann/Hot/Her
Hay/Nut/Her   Hey/Not/Her
N/In/Hen/Virgin   Hot/Hat   R/Her/Are/Whore/Heir/Sex
N/In/Hen/Virgin is Hot Under the Hat for Sex
N/Hooter   Her Goal is the Breasts
Remember that Her is   Letter R/Her/Hair/Are/Here/Hear/Ear/Whore/Or/Heir/Err/Air/Our/Sex
No Real Identity for Her here   Only Stupidity and Rejection Thrown at Her   The Word Another is Just being Another/Her   as   Whore   When it Comes to The Fems   Says The Code   It is Implied here that She is a Nut and is Hot

Answer: Ann/N   See/Letter C/See/Young Girl   R/Her/Whore/Are/Heir/Err/Sex
N/In/Hen/Virgin   is Looking at Herself as a R/Whore/Heir/Her/Are/Err/Sex   She has the Answer   Says The Code
It Enhances Her   Hence/Her
Ann/Soeur   Soeur is Sister in French   a Soft Sound
Ame Soeur is a Soul Sister
Add   F/Fem/Fuck   and Get Fencer   Fence/Her
Add G/Penis Penetration and He Gets a Gender
Add C/See/Young Girl/Young Girl and She Gets a Cancer   Because Letter C/See/Young Girl Cannot be in Front of the Word Answer   Too Much Info and Power to Her   Says The Code

The Dam Code The Damn Book

Answer is a Big Cover Word here
N   Sir
Ann/N/In/Hen/Virgin   Meet/Mate a   Sir
The   Donkey/âne/N   and the   Sir   is a Replica of Kingdom   the King and the Dumb   Kingdom
Ants/Her   Being So Small and Working So Hard   She Sees Nothing
Aunt/S/Her   Other Heavy Weights Put on Her   It Haunts/Her

Ant: NT   2 Fem Sounds Letters
Aint   Aunt
N/In/Hen/Virgin   is with   T/Fem Cross
She has Her First Loss of Blood
It is Not Important at All   It is Small As an Ant
And it Aint (Happening)   So Now She Starts to Feel Fragmented by that Huge Reality that Fell on Her   She has to Compress it All   And be Nothing   Move on   As an Ant

Antenna: Ant   Hen   A/All Men
She is an   Ant   and a   Hen   here   With All Men
There are 2 Fem Symbols in that Word   Hunt/Anna   Says The Code   Or   Hunt/Hen/A   Now the Hen (Chick/Young Girl) is being Chased by All Men
Hunt   N/In/Hen/Virgin   A/All Men   All Men Hunt that Virgin   That is How Men Use Antennas
Ann/Ten/A
Ten is the Age for The Fems to Prepare for Sex in The Code
Aunt   N/A   Be Careful about Her   She is Aging   (Aunt/Anna)   So Hunt Her Too
She Knows (But No) a Little Better Now   She is Seeing the Big Game a Little
But No   She does Not have Antennas for That Code

Anus: Ann/Ass   Ann/Us   N/In/Hen/Virgin   Ass
Anus is Almost Made Entirely of Fem Letters
Except for   S/is/His/Us/Ass/Hiss/Serpent/Penis   or to Indicate Plural as in   All Virgins
Letter S/Ass/Has/As/Is/His/Us/Hiss/Serpent/Penis   Big Biz Going On with   Anus

Âne is French for Donkey/Ass
Donkeys are Slow and Bucked Head   but   Pretty and they   Work Hard
Men Had Sex Commonly   with them   in the Past
Anne/Ann   is an Old Fem Name
It is the Letter   N/In/Hen/Ann/Virgin
Out of the Ann/Us   are   Feces
Feces is   F/Fem/Fuck   2 CC s/Young Girls/See
Feces is   Several Fems Alone Together   Says The Code
So   a Place to Hide is a Place Where No One looks
No One Wants To Look at an Anus
NS   N/In/Hen/Virgin   is in Front of   S/Is/His/Us/Ass/Hiss/Serpent/Penis
A Big No Says The Code   So   it is Anus
Switch U/You/Ovulating for O/Fem Hole   And She Gets A/Nose   which we want the Least Close to Anus
A Nose   is   Knows (for Him) and   No s (for Her)
Nose is   N/In/Hen/Virgin   Hose (His Hose (Slang for Penis) is in the Middle of Her Face Now
Know that the   Olfactory Sense   is the Oldest and Most Psychic One   and a   Powerhouse of Memory   As Your Grandma Soups Aromas etc   Someone that Has a Nose for Something
The Code Planned on that   Planet (Plan/It)   Uranus (Your/Anus)   Your Highness
Anus and Nose are Cover Words here

Any: NA   Annie
Ann/An/Âne/N/In/Hen/Virgin   and   A/All Men
Any as in   Any Virgin for All Men   Says The Code
No   N (Fem)   Can be in Front of   A/All Men   So
N/A   Means   Not Applicable
How Convenient for The Code

Anybody: N/He/Buddy   Annie/Bud/He
N/In/Hen/Virgin   is Next to   Buddy (A Buddy is a Masc Entity   Says The Code)   She is Anybody
N/He/Bud/He   A Virgin for One   A Bud for the Other
N/He/Butt/He   That Is for Her She Gets to be with Two of Him and Their Butt

The Dam Code The Damn Book

Anyhoo: Annie/Who   Any/Who
Anyhoo Sounds As Fun   But   The Fems Cannot be there   Annie (The Hen   That is The N/Virgin has No ID)
anyhoo: humorous alteration
Anyhoo in the Dictionary   is in between   Anybody   and   Anyhow
Anyhow N/In/Hen/Virgin   He/E   Ow
Annie/Ow
ow: used especially as an expression of intense or sudden pain
The Code Never Ends   The Fems Pains
Add Another   N/In/Hen/Virgin and She Gets Own Annie/Own   Ow   All These Under Intense Sudden Pain

Anymore: Ann/N/In/Hen/Virgin   Him/M/Motherhood   Whore/R/Her/Are/Heir/Sex
N/In/Hen/Virgin   E/He   More   More Virgins For Him
More is   M/Motherhood   as   Whore   or   Him/M as Whore
More of   Ann/N/In/Hen/Virgin   as Donkey (D/Pregnant   On   Key   Pregnant/On/Key)
NMR   N/M/Whore
N/In/Hen/Virgin   and   M/Motherhood   As a   Whore/Are/R/Her/Are/Whore/Sex
A Dirty Offensive and Mean Word for The Fems Here
The Code Hides its Tyranny   in Innocent Words
anymore: any longer   nowadays   presently
Here Contraries are Meeting Heavily (Eve/He/Lay)

Anything: Ann/N/In/Hen/Virgin   He   Thing/Thin
All Things Belong to Him (a Thing is Slang for a Fem)
Keeping The Fems Thin and Little   Weakens Her   A Good Thing   Says The Code
Switch T/Fem Cross for D/Pregnant and She Gets
Ann/He/Ding   D and T are Interchangeable in The Code
To Ding is to Dent   Dent is Tooth in French   Biting Implied
The 21st Jewish Letter Tooth is Shin (She In/N)   and it is Also the 13th Arabic Letter
A Shin is the Front Part of the Lower Leg
Switch T for R/Her/Whore/Are/Heir/Err/Sex and She Gets Any/Ring (See The Many Meanings of Ring in The Words Chapter)

43

Lise Rochon

She Enter a Ring to get a Beat   or   a Church Bell Rings   for Her for Different Reasons   Ring That Bell (Belle)

Anyway: N/He/Way   Ann/N/In/Hen/Virgin   He/E   Way   Annie/Way
The Way to the Virgin   is
anyway: in any case   anyhow   nonetheless   regardless
Any Way is Permitted   to Get to that   Virgin   The Code
Says   Get   In/N

Anywhere: Ann/N/In/Hen/Virgin   E/He   Wear
N/He/Where   Annie   Where
Wear
WR   W/All Fems Sex Active   R/Air/Her/Our/Hair/Are/Here/Hear/Ear/Heir/Or/Whore/Err/Sex
N   He   Where   Where   N   and   E/He   Meet for   R/Her/Hair/Are/Here/Hear/Ear/Whore/Or/Err/Sex
Anywhere   Says The Code

Apocalypse: Ape   O/Fem Hole   Call   Hips
Apocalypse is When   Her   as Ape with   Her Hole and Hips   are Calling
Ann/Letter N   is Also the   Donkey/Ann/N
apocalypse: any revelation or prophecy   any universal or widespread destruction or disaster
More Bad News from The Code for Her   She Cannot Call on a Male Sexually   It is Apocalyptical for Her

Appealing: Ape   He   Laying
The Code Says   What is Appealing about The Fems   is She is
an   Ape   That   Lays
appealing: attracting desire interest
Switch E/He for O/Fem Hole and She Gets   A/Pole/In
One that will Hop   Up/Hole/In
Apple and Appeal (ing)
If Not   Hops are good for that

Apple: Ape/All   Hop/All   Hope/All (Opal)   Up/All
Apple is a Cornerstone Word in Genesis

The Dam Code The Damn Book

The Apple has been a Grand and Mysterious Symbol of Knowledge for the Initiates   Since the Beginning of Our Age
Ape/All   is the Simplest Concept Apple Represents   but Not to Her   She Never Gets it
The Apple was the Chosen Code Word by the Good Symbology Professor Langdon (Long Done) Played by   Tom Hanks   in the Movie   The Da Vinci Code
Other Symbolic Names in that Book/Movie are the Corrupt Bishop Aringarosa   Literally To Ring A Rose (Rosecrucians   The Cross and The Rose)
The Ring has Other Deeper Meaner Meanings (See the Word Ring in the Words Chapter)   Another Good Professor is/was Sauniere (Son/He/Heir)   The Bad Chief Police Inspector Name is Faché which Means Angry in French and He is an Angry Man who wants to Criminalize Prof Langdon   It is the Bishop Ringarosa that is Commanding Him to do that   Sophie is Just a Tender/Innocent Name for Her Innocence/Ignorance
A Great Symbolic Movie
Cut an Apple in Half   When the Apple is Up
It is a Heart Shape (The Fems As it)
When the Apple is Turned Down
It is in an Ass Shape (the Masc As It)
Where there is a Hop   There is Hope
Hope is a Cover Word Here
Switch A for O/Fem Hole and She Gets Hope/All   Opal
Switch O/Fem Hole for i/Marriage Act and She Gets Hips (Letter i being the Sex Union   She Ends in Pregnancy with the Larger Hips)
Add W/All Fems Sex Active to Hip and She Gets the Whip
So   Better Hop   Hop/On   Upon   on it
The Code Says to Her   Better be a Good Ape   Ape/All   And April is So Close   Time for Sex in The Spring
Apple is The Fruit of Knowledge that was Forbidden to Humans   Where would we be if Not Knowledge be with us
Apple is Part of The Rose Family

Appease: Ape/He/Is   Ape/Ease   Hop/He/Ease   Hope is
Hope and Hopping are Appeasing   and   Are Good Things   Happy/Is   So   The Fems being Barred from Well Being in The Code   There

are No Fem Letters in Appease   So We are Only Talking about The Masc   Here

Apply: Ape/Lie
Applied: Ape/Lied
The Code   Demands that Man   Pretends   and   Aims   at Being an Ape
A/P/Lie   A/All Men   P/Man Power   Lie
And Lie About it
Ape/Lied   Happens in the Past Also   So   It is Already a Repetition   Part of Our Education   A Created Unconscious Habit   That Splits Our Mind
Hope/Lie   Ape/Laid

Approve: A/Proof   A/Prove   Up/Roof   Ape/Roof   Hop/Roof   A/Pro/V
Proof is a Legal Document
The Code Approves When She   OV/Ovulates   and Hop to the Roof   Hop/Up/Her to the Roof
Approve is Also The Power of The Pyramid that Proves That Message   It Also Starts from A   Barely Audible

Apron: Ape   Are   On   He/Prey/On   He/Pray/On
The Free Masons Use Lambskin Aprons (the Sacrificial Lamb Comes to Mind)
Ape/He/Run   And The Code   Ran Away with that too
The Best Pics of Aprons on the Internet are Mapron38c.jpgimages
Found Under Freemasons Aprons
This One is Hemmed with a Blood Red Fabric All Around
The Compass/Cuntpass (See Compass in the Words Chapter) Represents Her Open Legs
Letter   V/Fem Sex Active   is Between Her Legs
That Compass Stands Still Tall on Top of a Throne
On Top of that Throne Also Stands   a Letter V   Tool
On Top of a Pyramid which Stands on Top of the Throne   In Between Her Legs   Her Blood is Coming Out in a Chalice (See Chalice in The Words Chapter) Below

Still In the Middle of the Pyramid   The Blood Arrives in Between the Legs of the Throne
In a Shape of a Heart Right Above Two Hands with Arms Shaking in Clouds (More Secrecy)
The Hands Hold the Egg (Ov/Ovulation) on a String Ready to Fall on the Nest Below (Endless Pregnancies)
Above Her is a Star Which Represents The Fems
With Letter C/See/Young Girl   in the Middle
Above All and Around is a Rich Decorum   With Nice Swinging Forms
On the Left of the Compass
Is the Tree of Life on a Mountain (Mount/In   Month/In) Top (T/Hop)
There is a Cavern inside the Mountain
It is their Secret Meeting Place
A Sword is Lying at the Door
That Sword is in a Shape of a Cross (T/Fem Cross/Great Curse) (Jesus Cross Comes to Mind)
Hiding it All in Plain View
Ruling On Top of that Mountain is a Flamboyant Sun/Son
On the Right Side of the Apron are Columns and Columns Rings (See Columns and Rings in The Words Chapter)
On the Right Side is a Stairway with Old Secret Books In a Pile
The Last Column Up Touches a Smiley Man Head in the Clouds (Secrecy)
Both Suns are Touching the Banner (Ban/Her) Under the Stars (See Asterisk *   or   the Triple Cross for Her)
On the Banner Left Side is a V/Fem Sex Active
And a V Reversed Along the G/Hymen Perforation Letter or the God Letter   Letter G is Usually in Between the Legs of the Compass   Except In the More Modern Aprons
On the Right Side of the Banner
Symbol V is the # 5 in Roman Numerals (See the Roman Numerals Chapter)   Is a V/Fem Sex Active   Again here Also
The 3 Dots are in a Pyramid Shape (Dots are Fems)
Those Secret Societies are Only and Entirely Masc   The Dots Represents Only Fems as Drop of Bloods and Pregnancies   Which Creates the Foundation of the Shape of The Pyramid
There Were/Is so Much Shame about the Great Curse in the Past to Now   The More Time go Back   No One Could Talk about that Subject   It is/was a Shamed Unauthorized Subject

Arc: RK
R/Her/Hair/Are/Here/Hear/Ear/Whore/Or/Heir/Err/Air/Our/Sex   K/Broken Fem Warrior
The Arc Represents the Arches of Her Legs   In the Compass (Cunt/Pass) (See Letter G in The Letter Chapter) The Compass Opens Her Legs   for the Sex Act with the   G/Penis Penetration Which is There (See Pic on the Free Masons Link Apron Above   in the Apron Word)
The Word Arc is a Very Important Word for The Code (See Bow and BB)
arc: anything bow shaped
In Old Buildings the Entrance Doors were Round at the Top   So Walking Through is As Walking in Between Her Legs
Here   K/Broken Fem Warrior Letter   Transits into   Her/R/Whore/Sex Letter   After   When that Battle of The Sexes   Ends
Notice the Physical Similarities Between K and R
And   See Letter R and K in The Letter Chapter
Switch C/See/Young Girl for T/Fem Cross/The Great Curse and She Gets Art (See Art)   Art is a Cornerstone Word of the Secret Code
Switch C for D/Pregnant and She Gets Hard
Switch C for M/Motherhood and She Gets Harm or Arm
Switch C for K/Broken Fem Warrior and She Gets Ark (Not Much help Here for Her   A Farm Animal on a Ship 2000 Years Ago)
Switch C for S/His/Is/Penis and He Gets Arse (the buttocks   sexual intercourse)
Switch A/All Men for O/Fem Hole and She Gets an Orc   No Fem Allowed in The Art Secrecy   So
orc: any of the various whales such as the killer and grampus   a mythical monster as an ogre
The Code Says Kill that Big Fish (Her) with a Harpoon (See Harpoon and the Harp/On at Noon in The Words Chapter) She is a Monster
Switch C for P/Man Power and He Gets a Harp
That is The Art   On   Harpoon

Arch: Arc   She/Shh
The Arc is the Inner Curve of The Fems Legs
Arches in Buildings   All the Way   from Greek Roman   and   Ancient Old Cities   to Now
Especially in Old Official Buildings   Universities   State and   Religious Buildings With Round Arches (Many of Them Extremely High)

The Dam Code The Damn Book

It is Symbolically Walking Through Her Opened Legs as You Go in
We Go Through Arch Doors Imitating Sex
Arch is Modern for   Bow as in Bending
Bow and Arrows   Bow   Hand   R/Her/Hair/Are/Here/Hear/Ear/Whore/Or/Heir/Err/Air/Our/Sex   and   O/Fem Hole
The Arrow   R   O   R/Sex and O/Hole   Points and Penetrates   The Bow Bends for The Arrow to Go
Arc and Ark are Similar in The Code Language
The Arcane (Arc/Ann/N) of the Tarot   The Arch/Angels   Noah   Ark   Jane Of Arc   The Monarchs
A is Entirely Silent here   Arch Falls on   H/The Code   and   R/Heir/or/Whore/Her   and   C/See/Young Girl   Are There   C   is becoming   R Harsh
There are Several Definitions in the Dictionary for Arch

Archenemy: Arch   N/In/Hen/Virgin   Amy (A/Me)   Arch/Enemy   Arc/Enemy   R/Are/Her/Hair/Hear/Ear/Here/Whore/Or/Heir/Err/Our/Air/Sex   K/Broken Fem Warrior   Enemy
Letter K is the Enemy here   She (Her Stick) is being Split in Half (See Letter K in The Letter Chapter)
Archenemy: a chief enemy   Satan   the devil
Arch is a Cornerstone Word   in The Code Fabrication
And Now Learn   it is Related to   Satanic Forces
A Most Frightful Nightmare for Her   She is the Arch to be Bended here
See BB in The Words Chapter   Thread Especially Carefully there

Archer: Arch/Her   Whore/She/Her
The Forceful Opening of Her Legs for Sex is Done by   the Archer
An Archer is With the Bow and the Arc
Archer is A Code Cover Word here
The Arc Bends as in Obedience
The Arrow (R/O   Whore/Row   Whore/Ow   R/Ho)
Is the Complement of the Arc (Arc is a Bow in French) or the Bow (See Bow in The Words Chapter)
Bow Down to That
The Arrow   Is   R/Whore/Heir   O/Fem Hole
Arrows   Are   Rows   Are/Hos   Hos are Prostitutes (Another Dead End for Her)

49

The Secret Code Art Hides and Thrives   in Symbols As These Above
Arches and Domes (The Ever Expandable Breasts)
Doom   is All Fems Letters   and in Dome the   E is Silent   as in being
Anonymous   or   a Spy for The Code

Archive: Arc/Eve   Arc/Hive   Arc/I/V   (See Arc and Arch in The Words
Chapter)
The Goal of The Code is to Integrate All Fems   as in being Arched   and
in a   Hive (Bees   Workers are Fems)
When All Fems are Arched   It is Part of The Code Archives
Switch i for A/All Men and He Gets Our/Cave
archive: documents or records relating to the activities business dealings
etc of a person family corporation association community nation

Arctic: Art/IC
IC   Means   Integrated Circuit   such as   Workaholic   Alcoholic   So
The Secret Art (See Art in the Words Chapter) is/as an Integrated Circuit
It is Hidden Far Away Where No One Goes   in The Arctic of Our Mind
The Arctic is Very Cold   Few Go There
So is   Mount Everest   Where   Eve/Rest   on a Mount (Time of the
Month   When there are No Mounting) Read That Again
here is an Impossible Concept in The Code   For The Fems to Rest
So   She is Frozen Far Away   Not being Able to Move   Under The Arc/
Arched
Only Climbers (Climb/Her) go there
Arctic is a Cover Word Here

Ardor: Herd/Her   Hard/Her   Hurt/Her   Whore/Door
Her/D/Pregnant/Her
For The Fems   The Code Says   it is To Work with Ardor/Harder   to
be Part of the Herd   Where She Will Get Pregnant   To Accentuate
that Concept is the Sound Syllable   R/Her   Starting the Word Ardor
and Finishing it too   Conclusion   A Whore at The beginning   and
a   Whore   at The End
What Happened of All This Work and Ardor
ardor: great warmth of feeling fervor passion   intense devotion
Ardor is a Cover Word Here

The Dam Code The Damn Book

Are: The   Letter R
R   One of The Most Important   if Not the Most Important Letter   of Our Alphabet
Letter R has   13 Different   Connotations   and   Definitions from The Code   That I Know
Letter R/Are/Her/Hair/Here/Hear/Ear/Whore/Or/Heir/Err/Our/Air/Sex
The Code Uses those Short Words to Interfere with Our Thoughts Processing
R/Are   is in the Present   and   Plural
Switch One Whore for Another   it is Gold/Or   For The Code
Or In French   Oro is Gold in Spanish (R/Whore/Heir   O/Fem Hole)
Making   Gold/Or/Oro   a   Cover Word (How Convenient for The Code)
Add T/Fem Cross at the End and Get Art (See Art in the Words Chapter)   close to Hurt
Add 2 TTs/Fem Crosses/Great Curse and She Gets a Tart
She Must Never Know   She is That Cross   So
A Tart Means Stupid and Not Too Good at Taste
It is Also a Pie/a Tarte (So Delicious) in French   (See Pi in The Words Chapter)

Area: REA   Made of 3 Masc Letters   With   R/Sex/
Are/Her/Hair/Here/Hear/Ear/Whore/Or/Heir Err/Our/Air/Sex   E/He   A/All Men
Sex from   R/Whore/Heir   for   He/E   Individually   and   A/All Men   Globally
Any Particular Space Surface or Area will Do to Perform
The Fems has No Identity Here   Except as the   R/Whore/Heir
The A is Silent here   Anonymity   is What The Code Need
Add N/In/Hen/Virgin and She Gets Arena (Where She is Probably Sacrificed)
A is Silent here Again

Arena: RNA
R/Are/Whore/Heir/Her   Ann/N/In/Hen/Virgin
   A/All Men
The Arena is Where the   N/Virgin   as a   R/Whore/Heir   meet with   A/All Men (And One A   Spying or Organizing)

51

arena: the oval space in the center of an Roman amphitheater for gladiatorial combats or other performances   a central stage a ring area or the As used for sports or other forms of entertainment surrounded by seats for spectators   a field of conflict activity or endeavor
A Sphere is a Fem Shape   Therefore a Fem Symbol   Oval (Ov All   Ovulation For All Fems)
Arena   A/Reina   Reign   Reine is Queen in French
The Fem is the Queen of the Day   When
N/In/Hen/Virgin   is being Transformed into a   R/Whore
A Big Game   Where She loses Her Battle   to A/All Men in The Arena to the Unknown Code
A Bigger Shame (She/Aim) for Her

Argue: R/Her/Hair/Are/Here/Hear/Ear/Whore/Or/Heir/Err/Air/Our/Sex   G/Penis Penetration   U/You/Ovulating/Holy Cup/Chalice
Take Away R and She Gets Hag/You   (See Rag/Nag in The Words Chapter)

Ark: Noah Ark and the Flood
Men could do Nothing   to Stop   the Red Fem Blood Flood
So   they Built a Ship (She/P) to Float on it   Symbolically
Switch K/Broken Fem Warrior for B/Boy Holding All Fem Breasts   and He Gets a Bark   (He is Too Young for The Code but He can Scream/Bark at His Mother and Sisters   It Helps The Code to Weaken Her Some More)
Add D/Pregnant and She Gets Dark   The Code Keeps The Fems in the Dark   (See Night in the Words Chapter)
Switch K for M/Motherhood and She Gets Harm
Switch K for She/Shh and She Gets to Arch (See Arch   R/Her/Hair/Are/Here/Hear/Ear/Whore/Or/Heir/Err/Our Air/Sex   She/Shh)
arch: a chief   a mischievous person
Switch K for T/Fem Cross and She Gets Art (T/Fem Cross/Her)   Hurt is Close
The Arts are The Secret Society Code Rituals

Arm: RM   Harm   When The Code (Letter H) Hits Her   It Harms Her
There are No   Arm/Her   in The Words Code for Her   Except the Armor in Which Case   Only Men Gets to Wear It
Again A is Silent   The Code Rules from Far

The Dam Code The Damn Book

Army: Harm/He   Arm/He
The Language Never Created Fem Words for that Purpose
We Could Have had a Fem Army Called Arm/Her   or   Arm/
She   But   No Says The Code
Take Away Letter R/Her/Hair/Are/Here/Hear/Ear/Heir/Or/Whore/Err/Air/Our/Sex
And Get   Ham/He   That is Her as   Ham   and   He/E
There were No Fem in the Military for Thousand Years
Especially No Fem Army   The Amazons got Extinguished Fast
Amy Survived as a Fem Name

Around: R/Heir/Her/Whore/Are/Sex   Round
She is Round When   D/Pregnant
D   Ends the Word   Around
A   Round   A/Whore/Hound   Her/Hound   Are/
Hound   R   Hound   Are/On/D
hound: breed of dogs   any dog   a despicable person
From the Word Hound   Take   H/Secret Code Letter Away Add R That
Dog Gets to be Round (Pregnant) too
Again the Innocents (Animals and Her) are Mixed with Something that
Conceptually Make it Shadowy and Ugly   So   No One Wants that
In The Code   the Dog is the   Fem/Bitch   and   a Bad Person to be
With   It is Another Curse on Her   It Surrounds (Sure/Round) Her
around: in circumference   in a circle   to surround
Circles are Entirely Fem

Arouse: A/Rose
When The Fem has Sex   or   Is/His   Aroused
Her Loins Looks As a Rose (See Rosicrucian)
A Rose   Arose   Arrows   Arrow/Us
R   Us   More Than One Rose
R   Rose (See Rosicrucian   The Rose and The Crux/Cross)
A/All Men   Rose (From That Rose)
R   Hose (R and the Hose (Penis in Slang)

The Arrow and its Bow (See Arc in the Words Chapter)
Are/Rows   Whore/Rows   Her/Rows   R/Owe
Keep those Fem in Rows   The Enemy has Arrows

Lise Rochon

RS   Letter R/Her/Hair/Are/Here/Hear/Ear/Whore/Or/Heir/Err/Air/Our/Sex   and   S/is/His/Us/Ass/Hiss/Serpent/Penis   Together
The Fems as   R/Whores/Sex   with   S/His/Serpent
RS   Whores are In Plural
arouse: to stimulate sexually   stir to action
Arousal: A/Rose/All
R/Whore/Her/Or/Heir   Hose   All/Letter L/Ill/Ail/Sweet Fem Love Life
The Hose is in Action with the   R/Sex   to All
A/Ross/All
Ross is the Color of Dry Red Blood   The Fems Knows That Color   For Many Generations
Switch R for L/Fem Light/Ill/Ail/Hell/Elle and She Gets Allow (All Owe)

Arrangement: R/Whore/Her/Are/Our/R/Her/Hair/Are/Here/Hear/Ear/Whore/Or/Heir/Err/Air/Our/Sex   Hinge   E/He   Meant
Sex is the Hinge   The Code   Meant It that Way
hinge: a jointed device   pivot
pivot: a pin point or short shaft on the end of which something rests and turns or upon and about which something rotates or oscillates
The Pivot Turns the Wheel (See Wheel of Time)
It is this Pivotal Effect that Perpetuate the Wheel (W/All V/Fem Sex Active   Hell/Ill/Elle)   of Time   on a Dime
With   N/In/Hen/Ann/Virgin   and   G/Hymen Perforation
The Virgin is in for a Sure Hymen Penetration
To Make that Wheel of Hell Continue (Cunt/He/Knew)
The Pivot   The P   Keep the V/Fem Sex Active Hot

Arrest: Letter R/Her/Hair/Are/Here/Hear/Ear/Whore/Or/Heir/Err/Air/Our/Sex   Rest
The Code Says   If the Whore Rest   She Gets Arrested
S/Is/His/Us/Ass/Hiss/Serpent/Penis   T/Fem Cross   Many Words Ends in ST   a Direct Connection Between 666 and The Great Curse   (ST   is The Serpent Hissing)

Arrive: R/Her/Are/Hair/Are/Here/Hear/Ear/Whore/Or/Heir/Err/Air/Our/Sex   Hive
R   and   Hive (All/Eves   Letter V/Fem Sex Active   In Plural)
R   Hive   The Hive is Where Whores Live

The Dam Code The Damn Book

It is a Rêve (Rêve is Dream in French)
Lots of Arriving Points   Here for   Him
Bees are an Important   Working Fem Symbol in   The Code
Letter A   The Boss   Is Silent   Almost   Invisible   Blending in with R
Arriving: R/Her/Hair/Are/Here/Hear/Ear/Whore/Or/Heir/Err/Air/Our/
Sex   i/Marriage Act   V/Fem Sex Active   N/In/Hen/Virgin
From Virgin to V as Whore   Where She Arrives with Him
Are/Hive/N   R/Hive/N
A/Rêve/N
That would be a Too Close and Dangerous Meet for Her for The
Code   Even in a Dream   So it is a
ravine: steep valley eroded by running water
Water (Fem Symbol) is Powerful   It Creates Ravines   Few Dare to Go in
Ravines   No Fem there   The Code is Safe
R/Eve/Vin   Vin is Wine in French   Here The Wine Just Appeared   Along
with Eve (See Blood and Wine in The Words Chapter)

Arrow: RO
R/Her/Hair/Are/Here/Hear/Ear/Whore/Or/Heir/Err/Air/Our/Sex   Is to Aim
(Letter M/Motherhood) that Arrow at the   O/Fem Hole

Arse: Ours   Whores   Are   Horses   Hours
arse: origin is ass   sexual intercourse   anus   buttocks   a stupid person   fool
In The Code Letter   S/Is/His/Us/Ass/Hiss/Serpent/Penis   is   Ass/Us/
Asses   All those SSSS
Ass as in   SSS/Serpent   it Hiss   Sex/Sex/Sex (SXSXSX   See Letter   X/
Fallen Fem Cross)
Plus   Letter S   It Pluralizes
Ass is   A/All Men   with   2 SSs/Is/His/Us/Ass/Hiss/Serpent/Penis
Twice a Letter Indicates Plural or All of Them
There are Only Masc Letters in Ass
The Code Often Associates Sex in the Same Word with Concepts of
Vulgarity and Stupidity
There is a Jump here from S/Ass   being Masc   and   Arse   being a
Donkey Letter   N/Virgin   and Defining itself as a Fem   N/In/Hen/Ane/
Ann/Virgin

The Arse/Ours/Horses/Whores/Hours (See Clock) are All in the Same Category here   They are All Fems
Here All the Words Definitions Acts as Cover Words for Each Other Covers   And Create a Bigger Stronger Hypnotic Picture of   The Code   in the Same Time
A is Silent as Usual   here with R   And So Close to Art (See Below)

Art: RT
Art   Earth   Hearth   Heart   Hurt   Those
are   Important   Inspiring   Humanistic Words
They Follow Along   Under The Code Sound World Control   of that Important Word   Art
Art is One of the Biggest Cover Word in The Code
The Art or the Ancient Arts is the Name Given to the Rites of the Ancient Secret Societies
Those Initiates Were Permitted Over Time to Know
More of the Great Curse Secrets
The Code Meaning for The Code is Art   RT   The R/Whore/Heir   and T/ The Fem Great Curse
R/Her/Hair/Are/Here/Hear/Ear/Whore/Or/Heir/Err/Air/Our/Sex   and   T/ Fem Cross/Great Curse
Adding Different Letters to Art Attaches Other Concepts
Those Narrow Down the Word Meanings in Smaller Affiliates Concepts
Add Letter B/Boy Holding All Fem Breasts and He Gets to be Bart (Too Young for The Code)
Add C/See/Young Girl and She Gets a Cart   To Get there   to the   T/ Fem Cross   Faster   She is Ready for it   Says The Code
Add D/Pregnant and She Gets a Dart
Add F/Fem/Fuck and She Gets a Fart (She is Not Allowed in The Art)
Add M/Motherhood and She Gets Mart
mart: a cow or ox to be fattened for slaughter   a fair
Add S/Is/His/Us/Ass/Hiss/Serpent/Penis and He Gets Smart
Add P/Man Power and He Gets a Part
Add a Second T/Fem Cross that Makes Her a Tart
Add W/All Fems Sex Active and They Get Warts
Dart   Fart   Tart   Wart   are Code Symbols to Keep Her Out From Looking/Hearing Anything from The Code

The Dam Code The Damn Book

Switch A for U/You/Ovulating/Uterus and She Gets Hurt (Her/T)   a Normal Situation for a Uu   Says The Code
Art for Him   Hurt for Her
Add   ST   S/is/His/Us/Ass/Hiss/Serpent/Penis and T/Fem Cross at the Beginning of Art and it Becomes a Start   Always Restart   The Art (with S and T)
st: variant of –est   *first least*   a suffix forming the superlative degree of adjectives and *adverbs*   *shortest fastest*
Switch T/Fem Cross (T The Pivoting Letter   That Eventually Creates a Wheel) for S/Is/His/Ass/Hiss/Serpent/Penis and He Gets Arse (Ass/Sex)
That is an Example   on How   The False Magic of that Art
is   Activated   and   Applied
The Art Turns into a   Ass/Donkey   (See   Ane/Anne   and Arse   in The Words Chapter)
Basically That Code would   Not Exist if   The Fem Cross/Great Curse   would Not   be there
Note RS/Arse Ends with a Silent E   Which Indicate Secrecy   2 Silent Letters in   arse   A and E

Artery: Art   Hear   He
Someone that Can Hear the Art in the Word Artery has Lost its Way in Trying to Decipher That Code   Unless They are Talking about Her Blood Loss (See Body Parts in Words Chapter)
An Artery Carry The   Blood
Wine   and   Chalice   Follow/Flow
Hurt   Her   He
For Her The Hurt   For Him The Art
Art/Her/E   The Great Art is About Her
Get to the Artery   The More The Blood Loss   the More The Better   Says The Code
Arthur/He   Heart/Her/He   See King Arthur in The Holy Grail Book (The   Hole/He   Girl)
See Arthur below

Arthur: Art/Her   Hurt/Her
Arthur is a Very Old Name
Britain 5th Century King Arthur is Known to Us from Chretien de Troy's (12th Century) who Wrote The Holy Grail Story

The Story of The Excalibur the Sword (Masc Symbol) Stuck in the Stone (Fem Symbol   The Roc)   The King Bleeding Lance (The Blood Loss on His Penis) The Knights Of the Round (Fem) Table and the Holy Grail (Holy/Girl) as a Chalice (See Chalice   Blood   Wine) or a Cup (Fem Symbol for the Cups which also Represents the Hearts in Cards
The 3 Crowns Ornaments on King Arthur Blazon are the Fleur de Lys Symbols (See Fleur de Lys in The B3 Chapter in Words)
The Holy Grail is a Metaphorical Novel and a Symbolistic Translation for The Fems Loss of Blood   Tragedy   That King Arthur Experiences in The Novel
A Very Powerful Book
Think Back Then There was No Electricity Little Running Water Very Little Education and a Lot of Superstitions
Clothes and Cotton were Rare and Home Made
But The Fems was Bleeding   Regularly then too
And Always a Little More and a Little Earlier in Life
A Nightmare (Night/Mare) for Any Fem and Masc
A Death Sentence for Many Fem
There was No Hygiene then
And The Great Curse was Already on Her   from the Catholic Church
The Fem was Called Satan Cursed   Evil (When in Fact it is   Eve   that is   Ill   Eve/ill) etc
The Bleeding Lance was Arthur Penis when it was Coming Out from Her After Sex   His Organ was Covered with Blood and He was Freaking Out   Read the Book   Imagine that in the 5th Century   For All The Fems The Same

Artisan: Art   He   San/Sun/Son
Heart/He/Son   Hurt/He/Sun
san: extremely religious person   righteous person   a Saint
Men Titles in The Code are Strong and Clean In Definition
Here   Being an Artisan Makes That Man Not Educated to Understand The Code   But   He as a Man takes Advantage of all The perks   such as being   A Son   A Sun   A Saint   Etc
The Fems Gets Nothing of That   She is the Daughter Dot/Her (See Letter i l/The Dot/Dowry   in The Letter Chapter)
Thee/D/Pregnant   Dough   T/Fem Cross   Her/R/Whore/Or/Heir/Sex

The Dam Code The Damn Book

As: AS
A/All Men   and their   S/Is/His/Us/Ass/Hiss/Serpent/Penis
as: to the same degree amount or extent   similarly   equally
Add Another S/His/Us/Ass/Hiss/Serpent/Penis and He Gets an Ass/
Donkey   Which is a Hen   N/In/Hen   Ann/Ane   He Gets Both here   a
Donkey and a Hen   or a   Donkey as a Hen
Ass is 2 Masc Letters   and a   Repeat
Ascend: Ass/End   Ass/And   Ass/Hand
The Word Ascension Starts with an Ass/S Sound   Then Another   If it
does Not Work   The Hand will do it   Ascend/Rise to That   Says The
Code
Ascending: Ass/Ending
Ass   End   In/Ann/N/In/Hen/Virgin   The Ass Ends with the
Virgin   Ending in   D/Pregnant
Ass   And   Ding   Here is the Hurt for Her
Ding That Thing   Ping/it   Ring/it   Thing/Tin/it   Sing it   Sign it
When   S/Is/His/Us/Ass/Hiss/Serpent/Penis   is   in/N
ping: to produce a sharp sound As that of as bullet striking a sheet of
metal
No Ascending for Her   That Code is Serious

Ashes: HS
The   H/Secret Code Letter   and the   S/Is/His/Us/Ass/Hiss/Serpent/
Penis (All of Them or Plural)
A/All Men   She/Shh   S/Is/His/Us/Ass/Hiss/Serpent/Penis
When She as Shh (Silence) Is Surrounded by All Men Penisses in Secret   It
is Ashes   Nothing to Recover

Ass: A/All Men   and   2 SSs/Is/His/Us/Ass/Hiss/Serpent/Penises
Asses has   3 SSS s   in Plural
Ass is Made Entirely of Masc Letters
All of Men of The Pyramid and their Penisses are All Equal
Ass is a Cover Word here
The Ass is the Donkey   The Ass is Transferred to Her as Âne/Ann/N/In/
Hen/Virgin The Donkey
She Belong to   All Men Asses/Is/His/Hiss/Serpent/Penisses

Ashamed: She/Shh   Aim   She/Âme

Lise Rochon

The Code Says   The Fems Aims   in Silence   In Her Soul   in Shame   Until Her Death (Ashes   A/She/Is) (The Fems are Never Anything in That Code   Ashes here)
The Fems is the   One Being   Blamed for the Great Curse of Humanity   She Carries that Word Shame as a Shadow
The Fems are Taught   Aim at being Dolls and Dull   Then She Gets Blamed for being Stupid
Her Sense of Aim in Life is Blurred from the Start from That Code
Âme is the Word Soul in French   It is Alma in Spanish   Alma is a Fem Name   The Code Says   All/Ma   All Mothers
The Code Diminishes The Fems in Every Aspect   to   No Worth   Until She/Is Totally   Invisible   or/and   Non Existent

Aside: Ass/Hide   As/Hide   S/Hide   A/Side
He Hides   His   Hide/Saddle/Ass/Penis
aside: apart from   except for

Ask: SK   S/Is/His/Us/Ass/Hiss/Serpent/Penis/Plural   K/Broken Fem Warrior
It is Basically a Fight Involving Her Sexual Organs and the Ass (Homosexuality for Him if He Loses)
Ass/K
Letter K is the Axe Sound (Letter X/Fallen Fem Cross is Under the Axe)   She Dies here to be Reincarnated as R/Her/Hair/Are/Here/Hear/Ear/Whore/Or/Heir/Err/Air/Our/Sex   Where She is Represented by that Top Circle Being Held by Her Broken ½ Stick (See Letters K and R in The Letter Chapter)
Ass/Kick   S/K/K
One   S/Is/His/Us/Ass/Hiss/Serpent/Penis   here can Fight 2 KK s   and Win
For Her No Asking Allowed   If She Ask She Loses to Death
Switch S for R and Get Ark

Asking: S/King
S/Is/His/Us/Ass/Hiss/Serpent/Penis   and the   King
Men Are Always Close to their Penisses   All the Way to the Highest King In All Ranks   The Code is Being Endlessly Flattering Itself   You will Not Find that Anywhere about The Fems

The Dam Code The Damn Book

Asleep: Letter S/Is/His/Us/Ass/Hiss/Serpent/Penis   Leap
When All is Asleep   He Leaps Out
leap: to move or act quickly or suddenly

Aspire   SPR   A/Spear
S/Ass/His/Is/His/Us/Ass/Hiss/Serpent/Penis   P/Man Power   Higher
(High   R/Her/Hair/Are/Here/Hear/Ear/Whore/Or/Heir/Err/Air/Our/Sex
Ass   Pire   A Pire is a Fire
Aspire is   The Man Penis in Fire   Gets Him Higher
Take Away P from Pire and Get Ire
i/Stick   R/Her/Hair/Are/Here/Hear/Ear/Whore/Or/Heir/Err/Air/Our/Sex
Because the Word ire Starts with i which is the Sex Union Letter and The
Fems there are   The Dot   Followed by   R/Her/Hair/Are/Here/Hear/
Ear/Whore/Or/Heir/Err/Air/Our/Sex   Again   She cannot Start a Word as
Powerful as ire   A Big No Says The Code   So
ire: intense anger   wrath
And The Code has the Pire (Has/Pire   Aspire) for that
Pire in French Means Worst
S/Ass   P/Man Power   R/Hire   And Bringing Prostitution Along

Assassins: SSNS   Ass/S/Is/His/Us/Ass/Hiss/Serpent/Penis   N/In/Hen/
Virgin   S/Ass
5 SSSSSs/Is/His/Us/Ass/Hiss/Serpent/Penisses   here   Surrounding
that   N/Virgin   and Coming at Her As Assassins   Until   S/
Penis   is   In/N/Virgin
A Cover Word for Homosexuality or/and
Too Many S/Is/His/Us/Ass/Hiss/Serpent/Penisses Together As in an
Army   Testosterone Levels are High
Not Enough Love   Kills

Assault: S/Ass/Is/His/Us/Hiss/Serpent/Penis   Halt
S   L/All/Ill/Sweet Fem Love Light/Hail/Ail/Hell/Elle   T/Fem Cross
If Sex Stops She Gets an Assault

Asset: S/Is/His/Us/Ass/Hiss/Serpent/Penis   Hit
Ass/It   As/It   S/Hat   Asses/Hit   Ace/It
When S and the Hat (Secret Code Symbol) from Art   Meet (Mate) it Hits
an Asset (Ace/Hit)

61

asset: a useful and desirable thing or quality

Asshole: S/Is/His/Us/Ass/Hiss/Serpent/Penis   is with   O/Hole
Ass/Hole   Has/Hole   Has/Whole   S/All
Letter O (and The Word Hole) is Depicted Here   as a Hole Only   No Gender Identity
Homosexuality is Common at All Times in Our History
And so was Sex with Animals (See   the Arse/Ass   the Horse/
Whores   The Donkey/Ann   The Sheeps   etc)
Although According to The Secret Code Symbology of Letters   The Letter O/Hole is Fem   So here   She is the Ass   and   the Ass/Hole (See Donkey as N/Ann/Ane/In/Hen/Virgin)
And The Code Calls it   A/Soul   Same for the Sole   it is Under The Feet and is also Called a   Flat Fish

Assess: 4 SSSSs   And Only One Sound   The   S/Hiss
S/Is/His/Us/Ass/Hiss/Serpent/Penises   in Plural
Ass   in Plural is   Asses
A/All Men   Sys/Sis as in Sisters   Sissies   It is Systemized
All Men with Sisters   or   All Men with Asses   Evaluate before Choosing
assess: to estimate officially the value of (property income etc) as a basis for taxation   to estimate or judge the value character etc of   evaluate
Assess   is a Decision Maker Word   So   The Word is Entirely Masc
The Hiss Keeps it Well Guarded

Assist: Has 3 SSSs/Is/His/Us/Ass/Hiss/Serpent/Penisses
Asses   with   T/Fem Cross
S   is to   Assist   The Fem Cross with   Many More Penisses (Which means More Pregnancies And More Decadence for Her) to The Way of the Fem Cross/The Great Curse
assist: a mental or emotional position adopted with respect to something

Assistance: S/Is/His/Us/Ass/Hiss/Serpent/Penis   He/E   Stance
It is All About the Masc   The Code and What it Stands for
S/Is/Stance   Penisses are the Standard to get Assistance

The Dam Code The Damn Book

That is His Tent   and He Stands for it
The Code Hide in Tents (Intents)   A Tent is in a Pyramid Shape
As Usual Letter A is Hiding in Silence   After Starting the Word

Associate: S/Is/His/Us/Ass/Hiss/Serpent/Penis   Us/Penis   He/Ate
That is a Close Body   Especially to do it Twice
In That Code   The Associate   is the   S   that   Eat   Penis   a Blow
Job   Some Associates Will do that
Ass/S   O/Fem Hole   She/Shh   Ate/Hate   She Gets to Eat it Too   As
the   Ass/Arse/Donkey/Ane/Ann/In/N/Virgin

Association: Ass/O/See/A/She/On
The   Ass/N/Donkey/Ane/In/Hen/Virgin)   is What a Fem Gets to
See   from   A/All Men   in the Words Association
That Association Is   The Union   Presented to   Her/R   by   The Code
Being   Her Marriage to   Him/M/Motherhood   Via   That Code Rules

Assume: Ass   You/U/Ovulating   M/Motherhood
Assume Being a Fem an   Arse/Ass   When Mother   Says   The
Code   As/You/M

Assumption: Ass/S/Is/His/Us/Hiss/Serpent/Penis   Hump   She/On
The Code Assumption is That Humans will Continue to Think About
themselves   as Asses   The Fem Ass   N/Donkey Ass/Ane/Ann/In/Hen/
Virgin)   and the   Masc Ass/His/Hiss/Penis
They have been Humping Animals for an Eon (He/On)   It will Happen
(Hop/In) to Continue
That is Why Consciousness is Important to Our Development   So We
can Build a World that Resembles Us   and Can Grow   Happy and
Satisfied   Living In It

Assure: Ass/Sure   As/Sure   Ass/Your   As/Your
S/Is/His/Us/Ass/Hiss/Serpent/Penis   To The Fems   Be Sure   that They
are as   Asses (Donkey)
as: similarly
If   Ass   Loses an   S   it is the Same Anyway   with As   Be A/
Sure   Be Assured   With D/Here Added   Pregnancy is On The Way

At: A/All Men   T/Fem Cross
All Men and the Great Curse
at: to indicate
A   The Pyramid Letter   Points   at the   Great Curse
The Word Hat (H/At) is a Cover Word for the Secret Arts   This is Where it is At
Hat   Had   and   Add (See the Plus Sign in the Keyboard Chapter)
From   As/Ass (S/Penis (Above)   to   At (T/Fem Cross)   In The Hat   It is The Art Talking
Note here that ST Connected makes the   -ist   which is Defined Below in Atheist

Atheist: Hate/He/Ist   Hat/He/Ist   At/He/Ist
-ist: a person who performs a certain action   a person who advocates a particular doctrine system or relating to such a person or the doctrine advocated
Atheists are Not Necessarily Haters   It Comes Out that Way in The Code World   The Code Hates the Atheists They Do Not Belong to Their Religions   And   They Stay Close to Their Hat
Flutist   Harpist are Artists   (The Code Steal Words and Keep the Meaning for Themselves)

Attack: Hat/Hack   At/Hack   At/A/K
A Hack from the Hat
The Attack is Towards   K/Broken Fem Warrior   By   A/All Men   Twice   Which are Circling that Cross the   T/Great Curse   And are Pushing on to K   Under Attack
The Mean Code   Creates Mean/Men (Add T/Fem Cross and She Gets Meant   As in The Code Mean it   (See Hack Definition below)
It was   Meant in the Past   as it is   Meant Now   The Code Attacks   Do Not Get Close to that Hat (See Hat in The Words Chapter)
hack: to cut notch slice chop or sever something with or as with heavy irregular blows

Attention: Hat   N/In/Hen/Virgin   She   On   A/Tent/She/On
Under The Code Hat   She Has been Kept   Under that Tent/Veil/Pyramid Shape   for an Eon

The Dam Code The Damn Book

The Tent Shape Represents the Veil   Not Only The Veil of Secret Knowledge Which I Rip Here   Also That Veil That The Fems are Always So Close to Fall Under
The Tent is Also The Separation of Knowledge Between The Fems and The Mascs   A Form of   The Glass Ceiling
That is 2 Coverings on Her Head
The Code Ordering   Attention   She Better have Her tent On   The Mullahs Used to Beat the Fems at the Market Just for Showing an Ankle   That Veil has been a   Serious   Damaging   Experience for the Fems Especially
Attention   is a Military Command   A Tent She On

Attic: A/Dick   (See House)   Add/Dick   Hat/IC
IC is an Integrated Circuit (Hic)
T/Fem Cross (Twice as in Several of them or Plural)   and   D/Pregnant   are Interchangeable in   The Code   So   D/Pregnant   will   become T/Fem Cross   Says The Dick/Code in The Attic   It is an   Integrated Circuit
Ticks

Attitude: Hat/He/Tude   At/He/Tude
tude: suffix indicating a state or condition
The Code Hat is/His On
Switch T for L/Sweet Fem Light/Ill/Ail/Hell/Elle and She Gets Altitude   Above as/and Below is The Code   so   Nothing There For Her)

Attract: Hat/Rack   At/Rack
A Hat (See Art/Hat) on the Rack (Her Breasts)
A/Track is the Way to Follow
Switch A/All Men for O/Fem Hole and She Gets a Hot/Rack
Switch last T for K/Broken Fem Warrior And She Gets on Track   with Racks   Which is Breasts In Slang
The Attraction is on The Rack

Attractive: A/Tract/Eve   Hat/Rack/Eve
All V/Fem Sex Active on the Same Tract
Big Breasts is the Way to be Attractive   Says   The Code
Keep that on Tract

65

tract: a brief treatise or pamphlet for general distribution usually on a religious or political topic

Audience: Odd/He/Hens   Ode/He/Hence
Note that   Odd   Spells with All Fems Letters
To Make Her Odd   is Another Way to   Weaken Her
Making Her Lose Her Human Individuality and being Assimilated as a Conceptual Hen
And   Taking it as a Compliment from the Audience
hence: from this time   for this reason
The Fems are Chickens (Hen/N/In/Ann/Virgin   Chicks)   Horses (Whores)   Dogs (Bitches)   The Code List of Her Animal Names is Long   That is How it is Played in The Code
Ode/He/Hence

Aunt: Haunt   Hunt
The Shadow of Fear is Always with The Fems   Even When She is The Loving Kind and Full of Wisdom   As an Auntie Is (I Learned That in Hawaii)   Children Love Those
But No   The Code Says   It Haunts and Hunts Those
Compare to Uncle   On/Call   One/Call
One Call and He is Gone
The Code Stays Away from those Shadowy Figures Depicting The Fems

Austere: S/Tear   Us/Dare
Austerity: S/Tear/Hit/He   Us/Tear/Hit/E   Oust/Her/He/T
If it is About Hitting Tears and Rejection   Then It is All About Her Esther   All Fems Names   are Connected to a   Form of oblivion: the state of being completely forgotten or unknown   the act or process of dying out

Authority: O/Tore/Hit/T
The Fem   as   O/Fem Hole   is Torn   Being Hit   to be a   T/Fem Cross/Great Curse   Or
A/Hot/Whore/Hit/He
O/To/Rite/He   How to Write He   How to Rite He
The Rite for Him Is to Tear Her
Rite/Write/Right   All Powerful Code Words

The Dam Code The Damn Book

Hot/Whore/He/T
When The Fems is a Hot Whore and a Cursed T/Fem Cross
The Authority of The Code is in Action Here
Hot/R/Hit/E
When the Whore is Hot there is a Hit
Hot/Her Author   Fits with Rite and Write   and Hit/T
Hit/Her   Hat/Her   Hut/Her   Out/Her   Finish those Words with Rite/He
(Poor Situation for Her)
Ut is a Musical Tone that Gives a Tone As a D (Re) (D/Pregnant)
All Are Cover Words here

Avail: A/Veil
avail: value   advantage   to be of use   to profit   to serve
Avail is a Very Scary and Dangerous Word/Concept for The Fem
The Code Tries Endlessly to Put Her Back Under that Veil   And Presents it
as an   Advantage or Extra value   in Her Life (See Veil)
A/Veil   V/Ail
ail: to cause pain   trouble
That Veil Destroys Her Freedom Her Power and Hides Her Face
The Code is Adamant (See Adam   A/Dam) about the Veil   She Will
Always be Under the Veil
pre: earlier than   an advance
Prevail (Pre/Veil) is in the Present Past and Future
prevail: to succeed   become dominant   to be widespread or current

Available: A/Veil/Able
A/All Men   Able the Veil   Says The Code

Average: Every/Age   Eve/Her/Age
Every Fem is Average   Says The Code
ave: hail   welcome   farewell   goodbye
Eve/Rage
Welcome to The Age of Eve   Where Eve Rages   That is Why it is So
Average

Avoid: A/Void
A/All Men   The Code Create Voids   to Avoid   Hot Potato
Subjects   Such as   AVD (All Fems Pregnant)

Aw: A/All Men   W/All Fems Sex Active
When   A/All Men   Meet/Mate   All Eves
aw: protest   disbelief   disgust   sugary or sentimental approval
Add E/He to Aw it Becomes Awe
awe: power to inspire fear or dread   an overwhelming feeling of reverence admiration produced by what is grand sublime extremely powerful or the As
Because   W/All Fems Sex Active   is in Between   A/All Men   and   E/He   in Awe   It is an Expression of Fear Dread Veneration and Wonder for Her   Says The Code
Awe   HA
H/Secret Code letter   A/All Men
The Secret Code Says   it Keeps All Men   in Awe and Hope   Instead it Bring Desperation to All

Awake: A/Wake
A/Way/K
A   Way   for the   K/Broken Fem Warrior   But No
A/W/Ache
A/All Men   and   W/All Fems Sex Active   Ache
Awakening as the Ultimate Liberation   Buddha Said   That First
wake: watch   rites   vigil   funeral
Awakenings   should be About Experimenting Life   Not Framing it   Around Rituals For The Fems Especially
To Awake to That Code is Not   A/Walk   in the Park
Awake is a Strong Word

Award: A/Word   is a Code Word   Guarded Closely
A/Ward for Her   A/Word for Him
ward: the action or process of guarding
If Someone Understand The Code Even Just a Little   It is Awe/Heard   Or   Ow/Hard   Depending on How The Code Acts
It Becomes a Reward   When Letter   R/Her/Are/Ear/Hear/Our/Whore/Or/Heir/Err/Air/Our/Sex   Starts the Word

Away: A/Way   Hey/Way   Hay/Way   He/Way
Letter A as in   A/All Men   for Him   Hay as in Cattle Food for Her
Hey is a Common Greeting Expression

The Dam Code The Damn Book

So The Code does it   Infiltrating Itself inside Our Brains
The Way of   A/All Men   is to be Away

Awful: A/Fool   A/All Men   are with   Fools (Fems)
Full/Fool is Made of All Fems Letters
Awe/Full   The Fem is in Awe   When Full (Pregnant)   But No Says The Code   it is Awful

Axe: X/Fallen Fem Cross   is   T/Fem Cross Fallen   on Its Side
A/All Men   X/Fallen Fem Cross   E/He
In the Word Axe Letter   A/All Men   Starts the Word as a Group and the Letter E/He Closes the Word as One Man (A/All Men   and   E/He)   So X is Surrounded
The   X/Fallen Fem Cross/Fem Sacrifice/Great Curse   Has Perished   She is Now Dead
Letter X is the Last Letter of the Alphabet that Deal with that Cross
Y was added there as a New Letter and Z is the Last Symbol from The Code   As in Sleep on it
It is Indicated by the Shape of Z   As Above as Below
Letter X is the Sound of an Axe
She Fell Under that Axe Under Letter X
Switch X for K/Broken Fem Warrior
And She Gets Hacked
Always Back to the Deep Hurt for Her
The Whores and the Animals
hack: to cut with repeated irregular or unskilled blows   a horse let out for common hire
To be X Out of Somewhere   Ex   Ex/Spouse   Executed   Letter X is Terminal
Letter X is the Sign Symbol for those Who Cannot Sign Their Name   And The Code Loop is Complete   All the Way to ID Yourself

Axis: Axe/His   Axe/Is   X/Is   X/His
X/Fallen Fem Cross/Great Curse   is On with Axis
This is When The Fems Is Programmed to Turn on an Axis
As in Going in Circles (Cycles)
It is The Menstrual Cycle Always Repeating Itself
Axis is a VIP Word in The Code

axis: the line about which a rotating body such as the earth turns
That Line can be Real or Imaginary
Then there is the Deer Axis (Dear/Her)
Clock Needles Rotate Around an Axis
Anything Round is Fem in That Code

Axle: Axe/X/Fallen Fem Cross   All/Ill/Ell/Sweet Fem Love Light
axle: pole or pin upon a wheel revolves
(See Wheel of Time in The Words Chapter)

Azure: As/Her   Ass/Her
A Perfect Day for That   Says The Code
azure: a clear blue sky   a light purplish blue
Purple is the Mix of Color   Red/Blood/Fem Color   and   Blue/Masc Color
A Dream for   The Code

B b
Intro
B Is a Masc and Fem Letter
It is a Stick that Holds 2 Half Circles
B is the Young Boy Letter (Baby Boy)
B (He) is the Stick Holding Her Breasts to Keep them Full
As a Domesticated Cow has/is
Letter B is the Number 3 Symbol (Her 2 Breasts and a Stick Holding it   Makes a 3) the Bar/Stick Barring it   How Convenient
B is The Second Letter of the Alphabet but is Not Fem As it Should to Maintain Equilibrium Between Sexes   But No   Says The Code
B is a Powerful Letter that Reaches Many Places
There is a Soft Mellow Positive Aspect to it   For the Boys Only Though   B is the Letter that will Be   B
Growing Up Eventually into a Full Grown Man the   P/Man Power
Words with Letter B are   Baby (BB)   Be   Bee
B b Words
Baby Boy: B/B   Oy
oy: a grandchild   an exclamation of multiple significance *oy may be employed to express anything from ecstasy to horror*
hoy: a heavy barge

The Dam Code The Damn Book

O/Fem Hole   Y/Wounded Fem   With the Secret H/Code Letter   Not a Good Combination for The Fem
The Boy Gets Carried   See Ship (Her as   She/P   Sheep)
Baby Girl: Bay/be   G/Hurl
Bay/Be   G/Penis Penetration   Hurl
hurl: to throw or fling with great force or vigor
Switch B for M/Motherhood and She Gets May/Be
The Code Mind Control (Cunt/Roll) Starts at Birth

Back: B/Baby Boy   Hack

Background: Back/G/Round
Back into Another Round of G/Penis Penetration
Back   G/R   Hound
Back to the Dog (Bitch) for Her

Bad: B/Add
B/Boy Holding All Fem Breasts   Add
Meaning More B's Coming Up
Switch B for D/Pregnant and She Gets Dad
Switch B for F/Fem/Fuck and She Gets to be a Fad
Switch B for L/Sweet Fem Light and She Gets a Lad (The Baby Boy)
Switch B for M/Motherhood and She Gets Mad
Switch B for P/Man Power and He gets a Pad (a Bed)
Switch B for R/Her/Hair/Are/Here/Hear/Ear/Whore/Or/Err/Our/Air/Sex and get Rad as in Radical   Rad is Slang for Wonderful
Switch B for S/Is/His/Us/Ass/Hiss/Serpent/Penis and he Gets Sad (B is too Young to think about Penis and Sex)
Switch B for T/Fem Cross and She Gets a Tad (A Child or a Bit of Something)
Switch B for W/All Fems Sex Active and She Gets a Wad
A Wad of Bank Notes would Imply Prostitution here   or it is a small mass lump or ball of anything   a bundle
Add N/In/Hen/Virgin to Bad and She Gets Band
More Power to the Boys

Bag: B/Boy Holding All Breasts Stick Holding Fem Breasts   A/All Men   G/Hymen Perforation

71

Bag is Slang for The Fems Genitals
Switch B for F/Fem/Fuck and She Gets Fag
Switch B for N/In/Hen/Virgin and She Gets Nag
Switch B for R/Are/Her/Hair/Are/Here/Hear/Ear/Whore/Or/Heir/Err/ Our/ Air/Sex and She Gets a Rag
Switch B for T/Fem Cross and She Gets a Tag
Weak Words for Her from The Code

Bagdad: Bag/Dad
The Bag is Slang for The Fems Genitalia
The Code is Ancient
Looking at Old City Names Will Educate You in Ways you Never Imagined
Bagdad is the Capital of Iraq (I/Rack)

Bagel: Bag/All
A Bagel Has a Hole in the Middle   And You Grab Them from That Hole
Bagel is a Cover Word here for this   Bag/All   Concept
Big/Girl   Bag/Hurl
hurl: to throw with great force
The Code is a Constant Source   Looking

Baggage: 3 GGGs/Hymen Penetration
Bag is Slang for Fem Genitals
Bag/Cage
Bag/Age   As She Ages   She Becomes Baggage
Bag/Gage   And a Challenge Because She Knows More
gage: a challenge

Balance: Ball/Hence
When the Balls Are Henced (Searched For)   All Is in Balance

Ball: B/All
Balls are Men Trophies
B/Stick or Penis Holding All Fems Breasts   All in the Hall
A Ballroom would be   A Room for the Balls to Play
Nothing Wrong with that   All in a Good Context

Ballerina: Ball/He/Reina

Reina is Queen
The Queen of the Balls
The Code Creates Absurdities about The Fems   So at the End   She has Nothing at All
She is a Reina   But Only When She Can Walk on Her Big Toes Wearing a Tutu (Two/Too)
Ball/He/Reign/A   No Fem here as He Reigns   Having a Ball

Ballet: Ball/A   No Fem There

Banal: Ban/All   ban/L/Sweet Fem Love/Ill/Ail/Hail/Hell/Elle
The Bar or the Ban from   The Code   is Towards All Fems
It is a Banality   Says it
banal: devoid of freshness or originality

Banality: Ban   All   He   T/Fem Cross
Because   The Fem is   The Cross   She is Banned   and Hit for it Ban/All/Hit/He
It is Still Insignificant   Says The Code
Banality   almost as Delicious as Banana   That Power of Hypnotism   from That Code

Bang: Ban/G
To Ban   G/Penis Penetration   Would Ends in a Bang for Her
Switch B for H/Secret Letter and She Gets Hang
And   B/Baby Boy   Needs to Hang to Her Breasts as in B/Hang
bang: slang for sex   to strike

Banger: Bang   R/Her/Hair/Are/Here/Hear/Ear/Whore/Or/Heir/Err/Air/Our/Sex

The Banger is the One that Bangs
The Word Banger is Slang for Sausage which is Slang for Penis
banger: a person or thing that bangs
Take the G/Penis Penetration Away and Get a Banner Ban/Her   All Fems are Under that Banner

Bank: B/Ankh

Ankh is the Egyptian Key for Eternal Life
Ankh is in a Cross Shape   with a Handle or a Loop   at the Top
The Cross is the Letter T   and   is the Symbol for The Fems Curse
B/Boy Holding All Fem Breasts is Holding the Key
Change K for G/Penis Penetration and Get Bang

Banker: B/Ankh/Her
You Can Bank on Her   Says The Code

Baptism: B/Apt/He/Ism or Seem   Be/Apt/He/Seem
apt: inclined   disposed   given
ism: a doctrine   a system   a practice
Baptism   is a Ritual   Accomplished with the Power Water Purification from (A Fem Element)
The Fem   is the One Cleansing the Sins of the World   by Being the T/Fem Cross/Great Curse
Catholicism   Judaism
The Only Fem Letters in Baptism are T/Fem Cross and M/Motherhood

Bar: Is Made of 3 Masc Letters
A Bar is a Stick
It is the Letter I/Eye/High (See Eye)
B/Boy Holding All Fem Breasts   with   His Stick   A/All Men
R/Her/Hair/Are/Here/Hear/Ear/Whore/Or/Heir/Err/Air/Our/Sex
Switch R for N/Virgin and She Gets Ban
That Bar Starts in Childhood with that Boy
To Bar   is to   Eliminate
Bar   as in a   Rod   Pole
Fem Have Been Barred   from the Life of Men   Since Ever (We Miss Them So Much (Dedicated to All The Men I have Loved   Especially My Dear D)
In Greek Times   The Fems   that Sometimes Were Invited to Public Functions or Parties   were Only   Concubines
Mothers Stayed Inside the House   Almost the Same as   The Arabic System   Nothing I Would Have Chosen Personally
A Bar is Where Men Drink Alcohol (All/Cool/Hall)
A Bar Was a Place Where The Fems were Not Allowed Unless they Worked   or   Slaved there

The Dam Code The Damn Book

A Bar as Rank
A Bar in Music
A Bar as Measure
A Bar as in Stripe of Honor
The Bar as in the Law
The Word Bar is in Many Places
A   Bar   Separate One Side from the Other   a Dam (Damn)
Note that the Word Ill has 3 Bars which Makes it Infinite They Look As Prison Bars   The Men Symbol is the Bar/Stick   The Fem   is a Dot (Circle)   Note That The Word   Dot   is Made of All Fems Letters
Note that   Bar   is Made of   B/Boy Holding All Fem Breasts   A/All Men   and   R/Whore/Or/Heir (From Boyhood to Manhood   The Whore is The Way   Says The Code)
Add E/He to Bar and He Gets a Bear
Switch A for O/Fem Hole and She Gets Bore (B Whore/Or/Heir)
Switch A for U/You/Ovulating and She Gets a Bur   Sticky Prickly Stuff   Do Not Touch
Switch A for Another R/Her/Hair/Are/Here/Hear/Ear/Whore/Or/Heir/Err/Air/Our/Sex   and She Gets Brr (Cold)   2 Whores Together with a Baby Boy   Is a Big No from   The Code   So   Bear that Cold

Bar Code: The Infiltration of Modern Words/Concepts
Changes or Replaces the Old Word Meaning
Such as the New Tarot Cards Decks
Their Meanings is Altered from the Original Messages
Which Few Understood Anyway   Making it More Confusing   Which is the Plan from   The Code Acts   The Code Reacts   The Code Says

Barbell: Bar/Belle
The Fem is Barred Everywhere   in Any/Way   Any Time   in History
A Barbell is a Rod with Many Interchangeable Discs to Put on as Weights   They have Holes in them   You Grab Them By The Middle   How Convenient for The Code
Anything Round is Fem   Especially if it has a Hole in the Middle
A Bar Belle Could be a Pretty Fem in a Bar   But No   She is a Weight   and   a Fem of a Doubtful Reputation
Bar/Belle   The Rod/Bar   Homosexuality   In The Code   Hides in Many Facets

Barely: Bear/He/Lay
Never Enough Lay for The Code   Bear   Man
Bar/He/Lay   The Code Sets the Bar   And Minimizes its Impact   When He Wants   It Depends Which Bar and Which Man   The Code Decides

Barge: BRG
When Boy Discover Sex with Hymen Penetration   He is on that   Boat/Vessel/Ship   Barging in (Rape Style)
barge :   to carry or transport by barge   to intrude especially rudely   to force oneself upon   to bump into collide with
Barge goes on Water therefore is Related to The Fems

Baron: Bar/On
The Bar is On   here   with that   Honorary Masc Title   That Gives Him   The Power   to Establish that   Bar)
Baroness: Bar   N/On/In/Hen/Virgin   Ass/S/Is/His/Us/Ass/Hiss/Serpent/Penis
All is Lost for Her   Here
Bear/On/Ass   Bar/On/Ass
Beer/On/Ass   For The Adepts of Deeper Research which will Keep on being Weirder   Bier   On it
Another of Those Fun Concepts Here For Some Men
And a Heavy Load for Her   As Usual   Says The Code

Barrel: Bar/All
Bar   L/Fem Sweet Love Light/Ill/Ail/Hail/Hell/Elle/All
Barrels of Them   Bear Them All   And   Bier with Them All   Too
B/Are/All   Boys Get it All

Barren: Bar/N/Virgin   Bear/In
The   Bar   from The Code   is   In   When   N   is
barren :   unproductive   unfruitful
Not Allowed to Her By   The Code   So   Back Then   They Would Abandon those Fems in the Desert   By Themselves with a Loaf a Bread
It is Either   The Bear   or The Bar for Her   Both Words Ends with   R/Whore/Or/Heir   No Improvement here for The Fems

Barricaded: Bar/He/Gated

The Dam Code The Damn Book

To Keep   The Bar   Going   The Code   Gates it (See # 11 in the Clock Chapter)   Barricader (Bar/He/Gator   has the word Gator in it)

Barrier: Bar/He/Her
Another Fence or Ban (It is on the Banner (Ban/Her) for The Fems
Bear/He/Her   is Always There to Push Her Along that Nightmare
Bare/He/Her   Be/Here/Her

Basement: BS (Bull Shit) He   Meant
The Basement in a Home Represents the Unconscious
And that would be BS (Bull/Shit) as Given from The Code
BS is B/Boy with Penis   Being too Young for that S/Penis It is in the Basement for Now

Basic: B/Ace/IC   Base/IC
IC is an Integrated Circuit   it Aces the Bases (See Bases in Baseball) It is Basic in   The Code   to Have the Boy Ace

Bastard: B/Ass/Tard
tard: acting as retarded
Tart is Close to Tard   D/Pregnant   and   T/Fem Cross   are Interchangeable in The Code
Note that Tart Starts and Ends with T
Tart:

Bat: B/At   B/Hat
The Hat is Where the Secret Hides the Secret Art   With a Big Stick
bat: heavy stick
Shorts Words with   At   are More Evident   Code Covers   They are Often Older
Adding E/He   Silent at the End of At Words Creates Secrecy
Bat Bate   Cat Cate   Fat Fate   Gat Gate   Hat Hate Lad Late   Mat Mate   Gnat Nates   Pat Pate   Rat Rate   Sat Sate   Etc
Switch A for i/Marriage Act   And She Gets It (Hit)
The Code is Clear here that   H/Secret Code   Creates the Hit in It
Switch A for O/Fem Hole and She Gets Ot (Hot   Out)

There Cannot be a OT Word   because that would Imply O/Fem
Hole   and   T/Fem Cross   are Together Alone   A Big No from The
Code   So   She is Either Hot or Out
Switch A For U/You/Ovulating and She Gets Ut
When   U/You/Ovulating   and   T/Fem Cross   are Together   It is Music
Says The Code
Switch A for E/He and He Gets -Et
-et: a noun suffix having properly a diminutive force
So   et   as E/He   with   T/Fem Cross   is Safe for Him here   Her being
Diminished

Bathroom: Bat/Room
The Bat is Another Slang Word for Penis
To Strike with His Bat in a Room
Batman: B/Hat/Man
The Hat is the Secret Word for The Code
The Secret Art Lives Under that Hat
The Bat and Him
So Many (Man/He) Movies and Heroes (Her/OOs) about the Man and
His Bat
A King Kong Movie with its Gigantic Ape Kidnapping that Fem   How can
a Man/Ape be Attracted by a Fem the Size of a Squirrel

Batter: Bat/Her   But/Her   Butt/Her   Bet/Her
Beating Her to Get to that Butter (Butt/Her)
Makes it Better   Says The Code   Bet on it
batter: to beat persistently or hard   pound repeatedly
That is Not the Butterfly Effect She Dreams of (Butter/Fly   Butt/Her/Fly)

BB or Belly Button: Bell   He   Butt   On
The Shape of the BB Influences the Rest of The Body Growth
It Can Cause Scoliosis of the Spine and Put the Insides Located in the
Font   in a Slightly   or   Gross   Forced Shape that Eventually Cause
Certain Organs to be Weak   Collapse   or m Cause All Kind of Problems
Because the Waist Cannot Expand Normally after that BB is Wrongly
Cut   Or   Pushed Inside Too Deep After Birth
The BB Influences the Body Shape and Forms Internally

The Dam Code The Damn Book

The BB Starts Pulling on the Back of the Spine Early in Life   Causing Low Back Pain   Where the Weakest Point is
Even the Very Strong Spine Cannot be Strong Enough to Grow Normally Under the Pressure of a Too Short BB that is pulled on Day after Day Minute after Minute as that Baby Grows Into a Child and goes on to Grow Again and Again to be Bigger   The Pains Intensifying Because the Stretching is Abnormal and Painful All the Way to Create Scoliosis in Worst of Cases   It is Mostly Fems that have Scoliosis   Scoliosis would be Caused by the Extreme Shortness of the BB Causing the Whole Spine to Bend Helpless   Because The BB Acts as a Wire That Prevent the Growth Upward   The Whole Body Cannot Expand Normally   As a Normal Child Growth Happens   The Scoliosis Body is Now Cemented as The Bones have Place Themselves in That Curved Spine
Babies are Not Sleeping and Having Nightmares and Are Being Problematic   Those Imposed Subtle Internal Malformations Caused by the BB are Painful
How To See How Bad Your Baby or Yourself BB Cut is
Lay Down the Naked Baby on its Back and Check How the Stomach Respond to the Natural Breathing Progress
I See Especially in Girls that the Breathing is Unnatural or Forced as in being Pushed and Pulled Fast
In that Kind of Breathing the Stomach is Pulled Back in and Shakes Slightly When Breathing and Goes into a Quick Withdrawal   There is a Block There caused by that General BB Constriction
Often Those Babies Have No Patience   Will Cry Often   Get Sick Easily   Develop Allergies from Food   Will be Constipated Endlessly   Or   have Other General Gastric Problems
I See Babies with Full Round Stomach that Breathes Normally Up and Down Naturally Without Jerking
Those Babies with a Natural Breathing are Happier with Quieter Sleep   Those babies have Loser BB   Their Stomach is Not Constricted

The BB is the Original Sin   and is   Represented in Symbology with the Fleur de Lys
Where the 2 Fallopian Tubes/Ovaries and the Cervix/Uterus   Are Squished As that Fleur de Lys Ties/Rings
1 2 or 3 Rings from the BB are Causing That

Lise Rochon

A Lot of Movies and According to Old Beauty Society Rule Women Must   They All have an Abnormally Small Waist
And They Often Wore/Wear Tight Corsets to Reinforce that Imposed Fem Anomaly
The Pain from the Too Tight BB   Blocks Most People from   Having a Normal Human Life   Always Tired   Not being What they are and Knowing it
We Humans have too Much Pain in the Body from that Abnormal BB to Function at Our Best   We had it from Birth We do Not Feel it as is   Only Symptoms
Blacking Out is a Symptom and the Permanent General Weakness of The Fems is Another   Our Pale Lips   Frail Joints   All These from Lack of Nutrients   from Not Eating Enough Etc
Those Fems have Little or No Energy   The BB is So Tight Pushing Everything Towards Her Insides   She Can Hardly Breathe (Only Breed)
That Squishing of the Waist Makes Breasts Grow Larger Meaning More Estrogen/Emotions for Her   And More Weight (Breasts are Heavy) Pressing On All Her Front Organs/The Muscles   Which will Amplify that Already there Heavy Pain
The Code that Way has Kept The Fems Waist Tighter than Any Man
For Most Initiates Those Words are New   There are Good People everywhere
For a Few Years   Now Life is Changing
We See More Masc with a Smaller than Normal Waist
And They Act as it is a New Fashion
We can See the Muscles Pressure on the Back and the Sides   It Makes them Uncomfortable   And they Carry that Pain on their Face   (See The Arc/Arch in The Words Chapter)

It Happens to All of Us   and at   Birth
Our Lives are Already Cursed from Being Born
Because the First thing that Happen to a Newborn
Is to have their BB Cut and that Cut Shape His/Her Life and its Tightness will Alter His/Her Life for Ever
The Bending of the Feet in China for ther Fems Is/Was a Representation of Imposed Pain to All Fems   It Prevented Her from Walking Fast   Then She Could Not Escape from the Beatings/Abuse   According to Testimonies

The Dam Code The Damn Book

Depression: press to compress or force to alter a shape
Mental Illness   they Call It
Yes depression has a Proper definition   Mental Depression is a Symptom of All Pains There is
Deep/Pression   I would Compare it   to the Pains from That Faulty BB   It keeps Everything Inside in a State of Malfunction and There are All Kinds of Maladies Resulting from Those Pressures which   Accelerate or decelerate   Different Organs   being pressed On
When the Pressure of the BB is So Strong Towards the Inside of the Body   It Attains then the Point of No More Stretching   Then as Child Growth Happens At Some Point of The BB is So Elongated It Becomes an Overstretched Leather Bands   Feel That Cutting Knife Pain 24 Hours a Day for Ever Coming Directly from Your BB   A Few Fems Have Complained about that Knife   Or/And   Pins and Needles Pains Around Their BB   Then The Body/Spine Starts to Curve In from the Back From That BB Straps Frontal Physical Pressure and Slowly Slows Down Many Physical Functions Such As Heart/Lungs/Pancreas/Liver   Going All Around to the Back With The Sides All Collapsed Muscles (Still Working Full   Or   Partly Despise The Pain) they have Developed That Way being So Pulled by this Fixed Bad BB
Those Muscles Have Created Her Thin/Small Waist
Which by the Enhancement of Corsets Weakened/Destroyed The Fems Energy by Simple Compression that Never/Ever (Eve/Her)   Ends
Also Causing Lots of that Common Back Pain that the General Population Suffers From
The Fems as L/Sweet Fem Love Light/Ill/Hail/Ail/Hell/Elle are Represented in a Pure Form in L   It is Elle
From the Weakness (Soft Tissue) of The Lungs Those Constraints in Time Will Compress Also on The Rib Cage
Now Limiting All The Front Organs as in a Corset
One Way/Direction   Or   Another The BB   Has a Different Form of Attacking Depending on How is was Pushed Inside The Body at Birth And Now   The Rib Cage Is The Inner Corset   The Rib Cage Cements in Late Childhood   Therefore after That   The Human Permanent Body is Stabilized   And   Will Stay that Way for the Rest of Our Life   The Compressions are Felt All The Way to The Neck   Which by Nature is Fragile and Easily Malleable   The Neck Starts to Bend Down (And Will Stay That Way (If Not Stopped Manually By Exercises Massages and Other

Lise Rochon

Means)   Or   has had Not a Chance by The Muscles Contracting From Everywhere To Grow Properly   Causing Again All Kinds of Different Pains/Problems Around The Area

The Fems Most of the Time are Given a Tight Innie BB Which is Very Bad for Her   The Masc Gets Often an Outie Which is Way Better for His Breathing Posture and General Health   There are Several Kinds Of BB that Needs to Be Looked at Because of Their Lifetime Repercussions Again Any BB Configuration will Shows Health Problems
A Deep Pushed Innie Inhibits Circulation and Block Many Passages in Different Ways   As the Small Intestines Blocking Feces in Different Places   Causing Constipation Or the Opposite   Then The Large Colon Suffers from Pockets from Accumulated Feces   Probably From One of Those Cutting Wires Areas Originating from That Bad BB Trapping/Pushing/Cutting on It   Slowing Down the Passes of Feces and Creating All Kinds of Other Health Problem in Its Way   The Human Body Can Only be Aligned and Live Natural in Order to Maintain a State Of Well Being
There at Birth is/Was a Pull Up from the Anus Too That Starts Right Away as The Baby Develops and Need More Inside Space To Do it   The BB is Already There Blocking The Inside a Second at the Time on These Very Soft Tissues from Babyhood and are Easily Manipulated   Naturally   Babies in Lactation do Very Little Poop   So Nature Makes This Area Stronger Later
Those Inner Pulls/Pushes are Felt All the Way Up to the
Neck   Headaches   Numbing Pains   A Soft Spot Especially as a Child
The BB has a Powerful Grip Over the Health of That Growing Baby Body   For Thousands of Years   No One Looks at it as A Problem
These BB Pulling Hard Lines Create Pressure All Over The Guts   Then Create Gas Pockets   Many People have Them
Those Hard Lines Pressures All Around The Waist Line All The Way To The Back   On The Spine   Creating Problems There
Those Spots (Around The BB) Are Where Fat (Fat is Heavy)   Accumulates Easily Creating More   Weight/Gravity   Pulling/Down/Tension/Pressure On the Way
The Fems Skin is Very Tight Around the Hips   She Will Fatigue Easily from that
Depending on the Area of Binding People Insides

The Symptoms Will be Different
Women Love to Cook themselves Under the Sun   it Numbs their Stomach Pain   Even Older They are Still having Erratic Breathing   Most Men As the Shade Better   Most Men Do Not have a Waist   They Do Not have a Deformed Waist
Being Ticklish Can be a Result of those BB Tie   As in Oversensitivity

Be: B/Boy Holding All Fems Breasts   E/He
Be   has a Redundant Symbolic Word Meaning   B/Boy   E/He   As in growing Towards it   for the Boy Which is to Be
"To Be or Not to Be" takes a New Meaning "Not to Be" is for Us The Fems   Says The Code
The Bear (A Powerful Masc Symbol)   Be/Here

Beach: Anything Related to Water is Fem
B/Each   B/Boy Holding All Fems Breasts   and   Each of Them
A Beach is a Wonderful Place to be   Add T/Fem Cross and She Gets   The Code Shadowy One   It Kicks in   That is the Bitch   Another Bad Thing for The Fems

Beacon: Beak/On   Be   K/Broken Fem Warrior   On
beacon: a guiding or warning signal
Watch Out On that Signal   It Indicates that this Fem Warrior Fem Is
That would Explain that Beacon Signal
Add R/Her/Are/Hair/Here/Hear/Ear/Whore/Or/Err/Our/Air/Sex   to Beak and get   Break/On

Bear: B/Boy Holding All Fem Breasts   R/Whore/Her/Are/Err/Sex
B/Heir   B/Hair   Be/Here   be/Whore   Be/Our
The Bear Heir is Also Masc   Hair Always Attracts the Attention of the Girl   It is called a Bait
When Baby Boy is with 2 RRs/Whore/Heir/Her   Brr   it is Too Cold for The Child
It Makes No Sense for The Man Code   So   (As in Too Far Away) it is for that Baby Boy
Take Away E/He from Bear and Get a Bar (The Code Bars) or B/
Are   Reinforcing the Concept   A Gold Bar

83

bear: animal of force often used to represent man strength in code of honor
The Masc in   The Code   is Always Up there in the   Honors
All what She Gets is   Horn/Her
To be a Bear Implies Responsibility to The Code
B/Ear   So The Message is do Not Mess with the Bear Ears which is The Sound Code

Beard: B/Boy Holding All Fem Breasts   Herd
B   Her   D/Pregnant
To Be/Heard Cannot Belong to a Fem Power   So it is a Beard   The Fems Abhor Beards on Herself   The B/Baby Boy will Pick it up   He will be Heard   And She can be Part of that Herd

Beast: The Mark (M/Motherhood   Arch/Ark) of the Beast
The Mark of the Beast is the 666 is   Sex/Sex/Sex
That Sex Mark Prison Stands Right on Top of the Third Eye   Blocking its View
Be/East
All those Code Traditions and Old Languages Come from the Far East
Easter   East/Her   Only the Letter B/Boy Holding All Breasts is Missing here to Complete that Beast/Her   666   The Number of the Beast
Add a Y/Wounded Fem and She Gets Yeast
Yeast is a Mold   It is Necessary to Rise Bread (Bred)   It is Also a Vaginal Infection that The Fems can get Easily
Add R/Her/Hair/Are/Here/Hear/Ear/Whore/Or/Heir/Err/Air/Our/Sex   to Beast and it is Her Breast

Beat: B/Boy Holding All Fem Breasts   E/He   A/All Men   T/Fem Cross
Be/Hit   So   Be It
B/Eat   Be/Hit
Adding or Taking Out One Letter Still keep the Word its Meaning   and Add Another Function or Dimension to it
A Beat is a Rhythm (Rite/Him)
Rhythm has 2 HHs/Secret Society Letters

Beaten: Beat   N/In/Hen/Virgin   B/Hit/N
B/Boy Holding All Fems Breasts   Hit or Beat   N/In/Hen/Virgin

The Dam Code The Damn Book

Beautiful: Boot/He/Full
Botte is French Slang (Take Your Boot   Prendre sa Botte) for having Sex
Life is Beautiful When His Boots are Full   Says The Code   or   When His Boot is Full of Wine
Add N/Virgin   and She Gets Bountiful (She Gets Plenty of Sex here A Good Thing for The Code)
Now Many People Uses the Word Great Instead of Beautiful

Beauty: B/U/T
Beauty is a Word that Generally Relates Positively to The Fems   That would be   a Big No from   The Code   So
Butt/He   But/E   Bet/He   Bite/He   Bee/T/He   Bid/He
Bet   Beat   Bite   Bid   on That Bee
Working Bees are All Fems   Nothing Nice for Her   here again   Even if She is Blessed with Beauty
La Beauté n'Apporte pas a Manger   (Beauty does Not Bring Food) Says an Old Adage

Because: B/Be/Cause
The Cause is that   B/Baby Boy Holding All Fem Breasts
Do Not Ask Questions   It is Meant to Be   He is the Cause

Bed: B/Head   B/Ed
When   B/Boy Holding All Fems Breasts   Is the Head   His Name is Ed   He Adds to the Masculinity of the Ownership of The Code Concept of Bed
Switch E/He for A/All Men and He Gets Bad   B/Had   B/Add   It is In the Past   and   The B/Boy Adds by being Bad in Bed   Says The Code
Add R/Her/Hair/Are/Here/Hear/Ear/Whore/Or/Heir/Err/Air/Our/Sex   and He Gets   Bred   Bread   Beard   The Fem Will Stay Away from   if Only by the Beard

Bedding: Bed   N/In/Hen/Virgin
Switch E for A/All Men and He Gets Bad/In
Switch E for i/Marriage Act and Get a Bid for N/Virgin
Switch E for U/You/Ovulating (Open as in Ov) and She Gets Bud   Budding in Bed   to be a Bad Boy
The Code Makes Him Proud to be Bad   And   He Gets a Bed
There are   43 Different Meanings   for   Bed   in the On Line Dictionary

Bedded: Bed/Head   Bad/ID
ID   is Identification Data   ID has a total of 102 Definitions   A Must Read

Bedfellow: Bad/Fall/O   Bid/Fell/O
O/Fem Hole   Falls in The   Bed/Bad/Bid   it is All Good   Says The Code
Switch E for O/Fem Hole and She Gets The Bed/Follow   The Code here
Enhancing its   Obedience   from The Fems to That   In The Future Also

Been: BN   Be/In
B/Boy Holding All Fems Breasts   is with   EE/Many Men   Going at
the   N/Virgin
As a Sex Ritual When Men Hold a Girl and Let the Boy have Sex with
Her   The Ancients Terrible/Horrible Ways are Very Much Unknown to Us
in a Modern Civilization
It is In the Past (Been) When   B   Mates with   N/In/Hen/Virgin   It is an
Event as Small as a Bean   Says   The Code   So   No One Looks at It   It
is in the Past Anyway
The Word Being/Bean/Been Could have been a Very Alive Word in a
Natural Language   Especially   Because it has an Important Word in
it   Being   as in   Supreme Being   But No Says   The Code   So
Switch E/He for A/All Men   The Code Bans it
Put it All in a Bin As Beef or Beets   and it is a Been Be/N   N/
Virgin   Cannot be a B/Boy   So   Nothing for Her Here Again   And it is
in The Past Already   Says The Code

Beer   BR   B/Hear   Be/Here
With   B/Boy Holding All Fems Breasts
Hear/Here is Something Men from   The Code   Make Sure   That   The
Fems Cannot Not Follow Conversations   Keep Her Eyes Down   So   She
Cannot See Around Her
Switch E/He for A/All Men and He Gets a Bear   That is a Serious Cold
Minded Matter   BRR
The Code Says   B/Boy   Cannot be with   R/Whore/Heir   and   Drink
beer   So
A Beer is a Coffin too
Beer   a Word being with Us For Millenaries   Is an Important Word in
Our Vocabulary   Worth Looking at It   Closely   The Code Did it a Long
Time Ago

The Dam Code The Damn Book

Before: BFR
B/Boy Holding All Fems Breasts   F/Fem/Fuck   R/Whore/Heir
It is in the Past   So   It has been Done
Be/For   is an Acceptation   That is How this Code Symbolism from   The Past is   Accepted   in The Present   by Our   Subconscious/Unconscious Mind

Beg: B/Boy Holding All Fems Breasts   Egg
When the Young Masc Get Close to Her Egg (Ovulation)
He Begs
Switch E/He for U/You/Ovulating She Gets a Bug
Switch E for A/All Men He gets a Bag
Switch E for i/Marriage Act and He/She Gets Big

Begin: BGN   Bag   N/In/Hen/Virgin
B/Boy Holding All Fems Breasts   G/Penis Penetration   N/In/ Hen/Virgin   The Boy and the Penetration of the Virgin is How it Begins   Says   The Code
B/Egg/In   Bagging the Virgin from the Beginning   Bag is Slang for Loins   It Begins with the   Egg/in
Eve (V/Fem Sex Active) and Adam (A/All Men   Damned)
Add R/Heir/Whore and She Gets Bragging
That Looks As   First Time Sex   and   Pregnancy for Her   from a Boy   in the Word Begin (Beg/In)

Begun: Bag/On   Be/Gone
When the   Gun   is/has   Gone
When the Bag is On (Bag   On   Pregnancy)   He is Gone and   Done   Says   The Code   It has Already Begun in the Past

Beginner: Bag   N/In/Hen/Virgin   R/Her/Hair/Are/Here/Hear/Ear/ Whore/Or/Heir/Err/Air/Our/Sex
B/Egg/In/R   The Beginner Boy has Succeeded   The Egg is in with the Whore   She is Not Virgin Anymore   It comes with it   Says   The Code

Behave: Bee   Hive
The Fems are the Bees in The Code   Behave   So   She Works More   So   B/Boy Holding All Fems Breasts have it All   B/Have

Behind: Be/Hind
hind: the back of something   fem deer   fishes   peasants
Peasant is the Slang Used for the Red Collar Blue Collar and White Collar
Workers (the People that are Behind) Says   The Greedy   Code
We are All Under   The Code   Spell   We are its Butt Joke The
Behind   Where   The Code   Kicks Us
Men Think they have the Upper Hand   But No   We
Stand   Between   and   Behind   Fishes   Deer   Butt   and   Very
Little People

Behold: Be/Hold   B/Boy Holding All Fems Breasts   Hold
Hold that Boy   Boy/Be Hold
behold: often used as an imperative to draw attention to something   to
look (at)   observe

Belch: Belle/She
For a Fem To be Beautiful and   Knowing it   Would be a Big No
from   The Code   So   it is a
belch: to eject gas spasmodically and noisily from the stomach through
the mouth
No One Especially The Fems is Interested in that
Belle/Shh   And Not a Word about it

Believe: Belle/Eve   Bell/Eve   B   L/Ill/Hell/Elle/All   V/Fem Sex Active
Believe   Makes Her Believe that She is a Belle (Isabelle)   So   Ring/That/
Belle (Since Eve)
When the Sound/Word   Letter L/Hell   is Part of a Word
Not So Good for Her   Hell/Ill/Ail/Hail/Elle   She Goes Back to Evil as
in   Eve/Ill   Again
B/Hell/Eve
B/Leave   The   B/Boy   Leaves   because   He is too Young for The
Code
After   B/Boy Holding All Breasts   is on the Leave
She Gets the Bill   Bill/Eve   Bill/V
Believe in   Bill   and   Eve
B/Boy is Ill with   Eve/V   Says The Code
Ball/Eve

Bell: BL
B/Boy Holding All Fems Breasts   L/Sweet Fem Love Light/Ill/Elle/Ail/Hail/Hell
B/Hell   B/Elle
Bell/He   Is Her Belly   Where BBs (See BB   in Words) Is She is a Belle at the Belly   But No   The Code   Stole that Too   Ring That Belle   She is a Belle in the Belly for   The Code   Heirs   B and B   More B/Boys
Switch E/He for A/All Men and He Gets Ball (s)
Switch B for F/Fem/Fuck and She Gets Fell (F/Hell)
Switch L for G/Penis Penetration and He Gets Beg   So Close to Bag In Sound
Switch B for P/Man Power and He Gets the Pal Sound
Add T/Fem Cross   and He Gets a Pelt (Her Death)
Switch B for H/Secret Code and Get Hell (Where   The Code   Hides The Fems)
Switch E for i/Marriage Act and Get a Bill   or   Tell Bill
Switch E for O/Fem Hole and She Gets a Bowl
Switch E for U/You/Ovulating and She Gets the Bull (Ovulation Time   Males Smells that)
Switch L for T/Fem Cross and She Gets Bet or Bat or Beat Butt Bit Etc   is Under The
Add T/Fem Cross and She Gets the Belt because She Cannot Get Close to   That Understanding of The Code   that Says   She is a Belle   because   She is a Bell in The Belly (Belle/He   Pregnant)

Belladonna: Bella/Donna
Belle Dame   or   Beautiful Lady
A Gracious Fem Name
That Great Could be Fem Name Has a Title (Don is Masc   Donna is Fem)
But No Says   The Code   As Usual   So
She Was Named a Poisonous Plant   Bella Donna
belladonna: also called deadly nightshade   a poisonous plant
Belladonna is also Used in Pharmacology for Specific Symptoms
Amaryllis (Which is So Close to My Adopted Name) is also Called Belladonna   and   Naked Lady   is a Related Plant
What can do a Beautiful Naked Fem All alone   Nothing at All Except being at the Merci of Her Environment
Same as for the Word Heroin   The Fem Name for Hero

Lise Rochon

It Is Now Called a Forbidden Drug   Why
The Fems Never goes Anywhere in That Code
It Makes Her Weak in Many Ways
That Code Language Creates Only Negatives Life Patterns for Her   Bringing Mental Slavery in All Areas of Her Life   Therefore Influencing Everyone Around

Belong: Blown   Bell/Belle   On   Bell/On
She is (Belle/On) here to Belong
Be/Ill/On   To be Ill is Where She Belong   It will Be/Long (Not Much Hope here for Her)
And Bill Her On (Bill/On) for That   And Bill is On for the Ride   Says The Code

Below: Be/Low   Belle   O/Fem Hole
The Low Blow That Keeps the Belle Below is that She The Hole is in That Belle in That Bell
Belle/Owe
The O/Fem Hole of the Belle being Below   She Owes it All   Also
The Bell Rings because a Belle Is Ringed In Marriage (Men as a Custom do Not Have to Wear their Wedding Ring   as Women did)
There are All Kinds of Rings for Her   Visible and Invisible
Add Another L/Sweet Fem Light to below (Which should be a Good Thing   But No Says   The Code) and She Get Bellow
bellow: to emit a hollow animal cry as a bull or a cow
More Pain for Her   here   Again   As Animal   A Cow   That One   That Provides Milk   M (as in Mom/Mum/Maam)
Switch E for O/Fem Hole and She Gets Bolo   Bowl/O (Chalice/Bowl/Bag   The Same) Back to the Animals and the Crying for Her   Again

Belt: Belle/T   Bell/T   Built
From Belle   Build   L/Fem Sweet Love Light   into a   T/Fem Cross   Says   The Code   It is done With a Belt to Her
The Amount of Beatings to The Fems (Children and Other Weaker People   of All Ages) Behind Us   For Ages   Proves That
The Code   Programs Us That Way

The Dam Code The Damn Book

Switch B/Boy Holding All Fems Breasts with W/All Fems Sex Active and She Gets Wealth   The More The Fems Under That Belt   The More Better for That Code

Belly: Belle/He   She is Never Left Alone   Says   The Code   Bell/He Where She is Beautiful   is in the   Belly (Ball/He)
A Fem in   The Code   Is a Belly for His Balls   As in Her Pregnancies

Berry: Bear/He
B/Boy Holding All Fem/Breasts
R/Her/Hair/Are/Ear/Hear/Here/Whore/Or/Heir/Err/Air/Our/Sex
Berries are Commonly Associated with Girls and Poetry Her Lips as Sweet as Berries Etc
But No Says   The Code   She will Not Enjoy that Either   So
When the Vigorous Boy Arrives as a Bear   The Berry (Her) has Not a Chance   She will be Eaten   Bears Love Berries
A Berry is a Fruit   The Fruit of Her Belly   is So Close
A Tree Bears Fruits   No Chance for Her here Also   The Code has given the Name Bear for the Action of the Tree Growing those Berries
The Word Err is in Here   It Indicates Danger for Her   As in an Erratic Action from that Bear or that Girl/Berry is Erring (Herring (See Fish in The Words Chapter))   (R/Ring   2 Whores In   here) as in   Hurry/In   for R/Her/Err/Whore
If it Smells As Herring   Must be it
err: to go ashtray morally   sin   be mistaken   be incorrect   to transgress
Note that the Sound Letters of Berry are   BRE   and are All Masc Letters   Brr
Always   The Code Switches Fems Identities Around in   His   Favor   So The Masc Always Win   and She takes   Losing or having Nothing   as a Normal Part of Life

Beside: B/Boy Holding All Fems Breasts   Side   Be/Side   Bees/Hide Bees Cannot Hide   But it is Beside the Point for Her   She does Not Know Anything About   The Code   That Rules Her   It is Beside The Point She Says   She has to Keep on Working

Best: BST   B/Boy   S/Penis   T/Fem Cross

Beast   Be/East   The Beast from The East   Close to Best
B/Stay   B/Boy Holding All Fem Breasts   is Meant to Stay   Says The Code
To Best Add R/Our/Air/Her/Hair/Ear/Hear/Here/Are/Whore/Or/
Heir/Err/Sex   Makes a   Breast   (A/All Men   is Anonymous and
Silent   here)   Reinforces that All Fem Breasts Belong to All Men   Not Only One Man as   E/He
Letter B/Boy Holding All Fem Breasts   Starts The Word
Back to the Domes for Her (See Doom and Domes in The Words Chapter)
That Ever Expending Breast Cup   It is the Fastest Enlargement of The Human Fems Breasts (and Some Males) in Our History
It is the Mutation of the Millenary   Accelerating Fast in this Last 50 Years with Fem Events such as Sophia Loren Gina Lolobrigida and Brigitte Bardeau   Early Most Loved Fem Hollywood Models   Those Breasts Look So Appeasing   Yet Close to it is that Tiny Atrocious Waist Line (Often Encircled with a String) Which Looks As Torture on Her   Do Not Try That   It Strangles Her Body   Weakening Her   The Code   Calls it a Corset (Core/Set   A Horrific Word)
Much Needs to be Said about Her Artificially Enlarged Heavy Mamma or Mammary Glands   Creating All Kinds of Weight Imbalances and Stagnancies on Her Body   Therefore   Pains   and   Weakening in Strength

Bet: Beth   Bat   Bath   Bit
Switch E/He for i/Marriage Act and Get Bit
B/Boy Holding All Fems Breasts   Hit   So   B/Be/It   The Boy Does it   He Hits   B/Boy/Hit
Switch E for A/All Men and He Gets a Bat (a Weapon) or a Bath (Easy it is)
Switch E for U/You/Ovulating and She Gets a Butt or
But
Beth (a Fem Name to bet On) and Bath are Cover Words here

Better: Bet/Her   Bat/Her   Bite/Her   Bed/Her   Beat/Her   B/Hit/Her.   Bitter
All those Negative Actions are Coming Towards Her
To Create the Word Called   Better
"And Make it Better Better Better" a John Lennon Song
Some Men Have So Much Heart

The Dam Code The Damn Book

That Code World   Often Kills those with a Big Heart One Way or Another

Between: B/Baby Boy Holding All Fems Breasts   Hit/It   When/Win
Bet/Win   B/Hit/Win   Bit/He/Win   Bit/Bet   We   In/N
A Man Life in   That Code   is about When to Hit and Win that
Virgin   The Bet is About the N/In/Hen/Virgin   The Word Between Ends
with N/In/Hen/Virgin   Therefore it is the Result
The Bet to Win that Virgin with a Bat (No But   Only Butt) is in the Word
Between   So Few Can See it
Bat/We/In/N   Bat/Win   The Stick Keeps on Beating   So His Bit Can Win
Itself   In/N/Virgin

Bewitch: Be/Witch   B/Baby Boy Holding All Fems
Breasts   Be   With   Shh
The Code Holds the Silence on Witchery
Respect and Revere those Wizards and Magicians (Mage/Ic)   Says   The
Code   But   Burn those Witches
bewitch: to affect by witchcraft or magic   cast a spell over

Bewitched: B/Be/Boy Holding All Fems Breasts   Witch   D/Pregnant
When a Witch is D/Pregnant   She is Bewitched Enchanted and
Charmed   Says The Code
bewitched: enchant   charm
Which is Which is a Common Expression   The Fems has No face or
Identity in The Code   The Fems are a Bunch of Sheeps with a Man
Holding a Stick (Sheppard) to Push them Around

Bible: Mathew 26 28:   "This my blood of the New Testament Which is
Shed for the Remission of Sins"
From the Church of Latter Day Saints Joseph Smith Who was a Free
Mason Said Being Anointed into the Endowment "To Become Clean from
the Sins and Blood of this Generation"
Why is it About Blood and Not Any Other Part of the Body   And   Which
Justice would Forgive the Responsible and Allow them to Walk Free
endowment: an attribute of the mind or body   a gift of
nature   gift   bequest   capacity   faculties   ability   capability
NDOMNT (In Dome/Doom   Meant   See Dome (Breast) in the Words
Chapter) Is Made Entirely of 6 Fems Sounds Letters

Well Endowed is a Common Term about a Woman having Large Breasts   Not Much Else
This is Where   The Code (That Never is Positive to Her at All   it is All Part of   The Code   Plan)   Dares to Call Her a Gift of Nature   Because of Those Breasts   Which is the Central Plan for Her   To have More Breasts Size (More Hormone Lactation   More Estrogen   More Sluggish Mind and Body for Her)
That Word Endowment Says   The Code   Uses Her as The Sacrificial Lamb
The Code   Steals Diminishes or Ignores Her Gifts and Capacities   She is The One Pouring the Blood   She is The One Blamed for Those Sins   And   Is The One being Cursed Also
Sins or Mistakes that could be Avoided by Everyone of Good Clear Conscience in a Normal World
In The English Standard Bible Version Exodus 24 8 " and Moses took the blood and threw it on the people and said "Behold the Blood of the Covenant that the LORD has made with you in accordance with all these words"
Those Words would Mean   Her Lost Blood is The Blood of the Covenant
Covenant as a verb is a binding agreement
covenant: *Law*   an incidental clause in such an agreement
Covenant in the Bible is an Agreement Between 2 Parties
Covenant Sounds As Government   The Blood of the Covenant   The Word Blood is a Very Important Word
Jesus is the Biggest Example for   The Code   to Implant in Our H   The Curse of The Fems Loss of Blood
In John 1:1:   "in the beginning was the Word and the Word was with God and the Word was God"
From One Concept Jumping to Another   First Phrase Saying   The Word (as in a Language) had Already Happened in the Past   Then   It is with a God (The Ultimate Figure of Creation and Power   Now   The Word has become that God in the Third Concept   As   The Code   Says   That God Was Taught from That Word (Language)   Which is Impossible Because The God Source (No Matter The Name) is Supposed to be The Great Starter of All Life
In Revelation 21:6: "It is done I am the Alpha and the Omega the beginning and the end.   To the thirsty I will give freely the water of life without payment"

The Dam Code The Damn Book

The Entire Letters Chapter in this Book Explains the Symbolic of Letters
Water is the Universal Fem Symbol   Free Water   it Says here   No Need to Pay Her or for Her
Mental Mazes Created by The Code   Her Water   Which has been Transformed into Tears (Her Constant Loss of Water)   Then   Is Transformed into Wine (Whining)   That Wine is Now Symbolically Her Blood   Then   Breaking (Hymen   I/Marriage Act   Men   High Man) Her Body (Calling it Bread)   to Breed Her   Add Butter (Butt/Her)   or   Cheese (Slang for Fem Juices   She/Is)
In Luke 34 35"Forgive them they do not know what they are doing"
That Happens When Someone Else Rules Your Life   Or are Children Minded

Big: B/Boy Holding All Fems Breasts   i/Marriage Act   G/Penis Penetration
When   B/Baby Boy   Gets Big   He/E   will Have   I/Marriage Act   with His/S/Serpent   G/Penis Penetration   Then   Her G/Hag/Egg Comes
hag: an ugly old woman   especially a malicious or a vicious one   a witch or sorceress   a hagfish
A Hagfish is Ugly
Switch I for E/He and B/Be/Boy Gets Beg B/Egg   (See Egg in The Words Chapter) Surprise   B/Boy is Now with Her Egg
Switch I for A/All Men He Gets   it is in The Bag   No Begging for Him
Switch I for U/You/Ovulation and She Gets a Bug   (The Code   Says No to The Fem to Get Big)
Switch I for O/Fem Hole and She Gets Bog
bog: a slang word for lavatory   Australian slang the act or the instance of defecating   a place or thing that prevents or slows progress or improvements   wet spongy ground

Bigger: Big/Her   Bag/Her
Big/Her   is Pregnancy
Bag/Her   would be   The Bag (Her Genitals in Slang)   and   R/Our/Air/Her/Hair/Are/Here/Ear/Hear/Whore/Or/Heir Err/Sex
A Bag is a Handbag or a Fem Purse
Switch P/Man Power for C/See/Young Girl and She Gets
The   Curse   The Great Curse   The T/Fem Cross
The Code Ties Her L/Hell/Ill/All/Elle/All Together   Seamlessly

Switch I for U/You/Ovulating and She Gets a Bugger (Something Annoying)
booger: *Informal*   any person or thing   a piece of dry mucus in or from the nose

Bigot: Big/Hot   Beg/It   Bag/Hit   Big/Hit
The Code Hides its Horrible Messages in All Forms
bigot: a person who is utterly intolerant of any differing creed belief or opinion
Bigot Ultimately would be a Most Accurate Name for that Ugly Code Because the Bag is The Fems in All the Degrading Aspects of   The Code   and they Know it   They are the Bigots (Bag/Hot)
Switch Letter B/Boy Holding All Fem Breasts for P/Man Power and He Gets Pig/Hot (Hot Pigs is What they Become When He Grow up)

Bill: B/Ill   Belle (Beautiful In French
The Fem Always Pay or Pay More   Beautiful (Belle) or Sick (Ill)
Bill is a Masc Name   The Code Invades Her in Every Way

Binger: Binge   Her
Here   She is the One Associated with that Concept
binger: a period or bout usually brief of excessive indulgence as in eating drinking alcoholic beverages etc   spree

Birth: B/Boy Holding All Fem Breasts   Earth
Let it be Said that by Birth on this Earth   Says   The Code   B/Boy   is The Owner of the Fem Breasts
Be/Hurt   Be   H/Secret Code Letter   T/Fem Cross

Birthright: B/Be/Boy Holding All Fems Breasts   Hurt   Rite/Right (See Rite in The Words Chapter)
B   R/Her/Hair/Are/Here/Hear/Ear/Whore/Or/Err/Sex   T/Fem Cross   Right/Rite
From Birth to Bondage   Just As We do with Cattle   Do what is Right and Forget about the Left (Fem Side)

Bit: B/It   B/Hit   Be/It
B/Boy Holding All Fems Breasts   and the   Hit

It   Is of Small Importance   No One Looks at It
Add E/He and He Gets a Bite
Switch i/Marriage Act for E/He and He Gets to Bet
Switch I for A/All Men and He Gets a Bat
Switch I for O/Fem Hole and She Set the Boot
Switch I for U/You/Ovulating and She Gets But (t)
Beat (Be/It/Hit) that

Bitch: B/Boy Holding All Fems Breasts   and   Itch
B   Hit   and then   She/Shh (Silence to Her)
A Bitch Is a Fem Dog   Back to the Animals for The Fems
Bitch is Used Regularly Describing a Fem that does Not Fit the Criteria of the Passive Silenced Powerless Type of Fem
The Word Bitch is Used Often in Our Daily Speech
The Bitch is Blamed for Every Existing Calamity
"What a Bitch of Weather"   "Life is a Bitch"   "Work Sucks as a Bitch"   "That Bitch Sucks"   And More
In France it is the Same Mental Attitude to Her with the Same Word Translated in French   La Putain
La Putain   A Popular Term to Describe The Fems as Putain Means Whore
It is Used Widely at the Drop of a Hat to Blame Her   Calling Her Whore about Anything   Anything Goes
The R/Whore is Responsible for Everything   It is a Daily Put Down on Her (Since She Was Born and Before
That is Another Facet of Her Great Curse   Blaming The Fem   When She Has/Had So Little Decision Power   in Our History
These Words are Just a Few Examples
The Code Pictures The Fems as   Bad Poor and Stupid   No Power No Money No Hope for Her (Barefoot and Pregnant)
What Can She Do   The Code   Says   Be Pregnant/
Heir/R   or   Whore/R   or   be Rejected and   Err/R
Hope is a Fem Name
Poverty is Always Lurking in the Corner of Her Eyes Until it Makes Her Lose Her Dignity when Falling in It   It is the Same for Many Men   That Code Impoverishes Too Many
Puta is Whore in Spanish   More of the Same Insult to Her   Puta as Slang is a Very Much Used Word

Seeing The Fems as Whores is an Old International Concept   An Unconscious Model Pushed on Us   and   that for an Eon (He/On)
That Code of Letters Words Symbols Expressions and Signs Is Terribly Positive and Power Giving to All Men   Only
The Usual Bastard Name for Him will Come Up Once a While in Wordily Conversations   But Mostly that System of Words is So Deep and Strong for Him that The Fems Took Thousands of Years Just to Begin to Think   That they Also Could be Worthy (Worth/He)
In French Quebec We Have la Vache (She as   Cow) as Expletive in the Hiding for Blaming (When B is Lame) Her

Bite: B/Boy Holding All Fems Breasts   Height   Or   Be/Height   As in a Kite
When Switching B for K/Broken Fem Warrior She Gets a Kite
Switch i/Marriage Act for A/All Men and He Gets a Bate   or   B/Hate/Ate   Eating Hatred is a Vile Term
Take Away E/He and He Gets a Bit (B/Hit)
Switch T/Fem Cross for D/Pregnant and She Gets to Bide While B/Hides (He does Not have to Bide)
Switch B for F/Fem/Fuck and She Gets a Fight
Switch B for L/Sweet Fem Light/Ill and She Gets a Light (The Light is here for Her here Says   The Code   because the Word Bite Implies Pain for Her)
Switch B for M/Motherhood and She Gets to be a Mite (So Small No One Sees Her)
Switch B for N/In/Hen/Virgin and She Gets to be in the Night (No One Sees Her in the Night   All Sleeps)
Switch B for R/Her/Hair/Are/Here/Hear/Ear/Whore/Or/Heir/Our/Err/Sex and She Gets a Rite/Right (The Rite is When Her Initiation Happens   Her Transformation from a Virgin to a Whore   That is The Right Thing to do for Her Says   The Code
Switch B for S/is/His/Us/Ass/Hiss/Serpent/Penis and He Gets a Sight (Always an Advantage to have that Gift)
Switch B for T/Fem Cross/Great Curse and She Gets Tight (It is Tight for The Code here   The Word Starts and Ends With T   And has the Sound Height in The Middle   No Says   The Code   the Fem Cannot have Any Height   So   Tight it is)

The Dam Code The Damn Book

Switch B for W/All Fems Sex Active and She Gets White   Nothing there   Says The Code   It is All   They Immolate People in White   White Sheeps   Jesus as a Sheep   Losing His Life for That Sheep (See Sheep in The Words Chapter) White   White from Fear
Add R and She Gets Bitter (Mary in Italian   See Merry/Marry in The Words Chapter)

Bitter: Bet   R/Her/Hair/Are/Here/Hear/Ear/Whore/Or/Err/Our/ Sex   Bite/Her   Beat/Her   Bate/Her   B/Hate/Her
Any of those Actions would Make Her Bitter
Beat Her Until She is As Butter (Butt/Her)
That Popular Fem Name Mary Means Bitter in Old Roman Language
Bitte Means You Are Welcome in German
Better is The Cover Word here   The Code Feeds on Stuff As that

Black: B/Lack
Black is the Color of the Dry Blood in Alchemy
Black is the Color the Boy Lacks   being Too Young
The Fems that Represents Evil is Often Dressed in Red (Blood) and Black
Evil is the V/Fem Sex Active Letter as in Eve that is Ill
She is Often Represented as an Ugly Fem in   The Code
The Word Ill is Made of 3 Bars (See the Word Bar and # 11 in The Numbers Chapter)

Blah: B/Law
B/Boy Holding All Fem Breasts   Law
Boys are the Law   Repeat it Over and Over
blahblahblah: and so on so forth
When that   B/Baby Boy Holding All Fems Breasts   is with   L/Fem Light/ Ill/Hell/Elle   in the Company of   A/All Men   It is Big for Him almost as an initiation to   The Code   So   The Fems will Hear it as Blah
blah: a slang name for   nonsense   rubbish   a feeling of physical uneasiness   a general discomfort or a mild depression
Note that   H/Secret Code Letter   is Silenced here   Implying Secrecy   Same as in Law   Where   W/All Fems Sex Active   are Silenced

Blame: B/Lame

99

When   B/Boy Holding All Fem Breasts is Lame
The Code here Blames the   Belle (Her) Âme (Soul in French)

Blank: Switch   N/In/Hen/Virgin with C/See/Young Girl   And She Gets Black
Another Blanket   Blank/Hit   Blink/It

Blast: B/Last
When   B/Boy Holding All Fems Breasts   Last for Him   It is a Blast

bleat: to utter the cry of a sheep goat or calf or a sound resembling such a cry
Bleed (See Blood of the Lamb in Blood in The Words Chapter) is Close
Blate (Be/Late)

Blemish: Blame   Shh/She
(See Acne in The Words Chapter)   Blame Her for Things She Cannot be Responsible for

Blend: B/Boy Holding All Fems Breasts   Land
blend: to mix smoothly and inseparably together
Another Sweet Initiation to Sweet Living for the Heir

Blender: Blind/Her   Blend/Her
Blind Her   So   She Can Blend with the Others (Odd/Her)
Blind Her By Shaking and Spinning Her Really Hard

Blessing: B/Boy Holding All Fem Breasts   L/Sweet Fem Light/Ill/Hell/Elle   Ass   N/In/Hen/Virgin
A Blessing for that Boy   is   When He Gets some Ass (S/Sex) from that Sweet N/Virgin

Block: B/Baby Boy Holding All Fems Breasts   Lock
Here is B/ Boy Locking His Luck Away
Block is a Powerful Word
The Code Locks Its/His Luck and Blocks it to Her
The Code Holds The Keys of the Locks

The Dam Code The Damn Book

Blood: B/Boy   Holding All Fems Breasts   L/Sweet Fem Love Light
Knowledge/Ill/Elle/Hell   2 OOs/Fem Holes   D/Pregnant
It is in the Blood that that Boy will Impregnate All Fems
Bram Stoker the Author of Dracula was a Member of the Secret Golden Dawn Society which was a Breakaway Movement from "Societas Rocinciana" (Note the Words Rose Sin and Anna (See Letter N in The Letters Chapter and the Word Rosicrucian in The Words Chapter)
It Was Founded by Robert W. Little in 1865 who was a Freemason in Rocinciana
"Le Serpent Rouge" by Pierre Feugere and Louis St-Maxent Gaston de Koker (Plantard) Said "Some named Her Isis Queen of All Sources Benevolent"   That Remind Us of the Tibetan Goddess Tara   She Allow All Benefits to Her Devotes When Asked
"Come unto Me all who suffer and are to be afflicted and I shall give you rest"
She is the Mary Magdalene of the Celebrated Vase Filed with Healing Balm   The Initiated Knows Her Real Name She is Notre Dame Des Croix"(Our Lady of the Crosses)
The French Which were Still Very Much Sane about Religion Then   Many Years Ago   Researched   That Code   and Planted a Huge Church in the Middle of the Meeting of Many Meridians which were Calculated by the Franc Masons or the Freemasons (Free/My/Sons)
French Franc Means Frank in English Which is a Beautiful Word   The Franc is the Currency in France
Here is a Word that Seems to be Contrary to The Code
The Templars and the Sion have had the same Grand Master   Note the Resemblance Between the Word Zion (Z/On) and Sion
This is When   Z/Sleep   the Last Letter of the Alphabet was Replaced by   S/Is/His/Snake/Penis/Stick   with Almost the Same Meaning   but   in a Different Letter Identity
The Code is All About 666/Sex/Sex/Sex   It is Represented Clearly in The Letter S
The Rosicrucian's were Pronounced Enemies of the Roman Church
Sang is Blood in French
Sans Means Without in French and Both have the Same Exact Sound   The Word Goes from   Without   to   Blood
Saying   Without Blood The Blood Loss of All Fems makes Her Empty of Her Blood Over Generations   One of the Greatest Fear inside Any Man

Lise Rochon

In The Fems Diet In Ancient Times   Many Foods Containing Iron were Given First to Pregnant Bleeding or Weak Fems   Liver Kidneys Ligaments Blood Root Vegetables etc

Bloom: B/Boy Holding All Fems Breasts   Loom
When Boy Dominates as He is Supposed to in   The Code
He Blooms
Loom is Made Entirely of Fem Letters   and   Blooming is Usually Reserved for Flowers   which is a Fem Symbol for Her Sexual Opening
loom: to dominate or overhang
Switch M/Motherhood for D/Pregnant and She Gets Blood
Take Away L and He Gets Boom

Blow: B/Boy Holding All Fems Breasts   L/Sweet Fem Love Light/Ill/Hell/ Elle   O/Fem Hole   W/All Fems Sex Active
Blow (Below) is a Blow Job
Blown (Oral Sex for Him)   Balloon/Ball/On (Pregnancy for Her)

Blowhole: Blow   Air/Heir/R/Whore   in that Fish Hole (See Fish and Sea in The Words Chapter)

Blunder   Blond/Her
blunder: a gross stupid or careless mistake
A Blond Fem is/was Said to be Prettier   But She will Gain Nothing from that Either   Says The Code
Many Blond Fems Tried to Become Stupid (Dull as a Doll) to make themselves Interesting   Stupid Blond Jokes are Always Popular

Blown: That Blow Job is on with   N/In/Hen/Virgin

Blustery: B/Lust/R/He   B/Lust/Are/He
B/Boy Holding All Fems Breasts   is Lusty and Feeling it
blustery: to roar and be tumultuous

Board: B/Boy Holding All Fems Breasts   R/Her/Hair/Are/Here/Hear/Ear/ Whore/Or/Heir/Err/Our/Sex   D/Pregnant
The Boy The Whore and The Pregnant   All Across The Board
board: a sheet of wood

Not Much Life There
Bore/D
bore: to make a hole with an instrument by drilling
Drill that Hole to Make Her Pregnant
Border   Board/Her
A Border is a Limitation of Space
Wood is a Fem Element in Chinese   Along with Air Water Fire and Earth

Boat: B/Oath
The Only for Men Oath of the Secret Societies   Or   Get the Boot   Or Both
Both   The Code   is Often About Having More than One Fem per Masc
Boats and Ships are Related to Water therefore Fem
In French it is Bateau (Bat/O   Beat Her Hole)
Eat it As Oats

Bodacious: Beau/Bow   D/Pregnant   She/Shh   S/Is/His/Us/Ass/Hiss/Serpent/Penis
The Beau   The Silenced Pregnant   and   The Penis
Body/She/Us   Her Silenced Body Belong to His Penis   With a Bow A Bow is Meant to Tie/Attach
Bud/He/She/Us
Synonyms for Bodacious: remarkable   outstanding   sexy   voluptuous   impressive   remarkable   excellence   a male companion   a lover   a dandy
That One Word Bodacious is   a Grandly Positive and Reinforcing Message   a Gift to Man   Only   Voluptuous is here because She can Only be Remarkable When Her Sexuality is Involved
Bodacious Starts with Entirely Masc Words   Beau (Masc for Belle)   or   a Bud as in a Buddy
An Abode (A   Bod/Bud) is Where a Brother Stay   or   is Safe   Says The Code   The Fem has No Space There

Body: Bud/He
bud: a man given name   a brother   a buddy
Always Budding (Body/In) Something That Men Code
The Fem has None

Here are Different Parts of the Human Body   and   What I could Find   As Their Meaning According to   The Code
Body: Achilles Tendon (A/Kill/Us   Tend/Tent   On (Here in a Rare Occasion   The Code is Negative to a Man   A/All Men   Kills   S/Penis   If a Man is the Weakest Point (Talking Too Much) He Gets Killed   It is Done in Secret (The Tent) and is   On)   Arch (See Arc and Archer in The Words Chapter)   Artery (Art   Her/Hear   He)   Arteries (Art/Her/His/Is   See Art and Blood in The Words Chapter)   Belly (Belle/He   Bell/He)   Chin (She/Shh   In) A Chin that is Pulled Back is Interpreted as a Sign of Obedience Weakness or Fear)   Calluses (Call   Us/S)   Coccyx (Cock   X/X   The Coccyx is the Triangular Bone at ther Base of The Spine Where the Fire of Kundalini Process Starts   The Eye of God is in That Pyramid   That Triangle)   Colon (Call   N/On/Virgin   Back to The Feces for The Fems)   Coma (Come/A   the Comma   See Comma in The Punctuation Chapter)
Digits   (Dig   Hit/It)   Face (F/Ace   F/Ass) When F/Fem/Fuck   is in Front of Ace (Masc)   it is on Her Face   Faces   Become   Feces   Facial   F/She/All)   Feet (F/Heat Fit   F/Hit   The/Feet (Defeat)   Foot (F/Fem/Fuck   Hoot) hoot: to cry   to shout
The Sole (Soul) is Under the Foot
Femur (F/Fem/Fuck   M/Motherhood   U/You/Ovulating   R/Her/Hair/Are/Here/Hear/Ear/Whore/Or/Heir/Err/Our/Sex
Genitalia (Gene/He/Tail/U)   Heart (Herd/Heard with T/Fem   Cross   Crossing Over   from   D/Pregnant)   Fingers (Fin (Fish)   G/Penis Penetration   He
Heel (Ill/Elle/Hell/All/Sweet Fem Light/L)   Knee (N/He   On Her Knees for The Virgin   Neigh)   Leg (Lay/Egg   it is Between Her Legs)   Liver (Live Her/R/Whore/Heir)   Mouth (M/Out   The Mother is Out   here   as She/Shh is being Silenced)   Navel (Naïve   All/Ill/Hell   N/V/L   are All Fems Sound Letters)   Nose (N/In/Hen/Virgin   Hoes/Hose   Knows/No(s)) (The Nose is the Oldest Memory Sense Organ (Whore/Gang   Or/Gain   The Metal Or is Gold in French)
(Whore   G/Penis Penetration   Ann/N/In/Hen/Virgin)   Shin (She/Shh   N/In/Hen/Virgin)   Shoulder (Should   R/Her/Hair/Are/Here/Hear/Ear/Heir/Or/Whore/Err/Our/Sex There are 2 Shoulders   An Indication Again of the Openness of The Code to Polygamy   Sinew   (Sin/You   a Sinew is a Source of Strength and Power   it is a Tendon   The Code   Says Find Strength   by Sinning)   Sole (Soul   Sow/All

The Dam Code The Damn Book

(Sowing His Oats)   Spine (S/Is/His/Us/Ass/Hiss/Serpent/Penis   P/Man Power   N/In/Hen/Virgin   E/He) has the Same Letters as Penis (a Column too)   Many Animals Pee/P to Mark Territory (Men Love to Pee)   (Spy Ann/N/Virgin) Take E/He Away and Get a Spin
Tendon (Tend/On)   Teeth (Tit)   Tumor (T/Fem Cross
Humor)   Hormones were Called Humors and were an Important Term in Medicine in Older Times
Switch M for N/In/Hen/Virgin and Get Tuner (Being in Tune with a Tumor)   Urine (Your/N   You/Are/In/N   Your/Ring   Year/In/N   Hear/In   Herein)   Uterus (You/Tear/Us   Tears and Tears Us)   Uvula   (You/Veil/A   You/View/Law   You/Voila   All Americans Know Voila   The Code is As a Little (Big) Rat that Infiltrates itself into the Core of Our Brain and Grow from there Using Us as the Host)   Vein (Vain/Vine   (See Blood and Wine in The Words Chapter)   Vulvae VLV 3 Fem Sound Letters in French Vulve (Valve) (V/Sex Open Fem   L/Sweet Fem Light/Ill/Hell/Elle and   V Again)   Wrist (Risk it as a Hand Job)   Zit(Z/Sleep   on   It/Hit)

Bold: B/Hold   B/Old
B/Boy Holding All Fems Breasts   is Holding On to Them Until He is Old That Is Bold   Without the Boy She is Old or on Hold
Switch B for C/See/Young Girl and She Gets Cold   She does Not Want to be in the Front   being Too Young)
Switch B for F/Fem/Fuck and She Gets to Fold
Switch B for G/Penis Penetration and He gets the Gold
Switch B for H/Secret Code Letter and He gets a Hold
Switch B for M/Motherhood and She Gets Mold
Switch B for S/is/His/Us/Ass/Hiss/Serpent/Penis and She Gets Sold
Switch B for T/Fem Cross and She Gets Told
Switch B for V/Fem Sex Active and She Gets a Volt or be in a Vault
In Volt   D/Pregnant   Transforms into   T/Fem Cross There is High Electric Tension Here and it is Also Secret
Switch B for W/All Fems Sex Active and They Get Wold
wold: an elevated tract of open country
How Convenient

Bond: B/On/D   Be/N/D
B/Boy Holding All Fems Breasts   On to   D/Pregnant
B/Boy Holding All Breasts   O/Fem Hole   N/In/Hen/Virgin   D/Pregnant

Lise Rochon

The Bond to Be is   The Boy   The Virgin   and   The Pregnant
bond: something that binds   a tie

Bone: B/Boy Holding All Fems Breasts   Own/On
Here B/Boy Owning The Fems Breasts Concept is
Repeated   Being   Accentuated with Own/On
A Bone (Bonus) is Something Good to Look for a Boy
Own that Bone   On With That Bone   Be/One
Add R/Her/Hair/Are/Here/Hear/Ear/Whore/Or/Heir/Err/Our/Sex   And it is
the Word   Born   She From being a N/Virgin has becomes a R/Whore or
with Heir   That Bone is Big Change For Her
Switch B for D/Pregnant and She is Done
Switch B for F/Fem/Fuck and She Gets Fun   The Code   is All for
That   With The Boy Bone (Slang for Penis) in Erection   She Comes at
The Rescue (it is Done with D/Pregnant)
Switch B for G/Hymen Penetration When Done He is Gone
Switch B for J/Sheppard and He/She Gets a John (Prostitute Client)
Switch B for K/Broken Fem Warrior   or   Hard C/Conne   or   Q/
Bleeding Fem and She Gets Con (Stupid in French) (See Con and Conne in
The Words Chapter)
Switch B for L/Sweet Fem Love Light/Ill/Elle/Hell/All and She Gets Loan
(Alone to be Loaned to The Bone)
Switch B for S/Is/His/Serpent/Penis and He Gets Sown (To Sow His Wild
Oats)
Switch B for T/Fem Cross and She Gets Tone (The Tone to Adjust to Meet
that Bone)
Switch B for Z/Sleep on It and She Gets The Zone to be at When That Boy
Bone Comes to Her

Boner: B/Own/Her   Bone/Her
Boner is Slang for Erection
(See Bone for More Explanation on a Boy Bone)

Bonus: Bone   S/Is/His/Us/Ass/Hiss/Serpent/Penis
Double Bonus   Ye   Says The Code   Penis is here Twice
Bone/Us

Boo: B/Boy Holding All Fems Breasts   2 OOs/Fem Holes

The Dam Code The Damn Book

If a Boy would be with 2 Holes or 2 Fem Holes   No
boo: an exclamation of contempt and disapproval
Add Another B/Boy and She Gets Another Boob
Because Boo can be a Scary Thing   She does Not Look at it   So   The Code is Safe here

Boobs: 2 BB s/Boy Holding All Fems Breasts Starts and Ends the Fem Boob Word with 2 BB s/Boys   and   2 OOs/Fem Holes in its Middle   2 for 2   One Boy for Each Boob   Just Saying
According to   The Code   the Boys are the Ones Responsible for Maintaining All The Fems with Large or Unnatural Breasts   Keeping that Hole Open Permanently as in the Artificially Code Made Letter V/Sex Open Fem and W/All Fems Sex Open
boob: a stupid person   a blunder   a mistake   a feminine breast
Big Boobs are Confusing Stupid Mistakes   The Code   Says
But In Nature Mammals have No Permanent Breasts   Except on Cows which are Artificially Maintained for Milk Production and Commerce by Humans   Cow is a Slang Term for The Fems
That Word Boob Would be the Ultimate and Perfect Example and Proof if Possible (Puss/Able) on How the Language Code/Grid Secret Code Works its Stupid Way Inside The Fems Mind As a Parasite   Making Breasts Stupid
Take Away the Ending B/Boy and She Gets Boo

Booboo: When   B/Boy Holding All Fems Breasts   Has too Many(4) O/Fem Holes   Around Him   It is a Booboo   He Cannot Handle it
booboo: a silly mistake   a minor injury
Be/Oo   Twice   Or   Be/O   As in to Her   Just be a Hole
O and O: owned and operated
How Convenient for The Code
B/Who   Be/Who   The Code Says it is a Bad Question to Ask   And It Says it Twice   It May Bring a Small Injury and be Laughed at
boo: to show disapproval by booing   to cry boo in derision
Then The Code Hides in Disapproval

Book: B/Hook
The   Secret Code   Concept of a Book is   The B/Boy Holding All Fem Breasts with a Hook (A Hooker is a Whore)

Booster: Boos/T/Her   Boo/Stay/Her
Boos is the Plural of Boo
The Code   Says Here What a Boost for Her it is to Remain Scared as She Gets Busted (Bust/Her)   Really Big
Busted Also Means Getting Arrested/Cut   Another Double Edge Knife for Her From The Code   Trying to do Something that She is being Told to do   And Getting in Trouble for it
buster: something really big   someone that breaks something
T/Fem Cross/Great Curse   Adds Another Boost   Without   T   She Would be a Boozer
Booster Her Some More Breasts   A Booster Bra

Boot: B/Boy Holding All Fems Breasts   2 OO s/All Fem Holes   and   T/Fem Cross
The Boot here is   All Fem Holes Get to be Crucified/fem Cross   With B/Boy Starting Early that Boot
boot: an instrument of torture   to kick   any shoe
(She/Shh   Who)

Booty: Boot/He
booty: a small temporary structure
Booty is Sex in Slang   How Convenient for The Code
He B OOs Her until T/Fem Cross   Then   Give Her the Boot (a Kick in the Butt)
Switch O/Fem Hole for U/You/Ovulating and She Gets a Butt

Boot Legg: Boot/Leg   L/Sweet Fem Light/Ill/Hell/Ail/Elle   and the   Egg (Ov   Ovulation)
Kick those Legs   It is Time for Pregnancy
The Code Calls it Legs and Lays
Boot that Leg and Keep it Secret because it is Illegal
boot Legg: something that is made or sold illicitly
Leg/A/C   Legacy   Giving or getting The Boot (See Boot)
There are Secrets in that Word

Border: Bore   D/Pregnant   R/Her/Hair/Are/Here/Hear/Ear/Whore/Or/Heir/Err/Our/Sex
B/R/D/R

That is Why The Fems Get to be a Dull Doll   She has Borders Put on
Her   And it Bores Her too
Being Pregnant (Bearing a Child)
or a Whore can be Part of them

Bore: B/Boy Holding All Fems Breasts   and   R/Her/Hair/Are/Here/
Hear/Ear/Whore/Or/Heir/Err/Our/Sex
It is to Bear in Past Tense as in BRR (Cold)
When Boy is Done with the Whore   He is Bored
Bear or Boar   He Can Bear it
bore: a dull person   to make a hole bigger
A Boar   A/All Men   BRR   A Boar is a Pig

Boring: Boar/In   Bore/N   Bow/Ring   B/Whore/In
When the Boar is with N/In/Hen/Virgin   He Gets to Bore the Hole
bore: to increase the diameter of a hole
Was it Boring

Born: B/Horn
B/Boy Holding All Fems Breasts   and a   Horn
A Baby Born Without a Horn is a Girl   She is Not Represented here
in   Born
Switch B/Boy to T/Fem Cross and She Gets a Thorn or be Torn

Boss: B/Us
Be   U/You/Ovulating   S/Is/His/Us/Ass/Hiss/Serpent/Penis
B is the Boss   When a Uterus is in Between a Boy Penis and Him   it
is   BS
BS is Slang for Bull Shit   Back to the Feces For Her
Bus is the Cover Word here

Both: B/Boy Holding All Breasts   Oath   Boat
A Boat is a Small Vessel   Any Word Related to the Sea or Water is Fem
An Oath is Related to The Code   The Initiates of   That Code   have to
Pronounce Oaths as they Gain Power and Knowledge
Oath may Refer to a Profanity or a Swear Word
B   O/Fem Hole   T/Fem Cross/Great Curse   H/Secret Code Letter
Here   B/Boy is with   T/Fem Cross   O/Hole   in Accordance to The Code

One of the Hidden Message of the Secret Societies is to Separate Loving Couples by Creating Polygamy   Or   Sex with Animals
He Gets to Keep them Both
Une Botte   Is a Boot in French   To Take your Boot is to have Sex
both: the one as well as the other
Both Cannot be Both without the H Letter for the Secret Code   Then It would be a Boot Instead   or a Butt   But
The Word Both is   Which Witch is Witch With   All Over Again

Bottle: Butt/All
Bottle is Slang for Breast   Jugs
The Reward for Having Jugs or Giving the Bottle   is   Something On the Butt   or   a But

Bottom: Butt/On
Bottoms Will Always Go On   with Butt/On   Because The Fems Can Only go Down One Direction   Till Bottom
No But and No Butts
The Bottom is the Ass   Where the Anus is (Ann/Us)

Bouquet: Boo   K/Broken Fem Warrior
Kay is a Fem Name
A Bouquet of Flowers is Several Cut (Half Dead) Flowers Tied All Together   As   The Code   would Say   Tie those Dead Fem Together and Boo Them

Bouncer: Bounce/Her
bouncer: an employee that get rid of disorderly persons in a bar
Bounce R/Her/Hair/Are/Here/Hear/Ear/Whore/Or/Heir/Err/Our/Sex
Bounce Her as a Ball

Bow: B/Boy Holding All Fems Breasts   O/Fem Hole   W/All Fems Sex Active
B/Boy   Holds Fem Holes   Also
From a Ribbon Bow to a Bowing Gesture   It Implies to Twist or Bend Something (See BB in The Words Chapter)
An Arc and a Bow
bow: to curve

The Dam Code The Damn Book

To Curve is an Old Word for Arch
When the Bow/Beau is Here   All Fems Sex Active Holes Falls or Bow for the Beau   Says The Code

Bowel: Bow/Well   Bow/All
Bow/Well   All Fems   from the Bowels (See BB)   Needs to Bow to The Boy
Back to The Feces For   Her/R   Bow   Hell/Ill/Ail/L/All

Bowl: Bow/All   BL
Switch O/Fem Hole for A/All Men and He Gets a Ball   B/All   Be/All   (That Includes All Masc)   Add i/Marriage Act Union and They Get Bailed
A Bowl of Food   For Him   B/Whole   B/Hole
Switch O/Fem Hole for i/Marriage Act and They Get Bill (a Masc Name   and Money)

Box: BX
B/Boy Holding All Fems Breasts   O/Fem Hole   X/Fallen Fem Cross
When B/Boy is with a X/Dead Fem Hole   It is a Box Called a Grave
Watch More for Words with an X in It   Especially When Ending the Word
Boxing   Box   N/In/Hen/Virgin/In
Switch X/Fallen Fem Cross for T/Fem Cross and She Gets   Boot/In

bra: a female underwear
A Bra is a Brother in Slang
The Code   Stay Close to The Fems Breasts   in Every Way
A Bra is a Brassiere in French (Bear/Ass/Here   Brass/Here)

braw: fine looking   excellent
If the Braw and the L/Fem Sweet Light   Meet
It is a Brawl   Bra/All
No One Pays Attention here because the Bra is Braw   It is Beautiful   But
No   It is a Brawl   Get Out or Get Hurt

Brag: B/Boy Holding All Fems Breasts   Rag
When Boy Meet the Rag   He
brag: to boast   to vaunt

Braid: Bread   Bride   Bred   Same Formula and Progression as in the R Letter/Her/Hair/Are/Here/Hear/Ear/Whore/Or/Heir/Err/Our/Sex   As in from Hair to Hear it to Have a Heir or be a Whore or to Err as Her Sex Options
With Her Braid   The Bride   is Bred
The Bribe is the Dowry/Dot
Bred   The Bread Comes with the Wine/Blood
The Braid is Another Way for   The Code   to be with Her/Hair/Heir/Or/Whore/R (See Letter R in The Numbers Chapter)
It is the Bread and Butter (Butt/Her But/Her) of Our Societies   The Code   Speak
Br/Aid   The Bear/Aid
Switch B/Boy Holding All Fem Breasts for P/Man Power and He Gets Prayed
Switch B for T/Fem Cross and She Gets Trade (d)
Add S/Is/His/Us/Ass/Hiss/Serpent/Penis and P/Man Power and He Gets Sprayed

Brave: B/Rave
rave: extravagant praise   to talk wildly   a sound
When Boys are Brave   There is a Lot of Loud Praise
Nothing is Neglected in the Language Code
B/R/V   B/Boy Holding All Fems Breasts   R/Her/Hair/Are/Here/Hear/Ear/Whore/Or/Heir/Err/Our/Sex   and   V/Fem Sex Active/Open Legs
The Brave Boy is having Sex with a Fem Called Whore

Bread: B/Red   Bred
Drink the Wine (Blood) and Break the Bread (Bred)
The Way to Breed   Says The Code   Is to Break it
Do it Just As Natural Breathing   It is a Fundamental Need   Contraceptives were Forbidden Until Lately   So No Chance for Her

Break: B/Boy Holding All Fems Breasts   Rake
The Boy Rakes It in When He Brake/Break Her (See Broke) Her Hymen

Breaker: Break/Her

Because it Means to Break Her Literally   She Cannot Know That Before it Happens   Therefore the Electric Discharge   Do Not Touch
Breaker is a Cover Word

Breast: B/Boy Holding All Fems Breasts   Rest
Breast is a Beast without R/Whore/Are/Her/Heir/Err/Sex
The Breast Shape or Dome/Doom is on Top of Many Old Religious or Important Buildings
Breasts Are the Ever Expendable Cups   Says The Code
And it is a Complete Success
The Code has Been Working on that for Thousands of Years
Now so Many Fem are Full On Carrying Super Big Breasts
From Surgery   too
The Great Curse   Secret Code   Web is Tightly Knit
Very Few Can See through
We All Abide by it   All Day Long
In French Breasts is Sein and Pregnant is Enceinte
The French Language is Closer to the Natural Way of Being
The Influence of The Code was Less and Different Over there

Breather: Breed/Her
In Ancient Times They Used to Breed The Fems for Size
breather: short pause for rest   a person who breathe
B/Read/Her
When Boy can Read Her   It is Time to Breed her

Breathing: Breed/In
Bread/Breed/Bred
The Code   Associates Its Most Important Symbols with the Most Important Factors of Life   Such as to   Breathe
A Boy/Man Ejaculation   Is almost As Breathing   There is a Lot of it   and   Often   It just Happens   The Every Morning Erection
Bread is Made of Dough   Daughter   Dot/Her   Do/Her   Dough/Her   Then   Do/Other
D/Pregnant   Goes from Being   C/See/Young Girl   to being   D/Pregnant   C is Now being Attached to the I/Stick
She is Attached To Him But   Looking in the Past (Left) Instead of the Future (Right)   How Convenient for The Code

Lise Rochon

That Change of Direction of C Half Circle When She Turns into D/ Pregnant   Letter C has gone Backward   But Her Belly is Facing Forward in Letter D

Breed: Bread   Brad   Beard
BRD   When Boy has Sex with D/Pregnant as a Whore
Be/Heard   Brad Boy Bear a Bred Beard
Bread   Adding a Man Name is Almost Adding a Title   It Brings Importance and Stability
The Code   Says No Fem Presence Needed here in Breeding   Except for the Letter R/Whore/Heir
In Antiquity Men of Power Were Breeding The Fems for Size

Brr   A Beer   Words with B/Boy Holding All Breasts and are Positive to The Code
Especially with 2 RR s/Her/Whores/Or/Heirs/Sex
Add D/Pregnant and She Get a Brat with Beard that Breed a Bride
Bird is the Cover Word Here

Brew: B/R/U
B/Boy Holding All Fems Breasts   R/Her/Hair/Are/Here/Hear/Ear/Whore/Or/Heir/Err/Our/Sex   U/You/Ovulating/Chalice/Cup
Here is The Code Brew from   A Receptive Whore

Bride: B/Boy Holding All Fems Breasts   Ride
Ride that Bride   Says The Code and Breed   How Convenient
Another BRD Word Here
Braid   Beard   Breed   Bred   Brad   Bride
B/R/Hide That Pride

Bridge: B/Ridge
B/Boy Holding All Fems Breasts
ridge: a long narrow elevation of land   a chain of hills or mountains   the back of an animal
The Ridge is here Depicting The Fems Breasts in Rows and the Ass Together in the same Concept   A Common Concept in That Code is to Associate The Fems with the Ass (See Ann/N/In/Hen/Virgin/Donkey)   Don/Key   Titles have a Lot of Unknown Powers)

The Dam Code The Damn Book

The Bridge in The Code is the Separation Between the Masc and what She Sees
The Bridge is a VIP Word in The Code Symbology
In the Holy Grail Story Percival Crosses Several Bridges
They All have a Meaning as in Advancing into New Territories   Where Others will Not   In the Very Beginning He leaves His Mother   and   He Crosses the First Bridge
As He look Back   She is Lying on the Ground before the Bridge   May be Dead
He Goes On Anyway on His Journey Without Looking back   He has Shed (She   D/Pregnant) Her

Bring: B/Boy Holding All Fems Breasts   and the   Ring
Bring that Ring to All Fems from Childhood

Brink: B/Rink
G/Penis Penetration   has been Replaced with   K/Broken Fem Warrior   (See Letter K in The Numbers Chapter)
Going from   B/Ring the Ring   to   Bring/K
brink: the edge   a point of unset   threshold of danger
It is Dangerous for Her   Because She (K) Will Die here and be Resurrected   As the R/Her/Hair/Are/Here/Hear/Ear/Whore/Or/Heir/Err/Our/Sex
Kay is a Fem Name
When Kay is D/Pregnant- There is D/Kay   Decay
The Fem Never Wins in   The Code

Brisket: B/Risk/It   Be/Risk/Hit
Cooking Breasts   To Cook Something is Also Planning Something   with a Risk
brisket: the breast of an animal or the part of the breast lying next to the ribs   a cut of meat especially beef from this part
To Cook a Brisket is Generally a Happy Event
As Long as The Fems Loses Something   It Fits   The Code

Broad: B/Boy Holding All Fems Breasts   Road
The Road Ahead is Broad for Him (for Her it is M/Motherhood)
B   Rod   A Boy and His Rod (Penis)

Lise Rochon

Not for the Broad   She got to be a Largely Opened Promiscuous Tolerant Mainstream Whore
broad: of great breadth   measured from side to side   of great extend large   widely diffused   open   full   liberal tolerant   main and general   a term used to refer to a woman   *Slang usually offensive*   a promiscuous woman
A Promiscuous Man is Loosely Called a Seductor Bachelor or a Beau
A Bachelor Degree is a (Another) Free Title for the Masc   It Associates Him Well with Power   Unconsciously
In The Code All Fems are Beasts   (Whores/Horses/Chickens etc)
No Title for a Fem Unless there is an Ass Attached to it as in in Mayoress Actress Baroness   or   Something Unfair or Ugly
Switch A/All Men for Another O/Fem Hole and She Gets Another Brood
brood: a family of offspring or young   a breed species group or kind   to incubate   to think or worry persistently or moodily about   ponder
It is the BR/Hood   The B/Boy   The R/Whore   and   The Code/Hood

Broom: B/Boy Holding All Fems Breasts   Room
When the Boy Stick is in a Room   it is His
BRM   B/Boy   R/Sex   M/Motherhood
Switch B for V/Fem Sex Active and She Gets to Vroom
vroom: the roaring sound made by a motor at high speed
Switch B for G/Penis Penetration and He Gets a Groom

Broke: B/Roc/Her
The Stone was/is an Important Symbol in the Philosopher Stone History
Jesus Left Peter with "on this rock I will build my church"
A Rock is Une Pierre in French which is Peter in English
Une Pierre is Also a Stone/Rock
And the Rock/Stone is The Fem
The Code   Says here   Breaks that Stone/Rock
Broke is in the Past   so   it has Already Happened
B/Boy   that Rakes the Benefits   B/Rake   As Usual

Broker: Broke/Her
A Broker is a Serious Financial Word   Beware
It Comes With Studies and Diplomas

The Dam Code The Damn Book

Another Cover Word for the Breaking of Her

Brothel: Brought   L/Sweet Fem Light/Ill/Ail/Hell/Elle
Hell is Brought in the Brothel
Switch L for R/Her/Hair/Are/Here/Hear/Ear/Whore/Or/Heir/Err/Our/Sex and He Gets a Brother
Without R/Her/Hair/Are/Here/Hear/Ear/Whore/Or/Heir/Err/Our/Sex   She Becomes a Bother
Brothels Brothers and Broads   The Code   Speaks
Brought/Hell   Brought/Her   Brought/D   It is the B/Rod
Bro/Bra   T/Fem Cross   Hell/Ill
A Brothel is When All Brothers are with   T/Fem Cross/Curse   in   Hell/Ill   The Bro/Tell

Brother: Broad/Her (See Broad)
A Brother Does That
broad: of great extend   large   a promiscuous woman
Brother is an Important Word in The Bible

brooder: a device for rearing young chickens
Chick/Chicken is The Code Slang for The Fems
Broth/Her   Brothel (Brought/Hell) is Close
Switch 2 OOs/Fem Holes for A/All Men   and He Gets
Brat   R/Her/Whore/Are/Our/Heir) Err/Sex
Bra/D/Her   Back to the Pregnant Breasts for Her
Take Away R/Her/Hair/Are/Here/Hear/Ear/Whore/Or/Heir/Err/Our/Sex   and He Gets a Bother
Brother/He   Broidery Would be the Cover Word Here
The Broader Her   O/Fem Hole   Makes Sex More Accessible   It Is to Make Her a Whore (Broad)   Says The Code

Bruiser: Bruise/Her
bruiser: a strong tough person
She can take it   She was Bruised before
The Code   takes Advantage of Those Double Meaning

Brute: B/Root
Brutal: B/Root/All

Brutality: B/Root/All/He
The Code   Says Man is a Brute is His Roots

Buddy: Bud/He
U/You/Ovulating   Makes it a Friendly Open Hole (Natural Ovulation)   But No Says The Code   No Buddies for The Fem   Buddies are for Men Only   Including the Ones Budding (The Boys)   Her She is the Nobody
Add L/Sweet Fem Light/Ill/All/Ail/Hell/Elle and She Gets Bloody (Fem Blood Loss)

Bug: B/Hug
Boys do Not Hug that Much   Same for Men Unless Sex Is involved   Otherwise it Bugs Them
Many Boys are Fascinated By Bugs

Bull: B/Boy Holding All Fems Breasts   Hull
Bull/He   Bully
Switch U/You/Ovulating for A/All Men and He Gets Balls
B/All   All Boys are Bulls in the Hull
When   B/Boy Holding All Breasts   will be   P/Man Power   He will Pull
Boule Is French for a Ball   Boules is Slang for Breasts in French

Bullet: Bull/Hit
Switch B for P/Man Power and He Gets Pull   Hit/It (Pull The Trigger for a Bullet Hit)

Bullshit: B/Boy Holding All Fems Breasts   You/U/You/Ovulating   L/Sweet Fem Love Light/Ill/Hail/Ail/Hell/Elle   She/Shh   It/Hit
Bullshit here is Her Beaten Up   Silenced in Sexual Hell Held by   The Code   from Boyhood
Bull/Shit   (See Shit (She/It) in The Words Chapter)
When Looking at Feces Words   Look for The Fems Relationship With it
Here is a Bull (a Cow) and Feces
In Bull Shit   She is His Shit

Bunch: B/Boy Holding All Fems Breasts   Hunch

hunch: to thrust out or up in a hump   to shove push or jostle   an intuitive guess or feeling
The Boys All Know Each Other in Many Ways   Says The Code   The Girls   No   Not Allowed

Burden: B/Boy Holding All Fems Breasts   Herd   N/In/Hen/Virgin
burden: that which is carried   that which is born with difficulty   a load
That Burden is On Her from Early Age   She is the One being Herd (See Sheep in The Words Chapter)   It is Heard   Says The Code

Burial: B/Holding All Fems Breasts
R/Her/Hair/Are/Here/Hear/Ear/Whore/Or/Heir/Err/Our/Sex
L/Sweet Fem Love Light/Ill/Ail/Hail/Hell/Elle
That Burial is Where All Fems Are Whores
Bury/All   Bore/He/All   For The Fem
Burr/He/All   Bear/He/All   Brr/He/All   For The Masc

Burn: B/Boy Holding All Fems Breasts   and the   Urn
Urn is   U/You/Ovulating   R/Her/Hair/Are/Here/Hear/Ear/Whore/Or/Heir/Err/Our/Sex   N/In/Hen/Virgin
R/N   Are/N   Her/N
An Urn in Antiquity was a Receptacle Common for Grains Wine Water and Ashes
When B/Boy Holding All Breasts is with the Urn which is The Fem Receptacle/Vagina   It is a Burning Subject for Him   He Wants In   Cannot   being Too Young   Brr/N   Bear/N   Burr/N
Having Sex   Be/Earned   Implies Paying for it as in Prostitution   Says The Code
Switch B for T/Fem Cross and She Gets a Turn (to Play with the Boy)
Switch B for F/Fem Fuck and She Gets Fern (Easy on The Boy)
Switch B for L/Sweet Fem Love Light/Ill/Ail/Hail/Hell/Elle and She Gets Learn
Switch U for O/Fem Hole and She Gets Born (a Baby)
Switch U for A/All Men and He Gets a Barn (Back to The Animals for The Fems)

Bury: Another BR Sound Sad Word
Bear/He   Burr/He   Brr/He

Nothing Friendly here
Bury is a Strong Code Cover Word that Holds to the Story of the Holy Grail (Hole/He/Girl) King Arthur the Bleeding Lance and the Sword In/Out of the Stone
The Bear was King Arthur (Art/Her)   His Flag Is a Red Dragon (Red Rag/On   with D Pregnant) with its Tongue Out
Bury It is a Powerful Word in The Code
bury: to cover and put in the ground   to immerse oneself   to entomb   to hide   to secrete   to cover in order to conceal
B/Hear/He   Boy Can Hear   Girls are Berries/Fruits to be Picked   By the Big Bear He is   No Says The Code   Too Young
B/Be   Hurray   B/Boy Holding Fem All Breasts   is with R/Her   He Hurry   and then   He Buries/Hides It
burry: a rough covering of a nut or a seed
A Fruit Needs a Bush (Slang for Pubic Hair) or a Tree to Grow From (Tree of Life)
Tree and # 3 Are Important Signals/Symbols
The Burning Bush is an Old Heavy Concept   Bush is a Well Known Old Powerful Family Name in America

Bush: BSH   B/Boy Holding All Breasts Holding All Fems Breasts   S/is/His/Us/Ass/Hiss/Serpent/Penis/SSS/Snake   H/Secret Code Letter
The Boy Penis here is with H as One   S and H are Together in Sh (She/Shh)   A Coveted Concept
Bush in The Code is an Important Word
bush: a large uncleared area thickly covered with mixed plant growth trees etc as a jungle   mediocre   second rate   amateur   the pubic hair esp of a Female   beaver a woman pubic area   *offensive* a term used to refer to a woman
She is Called a Bush but She has to Find that When in that Jungle
Being Called a Beaver is Just Another Insult to Her Constant Work
Switch B for C/See/Young Girl and She Gets Cush (Cushion)
The Code Loves it When She is Ready for Sex
Switch B for G/Penis Penetration and She Gets a Gush (Sperm)
gush: a sudden copious outflow of a fluid   the fluid emitted
Switch B for H/Secret Code Letter and He Gets Hush
hush: to become silent or quiet   to make silent   silence
That is How The Code Speaks

The Dam Code The Damn Book

Switch B for L/Sweet Fem Love Light/Ill/Ail/Hail/Hell/Elle
and She Get Lush
lush: drunkard   alcoholic   sot
Add L and She Gets Blush
That is What Happens When She is Sweet   The Code Eats it All
Switch B for M/Motherhood and She Gets a Mush
Switch B for P/Man Power and He Gets a Push
Switch B for R/Her/Hair/Are/Here/Hear/Ear/Whore/Or/Heir/Err/Our/Sex
and He Gets a Rush
Switch B for T/Fem Cross and She Gets a Tush
Push on that Tush
tush: an exclamation of impatience disdain contempt   horses
teeth   Us *Slang* for Buttocks
Tush and Tushie (Touch/He)
tosh: nonsense   bosh   neat   tidy
Toucher in French is to Touch
Tush Touche and Tosh have the Same Sound

Busy: BZE   Bee   Is/His   He/E   Bee/See   Biz/He
While She (Bee) Works   He is Bossy and Boozy
Buzz/He   Boss/He
busy: not at leisure   occupied
Busier: B/See/Her

Bust: A Bust is Also   The Fem Breasts/Rack
This is One Thing That Dignifies Her in The Code   Is to have Breasts
On the Other Hand   The Code Says
bust: to collapse from strain   to bankrupt   to place under
arrest   to hit
A Busy Word for Her   The Code   in Full Action   She is in
here   Placed at The Usual Bad Place   Collapsing   Being
Arrested   Impoverished   Hit   Etc   Being Destroyed   If you have to
Bust Someone   Bust/Her   Buster
The Man in The Code   He Gets His Bust in having Honors   as   a
Sculptured Representation of Himself from Shoulders Up
How Convenient for The Code
B/Be   Us/S/Penis   T/Fem Cross   The Code   is Laughing All The Way
to   The Fems

But: B/Boy Holding All Fems Breasts   U/You/Ovulating/Uterus   T/Fem Cross
Here   B/Boy   is with   T/Fem Cross   and Her   U/Uterus (You/Tear/Us)   A Serious True Concept for   The Code
but: on the contrary   except   save   otherwise than
Add Another T/Fem Cross and She Gets Butt
A Butt is a Derrière   D   Err/R   He/E   R/Err   in French D/Pregnant   R/Err   He   R/Err   Lots of R/Whore   or   R/Heir   or   R/Err   in Derriere
The Code Keeps Her there   Back to Feces for Her   Where it Comes Out of Our Derrière
Switch U for A/All Men and He Gets a Bat
Switch U for E/He and He Gets a Bet
Switch U for i/Marriage Act and They Get a Bit
Switch U for 2 OOs/Fem Holes (Prostitution   Polygamy   or   Infidelity)   and   While He Gets That   She Gets the Boot   No Reward here for The Fems   No Matter What She Does

Butcher: But/Butt   She/Shh   R/Her/Hair/Are/Here/Hear/Ear/Whore/Or/Heir/Err/Our/Hour/Sex
Butt/She/Her   A Fem Concept Just for Her   As Simple as
She has a Butt   But No The Code does Not Allow Her to have Anything   So   Butcher/Her   or   Botch/Her
botch: to spoil by poor work
The Word Butch was Integrated as a Lesbian Word in the last 20 Years

Butter: Butt/But   R/Her/Hair/Are/Here/Hear/Ear/Whore/Or/Heir/Err/Our/Sex
Butter is Made from Whipped Cream (Her Sexual Juices)
That Cream Need to be Whipped   A Bad Word
That Makes it Easier to   Beat Her   Bet/Her   Batt/Her   B/Utter
utter: to give expression to speak to pronounce
When She Makes Butter   She can Speak about it
She can Say it Comes from Her Butt   As a Batter

Buttercup: Butter/Cup   Better/Cup   Bet/Her/Cup   Bate/Her/Cup   Batter/C/Hop   Butt/Her/Cop   Ha
So Many Things She Can Do with Her Buttercup   Going Nowhere

Butterfly: Her Butter (Butt/Her)   But/Her)   Fly
Butter is Slang for Fem Sex Juices
Fly as in Psychic   By the Thought

Button: Butt/But   On/N/Hen/Virgin
The Code Uses Words to Exaggerates One Way or Another   here   A Button is So Small   To   Butt/On   is a Very Big Concept   with Big Negative Consequences for The Fems
A Cover Word for The Code

Buy: B/Boy Holding All Fems Breasts   I/High/Eye of the Pyramid
B/Boy   having a Look in the Secrets of the Eye   Would be Too Young   He Cannot Buy   He Cannot Enter   so   He Says Bye   as   He Passes (P/Asses) By
Bye   By
To be Part of those Secret Societies   You Need to have Money and Power   Only on Invitations   A Passerby will Not Enter

By: B/Boy Holding All Fems Breasts   Y/Wounded Fem Warrior
By and By   Buy and Bye
Buy it Says   The Code   By/Hit
To be By   is to be Gay Also
Bi   Means Two or Twice
B/High   B/Eye   B/I
B/Boy Holding All Breasts   is High and Healthy   The Eye is Watching Over Him   B/Boy Holding All Breasts   and   I are 2 Masc Letters   That Carries The Dot (See Dot in The Words and The Punctuation Chapters) For The Fem She Gets   Y/Wounded Fem Warrior   with   By   And   Good   Bye (E is Silent and Almost Invisible)
In Strong Coded Words/Letter I Often Hides as Y   As in Bicycle (B/Boy Holding All Breasts   and   Cycle)
A Bicycle has 2 Wheels (Fem Symbols)   In The Code Symbolism it Means Polygamy
Bicycle is a Cover Word here
by: near or next
Keep Close to that Cycle   Says   The Code

C c
Intro
C/c   is an Entirely Fem Letter
It has a Round Shape in Small and Large Caps
C is The Letter of Youth for a Girl in   The Code
C/See/Young Girl
C as in See   or   Sea   All Water Symbols are Fem   and Connected
In The Sea   The Code   Can See All (The Seal   An Animal   and   a   Pact in   The Code)
She is C   The Sea   and She is   All Fishes   Fishes Do Not Talk   She is   F/She (F/Fem/Fuck   She/Shh)
The Fish Symbolizes All Fems   A School of Fishes   Always Learning/Seeing   The Code   Way
Jesus Symbol is The Fish
Close to the Fish Symbol in   The Code   is the Very Small Pi   ∞ or the Eternity Symbol   It is Said   ∞
It is Number 8 (# 8 is for Pregnancy) Sideways   So Small   We Often Miss it   ∞   She is Laid Horizontal   Eternally Pregnant   Says   The Code   Who is Wearing that Mask
Letter C Shows   Her   O/Fem Hole   Open To The Right   To the Future   She is Not   D/Pregnant   Yet   Which She Will Be   Says   The Code
D   is   C   with The Stick (Letter I/i   Penis/Any Man Stick   and   i/Marriage Act   The Eye/I   in The Pyramid) Blocking the Entrance of   C   Creating   D/Pregnant   C is Now Turned Around   and   Attached to That Stick (Penis or Sex Letter)   The   I/i/High/Eye (Anything from the High is   The Code   in Action from the Pyramid Eye)
C is the One that Meet that Stick in Letters   b   d   q   p
C is Painted in Different Personality Structures   Imposed by   The Code
Hard C in   Can   Carole   Carrol   Cane Cure   etc
Same Harder C Sound in C/Catherine   K/Kathrin   etc   Associates itself with   K/Broken Fem Warrior
The Super Soft C is ç (That Appendix Under   Small C   is Called Cedilla/Cedille   Cedille is Used Especially in Spanish and French (Older Languages Than English   Therefore   The Symbols from   The Code   are Generally More Obvious)
Cedille ç is   The Code   Symbol for Her Monthly Bleeding   Which will be Reincarnated in Large Caps in   Q   The Queen Letter

The Dam Code The Damn Book

Q   The Letter for   The Fem Loss of Blood   in   The Code   From
Queen to All Fems   Is Direct
Because of that   So   Only Fem Communication   Q Words are
Quite   or   Quit   Rare   in   The Code
There are No Clues   Be in The Queue   Q Tips Necessary
Letter S/Ass/Us/Is/His/Hiss/Serpent/Penis   Could be Interchangeable with
C in Many Words as Ascendre   And the Word Sound Would Remain the
Same   As Silence could be Cilence   But No Says   The Code   (That
would Be Too Much/Many Info to The Common Man here)
C is in the Shape of the Smallest Possible Segment of the Moon   The
One that Shines the Less Light (Sliver   Silver   Another Strong
Weak Fem Symbol) Therefore has the Least Light   but   it Does Not
Matter   Because   It is Reflected Light   The Moon is Not a Planet   It is
a Piece of Mud Ratting Around Earth That Reflects The Light of the Sun
It is Called The Fem Planet
The Code   Lunar Terms are Plain Weird
Waning   WNN   3 Fems Sound Letters
W/All Fem Sex Active   N/In/Hen/Virgin   N/In/Hen/Virgin   Again)
Waning Moon is When Her Light is Diminishing   The Code   Calls it
Winning   WNN   in The Sound World
Waxing   WXN   3 Fem Sound letters
Wax/In   Moon   Wax Synonyms are to Enlarge and Dilate   Waxing
is When She as the Bee Secretes the Honeycomb   Preparing that
Nest   Becoming Larger Dilating More
Full Moon is When She is D/Pregnant   Full Moon is the Letter O/Fem
Hole   or   Zero/o   Which has No Value in Math
The Official Name for the   No Moonlight   Phase is Called New
Moon   Why is it Called a New Moon   When There is No Moon at All
Showing   Because in   The Code The Fem Never Gets a Break   She
Must be on with Sex   and Wax at Any Time   On Demand
The Moon Shines in the Night   We Sleep in the Night   There is Little
Action there   Except for Sex and   Procreation
For The Masc in   The Code   there are No Phases   He is the Son of the
Sun   The Planet Men have Attributed to Themselves   Its Light Shines in
the Day   When We are Awake   Where Life Happens
There Can be No Fem Fishing on the Sun   As that Boy/Man Fishing on the
Moon

Lise Rochon

The Fish Being a Fem Symbol   She Would Probably Choose Another Sport than Having a Hook (Hook/Her) in Her Mouth to be Caught with and Die there on Her Own Moon
There is No Fem Face on the Sun   either   as the Fat Sleepy Man on the Moon
The Moon is a Popular Image   But the Moon is   Not Made   of Cheese (Sex Juice)
C is Almost a Half Circle   The Word Circle is Her (Bleeding) Cycle Word   After Adding   Her/R/Hair/Are/Here/Hear/Ear/Whore/Or/Heir/Err/Our/Sex   in it   So   She can go Around Circles with that
In Modern Greek Letter C is Letter # 22 (Polygamy)
The Letters in Our Alphabet Picture The Fems as Weak   In the Big and in the Small   We are to be X/Extenuated/Extinguished/Exterminated/Exiled   etc
In All Fem Symbols Letters   X   is   Ultimately   The Code   Goal
Letter C is the ¢   It is a   One Cent   or   Scent
Here that   C/See/Young Girl   is Crossed (Vertically)   But   The Font Does Not Show it Entirely
A Cent is a Penny
For Her   Very   Little Bits of Money
Penny is a Popular Fem Name in The US

C   c   Words
Caca: Because   C/See/Young Girl   is in Front of   A/All Men   Twice   it Makes it   Caca (Shit   She   It/Hit)
In   The Code   the First Sound Letter Starts the Concept   Creating the Whole Word Concept Most of the Time

Cage: K/Age
K/Broken Fem Warrior   Ages   She is in a Cage

Cake: CK   2 Fem Sound Letters
C/See/Young Girl   is with   K/Broken Fem Warrior   She/Ache   But it is a Piece of Cake for Her   Says   The Code
Switch A/All Men for O/Fem Hole and She Gets Cook   Cook that Cock
The Second C in Cock is Silent as in Non Present   Polygamy Cannot be that Obvious   Says   The Code
cake: to be formed in a compact mass

Mass/Mess (See Mass in Religious Terms)

Calculator: Call/Cul/Ate/Her   or   Hate/Her
Cul is Ass in French
He Calls for Sex/Ass   He Eats/Her   and   He Hates/Her
A Cul de Sac in French (Dead End Street) Makes you Go in a Circle on a Street with No Way Through

Calendar: Call/End/Her   Literally
All Numbers and Letters Call for an End to Her
Call/Hen/D/Her
Call Her   N/In/Hen/Virgin   and Impregnates Her in   D/Pregnant
C   All   N/Hen/Virgin/In   D/Pregnant
The Code Call All the Virgins into Motherhood as Sex Whores

Call: C/All
The Call is that All   C/See/Young Girls   are Called
Called: In the Past All C became D/Pregnant
Caller: Call   R/Her/Hair/Are/Here/Hear/Ear/Whore/Or/Heir/Err/Our/Sex

Calm: Call   M/Motherhood
When in Need Call Mother to Calm Yourself
C/All/M   All Girls to be Mothers
Switch A/All Men for i/Marriage Act and Get Kill M/Him   Kill/N
kiln: an oven firing or cooking

Can: C/See/Young Girl   A/All Men   N/In/Hen/Virgin
All Men are Available (Can) to the Virgin When She is Ovulating
Switch A for O/Fem Hole and She Gets a
con: is a convict   to direct the steering of a ship   to persuade by deception cajolery   to hammer a nail or a peg   to beat or trash a person with the hands or a weapon
The Con is in the Can   Even More so because   Con Means to Steer a Ship   The Con is what Direct the Ship (She/P)   And it is done by Deception and Cajolery   Or   it will be Hammered in with Nails or Beaten into Her
Switch A for U/You/Ovulating and She Gets Cun which has the Same Ancient Root as Can   How Convenient for The Code History

Canal: Can/All
canal: channel   watercourse
Just Follow that Channel   The Code   Says to Her   And All The Fems will be in That Can (See Can in the Words Chapter)

Cancel: Can/See/Ill
If She can See that She is Ill as in The/Eve/Ill (Devil)
It is Canceled Automatically   Says The Code

Cancer: Can/Serve   Can   See   R/Her/Hair/Are/Here/Hear/Ear/Whore/Or/Heir/Err/Our/Sex
Can/Sir   A Man in a Can   A Weird Name for a Weird Illness

Candidate: Candy/Date
A Political Term   Can/D/Date   Is She a Candidate   No Says   The Code   Only a Candy

Candle: Can/D/All
All Fems Pregnant   It is Her Light Says   The Code
Switch C/See/Young Girl for H/Secret Code Letter and He Gets a Handle
Switch C for S/is/His/Us/Ass/Hiss/Serpent/Penis and He Gets Sandals

Candy: Can/D
When D/Pregnant   Life Can be Sweet   Says   The Code
Can/D/He
He Gets a Girl D/Pregnant   It is As Candy
C/See/Young Girl   Ann   D
C is a Hard C here As Carol

Canker: Can   K/Broken Fem Warrior   R/Her/Are/Whore/Sex
Canker is a Terrible Word
It Implies Transforming a Weak Fem (See Broken K   in The Letters Chapters) into a Whore
A Big No from The Code   So   it is a
canker: a disease   to corrupt destroy slowly
And   Cancer is Close   So   is Conquer
The Fem Zodiac Sign Cancer (Which Represent Motherhood) Is Represented by the Moon   Its Logo is a Crab (it Bites)

The Dam Code The Damn Book

The Code Makes Sure She Stays in Line
The Tarot Card # 18 The Moon (Blood Loss) Shows Barking Dogs   a Scorpion   Gloom All Around   It is for Difficult Times to Get that Moon Card
No Fem Never Wins   The Code Game

Cannon: Can/On
K/Broken Fem Warrior   N/In/Ann/Hen/On/Virgin
All   N/Hens/In/Ann/Virgins are Defeated That Way   Virgins To become Whores
It is Not a Choice   It Arrives to Her As a Cannon
Switch A for O/Fem Hole and She Gets a Con
(See Con In The Words Chapter)

Cannot: CNOT   Is All Fems Letters Sounds
Even When She is Hot   She Still Cannot Have Any Power
No (No is Made of 2 Fem Letters) She Cannot
No/Can   Can/Hot   Can/Hut   Count   Cunt   Cant

Cap: C/See/Young Girl   Hap   K/Wounded Fem Warrior   Hap
cap: a close fitting for the head   a headdress denoting rank   to cover   to top   to limit
hap: to cover with   one luck or lot   an occurrence happening   or accident
The Rank from that Cap Says   Cover or Limit Her Vision   It is in His Luck   And if Not   Picture for Her When   C/See/Girl   Becomes   K/Broken Fem Warrior
She will Die here Where She is Transformed From K into   R/Her/Hair/Are/Here/Hear/Ear/Whore/Or/Heir/Err/Our/Sex   Later
(See Letters K and R in The Letters Chapter)
Switch P/Man Power for R/Whore/Heir/Err and She Gets a Car (R is When The Fem as R/Whore and The Masc are Having Sex   This is Where the Rewarded Car is from)
Cap is Also the Word Capital (Caps) the Large Size Letters Called Majuscules   Cap Must be an Important Word in   The Code
Switch A for U/You/Ovulating and She Gets a Cup (Chalice   Bra Size) This Cup has Her Blood in It   How Gross

129

Switch A for O/Fem Hole and She Gets The Police   The Code Keeps Out
The Fems Out of those Hot Zones for   The Code

Cape: K/Kay   With an Ape   Or   As a Hard   C/Ape
The Code Hits 2 Fem Letters here   C/See/Young Virgin Girl   and   K/
Broken Fem Warrior
Cape is a Cover Word from   The Code   Insinuating   She is an
Ape   And   it Hides it Under that Cape
The Franc Masons (My/Sons) Apron   Sits on Their Genitals (Ape/He/Run)

Caper: C/Ape/Her
caper: to behave playfully   a fish
When   She/The Fem   is a Fish   It is Happy Times for   The Code   It
Implies Her being Treated as an Ape   In a Horror Picture of Ending as a R/
Her/Whore/Heir/Err   That Cape/Veil has been Put Over Her   The Code
Calls it a Keeper (Keep/Her)
In The Code   The Fems are Together in   Schools of Fishes   Those
Coded Fems are Always Learning and Moving Together as One as The
Code Wants
Men are Free to Move Alone   The Fems No   Says   The Code
No Matter What   The Code is Always Condescending   or/
and   Damaging/Destroying Towards The Fems
Caps are Waves Tops   Anything Related to the Water is Naturally Directly
Powerful To Her   Positive or Negative

Captain: Cap   T/Fem Cross   N/In/Hen/Virgin/Ann/Virgin
The Code Cap is On Her   The Virgin has become The Fem
Cross   and   The Carrier of The Great Curse

Captor: Cap   T/Fem Cross   R/Her/Hair/Are/Here/Hear/Ear/Whore/Or/
Heir/Err/Our/Sex
She is Captive as the Cursed Fem in The/Her/R/Heir/Or/Whore/
Err   Secret Code

Capture: Kept/Her
The Code Keeps Her Captive by   Capping Her   as in a Curse (T/Fem
Cross/Great Curse)

The Dam Code The Damn Book

As   Her/R   Be a   Mother (Heir)   a Prostitute/Whore   or   Get Lost/Err
That Capping Involves Sex   Anyway
V/Fem Sex Active is Open for Sex Any Time
capping: overburden

Carbonari: Members of a Military Religious Secret Society in the Early 19th Century in Italy France and Spain

Care: K/Broken Fem Warrior   R/Her/Hair/Are/Here/Hear/Ear/Whore/Or/Heir/Err/Our/Sex
Kay   As   R/Heir/Whore/Her

Carnal: CRNL   4 Fem Sounds Letters
Care   N/In/Ann/Hen/On/Virgin   L/Ill/Ail/Elle/All/Hell
carnal: relating to the appetites and passions of the body   sensual   fleshy
That is What is Put in the Care of The Fems   The Carnal
The Word Carnal could have been a Good Meaning for Her with The 4 Fems Caring for Their Ills
But No Says   The Code   That Would be too Much Care for Her   So   Carnal it is for Her   Be at The Code Mercy

Carousel: Care/Us/Hell   Care/U/Sell
Care for The Fem in Hell   Put Her on a Carousel
carousel: merry go round   a revolving belt
Fems and Children are Afraid of Belts   Especially One that Constantly Comes Back
The Carousel is Emblematic for Pregnancy   Mary Go Round
The Carousel has 2 or 3 Rows of Horses/R/Her/Hair/Are/Here/Hear/Ear/Whore/Or/Heir/Err/Our/Sex   (See Horse in The Words Chapter)
The Horses/Whores on the Carousel are The Carriers
Watch the Old Movie The Carousel   Study its Symbolism
She Wears the Red Rag Sometimes On Her Butt
Pregnant She Gives Away Her Food to the Bad Abusive Man

Caress: Care   2 SSs/Is/His/Us/Ass/Hiss/Serpent/Penisses

Lise Rochon

Hard C/Young Girl   as   K/Broken Fem Warrior   as   R/Whore/
Heir/Sex   S/Is/His/Us/Ass/Hiss/Serpent/Penisses (Plural   or   All
of Them)   The Fem is Always a Whore   Says   The Code   No
Matter   Even when Lovingly Caressing

Carve: CRV   C/See/Young Girl   R/Her/Hair/Are/Here/Hear/Ear/Whore/
Or/Heir/Err/Our/Sex   V/Fem Sex Active
From Childhood C to Adulthood   Be Sex Active as a Whore   Have a Heir
or be Rejected says   The Code It is Carved in Her

Carryon: Care/He/On
carryon: a small piece of luggage
The Code   says the Masc Cares for The Fems As a Piece of Luggage
K/Broken Fem Warrior   Err   On

Cash: K/Ash   K/Shh/She
When Kay or Hard C/Young Girl   are in Ashes   or   Silenced   They
Cannot Bring that Much Cash
Cache is the Cover Word here   As in Hidden (from The Fems)
Cashier: K/Ash/Her   Cash/He/Her

Cast: K/Broken Fem Warrior   Ass   T/Fem Cross
When K becomes Fem Cross   She is Cast into it
K/Kay as T/Fem Cross
Those 2 Concepts are Highly Forbidden by The Code to be Known to
Her   So She is Hurled Out and Placed in a Different Angle or Position
cast: to throw   to hurl   to fall in a certain direction
The System of Castes in India is a Cast System
Casser in French is to Break

Castle: Cast   All/L/Sweet Fem Love Light/Ill/Hail/Ail/Hell/Elle
Back to the Sweet Fem Love Princesses World and their Castles with
Towers in Shape of Penisses   Casting Hell/Ill on Her
cast: a rigid system of social classes   to take away
The Fems Are/Were Second Hand Citizens   Even in
Castes   and   Castles Times
C/See/Young Girl   Ass/S/is/His/Us/Ass/Hiss/Serpent/
Penis   or   Plural   All/Ill/Elle

The Dam Code The Damn Book

The Code   is Smokes and Screens

Cat: C/Young Girl (Young Pussy)   K/Broken Fem Warrior   At/Hat
Letter K or Kay as the Cat in the Hat
The Code   Hat   Hides Secrets
Hat/At   and Art   (Add R/Her/Hair/Are/Here/Hear/Ear/Whore/Or/Heir/
Err/Our/Sex   and Read Art) are Together in the Ancient Arts Code Secret
Language
Men of Power are Afraid of the Cat   Because The Fems
Identifies with Cats   Smart Curious and Cuddly
Those are Dangerous Qualities for a Fem Under   The
Code   Rule   Curiosity Killed the Cat
Switch C for B/Boy Holding All Fem Breasts and get a Bat (Penis in Erection)
Switch C for D/Pregnant   and She Gets That (Nothing)
Switch C for H/Secret Society Letter and Get Hat (Keep Secrets in The Hat)
Switch C for K or Hard C or Q and She Gets a Cat (No Secrets here Given to Her)
Switch C for M/Motherhood and She Gets a Mat (Poor Her)
Switch C for N and She Gets a natte
Switch C for P/Man Power and He Gets a Pat (Always Good to Receive Comfort)
Switch C for R/Her/Hair/Are/Here/Hear/Ear/Whore/Or/Heir/Err/Our/
Sex   Even if She Has a Heir or is a Whore or Err   With or Without
Hair   She Will Still be Called a Rat
Switch C for S/Ass/Is/Us/His/Hiss/Serpent/Penis and He Sat
Switch C for W/All Fem Sex Active and The Fems Get What   a Question
that will Remain Unanswered to Her
Switch A/Al Men for U/You/Ovulating and She Gets a Cut (Cut as in Losing
Virginity)   or   She Gets Caught
Caresser la Chatte   a French expression   is to Caress the Puss
Chat in French is Cat   To Chat in English is Having a Small Talk
Anything Fem in   That Code   is
Either   Bad   Destroyed   Diminished   or does   Not Exist

Catastrophe: Cat/Ass/Trophy
If Anything that Belongs to Her is Given Value or Importance in Any Way
It is a Catastrophe

But Her Trophy is Some Ass
When a Cat (Her) Think Her Ass is a Trophy   Here comes a
Catastrophe   Says The Code   Nothing Good Comes to Her   Never

Catharses: They Refused the Communion and the Baptism
Which Means to Me They Understood Those
As the Acceptation of the Sin as Communion
And its Forgiveness of it in Baptism (With Water a Fem Symbol) and did
Not Allow those in their Lives
Catharsis is a Demolished Word in Cathartic

Catch: K/Broken Fem Warrior   Hatch
Cat   She/Shh
A Cat is a Symbol for an Independent Fem
A Cat Never Submits   It is a Free Animal and   The Dam Code   Hates
that
Mean People Burned Cats Along with the Accused Witches during the
Inquisition   Read the Book The Drone   An Excellent History about The
Fems Presented in an Original Angle

Caught: Cut
The Cut in   The Code   is Her Loss of Virginity   Or
Barbers Used to do Clitorectomy
All The Fems Get Caught   Then   The Cut

Caveat: Cave/He/Hat
caveat: a warning of caution
When   The Code   is in the Cave   With His Hat (Art) On   Caution   The
Regular Human Never Witness that   Those Caves are their Secret
Meeting Places   When they Wear Their Special Clothes and Hats

Cavity: KVT are All Fems Sounds Letters
K/Broken Fem Warrior   V/Fem Sex Active   T/Fem Cross   Those 3 Fem
Create and Attract Desire
But there is a Separation   The Cavity
Cave/He/T
cavity: unfulfilled space between a mass
Caveat and Covet/He are Close

covet: to desire
Cavity is a Good Word for The Code   It Need to Fill Spaces in the Language   So it is All Evenly Cloaked in Invisibility with Scary Words As a Cavity   He/Cave/T   As Her All Alone in a Dark Place

Cedar: Seed/Her
Another Innocent Looking Filling Word from   The Code   Another Bate   that Says   Impregnation
Cedars are Magnificent Trees   Cedars are Popular to Make Bug Free Wardrobes
Cedars are Expensive   Seeding Her Can be Costly

Ceiling: CLN   All Fems Sound Letters
C/See/Young Girl   L/Sweet Fem Love Light/Ill/Ail/Hail/Hell/Elle   N/Hen/In/Virgin
L/Sweet Fem   is a   C/Young Girl   and a   N/Virgin   (Redundant)   Reaching   The Code   Ceiling
Seal/Ill/In   See/Ill/N
Every House Part Word is a Symbolic One   to   Keep Her in   The Prison Code
When the   Seal/See/Hill   is In   Literally   It is on Top of Walls (W/All Fems Sex Active   All/L/Sweet Fem Love Light/Ill/Ail/Hail/Hell/Elle)
A Wall is a Barrier (Bar/Her) that Blocks the View

Cell: CL   is Made of 2 Fem Sound Letters
C/See/Young Girl   L/Sweet Fem Love Light/Ill/Ail/Hail/Hell/Elle
See   Hell
C   Hell/Ill/All/Hill/Hall
See   C/Young Girl   in   L/Hell
cell: a small room in a convent or prison
The Code Confines Her in Every Way   Always Confined in Something Small   A Cell is a Very Small Starting Entity for Her to be Confined to   The Code
A Cell is Also Part of a Secret Organization Building Block
Seal   If you have Money and Interest it can be a Sell
Celles is the French Word for Those as in The Fem Gender   Ceux is The Masc Gender for Those

Lise Rochon

Cemetery: See/C   Me   Tree/Three
The Code Hides itself from Most Men   The Initiates (Men Only) Get to Learn   Ordinary Men Would See   The Tree of Life   in a New Light   That Would be   a Big No   from   The Code   So   It is Where   No One Talks   a Cemetery
Symmetry

Center: Cent/Her   Sent/Her   Scent/Her
The Center Concepts in   The Code   are to Keep All Fems   Poor   Focused on Sex   and to be Able to   Send Her   or   Keep Her Away   On a Dime
The Scent is There to Remind Her That She is Only an Object for Sex   At The center   too   All The Way from The Periphery because of its Ending in R/Her/Hair/Are/Here/Hear/Ear/Whore/Or/Heir/Err/Our/Hour/Sex

The Sound Scent here Adds a Cover Sound

Century: Cent/Hurry
Working Hard   Hurrying   and   Being Poor   We Remained for Many Centuries   and Worse   With Slavery
Everyone Loses with   The Secret Word Code
Scent/Her   A   and   Sent/Her   A   Make The Word Center as Described Above   A Center with   A/All Men   In The Center   and that   for a Century   How Convenient for   The Code
It is Actually Way Longer Than That   But For This Word Specifically it Describes For a Century   Every Word has Its Own Purpose   Some Large Some Small
All This (Century) for a Cent (So   Very Small   Puny)
Shallow Sad Cover Words   Here/Are   Center   and   Century
A Cent is a Penny   Penny is a Popular Fem Word in The US   Hurry to Your Penny   Says The Code

Ceremony: Sir/He   Money
Naturally   Says   The Code   Money Is   His/S/Is/Penis   and   He has a Rank   He is Called a   Sir
Secret Societies   Need a Ceremony   in Order to   Seal Their Secrets Sir/He/Moan/He   As in a Sex Act   HoHo

It Gives Him Great Joy (Sire/He/Moan/E) and Power (Pow/Her) to be Flattered and Rich   So   it is Their Ceremony   It Imprint in Our Heads   Even Not Knowing About it

Certain: Sire   T/Fem Cross/Great Curse   In/N/Hen/Ann/On/Virgin   S/Penis   is/as a   Noble Man (Sir/Sire   Children) here   and   T/Fems Cross   is in Every N/Virgin   Such as   Ann   An   In   On   Hen   N/Virgin
Certainly: Sire/Thing/Lay   Sure/Thing/Lay
The Code   Says   Sire   Certainly   Stay Laid

Chafing: She/Shh   F/Fem/Fuck   N/In/Ann/Hen/On/Virgin
When   Shh as She   and the   N/Virgin   F/Fem/Fucks   She Gets   to be Called a Lesbian   Then   The Code   Says No   and   She Gets chafing: to become worn by rubbing

Chain: She/Shh   Ann/N/An/In/On/Hen/Virgin
The She/Silenced Virgins   are   Made of An Ann   on That Chain (She/Ann/In)
The Fems Were the Cheapest (See Sheep   She/P)   And Most Expendable Meat (M/Motherhood   It/Hit) of All to Sell
Virgins (Were Offered (Off/Ov   R/Her/Hair/Are/Here/Hear/Ear/Whore/Or/Heir/Err/Our/Sex
As Sacrificed Lambs in Antiquity to Gods (Aries   Heir Is/His)
And Some Goddesses   Were Trashed into Depravity (Fem Slavery to Death)
Venus is the Goddess of Love   Natural Opulence and Goodness of nature
Venus Temples became Blood Houses for the Virgins   and Animals Representing Her
Chains and Rings are Mostly Fem Jewelry
A Chain (She/N) is Made of Metallic Circles Called Rings (R/In) Letter O/Fem Hole   All Tied Together
As the Others (Odd/Her)   The Fishes   Cows   Sheeps   Chickens (Chicks/Hen/N/Virgin) are
Ring (Marry Merry Mary) That Bell (e)   Is an Untold Concept Link from The Code Chain of Rings

Chainsaw: She/Ann/Saw

Lise Rochon

She   N/In/Ann/Hen/On/Virgin
If a Fem would See the N/Virgin   or   the Virgin would See Herself (R/Self) in the Mirror of That Code
She would be In Pure Torture
Any Knowledge for The Fems is a   Big and Only No (See No in The Words Chapter)   From The Code   So it is
To Cut Out with a Chainsaw if   She (Ann) Saw
So Scary No One goes there

Chair: She   Heir/Whore/Err
Shh   and   R/Her/Hair/Are/Here/Hear/Ear/Whore/Or/Heir/Err/Our/Sex   Be Silent   about being Treated of   R/Whore   or   Forced in Pregnancy (Heir)   or   Err for Ever (Eve/R)
Chair and Table   T/Fem Cross   Able   She   Err/R
T/Fem Cross   with The Other Fem   She/Shh   as   Table and Chair   Go Together   Says The Code
This is   Where   The Fem as Cross   is Able to do Something   Says   The Chair (Boss)   be a Chair

Chalice: She/All/His   Or   She/Is/All/His
The Chalice is Where Jesus Blood/Wine Is Transformed from One to the Other
Shall/Is
The Chalice is the Symbol of Refining in Alchemy
Her Loss of Blood for a Couple of Thousand Years   Doing Just That
All/She/Me   The French Pronunciation for Alchemy in English
The Chalice is the Vase   The Vessel   Vase/All
V/S/L   Vase/Penis/Light
It is the Uterus or the Open O as the U
The Chalice Top Round Cover has a Cross on Top
The Code Need The Fems Blood Loss/Great Curse
In Order (Whore/D/Her) to Give The Man   The Power to Breed Freely with Her   as an Object   The Code Encourages Her   To do That   They have been Doing That for Millenaries
Buying Fem for Sex is Just a Part of it
She/Is/All/Ice   as the Frigid Fem   She has becomes   With That Stupid Code

The Dam Code The Damn Book

Challenge: She/All/Hinge
She is Always Tied to Something Says   The Code
hinge: a jointed device that turn and swing

Chamber: She/Shh   M/Motherhood/Him   Be/B/Boy Holding All Fem Breasts   R/Her/Hair/Are/Here/Hear/Ear/Whore/Or/Heir/Err/Our/Sex
Chamber is   Shh/She (The Silenced)   M/Motherhood/Him   B/Baby Boy   R/Her/Hair/Are/Here/Hear/Ear/Whore/Or/Heir/Err/Our/Sex
chamber: a room usually private in a house or apartment especially a bedroom
She/Amber   Amber is a Fem Name   The Fem is in Fire in   The Chamber   She/Shh   has No Place in   Chamber   The Amber Alert (All/L   Hurt)
Chambers are Big Institutions   The Chamber of Commerce

Champion: She/Hump/He/On
The Code   Says When She goes On   Humping Him/M   She is a Champion
What a Reputation to build Up for The Fems
hump: *Slang   Vulgar*   to engage in sexual intercourse   the back of a camel   *Informal*   to exert oneself hustle or hurry
Joke: Now We Get it   The champion is the one that has to engage as fast as can in sexual intercourse with the N/Virgin
Close to Champignons   (Mushrooms in French)   Mushrooms Grow in The Dark with their Magical Properties of Any Kind   So Few Are known

Chance: She/Shh   Hens   So Sad Say I
She N/In/Ann/Hen/On/Virgin   Twice   In 2 Different Syllables   She is Mentioned as the Sound Hen   and the   N/Letter for Hen   So She/Shh   Hence
hence: for this reason   from now
Here   She as a Hen   is The Reason for Her Chance
Switch C/Young Girl for N/In/Ann/Hen/On/Virgin   and She Gets Enhanced   Soft Words For Her Here from   The Code   Which is Seeing The Forwarded Situation of that Kind of Chance   Coming to Her
The Code   Knows in Advance   The Passages of Life and Ages   and it Plays on That
The Code   Says   She is Starting to Hatch

139

The Code   Makes No Sense to the Natural Mind of a Human
Chains (She/N) is Close to Chance   She/Ants   She/Aunts

Change: She/In/G   Shh/N/G
G/Penis Penetration   is Done to The Silenced   N/In/Ann/Hen/On/
Virgin   It is Time for a   Change
She/Hinge
She is the Hinge   That Part Swing (Sex) the Door (See Adore   A/Door)
For Opening or Closing

Chapel: Chop/All   She/Ape/All   She/Apple   She/Hope   L/Sweet Fem
Love Light/Ill/Ail/Hail/Hell/Elle   Not a good Thing to Hope for
Sorry About that One too   I have Loved the Word Chappelle in French
Since Childhood   Its Sounds are Soothing   It is Something Good
But No   The Code Stole That One Too   a Long Time Ago

Character: Care (KR)   Actor   Care/Act/Her
The Care in   Character   is When   K/Broken Fem Warrior   has
Sex as a   R/Heir/Whore/Err/Sex   As an Actor of Character (Act/
Her   Actress   Act/R/Ass   Back to The Feces for Her)

Charge: She/Arch
She Arch When He Charges

Charity: Share/He/T   Which is Not that Different from Care/He/T   But
Sharing Her   T/Fem Cross   Would be Charity
She/Art (RT) Is   The Secret Code   Art Goal
She/Shh   R/Her/Hair/Are/Here/Hear/Ear/Whore/Or/Heir/Err/Our/
Sex   and   T/Fem Cross
R/Her   as The Cursed Whore Should be Given as a Gift (Charity) from The
Fems   And   be Silent/Shh about it
Hurting Herself and Other Fems   For Free says   The Code
Charity is a Fem Name
Care/He/T   As if   The Code   Ever Cared about Her   T/Fem
Cross   No   That would be a First
The Confusion here Resides that Charity should be Pronounced as
a   Sh   Not a Hard C   That would be

Charm: Shh/R/M   She/Arm   She/Harm
Her Charm is Her Weapon (Weep/On) with Arms and Harms on the Way for Her   But No Says   The Code   it is Only a Charm

Charmer: Charm/Her   She/Harm/Her   Shh/Arm/Her
The Fems Arms would be Her Charms   That would Harm Her
She/Shh/R/M/R   Twice   She is a R/Her/Hair/Are/Here/Hear/Ear/Whore/Or/Heir/Err/Our/Sex   here   For More Charm

Chart: She/Art
chart: a map showing information
She   as the   Secret Art Product   Follows that   Art Code Chart

Chase: She/Ace
She Feels   as   She Got an Ace
During   The Chase   it Makes Her Feel   as   a Million Bucks (Buck is a Male Horse   Nothing here for Her)   or
Chaser: Chase/Her
chaser: a hunter   a gun   a person or thing that chases   a drink of a milder beverage taken after a drink of liquor

Chasm: K/Broken Fem Warrior   or   Q/Bleeding Fem   or   Hard C/See/Young Girl
All those Fem Letters   and   Ism
ism: a distinctive doctrine theory system or practice
That would Definitely Not be Allowed to Her
So   it is a   Chasm
Ism Would Mean   She is Powerful and Independent   Not a 4 Fem Letters Tool
So   No   it would Create a Chasm
chasm: a wide fissure   a breach of relations   a marked interruption

Chastise: Chaste/Ice   Chaste as Ice   That is a Good One
Chase   T/Fem Cross
chaste: not having sex
No Sex is to Put Sex on Ice   As Frigidity
Is a Big No from   The Code   So   it is Chastised
chastise: to inflict punishment

Lise Rochon

Chest/Ties   Enough to Give You a Heart Attack   Think for Yourself

Chat: She/Hat   Shh/At
C/See/Young Girl   is in the Hat (Code Word)   Or   Wearing   The Code   Hat
Chat   is a Cat in French   Pronounce Shhhh   A Cat
chat: casual informal conversation
The Code   Reduces Her/R   as Casual Conversation
The Word   Chat   Starts   with   C/See/Young Girl
It is Not Good News for Her   She Cannot be in Charge of that
Word   The Words   Hat/At/Art   are Dangerous Words for Her
Keep the Fem Conversation Light and Superficial by   Chatting
Because   it is Where the Secret Art is   Without the R/Her/Hair/Are/Here/Hear/Ear/Whore/Or/Heir/Err/Our/Sex
Which it Needs to Survive
The Code   Has Perverted Our Sex Life   By Messing it Up for   All Fems   and   All Mascs   That is How   it is Done by the Secret Societies   For Millenaries
A Chat is A Cat in French without the T/Fem Cross   Sound
Cats/Kill/Eat Rats   The Code   Does Not Accept it
There is Much Hatred Against Cats
Words with Hat/At are Diversified and there are Many of them: Bat   Cat   Fat   Ghat   Kat   Lat   Mat   Nat   Knat (a R/Her/Hair/Are/Here/Hear/Ear/Whore/Or/Heir/Err/Our/Sex
L/Sweet Fem Love Light/Ill/Ail/Hail/Hell/Elle   S/Ass/Is/Us/His/Hiss/Serpent/Penis
N/In/Ann/Hen/On/Virgin
Fly)   That   Rat   Pat and Path (a Cover Word)
The Rat is One of the Most Hated and Feared Animal
Why is this One Especially Hated When there are so Many Vicious Animals that Would Kill a Human Even Faster
Because   The Code   Protect Its Words   The Rat   is The Code Cover Word for the   Hat/Art (Art has the Same Letters as Rat)
The Hat and the Rat   R/Her/Hair/Are/Here/Hear/Ear/Whore/Or/Heir/Err/Our/Sex   At/Hat
To Keep People (Peep/Holes) Away from Thinking about that Hat or the Art

Cat Hat and Rat are Almost Similar   C/See/Young Girl   R/Whore   H/
Secret Code Letter   It is All About The Fems and Secrets

Chatter: Chat/Her   She/Hat/Her/R
She   Hate/Ate   R/Her/Whore/Are/Our/Err/Sex
She Hates Herself as a Whore   Still She Ate that Chatter as Cheddar
Anyway   Not Knowing   What That Chat Really Implies
chatter: to talk rapidly in a foolish or purposeless way
jabber

Chatty: She/Hat/He
That would be a Big No from   The Code   for Her to be in the Hat/Art
Secret   So
chatty: characterized by friendly and informal talk or writing often about
minor or personal matters given too much talk
Chatter (Chat/Her) Definition is a Foolish Conversation and Chatty (Chat/
He) is a Casual Conversation   There is a Difference   The Fem Goes
Down here   as Usual
The Fems in History do Not Check Charts   A Chat   with R/Her/Hair/Are/
Here/Hear/Ear/Whore/Or/Heir/Err/Our/Sex

Cheap: She/P   She/Shh   and   P/Masc Power
Because the Sound Word She Starts the Word Cheap
She is in Front of P/Man Power   or   She would be the P/Man Power
That Would be a Super Big No from   The Code
So   She is a Sheep (The Lamb of God)
A Sheep is Cheap   It is C in a Heap (Multitude)
cheap: of little account   of small
value   mean   shoddy   embarrassed   sheepish
All Fems Sheeps are Under the Sheppard (She/Shh   P/Man Power   R/
Her/Hair/Are/Here/Hear/Ear/Whore/Or/Heir/Err/Our/Sex
D/Pregnant) Stick
Switch P/Man Power for T/Fem Cross and She Gets Cheat   She/It (Shit)
and Sheet (Bed Sheet)
Puny Money and a Poop on T/Fem Cross for being Cheated
Cheaper: Cheap/Her   Sheep/Her   Shh/Hip/ R/Her/Hair/Are/Here/Hear/
Ear/Whore/Or/Heir/Err/Our/Sex
Make a Sheep Out of Her   Get Her Cheaper

C/Young Girl   Heap   R/Her/Hair/Are/Here/Hear/Ear/Whore/Or/Heir/Err/Our/Sex
Multitude of Young Girls to become R

Cheat: Sheet   Shit   She/It/Hit
C/Heat   C/See/Young Girl   In Heat
The Code   Mental Associations to Diminish The Fems are Endless
Cheating: Cheat   N/In/Ann/Hen/On/Virgin
Shit/In   She/Hit/N
Shush about   N/In/Ann/Hen/On/Virgin   being Hit   and   being Poop on

Check: Chick   She/IC
IC Means Integrated Circuit
The Check is in the Mail   The Chick is in the Male
Chick and Chicken are Well Known Slang Words for Describing   The Fem is So Smart   She will Make Anything Chic
Chic is the Cover Word Here

Cheek: She/IC
IC   Means Integrated Circuit
She   as the Buttocks   Men Check on it   Chic
A Sheik is a Title of Honor for Men Only
The Same Sound Word   Cheek   Refers to The Mascs as a Powerful Name Title   and   For The Fems it is a Reference to an Ass   The Code as Usual S/Ass/His/is/Serpent   Penis

Cheer: She/Hear   She/Here   She/Shh   R/Her/Hair/Are/Here/Hear/Ear/Whore/Or/Heir/Err/Our/Sex
If She Hear R She Better Cheer   R is Only what She Can Hear
Switch R for T/Fem Cross and She Gets Sheet and/or Shit (She   it/Hit)

Cheese: She/Is   Shh/His
When She is His   It is All Cheese for The Code

Cherish: Share (She/Heir)   She   R/Her/Hair/Are/Here/Hear/Ear/Whore/Or/Heir/Err/Our/Sex
She/Rich   Shh/She   Reach

The Dam Code The Damn Book

There are No Words in   The Code   as Her being Rich   or   to Reach Her Goals   and   Loving it/Cherish   in   The Code
The   Cher   Sound Feel Soft Gentle and Safe
Cherry   Some would Say
But No Says   The Code   Cherry/She is (Cherry is Slang for Her Clitoris)   So   To Cherish Says   The Code   to Her   is to have a Clitoris   Talk about going Nowhere for Her Except to Sex   Where   The Code   Wants Her to be   and
She/Shh   Be Silent/Silenced about it
Cherry   also   Implies here   Share/He So   When Done   He is gone
Sh/She   R/Her/Hair/Are/Here/Hear/Ear/Whore/Or/Heir/Err/Our/Sex   ish
While She is with   Heir   or   being a Whore   or
is   Erring   (Herring   a Fem Symbol) in Poverty

Cherry: Share/He   She/Err/He
She   R/Her/Hair/Are/Here/Hear/Ear/Whore/Or/Heir/Err/Our/Sex   He
Shh   Her/Heir   He
When a Fem has an Heir with Him   or   is a Whore   or   Err in Poverty   that is Cherry   Says The Code
cherry: virginity   the hymen   virginity   an innocent novice
So   Cheer on that   A Cherry is a Splendid Fruit
But it is Just Another Painful Symbol for Her
She/Hairy would be   The Code   Cover Concept here Against Her   So   She Stays Away
Take Away Sh (She) or Ch and She Gets Airy/Hairy   Heir/He   or   Harry
Switch Ch for B/Boy Holding All Fems Breasts and He Gets a Berry (Bear/He) Too Young to Understand The Code
Switch Ch for D/Pregnant and She Gets Dairy (Feed That Baby   Dear/He   The Fems Owns The Breasts   The Mascs Owns the Dairy)
Switch Ch for F/Fem/Fuck and She Gets Fairy Furry or Get on the Ferry   Far Away
Switch Ch for G/Penis Penetration and She/He Gets Gary
Switch Ch for L/Sweet Fem Love Light/Ill/Ail/Hail/Hell/Elle and She Gets Larry or Leery
Leery: wary   suspicious   *archaic*   knowing   alert
Switch Ch for M/Motherhood and She Gets to Marry and be a Merry Mary
Switch Ch for P/Man Power and He Gets Perry (Pear/He   Homosexual Content here) Pair/Pere   Both Words are Strong

145

Switch Ch for S/Ass/Is/Us/His/Hiss/Serpent/Penis
and He Gets Sir/He   Enhancing The Masc
Switch Ch for T/Fem Cross and She Gets Teary (Tear)
Switch Ch for V/Fem Sex Active and She Gets to Vary Sex Partners
Switch Ch For W/All Fems Sex Active and They Get Weary
weary: tired or exhausted   causing fatigue or exertion
Chest: She/Shh   Ass/S/is/His/Us/Ass/Hiss/Serpent/Penis   T/Fem Cross
For The Fems the Chest is All in The Breasts   Says   The Code
A Chest for a Man is His Torso   it is a Bust   He is Proud to have His Face There

Chew: She   as   U/Vase/Uterus/Holy Cup
The Fems have been Chewing on that for Millenaries

Chicken: The   Check/Chick   is   In/N/Hen/Ann/On/Virgin
A Chick is Common Slang Name in American English for a Fem or a Girl
That Chick is All Over The Kitchen   As in Food to Order or Serve
Ask for Her Fried Breasts Legs Thighs or Wings
Chicken Wings are so Small and the Breasts are so Large
No Flying with those
Compared to that Flying High and Fast Bald Eagle on the US Flag
The Chicken is a Bad Code Joke on The Fems
Order Beef a Masc Symbol for Horns   When in Fact it is Cow
See the Differences in Parts Names and Cuts
As Sirloin (Sir/Loin   (Sire/Loin)
T (Fem Cross)/Bone is Another Cover Word Here
Skulls and Bones (Secret Societies Logo has an X (See Letter X) or Fallen Cross Behind a Skull
A Bone is also an Erection
Because the Name of their Logo is Death   it is Illustrated by Bones in a Pattern of a T   It is a Clear Image of Her (and Him Too in the Rebound)
Great Curse   Letter T/Fem Cross/Curse is the Great Curse Letter
Same Concepts for Pig Cuts
PG   When P/Man Power Faces G/Penis Penetration   Pig
Rack Of Lamb   Many Lambs (Baby Sheeps   The Lambs of God to be Slaughtered Right to Your Plate
Rack is Slang for Fems Breasts
About Eggs (Hers Always in 2) and Sausages (Him) as Symbols

The Dam Code The Damn Book

Pollo in Spanish is Chicken   Pole/O   The Pole (Penis/Code) is Always There
Rooster   Roaster   Roast/Her   Rose/T/Her   R/Host/Her
Sex is with Her Continually
How About the Perfect Combination of Bread and Cheese
Bred with Fem Sex Juices
Now Insert the Butter (Butt/Her) in Between the Two and Imagine the Rest
The Code   is So Old and We are All So Lost in It (Hit)

Chief: She   F/Fem/Fuck   She/If
The Code Presents Her here   as a Chief   Because   She is The Fem That Fucks   A Chef in French
Chief is a Cover Word Here

Chiffon: She/Fun
When She is Having Fun   It is Not Going to Last   Says   The Code
Chiffon is a Very Fragile Fabric   Easy to Rip

Chignon: She/Shh   Neigh/Nay   Eon
A Chignon is a Fem Type of Hair Do
The Code   Says   Neigh   Silence   No   to Her   for an Eon   Or   She/Shh   N/In/Hen/Virgin   On
On with the Silence of the Virgin

Children: She/Ill/D/Pregnant   R/Her/Hair/Are/Here/Hear/Ear/Whore/Or/Heir/Err/Our/Sex   N/In/Hen/Virgin   Shield/Ran

Childbearing: Child/Bear/In   Child/Be/Ring
The Bear is In The N/Hen/Virgin   Baby Boy is Coming   It is the Ring (See Ring)

Chill: She/Ill   Because of   The Code   Situation She is Ill   Men would Tell Her   Chill   It is All in Your Head

Chime: She/Aim   She/Ame (Soul in French)   She/M/Motherhood   Shame
Aim to Shame the Belle

147

She Shine being Shamed   She Does says   The Code
And Music Come Out of that it (Hit)
chime: a sets of bells or slabs of metals stone wood etc producing musical tones when struck
To Strike a Bell(e) is No Coincidence here for   The Code
It is Business as Usual
Chime is a Cover Word here

Chirp: She/Shh   R/Her/Hair/Are/Here/Hear/Ear/Whore/Or/Heir/Err/Our/Sex   P/Man Power
When The Fem Chirps it is because   She as   R is with P
Chirping is a Soft Sound   Not Too Fast Says   The Code
Cheer/Up   She/Urp
urp: vomit
Chisel: She/Shh   His/Is   Ill/L/Hell/Sweet Fem Love Light/Ail/Elle
chisel: to cut shape or fashion by or if by carving with a chisel   to cheat   to trick
She is Carved that Way to Stay Ill/Hell (See Evil   Eve/Ill)

Chitlin: She   TLN
All Fem Concepts or Letters
She/Shh   T/Fem Cross   L/Sweet Fem Light   N/In/Hen/Virgin
The Code Hates it When Different Fem are Together Alone Without Any Masc Presence   So
chitlins: the small intestine of swine especially when prepared as food
Back to Animals and Feces for Her   And Shh about it
Cheat (She   Hit/it)   R   L   In
Chitterling: Cheat   R/Her/Hair/Are/Here/Hear/Ear/Whore/Or/Heir/Err/Our/Sex   L/Sweet Fem Love Light/Ill/Ail/Hail/Hell/Elle   N/In/Hen/Virgin

Chivalry: She/V/All/R/E
She/The Fem   as   V/Fem Sex Active   and as   R/Her/Hair/Are/Here/Hear/Ear/Whore/Or/Heir/Err/Our/Sex   with   E/He
She/Val/Her/He   She/Val/R/He
She is in a Valley (Troubles) While Being a R with a Masc
The Code   Meaning of Chivalry is Far Away from the Noble Concept We Imagine

The Dam Code The Damn Book

Chop:
To Chop is to Cut Finely
The Code has Dissected Her so Finely that   She Keeps on
Hopping and Hoping   and Sees   None of it
She/Hop   She/Hope The Difference of Sound is From Shop and Chop
is   One a Young Girl is with Chop and The Other is   S/Serpent   doing the Shopping

Choose: She/Ooze
The Code   does Not Allow   The Fems   to Make Choices or Decisions for Themselves   So
ooze: to exude slowly   to over flow   to disappear gradually

Chore: She/Whore
Because All Fems are Whores and are Cursed
They Get to Do the Menial Chores

Chosen: She/Shh   Hose   N/In/Hen/Virgin
The Fems are Chosen to Serve that Hose   Since Youth

Church:
Church has been the Most Difficult Chapter to Write
Thread Carefully   Please   Remember   Please   I did Not Create   That Code   I Listened to it   After it Appeared to Me in a Small Door of Consciousness that Kept on Unfolding   It has been a Road Paved with My Tears
Back to   The Code   Hell/L (See L in The Letters Chapter)
Adore: Add/Or   A/Door   Add/Whore   Add/Heir   Add/Err   Add/Her   Add/Our   Add/Hour (See The Clock Chapter)
Such a Sad Word For The Fems   Because   It has All to Do with The R/Her/Hair/Are/Here/Hear/Ear/Whore/Or/Heir/Err/Our/Sex
Switch A/All Men for O/Fem Hole and She Gets Odd/Her
Other   Identifies to Anything says   The Code
It Is Saying that to   Add   R/Her/Hair/Are/Here/Hear/Ear/Whore/Or/Heir/Err/Our/Hour/Sex
Add/Or   Or is Gold in French   Gold is Richness   Gold is an International Word

The Word Gold is Made with   G/Letter of God/Penis/Hymen
Penetration   With   3 Fem Letters   O/Fem Hole   L/Sweet Fem Love
Light/Ill/Ail/Hail/Hell/Elle/All   D/Pregnant
For   The Code   To Identify to   God   and   The Public   It has to Carry
(Care/He) those 3 Fem Attributes (No Masc here)   Read Above Again
To   Add/R   is to Add
R/Her/Hair/Are/Here/Hear/Ear/Whore/Or/Heir/Err/Our/Hour/Sex
So   Adore   Implies   Add/Her   Add/Whore   Add/Heir   Add/
Err   Add/Our   Add/Hour   Add/Ear   Etc
It is All Directed to The Fems   And Their Fem Curse
Adore in my Mind is a Word Made from   The Light of The Sun   Adore is a Luminous Vibrant Word on Sound Level
But   No says   The Code Blasphemies   that Destroys Church: She/Her/She   (3 Fems)
Shh/She   R/Her/Hair/Are/Here/Hear/Ear/Whore/Or/Heir/Err/Our/Sex   Shh/She
A Double Shush for Her as Whore Here
SHH: interjection   order to be silent
Shh is Made of 3 Masc Letters   2 of Them being a Repeat of H/Secret Code Letter
shush: command to be silent
Add R to Shush and She Get Church   She/Arch   (See BB   and   Arch in The Words Chapter)
It is the Close of the Loop (See Arc)
Churches Use Lots of Cut Flowers (See Flower   Flaw/Her in The Words Chapter) for their Rituals (Baptism) and   Fountains   (More Fem Symbols)
They could have Used Other Objects
Chapel: She/Apple   She/Ape/All
A Chapel is Something Sweet in The Mind of a Fem   But No   Another Bate from The Code done to Her
circumcision: an Incision with a Small Scythe
circum: round about   around
A Round About is a Place Where you Can Turn in Circles for a Long Time   The Code Loves that Kind of Strategy When it Comes to Talk about their Secrets Rituals   Circumcision being the Most Important of Them Everything   and   Keeps Its Secrets Hidden in Plain View/Sound from   The Average Citizen

The Dam Code The Damn Book

Deer/Dear are the Sounds Cover Words here
Altar: Halt/Her (Stop Her)   Halt/R
The Alter is Where Her Sacrifice (Blood and Flesh) Happens   Because She has been Transformed into a   R/Her/Hair/Are/Here/Hear/Ear/Whore/Or/Heir/Err/Our/Hour/Sex
This is When   She Becomes   R/With Heir   or   Will R/Err   or   will be a R/Whore
All/T/R   All Fems T/Fem Cross to be R/Her/Hair/Are/Here/Hear/Ear/Whore/Or/Heir/Err/Our/Hour/Sex
Amen: A/Man   A/Men
Come from the Egyptian Amun Ra
Note here   Amun   and   A/Moon
As the Chief Deity of the Egyptian Empire   Amun Ra   Also Came to Be Worshipped Outside of Egypt in Ancient Libya and Nubia   and   Ammon Came to be Identified with Zeus in Ancient Greece
Amun   He was the champion of the poor or troubled and central to personal piety   his position as King of Gods developed to the point of virtual monotheism where Other Gods became Manifestations of Him
Wikipedia   Says Amun Offspring was Khonsu
Khonsu   is an Ancient Egyptian God   Whose Main Role was Associated with   The Moon   His Name Means Traveler
Khonsu   Cons/You   Pops Up here   in Sounds
Traveler would Mean that   The Fems   Back Then would
Go   from   One to Another Place for Commerce
Communion: Come/Union   K/Broken Fem Warrior Home   U/You/Ovulating/Chalice   Neigh   On
Come   You   N/Hen/Ann/Ane/Donkey/Virgin   Eon
At a Certain Age   The Code   Make the Girls Ready for that Transformation   Be a Donkey   a Hen   and be   a Nag about it
Angels: the Angle of the Freemasons   The Broken Wing of the Fifth Corner
Blessing: B   Less   Sin   B/Less/In
The Blessing is there are Less Sins for that Boy
B/Boy Holding All Fem Breasts   Less (L/Ass)   N/In/Hen/Virgin)
The Reason is That He is a Child   He knows Less about Sins

Canonic: Can   On   IC/Integrated Circuit
Can   O/Fem Hole   IC

Switch A/All Men for O/Fem Hole and She Gets Con/On/Ic   Not a Word in   The Code
Chalice: She/All/His   Shall/She All   His/Is   The Code   Says   She is All His   Chalice (Her Blood Loss)
Cherub: She/Rub   That Code   is So Ugly
Creator: Create   Her R/Her/Hair/Are/Here/Hear/Ear/Whore/Or/Heir/Err/Our/Sex   The Code   History in Our World Revolves Around R
Devil: The/Veil   The   Eve   that is   Ill   is Under That Veil   She Cannot See
D/Pregnant   Eve   Hell/Ill   D/He/Veil
Divine: The/Vine (Her Blood Loss)
Ecstasy: XTC   3 Fem Sound Letters
X/Fallen Fem Cross   T/Fem Cross   Letter C/See/Young Girl
Churches are Based on The Fems   A Fem Cannot Serve as a Priestess (Priest/Ass) and Give Communion   Because   Basically   She would be Doing the Ritual Herself of Transforming Wine into Her Own Blood/Great Curse   and   Advocating The Breaking of the Bread (Bred) as Her Own Body
Evangelical: Eve/An/Angle/All
Angels can Only be Masc   How Convenient for   That Code
The Right Angle is When Her Stick is Broken   but   Still Attached   The Letter L/Sweet Fem Light/Ill/Ail/Hell has that Shape
In Small Cap   Letter l   Her Stick is Not Broken Yet
Eve/V/Fem Sex Active   Is Put at a Certain Angle in The Code   To Keep Her Weak
Evil: Eve that is Ill   Eve/Ill   He/Eve/Ill
Close to   He/Veil   He/Vile   He/Villain (He/Veil/In   He/Vile/In)   The Code   Associates Her with Anything Bad
Faithful: F/Fem/Fuck   Hate   U/You/Ovulating   All
Fate/Faith   Fool/Full (Full is Pregnant)
F/Fem/Fuck   Hate/Ate/# 8   (# 8 is Pregnancy)
Faithfulness is a Great Character Quality   But   The Code   Destroys that too
God: G/Penis Penetration   O/Fem Hole   D/Pregnant
GD   G/Hymen Penetration   and   D/Pregnant
God is Dog Written in Reverse (The Bitch is her)
G is The God Letter from   The Code   and is on the Apron that Cover the Genital Area of the Freemasons Costume

The Dam Code The Damn Book

Heaven: Oven
Add W/All Fems Sex Active and They Get Woven
The Code has Woven it All
In Our History   It is Mostly The Fems Who Weave
It is Woven   All Women are Woven   in that Pattern
Woven   and   Women   The Difference is that One has   M/Motherhood as its Center   and The Other has   V/Fem Sex Active as its Center   One Brings the Other Along   as Implied in   Woven
Hell: L/Sweet Fem Love Light/L/Ill/Ail/Hail/Hell/Elle   is Considered by   The Code   as Fem   When She is at Her Sweetest
Holy See: The   Hole   He   See
Holiness: Hole   He   N/In/N/Hen/Virgin   Ass   The Whole in The virgin Ass   Such Horrible Concepts   Especially for Holy Words   Such as Holiness
Mass: M/Ass   MS
Him/M/Motherhood   Ass/S/His/Is/Serpent/Penis
Because M is in Front of S   And Him as Letter M is the Same as the Mother Letter   This is a Pure Oedipus Complex Example Unfolding here
It is M with All Men and the 3 SSSs/Is/His/Us/Asses/Hisses/Serpents/Penisses
M as in Aime   To Love in French   To Aim is the Closest in English
The Code   Uses Cornerstone Words   Especially in English
Such as   Pope and Poop   to Keep Us Away from being Curious and/or Understanding How   The Code   Works
Mass/Mess is One of the Big Ones
One of the 17 Meanings of Mass in Internet Dictionary
The main body   bulk   greater part of anything
Read the Other Ones for a Clearer Understanding of   The Code
Then Separated is a Definition of the Eucharist
Change A for E/He and He Gets a Mess
mess: a group regularly taking their meals together   the meal so taken   a dirty untidy or disordered condition
In The Code   a Meal is Bread and Wine
In Mass Switch A/All Men to Letter E/He and Get Mess
The Communion has Happened here   That is   The Code   in Action
By switching A for i/Marriage Action   the Dot Bring in a Fem as the Sex Union   So   The Miss Get to Miss it   Since that Story of the Transfiguration of the Wine into Jesus Blood

Mass   Add R/Heir/Or/Whore/Here/Are/Our/Hair/Sex and Get Mars (a Month of the Year in the Sign of Aries (R/His   A Masc Sign and the God of War Mars   More Fighting)
(See Calendar)
Switch A for O/Fem Hole and U/You/Ovulating (2 Fem) and She Gets a Mouse in the House   M for Mother and H/Secret Code Letter for the Omnipresent Code   Back to the Animals for Her
Add N/In/Hen/Virgin and She Gets Menses (Men   Sees/Seize) Menses is Always Plural as in All of Them
Switch M for S/Is/His/Us/Ass/Hiss/Serpent/Penis and He Gets His Senses   Compare to Synagogue   Sin   A/All Men   Go   G
All Men Sin by Perforation of the Hymen   Twice here   as they are   2 GG s/Penisses Penetrations   in Synagogue   Surrounding O/Fem Hole
Mas Means More in Spanish   Yes   Give Us More of That Says   The Code
Messiah: Miss/He/A   Miss   He   Hey/Hay
And the Girls Misses it All   She will be a Miss   Until She Get Married   When She becomes a Madame (Mad/Ame/Aim)   A Madame is Also a Whore in   The Code
Or   a Ma'am (Maim)   She Never Gets Out of   That Code   Program
Nave: Naive
Add R and She Gets Never   NVR   N/In/Hen/Virgin   Eve/V   R/Her/Hair/Are/Here/Hear/Ear/Whore/Or/Heir/Err/Our/Sex
The Code   does Not Allow Her to Know   What will Happen to Her   So   It Makes Her   Naïve/Her
Nave or Nef in French
A Nave is an Entrance to a Church   The Public Area   it is Also   A Part of a Ship (See Ship in The Words Chapter)
Naïve is N/Eve   See Navel in BB in The Words Chapter   Naïve is a Soft Minded Word   as in   Innocent (Ignorant)
The Traditional Church Building Shape is in a Cross   Looking Closely it is Round at One of the Ends   The Right (Masc) Side has a Longer Arm In French   The Church Parts Names are Puzzling   Words that Seemed Not to Fit with Each Other   Or   Weird
Such as   Messe   Mass   Messes   Masses   Mess   Miss
For the Masses (a Mass is   a   Weight (Wait)   That Daily Mass is M/Motherhood with the 2 SS//Is/His/Asses/Hisses/Serpents/Penisses

The Dam Code The Damn Book

You Deal with this with Grief
Oil: O/Fem Hole   All/L/Ill/Hell/Ail/Whole/Fem Love Light
Holy: All/He/E   Hole/He   The Code   Owns Her Hole
The Oily/Holy See (Hole/He/See) of the Catholic Tradition
Hole/L/All/Ill/Hell   and   O/Fem Hole   Starts   Oil
But   is Masked by   The Silenced H/Secret Code Letter Society   in Holy
Think   The Virgins and the Oil in Bible
Ordain: R/Heir/Or/Whore/Err/Our/Sex   Den/Then   Whore   D/
Pregnant   N/In/In/Hen/Virgin
The Code Desecrate   The Real Human Soul and its Possible Natural Religion
In a Real Felt Religion   The Fems and Mascs   would Practice Love   as in Amour (Love) and Ame (The Soul)
The Code   Puts the Soul (Sole   Sol   Solo   Seul/e)   Under Our Feet in the Dirt   DRT is Made of 3 Fem Sounds Letters
D/Pregnant   R/Her/Heir/Or/Whore/Our/Err/Here/Sex   T/Fem Cross
Always the Same Message from that   Dam Code
From the Church of Latter Day Saints   Joseph Smith was a Free Mason   He was Anointed into the Endowment: "To Become Clean from the Sins and Blood of this Generation"
They Always Put Blood and Sins Together   and   Suck/Drink on it   Why   Those are Scary Words
Order: RDR   R/Heir/Whore/Or/Err/Her/Are/Our/Sex   D/Pregnant   R/Her (again)   R/Her is Said Twice (Indicating Polygamy)   As in to Focus on   That is an Order   Herd/Her
Pastor: Past/Her   Put Her in the Past   So   She Will Not   Exist in the Present
P/Man Power   S/Is/His/Us/Ass/Hiss/Serpent/Penis   T/Fem Cross   R/Her/Heir/Or/Whore/Are/Err/Our/Sex
Pass/T/Her   He Passes that Cross to   R/Her (Pass   Her   With the T/Fem Cross in the Middle)
Past   Whore   P/Ass   Pass   The R/Heir/Or/Whore/Err/Our/Sex
It is in The Fems Past to be a Whore   And to have Passes Made at Her   And   to be Passed Around   Says   The Pastor   to His   Sheeps (See Sheppard   or   The Letter j/J the Shepherd Stick   and   The Dot   as Her in the   i/Marriage Act Union)
pastor: an archaic word for shepherd   from *pascare* to feed

Lise Rochon

The Pope is the Top Pastor   He Wears White Representing the Sheeps (The Fems/Jesus in The Secret Code) before They Get Slaughtered
Bishops Wear Magenta (Mage/Enter)
Archbishops Wear Amaranth (A/Mare/Ant   A/Mère/Aint)
Red is The Color of Blood   The Cardinals Wear Red
Red   or   Purple (When Blue Mixes with Red)
Depending on the Occasion
Magenta is a mix of 50% Blue and 50% Red
Magenta is a complicated Color
It changes into Many Other Colors from Carnation Beige to Fluorescent Pink to Chocking Pink to Rust Color to Amaranth to Hollywood Cerise to Orchid to Dark Byzantium to Purple Taupe
You Can Find on Wikipedia All of the Hundreds of Variations of that Magenta Color
It goes from the Sweetest Innocent Pink (Virginal) to Blood Red (Blood Period) to Dark Dry Blood (The Red Substance of the Alchemists)
Passion: Pass/He/On
P/Man Power   S/Is/His/Us/Ass/Hiss/Serpent/Penis   N/In/Hen/Virgin
Even in Passion   He Passes Her to Another
P/Ass/He/On   P/Man Power   S/Is/Ass   E/He   On
Passion does Not Fit   or   is Not the Proper Word/Term for When a Worshipped by Millions Christ   Was Executed by Crucifixion   And That They Call it Passion of Christ
Pity: PT   P/Man Power   T/Fem Cross
That would Put Him in a Pit   if He would Pity Her
P/Man Power   Hit/He
Pope: P/Man Power   O/Fem Hole   P/Man Power   E/He
Power to All Men Over   The Fems Loins
2 PP s/Men Power Surrounding Her O
Add Another O and She Gets Poop
Take E/He Away and He Get Pop   to Pop a Fem is to Have Sex   Or   He can Just Pop Out
pope: father   origin   leader
Praise: PRS   3 Masc Sound Letters
P/Man Power   Raise   Man Power   Rise
The Power of Man Rises When Praised
There are No Fem Power Letters Here and Never a Praise for Her in   That Code   Either

Pray: to Prey   P/Man Power   Ray
Add S/Is/His/Us/Ass/Hiss/Serpent/Penis and He Gets to Spray
Prayer: Prey   R/Her/Are/Heir/Or/Whore/Err/Our/Sex
Priere is Prayer in French
Add S/Is/His/Us/Ass/Hiss/Serpent/Penis and He Gets a Sprayer
Preach: P/Man Power   Reach
Purgatory: Purr/Gate/Whore/He   Pure/Gate/Her/He
Rapture: Rape   T/Fem Cross   R/Heir/Or/Whore/Her/Are/Err/Sex
Rupture that Hymen   Hi/Men   In Plural   Indicating   Rape
or   Polygamy   The Code Presents it to Her as
rapture: ecstasy   joy or delight   joyful ecstasy
Rosary: Rose   A/All Men   R/Heir/Or/Whore/Her/Are/Err/Sex   He/E
The Red Rose is the Ultimate Symbol for The Fem Genitals in   The Code
(See Rosicrucian)
Satan: STN   Sat   N/In/Hen/Virgin
Sat/Anne   Sat/In
Satin is the Cover Word here
In Ancient Time   The Fems   Would Sit   To Bleed on a Rag or Rug
Satanic: Sat/N/IC
IC: Integrated Circuit
Sermon: Sire/Mon
Mon   Means   Mine   in French (Monday   Moon/Day   Once a Week
Makes 4-5 a Month   Her Bleeding Days)
Sin: S/Is/His/Us/Ass/Hiss/Serpent/Penis/Serpent   In/Ann/N/Hen/Virgin
Sin is S/Penis with a N/In/Hen/Virgin
S/is/His/Us/Ass/Hiss/Serpent/Penis   is   In

Synagogue: Sin/Seen   A/All Men   Go   G/Hymen Perforation/
penetration   The 2 GG s in this Word Makes it a   Rare   Word   O/Fem
Hole is Surrounded by those 2 GG s
The Missing Corner on the Open Book Above the Door Outside a
Synagogue   Is at the Bottom Left (Fem**)**
Temple: T/Fem Cross   Ample
Lots of Fem sacrifices   in Old Temples
Tomb: T/Fem Cross   Wound
The Fem Wound is Sealed in Secrecy   The Tomb is a Reference to the
Dark Places The initiates Meet

Truth: Truth as the Route to Higher Knowledge Should have been a Good Word   Not in   That Code
There are   2 TT s/All Fems Crosses   Surrounding R/Heir/Or/Whore/Her/Err/Are/Sex   and   U/You/Ovulating   Which Ends with   The Code   H/Secret Code Letter
The Only Truth here is   Crosses for Her as a Whore
Thee: Letter D/Pregnant
Vigil: VGL
V/Fem Sex Active Since Eve (He/V   The Fem is Never Left Alone In The Code   Since Eve)   G/Penis Penetration   Ill/L/Elle/Hell/Ail/Sweet Fem Love Light
For All Fems Penetration and Sex is Her Vigil
vigil: devotional watching   or keeping awake

Mount Sinai: Mount (Sex)/Month (Time of the Month)   Sin   I/i (Sex Union)   The Place to Sin   Is on That Mount
Wedding: Wet/Ding   Way/Ding   Wet   N/In/Hen/Virgin
ding: to make a ringing sound   minor surface damage
A Thing is Slang for a Fem (Some/Thing   Something)
Worship: Whore/Ship   Or/She/Shh   P/Man Power Ship (She/P)
There are Many Other Words that could be Added here

Churn: She/Urn (See/Urn in The Words Chapter)   She/Earn   She/R/N   The More She Churn   The More She Earns Says   The Code   Back to The Animal Rank For Her
churn: a machine in which cow breast milk is agitated to make butter
Note That the More The Mammal Glands are   Stimulated/Touched/Pinched/Compressed as in a Bra/Etc   in Early Age   The More That Fem will Have Bigger Breasts Later in Life
In Our Modern Life   Being Agitated   is a Bad Emotional Term for Her   The Code   Will Prevent Her to   Go to The Comprehension of   Churn   By Having Her Spending Most of Her Life Time Earning for Her Basic Needs (Being Pregnant/With Children   Often Abandoned (especially if She had a Girl) etc
That   Churned Milk   Comes from a   Cow (C/See/Young Girl   How)   Butter (Butt/Her)

The Dam Code The Damn Book

The Land of Milk and Honey is Made Entirely of Fem Symbols   The Code   Took it by Force   Used/Abused it
The People that Won   That Code   War   Never Cared for that Land   Now it is a Huge Desert   Another Desert in The Far East   Where it Used to be Luscious and Opulent   and Life was Easy   then   The Water Left
The Musical Album of   Land of Milk and Honey   by John Lennon   Told Us in a Modern Way of that Sweetness of Life
We as Humans We Love Sweetness of Life   so   we must have a Direct Connection to it   But No We are Lost In   The Code
It Could be Easy to Recuperate

Ciao: She/Ow   She/Owe
ow: expression of sudden pain
Ciao is a Sweet Way to Say Good Bye in Italian
In All Languages Hidden Under Poetic Words   Is That Mean Code   How Can a Fem Owe   That Non Existent Pain (Ow)that is Hidden Behind that Sweet Word Ciao
Note That Ow is Made of 2 Fem Letters

Cinch: Sin/She
cinch: something sure and easy
The Code   Tells here that Sinning for Her is an Easy Sure Thing (Thing is The Fem In American Slang)

Cipher: Sigh/For/Her   Psy/For/Her
Anything Nice for Her in The Code Words would be Plain Wrong   So
cipher: any of the Arabic numerals   a person of no influence or importance   the key to a secret message
(See Number (Numb/Her) Chapter)
Decipher would be D/Pregnant and the Cipher
But   The Code Says it is of No Importance
Cipher Sounds As the Word Safer

Circle: CRCL
C/See/Young Girl   R/Her/Hair/Are/Here/Hear/Ear/Whore/Or/Heir/Err/Our/Sex   C/See/Young Girl (2nd Time   as in Polygamy)   L/Sweet Fem Love Light/Ill/Hell/All/Ail/Elle

See/Her/Call
Circle   is a Sire/Sure   Call
E/He   Made His Way Inside The Circle   as a Sure Thing   Sir   is a Sign of Male Respect (Giving Him Priority)
Encircle: In/Circle   In/Circ/All
Circ/All   Circ/Hell   Circ/Ill
In The Code   The Word   Encircle   Reinforces the Word   Circle
Make Sure Sir   that   All Fems Arch (See Arch and Arc in The Words Chapter)
The Circle is a Powerful Symbol for All Fems
From Breasts to Pregnancy   She is Rounded and Surrounded (Sure/Rounded)
The International Fem Symbol is a Circle with a Cross on Top   or   All The Way Around   She Cannot Move   being Afflicted/Stagnated by   T/Fem Cross/Great Curse
The Masc Symbol is an Arrow with a Circle on Top   or   All The Way Around   The Arrow Flies   He has Plenty of Movement
From Inertia (Fem) to Movement (Masc)   Says The Code
I Say   There Can be No Real Masc Without a Real Fem

Circumference: Sire/Sure   Come   Fear   Hence
Circ   M/Motherhood   Fear   Hence
hence: for this reason
Obviously

Circumcision: Circum   Seize   He   On
Circ is the Abbreviation for Circumcision
Circ   Him   C/See/Virgin   Eon
Circ as in Circle/Cycle
Circumcision has Invaded the Populations at Large by being done in the Hospitals Automatically at Birth   Just Until about 10 years Ago   The Medical World do Not Recommend it as a Necessary Procedure Anymore   A Big Win for The Gentles
Some People Pretend that Sex is Better with Circumcision It is a Lie   or   they are Ignorant on the Subject
It Actually Brings Numbness to the Tip of the Penis because it is Constantly Abnormally Exposed   and in the Same Time   Makes Him More Vulnerable   to be Excited Sexually

That Circumcised Penis has its Most Sensitive Tip in the Open (Because of The Missing Skin Piece)
Exposed
Without Circumcision that Part Wraps the Penis Therefore there is Less Sexual Stimulation Perceived   from the Outside   Making Life More Comfortable with Others for Him
Most Male Animals Have their Genitals Inside or Almost (It is a natural Protection) Until Mating Time
That Uncovering of the Penis (Circumcision) at Sex Time Brings a Lower Natural Ecstasy Sensation
It is As having Sex in Black and White   Instead   of in Color   I heard it Reduces Fertility   It could have been Believed as Another Mean of Contraception in that Time Where there was So Much Poverty and Food Deficiencies   And No Contraceptives Allowed by Religion   Or Not Yet Invented   Do you Really Want that in Your Life
We Need to Reflect a Long Time on that VIP Rite   Because   We are Following the Blood Trail Here and that Rite Draws Blood Too
The Answer came to Me in a Dream Awake or Sleeping
It was for the Man to Help Carry Part of That Fems Curse
    By Carrying that Curse/Memory with Him   by   being Circumcised   Therefore Altering His Sexuality   Numbing it
circumcision: an act   instance   or the rite of
circumcising   clitorectomy   spiritual purification   a surgical removal of the foreskin of males   the cutting around of an anatomical part   the act of circumcision performed as a religious rite by the Jews and Muslims
The Way the Dictionary Presents the Cutting of Our Men and Fem Genital Parts is Different   They Call it a Ritual and a Spiritual Purification   No Thank You
The Surgical Removal of Part or All of the Prepuce is also Called   a Church Festival in Honor of the Circumcision of Jesus Observed on January 1
They Make that a Holiday on that Very First Day of the Year in Our Calendar that Says that is the First Thing to Do When Starting a Brand New Era of Life
Now did Anyone Asked Jesus if he had had a Choice of Yes or No to that Mutilation   What would He have Said
Circumcision Causes Traumatic Pain from Altered Genitals for Ever   (The Word Seize is in Circumcision)

Lise Rochon

Circumcision Changes The way of Natural Life by Inflicting Physical Emotional and Mental Pain for a Whole Lifetime   And   Who Knows What it does to the Soul

Citation: S/Is/His/Us/Ass/Hiss/Serpent/Penis   Hit/It   E/He   On (Eon) Penis Hits for Eons   it is a Must
citation: a summons   especially to appear in court   a passage cited   quotation
That is an Important Notation
Letter C/See/Young Girl   High/i/Marriage Act   T/Fem Cross   She/ Shh   On
The Citation   or   the Summons here are that a   C/Young Fem   Has i/Marriage Act   And is a   Shh (Silently)   T/Fem Cross   that Keeps going   On/N/Virgin

City: Cite/He   Seat/He   See   T/Fem Cross
See/T   Under that Authority   All She Sees is Her   T/Cross
He/E   is the One in Authority in this City   He Cites   and   Sits On it C/Young Girl   Hit/it   He/E
The Masc Relationship with   T/Fem Cross   is C/See/Young Girl   Hit   He   Hit on that Fem

Civilian: See/Villain
See   Vile   He   N/In/Hen/Virgin
The Code   Says   To Be a Civilian is to   See The Vile/Villain   In Her(Since She is Young)
That Code   is Corrupt to its Deepest Roots

Civilization: See/C   Veil/Vile   Is/His   A/All Men   Shh/She   On

Clap: C/See/Young Girl   L/Sweet Fem Love Light/Ill/Ail/Hail/Hell/ Elle   Hap
hap: one's luck or lot   an occurrence   happening   or accident
Clapped is   C/See/Young Girl   Lap   of   P/Man Power
When C is Sitting on His Lap   Clap on That
Note here it can Turn Wrong on Her because of a Mishap
lap: portion of the body between knees and waist when in sitting position

Class: C/L/Ass
No Matter the Social Class S/Ass/Is/Us/His/Hiss/Serpent/Penis   is There (Twice here)
K/Broken Fem Warrior   Lass
lass: an unmarried girl
Once K has Lost the Battle   She is a Class by Herself
Tied with a   Lass   O (Fem Hole)

Classy: C/Lass/He
C/See/Young Girl   is with   He/E   It is Classy Says   The Code   Marry That Girl as Soon as Possible
Q   K   and   Hard C   have The Same Sound Meaning

Clean: C/See/Young Girl   or   K/Broken Fem Warrior
Lean
When C is lean She Looks Clean   it is Difficult for a Fem to Remain Lean After Giving Birth and Breast Feeding

Cleaning: Cling/In
The Code   does Not Allow Her to Cling to Anything
But   When it Comes to Cleaning   She can Cling to that
Clean   N/In/Hen/Virgin
From Youth   She is In with Cleaning   Says   The Code
Change N for R/Her/Hair/Are/Here/Hear/Ear/Whore/Or/Heir/Err/Our/Sex   and She Get Clear   in a Clear Message   for Her   be with Heir or a Whore or Err

Clear: K/C/Q   L   R   All Fem Sound Letters
clear: free from darkness   light   transparent
She is in the Clear as Long as She is being Transparent
Switch R for N/In/Hen/Virgin and She Gets to Clean
C/Lair
Lair:

Clearing: Clear   N/In/Hen/Virgin
To Stand Clear of Somebody is to Stay Away
Clear/Ring
The Ring Word is Popping Up in the Word Clearing

clearing: a tract of land   as in a forest   that contains no trees or bushes
A Clearing is Also a Financial Transaction
There is Nothing here for Her Except Checks and Balances Happening in a Bare Land Where Nothing Grows

Clink: C/See/Young Girl   Link
She (C) is Getting a Link
She is in the Clink   Says   The Code   No Hope for Her Here
clink: a prison   a sharp ringing sound
The Ring Word Made its Ways here to Her   Again

Clout: Cloth
Note that One of the Many Definitions of Clout (Archaic) is
clout: any worthless piece of cloth   rag
Also
clout: a blow with the hand   *Informal*   pull strong influence   muscle especially political power   *Archery*   the mark or target shot at especially in long distance shooting   a shot that hit the mark
She is in the Clouds during that Time   being Lost in False Cloud Fashion Clout

Club: Claw/B
The Fems were Kept Out of Men Clubs   Men Kept Only to Themselves   and   Their Boys
In the Past   A Club is For Men Only
A Club is Also a Weapon
Clubber: Club/Her
Towards Her as Usual in   The Code

Cluck: 5 Fem Letters   Clock (Another 5 Fem Letters)
A Hen (N) Clucks Loudly after Laying an Egg
C/Luck   The Code Tells Her   it is Luck   and   She is C/Lock In
cluck: a hen call her chicks by clucking
A Very Maternal Concept That One
It is When   C/See/Young Girl   is in Luck   or   Under the Lock
Cluck on That   And   Clock on That   Just As a Punch Card at Work   (See Clock)

The Dam Code The Damn Book

Clue: K/Broken Fem Warrior   Lou
Back to the Bathroom for The Fems
Switch C for G/Penis Penetration and She Gets Glue (Glued to The Code)
Un Clou in French is a Nail (See Cross and Nail in The Words Chapter)

Clueless: K/Broken Fem Warrior   Lou   Less
Clue L/Sweet Fem Love Light/Ill/Ail/Hail/Hell/Elle
    Ass/S/Is/His/Us/Ass/Hiss/Serpent/Penis
The Only Sweet Clue She Gets from   That Code   is to Focus on the Ass

Cock: 4 Fem Letters   KOK   3 Fem Sound Letters
cock: a male roaster   part of a lock that discharge
The Word Discharge is in its Definition
Cock is a Strong Word for the Man Penis/Stick
cocky: arrogant   conceded
And Proud of It
Add R/Her/Hair/Are/Here/Hear/Ear/Whore/Or/Heir/Err/Our/Sex   and She
Gets a Croc   That is a Man Says   The Code
The Cock and the Cunt

Cocoon: 6 Fem Letters   3 CCCs/See/Young Girls   and   3 OOOs/Fem Holes
Cock/On
cocoon: a protective covering
The Code Holds its Secrecy in Many Layers   It Keeps its Virgins in Cocoons to Hide Her Ignorance to Herself   So She can be Ringed Asap When Her Butterfly (When Her/Butter/Flies) Opens

Cod: Made of All 3 Fem Letters
Add E/He and He Gets a Code   She Remains the Fish to be Caught   As The Code Says (See Fish in the Words Chapter)
The Fish is One of the Most Extended Fem Symbols in   The Secret Code Along with the Cows   the Chickens   the Ants   the Donkeys   the Horse   etc
Switch C/See/Young Girl for G/Penis Penetration and They Get a God
Switch C for N/In/Hen/Virgin and She Gets a Nod (Very Little)

Code: COD   or   KOD

All Fems Sounds Letters   With the Silent Anonymous   E/He
Could   All Fem Letters
Switch D/Pregnant for T/Fem Cross and She Gets a Cut (Clitorectomy)
Do Not Get Caught   or   Get that Cut
Caught and Cut have the Same Sound   it is a Message to Her
C/Ode   K/Ode
K/Broken Fem Warrior   The Letter for the Sound of The Axe (X) is to
Come (See X in The Letter Chapter)
I Do Not See Any Words with KX
ode: poem to be sung   exalted emotion
Sing an Ode to C   Find it Odd   It is for a Cod (Her)   Cod is a Fish   Cod/
He   Could/He
cud: portion of food that a ruminant returns from the first stomach to the mouth to chew a second time
Few Fem would Look at that   Yuck   So   The Code   Survives
Secretly   because   of those Disgusting Mental Images presented to Her by   That Code
The Code Knits Extravagant Patterns of Sounds to Confuses Us   Only a Few Take/Have Time to Reflect on That Language that Brings that Human Mental Slavery
On   All of Us

Code X: Codex   (Archaic Code)
A Very Important Word that Carry the Name of the Art
About having All Fems as   X/Fallen Fem Cross   because of   The Great Curse   Which is Her Immense Loss of Blood   T/Fem Cross/Great Curse
The Code   Clouds Her Mind into Accepting Something More Positive More Acceptable Than it is in Reality

Coffer: Made of All Fem Letters   Except for The Silent Anonymous and Generally Spying on Her   E/He
Cuff/Her   C/Ov/Heir   C/Off/Whore
C/Young Virgin   is Ovulating Here (She Knows Nothing About The Whore)
The Code Says   It is Time to Get Her Off   by Cuffing Her in a Situation   Where She Finds a Coffin   Where/When   She Thought (Since Childhood) She Would Find a Coffer Full of Gold
coffer: a chest esp to store valuables   usually plural   a store of money

The Dam Code The Damn Book

The Secret Code   Remains

Coil: KL   Made of All Fem Letters   Including One Having Sex (i/Marriage Act Union)
K   Oil/All
K/Broken Fem Warrior   All/L/Sweet Fem Love Light/Ill/Ail/Hail/Hell/Elle
When with Oil   She Coils   in a Serpent/Penis Shape
Why
C/All   Call (She is On Call)
C   here is a   Hard C   as in   Coil (Carole is an Example)
The Virgins and the Oil in The Bible   Another Mysterious Story

Coin: Con/In
The Con   The Famous Fems Loins   is Something Small or Not Important as a   Coin   Says   The Code
A Coin   without   i/Marriage Act   is a   Con   (See Con In The Words Chapter)

Coincidence: Con   In/N/Hen/Virgin   See   Dense/Dance
Coin/C/D/Hence   Con/N/C/Dense
Being Dense is being Stupid
So   Dance with it   Girl/Con or be Dense About it
Con/In/See/Dance
Con   Rhymes with   Coin   Has a Small Value

Coitus: Quiet/Us   Quiet   S/Is/His/Us/Ass/Hiss/Serpent/Penis
Coitus Calms the Penis   Being Coy

Cold: C/See/Young Virgin   Old
When   C or K/Broken Fem Warrior   is Old
The Code Gets Cold to Her   Such as Calling Her   Old Maid   Etc

Collar: Color   Call/Her   Kill/Her   Cool/Her
K/L/R   K/Broken Fem Warrior   L/Sweet Fem Love Light/Ill/Ail/Hail/Hell/Elle   R/Her/Hair/Are/Here/Hear/Ear/Whore/Or/Heir/Err/Our/Sex   She is On a Collar
That is Her Collar   Once the Collar is Called on Her   Cool it or be Killed
"Dogs Must be on Leash" Is a Common Sign at the Beach or Parks

Lise Rochon

Color is the Cover Word here

College: Call/Egg   Call/Age
College for   The Fems   is to Produce Eggs   When at Age

Colon: All Fem Letters
Call/On   C/All/On   Call   N/In/Hen/Virgin   Cool/On
Because   Colon is Made of Entirely Fem Letters   It has to be Ugly by   That Code   Especially if it is a Cool Call   on the N/Virgin   So   it is Full of Poop
Ugly it is

Color: Call/Her   Cool/Her   C/Young Virgin   All/L/Sweet Fem Love
Light/Ill/Ail/Hail/Hell/Elle R/Her/Hair/Are/Here/Hear/Ear/Whore/Or/Heir/Err/Our/Sex
Yellow: Yell/O
Yellow is a Cool Relaxing Color   It Should Not Mean for Her to be Yelled at   But it Does Says   The Code
Orange: Whore/Ange   The R/Whore is the Angel here in   That Code   So Sorry for that
The Angel   or   The Right Angle   of the Free Masons
Green: GRN   G/Penis Penetration   R/Her/Hair/Are/Here/Hear/Ear/Whore/Or/Heir/Err/Our/Hour/Sex   N/In/Ann/Hen/On/Virgin
For   N/Virgin   it Goes Green with   G/Penis Penetration   as a   R/Her/Hair/Are/Here/Hear/Ear/Whore/Or/Heir/Err/Our/Sex   with   N/In/Hen/Virgin
Gear   Ann/N/Virgin   Gear in Virgin   The Light is Green for G/Hymen Penetration   And   it Makes Her a Whore   to All Men (2 EEs/He)
Red: Read   R/Heed (Pay Attention to Sex)
Purple: Purple is a Mix of Red (Fem Symbol) and Blue (Masc Symbol)   Purple is the Color the Bishops Wear
The Archbishops Wear Amaranth (the Color of Her Blood Loss)

Colt: Cold is a Gun as   D/Pregnant   and   T/Fem Cross   are Interchangeable by Sound in   The Code
A Colt is a Weapon

Column: Call   M/Motherhood

column: cylindrical shaft
A Slang for Penis
In Old Architecture   the Column Shapes and Their Numbers are Important in The Ancient Secret Code Symbolism

Coma: K/Broken Fem Warrior   Home   A/All Men
No Such a Thing as Harmony in   The Code
A Home with Parents   No   So   in the Coma it is
Come/A
If   A/All Men   would Come to C/See/Young Virgin   or   K/Wounded Fem Warrior   That would be a Big No from   The Code   So   Put that in a Coma
Come/Ma
If Ma would/could Come   That would be Another Big No from The Code   So   It Will be as Small as a Comma   No One will Notice   And 2 Mm s at the Time can Come too (Polygamy)
coma: a state of prolong unconsciousness   including a lack of response to stimuli from which it is impossible to rouse a person

Coming: Come   N/In/Ann/Hen/On/Virgin
Is that the First or the Second Coming

Note   All Those Important Words from   The Code Starting with C and Having 2 MMs/Motherhood in Plural   or   All of Them (Fems)   Coming Up

Command: Come   End/Hand
An Allusion to Happy Ending Masturbation
Commander: Command/Her
Come/Hand/Her   Come/End/Her (R)
Clear is   The Code   here   A Follow Up on   Command
Commando: Come   End/Hand/And   O/Fem Hole
Come   N/In/Hen/Virgin   Dough (Daughter   Dot/Her)
The Virgin Is as Dough   Says The High Order of   The Chain (?   She/N/Virgin) of Command

Comment: All Fem Letters   Except a Discreet Almost Invisible   E/He   Come/Ant

That is What is Her Comment is Worth   As Big as an Ant
Commenting   Come/Meant
It is Meant Says   The Code

Commentary: Cow (C/How)   Meant   Hairy/Harry
Come   Mentor (Meant/Her)   Harry/Hairy
The Mentor Harry Says   Come
Come/Meant/Her/He
Coming here is Her as   T/Fems Cross   for Him   It is Meant that Way
Says   The Code
Come/Ant/Hairy   Come/Aint/Err/He
As Small as an Ant   No Fem Sees it

Commissioner: Come   He/E   She/Shh   N/In/Hen/Virgin   R/Her/Hair/
Are/Here/Hear/Ear/Whore/Or/Heir/Err/Our/Sex
A Couple here is Him With She as the N/Virgin R/with Heir or Whore
Come/Mission/Her
Her Mission is to make Him Come
A Commissioner is an Official that is in Charge to Rule
She Gets Ordered in that Reality

Commit: Come   It/Hit
That is What   The Code   Calls a Commitment

Commitment: Come   Hit   Meant
Rude Awakenings for the One Committing

Committee: All Fem Letters   except for The Elusive Almost Invisible
E/He
Unusual here is   The Double EEs/He/E   Letter E is Not Even Needed
here   as Letter T has The Sound He/E in it Already   So More Surveillance
T/Fem Cross   She is the One Coming to the Committee
Commit/He   Come/He/T   He Commits to The Law Says   The Code
committee: *Law*   an individual to whom the care of a person or a
person estate is committed

Common: Made Entirely of Fem Letters   Come/On
When Her Loins Are On and Coming   That is Common

The Dam Code The Damn Book

C/See/Young Girl   O/Fem Hole   with   2 MM s/Mothers O/Fem Hole (Again)   N/Ann/Hen/In/On/Virgin
The Common Thing is to have All Ovulating Girls become Mothers
2 OO s/All Fem Holes and 2 MM s/Motherhood in Plural   Ensures that it is Commonly done

Communicate: Commune/He/Gate
Come/U/Neigh/Gate
Communication is Gated   or Negated   to Her   Neigh
Communication: Come/U/Neigh/Gate/Eon   or   He/On
That for an Eon

Communion: Made Entirely of 9 Fem Letters
2OO s/Fem Holes as in Plural   or   All of Them
2 MM s/Motherhood in Plural   or   All of Them
2 NN s/Virgins in Plural   or   All of Them
The Code Makes Sure All Fems Virgins are There   for Her First Initiation to The Ring of Marriage
Come/Union   Come/U/N/Eon
For an Eon   at a Certain Age   The Code   Marks the Girls to be Ready for Something New
The Communion is the Preparation for the Virgin to have Sex Eventually   In The   Coming Union   Therefore   She is Wearing that White Virginal Veil (Same as on Her Wedding Day)

Community: Come/You/Knit/T
Come/You/Knight/He   Come/Unity
The Unity of the Community Says   The Code   is for Her to be Knitted as   T/Fem Cross
As We See We Never Completely Get Out of   The Secret Code because it is Deep in the Small and Big in Our Lives

Compare: Con/Pair   Or a   Pair of Cons   or 2 Coins
She is Not Allowed to Compare
She Needs to Concentrate on that Con being Cheated (To Con) (Polygamy) or Sold for Cheap
Concentrate on the Small Stuff of Life   As Coins or Pennies (Penny is Fem Name)

Comparison: Come   P/Man Power   Reason
The Comparison here is   Only   Between   Men Powers
Compare/His/Own   Compare/His/Sons   Come/Pair/His/Son   Come/ Père/His/On   Come/Père/His/Son   From Father to Son   The Comparison goes On
The Code   Is Clear here about its Real Intentions
Père is Father in French   A Pair is Two (Polygamy   is a Staple in   That Code   as a Pair of Shoes (She/Us)
Con   P   Reason   Con and Come Are Interchangeable in The Code (Because   N/Virgin   will become a   M/Mother)
The Con   and the   Reasonable Man Power   Meet in Comparison   Come/Prison is So Close   No Happy Ending with   That Code

Compassion: Come   Passion (Pass/He/On)
Con/Passion   When Comes The Passion   be an Ass and P/Ass   it On To The Code   Compassion is Nothing Else   than to   Pass that Con On
Con   Means   With   in Spanish   Enhancing the Concept as in being Together to do it
A Terrible Situation Where   The Code   Won Over   Real History   as in So Many Times
Pass it on

Compass: Com/Pass   Con/Pass   Cunt/P/Ass
That is What a Compass does in   The Code
The Compass is the Rosicrucian Logo on Their Apron
It Must be Very Precious   They Wear It   In Front of their Penisses and Balls
It is   V/Fem Sex Active   In Reversed as The Compass   The G/Penis Penetration   is inside That   V
Opposite Down is   The Letter V Called the Lever
G/Penis Penetration of the S/Is/His/Us/Ass/Hiss/Serpent/Penis   which will Go in the O/Fem Hole   or   Loins   as in to Go
G is the Letter for God in   The Code
Not Too Many People Especially a Fem Will Look in that Area Even When in Public Ceremonies
The Code Men   are Masters of Hiding   having Centuries (Millenaries) Experience at it

172

Compel: Con/P/Hell
When Her Genitals (Con) are in   Hell   from   P/Man Power   She is Compelled to Subdue Says   The Code
compel: to subdue

Comprise: Come/Prize   Come/Price
Coming is the Prize that Comes with a Price for Her
comprise: to include   to contain

Computer: Come/Put/Her   Con/Put/Her
M and n are Interchangeable in   The Code   M/Motherhood   N/Virgin   waiting to be Mother
There is a Large Amount of Words Starting with Con (See Con in The Words Chapter)
Con is an Insult to The Fems   But   is Still Alive in the Everyday World   to Put Her Down
con: against a proposition opinion etc   to learn study peruse or examine carefully   to commit to memory   the act of conning   to persuade by deception   a lie exaggeration or glib self serving talk   to hammer a nail or peg   to beat or trash a person with the hands or a weapon   a convict   to direct the steering of a vessel   a scam
Basically what   The Code   Says here with the Word Con is   Learn your Message Under the Nail (Crucifixion) or any Weapon If Necessary   In the Meantime you are just a Con (Vict) that Needs to be Directed as a Ship (She/P) All Fems to go Through those Pains
The Dictionary does Not List Con as a Fem Genitals Insult   But Because Cunt is and Cunts in Plural Sounds the Same as Cons   it Fits here for Me to Incorporate Con as that too
The Word Con is also Part of that Definition to be a Convict   The Code Nails that Peg on that Word

I Suggest Reading The Dictionaries Definitions of Con and Cunt before Entering those Words Section
Con: All 3 Fem Letters
C/See/Young Girl   O/Fem Hole N/In/Ann/Hen/On/Virgin
A Con (Masc) and a Conne (Fem) is Slang for Genitalia in French
Replace O/Fem Hole with A/All Men and He Gets Can   As the Accessibility to that Con for All Men

Con and Cunt are Translatable as the Same Word
Con is Also Part of the Word Count as in to Count   Numbers (See The Numbers Chapter) Therefore is a Forerunner Word
Con Means With in Spanish and Against in English
as   The Code   Evolves into Contraries to Hides its Presence
The Code   Says Eliminate or Use   but No   to Join Her as in with L/Sweet Fem Love Light/Ill/Ail/Hail/Hell/Elle
The Pro and Cons   The Professionals (Code Men) and the Cons (Vaginas   Convicts Etc)
Switch N/In/Hen/Virgin for C/See/Young Girl and She Gets a Cock (Scary Picture to Look at for Her)
Switch N for P/Man Power and He Gets a Cop (Law) or Drink from that Cup
Switch N for R/Her/Hair/Are/Here/Hear/Ear/Whore/Or/Heir/Err/Our/Sex and She Gets a Core (C/See/Young Girl   R/Heir/Whore)
Switch N for D/Pregnant and She Gets a Cod (She is The Fish in   The Code)
Switch C for G/Hymen Penetration and Get God or be One
Switch N for S/Is/His/Us/Ass/Hiss/Serpent/Penis and He Gets a Cause (A Virgin Meeting a Penis Gives a Cause to Move)
Switch N for B/Boy Holding All Fem Breasts and He Gets a Cub (a Child   Too Young for The Code)
Switch N for W/All Fems Sex Active and She Gets a Cow or to be One
The Core or Cause of   The Code   is Her as the Con   or the   Cup   or the   Cod   or   the Cow   to Create the Cub
The Con is the Core of   The Code   Its Cause

Conceal: Con/See/Ill
The Fems Must Not Know or   See/C/Young Girl   that Her Loins are All Ill and in Hell
That Council is to Seal the Con (Con/Seal)
council: an assembly of persons summoned or convened for consultation deliberation or advice   an ecclesiastical assembly for deciding matters of doctrine or discipline
Even Today   The Fems are Not Permitted Contraceptives by Churches   and   She Cannot be a Priest and give Communion because it is the Root of those Rituals   that Keep Her Pregnant and in Poverty   It is All About Her
The Seal is Just Another Form of Keeping   The Code   Secret (Con/C/Ill)

The Dam Code The Damn Book

When Her as a Con is with Another C   and are Ill Together   Conceal That

Concentrate: Con/Center/# 8/Hate   or   Ate (Cover Words)
Concentrate is When Her Loins are Fixed Upon the Center which is # 8/Pregnancy   Hate it or Not She Will have to Eat it

Concept: Con/Cept
The Con and the Scepter
The Con here is with The Penis Seen as a   Scepter
C/On/C/Apt
All or 2 CC s/Ovulating are On and Apt to that Concept
apt: inclined   disposed   given   prone
Con/Fem Hole   Cept/Scepter (Stick)
Cept Means Also Except
Con/Accept
So No Con Accepted   Only the Scepter is Accepted and the Scepter is the Penis

Conceptor: Con   Scept/Cept/Sept   R/Heir/Her/Whore/Err/Are/Sex
The Sept/Cept is # 7 in French   A Number of Luck (See # 7 in The Numbers Chapter) for Him
conceptor: a person who generates or conceives ideas or plans

Conception: Con/Sept/He/On
Sept is # 7 in French   We are Told Seven/Sept is a Lucky Number   Also a Scepter (Masc/Penis)   The Scepter and the Con for an Eon
Con/Sap/Eon
sap: to undermine weaken or destroy insidiously
Sap is Sève in French (The Blood of The Tree)
Conception is to Destroy Her   That is the Concept of   The Code   for an Eon (He/On)   Which is Bad for Child Conception
Concept/He/On   The Conception of A Boy   is The Concept that Stays On   Says   The Code
Con   C/See/Young Girl   Option   or   The Young Virgin   Option
conception: act of conceiving
Conception Should be a True Act of Love as in to Conceive   But No Says   The Code   Con/See/Eve   Con/Sieve   Her Genitals Compared to a Sieve   Since Eve

175

Concern: Cons/Urn   Con/C/Urn   Con/See/Earn   Con/See/Her/N
It is a Concern   The Fem is Said to be an Urn and a Con in   The Code
but   She Cannot Know it   So   it is of Concern   Few Want an Extra
Concern   They will Look Away
Con/See/Earn
Earning Anything for Herself   even as a Con (Prostitution) is a Big No
from   The Code   So   It is Hidden in a Concern

Concierge: Con/See/Urge
Con/See/Her/G/Penis Penetration
That is a Special Kind of Concierge Service   Just for That Urge

Concoction: Con/Cock/She/On
When the Con and the Cock are Together   She is On
concoction: to make by mixing different things
Again Here the Concept of Polygamy is Infiltrated

Concubine: Con   Q/Bleeding Fem   Bind
The Code   Defines a Concubine as   Binding the Vagina   and Relates it
to   Her Loss of Blood   In and Along with the Concept of Polygamy
concubine: a secondary wife
bind: to fasten or secure with a band or bound

Condemn: Con/Dame
The Fems as a Dame (a Presumed Respectful Term for a Fem) is Still a Con
and She is Condemned Anyway to be a T/Fem Cross from that Con (Loins)
Condemnation: Con/Dame/Nation
The Code Makes it a Common Knowledge Among Nations

Condom: Made of All 6 Fem Letters
Con   Dumb/Doom/Dome
The Con as the Dumb is Doomed Under that Dome   (Continued
Enlarged Breast Shape Over the Last 2 Millenaries   Creating More
Estrogen   More Weaknesses)
Con   D/Pregnant   On
Here   Her Con is Pregnant Anyway   Even with the Condom   That is
How it Works Says   The Code

Condoned: Con/Them   Condemned
Con   Damn/Dam   Con/Dame
The Con of that Dame is Done and Damned   So   Disregard the Entire Concept
condone: to disregard or overlook
To Con Someone in French is to Cheat on them
Con Means With in Spanish as to Attach Something with Something Else
Con as With do Not have its Own Identity   As in the
Words   And   or   Or (Heir/Whore/Err/Her/R)   Or the Word   The   D/Pregnant (Thee)
Those In Between Words   They are The Same as the Zero (Fem) in Numbers (See Zero in The Numbers Chapter)
A Zero has No Power by itself   Unless it is Affiliated With a Number in Front of it
Con Translates as Idiot Stupid and Bloody
"So Dark is the Con of Man" Is a Cornerstone Sentence Riddle from the "Da Vinci Code" Movie and Book by Dan Brown
That Movie is a Direct Hit to The Code

Conduit: Con/Do/It
conduit: a passage
According to The Code the Passage to the Con is Just to Do it (Rape)

Cone: Con   Her Loins are in the Shape of a Cone

Confine: Con/Fine
The Code   Says All is Fine for The Fem When Her Con/Loin is Confined or Fined
When Her Sexuality is Confined   She Can Not Win   Says The Code

Confess: Con   F/Fem/Fuck   Ass/S/Is/His/Us/Hiss/Serpent/Penis
Con/Fesse   When the Con is Being Fucked in the Ass
Fesse is French for Buttock
(Cheek)   and   Con   Means   With   and   Vagina
Ass Fuck is a Sin According to Many Religions   But They Confess it   and are Forgiven

Confidence: Con   F/Fem/Fuck   Dance/Dense

Lise Rochon

When The Fems Loins are Dancing or being Dense While Fucking Her Confidence is On
confidence: full trust
The Code   Speaks and Means Differently   Talking about the Full On Thrust of that Stick/Penis

Confirm: Con/Firm
It is a Must for Him to Confirm that that Con is Firm

Confound: Con/Found
No   She Cannot Find Out She is The Con   Her Code Identity
It would be a Sudden Disturbance to The Code   So
confound: to throw into confusion or disorder   to treat or regard erroneously as identical

Confuse: Con/Fuse
If Her Con were to Fuse with Her
That would Be an Opening to Communicate with Herself
So   No Says   The Code   She is Confused to think That
Con/F/Use
When F/Fuck or Fem   Con   Use   Are Together without a Masc Attendance   It is Confused Says   The Code
Con/Few/S
Not a Good Idea for The Code to Have Few or Less Cons at its Service
So   The Code   Says to Her   She is Confused here Too

Congenital: Con/G/Knit/All
The   Con/Fem Hole   and the   G/Vaginal Perforation/Penetration   are Knitted Together for All Fems
Con/Gene/Hit/All
Cons   Genes   and   Gents
congenital: innate   having by nature a specific character
The Applications of   The Code   have Gone Congenital

Conic: Con/IC
IC Means Integrated Circuit
Switch O/Fem Hole for A/All Men and He Gets Can/IC   Canonic is So Close

The Dam Code The Damn Book

Coincidence: Con   In/N/Hen/Virgin   See   Dense/Dance
Go   In   See   D/Pregnant   Hence
Pregnancy is a Certitude in   The Code   But   The Code   Defines It as a   Coincidence

Conman: Con/Man
The Code   Says The Fem Does Not Own Her Genitals
The Word   Con   is Made of 3 Fem Letters   it also Refers as the   Cunt   Which is Made of 4 Fem Letters
In French Con is a Popular Swear as Bitch is in English
Connarde   and   Conne   are Fem Terms
Connard and Con is a   Masc with a Vagina (an Insult to Him and Her)   Which Basically Mean Deception
Also is Le Con   Her Vagina in the Masc Form   Used to Insult a Man
Con Col and Com are Together Jointly According to Dictionary
Con   Col   Com and Cun are All 3 Fem Letters Words
cun: to inquire to learn to study
The Study here that   N/In/Hen/Virgin   Learns How to Use Her   U/You/Ovulating   When N/Ovulating
con Man: a person who uses a fraud method known as confidence trick
Conman is a Strong Cover Word in   The Code

Connect: Con   IC   T/Fem Cross/Great Curse
Con   Means   With   in Spanish (As One   Says   The Code)
The Code   Says to Her   Connect Means   Her Vagina Is Connected to   T/Fem Cross/Great Curse

Connection: Con   IC   She/Shh   On
IC   Integrated Circuit
The Con is Her (See Con in The Words Chapter)   It is an Integrated Circuit   She is On with that Connection   and in Silence Also
Cannot/She/On   No Other Connection For Her
Con/Hit/She/On
Terrible is That Code

Conned: to be conned   to be cheated
Con/Fem Genital Organ (Whore/Gain)
Con/D

Add Another O/Fem Hole and She Gets a Coon or Get to be Accused of being One (Coon is All Fems Letters)
coon: a rustic or undignified person
She never Wins   Anything Fem/Genitals Suffers Total Humiliation   in That Code   With Either Blame Dishonesty Stupidity or Illnesses
The Fems is So Small and Helpless   She Cannot See The Code Cunning Her
Add Another N/In/Hen/Virgin to Con and She (They) Gets to be Conned
conn: the place where a person who cons a vessel is stationed   responsibility for the steering of a ship
Her Con is Nothing but a Wheel (Wheel of Time) to be Turned (T/Urn/Earn) to Move that Ship (She and the P/Man Power Over Her) Upon (Hop/On) Her Waters

Conner: Con/Her
Con is Slang for Vagina
conner: a small fish
The Fish is an Universal Symbol for The Fems in   That Code
Switch O/Fem Hole for A/All Men and He Gets Can/Her
In the Can goes the Small Fish

Conquer: Con/Cue/Her
cue: a hint   a guiding suggestion
The Code   Says She can Win if She takes Her Con as Her Guide (Which would Make Her a Whore)
Con   K/Broken Fem Warrior   R/Her/Hair/Are/Here/Hear/Ear/Whore/Or/Heir/Err/Our/Sex
Con   Queer
When the Con is with the Queer She can Win   More Foolish Fallacies from The Code
Replace R with N/In/Hen/Virgin and get a Queen
The Closest Word for Queen is Queer
Another Way to Diminish (Dim/She) The Fems
Conqueror: Con/Queer/R/Her
Con/C/Err/Her/R   Con/Q/Her/Her   Con/K/Error
The Con/K is Her Losing the Battle   She will Not be the Conqueror here being Already Defeated (See Letter K)
Lots of Rolling R/Whores Sounds here

The Dam Code The Damn Book

The Sound Q Already Says   Blood Loss for Her
Old Long Words are Harder to Read
But Often have More Meanings than the Little Words which are Straight Clear

Conscience: Con/Science   Con/She/Hence
The Code   Says   Conscience   is the Science of the Cons and   Affirms/Amplifies/Secures itself with the Word   Hence   in it
hence: therefore
Conscience   here   Is the Presumed Light of the Soul for Most of Us   Presented as an Insult   to Real Clear Consciousness
The Dictionary is Particularly Poor on that Definition here
conscience: a feeling that something you have done is morally wrong   moral goodness of one conduct
Conscience to Me is   The Endless Search for The Eternal Truth of The Universe   Through The Small Means We Humans   have
Conscience is a Huge Spiritual Word
The Code Appropriated It a Long Time Ago
Conscience is a Cover Word

Consider: Cons/Fem Vaginas   ID   Her/R   Con/See/D/Her   Con/See/Dear
ID is from The Freudian Age (Beginning of the 20th Century)
ID is a Difficult Psychological Concept to Grab   Somehow   it is   Instincts Under Control Would Be the   ID   We All have One
ID is   i/Marriage Act   or   The I/Stick   with   D/Pregnant
We Do Need to have a Social Identity Entity
So   We can Know Who We are in Between Us
Vote and Organize   So   We can Get a Better Life   But it does Not Work that Way (Wrongly) Says   The Code

Consciousness: Con   She   Us/S/Is/Has/Ass/His/Hiss/Serpent/Penis   Nest
The Con   as Her (She) Genitals   S/Is/His/Penis   and a   Nes t (With a Hidden T/Fem Cross/Great Curse   to Her   at The End of What She Think is Real Consciousness) Says   That Code

Consecration: Con   Seek   R/Her/Hair/Are/Here/Hear/Ear/Whore/Or/Heir/Err/Our/Sex   Ray   She/Shh   Eon (He/On)
The Fem here is   The Con   that Seeks   R/Sex   as R/Her/Hair/Are/Here/Hear/Ear/Whore/Or/Heir/Err/Our/Sex   for Ever
consecration: the part of communion where the bread and wine are consecrated
Consecration is a Catholic Religious Word   Not a Natural Word
It Tells Humans What to Believe as a Religion
On a Second Level of Reasoning
As   Teaching the Little Girls   to Wear a Veil   at First Communion   By Making them Getting More Attention Around that Special Event for Her   Try That on a Boy
The Veil is the Abyss   The Fems Falls in   and   Becomes a Shadow

Consensus: Con   Scents   S/Is/His/Us/Ass/Hiss/Serpent/Penis   Con/Sense/Us
consensus: majority of opinion
Everyone   Agrees in   The Code   that   The S/Penis   is with the   Con   it Smells (Scents) it
Con/Sin/She/Shh   Us/S

Consent: Con/Scent   Con/Sent
The Word   Consent (Obviously) is an Important Word in   The Code
Consent: agree   concur   conform   ascent   comply
It Acts (Consents)   on a Different Level of Language   and   Therefore   has a Different Level of Understanding*
"For those Who Can Understand   Understand"
Said a   Very Long Time Ago   Someone Very Much Loved to Us (Jesus)   He Understood That
Proceed
The Code   System   Reflects   Sex   in Only One Light
The Love Kindness and Fun of   The Fems as   One
Fem   and   Mother   or   Wife is   Not   in   That Code
Having a Good Clean Life and being Happy doing it and Not Hurting Others in the Way is Not Part of   That Code
That Code Enslaved   The Fems   Into being   Cons
She does Not See   it Coming   And   The Abuse Cause Mental Illnesses
Lack of Love for Others Diminishes a Civilization

The Dam Code The Damn Book

The Code Counts (Cunts) on that

Conservative: Cunt/Serve/At/Eve   Cunt/Serve/Hat/V
Cunt/Serve/T/Fem Cross   Eve (He/V)
The Fems Hole is Serving The Code Since Eve
With that Fem Cross   The Great Curse
See Hat in Words

Consider: Con   See   D   R/Her/Hair/Are/Here/Hear/Ear/Whore/Or/
Heir/Err/Our/Sex
Consider   is Her   Seeing Herself as a   D/Pregnant   R/Heir/Whore/Err

Consistency: Con/Sees/T/Hen/See
Because of   T/Fem Cross
All the Cons and Her Sisters are Under that Tent
Con/Sees/T/And/See   So
All What The Fems Sees is Her Bloody Cross
That is Called Consistency in The Code

Consistent: Con   Sys as in System   Sis as Sisters   Tent See/C/See/
Young Girl
All Fems are Under   That Code   Tent

Consonants: Con/Sonnets
Sweet Music for the Cons (Fem)
Strauss Said About His Waltzes   His Music was As Churning
Butter   More As Making Ice Cream to Me
It was in Vienna that Freud Discover that Neurosis from   The
Fems   Coming to Him with Neurotic Behaviors   He then Published in a
Medical Journal that it was Sexual Abuse done to Her that was Causing Her
Neurotic Behaviors   Then   the Pressure from those High Class Families
was So Powerful on Him   that He had to Change His Theory for the
Famous Oedipal Complex that Makes The Fems Desire to have a Penis and
that is What Created Her Neurotic Behaviors   A Weird Concept here that
Makes No sense to a Normal Fem

Conspiracy: Cons/Piracy

Any Form of Upheaval from the Cons is a   Big No in   The
Code   So   Cons/P/Racy   It will Be Racy for Her
Cons   P/Man Power   R/Her/Hair/Are/Here/Hear/Ear/Whore/Or/Heir/Err/
Our/Sex   Ace/Ass/As   C/See/Young Girl
Because   P/Man Power   in its Coded Sex Enslavement is the Ace in
Conspiracy   with its Ass/Arse/Donkey/N/Ann/Ane/Virgin   as   R   to
End   Including   C/See/Young Girl   She Loses here Because of Her
Animal Status
Con/Space/R/See (C)
According to   The Code   She has to Create Space for   R/Her/Hair/Are/
Here/Hear/Ear/Whore/Or/Heir/Err/Our/Sex
Cons/Père/Ici   Ici Means Here in French   Père is Father in French
More of the Same Concept   Except   it Comes from The Authority
Channel   A Father Figure   or   a Guide
In this Case it is   The Code
conspiracy: an agreement among conspirators
How Suitable for   The Code   The Agreement of the Conspirators   is
the Pirating of the Cons

Conspiration: Con   S/Is/His/Us/Ass/Hiss/Serpent/Penis or Plural   P/
Man Power   R/Her/Hair/Are/Here/Hear/Ear/Whore/Or/Heir/Err/Our/
Sex   She   Eon (He/On)
An Eon is an Indefinite Long Period of Time
conspiration: joint effort
From   The Code   She had Sex Since an Eon as a Con
Conspirator   Cons/P/Rate/Her

Constantly: Cons/Tent/Lay
The Cons (Her) Stay in the Tent and Lay (Eggs/Ovulation) there Constantly

Constellation: Con   S/Is/His/Us/Ass/Hiss/Serpent/Penis   T/Fem Cross/
Great Curse   Hell   He   On (Eon)   Con/S/Tell/He/On
The Stars Too Tells Us About   The Code   Power Over that Con
The Stars Above Us Were Named by the Greeks for Us   According to
Their Mythology   Astrological Records   Dates Back to Babylon 1645
BC   and   Earliest Horoscope was 410 BC
Those Men Recreated a World Above US   of What They Knew or Feared
Below   In Our World

The Dam Code The Damn Book

Astrology Uses 2 Goddesses Planets   Venus (Beauty) and Moon (Emotions Pregnancy and The Bleeding Cycle)
Venus has No place in the Night Sky   Except She Comes at Sunset   and   Disappear When it gets Dark at Night
The Other Fem Planet is the Moon   She Has No Name
The Moon Card is a Bad Card in The Tarot Deck (Dick)

Constriction: Con/Strict/Eon   or   He On
Constriction of the Con is Important for   The (Man Only) Code
A Fem Canal after a Child Birth is Not Constricted Anymore   It Makes Her Lose Power Because Her Identity is That Con   So   When it has Become Deficient   She is Done and Out
The Code is Strict about that Loss of Her Power   Because that Tightness Goes Away Early in Life for Her   Therefore Weakening Her More   Ahead in that Alley

Construction: Con/Struck/He/On   or   Eon
When the Con is Struck that is Called a Construction (Children) in the Mind of   The Code   Since an Eon

Consulate: Cons/All/Late
The Fems are Kept Away from All Positions of Power   in Any Way Seen by   The Code

Consult: Con/Salt
Salt was Part of the Alchemical Works
Cons/Halt
The Code   does Not Consult the Fems (Cons) for Nothing   The Code   Obeys   The Code   or   Out

Consume: Con/Sum
Con/S/U/M   is   Con/Her Loins   S/Is/His/Us/Ass/Hiss/Serpent/Penis   U/You/Ovulating   M/Motherhood
The Total and Only Thing to All Cons Says   The Code   is to Get Consumed   and   Fall into   M/Motherhood   as in   No Other Choice
Contraceptives were Outlawed by Religions   Until Recently in Modern Countries   and are Still Outlawed in Many 3rd World Countries
sum: total

Lise Rochon

Consumer: Con   Sum   R/Her/Hair/Are/Here/Hear/Ear/Whore/Or/Heir/Err/Our/Hour/Sex
The Code   Says   The Sums of All Cons are to be   All/Whores
The Only One Buying that   is The Con (Her) Being   so   Ignorant

Contact: Cunt/Act
Contact Here is Made by Narrowing Down   The Sex Act to a   Cunt (Insulting Her)   Act
Every Contact in   The Code   Brings in that Con   See Con and Cunt in Modern   and Old   Dictionaries
Con is also a Convict   etc

Contagious: Cunt/Count (See The Numbers Chapter) Age/Egg   Us/S/Is/His/Hiss/Ass/Serpent/Penis
Fact is   We All Grow Old   Although Here in   The Code   Age is Related to Her Pregnancies/Children   or   Her Eggs
It is Contagious   Says   The Code   All Fems Get to Go Through it   If Not   It will Haunt   You/U/Ovulating Time from C/See/Young Girl C/Haunt   Age   He   Us

Contain: Cunt/In
Cunt   N/In/Hen/Virgin   R/Her/Hair/Are/Here/Hear/Ear/Whore/Or/Heir/Err/Our/Sex
Letter N is Ann/In/Donkey   Âne in French

Container: Contain/Her
Cunt   N/In/Hen/Ann/Virgin   R/Her/Hair/Are/Here/Hear/Ear/Whore/Or/Heir/Err/Our/Hour/Sex
Con   T/Fem Cross   N/In/Hen/Virgin   R/Her/Hair/Are/Here/Hear/Ear/Whore/Or/Heir/Err/Our/Sex
Her Loins from   N/Hen/Virgin   to   T/Fem Cross   to   R/Heir/Whore/Err/Are/Sex   It is All Contained   Says   The Code

Contempt: Cunt/MPT   Con/Tempt

Contend: Cunt/End
That Would be a Big No from   The Code   to End that Fem Enslavement of The Cunt (Con/T)   So

contend: to struggle in opposition   to strive in rivalry
Contender   Cunt/End/Her   She will Not Win That One   Con/Tend/Her   Always Helping   That Con
contender: a person who tries to win something in a contest

Content: Con/Tent   Cunt/End
The Code   is Hiding   The Code Content of Her   Con/Cunt   Under that Tent   Which is the Shape of the First Letter A (See A in the Letters Chapter)

Contest: Con   Test   as a Horrible Word/Concept as can Be   Figure it Out
The Code   Suggests here that the Word Contest is
To Try   As Actually Part of that Contestants Game
Contestant: Con/Test/Ant
Ants are So Small   and   they are So Many of Them   And are All the Same Too as   The Code   Says
Ants Are One of The Conceptual Patterns Chosen by   The Code   Targeting The Fems as   Hard Working Self Motivated Focused Workers

Context: Cunt   X/Fallen Fem Cross   T/Fem Cross
Count   X/Fallen Fem Cross   All Fems Sound Letters
Accountability is Important here
That is the Context of   The Code
Count and Cunt are   No Sound Coincidence (See The Numbers Chapter)   M/Motherhood   and   N/Virgin   are Interchangeable in   The Code

Continent: Cunt/He/Meant   Count/He/Meant
N/In/Hen/Virgin   and   M/Motherhood   are Linked Together as One
M/Motherhood   and the Other is   N/The Virgin that waits to be a Mother   When N   Becomes M

Continue: Cunt/He/Knew   Count/He/Knew
The Code   Means   All Cunts Must Be Known   In the Biblical Sense   it is Known that to Know a Woman is to Have Sex with Her
As If There was Nothing else to look for as a Life Partner

continue: to go on to continue
It Must Go On   Says The Code

Continued: Cunt/He/Knew   D/Pregnant
You may Want to Check All Words in Con or Cunt in Any Dictionary (Dick/She/Horney/Honey) for a Special Mental Ride   Then   Meet Words   As Constitution   Feel the Power of The Code On Us   It is Enough to Make a Grown Up Cry

Contract: Cunt   R/Her/Hair/Are/Here/Hear/Ear/Whore/Or/Heir/Err/Our/Sex   Act
R with the Cunt   That is   The Code   Contract for The Fems
Cunt/Rack
Rack is Slang for Fem Breasts
Con/Tear/Act   That Contract is to Tear About
The Code   has it All Planned   It Knows the Grief it Brings

Control: Cunt   Roll
Roll that Cunt to Keep   The Code   Order (Whore/D/Her)
Con/T/Roll
Control is to Roll In and Out The Fems Genitalia for Better Control of The Fems and Keep that T/Fem Cross Unfolding Forward

Controversial: Cunt/Reversal   Cunt/R/Verse/All
If In Any Way   She Sees and Wants to   Change/Reverse   Something   As a Cunt Reversal to Normal   that Would be Controversial to   The Code   Verses   So   No   The Code Declares it Controversial and therefore is Dangerous for Her   Another Weak Spot to Add on Her Shoulders
Count/Her/V/See/All
V/Fem Sex Active   would See All about the Cunt and that is Also Not Admissible for   The Code

Convent: Con/Vent
Her Con (Her Loins) Gets a Break from Sex in a Convent
As Long as that Convent is Not Invaded by Barbarians Where they Rape All Fems/Nuns and Burn their Place Down
It has been the Message for   The Fems   Not to Do that

The Dam Code The Damn Book

Conversation: Con/Verse/A/She/On
A Conversation is the Con (Her Loins) Going Along with the Verses of   The Code

Convert: Con/V/Hurt
When the   Con of the   V/Fem Sex Active   is Hurt   She convert: to transmute   to transform
Con   V/Fem Sex Active   R/Her/Hair/Hear/Ear/Here/Heir/Or/Whore/Err/ Are Our/Sex
T/Fem Cross
Here The Fem Sexuality is Transformed into being a   T/Fem Cross

Convey: Con   V/Fem Sex Active
The Con   and the   V/Eve/Fem Sex Active   Together   That is The Only Match Possible Accepted by   The Code   For Her is to   Convey from One to the Other
convey: to take from one place to another   to transport   to communicate   make known to transfer pass the title to
archaic   steal   purloin   *Obsolete*   to take away secretly   to lead or conduct as a channel or medium
Convey Gives a License to Steal and Cheat
Con Mean With In Spanish Which Corroborates with the Meaning of Convey
In The Code   Con is a Bad Word for   The Fems
Words as   Connard(e)   La Conne   Are Degrading to Her
Add N/In/Hen/Virgin and C/See/Young Girl and She Gets Convince

Convince: Con/Vein/C
Vein/Venus/Vein/Us are Related to the Menstrual Cycle
Con/V/Hence
Hence Enhances the Action of Convincing Her
hence: therefore
Hence   is   N/In/Hen/Virgin   and   C/See/Young Girl
Con   Vin   C/See/Young Girl
Vin is Wine (Fem Blood Loss) in French
With Wine   A Young Girl Con   Gets Softer
Rape is Always in The shadow of   The Code
Con/V/In/C

Lise Rochon

In Convince   The Con of   V/Fem Sex Active   N/In/Hen/Virgin   and C/See/Young Girl   are Held Together in a Convincing Mode
convince: to move by argument or belief   agreement   consent   or a course of action

Coo: Made of All 3 Fem Letters
C/See/Young Girl is with   2 OO s/Fems Holes (Plural or All of Them)
coo: to utter or imitate the soft murmuring sound characteristic of doves   to murmur or talk fondly or amorously
Cooing: Coo   N/In/Hen/Virgin
Attract That Virgin   That is The Language Sounds that   The Code   Finds Appropriate for The Fem When   She is Communicating   and That   From Childhood
Cooing Puts to Sleep and Keep Babies Sleeping   Not Much of a Strong Adult Voice to Express Herself
Coo Makes a Low Comforting Back Ground Noise it is Another of Her Code Sounds Pushed on Her   Such as Bitch   B/Boy Holding All Fem Breasts   Itch   Etc
Close to Coo is   Coucou Which Means Crazy in French
cou: a woman a person esp a woman viewed solely as a sex object   the female genital   vulva
That is   The Dam Code   The Code   of the Damned   It Turns On a Dime   A Dame Said
Switch C/See/Young Girl for B/Boy Holding All Fem Breasts and He Gets a Boo   A Boo Boo for the Young
Learning the Dam Code with Sweet Sounds
The Code Steals/Sucks from The Love and
Dehumanizes The Humans Soul
Animals do Not Even do that to Each Other
Switch C for G/Penis Penetration and She Gets Goo
goo: a sticky or vicious substance   coy sentimental language or ideas
That would be The Love Juices
Switch C for L/Sweet Fem Love Light/Ill/Ail/Hail/Hell/Elle and She Gets Loo
loo: toilet   the forfeit or sum paid into the pool   the fact of being looed
Note Loo is 3 Fem Letters
Add T/Fem Cross and She Gets Loot
loot: spoils or plunder taken by pillaging as in war

The Dam Code The Damn Book

Switch C for M/Motherhood and She Gets Moo
Back to the Cows and Animals for Her   Especially as a Mother of those
Men and Their Children   The Code   Ignores That
Switch C/Young Girl for N/In/Hen/Virgin and She Gets New   The Code
Sound Barrier will Work here for Her   She will Not Make   The Sound
Connection   There is No Word Called Noo
The Code   Interprets   The Past   Present   Future   Together (To/
Get/Her)
What Can be New Now for C and N   They have Almost The Same
Definition   That is Their Connection
When C/Young Girl Becomes Old Enough   She Transforms from N/Virgin
into a M/Mother   When One More Bar is Added to N (See Bar in The
Words Chapter   and # 11 in the Numbers Chapter)
As the Example here   New (Knew) Means   Already Used in the Biblical
Sense   A Man Knew Her   for Example
Switch C for P/Man Power and He Gets Poo
poo: excrement
The Man Code wants No Connection to be Made here with Any
Men   Whatever it is Poo or Coo
Poo Smells Bad and Should be Avoided   So it is   She will Stay Away
from That
Switch C for S/Is/His/Us/Ass/Hiss/Serpent/Penis and He Gets Sue (A Girl)
For Her it is Stay Away from that Knowledge or Get Sued
Switch C for T/Fem Cross and She Gets Too/Two/To
Number 2 Tells Her there is Always Another Hole to Go To Too for
Him   And That it is All Poop Anyway
Switch C for W/All Fems Sex Active and She Gets Who
The Code   Says She Cannot Know   She is a Nobody
Add R/Her/Hair/Hear/Ear/Here/Heir/Or/Whore/Err/Are Our/Sex   to Who
and She Gets R Again
That R Identities Her in   The Code
The Root of   The Code   is The Cross (Her Bloody Cross/Great Curse)
With the Letter T   Now Known as The Nail (N/In/Hen/
Virgin   Ill/L   Nil   Nell in Hell/L   etc)
The Code   does that by Nailing All Fems that Way
Switch C for Z/Sleep On It and Get Zoo
Nail   Polishing   is The Cover Word Telling/Showing   The Deadly Irony
of That Code

191

Lise Rochon

Cook: C/See/Young Girl   Hook
All Fems   Starting in Childhood and Under   The Law of The Secret Code of The Hook is on Her
The Code   Calls it Cooking   Here From   C/Young Girl
Ook has a Special Letter Arrangement   It is 2 Fems   as   O/Fem Holes   Ending in   K/Broken Fem Warrior   Meaning All Fems are on The Way to End Up Broken
The Hook   is for the Fish (See   Fish   Ship   Ocean (O/Fem Hole   She/Shh   N/Ann/In/Hen) in The Words Chapter)
Take Away C and Get a Hook (A Hooker (Hook/Her   R/Heir/Whore/Err   Hooks))   H/Secret Code Letter   is Silent   so   the Impression done is That   The 3 Fem Letters   are Acting Alone   But No   H is in The Front
Switch C for B/Boy Holding All Fem Breasts and He Gets a Book (The Teaching of   The Code)
Switch C for L/Sweet Fem Love Light/Ill/Ail/Hail/Hell/Elle and She Gets Looks (Smoke and Screens for Her)
Switch C for R/Heir/Or/Whore/Are and She Gets a Rook (a Crow)
rook: to cheat   fleece   swindle
A Rook is Also a Chess Piece
Add R/Heir/Or/Whore/Err and She Gets a Crook
This is Where   R   Err   She Gets The Looks (Hair)   Then She Gets Through   R   Prostitution was Never Legal   So between a Crow and The Rook is Where She Arrives

Cool: All 4 Fem Letters
C/See/Young Girl   2 OOs/Fem Holes (Plural or All of Them)   L/Sweet Fem Love Light/Ill/Ail/Hail/Hell/Elle
This is Not an All Positive Fem Word for The Fem
C/See/Young Girl   Knows that it Takes 2 Holes/Loins   or   More to be Cool   Polygamy is Understood
Polygamy is in Many Words in the Language Code
Not   So Cool   Icy   Frigidity Follows
Switch C for T/Fem Cross and She Gets to be a Tool
Switch C for R/Heir/Or/Whore/Are/Her and She Gets The Rules (Règles in French is Her Period)
Switch C for F/Fem/Fuck and She Gets a Fool

Switch L for K/Broken Fem Warrior and She Gets to Cook   or   be Cooked
("We are going to Cook Some Poodles in the Mountains Over the Weekend"   A Rush Limbaugh Nasty Quote on His American National Daily Radio Show)
You can Figure that One Out

Coon: All 4 Fem Letters
The Con (See Con Cunt and Count in The Words Chapter) with an Extra O Adds More Cons   Polygamy being Again in The Cards
coon: a rustic or undignified person

Cop: The Sound Relationship Between Cop and Cup is Not a Coincidence
cop: a police officer   a person who seeks to regulate a specified behavior activity practice etc
In   The Code   Sound World a Cup is a Good Drinking Tool
A Cup Usually Serves Something Good as Tea which is T/Fem Cross
Often   The Code   Serves The Fems These Bad Teachings
in an Attractive Package to Her   As the Syrup that Hides the Medicine   Although in   The Code   World She is being Served Poison
The Cups is a Suit (Something Nice to Wear) in Tarot   and   in a Regular Deck/Dick of Cards
A Cup is Considered a Fem Aspect
In Tarot   The Cup Represents the Heart or the Emotions of Love
The Cup is Also the Holy Grail Cup   A Center Item in The Well Known Mysterious Symbolic Book   The Holy Grail (Hole/He   Girl)   It is Said to be The Chalice from Christ Last Supper   It Could have been Any Other Object than a Cup   But No   because The Book Subject is That Cup
The Cup is Also a Bra Size
Stimulating Young Girls Breasts Can Actually Make them Faint
Those Cups are Cupped/Seized in Early Age by   The Code   Order
seizure: the act or instance of seizing   sudden attack of illness
It is   The Code   Law of the Ever Expandable Breasts
One of The Code   Laws   for Her to Obey
When Letter   C/See/Young Girl   is Up in   U Letter   Form She is to be Grabbed/Seized   by P/Man Power

Lots of Men are Focused on those Breasts   Which Seems to be an Anomaly of Her Anatomy   All Other Mammals have No Breasts Showing   Once Feeding Babies is done
Cup and Cop are Important Words in The Code
On a Symbolic Level it Represents   The Code   Surveillance Focusing on Those Cups
cop: to seize   catch or steal
This Definition Brings the Element of   Sexual Abuse   as in   Just Do Not Get Caught
And the Word Cub is So Close   Switching P/Man Power for B/Boy Holding All Fem Breasts   A Smooth Transitional State of Mind to Babyhood

Cope: K/Hope
C/See/Young Girl and K/Wounded Fem Warrior are Both Fem Letters
One Hops and the Other Hopes in Order to Cope
Cope: to face or struggle with responsibility
C/Hop

Copulation: Cup/He/Lay/She/On   Cup/U/Lay/She/On
Both Sexes are Represented in the Copulation Word Sound
It is an Example of When   The Code   Infiltrates itself and Attach itself to a Natural Phenomenon (as Sex) and Impose/Stamps a Religious Belief or Principle on it   Here   it is Associating Her Sexuality with a Cup (See Cup in The Words Chapter)   Cup is an Important Symbol in Religions   From Common Knowledge   All the Way   to Secretive Esotericism
Cope   U/He   Lay   She/Eon

Copy: Cope/He   K/Hope/He
More Subtle here is   The Code
Hope and Cope are Part of Almost Everyone Life as We Struggle with   That Code   We are Just Copies of Each Other that Way
But   The Real Ending here is with   K/Fem Broken Fem Warrior   Where She Loses the Battle Every Time   That is the Real Copy
Cup/He   Cop/He   Cape/He   Cap/He
Here is the Subtle Code Presence of the Hearts/Cup and Surveillance/Cop   and it is Hiding Under a Cape
The Cop as in a Policeman is Not Represented Physically here   He Just Represents Our Fears

Core: C/See/Young Girl   O/Fem Hole   R/Her/Hair/Hear/Ear/Here/Heir/Or/Whore/Our/Err/Are/Sex
K/R   K/Roar   C/R
The Core/Center of   The Code   is When   C/See/Young Girl   or   K/Broken Fem Warrior   Roars Having Sex with Him   Under The Supervision of The Very Quiet   E/He
She is Still a   R   at the Core   Says   The Code
core: center
Switch O for A/All Men and He Gets Care
Switch O for U/You/Ovulating and She Gets Cure   The Cure for Her is When C is Transformed into R

Corn: C/Horn
C/See/Young Girl   is with the   Horn/Penis   as in Giving a Hand Job   It is Just Corn   a Banal Callosity   Says The Code
K/R/On
K/Fem Broken Warrior   is Defeated When She has become a R/Hair/Are/Here/Hear/Ear/Heir/Or/Whore/Err/Our/Her Sex   It is as a Piece of Corn
corn: a cereal   a grain   banal and sentimental   callosity   slang for money   maize
Amazing (A Maize/N   A/Maze/In) Corn has Many Facets
The Maze here is that The Fems Cannot Hold Any Power Position
When She is Holding the Horn it is as Little as a Grain   It is Banal and has No Importance (Being Sentimental) and it can be Bought for Money Bringing the Whore Concept Along
The Word Corn is Old Symbolism from Ancient Greece
Demeter (The/Mother) is the Goddess of Corn and Agriculture
Demeter   Diameter   Die/A/Mother
Demeter Went to Save Her Daughter Persephone (Pierce/the Phone) as in Decoding the Sound Code) from the Abyss of Hades (Hide/His) the God of Death and Hell
Persephone did Not Come Back and Corn Started to Grow Where She Went Missing
Corn has Ears
Switch C for H/Secret Code Society and He Gets Horn (Penis)
Switch C for P/Man Power and He Gets Porn   Or What a Man Should Think About Sex According to   The Code
Switch C for B/Boy Holding All Fem Breasts and He Gets Born

Switch C for N/In/Hen/Virgin and She Gets Norm   Virgins are Supposed to be All the Same   The Code Aim (M/Motherhood) at That
Switch C for W/All Fems Sex Active and She Gets Worn as in Being Too Old or Too Used (Sexually)
Take Away R/Whore/Her and She Gets Con (Female Loins   Vulgar   Cunt)
Corn on the Cob   Sex and a Cub (Baby)
Pushing Pregnancies is One of the Roots of   The Code
Organic Corn is a Fantastic Food   But the Word is Just Another Way of Hiding Her as a Whore
corny: banal   stale   pertaining to or affected with corns of the feet   of or abounding in corn   old fashioned trite or lacking in subtlety   sentimental
The Code Says   Corny it the More the Corn the More the Lack of Subtlety and Banal it is

Corner: Corn/Her   C/Horn/Her   K/Horn/Her
Corn is Great Food   so   it is a Place to Hide   The Ugliness of   The Code
Corn/Her/Her   Says   The Code   so   He can Horn/Her   and   Con Her (See Con in The Words Chapter) Out of Her
In the Corner the Con (Fem) is Playing the Horn and it Pays Corn
Research the 5th Corner of the Freemasons
K/Broken Fem Warrior   Horn   R/Her/Hair/Hear/Ear/Here/Heir/Or/Whore/Err/Are/Our/Sex
K/Broken Fem Warrior Gets Horned When Cornered to become a R/Heir/Or/Whore/Err

Corny: Corn/He
C/See/Young Girl   is Horny   it is Corny
corny: old fashioned   sentimental   calluses
C/See/Young Girl   R/Her/Hair/Hear/Ear/Here/Heir/Or/Whore/Err/Are/Our/Sex
N/In/Hen/Virgin   He/E
Always the Whore or Motherhood Shadows for The Fems
K/Horn/He   When   The Code   Horns that K/Broken Fem Warrior to Achieve Her   It is Corny (Small Importance) Says   The Code

Corpse: Core/Puss   C/Whore/Puss   K/Whore/P/S

The Dam Code The Damn Book

The Core of Corpse would Be Her   Puss/Pussy
That would be a Big No from   The Code   So
No One Wants to Look at a Corpse   Especially a Fem (Core/Piss)
corpus: a large or complete collection of writings   the body of a person or animal especially when dead
According to   The Code   Her Puss has a Long List of Books Written about it (?)   but   Dead it is   As a Corpse   Core/Piss   or   C/See/ Young Girl   R/Heir/Whore/Err   Puss (Close to Plus)Which is probably Her Love Juices

Correct: C/Young Girl   R/Heir/Or/Whore   Act
What is Correct Says   The Code   is to have   C/See/Young Girl   Be Called a   R   in the Act (Sex)
C/See/Young Girl   Whore   Wreck
Make a Wreck of that Little Girl Whore (Whore/Her   Horror) It is Correct Says   The Code

Corset: Core/Set   Core/Sit   C/Young Girl   R/Her/Hair/Hear/Ear/Here/ Heir/Or/Whore/Err/Are/Our/Sex   Set
That Core is Her Middle Section   (See BB in   The Words Chapter)
The Code   Sets Her Core   by Making Her Waist Very Small   Represented Uniquely in the   Fleur de Lys   Flower Pics
Waste   as in   Her Waist   Waste   is the Cover Word here
Her Core becomes So Small/So Tight It Impairs Her Health   Her Life   Her Judgment
It is the Chinese Feet Binding All Over again   Hurting The Fems Feet so   She Cannot Run Away   This is Worse than that   The Binding Comes from The inside
That Waist Binding from the BB   Contracts All Her Inner Organs   Slows and Disturbs Her Digestive System   and   Other Functions   It Weakens Her in Many Ways   That is   The Code   in Action
Many Generations Now The Fem has Complied with that Small Waist Syndrome   So   So Bad for All Fems
So Many Hollywood Movies are Fascinating   But   Hollywood is the Great Carrier of That Monstrous Message to The Fems   To have   Big Breasts   Small Waist   Long Legs   Perched On   Small Feet   Hooked on   High Heels (Hell)   Big Eyes   Big Lips   Big Hair   Small Nose   Small Ears   High Cheeks   Porcelain Skin   Rich   Smoking   it

is Endless   The Amount of Time Needed to Try to Reach That
Mirage   Prevents Her   from being Interested in anything Else in
Life   Then   The Children Comes   The Mirage is Gone   Another
World Opens   Then   She is Called Funny Looking   A Thing   by Many
Men   Who are Plainly Scared from That
Every American Made Medieval Movie Teaches   The Fems How to
Use that Bed Pole to Hang On   While the Waist Strings from Her Dress
are being Pulled from Her Back (it Cannot be Seen by Her that Way)
to Constrict Her Waist   Now   from The Outside   It is Still with Us
Today   Those Tight Clothing with Elastics Around Her Waist   Have been
there   Since   We were on Diapers   That Tightness That Maims The
Fem Never Left Her
Eventually The Fem Develop an Inner Corset
K/Broken Fem Warrior   R/Heir/Or/Whore/Err/Her/Sex   Set
The Corset is How the Syndrome is Set (From Pain)

Cosmos: CSMS   C/Us/M/Us
C/See/Young Girl   is with   S/Is/His/Us/Ass/Hiss/Serpent/Penis   M/
Mom   and again   S/Penis   It is The Never Ending Story of   The
Code   for The Fems
C/Young Girl is Surrounded with S/Penisses Until Motherhood   That
Chain Continues   The Code   Cosmos   Nomenclature
Take C Away   Add Another S/Penis   and Get   Osmosis   We Bath in
That Code

Could: C/Hood   K/Hood
C/See/Young Girl   and/or   K/Broken Fem Warrior   in the Hood (Secret
Societies) can Only be a Possibility for Her Because in   The Code   Mind
it Will Never Happen

Council: Con/Seal   Cons/Ill
C   On   Seal
council: a group of people who are chosen to make rules laws decisions
Fems are Represented here as Cons   and   They are Sealed Out
C/See/Young Girl   On   See   Ill   The Fem in Council Rules can Only See
Herself as   Ill/L/Sweet Fem Love Light/Ill/Ail/Hail/Hell/Elle   Therefore
Inept to Conduct Business There
Seals is Big Secret Business in   The Code

The Dam Code The Damn Book

Count: Count Numbers   Or   Cunt/Numb/Her (Numbing Her Con/Cunt) in S/Plural   or   All of Them
cunt: the vulva or vagina   extremely disparaging and offensive   a contemptuous term used to refer to a woman   a term used to refer to a contemptible person   sexual intercourse with a woman
From Contemptible to Vaginas are the Cunts
To be a Count is a Masc Honor Only   The Code   Protects Men with Titles   There are Many Instances   It Separates Them from The Situation
If it would be a Fem Count   She would have a Different Name   a Countess is a   Count/Ass
Count/Cunt is a Powerful Name in   The Code
Count the Days   The Time of the Month   Anything Related to Numbers is a Lead
Count is a Cover Word Here

Counter: Cunt/Her   Count/Her
(See The Numbers Chapter)
counter: table or display case in which food can be shown   business transacted   etc   an imitation coin or token   money
Not Even knowing about it   The Fem is Being   Counted (Cunt   Hit/It)   She is on Display for Sale   Cheap
As a Countertop She is Being Topped (See Top in The Words Chapter)   Business as Usual for   The Code
Counter is a Cover Word here

Contour: Cunt   Our/R/Heir/Or/Whore/Err/Her/Sex
Her Genitals Belongs to   The Code
Contour Says   The Fem Cunt is Defined as R
C/See/Young Girl   Hunt   T/Fem Cross   R/Heir/Or/Whore/Err/Her/Sex
The Line that Defines Contour is   Hunt C as R   Put Her in That Cunt/Con Tower   Give Her a Tour   Tour is Tower in French   Count on That
contour: the outline of a figure a body   the edge or line that define bounds   a shape or object
Switch T for D/Pregnant and She Gets Con/Door   A Condor would be The Alternative   But it is Impossible to Find for Most of Us

Country: Cunt   Her/R/Hair/Hear/Ear/Here/Heir/Or/Whore/Err/Are/Our/Sex   Hey

Hey is Food for Horses/Whores
Count/Her/Hey
Con/Tray
Her Con/Cunt on a Tray is Her Country
Cunt/Ray   Her Loins are Radiating All Over   When She is on a Tray
But No Says   The Code   Can/T/Ray
The Proposition has been Cancelled   T/Fem Cross   Cannot be a
Ray   Not in Her Country
The Fems has No Value in Every Nook and Cranny of   The
Code   Language
That Code   is Only Hard on Her   But   Presents itself Often as
Something Nice   Here   the Country is a Nice Place to Visit
Country is a Cover Word here

Couple: Cop/All
cop: to catch   nab   to steal   filch   to buy (narcotics)   to cope
out   cope a plea
Those Boys doing Just that to Girls   Grabbing Us
Cup/All
Her Breasts Must be Cup Size
Hop   All Fems
Make Sure   She Shows Bigger Breasts than Natural   C/See/Young
Girl   Hop/Up   with   All/L/Sweet Fem Love Light/Ill/Ail/Hail/Hell/Elle
C/Hop/All
Cup/Hold   Hold that Cup Size
cup: to form into a shape of a cup
To Cup is to Give Shape   and   That is what   The Code   Does to The
Fems   Wanting to Enlarge Her Breast Size   Ad Vitam Aeternam (Among
Other Things to Change)
Cups is a Suit in a Tarot Deck   Cups Represents The Affairs of The
Heart   or   The Fems Emotions   So   are the Breasts on a Symbolic
Level (See Dome and Doom in The Words Chapter)
Switch P for T/Fem Cross and She Gets Cut (Blood) or a Cot (Poor Bed)
Switch P for B/Boy Holding All Fem Breasts and He Gets a Cub (Too Young
for   The Code)
Switch C for M/Motherhood and She Gets a Mop
Switch C for P/Man Power and He Gets Pop or Pup That Cup
Switch P for L/Sweet Fem Love Light/Ill/Ail/Hail/Hell/Elle

The Dam Code The Damn Book

And She Gets Cul (Ass in French Cul de Sac (Dead End)
Couple is a Cover Word

Courage: Coeur/Core   Age
C/See/Young Girl   R/Her/Hair/Hear/Ear/Here/Heir/Or/Whore/Err/Are/Our/Sex   Age
Coeur is Heart in French
It is for   C/Young Girl   to Know About That   R/Heir/Or/Whore/Err/Her/Sex   at The Due Age Says   That Code   Starting Young here With   C/Young Girl
The Word Rage Ends Courage
That Courage Starts with/in/at   Her Core

Cousin: Cuss/In   C   Us   Sin   or   In
C/See/Young Girl   and Her   U/You/Ovulating   are with Sin   or   In
cuss: to use profanity   curse   swear
Add R/Her/Hair/Hear/Ear/Here/Heir/Or/Whore/Err/Are/Our/Sex and She Gets   Curse   N/In/Hen/Virgin   or   Cursing
Endless is   The Code Curses on Her

Courtesan: Court/He/Sin
A Self Explained Image here   Men in   The Code   can have Fancy   or/and   Legal Names Associated with   Cheating Easily on their Wives

Cove: C/Ov
C/See/Young Girl   is with Her Egg   She is Ovulating   She is Alone there Too in The
cove: a narrow pass between woods and hills   a cave   a cavern
Switch O/Fem Hole for A/All Men (The Pyramid Letter) and He Gets a Cave   Which is Part of the Definition of a Cove   And   A Place for The Initiates

Cover: Cove/Her   C/See/Young Girl   Ov   R/Heir/Or/Whore/Err/Her/Sex
C/See/Young Girl   Ovulates   and has   R/Sex (Under the Cover)
C/Over   After C/Young Girl has Sex   it is Over
cover: to top   to bring warmth   to place something over
To Cover as to Veil

201

cove: a narrow pass
Switch R/Heir/Or/Whore/Her/Err   T/Fem Cross   She Gets Covet (See Below)
Cover is a Cover Word Here   Ironic

Covet: C/Ov/T
C/See/Young Girl   is   Ov/Ovulating   to Transforms into   T/Fem Cross/ Great Curse
covet: to desire wrongfully
Une Couverte in French is a Blanket   It is to Cover in Present Tense in English   or a   Cover (Blanket)
Another Cover Word from The Code

Cow: C/See/Young Girl   O/Fem Hole   W/All Fems Sex Active
The Fems are Often Represented as Cows in   The Code
A Cow in Slang is a Large Fem or a Fem that is Always Lactating
Husbandry is the Term for the Men that Raise Farm Animals   It Used to Includes The Fems
In   The Code   The Fems Were/Are Identified as Many Animals
In   The Code   The Fems are Associated to Cows   also because   Cows are the Only Mammals that Have Artificially Maintained Permanent Breasts   Just As Us The Fems
The Cow is a Definite Symbol that Influences The Fems into Growing Big Breasts (Jugs) that Provides Milk to   That Boy Code   Forever
In French People Say   La Vache (The Cow) as an Exclamation for Instant Disgust or Rejection

Coward: Cow/Hard
Here is a Conceptual Opposition that   The Code   Projects on Her   To Confuse Her Mind
When the Cow (Fem) Gets Hard   That Concept Hides in a Coward Manner   And   It does Not Describe the Real Situation
So   When Cow/Girl is Hard   She is a Coward
That Code   does Not Allow The Fems to Get Powerful in Any Way

Cowboy: The Cow (Her) and the Boy
Cow   Bows   The Bows are the Girls (See Bows in The Words Chapter)
And Boobs are Close

The Dam Code The Damn Book

Cow Webs is What She Gets in   The Code
The Cowboy is Meant to Catch   The Cow (Her)   with a Lasso/
Gun   or   at The Abattoir   to Eat Her Later   as Steaks (Burned at The
Stake)   Which Most of Us Loves
In Any Way   She Gets Eaten

Cower: Cow/Her
cower: to flinch as in fear
So Much for All the Girls   Again   to Flinch in Fear is The Domain
Imposed to Her by   The Code
Collar is Close (Caller   Call   Her/R   The Collar is to Keep The Fem
Strangled in Obedience as The Feet and BB Binding   Etc)
Collar   Call/Her   Call R/Heir/Or/Whore/Err/Her/Here/Sex
C/See/Young Girl   L/Sweet Fem Love Light/Ill/Ail/Hail/Hell/Elle
R/Her/Hair/Hear/Ear/Here/Heir/Or/Whore/Err/Are/Our/Sex
He Calls on Her for Sex   She is on That Collar   Even as a Sweet
Girl   She Still has to Carry   That Code   R/Heir/Or/Whore/Err/Her/
Sex   Along   As She Will Always be Poor and Degraded   And Our
History has Done Just That
See Cowl Below

Cowl: Cowl is Made of 4 Fem Letters
cowl: a monk hood   the hood of a garment
The Fems Were Never Allowed   to be Part of Any Monkhood   So   They
Never Wore that Religious Hood (Buddhist   Christians   Hindus   Etc)
Men Always Wore Hoods   because   They were Cold at Night   or   to
Hid their Identities   or   to Practice Their Religions
The Fems   No   Not Allowed   She is a Cow with Lights (L)   N/
On   (Cow/L)   (Hindu Religions do that All The Time in Their Religious
Parades   Cows with Flowers and Lights)
For The Fem Unless She Innocently Went out   and   being Cold   She
Wore Her Own Fem Hood
Hood is Therefore a Cover Word here   being There and Not There in The
Same Time
But   No Says   The Code   This Popular/Common Word Belongs Only
to   The Secret Code

Hood Means Secrets   Or   Absences   Back to Sects and
Secrets   which   She Never has Access to   Being Not There in the First
Place (Absences in One of the Secret Meaning For Her here)

Cowslip: Cow/Slip   or   Cows/Lip
Falling/Slipping   for The Fems as Cows   to Come   The Code   Says
The Code Hides in Flowers
Cow   S/Is/His/Us/Ass/Hiss/Serpent/Penis   Lip (Lips   on   Penis)
cowslip: an English primrose   the marsh marigold
She Slips   as   She is being Named after a Flower Called   Prime
Rose   and another   Mary   that has/is   Gold   Just by being
Yellow   Not Much Gain here for Her
The Code   Will Not Allow Her to have Any Pleasure   or   Feel Good
About Herself   or   Gain Anything   Ever   in Any Circumstance   I
Looked Everywhere I could   Never Found Any

Crack: KRAK
Cannot be a Good Name for The Fems because   K/Broken Fem
Warrior   Starts and Ends   The Sound Word of Crack
C/See/Young Girl   Rack   See/Rack
In American Slang   Rack is Common Slang for Breasts   A Crack is a Fem
Vagina
Girls Always Under the Threat of a Boy Around to Play Tricks on
Her   because   He Learned it That Way
2 CC s/Young Girls/See   Implies   Again   Polygamy
To Crack a Joke   about that   is Common
Crack/Her/Jack
Cracker: KRAKR   Adding Another R to KRAK Indicates The Battle Is On
Crack   R/Heir/Or/Whore/Err/Her/Sex
To Crack is to   Break   Open   Split   Find the Hole
Nut Cracker   Safe Cracker   Cracker Jack   and More
C/Rack/Her   A Rack is The Fem Breasts in American Slang

Crap: C/See/Young Girl   Rap
K/Broken Fem Warrior   Wrap
C/See   She is Inside that Crap Wrap
rap: to strike with a light blow
C   Strikes   It is Crap Says   The Code

The Dam Code The Damn Book

crap: defecation
Nobody Especially a Fem Would Want to Look at That
crapper: toilet
Crap/Her   Grab Her
The Fems is Often Affiliated/Humiliated with Feces   for Example   Shit (She/It   She/Hit) is a Popular One

crappy: extremely bad   unpleasant

Crazy: Craze/He   C/See/Young Girl   Heir/R/Or/Whore/Her/Are/Sex   Easy
Sex with   C/See/Young Girl   is a Craze   Made Easy
craze: insanity   popular fashion   fad
That is Often How Babies are Made   She Does Not See it Coming   And Mom is Always Wrong

Cream: CRM   C/See/Young Girl   R/Heir/Or/Whore/Err/Her/Sex   M/Motherhood
Add   S/Is/His/Us/Ass/Hiss/Serpent/Penis   in Front   and it Becomes a Scream   When C/Virgin Scream   the Cream Comes
The Code Goes in Many Directions and Many Layers   Whipping the Eggs
The Language Code   is Her Destruction
Creamy: Cream/He
He Owns the Cream
Cream is a Cow (Her) Byproduct

Creator: Create   R/Heir/Or/Whore/Her/Sex
So Sorry
Take E/He Away and She Gets Crater
A Crater is a Big Hole   The Bigger the Less She Can See it

Creature: Create   Her/R/Heir/Or/Whore/Err/Are/Sex
creature: an animate being   a farm animal   a human being
In French and English
Take E/He Away and She Gets Crate/Her   it Puts Her in a Box   a Crater

Creepy: Creep/He   C/Rape/E

Lise Rochon

C/See/Young Girl is in the Front here She Starts the Action of that Word Which is Not Allowed by The Code for a Fem to be Ahead So it is Creepy C/Reap/He is Not a Possible Action from The Code Neither Can She Rape or Reap Anything from The Mascs

Cremation: Cream/He/T/Eon
Another Illusion Created by The Code Telling T/Fem Cross She will have Cream For Ever When Cremated (Dead) Cream/A/She/On

Crime: C/See/Young Girl Rhyme
A Rhyme Means there is an Affiliation
K/R/M
K/Fem Broken Warrior R/Heir/Or/Whore/Err/He/Sex M/Motherhood
She is Broken The Code has More Power Over Her So it is Sex with a Whore Then Leaving Her Alone with Motherhood Unless it is a Boy A Responsibility that will Last a Lifetime for Her
Switch i/Marriage Act for O/Fem Hole and She Gets Chrome
Cream that Chrome Make it a Crime and Hide it in a Rhyme So More Fems will Fall in That Trap

Crisis: Christ/Is Cry S/Is/His/Us/Ass/Hiss/Serpent/Penis His/Is
A Strange One
For Christ The Code was/is Certainly a Crisis To See that That Dam Code is Still Ruling Humanity
The Original Christians Had The Tongues of Fire
It was the Initiation to become a Christian in Christ Time
That is Why they were Hunted to Death
Paul Alone Killed 10 000 Christians in Horrible Torture
Then Roman Church Transformed their Secret into Rites as in R/Heir/Or/Whore/Err/Her T/Fem Cross
Baptism Are The Fems Tears of Forgiveness or that Christ Died for Our Sins Says The Commonly Used Sentence
That Communion (Come/Union) Sacrament (Sac/Remnant) is to Transform All Fems from Free Fems into T/Cursed M/Mothers
Where the Wine (See Wine) is Her Blood Loss and the Bread/Bred is Her Flesh
The Confirmation Sacrament Confirms that
She Will Bleed Before She has Sex

The Dam Code The Damn Book

When Her Con is Firm Enough
Her Blood Loss Confirms She Can have Sex Now
It Will be in Marriage (Mare/Mary   He   Egg/Age)
Which Brings Her Back to the Heirs   Horses   Whores   Or   to   Err   If
Not   She Gets to Lose Her Virginity (Verge/In/T) in Rape or Seduction
(See/Duck/Eon) Which Make Her Lose Her Soul Anyway   and
be   Repudiated According to the Rules of   The Code
Verge is Slang in French for Penis
The Code Starts The Fems Young   Men Remain in the Shade of   That
Code   While The Fems Gets Baked in that Sun/Son because it Avoids
those Shameful Pains to Fall on Him

Crook: C/See/Young Girl   R/Her/Hair/Hear/Ear/Here/Heir/Or/Whore/
Err/Are/Our/Sex   Hook
A Crook is the End Part of a Sheppard Stick   He Hooks Those Little Girls
(See Letter J/j in the Word Sheppard and His Stick J/j in The Letters
Chapter)
A Crook is a Dishonest Person
To Crook is to Bend or to Curve (See Arch in BB in The Words Chapter)
When C and R are Hooked   They Curves (See Arch in The Words Chapter)
C Rook
Rook: *slang* to overcharge   swindle or cheat
She Obviously is being Cheated in   Without Her Knowledge   and Will
Pay The Price   Accused of Cheating

Crop: C/See/Young Girl   R/Her/Hair/Hear/Ear/Here/Heir/Or/Whore/Err/
Are/Our/Sex   Hop/Up
A Crop is a Harvest
So   When The Fem has Sex as R and is Hopping   that is the Harvest
for   The Code   And She is Thinking She is Going Up
Switch O/Fem Hole for A/All Men and He Gets to Crap on it
For The Code Anything a Fem does has No Value   Or Worse

cross: to intersect   to move   to pass   a structure to execute persons
in ancient times   a signature   Jesus Cross   Christian emblem
The Knight Templars have a Red Cross Painted on their White Robe
The Rosicrucian Symbol (Sin/Bowl) is a Large Red (Blood Color) Cross on
their White Robe in Front and Back

The Sign of the Cross is a Basic Natural Pattern   We See it in Snow Flakes
The Secret Code   Presents The Cross/The Great Curse as the Plus + Sign Creating the Illusion of Gain
The Sign Plus + Gives a Positive Image (as in Adding/Gaining) of that T/Bloody Fem Cross/Great Curse   and Put Minds to Sleep About that Horrible Concept
This Mental Falsity is Now Integrated in the Cross Symbolic Meaning in Our Minds
The Sign + is an Horizontal Bar (See Bar in The Words Chapter   and   #11 in The Clock Chapter) which is Called the Minus Sign (How Convenient for The Code) and a Vertical Bar
Without its Vertical Bar (The I/Eye in the Pyramid) it is Only a Minus Sign (Mine/Us   Minimize   Us   The (MNS) Fems are Not Allowed in That Secret Pyramid Club)
For the   Plus Sign   or   Cross Sign   to be Complete it Needs Both Bars
Her Cross Manifests Her Minimization   It is One of The Code Goals   Reduce Her to Nothing   Then Cross Her
The Word Cross has been Used/Abused Extensively by The Secret Societies   The Only Resurrection for Her in   That Code   is in   X/Fallen Cross
The Word Cross has the Sound Word   Curse   in it   C R S
C/See/Young Girl   R/Heir/Or/Whore/Err/Her/Sex   S/Is/His/Us/Ass/Hiss/Serpent/Penis (All of Them   or   Plural)
O/Fem Hole   is Almost Silent   or   Omitted   Because   The Fems Cannot be there in Any Form as a Witness to Understand that Knowledge   Being   The One Being Cursed/Crossed   That is Why The Roman/Catholic Church Prohibits Fem Priests to Practice Their Rituals of Blood and Body   It is Her being Symbolized
The Cross Symbol/Letter T is the Letter Tau   It is the Last Letter of the Hebrew Alphabet   It is the T or Th
(H Being the Letter of the Secret Code   in My Book)   Tau Means that the Word of God has been Realized/Happened   Tau is Part of the Word Tarot and the Word Torah (The Old Testament)
In Ancient Hebrew the Tau Symbol is Letter X
(Letter X is the Fallen Cross in   The Code   (See Letter X in the Letters Chapter)
The Astrological Sign The Taurus   (The Cow   a Fem Symbol) Which Represents The Horn of Abundance in the Form of a Happy Cow (Always

Giving Milk   All The Way to The Milky Way) Originates from Tau   We are Told
The Cross Sign Meant Execution in Ancient Roman
In the Greek Alphabet it is the 19th Letter
(# 9 is an Entirely Fem Number)   # 19 is a Bad Number for Her   Because Next in # 20   She will be Back to   Zero   with 2 Opponents in Front of Her Instead of One
There are No Good Numbers for The Fems in   The Code
There is Nothing Positive about that Cross
Sumer Astrology Depicts   The T/Fems as a Cross on Top of a Circle (Both Fem Symbols)
The T/Fem Cross is a Pivotal Letter/Symbol in The Code
At the Top of Every Catholic Church Roof was a Cross
There is Often a Circle (Fem Symbol) a Tie Around the Center of   That Cross
There are Crosses with Flowers (Flaw/Her   S/Penis) at the 4 Ends
Draw Around All 4 Corners of the Cross its Makes a Circle   The Fem Symbol   Says   That Code

The Illiterates Put a T/Fallen Cross   Sign   The Common X/Fallen Cross   To Sign their Name on a Contract (Cunt/Rack)   That Cross (T and X) Represents Identity   And That is Since   A Long Time Ago
In The   "Holy Blood Holy Grail"   Book by Robert White P 95   He Writes "According to masonic traditions in A.D 46 Ormeus is said to have conjured on his newly "Order of Initiates" a specific identifying symbol – a red rose cross…in 1188 The Prieure de Sion l'Ordre de la Rose Croix VERITAS (Rosicrucian's)
-Holy Blood Holy Grail: P 97 The red cross was also a traditional symbol motif not only was it on the blazon of the knights Templar but also subsequently on the cross of George and as such was adapted by the Order of the Garter (British Knighthood)
-HBHP P 134: Pope John XX111 was secretly a member of the Rose-Croix. In June 1960 he issued a profoundly important apostolic Letter
The missive addressed itself specifically to the subject of the "Precious Blood of Jesus"
HBHG P 136: "Papal infallibility started in 1870"
HBHG P 158: "The Rosicrucian's were pronounced enemy of the Roman church

Sumer Astrology Depicts The Fems as a Circle with a Cross Standing on Top
The Red Cross Was the Emblem on Columbus Ships
On Every Sail was A Red Cross
The Red Cross was in Spain Too   Queen Isabella Wore a Red Cross on a Chain (?)Around Her Neck (Did She Know What She was Doing)
The Swastika Cross is a   T/Fem Cross Sign   or a   X/Fallen Cross Sign   with Added Feet and Hands   Giving it   to Whoever Saw That Velocity
So   That Cross Can Roll and Go Forward Fast   As it Starts to Roll Fast it Gives the Illusion of a Circle (Fem Symbol)
A Swastika was Sign of Luck in Ancient Times   We can See Them in India   In Old Buildings and They are Present in Their Spiritual Art
The Nazis Used it as their World Conquering Emblem
Christ Was Used as a Vehicle by   That Code   With That Cross
The T/Cross Symbol Implies   The Sacrificial Lamb   which is Her/R (See Sheppard and Sheep in The Words Chapter) in Which Jesus Represents Both   Believe it   or   Not
To Cross is Also to Go Beyond Something   See Bridges in The Holy Grail Book

Crossroad: Cross/Row/D
T/Fem Cross   as   D/Pregnant Girls   in Rows   Says   The Code
A Very Important Step in The Life of a Girl is that Crossroad   The Boy is Absent from that Situation Here   Totally   because   That Cross is Entirely Fem   Men do Not Bleed   So   It is a Fem Situation (JK Rowling Said it Right)
C   Ross (Dry Blood Color   Substance of The Alchemists)
R/Her/Hair/Hear/Ear/Here/Heir/Or/Whore/Err/Are/Our/Sex   D
At The Crossroad The Girls are in Rows   The Choice to be Made is Limited to Few Options for Her   The Bleeding Virgin   it is All About Pregnancy   D/Pregnant
Here   Are   With   Or   Without   Her   Great Hair   Hear   with Your   Ears   Bear   an Heir   Or   be a   Whore   Or   Err
A Fem Alone Erring in The Desert at Night would Not Survive by Herself Until Dawn

The Dam Code The Damn Book

Often   Outside Circumstances will Decide for Her at that Crossroad of
Her Life   as   Is She Fertile   Healthy From a Rich Family   Her Capacity
to Work   How Many Children Especially Boys Can She Bear   etc
That Has been Our History   And The World Population has been Growing
Exponentially Since   The Fem Lost Her Right To be Part of That Decision

Crossword: Cross   Word
An Innocent Puzzle   It Seems
Just Another Way   The Code   Hide its Work
The Word   Word   being Loaded with Significance with   That Code   is
Now Associated with Another Important Word in   That Code   The Word
Cross   T/Fem Cross
Which Hides here with a Game of Words   a Puzzle for The Innocent
Mind   Which Never Address   The Real Code Situation
Crossword is a Cover Word   here

Crotch: C/See/Young Girl   R/Her/Hair/Hear/Ear/Here/Heir/Or/Whore/
Err/Are/Our/Sex   Ouch
When C/Virgin Has Sex for a Heir   or   as a Whore   Ouch
crotch: slang for the genital area
Crush is the Cover Word here

Crown: Crone
Q/Her Blood Loss   R/Her/Hair/Hear/Ear/Here/Heir/Or/Whore/Err/Are/
Our/Sex   Own/N/On/Ann/Hen/In/Virgin
The Word Crown is Telling The Young Girl   That Her Blood Loss   Reigns
as Her Power
crone: a withered witch as old woman
That Shows Again that When a Fem Letter (as in C or K or Q Here) is in
Front of   R/Heir/Or/Whore/Her/Err/Sex   and Followed by Own/On   It is
a Big No from   The Code   Because it Would be a Sign of Power for Her
to Rule Sex as Her Own
So   The Code   Made it a Very Ugly Picture to Look at
That Crone is an Ugly Fem   Not an Ugly Man
Narrowing Down that Word Effect on Her Even More
To have a Word Close to The Ultimate Power as a Crown
The Code   Appointed a Double Meaning for that Word

211

In CRN/Crown   C/See/Young Girl   and   Owned by the Virgin   and   R/Her/Hair/Hear/Ear/Heir/Or/Whore/Err/Are/Here/Our/Sex   Ann/N/In/Hen/Virgin   is On Her Own and Owned in the Word Crown/Crone to Create an illusion of Power
Men Crowns Have Triangles Crosses and Dots All Around their Crowns   or   Circles with a Cross on Top (All those are Fem Symbols   or   Relates to Them)
Fem Crowns had Often Only Little Dots (Circles) on Them
Few Fem have Worn Crowns
That Fem Crown is the Crown of Thorns (The Rose an Entirely Fem Symbol   has Thorns   That is What is given to Us   The Fems with the T/Great Curse   Where its Symbols are on the Crown Itself
That is Her Crown to Wear
Although Little Modern Girls are Having Fun with Crowns and Princesses (Prince/Ass) Outfits in Early Age   It is The Code   Acting on a Subtle Level   The Code   Changes and Adapt Over Generations   Getting Deeper in Our Unconscious   from Babyhood
Some Crowns have Breasts Shapes with Fleur de Lys (See BB in The Words Chapter) on Top   and   Dots   or   the Pyramid Symbol

Crumble: C/Rumble
crumble: to break apart in small pieces
When   C/See/Young Girl   Rumbles   She Crumbles   The Code   Says
rumble: the sound of thunder   complain
No Positive Exit for Her in   That Code

Crunch: C/R/Hunch
Any Hunch about R/Her/Hair/Hear/Ear/Here/Heir/Or/Whore/Err/Are/Our/Sex   and   C/See/Young Girl   is a Big No from   The Code
So   She will be Crushed
crunch: to crush and grind noisily

Crusades: Crux/Aids
Who Helps   That Cross
crux: a vital basic decisive or pivotal point   a cross   something that torments by its puzzling nature   a perplexing difficulty
Strong Words from   The Code

The Dam Code The Damn Book

The Words   Aid/Aids   Could have been an Honorable Word   But   Then it Disappeared Under the Awful Aids Disease Name   The Code   New Subtle Definition/Conception Meaning Just As the Word Gay Used to be a Truly Happy Word Now   it Means Homosexuality

crusades: any wars carried on under papal sanction

Cry: KQC   3 Fem Letters
R/Her/Hair/Hear/Ear/Here/Heir/Or/Whore/Err/Are/Our/Sex
    I/Eye in The Pyramid/The Voice from The High/Eye/I
Crying is for the Fem Only   It is a Sign of Weakness and Vulnerability   Says   Common Knowledge
Here it Means that 3 Fems are Hit by Crying   K/Broken Fem Warrior   Q/Bleeding Fem   C/See/Young Girl

Crying: Cry   Ann/N/In/Hen/Ann/Virgin
K/Broken Fem Warrior   or   Hard C   or   Q/Bleeding Fem   Rye (R/I)   Ann/N/In/Hen/Virgin (Note here that Ing as in N Reflects the Action of it happening   Extending its Force)
When a Fem Letter is in Front of R   That is a Big No from   The Code   Especially if it is Followed by the Y/Wounded Fem   as a Consequence   She cannot Know the Unfoldment of   The Code   So
rye: a gentleman
The Masc in   The Code   is protected Against Crying here in the Word Rye

Cube: The Cube is an Important Figure in Building and Math Terms The Builders   The Masons   The Initiates   are Masters of Those
cube: raised to the third power   to cut meat to increase tenderness
Q/B
Q/Fem Blood Loss (The Great Curse)   B/Boy Holding All Fem Breasts The Fems are in Queue and Queued   To Get Pregnant with that Baby Boy   Says   The Code
Raise that to the Third Degree (a Painful Initiation) as in Cutting that Meat to Increase its Tenderness

Cuddly: Made Entirely of Fem Letters

Cod/Lay   Lay with a Fish (See Fish in The Words Chapter) How Convenient for   The Code   The Fish being a Big Important Fem Symbol in That Code
Code/Lay   The Code   Makes Sex (The Lay of   The Lady)
Cuddly   or   as an Ode to Sex   C/Ode/Lay
Could/Lay   Leaves the Door Open
C/Odd/Lay   Even The Odds Get to it (See Odds in The Words Chapter)

Cult: Q/Halt
That Interesting Concept of Stopping the Menstrual Cycle would Be Considered a Bad Cult (and be Bad for You) because She would be Out of   The Code   System to do that
cult: a particular system of religious worship
Her Loss of Blood is The Shameful Cornerstone in   That Code   She is The Sacrifice on The Altar (Halt/Her   or   Halt/R)

Culture: Cult   R/Her/Hair/Hear/Ear/Here/Heir/Or/Whore/Err/Are/Our/Sex
The Culture of having The Fems as   Mothers   or   Whores   or   To Be a Reject
La Putain in French is a Perfect Example of that Old Code Principle
Cul   T/Fem Cross   Her
Cul is Ass in French   Add T/Fem Cross and She Gets a Cult
Ass/S/Is/His/Us/Ass/Hiss/Serpent/Penis
Culture in   The Code   Means Sex in the Ass for Her
culture: a stage of civilization   that which is excellent in arts in manners etc
To me Culture Grows by Itself   It is an Integrated Human Growth Pattern   Culture is a Word for What One Knows
The Best Ones are the Ones that Take Real Good Care of Their Inhabitants   In Bhutan   They have an Index for Gross National Happiness   It is a Peaceful Country
But in Our Civilization That Dam Code Took Over so there is Only Distress for Us   All The Peace We have We had to Fight for It

Cunning: Con/In   Con/N/In/Hen/Virgin
cunning: trickery   finesse   artfulness   intrigue

Lies and Finesse are Part of the Art (See Art in The Words Chapter) in Luring that Con
To Con is to Cheat
That is What the Secret Art or Secret Societies are All About   Cheating on The Fems
To Keep The Fems Weak and Stupid to Maintain that Con/Cunt Easily Accessible
Millenaries of That and All of Us are Programmed Into it
Add Another O and She Gets a Coon
Con/Cunt/Count as in to Count Numbers (Numb/Her)   See the Numbers Chapter
coon: an undignified person
Coon Spells with All 4 Fem Letters

Cunt: C/Hunt
Hunt   that   C/See/Young Girl   to have Her Controlled
Control   Cunt/Roll
Cunt   R/Her/Hair/Hear/Ear/Here/Heir/Or/Whore/Err/Are/Our/Sex
All/L/Sweet Fem Light/Ill/Hell/Ail/Hail/Elle
Sex with All Cunts
Con and Cunt Are the Same
In French Un Con is for a Stupid Guy   and   Une Conne is a Stupid Girl
Con is Used for Anything Stupid
A Count is a Masc Title   It is All OK for Him Says   The Code   He Gets Protection
cunt: female genitalia   a contemptible person
In That Code   The Fems or Fem Parts   Are Never Represented with Strong or Good Aspects by Association   as Seen here Again

Cup: C/Hop
C/See/Young Girl   is   Up   and   Hopping
C   U/You/Ovulating   P/Man Power
Cop is Slang for Police   Implying Surveillance from Above
Cup is a Bra Size   A Bra Stimulates the Breasts
Switch P/Man Power to T/Fem Cross/Great Curse and She Gets Cut   That Cut is that Clitorectomy   or   Any Other Pain/Injury
Switch O/Fem Hole for A/All Men (In the Pyramid) and He Gets a Cape   To Hide it All Under (Hunt/Her)

The Cups is The Red Heart Suit in a Play Cards Deck
The Tarot Deck has Cups as One of its Suits
Love is the Cover Here   because   The Fems Respond to Cups as a Sign of Love   It is The Heart
Cups Hold The Wine/Blood and That Code Game Repeats itself Over Again

Cupid: QPD
Q/Her Loss of Blood   P/Man Power   ID/Unconscious Search for Pleasure   or   D/Pregnant   or the   ID   Identification Card
Stupid Cupid Can be Very Mean Too as Different New and Old Stories Tells
Cupid is Often Showed as a Blindfolded Winged Child
The Word Root of Cupid is a Cup (See Cup in The Words Chapter)
Cherub and Cupid are Related

Curator: Cure   At/Hat   R/Her/Hair/Hear/Ear/Here/Heir/Or/Whore/Err/Are/Our/Sex

curator: the guardian of a minor or an incompetent especially with regard to their property
Under the Hat of   The Code   She Gets Her Cure as an Incompetent   R   then Someone Else Owns Her Stuff
Which Is/Was Often the Case in Marriage (Dowry)
Keep that Fem Barefoot and Pregnant   While Spending Her Money   Says   The Code

Cure: K/Broken Fem Warrior   or   C/See/Young Girl   or   Q/Fem Blood Loss   Her/R/Hair/Hear/Ear/Here/Heir/Or/Whore/Err/Are/Our/Sex
The Cure for that Defeated Young Fem is to Bleed   And have   Her/R/Heir/Whore/Or/Err/Sex   Says The Code   No Honor For Her

Curious: Cure   He   Us/S/His/Is/Ass/Hiss/Serpent/Penis
The Cure for being Curious is in The Penis for Her
C/Young Girl   Your/R   He/E   Us/S/Ass/Is/His/Hiss/Serpent/Penis
Curiosity Killed The Cat is a Commonly Known Expression
The Code   Does Not Accept Curious Fems
Care   He/E   Us/S/Penis
Being Curious about the Care of that Penis

The Dam Code The Damn Book

C/See/Young Girl   Sex   He/E   Us/S/Is/His/Ass/Hiss/Serpent/Penis
The Fems Can have Sex for Pennies
In All Cases here Sex is Worth Pennies   Bringing the Concept of Prostitution All Along in the Word Curious
Whore in Plural is Whores   It is the Sound   Hearse   It Ends there for Her   She is Back to The Animals   as Usual Says   The Code   and   Curiosity Kill that Cat (See Cat   A Fem Symbol   in The Words Chapter)

Curl: Curls
Switch C for G/Penis Penetration and Get Girls
Among Surfers   The Girls are Known to be Curls in California   Girls Do Not know That
Switch C/See/Young Girl for H/Secret Code Society Letter and She Gets Hurl
hurl: to throw or fling with great vigor   a forcible violent throw
That Shows That   Girls   and   The Code   Do Not Mix
That is a Serious Beat for the Fems from   The Code
A Fling is an Affair and a Cover Word here

Curly: Curl/Girl   He
The Fem (With   or   Without Curls) is Never Left Alone in   The Code
Men Do Not Care about Their Hair With or Without Curls   They Actually Quite Often Flatten/Oil Them   or   Cut Them Short
The Girls Love Curls
Curly is a Flattering Man Name   Why   Where is Curl/She   It Does Not Exist   it is because   The Code   Uses Everything at Hand to Seduce Any Fem
This is How   The Code   Organizes Our Thought Processes (3 SSSs/ Penisses Needed Here by   The Code   in to Establish a Process in Plural   or   All of Them)

Curse: C/See/Young Girl   Hearse/Hers/Whores/Are
hearse: a vehicle that carry a coffin   a canopy over a tomb
Yes C is the Vehicle of   The Curse   and That Vehicle is
a   Hearse   or   a Coffin (C/Off/N   When C and N are Off   They are Dead   says   That Code)
The Ultimate Secret Place for   The Code   to End Her

In Any Way
The Sound Curse is the Sound of a Serpent KRSSS (Christ)
Without R it is a Cuss   Sex is on its Way   Says   The Code
Nurse   Purse   Verse   Worst
Add O/Fem Hole and She Gets Course
According to Thesaurus a curse is a ban   a bar   damning   evil   bête noire   shame and more
All of those Cause the Same Shame
She is   The Holy Grail   or   The Holy (Hole/He)   Girl
G/Penis Penetration   Her/R/Heir/Or/Whore/Err/Our/Sex   L/Sweet Fem Light
The Holy Girl Means R in Waiting
There is a Sense of a Curse in the Holy Grail Book

Cursive: Curse   Eve/Letter V/Fem Sex Active
Cursive is a Form of Handwriting   So   The Word is Engrained in Our Subconscious as Inoffensive   because
Cursive is When All the Letters in a Word are Joined Together   It is   All The Fems Holding Hands Together in Their Curse Since Eve   Wowowow to Me

Curtail: Cure   T/Fem Cross   Hell/L/Sweet Fem Light/Ail/Hail/Ill/Elle
According to   The Code   The Cure from Hell is to Minimize   The Fems into   T/Fem Cross
Cure/Tail   Tail is American Slang for Penis
Switch L for N/In/Hen/Virgin and She Gets Curtain
How Convenient for   The Code   The Virgin Cannot See that Tail   It is Behind a Curtain
C   Hurt   All/L/ /Ail/Hail/Elle
Q/Bleeding Fem   U/You/Ovulating   R   T/Fem Cross   Elle/L/Hell/Ail/Hail   or   Tail
Court the Tail   or   Court   T/Fem Cross   in   Hell/L/Sweet Fem Love Light/Ill/Hail/Ail/Heel/Elle
Only If you Make it Fast and Make it a Small Event
curtail: to cut short   to diminish
Court/Ail   Court/Hail
The Word Court brings an Impression of Surveillance and Punishment to the Word Curtail

Curve: CRV
C/See/Young Girl   R/Her/Hair/Hear/Ear/Here/Heir/Or/Whore/Err/Are/Our/
Sex   V/Fem Sex Active
When the Virgin has Sex as a R/Heir/Or/Whore/Our/Err/Sex   it Her Gives Her Curves Says   The Code

Cushion: Add   R/Her/Hair/Hear/Ear/Here/Heir/Or/Whore/Err/Are/Our/
Sex   and She Gets a Crush   He/E   On/N/Virgin
Couche   He   On
Coucher is to go to Bed in French
A Couche is Also a Diaper (Fem Products) in French

Cut: Is Made of 3 Fem Letters
C/See/Young Girl   U/You/Ovulating/Uterus   T/Fem Cross
That Cut here is   Clitorectomy
The Words Cute and Cut are   Close
She is Cute When Cut For   The Code   Not to get Caught
Switch C for B/Boy Holding All Fem Breasts and He Gets a But or Butt (Spanking)
Switch C for D/Pregnant and She Gets a Dot (The Dot is Pregnant)
Switch C for F/Fem/Fuck and She Gets Fought
Switch C for H/Secret Code Letter and He Gets a Hut (The Code Hide in Caves and Huts)
Switch C for K/Broken Fem Warrior and She Too Gets a Cut   So Does Q/Fem Blood Also by Sound Association (Here Blood Meets Blood)
Switch C for L/Sweet Fem Light/Hell/Ail/Hail/Elle and She Gets a Lot (of Cuts)
Switch C for M/Motherhood and She Gets a Mutt (Bitch Dog   and   Mute is Close) Mutt is Made of 4 Fems Letters
Switch C for N/In/Hen/Virgin and She Gets a Nut
Switch C for P/Man Power and He Gets a Pot
Switch T for L/Sweet Fem Love Light/Ill/Ail/Hail/Hell/Elle and She Gets Cul (Ass in French) Add Another T and She Gets a Cult
Switch C for R/Her/Hair/Hear/Ear/Here/Heir/Or/Whore/Err/Are/Our/Sex   and She Gets in a Rut
Switch C for She/Shh and She Gets Shot or Shut

Cutie: Cut/He
In Some Countries   He Cuts the Young Girl Clitoris to Make Sure Sex is Painful She will do it Only Under the Pressure of the Husband
C/Hot/He

Cycle: Something that Moves Around Endlessly in a Circle as Bicycle Wheels   Or   the Wheel of Time
C/See/Young Girl   Y/Wounded Fem   K/Broken Fem Warrior   All/L/Sweet Fem Love Light/Ill/Hail/Hell/Ail/Elle
2 CC s/Young Girls Sounds is a Rare Combination in   The Code   Especially this One has a Soft C and the Other has a Hard C
2 Girls Together is a Big No for   The Code   Except Here That Menstrual Cycle   Unites Them
It is OK   To Ride Together in That Wheel   But Not Talking about it   As Our History Tells
Cycle Sound Word is Psych/All
psych: to intimidate   to figure out
Psych   All/L/Sweet Fem Love Light/Ill/Ail/Hail/Hell/Elle
Bicycle is the Cover Word here

Cymbal: Sin/Bowl
A Loud Cymbal Deafens You for a Minute
Making you Forget About its Obvious Sound Meaning
Symbol is a Big Word in   The Code
Cymbal is a Cover Word

Cynicism: Sin/Is/Him   Sin/Is/In   Sin   S   N/In/Hen/Virgin   M/Motherhood   Syn/His/Him
syn: prefix meaning with
The Code   Premeditates that   Sin is with Syn   in a Context/Cover of   Cynicism
The Code   is Heartless and Cynical
Sin   Is/His   M/Motherhood
See   N   Is   M/Motherhood
ism: a distinctive doctrine theory system or practice
The Code   Doctrine here is to   Sin   That   N/Virgin   and be Cynical about it
Sin (S/Penis   In/N/Virgin) (Penis   In   Virgin)

The Dam Code The Damn Book

D d
Intro
The Letter D/Means Pregnant in   The Code   D is a Very Special Letter   because its Sound is Thee   The Sound of God   The Answer/Reflection   of God   She is D/Pregnant   Says   The Code
D/Pregnant is Especially Difficult for The Fem
D has been One of The Most Difficult   Part of this Work for Me   Because of The Abuse   I had to Witness   Writing This Book   as I Understood it
       d is b in Reverse   Dd/Pregnant   is   Bb/Boy Holding All Fems Holes and Breasts
The Word Detest is One Sad Example of The Power Given to   D/Pregnant   with Cursed   T/Fem   The Word Test in it makes it Dangerous
D   and   b   db   Joined Together make   an Illustration of 2 Full Lactating Breasts   or   a Large Fem Butt Cheeks Shape   Looking from the Backside
d b q   are   O/Fem Holes   that have Now Become Attached to a Stick of Power/Penis   The Stick is Holding   O/Fem Holes   from the Front and Back Top and Bottom in Different Concepts and Actions   As in
D   B   P   R   etc
Another Mental Picture for the Same Concept from the Secret Code is   The Breasts are the Ever Expanding Domes (Dumbs) in our Architectures   And   Big Boobs have become a Hollywood Fav   Because Men are Looking More Sexually at Those Fems in those Films
In Our Time Especially   The Fems Breasts   Are Growing Larger   Bigger   As in Expendable Cups (from Plastic Surgery   Etc)
D and T Sounds are Almost the Same   And   They are Connected on the Path of Her   Sacrifice   The/T/Fem Cross/Great Curse
In Ancient Greek D is The Pyramid Shape   Δ
In   The Code   Where there is a D   there is a T
Those 2 are Interchangeable   They Have Almost the Same Sound   D/Pregnant   Brings   T/Fem Cross   According to the Secret X Code Grid
Not Only Because Pregnancy Often in its Own   Is a Shame for Her   Especially Out of Marriage   Since Long in Our Past
But in Our Societies this Is   Where She Loses Her Power   Instead of Gaining More
It has been an Important Vital Element of Our Societies to Keep Her Powerless   Fem Voting is an Example Here   it Happened Only in the

1920 in The US After The Fems had been Trying Hard for Decades   She had to Wash Away Many Spits from Many Men to Gain that One Basic Right
Before that Time   Men Only   were Voting/Deciding on Everything/Everybody   In Their Powers   was to Keep The Fems   Powerless/Invisible   Under Control (Cunt/Roll) Says   The Code
Letters O/Fem Hole and D/Pregnant are Close in Shape
D is The Past Tense Letter in Sentences Construction in The American English Language   Add D at the End of Many Verbs and it Puts That Verb in Past Tense   As Wound and Wounded
So   it is All Hers   D is Pregnant   In The Past and Present
The Double DD Fem Sound is the Word Dead   or Deed   or   Did (Past)   Or   Dad (An Often Absent Figure in The Past)
Men Left Young Children to The Mothers
Dad is Still   A/All Men   in Between 2 DDs/Pregnants   Which Includes a Polygamy Concept Here
Often Men Kept that Lineage of having 2 Fems
Repetition of the Same Letter in   The Code   Words has Kept   Strongly Alive   That Concept
Why is there a Curse to that D Letter
Because   T/Fem Curse/Great Curse   is Coming Soon to Today   to   D/Day/Thee/The Name of God   D   is   The   or   Thou   The Dough of Our Daughters (Dowry)
D is a   Soft   Weak   Often Submitted Letter
With a Long Dead/Did/Dad/Done   Past
Being D/Pregnant Weakens a Fem and will Makes Her Often Dependent
Grade A   A/All/Men   is The Best Grade
Grade B   B/Boy Holding All Fem Breasts is Excellent
Grade C   C/See/Young Girl is Average
Grade D   D/Pregnant   is Day/Thee (God is The Cover Word)   They and   Die
Words with Double DD are   Dead   Dad   and   Did   as in Done
Letter D is a Sad/Weak Letter with its Doom Damn Dome Dumb Done etc
Grade E   He/E is Trailing and Barely Passing   But
Grade F   Failing Grade   F/Fem/Fuck   does Not Pass   F (Fail/Her   Failure)

Dad: A/All Men   are with   2 DD s/Pregnants

The Dam Code The Damn Book

In   The Code   a Double Letter in a Word Especially if   The Word is Very Short Indicates   Plural or All of Them
So   Dad here is a Polygamist Says   The Code
D/Add   D/Had   As in Add Another Fem   Pregnant
Note Had is the Past   so   it is a Repetition of the Past
The Code Hypnotize Men into Rocking and Rolling The Fems Out

Daddy: Death/He   Dot/He (See Dowry   Dot in French)
Dad is a Poor Word for a Father in   The Code   Because Children Should be a Fem Burden   Only
Dad   Dead   Death (See Death)   Debt
The Poorest is a Pig Slang for a Man   Pig/Hot   Bigot   There are Not that Many Bad Words for Men   Many More for The Fems

Daemon: Damn/Dame   On   Dame   He/On
The Whole Symbology of Evil (Eve/Ill)   and   Demon (The/Month) is an Adaptation from the Blood Loss Madness
The Fems have been Bleeding for Thousands of Years with No Real Tools to Help
Many Years Ago The Fems Were Bleeding on Home Made Rags (Isolated In a Special Hut for That Time of The Month for Her) Rags they had to Wash and Reuse
Seen on Rare Ancient Greek Tiles The Fems would Be Bleeding in Urns
The Fems are Blamed for The Great Curse   and   being Cursed for it   This is Where the Word Damn   Demon   Dame   Originates in   The Code
daemon: a demon   a subordinate deity as the genius of a place or a person attendant spirit   a god
The Dictionary Says it is a Power from Above implying that those Demons are in your Own Home   And They Are In The Fems Form
In the Far Past The Fems was Often Accused of Demonic Possession   and   Could be Burned/Stoned for that

Dairy: Dear/He   Dare/He
That Breast Milk is for Dear Boy   First
The Code   Dares (Dear/S)
Dairy Products come from the Dairy Farm   Where the Cows (Her   See Cow in The Words Chapter) Provides The Milk   Endlessly

Lise Rochon

Switch Letters Around and Get
diary: personal writings
Diary is the Cover Word here   For Her/Cow Breasts Slavery

Dais: DS
D/Pregnant   Is/S/Us/His/Ass/Hiss/Serpent/Penis
The Message is Clear   D/Pregnant   Is   Confirmed
Pregnant   with   Is/S/Plural   or   All Of Them
dais: a raised platform as in the front of a room for a
lectern   throne   seats of honor etc
The/Day/Pregnant   Is/S/His   Therefore   She will be in The Seats of
Honors for a While Under The Writings of that Church
lectern: a reading desk in a church on which the Bible rests and from
which lessons are read during the church service
Lectern (Leg/Turn)
Dais   Deesse is Goddess in French
Add E/He and He Gets a Dizzy Daisy
All is Cool in   The Code   for Her   While being Preached for being
Pregnant   The Constant Smoke Screens for Her

Daisy: Daze/He   Dizzy   D/Easy   Days/He (See Days in The Calendar
Chapter)
The Love of Flowers is Deep for The Fems   Something to Do with the
Natural Beauty and Harmony They Exudes   The Fems are Sensitive to
That
But   The Code   has Also Taken Over Our Botany Names a Long Time
Ago   The Fem is Cornered from Everywhere   All the Time in   The
Code   That Keep on Giving Her a Flawed Vision of Her Natural Could be
Reality

Dam   or/and   Damn: DMN   All Fem Sound Letters
Dam and Damn have the Same Sound   The N/Virgin Sound
being Attenuated   Because M/Motherhood is Victim of That
Code   so   is   N/Virgin
The Code Definition of The Word Dam is Important
D/Pregnant   A/All Men   M/Motherhood
That Code   Damns   All Men Having Daughters   and   Their Mothers
are Also   Damned

The Dam Code The Damn Book

That Code   Damns   Its been The Way to do that in Several Religions   being Excommunicated being One of Them
Damn   Dame   Dome   Doom   Down   Etc   Words with Mostly Fem Letters   Except When   The Code   Translates Itself   As in The Word   Damn with   A/All Men   Carrying   That Code   Message
Switch A/All Men for i/Marriage Act Union and She/He Gets a Dime   She Turns on a Dime   When   i/Marriage Act Union   Replaces A/All Men   She is Unimportant as that Coin (See Con in The Words Chapter)
The Code   Says
Madame (M/Damned   M/Dame is Mundane   Disconnected from Reality)
A Dam Keeps the Water (Fem or Emotions) on One Side Only (The Fem Side)
Dawn and Dune are Cover Words Here   For Damn
That Code   Is Mind Hypnotism

Damage: Dame/Age   Dame/Egg   Damn/Egg   Dam/Age
DMG   D/Pregnant   M/Motherhood   G/Penis Penetration
The Code   Sees   Sex   Pregnancy   Motherhood   Damaging to Her Instead of Giving Her Honor/Pride
Any Way is Used to Bring the Fem Down by   The Code
She Could Cause Damages When She Ages   A Little She Can Lift that Veil of Ignorance   Although Not a Lot   Just Enough to Get Bitter
Mary in Italian Means Bitter
Mary is the First Name Given to All Fems   When Baptized in the Roman Catholic Church   Marry/Merry/Mare/He (See Horses/Whores in The Words Chapter)
Damage as in   The/Mage   The # 1 Tarot Card in The Tarot is   The Magus   He is The Magician   He is the One in Charge of The Manipulations   He has All the Elements in Hand to Manipulate the World Desires
The Code   Uses the Word Eggs as Synonym with Age Because   She has to be of Age to Carry the Egg in Pregnancy   and When Eggs are gone   The Menopause Changes Her   All Over Again

Dame: DM   2 Fem Sound Letters
D/Pregnant   and   M/Motherhood
Damn   D/Aim   D/Âme   Deem

225

On a   Dime Damn Them Dumb Dim Doom Dame
Switch A/All Men for O/Fem Hole and She Gets a Dome (See Dome in The Words Chapter)   Add 2 OO s/Fem Holes and She Gets Doom
Switch D/Pregnant for   S/Is/His/Us/Ass/Hiss/Serpent/Penis and He Gets Same (of Course)
As The Fishes in the Ocean   The Cows   and   The Sheeps (She/P)   All Fems are Under J/Sheppard Stick   Until They are All the Same   and   as Small as an Ant (Aunt)
The Fems are Kept in Sight Under   The Code   Watchful Eyes
Dame/Hit   A Dame Cannot Hit   But Can be Hit   So   Dammit   Damn/Hit

Dance: DNC   3 Fem Sound Letters
D/N/S   D/Pregnant   N/In/Hen/Virgin S/Is/His/Us/Ass/Hiss/Serpent/Penis
There is No S/Is/His/Us/Ass/Hiss/Serpent/Penis in Dance   But   it is Implied by Sound
Then it is Dense   on Her
D/Hence   Therefore Pregnant
hence: from now

Danger: D/Pregnant   Anger
When The Fems is Pregnant and Angry   Dang/Her
Dang: euphemistic word for damn
Switch N/In/Hen/Virgin for Another G/Penis Penetration and Get Dagger

Dangerous: Danger/Us
Dang Her/R/Hair/Hear/Ear/Here/Heir/Or/Whore/Err/Are/Our/Sex   Is/S/His/Us/Ass/Hiss/Serpent/Penis

Dare: D/Are   D/Hare   D/Heir   DR
D/Pregnant   R/Her/Hair/Are/Here/Hear/Ear/Whore/Or/Err/Sex
A Hare is a Rabbit   A Sweet Symbol for Many Children
dare: to be bold
The Message here for Her is Be Bold and Dare   Have Sex and be Pregnant

Dark: The   Arc (See Arc in The Words Chapter)
D/Pregnant   R/Her/Hair/Hear/Ear/Here/Heir/Or/Whore/Err/Are/Our/Sex
Darker: D/Arc/Her

The Dam Code The Damn Book

Darling: Dare   L/Sweet Fem Love Light/Ill/Ail/Hail/Hell/Elle   In/N/Ann/Hen/Virgin
Dear   All/Ail/Elle/Hell/Ill   N
D/Pregnant   R/Her/Hair/Hear/Ear/Here/Heir/Or/Whore/Err/Are/Our/Sex   Laying/Lying
The Code   Says All Pregnant Fem are Laying/Lying   R/Heir/Or/Whores/Err
lane: a passage   track   channel or course
The Word Darling is the Passage to have that Done

Darn: That Would be Another Word for Damn
darn: to mend   to curse
Who Gets it
Dear   Ann/N/In/Hen/Virgin   She Follows The Yarn (Woman Work)   The Sheep Way (See Sheep in The Words Chapters)
The Yarn is The Cover Word Here
Switch N/Virgin for M/Motherhood and She Gets The/Arm as in Getting Harmed   D/Harm   Being D/Pregnant

Date: D/Pregnant   Hate/Ate/# 8
Day/T   The Day/D/Pregnant as T/Fem Cross
8 is the Number of Pregnancy in The Code
A Date is a Sweet Fruit   A Date is a Rendezvous   The Date of the Day   Death and Debt Follows
D/Pregnant   Hated It   But did Ate it

Daughter: Dot/Her   Dough/Her
The Dot is The Fem Dowry   The Dot is Represented by a Small Circle on Top of The Letters i and j
The Dot is Also the Period (Blood Loss) at the End of a Sentence (The Blood Loss is The Sentence)
The Door for Her is a Cross Starting with D/Pregnant
Dough   T/Fem Cross   Her/R/Hair/Hear/Ear/Here/Heir/Or/Whore/Err/Are/Our/Sex
The Dough Makes the Bread (Bred   Bed with R/Heir/Or/Whore/Err/Sex)
Dog   T/Fem Cross   Her/Whore
The Code   Animalizes The Fem Often   Here by Making Her a Bitch/Dog   Another Humiliation Cross to Bear for Her

227

Lise Rochon

Compare Daughter to Brother: Bro/Bra   T/Fem Cross   R/Her/Whore/Sex
No Coincidences in   The Code
Take R Away and She/He Gets a Bother

Daily: Day/Lay   The/Lay
D/Pregnant   and the   Lay
The Daily Lay
Nothing Wrong About that in Loving Contexts   What is Wrong Too here is   The Fem is Ignorant about That Horrible Dream Around Her
Add i/Marriage Act and She/He Gets Ideally (ideally Starts with i/Marriage Act)   Hide The/D/Pregnant   Lay
Day is Letter D/Pregnant
Days   Daze   Dizzy   Days/He   Daisies
The Fems Love Daisies
Day   They   D/Pregnant   The Fems are Part of The Anonymous/Secluded Crowd in   The Code
She is The   Sheeps   Cows   Fishes   Ants   Horses   Dog Etc
Minimize The Fems by Considering and Treating Them as All the Same
Switch D for F/Fem/Fuck and She Gets Fey   3 Fem Letters
fey: *British Dialect*   doomed   fated to die
Chiefly Scot   appearing to be under a spell
Supernatural   unreal   enchanted   interested or believe in attuned to the supernatural   clairvoyant or visionary
A Fee in French is a Sweet Fairy   There are Bad   Fees   Also in the French Language
Switch D for H/Secret Code and She/He Gets Hey/Hay   Food for the Horses/Whores
Switch D for N/In/Hen/Virgin and She Gets Nay/Neigh a No
Switch D for M/Motherhood and She Get a May (as in May I   A Permission   The Answer for   May I   Resides in the Future   Which is Not to be Attained by Her in   The Code
Switch D for P/Man Power and He Gets Pay
Switch D for Q/Bleeding Fem and She Gets a Quai (Anything Related to Water is Fem) or   K/Broken Fem Warrior
A Quai in French is a Dock
dock: lay up in a dock   a place in a courtroom where a prisoner is kept during trial   to cut short the tail of a horse   the bony part of a tail of an

animal   the part of an animal tail left after the major part of it has been cut off
Dock is Another Dirty   Code   Interpretations   The Boat (Ship   She/P/Man Power) Arrives on Shore (She/Whore) Where Animals Mutilation Happens (Clitorectomy for Her   Circumcision for Him)   and   A Dock is a Courtroom Prisoners Space   a Scary Place to Be
Dock is Made of 4 Fem Letters
Switch D for   R/Her/Hair/Hear/Ear/Here/Heir/Or/Whore/Err/Are/Our/Sex and She Gets Ray (a Man)
Switch D for S/Is/His/Us/Ass/Hiss/Serpent/Penis and He Gets a Say   S/Hey/Hay
The Penis has a Voice in That Matter   And it Comes with Food for The Horse/Whores
In The Code   One Horse Includes All Whores
Duck is The Cover Word here   Duck is Also Made of 4 Fem Letters

Dead: DD   Made of 2 Fem Sound Letters
First and Last Letter are D/Pregnant
E/He   The Man as the Individual   and   A/All Men   are in the Middle Almost Silent
D/Pregnant   Head   The/Head
The Fem is There to be Pregnant   It is in Her Head
If E and A   Are In the Middle   or   Under the Power of   D (a Fem)   That is Not Possible Says   The Code   So   It is Called Dead
Take Away E/He (The Man as in The Individual) and Get a
Dad is Close   D/Add   Adding More   D/Pregnant
2DD s/Pregnants   Surrounds   A/All Men
He could be Powerless Losing Its War (or Dead)   but No   He is Protected   He is Under The Umbrella of being a Dad
A Real Dad to a Child was a Rare True Event Especially to a Girl

Deal: D/Pregnant   D/Hill   D/Heel   D/Ill   D/Hell   D/Elle   D/Ail
D is Under The Hail   All The Time in   That Code   It is Its Horrible Deal   The Code makes the Weather (Wet/**H**er)
Dealer is More of The Same   Because   Selling D is Involved
Dealer: Deal/Her   D/Heel/Her   D/Ill/Her   D/Ill/L/Elle/Hell   etc   R/Her/Hair/Hear/Ear/Here/Heir/Or/Whore/Err/Are/Our/Sex
D/Heal/Her

To   Ill   D/Pregnant   is the Deal
Here to   Heal   is with Her   That Would be Something Positive for Her
But No   The Code   Does Not Allow that
So   Heal and Her Can Only be Together   If the   Heel (Penis/S/
Serpent)   Is Coming Along (See Ill   Devil   Eve that is Ill   etc)
D/Pregnant is Present as The Fem Representative   and She is being
Pregnant   D Starts The Word   so   It is The Most Important Piece of
The Word

Dear: D/Here   D/Hear
O Dear   O/Fem Hole   Tear
D and T are Interchangeable in   The Code   Dear and Tear are
Interchangeable for The Fem

Death: DTH   2 Fem Sound Letters and   H/Secret Code Letter
Presence to Make Sure it Happens Their Way
D/Pregnant   and   T/Fem Cross   Are in Front of   H/Secret Code
Letter   as in Ruling Over the Next Letter   That is Not Allowed by   The
Code   so   it Death
D/Pregnant   E/He   A/All Men   T/Fem Cross   H/Secret Code Letter
Society
That Death is Her Death for   The/D/Pregnant   as She Develops into   T/
Fem Cross/Great Curse   Ending with H/Secret Code Letter
These Sound Words reflects The Reality of   The
Code   Debt   Dead   Deed   Did   Dad (I wonder Why Taxes are Not
Represented here   being a Product of All this   Code   Misery)
Dad is a Poor/Neglected Word in   The Code   Comparing to All Other
Masc Terms   That is Scary for All Fems
Dead/That   The/Hat
(See Art and the Hat with R/Her/Hair/Are/Here/Hear/Ear/Whore/Or/Err/
Sex   in The Words Chapter)

Debar: The/Bar   D/Bar
D/Pregnant   and   All Other Fem Types   Are Barred from   The Code
Add Another E/He and He Gets The/Bear (If The Bear Says it   The
Bar   it is)   The Bear is an Important Figure in in Dreams and
Religious Symbology   The Bear Along with The Bull   The Eagle (US
Emblem)   and   The Human Face (a Man   of Course Says   The Code)

The Dam Code The Damn Book

Debar:

Debt: DBT   3 Fem Sounds Letters
The Debt is   The Original Sin   The Code   has Attached on All Fems (Men Also   on a Way Smaller Scale than The Fems)
Switch B/Boy Holding All Fem Breasts for P/Man Power (and Adding H/Secret Code) and He Gets Depth
The Code   is Ancient and is Everywhere
Death is Close   DTH (2 Fem Letters and T/Secret Code Letter)
DTH   is   D/Pregnant   T/Fem Curse   H/Secret Code
D being Interchangeable with T   It Creates a Cycle of Self Regenerating/Repeating its Message   Which is Death to The Fems Through   The Great Curse   from Childhood to Maturity
Switch B for L/Sweet Fem Love Light/Ill/Ail/Hail/Hell/Elle and She Gets Dealt   It has been All Dealt   in Depth   to Death

Decade: DKD   Made of 3 Fem Sounds Letters
D/Pregnant   K/Broken Fem Warrior   D/Pregnant
Here   2 DDs/Pregnants   Surrounds K/Broken Fem Warrior in   Decay/D
Decadent is Close   Decay/Dent (Another Dent to Her)
A Decade is 10 Years
DKD could have been Good to The Fems here as in Protection   But No Says   The Code
Decay   D/Pregnant   K/Broken Fem Warrior
It is Always the Same Bad in   The Code   for The Fems   Here   Pregnant and Broken   She is in Decay
Deck/He   Duck/He   Dock/He   The Code   Avoids that for the Men   No Decay Here for Him   He will Dock it

Deceit: DCT   3 Fem Sounds Letters
D/Pregnant   C/See/Young Girl   T/Fem Cross
This/Hit   She Gets a Double Hit here   On Her Way to Her Cross After being   Young and Pregnant   She is Now Being Accused of Fraud or Cheating   It Never Stops for Her in   That Code
deceit: fraud   trick   cheating

Deceive: DCV   3 Fem Sound Letters   This/Eve   T/His/Eve
D/Pregnant   C/See/Young Girl   V/Fem Sex Active/Eve

The Concept of D/Pregnant and C/See/Young Girl to Become V/Fem Sex
Active Deceives Her
The Code   Does Not Allow Her to See Her Cursed Situation
deceive: to make believe of something that is not true
Dis/Eve is Mind Bugging
dis: a goddess   a lady   a woman   a prefix meaning
apart   reversal   negation   removal   intensive force
All those Words Together in an Assemblage of Different
Concepts   Making it Impossible to Read it Emotionally for Her
Talking about   This   Eve/V/Fem Sex Active   as a Deceiver   D/See/V/
Her   D Sees Herself as a Sex Deceiver

Decision: D/C/On   D/See/On   This/Is/On   Dis/He/On
D/Pregnant   C/See/Young Girl   Eon
So According to The Code it is Her Decision (This/is/On) to be Pregnant
When Ovulating (D/C/On) as The Code Sees It and Hit on Her for an Eon
dis: a woman deity promoting fertility   an insult

Decide: D/Pregnant   See/C/See/Young Girl   Hide
The/D   Side
2 DDs/Pregnants are being Sided by being Hidden/Not There When Time
to Make a Decision (See Veil in The Words Chapter)

Declaration: Dick/Lay/Ration   The Dick (a Penis   a Man Name)   Rules
in   The Code

Decrepit: D/Pregnant   Creep   Hit/It
The Code Says   D/Pregnant   is a Creep in Decrepit   and   is being Hit
decrepit: weakened by old age   feeble   infirm   worn
out   dilapidated

Deed: 2 Fem Sound Letters   DD   as in Dead   Did
Double D/Pregnancies   Here is Concept of Polygamy
deed: something that is done   accomplished
Death (DT) is that Also (D and T being Interchangeable in   The Code)
Did/He/D   D is Pregnant in Plural   He/E   Did His Deed

The Dam Code The Damn Book

2 DDs/Pregnants (as in Plural or All of Them) Surrounding 2 EEs/He (as in Plural or All of Them) D/Pregnant with E/He in the Middle could have been an Interesting Loving Concept in A Code Free World But No Says The Code 2 Men or All Men Cannot be Surrounded by Pregnant Fems so It is a Dead Deed In/Deed/ Naturally Dad Did Hit/It
Dad and Did are The Cover Words here

Default: DFLT   4 Fem Sound Letters
D/Fault
default: failing   inaction or neglect
It is D/Pregnant Fault Says   The Code   When According to   That Same Code   She has No Power of Action

Defeat: DFT   Made of 3 Fem Sounds Letters
Deaf/Heat   The/Feet
The/Feet   Under the Feet is   The Sole/Soul (Remember   The Code   Calls it That Way)
D/Few/Hit   D/Fit
D/Pregnant Gets a Few Hits   It Fits (F/Hits)   She is Defeated

Defecate: DFCKT   is Made of 5 Fem Sounds Letters
A Rare Code Word that Way
What to Expect from   The Code   When it Comes to Feces   The Fems is Always and the Only One Associated with Stools (Hiss/S/Is/His/Us/ Ass/Serpent/Penis   Tools) Another Tool for The Male to Aggress the Fems   Says   The Code   Call Her   Shit   She/It)
Kate as Fem Name is There   because   She is Dangerous that One   She is   K/The Fem Warrior   Wounded and Under   But   She is Still Alive   Which is a Big No from   The Code   so
To See   Deaf   and   Cake   Together in the Same Word is Obviously Disrupting Enough   but Associating it to a Word Called Defecate is an Insult to Our Intelligence   so   The Code   Wins by Keeping The Masses Away
This Word is an Assassination of Character to Her 5 Aspects (The Fives Sounds Letters of The Fems in that One Word (Defecate)   A Huge Negative Impact on Her

233

Defect: DFCT   Made of 4 Fem Sound Letters
4 Fems are Together   It is Defective Says   The Code
Defect/Eve   No Surprise Here
defect: fault   imperfection
Make Her Imperfect
Letter D being Especially a Difficult Letter to Approach/
Comprehend   being Hard on Her
Defector: Defect   Her/R/Hair/Hear/Ear/Here/Heir/Or/Whore/Err/Are/
Our/Sex
She Carries   Heir/Or/Whore (Most Important here is The Precious Metal
Gold   Or   in French and in Many Other Languages   Oro   Whore/O/
Heir)   In   The Code   Still She is Defected

Defend: DFND   Made of 4 Fem Sounds Letters
Defend Starts and Ends with a Double   2 DDs/Pregnants   so   it arrives
on a   Deaf/End
There is No Such Thing as a Defense for The Fems in   The
Code   So   No One Hear Her (a Deaf Ear) there
Switch F/Fem/Fuck for D/Pregnant and She Gets a Dead (Double D/
Pregnants) End (More Difficult to Defend for Her)

Defense: DFNC   Made of 4 Fem Sounds Letters
D/Fence
Here is a Rare Code Event   2 Sound Letter Words in the Same Word
Meaning the Same   Fence   and   Defense The Code   Pointing its
Offense   The/Fence (See Bar in The Words Chapter)   Against   D/
Pregnant
fence: barrier
Bury/Her   Bar/Her
Offense   O/Fence   Of/Fence   Off/Hence
In Defense   or   Offense   She is Off the Fence   being D/
Pregnant   Also

Defile: DFL   Made of 3 Fem Letters
D/Pregnant   F/Fem/Fuck   L/Sweet Fem Light
The Fem Can Only Go Down in The Code   so   The Code   Says   The/
File   is   D/File   D/Fail   Deaf/All

defile: to make foul dirty unclean pollute taint debase   to violate the chastity of   to make impure for ceremonial use   desecrate   to sully as a person reputation
Fille is Girl in French   Fil is Thread   Le Fil du Temps (Thread of Time Is   The Code   Grape Vine/Wine/Vino/Fem Blood)
Fill Her Up   With What
The File is Long   Heavy and Deep   on The Fems Being Defiled

Define: DFN   Made of 3 Fem Sound Letters
D/Fine
D is Pregnant   She is Fine as Defined by   The Code
define: to identify the nature or essential qualities
Deaf   Ann/N/In/Hen/On/Virgin
Deaf/Ann   to that Definition   So   She Cannot Hear That   So   She is Fine

Deft: DFT   3 Fem Sound Letters
Deaf   T/Fem Cross/Great Curse
deft: dexterous   nimble   skillful   clever
T/Bloody Cross   is Deaf
She is Deft   at Being that Cross   Which is Another Brain Wash from   The Code
DFT is   F/Fem/Fuck   D/Pregnant   T/Fem Cross

Delay: D/Lay
D is Pregnant   The Lay is Still There says   The Code

Delicate: D/Pregnant   Lay   Cut/Cat   D/Ill/Cut   Daily/Cut   The/Lid/Cat
D/Pregnant   is Ill from the Cut   Defloration/Clitorectomy
D/Pregnant   L/Sweet Fem Love Light/Ill/Ail/Hail/Hell/Elle He   Cat
The Fems is Often Compared to the Independent Cat
This One Needs to be Cut too

Delivery: D/Ill/Very
D/Pregnant   is Ill   When She   Delivers
D/Hell/Eve/R/He   or   Plainly Said   Hell is with Her/R   Since Eve

It is All About R/Her/Hair/Hear/Ear/Here/Heir/Or/Whore/Err/Are/Our/Sex
As Usual in   The Code
The/Ill/River (Reef/Her)   D/Hell/Every   D/Pregnants are in Hell for
Ever   Clearly Says   The Code

Delving: DLFVN   Made of 5 Fem Sound Letters
D/Hell/F/In
D/Pregnant   is in   L/Hell   with   F/Fem/Fuck   as   V/Fem Sex Active
delving: intense research
The Fem in All Her Aspects is Always Under Scrutiny   So   The
Code   Keeps All its Hypnotic Tricks to Hide itself from Her and has Kept
Her That Way in Their Slavery
A Soft Word   The Elf is In
Dolphin is The Cover Word here
D/Thee is The Answer/Reflection of God   Because   She is
Pregnant   Says   The Code

Demand: DMND   Made of 4 Fem Sounds Letters
D/Man/D   The/Man/The   Thee/Man/Thee   Thee/Man/D
The Code   Demands that   The Man is the Center of Attention   The
Fems Serve All Men (As Gods   Thee) with Pregnancy   First
In Demand The Masc Letters   E/He   and   A/All Men   are Surrounded
by   2 DDs/Pregnants   That Would be a Big No from   The Code   But
here An   Exception   M/Motherhood   and   N/Virgin/Future Mom   are
Inside Responding to The Demand   of   The Code   Which is to Be
Pregnant   or   to Bring Pregnancy
It is   The/Mound   of the Young   D/Pregnant
Month (Mount   See Mount in The Words Chapter) is Close   M/Hunt
(Blood Loss)   A Hunted House   Scary
The Month   or   The Mount is What   The Code   Calls   Her Monthly
Period (The Period   Comes After   The Sentence)   it is   T/Fem Cross/
The Great Curse   of Humanity
Switch A/All Men for O/Fem Hole and She Gets a Demon   (That Would/
Could Not have been   Her   Wish/Demand   But it is   DMN   3 Fem
Sound Letters   Says   The Code)
The Fems in   That Code   are Always   Surrounded   with Its Scary
Energy

The Dam Code The Damn Book

Demeanor: Demon/R   D/Mean/Her
D/Pregnant   Mean   Her/R/Hair/Hear/Ear/Here/Heir/Or/Whore/Err/Are/Our/Sex
The   Heir/Or/Whore/Or/Err   Here is Her Fem Demeanor   Demanded By   The Code
Damn   He   Her/R/Hair/Hear/Ear/Here/Heir/Or/Whore/Err/Are/Our/Sex
Dame/He/Whore   is Included here   At All Times in Her Life
D/The   Minor (Mine/Her)   Starts Early in Life for Her/R   The Code   Orders
D/Mine/Her
demeanor: conduct   behavior   facial appearance
The Thing about   R/Her   is   Heir   Whore   Or   Err
She will End Up having Sex   or   Die   Anyway
The Signification of That is in   T/Fem Cross   and   X/Fallen Cross   It is   The Progression   Anticipated by   The Code   Since The Beginning   of Its Time

Demure: DMR   3 Fem Letters
D/Pregnant   M/Motherhood   Together with   R/Her/Hair/Hear/Ear/Here/Heir/Or/Whore/Err/Are/Our/Sex
demure: reserved
That Would be a Reserved Situation for the Husband
D/Pregnant   Mur (A Wall in French)
D/The   M/Motherhood   Your/R/Her   Her as The Whore is Always there

Demolition: Dame/O/Lay/She/On   Damn/O/Lay/She/On   D/M/Lay/She/On
Because there is Not a Masc Sound here   Therefore Demolition is an Entirely Fem Word
If a Dame is Laying Her   O/Fem Hole   by Herself in the Future   She is Demolished Says   The Code

Demon: DMN   Made of 3 Fem Sounds Letters Damn/Dame   On   D/Pregnant   M/Motherhood   On
As in the Word Devil (See Devil in The Words Chapter) Demon Fits All Together in   The Fem Hell Code
Switch N/In/Hen/Virgin for M/Motherhood and She Gets Mom (Mum   Mam   Mame   Mine)

237

Switch O/Fem Hole for A/All Men and He Gets The/Man
Reverse the Syllables of Demon and Get Mon/D as in An Independent Pregnancy   It is Also Monday the Day of the Moon   Having Her Moon is Her Bleeding Time
Mon Means Mine in French   Mon as in Mine Making the Concept Stronger by Adding Another Unconscious Lien
It Does Not Exist in   The Code   Because   It Would Imply that 3 Fem Letters   Could have Something as Theirs

Denied: DND   Made of 3 Fem Sound Letters
D/Pregnant   Nigh   D/Pregnant
D   N/In/Hen/Virgin   ID
It is Some Kind of a Negation of Something Directed   to Her
The Word   Denied   Starts and Ends with   D/Pregnant   with 2 EEs/He in the Middle   with a   N/In/Hen/Virgin
E/He   Would Be Under the Power of a Fem   When Dealing with a N/Virgin   That is a Big No from   The Code   So   it is Denied
DND   becomes TNT (D and T are Reversible in   That Code
It is a Strong Way to Say No from   That Code

Dense: D/Pregnant   Hence
Hence She is Pregnant as a Result of the Density of The Code
Dense: stupid   dull   intense   extreme   compacted
Dance is the Cover Word Here

Deny: D/N/I   The/Nigh
nigh: near in space   nearly   almost
NI is the N/In/Hen/Virgin in Front of the I/Stick   or   Holding Her Own Stick (See il in the Letters Chapter)
Denied   Adding Another D/Pregnant   to That Word Starting with D   Its Adds Force to the Concept Therefore   That is a Big No From   The Code
No Words of Power for Her are Allowed Around Her
Add E/He and He Gets a Neigh
neigh: the cry of a horse
The Cry of a Horse/Whores is a Whine (Win/He)
whine: a feeble complaint
Everything Around The Fems in   That Code is Weak
Denote: DNOT   Made of All 4 Fem Sounds Letters

The Dam Code The Damn Book

So Again here the Energy is Heavy for The Fems
D/Not (4 Fem Letters)   D/Naught
Naught: obsolete   failure   zero   ruin
If D is Not Pregnant She is a Naught
Denote: the mark   the sign   the symbol of it
D/Note
Look at D/Pregnant Gloom   She is The Sign of Failure Denotes The Code

Deny: DNY   Made of 3 Fem Sounds Letters
D/Nigh   D/Pregnant   is Denied from Close by   The Code   too
nigh: near in space   nearly   almost
Ding Her (Ding/I   Ring) is Another Way to Force Her to Deny Herself and Her Beliefs (See R In The Letters Chapter)
(About Ding   See Bell/Belle in The Words Chapter)
Dean/High   The Code   Often Uses Innuendos   As High Position/Power Words to Enhance Her Fears About Her Safety Without Her Knowing Consciously

Derelict: The Relic   D/Relic   Dear/He/Lick   There/He/Lick
Derelict is a Shivering Word and a Cover Word Here
derelict: vagrant   bum   a vessel abandoned at sea   falling into ruins   guilty of neglect of duty
Again here   The Code   Reflects Several Bad Aspects on Her
Vessel   is   V/Fem Sex Active   Ass/S/Has/Is/His/Serpent/Penis All/L/Hell/Elle/Ail/Ill/Hail/Elle
D/Pregnant   Are/U/Lick   R/He/Lick   R/Her/Hair/Hear/Ear/Here/Heir/Or/Whore/Err/Are/Our/Sex   Lick
R/Her/Hair/Are/Here/Hear/Ear/Whore/Or/Err/Sex   E/He   Lay   IC
IC Means Integrated Circuit
relic: remains of a martyr   a surviving memorial of something past
A Relic is a Powerful Spiritual Word   And a Powerful Cover Word for The Secret Societies
Pious Men Avoided Those Code Concepts   Because of Great Fear of Insulting   Their God or Their Church
To be a Derelict is What She Gets as   D/Pregnant in Front of a Relic   Derelict is Ruin or/and Abandonment for Her
And   The Code   Goes Along and Gets Away with That Symbology in Front of Her Eyes

Derriere: D/Pregnant with 3 RRRs/Her/Hair/Hear/Ear/Here/Heir/Or/Whore/Err/Are/Our/Sex
There   He   Err   Dear   He   Heir
Sex in the Butt cannot Make a Fem Pregnant   No   but it is an Old Contraception Method
Or it could Exhibit a Rape by 3 or More Men
And Hide it in the Back
DRRR Could have been a Position of Power for Her
That would be a Big No from   The Code   So   Derriere Is The Ass   or   The Donkey   or   The Donkey Ass   Back to the Butt or/and Feces for Her   Again
Derriere is Backside or Butt in English

Deserve: Dis/Serve   D/Serve   D/Pregnant   Serves   This/Serve   Disserve   D/Sire/Eve
dis: a woman   a Female deity especially for fertility related to Di or Diana
Here the Goddess Serves   She Deserves it   Says   The Code
Dis Has a Hard Meaning too
dis: to show disrespect   affront   insult   criticism
Somewhat that Bad Name Goes to   The Goddess   of Agriculture and Fertility
The Code   Disqualify The Beauty of the Word
The Word Heroine Also   Has been Traded Down for a Deadly Drug Name
Dis is also This (A Cover Word)   It is in the Now
this: a pronoun used to indicate to point
This is Another In Between Small Words that Accentuates   The Belief/Concept That is Pointed at
D/Pregnant   is Serving Here as Being of Service   But She Does Not Deserve It   Says   The Code
The Merit that She Deserves   It is To be Disserved
Deserve   DSRV   is to Merit
Disserve   DSRV   is to Serve Harmfully
Those DSRV Words are Cover Words in   The Code
D/Pregnant   Serves   D/Pregnant
When D Serves D   She Deserve to Be Disserved
Mind Bugling That Ugly Code

The Dam Code The Damn Book

Design: The Sign   D/Sign
design: to plan skillfully or artistically   to form   conceive
For The Fems that Sign or Design is to be   D/Pregnant   It is by Design
Says   The Code   So   True in Nature Too   They Say
Having Babies is a Natural Thing to do for Most of Us
The Problem Here is that the Word Design in   The Code   is   D/
The/Sign   that Count   When She Receives the Sign   It is Time to
Conceive   or Plan on it
The Code   has been Succeeding   so Much that We have
had Child Poverty for a Long Time and are Suffering from
Overpopulation   Because   The Fems Had had Little Power to Decide
about Her Natural Fertility Rights

Desire: D/Pregnant   Sire (S/Is/His/Us/Ass/Hiss/Serpent/Penis   R/Her/
Hair/Are/Here/Hear/Ear/Whore/Or/Err/Sex)
Her Desire According to   The Code   is to be   D/Pregnant   by a Man of
Value
Dis/Goddess   or   Affront/Insult   and   R/Her/Hair/Hear/Ear/Here/Heir/
Or/Whore/Err/Are/Our/Sex   The Code   Uses Bates As Syrup (Sire/Up) To
Achieve its Goal

Despot: D/Pregnant   Spot
The Fems Inherits All the Bad   or   Weak Concepts   from   The Code
D/Pregnant   is in that Spot   She is a Despot
With No Reason   It is Just The Way   That Code   Says
D/His/Pot   That is His Pot to Cook In
D   S   P/Man Power   Hot
Hot   D   and   Hot Man Penis   Makes Her a   Despot   The Spot

Dessert: DSRT
D/Pregnant Ass/S/Is/Us/His/Hiss/Serpent/Penis
R/Her/Hair/Hear/Ear/Here/Heir/Or/Whore/Err/Are/Our/Sex   T/Fem Cross
D is Hurt   This/Hurts   Dis/Hurt   That is Called a Dessert in   The
Code   For Her
Take One S/Ass/Is/Us/His/Hiss/Serpent/Penis
Away and Get Desert
Not Much Grows in the Deserts of the East   They would Throw a Fem in
the Desert with a Loaf of Bread Because She is Barren

Add Another R/Heir/Or/Whore and She Gets a Deserter   Desert/Her
desert: to quit one post or duty

Destiny: Dis   T/Fem Cross   Neigh
D/Is/T/Nay
In   That Code   Cross The Goddess Dis Dies   Whining   Says   The Code
nay: denial
neigh: the cry of a horse   whinny
Where there is a Horse there is a Whore (S)
There is a Real Neigh   But it is Denied in the Word Nay
D/Pregnant   Is/S/His/Penis   T/Fem Cross   Nay
From Pregnant to Fem Cross it is   The Law   of   The Code   for Her   It is Her Destiny   She does Not Know

Destruction: D/Pregnant   Is   Struck   On
So Obvious and So Hidden are the Horrors of   The Secret Code
Destruction Here Mean   a D/Pregnant Fem Struck On and On
(Eon   He/On)

Detail: The Tail   The Tale   The Tell
Tail is Slang for Penis
Tale   T/Fem Cross   All/Elle/Hell/Ail/L/Sweet Fem Light
The/Tale/Tell is that The Fem Cross is for All Fems
Tell All   T/Fem Cross   for All/L/Sweet Fem Love Light/Ill/Ail/Hail/Hell/Elle
More of the Same from   The Code
Tell the Details About So   The Code   Can Follow and Adapt
The Devil (The   Eve that is   Ill) is in the Details
The Fem Usually Takes Care of Details

Detective: Detect/Eve   Detect   He   V/Fem Sex Active
Detect which One is into Sex   A Joke here   The Code   Uses them

Detention: D/Tent/Eon   The/Tent/He/On   The/Tent/He/Own   D/Tent/Eon
Tent is T/In/T or TNT
T/Fem Cross   Surrounds   N/In/Hen/Virgin
She is Under a Tent   Which is Symbolically the Extension of The Veil

Detention Here is for The Fems Only
D/Pregnant   has been Under that Tent (The Veil Also) Since an Eon
For an Explosive Concept   He Owns the Tent   It is Not Hers   Detention is the Term Here
Here TNT as the Explosive Device is the Cover Word

Devastation: D/Vase/T/He/On
The Vase/Chalice is   T/Fem Cross   for an Eon

Devastated: D/Vase/T/T/D
The Vase as Her Uterus   (See Vase or Chalice in The Words Chapter) With 2 TTs/Fem Crosses   and   D/Pregnant   It is Stated Devastated   The/Vase/Stated   is Her Condition in   The Code

Develop: D/Veil/Hop   The/Veil/Up
D/Pregnant   Would Develop if She Hop Under that Veil Says   The Code
D/Veil/Hope   There is Hope Under that Veil
D/V/Lop
When D/Pregnant   and   V/Fem Sex Active   Get Cut Off   She Develops
lop: to cut off

Developer: The/Veil/Up/Her
When The Fem Gets   That Veil   She Goes Up with Hope   and   She will Hop More Says   The Code
Develop   R/Are/Her/Heir/Or/Whore/Sex
The/D   Veil   Up/Hop/Hope   R/Her/Are/Heir/Or/Whore/Sex
The Veil is Vile to Her   It Still Tells Her   That She is a Developer That Way

Device: The   Vice   D/Pregnant   Vice
D and V/Fem Sex Active are Both Fem Letters
device: a thing made for a particular purpose   a crafty scheme   trick
The Code   Plan here Is to   Own (By Trickery)   Craft   and   Keep   D/Pregnant   as a Source of Vice   Which is   The Code   General Rule with Her Identified as   Letter R/Her/Hair/Hear/Ear//Heir/Or/Whore/Err/Are/Our/Here Sex
She is Going Down in Any Way Possible   Says   That Code

243

D/V/Ice would Imply Frigidity   Another Reason to make Her Vicious   Says   The Code
Frigidity Often is Generated from Abuse in Our Modern Knowledge/Understanding
Common Known Terms Such as a   Vice President   Is a Term That Will Deter The Curiosity of The Common Man Towards   The Code   For a More Contemplative/Real Form of Understanding from   That Code   Universe (Uni/Verse That One Verse   At The Beginning was The Word   Etc   It is The Purpose of My/This Present Book)

Devil: The/D/Thee/Pregnant   Veil   D/Vile
According to   The Code   D/Pregnant is So Vile Under That Veil that She is The Devil
Devilish: Devil   Is   She/Shh
Another   Code   Association to give The Fems a Terrible Identity and be Silent   She/Shh   about it

Devise: The/Vice   D/V/Ice
D/Pregnant   or   V/Fem Sex Active   To Put Sex on Ice   That would be a Vice   Says   The Code   To Her
devise: to plan carefully
The/Vise
vise: to hold   to press   squeeze with a vise
Vise has the Same Sound as Vice
The/Wise (V/Fem Sex Active   and W/All Fems Sex Active are Interchangeable in   The Code   As M/Motherhood and N/In/Hen/Virgin) Switch i/Marriage Act for A/All Men and He Gets   The/Vase (Her Uterus   The Chalice)
Wise is WZ   A Sleepy Word for All Fems Sex Active   She is Asleep   When it is Time to Think   or   Being Wise
Comparing with Device   The Code
Devise is a Vise For The Fems

Devotion:
D/V/O/She/On
D/Pregnant   V/Eve/Ovo/Egg   O/Fem Hole   On for an Eon
Eve Hole Keeps on Staying Open for an Eon   That is Her/R/Are/Heir/Or/Whore/Err/Sex

Devotion   The/Eve/She/On
The Code   Repeats Itself in Owning The Fem Sexuality   in Minute Details   Using Religious Terms   Shamelessly   The/Vow/She/On   Imposing to Her a Vow   That She Pledge Without Knowing about it   before Birth
Deva is a Cover Word here   D

Dial: Die/All   D/Pregnant   I/Marriage Act   All/Hell/Ill/Letter i/Sweet Fem Light
(See Dead)
dial: a rotatable plate
If it Turns (See Urn) and Spins   it is Fem
The Code   has to Keep Her Dizzy   It Weakens Her
A Dial is Also an Instrument Use to Read the Time of the Day   (See The Clock Chapter for More Info about   That Code   Time Influence on The Fem)
diameter: a straight line passing through the center of a circle
Diameter: Die/A/Mother   Die/A/Mater
Anything Round is Fem   and   Is Meant to Die   One Way or Another   Says   The Code   As Long As   it is Still an Available Vagina to be a   Silent   Sex Giver   a Pregnant Donor   of Heirs   a   Whore on Call for Free   for Eons

Diabolical: Die   A/All Men   Ball   O/Fem Hole   He   Call
Die   A   Bowl (B/Hole) He   Call
The Bowl   Or   the Ball Game is the Receptacle   Her Uterus   and   it is On Call to be   Diabolical
diabolical: pertaining to or actuated by the devil
Here Again   The Code   Associates Her with Demons (D/Mon   Mon is Mine in French (Mine   D/Pregnant) Weakening Her at Every Turn
Diablo   Die   A   Blow (D/Pregnant   A/All Men   A   Blow)

Diamond: Die/Mound   Damn/On   Dame/On   D/Mound   Thy/Mound   Damned/On
A Mound is a Small Mount (See Month in The Calendar Chapter)
A Diamond on a Ring is Given in Marriage (Mary/Merry   Age/Egg) to a Fem as Wife to Be   it is   The Prize to Pay for the Man/Husband (Us/S/

Penis   Band)   so   He Can Mount Her Freely   As in Unlimited Sex in Marriage
Pussy Galore is in the Same Vein/Vain Says   The Code
She Dies on that Mound   So   Mary Go Round (Pregnant)
Since Ever (Adam   A/Damn   and   Eve/Ovo/Egg   He/V)

Diary: Die/Whore/He   D/Here/He   D/Hear/He   Dear/A/He
Many Fems Started Writing Diaries From Lack/Need of True Communication with Others/Husbands   or   Wanting to Leave a Fragment of Their Lives to Posterity Men   Not So Much
Add Another A/All Men and He Gets Diarrhea   Funny
Diaries are Often a Laughing Matter in   The Code   Being Generally Written/Created by a Fem   Another Example A Fruit Cake   A Old Nutritious Delicious Dessert is Ridiculed by   That Stupid Code   Again

Dick: DK   A Penis Letter is Absent
Instead Dick is Made of 2 Fem Sound Letters
D/Pregnant   K/Broken Fem Warrior
K will Become R/Her/Hair/Hear/Ear/Here/Heir/Or/Whore/Err/Are/Our/Sex   After being Defeated   (See K in The Letter Chapter)
D/IC
D/Pregnant   IC
IC: integrated circuit
Fem Pregnancy as an Integrated Circuit
That would be Questionable in Our Modern Civilization As We Know Now   Many Fem do Not Feel/Have that Call
Switch i/Marriage Act for U/You/Ovulating and She Gets a
Duke   An Honorary Title for a Man   The Code Honors Men in Many Different Ways   The Fem has None

Dictate: Dick   T/Fem Cross   Ate
Dick   T/Fem Cross   Hate
dictate: an authoritative order or command
Hate it or Not She will Eat it Anyway   It is Dictated   She Will be Crossed with the Great Curse   Says The Dick

Did: D/Pregnant   i/Marriage Act   D/Pregnant

The Dam Code The Damn Book

When 2 DDs/Pregnants Surround i/Marriage Act the Message is Clear   Where there is a Sex Union there are Pregnancies   In The Past   In The Future
2 DDs Means Plural or All of Them
Did is in the Past   It is Bound to Repeat Itself in The Future   Did as in Dead   The 2 DDs here Shows The Fem Her Place in   The Code
Double DDs is Also a Very Large Bra Size   One of the Goals of   The Code   To Expand Her Breasts Endlessly as in Endless Motherhood (See Domes and Doom in The Words Chapter)   Dad Said it

Die: D/i   D/Pregnant   i/Marriage Act   D/High   When Pregnant   She is High and Dead

Died: The Hide   The/High/D
i/Marriage Act   and   E/He   are Stuck Between   2 DDs/Pregnants
i/Marriage Act Union   is Happening here in the Word Died With   D/Pregnant   at Both Ends
The Word Died Starts and Ends with D/Pregnant
In   The Code   The First Letter Starts The Direction/Meaning of That Word   The Last Letter is The Pointer Towards Its Realization
The   Code   Says Here   D/Pregnancy   Means Death/Dead/Dad   or   has Died in the Past from it   but   She is High from it (A Lie)
Dyed is the Cover Word here

Diet: D/Pregnant   Hit
A Good Diet is Good for Your Health
The Code   Says No to that   so   D Gets Hit for That Too
The Word Diet Starts with D/Pregnant and Ends with her on The T/Fem Cross   That is Her Diet Says   The Code

Different: The/D/Pregnant   F/Fem/Fuck   Rant   D/If/Rant
D/Pregnant   and/or   Any Fem   Rants
That Would be a Different Situation According to the Normal Image Manifested for The Fems in   The Code
    so   it is Considered a Rare Situation   Not to Happen too Often
rant: to speak or declaim extravagantly or violently

Difficult: Deaf/Cult   D/Pregnant   F/Fem/Fuck   Cult

247

D/Pregnant   F/Fem/Fuck   In a Cult (Occult)   or   Separated in a Different Faith by   The Code
Any Way   The Code   makes it Difficult for Her
It would be Deafening   That would be Difficult as in Excommunication   or   Meet a Deaf Ear   and be   Locked Up in a Dungeon
The Code   Has Already Its Beliefs in Religions for Millenaries
Cults and Witches were Exterminated Fast Back Then
Difficulty: Deaf/He/Cult/He   D/F/Cult/E/He
Adding E/He Sound   Adds More Weight to Her Difficulty

Dig: D/Pregnant   i/Marriage Act   G/Penis Penetration
Dig and Dick (Masc Slang for Richard   (Rich/Hard))
Men Love to Dig Holes   Always Did   Anywhere   Anytime
I will Be at the Bar Darling

Dignity: Ding   He/E   T/Fem Cross
There is No Dignity Allowed for The Fems in   The Code
She Will be Dinged Until She is on That Cross

Dime: D/Pregnant   i/Marriage Act   M/Motherhood
A Dime is a Very Small Amount of Money
No or Little Value Follows The Fems Here in   The Code   as Usual
This Time it is   i/Marriage Act   D/Pregnancy   M/Motherhood The Fem is Valued   So Little   They have No Importance
The Fems Cannot Get Anywhere in Life   No Matter What She Does   That Glass Ceiling does Not Permit It
Switch i/Marriage Act for A/All Men and He Gets a Dame/Damn   At the Minute a Man would Part of a Dime   He is Gone and She is Left Behind with The Damn/Dame/Dime

Dimension: The/Menses/On
D/Pregnant   Men   See   On
Men See Bleeding and Pregnant as the Only Dimensions for All The Fems
Note Menses Can Only be in Plural
The Code   has it All Covered

Ding Dong: DNDON is Made Entirely of 5 Fem Sounds Letters

The Dam Code The Damn Book

Ding Dong is the Sound of a Bell Ringing
D/Pregnant   N/In/Hen/Virgin   D/Pregnant   On
Ring (Mary) that Bell (Belle is a Beautiful Fem in French)
dung: excrements   manure
From being Dinged   She is Now a piece of Dung
The Code Keeps Her Close to Any Kind of Excrements (X/Fallen Fem
Cross   Crime   Meant)
Some Words are Repulsive to Her Unconsciously Also
Down (D/Own) and Dong/Dung are Close
Ding and Thing are Close   Thing is Slang for A Fem
T/Fem Cross   and   D/Pregnant   Are Interchangeable in   The
Code   Because   One Becomes the Other
Same for   N and M   And   V and W

Dinner: Din/Her   Dim/Her
An Example Here on How   N/In/Hen/Virgin   and   M/
Motherhood   Can Blend into Each Other in The Code
From Being Din   A Loud Tumultuous Confused   Virgin   Into
Dim   Motherhood   She has Now Dimmed
din: a loud confused noise   a noisy clamor
dinar: gold coin issued by the Islamic Government
The Fems (Virgin   or   Mother) Cook and Serve the Family
Dinner   D/N/R
D/Pregnant   N/In/Hen/Virgin   and   Her/R/Hair/Hear/Ear/Here/Heir/Or/
Whore/Err/Are/Our/Sex Object   3 Fem Types   Are All In Together   It is
Dinner to be Served for   The Code
In the Greek Language there was No   N/In/Hen/Virgin   Only   M/
Motherhood   for The Fems

Dip: D/Pregnant   Hip   D/E/P
D   has   i/Marriage Act   with   P/Man Power   It is Called a
Dip
Deep   In the Hip   It is Hip   Sip On it   Tip It   Make it VIP   Rip It   On
the Lip   Whip It   Just a Beep   Skip it   Zip It
One Syllable Words with   P/Man Power   are Illustrated here in a Variety
of Options for Masc Letter P
dip: to plunge into water or other liquid and emerge quickly   to engage
slightly into a subject   a naïve foolish obnoxious person

A Ding (DN) for Her   A Dip (DP) for Him
Dip is Slang for Quick Sex

Dire: DR   D/Pregnant   R/Her/Hair/Hear/Ear/Here/Heir/Or/Whore/Err/Are/Our/Sex
That is What the DR Prescribes Says   The Code
dire: causing or involving great fear or
suffering   dreadful   terrible   trouble   disaster   misfortune
From D/Pregnant to R   it is Dire for Her
Doctor is the Cover Word here

Direct: Dire/Wreck
D/Pregnant   is being Wrecked Directly

Direction: The/Erection
D/Pregnant   Wreck   She   Eon
The Direction here is that   The Fem is Pregnant and a Wreck Since Eons
and Going Ahead for Another says   The Code
Take Away D/Pregnant and She Gets at the Next Erection to Keep Her
Focused on being Pregnant   It is That Direction Says The   Code

Dirty: D/Pregnant   Her/R/Heir/Or/Whore/Err   T/Fem Cross
From being   Pregnant to   Her   Fem Cross/The Great Curse   She is
a   Mother   a   Whore   or   Get Lost (Err) With   or   Without   Nice
Hair   She will Hear it All Her Life
D/Hurt/He   Dirt/He
When   D   Hurts it is Dirt
D/Heir/T
When D Mixes R and Her T/Fem Cross/Great Curse/Blood Loss   It is a
Dirty Subject   No Fem Wants to Look There
Her   R/Whore   Heir   Hair   Air

Disaster: This/Has/T/Her   This Has to Be Her
Dis/Aster
aster: Greek for star
A Star/Asterisk is a Symbol for The Fem Cross (See Asterisk in The
Keyboard Chapter) as in Multiplying it

dis: Fem deity (promoting fertility)   lady   woman   to show
disrespect   insult   criticism
dis-:   indicating
reversal   disconnect   negation   lack   deprivation   distrust
disgrace   removal or release   expressing intensive force   the Roman
god of the underworld Pluto (the abode of the dead)
Here are Some Words with
Dis: Disability   disaffirm   disbar   disbelief   discontent
dishearten   disown
Knowing   The Code   It Put The Fem as a Goddess   Forcefully in the
Line of Fire of Her Total Disgrace
Along with Dis as a Fem Deity   The Code   Added a God Along to make
it Levelled in All Dimensions   It Chose for Dis/Her the God of Death Hades
or Orcus (Whore/Curse)
It is Called a Disaster   it is All About Her

Discharge: T/His/Charge   Dis (See Dis Above) Charge
T/Fem Cross   is His Charge   He Let Go of Her in
discharge: to relieve oneself of a charge or load
This/Dis   She/Shh   R/Heir/Or/Whore/Err/Sex   G/Penis Penetration
Discharge is Another Slang Word for Ejaculation
She is the Whore   The Object of   The Code   Discharge

Discover: This/Cover   D/His/Cover   Dis/Cover   Disc/Over
D/Pregnant   Is/His   C/See/Young Girl   Ove/Egg R/Her/Whore/Are/Err/
Heir/Hair/Air/Sex
This/Cove/R
cove: a sheltered place
In That Cove   She is a   R/Heir/Or/Whore/Err/Sex
Dis is a Fem Deity   and   an Object of Rejection by Brutal Deathly Force
(Dishonor/Disavow/Distant/Destruct   etc)

Disdain: DSDN
This/Dame/Damn   D/Pregnant   Is/S   Damn   This/D/Ann   Dis/
This   D/Pregnant   Ann/N/In/Hen/Virgin
Letter N/In/Hen/Ann/Virgin   and   M/Motherhood are
Interchangeable   because   One will be the Other   Says   The Code

Add One More Bar to N   and   N Gets to become M (See Letter N and M in The Letter Chapter)
In Disdain   There are   2 DDs/Pregnants   with   His/S/Is/Hiss/Serpent/Penis
(As in Now   and   His Property) in the Middle   and   Ann/N/In/Hen/Ane/Virgin as the Ending   would be a Big No from   The Code   This Dame   Cannot Get Attention at All in   The Code   Even in Hidden Ugly Ways   Such as Disdain
This/Day/In   and   All the Other Days   She is The Victim of Disdain

Disgrace: T/Fem Cross   His/S/Is   Grace
T/His/Grace
T/Fem Cross   Grace is His
Dis (Fem Deity) is Graced here   That is Why   The Code   Calls it a Disgrace
Proof of That is All Around in   The Code   for The Fems
Grace as in G/Penis Penetration and Race
This   and   Dis   Have the Same Sound   (D/Is)

Dish: D/Pregnant   She/Shh
Dish Towel: D   She   Tow/To   All
The Dish Served to Her is   All Fems to be Towed in Pregnancy
Switch D for W/All Fems Sex Active and She Gets a Wish
W   Shh/She   As in Remaining Silent

Dismiss: DSMS
D/Pregnant   Is/S/His/Ass/Hiss/Us/Serpent/Penis   M/Motherhood   with   Another   S/Serpent/Penis
Pregnant   or   Mother   are to be Dismissed by   The Code
D/His/M/His/Is   She is   All His   Anyway   From Natural Love
Dis/Miss   She will Miss here
Miss   is Her Name Until   She is Married   All Fems Know That
In Dismiss   D/Pregnant   Becomes a   M/Mother
3 Penisses are Present Her to   make Sure   She is Pregnant   and/or   Mother

Dismount: This/Month   Dis/Mount

The Dam Code The Damn Book

Dis is The Fertility Goddess to be Destroyed (See Dis in The Words Chapter) Says   The Code
Time of the Month   and   The Mount is Related to Sex
The Code   Separates Those 2 Concepts in Dismounting

Disobedience: D/His/O/Bed/He/Hence
The Word Bed Already Tells The Fem to Watch for Herself for a Forced Pregnancy
Switch E/He for A/All Men and He Gets Bad
Switch E/He for i/Marriage Act and Get Bid   Sex is Always for Money or Power in   The Code
Switch E/He and He Gets a Bud (a Baby Boy)

Disorder: D/Pregnant   Is/S/His/Penis   Herd   Her
D/Pregnant   is Part of That Herd   It is Called
D   His   Heir/Whore/Her
This/Order   Is   The Order To Herd Her
as   Another   Heir   Or   Whore   Err
dis: to show disrespect   affront
2 DDs/Pregnants   Surrounds the Word Order
It is a Serious Matter for   The Code   The Fems Cannot Know Nothing about   The Secret (Sacred   Sac/Red   Her/Uterus) Code
The Sound Word Order is Her/R/Heir/Whore/Err/Sex   D/Pregnant Her/R
The Letter   R/Heir/Whore/Err/Her is Repeated Twice Here With   D/Pregnant   in Between
The Word   Order   is an Important Word in Secret Societies

Distorted: This/Dis   T/Fem Cross/Great Curse   R/Heir/Whore/Her/Sex   Turd
She   as a Cursed Whore   is a Turd   It is Not a Distorted Fact   It is Her Reality in   The Code   (See Feces in The Words Chapter)

Dive: DV   2 Fem Sounds Letters
D/Pregnant   V/Fem Sex Active
Dived: Die   V/Eve   Die
D/High/V   The Code   is High About Her Dive   in D/Pregnancy

253

Diverse: Die/Verse
That Code   Secret Plan would have Died   if   Diversity had been Allowed   But No   Says   The Code
Distance   Dismiss   Distress   Disrupt   Distort   Disorder
Divide   Destroy   and So Many Others   Letter D/Pregnant   is a Poor Weak Letter

Divide: DVD   Made of All 3 Fem Sounds Letters   D/Eve/D
V/Eve   is in Between   2 DDs/Pregnants
There could Be Communication Even Friendship
The Code   Rejects That Concept Entirely for The Fems   so   Divide Them to Conquer (Con/Queer) Them
D/Pregnant   V/Fem Sex Active   Hide
A Hide is also an Animal Skin
Getting Under Her Skin   to Divide   The Fems   or/and   Bring Her back to being an Animal   As a   Horse/Whore   Chicken/Hen/Ann   Ann/Donkey   Bitch Dog   etc

Divine: The   Vine/Wine   The/Eve/Vine   D/Vine D/Pregnant   and Her   Vine/Wine/Blood Loss
From that   Vine   Another   Vine   Follows   Its Fermented Fruit is Called   Wine/Whine   It is Made of Grapes (G/Rapes)   A   Single Grape   is from   a Grape of Grapes
Switch A/All Men for O/Fem Hole and She Get Grope
grope: to feel about with the hands   to feel ones way   an act or instance of groping   *Slang*   an act or instance of sexually fondling another person
Add U/Uterus and She Gets a Group
Grape/That   a Gang Rape from   The Singular   to The   All of Them   Rape is   The Code
Another Horrible Concept from   That Code
Note here that   W/All Fems Sex Active   is the Extension of   V/Fem Sex Active   in Singular   Add More Bars to V It is a W   or   put   2 VVs   Together   it is a W
divine: of or pertaining to a god   especially the Supreme Being   God as   characteristic of or befitting a Deity

The Dam Code The Damn Book

That Code   Has Made Its Way in There Too   Of the Vine   Grows the Wine   Jesus Blood at the Last Supper   That The Catholics Drink at Their Regular Mass Ceremony in The Form of Drinking Wine

Division: DVCN   4 Fem Sound Letters
D/The   Vision   The Code   Vision of D is   D/Pregnant   is Not Allowed to have Vision Except When Related to Children   and   The Husband   That is Why   They Veil   The Fems in Eastern Arabic Countries Mentality   or   Segregates Her   in Many Ways in Different Other Religions of The World   Jewish   Catholics   to Name a Few
D/Pregnant   V/Eve/Fem Sex Active   C/Young Girl/See   On/Eon or He/On)   It is Her Lot in   Division
The Fem has been Isolated in
Being   D/Pregnant   and   V/Fem Sex Active   Since Eve/V/Fem Sex Active
D/V/See/On
D and V Would See/Understand What Is going On in   The Code   Is a Big No   So   Divide to Keep on The Control   (Cunt/Roll)
division: to divide   to separate into parts

Divorce: DVR   The Fems (Pregnant   or/and   Sex Active) Are/R/Whores   if They Divorce
Switch V/Fem Sex Active for F/Fem/Fuck and She Gets The Force (Police) (F Letter is Not Necessarily Sex Active All The Time   or   At All   Naturally   She is More The Type of a Free Fem)
D/Pregnant   Force   Forced to be Pregnant   or   Forced Pregnancies   Nothing New for a Fem On Our Planet Earth (Hurt)
Dive/Whores   The/Eve/Whores

Dixieland: Dick   See   Land
Dixieland: a kind of jazz originating in New Orleans

Do: DO   2 Fem Letters
D/Pregnant   O/Fem Hole/Loins
To Do is to D/Impregnate   O/Hole
Do   T/Hat (Follow The Rat in The Hat Says   The Code
Do/Dad
Repeat Do Twice   It Becomes a Dodo

dodo: a clumsy bird   *Slang*   a dull witted slow reacting person   a thing that is outmoded or obsolete   a person with old fashioned conservative or outmoded ideas
Add More OOs/Fem Holes   and it   becomes Doodoo
(Feces   Poop   Shit   All those Important Fem Called Words in   The Sound Code)

Doctor: Duck/Dock   T/Fem Cross   Her/R/Hair/Hear/Ear/Here/Heir/Or/Whore/Err/Are/Our/Air/Sex
Take C Away and She Gets a Dot (She Is So Small in   That Code   Dot   3 Fem Letters) Dot/Her   Daughter (See   Dowry   Dot   and   Daughter in The Words Chapter) It is Her Destiny from   Daughter   to   Mother   to be a Dot   Says   The Code
The Way to Reach That is to   Duck Her   or to   Dock Her (The Fem is a Fish   if you Dock a Fish   It has been Fished and Is on its Way to The Fish Mart
Switch O/Fem Hole for E/He and He Gets a Deck
DR   Dear   The Code   Says   Is The Abbreviated Doctor Sound Name) Dear is The Cover Word here

Dodo: Made of 4 Fem Letters
D/Pregnant   O/Fem Hole   And   Repeat
It is Another Name for Poop as in Doo Doo With a Lien here to Unite The Fems Together as Dodo (and Do it Twice)
P/Man Power   Poops When He Meets   O/Fem Hole   in Plural
The   Do Do   Repetition of Do Accentuates Its Meaning
Dodo   To Do a Fem is to have Sex with Her Says   The Code   Implying here   Another Form of   Polygamy
dodo: dull witted outmoded obsolete   excrement
Doo-Doo is Shit   She/It
The Code   Gives here Another Example of The Fem Complete Degradation   Comparing Her to   Feces   Again
Reverse The RX Symbol Upside Down and it Becomes Letter P/Man Power   Extending its Shape into X/Fallen Cross

Dog: D/Hug
A Bitch is a Worldly Known Slang Word Defining a Fem
D/Pregnant Fem Hugs/Likes Herself as Being Identified as a Dog

The Dam Code The Damn Book

There are Many Small Important Code Words with   O/Fem Hole   and   G/Penis Penetration   Here are a Few
Bug (Small   Annoying)   Clog (Yuck)   Cog Cheat)   Dog (The Bitch (The Fem)   Fog (Confuse)   Fug (Stale Air)   Hog (boar or swine   a Filthy Person)   Hug (Hug That)   Log   Mug (Cup)   Nog (Drink with Eggs in It)   Plug (Aperture)   Pug (a Dog/Her)   Rogue (Scoundrel   Dishonest)   Rug (Slang for Period   Being on The Rag)   Slug   Tug
Those Words are of Small Importance   Annoying   or   Bad for Her
dog house: in disfavor or disgrace   a small cabin
it Seems Ideal in   The Code   for Her/the Bitch (Dog/Her)
dog shit: *slang* for a despicable matter   pretentious trash crap
Even Her Poop is Wrong
Dough   G   She/Shh   It/Hit
To Us The Fems   That Dog is God   in Reverse
That is   The Code   Language for You

Dodge: DODG   3 Fem Letters   with   G/Penis Penetration   with The Invisible Noiseless Spy   and   Participant   E/He
2 DDs/Pregnants   O/Fem Hole   in Between   Ending with   G/Penis Penetration
That would be Too Much Information for Her   And a Big No from The Code   so
dodge: to elude or evade by a sudden shift of position or with strategy
A Dodge was and a Not So Good Car at The Past

Dogma: The Dog   and   The Ma
The Bitch and the Mother   or   Mothers as/of Dogs
dogma: an official system of principles or tenets concerning faith morals behavior etc   as of a church
The Secret Societies Have Used those Discrepancies
As Unconscious Barriers to Hide   Their Code   so   No One Dare Look at   For example Pope and Poop Reinforces that
Dog/Her is Reverse of The Word God and No One Says Why
The Name of their Deity   Would also have an Animal Name in Its Name   Especially a Dog   Is plain Weird

Doing: DON   All Fems Sound Letters   As in Don   A Masc
Title   Which Add Power and its Respect
Do/In   Is to Do/N/In/Hen/Virgin
To Do a Fem is to Have Sex with Her
Dodo Would be its Repetition   Which Puts Her back to Feces
(See Dodo as in Poop in The Words Chapter)
Dodo here as in To Do it Twice   Which Implies Polygamy

Doll: Dull   i/Doll i/Dol
She Worship (Whore/Ship) the Doll/Dull as Her Idol
What a Doll Can do   Is to Be Dull and Put Up with the Pain   Be a Doll Will You and get Me a Drink
dol: a unit for measuring the intensity of pain
The Fems are   Russian Dolls   The Code Influence   All Fems in the Same Pattern   From Big to Small
As the Bee/Hive (B/Eve)   The School of Fishes (See Ocean   O/She/N)   The Chickens (Chicks/In/N)   The Sheeps (She/P) Kept in Rows   The Cows in the Field (F/Fem/Fuck   Yield)   The Horses (Whores) Symbol of Sex for The Fems   Etc
All Fems are Controlled (Cunt/Roll) to be Less than a Normal Human (You/Man) in   The Secret Code   The Language is Expressed Clearly   It Pays While in Power

Dollar: Dull/Her   Doll   R/Whore/Her/Sex
Making Her   A Doll/Her (A Dollar Whore) Dull/Her   by Not Telling Her Anything   That Matters
In Our History The Code has Always Kept Money and Power (Pow/Her   As in Finish   R/Her/Are/Whore/Sex) Away from The Fems in Different Ways According to Her Age

Domain: DOMN is Made of 4 Fem Sound Letters
Dome/N/In   Doom/N   Dumb   In/N
When Doom is the Dumb N/In/Hen/Virgin
The Code Pictures that as a Domain
A Domain for Him   For Her the Nightmare of being Doomed
Another Dome   Another Doom   Another Dame   Another Done

The Dam Code The Damn Book

The Glass Ceiling is What She Sees (2 EEs/He in Plural   or   All of Them   and   2 SSs In Plural or All of Them   S/Ass/Is/His/Hiss/Us/Serpent/Penis   Is Very Little (A Litter for Her)
She Does Not Hear it at All
Domain   Do/Man
The/D/Pregnant   Doom   N/In/Ann/Hen/Virgin

Dome: DOM   Made of 3 Fem Sound Letters
D/Pregnant   O/Fem Hole   M/Motherhood   Are Under that Dome/Doom/Dumb
Dome is the Original Image in   The Code   for the Ever Expendable Breasts Presented to The Fems as the Example to Be
It is Working Strong with Fems Aligning their Breasts
As 2 Loaves of Bread   or   Jugs
The Fems Breasts have been Expanding a Lot in Our History
The Code   Sees The Fems in Plural in   As 2 Eggs on a Plate   Two Holes in Wall Plugs   Etc   Always Implying Polygamy for Him
The Builders/Freemasons did Symbolic Work   for Example   In Eliminating The Fems Space on the Left of the Stove (Where the Fire is)   or   The Sink (Where Water Flows Down) Transferring it to the Right/Masc Side
There is Immense (Him   and The   Menses) Secret Symbolism   Where they Put Their Columns (Penisses) in Their Buildings   The Importance of Numbers   The Orientations of   Forms   Sizes   Colors   of   Walls   Doors   Windows   etc   are Parts of   The Code   Construction
There Are   Domes/Dooms/The Home   Everywhere in Ancient Buildings   Temples   and   Old Government Offices Buildings and They are Picture Perfect of a Large Breast with a Man (In Uniform) at Its/Her   Top/Tit
Examples   The White House Dome   Saint Peter Church Dome   The Muslim Gold Dome   Brunelleschi Dome of Florence Cathedral   The Cambridge University Dome   and   Many Other Old Structures Carry   Dome   Doom   The/D   Home   D/Pregnant/Home Doomed   In the Past Tense is   DOMD   4 Fems Sound Letters   Ending with D   so   That Code   Past Repeats Itself Through D/Pregnancy

Dominate: Dome   In/N/Hen/Ann/Virgin   Ate/Hate

Dumb/Hen/Hate
Ann/Hen/N/In/Virgin   is   The Code   Fem Chicken (Through All
of Us   The Code   Hypnotized Population) The Code   Calls The
Fems   Chicks (See Chick in The Words Chapter)
The/Dome   The/Doom   The/Home   is Everywhere
Under   The/D/Pregnant   Domination/Dominated   Word   She Hates
it   But   She has to   Eat it   Anyway   Says   That Code   Hate it or
Not   Eat That Abuse
#/Number (Numb/Her) 8 is   D/The/Pregnant   on The Code   Grid)
D/Pregnancy (#8   Top Hole (Her Head)   of   O/Fem Hole
The Other   O   or   the Baby Head O Below is Represented at Her
Belly Height   Which Creates   The Code   #/Number/Numb/Her/8/D/
Pregnancy
Ugly is   The Code   It Identifies   The Fem as Beast of Burden
(Husbandry)   and   How To Keep Her   That Way
Aleister Crowley   Understood   That Bloody Secret
Code   and   Identified It to Us   By   Breaking It into Smaller
Pieces   It Made it Simpler to Comprehend   Therefore   in being Able
in   Identifying it   Better/Clearer
It Made it a Little Bit Easier to Depict and Comprehend for   Code
Searchers   Professionals   and   Amateurs   like Me   and Great People
I admire   Mr Dan Brown (The Vinci Code and Mr Tom Hanks The Great
Magnet to Attract Us to That Complicated Secret Knowledge   Great
Heart Felt for you both and all helpers on The Way to Create The   Da
Vinci Code   Thank You)
The Aleister Crowley Tarot Deck Cards is An Extraordinary Illustrated and
Truly Magically Meaningful Tarot Deck Work
He was   So   Ahead of His Time   It Took Half a Century to Figure it Out
Without Screaming Witch
On His Cards Back Cover is a Large Brightly Colored   Cross   with a
Background that has Almost The Shape and Colors of of a Traditional
Chess Board   Somehow Visually Distorted   it has Rare Mystical Symbols
on its   Black   and   Red   Elongated Squares   Which have Direction
It is a Profoundly True and Scary Tarot Deck
That Crowley Cross has   2 Crowns/Couronnes of Flower Petals
Around   That Cross   Symbolic Neck (Une Couronne   is a   Crown/
Royal Order   in French   Une Couronne de Fleurs   A Crown of Fleurs/

The Dam Code The Damn Book

Flowers (Flaw/Her with S Meaning Plural or All of Them and/or Penis/S/Is/His/Hiss/Serpent)
Une Couronne de Noel is a Christmas Wreath/Reek))
A Double Crown of Flowers Each Flower Petal in a Variety of Colors Representing The Colors Symbolic Meaning System of That Code
Those Colored Petals are Connecting/Expanding to The Cross 4 Arms/Members (# 4 is The Pyramid Number See #4 in The Numbers Chapter) Here Their Code Color Depends on Their Members Direction
Left is Fem/Unattractive Weakening Colors Right is Masc/Attractive/Expanding Colors Going Up is Masc Going Down is Fem
In The Middle of Those 2 Crowns of Flowers is Another Crown of Only 3 Petals A Dark Blue A Bright Red and A Yellow One
In The Center of That Center is a Discreetly Looking Beige Cross with a Proportionally Large Red Dot in its Middle (See Dot and Color Red in The Words Chapter)

Dominion: Dome/Doom He N/Ann/Hen/In/Virgin Eon/He/On (See Dome Doom Damn Dumb Etc in The Words Chapter)
Doom is with N/In/Ann/Hen/Virgin for an Eon
Domain He/E On/Own or an Eon It is Masc
The/D/Pregnant Dome/Dumb/The Home is the Ever Expanding Breasts from The Secret Code to keep Her Dumb (Too Much Estrogen Makes Her More Emotional therefore Weaker The Larger The Breasts The More Estrogen)
For Ann/N/In/Hen/Virgin The Dome/Dumb/The Home of M/Motherhood Must Go On so
dominion: sovereign authority control domination

Domination: Dome/He/Nation
Obsessed with The Fem Breasts as Usual is The Code

Dominoes: Dumb/He/Knows Dome/he/Knows Dumb/he Knows All Over Again with The Code World of Dumb/Doom/Dome/The Home of The Fems
A Game of Dominoes for Us in The Code
Dominoes is a Cover Word here

Don: 3 Fem Letters   Representing a Looking Respectful Title/Image for a Man   from All Those Fems
D/Pregnant   is   On
don: a title of respect for a man   the head of a family   to put on or to dress in   to wrap around   a leader   from Latin Dominus or Lord   a goddess the mother of Gwydion
Don as Fem is Donna   As in to Give (A Don)   so   She Gives Herself for Free (Un Don is also a Gift in French)

Donate: Don/Ate   Don/8   Don/Hate
Hate it   or   Not   She will Eat it and be   D/Pregnant   #8 is Pregnant
(See Number 8 in The Numbers Chapter)

Done: D/Pregnant   is   On   Don has Done it   It is in the Past   It is Done
(See Down in The Words Chapter)

Don't: 4 Fem Letters
The Very Concept of Associating a Negative Command in a Symbol Makes it Unattractive
so   The Fems Sees Nothing   but a Gift (A Don) When
D/Pregnant   is   On   for Her to Be a   T/Fem Cross   Hiding in   Don't

Donut: Do/Not   Dough/Nut   Do/Nut   Do/Knot (Tie the Knot)
D/O/Not   D/On/Hut
A Donut is a Sweet Bread (Bred) with a   O/Fem Hole   In its Middle
Nut/Not   are Made of All 3 Fem Letters
The Dough is the Daughter   She /Raises/Rises in Pregnancy   Lies   The Code
Dough is Also Money   Same for Bagel (Bag/All   Big/Hole)
A Bagel is Part of a Jewish Favorite Sunday Brunch   Add Salmon
(The Wiggly Fish/The Girl Child from King Arthur (Art/Her) Bleeding Lance of the Holy Grail)   Spread (?) it with Cream Cheese (Her Sex Juices) and We have a Meal (M/Motherhood   Heel (Slang for Penis))   Motherhood   is   Ill

Doodle: DODL   All 5 Fem Letters   with   E/He   Discreet/Inaudible

The Dam Code The Damn Book

L/All   D/Pregnants   O/Fem Holes   L/Sweet Fem Love Light/Ill/Ail/Hail/Hell/Elle   That would be a Great Peaceful Concept for Humanity   But No Says   The Code

doodle: to waste time (time) in aimless or foolish activity   *dialect* to deceive cheat   to draw or scribble idly

The Code Hates Particularly   L/Sweet Fem Love Light/Ill/Ail/Hail/Hell/Elle   in Any Form   L/Sweet Love/Ail/Hell is the Most Dangerous Sentiment Against   The Code   Endlessly Ugly Greedy   a Dark Murderer Power

Some Men are So Sensitive to that Sweet Giving   L/Love   It makes it Even More Dangerous for   The Code   so   it Does Not Doodle with That

Doom: All 4 Fem Letters   DM
Dome (See Dome/Doom and Breast (Brr/East   Bear/East   Beast   Without R/Her) in The Words Chapter)
Dame   Damn   Dam   Dim   Dime   Dumb   Them   and   Many More That is   D/Pregnant   in Her Way to   M/Motherhood   She is   Damned   Dim   and   Cheap   That is The Making of   The Code Directed to The Fems

Domestic: Do/Me/Stick   Dome/He/Stick   Dome/Is/Dick   Doom/He/Stick   The/D/Pregnant   Home   His/Is   Stick
Domestic Rules   Includes   The Stick   for   D/Pregnant   at Home The/D/Pregnant   Home   He/E   Stick
The Dome/Doom is   The Fem Breast   or   the Cup/Chalice   as a Bra Cup Size
The Cup is The   Chalice/Uterus
What We See Here are Sticks Doing/Her   or   Dooming/Her
It is a Jumping Point Where Sticks and Breasts are Related as   Penis   Creating Breasts
We Lost The Fem Human Natural Mating Cycle   therefore   The Fems Developed Permanent Breasts   The Only One in Mammals to have Permanent Breasts Out   Once Grown   Once
The Longer I Write This book   The More Difficult it is to Write it

Door: Do/Her   The/R/Whore/Heir/Her/Err/Sex
D/Pregnant   2 OOs/Fem Holes   in Plural   or   All of Them With   R/Her

Lise Rochon

The   2 OOs/Fem Holes   here Indicates   Polygamy
A   Door   Adore (Add/Whore/Her/Heir/Or/Err)
Adore is The Cover Word Here

Doorbell: D/Pregnant   Her/R/Heir/Whore   Be/B/Boy Holding All Fem Breasts   Hell/Ill/All/Ail/All/Elle
D/Whore/Belle   Door/Bell   is The Message from The Code
Ring (Marry   Mary) That Bell (e) (a Belle is a Beauty in French)
Now We have   The Belle as a Door (The/Whore)   No Need   She is a Door Bell   Here is   The Code   for You

Dough: Do/Not   Do/Nut   Done/Hut
Dough is Slang for Money
Dot/Dotte/Her   Daughter
Une Dotte   is A Dowry (Money   Legacy for The Fem at Her Wedding) in French   The Dot is a Small Circle   As The Period at The End of a Sentence (See   The Non Indented Punt here) The Code   in Action
Dough/T/Her   Dough   Makes Bread (Bred   Daughter is being   Bread)
The Bread   and   The Wine of   Jesus   in   The Code   Symbolism
T/Fem Cross   Being the Reason for All this
Add   Nut/Not (Both All Fems Letters) to Dough and She Gets a   Donut   a Sweet Bread With a Hole   or a   Do/Not
The Dough (Daughter) has Now a Hole in the Middle   How Convenient for   That Code

Dove: D/Ov   D/Pregnant   V/Eve/Ovulation/Fem Sex Active
The Holy Ghost/Spirit is Represented by a Dove
The Dove Has Fems Qualities
dove: innocent gentle tender person
Switch V for L/Fem Sweet Love Light/Ail/Hell/Elle and She Gets Love from being   a Dove   Another Lie   to Her from   The Code
Love is Low/V Says   The Code   LOV Sound is Made of 3 Fem Letters
L/Ov   L and Ov/Ovulation
Switch V for F/Fem/Fuck and She Gets L/Of   or/and   L/Off
So   That Love is Off When a Fem does Not Necessarily has Sex (See Letter f/F) Says   The Code
Love is The Fems Intelligence Associated with Ovulation Says   The Code   Period

The Dam Code The Damn Book

Christ Was Not That Dove

Down: DWN   is Made with 4 Fem Letters
Done   and   on its Way to Die is the Way for Her in   The Code
Emphasizing Down More here in the Word Done   All Fems Go Down in the Past too   So   it is Done Already
The Secret Code/The Grid Code   Is Kaleidoscope
Where You See a Replica of the Others   but the Shapes in it Changes All The Time   so   it is Difficult to Focus on One Image
D/Pregnant   O/Fem Hole   W/All Fems Sex Active   N/In/Hen/Virgin
All Aspects of The Fems are Going Down here
Dawn is the Cover Word Here
The Fems Love that Word   The Dawn of the Day   It is a New Beginning   Soft as Dawn
don: a title of honor for a man   to wrap around
The Man Code is there Only as being Honored and Respected   Honor (Hon/Her   Horn/Her)

Dowry: Dow (3 Fem Letters)   R/Her/Hair/Hear/Ear/Here/Heir/Or/Whore/Err/Are/Our/Air/Sex   He/E
dow: to be able   to thrive
Dow/Dough   is Slang for Money
Money   Sex   Him and   are Doing Good in Dowry
The Dotte (a Point) is the Dowry in French
A Dot in English is an Unremarkable Very Small Symbol in   The Code   Same Size as a Period (See Period in The Words Chapter) at The End of a Sentence (Punt Intended here   Says   The Code)
It is the Dot on Top of Letters   i/Marriage Act   and   j/Shepherd/The Sheep Master (See Sheep in The Words Chapter)
Compare Those to Other Very Small Code Symbols
The Pi ∞ The Infinite Sign   Is   Number 8   Laying Down   It Represents   D/Pregnant   Pregnant   Infinitely
That Symbol Resembles an Eye Mask   The Code   Hiding Something   Again
The Star * (Stay   R/Whore/Are/Heir/Err/Sex) is Called Asterisk   (See Asterisk in The Punctuation Chapter)
The Word Risk is Part of Asterisk

asterisk: a sign in printing or writing to indicate a cross reference or an omission
The Code   Eliminates More of Her Here by Making those Important Code Symbols Minuscule   so   Few Fems Will See Them or Pay Attention to Them
Making Her Tiny is Just Another Way to Diminish Her
dowry: the money goods or estate that a wife brings to her husband at marriage
Compare that Trade to Persephone and Her Mother Demeter Story   When They Met Hades (Hide/His) in His Underworld (Hell)
Daughter   Dot/Her   Dot   R/Heir/Whore/Err/Or/Sex
Dow Corp is On The Stock Exchange Big Names
Dow Jones is The Cover here

Dozen: Does   Ann/N/In/Hen/Virgin
She Does it by   The Dozen   While She   Dozes   In/N/Virgin
Switch O/Fem Hole for A/All/Men and He Gets Daze/In   as in Being in a Daze with Half (F) a Dozen as in 6 (Sex   666) Eggs (Eggs has 2 GGs/Hymens/Vaginas Penetration   as   in Many   or All of Them)
Doze/N/In/Hen/Virgin   and   She is Sleeping on It
That Code   is in Every Part of Our Lives

Draft: D/Pregnant   Raft   The/Raft
That is Her Draft   On a Raft   Poor and Abandoned
The Rat is The Animal Representing The Ancient Secret/Sacred/Sac/Red (Red Sack   Her Genitals   Bleeding)   Art (Same Letters)
The Rat   The Cat (Cat is Fem) All in That Code Art Hat
draft: a system for selecting young men for compulsory Military System administered by the United States   a plan a sketch or drawing of something   a draw up an outline for something   a bill of exchange
Under That innocent Word Draft   We have Executive Orders Ready as a Draft to Go   A Draft is Also A Plan
Take Away F/Fem/Fuck and She Gets D/Rat (Pregnant of Rats)

Drag: The/Rag   D/Pregnant   Rag
Being on The Rag is a Common Expression Addressed to The Fems   When She is Losing Her Precious Blood
drag: to carry painfully   discomfort   poverty   unhappiness

The Dam Code The Damn Book

How Would She Have Known She would Get All those Drags on Her Life

Dragon: D/The/Rag/On
The Dragon is a Popular Mythic Figure
drag: to draw with force effort or difficulty   pull heavily or slowly along
In Mythology the Dragon takes Many forms
For Example
St George Fighting in the Dragon Paintings
Paintings of William Blake are Particularly Accurate in that Meaning
Especially The Red Dragon with the Woman Clothed with the Sun
Layers of New Subtle Symbolism have been Added to Old Symbols
in Modern Times (Mode/Urn   See Urn/Earn in The Words
Chapter)   Shading The True Light on Their Original Meaning   Although
if One can Interpret some of it   Those Layers can be Little Foot Steps
Towards More Understanding   But Not Says   The Code
D will Be Pregnant and on The Rag   Poor   On a Life Raft
Switch G/Penis Penetration for W/All Fems Sex Active and She Gets a
Draw

Dragon: A VIP Word for The Code
The/Rag/On
D/Pregnant   R/Her/Hair/Hear/Ear/Here/Heir/Or/Whore/Err/Are/Our/Air/
Sex   Hag On
hag: old woman or demon
Always Dark Scary Shadows on Her Shoulders from   That Code

Drain: The Reign   The Rain   The Rein
D/Reine (Pregnant Queen   All Over Again   See Q in The Letters
Chapter)
Drain is A Cover Word in   The Code   to Despise/Destroy The Fem in Her
Element   That Precious Water That Life Cannot Be Without
The Words   Queen   and   Reign   are a Drain   or   in a Drain
Rain is   So Clean   and   So Primordial   A Prime Source of Water/
Life   And   It Falls from Heavens/Sky   That Makes it Even More
Dangerous for   The Code
rein: a leather strap   any of certain other straps or thongs forming part
of a harness   to rein a horse or other animal

reins: the kidneys   (especially in Biblical use) the seat of the feelings or affections formally identified with the kidneys

The Code   had to Reach High   to Keep Her Asleep on that
One   Flattery Works   so The Code Put   Queen   and   Reign in it (A Reigning Queen   Reine/Reign   is Queen in French)   Those are Cover Words for Draining Her Emotions Down
drain: to become empty of a liquid
How Appropriate for   The Code   To Drain that Majestic Rain/Water (An Entirely Fem Element   Including   O/She/Ann (Ocean))
The Code   is Merciless and Subtle

Drat: The/Rat   Dear/Hat   Deer/Hat   D/Pregnant   Rat
In the Hat is Where the Secret Societies Hide their Secret Arts
The Rat is Known to be an Animal that Bring Diseases   So No One Wants that Close By   Therefore a Good Hiding Spot for The Code
The Cover Words here is   Deer   Hat   and   Dear
Such Inoffensive Sound Words for Damning   and   Confounding
In Drat   The Code   Rat Keeps the Fem Pregnant and on that T/Fem Cross
drat: to dam   to confound

Dread: When a Word Starts and Ends with D/Pregnant
It is Bad News to Her from   The Code   (See Dead/Dad/Did/DD in The Words Chapter)
Especially if Letters R/Her/Hair/Hear/Ear/Here/Heir/Or/Whore/Err/Are/Our/Air/Sex   With E/He   and   A/All Men   In its Middle
It is a Big No from   The Code (Cod/He   See Fish in The Words Chapter)   so
dread: to fear greatly   be in extreme apprehension   *Archaic*   to hold in respectful awe
Take R/Her Away from Dread and She Gets Dead (2 DDs/Pregnants)

Dream: D/Pregnant   R/Her/Hair/Hear/Ear/Here/Heir/Or/Whore/Err/Are/Our/Air/Sex   Him/M/Motherhood
Motherhood Happens with Him   so   Trailing to do It He is   The Code   is with Him

The Dam Code The Damn Book

Her Dream Says   The Code   Language is to have Sex   and   Be D/
Pregnant   D/Plural   or   as in The Past
D is on the Rim   is R/Her   with   M/Motherhood
On Another Note   REM is Rapid Eye Movement   Which Happens When
One is Dreaming at a Certain Stage of the Night
D/Pregnant is Kept On the Outer Part (Rim) of the Wheel (W/All Fems
Sex Active   Ill/L/Elle/Ill/Hell)   It is Called   The Wheel of Time   The
Will of Time   Says   The Code   The Will of Time being   The Saturnian
Time Definition which is   TM   T/Fem Cross/Great Curse   M/
Motherhood/Him
Dreamer: Dear   M/Him/Motherhood   R/Her
She Dreams of Him as Dear   Dear/Him/Her
D/R/M
D/Pregnant   R/Her   M/Motherhood as Him/M
Pregnancy   Sex   Motherhood are Facts Here
Not a Dream   The Code   Tells
Switch M/Motherhood for D/Pregnant and She Gets Dread   Another
Dream Gone Dread   for Her   The Code   Speaks

Drill: D/Pregnant   Reel
reel: frame turning on an axis   frames that turn on an axis onto which
film magnetic tape wire thread etc may be wound or spool   angling
device for reeling a fish   to sway esp under the shock of a blow dizziness
or drunkenness   a staggering or swaying motion or sensation   a lively
dance
Being   Reeled   is No Fun for Her   Being   That Fish (See
Fish in The Words Chapter) Especially With Words   such
as   Wound   and   Staggering   Around
A Frame Turning on an Axis (Axe/His/Is) is a Wheel (See Wheel of
Time   W/All Fems V/Fem Sex Active   Ill/L/I) and that Wheel Will Turn (T/
Fem Cross   Urn) Says   The Code
D/Pregnant   with   Drill is
D   R   Ill (They   Are/Heir/Whore/Her   Ill)   D   R   Hell   (They/D/
Pregnant   Are/Whores   in   L/Hell)   D   R   All (They   Are/
Whore   All   in There)   D   R   Heel (They   Are/Whore   Heels
(A Weak Spot on the Human Body)   D   R   Letter L/Sweet Fem
Light   And they Are/Whore are   so   Sweet About it All

269

Lise Rochon

That is How   D/Pregnant   is being Drilled   with   being R/Her/Hair/Are/Here/Hear/Ear/Whore/Or/Err/Sex   in that Word   Curse
Drilling Makes Holes   How Convenient for   The Code
Switch D for G/Penis Penetration and She Gets Grilled
Switch D for T/Fem Cross and She Gets Thrilled
The Fems Being Cursed is a Thrill for   The Code
Another Big Lie to The Fems
Take Away R/Her/Hair/Hear/Ear/Here/Heir/Or/Whore/Err/Are/Our/Air/Sex   from Drill and Get a Dill
dill: an aromatic plant   a fool an idiot
Not Much Happening for Her   When R/Her/Hair/Hear/Ear/Here/Heir/Or/Whore/Err/Are/Our/Air/Sex   is Not Part of that Drill
A Dill Pickle Maybe to Chew On (She Gets Chewed on)
    or   a Plant that Smells Good

Drool: D/Pregnant   is with R/Her/Hair/Hear/Ear/Here/Heir/Or/Whore/Err/Are/Our/Air/Sex   and 2 OOs/Fem Holes (Polygamy)   Plus a Sweet Attitude   It is to be Drooled Upon Says   The Code
Drool is Made of All Fems Letters   Except for Letter R/Her   which is a Half a Fem Letter
Take One   Hole Away and She Gets a Droll   A Droll is a Gross Word for a Fem   so   She Stays Away   And   The Code   Wins

Dry: The Rye   Dear/I   Deer/Eye (See Letter i/I   The eye in the Pyramid)   Dire/High
If She is Dry Give Her a Shot of Rye Says the Rye (a Gentleman)   It may give Her Deer Eyes or Feel Dear   Later She may Say it was a Dire/High D/Pregnant   R/Her/Hair/Hear/Ear/Here/Heir/Or/Whore/Err/Are/Our/Air/Sex   High is a Dry Word for that Fem
Letter i the I/High/Hi   or   Its Stick do Not Deal with The Fems At All Except When in Small Cap/Childhood as the i/Marriage Act Which She is Only the Dot on that i/High

Duck: D/Pregnant   Yuck
She is a Dock When D/Pregnant
Duke is a Masc Title   He Stays Out of that Quagmire
Duck/Her   Dock/Her

The Dam Code The Damn Book

Add T/Fem Cross to Dock and it is the Doctor Talking   A Person of Often Ultimate Authority on You

Dud: All 3 Fem Letters
That Could have been a Great Word for The Fems
Having 2 DDs/Pregnants with a Fem in U/You/Ovulating/Ovulation to get Advice or Simply Share
But No Says   The Dam Code
It will Not accept Any Form of Knowledge or Communication for The Fems   so
dud: a device person or enterprise that proves to be a failure
Add One Masc Letter E/He And He Gets Dude
dude: *slang*   a fellow chap
The Fem is Not there Either A Dude being Masc

Dude: DUD   3 Fem Sounds Letters   and   E/He   Do/ID
2 DDs/Pregnants   with   U/You/Natural Ovulating Time   in the Middle   Makes a Dude   Says   The Code
dude: fellow   a chap   a man excessively concerned about his clothes
Switch D for B/Boy Holding All Fem Breasts and She Gets a Bud
(A   Another   Baby)   Buddy/Butt/He/Boot/He   The Code   is Bad for Both Sexes (Although The Masc is Highly Protected from All Her Curses   Without Knowing it)
Dude is a Cover Word here in Our Modern Times
duke: a man honorary title
The Old Term for a Fem Duke is   Duchess   which is   The so   Humiliating   Douche   Ass/S/Is/His/Us/Hiss/Serpent/Penis
Dough (Bread)   She   S/Is/As/Has/Ass/His/Us/Hiss/Serpent/Penis   or   Duck   She   Ass
Same for Baron   Bar/On   Baroness   Bar (See bar in the Words Chapter   N/Hen/In/Ann/Virgin   Has/Ass/S/Is/His/Us/Hiss/Serpent/Penis Bar   On   N   S
N/Hen/Ann/Virgin   Is Barred from Owning Her Own Natural Stick of Power
I Say   and   The Me Too Movement   Say   Too   You do Not have to have a Penis to have a Stick of Power in Real Natural Life

271

Lise Rochon

Emperor   A Man of Power   Emperor has The Sound Word   Whore/R/Heir/Her/Are   in it   MPR
Empress   Is as in to   Impress (Him/M/Motherhood   Press)   He Presses for Motherhood
P/Man Power   His/Is   or   M/Him/Motherhood   P/Man Power   Is/His   She Does Not Get Any Stick of Power   Again

Dull: Dull is Made of 3 Fem Letters   One being a Double   2 LLs/Elle/Hell
D/Pregnant   U/You/Ovulating   All/L/Ill/Ail/Hail/Hell/Elle (Twice)   The/Hull
hull: the body of a ship   the shell of a pod of peas or beans
D/Pregnant   All   The Concept is Old and Sinuous
The Body of that Ship (She/P) is Her
It is Just a Shell (The Size of a   Pea   or a   Bean) Says   The Code   so   It has Little Value
Another Lie from   The Code   The Love for Peas and Beans   We Cannot Live without Those International Delicious Sources of Life
D/Pregnant   is   U/You/Ovulating   or   Shell
D/Pregnant   U/You/Ovulating   Her/R/Hair/Hear/Ear/Here/Heir/Or/Whore/Err/Are/Our/Air/Sex   (Twice) that Is Called   Dull   by   The Code Minimizing Her
Switch D/Pregnant for F/Fuck/Fem and She Gets Full (Pregnant)   D/Pregnant Started that Word

Dumb: When a Word Starts with 3 Fem Letters   Followed by a Masc Letter (B as in Boy/Baby) it Will be Bad News for Her   She is Dumb   because   Done/B   Down/Be
D/Pregnant   is done with   B/Boy Holding All Fem Breasts
Switch B/Boy for His Stronger Older P/Man Power   B/Boy   becomes   P/Man Power   in Adult Life   He Gets Dump   D/Pregnant   Humping
Dump is Related to Defecation   Another Old Word that Tells Us   The Code   System According to   Their Code   Rules
That Code   is That Sea (See   Hole/He/See) of Their Manipulated of Our Natural Sounds   In and Around Us   The Glass Ceiling   is the Real World of Sounds for   The Code

Dummy: Made Entirely of 5 Fem Letters

The Dam Code The Damn Book

Dome/He   Doom/He/E
Breasts Expansion and Doom Are Not for Men in   The Code   so   it is for Dummies (Her)
And it ther because it has to be there to Maintain The Balances of Letters   That   The Code

Dumbbell: Dumb/Belle   (See Bell in The Words Chapter)
dumbbell: an exercising weight consisting of a simple bar with a heavy ball or disc at either end   a stupid person   a small wooden object shaped as this used in dog training for the dog to retrieve
How Convenient for   The Code   She has Become   The Dog (Bitch)   being Trained Into Being   Dumb   and   Belle/Cute/To Cut/Clitorectomy
And it is What   The Code   Says   The Fems   Wants from Life
A Dumbbell is a   Stick/S/Penis   with 2 Interchangeable Bells/Belles   at it Ends   Indicating Polygamy here
It is the Way to Go for Him Says   The Code   Go Heavy (Eve/He)   Until Breaking the Record (Wreck/Her/D/Pregnant   Wreck Her Until She is Pregnant)

Dump: 3 Fem Letters Start this Word   P/Man Power   Is Behind and She Gets a Dump
D/Hump
D/Pregnant   Humps   She Falls in a Dump of Dump
dump: to fall suddenly   slang for defecating
Switch P for B/Boy Holding All Fem Breasts   and   He Gets Dumb (as The Mother   and   All Fem Letters   plus   a Baby   B/Baby Boy)   Too Young for   The Code   so   Dumb it is (Baby does Not Get it)
Switch D for N/Pregnant and She Gets Numb (3 Fem Letters   Plus   B/Baby)
Switch D for H/Secret Code Letter and Get Hump (Slang for Coitus)
Switch D for P/Man Power and He Gets Pump (Masc Word   Penis In Slang) (Begins   and   Ends   with P/Man Power)
Switch D for B/Boy and He Gets a Bump (Slang for Pregnancy and Coitus)
D/U/Hump   Do/You/Hump   Hump   Dumb   in a   Dump   The Code   Says

Dungeon: D/On/G/On

D/Pregnant   G/Penis Penetration   On (Twice)
Rapes were Common in Dungeons
Don/G/On   Don is Going On with   G/Hymen Penetration   in That Dungeon   on those   N/Ann/Virgins
Dong/He/On   Lots of Poop

Duo: Made of All 3 Fem Letters
DO/O   to Do   O/Fem Hole   is a Redundant Describing Way Pregnant   in American Slang   T/Fem Cross
This is   The Code
The Opening of the   O/Fem Hole   in a   U/You/ Ovulating   Shape   Becoming   The Chalice   Here   While being Under   The Code   Concept
To Do   the/D   O/Fem Hole
duo: two persons commonly associated with each other   couple   a pair
The Code   Makes Sure She is Not Alone   in Doing Her O   With Duo
It is Dodo (Poop) Anyway When Done   Twice
Dodo   4 Fem Letters

Dusky: DSK   He
D/Pregnant   with   Hard C/See/Young Girl/K/Broken Fem Warrior   with   S/Is/As/Has/Ass/His/Us/Hiss/Serpent/Penis   in the Middle
That would be a Big No for   The Code   so
dusky: something dark   gloomy   sad
The Fem Naturally would Stay Away from That

Dwell: DWL   3 Fem Sounds Letters   with 2 LLs/Sweet Fem Love Light/Ill/Ail/Hail/Hell/Elle   as in Plural   or   All of them
D/Pregnant   W/All Fems Sex Active   L/Sweet Fem Love Light/Ill/Ail/Hail/Hell/Elle
Do/Well/Do/Hell/Do/Elle/Do/Ill   D/Well   D/Pregnant   is Well   She is in a   Well
Add Another E/He   and   Get   The Wheel of Time (T/Great Fem Curse)   She Dwells in it Says   The Code
dwell: to live or stay as a permanent resident   reside
In the Well   She Dwells   Ill   Ailing   in Hell   Elle

The Dam Code The Damn Book

Oh/O   D is Well   All/L   is Well   Says   The Code

E   e
Intro
In   The Code   Letter   E/He   is a Masc Letter
E/He   is The Man as an Individual (Compare to A/All Men which is   All The Men)
He/E   Structure Stands Solid
E/He   is a   Strong   Straight   and   Popular Letter
E   With Its Vertical Stick/The Mental   Holding 3 Forms of Knowledge   The 3 Parallel Bars/Sticks   Spiritual   Emotional   Physical
E   Fits into   H   F   L   I   They Reinforce Each Other in   The Code   Grid Pattern
E/He   is Often Anonymous   and   Not Perceived as being there   Especially When it is at The Start of a E Word
E/He   is The Silent Witness   or   Spy   to All Forms of Fems Lives   With its Presence Almost Everywhere
Its Silence Presence Adds to the Mystery of That Letter
Silent   E/He   At the Beginning of a Word Indicates Anonymity   and   a Secret Agenda According to   That Code
Because   E/He   Words are More Complicated to Figure Out Because of that Wild Silent Card   To Understand this   E/He   Chapter Best   It is Especially Important to Rely on The Entire Word Letters Meaning
He/E   as a Man of   The Code   is There   Know it   or   Not
H/Secret Code Letter   is Also a Silent Letter
Superpose   E   to   H/Code Letter   it Creates 2 Squares Sealed Together in a Grid Pattern   With Double Reinforcement in The Middle and The Left Side (More Secrecy from   The Code   to Her)   and   No sound   or   so Little   Just as Real Spies
The Square is The Foundation Flat Shape of a Pyramid   (See # 4 in The Numbers Chapter)   The Square would be the Strongest Most Safe most Stable Form in   The Code
Superpose I/Marriage Act   on top of   E/He   It Also Creates 2 Squares   Creating a Grid Pattern   Also
F/Fem/Fuck   Fits in The Grid Itself   It Could Create 2 Full Squares   with   a Reversed Large Cap   L/Sweet Fem Love Light/Ill/Hell/Elle/Ail   Which is Not Possible because it does Not Exist in Our Alphabet

Lise Rochon

F/Fem/Fuck could have Felt Good about a Fem Alliance with L/Fem   But   No Says   The Code   With a Large Cap   L   Superposing   F   It makes an   E/He   She as a Fem (2 Fems) Still does Not Exist in   That Code
The Dot on top of Small Cap i (The/D/Pregnant   Hot   has Disappeared from   i   to Large Cap   I
Only His/S/Stick/Is/Hiss/Serpent/Penis   is Now Identifying that Letter   I   She Lost a Battle   Not Even Knowing it   Because   She is Too Young
I   is The High (The Eye in The Pyramid)   The Friendly Eye of God Unto Men   The Hi   from   The High   Sweet
I   is the Basic Symbol Used for   I/Stick/Penis   Shape in   The Code
H/Secret Society Silent Code Letter   Here   is 2 Vertical
Sticks   Connected Together in The Middle by a Lien   a Horizontal Bar   All Bars are Masc Symbols   All are Builders of   The Code   Grid Secrets   All United (See # 11 in The Clock and The Numbers Chapters)   Know it   or   Not
He/E   is The One that Carry The Knowledge   and   H/Secret Code Letter   Keeps That Pyramid Grid Together with That Lien
H   being before   E   Teaches it What to Do
In   The Code   The Fem Circle Letters   O   U   C   Supports as Bubbles from the Inside The Foundation of   That Grid Code
eE   fF   hH   iI   l/L   tT   These Letters Modifies When Switching into Large Caps   in Adulthood   When She is Being Assimilated by a   I/Stick
Bb   Dd   Pp   Rr   O/Fem Hole/Circle   have No Power Alone   She Cannot Stand Unless a   Stick/Bar/Masc/I   is Holding Her   as in   B   D   P   R
Q/Stands Alone (See Q in The Letters Chapter) because She is Bleeding Right Now   No One is there for Her
Her Curse Goes On Silently   T/Fem Cross/Great Curse
O/Fem Hole   The No/Number   The o/Zero   is The No Value Number When By Itself/Herself   It Gains Value Only When Placed Behind Any Number from   1 to 9
For Example   0001 Still has The Value of 1   Compare it to 1000   Where   Zero/o   is Behind the 1 with 3 other ooo (Polygamy Included Automatic)   An Immense Difference in Value
Lay Down   E/He   it becomes a   M/Motherhood/Him   It is The Greek Letter Sigma   Sigma has 2 Letters to Represent it   o/O/Fem Hole with a Upper Right Lien   and   c/C/Young Girl

Words with E Letter Sound are He and Letter I in French (i/ Marriage Act)
He/E   Sound   is an Extremely Commonly Used Sound/Word All Day Long in The English/American Language   She   Not so Much Only Specifically
EEE :   the widest proportional shoe width size
The Masc Always So Strong Wins in   The Code

Each: He/Itch   He   She/Shh
He Itch for Each She
Here She is Carried Along as The Silent Shh
There is No Real She in Each   Because there can be No Identity for Her
Only Whores/Horses and the Rest of the Menagerie are Hers
Add P/Man Power and She Gets Peach (Be a Peach/Bitch)

Eager: He/E   G/Penis/Hymen Penetration   Her/R/Hair/Ear/Hear/Here/Heir/Or/Whore/Are/Err/Our/Ere/Air/Sex
When   E/He   is that Close into Sex He gets Eager
eager: ardent in desire
He/Gears for That
Switch E/He and A/All Men for O/Fem Hole and She Gets an Ogre

Eagle: Egg/Hole   He/Goal
The Goal is that Egg that is in that Hole
Some People at the Time Were Angry that the Bald Eagle a Scavenger was Chosen Over the Wild Turkey which would have been a Great Beast (?) for The US Flag
To become Bald is Normal for Men   A Bald Fem No (That Brings Shame on Her)   The Eagle Remain an Entire Masc Identity

Ear: Hear   Here   R/Her/Heir/Or/Whore/Are/Err/Our/Hair/Ear/Hear/Here/Air/Sex
It Corroborates with   The Code   to be in the Present to Hear   That Code   in the Making Through the Flow of Our Words   Hear/R it Right Here
The Fem Does Not Hear The Glass Ceiling   Code
It is All about R/Her (See R in The Letters Chapter)

Earlier: Her/R   Lay   Her/R/Hair/Hear/Ear/Here/Heir/Or/Whore/Err/Are/Our/Air/Sex
Lay   Her/R/Heir/Or/Whore/Are/Err/Our/Ere/Air/Sex   Again
R/Lay/R   The Lay is Surrounded by 2   Heirs   or   Whores
Lay Eggs   Lay Down (Going Down as Usual for R/Her)
L/Sweet Fem Light/Ail/Ill/Hail/Elle/Hell   is With   A/All Men   as a   Her/R/Heir/Whore/Err/Sex
It is a Lay   Another Layer (Lay/Her)   Lying to Her
Watch Words Starting with   E/He   and   R/Her/Hair/Ear/Hear/Here/Heir/Or/Whore/Are/Err/Our/Air/Sex
Early: Her/Lay
When the Man   Comes/Ejaculates   Early   That is Her Lay
Her/R/Hair/Ear/Hear/Here/Heir/Or/Whore/Are/Err/Our/Air/Ere/Sex   Lay (L/Hey)
Err/Lay   As in Erratic Lays (Rape   Polygamy   A Fun Night   etc)
Lay/Her is its Reverse   Another Liar   Another Lawyer   Says   The Code   Lying   Lie/Her   Lay/Her   Lay/Here

Earn: URN   Made of 3 Fem Sound Letters   Urn (See Urn in The Words Chapter)
Her/R/Heir/Whore/Hear/Err/Sex   Ann/N/In/Hen/Virgin
Earn as in Sex   with   a Virgin
Make Her an Urn   A Receptacle (Pregnancy)
Add Y/Wounded Fem and She Gets Yearn (He/Earns from The Urn)
Add B/Boy Holding All Fem Breasts to   Earn/Urn/Rn   and Get Burn   B/Urn   She Cannot Earn from being a Mother   She Will Get Burned
Add T/Fem Cross to Earn/Urn and She Gets Turn (T/Urn   Does Not Earn Anything as an Urn and Being Crossed)
Nocturne is The/Urn in the Night
Modern is   Mode/Urn   For Her   The Code   Never Changes   There is No Escape   Always the Urn   The Earn (Poverty)   and   The Cross/Great Curse

Earrings: Her/Ring   Ear/Ring   Hear/In   Here/In   Plural   Hearings are Round/Circles   The Circle/O/Fem Hole Are Fem Symbols   Ring the Belle   Bracelets (Embrace/Let)   M/Brace   Mom Jewelry Holds Her Together   M/B/Race

The Dam Code The Damn Book

Earth: Hurt   Art
Earth is Made of 2 Masc Letters Except for   T/Fem Cross
E/He   A/All Men   T/Fem Cross   and   H/Secret Code Letter Society Letter
That is What the Secret Societies Secret Art Want to be the Planet Earth   About
Hurt on Earth   Her/T   Her Fem Cross/The Great Curse

Ease: His   He/Is
Ease is All Masc Letters
It Starts with E/He   and   Ends with E/He
Ease Has A/All Men   and   S/Is/His/Ass/Us/Hiss/Serpent/Penis in the Middle
Traveling Light   With Ease For   The Masc Says   The Code
Easy: His/E   Reinforce the Idea of Easiness with Another He/E   for Him   He/See   His/He   Is/He   He/Z
Easy Life for Him Says   The Code   and He Can   Z/Sleep   on it   He/Z   He/Sleep
He/C   Him   and   C/See/Young Girl
That is What He/Sees   Ease/He (Letting Go of a Load)
The Code Support the Man in an Easy Way Entirely

East: His/T   He   Is   T/Fem Cross
The Sun (Son) Rises in the East
Easter: East/Her   He/Is/T/Her
In the East Men   Veil The Fems and Keep Them Pregnant and Isolated
The Great Curse Comes from The East
We Have a Lot of History (His/Story) Coming from the East
Other Ones The Greek   The Romans   The British   The French   The Italians   The Germanics   The Norse   The Spanish   and   More   Have Influenced Our Civilization Also
The   Bible   Buddhism   Hinduism   The Jewish   Books and Many Others   All Influenced the American Language
Easter Date is Precisely Calculated   so   it Match with the Given Birth of Christ Date on Dec 25
Easter is the Celebration of the Egg
A Great Fantasy Day of for Children   A Fun Celebration in the Year   Along with Christmas   Easter is Presented in a Cute Package as

a Chase for Painted Eggs with Candy Inside   Left Behind by a Rabbit (Fertility)
The Egg Is Between Her Legs (L/Egg) as in Pregnancy
Just As Christmas is the Best Day of the Year for Children
It Is Essentially the Celebration of the New Born Baby Boy
As in Motherhood

Eat: It   Hit   Hate   He/It   He/T   # 8 (See Number 8)
He/E   and   T/Fems Curse   are Together
While She is Bleeding   He Hit/Her   Hate/Her   It/Her
Eat That Girl   The Law of   The Code   Jungle Here

Ebb: 3 Masc Letters
He/E   with   2 BBs/All Boys Holding All Fems Holes or/and   Fems Breasts   in Plural or in All of Them
ebb: the flowing back of the tide as the water returns to the sea opposed as flood flow
Ebb is a Formidable Word for   The Code   because
As the Water Recedes it Bring Back with it The Web of   The Code
The Carrying On of The Curse
thesaurus: decline abatement decay decrease degeneration deterioration etc
Ebb in is a Weakening Word for Her

Economy: He   Con   He   Me
Her Con Is His
Big Finance Groups Are Part of those Secret Societies
Few Share or Give Anything
Enslaving is the Word   (In/Sleeve   On the Arms/Harm)

Ecstasy: Egg   Stay   C
C/See/Young Girl Stays with Her Ovulation
It is Ecstasy to Her Says   The Code

Edge: Head   G/Penis Penetration   Had   J/Sheppard
When His Head or His Eyes are On the Hymen   She is on Edge
edge: sharp side of a blade   a line   a border   a brink or verge

The Dam Code The Damn Book

Verge is French Slang for Penis   A Verge is also a Measure   3 Feet of Fabric in a Verge   Never Too Long Says   The Stupid Code Jokes

Eden: ID   N/In/Hen/Virgin
The ID Card and the Freudian ID
The ID here is for Her to Remember Herself as Eve in Eden   Freudian ID is to Search Pleasure
Eve as Letter V/Fem Sex Active (Always Opened)
In Eden Hidden
Switch N for M (They are Interchangeable in   The Code)   And Get   Hid/Him   or   Hid/M/Motherhood
The Code   has Often a Door Where The Masc Escapes For Her Motherhood Stays

Educate: He   Duke   Ate/Hate/# 8   The Assumption is that She is Pregnant and Not Going to School While He Goes to School and Feel   or   is Treated As an Honorable and Respected Masc
ID/U/Gate   The Gate Where U/You/Ovulating Presents ID
Ed/You/Gate   Speaks for Itself   Code
Add Another D/Pregnant to ID and She Gets IDD   I/Died I Did   It Is Entirely Fem here Because   It is the Stick/The Eye in the Pyramid or the Eye/Letter I/i   and   D/Pregnant
She is Dead from the Stick here in IDD in the Word Education

Education: He/Duck/Eon
Him   and   The Duck/Her   for an Eon
Remember that Silly Goose   That Little Girl
The Message is Clear from   The Code   The Duck (D/ Pregnant   Yuck   for an Eon (He/On)

I Cannot Stop Crying in My Heart to have to Write That
Effective: He   Fucked   Eve
F/Fem/Fuck   Or   Fuck   IC/Integrated Circuit   T/Fem Cross   V/ Eve/Fem Sex Active (No Ovulation Time   Available anytime) since Eve   U being the Natural Ovulation   According to The Code (Cod (Fish   Her   with an   E/He
F/Fem/Fuck here Is T/Fem Cross as an Integrated Circuit Since Eve   That is What is Effective   We are Told by   The Code

Lise Rochon

F/Heck/T/Eve
heck: something remarkable of its kind or annoying
He Fucked Eve   That is Effective   Says   The Code
hack: cut   notch   slice   damage
The E/He is Silent here Hiding Behind F/Fem/Fuck

Effervescence: F/Fem/Fuck   R/Her/Heir/Or/Whore/Are/
Sex   Vase   Sense
The Fem as Whore with Her Vase/Uterus/Loins/Chalice/Blood Loss and Her
Sex Life Too   And the Word Sense as in Making Sense of All That
F/Fem/Fuck   R/Her/Heir/Are/Whore/Are/Air/Sex   Vase   Scents
Way Too Much Questions and Knowledge for Her   Here   to Get   so   it
is A Big No from   The Code
Effervescence is just a Bunch of Bubbles Popping Up in the Air/Heir   Not
Much Interest in The Stock Market (Joke) E/He   is Silent here Hiding
Behind F/Fem/Fuck

Effigy: F/Fem/Fuck   or   Fuck   E/He   G/Hymen Perforation/
Penetration
The Fems would be with Him as Sex Partner   A Big Yes from   The
Code   so
effigy: a representation or image especially sculptured as on a
monument   a crude representation of someone used for purposes of
ridicule
F/Fem/Fuck   is in Front of He/E (In Spite of Silent E in the Front)   It is Bad
Says   The Code
There is Always a Down Side   or   a Degradation for Her in the Meaning
of a Word as seen here in the Second Effigy Definition
E/He is Silent Hiding Behind F/Fem/Fuck

Effort: F/Fem/Fuck   F/Forth   F/Fart   F/Hurt   F/Art
The Secret Art for The Fems to go Forth in   The Code   is through
Effort   for Her   To be Hurt   To be Farted On
E/He is Silent here Hiding Behind 2 FFs/Fem/Fuck
The   Code   Says to Her   to make The effort to Go Forth   Bring Her to
be Fucked   or   Farted on   or   to be Hurt   Etc

Egg: E/He   Double 2 GGs/Hymen Penetration in Plural   or   All of Them   or   Him having Sex in Plural   or   Him with Different Fem Eggs   Another Sign   here   The Code   Integrating Polygamy from   He/ Egg   Eggs   are   X/Fallen Fem Cross   Sounds As Devilled Eggs   Eggs Represents   The Fems
The Fems is Always Presented in a Bad Light in   The Code   so   here it Associates Her with the Devil (The/D   Eve   That   Is   Ill)   so   Scary for   The Fems
The Code   Creates Another Concept of Mismatched/Confusing Concepts for Her   Devilled Eggs are Delicious   The Code   Wins in its Association of Adding More Bad Energy on Her   Through that Palatable Bait of Cooked Eggs with Mayo   Slang for Fem Juices in The American English E/G   He/E   G/Penis Penetration
Leg   Lay/Egg   The Code   Nightmare Continues That Way

Eggnog: Egg/Nog
nog: a wooden peg for nails to be driven In
Pierce   Her Egg   Use Something with That Peg (Penis)   that Taste Sweet   and   Sugary   The Fem Likes   Without Questioning Says   The Code   Then She is   The Egg/Her (Eager) Loins   To be Perforated by The Nail which is The Foundation of That Cross   T/Fem Cross/Great Curse   She will Face
Egg Nog is a New Year Celebration Drink   We Savor it in **B**ed   How Convenient for   The Code   Which Takes Advantages of Everything for Ages (Egg/S)   Forced Pregnancies for Her

Ego: He/Go
The Fems have No Ego and No Go (There is No Word Called She Go (Shag/O Is Close) or Her Go) by Themselves Says   The Code   so   He Goes in Full Ego   No Opposition

Einstein: I will Not get in Depth with Jewish Names here But the List is Long   Names Speak for Themselves   Those Names Carry Old History   A Lot of them have Stein (Stain) As Einstein and Rosenstein (The Stain from the Rose (Heavy Fem Symbol) in them
It was Part of the Message   Know It or Not
The Circumcision Carries The Fems Curse in The Masc

Circumcision Diminish His Sex Pleasure   It is As Having Sex in Black and White for Him   And Why would Any Grown up Man Agree to have Part of His Penis to be Cut and Diminished at Birth   and   Call that a Piece of Schmuck   a Loser   a Piece of Garbage   See Schmuck in Dictionary   Schmuck is a Word Full of Negative   Why a Penis has to be   so   Dirty in Signification   by a Religion   Sex being a Natural Phenomenon   as Long as All The Participants are Active in That Decision   Which in The Case of Our Religions is Fully in Charge of Our Sexual Lives According to Their Religious Beliefs

Either: He/T/Her   He/Hit/Her
Him Hitting   T/Fem Cross   R/Her/Are/Heir/Whore/Sex
The Usual Nightmare for The Fems Because
either: one or the other of two
2 Fems Hurt here   or   Hit Twice   Polygamy here is in the Cards for Him   Again
ether: a substance composing all heavenly bodies
(Heavenly as in   Eve/V/Fem Sex Active   N/In/Hen/
Virgin   Lay   Eve/V   N/In/Hen/Virgin   Lay   All Virgins to Lay and be Sex Active   Even/Lay is Close   The Heavenly Bodies are a Haven   Says   That Horrible Code)
Heather is a Fem Name   So Soft So Sweet
Before She Makes To The   Weather/Wet/Her   She has to be   W/Sex Active   as All of The Others
Add K/Broken Fem Warrior (Weakening Her More) and She Gets Kether
"Kether is the topmost of the Sephirot of the Tree of Life meaning crown   Kether is so sublime it is called the Zohar the most hidden of all things   it is also described as absolute compassion and is the source of the n13 Supernatural Attributes of Mercy"
Although I am Not of Jewish Fate   I Accept Religions   Here I Only Give an Example of Where   That Code   Brought Me/Brings Me as I Study/Studied it   This Book is Full Of Those Moments of Tears and Terrors   Jesus Said   Forgive and don't do it again
So   The Code Says to Get that Crown   She has to be a Broken Warrior   or   Lose Her Battles Be Sexual to All   Stay Hidden and be Totally Compassionate but Most   To Remains Hidden even if She is Most Sublime   And She Give Mercy for All That (That Veil Covering Her Face will do that)

The Dam Code The Damn Book

(Mercy   Mère/See   Mere is Mother in French   and   The Ocean is La Mer   See Ocean and Fishes in The Words Chapter)
Chokmah (Shock/Choke/Ma)   Tiphereth (T/If/A/Rate)
I Feel So Sorry about Describing All This   And   I
Apologize   Again   See Ea

Election: He/Lick/He/On   He/Lect/Eon
Lect is a Word Close in Definition to Dialect   Lecture   Those are Linguists Respected Words
The Code   Hides in those   Homosexuality among Men has been a Secret kept from The Fem in Our History   He/Lick/He/On is No Coincidence here   Only Men Voted Then in Elections   Those were Often done in Chambers (Une Chambre is a Bedroom in French) which had Many Secrets (See Either in the Words Section)

Element: LMNT   4 Fems Sound Syllables
Hell/He/Meant   The Code   Says Hell is Her Element
Hell/L/Sweet Fem Love Light/All/Ill/Ail/Hail/Elle   He/E/Meant   and Hell it has been for The Fems
The Dictionary Puts in First Definition of Element as the Sacrament of Communion in The Catholic Religion
element: the bread and wine of the Eucharistic Service   a rudimentary principle of an art   a natural habitat   one of the part of a whole
Elements are Very Important Concepts in Human Consciousness   There are 4 Classical Elements   Earth Air Water and Fire   Other Nations have Added More   The Chinese Added Wood   Others Added eather   "The nature and complexities of all matter in terms of simpler substances"   Also known as aether aither or ether and quintessence   Wikipedia Says   Eather is the material that fills the region of the Universe above the terrestrial sphere   The concept of eather was used in several theories to explain several natural phenomena
The   3 EEEs/He (Many or All of Them)   are Silent Hiding

Elf: LF   Made of 2 Fem Sounds Letters
Hell/L/Elle/Ill/All   for   Her   F/Fem/Fuck
Write it in Cursive (Curse/Eve) The Letter l/L and the F/f have Almost the Same Shape
Letter L is Only on Top of the Line

285

Letter F is Both on Top and Under the Line
Letter F Forming the Shape of a Bow (See BB in The Words Chapter) or # 8/Pregnant
Cursive is As Little Hands Joining the Letters Together
From the Past Into the Future   Also
The Lines Where We Write Separate 2 Different Code Worlds from One to Another
In   The Code   The Conscious is on Top of the Writing Line and the Unconscious is Under The Line   Letter F is Both
Elfish   Here Appears the Fish (See Fish)   It is One of Her Symbols in   The Code   (Fish   F   Shh/She   Ocean   O/She/N)
Elf is Her as   L/Sweet Fem Love Light/Ill/Ail/Hail/Hell/All/Elle   and as   F/Fem/Fuck   She/Shh   That is 3 Fem Entities Together   A Big No from The Code   so
elf: a one of the class of preternatural beings with magical powers given to capricious and often mischievous interference in human affairs   a diminutive person especially a child   a mischievous person especially a child
The Code   Hides LF in Fem Letters Scary Magical Powers
E/He is Silent here but He is a Real Presence
When in Large Caps Letter   Ll and   Fl   are on Top of Each Other   They Form Part of   The Secret Code   Grid Shape
Reverse F and they Make a Square   It is # 4   The # of the Law in The Code   # 4 is the Foundation of the Pyramid   Where the Eye/I/High is with the T/Fem Cross/Great Curse in the Middle   The Cross Inside a Square   The Grid   A Screen Door Pattern is a Very Small Example of the Amplitude of   That Sound Code
E is Silent here But in Full Action Hiding Behind the L and F

Elimination: Hell   He   M/Motherhood   In/N/Hen/Virgin   Nation (Neigh/She/On)
Here the Mother and the Virgin are In Hell as a Nation (Notion)
Hell   Him/M   He   Nation
L/Sweet Fem Love Light/Ill/Ail/Hail/Hell/All/Elle   M   Neigh   She/On
E is Silent here and Hides Behind L/Sweet Fem Light

The Dam Code The Damn Book

Eleusinian Mysteries: Ill/Hell/Ail/Hail/Elle/Letter L/Sweet Fem Light   U/You/Ovulating/Chalice   C/See/Young Girl/Ovulating   N/In/Hen/Virgin   Mysteries
Illusion is Close
Demeter (The/Mother   The Matter) and Her Daughter
Persephone (Pierce the Phone) Were Breaking or Understood   The Code   Here   And Got Punished For That For Ever After
Persephone was Tricked into Going to the Underworld/Hell and was Kept Prisoner there by Hades (Hide/His)
He Tricks Her Out of Her Powers By Stealing One Piece of Her Jewelry at the Time   Until She was Naked and Out of Power   Then He Stroke   He Threw Her in Hell
Here is   The Code   in the Light of Day
E/He is Silent Hiding behind that L/Sweet Fem Love Light

Elevator: Elevate/Her
That would Sound Good for Her
But No   The Concept of the Word Does Nothing to Bring Her Knowledge or Power   Therefore She is Not being Elevated
An Elevator Brings Everyone Up or Down Physically
But She is Not Going Anywhere   it is an Illusion   Commands   The Code
Elevator is a Cover Word here
E/He is Silent here and Creates the Concept of Hell

Elicit: L/Sweet Fem Love Light/Ill/Ail/Hail/Hell/All/Elle
E/He   Sit
elicit: to draw or bring out or forth   educe evoke   to bring to light
Comfortably Sitting   The Code   Brings Forth the Light to Her that Says Hell is for Her
E is Silent here Hiding behind L/Hell

Eliminate: Hell/He/Mean/Hate
The Code   Eliminates The Fems with Hate With L/Sweet Fem Love Light/Ill/Ail/Hail/Hell/All/Elle
E is Silent here   Hiding behind L/Sweet Fem Love Light/Ill/Ail/Hail/Hell/All/Elle

Elite: Hell/It   Elle/L/Hell/Hail/Ill/Sweet Fem Love Light   Hit

Lise Rochon

Hell Hits Her   She is Part of That Elite (Hell/Hit) Says   The Code
The 2 EEs/He (In Plural or All of Them) are Silent here

Else: Hell   See
Hell is Somewhere Else   She does Not See it Says   The Code   to Her
E/He is Silent here   Hiding Behind Elle/L/Hell/Hail/Ill/Sweet Fem Love Light

Elucidate: LUCDT   5 Fem Sound Letters
Hell/You/Sedate
Hell/Elle   U/You/Ovulating   Sedate
Sedated No Fem Can Elucidate or Comprehend Anything
elucidate: to make lucid or clear throw light upon explain
The Code   Means Contraries here to Confuse Her More
Hell/L/Ill   You/U/Ovulating   Young Girl/C/See   Date
Although She Sees Only a Date (A Sweet Dry Fruit   as   All of Them)
There   so   Nothing to Elucidate   No Light here for   L/Sweet Fem
Love Light/Ill/Ail/Hail/Hell/All/Elle   U/You/Ovulating   C/See/Young Girl   and   D/Pregnant
Pain and Abuse from   The Code   Sedates Her   Elle/You/Sedate   All The Way from being a   Young Girl   Ovulating   to   Pregnancy   in Hell/Ill
E/He   is Silent here Hiding Behind L/Sweet Fem Light

Embarrass: Him/M   Bare   Ass   If a Man Finds Himself Undressed He is Embarrassed
M/Motherhood   Bear   S/His/Is/Hiss/Penis/Serpent
The Fem is Embarrassed if She would Think/Wish about having a Penis (The Stick of Power In   The Code)   M/Brace   for That
Him   B/Boy Holding All Fems Breasts   Her/R/Hair/Ear/Hear/Here/Heir/Or/Whore/Are/Err/Our/Air/Sex   Ass/S/Is/As/Has/His/Us/Hiss/Serpent/Penis
The Word Embarrass Starts with   E/He   Silent
This is Not a Book for Children   It is   M/Him   having Sex with   Her/R/Hair/Ear/Hear/Here/Heir/Or/Whore/Are/Err/Our/Air/Sex   (as Whore Not Heir) with a Boy in the Ass   or   with His/S/Is/Us/Ass/Hiss/Serpent/Penis Embarrassing   In/Bar/Ass/Sin   Him/Bear/Ass/In
Him/Bare/Ass   or   His/S/Is/Us/Ass/Hiss/Serpent/Penis   In/N/Virgin

The Dam Code The Damn Book

Humanity Loses its Mind and Heart from being   in Need for
Sex   Not having it   or   Not Enough of it   Not Knowing Enough
about It   and   The Fems are All Bleeding (See Blood in The Words
Chapter)   Men are Afraid of That   and   Ashamed   Not Understanding
Why   Being Puzzled   They Called it   The Great Curse/Fem Cross/T
(See T in The Letter Chapter)
Men of Power in History Made their Own Rules
Sex with Boys was Allowed/Encouraged (See The History of The
Ancient Roman Army Culture) Who Say Sex was Simpler and Even More
Pleasurable with Boys
The Fems were Not Available to Men
Unless   Money   Rape   Marriage   or   Any Man Power   was Involved
The Word Brass (Military Term) is in Embarrass
Embarazada is Pregnant in Spanish
He/E   is Silent here Hiding Behind   M/Motherhood   or M/Another Man
Embarrassing: Him   Bare   Ass/S/Is/As/Has/His/Us/Hiss/Serpent/
Penis   In/N/Hen/Virgin
In His Bare Ass Something Goes In   or   It is Him in His Bare Ass   with
a   N/Virgin
E/He   is Silent here Hiding Behind   M/Mother   or   M/Him (as In
Another Man)
M/Motherhood   Bear   His/S/Is/As/Has/Ass/Us/Hiss/Serpent/
Penis   More Pregnancies for The Mother   Him/Bear/Ass/N   Says   The
Code

Embrace: Him/Brace
The Code   Says Brace Yourself When She Comes with an Embrace (M/
Brace)   No Love Allowed in   That Code   for Her
He/E   is Silent here Hiding Behind   M/Motherhood (His Own or
Others)   or   M/Him (Another Man)

Emotion: He/Motion
He Motions That
motion: power of movement
In Emotion He has the Power of Motion/Movement
E/He   M/Motherhood   O/Fem Hole   Shh/She   On
He/Moo/She/On   Emotions are for The Cows (The Fems)

M/O/She/On   M/Motherhood   O/Fem Hole   She   On   Him/O/She/
On   Him   O/Fem Hole   Shh/She   On
Emotions Are Not Much for a Man
Switch O/Fem Hole for A/All Men and He Gets He/Mate/She/On   He/
Mat/She/On
Emotional: He/Motion/All
E/He   is Silent Hiding Behind   M/Motherhood (His Mother)   or   M/
Him (as in Another Man)

Impair: M/Pair   Him/Pair   M/P/Err   M/Pyre
M/Motherhood   or/and   M/Him   are a Pair   That Could Have been
Good   But No Says   The Code   The Relationship is on a Pyre   or/
and   M/Motherhood   and   P/Man Power   Err   Are Impaired
impair: diminish in ability
He/E   is Silent here Hiding Behind   M/Him (Another Man)   or   M/
Motherhood (May be His Own)

Emperor: M/Per/Her   M/Motherhood for All Fems
Him/Poorer   (See Empire in The Words Chapter)
E/He   is Silent   Hiding Behind   M/Him (Another Man   His Own Father
Here)   or   M/Motherhood (His Own   or   Others)

Empire: M/Pyre   Impair/Her   M/P/Err   M/Pair   M/Père   Him/Père
In the Word Empire She is Erring and Impaired   and   on a Pyre (Fire)
from The Père (Father is a Code Word)   and   Kept in Pairs (Polygamy)
Says   The Code
She has No Chance of Survival in This Empire

Emulate: E/He   Mule   Ate/Hate/# 8 (Pregnancy)
Hate it or Eat it That Mule (See Ann/N/Ane/Virgin as the Donkey in The
Letters Chapter) is there to Emulate(Obey) Her into Pregnancy
E/He   is Silent here Hiding Behind M/Motherhood   or   Another M/Man

Encyclical: N/In/Hen/Virgin   Cycle   C/See/Young Girl   L/All/Hell/Ill/
Hail/Sweet Fem Love Light
Encircle those Virgins in Hell in that Bloody Cycle
Encyclical is a Bad Word for The Fems

The Dam Code The Damn Book

encyclical: *Roman Catholic Church* a Letter addressed by the pope to all the bishops of the Church   intended for wide or general circulation; general
Silent E   is Hiding Behind   N/In/Hen/Virgin here

End: And   Hand
An   Ann   Hen   In   with   D/Pregnant
Which in   The Code   is The End of the Road for Her   Being Pregnant   as a Hen a Donkey and a Nobody (An)
At Hand   or/and   Handy
He/E   is Silent here Hiding   Behind N/In/Hen/Virgin

Ending: N/Ding
To be Dinged is the End for   N/In/Hen/Virgin   The Code   Says
That is Easy because   N/In/Hen/Virgin is a   Thing   or   a Ding   T and D being Interchangeable in   The Code
ding: to cause to make a ring sound   to talk insistently
Switch D/Pregnant for R/Her/Hair/Ear/Hear/Here/Heir/Or/Whore/Are/Err/Our/Air/Sex   and She Gets An/Ann/Hen Ring (R/In   See R in The Letter Chapter)
E/He is Silent here Hiding Behind N/In/Hen/Virgin

Endure: NDUR   4 Fem Sound Letters
In/Dure
N/In/Hen/Virgin   D/Pregnant   U/You/Ovulating   with   R/Her/Hair/Ear/Hear/Here/Heir/Or/Whore/Are/Err/Our/Air/Sex
Dure: hard   severe
When N/In/Hen/Virgin   D/Pregnant and R/Her/Hair/Are/Here/Hear/Ear/Whore/Or/Err/Sex   are Together
It is Bad News here to The Fems from   The Code As Usual
She Will Endure Pain for That
E is Silent here Hiding Behind N/In/Hen/Virgin

Enema: NAMA
N/In/Hen/Virgin   and   Ma/Mother   are Together
With 2 AAs/All Men (The Pyramid Letter   Twice) as in to Join Those 2 Fem Together in   The Secret Code   Knowledge   That Would be a Big No for   The Code   so

enema: the injection of a fluid into the rectum to cause a bowel movement
The Fems is Back here to the Butt and Feces   Again   Ann/Ma
The Code   Says Here that   N/In/Hen/Virgin   is a Donkey   so   is Her Mother/Ma
E/He is Silent here Hiding Behind N/In/Hen/Virgin

Enemy: NME
N/In/Hen/Virgin   M/Motherhood/Him   E/He
N/Hen/Ann/âne/In/Virgin   He   Me
Here in Enemy   She is Both the   Hen/Ann/Chicken   and   Ann/Âne   the Donkey   He/Name/He
Switch N/In/Hen/Ann/Virgin for D/Pregnant and She Gets A/Damn/Dame/He
Nothing Else in   The Code   for Her than to be Damned   or   Shamed   Especially After being Pregnant
N/In/Hen/Virgin   E/He   Me   The Virgin is for Him
N/Virgin   and   M/Motherhood are Enemies of He
N/In/Hen/Virgin is in Between 2 EEs/He (in Plural or All of Them) Ending in M/Motherhood   with a   E/He (A Male Heir)   Being Enemies   The Whole Time
E/He is Silent here Hiding Behind N/In/Hen/Virgin

Energy: N/In/Hen/Ann/Virgin   Urge   He
N/Virgin Urges Him   it is
In/Her/G   Inner/G   In/Her/G
G/Penis Penetration   Gives Her Energy Says   The Code
NRG   N/In/Hen/Virgin   R/Whore/Sex   and   G/Vaginal Penetration
E/He is Silent here Hiding Behind N/In/Hen/Virgin

Engage: N/In/Hen/Virgin   Gage
gage: a challenge   a pledge   a pawn   to measure
Switch G/Vaginal Penetration for C/Virgin and She Gets a Cage   N/Cage
To Put That Virgin in   That Code   Cage is a Measurable Challenge
N/In/Hens/Virgins   Engages in   The Code   Cage   To be Engaged to be Married is a Common Expression Meaning being Fiancés
E/He is Silent here Hiding Behind N/Ann/Virgin
Engagement: N/Cage/He/Meant   More of The Same

N/In/Hen/Virgin in   The Code   Cages to be Engaged
E/He is Silent here Hiding Behind N/Virgin

Engine: NGN
N/Gene
2 NNs/In/Hen/Virgins   Surrounds the Area of   G/Penis
Penetration   They are the Engine of   The Code   here   as in the   N/
Gene
E/He is Silent Hiding Behind N/In/Hen/Virgin

Enjoy: N/In/Hen/Ann/Virgin   G/Penis Penetration   Oy
Add J/Sheppard to Oy
It Creates the Word Joy   Transforming the Oy Meaning from Bad to Good
in Joy (See Letter J   and   The Sheppard)
The Sheep (Her as the Sheep/Ship is   She/Shh   P/Man Power)
She has   The Code   Man Power Behind Her When She is that
Sheep   Sheppard   The Sheep and the Herd (R/Her/Are/Heir/Or/Whore/
Sex   D/Pregnant)
OY is Made of 2 Fem Letters   O/Fem Hole   and   Y/Wounded Fem   A
Wound in The Fem Genitals
Even in Pain 2 Fems Alone in   The Code   Without a Masc Letter
Presence   is Not Allowed   so   It is A Big No
oy: interjection used to express dismay pain annoyance grief etc
The Fems are Supposed to Enjoy Sex as They are Having Dismay Pain
Grief   and will Only Say Oy Oy Oy
E/He is Silent here Hiding Behind N/In/Hen/Virgin
Enjoyable: N/In/Hen/Ann/Virgin   G/Penis Vagina
Penetration   Oy   Able
joy: a state of happiness or felicity   rapture
Be Able to Rupture that Virgin Hymen   Enjoy it with a Joystick
E/He is Silent here Hiding Behind N/In/Hen/Virgin

Enormous: He/Norm/Us
The Code   as Masc Creates Forms and Norms for The Fems (See Domes/
Doom in The Words Chapter)
N/In/Hen/Ann/Virgin   R/Whore/Heir/Err/Sex   M/Motherhood   Us/S/Is/
His/Us/Ass/Hiss/Serpent/Penis

From N/Virgin to Whore to M/Motherhood with S/Is/His/Us/Ass/Hiss/Serpent/Penis as Ending   It is the Norm for The Fems Says   The Code
Makes   Us/S   Enormous (Pregnant)
E/He is Silent here Hiding Behind N/In/Hen/Virgin

Enough: N/In/Hen/Virgin   Off
Being N/In/Hen/Virgin/Ann   or   the Donkey/Âne is Enough for Her
Where there is Enough the N/Virgin is Not There
E is Silent here Hiding Behind N/In/Hen/Virgin

Enter: N/In/Hen/Virgin   T/Fem Cross   R/Are/Whore/Err/Heir/Sex
The T/Fem Cross Enters That Code Door Here as a N/In/Hen/Virgin   And Exit it as a Whore/Sex Object
Ant/Her as in Making Her So Tiny (Tiny is All 4 Fem Letters) No one Sees Her   She is as Small as an Ant
Switch Letter T/Fem Cross for D/Pregnant and She Gets End/Her   That Does it with T (and X)
Switch Letter E/He for U/You/Ovulating and She Gets Aunt/Her (Which Gives Her No Power)   and   Hunt/Her
In Nature the Masc Loves to go for The Fems   But The Code is Torture for Her and Slaughters Her   and it Follows Her Until Her End
The E is Silent here Hiding Behind N/In/Hen/Virgin

Enterprise: Enter/Prize   Enter   P/Man Power   Rise
The Prize goes to The Masc He   P/Man Power   Rises to Big Projects   He has Big Plans
While The Fem Her Gets   End/Her/Prize   (See Enter (End/Her) in The Words Chapter)   or   Hunt/Her/Prize   so   She has it Stolen
E/He is Silent here Hiding Behind N/In/Hen/Virgin

Entertaining: Enter   T/Fem Cross/Great Curse   N/In/Hen/Virgin (Twice   A Rare Event here)   In/N/Virgin
T/Fem Cross/Great Curse/Loss of Blood   Enter   The Virgin   or   Happen to Her   The Code   Calls it Entertainment
Enter/T/Meant   T/Fem Cross   was Meant
Enter (Ant   R/Her/Heir/Or/Whore/Err/Are/Hair/Air/Sex)   Ten/# 10 (See Number 10 in The Numbers Chapter)   Meant

The Dam Code The Damn Book

Around 10 Years Old for Her is Time to be Introduced to   That Fem Blood Loss Nightmare   Code   Game
Switch N for M/Motherhood and She Gets Tame (T/Aim/Ame)   Enter   Tame   N/In   Meant
Motherhood has happened to Her   She is More Tame Now for that Kind of Idiotic Entertainment   She was Meant for it Says   The Code   It is Fun   Hunt/Her   Ant/Her   End/Her
E is Silent here Hiding Behind N/In/Hen/Ann/Virgin

Entire: NTR   N/In/Hen/Virgin/Ann/Virgin   Tie   Her/R/Are/Here/Heir/Or/Whore/Err/Air/Sex
Tie is Letter Sounds   T/Fem Cross   and   i/Marriage Act
Enter/Her   Not Good   For a Virgin to be Tied to Sex
E/He is Silent here Hiding Behind N/In/Virgin
Entirely: N/Tie/Her/Lay   Entire/Lay
Ann/N   Tie   R/Her/Are/Heir/Whore/Sex   Lay
Ann the Virgin is Tied Up to Lay Entirely
Ant/Hire   She is So Small   No One Cares
Aint/Her   It is Not Her Says   The Code
Switch i/Marriage Act for O/Fem Hole and She Gets Into   R/Her/Are/Whore/Sex   Lay   Hourly
That Completes It Says   The Code
The Good Fun Sex for Responsible Adults   does Not Exist in   The Code
E/He is Silent here Hiding Behind N/In/Hen/Virgin

Entity: NTT   Made of 3 Fem Sounds Letters
N/In/Hen/Virgin   and 2 TTs/Fem Crosses (in Plural or All of Them)
For Her as an Entity   Only Crosses Ahead
entity: something that has a real existence
E/He is Silent here Hiding Behind N/Ann/Hen/Virgin

Entry: Ann/Tray   Ant/Ray   Aint/Ray   End/Hand/And   Tray   NT/Ray
Ann/N/In/Hen/Virgin Ray is No More than an Ant on a Tray   No it Aint
Even That Entry is   N/Virgin   as   T/Fem Cross Entering the   NT/Ray   On an Ant Tray
E is Silent here Hiding Behind N/Ann/Virgin/In

Envious: NVS

N/In/Hen/Virgin   and   V/Fem Sex Active   with S/Is/His/Us/Ass/Hiss/
Serpent/Penis   In Plural
Envy/Us   The Code   Says   but   Envious is Made of 2 Fem Letters
NV   with   S/Penis   Is it the Desire for The Penis for Her   or   a
Wish   Envious   Says She is
E is Silent here Hiding behind N/In/Hen/Virgin

Envy: NV   Made 2 Fem Sounds Letters
N/In/Hen/Virgin   V/Fem Sex Active
Envy will Make Her Go from   N/In/Hen/Virgin   to   V/Fem Sex Active
N and V The 2 Fems are Together   They could have a Chat or some
Fun   There are No Masc Letters   That is a Big No from The Code   so
Envy will Create Tensions Between those 2 Fems   They Cannot Really be
with Each Other
The Code   Says The Fems Must Not have Joy or Power in Any
Way   Divide (DVD is All Fems Sound Letters) to Conquer   She was/Is
Barely Aware of it Until Our Modern History

Eon: He/On
eon: 1 billion years   the largest division of geological time
E/He   and   On/N/Virgin
For a Billion Years   It is All About Him and His Manly Sexual Powers   on
N/Young Virgin/Girl   No Power here for The Fem

Ephemeral: Phem (or PHM)   Here Hides in The Sound Fem
E/He   Fem   R/Her/Hair/Ear/Hear/Here/Heir/Or/Whore/Are/Err/Our/Air/
Sex   All
He/Fem/Real
ephemeral: lasting a very short time
E/He is Silent here Hiding Behind Ann/N/In/Hen/Virgin

Equal: He/Quell
The Code Forbids Equality Between Sexes
quell: to suppress   put an end to   extinguish

Era: E/He   R/Her/Hair/Are/Here/Hear/Ear/Whore/Or/Err/Sex   A/
All Men
He   Ra (Egyptian God)

The Dam Code The Damn Book

Hear/A   Here/A   Her/A
It is All about the Masc
era: a period of time
Hera   The Goddess is The Ancient Queen of Heaven   The Daughter of Cronus (See Saturn)
Saturn being the God of Time and Era is   He/Ra   or   Era
Saturn is Bad   He Means   Restrictions Limitations and Authority
Saturn is the Ruler of The Astrological Sign The Capricorn
Saturn Symbol is   T/Fem Cross   with a Reversed Hook (Scythe) Attached to Its Bottom   Saturn is the Alchemical Name for Lead (Heavy)
Alchemy is All About Transforming Lead into Gold
This Symbolically Created The Fems as the Lambs to Sacrifice on the Altar (Halt   Her/R/Sex)

Eradicate: R/Her/Hair/Ear/Hear/Here/Heir/Or/Whore/Are/Err/Our/Air/Sex   Dick   Ate/Hate/# 8/Pregnancy
eradicate: to remove or destroy utterly
A Whore Eat His Dick for a Heir or Not   It is Eradicated   Nothing Happened   Nobody Remembers   The Code   Acts That Way

Eraser: He/Raise/Her   No Way   The Code   does Not Allow That
Her/Ace/Her   No Way (See Ace in The Words Chapter)
To be with   a Heir   or be a   Whore   or have   Nice Hair   does Not Ace Her
Her/Ease/Her   No Way   He/Race/Her   No Way   The Masc does Not Race with The Fems   He/Rise/Her   No Way   No Says   The Code   Not Allowed
R/Ass/R   Her/Ass/Her   No Way   Is it
Polygamy   Lesbianism   Homosexuality   As Whores too   No One Talks About   so   The Code   Erased Her All

Ergo: Go
Her as   Her   with   Heir   or as a   Whore   or to   Err   is the Sentence (Literally) Connector (Connect/Her   to The Sentence)   Here/Go
ergo: sentence connector   hence   therefore
E/He Is Hiding Behind Her/R/Heir/Whore/Err/Sex

Eros: He/Rose   He Unites with the Rose (See Rose Rosicrucian)   The Code   Uses The ultimate Fem Symbol   The Rose   To Represent His Own Male Sexuality
Eros: ancient God of love as physical love   sexual desire
He/Rose   Hear   S/Is/His/Us/Ass/Hiss/Serpent/Penis   Here/Us   Heir/S/Is   Heir/Is   Heir/His   It is All About Him and His Heir
He/Ross   Ross is Dark Red Color   Dry Blood Color (See Rosicrucian in The Words Chapter)
E/He is Hiding Behind R/Heir/Whore/Her/Sex

Erotic: Her/O/Tick
Her   O/Fem Hole   is On a Clock   And is Ticking Says   The Code
E/He is Silent Hiding Behind Her/R/Heir/Whore/Err/Sex
A Tick is an Annoying Blood Sucking Insect
Her Hole Says   The Code   is Blood Sucking

Err: R/Her/Hair/Ear/Hear/Here/Heir/Or/Whore/Are/Err/Our/Air/Sex   Hair   Heir   Air   Hear   Her   Our
The Glass Ceiling is Hiding in   Her/Hair
Some Fem Can See it a Little   But do Not Hear It (Hear   R/Her
err: hesitation   uncertainty   to go ashtray
(A/She/Tray)

Erratic: Heir/Hat/IC
The Heir is in the Hat (as in being Successful) as in an Integrated Circuit
It is the Art of The Secret Code
The E is Silent here Hiding behind R/Her/Whore/Are/Air/Err/Sex
Here/At/Hic   As in being Drunk   So   No One Remembers Especially The Fems

Error: RR   Err/Her
Here She is the Error   Err/R/Her   Some More   In the R/Her/Are/Heir/Or/Whore/Hair/Err/Sex   Code
R/Sex   Has Cemented the Existence of   The Code
Error is a Rare Word   Letter R/Whore/Her/Sex   Twice   Creates The Word
Here 2 RRs/Hers/Sex (As in Plural or All of Them)   is Called an Error   because   it Relates to   Her/Heir or   Heir/Her   or   Her/

Whore   Etc   That Would be a Big No From   The Code   for Her   to Know Anything or Own Anything   Not Even Air   Especially Not an Heir   on Her Own   No   so
Her/Hair   Her/Heir   Are/Whore   Etc   Those are Covers From   The Code   to   R/Her
R/Her/Hair   Is in Her Hair   It is In Her Heir   It is in Her Air   It is in Her Ear   Or   (Or is Gold In French)   Hear   It Ends with The Whore in the Air   to Err   or   Another Heir
The Word Whore has a Way of Appearing in Words
An Heir was the Most Important Thing to All Fems
To Give One to the Husband for Her Protection in Older/Ancients Civilizations
In Some Desert Tribes in the East The Fems were Abandoned in the Desert with a Loaf of Bread   if   She was Barren   It is a Prison The Fems Could Not Escape
Talaak Talaak Talaak Said 3 Times by a Muslim Man   and   He is Divorced Legally From His Wife   Thrown in the Street She is   No Access to Money   Loss of Honor   Repudiated by Family   Uneducated   That is a Long Time Error   Some Called it a Tradition From those Old Religious Beliefs
When Her Hymen is Broken   She is Dirty to Touch   Back then Was No Antibiotics   And Natural (Called Unsafe Sex Now) Sex was More Safe
E/He is Silent here Hiding Behind   R/Her/Heir/Or/Whore/Err/Sex
Error is a Cover Word here

Escape: S/Is/As/Has/Ass/His/Us/Hiss/Serpent/Penis   Cape   Penis Under a Cape   A Penis Cover   That is The Escape for Him in   The Code   A Superman
Both 2 EEs/He (Plural or All of Them) are Almost Silent   One Starts   and   One Ends The Word Escape   An Extra Escape for   The Code Man
Escape is a Cover Word here

Escort: S/Court
Courting   S/Is/Has/Ass/His/Us/Hiss/Serpent/Penis   That is the Job of the Escort
S/Score   T/Fem
Penis Scores with   T/Fem Cross

Lise Rochon

Escort   S/Is/His/Us/Ass/Hiss/Serpent/Penis   K/Broken Fem Warrior   or   Hard C/See/Young Girl   Her/R/Heir/Whore/Err   T/Fem Cross
S/Core/T
S/Is/As/Has/Ass/His/Us/Hiss/Serpent/Penis   goes to the Core of   T/Fem Cross   She is Escorted
E/He is Silent Hiding Behind S/Is/As/Has/Ass/His/Us/Hiss/Serpent/Penis (Plural or All of Them)

Escrow: S/Crow
Where There Would be a Crow   There are Many   Crows are Intelligent   The Code   Said They are Some Kind of No Good Old Dark Fem Symbol
A Crow With the Word S/Is/As/Has/Ass/His/Us/Hiss/Serpent/Penis Together would be a Big No in   The Code   for Her   So
escrow: a contract deposited with a third person promising the fulfillment of some condition
Escrow is a Safe Word in Business   No One Questions it
Un Escrow is a Criminal in French
Escrow is a Cover Word here
E/He is Silent here Hiding Behind S/Is/As/Has/Ass/His/Us/Hiss/Serpent/Penis   or   Plural   or   All of Them

Especially: S/His/Ass/Is/Us/Hiss/Serpent/Penis   Pay   She/Shh   All/L/ Sweet Fem Love Light/Ill/Ail/Hail/Hell/Elle
    He/E
More of the Same   His Penis Pays Silent She
E/He is Silent here Hiding Behind Ass/S/Is/His/Us/Hiss/Serpent/Penis (Plural   or   All of Them)

Essence: Ass/S/Is/His/Us/Hiss/Serpent/Penis   In/N/Hen/Virgin   C/See/ Young Girl
Hence   His Penis is with a Virgin   Hence it is His Essence   Ass is Slang for Sex (To Get Some/A Piece of Ass)
His/Sense   Hiss is S The Snake Sound Letter
His/S/Is/Us/Ass/Hiss/Serpent/Penis   Sense
S/Penis   is Making Sense Being the Essence
S/In/Since   A/Sin/C   A/All Men   Sin   C/Virgin

300

The Dam Code The Damn Book

Penis   In/N/Hen/Virgin   Since (Sin/S   Or   Sin   C/See/Young Girl)
His/S/Is/Us/Ass/Hiss/Serpent/Penis   Scents   His Penis Scents is as Incense Says   The Code
essence: basic inevitable nature
E/He is Silent here Hiding Behind S/Penis

Essential: His/S/Is/Us/Ass/Hiss/Serpent/Penis   Sin   She/Shh   All Mix Together   The Penis The Sin and All of She as Silent
The Code   Gets Essential Ingredients here to Maintain The Curse in Place
A   Scent   She/Shh   All
His/S/Is/Us/Ass/Hiss/Serpent/Penis   N/In/Hen/Virgin   Shall   Shawl   A Must to Veil
To Confirm   The Code   Concept here Add   E/He a Masc Letter at the End of Essential and He Gets
Essentially: S/Sin/She/All/He   or   Ass/Central
E/He is Silent here Hiding Behind S/Penis
Establish: His/S/Is/Us/Ass/Hiss/Serpent/Penis   T/Fem Cross   Ebb   Leash
ebb: a flowing backward or away   decline or decay   a point of decline
Ass/S/Penis   Tab   Leash
The Fems as   T/Fem Cross   is Leashed to that   S/Is/His/Us/Ass/Hiss/Serpent/Penis   and She is On Tab
For Her Being Established Says   The Code   Means to go Backwards and to Decay
E/He is Silent here Hiding Behind S/Penis

Esteem: His/Team
Us/S/Is/His/Ass/Hiss/Serpent/Penis   Team
How Appropriate for   The Code
esteem: to regard highly or favorably
Ass   T/Fem Cross   Him/M/Motherhood
His/T/Him   T/Fem Cross   is Surrounded by   A/All
Men   Penisses   Asses   and   Pregnancies
S/His Team has Esteem   and   Has Steam   TM   T/Fem Cross   and   M/Motherhood
STM   His/S/Is/Us/Ass/Hiss/Serpent/Penis   T/Fem Cross   M/Motherhood

301

Lise Rochon

E/He is Silent here Hiding Behind   The Code   S/Hiss/His/Serpent/Penis

Eternal: He/Turn/All
E/He   T/Fem Cross   Her/R/Hair/Ear/Hear/Here/Heir/Or/Whore/Are/Err/Our/Air/Ere/Sex
N/In/Hen/Virgin   A/All Men   L/Sweet Fem Love Light/Ill/Ail/Hail/All/Elle/Hell
He/T/Urn/All
The Code   Says All Fems   as   T/Fem Cross   are Urns (See Urn in The Words Chapter) and Are Turned Into Urns That Turns   He/T/Her/N/All   and   It is Eternal
Hate/# 8 (Pregnancy)/Ate/Hate   Her/R   In/N/Hen/Aâne/Virgin   L/All/Hell/Elle/Sweet Fem Light
Hither   Heather   Ether   Either   so Much   Code   Fem Energy)   Nell   All The Same to Her
E/He is Silent here Hiding Behind T/Fem Cross
Add W/All Fem Sex Active   and She Gets that Message as Sure as The Weather

Eternity: Hit/Her/Knit/He   Hit/Her/Knight/He   He/Tear/Night/He
He   T/Fem Cross   Her/Whore   Night   He
Eternity is a Long Time for Hitting and Tearing The Fems
Turning Her Since an Eternity into Urns and Whores
And Keeping Her in the Night of Ignorance About it All
The Knight Represents here a Figure of Authority
E/He is Silent here Hiding Behind T/Fem Cross

Ethic: Hit/IC
That Would Be Ethical According to The Code to Hit
C/See/Young Girl or K/Broken Fem Warrior
Hate/IC is Ethical too
Hat/IC   The Code is in the Hat (See Hat)   Attic
He/Tick   E/T/IC
E/He and T/Fem Cross are in a IC/Integrated Circuit   It is Ethical for a While (The Clock is Ticking)
To have More Ethical Natural Unions Between a Masc and a Fem Sounds Wonderful   But the Only Letter Chosen for that Role here is T/Fem Cross   Which Makes It Definitely Unethical

ethic: the body of moral principles or values governing a particular culture
Note that in Ethic E/He is Pronounced Clearly as in Governing Openly   Not Secretly
Ethical: Hit/He/Call   Hate/He/Call   Hat/He/Call
That Hate   and   that Hit Towards Her Come from   That Code   Hat He/Tick/All   For a While   A Tic is a Bug   Not Good to Stay there Long   and   The Clock is Tick/Ing Anyway

Eunuch: UNQ   Made of 3 Fem Sound Letters
eunuch: a castrated man
Here 2 UUs/Uterus/Open Loins Surrounding   N/In/Hen/Virgin Which Ends with Q/Her Loss of Blood (Period)
The Eunuch Watches the Virgin Until She Bleeds for the First Time   She will be   U/You/Ovulating   Soon After that   As in Not a   N/In/Hen/Virgin   Anymore

Euphemism: U/You/Ovulating Uterus   Fem   Is/His/S   M/Him/Motherhood
You/U   Fem   Ism
ism: a distinctive doctrine theory system or practice
Her Uterus is the Ism in   That Code
euphemism: an agreeable word or expression substituted for one that is potentially offensive
The Starting E/He is Completely Silent here

Evacuation: Eve/A/Queue/She/On
Eve is Always in Queue for Anything Good for Her   It is a Big No from   The Code   so   Evacuated She is
Eve is in a Queue to be Evacuated   Evacuation is a Word for Pooping Also   Evacuation Starts with Eve/V/Fem Sex Active   Ladies (Laid/S) First

Evaluate: He/Value/Hate
Eve   All   You   Hate/Ate
He   Val   You   Hate/Ate
He   Valley   Hate/Ate
E/He   V/Fem Sex Active   All   U/You/Ovulating   Hate

Eve is   V/Fem Sex Active   Since Eve (See The Parallel Between V/Fem Sex Active   and   U/Uterus/You/Natural Ovulation Time in The Letters Chapter)
The Word Evaluation Brings the Word Hate (as in Eating it too)
with   Eve   and (or in the)   Valley
Not a Positive Place for Her to be Evaluated
for The Fems It is All about being Hated   and   being Hit
The Code   is in Full Action here

Evasive: Eve   Is/S/His/Us/Ass/Hiss/Serpent/Penis   Eve
Eve   Is   Eve
The Code   is Adamant about Eve being an Ass   or   being
Treated   As   One
He/Vase/Eve
Eve as a Vase (See Urn in The Words Chapter)
Vase is Mud in French   and   a Vase Also
E/V/S/V
His/S/Ass/Is/Us/Hiss/Serpent/Penis   is in Between   2 VVs/Fems Sex Active
Eve is a Sieve
Evasive
Eve/Ace/Eve
Eve: Eve is the Letter Word for Letter V/Fem Sex Active as in the Ovulating Eve
E/He   V/Fem Sex Active   E/He
V/Eve   Is Surrounded by   2 EEs/He (Plural or All of Them)   She is Powerless Against that Force
V/Eve   and   2 EEs/He   Penetrates All Fems
Those are Strong Concepts for Eve
Eve is a Very Important Word   Eve being the Mother of All   Says The Catholic Religion
Eve has a Similar Shape as the Also Very Important Code Word Eye
Eye is I/High/Eye/The Stick in the Pyramid
EVE   EYE
The Code Pictures The Fems as a Real Natural Stick Too Which is the Letter I/Eye   Her Stick will be Axed into the Y/Wounded Fem as the First Step in Breaking Her Eye/Stick/Letter I Says   The Code   As The Split Continues   She becomes V/Fem Sex Active   Then Her Stick Splits

The Dam Code The Damn Book

More in   L/Sweet Fem Light/Ill/Ail/Hail/Elle/Hell   To Eventually Separate in 2 Separate Sticks that will Sticks Back to the Other in K/Fem Broken Warrior   (The Stick Broken in Two is The Fem Symbol   The Unbroken One   The Upright Stick is The Masc Symbol)   When the Battle is Over   She Will Have Sex for a Heir   or   as Whore in   R/Her/Are/Heir/Or/Whore/Err/Sex   or   She Will Err
Then   She Will be Nailed (Nail/Nell/Nil   D/Pregnant) (Nail NL is Made of 2 Fem Sound Letters) on the Cross in T/Fem Cross   and   She Will Die in X/Axe/Fallen Cross
In Aramaic   Eve Serpent and Instructions are Closely Allied   Hawahi   Ahawa   Hewya
That Code   Proves Again that it Has Infiltrated All Levels of Our Language Add   R/Her/Hair/Are/Here/Hear/Ear/Heir/Whore/Or/Err/Sex to Eve and She Gets Ever   Eve/R   VR   V/Fem Sex Active   and   R/Heir/Whore/Err/Sex   Unites for Ever
That Code   is a Chain of Symbols Repeating Itself Endlessly in Different Forms and Shapes   There is an Overwhelming Amount of Them   A Kaleidoscope of This Kind of Concepts   We are So   Surrounded by it   We do Not See it
Every   Eve/Ray
Eve   Her/R/Heir/Whore/Are/Err/Sex   A/All Men
Eve Has a Light as Long as She Has Sex All the Time with All Men
Every Day   Eve/Her/Day
Eve   R/Her   Day/D/Pregnant
Eve has Her Day as Long as She has Sex Every Day   and   Get Pregnant
E   V   R   E   D
Eve/Red/He   Eve/Read/He
Red is the Color of Stimulated Sex organs
Heave/Her/Day
heave: a fling   to rise or lift with force   a throw   a toss   a cast
To Heave Eve is Scary and Dangerous for Her Health and Sanity
Even if it was Just a Fling   Whores Cannot have Flings Says   The Code or Will be Outcast
And that Word Heaven is So Close   Just Add Another Virgin/N to Eve Switch Letter E/He for A/All Men and get
ave: hail   welcome   good bye   farewell
Just Arrived   And Gone Already
Ave Maria: Eve/V   Marry/Merry   A/All Men

305

Lise Rochon

All Fems Get Married Merrily with a Man that is Not there
An Eve is the Night Before an Event   As   Christmas
She is Again in the Night   and   Not a Part of That Event

Even: Eve   N/In/Hen/Virgin
Eve in   The Code   is Represented with   V/Fem Sex Active
Generally it would be VN   2 Fem Letters   But No   It is Subtle Here
Because   E/He   is Not Entirely Silent in   Eve/N
Eve/In   As in   V/Fem Sex Active   and   Ann/N/In/Hen/Virgin   Not
E/He   V/Fem Sex Active   N/In/Hen/Virgin   Yes
With the Help of   E/He   Ann/N/In/Hen/Virgin   is Now a   V/Fem Sex Active   It makes it Makes it Even Says   The Code   Almost Heaven
(Heaven being Where Everything is Equal   and   Happy)
Switch E/He for O/Fem Hole and She Gets Oven   (Lots of Heat on Her)
Reverse VN and She Gets Envy NV   Which is a Direct Contradiction with Even
E/V/N
E/He   is with   V/Eve/Fem Sex Active   as   Ann/N/In/Hen/Virgin   All Even
Even is Also   E/He   V/Fem Sex Active   E/He   N/In/Hen/Virgin   While
V is Surrounded by 2 EEs/He (In Plural or All of Them)   the N/Virgin is Alone (Therefore Weak)
With EVN   2 Fem Types   V/Sex Active   and   N/Virgin   are Following the Lead of   E/He
To Make it Even for Him (He Deserves More) The Code   Throws a Polygamist Symbol there   Again
In History The Fems Were Never Left Alone   Even in Tents   or   Going to the Market   Anywhere   In Some Countries It Is Still a Custom   Put a Sheet on Top of Her Head   Keep Her Weak (She Cannot Breathe/See in There) Under that Veil (VL   2 Fem Sound Letters)   She is Vile Says   The Code
Une Ville is a Town in French   Make it Popular and Known Says   The Code

Evening: V/Fem Sex Active   and   N/Virgin   are Together   with He/E
E/He   V/Eve/Fem Sex Active   In/N/Hen/Virgin   In/N/Virgin   Two Virgins are In   with Him

The Dam Code The Damn Book

EVNN   Eve   Ann/N/In/Hen/Virgin   Twice
V/Fem Sex Active   is with   2 NNs/Virgins (Plural or All of them   Almost a Ring   A Ning
It is Night Time Now   The Only Place Where The Fems Belong Says   The Code
Nothing Happens in The Night   Except Motherhood   and   Troubles

Event: Eve/Aint   Eve/Ant
Either She is as Small as an Ant   or   She Aint there   for the Event   Nothing Nice Never Happens to Her Says   The Code
On the Other Hand   Event is a Place Where   He/Vent (s)
Switch T/Fem Cross for D/Pregnant and She Gets Eve/End   Not a Good Event for Her   Again
Ave (Have He)

Ever: Eve/V/Fem Sex Active (Eve is Mother of All   Says   The Code)   Her/R/Hair/Ear/Hear/Here/Heir/Or/Whore/Are/Err/Our/Ere/Air/Sex
E/He   V/Fem Sex Active   Her/R
For Ever is   Eve/V/Fem Sex Active
E/He   is in Charge with   2 EEs/He (Plural or Al of Them) Encircling V with being   R/Heir/Motherhood   or   a R/Her/Whore   or   R/Her/Err
E/He   is Almost Silent therefore Almost   Invisible Hiding Behind V

Everest: Eve/Rest   on   an Icy Mountain   Reminds Us of the Popular Fem Frigidity Word
Frigidity is When a Fem Refuses Sex   because   of Abuse   or   is Overwhelmed by Something   or   She had Too Many Pregnancies   or   The Love Stopped etc
Everest is a Far Away Place   and   so Cold for Eve to Rest   She would Never Go/Get there   As a Fem I would have Chosen a More Accessible/ Warmer Friendly with More Possibilities But   The Code   Said No   A Long Time Ago
3 EEEs/He (All of Them) are almost Silent here Hiding

Every Day: Eve   Her/R/Heir/Whore/Err/Sex   Day/D/Pregnant
Days (Daze/Daisies)   Hours (Ours/Whores)   Minutes (Mine/ Hits)   Month (Mount)   and   Year (You/Here/R)
Targeted to All Fems   Since Eve

307

E is almost Silent here Hiding Circling   V/Fem Sex Active

Everywhere: Eve/V/R/Her/Heir/Whore   He/Letter E
(Ever/He)   Where/Were or Wear Are Interchangeable Here and Enhancing Each Other in Different Ways
Eve and Sex as a Whore with Him is Everywhere in The Code
E/He   is Part of   V/Eve   as in IC   Means Integrated Circuit   so   to   Postulate   All Words Starting with   E/He   and   V/Eve   Together are an IC
E/He is almost Silent here Hiding and Circling Around   V/Fem Sex Active   The Code   is Everywhere

Evidence: Eve/He   Dense/Dances
He/E   V/Fem Sex Active   D/Pregnant   Hence
The Code   Evidence is that   R/Her   is Ready for Sex   Hence She should be Pregnant   It is a Dense Dance for Eve
Dance with a Damsel (Damn/Dame   Sell)
Eve/V/Fem Sex Active   The/D/Pregnant   Ants
All Fems are Pregnant Ants   It is The Evidence Says   The Code
Eve/He/Dance
Double   E/He is   Almost Silent here Hiding and Circling V/Eve   Wanting Sex   It is Evident

Evil: He/Veil   He/Vile   He/Will
vile: repulsive   disgusting
This is What She Meets as Oppositions from   The Code
All the Way from E to the Veil   Evil is Disgusting and Repulsive   So is The Veil
Eve   Ill/All/Hell/Ail/Elle/Hill/Hail   Says   The Code
Eve that is   Ill   in Hell   Ailing
hill: small mountain
Mount/N/Ann   Mount/In   Mount/An   Month/N
An   as   In   or   Any   or   Ann/He   or âne/He   Annie
Annie is Any   Ann N/In/Hen/Virgin   She is the Donkey   All Over   Again
She is Back to The School of   Fishes   Hens   and   Cows
And Evil has Succeeded as in to   Avail   A/Veil
The Veil Makes Itself Present in Prevail (Pre/Veil) (See Prevail)   The Veil Appears Suddenly   or in Code   Time

Evil: EVL
E/He   V/Fem Sex Active   i/Marriage Act   L/Sweet Fem Light
Switch V for W (Which are Interchangeable in   The Code as is   M and
N   D and T   and Some Others) and She Gets
E/He/Will   (as in to   He/Veil   He/Vile   in the Future)
vile: depraved   despicable
To be Violated   That is Evil
Evil In Reverse Spells Live
Making the Word Live a Cover Word
Add D/Pregnant and She Gets Devil (D/Evil   The EveThat is Ill)
Devilish: Devil   Is   She/Shh
Make it Fun   So The Girls will be Attracted   it Works
Oval (is in a Shape of an Egg)   and   Ovule   are so Close
OVO   (Funny Face)
Eves   Holes   (See Lilith)

Evolution: Eve/V   Hole   U/You/Ovulating   She   On
Eve Ovulation   Is Evolution Says   The Code
She/On is Not a Word but Eon (He/On) will Absorb it (Her) Anyway   As Usual
Evaluation is so Close   The Solution
Evolve: He/Vulvae
vulvae: external female genitalia
He/E   is There   The Code   Never Allows The Fem to Be Alone   or   to Think or to Own Anything   Including Her Genitals
Her Vulvae is in the Shape of a Rose
The Red Rose Is the Symbol of The Secret Society The Rosicrucian (As the Name Says   The Rose   and   The Cross (Crux)) Together
The Goddess Venus Flower is the Rose
To Deflower a Fem is to
All those Terms Help Us Understand which Flower   The Code   is Talking About

Evolution: Eve   Hole   You/U/Uterus   She   On
Evolution Happen That for   That Code   Eve Holes and Loins are Opened Permanently (No More Ovulation Time for Her as The Other Mammals do)   as She Goes On

Exact: X/Act
Implying Anonymity   E/He   is Silent Hiding Behind X
The Code   Anonymity
X/Fallen Fem Cross Involves Death
A Dead Act here is What is Waiting for Her in Exact
As Exact as   That Code   Is   Eggs/Act
Add O/Fem Hole and She Gets an Exacto (a Sharp Cutting Knife)   Do Not Mess With   The Code
Letter E is Silent here   Letting The   X Act   Happen

Example: X/Fallen Fem Cross   Ample   Eggs/Ample   Axe/Ample
Plenty of   X/Fallen Fem Crosses   Examples for Her from   The Code
In Example   He/E   is Silent in Front of   X/Fallen Fem Cross   Implying Secrecy
XM (2 Fem Letters) Exam is Part of Example as in   The One Dead on That   X/Cross   is   M/Motherhood
E/He is Silent here Hiding Behind The Axe (X) of The X/Fallen Fem Cross

Excel: X/Fallen Fem Cross   Hell
A Dead Fem goes to Hell   Excel to That Says   The Code   To Her
Switch E/He for A/All Men and He Gets X/All (Kill Them All on That X/Fallen Cross)   or   Axe/All
Eggs/Hell   Eggshells (Walk on Those)
E is Silent here Hiding Behind X/Fallen Fem Cross   The Axe

Excellent: Excel   Aint/Ant
If She is an Ant   or   She Aint   There
To Excel Cannot Happen To Her
X/Axe/Fallen Cross   Hell/L/Ill/Ail/Hail/Hell/Elle   Ant/Aint   and   X
Denies it or is too Small to Understand it
Eggs   Hell/L/Sweet Fem Light   Aint/Ant
The First Letter of Excellent is E/He and is Silent
Implying Secrecy   or/and   Hidden Means

Exception: X/Ape/She/Eon
She as   X/Fallen Fem Cross Under The Axe   is an Ape for an Eon   It is an Exception Says   The Code
E/He is Silent here Hiding Behind X/Axe/Fallen Cross

Exchange: X/Change
The Code   Says to The Masc   Change One Older   or   Destroyed Fem   for Another Fem
Married Men Have Exchanged Fems/Wives from One to the Other   As it is a Natural Thing to Do
Medical Science   Ovarian Cancer is Caused by the Masc Partner Having Sex with Other Fems
Eggs/Hinge   Eggs/Ange (Un Ange in French is an Angel (See Angle as in the Fifth Angle of the Freemasons)
E/He is Silent here Hiding Behind X/Axe/Fallen Fem Cross

Exhibition: Eggs/He/Be/See/On   Eggs/A/B/C/On
X/Axe/Fallen Fem Cross   E/He   Be/B/Boy Holding All Fems Breasts   She/Shh   On
The Fems goes on as   X/Fallen Fem Cross Under The Axe
An Exhibition is a Public Display   How Convenient for   The Code
Showing Her Boy and Her Breasts in the Mind of Men and Boys   and   She is Mum (Shh) about it
E/He is Silent here Hiding Behind X/Axe/Fallen Cross

Excited: X/Cited
That Could have been a Positive Term for X/Fallen Fem Cross
But No   The Code   Says She is Cited here
X/High/T/ID   X is High about Her Fem Cross ID
X/Hide/Ted   Eggs/Height/It
E/He is Silent Here Hiding Behind X/Axe/Fallen Fem Cross
Exciting: X/Axe/Dead T/Fem Cross/Fallen Cross (See T in The Letters Chapter)   Hide   In/N/Hen/Ann/Virgin
What is created by   The Code   is   X/Fallen Fem Cross   Playing Hide and Seek with   N/Ann/Virgin   and   Both have No Idea What is going On   They are Excited
Eggs/Height/In   Eggs/See/Thing   The Code   Says Her Ovulation Brings Her to Feel Tall   She Sees Things
E/He is Silent Here Hiding Behind X/Fallen Fem Cross Under The Axe/X

Excrement: X/Cream/Ant
X/Axe is the Fem Fallen Cross Letter

Cream is Commonly Known as Sexual Fem Juices   or   Something
Nicer   As The Cream on The Cake
Ant   Aint   Aunt (Fem)   are Fem Nicknames in   The Code   for Her
Sex Known as Taking a Shit is an Old Vulgar Reference to having Sex with a
Fem Nothing New Here
Excrements here is a Dead Ant Cream   That is Little
Ant   is Also   Aint   So there is Nothing there at All for Her
Therefore   Erasing/Minimizing the Word Excrement Meaning into The
Fem Mind
The Code   Men Have Given Sex Very Little Importance   Not to Honor
The Fems   He is having Sex With
The Code   is All about Having Sex with All Fems as Soon As Possible and
make Them D/Pregnant   Poor   and   Powerless   as Soon as Possible
The Fem is Identified as   Whore/Her/Heir/R/Are/Err/Sex
She is Merely a Sexual Domestic (Dome/He/Stick   The Domes
are Her Ever Expendable Breasts) along with being a Maid without
Pay   Power   and   Being an Excrement (See Feces   Faces)
Letter E is Silent here Hiding Behind X/Axe/Fallen Fem Cross

Exist: Eggs/X/Axe   Is/His/S (Hiss of the Serpent as in Sex)   T/Fem
Cross
The Fem Cross Exist Through the Egg (Which is the X/Fallen Fem Cross
Under the Axe) or the Ovulation (Egg)
Letter E/He is Silent here Hiding Behind X/Axe/Fem Fallen Cross   to Exist

Excrete: X/Create
It is Impossible for X/Fallen Fem Cross to Create Anything at this Point
of Her Life (She is Dead in X)   so   it is Excreted   In a Crate (That is
Thick)   or   Eliminated   or   Separated   or   Discharged from an
Organic Body   The Code   Says
excrete: to separate and eliminate from an organic body   to
discharge   to eliminate
E/He is Silent here Hiding Behind X/Fallen Fem Cross (Dead Matter   Dead
Mother)
X/Eggs

Excuse: X/Q/Use   X/Q/S

The Dam Code The Damn Book

Q/Menstrual Cycle   and   X/Fallen Fem Cross Under The Axe   The Excuses for   The Code   to Use Her
X/Q/Us
Add Whore/R/Heir/Her/Are/Err/Sex and She Gets X/Curse   X/Fallen Fem Cross is Cursed
X/Cues   Are   Clues for the Excuse
E/He is Silent here Hiding Behind X/Axe/Fallen Fem Cross (Dead   Matter   Mother)

Existence: X/Is/Tense
X/Fallen Fem Cross   is Always Tense   It is Her Existence
    The T/Great Curse Deadens Her
Axis/Fem Cross   Hence (See Axis in The Words Chapter)   The Axe is The Axis (Axe/His/Is/S)
Eggs/Is/Stance
stance: the position or bearing of the body while standing   a mental or emotion position adopted with respect to something
E/He is Silent here Hiding Behind X/Dead Matter/Mother/Her Fallen Cross Under The Axe

Exit: X/Axe   Hit   X/Hit   X/It   Eggs/Hit   X/He/T
X/Fallen Fem Cross   i/Marriage Act   T/Fem Cross
After the Axe Hit   or   the Eggs are Done (D/Pregnant)   It is Time to exit: a way or passage out   departure
The Exit here is Through an Axe that Hits
E/He is Silent here Hiding Behind X/Fallen Fem Cross/Axe

Exited: Eggs/Hit/ID
ID is an Identification Card   She is Exited When Her Ovulation it/Hit Her

Exorcism: X/Whore/Sees/Him/M/Motherhood
A Fem Dares to See that All Fems are All Dead Whores Mothers   That Can Make Her Crazy   So   She Gets an
Exorcism: a calling up or driving out of evil spirits
E/He is Silent here Hiding Behind X/Fallen Fem Cross/Axe

Expand: X/Band

313

Lise Rochon

Keep Expanding the Separation Between X/Fallen Fem Cross and the Band (The Ban/The Bar/The Code)
In   The Code   B/Boy Holding All Fem Breasts   and   P/Man Power   P is an Extension of B (Note The Shape of These Letters Are Almost The Same)
Eggs/Pan   Eggs in the Pan being Cooked

Expansion: X/Pan/She/On   X/Pants/Eon   Expand/She/On
She can Only Expand through Her Pants
Letter E is Silent here Hiding Behind X/Fallen Fem Cross

Expert: X/P/Hurt
X/Fallen Fem Cross   becomes an Expert   P/Man Power will Hurt
Eggs/P/Her/T   Eggs Meaning Being Pregnant
E/He is Silent here Hiding Behind X/Fallen Fem Cross

Explain: X/Plain
Eggs/P/Laying   The Code   says   P/Man Power   Lays the Eggs   The Code   is Always Appropriating The Most Obvious Fem Qualities to the Masc Gender
E/He is Silent here Hiding Behind X/Fallen Fem Cross

Exploit: X/Plot
A Plot is a Conspiracy
exploit: a striking or notable deed   feat spirited or heroic act
X/Fallen Fem Cross Plot is in an Exploit Says   The Code That would be a Story with an Evil Plan
Plotte is Slang for Vagina in French
E/He is Silent Here Hiding Behind X/Fallen Fem Cross/Axe

Explosion: X   Plow   S/Penis   Eon (Eon)
X/Fallen Fem Cross   has been Plowed by His/S/Is/Us/Ass/Hiss/Serpent/Penis for an Eon
Eggs/Axe   Plows   He/On(Eon)
E/He is Silent Here Hiding Behind X/Fallen Fem Cross/Axe

Expose: X/Spouse

314

The Dam Code The Damn Book

If a Fem Wants to Divorce   The Axe is Ready for Her   Take the Pose   X/Pose   Axe/Pause
Eggs   Pose   Eggs   P/Hose
E/He is Silent Here Hiding Behind X/Fallen Fem Cross/Axe

Expression: Express   He   On (Eon)
Expression is a Masc Form of Communication for an Eon
Axe/Press/Eon   The X/Axe Has been Pressed on Her for an Eon (See Axe in The Words Chapter   and X in The Letters Chapter)
E/He is Silent Here Hiding Behind X/Fallen Fem Cross/Axe

Extend: X/Fallen Fem Cross   Tend
Eggs/Tend   The Fem Extends Herself by Taking Care of Her Eggs
Says   The Code   Pregnancies   Poverty   Powerlessness   Over and Over for Her   More than 2000 Years   No Contraceptive Permitted Then
Extender: X/Tender
extender: a substance added to another to increase its volume
X/Fallen Fem Cross/Axe   Tends and is Tender   When Extending Herself
Eggs/Tender   Eggs/Tend/Her   Always with it Says   The Code   More the Better
E/He is Silent Here Hiding Behind X/Fallen Fem Cross

Extract: X/Track
X/Fallen Fem Cross Under The Axe   is being Tracked and Extracted   She is Being Sucked Up of Her Energy Until She Dies in X
E/He is Silent Here Hiding Behind X/Fallen Fem Cross

Extreme: X/T/Rim
X/Fallen Fem Cross   T/Fem Cross   are on The Rim
Note that T Eventually Ends as X in this One Word (See Letters T and X in The Letters Chapter)
T becomes X When She as being Cross has Fallen Down
rim: the outer edge border margin or brink of something especially of a circular object
E/He is Silent Here Hiding Behind X/Axe/Fallen Fem Cross

Exude: X/U/D   All 3 Fem Sounds Letters
X/Fallen Fem Cross/Axe   U/You/Ovulating   D/Pregnant

The Code   Says Her Femininity Exudes When   Her X/Cursed   U/Ovulating Uterus   is   D/Pregnant
X/Fallen Fem Cross would be Too Close to The Hood as in Switching   U/Her Ovulation   for   O/Fem Hole   An Easy Switch to do from the Sound Level from O to U   Creating X/Hood   That would be a Big No to Her from   The Code   so
exude: to ooze or spread in all directions
The Code   Hiding itself as Usual in Ugly Words
E/He is Silent Here Hiding Behind X/Fallen Fem Cross as Usual

Eye: E/He   Y/Wounded Fem   E/He
The Wounded Fem is Surrounded here by the Eyes of the i/High/Eye   It is Letter i l (The Man Stick) The Eye/I of That God in That Pyramid on the Back of the American Dollar Bill in   The Code
The i/The High/The Eye
An Eye has the Shape of Circles within Circles which are Entirely All Fems Symbols
From   i/Marriage Act   She is the Wounded Fem
When i is in Large Cap it has the Shape of a Bar/Stick
Then l Splits in Yy/Wounded Fem   then More Split in Vv/Fem Sex Active Which Ends in W/All Fem Sex Active
The I Also Split in L/Sweet Fem Love Light/Ill/Ail/Hail/Heel/All/Elle/Oil/Hell
The Y or Why is for Her   Not for Him
The Eye is for Him as in Hi   Another Cover Word

F f
Intro
In The Code   Letter F Stands for Feminine   and for   Fuck   as We All Know
The Letter F could have been a Nice Letter for The Fems
If it was Not Called the F Letter of the Fuck Letter Which Diminishes Her (Whore) to a Fem Fucking Whore
F is a Masc Made Fem Letter
A Handicap for Letter F is that Its Structure has No Balance by Itself   It Cannot Stand by itself
Letters A/All Men and E/He Stands Solid on the Ground
Letter F Would Need a Big Cap Letter as Partner (Marriage/Obedience was part of the Vows until the Fifties) As L/Sweet Fem Light   or   E/

The Dam Code The Damn Book

He or H/Code Secret and Silent Letter as Examples to Stand and Stay Upright Solid
F Letter can be Only a Satellite or Under the Thumb of Another Letter Which All Operates Under a Different Program
One Horizontal Stick of Knowledge Is Missing in Letter F Compared to the Letter E
Note the Resemblance Between the Small Cap Letter f and the Small Cap t Letter
They Both are a in a Shape of a Cross and are Fem Letters
The f Hook is at the Top (Head)
The t Hooks is at the Bottom (Loins)
Both Curve to the Right or the Future Instead of the Past or to the Left (No need to Remember the Past) Making The Code Cross Concept Going Forward in that Mode -Another Weakness to The Fems Here
The Right Side or Right Hand (As in The Right Way) is the Masc Side and is Always Right The Left Side or the Left Hand is for Wiping Butt in Eastern Countries Left as in Left Behind Right for Him Wrong for Her
F/Fem/Fuck is The Key Letter Shape (Look at Its Shape Sideways) F/Fem/Fuck
Ph is also the F Sound As Phone Fun Fan are Innocents Words
P/Man Power H/Secret Code Letter There is No Fem Power here
Ph is the Letter F in Greek and it is a Circle with a Bar (Another Bar) Across it It is The φ (Creating the Pattern of a Cross) The Circle is an Entirely Fem Symbol
The Letter F is Also the "Fuck You" Letter/Words or the F Word as it is Called in American Slang
It is Important to Say that Now Because for Most of Us
When Someone Says the F Word it is Not Fem that Comes to Mind
It is Fuck in its Different Modes or Moods F for Fuck or Fuck You an in All Its Shades
The Reason is to Downsize Diminish Destroy (Those 3 Words Start with Fem D/Pregnant) that Fem F Letter
Any Power in a Fem Form on Any Level Must be Turned Off Says The Code Nothing Fem is Ever Given or Rewarded in That Secret Code We Live Under
F is for Failing Grade

Word with Letter F is   If   A word Making Her Uncertain Just As Her F Unstable Structure
Nothing Can be Solid for The Fems in   That Code
Especially in that Letter F which could Have been So Powerful for Her
F   f   Words
Fable: F/Able
That could have Been a Nice Concept to Able The Fems to Something but That is a Big No from   The Code   so
fable: a story not founded on facts
Not a Reality
Switch A for E and Get Feeble   Men do Not belong there   so   it is Feeble and Not Dignified of Interest

Face: F/Ace
F/Fem/Fuck   is in Front of an Ace
What is in Her Face   It is Feces in Plural
Feces   Those are Her Faces in   The Code   Feces comes Only in Plural

Fag: F/Fem/Fuck   A/All Men   G/Penis/Vagina Penetration/Letter of God
Anything in Ag is a Weak Word
Bag   Gag   Hag   Lag   Nag   Mag   Rag   Sag   Tag   Wag   And More
fag: to tire by labor
A Fag in its Newest Form is a Gay Person as in a Homosexual
It Diminishes The Fems Value even More as being Part of Something She does Not belong to

Fail: FL   Made of 2 Fem Sounds Letters
F/Fem/Fuck   as in   F/Ail   F/Elle/Her in French   F/Ill   F/Hell   F/Heel   F/Hail   (See Letter L in the Letters Chapter)
A Lot of Bad Concepts Around the Word Fail for Her to Absorb
She is Being   Failed   Hailed   Ill   Ailed   for the Same Fall
The Great Fall/Curse of Adam and Eve from That Jewish Tradition Including that Bible   Always Ending in Guilt and Suffering for All of Hers   The Fems are getting the Brunt of it All

Faithful: Fate/Full   Faith/Fool   The Code   in Full Action Here

The Dam Code The Damn Book

Feel: FL   Made of 2 Fem Sounds Letters
To Feel is Mostly a Fem Faculty According to Common Knowledge
Une Fille in French is a Girl   Une Ville is a Town
Switch F for V and She Gets The Veil/Vile/Val/Vial (Chalice/Blood)   To Veil in French is Voiler (To Sail in English)
Voler is to Steal and to Fly   here Implying Dishonesty
Une Vollée in French is also a Beat with a Belt or a Whip
In the Fifties Parents Used to Scare their Children with that Word Vollee Which was a Common Form of Punishment Back Then to Children   Beatings with Belts or Paddles Injures the Spine and Put Muscles in Shock for Ever Unless it is Relieved with Deep Tissue Massage
Beating Children Back then was a Normal thing to do   Especially in Farm Land where Being a Catholic was Strong and Guilt was the Word for The Common People
V   F   and   L   are Fem   The Fems Carries that Burden Having No Power in Marriage

Fairies: Fair/He   S/Plural and Penis
fairy: a feminine mythical entity
The Code   Steal the Identity Here by Inserting the Sound Word He as in Owning it
It Should Be "FairShes"   Being a Fem Entity
Ferry as a Ship (She/Shh   P/Man Power) (See Ship in The Words Chapter)
Fairy: Fair/He   Ferry
When it Rains it Pours for Him Says   The Code
A Fairy According to Tradition is a Small Delicate and Very Fem Entity
For/He   Another Steal from Her by   The Code
The Fairy (Fair/He)   is a Ferry for Him   Free/He   Not for Her   She Pulls the Oars Down there in the Dark to make That Ship Move

Faith: F/Fem/Fuck   Ate/Hate
Fate   F/8 (Pregnancy)
The Code   Keeps Strong Cover Words as Fate and Faith
Hate and Ate   so   people are Accustomed to Think that What they Think are Idiosyncrasies of the Language
There Are No Coincidences Here in   The Code
Fear Needs to Remain and Fate will Hit the Faith
Faith is a Terrible Word for The Fems in   The Code

Lise Rochon

Be Careful what you Believe
Faithful: Fate/Full   To Believe in Faith/Fate about Pregnancy   Being Full is being D/Pregnant
Switch A/All Men for i/Marriage Act and She Gets a Fit

Fall: Autumn (Hot/On)
A Common Word in Our Language   Time to Fall (in Love) and Pregnant

Falter: Fault/Her   Vault/Her
falter: to stumble
She Stumble All Alone   Being Blamed   or   Isolated by   The Code   It is a Vault Secret

Fake: F/Ache
F/Fem/Fuck   Ache   it is Fake Says   The Code

Family: F/Fem/Fuck   He/E   Lay
F/Fem/Fuck   M/Motherhood/Him   E/He   Lay
He Lays with   The Mother   and   The Fems   Polygamy is Implied Here
Where there is a Lay there is a Cover (Blanket)
Fem   Ill/L/Sweet Fem Love Light/Ail/Hail/Hell/All/Elle
    Lay
In   The Secret Code   All Fems are Always Sick as in L/Ill   or   Under Duress   as in L/Hail/Hell/Ail   Which are a Bunch of Bars/Sticks/Men   as Usual in   The Code
She Cannot See in Front of Herself   and   She has Always has Another Hill/Ill to Climb
Familiar: Fem   He   Liar   In   That Code   Everything is a Lie   The Fem Has been Transformed into a Weak Being   and   Her Beautiful Man (Mane) Her Half Has Been Transformed into a Liar   Which puts Him in Trouble with The Law   His Family   Friends   etc   He becomes a Shadow of Himself   Not Knowing it Before Many Years Later   If Lucky Enough for Consciousness to Makes a Breakthrough
Lying is a Form of Starvation

Famine: FMN   Made of 3 Fem Sounds Letters
F/Fem/Fuck   M/Motherhood   and   N/In/Hen/Virgin
A Fem is with a Mom and a Virgin

The Dam Code The Damn Book

It would be Too Much Info here for Her Says   The Code
A Big No to that   so
Starve them Girls in Famine
FMN is a Soft Gentle Sounds Word for Something that Scream the Pains of Starvation
The Code   Uses that Kind of Cheating to Keep The Fems Poor and Ignorant   It is One of Their Big Cover

Fan: FN   Made of 2 Fem Sounds Letters
F/Fem/Fuck   Meets   Ann/N/In/Hen/Virgin   It is Fun (3 Fem Letters) and Cool Under the Fan   Nothing Much is Said Because Life is Good in that Moment   No Thinking Here Only Pleasure for   N/Virgin   and   F/The Experienced Fem
Fannie s Fanny (Buttocks) is Next

Fannie: Fannie is a Fem Name   The Code   Traps The Fems
Fan/He   Fun/He   Funny
This Fem Name   here is a Given to the Masc   It Belongs to Her But No
The Masc Gets it All Says   The Code   The Fem does Not Exist
A Fanny Pack is a Good Thing   Same as a Pack of Fannies
Put a Pro in Front of Her here and She Get Profane   it is Not Aloud in That Religion
Profane: Pro/Fannie
Introducing to Her the Notion of Excommunication   Because of Her Genitals
Pro/Fan   Prof/Ann/N/Virgin
Profanity is Close By (Vanity)

Fantastic: F/Fem/Fuck   Ann/N/In/Hen/Virgin   T/Fem Cross/Great Curse   S/Is/His/Us/Ass/Hiss/Serpent/Penis   T/Fem Cross/Curse   IC/Integrated Circuit
S/Penis   is in Between 2 TTs/Fem Crosses   with   A/All Men
All Fems Into the Great Curse   It is Fantastic   Says   The Code

Fantasy: Fun/T/See   Fun/Fan   T/Fem Cross   Easy
It is Fun and Easy for Her as   T/Fem Cross/Great Curse   Says   The Code
But No   There is No Such Thing as an Easy Horrible Curse
Fun   Tease   He

Have Fun with a Man and Think Sex Says   The Code
Because there Can be No Friendship with a Fem
Fun/T/See   Fun/Tease/He   Fun/to/See
Fantasies: Fan/Fun   Daisies   Making The Great Curse   Sound
Attractive   The Fems Love Daisies

Far: F/Her
Here   Both Sounds Means the Same
F/Fem/Fuck   is   Her/R
FR   F/Fem/Fuck   Meet   Her/R/Hair/Ear/Hear/Here/Heir/Or/Whore/Are/
Err/Our/Ere/Air/Sex   could have been a Good Thing   But No Says   The
Code   so it is Far   Anything Good For Her is Far Away
F/Heir   The F/Fem/Fuck   and the   Heir
Switch A/All Men for O/Fem Hole and She Gets For (as in Go for it)
Add T/Fem Cross to End the Word Far and She Gets a Fart   The Fems
Ends Often in Feces in   That Code
Add D/Pregnant to Far and She Gets Fard (Make Up)

Farce: F/Fem/Fuck   R/Her/Hair/Ear/Hear/Here/Heir/Or/Whore/Are/Err/
Our/Ere/Air/Sex   C/See/Young Girl
She Sees None of that   so
F/Fem/Fuck   Heir/Or/Whore/Are   C/See/Young Girl
She is the Butt of the Joke Says   The Code   and is Blind to it
Far/C   Far/See

fard: to apply powder to the face or the powder itself
The Fems Do That Generally   and   The Theatre Actors (To Fard Also
Means to Hide   or   Transform)
Replace D/Pregnant with T/Fem Cross and She Gets a Fart (Back to the
Feces for Her   Again)   It Is Hidden in that Stinky Word   so   No One
Come Close to It

Fashion: F/Ass/She/On   F/Ace/She/On
F/Fem/Fuck   is in Front of an   Ace   or an   Ass   Giving Her a Position
of Power   It is a Fashion   It Will Not Last
Says   The Code

Fast: FST

S/Is/His/Us/Ass/Hiss/Serpent/Penis   is in Between a F/Fem/
Fuck   and   T/Fem Cross   It Calls for a Fast Action
Switch A/All Men for i/Marriage Act and She Gets a Fist
(Because with Fist F would have i/Marriage Act Union with T/Fem
Cross)   A Big No from   The Code   so   Add E/He and He Gets a Feast

Fatal: FTL   Made of 3 Fem Sounds Letters
Fate/All   Faith/All   Fat/All
It is Fatal For Her
F/Fem/Fuck   Hat   All/L/Sweet Fem Love Light/Ill/Ail/Hail/Hell/Elle
All   F/Fem/Fuck   in   The Code   Hat (See Art and Hat in The Words
Chapter)

Fate: FT   Made of 2 Fem Sound Letters
F/Fem/Fuck   Hate/Ate/Eight/At/Hat
The F/Fems   and the   Hate
It is Her Fate to be Hated Says   The Code
Switch A/All Men for 2 EEs/He in Plural and He Gets Feet/Fit
Feet that Walk Away from that Fem Fate
The Code   Feet Steps on the Soul   It is the Sole Under Our Feet   We
Walk on It All Day   It is The Dirtiest/Lowest Part of Our Body

Fault: F/Halt   Stop Her
To Fault Her is a Way to Stop Her Endeavors
Switch F/Fem/Fuck for V/Fem Sex Active and She Gets Vault (She Knows
Nothing About The Secrecy of   The Code)

Favor: FVR is Made of 3 Fem Letters Sounds
F/Fem/Fuck   V/Fem Sex Active/Eve   R/Her/Hair/Are/Here/Hear/Ear/
Whore/Or/Err/Sex
F and V are in Front of R   Here is a Sexual Favor for Him From Her
favor: something done or granted out of good will
Favor is a Soft Sounded Word   It Sounds Inoffensive   And it Comes as a
Free Service to Him
In   The Code   The Fem Importance of Work is Either
Diminished   or   has No Value   and   Deserve No Thankfulness
Add All/L/Sweet Fem Light/Hell/Ail/Hail/Elle and   She Gets a Flavor

Fever   Fewer   Not Much here for Her Here Except Dispensing/Giving Sex for free

Favorite: Favor   Ate/Hate
FV/Rite   The Rite of Becoming a   V/Fem Sex Active   from a   F/Fem/Fuck
The Favor/Rite   To Get Sex Favor from Her By Using Tricks Such as Compliments   Promises   Lies
favorite: a person or thing regarded with special favor or preference
A Favorite is Also a Concubine

Father: Fat/Her   Fate/Her   Faith/Her
Both Words Father and Mother (Mate/Her   M/Motherhood   Hat/At   Her/R/Are/Heir/Whore/Or/Sex)   Ends with Here/R/Her/Hair/Are/Hear/Ear/Whore/Or/Err/Sex
Father   F/Fem/Fuck   At/Hat   Her/R/Heir/Are/Whore/Or/Sex
That Father has Nothing to do with True Fatherhood   It is about Fattening (Pregnancy) Her with   Fate   and   Faith
(See Faith and Fate in The Words Chapter)
Switch A/All Men for i/Marriage Act and She Gets Fitter
fitter: a person or thing that fits

Fathom: Fat/M   Fate/M   Faith/M   Fat/Home
It is About Domestic
Work   with   Pregnancies   and   Children   and   Having Faith in that Fate   We have to Procreate All the Time Says   The Code
fathom: to discover the meaning of   to comprehend   unit of length equal to six feet
Number 6 (See # 6/Sex in The Numbers Chapter) is Present here as a Structural Number

Fault: FLT   Made of 3 Fem Sound Letters
F/Fem/Fuck   Halt
Stop that Fem   She is at Fault
Switch F/Fem/Fuck for V/Fem Sex Active and She Gets a Vault
Switch F for C/See/Young Girl or K/Broken Fem Warrior or Q/Bleeding Fem and She Gets Cult   No Fem was Allowed to Create Her Own Religion   and Pass in History

The Dam Code The Damn Book

Switch F for D/Pregnant and She Gets Dolt
dolt: a dull stupid person   blockhead
Add Her/R/Hair/Are/Here/Hear/Ear/Heir/Whore/Or/Err/Sex to Fault and
She Gets Falter (Fault/Her)
falter: to hesitate or waver in action   purpose   intent   etc   give
away   to speak hesitatingly or brokenly   to move unsteadily   stumble
That is a Weakened Fem   The Way   The Code   Ass/Has it
A Volt in The Vault

Fax: FX   2 Fem Sound Letters
F/Fem/Fuck   Axe   The Fems Under The Axe
An Innocent Term   Fax   is
Fax is a Cover Word here

Fear: FR   2 Fem Sounds Letters
A Fem Cannot be in Front of Her/R/Whore/Sex and
F/Hear   F/Here   F/He/Hear   The Fems Cannot Hear or be Here   Then
The Fems would Hear   The Code
So   a Big No from   The Code
Fear Keeps Her Far   and   Fierce (Fear/See) is So Close

Feces: FCC   3 Fem Sound Letters
F/Fem/Fuck   2 CCs/Young Girls   with   His   F/Asses   Faces   F/Aces
Ass/S/Is/Us/Hiss/Serpent/Penis   Also   in Plural   Because Feces Can
Only Be Plural   Bigamy or Polygamy (Dirty Filthy) is Implied here
F/Fem   is Together with   C/Young Girl   It is F/Fem   That
Sees   Poop   As in   F/Sees   Feces
The F/Fem   is Not Aloud To See   That would be a Big No from   The
Code   so   It is Shit   She/It   After All   Feces Come Out of Anus
Ann/N/In/Hen/Virgin   Us/S/His/Penis
Anneaux are Wedding Rings in French

Fee: F/Fem/Fuck   2 EEs/He
F/Fem/Fuck   Precedes 2 EEs/He   That would be a Big No from The
Code   so
fee: charge or payment for professional services
Une Fée in French is a Fem Good Witch (The Code   in English Says
No   so   She from Good Witch is Transformed into a Fee   Not So Nice)

325

Fee   Sounds Same as Fey in English   But   Because English has the Latest Form of the Language Code   Fey is
fey: doomed   fated to die   appearing to be under a spell   marked by an apprehension of death calamity or evil   being in unnaturally high spirits as were formerly thought to precede death
Follow Up in Dictionary.com for More Bad to Happen to Fee/Fey
Fay is Also a Fem Name
The Code   does Not Allow a Masc to be Fair   so
fairy: out of touch with reality
A Fairy is a Sweet Fem with Magical Powers and Wings
That Would be a Big No for   The Code   so
Fay or Fairy are also Slang Terms for Homosexuals
A Ferry is the Cover Word here
Add L/Sweet Fem Light to Fee and She Gets Feel
(F/Fem/Fuck   Ill/Hell/All/Heel/Elle/Hail/L)
Or   a Feeling When Adding N/Ann/Donkey

Feel: F/Ill
When She Feels   She Feels Ill/Hell/Elle/Heel/Hill/All/Hail/L
He/E   and   L/Sweet Fem Light/Ail/Hail/Hell/Elle are Together
That is a Big No from   The Code   so   She is   Ill/L/Ail/Hail/Hell   That Fem Light
The Code   is Entirely Against Sweet Fem Love Light/L/Ail/Ill/Hell   Between a Fem and a Masc
Because   That Love Would Melt that Faith to Fate   to Nothing
That is Not Interesting for Us Human Beings   That Want Prosperity   Peace   Love   Healing   for All
The Code   is Against it   Period (Also Fem Blood Lost   No Coincidence Here)

Feeling: Feel/In   Feel/N/In/Hen/Virgin
Feel the Inside of That Virgin
F/Eel/In   Feel the Eel (Penis)
Fil is Thread in French   Fille is Daughter in French   Le Fil du Temps   is The Thread of Time (The Vine/Wine/Her Blood Loss   T/Fem Cross/Great Curse)
The Code   Works into Creating Memory Threads   so   The Fems would Keep on Repeating Endlessly the Same Perturbed Life Patterns Keeping

The Dam Code The Damn Book

Her Pregnant   Poor   Powerless   It has been more than 2000 years for The Fems to be Silenced   The "Me Too" Movement in The United States has Created a Breach for Healing to All of Us Fems   Thank U   After 2000 Years of Trying

Fellow: FLO   Made of 3 Fem Sounds Letters
F/Fem   L/Ill/hell   O/Fem Hole
A Fem Cannot be a Fellow Says   The Code
That would Mean She would have Friends and People Liking Her Because She would have Power and/or Knowledge   or   Love   That would be a Big No from   The Code   so   here She Falls
Fall/O   F/Hell/O   F/Hello
Hello Is an Accepted Friendly Greeting But   The Code   Brings Its Hell on Her Through it
Switch E/He for O/Fem Hole and She Gets Follow
(Women in Marriage could Only Be Satellites Not Partners   Unless Money/Power Would be Involved)
W/All Fems Sex Active is Silent Here   and   Ends the Word Fellow   as in The Result of the Meaning of the Word by Having All Fems having their Legs Opened at All Times for Sex   Procreation   Etc   That is How She Follows as a Fellow in Silence as   W (See Letter W in the Letters Chapter) And that is the Normal Flow Says   The Code

Felon: FLON   Made of 4 Fem Sounds Letters
Another Load on The Fems from   The Code
Fell/On   Fail/On   F/Hell/On   Fell/N
F/Fem   Hell/L/Sweet Fem Love Light/Ill/Ail/Hail/All/Elle   On
The Fem Gets to Fall/Fail/Fell/Fill   Be in Hell and Be Called a Felon

Female: Fem   Hail/L/Elle/All/Hell/Ill/Sweet Fem Love Light
F/Male   F/He/Mail   F/He/Male
A Fem is Never Left Alone Anywhere in   The Secret Grid Code   Not Only She has No identity by Herself   The Code   Says She is a Male Here The Male is with Her with Letter F/Fuck/Fem as the Start of the Word The Code   Assembles Different Subtle Sounds

Feminine   FMN   Made of 3 Fem Sound Letters
F/Fem/Fuck   M/Motherhood   Ann/N/In/Hen/Virgin

327

All Virgins are Mothers with Fem/Fuck
The Code Says Here That is The Fems Definition
   The Code is Heavy on The Word Feminine
FMN   Lots of   F/Fems   and   N/Virgins   having   i/Marriage
Act   With   E/He   and   M/Motherhood is for All the Fems as   N/Hen
Fem/In/Hen   Fem/Ann/In   Fem/Ann/Ane (Donkey in French)
Fem/In/N   F/Fem/He/He/Knee/Knit/He/T/Fem Cross
F/M/He/Nine   (See Number 9 in The Number Chapter)
In The Code   An/Ann/Hen/In/N/the Virgin Letter   is the
Ane   or   Donkey (Arse/Ass)   or   Hen (a Chick)
The Which will Become M/Motherhood   When Another Bar Is Added
(See Bar in The Words Chapter) to the N
MNM   is a Succession of Up Down that Holds Hands
In The Moment N/Ann is Just an   an   Which is a Connecting Word
having Little Value in Itself   The Code   Works That Way

Fence: FNC   Made of 3 Fem Sound Letters
F/Fem/Fuck   N/In/Hen/Virgin   C/See/Young Girl
That Fence for The Fems from   The Secret Code is   Not for Her to See
fencing: the art practice or sport in which an épée foil or saber is used for defense and attack   a parrying of arguments avoidance or direct answers
Fence   Ann/N/In/Hen/Virgin   in with Something that will Pierce Her (A Penis) That Virgin
Add Another E/He and He Gets Fancy   (Fence/He/That)
Fancy is Behind the Fence   She has No Access to That

Ferocious: F/Fem/Fuck   Her/R/Hair/Ear/Hear/Here/Heir/Or/Whore/Are/Err/Our/Ere/Air/Sex   She   Us/S
Fair   She   Us/S/Ass/His/Hiss/Serpent/Penis
F/Err/She/Us
Fur   O/Fem Hole   She   Us
F/Here/She/Us   She is There Fair to Comply

Fervor: For   V/Fem Sex Active   R/Her/Hair/Ear/Hear/Here/Heir/Or/Whore/Are/Err/Our/Ere/Air/Sex
V/Fem Sex Active   Acts With Fervor Says   The Code
fervor: great warmth and earnestness of feeling
great intensity of belief or belief of ardor and zeal

The Dam Code The Damn Book

Ardor has Almost the same Definition as Fervor
ardor: great warmth of feeling   passion   intense devotion   burning heat
Ardor   Our/Door   Her Door   Heir/Door   Whore/Door   etc   She Ends There in   The Code
Ardor and Fervor are Cover Words Here

Ferry: Fairy   Fair/He   For/He
fairy: one of a class of supernatural beings generally conceived as having a diminutive human form and possessing magical powers with which they intervene in human affairs   *Slang* a male homosexual
The Fem does Not Own that Word
Ferry is another Cover Word to Make Him Look Sweet and Attractive in Our Heads as a Good Memory
F/Fem/Fuck   R/Her/Heir/Whore   E/He

Festival: F/Fem/Fuck   His/S/Is/As/Has/Ass/Us/Hiss/Serpent/Penis   T/Fem Cross   Val
Fast/He/Val
A Quickie at the Fair While He is with the Neighbor Wife in the Val   Feast/He/Val (V/Fem Sex Active   All
Add Another S and it is a Valse/Waltz   a Danse   Says   The Code

Fetus: FTS   2 Fem Letters in Plural
F/Fem/Fuck   with   T/Fem Curse   in Plural or with His/S/Is/As/Has/Ass/Us/Hiss/Serpent/Penis
D/The   Feat   Us (The Fetus) Defeat Us

Few: FU   Made of 2 Fem Sound Letters   Fuck You
F/Fem/Fuck   You/U/Ovulating Uterus
Even if F is the Letter for Fem and Fuck it has less Connection with Sex than Other Round Letters As   U O C and Code Letters   As the Open V   W   M   N
F as in Feminine   F Could have been the Intelligent One of All Fems Letters   A Letter of Power   But it Cannot Stand Alone by Itself It will Tilts (Tits without L/Sweet Fem Light)
The Word Few and the Word Fem are Close   Upside Down   W/All Sex Active Fem   is   M/Motherhood

Lise Rochon

View as VU   Here VU is V Viewing Herself as V/Fem Sex Active with U/ Opened Loins
The Code is Focused on That

Fiancé: FNC   Made of 3 Fem Sound Letters
In The Past   Marriage came as of Secondary Importance for The Masc   and   of Primary Importance as a Goal/Gold of/for Life for the Fems   Since Childhood   She Has Been Programmed/Educated That Way For the Last 2000 Years   The Modern Fem is Barely Coming Out of That Hypnotic/Intoxicating/Concept
F/Fem/Fuck   And   Sea/Say   That is What a Fiancé Is   Says   The Code
Fiancé(e)   FNC   Has the Same Sound in Masc and Fem
Add Another E/He it becomes Fem   The Fem does Not Exist by Herself in   The Code
F/Fuck/Fem   N/In/Hen/Virgin   Sea/C/See/Young Girl Back to Being a Fish in the Sea for Her
She is Engaged (In/Cage) Being a Fiancée
Fiancé is Mirroring Fiancée in Fem Because He has Nothing or Little to do with it Says   The Code
It is Quite an Empty Word
Back then Men Had Harems   Bigamy/Polygamy were Common   Marriages were mostly Business Deals
To the Muslim Religion a Man can have 4 Wives

Field: F/Yield
field: a piece of ground for sports
The Fems Was Not Welcome in Practice of Sports in the Past   Says   The Code   so
yield: barren sterile   to give up surrender
Add F/Fem to Yeld and it makes it Ground for Sports

Fight: F/Height
Here The Fem is Placed in a High Place   Because   It is a Fight   Where She Will Lose because of Her Height   or   Any Other Weakness   The Fems Never Practiced/Engaged in Real Man Combat   They Had No Real Chance in Any Compartment of Life   and   No Chance was Given to Her By Any Man   it Was/is a Man Thing

F/Fem/Fuck   Height
Take Away H/Secret Society Letter and She Gets Eight/# 8 (Pregnancy)
It is Fate(F/# 8) for Her   or/and a   Faith to Follow Says   The
Code   Hate it   or   Eat it

Fill: F/Fem/Fuck   Ill/L/Sweet Fem Love Light/All/Ail/Hail/Hell/Elle

Switch F for The Fems Letters C/K/Q and She Gets Kill
Switch F for G/Penis Penetration and She Gets Gill
(Back to the Fishes for Her (Ocean   O/She/In))
Switch F for H/Secret Code Society Letter and Get Hill (a Small Mount
(Sex)   or   Month (Her Blood Loss)   L/Sweet Fem Love Light/Ill/Hail/
Hell/Ail/Elle/Oil/Heel/All/Sex
Take Away F/Fem/Fuck and She Gets Ill
Switch F for M/Motherhood and She Gets to Mill
Switch F for N/In/Hen/Virgin and She Gets Nil
Switch F for Masc P/Man Power and He Get Pill
(Men Always Get Away in   The Code   When it Gets Too Hot for Him)
Switch F for Masc S/Is/His/Us/Ass/Hiss/Serpent/Penis and He Gets Sill
(Silly) (To See   C/Young Girl   Ill   is Fun and Silly Says   The Code)
Switch F for T/Fem Cross and She Gets Till
Add E to Fill (Fill is to Fill Something as in Pregnancy) and   She Gets a Fille
(a Daughter in French)
Add A/All Men and She Gets to Fail (The Fems   Ail   Weil and
Hail   Under That Veil) (See Letter F in The Words Chapter)
Fil is Thread in French   Le Fil du Temps (The Thread of Time) (See Time
and the Wheel of Time in The Words Chapter)
Le Fil du temps is Often Represented by a Grape Vine
A Grapevine is Also a Place Where People Exchange Gossips (The Fem
should have No Secrets Says   The Code)
Feel That

Fille: Fille is French for Girl   or   The Grail Herself
F/Fem Fuck   L/Ill   F/Hill   F/Hell   F/Ail
L/Sweet Fem Love Light/Ill/Hail/Hell/Ail/Elle/Oil/Heel/All
The Fem is Ill   in Hell   Early in Age
The Sang Real of The Girl   and   The Lance of The King Mean Real
Blood   Not Royal Blood

Find: FND   Made of 3 Fem Sound Letters
Fin   D/Pregnant
F/Fem/Fuck   N/In/Hen/Virgin   D/Pregnancy   is What She Finds for Herself
Finder   Fin   D/Pregnant   R/Her/Are/Heir/Whore/Sex
Back to the Fishes and the Horses/Heirs/Whores for Her to Find
Add E/He to Find and She Gets Fiend
fiend: Satan the devil   any spirit demon
See Dictionary for More Definitions of Fiend
Fiend is the Word here for Where Ends The Fems in   The Code
The Fems has been Annexed (N/N/X   N/Next) with the Devil (See Devil D/The   Eve   Ill   in The Words Chapter) Since Antiquity
Add Her/R/Hair/Ear/Hear/Here/Heir/Or/Whore/Are/Err/Our/Air/Ere/Sex to Fiend and She Gets Friend
Switch D/Pregnant for E/He and He Gets Fine
Men in   The Code   Do Not Get Involved in that Kind of Find
But   She is Fine with it Says   The Code
Finder Keeper   Find/Her   and   Keep/Her
Here   She/Shh Again Belong to All and None

Fine: FN   Made of 2 Fem Sound Letters
Switch i/Marriage Act for U/You/Ovulating and She Gets
Fune/Funny (She Loses it As it Gets Transferred to The Masc)
The Fine for Her Comes with The Guilt of   i/Marriage Act   It is Fine Says   The Code
Fun/He   Funny

Finish: Fin/Is/She
Back to the Fishes for Her   She is a Fin
The Fins Would be the Mermaid Unopened Legs in   The Code   as in FN   Letter N/In/Hen/Virgin   becoming Sexually Sex Active (V)   That Virgin Time is Over Says   The Code   Time for Sex
F/Fem/Fuck   N/In/Hen/Virgin   She/Shh   and be Silent About it

Fire: F/Her   F/R   F/Ire
ire: fury   rage   intense anger   wrath
F/Fem/Fuck   is With   Ire/R/Her/Hair/Ear/Hear/Here/Heir/Or/Whore/Are/Err/Our/Ere/Air/Sex

The Dam Code The Damn Book

There is Fire   The Fem is with Herself   She is in Fire   The Code   Knows Her Passion   Anger   Bitterness (See Mary in Italian)
Fired: Fire   D/Pregnant
As Passionate   or   Angry She is   She is Now with Child for the Rest of Her Life
Firemen: Fire/Men   No Fem There   Fire Stations were Men Fortresses   The Guardians of Her Fire

Firmament: Firm/He/Meant
The Stars (Stay/Whores) are Firm (Vagina)   He Means it   It is All Over The Sky/Firmament

First: F/Fem/Fuck   Her/R/Hair/Ear/Hear/Here/Heir/Or/Whore/Err/Are/Our/Ere/Air/Ire/Sex   S/Is/His/Us/Ass/Hiss/Serpent/Penis   T/Fem Cross
First for The Fem is Her Having Sex for a Heir   or   as a   Whore   or   to   Err   for   Air   in All   Her   Ire etc
Take Away R and She Gets Fist
F   Is   T/Fem Cross as in   All Fems Being Crossed   or   Get that Fist   It Comes First

Fish: FSH   F/Fem/Fuck   His/S/Is/Us/Ass/Hiss/Serpent/Penis   H/Secret Code Letter
F   Shh/She   Fishes   Fish/She/Is   The Fem is the Fish
F/Fem/Fuck   i/Marriage Act   His/S/Is/Us/Ass/Hiss/Serpent/Penis   H/Secret Code Letter
There is No Word to Represent Fish/Her (a Fisher) Compared to a Hunter (Hunt/Her)   Because a Fisher (Fish/Her) Would be that She Fishes Herself   Only a Fish/Her/Man is Allowed to do That   Jesus Symbol Is the Fish
Dish   Fish   Leash   Miche (The White Part of Bread in French   La Mie (The Softest Part))   Niche   Wish   The Fem   Ish   is Important here   Especially with Those Fem Starting Letters (D F L M N W)

Fish as   Cod (Doc)   Trout (The/Route)   Sole (Soul)   The Gill (Girl)   Fin (Fem   Ann/In/N/F/Donkey)
Jelly fish: J/Sheppard Stick   Hell/Elle   He   Fish
No Meat on Friday (a Fem Day)

333

Fish/Friday   or   Eggs/Easter Day   had Old Hypnotic Catholic Rules for Their Believers

Fist: F/Fem/Fuck   Is/S/His/Penis   T/Fem Cross/Fem Great Curse
Take His/S/Is/Us/Ass/Hiss/Serpent/Penis Away and She Gets a Fit from Him
The Fems is in Trouble here With   or   Without the His/S/Is/Us/Ass/Hiss/Serpent/Penis

Fit: F/Hit
A Fit is to have   F/Fem/Fuck   Being Hit
As Normal as Feet   it Fits   F/It
Feet is the Cover Word here

Fix: FX   Made of 2 Fem Sound Letters
F/Fem/Fuck   Become   X/Fallen Fem Cross
She is All Fixed (FXD) as in Dead and Good to Go   Says The Code She is Pregnant

Flag: FLG   F/Fem/Fuck   L/Ail/Sweet Fem Light   G/Penis Penetration
F/Lag
lag: to stay behind
The Fems Stays Behind when it Comes to Politics and Symbolism
Says   The Code
F is with L in Front of G/Penis Penetration
Flag as in   Flaw that Hag
The Flag as a Fem is Attached on a Rigid Pole (Penis)   and   It Goes Down at Night
I Will Not Expand in Details with Flags   Flags Colors and their Symbols
More Research to be Done
A Star is Multiple Cross Superposed   The T/Fem Cross is That Cross Says The Code
Color Red Represent Her Blood Loss and Blue is the Free Man as in the Blue Sky
I Love the American Flag   and I Respect All Peaceful Nation Flags
But Until   That Code   is Known to All People (Peep/Hole) People will be at Each Other Throat and Will Not Know Why
Many Short Words Starts with AG
You   Bag   Nag   Hag   On the Rag   Sag   Wag

They All Relate Closely to The Fems   and   None of them being
Nice   The Way   The Code   Words Works
AG is   A/All Men   G/Penis Penetration
The Code   Hides that in   Because it Means Basically Homosexuality   G/
Penis   and   A/All men
hag: a vicious old ugly Fem
The Code   is Old and Powerful   It Deters Normal People from Looking
at it Closely   by   It makes it Looks Uninteresting
That does Not Stop the Good People Allegiance to the Real Goals of Their
Flag
Anthem: Hunt/M/Motherhood/Him   Hunt/Them   Haunt/Them   Ant/
Them   Aint/M/Him
Hunt   D/Pregnant   M/Motherhood
So Much Application/Force from   That Code   into Making All Fems
Pregnant by Hunting and Haunting Her and Making Her Powerless for
Ages

Flake: F/Fem/Fuck   L/Ail/Ill/Sweet Fem Love Light   Ache (Fell/Ache)
When She Ache It is as Small as a Flake   No One Sees it Says   The Code

Flatter: Flat/Her   Oh No No
A Flat Chest for a Fem is a Big No from   The Code   Do Not Flatter
Yourself   Stay Away from that Thought Says   The Code   It is a Lie
flatter: to complement insincerely

Flattering: Flat/Her/In
flattering: to try to please by complementary remarks or attention
It Cannot Happen to Her   because   To be Flat is a Bad Thing for a Fem
Says   The Code   She cannot Win Here Neither

Flatulence: Flat   U/You/Ovulating/Uterus   L/Ill/Ail/Hell/Fem Sweet
Love Light   Hence
Flat (A Flat Chest) is Bad for   The Code   so   Make it Annoying and
Reject it
She Cannot Have a Flat Chest   The Code   Says If She Does   She Will
have Flatulence   Another Deterrent
Flatulence is a Cover Word Here
Flatulent: Flat/U/Lent

F/Fem/Fuck   L/Hell/Ill/Ail/Hail/Sweet Fem Love Light   You/U/Ovulating/
Uterus
The Fem is Sweet and Opened Sexually   It is Just a Bunch of   Air/Heir/
Whore/Her Says   The Code   Pompously to Her/R/Heir/Whore/Err/Sex
flatulent: having unsupported pretensions   inflated and
empty   pompous   turgid

Flaw: F/Law
F/Fem/Fuck   is The   Law
To Flaw The Fems is The Code   Law here
Flaw is the Base Sound for Flower   Flaw/Her   R/Her/Hair/Ear/Hear/Here/
Heir/Or/Whore/Err/Are/Our/Ere/Air/Ire/Sex
flaw: a feature that mars the perfection of
something   defect   fault   a defect impairing legal soundness or
validity   a crack   break   breach   or rent

Flawless: F/Law/Less   F/Law/L/Ass
F/Fem/Fuck   with   2 LLs/Sweet Fem Love Light/Ill/Hail/Hell/Ail/Elle/Oil/
Heel/All
For a Fem   The Law   is the   His/Ass/S/Has/Penis   In Plural for Her
(Polygamy or Bigamy)
If You do Not have a Penis You have a Flaw   so   You Cannot be Flawless
Flawless is a Cover Worde Here

Flesh: FLSH
Take Away L/Sweet Fem Love Light/Ill/Hail/Hell/Ail/Elle/Oil/Heel/All and
She Gets Fish (See Ocean   Fish   Sheppard (Letter J) in The Words
Chapter)

Fleur de Lys: It is The Priere de Sion Emblem
It Also Represents The Bible Holy Trinity   (Research the History of the
Fleur de Lys)   (See BB in The Words Chapter) The Fleur de Lys Represents
The Inner Formation of the Fem Stomach and Sexual System   Strangled
by Diminishing The Fem Waist   Manipulating/Twisting Her BB   Calling
it an Innie for The Fem   Men have a Normal BB Called Outie Cut lose
Enough with No Pressure on The Organs of His BB at Birth Which Gives
The Masc More Force   Clarity

The Dam Code The Damn Book

Contrary to the Fem which has to Fight All Lifelong All Kinds of Unbalances and Diseases and Pains Occurring from That   Keeping Her Weak is the Goal of   The Code   Keep Her Awake   and   Healthy Enough to Keep Pregnancies and Sex Going   Thousands of Years The Fem is Enduring That   and   More
Fleur de Lys is a Cover Word here

Flick: F/Fem/Fuck   Lick
flick: a sudden light blow or tap as with a whip or the finger
There is Always a Whip for Her in   The Code   Especially if it Involves a Light

Flicker: F   Lick   Her/R/Hair/Ear/Hear/Here/Heir/Or/Whore/Err/Are/Our/Ere/Air/Ire/Sex
flicker: unsteady light   a brief appearance   a sudden blow or strike
The Code   Says When a Fem Lick Him it is a Brief Encounter   And She better Go Away Fast Because there is Blow Coming   In Slang to Blow Also Means to Blow Him   And Her light is Flickering   so   She does Not See Much of What is Happening

Flight: F/Fem/Fuck   Light
Fucking is Her Light   Says   The Code   She Takes Off in that Flight Light
Letter F is Not a Sexual Letter (See Letter F in The Letters Chapter)   But Fuck is Her Code Shadow   so   That Flight is Only Sexual for Her   And Her Light is Focused on That
Not Much there for The Fems Here   Pregnancy is   The Only Outcome Because Contraceptives were Forbidden by The Law and the Clergy

Flip: F/Fem/Fuck   Leap/Lip
F/Fuck/Fem Can Jump from One Man to Another   Says   The Code   (Because Her/R/Hair/Ear/Hear/Here/Heir/Or/Whore/Err/Are/Our/Ere/Air/Ire/Sex)
leap: to jump from one to another
Flipper   Flip   Her/R/Hair/Ear/Hear/Here/Heir/Or/Whore/Err/Are/Our/Ere/Air/Ire/Sex
Flip/Her Accentuates Flip in Common Knowledge Because   The Code   Now Associates it to Her Exclusively   Although She is Not Allowed to Flip Him   Only The Masc Can Flip Her

flip flop: to make a complete change of opinion   to move with repetitive flaps
F/Lip   Mutates into the Word Flop (F/Lop)   and   Flap Appears as Part of the Flip Flop Definition

Flock   F/Fem/Fuck   Luck
The Code   Says The Fem Becomes Lucky When She has a Flock of Children (See Chicken in The Words Chapter)
F/Lock   The F is Locked in That
Fuck for Luck   The Code   Has a Multitude of Smoke Screens to Attract Her into Sex   and   Pregnancies
Fuck Starts with a fem letter F/fem fuck   and   Luck Also Starts with a Fem Letter L

Floor: Flaw/Her
Same as Flower   Flaw/Her (See Flower in The Words Chapter)
And Floor That Flower as in Stepping on it
A Floor   We Walk All Over it
Add U/You/Ovulating/Uterus and She Gets Flour/Flower
Flour and Water (Water is a Fem Symbol) Makes Bread (Bred   B/Read) With Yeast (He/East)
Eat and Drink   The Bread/Body   and   The Blood/Wine   Which is Cannibalism   and   Vampirism
Floor it   Fell/Whore   Hit

Flop: F/Fem/Fuck   Hop
When Her Light is On About Fucking and Hoping   It is a Flop   Nothing Good Coming Her Way Says   The Code   Only Failure   and   She Will Fall from it
flop: to drop with a sudden hump   to fall or plump down suddenly   to change suddenly   to sleep or be lodged   to fail
When He/E Hops F and L   2 Fem Letters here Implies Polygamy here   She will be Dropped

Florist: Floor/Ist
ist: practice of doctrines   principles
Florist is   Floor/Is/T/Fem Cross/Great Curse

The Dam Code The Damn Book

She is to Be Walked All Over It/Her (Animals and Things is What She is in   The Code)
She is   FL   Heir/Whore/Err   Ist   Her Doctrine to Follow is to Be with   Heir   a Whore   Or   Err   In Any Case She is to be Abandoned   Says   The Code
Flower   FL/Whore   Flaw/Her   Flow/Her   with All Those Hypnotic Lies   Floor   and   Flaw   Deteriorates that Flower as She Flows
Flowers are the Ultimate Fem Symbol of Beauty   and   Magic of Nature   But No Says   The Code   so   F/Lower   Fall/Her   His   T/Fem Cross   Back to The Great Curse with Flowers for The Fems

Flow: FLOW   Made of All 4 Fem Letters
F/Fem/Fuck   W/All V/Fem Sex Active   and   L/Fem Sweet Light Are Concentrating on their O/Fem Hole   Juices Flow
Switch O for A/All Men and He Gets a Flaw   The Code   Men Stay Away from Those Flows/Flaws   As Said Flow is All Made of Fem Letters

Flower: Flaw/Her   Flow/Her
The Fems Have Been Taught to Love What is of No Help   or   is Bad for Her
Cut Flowers Go Dead So Fast   and   Take Long to Grow   and   Cost so Much   Cut Flowers are Just Another Facet of Her Being
Dead   as   Deflowered   and/or   Flawed
Sorry Again and Again   Especially to Florists   and   Flowers Lovers   I am One of Them
Flower Petal   Flaw   R/Her   Pet/All   Pat/All   Pit/Her   Pot/All (Back to The Kitchen   and   being Petted for Her   as an Animal (Animal is Fem)   Une Patte is an Animal Leg in French

L/Sweet Fem Love Light/Ill/Hail/Hell/Ail/Elle/Oil/Heel/All

Fluff: FLUFF   Is Made of 5 Fems Letters
F/Fem/Fuck   with   L/Sweet Fem Love Light/Ill/Hail/Hell/Ail/Elle/Oil/Heel/All   U/You/Ovulating   Plus   2 FFs/Fem/Fuck   More
Fluff has 3 FFF s   Therefore Representing The Vast Majority of   F/Fem/Fuck   Says   The Code
fluff: something of no consequence   an error   a blunder   puff out   downy particles

The Code   Says to Her That The Search for Sex is Light and Fluffy   With No Consequence   It Means Nothing to Anybody   Being Fluff   Being Small   has Errors in it   Being a Bunch of Air and Particles (Down/
He   Particles)
Fluff as in For/Luv   or   Fou/Love   Fou Means Crazy in French (3 Fem Letters) and Loco (4 Fem Letters) in Spanish
The Code   Always Diminish/Destroy Love Between a Fem and a Masc   because   It Feeds from Hate and Greed
It is All Fluff Anyway   Puff it Up Says   The Code
It Empties The Fems in Every Small   or   Big Way of Life

Fluke: F/Fem/Fuck   Look
fluke: the part of an anchor that catches in the ground   a barb or the barbed head of a harpoon spear arrow or the as   either half of the triangular tail of a whale   an accidental advantage   stroke of good luck
If a Fem would have an Accidental Advantage or a stroke of Good luck
The Code Flips Concepts to Accentuate its Mechanism in Many Directions
Here The Fem again is being a Fish or being Fished (See Fish and Ocean in The Words Chapter) It Can be a Stroke of Luck to Kill One Says   The Code
It is Her   Luck/Lock   to be Hooked (Hook/Her   Hooker   Prostitute)
F/Fem/Fuck   L/Sweet Fem Light   Hook   Always Back to Sell Sex
for   Heir   or   Whore   if Not   Err

Flush: F/Fem/Fuck   Lush
When The Fems and Abundance are Together   Better Flush it Says   The Code
Switch F for B/Boy Holding All Fem Breasts and He Gets a Blush (Too Young to Understand)
A Rush of that Red Glow   Usually is from Being Guilty   Being Ashamed of Something   or   Being Intimidated
None of that That Attracting
Switch F and L for R/Her/Hair/Ear/Hear/Here/Heir/Or/Whore/Err/Are/Our/Ere/Air/Ire/Sex And She Gets Fresh

Flux: FLUX   Is Made of 4 Fem Letters
F/Fem/Fuck   Lux
flux: a flow
(See Flux   Flock   Influx   in The Words Chapter)

The Dam Code The Damn Book

flux: a flowing or flow   continuous change   passage   or movement
Nothing Stays With Her Says   The Code   Especially Lux which Means
Light   and   Luxury Comes to Mind
Flock in Plural is Flocks/Flux   The One with S/Is/His/Us/Ass/Hiss/Serpent/
Penis   T/Fem Cross
is The Luxury
flock: a number of animals of one kind especially sheeps goats or birds
that keep or feed together or are herded together   a large number of
people   crowd   a large group of things

Fly: F/Lie
F/Fem/Fuck   Lie   or   Lay   it/She is So Small it/She has No Value
Kill Her/It/Hit   Throw It/Her Out as a Fly
on the fly: to complete one action without stopping the first action
Married but Having Another Fem on the Side   On the Fly
The Code   is All Lies Working for the Lay   It Flies
A Fly is also a Man Zipper

Focus: Fuck/Us   Fuck   S/Is/His/Us/Ass/Hiss/Serpent/Penis
That is   The Code   for Her to Focus On   Not Even having Sex for
Love   Just Fuck
Letter F/Fem/Fuck is Also the Word Fuck

Foe: FO   Made of 2 Fem Sound Letters
foe: a person who feels hatred for another   enemy
The Code   Says   F/Fem/Fuck   Should have Hatred for Her Own   O/
Fem Hole
Faux Means False in French   The Code   Acts Erratic on Her   Its
Confusion Leads Her Nowhere
Lots of Mental Illnesses from that World of Lies Forced on Her by   That
Code

Fog: Is Made of 2 Fems Letters   and   Penis Penetration
F/Fem/Fuck   O/Fem Hole   G/Penis Penetration
Letter G Goes 3 Ways   The Fem   The Masc   and It is The Letter of God
It is All in a Fog for The Fems About Her Fem Hole Penetration   and   G/
God Letter/Penis Penetration

Lise Rochon

Add R/Heir/Or/Whore/Her/Hair/Ear/Hear/Here/Err/Are/Our/Ere/Air/Ire/Sex and He Jumps Over to Her as a Frog (The Prince and the Frog Story   When The Fem Kisses a Man That Does Not Attract Her)

Fold: F/Fem/Fuck   Hold
If The Fems Holds on to Something it is Folded   or   Gone Already   or   She can Hold on to that Fold Where Sheeps are kept   Look The Church is There too
fold: an enclosure for sheep or occasionally other domestic animals   the sheep kept within it   a flock of sheep   a church   the members of a church congregation   a group sharing common beliefs values
Back to the Animals/Sheeps for The Fems   or   Under a Church Ruler as The Sheppard (See Sheep   Ship   Letter J in the Words and Letter Chapter)
F/Old   When The Fem is Old   She Folds Says   The Code
She Holds and Folds According to   The Code
Being Old is Big for   The Code   so   The Code   Can Eliminate Her Often For Any Reason   It is All Set Since 2000 Years

Folk: Fuck
folk: people in general
That How The Secret Language Code Works

Follow: Is Made of 6 All Fems Letters
Fall   O/Fem Hole   Fell/O   Feel/O   Fool/O
Fool is Made of 4 Fem Letters
2 LLs/Sweet Fem Love Light/Ill/Hail/Hell/Ail/Elle/Oil/Heel/All (Plural or All of them)   and   2 OOs/S/Is/His/Us/Ass/Hiss/Serpent/Penis
Plural Makes Its Meaning Grows Stronger   or   Includes All Penisses
F/Fem/Fuck   O/Fem Hole   L/Sweet Fem Light/Ail   O Again
The Fem in   The Code   is to Follow that O/Fem Hole and Keeping that Hole Open to Go
Follow Ends with   W/All Fems Sex Active   (The Plural of V/Fem Sex Active   Singular)
Follow Means   O/Fem Hole(and Become Hollow) has to Fall in Order to Follow On for More
To be the One that Follows is What is Taught to Most Fems
Fellow (Friend) is the Cover Word here

The Dam Code The Damn Book

Food: Is Made of 4 Fem Letters
F/Fem/Fuck   2 OOs/Fem Holes   D/The/Pregnant
F/Hood   Food in The Fem Hood
All Fems Holes are   F/Fucking   2 OOs/Fem Holes (Plural or All of Them)
D/Pregnant   Several Fems Fucking to Get Pregnant   That is The Fem
Food Says   The Code
Food for Thought
Around The World The Fems Mostly   Grow   Prep   or/and   Cook Food for Millenaries
Same as Cleaning   A Job for Life (Wife/Strife/Knife) for The Fems Want it or Not   It has been
The MeToo Movement is Saving Millions of Fems
Switch D/Pregnant for L/Sweet Fem Light/Ill/Ail/Elle/Hell and She Gets Fool (4 Fem Letters)
Here is a Few Examples on How   The Code   Organizes Our Thoughts Around this Necessary Part of Life which is Food
Apple: Ape/All   The Forbidden Fruit of The Bible   The Apple   The Fruit of Sin   Coming from the Tree of Knowledge It a Sin to Want to Know More
Carrot: Care/Hot
Chicken: Chick/Chicken is a Common Slang Name for a Fem in The US
Check/Chick   Ann/N/In/Hen/Haine/Virgin   Wing (We/In   Oui is Yes in French)
A Chicken Cannot Fly having Too Small Wings (They have been Trimmed or Cut for Long for Domestication)
Cold Cut: is Clitorectomy   or   First Vaginal Penetration without Anesthesia it is a Clitorectomy
Egg: Broken   When a Fem is Sexually Aroused She is Ready to be Broken   In/N/Ann/Hen/Virgin
Eggs Usually come by 2   2 Fried Eggs   Insinuating Bigamy   or   More
Farm Eggs   F/Fem/Fuck   Harm/Arm   Eggs/Hag
A Farm is a Place for The Fems to be Harmed   and/or   Armed
(But Having Arms Was Never Allowed to The Fems   Only Sleeves
(That   They Gave to a Galant Chevalier to go to Go To Combat for Luck)   so   Only
Harmed is Left for Her Says   The Code

Eggs and Sausages with Toasts: 2   or   All Penisses With One
Egg   or   Two (Bigamy/Polygamy)   Ovulating (See How Many
Spermatozoids Needed to Fertilize a Fem Egg)
Heating   and   Cooking   The Egg (s) is Part of   The Code   Process
by Heating The Fems Eggs Such as   Toasting   Frying   Boiling   Etc
(Those are Different Types of Pains/Abuses That Fems Go through) To
Accentuates/Facilitates/Accelerates   the Process of Her Desiring a Man
Sexually   Which Should be a Natural Process   In a Natural Fem and
Masc World   Where They Both Feel Sex Energy for Each Other
In   The Code   The Masc is Endlessly Running After that   Her/R/Heir/Or/
Whore/Err/Sex   Which He Also Despises Mostly   Being Influenced from
Those Old Religions
Bacon and Eggs: Bake/On/End/Eggs   Bacon (Bake/On) is Pork
Fat   Which is Not Allowed to Eat in Those Eastern Religions
Scrambled Eggs: Cook The Eggs Whipped or Beaten or Whole (Harsh/
Bad Words here to Address Such a Soft Thing as an Egg Which is The
Embryo Food)
Banana: Ban/Anna   Although it is a Positive Symbol for a Penis   That
is How   The Code   Interprets Symbols   to Control The Fem
Senses   Anna/N/Ann/Hen/Virgin   is Banned
Cherry: She   Err/R/Heir/Or/Whore/Air/Ere/Ire/Sex   He/E
(Cheri(e)   Cher/He)
A Cherry is Slang for Clitoris
A Cherry Also is the Red (Fem Rose Color) Flame on a Cigarette   Hot Hot
Hot   Here She Comes with Her Hot Clitoris and She Gets Pregnant with
an Heir/Or/Whore/Are/Err/Air/Ire/Sex
Hot Dog   Hot She Is Says   The Code   When a Bitch/Dog for that   S/
Sausage/Is/His/Us/Ass/Hiss/Serpent/Penis
A Weiner (Whine/Wine/Win   Her) is a Sausage   She Whines for It
Says   The Code
Ketchup: Catch   Hop/Up for that Loss of Red Blood
Mustard   Mast/Hard   and   Catch/Hop
Most/Hard   On   Hot/Dog   Figure it Out
Leeks: Leaks
Lime: L/Sweet Fem Love Light/Ill/Ail/Hell/Elle   M/Mom/
Motherhood   In Lime Green this Time as a Green Light Saying to Go
Says   The Code   Be Sweet   and   Be a Mother

The Dam Code The Damn Book

Switch M/Motherhood for F/Fem/Fuck and She Gets a Life (as a Mother it is)
The Code Wants Mothers or Whores (See Letter R in The Letter Chapter) from The Fems
Mango: Man/Go A Sweet Fruit for Him (in The Hawaiian Islands The Fems were Forbidden to Eat Some Fruits (Bananas) and Some Meats (Pork)
Mustard: Mast/Most Hard Mast is Slang for Penis
Onion: On/He/On On/Eon He Will Make You Cry Says The Code for an Eon Onions are Known as an Essential Food
Pork and Beans: P/Man Power Orc End/Hand B/Boy Holding All Fem Breasts Ann/N/In/Hen/Virgin S/Is/His/Us/Ass/Hiss/Serpent/Penis (Plural or All of Them)
Rack of Lamb: From being a Sheep Which She is Represented by in That Code (See Ship Sheep and Sheppard in the Words Chapter and Letter J/Sheppard Stick in The Letter Chapter) A Rack is an American Slang Word for the Fems Breasts
Roast: Her/R/Heir/Or/Whore/Are/Our/Err/Air/Ere/Ire/Sex Host
R/Oust He has Sex as a Host (The Host/Ghost Holy Hole/He/E Ghost He/E as Letter G/Penis Penetration here Comes In the Middle of The Night) Then Departs in Oust
It is a Roast (See Roast on American TV Where Guests Get Insulted)
Salmon: Sell M/Motherhood On Or Sell/Mom
Salmon is that Wiggly Little Virgin Girl from The Holy Grail/Girl Legend The Word Code without E/He is Now a Cod
Cod is a 3 Fem Letters (Cod is a Food Friday as a Good Catholic would Tell You No Red Meat on Friday Friday being Venus Day a Fem Day Therefore We are Deprived of Precious Red/Blood Meat)
Cod/Fish The Secret Code Comes Back to Animals Fishes here (See Fish and Ocean (O/See/Ann O/Fem Hole Shh/She N/Ann) in The Words Chapter) to Describe The Fems
Switch C/See/Young Girl for G/Vaginal Penis Penetration and She Gets God (The Reverse of God is Dog a Fem Symbol That Always Bothered Me)
Sole: The Soul A Flat Fish (A Fem with a Flat Chest was/is Frowned at by The Code)

The Fem is Alone Here Too (Solo   Soul/O   Solitude for Her) as The Zero   or   The Hole (H/Secret Society Letter is Silent here Makes it Even More Dangerous)
Steak: Stay   Here She is as a Piece of Dead Meat   even if She is Only   K/Wounded
S/His/Is/Us/Ass/Hiss/Serpent/Penis   It is His Take
He Takes a Steak
STK   S/Penis   T/Fem Cross   K/Broken Fem Warrior
T Bone: T/Fem Cross   The Code   Made its Way into Something Delicious   It Makes that Bloody Cycle Attractive to The Bone (a Bone is a Male Erection in American Slang)
Stay/Ache
toast: *slang*   to be doomed ruined or in trouble
Toast Bread (To/Host/Bred) Cheese (She/Is) with   Butter (Butt/Her (as in Penis Penetration in The Anus   Sodomy) But/Her (as in Stopping Her))
Trout: T/Fem Cross   Route   The Fem Curse   is The Route to be a Fish (F/Fem/Fuck   Is   She/Shh) for Her says   The Code
There are Many Many Other Examples of   The Code   in Action in The Food Section   and All   The Others
Food   for   The   Fool (All Fem Letters and 3 FFFs/Fem/Fuck as in All of Them   or   a Massive Amount of Them)   and   All of Them D/Pregnant

Fool: Is Made of All 4 Fem Letters
fool: a silly or stupid person
F/Hull
hull: the main part of a ship
(See Ship and Sheppard in The Words Chapter)
FU   (Fuck You in American Slang)   Elle/L/Sweet Fem Love Light/Ill/Hail/Hell/Ail/Oil/Heel/All/Elle/Sex
Switch O/Fem Hole for U/You/Ovulating and She Gets Full/Pregnant
Foul   Fowl (Chicken) are The Cover Words Here

Foot: Is Made of 4 All Fems Letters
F/Fem/Fuck   2 OOs/Fem Holes (Several or All of Them)   T/Fem Cross/Great Curse
The Code   Stands on Those   Legs/Lay/Eggs   and   Feet/Fit   to Hide/Step on   The Soul/Sole
For   Is made of 3 Fem Letters

The Dam Code The Damn Book

Take Heir/R/Whore/Her/Sex Away from For and She Gets Foe
foe: a person who feels enmity hatred or malice toward another
Foe is Made of 2 Fem Sounds Letters   FO   F/Fuck/Fem   O/Fem Hole
What is Foe   or   Faux Says   The Code   is Her Vagina/O
Faux   Means False in French   As a Copy of a Painting for
Example   or   Something Wrong   Fake   Artificial
From For to Faux and to Enemy in One Step   Because Her/R/Heir/
Whore/Sex is Missing   so   The Fems are The Enemies/Foe of   The
Code   Being Accused of Being False

Forbid: For/Bid   F/Fem/Fuck   Her/R/Hair/Ear/Hear/Here/Heir/Or/
Whore/Err/Are/Our/Ere/Air/Ire/Sex   Bid/Bed
What is Forbidden is Often for a Bid   or for   a Bed in Our World of
Financers
Bid that The Fem Is a Whore in Bed Says   The Code
bid: to command order direct

Force: FRS   F/Fem/Fuck   Horse
F/Whores
All Fems are Forced into being With Heirs   or   Being Whores   or/
and   Animals in   That Code
For   Her   Ass/S/Is/His/Us/Hiss/Serpent/Penis
For/Her/S   Means to Her   See the Penis/Ass   and   It is in Plural
Says   The Code
Switch O/Fem Hole for A/All Men and He Gets a Farce   An Example here
On How Different The Mascs Education/Outlook Compared to The Fems
in   That Code
Foresee   For   C/See/Young Girl   is the Force Pushing in   That
Code   to All Fems   It Starts Young Virgins Visions

Foreign: For/Reign   For/Reine
Reine Means Queen in French
Keep that Power Away (Foreign) from Her   so   She is Not Thinking of
Any Kind of Power for Herself

Foreplay: F/Fem/Fuck   Her/R/Hair/Ear/Hear/Here/Heir/Or/Whore/Err/
Are/Our/Air/Ire/Ere/Sex   P/Man Power   Lay
The Code   Says it is Fair/Play   For/Play

347

Lise Rochon

To Play is Not Very Often with Her   But Because She is Involved with Sex with a Man here   It Works for   The Code
Take L/Sweet Fem Light/Ail/Hell/Elle Away and She Gets For/Pay   Bringing Prostitution Along in The Foreplay

Forever: For/Ever   For/Have/Her
F/Fem/Fuck   Heir/R/Her/Are/Whore/Err/Sex   Eve/Have   R/Her/Are/Sex   Again
Here there are 2 RRs as in Plural or All of Them
F/Fem/Fuck   R/Heir/Whore/Her/Are/Err/Sex   V/Eve/Sex Fem Active   Her/R/Hair/Are/Here/Hear/Ear/Heir/Whore/Or/Err/Ere/Sex

Forfeit: For/Fate   For/Faith   For/Fat
There are 2 FFs/Fems/Fucks (Plural or All of Them) in Forfeit   and   F/Fem/Fuck Starts both of a 2 Syllables Word   It is a Forfeit for The Fems Says   The Code
forfeit: a fine   a penalty   a loss of right
F/Fem/Fuck Code Concept Starts the Word here   it Ends in   T/Fem Cross/Great Curse   Reread the Def of Forfeit
That is Too Much Information to Her Says   The Code   In This Word Forfeit She is Penalized for Her Faith/Fate (It is Fatal Fate/All for Her) T/Fem Cross   is Associated with F (Letter f in Small Caps is Also in the Shape of a Cross) as is   t/Fem Cross   Fate
Which is Her Fate   and   Penalized for being Fat
That would be a Big No from The Code   so It is a
Forfeit   and   it is a Cover Word

Forge: F/Fem/Fuck   Her/R/Heir/Whore/Err/Are/Air/Ere/Sex   G/Vaginal Penis Penetration
forge: beat into shape
The Message Here from   The Code   is to Beat into Shape/Forge Her   G/Vaginal Penis Penetration   the Way it Wants it as in   F/Fucking   that   Her/R/Heir/Whore/Air/Sex   for an Heir or Else

Forget: F/Fem/Fuck   Or/R/Her/Heir/Whore/Err/Ere/Air/Sex   Get The Code   Says to The Fems   Forget that Heir/Whore/Fuck   Role   that is there To Get Her (Together)

348

The Dam Code The Damn Book

For/Get   or   For/Give   Both are Still a Give from The Fem   She Takes on Doing The Giving   And Forgetting About it
F/Fem/Fuck   Heir/R/Whore/Her/Are/Err/Sex/Her   Give   The Fems Keep on Forgiving
Forgiven: F   R   G/Vaginal Penis Penetration   Eve/V/Fem Sex Active   Ann/N/In/Hen/Virgin
All Eves are Penetrated   It is Forgiven or/and   It is a Given to Her Says   The Code   But No
Forgotten: F   R   Got   N   to Her
The Whore is In Her   It is Forgiven Says   The Code   But No Says the Religions Below   She Will be Punished/Persecuted

Foresee: Force/He   For/See
He Forces   His/S/Is/Penis   Way   and   The Code   Foresees that F/Fem/Fuck   Her/R/Hair/Ear/Hear/Here/Heir/Or/Whore/Err/Are/Our/Air/Ire/Ere/Sex   See
foresee: to know in advance
Damn   DMN   Carries   The Pregnant   The Mother   The Virgin   In That Order   so   Rebirth of that Repetition into The Future Keeps Going On   Foreseeing   That it is How it Works

Former: Form/Her
As in to Shape Her
former: preceding in time   in the past
That Formation Happens from the Past   She is Not Aware of it   Not Being there   it is as a Tight Corset that Takes Her Breath Away and Weakens Her All Day   Making Her Sick   Not Knowing it Because it Is/Was there for so Long
The Code   Works In the Past Present and Future   so It Can Keep Its Hypnotic Grip on The Fems

Fornicate: F/Fem/Fuck   Horn   He   Gate/Get
For/Negate
F/Fem/Fuck   Her/R/Heir/Or/Whore/Err/Air/Sex   Negate
Negating is a Form of Forgetting
fornicate: voluntary sexual intercourse outside marriage
Adultery   A/All Men   Dull/Doll   Tear   He

349

Forth: F/Fem/Fuck   Whore/R/Her/Heir/Or/Err/Are/Our/Ere/Ire/Sex   T/Fem Cross   H/Secret Code Letter
Letters T and H are Together here as in One Breath   TH
TH   Assimilates T/Fems Cross   with   H/Secret Code   in a Secret Silent Manner
H/Secret Code Grid Letter   Is Here in a Silent Mode as Usual
What is Going Forth Here Says   The Code
Is That The Fems are Damned By   The Code
forth: inward or onward in place or space

The Code   is Fully Capable to Hold That Fort   It has been Holding It for a Couple of Thousands Years
Only Knowledge about It Can Make Us Above it
Forth is a Big Silent Cover Word

Fortress: Forth   Her/R/Heir/Or/Whore/Are/Our/Err/Ire/Sex   Ass/S/Is/Us/His/Ass/Hiss/Serpent/Penis
Fortress is to Bring Forth Sex in Plural   Fort/Rest
Fortress Could Be a Homosexual Word too   When Penis Bring Forth the Ass   For/Their/Ass   with 2 Asses Here
There was No Fems in Fortresses Back Then Except for Sex or Trade

Forward: For   Ward
4   Word (See # 4 in the Numbers Chapter)
4 is the Number of Stability   Justice   THE LAW   Jupiter
Jupiter Brings Fortune   Not So Fast   Fortune Oh NO Not for Her   Depravity to The Fems Oh Yes   Is the Power of That Word   For/Whore/D   FRD   F/Fem   R/Whore   D/Pregnant
Forward is here as in   For   The   Word
That   Word Sentence   Is the Foundation Concept of The Secret Grid
"At The Beginning Was The Word"
That First Sentence in That Bible is the Only One We Need to Remember   After that it Is All Repetitions of That Sentence/Concept in So Many Forms and Manners in That Book   A Huge Form of a Kaleidoscope It is
Forward is a Word That Starts with F/Fem Letter
Meaning

According to   The Code Grid   the Rest of the Letters in that
Word   Destroys   Ridicules   or   Diminishes   its Common Meaning
Here the Word Pushes   The Code   Grid Ahead   It is Spared Destruction
Even when Starting with F
The Word Forward Remains an Impersonal Word
Forward Means to Go Ahead   It is Guarded   Subtly   and   She is There
as The   F/Fem/Fuck   Whore/R/Heir/Or/Err/Her/Hair/Are/Here/Hear/Ear/
Sex   Ward
ward: process of guarding   to keep watch
The Word   is Guarded from Her Knowledge in the Same Time   To
Project Its   Code   in the Future in a Good Light   Is Another Way   The
Code   Works To Keep the Order (Herd/Her) To Continue (Cunt/He/Knew)
the Process of   The Secret Language Code
To Demolish The Fems by Making Them (Damned)   All Pregnant/
Whores/Or/Err/Sex
The Code   Goal is to Own Her Sexuality

Foul: All 4 Fem Letters   Foul is Bad Word for Her
Switch U/You/Ovulating/Open Loins for Another O/Fem Hole and She
Gets a Fool
Take Away O and Add Another L/Sweet Fem Love Light/Ill/Ail/Hail/Heel/
All/Elle/Oil/Hell and She Gets Full (Pregnant)
Switch U for W/All Fem Sex Active and She Gets a Fowl   Another 4 Fem
Letters Words
Fowl is a Soft Cover Word here   Along with the Autumn Season   The
Fall/Feel (A Fem Emotion) is So Close

Foundation: F/Fem/Fuck   Hound   A/All Men   She   On
As a Dog (Bitch) She Is The Foundation Says   The Code   and on with it

Fox: All 3 Fem Letters   FX   Fucks
She is a Fox   She Gets to Fuck   A Fix for a Fox
Now that is a Poor Word for Her   Again from   The Code

Frat: F/Fem/Fuck   Rat
Secret Societies have Frats (Only for Men)
frat: fraternity

Even if it Starts with F a Fem Letter   The Fem has No Place there in a Frat   being a Rat Fucking   or   a Fucking Rat Says   The Code

Fraud: FROD   Is Made of 4 All Fems Sounds Letters
The F/Fem/Fuck   and   The Rod
If a Fem Own Her Stick (As in Personal Power) or be in Front of a Masc or have Her Own Path in Life   It is a Fraud
Same as   F/Fem/Fuck   Road   Is a Big No from   The Code   so   That would be Fraud
Switch D for T/Fem Cross and She Gets Froth (See VIP Word Froth in The Letters Chapters)

Free: F/Fem/Fuck   R/Heir/Whore/Her/Are/Our/Err/Sex   2 EEs/He (Plural or All of Them)
The Code   For The Fems To be Free Would Be   Her/R Giving Sex to All Men   and for Free

Freedom: The Free and the Dumb   Free/Doom   Free/Dome
freedom: the state of being free or at liberty rather than being in confinement or under physical restraint
Here is a Double (2 Breasts) Message from   The Code
Freedom is in the Dome/Breast (See Dome/Doom in The Words Chapter) and She is Stupid Says   The Code

Free Masons: Free/My/Sons
All the Way from the Beginning of Our Time
People have been Fighting Slavery
Freemasons Found   Wealth   Power   Knowledge in Discovering Building Codes   Girls not Invited

Freeze: Free   Z/As Above As Below/Sleep on it
Says The Code   ZZZ   The Past Is Just As the Future   Says The Code   No One will Free Z   No Need   It is Sleeping
Freezer: Freeze/Her   Free/Is/Her   Free/Z/Her   Oh No Says   The Code   Freedom is Not Allowed for The Fems   so   it Puts Her in the Freezer

Friday: Fry/Day   Fry/Her/Day   Friar/Day

The Dam Code The Damn Book

Nothing Good for The Fems here
Friday was Used as a Day of Sacrifice by the Roman Church
No Meat on Friday for Catholics   Only Fish or Eggs as Protein that Day
Friday is Goddess Venus Day
Friday the 13th is a Bad Omen Day (See # 13 in the Numbers Chapter)
Says   The Code

Friend: For/End
There is No Such a Thing in   The Code   as Friendship for The Fems
F/Fem/Fuck   Whore/R/Her/Err/Are/Heir/Sex   End
Take Whore/R/Her/Are/Whore/Sex Away from Friend and Get a Fiend
Fiend: satan   evil   diabolically cruel or wicked person
FND is Also Made of 3 Fem Sound Letters

Friendship: Friend is on a Ship Here (See Ship and Sheppard in The Words Chapter)
Ship: "Old English *scip*   related to old Norse s*kip*   Old high German *skif*
ship scipfi cup
Cup and Ship are the Same   Cups Being The Fems Breasts Loins and Heart   as in   Christ/Cup/Chalice
Ship/She/P   Would be Her Body
Friend does Not Touch the Water being on a Ship
Separated from Her by   The Code
The Code   Says   Skip it by Replacing H/Secret Code Letter with K/
Broken   or   wounded fem Warrior Fem Warrior ?

Frigid: F/Fem/Fuck   is Rigid
That is from Lack of Love and Trust
She Was Obligated to have Sex According to the Law of Marriage with that Husband (Us/Band) Any Time He Wanted it   Frigid She Became   Also Not Wanting to be Pregnant Again

Frill: Free   Ill/L/Sweet Fem Love Light/Elle/Ail/Hail/All/Hell
To Free The Fems from The Curse   Would be a Big No from   The Code   so
frill: ruffle   something superfluous   affection of manner style etc   *slang*   a woman especially a young woman *frail*   a trimming as a strip of cloth or lace gathered at one edge and left loose at the other

Lise Rochon

In The Code Frail Is a Favorite Term for Her   It Says No Focus or Energy for The Fems   That Kind of Symbolism Has been Designed for Her The Masc Is Educated in a Different Angle of Life and Can Pass Right Through Those Bars and Go on Unattached to that Fem Angle

Fringe: F/Fem/Fuck   Range
fringe: an outer edge   a margin   periphery
range: the extent to which or the limits between variation is possible
Every Word has Always Limits with   The Code   for The Fems
This Word Range has 33 Different Definitions in The English Dictionary
So   When F Has the Head Up on Range   She is in the Margin or at the Periphery   So Not Much Happens for Her There

Frolic: F/Fem/Fuck   Her/R/Heir/Or/Whore/Are/Our/Err/Ire/Sex   Lick For/All/Lick
frolic: merry play   merriment   gaiety fun
Here She Goes Licking Thinking it is Frolicking as Says   The Code
A Licking in American Slang is a Solid Beating

From: FRM   is Made From All Fems Sound Letters   R/Her/Ear/Hear/Hair/Err/Here/Heir/Or/Whore/Are/Our/Ire/Air/Ere/Sex (Letter R being Half Fem and Half Masc (See The Battles of Letter R in the Letters Chapter))
F/Fem/Fuck   R/Her   O/Fem Hole   M/Motherhood
F/Fucking Fem   as the   R/Heir/Whore with Her O/Fem Hole Ends in M/Motherhood Says   The Code
The Word From is Another in Between Word with No Real Identity than to Point a Direction   The Code   Decides of Which   From the Origin (Whore/He/Gene)   To Our Age

Froth: F/Fem/Fuck   Rot
Froth would be F in Front of R/Her/Ear/Hear/Hair/Err/Here/Heir/Or/Whore/Are/Our/Ire/Air/Ere/Sex   with Her O/Fem Hole   T/Fem Cross   Next to   H/Secret Code Letter   Closing the Word
A Big No from   The Code   to have Her in Charge of Her Own Sexuality with Knowledge of   The Code   so
It is Froth at the Mouth   Very Unappealing
th: a suffix forming nouns of action (*Birth*) or abstract nouns denoting quality or condition

The Dam Code The Damn Book

TH is a Dangerous Mixture of Letters for Her Says   The Code   Because T/Fem Cross is Tied to H/Secret Code Letter   As in One Item
froth: an aggregation of bubbles as on agitated liquid or at the mouth of a hard driven horse   foam   spume   something unsubstantial trivial or evanescent
Water (All Water is Fem) Here is as Foam (FM 2 Fem Letters)   or   Saliva   or Fluid (5 Fem Letters) Coming Out of a Horse/Whores Mouth   A Revolting Sight   Resulting from Agitation or Abuse and   It is Evanescent (Eve/In/A/Scent)
Evanescent: vanishing   fading away   fleeting
Not Much For Her here so   the Memory of it All is Gone Fast   How Convenient for   The Code
Switch O for A/All Men and He Gets Frat   Short for Fraternity or Brotherhood   Now That is a Big Yes for   The Code   More Secrets to Keep Her Enslavement Going
The F and the Rat (See Hat In The Words Chapter)
Switch TH for G/Penis Penetration and He Gets a Frog   Kiss that Frog   It is a Prince Says   The Code

Frugal: For/U/Girl   For   U   Girl
Girls are Anemic   Already at 16 Years Old from Too Much Blood Loss   Girls Bleed Out   They Get Weak and Emotional   so   the Rest of   The Code   Story Continues
For Us Girls Anemia through Being Frugal is to Keep Us Weak Says   The Code

Fruit: F/Fem/Fuck   Root
F and Her Roots are the Fruit of Her Loins   No Says   The Code   so R/Her/Ear/Hear/Hair/Err/Here/Heir/Or/Whore/Are/Our/Ire/Air/Ere/Sex   2 OOs/Fem Holes   T/Fem Cross
It Takes 2 Holes (Polygamy) and a T/Fem Cross for R/Her/Heir/Whore to Root in   The Code

Fry: F/Fem R/Her/Ear/Hear/Hair/Err/Here/Heir/Or/Whore/Are/Our/Ire/ Air/Ere/Sex   Y/Wounded Fem
When Wounded and Fried The Fem is a Fucking Whore with or without a Heir Says   The Code

355

Fuck: FOK   3 Fem Sounds Letters
Switch F for L/Sweet Fem Love Light/Ill/Ail/Hail/Heel/All/Elle/Oil/Hell and She Gets Luck or Lock   which will Not be there for Her
Buck   Bock
(Beer)   Cock   Dock   Duck   Knock   Mock   Nock   Suck   None of those Words Except Buck and Bock (Which Starts with B/Boy Holding All Fem Breasts) Are Really Positive for Her
fuck: to have sexual intercourse   to meddle   a despicable person
The Fems Always go Down in   The Code

Full: Is Made of 4 All Fems Letters
F/Fem/Fuck   U/You/Ovulating   L/Sweet Fem Love Light/Ill/Ail/Hail/Heel/All/Elle/Oil/Hell
F/All   Fuck them All   Until Full (Pregnant)
Switch U for A/All Men and He Gets Fall
A Masc Letter Cannot be Surrounded by   The Fems   There is a Punishment Says   The Code
so   Autumn (Hot/On) as in Her Fall Season (Seize/On) is the Cover Word here
seize: to take hold of suddenly or forcibly grasp   to take possession of by force or at will   to grasp mentally understand clearly and completely

Fun: FN   2 Fem Asexual Sounds Letters
F/Fem/Fuck   U/You/Ovulating   N/In/Hen/Ann/Virgin
The Code   Says Fun is having the Virgin Open Hole Fucking
Switch U for A/All Men and He Gets a Fan
Switch U for i/Marriage Act and She Gets a Fin (Back to the Fish for Her)
Funny   Fun/He   Phone/He   Phony it Is

Function: F/Fem/Fuck   On   She/Shh   On   Fun/She/On
Because All Sounds Must be Used in All Ways in   The Code   A Word with   Fun The Fems   and   On would have to be Mapped Also   so function: the kind of action or activity proper to a person thing or institution   the purpose for which something is designed or exists   role
The Future is Hidden to the Young Fems   The Code   Makes Her Think That Her Function is to have Fun

The Dam Code The Damn Book

Funnel: Fun   L/Sweet Fem Love Light/Ill/Ail/Hail/Heel/All/Elle/Oil/Hell
Funnel Keeps All Fems Going in One Direction   Down   With the Word
Fun in Mind We All Fems Funnel Down

Funeral: Fun/Her/All
When Something Fun Happens to Her it is a Funeral Says   The Code
Phone/R/All
The Phone (Phonetics   The Purpose of this Book)
and its Glass Ceiling is Where The Fems can See a Little But do Not
Hear Any

Furnace: F/Fem/Fuck   Her R/Ear/Hear/Hair/Err/Here/Heir/Or/Whore/
Are/Our/Ire/Air/Ere/Sex   N/In/Hen/Ann/Virgin   Ace
When N with F and R are Aces   It is All Burning Up in a Furnace (Hot Sex)

Further: For   D/Pregnant   R/Her/Ear/Hear/Hair/Err/Here/Heir/Or/
Whore/Are/Our/Ire/Air/Ere/Sex
To Go Further in   The Code   is To Make Her Pregnant
Fur/D/Her   or   to Animalize Her
F/Fem/Fuck   R/Her   T/Fem Cross   R/Her
All F and T are with Heir or Whores
Also   The Code   Create a Constant Disfiguration of the Fems Mental
Plane   Fart/Her   F/Art/Her (See Art and Hat/Hate in The Words Chapter)

Fuse: F/Fem/Fuck   Use
The Use of The Fems is to Fuse with   The Code
fuse: to blend by melting together
A Fuse Box is Her in a Box

Fuss: FS
F/Fem/Fuck   S/Is/His/Us/Ass/Hiss/Serpent/Penis
fuss: to worry unnecessarily   unnecessary agitation
When a Fem Letter is in Front of a Masc Letter   It is Always Something
Unwanted Wrong Unnecessary or Little as a Baby Fussing Says   The
Code
Letter F has Nothing to Do with Sex or Children   But Is Forced into it
by   The Code   Definition

Both F and E Are Grid Parts with The H/The Silent Hiding Letter of   The Code

Futile: Few/T/Ill
The Code   Says Few   T/Fem Cross   are Ill (See Devil   Eve that is Ill)   Is a Flat Lie   The Fems Has had Many More Health Issues Often from Unknown Causes than Men
Few/Till   The Code   Says Few Fem Works   Another Lie   Women Always Worked Hard
till: to labor
Few/Tell   No One Says Nothing About it   No One Thinks about It   Because It Is Futile
Futile Here Convinces Us   That Us T/Fem Cross   Do Not   Work   and are Not Ill   and   We do Not Talk about It   It is Futile
Futility: Few/Till/He/T   The Code   Repeat the Meaning of Futile as in Accomplished

Future: F/U/T/R
FU is Fuck You in American
FU   T/Fem Cross   Her/R/Hair/Are/Here/Hear/Ear/Heir/Or/Whore/Err/Sex
Few/Chore   As if the Future would be Fewer Chores when There is Actually Always More

G   g
Intro
Letter G in Big Caps is the Hymen   Hi/Men/Man Penetration
The G Symbol/Letter Shows the O/Fem Hole Perforated by the Stick/Penis
Small Cap g Is the Fertilizing of Her Egg
G is the 7th Letter   It is   The Code   Lucky Number (See # 7 in the Numbers Chapter)
G is Also The God Letter   Part of those Secret Society Systems Is that   The Code   Established Strong Mental Emotional Barriers Between Symbols   Which Makes People Look the Other Way Fast   In Fear of Being Sacrilegious to Their Beloved God   Example   Pope   Poop   Pop (a Girl)   God and Dog   Those Gross Associations makes People Abandon   That Kind of Search
Letter G is Shown Between the Compass Legs
The Compass (Con/Pass) is the Logo of the Freemasons

Those Legs Always Look Fem   and they are Kept Opened on That Logo   They are a Manipulated Tool on a Map   Those Compass Legs Have a Hole at the Top where the Vagina would be
In Greek A Alpha Letter is in the Shape of an Old Compass   (See Letter A in The Letter Chapter)
Compass Word Sound and Con/Pass Sound are Almost the Same   When   N/Virgin   is Shifted into the M/Mother Role   N becomes M   and More/Mare is on   More/On   Moron   All for Her
In The Chi Rho Symbol Image   An Earlier Form of Christogram   The Compass is the Perfect Shape of the Ancient Greek Alpha Letter It has also the Omega Symbol on the Right   There are 2 Letters Omega   ω and Ω   ω is in the Shape of a Butt   And Ω is a Very Pregnant Belly   The Old Symbols are Often More Visuals
In The Wheel of Chiro   T/Fem Cross   is There   X/Fallen Cross   is there (T becomes X   as N becomes Next M)   P/Man Power Is there in a Sword Shape
The Earlier Version of the Chi Rho Logo   The Staurogram
Had a Cross Similar to the Egyptian Cross of Life
Staurogram was First Used to Abbreviate the Greek Word for Cross
The Ankh   The Tau (Taurus is an Entirely Fem Astrological Sign) are Other Versions for the Greek Word Cross
All the Way from Egypt Before Christ was Crucified
In the Ancient Hebrew Language the Letter Tau is the Cross
There was Greek Theta the Double TTs (Tits) For the th Sound T/Fem Cross   and   h/Secret Code Together   h is so Small here it is almost Incognito
Attached to the Upper t
The Earlier Version is The 1X Monogram
It is a Superposition of the I   T   X
Creating the Spikes of that Wheel again   So It Keeps on Turning From its Axis (X the Axe is the Fallen Cross)   X/Is Axe/His   Ass/His   As/His Once   I/Stick/Penis   is Inserted in O to become G   The Very Quest of the Secret Societies Code is Attained   The Transformation of Her Natural Fem Power Stick Sinks into T/Fem Cross/Great Curse   Then Falls in X/Fallen Cross
Those   Secret Code Secrets   Systems Have Manipulated Us for Millenaries

Lise Rochon

Words with Gg are   Gee and Letter jJ (See Shepherd in the Words and J in The Letter Chapters) Jay as in a Blue (Masc Color) Jay

G   g
Gag: A/All Men   is in Between   2 GGs/God Letter/Hymen Penetrations
Gag is the G/God Letter with A/All Men in the Middle or/and   G/Penis Penetration to A/All Men   That would be Bad for   The Code   to Have this Information Revealed   so
gag: to stop the mouth by putting something in it
A Gag is Also a Joke   Gag Implies Homosexuality Also

Gain: G/Penis Penetration/God Letter   is with   N/In/Hen/Ann/Donkey/ Virgin   The Code   Says that if the Virgin has Sex it is a Gain   Even a Spiritual One

Galaxy: G/All/X/He
G/Penis Penetration/God Letter   All/L/Ill/Ail/Hail/Sweet Fem Love Light   Axe   He/E
X/Fallen Dead Cross for Her Is the Ultimate End for All Fems Says   The Code   It Is as Big as a Galaxy
Those Secret Societies Codes Think Far   Close   Big   and Small
Gal/Axe/He   All Girls through the Axe/X
Then Comes the Milky Way   Milk/He/We   The Milk is On Its Way   Then Comes the   Planet (Plan/It)

Garden: Guard   Ann/N/In/Haine/Donkey
Grr   D/Pregnant   In/N/Ann
Guard that Virgin in an Illusion of a Garden as a Donkey Until Pregnant

Gas: Gay/Ass
G/Penis Penetration/God Letter   Ass
A Gay Ass   That is a Gas (Fun) Says   The Code

Gasbag: G/Penis Penetration/God Letter   Ass/S/Is/His/Us/Ass/Hiss/ Serpent/Penis   Bag
Gasbag Implies Homosexuality   A Hidden Meaning Only for Certain Men to Understand   The Code   Hides in It

gasbag: a bag holding gas as in a balloon or dirigible   a talkative person   windbag

Ghastly   G/Penetration/God Letter   S/Is/His/Us/Ass/Hiss/Serpent/Penis   Lay
Another Big Secret Implying Homosexuality in The Code Here   So   CHECK
ghastly: shockingly frightful or dreadful horrible

Gate: G/Penis Penetration   Hate
Hatred and Greed are Themes in   The Code
Here Hate is a Gate or a Bridge to Sex
Because it Implies there Must be Hate to The Fems to Get to Have Sex With Her   so   There are No Attachment to The Fems

Gather: Get/Her
gather: to bring together in one group
The Code   says Put Them All Fems Together
Gath/Her
Gath: a wide set of steps descending to a river   a mountain pass   a mountain range   escarpment
A Gath can be a Dangerous Place too
G/Hate/Her   because of the Hate Also

Gay: G/Penis Penetration   Hey
Penetration is Calling Here
G/Hay
hay: grass coming out of the ground
hey: used as an exclamation to call attention or to express pleasure surprise bewilderment   *Informal* Hello used as a greeting
To be Gay Now is The Word for Homosexuality   The Code   Says It is a Calling that Comes Right Out of the Ground   as in Natural

Gender: G/N/D/R
G/Penis Penetration   Impregnates   N/In/Hen/Virgin/Ann/
Donkey   by   Her/R/Ear/Hear/Hair/Err/Here/Heir/Or/Whore/Are/Our/Air/Ire/Ere/Sex
The Code   Says   Gene/D/Her

Gene: GN
G/Penis Penetration   of the   N/In/Hen/Ann/Virgin is the First Step to have Access to the Gene Pool
gin: a trap or snare for game   to begin   if whether   a primitive engine in which a vertical shaft is turned by horses driving a horizontal beam or yoke in a circle
In/Gene   Engine   See Pics of a Horse Gin
The Horses/Whores are Moving around in a Circle (Cycle/All) from a Made Cross (Fem Cross) Rotating on a Shaft (Penis) to Create Power/Pow/Her) And It is a Trap Too Says   The Code

Generation: Gene   E/He   Rate   On
Gene   He   Ration
The Secret Code   has Manipulated the Gene Pool for Ever   As far as in the Time of Solomon They Used to Marry Tall Fems to Short Men   so   the Daughters would be Smaller
Gene   He   Ray   She/Shh   On   Silence Is For Her   He Advances on a Ray and He Rates it and Rations It
Generation Has Nothing Fem About it   She does Not Exist There
Gin/He/Ration
gin: a trap or snare for game   to begin   if whether   a primitive engine in which a vertical shaft is turned by horses driving a horizontal beam or yoke in a circle

Genesis: Gene/He/Is
G/Penis Penetration/God Letter   In/N/Ann/Donkey
He/E   His/Is/S/Serpent/Penis
Ther Fem Is here Invisible as Usual in the Most Important/Vitals Functions of Life   Such as Procreation (!) She Had to be There According to The Laws of Nature   But No Says   The Code   She Is Not   Only as a   Virgin/N/In/Ann   which Knows Nothing about Sex   how can that be procreation: to beget or to generate   to produce   bring into being
Jeans is the Cove r Word here   Jeans/He/Is (Jeans were Mens Clothing Only for a Long Time)

Genital: Gin/it/All
G/Penis Penetration/God Letter   N/In/Ann/Donkey   He/E   Tail (Penis)

362

gin: a trap or snare for game   to begin   if whether   a primitive engine in which a vertical shaft is turned by horses driving a horizontal beam or yoke in a circle
Gene/He/Tall   His Genes will Make Him Tall
Gene/He/T/All   The Genes will Create T/Fem Cross In All Fems (See Letter L in the Letter Chapter)
No Fem Connection Here at All with Genes Says   The Code   Except through   T/Loss of Fem Blood

Genius: Gene   He   His/S/Is/Us/Ass/Hiss/Serpent/Penis
No Fem Here Either   The Code   Speaks here about The Masc and His Penis Connecting His Genes and Genius Together
gin: a trap or snare for game   to begin   if whether   a primitive engine in which a vertical shaft is turned by horses driving a horizontal beam or yoke in a circle
Gin/Is/Us

Gently: Gent/Lay
G/An/Aint   Lay
gent: *informal* gentleman   elegant   graceful
The Code   has it All Covered   It Says to The Fems It is Gentle in Bed   Count All the Rapes and Murders of Fem
Men Under   That Code   Create Wars to Rape The Fems
Switch G for C/Young Virgin and She Gets Cent/Lay   So She can do it for Pennies Too
Switch G for B/Boy Holding All Fems Breasts and He gets a Bentley

Girth: G/God Letter   Hurt
girth: the measure around anything circumference   something that encircles a band or girdle
As a Corset that keeps Going Smaller on Her   She can Hardly Breath   or   Focus
Switch G for B/Boy Holding All Fems Breasts and He Gets Birth (B is Too Young for The Code)
Switch G for M/Motherhood and She Gets
mirth: amusement   or   laughter
The Code   Hides The Pain from the Girth to The Fems
Switch G for H/Secret Code Letter Society Letter and Gets That Hurt

Get: Gate
G/Penis Penetration/God/Letter   is Hot (as in Got) in the Common Words Get/Got
That Gate is there as a Clear Garrison Word Because of A/All Men in it
Switch E/He for O/Fem Hole and She Gets Got
G/Hot   G/Penis Penetration/God Letter Is Hot   Therefore it is a
Go   with   T/Fem Cross
The Fem as a Person (Per/Son) is Not Involved   She Does Not Exist   She is in Here to be Got
She Is Kept Away from It/Hit by The Gate   Until Got It/Hit   Which Is For Her Says   The Code

Ghost: G/Host
G/Penis Penetration/God Letter   with a Host
That Host Can be Any Man Says   The Code

Gift: G/F/T
G/Penis Penetration/God Letter   I/Marriage Act Union   F/Fem/Fuck   T/Fem Cross
The Gift to Her is the Penetration/Sex Union   as   T/Fem Cross
Gift is also Gay/F/T   That is a Cornerstone Word   Gay/Fit   Homosexuality Made its Way in Gift

Giggle: G/Girl
Words with 3 GGGs are Rare
3 GGG s/Penisses Penetrations in Writing   and   2 GGs in Sound Letters   Penetrate All Girls
Only Girls Giggle   Gig/All
gig: a spear for catching fishes   a part time engagement   a punishment
Catching Fish (a Fem) takes Time   and   the Punishment for Her   To be Speared

Gigolo: GGLO
Words with 2 GGs or more are a Rare Occurrence   G/Penis Penetration/God Letter   Glows   This is a Petty Word Too
Gig/O/Low   Another Gig to Keep Her Low
With 2 OOs/Fem Holes   it indicates Plural or All of Them

gigolo: a man living off the earnings of a woman   an escort

Gill: A Fem Name
gill: to catch(fish) or (of fish) to be caught in a gill net   to gut (fish)   a narrow stream   rivulet   a wooded ravine   *archaic* a girl or sweetheart
Here   The Code   Compares Girls to Fishes to be Caught/Gutted by The Net   A Rivulet/Water Represents The Fem   Few Escape from that Ravine
Add   R/Her/Ear/Hear/Hair/Err/Here/Heir/Or/Whore/Are/Our/Ire/Air/Ere/Sex   and She Gets Girl

Girdle: Girl   D/Pregnant   All/L/Sweet Fem Love Light/Ill/Ail/Hail/Heel/All/Elle/Oil/Hell
All Girls Pregnant as in Confined/Limited in a Girdle   Corsets are Damaging and Painful   Only The Fems Wear them for the Illusion of Having a Smaller Middle Waist   as in Looking Non Pregnant
girdle: a belt coed sash or the As worn about the waist   anything that encircles confines or limits   a woman elastic corset covering the waist to the thigh   anything that encircle confines or limits
See Girl Below

Girl: G/Penis Penetration/God Letter   i/Marriage Act Union   R/Her/Ear/Hear/Hair/Err/Here/Heir/Or/Whore/Are/Our/Air/Ire/Ere/Sex   L/Sweet Fem Love Light/Ill/Ail/Hail/Heel/All/Elle/Oil/Hell
In   The Code   The Word Girl Means   i/Marriage Act Union   as   L/Fem Sweet Love   for   R/Heir or be a Whore
G/Penis Penetration   with Hurl/Herl/Earl   RL   Her/L
hurl: to throw or cast down   to fling with great force
The Girl is to be Destroyed Completely (Complete/Lay) and Utterly (Hot/Her/Lay)
Why   Why   Why   YYY (Y is the Fem First Stage Breaking Fem Letter   See Letter Y in The Letter Chapter)
Earl is the Cover Word here   It Mellows That Which Hides in the Word Girl
The Roots of the Word Girl are Ancient
herl: false feather for the making of fishing hooks
Hook   Hooker   Whore as the Hooker
The Hook Catches the Fish (Fem)
The Code   is Old and Nothing is Left to Coincidence

Girl   Curl   Gill   Guile   Grail
The Girl is the Grail and the Grail is Her Blood
As in "Le Sang Réel"   The Real Blood   Not Royal Blood   That would be Sang Royal   Although One is the Cover for the Other
The Grail is a Popular Literary Theme
Take R/Her/Heir/Whore/Sex Away from Girl and Get a Gill (Back to the Fishes Pool for Her)
It is Difficult to Understand   In the Holy Grail Book   That it Refers to Little Girls as a Salmon   A Wiggly Wet Fish   When they Rape that Young Virgin the First time   She was Held
And That Bleeding Lance from King Arthur (Art/Her   See Art in The Words Chapter)   The Bleeding Lance Would be His Own Penis   When it Come Out of Her Vagina at His Sex Time   He thought He was the One Bleeding   He could Not Handle All That Bleeding Anymore   Therefore The Great King Depression/Sadness   His Lance was Bleeding   No

It was in Between the 5th and 6th Century   Any Knowledge was Under The Empire of The Roman Church   Ignorance was common   Several of Arthur Many Loved Wives/Concubines Had Hemorrhages at Childbirth   or   had Constant Bleeding Cycles   Many Died
Perceval (Pierce/A/Wall   Pierce/Ov (Ovo)/All)
Girl   GRL   Grail   She is the Cup   The Cup is The Chalice   The Uterus that Bleeds   She is the One Bleeding   The Blood of Christ Is That Story
G/R/All   G/Penis Penetration   R/Her/Ear/Hear/Hair/Err/Here/Heir/Or/Whore/Are/Our/Air/Ire/Ere/Sex All
G/Penis Penetration/God Letter with Earl   or   be Hurled
earl: a male given name from the old English word meaning Noble
Men have So Many Titles (Sire   Count   Bishop   etc)
She is the Breathing/Breeding Part as the Fish
The Fish (Fem) Breathe (Breeds) Though the Gill (Girl)   Any Thing Related to the Water is Fem
gill: a stream   a brook   a rivulet
Stream Brooks and Rivulets are Sweet and Soft
Switch G for C/See/Young Girl and She Gets Curl
Curls are Waves on The Ocean   The Girl is the Fishing Goal   For the Score (S/C/Whore)
Switch L for T/Fem Cross and She Gets Girth
girth: the measure around anything   circumference

The Dam Code The Damn Book

Back to the Waist/Waste for Her

Girth: G/R/T
G/Penis Penetration   R/Her/Ear/Hear/Hair/Err/Here/Heir/Or/Whore/Are/Our/Ire/Air/Ere/Sex
Switch TH for L/Sweet Fem Love Light/Ill/Ail/Hail/Heel/All/Elle/Oil/Hell and She Gets Girl
girth: to encircle   a band around the horse belly to hold the saddle
Back to the Horse/Heirs/Whores for Her   In a Twist Here   The Code   Adds Her the Corset   (See BB in The Words Chapter)   She is Encircled Here   Specifically Around the Belly (Bell/He   Ball/He) (See Bell/Belle in The Letter Chapter)

Gist: G/His/T   G/Is/T
G/Hymen Penetration/God Letter   Is/His   T/Fem Cross/Great Curse
gist: the essential part of a matter
This Word Tells (Tails) a Lot   The Matter is to Mate/Her Which in Essence Curses Her

Give: G/Penis Penetration   Eve
Eve/V/Fem Sex Active has Given Up Her Virginity as a Given
Give Up: G/Eve/Hop
She Gives a Hop   It is Free too

Glad: G/Hymen Perforation/God Letter   and   the Lad
lad: affectionate term for a boy   a chap
Hymen Perforation Makes Him Glad
G/L/Add   And it Adds to Him Too
G   L/Sweet Fem Love Light/Ill/Ail/Hail/Heel/All/Elle/Oil/Hell   Add
It Adds to Him to Perforate Gladly the   G/Hymen   of   L/Fem Sweet Love/

Glamour: Girl   Amour
Love is Glamorous to The Fems Says   The Code   to Young Girls
Switch G for C/Young Girl and She Gets Clam/Her   Claim/Her
There is Nothing Nice for The Fems in   The Code

Glare: G/Lie/Her   G/Liar

glare: piercing stare
G/Lair
lair: a secluded place   a den
G   Lay   R/Her
Girl and Glare are So Close   Claire Is a Fem Name

Glimpse: G/Limps/In
glimpse: a very brief passing look sight or view   a momentary or slight   appearance   a vague idea
It takes Just a Moment Says   The Code   for   G/Penis Penetration/God Letter   to Limp   N/In/Ann/Virgin

Glory: Glow/Ray   Glow   R/Her/Ear/Hear/Hair/Err/Here/Heir/Or/Whore/Are/Our/Ire/Air/Ere/Sex   E/He
All this High Self Esteem Makes Him Glow
Her/R/Heir/Or/Whore is There as a Tool

Glove: G/Penis Penetration/God Letter   Love
That is How the Girl Fall (F/Fem/Fuck   All) in Love   with G Penetration
It Fits as a Glove Says   The Code
Glow   Ov (Egg)
A Glow for Eve (As an Egg Carrier Only) here because of Ovulation Fitting Her   As a Glove

Go: G/Penis Penetration/God Letter   O/Fem Hole
Goes/On: Go/Son
It is a Go When the Hole is With G/Hymen Penetration (Hi/Men)

Goal: G/Hole
G/Penis Penetration/God Letter   O/Fem Hole
Go Hole   It Is The Goal
Switched L/Sweet Fem Love Light/Ill/Ail/Hail/Heel/All/Elle/Oil/Hell with M/Motherhood   It is Go Home for Her Says   The Code

Goat: Go/At   Go/Hat
Men Cannot Live Without Sex
The Tarot Card # 15 is The Goat The Ram the Devil Card   It is a Card of Deceit   He Shows the Sign of Saturn in His Right Palm Hand

The Dam Code The Damn Book

Sex with Goats and Other Animals were Forbidden by Religious Laws Since Ancient Times
Even Masturbation was Forbidden by the Roman Church

God: I am Sorry Here Again   I did Not Invent Those Concepts   I am Relating Them
G/Penis Penetration/God Letter   O/Fem Hole   D/Pregnant
The Code   Says Here that in The Name of That God The Fems Get Pregnant Through Her Hole and Her Hymen (High Men) Penetration
In Reverse God is Dog
Dog   Do/Hug   Hugging the Concept of Hugging That The Fems Is Being a Dog (Bitch)   It is For Us The Fems to Do Says   The Code
The Code   is Not Ours/Her   It was Implanted Into Us to Maintain Itself and Keep Us   Poor   Stupid   Violent   so   The Code   Can Use Us More
Poverty is Degrading Us Humans Through Ignorance   Lack of Real Benevolence   Power   True Religion
The Usual Here from   The Code   for Her and All of Us
Jesus is an Example of a Pure Heart   He was an Enemy of   That Code
Take Away D and Get a Go   It is a Go
Switch G for B and He Gets Bud (Too Young for   The Code)
Switch G for P/Man Power and He Gets a Pod
Switch G for Her/R/Ear/Hear/Hair/Err/Here/Heir/Or/Whore/Are/Our/Ire/Air/Ere/Sex   and She Gets a Rod (Penis)
Switch G for S/Is/His/Us/Ass/Hiss/Serpent/Penis and He Gets a Sod
sod: sodomite   homosexual   chap   fellow   guy   child   brat
Switch G for T/Fem Cross and She Gets a Thud (As Usual   The Code   has The Fems at the Bottom of the Dirty Pile)

Goddesses: God/Asses
God   As/S/His/Is/Us/Ass/Has/Hiss/Serpent/Penis
The Fem is Never Left Alone with Any Form of Her Personal Power
in   That Code There is No Such a Word as Goddess (God/Ass) in the Mind of the Fems Until Lately
In That Code   It is/Was Either Insulting The Fems to Make Her Cry and Forget/Forgive   Or   Putting Sex in Front of Her as the Only Form She can Fit In in Life

Gold: G/Hymen Perforation/God Letter   O/Fem Hole   L/Sweet Fem
Love Light/Ill/Ail/Hail/Heel/All/Elle/Oil/Hell   D/Pregnant
Gold is Or/R in French   Oro is Gold in Spanish (Whore O/Fem Hole)
R/Her/Ear/Hear/Hair/Err/Here/Heir/Or/Whore/Are/Our/Ire/Air/Ere/Sex
Or/R Means One or the Other   Which is Witch   Which is Which   The Interchangeable Ones   One Fem or All of Them   They are All the Same Witchesm Cursed They Are/R
Gold is for Men   Silver is Fem
The Gold on the Stock Market Has a value of About $1325 per Once   Silver is about $20 per Ounce
So   there is No Comparison in Value
Switch G/Penis Penetration for C/Young Girl and She Gets Cold (Frigid) Subtle or Bold   The Code   is Continual

Gonads: Gun/Adds   Go and Add (In Plural)
Go and Add (Advertise) (In Plural)
Go/N/In/Hen/Ann/Virgin   Adds   Go and Add Virgins
In Between Gonads and Gone Mad When Switching Letter M/Motherhood for N/In/Hen/Ann/Virgin Letter
The Code   Here Says That Gonads are Related to Guns
The Word Gonads Origin is 1875 and Is Both for The Fems and The Mascs

Good: Same as God
But the God of   The Code   is Not Good
God is Jealous Punishing and Seems to Want to Destroy People as His Simple Joys of Daily Life
Wars Jalousie Hatred Greed Have been Ways of Life On this Planet Secret Societies Have Taken Over the Powers of Men and Called It God and here We Are

Google: Google is a Familiar and Powerful New Word on the New Wonderful Communication Medium Called The Internet
G/Penis Penetration/God Letter   2 OOs/All Fem Holes
All Fems are here to be Holes Says   The Code

Gore: Go   Heir/Or/Whore/R/Her/Ear/Hear/Hair/Err/Here//Are/Our/Ire/Air/Ere/Sex
G/Vaginal Penetration/Letter of God   Her/R

gore: blood that is shed especially when clotted   to pierce with or as if with a horn or tusk
Get it   or   Get/Hit   by it
Blood Often comes with Shed (She/Aid) or Shedding Hair (Heir/R)   She/ID (See ID in The Words Chapter)
The Code   is Chillingly Obvious in its Immense Contempt for The Fems   It is Sickening for All of Us   For Thousands of Generations
Switch G for B/Boy Holding All Fems Breasts and He Gets Bore/Boar (The Boy is Too Young for The Code)
Switch G/Penis Penetration for C/K/Q/Bleeding Fem/Broken Fem Warrior Again Fem and She Gets Core
(The Menstrual Cycle and the Breasts are the Cores of   The Code   for Her)
Switch G for D/Pregnant and She Gets Door (A door can be Closed or Opened   Adore   A/Door   Aid/Add   Whore/Heir/Her)
Switch G for F/Fem/Fuck and She Gets For/Four (All for it Says   The Code)
(Number 4 is the Numbers of Corners of a Pyramid   Not 3 as Shown on the American Dollar Bill)CHECK
Switch G for H/Secret Code Letter and She Gets Whore   Ha
Switch G for J/Sheppard Stick and She Gets Chore (She/Whore as being a Small Job to do)
Switch Letter G for L/Sweet Fem Love Light/Ill/Ail/Hail/Heel/All/Elle/Oil/Hell and She Gets Lore (Something to learn   Lure (Bait)
Switch G for M/Motherhood and She Gets More Says   The Code   in its Endless Hypnotic Way
Switch G for N/In/Hen/Ann/Virgin and She Gets Nor
nor: *Archaic* (used instead of neither as correlative to a following
nor)   *Archaic* (Used without a preceding *neither* the negative force of which it is understood)
Switch G for R/Her/Ear/Hear/Hair/Err/Here/Heir/Or/Whore/Are/Our/Ire/Air/Ere/Sex and She Gets Roar (The Word Roar Starts and Ends with R/Her)   The Whore/Roar   The fem is not Allowed to have a voice unless Now to proclaim Her/R/Whore/Or/Heir)
Switch G for S/His/Is/Us/Ass/Hiss/Serpent/Penis and He Gets Sore (Sore from the Whore or is it a Sore (From...)
No Man Wants that so Lets Snore with N/In/Hen/Ann/Virgin   She Knows (Nos) Nothing

Switch G for T/Fem Cross and She Gets Tore
(A Tour in French is a Tower in English   Get a Tour   See The Tarot Card
The Tower where It All Fall Down)
Switch G for W/All Fems Sex Active and She/They Get Wore (W/
Whore   W/Heir   Worn   We/Her/On)
Take Away G/Penis Penetration and Get Her/R/Hair/Are/Here/Hear/Ear/
Heir/Whore/Or/Err/Sex Again
Switch G for P/Man Power and He Gets a Pour of being Poor   He will Get
Poor if He Goes That Way   so He will Go for the Gore Instead of being a
Natural Good Man
With All the Wars Engendered by   That Mad Code
The Loss of Men in Horrible Deaths and the Sorrows of Their Families is
Immeasurable for Humanity

Gory: Go   R/Her/Ear/Hear/Hair/Err/Here/Heir/Or/Whore/Are/Our/Ire/
Air/Ere/Sex   He/E
gory: bloody   unpleasant disagreeable
No Body Wants to Look at That   But   Go/Whore/He   or   Go/Heir/
He   Says   The Code

Gospel: Go/Spell
Have a Different Point of View here of The Tongues of Fire (See Spell
in The Words Chapter) T/N/G as in T/Fem Cross   N/Virgin   G/God
Letter   All Fems are from God Cursed   The Word Spell is Important
in   The Code   because It Creates the Lien with The Letters Which Forms
Words Which is The Subject of This Book

Got: G/Hot
G/Hymen Perforation/God Letter   When Hot
You Got It   (See Get in The Word Chapter)
Goat   Got   Coat
goat: the constellation of Capricorn   the tenth sign of the Zodiac
Capricorn is Ruled by Saturn The God of Time (Time of the Month) and
Sorrows   The Code Loves The Goat
(((Satan))) is Personified as the Goat with its Horns and Fur
Switch G for C/See/Young Girl and She Gets Cot (Small Bed)
Switch O for U/You/Ovulating and She Gets Gut
gut: the bowels or entrails

The Dam Code The Damn Book

Back to the Butt/Feces for Her Says   The Code

Gotha: Got/She/U
Her Open Loins She Got
Got/U

GR: G/Hymen Perforation/God Letter   R/Her/Ear/Hear/Hair/Err/Here/Heir/Or/Whore/Are/Our/Ire/Air/Ere/Sex
GR is a Word with Many Faces   It is the Law of God and it is Cold   GRR

Grab: All 4 Masc Letters
Steal from The Fems Says   The Code

Grace: G/Race
The Race for G/Penis Penetration/God Letter is a Grace
Gear/Ace   Gear for the Ass
Homosexuality is Insinuated here Says   The Code

Grail: Girl
Robert de Boron is The Second Writer of the Holy Grail After De Chretien in "Perceval Le Conte du Graal"
He Portrayed the Holy Grail as The Vessel of the Last Supper
"A Cup A Bowl of Earth" (Her/T/Fem Cross)   A Vessel
A Single Mass Wafer Provided Sustenance for the Fisher King
Robert De Boron Tells the Story of Joseph of Aramethia Acquiring the Chalice of The Last Supper to Collect Christ Blood Upon His Removal from the Cross
It was in the Work of De Boron that The Grail became the Holy Grail
White Flower Blanche Fleur is the Beloved One of Perceval And the Mother of Tristan and Iseult   Another Legend   But of Secondary Importance to The Grail Here

Grave: Gear/Eve   G/Here/V   GRV
G/Penis Penetration/God Letter   and   R/Her/Ear/Hear/Hair/Err/Here/Heir/Or/Whore/Are/Our/Ire/Air/Ere/Sex   with   V/Fem Sex Active
The Code   Gives Her Nothing and Takes Everything   All The Way to The Grave for Her

Gray: G/Ray   God/Ray

Lise Rochon

If the Ray of God is Grey
It Does Not Attract Attention Says   The Code

Grave: When G/Penis Penetration/God Letter is the Rave
rave: to talk wildly as in delirium   to talk or write with extravagant enthusiasm   to evangelize   to speak authoritatively on a subject about which one knows very little
See More Definitions in the Dictionary for Rave
grave: an excavation made in the earth in which to bury a dead body   any place that becomes the receptacle of what is dead lost or past   death
Grave in French is Cerceuil (Circle/All   See Circle in The Words Chapter)
Switch G for B/Boy Holding All Fems Breasts and She Gets Brave (As having a Child)
Switch G for C/See/Young Girl and She Gets a Crave
Nothing Here for Her Says   The Code   As Usual

Great: G/Rate
G/Penis Penetration/God Letter is the Rating to Make Great in   The Code
Grateful: Great   Full (Pregnant) and   Grateful
Another Code Sweet Way to Call Pregnancy Great
Many Fem Died in Childbirth from Infections
then   Poverty   Ignorance   Silence   are the Always The Words of the Day Says   The Code
Switch T/Fem Cross for P/Man Power and He Gets Grape (See Wine/Blood/Chalice in The Words Chapter)
Grateful: Great   when   Full   Says   The Code   to The Fems   Being Full Means Pregnant

Greedy: Greed/He
It Is All For Him   Nothing For Her Here Says   The Code
Switch G for C/Young Fem/See and She Gets a Creed
(That is Quite an Obstacle for Her)
creed: any statement or system of beliefs or principles

Greeting   Great/Thing   Greed/Thing   Greed/In   The Code   Again Presenting Greed Under a Good Light   But here it is in the Form of a Greeting   and   Great is made of All Masc Letters which

Associated with   Sex/R/Her   and   T/Fem Cross   as the Ending to make HimThe Masc Great

Grid: G/Rid   G/Read   GRD
G/Penis Penetration/God Letter   R/Her/Sex   D/Pregnant
grid: a grating of crossed bars
The Grid is   The Code   Symbol of the Secret Societies

Grief: G/Penis Penetration/God Letter   Reef
G   R   F
R/Her/Ear/Hear/Hair/Err/Here/Heir/Or/Whore/Are/Our/Ire/Air/Ere/Sex   is   Iffy   or/and   on the Rocks   Not Good   Grief Starts with   That Code God
reef: a ridge of sand rocks and coral debris

Grin: GRR   N/In/Hen/Ann/Virgin
G/Penis Penetration/God Letter   R/Her/Ear/Hear/Hair/Err/Here/Heir/Or/Whore/Are/Our/Ire/Air/Ere/Sex   In/N/Ann/Hen/Virgin
Smiles are Upon Her   When the Virgin is Acting as a Whore
Grr is a Cold Word

Grizzly: Crazy/Lay
G/Penis Penetration/God Letter R/Her/Ear/Hear/Hair/Err/Here/Heir/Or/Whore/Are/Our/Ire/Air/Ere/Sex   2 ZZs/Sleep on it   Keep On Laying Eggs   Says   The Code   to The Fems
Craze/Lay

Groan: G/R/N
When G/Penis Penetration/God Letter   and   Her/R/Ear/Hear/Hair/Err/Here/Heir/Or/Whore/Are/Our/Ire/Air/Ere/Sex   are On
Grr/On
groan: mourning sound   a prolonged stresses dull cry expressed in agony
Are We Talking about Sex or Rape Here

Groom: G/Room
G/Perforated Hymen (High Men   I/Man)/God Letter   Eye/Man   in   a   Room

Grr/OO/M   All Fems Mothers Says   The Code
Groom the Broom in the Room

Ground: G/Round
G/Perforated Hymen/God Letter   Is Round   Which Is its Natural
Shape   or   When Pregnant
It is to Walk On it Says   The Code   Anything Round is Fem

Grovel: G/Rove/All
rove: stray

Grow: G/Penis Penetration/God Letter   Row
All Fems in a Row   All Rowing
Take   Her/R/Ear/Hear/Hair/Err/Here/Heir/Or/Whore/Are/Our/Ire/Air/Ere/
Sex   Away and Get a Go Anyway

Grunting: G/Penis Penetration/God Letter   Runt   or   Run/T/Fem
Cross   N/In/Hen/Ann/Virgin
grunt: to utter the deep guttural sound characteristic of a hog   to
grumble   as in discontent
The Sound of a Pig Runt
runt: the smallest or weakest of a litter especially of pigs and puppies

Guaranty: GRNT
G/Penis Penetration/God Letter   Her/R/Ear/Hear/Hair/Err/Here/Heir/Or/
Whore/Are/Our/Ire/Air/Ere/Sex   N/Young Girl   T/Fem Cross
It is a Guaranty Says   The Code   to The Fems Through Sexual
Penetration She Will Be a Whore and be Cursed With The Great Curse of
Blood Loss

Guard: GRD   G/Penis Penetration/God Letter   Hard
When a Girl has Sex for the First time   It Goes Hard Says   The
Code   and   The Code is on Guard For That

Guess: G/Ass   G/Penis Penetration/God Letter   and   Ass/S/Penis
It is a Gas   G/Ass   To Guess about the Ass
gas: to amuse or affect strongly
A Gas is Also a Fuel

Guilt: GLT
G/Penis Penetration/God Letter   L/Sweet Fem Love Light/Ill/Ail/Hail/Heel/All/Elle/Oil/Hell   T/Fem Cross/Great Curse
Take Away U/You/Ovulating   and Get Gilt
gilt: the thin layer of gold or other material applied to in gilding
Guilty: Gill/T
gill: sweet girl   fish organ for breathing   narrow stream
All Water is Fem Says   The Code   The Fems is Back Here to the Fishes/Cows/Sheeps/Chicks etc Again
When Breathing is as Breeding
Switch Her/R/Ear/Hear/Hair/Err/Here/Heir/Or/Whore/Are/Our/Ire/Air/Ere/Sex   in Breathing for   L/Sweet Fem Love Light/Ill/Ail/Hail/Heel/All/Elle/Oil/Hell   and She Gets Bleeding
Switch G for B/Boy Holding All Fem Breasts and He Gets Built/In
Switch G for Q/Bleeding Fem and She Gets Quilt (Because She is Told She Is Guilty)
Even if She is Very Narrow the Young Girl Gets to Breed
To the Gills   Fully   Completely   Totally
Fill Her Up (Hop) as Much as Possible
gill: to catch (fish) by the gills in a gill net
No Guilt   On our Sweet Girls   No Quitting Says   The Code   to The Fems   Keep On being Guilty You The Fems

Guitar: GTR   Guy/T/Whore/Are
A Guitar is in The Shape of a Fem Body with a Stick
Men/Artists Play/Compose with It for a Long Time
Gay/Tar is Always Around the Corner

Gun: G/On   G/One
When G/Penis Penetration/God Letter   Is On His Gun   He is On   and   He is Gone
G/Own   G/Penis Penetration/God Letter Owns The Gun
For the Masc is a Gun   For The Fem is a Gown (G/Own)
To Go/On   To Continue
Son of a Gun Sounds   Is it Better than Son of a Bitch
A Gun is a Positive Male Image for Penis Says   The Code
Gay/On

Gut: Got   God   Good
G/God Letter/Hymen Penetration   Hut   G/Hot
G/Sex Penetration/God Letter
In the House/Hut   G Is Hot   Gay/Hot   too
Switch T for D/Pregnant and She Gets Odd (All Fem Letters)

Guy: G/Eye   G/I
G/Penetration/God Letter   and   I/Marriage Act   or   High is what
Make   a Guy   a GI (Soldier)   Guys
Disguise   This/Guy
Gay/Guy   Guy is a Man Name   Here is Another Hint of Provoked Homosexuality to the Masc from   The Cod

H h
Intro
H Is a Masc Letter   H is a Silent or Almost Letter   H is The Letter of The Alphabet Grid of   The Secret Code
H is the Basic/Primary Letter that Carries The Secret of The Initiates of the Brotherhoods   Only Men Enter Says   The Code
No Fem Can Pass or Trespass that Very First Bridge to that Knowledge of That Grid that Teaches about The Great Curse or The T/Fem Cross and How it Happens
Letters T and D are Interchangeable in   The Code   Here D Transforms into The Common Word The or Most Important Thee
Superposing   H/Secret Code   with   T/Fem Curse (Th is a Common Combination in Words)   and   I/The Man Stick of Power   and   E/He They All Duplicate Squares (See # 4 in The Numbers Chapter) One Way or Another
Every Letter Enters the Grid/Square One Way or another   Some Letters are More Important than Others in   The Code
Letter h in Small Cap is of Minor Importance in the Grid (Children are Not Allowed in   The Code)
Small Cap h is n/Virgin with an Elongated Top Stick (Penis)   Add a Stick/Bar Crossing the Top Bar   It is The God Saturn   The Reaper The Death Card in Tarot # 13
ℏ Saturn is The God of Time   A Crossed Symbol   Close to t/Fem Cross/Great Curse

The Dam Code The Damn Book

Time is a Key Word in   The Great Curse Code   That   Time of the Month   being Its Cornerstone
Secret Letter hH Starts with n/Young Virgin   She Subtly Grows Into the Small h   The Secret Society Plan Letter   Where She Loses Herself In from Youth   The Plan is Completed in Letter H   Where She has Become Part of The Grid   Which is Endless Repetitions of Barriers for Her
Pay Attention on Words with H in it   Many Contains Even More Precise Info   On how   The Secret Language Code   Operates on Her   Important Concepts are Often Hidden in Words that are Not Attractive to the Mind
The H Sound Reminds of an Axe before it Hits the Tree
The Tree of Life is Part of Our Common Knowledge
Letter H is a Silent Quiet Letter that Infiltrates itself Often in No Apparent Need Disguised as a Spy in a Word   H can Add Power or Doubt into a Word
Words in H are   Age   Each   Itch   Ache Nothing Interesting or Worth   so   No Interest from any Curious Crowd

H   h
Habit: A/All Men   Bit
Bit is Slang for Penis   The Code   Wants to Keep The Fem Love Away from The Mascs by Making Homosexuality and Closeness Easier with Men

Hack: AK is Ass Kisser
hack: to cut notch slice or sever
Here   A/All Men   Left Alone with   K/Fem Broken Warrior   The Battle is On Says   The Code   and She Will Lose for Sure Alone Against All Men
Axe/X/Fallen Cross is so Close   A Terrible Word Hack is

hag: an ugly old woman especially a vicious or malicious one   a witch or sorceress
H/Secret Code Letter   Where The Code Hides
A/All Men   G/Penis Penetration/God Letter
A Very Dangerous Word for a Fem or a Layman to Look at
The Code   Hides as Usual in a Very Ugly and Discrediting Word for The Fems
hog: a domesticated swine weighing 120 pounds or more raised for market

Switch A for O/Fem Hole and She Gets Hog
(Back to the Animals for Her   Swine is an Especially Dirty One for a Fem)
Chiefly Scot   to reap with a sickle
Now That is When Clitorectomy Enters the Door and it is the Barber Next Door with its Dirty Blade To Cut Her For a Life of Pain Every Time Having Sex   and   Infections   and   Permanent Physical Mental and Emotional Pains
(See Sickle in The Words Chapter)

Hah: 2 HHs/All Secret Code Societies   Surrounding   A/All Men   Having a Laugh about It
Ha-ha: H/Secret Code Letter Society Twice or/and On Going A/All Men
Keep on Repeating after   Ha Ha Ha Ha Ha
As is if   The Code   Great Curse is Funny   It is All Smoke Screens to Her

Hair: Hair as in Letter R is Part of The Long List of R Meanings
R/Her/Ear/Hear/Hair/Err/Here/Heir/Or/Whore/Are/Our/Ire/Air/Ere/SexFem
Her Hair is an Important Matter therefore a   Code   Bait to Her
Hairdo: Heir/Do
To Create an Heir
In Her Hair is an Heir Here Breeding as Breathing Air
All are Cover Words for the Others
Her/Do   No No   She just Think So

Half: Letter F
All Fems are Always Shown is a Weak Position   So a Half She is Here

Hamper: Hump/Her   In The Basket of Dirty Clothes
There is No Love in   The Code   in Between the Sexes

Hand: H/Secret Code Letter Society Grid   And/End

Handkerchief: Hand   CQK   R/Her/Ear/Hear/Hair/Err/Here/Heir/Or/Whore/Are/Our/Ire/Air/Ere/Sex   Chief
Being a Chief of any Kind is Forbidden to Her by   The Code   So End   C/Q/K   Her   Chief   Blow that Snot Out of Your Snout on it

The Dam Code The Damn Book

Note here that Both Snout and Snot is S/His/Is/Us/Ass/Hiss/Serpent/Penis   with The Fem Word   Not/Nut (All Fem Letters)

Happen: Hop/In   Hope/In   Ape/In
All Connecting to Each Other as Holding Hands
It All Happen/In in the Hop/In   The Code   Says She Should be as a Rabbit Hoping All The Time

Happiness: A/Penis
Hop/He/Nest   Hop/Penis
Happy in Bed   That is Happiness Says   The Code   to The
Fems   Hopping from One to the Other Penis
A/Pea/Nest   Happy With these Tiny Peas
Pea is the Cover Word here
P/Man Power   He is Not a Pea
A/Pee/N/Is
Men Thought of Sex as if Going to the Bathroom   It is Done Often and Needs to Be
And Endless SS S/His/Is/Us/Ass/Hiss/Serpent/Penis Sound Ends in Happiness For The Mascs

Happy: Hop/He   Ape/He
Happier: Hop/He/Her
A Man is Happy when He Hops   Happier (Happy/Her/R/Whore/Sex)

Harass: Her   Ass   (Arse)
arse: *Slang Vulgar* ass   the buttocks   the anus   a stupid person   sexual intercourse   also called arse hole or asshole
Letter N/Young Virgin is The Arse/The Donkey/Ann
R/Her/Ear/Hear/Hair/Err/Here/Heir/Or/Whore/Are/Our/Ire/Air/Ere/Sex   Ass
When R and S Both Strong Sex Letters are Together   There is Bold Action   Because there is harassment

Hard: RD   R/Her/Ear/Hear/Hair/Err/Here/Heir/Or/Whore/Are/Our/Ire/Air/Ere/Sex   D/Pregnant

381

When R/Her/Sex Is in Front of D/Pregnant and Alone with Her   The Code   Says No   Because Later D will Be T/Fem Cross   She will be T/Fem Cross in Art (See Art in The Words Chapter)
H/Art   H/Secret Code Society Letter   The Art is The Practice of The Secret Rites
The Heart Is for The Fems (T/Fem Cross)
The Hard is for The Masc and Getting D/Pregnant

Harder: Hard   Her/R/Ear/Hear/Hair/Err/Here/Heir/Or/Whore/Are/Our/Ire/Air/Ere/Sex   Hard Sex
Hard/Her   Herd/Her   Heard/Her   Hurt/Her
Same as Usual Hard Treatment from   The Code   More Pain For The Fems

Hardly: Hard/He/Lay

Harem: RM   R/Room   R/Him   R/Aim
Her/R/Ear/Hear/Hair/Err/Here/Heir/Or/Whore/Are/Our/Hour/Ire/Air/Ere/Sex   M/Motherhood
Sex for Heir Or Whore Are and Motherhood Makes a Harem Says   The Code
RM in D/The/Pregnant   Room

Harmony: Heir/Or/Whore   Money   Heir/Whore   Many   Are/Many   Ere/Many
Her/R/Ear/Hear/Hair/Err/Here/Heir/Or/Whore/Are/Our/Ire/Air/Ere/Sex   Man/He
Are/Manny   Manny is a Man Name of Hebrew Origin
Man/He   No Place for Her in Harmony Says   The Code
Arm/On/He   Harm/N/He
Harem   N/Virgin   He/E
H is a Difficult Letter   it Implies Secrecy

Harness: RNS
Her/R/Ear/Hear/Hair/Err/Here/Heir/Or/Whore/Are/Our/Ire/Air/Ere/Sex   N/In/Hen/Virgin   His/S/Is/Us/Ass/Hiss/Serpent/Penis   in   Plural or All of Them

harness: the combination of straps bands and other parts forming the working gear of a draft animal
ness: headland   promontory   cape
She is Harnessed by   The Code   to being   Her/R/Heir/Or/Whore/Err/Are/Our/Ire/Air/Ere/Ear/Hear/Hair/Here/Sex   or   as a   N/Hen/Ann/Arse/Young Virgin   with   2 SSs/His/Penisses to make Sure it is Strong Enough and Always Close By   Says   The Code

Harpoon: R/Her/Ear/Hear/Hair/Err/Here/Heir/Or/Whore/Are/Our/Ire/Air/Ere/Sex   Poon
R/Her/Hair/Are/Here/Hear/Ear/Whore/Or/Err/Sex   P/Man Power   On/On
poon: a stupid or ineffectual person
P/Man Power   Is in Front of 3 Fem Letters
Harpoon are Used to Kill Large Fishes as Whales
The Dictionary tells us that Harpoon has Roots in:
Greek *harpagon* related to *harpe* sickle and in Latin *harpahook* cf *harpagonem* grappling hook
(See Sickle in The Words Chapter)
harpoon: to strike catch or kill with or as if with a harpoon
The Code   Madness Says   Play Harp Along with it to Hide
Boom   Coon   Doom   Moon   Room   Spoon
Balloon   Buffoon etc
Words with   2 OOs/Fem Holes   and N/In/Hen/Ann/Virgin   or   M/Motherhood   Are Weak Unimportant Destructive or Shameful   Says   The Code

Harvest: Heir/Feast   Whore/Fast

Has: Ass   is Still   S/Is/His/Ass/Hiss/Serpent/Penis
He still Has it   as the Ass/S in The Past   The Code   is Safe

Hat: The Hat is a Very Important Cover Word in   The Code
H/Secret Code Letter   A/All Men   T/Fem Cross/Great Curse
A Place to Hide is Under an Innocent Hat
Hat is an Important Word because   It is Connected to The Great Art   The Secret Societies Teachings   Hat is the Cover Word for the Secret Teachings
It Hides/Covers the Head (ID) Figuratively

383

At   A/All Men   T/Fem Cross   This is Where it Hides   The Hat/At   She Has No Idea
Then Comes The Art When Including the Letter for Sex/R

What: W/All Fems Sex Active   Hat
All   V/Fem Sex Active   Under That Hat/Hate
Add C/See/Young Girl and She Gets Cat   The Code Hates Cats They Are Friendly Sensual and Independent   They are a Strong Fem Symbol
Add F/Fem/Fuck and She Gets Fat   That Will Make Her Run the Other Direction
Add M/Motherhood and She Gets Mat (Because She Is Pregnant)
Add N/In/Hen/Ann/Virgin and She Gets a Gets Knat (a Mosquito   She Is Not Allowed to be There   Being Too Young)
Add P/Man Power and He Gets Pat (More Power To Him)
Add Her/R/Heir/Or/Whore/Err/Are/Our/Ire/Air/Ere/Ear/Hear/Hair/Here/Sex and She Gets Rat (Scary for Her   So She Runs Away)
R/Sex Cannot be in Front of The Hat because it Would Imply The Fems as R/Her/Are/Heir/Or/Whore/Sex is Being Conscious of That   No Says   The Code
Only Men Control (Cunt/Roll) the Secret Art
Because the Art is to get All Fems into T/Fem Cross

Hate: Number 8   Pi is a Miniature ∞ Lying Down
8 is the Number of Pregnancy   8 is considered the Number of Decay Death and Extinction in The Kabala
The Kabala is 2 thousands Year Old
Hater: Eight (8)/Her   Eat/Her   Making Her Pregnant Is That Too   Time to Eat Time to   Hit/Her   It/Her   Hate/Her   The Code   Reeking of its Violence and Depreciation to The Fems in General

Have: H/V   A/V
H/Secret Code Letter Society   V/Of/Ovo/Eve/Ave
When H/Secret Code   Meet With V/Fem Sex Active   A Done Deal   They Have It/Hit
They Have Had That Always
According to the Brotherhood of the Light "Secret Tarot" by C C Zain   P 337 "There is but one LAW in the Universe, and this is sex manifesting

The Dam Code The Damn Book

as male and female" "There is but one principle which manifest under 2 modes of motion as force and will"

Haze: HZ   Is   His   Ease
Add D/Pregnant and it Becomes   Days/Daisies   For The Fems   Men and   The Code   Do Not Care for Daisies
Add M/Motherhood to Her and She Gets Maize (Maze)
Now It is All Hazy and Lots of Work To get Out   if She Can
hazy: vagueness   obscurity
It is Easy To Read   The Code   When You have   The Code
It Keeps itself in Obscurity

He: Letter E
H/Secret Code Letter   E/He
The Symbols E and H (and A) Weight Heavy in the Grid
Imagine a Summer Screen Door   With All of Its Little Squares   This is How   The Code   Influence is Upon Us
T/Fem Cross/Great Curse is Hidden in Every one of the Grid Squares Between Him/He/E and Her/R   The Difference is She is a Sex Act   Not a Person (Per/Son   No Chance here) There is No Fem Letter in Her (R) Only a Sex Object Says   The Code   (See R Letter in The Letter Chapter)

Head: HD   ID   Hide   Had
H/Secret Code Letter   D/Pregnant
Hide The Head   Hide The ID   Because All What is in it is Pregnancy for Her   as Her ID Says   The Code
Headphone: Hid/Fun   Aid/Fun   ID/Fun   That is for The Masc

Heal: Letter L
Elle/L/Sweet Fem Love Light/Ail/Hail/Heel/All/Ill/Oil/Hell/All/Ill Elle
He/Ill is here Also
Hel: the Goddess of Nifheim the home of the dead
Heal would be Another Cover Word here
Healer: Ill/R   Hell/Her   All/Her   Heal/Her

Heap: EP   2 Masc Letters
E/He   and   P/Man Power   Are Together   It is Big
heap: to accumulate   to amass   a great quantity or number

385

Lise Rochon

The Code   In Action Totally for the Masc

Hear: Another Code Manifestation of Letter R for Her
A Fem has to Hear to Know What   The Code   Wants from Her   It has to be in Her Ear and Hair   (See Letter R in The Letter Chapter) Here/R/Her/Are/Air/Ear/Hear/Err/Heir/Or/Whore/Ere/Ire/Sex
Add D/Pregnant and Creates Past Tense   She Becomes Heard/Herd   So   She Cannot Reach its Understanding   Because Part of the Past and Part of The Herd She is Now   Back to The Animals for Her as Usual
Add A/All Men and He Gets Era
era: a period of time marked by distinctive character events etc
The God Ra in The Egyptian History   Powerful The He/Ra   See Hera the Greek Goddess in Dictionary   and Even If She had Nothing to do there as a Fem Her Name is There   This is How The Code Works   A Fem Cannot Find Her Tracks of Her Achievements

Heard: herd
herd: a number of animals kept feeding or traveling together   any large quantity   the masses
Switch D/Pregnant to T/Fem Cross and She Gets Hurt
Herd the Heart   Then She Gets The Hard (Erection)   The Hard is for Her Because of D at the End of The Word

Hearing: Hear   N/Ann/Hen/In/Virgin   Here/Hen   Her/Ann   Here/In   R/Her/Ear/Hear/Hair/Err/Here/Heir/Or/Whore/Are/Our/Ire/Air/Ere/Sex
Ring (See Ring in The Words Chapter) Ring That Bell (e)
Such Soft Sounds   and   Starting With H/Grid Code   Adding   Mystery   Her/Reign   The Code   Says Her Reign is Based to have Heirs   and/or   be a Whore   or   Err   Better Hear That
It is Her/Ring   and   He/Rings   She is The One being Ringed   as Bulls Camels Etc   Back to the Animals as Usual for The Fem

Hearse: Her/See
In The Code   For The Fems to See would Be a Big No   so It does Not Happen   The Word Hearse Proves that
And   If She would See Herself She is in the Hearse Already

The Dam Code The Damn Book

Her with S/Penis in front of Her is a Position of Power so No says The Code it is in a Hearse
When S is Behind Her it is Very Bad Says The Code So It is Not going to Happen
hearse: a vehicle for conveying a dead person a canopy erected over a tomb
Add N/Virgin and She Gets Nurse (The Only View for Her to See Herself Ahead is to Nurse

Heart: H/Secret Code letter E/He A/All Men R/Her/Ear/Hear/Hair/ Err/Here/Heir/Or/Whore/Are/Our/Ire/Air/Ere/Sex T/Fem Cross/Great Curse Sacrifice
Switch the A Sound for the U Sound and She Gets Hurt
Often The Mascs Does Not Understand the Heart as The Fems Do
The Art (The Heart Arthur Art/Her) is The Secret Knowledge Code in Action
The Heart Symbol has The Fem Buttocks Looks
The Adam (A/Dame A/Damn) Apple (Ape/All)
The Apple Reminds Us of Sin it is a Biblical Creation Mystery
An Apple Cut in Half is in the Shape of a Heart (for Her) and Upside Down it has the Shape of a Butt (For Him)
A Very Long Time Ago When Humans Started to have Sex Outside Her Natural Estrous Mating Time She Started to Bleed then More and More
In the Early 1900 Girls Bled at 16 Years Old and Less Quantity and Less Days than Now Now Girls Starts to lose their blood at 9 or 10 Years Old That is Shocking
Some Fem Bleed All the Time or Weeks at the Time Doctors Tell Her to Wait until it Ends So they can Look at it What I Know There Is No Medical Treatment to Stop it Immediately That is a Lot of Blood Loss on One Person
There is Little Research to Cure that Terrible Gene Drain
Natural Formulas Have Terminated My Many Hemorrhaging/Bleeding

Hearth: RT
Hurt Her/R/Ear/Hear/Hair/Err/Here/Heir/Or/Whore/Are/Our/Ire/Air/Ere/ Sex T/Fem Cross/Great Sacrifice
hearth: floor of a fireplace
In the Hurt She Builds a Fire for Him and Her Says The Code

Heave: Eve
He/E   V/Fem Sex Active
The Fem is Never Left Alone in   The Code   Even if She is Eve (See Letter V in The Letter Chapter)
heave :   to lift   hurl   to throw with force   to vomit   fling   cast
Heaving: Eve   In/N/Hen/Ann/Virgin
heaving: to move forcefully
No Coincidence   The Code   Sounds Reigns
It is in Heaven (Eve/N   and   Hurt/Earth) That She (V) is Thrown Forcefully and Cast Away
Sweet Sound Letters for Such Great Violence   Ovo is Close

Heaven: Have/Ann   Eve/In
Ov/Egg   In/N/Hen/Ann/Virgin
Add O/Fem Hole and She Gets Oven (A Bun in The Oven is Heaven Says The Code to Her)
Have/Him
Haven is the Cover Word here
Oven/Heaven/Ovo/In   and Earth   Hear it from   The Code

Heavy: EV
Eve/He   Eve/Hey   He/V
He/E   is with   V/Fem Sex Active Alone   It is Heavy   Then it Becomes a Lay as in
Heavily   Eve/He/Lay   Heavy/Lay

Hebrew: He/Brew
The Code   is Always Brewing

Heed: Hid   ID   Head
ID: part of psyche that seek satisfaction limited by the ego and super ego   dynasty
heed: to give careful attention
Hide that in your Head Says   The Code   That is The Idea

Heinie: NE
H/Secret Code Letter   In/N/Virgin   He/E
N/In/Hen/Ann/Virgin   is with   E/He

The Dam Code The Damn Book

heinie: the buttocks
Back to the Butt/Feces for The Fems   As Usual
With   H/Secret Code   Starting the Word Heinie It Adds Mystery and Secrecy
It is About The Fems Being
Heinous   NS   Haine/Us   Ann/Us   In/Us   Hen/Us
Ann/N/Haine/Hen/Ann/Virgin   is with   S/Is/His/Penis/
Serpent   says   The Code
Food for Thought   Why is it Heinous
Along with That   More Insults to Her   Anus   Ann/Us
Who Wants to Look There   Not Many Fems
Switch H/Secret Code for V/Fem Sex Active and She Gets Venous/Venus/Vinous (See Venous   Venus and Wine in The Words Chapter)

Helix: LX   2 Fem Sound Letters
/X
Hell/L/Sweet Fem Love Light/Ill/Ail/Hail/Heel/All/Elle/Oil/Hell   is with   X/Axe/Fallen Fem Cross (From T/Fem Cross)
Anything Round is Fem in Essence in   The Code
No Chance here for The Fem
helix: a spiral   a garden snail
Not so Fast   Her Helix goes as Fast as a Garden Snail
If   He/E   Goes There He is   Ill/X (He/Will/X)
Exile is XL   the Same Sound Letters as LX
In   LX   She Goes from Ill to Dead   In   XL   She goes in Exile   as in   Exit/All   When Adding T/Fem cross/Great Curse

Hell: L
Letter L is for Sweet Fem Love and the More Delicate Fem
Knowledge   But L is also   Elle   All   Ill   Ail   Hail   Hell
Wail/Well are Also Part of Her says   The Code
Hide (ID) the Ills of Hell of the Great Curse from Her
H/Secret Code   E/Man   2 LL s/Sweet Fem Love Light/Ill/Ail/Hail/Heel/All/Elle/Oil/Hell
Nell Mel Gel Belle Fell in the Well of Hell No Bell in the Dell
L Often Comes in Double as for   M/Motherhood   T/Fem Cross   and S/His/Is/Us/Ass/Hiss/Serpent/Penis

Lise Rochon

L is Called The Fifth Angle that Never Fitted   It is The Letter of the Freemasons   Hiding behind The Word Angel here

Hello: LO   2 Fem Sound Letters
Hell   O/Fem Holes   Elle/O   Allow   Ill/O   All/O   A/
Low   Heel/O   High/Low   Eel/O
O is Owe   She Owe   and   is Own (On)
Hello Has Many Aspects of The Same Meaning   And they All Are Low in Energy
Hello is one of Our Favorite Greetings

Help: LP   L/Fem Love   P/Man Power
Ill/P   P/Man Power   Hell/P   Elle/P
Ill   Elle   Bell   Belle
Helper: Ill/P/Her Hell/P/R
Help: ALP   Hell/P   Hail/P

Hemorrhage: M/O/Rage
When M/Motherhood and the O/Fem Hole Are in Rage
Him/O/Rage
Him/He/Rage
When M and O are in Age the Bleeding Starts Strong
Hemorrhage:

Hen: Letter N
Ann/N/In/Hen/Haine/Ann/Virgin
Letters are Words
In: i/Marriage Act   N/In/Hen/Virgin
The Hen/N is the Chicken (Chick and Chicken are Slang for Fem)
E/He   N/In/Hen/Virgin/Ann/Donkey   He is In the Virgin Here Says   The Code   With H in The Front it Adds The Secret Leadership of   The Code
E is Also Silent here   Hen Sounds Only as a N/In/Hen/Virgin
Here The Code   Brings N into M/Motherhood
The Code   Lives Inside the N/Hen   Heinie   Hen/He
Ann/N is also the Donkey
heinie: *Slang*   the buttocks
Back to the Butt and Feces for Her
Haine is Hatred in French

The Dam Code The Damn Book

Compare   He/E   Made of 2 Masc Letters with She   She   Is made of 3 Masc Letters   The Secret Code   is with   Him   She Has No Individuality in   That Code

Hence: NC
Hen   C/See/Young Girl   N/Hen/Ann   See
The Hen is what She Sees
hence: for this reason   from this time
Add F/Fem/Fuck and She Gets a Fence
She See Nothing as Usual
Add T/Fem Cross and She Get Tense
Add M/Motherhood and She Get Menses
Add S/His/Is/Us/Ass/Hiss/Serpent/Penis it Make Sense To The Masc
Add L/Sweet Fem Light and She Gets Lance
(The Bleeding Lance of King Arthur from The Holy Grail
One of The Greatest Mystery Book)
Add D/Pregnant and She Gets Dense or a Danse (She Cannot See there)

Her: R
The Letter R/Her/Hair/Are/Here/Hear/Ear/Whore/Or/Err/Sex
H/Secret Code   E/He is Silent (But is Here Anyhow) R/Her/Ear/Hear/Hair/Err/Here/Heir/Or/Whore/Are/Our/Ire/Air/Ere/Sex
H/Secret Code Letter   E/He   R/Her/Hair/Are/Here/Hear/Ear/Whore/Or/Err/Sex
She Has No Fem Personal Representation Except for Sex
H/R Makes Also the Sound Her Without the E/He
Add a T/Fem Cross and She Gets Hurt

Herald: Her/Halt
herald: forerunner
She Has No Chance here Also says   The Code

Herd: Her/D
Let it be Heard   D/The/Pregnant   is   T/Fem Cross in the Making
(Hurt   Her/T)
Sheppard (Ship/Herd) (See Ship and Sheppard in The Words Chapter)

391

Sheppard Without the Double P/Man Power would be She/Heard   A Big No from   The Code   It is Not Allowed to Hear The Code   so   Unheard (N/Heard) it is
Hard

Here: Hear
H/Secret Code Society Grid   E/He   R/Here/Hear/Ear/Her/Hair/Are/Whore/Or/Err/Sex
E/He   That is   H/Secret Code   with   R/Sex   with   2 EEs/He (as in Plural or All of Them)   Hear That
Here is Similar to Her   Although Her has Only 1 E/He   It is Monogamy for Her)
The Code   says it is Always Here/Hear for Her
Here and There (Their   T/Heir   DR)
The Difference Between Here and There is T/Fem Cross
Add T to Here and Get Something that is Far   She Cannot See It/Hit
Keep on Recreating T/Fem Cross to Get There
Deer is the Cover Word Along with Dear (D/Hear   Daughter Learns/Hears She is Pregnant) here
Add B/Boy Holding All Fem Breasts and He Gets Beer (No Too Young for Either)
Add D/Pregnant and She Gets Dear (Being Pregnant)
Add F/Fem/Fuck to here and She Gets Fear
Add G/Penis Penetration/God Letter and She Gets in Gear For That
Add H/Secret Code and He Gets to Hear
Add L/Sweet Fem Love Light/Ill/Ail/Hail/Heel/All/Elle/Oil/Hell   and She Gets Lear
lear: learning   instruction   lesson
Add M/Motherhood and She Gets Mire
Add Y/Wounded Fem and She Gets Year (See Year in The Time/Calendar Chapter)

Hereby: R/Her/Sex   Buy/By/Be I/Be High/Eye/The eye in the Pyramid   Where   as a   Sacred Code   Symbols on The Dollar Bill
hereby: by this or the present declaration action document etc   by means of this as a result of this
Here/Bye Says   The Code   To Take as Is
Her/Bye   No Invitation to the Fem here

The Dam Code The Damn Book

Herein: Here/R/Her/Ear/Hear/Hair/Err/Heir/Or/Whore/Are/Our/Ire/Air/Ere/Sex   is With   N/In/Hen/Ann/Virgin
It is Time for   N/Virgin   to Make The Change from Virgin to R/Sex Says   The Code
herein: in or into this place
Heroine   Her/O/In   (See Heroin in The Words Chapter) He/Row/N
Heroine is Another Great Word the Fem Lost that Acknowledge The Fems in a Uplifting Way   By Calling it an Illegal Drug   Heroine   Boring

Heresy: Her/He/See
Back to the Devil for Her Says   The Code
Devil is Eve that is Ill   The/Evil   D/V/L   (3 Fem Sound Letters)
R/Her/Ear/Hear/Hair/Err/Here/Heir/Or/Whore/Are/Our/Ire/Air/Ere/Sex
He   See
He Sees Sex with Her as a Sin

Heretic: Her/He/T/IC
IC Means an Integrated Circuit
T/Fem Cross   is an Integrated Circuit in the Masc and Fem
It is Heretic to Think or Look Says   The Code
R/Her/Ear/Hear/Hair/Err/Here/Heir/Or/Whore/Are/Our/Ire/Air/Ere/Sex   He   Tick
A Tick is a Bug   It Keeps Her and Him as Far as Possible from Those Concepts

Herewith: R/With
Here/R/Are/Ear/Hear/Hair/Err/Heir/Or/Whore/Our/Her/Ire/Air/Ere/Sex   With v Mystery here
herewith: along with
She has To go Along with the R Program says   The Code
Add C/Young Virgin Girl to With and She Gets Witch (Which in All Religions was Banned to Death)

Hermetic: Air/R/Hair/Heir/Err/Ere/Are/Her/Ear/Hear/Here/Heir/Or/Whore/Our/Ire/Ere/Sex   M/Motherhood/Maim   T/Fem Cross   IC/Integrated Circuit
Hermetic (Her/Meet/IC) is a Secret Code Word and it Means Here What The Letters Are Saying

393

hermetic: made airtight by fusion or sealing   not affected by outward influence or power characteristic of occult science especially alchemy

Hero: RO   2 Fem Sounds Letters
Her/O   Here/O   He/Row
Her/R/Ear/Hear/Hair/Err/Heir/Or/Whore/Here/Are/Our/Ire/Air/Ere/Sex   O/Fem Hole
He/E   is a Hero says   The Code   with Any O/Fem Hole
For Her Her/O as in Her Vagina is Non Existent because We are Talking about a Man Only   Hero

Heroine: HRN
Err/O/In
Hero/In   Her/O/In   He/Run/In   Here/On/In
Her/R/Hair/Are/Here/Hear/Ear/Heir/Or/Whore/Err/Sex
O/Fem Hole   In/N/Hen/Ann/Donkey/Ann/Virgin
She is The Heroine   The Fem of Hero   A Clean Word for a Masc   The Heroine Word is Prisoner of a Bad Rep from an Addicting Drug   Heroin   Heroine (Her/O/In)   It Wounds Her Name and Reputation as a Real Fem Meaning of an Heroine   Something else to be Ashamed of for Her   Both Words have Exactly the Same Sound   and That is How   The Code   Works

Herpes: Her/Peas
Peas are Feminine Symbols and are Part of The Fems Mythical Children Stories
The Code   Transformed it into in a Disease
R/Her/Hair/Are/Here/Hear/Ear/Err/Heir/Or/Whore/Sex   Pees
herpes: herpesvirus
Her/Peas   Herpes is a Cover Word here
Just Pee on it says   The Code   Because Her Peas/Pees Which were Planted to Nurture Nature/Her family is an Infectious Disease Sexual Also

Herself: R   Self   Her/Self   Her/R/Ear/Hear/Hair/Err/Heir/Or/Whore/Here/Are/Our/Ire/Air/Ere/Sex   Sell   F/Fem/Fuck   Nothing Good to Identify with for a Fem

Him/Self   is M/Motherhood   Self as in Sell   F/Fem/Fuck   A well Ordered Name for The Masc to Identify with His Mother says   The Code   It is still about Selling F/Fem/Fuck
Letter M as Him/M   Mothers as His Self   As if He was a Mother on That Code Level
That is How   The Code   Works in The Psyche of Humans
It Steals The Identity of The Fems In Any Way   and Makes it be So Bad

Hew: The Letter U
With H/Secret Code Letter and E/He in Front of W/All Fems Sex Active   It Spells Danger to Her
Hew: to strike forcefully with an axe sword or cutting instrument   to shape with cutting blows
Literally an Axe
You/U   Phew (On Cue A/Few/No)
Hew is so Soft of a Word as Dew or Cue or Few
The Fems has Soft Ears for that

Hex: The Letter X/Fallen Fem Cross in The Secret Code
hex: spell   charm   a witch
No Says   The Code   so   X/Hit/It   and   Exit
The Code is Treacherous   Immoral   Suicidal   for the Human Race

Hey: The Letter A Sound   Calling on   A/All Men
hey: hello   used as a greeting   used as an exclamation to call attention
Switch E for A/All Men and He Gets Hay
hay: horse or animal food
From One Man to Another (from He/E to A/All Men) a Smooth Transition as Usual

Hi: Letter i/I Sound   The Man Stick   The Eye in the Pyramid   The Voice from The High   Hi is a Calling

Hic: IC
IC Means Integrated Circuit
Something that Come with the Package   As Eyes or Ears or Feet or Something Integrated as Workaholic   Alcoholic   Addict   etc

Letter i/Marriage Act is in Small Caps   The I/The Stick in Large Caps has a Different Meaning (See Letter iI in The Letter Chapter)
C/See/Young Girl
IC Hides Under Hiccup   IC/Cup
The Cup is the Ever Expansible Breast of The Fems Breasts as Domes   And Doom Comes With it (See Dome/Doom in The Words Chapter)   He/Kick

High: Letter i/Marriage Act   I/High/Eye/Hi   of   The Code   Stick
It is The Eye on Top of the Pyramid on The American Dollar Bill
Anything that has a Penis/Stick
This Word High is Important in   The Code   Symbology
High has 2 HHs/Secret Code Letter   Twice   More Secrets

Highbred   I/Stick   Bred
High/Bread
highbred: of superior breed
When   The Code   Talks about a Highbred it is a Son/Sun/Man   A Heir in the Making   Not a Dough
Bread/Bred is one of the Source of Primal Modern Life   Ha

Highest: I/Haste
As Usual   The Code   is Ahead of Her

Highness: INS
I/High/Eye   N/In/Hen/Donkey/Ann/Virgin   S/Is/Us/His/Ass/Hiss/Serpent/Penis
The Virgin/N/Donkey   is in   i/Marriage Act   with   with S/Serpent
The Fem is Elevated here to Highness because   The Code   says She is with   S/Penis

Hill: Letter L
Everything goes Upward with Efforts for the Fems
L/Sweet Fem Love Light/Oil/Elle/All/Ill/Ail/Hail/Heel/Hell   goes Up the Hill
Small Mount/Month Time of the Month

Him: H/M   H/Secret Code Letter   With   M/Motherhood
That is The Reason For   The Code   To Exist

The Dam Code The Damn Book

H/Secret Code Letter   i/Marriage Act   M/Motherhood
Switch Letter I for Letter E and He Gets a Hem
H/Secret Code Letter   E/He   M/Mom
As Says   The Code   the Masc is The Mother Too
Stealing The Fems Identity   All the Way as Usual
Aim   Am   Ham are Cover Words Here
hmm: hesitation   perplexity   doubt
The Code Does Not Want You To Look at It

Hinge   NG   N/In/Hen/Virgin/Ann/Donkey   G/Penis Penetration/God Letter
hinge: that on which something is based or depends   pivotal consideration or factor
The Relation Between   N/Virgin   and   G/Vaginal Penetration   is vital to The Hinge of   The Code

Hiring: RN
Her/R/Ear/Hear/Hair/Err/Heir/Or/Whore/Here/Are/Our/Ere/Ire/Air/Sex   N/Hen/Ann/Virgin
R/Sex   is with N/Virgin   The Code   is Hiring
Earring   Ear/In   Earing it All She is as Usual from   The Word/Letters Code

His: Letter
Is   Hiss   Ice
H/Secret Code Letter   I/Stick/Sex Union   S/Is/Us/His/Ass/Hiss/Serpent/Penis   He/Is
Her is   Her/R/Ear/Hear/Hair/Err/Heir/Or/Whore/Here/Are/Our/Ere/Ire/Air/Sex
Big Difference Here Between the 2 Sexes
From His   He/Is   To Her   Heir/Whore   And a Heir in the waiting

Hissing: His/In   S/In   SSS/in
S/Is/Us/His/Ass/Hiss/Serpent/Penis   N/Ann/Hen/Donkey
The Code   Always Compare the Penis to a Snake   It is Not   The Penis is an Organ for Pleasure and Reproduction
It has been altered by Circumcision   Which Is an Awful Mutilation to The Masc   As Clitorectomy is to The Fems

Lise Rochon

History: His/Story
She is Not There as Usual

Hit: He/It   He/Hit
Hit/Hit   It/It   It/Hit   Hit/It
i/Marriage Act   and   T/Fem Cross/Great Curse
Hit is a word that Hides in The Code   Hid/It
It Does it in   D/Pregnant (Hid ID   i/Marriage Act   D/Pregnant) Before
She Gets it (Hit) in T/Fem Cross/Great Curse
Switch H or B/Boy Holding All Breasts and He Gets a Bit (Too Young for the Code   He Stays Away)
Switch H for CKQ and She Gets a Kick
Switch H for F/Fem/Fuck and She Gets a Fit
Switch H for L/Sweet Fem Love Light and She Get a Lit
(See Letter L In Letter Chapter   L as in Light)
In French a Lit is a Bed
Switch H for M/Motherhood and She Gets a Mate/Meet   of Course She Needs One to get Pregnant   So here Is   The Code   Providing One
Switch H for N/In/Hen/Ann/Virgin and She Gets a Knit/Night/Knight
Switch H for P/Man Power and He Gets Pete (a Friend)
Switch H for Her/R/Ear/Hear/Hair/Err/Heir/Or/Whore/Here/Are/Our/Ere/Ire/Air/Sex   and   She Gets a Rite   Something from The Code   To Exploit Her Some More
Switch H for S/Is/Us/His/Ass/Hiss/Serpent/Penis
and He Gets a Sit/Site/Sight
Switch H/Secret Code Letter for T/Fem Cross and She Gets Tit   She Needs Those while Pregnant   Which is the Goal of   The Secret Code   Why   Why   Why   I do Not Know   There Can be So Many Reasons
Switch H for Z and Get a Zit   The Code   Does Not want Anyone to Look at it closely
Add N/In/Hen/Virgin and She Gets a Hint
Hint is the Cover Word for Hit

Hits: Hit/Is   Hit/His   High/It   He/T   I/Hit   Eye/Hit   I/Hit   Switch the i Letter for A/All Men and He Gets to Hate/It
Hit is the Word for Her Transformation into   The Code   By th Force of The Hit

The Dam Code The Damn Book

From the Dot on Top of the i with the i/Marriage Act
Greatest Hits Would be Cover Words here for   The Code

Hmm: H/Secret Code Grid is with 2 or All MM/Motherhood/Moms
All M/Motherhood is Under The Power of H in Hmm   Because it is The Word Him   The Code is Running Motherhood
Such a Soft Sound in Hmm   For Such a Curse to Humanity
The Secret Code   is Very Careful in the Presence of Many Mothers (Mate/Hers)
hmm: interjection   to express thoughtful
absorption   hesitation   doubt   perplexity
The Code   Keeps Us Far Away with its Definition of Hmm
Which is Close to The Cosmic Sound   Om   Or   Oum Which Millions people Practice Every Day
Homme in French is Man   Which is a Powerful Noun

Ho: The Letter Sound   O/Fem Hole
When   H/Secret Code   is Alone with O/Fem Hole   It is a Big No from The Code   so
ho: derogatory term for a Fem (Prostitute)
an exclamation used to attract attention   laughter
Compare Here to   Oh Sound When that   O/Fem Hole is in the Front of H
oh: expression of pain   surprise   disapprobation
And That is For the Fems Says   The Code   The Fem is a Hoe

Hoard: Her/R/Ear/Hear/Hair/Err/Heir/Or/Whore/Here/Are/Our/Ere/Ire/Air/Sex   D/Pregnant
Whored   to Whore in the Past
hoard: a supply or accumulation that is hidden or carefully guarded for preservation future use etc
The Code   Says Pregnancy Must Go On

Hoax: The Sound Letters for Ox
hoax: too deceive   to play tricks
Take Away A/All Men and She Gets the Axe   Because H/Secret Code is Now in Front of O/Fem Hole   and   X/Axe/Fallen Fem Cross   The Fem Cycle of   The Code
Hoe/O is a Prostitute here   Which Falls Under the Axe/X/Fallen Fem Cross

Lise Rochon

Hold: Hole/D   Old
The Hole of D/Pregnant   Hold on to That Says   The Code

Hole: H/Secret Code   O/Fem Hole   L/Sweet Fem Love Light/Oil/Elle/All/Ill/Ail/Hail/Heel/Hell/All
Whole
"Love your sons and raise your daughters"   Illustrate just that Whole
Is the Hole Added with a W
Which We are All Perforated as a Whole
Add P/Man Power and He Sees a Pole (Penis)
The Code   Hypnotism Works on Both Sexes   But The Fem Suffers Most   The Code   as The Masc is Constantly Reinforced Positively

Holiday: Hole/He/Day
A Holiday is His Hole Day
Hole/He/They
Many Men Can Enjoy Her Hole Says   The Code

Hollering: Hole/He/Ring   Hole/Her/In
hollering: a loud cry to express pain or surprise

Hollow: 2 OOs/Fem Hole/Loins   with   2 LLs/Sweet Fem Love Light/Oil/Elle/All/Ill/Ail/Hail/Heel/Hell Plural or All of Them
There are No Man Here Except Letter H/The Code
All/O   Hole/O   The Code   says No to That   so
hollow: cavity within or inward curve   lacking in real value sincerity or substance
Never Anything Positive About The Fems or Her Sex Organs in   That Code
Halloween (Hollow/Win) is The Cover Word Here

Holocaust: Holocaust   Hole/Cost
Mid 13th Century Word Origin
holocaust: sacrifice by fire   great destruction
That Is What   The Fem Hole/All/O   Cost to The Fems   We Lost Our Natural Sexuality Between The Fems and The Masc When Circumcision Was Created   Physical Mutilation is What it is for Him   and   The Blood

Cycle for The Fems   Another Abnormality   The Great Curse From The Code
That is what The Hole/Cost Under the Great Curse
It Makes People Kill Each Other with Saturn at The Head (See Saturn in the Astrology Chapter   The God of Bad Times)

Please Note
To be Careful as You Enter this Section Here
The Holy Word Series of Words Terms is Exceptionally Insulting to People of Faith
Believers have been Using those Godly Words for
Millenaries   and   Suddenly Those are in the Dump with the Filth
Approach with Awareness

Holy: Hole/He   Oil/He
The Virgins and the Oil in the Bible Are Nebulous Passages   The Oil Being Perhaps is Her Honey Here
holly: red berries used during the Christmas season
Berries are Red as Fem Genitals   and   Easy to Pick

Holy Blood: Hole/He   Blood
Blood   Flood   the Red Flood
The Legend of the Flood All Over the World Finds Its Meaning here
Loosing Blood in that Amount Every Month for Us Fem
Is a Flood of Blood
For 2000 Years For Her   Especially with No Fem Hygiene Tampons and Pads in The Past etc   Another Shame for Her

Holy Cross: Hole/He/Cross   The Hole He Cross
The Code   is the Master of Her Sex Life   It Created   The Fems Cross/Curse for That
Hole/He/Cross is a VIP Word Here in   It Hides Under Religious Beliefs

Holy Grail: Hole/He/Girl
Sang/Real Yes   Royal Blood No   Real Blood Yes
It is Not Royal Blood it is About Real Blood
The Holy Girl from the Holy Grail   Girl is Fille In French
See King Arthur Bleeding Lance in The Holy Grail

Holy Land: Hole   He   Land
Be Aware of False Preachers of this Word
If it Is The Hole He Wants to Land It Is so Wrong
The Code   Says it is The Way

Holy Man: Hole/He/Mean   Hole/He/Man
No Discussion Here
Hole/M/N   Mothers and Virgins Holes
O/Fem Hole   He/E   M/Motherhood   N/In/Hen/Ann/Virgin
All Holes are His Says   The Code   It could Include Homosexuality here
because the   Hole/He   has No Sex   Except for the   O/Fem Hole
The Making of a Holy Man Says   The Code

Holy Spirit: Hole/He/Spear/It   Hole/He/Spare/Hit
The Code   Strangely and Rarely Ambiguous is
Ghost   Calling Her a Holy Ghost
The Holy Spirit is the Only One of the 3 of the Holy Trinity that Can be
Fem   She is a Veiled Ghost
The Father God The Son and The Holy Spirit/Ghost
Naturally You Need a Fem in Order to have a Child
But in   The Code   You Need to be a Virgin Mother to Be Barely
Respected   As in the Role of Mary Called The Mother of Christ/
God   The Mother of God   She is Not a Saint Enough
The Catholic Church has Never Given Any Form of Power to The Fems
She Failed to the Existence of The Fems as a Religious Power When She
is Called a Virgin and a Mother and a Ghost Instead   As in The Holy
Ghost   The Ghost That has a Hole In Her   Therefore Giving The Fems
No Power Again At All   A Ghost Cannot do Nothing
Picture Her as a White Dove   Again a Christ Symbol
The Dove is an Old Jewish Symbol (Which is a Fem Symbol Entirely)   (All
Fems Sounds Also   DOV)
The Spirit of God Descends in Jesus In the Form of a Dove
When He Was baptized In Mathew 3.16
Be Baptized With Water (Fem Symbol)
The Dove is a Metaphor of Sacrifice and Rebirth   As the T/Fem Cross/
Great Curse   Noah Sends a Dove   it Comes Back with an Olive Branch
(Peace Symbol) All/Eve

The Dam Code The Damn Book

The Dove is The Illuminati Symbol of the Fems Sacrifice And Because the Dove is White and Pure   It is Another Metaphor for the Sacrifice of the Virgin (As in Christ)   Get That
According to Wikipedia a Dove is as the White Lamb
It is to Be Sacrificed   Also a Blood Sacrifice As The Fems Have to have Says   The Code

Holy Water: Hole/He   Wet/Her
Water (Entirely a Fem Symbol) Transformed into Wet/Her   It is so Offensive to The Fems   A Religious Crime to Me   The Code   Says It is All a Go For Her   Talking about High Spirituality Used to Fool The Fems from The Code

Hollywood: Hole/He/Would   Holy/Wood (Wood is a Common Symbol for an Erection   and   a Name for Religious Sanctity)
But The Code Says No It is Really a   Holy/He/Wood
Wood (A Stiff)
Hollywood Creators of Entertainment Seems to Know Quite a Lot about   The Code   and are Using those Symbols in Many Hidden Ways in Movies to Influence The Fems with Its Grandiosity   Anyhow We Love Movies from Hollywood   They Puts Stars in Our Eyes
Hollywood has Created So Many Pieces of Great Art Films   Hollywood Entertainment is Priceless
But There is Sex Abuse More than Ever There in The Corridors of Movie Making and Elsewhere   Because That Code   System is Flawed Because That is What   The Code   Creates as a Direct Effect
To Understand for the Ones to Understand   Not to Understand for the Ones Who do Not Understand

Home: Om   The Mystical Sound of The Universe   2 Fem Letters M/Motherhood   with   O/Fem Hole
Homme is French for Man   Even Here She is Non Existent   She is Absent from The Concept of Home Maker (A Mother Being The Center of The Home Naturally) Homemaker   O/Fem Hole   M/Motherhood   Ache/Her
It is a Big Job   and   N/Virgin   The Daughter of M/Motherhood   Works a Full Day to Prepare Herself for Motherhood (in Older Times Daughters had No Choice but to Follow in Maternity as Soon as Possible It is still the Same in Many Countries)

403

Honest: On   His/Is   T/Fem Cross
T/Fem Cross   is On   In His Nest
N/Nest   N/Virgin   is Preparing The Nest
On/Est   That Come from The East Where   The Code   Still Rules Over
The Fems in a Hard Way
H   On/N   S/Is/Us/His/Ass/Hiss/Serpent/Penis   T   H/Secret Code
Society   is On with   T/Great Fem Curse
On/Haste   And Hurry Up   N/Virgin
Honestly   Honest/Lay   The Code   Called it Honest
Add Her/R/Ear/Hear/Hair/Err/Heir/Or/Whore/Here/Are/Our/Ere/Ire/Air/Sex
and She Gets a Horn Nest (Not Good as Usual)
Is That Honest No But   The Code   Says Yes
We need To Think and Reflect on Ourselves   So We can Find The truth
and Have a Peaceful and Better Life for All

Honey: N/E   N/A   On/He   Hon/He
N/Virgin   is with   He/E   And/Or   N/Virgin is with   A/All Men   No
Choice For Her here
Honey is Slang for Sex Prep
It Feels Homey Says   The Code   (M/Motherhood   and N/Virgin in
Waiting   are Interchangeable   One is a Mother the Other is Being
Trained for it by Adding One More Bar   (See Bar in The Words Chapter
and The Clock Chapter # 11 (a Double Bar)
Add Her/R/Hair/Are/Here/Hear/Ear/Whore/Or/Err/Sex   and She Gets
Horny (as Wanted by The Code Either Pregnant (Heir) or Whoring or Err/R)
Honey Made from The Bees as in   B/Baby Boy Holding All Fem
Breasts   for His Honey (Milk) Also
Honeycomb is When the Honey Come
honeycomb: the reticulum of a ruminant
Back to the Cows/Animals for The Fems as Usual

Honeymoon: Honey/Moon
Honeymoon is a   Code   Cover Word for Her Menstrual Cycle
Being Called Her Moon which has No Relation to Reality   The Fems
Do Not Bleed All Together in The World at Every New Moon or Full
Moon   Although They are Influenced by Fem Pheromones Easily and
will it will Influence The Time of Her Monthly Bleeding Until The Fems are

The Dam Code The Damn Book

Aligned All Together   For Example Moving in with Other Fems Totally Influences that Imposed Fem Calendar   A Mystery Still for Science (See Moon in The Words Chapter The Tarot and Astrological Chapters) Honeymoon as Nice of a Word it is Wrong   The Fems are Not Moons (A Moon is a Satellite it Rotates around Another Planet as an Obedient Fem) Honeymoon does Not Produce Cheese (Cheese is Also Known as Fem Honey)
A Moon does Not Produce Honey and She is Not a Bee Either

Honk: On/K
K/Broken Fem Warrior   is On
It Attracts Attention   so No says   The Code   to The Fems A Horn is Meant to Attract Attention in Order to Stopped or Attract Attention
If K as Broken Fem Warrior is On   The Code   Needs to Know to Accelerate That Processes of Her Destruction
honk: auto horn

Honor: Hon/Her
Hon is Honey   Back to Sex for Her and The Bees (See Bee in The Words Chapter)
Add R/Her/Ear/Hear/Hair/Err/Heir/Or/Whore/Here/Are/Our/Ere/Ire/Air/Sex and She Gets Horn/Her
Back to Sex for Her to Finding Her Honor
Honoring   Horn/Her/In   Honor/N   O/No/Ring   On/Her/Ring   here
She Gets or Not Get that Ring (See Ring in The Words Chapter   Ring That Bell/Belle)
Not Much for The Fems Says   The Code   As Usual

Hood: The Hood that Could
The Hat   The Secret Art is Part of the Same Disguise Here
The Only Hood for a Fem is Motherhood
Switch H for W/All Fems Sex Active and She Gets Wood Wood is Also a Masc Erection   She Would   If She Could   But No way The Code is Entirely Masc

Hoo-hoo: 2 HHs/Secret Code Letter   with   4 OOOOs/Fem Holes/Loins
That is a Weak Position for The Code   so No

hoo-hoo: bad luck   a person that bring bad luck
(See Letter H in The Letter Chapter)

Hook: The Hook Catches the Fish   Fishhook
hook: to snare to steal by stealth   to trick with artifice
Hooker (Hook/Her)   The Fish is The Fem in   The Code
Once She is Hooked   She is a Hooker
a Whore (See Letter R in its Many Forms in The Letter Chapter)   That
Hurt (Her/t) Her to Death (Death of Her Freedom   Free Thinking   To
have the Choice of Having or Not Children and Get Married or Not etc)
The Hook   The Ankh   The Anchor (Ankh/Her)   as In Bank   Ankh
Means Soul   or   Life in Egyptian
It Rhymes with Bank A rare Combination   Where the Money is Held is
Often Where Real Power is

Hoop: H/Secret Code Letter Society   with   2 OOs/Fem Holes (In Plural
or All of Them)   with   P/Man Power
H/The Code Grid   with   P/Man Power   Takes Over (Ov/Her) O/Fem
Holes/Loins   It is a Hoop done to Her
hoop: a ring of iron   a circular band of stiff material
The Code   is Closed to Her as a Fortress
It is Unbearable Injustice for Many Fems
Add S/Is/Us/His/Ass/Hiss/Serpent/Penis   and He Gets Oops (Another
Chance Given to the Man Novice)
Oops is the Cover Word Here

Hoot: Hot and Out
hoot: to cry or shout especially in disapproval or derision   the cry of
an owl
Owl/All
The Owl is Active at Night   The Night/Knight is a Fem Symbol Along with
the Moon etc
Hooter: Hoot/Her   Hot/Her   Out/Her
An Outhouse is a Toilet   That Is What She Gets Says   The Code   As
Usual The Fems Finds Herself in Feces

Hop: H/Secret Code Letter   O/Fem Hole   P/Man Power
Men Hop   When Up   Hop is Slang for Sex

hopper: a person that hops
Hop/Her
hops: the dried ripe flowers esp female flowers of the hop plant used to give a bitter taste to beer
Bitter (Bit/Her   Bate/Her   Boot/Her   Butt/Her   Butter)
Switch H/Secret Code Letter Grid for C/See/Young Virgin and She Gets Cup (Cups are The Fems Symbols for the Fems Emotions in Tarot Cards)

Horcrux: Sound Word Created by Author J.K Rowling in the Harry Potter Books   Wonderful Imagination to Me   But it is Says   The Code   A Whore and A Cross   That is Why it Sounds so Bad
It Is The Nightmare Created by   The Code   Now for 2 000 Years

Hormone: Whore/Moon   Whore/Mom
M and N are Interchangeable in   The Code   as in is The Letter N/Virgin Daughter   and   M/Motherhood   Are Related by The Daughter Adding Another Bar (See Bar in The Clock and Words Chapters)
Her/R/Hair/Are/Here/Hear/Ear/Whore/Or/Err/Sex   M/Motherhood   O/Fem Hole   N/In/Hen/Ann/Virgin   Makes The Fem a Whore/Heir/Err   She Has a Hole To Procreate for a Heir or for Men Fun or if Not She will Err with Hair or Not

Horn: R/N   A Nurse is a RN
Or/In   Her/R   N/Virgin
H/Secret Code Letter Society Code   O/Fem Hole   Her/R/Hair/Are/Here/Hear/Ear/Whore/Or/Err/Sex   N/In/Hen/Ann/Virgin
Sex is The Horn of Abundance   It is a Long Basket in a Shape of a Curved Bell
Horn is Slang for Penis in The American Language
HRN   Earn   We Would Think it is an Honorable Concept   But No Says   The Code
The Urn Is the Bottom of the Story Here
The Urn is a Container (Contain/Her   Cunt/N/R) in a Shape of a Pregnant Fem in Antic Egypt   Greece   Rome
Switch H for W/All Fems Sex Active and She Gets to be Worn
Switch H for T/Fem Cross/Great Curse and She Gets Torn
Switch H for C/See/Young Virgin Girl and She Gets Corn (C/Horn) (Corn is Sex in Slang)

Switch H for D/Pregnant and She Gets a Dorm (Being Pregnant She Gets a Bed in a Dorm Says The Code)
Switch H for M/Motherhood and She Gets to Morn (Motherhood is That Says The Code)
Switch H for N/In/Hen/Ann/Virgin and She Gets to Be The Norm
To be Torn and Morn is the Norm for The Fems Says   The Code
It Makes M and N and D and C Feel Worn
It is The Fems in the Dorm   Or   On the Horn
Switch H to B/Boy Holding All Fem Breasts and He Is Born
All This from The Horn
Horny   Horn/He
Ornament   Horn He   Meant is The Cover Word Here

Horrible: Whore/Heir/Err   He/Able
That Is What She is Allowed to Do and Has since Ancient Times   According to   The Code
The Oldest Jobs in the World for The Fems   Her Only Avenues   That being a Mother a Wife Through and being a Whore

Horror: RR   ROR
Whore/Her   With 2 RRs/Her/R/Ear/Hear/Hair/Err/Heir/Or/Whore/Here/Are/Our/Ere/Ire/Air/Sex (as in Plural or All of Them   O/Fem Holes)   Meaning Here All Fem Holes become Whores in Horror
Or/Whore   as in One Or the Other   Which is Witch   She is a Witch again says   The Code
Whore   Roar   Or   Her   Rear
Switch Double O/Fem Holes for He/E and He Gets a Heir/Her (Err Her) It is a Great Pride for a Masc to have a Boy/Heir
O/Fem Hole   with Her/R/Hair/Are/Here/Hear/Ear/Whore/Or/Err/Sex   with Silent   H/Secret Code   Starting the Word
The Code   says to Her   Her/Her   is Horror   The Whores Roars of Horrors
Ride That Horse Girl   The Horse/Whores is a Powerful Sex Symbol for the Fem and Masc in Our Human Mythology and Symbology
It is the Opening of Her Legs and The Start of The Banging on Her Genitals   That and the Feeling it Gave to Men to Watch it
It is the Same Unconscious Processes that Disney Serves Us on a Pretty and Sweet Dish for the Young Children Girl Story   The Little Mermaid

The Dam Code The Damn Book

Aurora (A/Horror   Whore/A   etc) is a Fem Name
This is When that Code Symbology is Easier to Understand
Men Take Pride in their Sexuality   It is Not Repressed or Humiliated as in with The Fem Sexuality
It is All the Way from The Veil to the Elimination of All Her Natural Powers (Read Persephone/Hades Mythology Story)   Horrible
The Code   Word Definition of Horrible is Something You do Not Want to Go Near   It is as a Nightmare (Mare/Mère/Horse   in the   Night/Knight)
That Would be Too Much Power for The Fems to Know says   The Code   so
Horrible   Night/Mare   in the Night it is

Horse: Whores (See Whores in The Words and Letter R Chapters)
One Horse is a Mix of Several Whores   Something to Mount   One or The Other

Hostage: Host   Egg/Age
The Ovulation is in the Host (Her   She is The Holy (Hole/He)   Ghost (G/Host) and is Kept Hostage by   The Code
This Language Secret Code is Ancient   It Has Evolved From and Since Mesopotamia and Before
Thorough Many Eastern and Western European Influences Over Thousands of Years
To be transformed Again by the British/English
Navigating to Become the Most Evolved Language on the Planet   The American English Language
We Need that Language Clean On All Levels of Understanding/Consciousness   To have a Chance of Succeeding in Our Lives

Hostile: Host/Hell   (See Devil in The Words Chapter)
Host/Ill   Host/Elle
Host He/E   L/Sweet Fem Love Light/Oil/Elle/All/Ill/Ail/Hail/Heel/Hell   He Lives Inside
Us/S/Till
The Code   Says The Fems Curse Makes The Fems Ill (Hell)
Hostel is the Cover Word here

Hot: H/Secret Code Society   O/Fem Hole   T/Fem Cross

409

H The Secret Code is in Front of O/Fem Hole and T/Fem Cross
A Big No from The Code   so   Make Her Hot and Hit it
Heat   H/It
Hot is Where   The Code   Hit   at The Hut (Home for Fems and
Children)   Hot/He   A Hottie is Someone Looking for Sex
And that is How   The Code   Gets Her   Out of Naivety and Ignorance as
Usual

Hotel: Hot/Elle   Hot/Hell   Hot/Ill   Hot/All
At/Hell   Hat/Hell   O/Tell   Ho/Tell
L/Sweet Fem Love Light/Oil/Elle/All/Ill/Ail/Hail/Heel/Hell
To The Fems it is The Usual from   The Code   A Ho is a Prostitute
A Hotel should be a Nice Place as an Inn Used to be in The Past   But Not
For Her Anymore
Inn (I/Marriage Act   2NNs/Virgin)

Hotter: Hot/Her   Hat/Her
(See At and Art in The words Chapter)
utter: complete   total   unconditional
She Can Only be Hot   It is in the Hat for Her Says   The Code   Being too
Hot could be a Cause for The Fem Loss of Blood

hottie: a sexually attractive person

Hour: Our (See Hour in The Clock Chapter)
Also Refer to   Month (Mount)   Week (Weak)   Days (Dazed   Daisies
(Days/His))   Hour (Our)   Minutes (Men/Huts   Mine   US/S/Is/Us/His/
Ass/Hiss/Serpent/Penis)   Seconds (S/Cons   Sex/Cons) etc
Our as in it is Us   The Fems as in Us/S/Penis   The Code   Misleads
Humans All The Time for Ever

Hour Glass: The Hourglass Is One of The Symbols for The Tightening
of The Waist On The Fems   The Number 8 Shape Represents the
Idealized Shape of a Fem Body According to   The Code   as in The
Bee Waist   or   The Fleur De Lys Symbol (See BB in Words)   or   The
Hourglass Shape   They are All The Same   It is The Non Real Fem
Waist with Big Breasts and Large Hips   Long Thin Legs   Small

Feet   Etc   Anything to Make Her Body Weak   Off   Unbalanced   One Way or The Other
She has No Waist to Breathe In/Out to have a Comfortable Living for Her Laying Down # 8   it is Pi ∞Symbol of Infinity   in Very Small   So Small it is Little Seen   How Accommodating for   The Code
A Reminder from the Glass Ceiling   All Fems are Prisoners of The Fems Curse   To Keep Lying Down for Eternity   Put That in Your Pipe
Lise is a Fem Name and Flowers are Fem Symbols Entirely
Our/Glass Shape is The Fems Glass Ceiling
She Stands (# 8) and Lays (∞)
The Sign of Jesus Fish Symbol is Similar
Whore   Hour   Our   Or   Her   Glass (Glass Ceiling)

House: Owe/S   Owe the S/Is/Us/His/Ass/Hiss/Serpent/Penis
How/S
S/Is/Us/His/Ass/Hiss/Serpent/Penis   How is the Hose   S/is/His/Us/Ass/Hiss/Serpent/Penis
Switch H for or C/See/Young Girl
There are Several Layers of Meanings Here
Switch H for M/Motherhood and She Gets a Mouse (Not Much Here for Her to Help Her)
∆ ∆ ∆ Erected Penisses (See Letter A in The Letter Chapter) as Houses
The Old Builders (Especially from Liban   The Masons) Knew and Used the Hidden Symbolism of   The Code
It Gave the Masc More Man Power in The House
Who/S   Whose   Woes   Who/Is
The Code   is Vague with Identity When a Fem is Close
Table: T/Fem Cross   Able   She is Able to Do Something Here for Once Says   The Code   It is to Serve Food   It is a Staple at This Table   This Table is Stable (S/Table   S/Penis   is With   T/Fem Cross   Able
Counter: Cunt/Her   Count/Her
Chair: She Err   She   Her/R/Ear/Hear/Hair/Err/Heir/Or/Whore/Here/Are/Our/Ere/Ire/Air/Sex
She is Not Allowed to Sit Says   The Code
Plate: P/Late   Play/Hate   P/Lay/Ate   He Will be Late or Not There To get Home
Dish: D/She   D/Pregnant   She is
Dish Towel: D/Pregnant   She   Two/To/Too   All

Towel   T/Fem Cross   O/Fem Hole   All/Ill/Hell/Elle/Letter L   While She Dries the Dishes with the Dish Towel (All Tow/All)   D Itches for That Too
Sheet: She/It   Shit
Bed sheet: Bad   Shit   Back to Feces for Her Says   The Code   as She Tries to Organize Life For Him and Her
Broom: B/Boy Holding All Fem Breasts   Roam
Every Word for a House Part is Bad For The Fems
Threshold: TRS (Threes or Trees   See Tree of Life) Hold
A Door: Adore   Add/Whore   A/Do/Her   D/Whore
A Very Important Old Religious   Code   Term Here
D/Pregnant   2 OOs/Fem Hole Loins Horses   Whores/Arse/Ass (Donkey/N/In/Hen/Ann/Virgin)
Back to Sex with Animals for the Fems Here
Door/Bell   Adore the Belle   Then Ring that Bell (Clitoris)   or   Put a Ring Around Her Finger   Which Means She Will Serve That Man For The Rest of Her Life Says   The Code For 2000 Years
Window: Win   The/D/Pregnant   O/Fem Hole   Win/Dough (Dough is The Breed/Bread Making   As in Daughter (Dough   T/Fem Cross   Her)
Win   D/Pregnant   O/Fem Hole/Ow/Owe
Win/The/O   Wind   O   Win/Wind   in the Window
Take N/In/Hen/Ann/Virgin Away and She Gets We/Dough
Ceiling: Seal/In   See/All/In
Wall: W/All
Hall   All/Ill/Hell/Ail/Hail/Helen
Room/In: Roaming
roam: to ramble   to wander
A Man Comes and Go in Any Room
Attic   Hat/IC (See Art/Hat in The Words Chapter)   A/Dick
Roof: R/Ov   R/Off   R/Of   Rough
Around the House
Garden: Guard/Him   G/Penis Penetration/God Letter   Hard   M/Motherhood   For Her is the Hard Road to Motherhood
Road: Red   Rod   Route (The Blood Flood is The Road for Her)
Boulevard: Bull   V/Fem Sex Active   Hard
Avenue: Ov/Of   He/E   Nu/Knew   Eve   He/E   Knew (In the Bible Sense)
Street: Stray   T/Fem Cross   Stay/Rite   Add a Pole and it is a Penis as in a   Street Pole

Tower: To/Owe/Her   Two/O/Her   T/Her   S/Is/Us/His/Ass/Hiss/Serpent/Penis   T/Fem Cross   Her/R   To   Owe   Her
Village: Vile/Age   V/Ill   Age
City: Cite/Sight   He   Nothing for The Fems Here
Town: All 4 Fem Letters   T/Fem Cross   is   Owned
Country: Cunt   Her   Hey/Hay (See Hey in The Words Chapter)   Cunt on a Tray for The Fems to do Says   The Code
Continent: Containment   Cunt/He/Meant   Count/He Meant (M/Motherhood   and   N/Virgin are Interchangeable in   The Code)
Island: I/Masc   Land   His/Land
The List is Unfinished and Seems Endless
No Matter (Mat/Her   Meet/Her   Mate/Her   Meter) How Far She Is/Goes
The Code   Never Goes Away for   The Fem   It Keeps at it by Constantly Being on It   Since at Least 2 000 Years   That is How it Worked on The Fem   She has Nothing Else to Compare to   Some Countries Far Away have Escaped it in Some Ways   Sweden   Norway   Denmark etc

How: O/Fem Hole   Ow
H/Secret Code   O/Fem Hole   W/All Fems Sex Active
When O is with H it is a Danger Territory for   The Code   so
ow: exclamation of pain
Owe   It is The Fem to Owe   Again
With H being in Front it is Minimized in a Simple Question   How Owe/O/Fem Hole
How is the Penis/Hose   Which Would be Hows in Plural   It Is Not in The English Language
⌂ Here it is   A Penis Symbol as a House   It is an International Symbol   We All Know it
Words in O/Ow   O/Fem Hole   and   W/All Fems Sex Active   Together are the Combination for   The Code   Here
To Make All O/Fem Holes Activated   In Ho (e) (Whore) with   W/All Fems Sex Active
Always   The Code   Hides its Power or its Actions   As in Some Letters have a Different Sound   Meaning   or   Spelling   Such as   Bow   Dough   Faux   Go   Ho   Mow
Row   So   Sow   Tow   Vow   Note those (Fem) Words are Weak/Feeble

413

in Meanings   Most having Fem Letters   or   a Masc Letter to Make The Fem Go in a Wrong Way
As for Wow   Cow   Now   Dow in a Different Sound Form

Hover: Ov/Ovulation   Her/R/Ear/Hear/Hair/Err/Heir/Or/Whore/Here/Are/Our/Ere/Ire/Air/Sex
hover: to hang fluttering or suspended in the air   to keep lingering about   wait near at hand   to remain in an uncertain or irresolute state   waver
Ov/Egg Normal Fem Sexual Cycle   R/Her   is on Anytime Because   It is From Above Her (See Letter Z in The Letter Chapter as Her Ending)
Her Ov/V/Egg is Always there and Ready to Go Says   The Code   She has No Normal Mating Natural Cycle Anymore says   The Code

However: OVR   How/Have/Her
How   Eve/V   Her/R/Ear/Hear/Hair/Err/Heir/Or/Whore/Here/Are/Our/Ere/Ire/Air/Sex
How to Have Sex With All Fems says   The Code   is to be Aloof about it   However
V is Also for Conception   as in Ov/Ovulation (Egg)

Huh: 2 HHs/All Secret Code Societies Letter   with   U/You/Ovulating   in the Middle
U/Uterus/Naturally Open Fem Hole   is Surrounded by   H/Secret Society Code Letters   A Big No from   The Code   She Being there is Too Much Information   Being too Close   to That U/Fem   so
huh: bewilderment   contempt   exclamation of surprise disbelief interrogation
No One or Few are Interested

Hull: All
hull: the husk   the shell covering of a fruit
Cracking the Nut to All is Slang for having Sex Says   The Code

The Dam Code The Damn Book

The Code   Says Humanity is Basically the You/U/Her Sacrificed into the   T/Great Curse and   Him

Humble: Him/B/All
Him   Holding   B/All Boys Holding All Fems Breasts
Him/Ball   M/Motherhood   and the   Ball (S)
Humble is a Word of Power   Hiding it Behind Something else as Usual for   The Code
Humble is a Cover Word Here
Humiliation: He   Mule   A   She   On   A Donkey She is

Hump: M/Motherhood/Hum   P/Man Power
hump: slang   instance of coitus
amp: to excite or energize
Take P/Man Power Away and She Gets
hum: to sing with close lips
Her Lips Are Closed here Too
Hump is a Happy Energetic Word
Add Her/R/Ear/Hear/Hair/Err/Heir/Or/Whore/Here/Are/Our/Ere/Ire/Air/Sex and She Gets a Hump Also
romping: to play or frolic in a lively or boisterous manner   to win easily   victory
When Sex and Hump are Together   It is the Usual Victory for   The Code
Switch H/Code for L/Sweet Fem Love Light/Oil/Elle/All/Ill/Ail/Hail/Heel/Hell and She Gets a Lump
Hungry: N/Grey   On/Grey
Grey is the Color of Hiding for   The Code   It is also the Color for Passing Away
As example There Is No Such a thing About White and Black People (When They Mix it Makes it Makes Grey Children) White Are Different Shades of Beige and Black are in Shades of Darker Beige Skin Depending on Their Origin   So When They Mix Together They Make a Nice Shade of Pale or Dark Shade of Beige Not Grey

Hunt: U/You/Ovulating/Chalice   N/In/Hen/Ann/Virgin   and   T/Fem Cross   together with   H/Secret Code in Front of Them   It Brings to be Hunted says   The Code

415

T/Fem Cross and Her Fem Friends would Be On as One   But They would be Hunted says   The Code
NT (Not)   On/T   Ant (Small)   Aunt
The Code   Keeps Her Small   as Always
Hunter: Hunt/Her   There is No Fisher for Fisherman
Because It Means She Would Be Fishing Herself with a Hook (Hooker)
In The Roman Catholic Religion and All   There Are No Fem of Religious Power Allowed For Her   No Matter How Saintly a Fem Can Be   She Cannot Represent a Church as a Priest   Because She Would Be The Secret Keeper of Her Own Sacrifice   Making it an Impossible Concept says   The Code
Religions are Entirely Male in Power and are   Mostly for The Fems to Follow According to   H/Code/Grid

Hurry: RA   or   RE   All Masc Letters Her/R/Ear/Hear/Hair/Err/Heir/Or/ Whore/Here/Are/Our/Ere/Ire/Air/Sex   and   E/He   or   A/All Men
R/Her   for   A/All Men   in Singular and Plural
Her/E   R/Her   and   He/E
There is No Her Says   The Code   so
Only R/Her
Because   R/Her   Are as One from having the Same Sounds
Here is an Easy Example on How to Read   That Code
Her/R   Hay   or   Hey   or   A/All Men
Her and the Hay/Hey
Back to the Horse (Whores) for The Fems
Her/Hey   Her/R   Calls says   The Code   Better Hurry
If Not   U/Hole/Loins   Does Not Get Hay/(Food)

Hurt: RT   Her/R   T/Fem Cross
T/Fem Cross/Great Curse   Brings Hurt
All of Humanity Is Hurt by   This Language Code
Here the Message is Sex and The Cross On it
Earth   Hurt and Heaven   Oven   Even   Eve/V   In/N/On/Hen/Ann/Virgin
More Hurt for The Fems

Husband: Us/Band   Os/Bend
os: zoology   a bone

Os is Bone in French
The 17th Meaning of Bone in Free Dictionary is *Slang*   to have sexual intercourse with
husbandry: Husband/Ray   The Code   is Always Good to The Masc

Hybrid: I/Bred   I/Bread   High/Bred   The I is the Masc Stick   He Breeds   No Fem Here as Usual

Hymn: The Letter M
H/Secret Code   Y/Wounded Fem   M/Motherhood   N/In/Hen/Ann/Virgin
A Catholic Song is a Hymn
He/Hymen (High Men) Sounds Nice and Soothing   Sounds as Him says   The Code   as Usual
M/Motherhood   and   N/In/Hen/Ann/Virgin   are with H/Secret Code   and   Y/Wounded Fem   is Added   so   It is All Him with   N/In/Hen/Virgin   Trailing
High/Men   I/Man   Eye/Man   A/Men   Hymen   Amen (AMN)   It is All about Him/The Masc

Hysterectomy: Operation where a Fem Loses Her Procreative Organs   Hysteria is close   In older times The Fems were easily Called Crazy/Hysterical Fast and the Hysterectomy was A Way to Cure Hysteria   and make   Money for The Medical System of The Time   Therefore the Name   Easter

Hysterical: His/T/Wreck/All
T/Fem Cross   Gets Crazy   She Wrecks it All
His/Sister/He/Call (The Code   Calls Her a Sister When She is Hysterical)
Easter/He/Call (Then She Resurrects from it)

I   i
IC: Integrated Circuit
An Important Word in   The Code
I/Marriage Act Stick   C/See/Young Girl
The Integrated Circuit From   The Code   Here is to have Sex with the Virgin and Hide it as Natural

IC can Only be Written in Big Caps therefore Eliminating the Small Cap of the I as The Dot (Her)
A Complete Integration and a Closed Door   IC
Hic (Burp) is a Cover Word here for   The Code

Ice: I   See
Dice   Lice   Mice   Nice   Rice   Spice   Vice
Ice is The End of the Word Chalice
Shall/He/Is

Icon   I/Con   I/Cone
A Cone is in a Shape of Letter O Looking at it from the Top
The Con(e) is the Shape of a Egg   (See Con In The Letter Chapter)
From N/In/Hen/Virgin to M/Motherhood   I/Come   Says The Code
An Icon is as an Idol   I/Doll or I/Dull
Add IC/Integrated Circuit and Get   Iconic (I/Con/It/Hit)
The Code is Always Violent on The Fems and More Horrific (Whore/He/Fuck) than Thought

ID: In Psychoanalysis it is the Part that Seeks Satisfaction to Pleasure
I/Marriage Act/Stick   D/Pregnant
Sex and Pregnancy as Pleasure Search says   The Code
It Makes Sense for It
An ID is Also Identification Card Which Reinforces that
It is The Cover Word here

Idea: I/D/A
I/Marriage Act   D/Pregnancy   with   A/All Men
That is the Idea says   The Code

Idiot: He/D/He/Hot
Switch O/Fem Hole for P/Man Power and He Gets a Dip
Idiot   He/Do/It   He/Do/Hit   He/Did/Hot   He/D/Hot
He/Dot (Dowry)   Hide/Hot   He/Did/O/T

Idle: Hide/All   Hide/L   Aid/All   Idol   I/Doll   I/Dull
idle: not active

It Could have Been a Positive thing for Her as in a Vacation or Thinking or Negative as Being Lazy
It was Forbidden in Chinese Law to be Idle

Idol: I/Dull   I/Doll
Making The Fems Dull or a Doll is Another Way to Keep Her Ignorant and Not Caring about It   Be A/Doll   Be Idle says   The Code   to Her   It is The Way to be an Idol
Idolatry   I/Dull/Doll   A   Three/Tree
Tree is a Powerful Word in The Secret Art   It is The Tree of Life   People Are Supposed to Live by That says   The Code
Idolatry is Forbidden by the Catholic Church   Another Dead End Road for Believers
Dolls are Boring/Dull

If: Word for Letter F/Fem/Fuck
If is a Tilting Word as the Letter F is
F Cannot Stand by Herself Compared to E/He

Ignition: He/Knit/On   it Is All About The Masc says   The Code   to Start Anything (Any/Thing   See Ding/Thing in the Words Chapter) as in a Masc God   a Starter   An Ultimate Creator

Ignore: In/Whore   with   G/Hymen Perforation/God Letter
She Does Not Know it
Ignorance: In/Whore   With   Hence/Therefore   She Gets To Know Nothing   as Usual in   That Code

Ill: Ill is an Important Word in   The Code   Symbology
Ill is Made of 3 Bars   The Bars Create the Grid (See Bars in The Numbers Chapter   Under Number 11 on Any Clock) It Creates Jail For The Fems says   The Code   L/Sweet Fem Love Light/Oil/Elle/All/Ill/Ail/Hail/Heel/Hell   She is at All Time Behind Bars

Evil Eve/Ill   as in   Eve that is Ill
Devil   The/D/Pregnant The/Eve/Ill
Devil is Ruler of Hell says History (His/Story)

Lise Rochon

Devil Eggs are Cover Words Here Because they Ally Ov with   Devil   and   Food   in a Succulent Way
A Hill/Ill is a small Mount (Sex)/Month as in Her Time of the Month   or   Time for Sex
heel: shabby appearance   the back of the human foot   kicking the heels   down at the heels   to follow at the heels   heel of a club   to arm with spurs
Nothing Appealing Here for Her
Add J/Sheppard Stick and She Gets a Jill
jill: a young woman   a sweet heart   a feminine name
Note here the Double Dots on the Word jill   and the 2 LLs/Ill/L/Sweet Fem Love Light/Ill/Elle/Oil/All/Ail/Hail/Heel/Hell (as in Plural   or   All of Them)   Making it an Uncommon Word   Because those Very Young Girls   The Dots   as in Girls Ready for Sex says   That Code (Making it an All Fem Word with   L/Hell/Ill   Except for the Mean   j/J (The Sheppard Letter with His Stick)
Little   Girl/Sheep   Follow   or   Get Beat   Little Sheep Girls (See Letter i/I in The Letter Chapter)
Add G/Penis Penetration/God Letter and She Gets a Gill (Another Fish Story Again For The Fems Says The Code to Her)
gill: the respiratory organ of aquatic animals as fish that breathe oxygen dissolved in water   a stream   a rivulet   a wooded ravine
The Code   Compares/Uses   a Stream to a Gill (Girl)   Even a Rivulet Loses itself in a Wooden (Wood can Only Grow with Water) Ravine Streams and Rivulets are Tender and Sweet in Reality for Our Feet to Walk On   But No Says   The Code
Add M/Motherhood and She Get to Mill (Work)
Add N/In/Hen/Ann/Virgin and She Gets Nil (She Gets Nothing as Usual from The Code)
Add K/Broken Fem Warrior and She Gets Kill
Killer   Kill/Her   K/Ill/Her
In The Code It is Always about Her to Get Ill/Weak   or/and   Killed in So Many Ways   Along with Unconditional Sex
Add P/Man Power and He Gets a Pill (Lucky Him   He can Forget About The Whole Situation)
Add R/Her/Hair/Are/Here/Hear/Ear/Whore/Or/Err/Sex and She Gets a Rill
Add S/His/Is/Us/Ass/Hiss/Serpent/Penis and He Gets a Sill/Seal
Add T/Fem Cross and She Gets a Till

Add W/All Fem Sex Active and She Gets a Will (She Will go On Doing Just That Says   The Code   There are No Exit For Her   She Has To Stay in The Code Maze)
Ill is Part of the Word Devil   D/V/Ill
Ruling   on   All/L/Sweet Fem Love Light/Oil/Elle/Ill/Ail/Hail/Heel/Hell

The Code is Rules The Fems   The Code Does that With Hades in Mythology When He Takes Away All Persephone Jewelry (Her Powers and All Her Richness) by Misguiding Her Telling Her More Powers will be with Her
And When She is Naked   He Imprisons Her
That is Against the Law Now   But We Still have to Obey   The Code   Rules says   The Code
V/Fem Sex Active are The Wheel Spikes (See Wheel of Time in The Word Chapter)
They All Turn (T/Urn   See Urn in the Word Chapter) Around the Middle Stick (Penis)
Looking at a Wheel From the Top it is Also in a Shape of a Piece of a Pie (See Pi as # 8 in The Numbers Chapter)
Here V is being Encircled (N/In/Hen/Ann/Virgin   Cycle) Attached to That Wheel of Time
Letter V has a Top in a Round Shape (Pregnancy) Looking at The Wheel from The Top   It is now in a Shape of an Ice Cream Cone (See Con in The Words Chapter)
Several More or All of Her Creating The Double V as in W) (W/All Fem Sex Active) in That Wheel Attached to That Stick
The Wheel of Time Includes the Letter I V X and the Deformed T
Also W/All Fem Sex Active   but Only When in Writing which is a V with Another V   Together   as in W/All Fems Sex Active
N is a Derivative of V   Adding a Stick/I in Front   It Gives it Balance   V/Fem Sex Active Now Carries a Virgin
They All are the Spikes of the Wheel of Time   or
as the Tarot (Rota/Wheel) Calls it the Wheel of Fortune Card)   Ruled by Jupiter   The Law   The Number 4 (See # 4 In The Numbers Chapter)   Jupiter Bring Good Fortune if you Follow the Rules of   The Code   But it is a Lie
The Code   Brings Wars and Tears   We All are Isolated in That   Which Is   The Code   Way To Keep Us Weak

Lise Rochon

Letter V (The Most important Letter Supporting The Wheel)
Letter V (# 5) is the Base of the Pyramid (The Law # 4) Shape Turned Upside Down
It is Part of the Star of David Shape

Illness: LNS   2 Fems in Plural
L/Sweet Fem Love Light/Oil/Elle/All/Ill/Ail/Hail/Heel/Hell
    is with   N/In/Hen/Ann/Virgin and with   S/Is/Us/His/Ass/Penis Hiss/Serpent   Adding Plural
L/Sweet Fem Light   is with   N/In/Hen/Ann/Virgin   and   S/Is/His/Us/Ass/Hiss/Serpent/Penis   It is a Big No from   The Code   so
ass: buttocks   anus   a stupid person   sexual intercourse
No One Wants to Look at That

Illuminati: Ill/You/Mean/Hat/He
Illuminati: a Masonic sect   a rare name for the Rosicrucian   persons possessing or claiming to possess superior enlightenment
We Need To have A Clear Understanding of Life so We Can Go back to Love Each Other Again and have a Prosperous Fine Life   For Us And All Of Our Family And Friends   The Way We All Want it to Be   We have been Working So Hard to Build it   All the Way with Our Ancestors But We have to Come Out Honest First   With All Facets of Life   And That Includes Understanding The Code   So We Wan Let Go of It   Including
The Work Place   The Family Place   The Friendly Place   The Neighbor Place   The Sex Place   The Fems Place and the Masc Place   And How We Teach the Children to Be Good Adults   So We Can be Proud of Them All Life Long And They Can Feed Us back Life Too   But No Says   The Code   It is Not the Way and it has Not been

Illusion: Ill/You/See/On
Being Ill is What She Sees On Going for Her as Her Illusion Says   The Code

Image: He/Mage (Magus)   I/Mage
Is the picture of the I/Stick and the Magus
The Mage   or   The Magus   or   The Magician   As Him

The Dam Code The Damn Book

The Magician is the First Card of the Tarot   He Rules Over The World of Illusions
He Has The Power Over The 4 Suits
Casting a Spell with One Hand and Pointing to the Ground with the Other   He has the Sign of Infinity ∞ Above His Head (See Pi in The Words Chapter)
The Code   In Full Clear Action Here

Imagination: Him/He/Mage/In/A/Eon
He/Mage/Nation   Him/A/Gene/Nation
Images We Carry in Our Subconscious
Images Are Important
I/Him/Gene   I/Am/Gene   It is All About Him
Him/A/Gene   that

Imitate: He/Meet/8
He/Meet/Hate   He/Meet/Ate
(See The Numbers Chapter For Number 8)
The Code   is Always In Action When it Comes To Hypnotize The Population

Immerge: Him/Merge   Him/Urge
The Way   The Code   Presents Sex
M/Motherhood   R/Whore   J/Sheppard Stick
immerge: to plunge
merge: to unite

Immense: Him/Menses (Immense Cannot Be in Plural and Menses Comes Only as Plural   So The Mental Connection is Not Made)   Him/Hence (It Enhances Him Says   The Code
Him   Men   Sense   Starts With The Sound of Motherhood   the M(Mom) Letter
The Code Says   it Is Ok   it Makes Sense   Motherhood is Immense   so are Menses

Immoral: M/Motherhood   Her/R/Ear/Hear/Hair/Err/Heir/Or/Whore/Here/Are/Our/Ire/Air/Ere/Sex   All

423

Lise Rochon

The Code   Says Her as M/Mother with R/Sex for Heir or as Whore is Immoral   Making Her Again Ashamed for being a Fem
Him/Oral   Him and Oral Sex   For Him Sex with All Holes Says   The Code

Immunity: Him/U/Not/He/T
M/Motherhood   U/You/Ovulating   Not   He/E
Motherhood and U are Not for Him says   The Code
M/U/Night/He   Good Night on That
Him/U/Knit/He
The Result is T/Fem Cross/Great Curse   But   The Code   Says He is immune To That Too

Impact: Him/Pact
M/Motherhood   P/Man Power/Act
A Pact is an Important Word in The Code   They Made Pacts Together To keep Their Secrets
One of the Pacts is to Keep The Fem Pregnant

Impervious: Him/Pervious
impervious: impenetrable
pervious: penetrable
Him/Perverse   M/Motherhood/Per/Verse Says   The Code   Verses Are Important in Religious Codes   Although Impenetrable for Most of Us

Imply: M/Motherhood   Ply
imply: to carry on to pursue   to involve as a necessary circumstance   obsolete
Ply to be a Mother says   The Code   It is Implied et Absolute

Important: Him/P/Her/Tend
She has To Tend to Him   It is Important for Her says   The Code
M/Motherhood/Per/Tent
Him/Poor/Tend

Impossible: Him/Possible   M/Motherhood/Possible
Him/Puss/He/Able

The Dam Code The Damn Book

It is Always Possible says   The Code   To Get to That Pussy for Motherhood

Impress: Empress   Him/Press   M/Motherhood/Press
To try to Impress Someone Can Go Both Ways   The Sound of Impress/Empress   Has Not Much Power over Her Here   says   The Code   Because it is All to do with Motherhood

Improvise: M/Motherhood   Pro   Vice
Here   The Code   Is Hiding its Ugly Ideology into a Great Word Improvise   It is inspiring   But No says   The Code   it has the Word Vice in it   and is being a Pro at it with Motherhood in the Front just For Her   That is Her Only Improvisation

In: Sounds as in one Letter   N/In/Hen/Ann/Virgin i/Stick/Sex Union/High/Eye   N/In/Hen/Ann/Virgin
The   i/Stick   is in with   N/In/Hen/Ann/Virgin
The Code   says N and M are Interchangeable   so   M/Pregnancy   is   In/N For Her The   N/Ann

Ina: a suffix in the formation of nouns of various types especially female proper names musical instruments compositions etc
It is All Music for Her says   The Code   (We do Not Catch Flies with Vinegar)   in Fact No   so far from that is Her Story/History
I/Stick   N/In/Hen/Ann/Virgin   A/All Men
All Men Penisses/Sticks are Surrounding the Virgin
The Sex Union is Made in Childhood for Her
In Adulthood the Large Cap of Letter i is now a Longer Stick   Letter I Which is also The Bar From   The Code   to Her   and   it becomes Her   It is that/Her Connection From Childhood to Adulthood
Series of Bars will Follow All The Fems All Her Life (See 11 PM in The Clock/Time Chapter)

In Small Cap Letter i is Her Young/Little Fem Stick Letter with That Dot on Top of Her Head Which Means Pregnancy   or   Fem Hole/Letter O)   This is Where She is Going says   The Code
Then Later Her Letter i is in the Shape of a Longer Bar When in Large Caps   Then She Becomes   L/Sweet Fem Love Light/Oil/Elle/All/Ill/Ail/

425

Lise Rochon

Hail/Heel/Hell   That Is What She becomes (See Letter L/Hell in the Letter Chapter)
Anna/Ann/Donkey   A Fem Name is Close
Cin (Circumcision Information Network)   Sin
Dina   Fina   Gina   Hina   Ina
Lina   Add D/Pregnant and She Gets Linda (Fem Name)
Mina   Nina (Nana)(Fem)
Pin/A   With P/Man Power a Masc Letter Starting that Fem Suffix   it Cannot be a Fem Word Here So He Gets a Pin/A or
penia: a combining form in the formation of compound words that have the general sense of lack deficiency
He Is Out   She Is Still   In/Letter/Ann/Donkey
Switch A for S/Is/His/Us/Ass/Hiss/Serpent/Penis in Penia and He Gets a Penis
Note Here that by Just Adding that One Letter S/Is/His/Us/Ass/Hiss/Serpent/Penis The Whole Word Identity Change into the Penis Itself
Reina A Queen In Spanish
Sina is a Female given name (as in Sinner)
Tina   Ten/A   Teen/A   Thin/A
Ten is the Time for the Girl (Thin/A) Says   The Code   to get Acquainted with Sex   And Her Bleeding Starts at This Time so Get Ready
vina: musical instrument made with a stick and 3 bags How Convenient for The Code   That would be The Wine/Vine/Whine   for A/All Men   An Impossibility   Says The Code
(See Wine/Menstrual Blood)
Switch A for O/Fem Hole in Vina and Get Vino   Vin/O/Fem Hole
vino: a derelict   a person addicted to wine
Wine   Win/He
The Usual Degradation from   The Code   to The Fems
Vino is also Wine (See Wine and Blood in The Words Chapter)

Incentive: In/Scent/Eve
V/Fem Sex Active   Scent/Sent   V/Fem Sex Active   is the Incentive for Sex says   The Code

Incest: In   Zest

Incise: N/In/Hen/Virgin   Size (Seize)

incise: to cut into   cut marks figures etc upon
When Her period Starts   The Code   Says She is Ready for The Cut   That Is The One With The Razor Blade from the Barber   It is Called a Clitorectomy   Which Is Illegal Now But still Practiced in Some Countries And had been Forced on The Fems for at least a Thousand Years   It Gives Her Infections and Chronic Pain   Diminishing Her in Another Different Angle
Cute   QT   Letter Q is The Fems Bleeding   Next to T/The Fems Cross   Which is The Great Curse (The Fems Loss of Blood)   A Double Clue here   so   He/Cut
Circumcision is the Same Body Mutilation   It Changes The Sexual Rhythms of The Masc Body for His Life Time also

Incontinence: In/N/Cunt/In/N/Hence
Hiding The Word Cunt (a Deep Insult to The Fems Vagina) here Which is a Virgin   Hence   It Works says   The Code
Incontinence is The Cover Word here   Nobody Wants to Think or Look at That

Inconvenience: In/Con/Vein/Hence
A Con is Also a Cunt   Being Next to N/In/Hen/Ann/Virgin and Vein/Vain/VN   (Venus Is Derived from Vein/The Blood Flows in it)   The Code says it is Too Close for All Those Fem Sounds to be Together   So   It is an Inconvenience and a Cover Word here   For The Code

Indeed: In/Did   In/D/ID   N/Did
indeed: in fact   in truth
ID is the Unconscious Search State for Pleasure For Freudians and is also an Identification Card (ID) Making it Powerful   Bringing it to The Law Level
N/In/Hen/Ann/Virgin is in with D/Pregnant
It is Her ID   N/In/Hen/Ann/Virgin Did It and Now She is D/Pregnant Indeed   The Code   says

Index: NDX   Is Made of 3 Fem Sound Letters
N/In/Hen/Ann/Virgin   D/Pregnant   X/Fallen Fem Cross
End/X says   The Code   Pointing the Finger to Her   Giving Her the Index
index: a sequential arrangement of material especially in alphabetical or numerical order

Lise Rochon

It is All Organized Precisely by   The Code

Infinity: NFNT   Made of 4 Fem Sound Letters
In/Fem/He/T
The Fems Curse Says   The Code   is For Ever for The Fems In/Finn/He/T
Back to the Fishes for Her with Finn (Her Unopened Legs/
Her Virginity)

Inform: In/N/Hen/Ann/Virgin   Form
To Shape (She/Ape) Her Form (Corsets   Uncomfortable Tight
Clothing)   Then The Fem is N as In/Form   For Her Information

Informatics: Here with the Binary System   The Code   Reacts to itself
with Only the Possibility of 1/Masc and 0/Fem Number

Inhale: N/All
Exhale: X/All
The Picture is All N/In/Hen/Ann/Virgins are Sucked in Their Air (Heir)
Then She Comes Out as Letter X/Dead/Fallen Cross
The Word In is the Letter i/Marriage Act   with   N/In/Hen/Virgin   Which
Starts In Childhood

Inherent: In/N/Ann/Virgin   He/E   Rant
The Code   does Not Want Her to be In Front of Him
so it is a
rant: violent declamation

Injure: Hinge/Her   Ange/Her
Ange is Angel in French   That would Make Her too Important so it is a Big
No From   The Code   No One Wants to be Injured or on a Hinge
Injure is a Cover Word Here   People Walk Around Carefully

Ink: NK   2 Fem Sound Letters
N/In/Hen/Ann/Virgin   K/Broken Fem Warrior
Le Code   Puts in Ink that Every Virgin is a Broken Fem
Add a W and The Girl Get a Wink   WNK   Made of 3 Fem Sounds
Letters   Girls Meeting So Fast No One Sees it

The Dam Code The Damn Book

It is Gone in a Wink   Another Form of Invisibility From   The Code   to Her

Initiate: In/Ann/N   Hit   She   Ate/Hate   In/He/She/8
Becoming Pregnant is The Initiation for N/Virgin   and   it Comes with a Hit for Her   and   Hatred Towards Her
(See # 8 in the Number Chapter)
Initiation: He   Ann (N)   He   Hate   On
Ann is being Separated from The Real Initiations of Life by Hatred also from   The Code

Inner: NR   In/Her
N/In/Hen/Ann/Virgin   is in Front and Alone With   Her/R/Ear/Hear/Hair/Err/Heir/Or/Whore/Here/Are/Our/Ire/Air/Ere/Sex   That is 2 Fems Together Alone Without a Man Around
A Big No from   The Code   So
inner: situated within   not obvious   hidden   obscure

Innocent: N/O/Scent   In/A/Scent   In/No/Scent   N/Know/Scent
N/In/Hen/Ann/Virgin   The Scent of The Virgin is Innocent   or   She Does Not Know She has a Scent   or   She has No Scent Yet   or   He can be in Her Vagina/O without Her having the Scent   or   Consent (Con/Scent)
That Scent would be the same as The Oil from the Virgins in Bible

Innovator: N/Hen/In/Ann/Virgin   Ov   Hate   Her/R/Ear/Hear/Hair/Err/Heir/Or/Whore/Here/Are/Our/Ire/Air/Ere/Sex
Innovation Should be a Good Word for All   But No Says   The Code
It is a Cover Word For Deeper More Hateful Secrets That Keep The Fems Enslaved to That World of Sounds   It is The Glass Ceiling
Innovation: N/Ov/Hate/Eon
Innovation Enhances the Concept by Telling Us that it Has been Happening for Eons   or   The Code   Wants Us to Believe that Now and in The Future

Inquisition: In/Q/See/On
Q is the Letter for The Fem Losing Menstrual Blood

Lise Rochon

Inquisition is a Very Heavy and Mean Word in a Religious War a long time ago   That is When they Burned The Fems Telling Them they were Witches because They Flew in The Sky on a Stick

Insane: Here is a Word that Starts and Ends with the Letters Sound   N/In/Hen/Ann/Virgin   with A/All Men in The Middle
The Code   Says No to That so It is Insane
In/Sin   is Close

Insecure: N/In/Hen/Virgin   C/See/Young Girl/Virgin   Cure
In/See/Cure   C and N are Together as a Cure
That is a Big No From   The Code   The Fems Cannot Do/have Nothing   so it is
insecure: subject to fear   doubt

Inside: In/N/Ann   is on the Side here Not   Inside

Insight: In/Scythe
scythe: a blade
Clitorectomy is Done with that Barber Blade That is The Symbol for the Scythe from Those Old Traditions

Instead: NSTD   4 Fem Sound Letters
N/In/Hen/Ann/Virgin   Is/S/His/Us/Ass/Penis/Hiss/Serpent   Dead   Ann is Dead
N/virgin   Stay   D/Pregnant   Ann Stay Pregnant
Ann/Stay/Dead   N/Stay/Head
N/Virgin   S/His   Dead   N/Ann   is with   S/Penis   it is Dead for Her
All are a Big No from   The Code   so
Instead Makes a Switch to Something Else   Instead Says   The Code

Institute: N/Stay/Toot
The Virgin is There for a Toot
toot: to make a sound resembling that of a horn whistle or the as
institute: to set   to establish
Institution: In/Stay/Toot/He/On or Eon
Radical but Clear Terms about Goals of Our Institutions
No Fem Was Allowed to Be Part of Them as a Person (Per/Son)

430

3 TTTs/Fem Crosses in the Word Institute   Making it a Solid Grid here
Institution: N/In/Hen/Virgin   Stay   Two   She/Shh   On
Has a Hint of Polygamy

Instructor: N/In/Hen/Virgin   Struck   T/Fem Cross   Her/R/Ear/Hear/
Hair/Err/Heir/Or/Whore/Here/Are/Our/Ire/Air/Ere/Sex
3 Fem Sound Letters being Struck in This Word as Their Instruction

Integral: Anti/Grail
integral: of pertaining or belonging as a part of a hole constituent or component

Intelligence: Intel/He/Gents
Intelligence is Given to Men Only Through Inside Info   as in In/Tel
Intelligent   N/In/Hen/Ann/Virgin   T/Fem Cross   L/Hell/Ill/Elle/All/Ail/
Hail   A/All Men   Gent (Gene with T/Fem Cross)

Intercourse: communication between individuals groups
countries   sexual relations especially intercourse
Haunt/Hunt/Enter   Her/R/Ear/Hear/Hair/Err/Heir/Or/Whore/Here/
Are/Our/Ire/Air/Ere/Sex   Course   It is as Halloween for   The
Code   Haunting/Hunting The Fems to Transform Them Into a Planned
Sex Course

Interest: Enter/Haste   Enter/East
Our Letters Numbers and Many Symbols Come from the East (Arabic Numbers)
haste: urgent need of quick action   a hurry   or rush
Interesting: Enter   His   Thing
In   T/Fem Cross   Rest   In
She Can Rest   S/Is/His/Us/Ass/Penis/Hiss/Serpent
is In
It Is Interesting to Her says   The Code

Internal: Enter/N/All   N/Turn/All   N/T/Urn/All
N/In/Hen/Virgin and T/Fem Cross in the Shape
Of an Urn (Pregnant)
It is All Internal (as in an Integrated Circuit) says   The Code

Lise Rochon

Interrupt: Enter/Hop   Ant/Her/Up   Haunt/Her/Hop
To Interrupt is to Stop   so to   Ant/Aunt/Hunt   Her Up would be a
Possible Upgrade for The Fems but   The Code says No   so   She is
being Haunted and Interrupted   for   The Hop (as in Hoping for Sex) Can
Enter

Interview: Enter/View   Aunt/Ant/Haunt   Her/View
Being an Ant or an Aunt for The Fems is being Very Small
Especially When She is being Hunted/Haunted in an Interview

Intruder: In/Through/Her
N/In/Hen/Ann/Virgin   Through   Her/R/Ear/Hear/Hair/Err/Heir/Or/
Whore/Here/Are/Our/Ire/Air/Ere/Sex
N/In/Hen/Ann/Virgin Becomes With Heir or a Whore by an Intruder

Inverse: N/Verse
No Verse for The Fems N/In/Hen/Virgin   Especially When She is Starting
That Word
So   The Code   Inverses it Making No Sense of It for Her
inverse: reversed in position   upside down

Invited: NVTD   All 4 Fem Sound Letters
N/In/Hen/Ann/Virgin   to   V/Fem Sex Active   to   T/Fem Cross   Then
to D/Pregnant
Invited to That is so Soft from The Code as it can Be
Then She Gets Involved into Motherhood

Involved: N/In/Hen/Virgin   Vulvae   V/Fem Sex Active   D/Pregnant
The Code   Way for Her to get Involved is   from Her N/In/Hen/
Virgin   Vulvae to   V/Fem Sex Active into   D/Pregnancy   And So
Forth   That is Where She Is involved
Involvement   In/Vulvae   Meant
V/All/V   All V/Fem Sex Active   are   All V/Fem Sex Active Twice
The Vulve With   U/Uterus   is Prisoner in the Middle
Insane: In/Sin

Intervene: Enter/Vein
See (Vein/Venus)

Integral: In T/Fem Cross   Grail/Girl
integral: of pertaining to or belonging as a part of the whole constituent or component
See   Girl/Grail   Holy/Hole/He   Girl/Grail
In/Tag/Rail   In/Tag/Roll   In/Tag/Rule   N/In/Hen/Ann/Virgin is All Tagged and on a Roll to Be on That Rail   An It is Integral says   The Code
Bag   Dag   Fag   Hag   Lag(L/Egg)   Nag   Rag   Sag   Tag   Wag
Words in Ag are Poor Weak Because They are Related to Her Menstrual Cycle   Symbolically or Physically

Intimacy: N/In/Hen/Ann/Virgin Time   He/E   See/C/See/Young Girl
The Time of the Month He Sees/Seize/Size   Ann/N/In/Hen/Virgin Into/Me/See   The Code   says No matter Where She is She is Always Under   The Code   Spying on Her

Invade: NVD   Made of 3 Fem Sound Letters
The Fem is in Alert to be Invaded as Usual
Another Weakness Thrown to The Fems from   The Code

IQ: The Small Cap i/Marriage Act is Never Present Here
IQ can Only Be in Large Caps
Letter i and the Identity of the Small Cap is integrated in the Adult I (The Stick) Here
Same for B when it becomes P   and   N becomes M   and   V becomes W   and   T becomes X   and   O becomes Q etc

Iron: I/Eye/High   Run
I/   R/Heir/Whore/Err/Sex   On
Iron Rod: I/Run/Rod
Iron is a Hard Metal (Meet/Mate/All)
A Rod is Also a Penis   He Rules Hard with His Dick says   The Code

Ironic: Her/R/Ear/Hear/Hair/Err/Heir/Or/Whore/Here/Are/Our/Ire/Air/Ere/Sex   N/In/Hen/Ann/Virgin   IC
R/Sex   and   N/In/Hen/Ann/Virgin
Heir/On/IC
The Heir as an Integrated Circuit for Her
I/Run/IC

Lise Rochon

The Code   Runs it as an Integrated Circuit

Is: It is The Letter for S/His/Is/Us/Ass/Penis/Hiss/Serpent
It is   I/High/Eye/Stick   With   S/Penis/Is/His/Us/Ass/Hiss/
Serpent   Making it His
The Masc Letters Carry Power and Positive Reinforcements says   The Code
To Be Is is to Be Masc Only   She Gets None of that
Switch i/Marriage Act for A/All/Men and He Gets As (Ass)
Switch i for U/You/Ovulating and She Get Us (Baby or Marriage)

Isabelle: Is/A/Bell   Is a Belle   Ring (Marry) That Bell (Belle)
In   The Code   People Names Follow that Same Pattern (See The People Names Chapter)

Isis: Is/Is   His/His
Isis: Wife and sister of Osiris
Isis Name Is been Tarnished by Being Compared to a Terrorist Group Called an Entirely Different Name (ISL)
But People Are becoming Aware and Not Calling it Isis
Anymore   President Obama Called That group ISL Which is its Real Acronym

Island: S/Is/His/Us/Ass/Penis/Hiss/Serpent   Land
It is His/Land says   The Code

ism: suffix   a distinctive doctrine   a system   a cause   a practice
Is/Him   His   M/Motherhood
The Doctrine or the System of   The Code   Is Clear on
That   Motherhood is The Only Endocrine System in Ism

It: I/Eye/Stick/High   T/Fem Cross/Great Curse
Hit   He/Hit
Small Cap Letter i is Sex Union   Large Cap Letter I is a Stick Only
It is a Hit on T/Fem Cross

Itch: Hit/She   Hit/Shh   He/Teach
I/Stick   T/Fem Cross   She

The Fems Cross is an Itch   It is a Hit and a Shh
Other Words with Itch: Rich   Witch   Bitch   Ditch   Fish   Hitch
Leech   Mitch   Niche   Pitch   Stitch etc
Note the Difference in the Meaning of those Words when a Fem Letter
Versus a Masc Letter Starts the Word
itch: restless desire

J j
Intro
Letter J is a Mix of Masc and Fem Symbols Letters
J is the Shepherd with The Stick   The Sheppard Rules Over the Sheeps
(She/P   Ships) which are The Fems Considered as Animals in   The Code
Sheep/Her   Ship/Herd
The Ship is a Word of Many Meanings such as Ownership
A Ship Floats and Moves on the Water Where Fishes (The Fems) Live (See
Ship in the Words Chapter)
Ship is a VIP Word in   The Code
A Fem Cannot Have P/Man Power   so   when She is with P She is
a Sheep and a Sheep is said to be Stupid and that is Part of   The
Code   Ownership of The Fems
Letter J is The Man Shepherd Ruling With His Stick
The Curve on the J of His Hook is to Grab The Sheep Around Its Neck
That is How the Sheppards Caught their Sheeps then (See Hook in The
Word Chapter talking about Hooking Fishes (The Fems Again)
Hook/Her (A Hooker) is No Coincidence Here
J s The Ultimate Power of Man and God Over All Fems
The Shepherd Stick is the Authority Connection from
God to Man   and   it Excludes All Fems All the Way OUT
of   Power   Intelligence   and   Independence
A Sheep does Not Decide Where and When to Go
Letter j Starts Under the Writing Line as on the Unconscious Level
(Advantageous for Him)
Letter i for Her (the Other Letter with a Dot) is on the Top of the Writing
Line Only
The Code   has it all Figured it Out on Many Levels
For Our Eyes and Ears to Soak it in All Day

J/Sheppard and G/Hymen Penetration Sounds Are Almost the
Same   One is Close to the Other   The Sheeps are Hooked to Go
Towards That
In French the G Sound is the J Sound and Vice Versa
J   j Words
Jack: J/Hack   JK
jack: fellow   device for lifting objects
J/Sheppard   Stick is Connected to   K/Broken Fem Warrior
It is a Lift or a Fellow in that Moment that comes for Him
Because it is the Sheppard Stick that Will Defeat K says   The Code
Jackass: Jack/Ass   J/Ache/S
jackass: male monkey   stupid
Adding an Ass Often behind a Male Tem Such as Prince/Princess   Mayor/
Mayoress   Actor/Actress   etc   makes it Fem

Jail: JL
J/Stick   is with   L/Sweet Fem Love Light/Oil/Elle/All/Ill/Ail/Hail/Heel/Hell
(See Letter L in The Letter Chapter)
She as The Broken I (Stick) is Now a Prisoner of The Sheppard Stick
Jj/Sheppard Stick   Small Cap j has the Fem Sex Union Dot
Such Soft Sounds
Letter J is Responsible to Keep the Sheeps (Us The Fems the She/P) in Line
(Pregnant and Bleeding)
Jailer: Jail/Her   J/Ill/Her   J/Hell/Her   etc

Jar: J/Sheppard (Sheep   Her   D/Pregnant) and his Stick   to   Her/R/
Ear/Hear/Hair/Are/Heir/Or/Whore/Err/Here/Our/Ire/Air/Ere/Sex
Jars and Jugs Keep Her Inside them so   The Code   with its Sheppard
Stick Can Keep Her as a   Mother   a   Whore
    or to   Err   with or without Nice Hair   Ear/Hear   It/Hit

Jealous: Jail/Us
Jealousy: Jail   U/Uterus   See/Letter C
The Fems are Too Curious   Too Suspicious   Too Analytical   So   Jail it
is for Her   When She is Jealous   Which Evidently is a Normal Thing to Do
for The Fems   Looking at the Immense Discrepancy in Between Sexes

Jewel: Gel/Her   Jail/All   Jew/Ill

Jewelry: Jail/Her/He   Jew/Well/R/He
Jewish: Jew/Wish   You/Wish
Jew/His/Is/She   Jew/Ish
J/Sheppard Stick   U/You/Ovulating   Wish
The Pattern and Goal of   The Code   Here Is
To Get to Her Jewel (With Gel   In Jail Anyway) With The Sheppard Stick
and Get Her Uterus Open   According to The Wish of   The Code   Which
is Supposed to Make it Her Wish it Too For Herself says   The Code   so it
becomes a Self Supporting System by having Her doing The Work of Her
Own Destruction
Jewish Names Always Fascinated Me   Rosenstein
(Rose   And   Stain)   Hellerstein
(Hell   Her   Stain)   Goldstein   Silverstein   So Many of Them have the
Word Stein (Stain as in Blood Stain)

Job: J/Sheppard Stick (It Moves the Sheeps (She/P))
O/Fem Hole   B/Boy Holding All Fems Breasts
J/Stick   O/Loins   B/Boys (Young or Old)
The Job is Done says   The Code
The Boy with the Stick   and   His Sheeps Can Do The Job   Just as The
Sheppard Does with His Stick   Now a Child Can do It   And This is How it
Works   Children Guards the Sheeps While in the Pasture (Pastor)

Join: J/Own   John/On
J/Sheppard Stick   is His Sheeps Keeper
John The Sheep Keeper Join with His Stocks (Sheeps/Her)
A John is a Toilet in The American Language   The Code   does Not
Accept Any Form of Join/Love Etc

Joker: Joke/Her
Another Big No to Her says   The Code   She is Not Allowed to Play Cards
(Poker)   or   She will be Joked on   Until She Loses
Switch J for P/Man Power and He Gets Poker (to Poke/Her)
Poker is a Fun Game for All

Joy: J/Sheppard Stick   Oy (Pain   Affected Shyness)
Boy   Coy   Toy   Not Much Happening here says   The Code   About
Joy   Because There is No Joy in   The Code

Lise Rochon

Jubilee: J/Sheppard   You   Be   Lay
jubilee: the celebration of any of certain of anniversaries

Jump: J/Hump   J/Home/P
J/Sheppard Stick is Humping at Home   or   Jumping Another

Jury: JURE
J/Sheppard Stick   Hurry
Jerry   A Masc Name
No Fem Here for This Important Term/Life Event

Just: Only
joust: a combat on horseback with 2 knights and lances
Switch J/Sheppard Stick for L/Sweet Fem Light and She Gets Lust (A Sin in The Code)
Bust   Cost   Dust   Lost   Must   Rust   Not Much to Gain here for The Fems

Justice   Just/Us
Just   His/S/Is/Us/Ass/Penis/Hiss/Serpent
A Perfect Combination says   The Code   It is Just
No Fem here
Just/S/Ass   Insinuating Homosexuality as Just

K   k
Intro
Letter K is a Masc Made Fem Letter
K Depicts a Step in the Process of Breaking the Fem Psyche in   The Code
The K is the Sound of the Axe
Letter K is an Action   A break   A Change   A New Bonding

K is the Fem Warrior   The One that Fights for Her Rights
She is Doomed to Fail/Fall   (F/All FL are 2 Fem Letters)   She Does Not Know It (The Axe Hits Fast)
She is the Fem as The Broken Stick   Her Fem Power Stick is Broken in Half and is Attached to the Other Unbroken Masc Vertical Stick/Penis
The Eye   The High   Letter I   The Ultimate God Power
Her Broken Fem Personality is Focused/Attached on Him Now

The Dam Code The Damn Book

In Childhood the Boy Stick Continues His Normal Evolution
The Girl Stick of Power is Funneled Early in Life into the Roles of Mothers and/or a Whore or to Err as a Secondary Tool
The Way it is Done is Through Life Opportunities   She Gets None (None is a Fem Word   See Also Nun Non No and Noon) Except marriage Etc
After Fighting   and   Suffering   and   Losing   Her I Her Stick of Power becomes Y/Wounded Fem
She is Then Changed into the V/Fem Sex Active
After When She is More Opened She Becomes the L/Sweet Fem Love Light
L Breaks Again   and   Split in   K/Fem Broken Warrior
She is a Different Kind of Fem Now
She Has Sex in R/Sex
But Not in that Order
R/Sex can only be in One place at the Time
She Has had R/Sex also in Letters
B D E F G H I J O M P S T U V W X Y Z
By then She Will Be   N/Virgin   becoming a   M/Mother Just by Adding a Bar to N (Another Bar)
There Were Little Contraceptives Until Lately
The Roman Catholic Church is Against Contraceptives
The Fems are Often Forced to have Sex in or Out of Marriage
She is Pregnant and Her Life is Given to take Care of
Children   This   or   be an Old Maid (See Maid/Made in The Words Chapter)
The Word Kill starts with K/Broken Fem Warrior that is attached to the word Ill K and the Heel (Heel is Under the Foot or the Foot of a Horse/Whores)   In a Spiral of Concepts
Sounds Words with Letter K are   Quai in French (Quai is a Dock/Duck) Dock and Duck are Acting as Cover Words here
The Dock Where the Ship (a Code Tool) Touches the Water
The Code   does Not Accept that Kind of Communication Between the Sexes on Any Level of Consciousness   So It Cuts it out With a K
Words with Double K Sound Reinforces That Word Concept   KK for Kick K k Words
Kabala: K/Ball/A   K/Broken Fem Warrior Ball/Masc Genitalia   A/All Men

C/B/Law   C/See/Young Girl   B/Boy Holding All Fem Breasts of All Fems   Law
Broken Fem Warrior   and   Fem Breasts are the Law
Oculists Connects the Path of the Tree of Life
With the 22 Trumps of the Tarot Deck Major Arcanes (See Tarot in The Tarot Chapter)
The Kabala Also Uses the Same Astrological Symbols as We Know Them Now in the West
We are Largely Influenced by those
kabala: a medieval and modern system of Jewish theosophy mysticism and thaumaturgy marked by a belief in creation through emanation and a cipher method of interpreting scripture   a traditional esoteric occult   or secret matter
Yes it is All Secret

Keel: Kl   2 Fem Sound Letters
K/Broken Fem Warrior Ill/L/Sweet Fem Love Light/Oil/Elle/All/Ail/Hail/Heel/Hell
keel: a ship or a boat
Kill Follows Her in   The Code

Keen: KN   2 Fem Sounds Letters
K/Broken Fem Warrior   In/N/Virgin
Key/In
The Key is In When the Virgin is Broken Down
keen: extremely sharp

Keep: KP   CP
K/Broken Fem Warrior   or   C/See/Young Girl   or   Q/Fem Loss of Blood   with   P/Man Power   is a Keeper says   The Code
C/Hip
Keeper: Keep/Her
Jail Keeper: J/All   or   Hail or Ail   Keep/Her
hail: to acclaim   to greet
ail: to cause pain

Ketchup: Catch/Up
Even if the Word Comes from a Chinese Dialect

The Dam Code The Damn Book

There Are No Coincidence in the Language Code
In the words It Keeps
Those Concepts Have Been Implanted in Us for a Long Time
Ketchup has the Color and Consistency of Menstrual Blood   Catching Up

Kettle: Get/All   Cat/All   Kit/All
Back to Cattle and other Animals for The Fems says   The Code
Boil the Water (What/Her) in the Kettle (Get All)

Key: K/Broken Fem Warrior   E/He   Y/Wounded Fem The Key is to Wound/Break (B/Rake) All Fems
Letter K Shares the Sound with Hard C and Q
K/Broken Fem   and He Are the Key to the   Y/Wounded Fem
Key Chain: K/Broken Fem Warrior   She   In
Key Ring: K Her/R/Ear/Hear/Hair/Err/Heir/Or/Whore/Here/Are/Our/Ire/Air/Ere/Sex   In/N   G/Hymen Perforation
Key Hole: K   All   Key   All   Holes
Jingle Keys: The Belles Jingles Making Repetitive Sounds While they are being Ringed
jingle: to ring or cause to ring lightly and repeatedly
G/Penis Penetration   N/In/Hen/Ann/Virgin   Girl
Qui is Who in French   Que in Spanish

Kick: KK twice or Hard C twice
2 KKs/Broken Fem Warriors
Kick them Some More says   The Code

Kid: K/ID
Her K/Broken Fem seen as Child Pleasure   and   as Her ID
Kid Yourself   or   Do Not Kid Yourself   It Is says   The Code

Kidnapper: Kidnap/Her
She is Always in Danger says   The Code   It Keeps Her Weak   and Ignorant
Kid/Nap/Her   Innocent Sounds

Kill: Cl or Kl   2 Fem Sound Letters
K/Ill   C/Ill/Hell/Elle   K/All   K/Ail

Hard C/See/Young Girl and K/Fem Broken Warrior Or C or K and Q are Close
Killer: Kill/Her   K/Ill/Her
The Fem Warrior is Weak/Ill   so Kill Her says   The Code
keel: a ship or boat
keel over: to turn upside down   to collapse suddenly
Keel Over   The Kill of Her
Kill: K/Broken Fem Warrior   Ill/L/Hell/All/Oil/Hail/Ail
Ov (Open Sex Fem with Holes/Ovulation/Egg)   Her/R/Ear/Hear/Hair/Err/Heir/Or/Whore/Here/Are/Our/Ire/Air/Ere/Sex

Kin: KN   2 Fem Sound Letters
C/In   or   K/In   or   Q/In
C/See/Young Girl   as   K/Broken Fem Warrior   or as   Bleeding Fem
kin: a group of persons descended from a common ancestor or a family clan tribe or race
It Follows The Fems Everywhere says   The Code

Kind: KND   3 Fem Sound Letters
K/Broken Fem Warrior   N/Ann/Hen/Virgin   D/Pregnant
K/Hind
Kay   and   Ann   are   D/Pregnant
And Kind about says   The Code

Kindred: Kin/D/Red
The Fem Kin is   D/Pregnant   and   in the   Red (Under)
Red is Her Blood Loss/Great Curse
kindred: a group of persons related to each other
kin: family relationship

King: K/N/G
K/Broken Fem Warrior   N/In/Hen/Ann/Virgin   G/Penis Penetration
At This Place of Ultimate Power It Means   That a Man is a King because He Brings a Broken Fem Warrior and a Virgin into Sex
Key/In   The Key is In
The King of Things (See Ring in The Words Chapter)
A Kingdom in   The Code   is the King (Him) and the Dumb (Her)

The Dam Code The Damn Book

Kiss: K/Hiss   K/Is   KS
K/Broken Fem Warrior   Hiss   Is/His   S/Us/Ass/Hiss/Serpent/Penis
A Serpent Hiss
C/Is   C/His
C/See/Young Girl   Is His   When She Kisses His   His/S/is/Us/Ass/Hiss/Serpent/Penis
Switch S for L/Sweet Fem Love Light/Oil/Elle/All/Ill/Ail/Hail/Heel/Hell and She Gets Kill
Switch S for D/Pregnant and She Get a Kid
Switch S for C/K/Q and She Gets a Kick
Switch S for N/In/Hen/Virgin and She Gets a Kin
Switch S for M/Motherhood and She Gets Kim (a Fem Name)

Kit: K/Broken Fem Warrior   i/Marriage Act   T/Fem Cross
A Broken Fem is a Weak Fem   With Being a Dot She Embarks on the Path of T/Fem Cross   That is the Kit for Her Here says   The Code
A Kitten is a Baby Cat   A Soft Approach Here from   The Code   To make Her Absorb That Kit (Code)

Kitchen: K/Itch/N
Chicken   Fem Slang for a Fem   A Chick

Knight: Night   Knit
The Night Represents The Fems   Where the Moon Shine   Which It Says Represents The Fems
Everything is Born from in Darkness Says the Sage
In the Day Time The Sun/Son Shines For The Man   Life Happens During The Day
In The Night Not Much Happens   That is Why   The Code   Put Her There

Knife: NF   2 Fem Letters
Girls going Under the Knife at Very Young Age
It is Called Clitorectomy

Knocker: Knock/Her (To Make Her Pregnant)
A Knocker is Slang
Even the Word Breast is Under Attack by   The Code

443

knock: to strike

Know: NO   2 Fem Sound Letters
To Know for Him   and   a Big No for Her says   The Code
The Fems are Not Allowed to Any Knowledge Since Ever (Eve/R)
Yes is for The Masc   Everything that is Negative is for The
Fems   Everything that is Positive is Masc
Get It or Get/Hit
Nothing (For Her)   and   Know/Things (For Him)

L l
Intro
Letter L is a Masc Made Fem Letter
L is for Light (Lit is a Bed in French)
L Starts the Word Love (The LV Sound is Entirely Fem)
L is in Many Words that Bring Knowledge and Kindness
L is a Soothing Letter   A Soft Letter
L is for Sweet Fem Love and the More Delicate Fem Knowledge
L is a Sweet Letter that Carry itself Lightly
L is Generally Married at that Stage
L can also be Too Weak
Letter L Portrays the Love/Light of the Fallen Fem
L is the First Letter of Lord   Ultimately an All Men Attribute
The Small Cap of Letter l/Fem Love is Longer than the I in Big Cap (ll)
Because Big Cap L (l) is a Masc Made Letter for the Fem
When She Grows up Her Stick is Bended Down in an Right (Masc Word)
Angle so L is Shortened to the Height of the Other Letters
She Shines the Light But She Must be Broken Anyway
Because She Stands Bigger than I   That is Why (YyY)
Join Letter l to Letter V to Letter T   They form the Image is the Spikes of a
Wheel (We/Ill   See The Wheel of Time in The Words Chapters)
Letter L is Used in Other Words   Ail (Weak)   All (of them Fems) Elle
(Means She in French)   Hall (She Provides a Large Entrance)   Hail (is
Hard Water Falling)   Heel (Under the Foot)   Hell (Where The Code Puts
Her)   Hill (Breast or Pregnancy) Ill (Sick)

Hidden (ID/In) are the Ills of Hell of the Great Curse to Her

The Dam Code The Damn Book

The Word Hell (Ll) is   H/Secret Society   E/He   and   2 LLs/2 Sweet
Fem Love Light/Oil/Elle/All/Ill/Ail/Hail/Heel/Hell
Meaning in   The Code   a Man Can be with 2 Fems
Which is Common in Our Societies for a Man to Do and Accepted
Letter L Often Doubles in Words (Indicating Polygamy)
Letter L is the Knowledge Torch Light Letter of the Kabbala
It is the Right Angle of the Freemasons   L was the Right and Fifth Angle of the Freemasons
There are 4 Right Angles to Form   a Cross   or   a Grid   or   a Pyramid
L is the Broken Corner in The Jewish Tradition and is Called The Fifth Angle Corner   The One that Does Not Fit According to Old Esoteric Tradition
I read about it in Several Books Several Years Ago   I Found Nothing about it on the Internet Now
The Fifth Unfitted Corner Meant Something was Wrong
On Top of the Entrance Door Outside the Jewish Synagogue in my Town there is was a Mold of an Open Book with its Bottom Left Corner Page Cut in a Half Circle
She has been Wounded Internationally on All Levels by The Misery and Rejection from Her Loss of Blood and its Shame
When Put on Top of Each Other Letter F with the Letter L form an E   But it Would Takes 2 Fem Letters to Do That Solid Standing that E Has
Bell   Belle   Dell   Elle   Fell   Hell   Nell   Well
The Belle Nell Fell Well in the Well of Hell in the Dell
(Words with Letter L are   Hell   Ill   Elle (She)   All   Heel Heal)

L l
Labor: Lay   B   Her/R/Ear/Hear/Hair/Err/Heir/Or/Whore/Here/Are/Our/Ire/Air/Ere/Sex
B/Boy Holding All Fems Breasts
Sex as in Lay Being Part of Her Labor   Labor is Also Giving Birth

Lace: L/Sweet Fem Love Light/Oil/Elle/All/Ill/Ail/Hail/Heel/Hell   is an Ace
She is Making Lace   or   Wearing it
In the 19th Century England they were Many Many Fem Sitting and doing Miles of Lace as Lace was being the Big Fashion of the Time   While the Masc were Busy Otherwise Making Money and Being Powerful Ruling The World says   The Code

Lad: Laid   Lay   D/Pregnant
When The Fem is Laid She is with Child
lad: affectionate term for a man
Ladder   Lad/Her
She is Going Up or Down Depending if it is before the Lay or After
She Feels as a Lad for a while to Him But No Says The Code
Ladder: Laid/Her

Lady: Laid/He   Lead/He
She is Nowhere to be Found Inside Her Own Name   Lady
Because The Fem as an Entity in   The Code   does Not Exist   Except in Terms of   Sex   Children   Obedience   and   Prostitution   And Better Shh (She/She) about it
Another Way of Leading Her is by Ignoring Her Totally
Not Only by Making Her the Laid Object   Also by Putting a Masc in Her place
That is a Common Theme in   That Code   Symbology
M/Motherhood and Him is an Example
Lad/He   A Man Friend
Ladies: Laid   S/Is/His/Us/Ass/Penis/Hiss/Serpent
Laid/His   His Lay

Lady Bug: A Lady (Laid/He) that is a Bug
bug: a microorganism
Small is She as usual as a Bug   So Pretty All Children Knows it   She is Black with Red Dots (As the Devil from The Code)   The 2 Colors of Blood Since a Millennium   The Colors of the Great Curse   And The Pattern Continues
Lady Bug is The Cover Word here

Lady Luck: Laid   He/E   Luck/Lock
How Convenient says   The Code   He is Lucky with the Laid   and   can Lock it too (as in jail it)

Laid: L/Aid
L/Sweet Fem Love Light/Oil/Elle/All/Ill/Ail/Hail/Heel/Hell
   Helps   When the Lad is Laid   and   To Lay an Egg as in D/Pregnancy
She Is Led There says   The Code

The Dam Code The Damn Book

Lair: LR   Her/R/Ear/Hear/Hair/Err/Heir/Or/Whore/Here/Are/Our/Ire/Air/Ere/Sex
L/Air   L/Heir   L/Hair
lair: a den   a secluded place
L/Sweet Fem Love Light/Oil/Elle/All/Ill/Ail/Hail/Heel/Hell   is with
Heir   or   having Sex   in a Den   a Secure/Secluded Place

Lake: L/Ache
L/Sweet Fem Love Light/Oil/Elle/All/Ill/Ail/Hail/Heel/Hell
   Ache (See Letter L/Ill)
Anything to do with Water is Fem
Add C/See/Young Girl and She Gets a Lack (Not Much for Her here)
Add N/In/Hen/Ann/Virgin and She Gets a Link

Lamb: L/Fem Light   A/All Men   M/Motherhood   B/Boy Holding All Fem Breasts
Lamb is the Virginal White Wedding Dress of the N/In/Hen/Ann/Virgin
The Lamb of God
About Agnes Dei   Go look at a picture of the Symbol for Christ and you will See a Lamb (Jesus was anything but a Sheep) Bleeding from His Torso Blood in a Chalice with a Banner in the Back Picturing a Red Cross with Another Cross at the End of The Stick Holding it
Christ was Not the Icon He is now because He was Married   or   because He forgave People (Fem) for their Sins   or   because He did Miracles
The Early Christians were given the Secret of His Teaching
and it was He that Dared to Talk about the Anomaly of The Fems
Blood Loss and it was Sacrilegious at the Time to Talk about that (Mary Madeleine being Cursed as a Sinner)

Lame: LM   2 Fem Sound Letters
L/Aim
If L/Sweet Fem Love Light/Oil/Elle/All/Ill/Ail/Hail/Heel/Hell   would
Aim   or   be a Mother by Herself as L   That is a Big No from The Code   so
lame: impaired or disabled   weak   inadequate
L/Âme
Âme is Soul in French
If L/Fem Sweet Love Light would Seeks Her Soul   That would be Lame

Switch A/All Men for i/Marriage Act and She Gets Lime (Sour Fruit)

Lamp:
Switch P/Man Power for B/Boy Holding All Fem Breasts and He Gets a Lamb
The Lamb has becomes a Light Now After being a Small Mutton (Mutt/On) going to Abattoir   (A/Bat/Whore)   (See Lamb)

Land: LND 3 Fem Sound Letters
L/Sweet Fem Love Light/Oil/Elle/All/Ill/Ail/Hail/Heel/Hell   End
L   N/In/Hen/Ann/Virgin   D/Pregnant
It is All Hers But All What She Gets is To be Pregnant

Lane: LN   2 Fem Sound Letters
When L/Sweet Fem Love Light/Oil/Elle/All/Ill/Ail/Hail/Heel/Hell   is with   N/In/Hen/Ann/Virgin   They are Kept in a Lane says   The Code   L/Ill/Hell/Ail   In

Large: L/R/G
L/Sweet Fem Love Light/Oil/Elle/All/Ill/Ail/Hail/Heel/Hell   Her/R/Ear/Hear/Hair/Err/Heir/Or/Whore/Here/Are/Our/Ire/Air/Ere/Sex   G/Hymen Penetration
Her Sexual Entrance is Large for The Masc
Larger and Largest is Even Better/Bigger   He Gets all Sizes

Lately: Late/Lay
All is Sex Says   The Code
Later: L/Sweet Fem Love Light/Oil/Elle/All/Ill/Ail/Hail/Heel/Hell   Hate   Her
In the Past or/and in the Future
The Code   Always Hates Her Light   or   Hates for Her to Know about Her Light   (See # 8 in Numbers)
Sweet Fem Eats or Hates Sex
L/Ate/R   Late/Her   Late in Her Period   Let/Her   She is Late
There is No such Thing as Letting Her Doing Anything In the Language Code Except Sex Pregnancy or being a Whore   If Not She Err (See letter R in The Words Chapter) so

The Dam Code The Damn Book

After She is Late She is then Pregnant and the Milk is there   Lait/Her   Lait in French is Milk
Switch L for H/Secret Code Letter and Get a Hater
A Letter is the Cover Word Here

Laugh: LF   2 Fem Sound Letters
L/Sweet Fem Love Light/Oil/Elle/All/Ill/Ail/Hail/Heel/Hell   F/Fem/Fuck Love
Laughter: Left/Her
And To Makes Her Gauche
gauche: inept   clumsy   crude   tactless
La Main Gauche is the Left Hand in French
Gauche is Clumsy in French also
The Fun is Never Long with that Language Code
Laughing: LFN   3 Fem Sound Letters
L/Sweet Fem Light   Ov/Have   N/In/Hen/Ann/Virgin Love/In   L   Ov   In
La/Fin (See Fish in The Words Chapter)
Laughter: Left/Her   The Fem is Not Allowed to Laugh/Be Happy One Way or Another in   The Code

Law: L/Sweet Fem Love Light/Oil/Elle/All/Ill/Ail/Hail/Heel/Hell   A/All Men   W/All Fems Sex Active
All Men to have   All Fems Sex Active   It is The Law
Laws for Justice/Just/Us(S/Is/His/Us/Ass/Penis/Hiss/Serpent)
Switch the Masc Letter A/All Men for the Fem Letter O/Fem Hole and She Gets Low
Some Difference Between Law (Masc) and Low (Fem) Lawyer: Law/Her   Lay/Her   Lie/Her

Lay: LA   L/Sweet Fem Love Light/Oil/Elle/All/Ill/Ail/Hail/Heel/Hell   A/All Men
L/Hey   L/Hay (See Hey and Lay in The Words Chapter)
L/Fem Love   and the   Hay/Hey
Many Casual Expressions with Lay
lay: position of rest   lay eggs   instance of sexual intercourse   nonstandard lie   the way a thing is laid
Switch Y for D/Pregnant and She Get a Lad

Lad: affectionate term for a man
A Friendly Lad for the Lay
Switch L for B/Boy Holding All Fems Breasts and He Gets a Bay (the Boy is Kept at Bay being Too Young for the Lay)   Add 2 B/Boys   And She Gets a Baby
See Other Bay Definitions in a Dictionary of the Safe Word Bay for the Young Him (M/Motherhood)
Switch L for C/See/Young Girl and She Gets a Cay
cay :   a small low island   key
Isolated Small and a Key   She is says   The Code   Kay is a Fem Name
Switch L for D/Pregnant and She Gets a Day (Letter D Sound in French) (See Day in The Clock Chapter)
Switch L for F/The Asexual Fem (F is also the Given Letter for Fuck) and She Gets Fey/Fay/Fee More Bad Words for Her
Switch L for G/Penis Penetration and He Gets Gay
Switch L for H/Secret Code Letter Grid and Get Hay/Hey
That Call Sound Hey is for Her to get Food as Whores/Horses Etc
Switch L for J/Sheppard Stick and He Gets the Singing Noisy Beautiful Blue Jay (A Man Name)
Switch L for K/Broken Fem Warrior and She Gets Kay
Add D/Pregnant and She Gets Decay because She is too Close to That Key
The F/Fem/Fuck Letter Up Side Down or Horizontal is   The Code   Key Shape
There is No Poetry or Rhyme (R/Her/Hair/Are/Here/Hear/Ear/Whore/Or/Err/Sex with M/Motherhood) here
It is Hell/Ill/Heel/Elle/Letter L on Earth (Hurt/Her   Her/T/Fem Cross)
Switch L for M/Motherhood and She Gets May (May or May Not)   A Fem Name and an If (Letter F)
Switch L for N/In/Hen/Virgin and She Gets a Nay
She is Too Young for the Lay but still a Neigh/Nay   Still a No for the Young Horse (Whore (s))
Switch L for P/Man Power and He Gets a Pay
Pay the Whore for the Lay says   The Code
Switch L for Q/Menstrual Blood and She Gets a Quay
quay: public path beside a waterway
Switch L for R/Her/Hair/Are/Here/Hear/Ear/Whore/Or/Err/Sex and She Gets Ray(A Man Name and a Sun/Son   Ray)
Switch L for S/Is/His/Us/Ass/Hiss/Serpent/Penis and He Gets to Say

The Dam Code The Damn Book

Switch L for W/All Fems Sex Active and She Gets a Way (A Way to The Lay   Being Sex Active)
Lay   the Neigh   in May   on a Quay   without a Nay   Say Ray   He Pay   it is the   Way

Layer: Lay/Her
Lay Her   Layer After Layer says   The Code

Lazy: Lay/Z   Lease/He   says   The Code   Give Him More Even if He is Lazy   Till The End in Z   and Sleep on It

Lead: Led   Laid   Lied   L/Head
For Once a Fem Letter L/Sweet Fem Light Would Have a Head   But No says   The Code
The Alchemical Lead Represents Saturn
She is Led by Saturn the God Of Time (Time of the
Month)   Hardship   and   Restrictions
Saturn is associated with Death with his Scythe (Clitorectomy)
And Satan (See Pics of Satan) is Close to his Looks
Saturn (Sat/Urn   See Urn in The Words Chapter) is The Hebrew Letter Tau Which is The Goddess Venus in Her Taurus Astrological Sign of Beauty and Plenty
The Code   Connections are Obvious When Knowing Where and How to Look   here The Goddess Venus is Transformed into a Cow   A Domesticated Animal Harnessed for hard Labor and to Produce Milk

Leader: Lead   Her/R/Ear/Hear/Hair/Err/Heir/Or/Whore/Here/Are/Our/Ire/Air/Ere/Sex
How to Bring Her to Sex is by   Letting Her be a Lad or on The Lead Until on the Leather (L/Heather) L is then Laid

Leather   Lad/Her   Let/Her   Letter   Lait/Her
Lait is Milk in French
Leadership Pops as a Sound Word Here   Lead/Her/Ship   Back to   The Sheppard/Ship/Sheep Herd   for Her

Learning: L/Urn/In   Learn/N

L/Sweet Fem Love Light/Oil/Elle/All/Ill/Ail/Hail/Heel/Hell Learn to be an Urn (See Urn in The Words Chapter) to integrate The Concept inside Herself   In/Ann/âne/N/In/Hen/Virgin says   The Code

Leash: L/Sweet Fem Love Knowledge   She/Shh
Always on a Leash and Silenced She Is
Dogs on Leash Signs at Public Parks are Cover Words Here
L/Each   and   Each of The Fems to Be on that Leash
Each   Is/She
Unleash: On/Leash   Here She Goes Again Either Way says   The Code   That Bitch (a Fem Dog) is on the Leash Even When Unleashed

Leather: Let/Her
When She is in Leather   He Let/Her
leather: animal skin
When She is Related to an Animal He Let/Her
Letter is the Cover Word

Leave: LV   2 Fem Sounds Letters
L/Sweet Fem Love   Eve/V/Sex Fem Active
L/He/V
Love from Eve to Him Means it is Time to Leave says   The Code   There is No Love Allowed in   The Code
Leaving: Leave   Ann/N/In/Hen/Virgin

Leech: L/Itch   Lick/She
Leech is Slang for Penis
Bloodletting was Used in Medicine with Leeches

Left: LFT   3 Fem Sound Letters
The Left Side is the One that is Left Behind   Also Called The Wrong Side   It is Called The Fems Side   In the East They Wipe their Butt Specifically with their Left Hand and It is Called the Unclean Hand
The Right Side Is The Right Way To Go and is Called the Masc Side   They Eat with Their Right Hand   The Clean Hand as They Call it

Leg: Lay/Egg   L/Egg   Lay/G
That Egg is Between Her Legs

League
league: an association
(Ass/O/See/Eon)

Legacy: Leg/Ass/He   L/Egg/Has/He
A Clear Concept Here from   The Code   The Egg Is His   It is His Legacy

Legal: Leg/All
L/Sweet Fem Love Light/Oil/Elle/All/Ill/Ail/Hail/Heel/Hell
Egg/Ov   All
What is Legal is the Love of Fem Related to Ovulation and Him says   The Code
Lay/Egg/All
Legally: L/Egg/All/He   Leg/Alley (Promiscuity)
Leg/All/He (He Looks at All Fems Legs)
All Legal   All/Leg/All   All/Lay/Egg/All
Legalize: Leg/All/Is   League/All/Eyes   Legal/Eyes
L/Egg/L/Eyes   All/Eggs/All/Eyes
The Egg/Ovulation is in Between L/Love Light and Eyes (The Code)
Leg/All/Sizes   All Sizes Fits

Legend: Leg/End
The Legend Ends With the Legs When She Lay/Egg
Leg/In/D
With the Legend She is D/Pregnant
Legendary: Leg/End   Her/R/Ear/Hear/Hair/Err/Heir/Or/Whore/Here/Are/Our/Ire/Air/Ere/Sex   He
That is Her Past Legends says   The Code

Lemon: Lame/On   Lay/Mom   L/M/On
L/Sweet Fem Light   M/Mom   On
When L/Sweet Fem Light is with M/Motherhood
It does Not Matter (Mate/Her)
It Should be a Marvelous Successful Event to be Pregnant in   The Code   But No   The Fem is a Lemon
The Code   is Lame/On
lemon: a yellowish acid fruit   a useless or defective person

See others as Banana (Positive Erect Symbol for Penis)   Mango (Man/Go)   Cherry (She/Heir/He   or   Her Genitals) Apple (Ape/All)   Lime (L/Sweet Love   M/Motherhood again   In Green this Time)

Lesbian: Less   Be   Ann/N/In/Hen/Ann/Donkey
She is Worth Less Because She is a Lesbian

Less: LS
L/Sweet Fem Love Light/Oil/Elle/All/Ill/Ail/Hail/Heel/Hell
S/Is/His/Us/Ass/Hiss/Serpent/Penis
When L/Elle is with S/Penis it is of a Less Value says   The Code   Too
Always Lessen the Value of The Fems
Lesser: Less/Her
lesser: small in importance
Lesson: Listen   Less/On

Lethal: L   All/Ill/Elle/Hail/She
To Lit All would Bring Light to All Fems   But No that would Be Lethal   Says The Code
Lit is a Bed in French

Letter: Let   Her/R/Ear/Hear/Hair/Err/Heir/Or/Whore/Here/Are/Our/Ire/Air/Ere/Sex
To Let Her Do Anything on Her own is Against   The Code so   It is Litter
litter: scattered rubbish
To Give Birth to a Litter (Animalize Her)   Let/Her be Pregnant
Lit is Bed In French
Letter is a Cover Word here

Level: Leave   All/L/Sweet Fem Love Light/Oil/Elle/Ill/Ail/Hail/Heel/Hell
level: having no part higher than another
The Code   Levels it All   All Fems are Rejected as Usual

Liar: Lie/Her   Lay/Her   L/Hey/Her   L/Hay/Her
Her/R/Ear/Hear/Hair/Err/Heir/Or/Whore/Here/Are/Our/Ire/Air/Ere/Sex
L/High/Her
L/Sweet Fem Light   should be High(I) here   But No says   The Code   All this is a Lie

The Dam Code The Damn Book

Liar is a Cover Word Here to make it All a Fem Word

Libido: Lib/He/Dough
Liberty to Him with the Dough/Daughter/Dot/Her/The Breeding Element   The Dot on Top of the Vowel is i The Sex Union

License: Lie/Sense
The Permission to Lie

Lick: L   IC/Integrated Circuit
L/Sweet Fem Love Light/Oil/Elle/All/Ill/Ail/Hail/Heel/Hell   is the Master in the Art of Licking Here says   The Code

Lie: L/I   L/High   L/Hi
Lie to Lay

Lien: L/Sweet Fem Love Light/Oil/Elle/All/Ill/Ail/Hail/Heel/Hell   In/N/Hen/Ann/Virgin
When Her Sweetness/Weakness is with   N/In/Hen/Ann/Virgin   She is in Debt Already says   The Code
lien: a right to retain someone property pending discharge of a debt

Lier or Liar: LR   L/Fem Sweet Love   R/Her/Hair/Are/Here/Hear/Ear/Whore/Or/Err/Sex
Lie/R   Lie/Her
Lie for Sex or Lay for Sex
Where there is a Lie/Lay there is a Cover

Life: L/Sweet Fem Love Light/Oil/Elle/All/Ill/Ail/Hail/Heel/Hell   i/Marriage Act   F/Fem/Fuck   E/He
Knife   Strife   Wife
Here The E/He is Silent as He is Not Part of Life
In   The Code   Essentially the Masc is Attenuated   It is The Fem That is in the Front because She is The Main Subject of   The Code
Life Says   L/Sweet Fem   has   i/Marriage Act   as in   F/Fucking

Light: Lite   L/Height

Lise Rochon

L/Sweet Fem Love Light/Oil/Elle/All/Ill/Ail/Hail/Heel/Hell   Intelligence Has Weight here   Because She Carries Light
The Fems are called in Certain Clubs   The Lights

As: See Ass in The Words Chapter   and   Letter S in The Letter Chapter

Lilith: Lilith was Adam First Wife
Lay/Lit   Lit is Bed in French   Which Means to Lay in a Bed
The First Part of the Word (To Lay) Continues the Meaning of the Word in The Second Part (In Bed)
Lilith is an Interesting Word Being The Oldest Fem Name Known in The Bible
L/Sweet Fem Love Light/Oil/Elle/All/Ill/Ail/Hail/Heel/Hell   L/Sweet Fem Knowledge   Hit/It
Also a Sign of Bigamy   Besides being Hit Twice as a It It has No Significance with being a Human
May be Before the Age of Adam and Eve Humans were More Free Sexually Naturally in a More Animalistic Way Closer to Seasons Natural Cycles More Ancient Traditions etc
And There was No Menstrual Cycle With its Immense Loss of Human Blood Through Her   The T/ Great Fem Curse
The Sound Lil Sounds Nice Almost as Lilacs   Another Illusion from   The Code

Limit: Lay/Meet   Lay/He/Meet   Lay/He/Mate   L/Mate   Lame/It   L/Âme/Hit
L/Sweet Fem Love Light/Oil/Elle/All/Ill/Ail/Hail/Heel/Hell   for Her Loving Light Intelligence   Starts That Word Limit
Limit is a Cover Word Here Because Its Sound Meaning Defies Its Common Definition

Line: LN   2 Fem Sound letters
L/Sweet Fem Love Light/Oil/Elle/All/Ill/Ail/Hail/Heel/Hell   N/In/Hen/Virgin/In/Virgin   Follow the Line Virgin
The Code   says the Fem are All   Ann/Âne/Letter N/Hen/Donkey   Sorry for All the Ann Girls

The Dam Code The Damn Book

Lion: Lay/On   Lie/On   Lie/N
The King of the Beasts
The Lion is One of the 4 Corners of God   and   Part of Many Royal Emblems
The Taurus (Venus) is Another   The Tau is The Fems Cross

Lipstick: Lip/Stick
The Stick is Everywhere on Her Even on Her Face To Her Pale Lips to Give Them More Color (Which is Caused by the Incessant Loss of Her Blood   An Enormous Lifelong Blood Lost that is Lasting for 2 000 Years Now)
A Fem is Never Alone in   The Code   And The Stick is Always Close By

Liquor: Lick/Her   Liquor Will Want a Man to do that
Liquor in Good Society was Not Allowed for The Fems to Drink in General Until Lately
Smoking Pot was Not Allowed For The Fems in India as Men Smoked it Freely All Along

List: Lease/T   Less/T   L/Is/T

Listen: LSN   3 Fem Sound Letters
To Listen to Sounds is a Big No to Her   Because the Language Code is Hiding There so
Lessen   Less/In
The Lesson is What is More important for Her says   The Code
Lease/T/N
Lesson is the Cover Word Here

Litter: A Letter as in the Letters of the Alphabet
Let/Her   Lighter   Lit/Her
Lit in French is a Bed   Lit/Her/Bed
Litter has Multiple Meanings from   Feces   to   Rubbish   to Giving Birth
litter: to scatter objects   to supply a bed for an animal
a Litter in the Male (A Letter in The Mail)   That is Her to The Code
Letter is Not a Fem Positive Word as in to Let/Her (Do Her Thing)   No Let Her have a Litter is What it is
Rubbish and Shit (She/It) are Not Too Far to Her

457

Letter is the Cover Word here

Little: Let/Her
L/Sweet Fem Love Light/Oil/Elle/All/Ill/Ail/Hail/Heel/Hell   Hit   All
Lit/All   Let/All (See Letter L in The Letter Chapter)
Litter is Garbage   Let/Her
Lait/Her (Milk/Her)   Lait is Milk in French   Lit/L
Late/Her   Making Her Late in Her Period
2 LLs/Sweet Fem Love and 2 TTs/Fem Crosses
Making it Plural or All of Them to be Little   Light/All   Little All   A Letter in The Litter to Lit to Stay Little
Letter is The Cover Word) Here

Live: LV   2 Fem Sound Letters
L/Sweet Fem Love Light/Oil/Elle/All/Ill/Ail/Hail/Heel/Hell
   V/Eve/Fem Sex Active
Leave   Live is Fem But She has to Leave it says   The Code
As a Leaf of a Tree   The Tree of Life   Back to the Old Traditional Religious Book

Load: Low/D
D/Pregnant   is Feeling Low   She has a Load
L/Owe/D
L/Sweet Fem Love Light/Oil/Elle/All/Ill/Ail/Hail/Heel/Hell
   is Own by   D/Pregnancy
She is a Load (Also Slang for Poop)
lewd: obscene

Loan: LN   2 Fem Sound Letters
L/Sweet Fem Love Light/Oil/All Elle/Ill/Ail/Hail/Heel/Hell
   N/In/Hen/Own/Ann/Haine/Virgin
N/Virgin and L/Sweet Fem Light are on Loan She Never Owns Her Own says   The Code

Lock: LCK   3 Fem Sound Letters
Luck is Also 3 Fem Sounds Letters
Buck   Cock   Dock   Duck   Fuck   Mock   Rock   Suck   Wok

The Dam Code The Damn Book

L/ L/Sweet Fem Love Light/Oil/Elle/All/Ill/Ail/Hail/Heel/Hell   is Yuck so   She is in Luck because of That
Look at your Luck   It is Locked
Locker: Lock   Her/R/Ear/Hear/Hair/Err/Heir/Or/Whore/Here/Are/Our/Ire/Air/Ere/Sex

Lonely: Low   In/N/Hen/Ann/Haine/Donkey   Lay
Lone/Lay
It is Lonely for the Fems   When there is Not Enough Lay   or   When She Is Alone with No Lay says   The Code

Long: L/Sweet Fem Love Light/Oil/Elle/All/Ill/Ail/Hail/Heel/Hell   On
L/Fem Sweet Love is on it is for Long
G/Penis Vaginal Penetration   is Almost Silent here
G Ends the Word as Reinforcing the Result for the Sex to be Done Concept to Her

Look: L/Sweet Fem Love Light/Oil/Elle/All/Ill/Ail/Hail/Heel/Hell
  2 OOs/Holes/Loins   K/Broken Fem Warrior
L/Hook (Bringing the Hooker In)
Double OOs Represent the Pair of Eyes (Look for Words with Double OOs Affiliated with Other Letters to profile Code Words to Look at for More Hypnotic Words)
Double Letters Mean Plural or All of Them
(See Luck/Lock)

Loop: L/Sweet Fem Love Light/Oil/Elle/All/Ill/Ail/Hail/Heel/Hell
  2 OOs/Fem Holes/Loins   Ending with   P/Man Power
Here the Masc Needs to Exit says   The Code   Because there is too Much Fem Force With Him so
loop: a portion of a cord ribbon etc folded or doubled upon itself so as to leave an opening between the parts

Loose: L/Sweet Fem Love Light/Oil/Elle/All/Ill/Ail/Hail/Heel/Hell
  2 OOs/Fem Holes/Loins   S/Is/His/Us/Ass/Hiss/Serpent/Penis   Letter E/He is Silent Here (Only His Penis Is There Implying Prostitution or Sex Only)
Loose Would be When 2 Loving Fem Vaginas are having Sex with His Penis

loose: free or relieved from fastening or attachment   not bound together
He is Free of Attachment says   The Code
L/Hose is   L/Her Sweet Love   and   His Hose
Ose in French is to Dare   Hose in French is Also a Hose   a Garden Hose or a Man Hose

lose: to be without
Loser: Loo/Z/Her   Lou (Toilet as in Her)   Luz is Light in Spanish
L/Sweet Fem Love Light/Oil/Elle/All/Ill/Ail/Hail/Heel/Hell
Meet with   O/Fem Hole   and   Z/Snooze Letter/As Above As Below (ZZZ)   Forgot About it All says   The Code   And Sleep on It

Loot: All 4 Fem Letters
It is a Lot More with Another O/Fem Hole
L/Sweet Fem Love Light/Oil/Elle/All/Ill/Ail/Hail/Heel/Hell
   2 OOs/Fem Holes   T/Fem Cross
The Fems is Usually More Vulnerable in Time of War   And here in Loot/Lot   She is Alone so   She becomes the
loot: spoils or plunder taken by pillaging as in war   says   The Code

Lord: Lord is Made of 3 Fem Sounds Letters   and   Lord is Made of 4 Fem Letters
L/Sweet Fem Love Light/Oil/Elle/All/Ill/Ail/Hail/Heel/Hell
Her/R/Ear/Hear/Hair/Err/Heir/Or/Whore/Here/Are/Our/Ere/Air/Ire/Sex   D/Pregnant   as in Sweet Fem having Sex and becoming Pregnant
A Lord is Another Way to Call a Man Honorary
Switch O for U/Uterus and She Gets Lure
lure: anything that attracts entices or allures   the power of attracting or enticing
Lured: Lure   D/Pregnant
The Fem has No place in those Punishing Religions Except as a Sinner (Sin/Her) or a Looser with   S/Is/His/Us/Ass/Penis/Hiss/Serpent   or   Plural
It is the   Damning Code   for Her

Lordship: Lure   She/Shh   P/Man Power

The Dam Code The Damn Book

What is a Ship doing with a God   (See Ship and Ocean in The Words Chapter)

Lose: L/Sweet Fem Love Light/Oil/Elle/All/Ill/Ail/Hail/Heel/Hell   Ooze
ooze: to exude slowly
As a Queen Bee Making Babies or Honey All Day   But Still Losing it All
Loser: Lose/Her
Add Another O/Fem Hole and She Gets Loose   Back to being a Loser for being Loose says   The Code
Loser   Lose/Her   And She is Gone   Be Lost   The Fem is Loose Until After Sex   then He Tells Her She should be Gone (G/On   Be/Gun)

Lost: Lust
When She is Lost   Lust Rises Right Up

Lot: All 3 Fem Letters
L/Hot   Low/T
L/Sweet Fem Love Light/Oil/Elle/All/Ill/Ail/Hail/Heel/Hell
    is Hot (and Low) it is Her Lot
Switch T for W/All Fem Sex Active and She Gets Low (Low is Also Entirely Made of Fem Letters)
Add U/Uterus and She Gets Lout
lout: an awkward person stupid person   clumsy   treat with contempt
Lout is Also Made of 4 Fem Letters
Add B/Boy Holding All Fem Breasts and She Gets a Blot
blot: a spot or stain   especially of ink on paper   a blemish on a person character or reputation
(Blood/Spot   Blemish   Blame/She   It is All For Her)
Add C/See/Young Girl and She Gets a Clot or a Cloth (a Menstrual Pad) because She is on a Clock (See Clock in The Clock Chapter)
Add G/Penis Penetration and He Gets Glot
glot: having a tongue
Add S/Is/His/Us/Ass/Penis/Hiss/Serpent   to Lot and He Gets a Slot (a Prostitute in American Slang)
Add P/Man Power and He Gets a Plot (a Plotte in French is Slang for Fem Loins or a Small Type Whore)
Add Another O and She Gets Loot (All 4 Fem Letters   Again She gets No Power Over Her Life)

loot: spoils or plunder taken by pillaging as in a war

Love: L/Sweet Fem Love Light/Oil/Elle/All/Ill/Ail/Hail/Heel/Hell   Ov (Ovulation)
L/Fem Sweet Love Light   Meets (Mate) with Love with Ovulation   She Aims to be Pregnant in the Word Love   and   that is how   The Code   Defines Love   The Kind Intelligent Intuitive Love Light from the Mother or a Fem in Love Meets/Mates at Ovulation Time
Love and Lay   Lovely to The Masc
Lover: L/   Ov   R Her/R/Ear/Hear/Hair/Err/Heir/Or/Whore/Here/Are/Our/Ire/Air/Ere/Sex
Switch L/Sweet Fem Love for D/Pregnant and She Gets a Dove (Dove is Christ and the Peace Sign)
Switch V for C/See/Young Girl and She Gets a Lock   or   Did She Gets Lucky in Bed
Switch V for D/Pregnant and She Gets a Load
Switch V for F/Fem/Fuck and She Gets a Loaf
Switch V for G/Penis Penetration and He Gets a Log/Lug
Switch V for S/Is/His/Us/Ass/Penis/Hiss/Serpent
and He Gets a Loss
Switch V for T/Fem Cross and She Gets a Lot (By Being Crucified)
Switch V for W/All V/Fem Sex Active and She Gets Low
The Code   Says It All   The More She Does What   The Code   Wants   The More She Looses

Low: 3 Fem Letters
L/O   L/Owe   Hell/Owe

L/Sweet Fem Love Light/Oil/Elle/All/Ill/Ail/Hail/Heel/Hell
e   O/Fem Hole   W/All Fems Sex Active
Add S/Is/His/Us/Ass/Penis/Hiss/Serpent   In Front of Low and She Gets Slow
Lowest: Low/Haste
Aim Low and Hurry says   The Code
Low/Ass/T

Loyal: LLLLOOOLLLL   3 Fem Sound Letters
Low   You   L/Sweet Fem Love Light/Oil/Elle/All/Ill/Ail/Hail/Heel/Hell

The Dam Code The Damn Book

In Order to be Loyal   The Fem Keeps Low (as a Dog)
L/Hell/Elle   O/Fem Hole   All
Be Loyal says   The Code   All Fem Holes Stay in Hell
It is Almost as Singing a Lullaby

Lucifer: Is Represented by the Planet Venus in the Sky
Venus is the Only Fem Planet in the Night and She is there Only at the Beginning and End of Night for a Short Time
Lucifer is Called The Morning Star Falling (of Course) From the Stars
Lucy/Fur   Lucy/For/Her
Lucifer (Lucy with Furs) could have Ruled in the World Before Our Time

Lunatic: Lune/Moon   A/All Men   T/Fem Cross   IC/Integrated Circuit
(Alcoholic   Workaholic)
Another Subtle Way of Diminishing The Natural Fems Power is to Associate the Planet She is the Most Associated to (The Moon)
with   Stupid and Lunatic
Looney: Lune/He   Men Will Have Nothing with That
Lune/Hat/IC is   When She Is Under the Hat/Art as an Integrated Circuit
Lune is Moon in French

Lure: L/Your   Lou/Her   L/Her
   Is thinking She is Having Loving Sex
Her Fem Love Gets Derailed   Especially When She Wants to Share Herself   Because it is a Lure
Lower   Lear
LWR   Low/Her
lure: the power of attracting   a decoy   anything that attract

Lush: L/Sweet Fem Light   She/Shh
lush: luxurious   opulence   succulent
Here Sweet Fem Love is Kept in Silence
LETTER L STARTS AT   P
END OF LETTER L   P 708

M   m
Intro

Letter M is an Important Letter in   The Code   Therefore it is Widely Used
M Is a Masc Made Fem Letter
M Portrays Motherhood   and Him/M
M in the Alphabet is a Comfortable Letter to be with as a Mom   and   Him
M Letter is Here to Nourish the Heir/R/Her/Ear/Hear/Hair/Err/Heir/Or/Whore/Here/Are/Our/Ire/Air/Ere/Sex   Through/From Herself
Add Another Stick at the End of the Letter N (Virgin)   M/Motherhood is Born From N to M
Small Cap n and m Start with a Stick   The Masc Stick Keeps Bended Her(s) Fem Stick
She is The n (See Anne as the Donkey in the Letters Chapter)
Same for Letter m   The Sticks Makes the Bending of Her Second Stick the Child Girl
When in Big Caps She is M   and   She Stands as a Mother
Because m stands with 2 Curves it can be Seen Again as a Bigamous Symbol
M and N are Sticks that Go Up and Down   There is Chaos in Her Life
Inverted Letter M/Motherhood is Letter W/All Fem Sex Active   Same Zigzag Pattern for Ever from V/Fem Sex Active   and   W/All Fem Sex Active
From Virgin in n/N   She is having Sex in v/V   As All the Others in w/W   and   She is a Mother in M/m having a Daughter Letter N/n   and   Continuing That Up Down Pattern Way
MNWVM
Those Letters Put in a Slant Font Type Will Draw the Zigzag Form as a Zigzag Fence in an a Uniform Shape
That Way All Those Fem Letters Loses their Identity
As the Fishes in the Ocean (Water is Fem   O/She/N)
Being in that Up Down Pattern She Never Rest
M is One Mountain to Ascend (Mount/In) After Another   and   Fall Down In   W/All Fem Sex Active   The Fems are Totally Open to Receive Sex Anytime says   The Code
The Constant Pattern for the Fem According to   The Code   is Motherhood   or   Whorehood   or   Err
M is close to a Double Letter A   But No says   The Code   Letter A has the Men Connection in the Middle   And that is The Brotherhood of Men

The Dam Code The Damn Book

And Him the Ordinary Man Understanding More or Less the Implications of   That Code   in His Life
The Man is a Representation of the Only God Power
All the Way from Ancient Letters Aleph (First Letter of the Hebrew   Alphabet (Bet/Beat/Beta is the Second the Beast) and   Alpha the First Greek Letter
A/All Men   and   E/He   are Strong in Many Other Different Letter Shapes also   B/Baby Boy Holding All Fem Breasts   G/Vaginal Penetration   J/the Shepherd   P/Man Power   R/Her/Sex   and the Powerful and Sinuous (Sin/U/Us) S/Is/His/Us/Ass/Penis/Hiss/Serpent   It Can Change Shape at Will and Become the Z/Sleep on it
That is a Different Picture from the Endless Same Up Down Zigzag of the Fem Letters MNVW
Letter M is Ma/Mama/Am/Ham/Mam/Maim/Mem
Mem is a Hebrew Letter   It Means Water Chaos and Blood   Mem is the 213th Letter of their Alphabet (Unlucky)
Mem cannot be Alone with Another Fem   In the Middle of Letter Mem is a Man   E/He
That M/Mother Letter is Tarnished
Mother: Meet/Her   Mat/Her Mate/Her Met/Her   Mute/Her: M/You/T/Her
The Mating   That Is What Matters Here   Meet and Mate
matter: the substance of which any physical object is composed
Letter M as in Mine MN (M/Mother   and   N/Virgin)
Her Mine is MY Mine says   The Code   The Word Man is Made of Only Fem Sound Letters   M as in MN (2 Fem Letters)
M   Him Sounds as Homme (Man) in French
The Fem is Never Left Alone in   The Code
Same for Him/M or Am (Only Him Can Be)
He the Man is There as   Code   and Command the Space
Him (M) is being   M the Mother Power
The Man (MN) Get to have the Mother M and the Virgin N Together in the Package of Being a Man
M is the Upside Down Letter of W/All Sex Active Fem
How Convenient for Endless Motherhood
Letter W is Called The Double U in The American Language When it should be called a Double V as it is

That Concept Switches from a Natural Open   U/Uterus/Naturally Open Hole   Concept to the   V/Fem Sex Active   Concept after the U has been Elongated in a V Shape by The Constant Hits of The Stick/Penis Since the Fems have No More Natural Mating Sexual Cycles
The Shepherd Letter j/J and i the Sex Act Teaches that Only
The U is the Natural Open Loins   It is in a Shape of a Cup
The Chalice   and   The Cup   and   The Grail   and   The Rose of The Rosecrucians
The Code   is About Her (as R/Sex) and Not Him M
The Man is Only Presented Here as the Object of Power
As in a Cinderella and Many Other Little Girls Stories
The Prince is Almost Invisible and Has No Name
The Code   says Because He has Total Power Over Her Therefore He is Her (R/Sex) as an Extension of Him (Her Obedience in Marriage)
Over Time   The Secret Code   got Pompous and began to Outline Itself More Precisely
It Sharpened Itself too   or/and   was Helped again and Again by Many Men that had often No Choice to Refuse
The Secret Code   was Carried by Some Invisible Powerful Ears and Voices to More Men Who Helped in a Subtle Way to Gain Power When it was Needed
They Pushed The Power of the Word into a Specific Symbolic Direction According to   The Code   Specifics of The Time   Making the Code More Obvious Over Time in Certain Places (See the Names Chapter for Example)
Many Letters from All Languages have Changed Over Time   Some Stayed   Some are Gone   It Makes a Difference Influencing the General Comprehension of a Language
In Greek Letters M Mu and N Nu have almost the Same Shape   M s the 12th Letter   # 12 Being the Number of Achievement/Completion   M as in Motherhood
It is Shaped as 2 Horizontal Sticks with a slightly Larger Flat top   as a Roof on Top
N Nu (New as a Virgin
Nu Means Naked in French for a Man   Nue is The Fem
Nous is We in French
Nu is the Thirteenth Greek Letter and Starts the Next 12 Letter Cycle Ending in Omega (M/Mother   G/Go God   and it is for   A/All Men) The Second Cycle Ends #24   A Number that can Double itself Infinitely

The Dam Code The Damn Book

The First Greek 12 Letters Cycle Ends With #12 M or Mu (Cow Sound) Motherhood
12-13 was the Age Known then for Her First Blood Loss
And the Time to Get Married
Words with Letter M
Hymn   Am   Hum   Aim   Him   Ham   Aime (Love in French)
Home   Hem (Cover Word)   Om Ame (Soul in French)
Double M Words are   Mom   Mum   Maim   Mam   Mame
2 Same Letters Words Accentuate   The Word Code   Concepts

M   n
Ma: M/Motherhood   A/All Men
Mama is the Chain/Link (Missing Link) On Going
Ma is Mom/Mum (Shh) M/Motherhood Encircling   You/U/You/Ovulating
Mum and Shh About That

Maam   The Double M
M/Motherhood   A/All Men Twice as in Plural or All of Them
Switch A for U/Uterus and She Gets Mum(or Mom)
Maam is   All M/Mothers are Surrounding A/All Men Twice as Mothers
Mam or Maam is Mother in British Informal   and   a term used in addressing the queen or a royal princess
Maim is Close
Change the Ending M/Maim for N/In/Hen/Ann/Virgin and She Gets a Mane   Girls of all Ages are Attracted to it   The Hair/Her/R/Ear/Hear/Err/Heir/Or/Whore/Here/Are/Our/Air/Ire/Ere/Sex   is a Powerful Symbol Related to Sex and Children
Mam   Mom   Maam   Maim Are Names for Mothers (Même in French Means Same as)
The Code   Does Not Want Her to Know that on a Deeper Level   That is Why She has No Power Over Her Children for 2000 Years or More
Maimed She is When Adding Letter i/Marriage Act in Her Life

Machete: Ma   Shit (She/It)   He
The Fems did Not Touch or Came Close to a Machete

Machine: M/Sheen
When M/Motherhood has a Sheen She is a Machine

Lise Rochon

Another Trap from   The Code
So close to Chain (She N/Hen/Ann/In/Ann/Virgin   She/Haine)

Mad: M/Add
If M/Motherhood would be Adding and Being the Starting Letter in a Word that would be Different than Mad   She Could have had a Chance   But   No says   The Code   She is Mad   and   It Adds to the Odds being Odder
The Fems Cannot Own Anything says   The Code   Not Even Her Mind
M/Had   It is Also in the Past says   The Code   The Past is The Foundation   The Code   Uses it a Lot
Mother was Already Told She was a Mad Maid
Madness: Mad/Maid/Made/Mat/Mate/Meet   Ann/N/In/Hen/Ann/Virgin   Ass/SSS/Is/His/Us/Ass/Hiss/Serpent/Penis
Maddening: Made/Maid   He/E   N/In/Hen/Ann/Virgin
Made to be Mad That Virgin is says   The Code
Mad is a Very Important Word in   The Code   because it Relates All Fems Under That Word MAD

Madame: a married woman
Mad/âme   Ame is Soul in French
A Mad Soul is a Madame says   The Code
M/Motherhood   Dammed   No Outlet for The Fems
A Madame is Also a Prostitute or an Escort
Not to Forget   At First it was an Honorable Title for a Fem   But in   The Code   She is Always Tarnished One Way or Another

Madness: Mad   N   Is/S/His/Penis
N/In/Hen/Ann/Virgin is Mad says   The Code
Women are Often Called Mad for No Reason

Madonna: My/Donna
A Word with M/Motherhood   D/Pregnant   and   2 NNs/Virgins   ending with   A/All/Men
M/Don/A   M/Motherhood   Gives to   A/All Men
A Madonna is Almost a Saint According to Common Knowledge   But Here in   The Code   it Only Means That Mothers   Daughters   and   All Virgins   are to be in that Circle of Motherhood says   The Madonna Word

The Dam Code The Damn Book

See Madonna Mary of the Rocks Painting by Leonard Da Vinci   It Was a Piece of Contested Work   He had to Do it Twice   Being Refused by The Buyer
Add a T/Fem Cross and She Gets a Donut (A circle (Fem) with a Hole (Letter O/Fem Hole) in The Middle)
Maid: M/Aid   Made
It is Motherhood in the Making by Making Her a Maid/Aid
A Fem Servant or a House Cleaner
This Concept Represents Us The Fems from Early Age to Old Age
All Fems Were/Are Considered Mothers or Maids at All Ages
It is a Must in   The Code   History that N/Ann/Virgin Transforms into The M the Mom
Why Force Motherhood On All Fems   I do Not know   Many Fems Love to have Children
She is Called the Sweet Maiden from Her Young age   Then She is a Maid for Life/Wife/Strife
Her Name in the Middle Age was Old Maid if She was an Unmarried Fem   The Old Maid is Presented in a Witch Black Dress with Warts on Her Face Wearing the Black Pointed Hat of the Bad Witch (The Black Hat is Part of the Secret Code Societies Rituals)
Maiden/Young Virgin   or   Maid/In   It is All Made in Advance for Her
Take i/Marriage Act Away from Maid and She Gets Mad (says The Code)
Mermaids (Mere/Maids) are Little Maids with their Legs Not Opened Yet by Sex   They are still Mothers in Potential Though   Mère being a Mother in French
Disney Plays it Very Well in the Movie The Little Mermaid

Magic: M/Egg/IC
M/Motherhood   G/Vaginal/Penis Penetration   IC/Integrated Circuit
A Mage is a Respected Masculine Sorcerer   and   IC Empowers it More
The Fem of Mage would be a Witch says   The Code   and as Much as a Magus Gets All Respect   Her so Called Witch Gets None   (See the French Inquisition in History) Learn the Horrible Details of What has been Done to Women

Maim: M/Motherhood   A/All Men   I/Marriage Act   M/Motherhood

Maim Starts and End with the Same Letter M/Motherhood   with   A/
All Men   with   i/Marriage Act   in the Middle   Ending with M/
Motherhood   Again
It Cannot Be says   The Code   The Fem Cannot Encircle All Men with I/
Marriage Act   That is Too Much Information and Power   so
maim: to wound or a serious Loss
Wound is Made of All 5 Fem Letters
Switch the Ending M/Motherhood for N/In/Hen/Ann/Virgin and She Gets a
Main/Mean/Man there to do the Job

Main: Mane/Horse Hair   Mine   Man
The Main Road is for The Mean Man   Says The Code

Mainland: Man/Land
Not Much here for The Representation of the Fems

Mainly: Manly   Man/Lay
To be Manly is Mainly to be Able to Lay says   The Code

Majestic: Mage/He/Stick
How the World is Ruled   By Creating Illusions
No Place Here for The Fems
Majesty: Mage/He/Stay
He is Here to stay says   The Code   That is a Position of Extreme
Strength From   The Code   Because it is Majestic
There is No Fem to Majestic

Major: Mage   R/Her/Heir/Or/Whore
Image/Her That Way

Make: M/Ache
M/Motherhood   K/Broken Fem Warrior
The Fem as Broken Mother and Warrior is Painful To Her
Make is a Common Word   No One Looks at it That Close
Maker: Make   Her/R/Heir/Are/Whore/Err/Sex says   The Code

Mal: M/Motherhood   All

The Dam Code The Damn Book

My Question is How Can Motherhood Be Mal   Because it is so says   The Code

Male: M/Motherhood   All
Note that Mal Male and Mail have the Same Sound
The Letters   ML   are 2 Fem Sound Letters M/Motherhood and   L/Sweet Fem Love Light/Oil/Elle/All/Ill/Ail/Hail/Heel/Hell
Mail and Male are Cover Words Here for   The Code

Malice: Mal/Is   Mal/His   Mal/He/See   Mal/Ace
M/All/He/See   Mail/His
M/Motherhood   L/Sweet Fem Love Light/Oil/Elle/All/Ill/Ail/Hail/Heel/Hell   He/E   See/C
All Fems Heading to M/Motherhood   The Cover Word is Malice
The Code   Sees to That Madness

Malign: Male/He/In
No Choice here The Male Must come Inside N/Virgin   It is Malign   As in Powerful   Inevitable
Mal   In/Ann/N/In/Hen/Virgin/Donkey

Mammon: riches or wealth regarded as a source of evil and corruption   avarice or greed according to Matthew 6 24
From Aramaic Mammon is Wealth   Riches   Gain
There is a Definite Switch Here from Good to Lust for Money
May be they Believed More in The Fems Back then as Providers of Wealth
The Meaning of that Word was Changed When Translated to New Testament
M/Motherhood   A/All Men   On
3 MMMs/   N/In/Hen/Ann/Virgin   O/Fem Hole
A Hidden Meaning for Polygamy   or   Forced Motherhood
But the Most Important Part Here Is that All those Mothers Together   A Virgin   and   Their O/Fem Hole   re Doing Something that is Very Wrong Instead of Very Good for Them and Their Loved Ones in that Word
Maim/On   Mam/On
Switch M/Motherhood for D/Pregnant and She Gets Demon   Dam/Dame   On   The Dame sound is Part of demon   So Sad

471

Man: MN   2 Fem Sound Letters
M/Mom   A/All Men   N/In/Hen/Ann/Virgin
From Mother to Virgin with All Men in the Middle
A Chain of Men Passing Through Virgins to Make Them All Mothers
Men: M/Motherhood   E/He   N/In/Hen/Ann/Virgin
Same Symbolism Meaning in Plural Men or Singular Man
Replace Letter A by Two OOs/Fem Loins and She Gets a Moon (Period)
Man to Moon
Moon is The Fems Cycle/The Great Curse   Her Moon
Man and Men   but no   Mens/Through/All
Mens would be Plural Twice Here
No Coincidence with   The Code
A/Men Means The End

Manage: Man/Egg   Man/Age
Manager: Manage   Her/R/Ear/Hear/Hair/ Heir/Or/Whore/Here/Err/Are/Our/Ire/Air/Ere/Sex
Man/Egg/Her   That is How   The Code   Manages the Fem   Keeping Her Pregnant

Manhood: Man/Hood
See in Dictionary.com the Difference between Manhood (7 Qualities)
Compared to Womanhood which is Vague and Almost Empty
Where there is the Word Hood   There is a Secret
Hoodie (Hood/He) would be the Cover Word here Because it is a Comfortable Piece of Clothing   but Only for Him   as usual in   The Code

Mannequin: Man   He/A   Kin
The Absence of Fem in Naming is Everywhere

Manner: MNR
M/Motherhood   N/In/Hen/Ann/Virgin   Her/R/Ear/Hear/Hair/Heir/Or/Whore/Err/Here/Are/Our/Ire/Air/Ere/Sex   A Fem Word

Mantle: Meant   L/Sweet Fem Love Light/Oil/Elle/All/Ill/Ail/Hail/Heel/Hell
Man   T/Fem Cross   Letter L Again
Conceal with a Mantle   T/Fem Cross   to   L/Hell/Elle

The Dam Code The Damn Book

And   The Code   Meant   All/Letter l/L/Ill/All/Hail/Hell
Mental (Meant to All/L)
To be told Being Mental is Not a Compliment
Man/Tell   Men Talk to Each Other   Mantle/Cloak In Secret   Under the
Cloak/Clock (See Clock)
Man/T/All
mantle: something that covers envelops or conceal
cloak: to hide or conceals   disguise   pretense
A Clock (See The Clock Chapter)
The Secret Organization of Skull and Bones
And All of them Secret Societies are based on those Secret Systems
Meant/He/All   Meant/Hell/Ill
mantle: the façade of a fireplace
Mantle is the Cover Word here

Many: MNE   Man/He   Men/He
Man/Men Words are Words of Plenty
M/Motherhood   N/In/Hen/Ann/Virgin   E/He
Virgins Into Motherhood for The Masc says   The Code
Mine/He   Minnie (a Diminishing Fem Name)
Minet is a Cat (a Fem Symbol)

Map: M/Motherhood   Ape
The Map to Motherhood for Her is to Follow the Lower Intelligence of an
Animal   Again

March: M/Arch (See The Calendar Chapter)
Mare/She   M/Whore/Shh
The Connection Between The Fem and the Heir/Whore/Err has been
Continual in   The Code
Switch The She/Shh Sound for K/Broken Fem Warrior and She Gets a
Mark   The Cows and Horses Get marked

Mare: M/Motherhood   Her/R/Ear/Hear/Hair/Heir/Or/Whore/Err/Ire/
Here/Are/Our/Air/Ere/Sex
mare: a fully mature female horse   huge dry holes on the moon   an
evil preternatural being causing nightmares
Moon Holes are Dry and Dead   Nothing Grows There

473

The Fems are Still Horse/Whores and a Nightmare (Night/Mare)
The Code   Takes All Precautions to Keep The Fems as Weak as Possible and One of the Ways to Do that is to Encircle Her with Bad Elements
Another is to Convince All Fems they are   Whores   or/and   Animals as we are Proving it in This Book
Mère is Mother in French (What can be wrong with that)
Mer is Ocean in French (What can be wrong with that)
Mare Ad Mare: From Sea to Sea in Latin
Once a Popular Term   It is Now Difficult to Find on the Internet   It is Too Much of a Compliment for Her The Mother says   The Code
Switch A for I/Marriage Act and She Gets a Mire
Switch A for U/Ovulation and She Gets Mur (a wall in French)

Maritime: Mary/Merry   Time
More   T/Fem Cross   N/In/Hen/Ann/Virgin
Merit/Him
Mare   It   Him
More to HiM/Motherhood
M/Whore/T/Him
All Water Related Words Concern The Fems but   The Code   takes it All in so here Maritime has Everything to do With Him being Merry with Mary and Getting All The Merit Etc

Mark: M/Motherhood   Arc
(See Arc)
Marker: Mark   Her as a Her/R/Ear/Hear/Hair/Err/Heir/Or/Whore/Here/Are/Our/Ire/Air/Ere/Sex
Marking: The Mark is In/N/Hen/Ann/Virgin
The Mark of the Beast for Example
Take Away S/Is/His/Us/Ass/Hiss/Serpent/Penis from the Beast and He Gets Beat says   The Code
In the Animal mammal Kingdom the Male is Not in Charge of the Mating Time   It is Often The Female Estrus that Guides it
Only Us/S the Humans have the Men and their Sex/Religious Laws ruling The Fems Sexuality   They Took That Away from Her
Making Her Sick Emotionally Weak   With Permanent Breasts and Bleeding a Sea of Blood   So Few Dare to Look at that Immense Human Dysfunction

The Dam Code The Damn Book

The Code   got its Hands Stained with All this Lost Blood
In All Themes and Variations

Mary   Marry   Merry
Marie: Mare/He
A Mare is a Mature Fem Horse (A Beast)   A Mare is a Hole on The Moon   In French Une Mare is a Dirty Spot of Water
Marie Means Bitter in Italian
All Fems Are Named Mary (Marie Maria) in the Roman Catholic Religion as a First Name When Baptized
Maria: bitter   sea of bitterness
Mariah a Form of Mary
Marilyn: Mary s line or descendants
Marah: bitter the sea
Une Mère is a Mother in French   Un Mari is French for a Husband   And be Merry About that
Marry that Mary (Mer/Mere/He)   Back to The Ocean for Her
Mare/He/A   Back to the Horses/Whores for Her

Marriage: Mary/Age   Merry/Age   Mary/Egg
Men do Not Raise Their Penis According to   The Code
When it Come to Sex and Marriage for The Fem It Comes at Young Age in Old Traditions
Mare/He/Egg
A Mare Hatching an Egg is as a Rabbit Hatching a Rainbow Color Painted Egg on Easter Day   The Code   Creates Fantasies so its Reality Remain Unknown to Us   and it Starts Early in Life
Marry/Egg: A Man Marry so He can have Descendants
Married: Mare/He/Hide   Infidelity is in the Cards Here

Married: Mare/ID
M/Motherhood here is a Mare
She Has the Identity of the ID (I/Stick of Power   D/Pregnant)
Mary   Aid   Mare/He/Add   Mare/He/Aid   Mère/He/Did   More/D/Pregnant
ID is The Search for Pleasures According to Certain Standards said Freud

Marry: Mare/He

475

Back to the Horse/Whores for Her
Mère/He   Mère is Mother in French   Mer is Ocean in French
The Mother and Him/M/Motherhood
Strange Here the Kaleidoscopic Effect of the Word Marry
It is Mother Meeting/Mating Mother
As in Polygamy
Merry/He   He is Happy
When She Marry   She is a Mother Already because of the Name Itself   Marry/Mary
Mary the Mother of Jesus was Never Canonized
Mary: Be Merry and Marry with All those Her/R/Ear/Hear/Hair/Err/Heir/Or/Whore/Here/Are/Our/Ire/Air/Ere/Sex
Mary is # 1 Fem Name in the Catholic Church
It is the First Name of All Baby Girls
When They Get Baptized (With the Water/Old Fem Symbol)
Mary: M/Motherhood   A/All Men   R/Sex   Y/Wounded Fem Name
Rose/Mary   Easy Symbolism Here   Rosemary is Also a Spice Called by 2 Fem Names   Rose a Flower (Flaw/Her) and Mary is to Marry The/Flower (Deflower   That Rose   and   Mary/Marry   Her   to Create More of that Mare)
Another One of those Closed Loops from   The Code
Call Him   MR/He

Mars: God of War
M/Motherhood   A/All Men Her/R/Ear/Hear/Hair/Err/Heir/Or/Whore/Here/Are/Our/Ire/Air/Ere/Sex   S/Is/His/Us/Ass/Penis/Hiss/Serpent
M/Mother is in Front of A/All Men   and   His/S/Is/Us/Ass/Hiss/Serpent/Penis   Having Her/R/Ear/Hear/Hair/Err/Heir/Or/Whore/Here/Are/Our/Ire/Air/Ere/Sex
A God of War will Stop that says   The Code

Marshall: Mare/She/All
She Can Only be An Animal Says The Marshall   By The Code Book
The Code is Scary to Look at for a Fem

Masculine
Mask/You/L/N   Mas/Cul/In
Mas is More in Spanish   Cul is Ass in French   Add a Mask

The Dam Code The Damn Book

As   The Code   is Hiding The Powers of The Masc

Mash: M/Shh
M/Motherhood   It is a Mash to Her and She be Quiet about it
mash: to crush

Mason: My/Son
2 Million Members in USA
Freemasons is an Ancient Society that Dates Before Salomon   The Builders with Codes

Master: The Mast (Rod/Penis)   Her/R/Ear/Hear/Hair/Heir/Or/Whore/// Err/Here/Are/Our/Ire/Air/Ere/Sex
Mast/Her   Bedroom   Here again She Is Inexistent in Her Bedroom
Master is The Mast and Sex With R
Must/Her   She/Must   Mustard (Mast/Hard)
Master is a Verb and a Noun
Switch A for U/Ovulation and She Gets Muster Muster to get Pregnant   the goal of   The Code
muster: to come together
Master is Powerful Word in   The Code
Mastery: Mast   Her   He/E

Masturbate: Mast   Her/R/Ear/Hear/Hair/Err/Heir/Or/Whore/Here/Are/ Our/Ire/Air/Ere/Sex   Bait/Bite
Master   B/Boy Holding All Fem Breasts   8/Hate/Ate
Masturbation: Master   B/Boy Holding All Fem Breasts   A/He/ On   or   Eon
That is a Long Time Trying to Master Her Without Positive happy Results

Material: Mat   He   Real
The Mat/The Math/The Meet/The Mate   it is all Real says   The Code

Match: M/Him/Motherhood   Hatch
To Hatch an Egg   is The Goal of M/Him/Motherhood
He Matches it   A Match is a Game
By Adding C/See/Young Girl to Math it is Now a Different Concept in Match   This One is For Her

Lise Rochon

Switch A for O/Fem Hole and She Gets Outch (Pain)
The Code   as Usual Puts Pain on The Fem
Take The C/young Girl Away and She Gets Math Which   The Code Keeps Her Away From

Math: M/Motherhood   at/or   M/Him/Motherhood   Hat
The Hat is the Cover Word for The Art of the Secret Societies Practices

Matrices: Mate   Her/R/Ear/Hear/Hair/Heir/Or/Whore/Err/Here/Are/Our/Ere/Ire/Air/Sex   Ice/Is/His/Hiss/Penis

Mature: Mate/Your   Meet/Your   May/T/Your
The Time to Meet and Mate says   The Code

May: May is a Lovely Fem Name   and   The Time for Early Fertility in the Land
May Mary Marry May in June
2 Lovely Fem Names   May or May Not   There is Always Uncertainty for The Fems

Mayday: Made/A   Maid/A   Maid/He
A Day In May
mayday: International Distress Signal
It is Atrocious to have a Distress Signal Called a Day in May
May is The Nicest Month of the Year and a Sweet Fem Name for a Fem
Another Fem Beautiful Name is Lost just as the Word Heroine is Lost
Nothing Can Be Positive for Us Fems says   The Code
Not Even a Day in May
Although Mayday Fits the Cry for Help from The Fem Experience   The Code   Experience   Yes She is Crying for Help but   The Code   says No

Mayhem: May   Him/Motherhood
She is Never Alone and at Peace in   The Code
mayhem: random or deliberate violence or damage
May/M   May is Time to be Mothers or to be with Him   says   The Code   But It is a Mayhem for Her
May is a Great Fem Name and Month   but The Greatness is Only for Him
hem: border of a garment

Hem is a Cover Word Here

Mayor: May   Her/R/Ear/Hear/Hair/Err/Heir/Or/Whore/Here/Are/Our/Air/Ire/Ere/Sex
For a Long Time it was Only a Man Job
The Name Alone is Scary for a Fem   Mayoress   Mayor/Ass
Mayor is a Cover Word here Implying that a Fem can be There also

Maximum: Max/He/Mum   Max is a Man Name
mum: silent   not saying a word
Here is Max (Masc) and Mum (as a Silent Fem with All 3 Fem Letters to Prove it)
The Code   says here that Maximum is Not for Her Either

Me: M/Him/Motherhood   He/E
Again   The Fem has No Definition or Identity Except as being a Mother

Meadow: Made   O/Fem Hole   Maid   O/Fem Hole   (See Maid)
Where Cows (Fem Milk Symbol) are Contained

Meal: ML 2 Fem Sound Letters
M/Motherhood   L/Sweet Fem Love Light/Oil/Elle/All/Ill/Ail/Hail/Heel/Hell
M is in Front of   Ill/L/Elle/Hail/Hell   Making Her a Mother
The Code   Calls it a Meal   Is it the Last Meal of Christ   The Ritual
of Breaking The Bread and The Drinking of Blood Ritual Repeated in Communion
Ill/L is Another Powerful Bad Word/Letter (See Devil in The Words Chapter)
It Hides Inside a Good Word   Meal
mill: a machine   a factory
The Meal Factory/Machine   Here She is

Mean: MN   2 Fem Sound Letters
And 2 Meanings Too
mean: offensive selfish or to intend
From   M/Motherhood   to   N/In/Hen/Virgin   Going in that Circle   It is
Mean and It Makes its Way In   as   in Me/In says The Code
Mine   Mein   Mine (As a Gold Mine)

Meddle: Meet/Mate   L/Sweet Fem Love Light/Oil/Elle/All/Ill/Ail/Hail/Heel/Hell
Next to Mind comes Middle
There is No Middle in   The Code   and it says that is None of Our Business (See Def of Meddle Below)
Anything in the Middle would Mean Some Kind of Equality   Equal Rights is a Scary One for   The Code
It Means Balance   Harmony   No More Wars
A Big No from   The Code   so
meddle: to involve oneself in a matter without right or invitation   interfere officiously and unwantedly

Medical: M/Addict/All   Med/IC/All   Med/He/Call   Medic/All
Doctor World is a Powerful Independent Structure with its Own Language

Meet: Mate   Meat
Nice to Meet/Mate You   N/Ice to Mate U   says The N/Virgin
By the Time She is on That Cross/T/Fem Cross/Curse   Her Power is All Gone
The Fem is Often Considered as Meat   As a Nice Piece of Meat
Meet and Mate

Melee: M/Hell/He   Male/He   Mail/He   M/Hail/He
hail: to cheer   to salute
Une Mêlée in French is a Bagarre   a Combat
M/Motherhood   is in Front of   Hell/L/Elle Sweet Fem Love Light/Oil/All/Ill/Ail/Hail/Heel   Followed by   He/E
That is a Big No in   The Code so
melee: confusion   turmoil   jumble

Member: Maim/Mame/Mom/Mum   Be/Letter B/Boy Holding All Fem Breasts   Her/R/Ear/Hear/Hair/Err/Heir/Or/Whore/Here/Are/Our/Air/Ire/Ere/Sex   as in Maim The Fems to Feed The Boys and have R/Sex for Heir or for Money
maim: to wound or a serious loss
Membership: Maim/Be/Her/Ship
There is No Membership for Her says   The Code   Her Ship is to be The Maimed Sheep (See Ship and Sheep in The Words Chapter)

The Dam Code The Damn Book

M/Aime/Her/He
Member is Another Slang for Penis

Memory: Mame/Maim/Maam   Her/R/Ear/Hear/Hair/Err/Heir/Or/
Whore/Here/Are/Our/Air/Ire/Ere/Sex   E/He
M/Motherhood   R/Her/Whore/Or/Heir/Our/Err/Sex   He
That is What We Keep in Mind as Memories says   The Code
M/Motherhood   Aime   Are   He/E
That would be a Better Sign for Mental Peace but   The Code   says
No   it is Only a false Memory   Only Mothers Love
Aimer is To Love in French

Menial: MNL   All 3 Fem Sound Letters
Where there is   M/Motherhood   N/In/Hen/Virgin   and   L/Fem Love
Light Together   There is Menial for Her
menial: servile   submissive   degrading
That Could have been Sweet Love Light/Elle/Hell   for/from   M/
Motherhood   to   N/In/Hen/An/Virgin   That is a Big No from   The
Code
M/N/He/All   Motherhood for All
Mean/He/All
Switch M/Motherhood for G/Penis Penetration and He Gets Genial

Menses: MNSS   Men/S/S   Men/Sees
menses: menstrual flow
Menses As Feces Come Only in Plural
Mense: propriety   to honor   to grace
That Mense is in a Different Area of Life for The Masc Only

Menstrual: Men   S/Is/His/Us/Ass/Penis/Hiss/Serpent
Through   L/Sweet Fem Love Light/Oil/Elle/All/Ill/Ail/Hail/Heel/Hell
All Men and Their Penisses are here   and   in Double Plural Meaning
Really All of Them is Going   Through   All   Fems
Mens   Tear   All
Monster   All
A Bizarre Word Menstrual

Mental: MNTL   All 4 Fem Sound Letters

481

M/Motherhood   N/In/Hen/Virgin   T/Fem Cross   All/L/Sweet Fem Love
Light/Oil/Elle/Ill/Ail/Hail/Heel/Hell
Meant to All   Mean/To/All
All   A/All Men   2 LLs/Sweet Fems Love Lights
Plural Makes it All or Twice as   The Code   Meant/All
Mental as in Not so Smart

Mentor: Man/Tore
Meant   Her/R/Ear/Hear/Hair/Err/Heir/Or/Whore/Here/Are/Our/Air/Ire/Ere/Sex
Men/T/Whore   Mean/T/Her   Mount/Her   Month/Her   MNTR
R/Her/Hair/Are/Here/Hear/Ear/Whore/Or/Err/Sex   Come Last after M N
and T   It is Too Much information for Her says   The Code
Mentor is a Powerful Word Against Her and Him Too
To Have Incentives as that and being a Mentor
It Would Mean there is No Love Left to Live For

Menu: MNU   3 Fem Sound Letters
Man   You/U/Ovulating
On The Menu for Him is Her Ovulating
Main   U
Mean   U   The Mean/Man and The U

Mercy: MRC
M/Motherhood   Her/R/Ear/Hear/Hair/Err/Heir/Or/Whore/Here/Are/Our/Air/Ire/Ere/Sex   C/See/Young Girl
Mother   Sex   Girl
Mère/See   Mothers Always Forgive
That Is what She Sees
Mère is Mother in French
Mer is Ocean in French
Mère/See   Motherhood as Mercy
M/Motherhood   Her/R/Ear/Hear/Hair/Err/Heir/Or/Whore/Here/Are/Our/Air/Ire/Ere/Sex   with C/Girls   He Sees that As Mercy
Asking for Mercy is the Last Begging
Remember that Fem Had No Way of Refusing Pregnancy
They could be Pregnant until Death Came

Anemia the Lack of Hygiene and No Antibiotics Back Then Made a Shorter Life for Her
Then the Man Could Choose Another or a Younger Wife
In Tibet Many Fems are Polyandrist   Calling it Advantageous

Mère: MR   M/Motherhood   and   Her/R/Ear/Hear/Hair/Err/Heir/Or/Whore/Here/Are/Our/Air/Ire/Ere/Sex
Une Mère is a Mother in French
La Mer is The Sea in French
M/Here   Myrrh   M/Err
Add D/Pregnant and She Get Merde (Merde is French for Shit (She/it))
Back to the Feces for Her Even in Bilingual

Merit: Mère/Mother   Hit/It   No Positive Space for The Fem Here

Mermaids: Mère/Maids   Mothers as Servants
She is a Maiden When She is Young   A Maid when an Adult   and She is an Old Maid when as a Fem She is Not Married Early in Life
Mere/Made
The Married Fem with Children do Not Escape The Curse
She Should be in a Position of Honor being a Mom
Instead She Become the Mother in Law
Putting on the Mantle of its Heavy Bad Reputation from   The Code

Messiah: Mess/He/A
The Girl Misses it as a Miss Herself
Messy: Mess/He   Mass/He   Miss/He
It is a Mass of a Mess but She Misses it
As in Not being Part of the Mass/Mess
And Missing Him in Her Heart
Mass: a body of coherent matter   a collection of incoherent particles   mass Roman Catholic Ceremony   the Celebration of the Eucharist
Army Mass Where people Meet to Eat   (Mass has more than 15 Definitions in the Dictionary
It Always Made me Tick that the Word Celebration was Used for the Sacrifice of the Body and Blood Ritual
Research says Only 3 times the Word Celebrate

Is Mentioned in the Bible King James Translation in its 1274 pages or 823,156 Words

Met: Meet   Mate
Almost as a Song
M/Ate   M/Hate   M/8 (Made Pregnant)   Me/Hit
Once Mated the Fun is Gone says   The Code
Met is Past Tense for Meet (M/Heat   Mother in Heat)

Metal: Meet/Mate/Mat (Rug/Rag)   All
And that is Solid as Metal says   The Code
Metal was the Base to Work with in Alchemy
Transforming Metal into Gold
In French they Pronounce it   All/She/Me

Meter: Meet/Her   Mate/Her
Always Measuring Her and Surveilling Her says   The Code

Method: Met/Odds(See Odds in The Words Chapter)

Mew: M/Motherhood   E/He   W/All Fems Sex Active
All Fems Sex Active Be Mothers
Mew is a Soft Sound   Cats are Very Close to The Fems

Milk: To Milk Someone   As in to Suck on Somebody Life
As We Do with The Cows   We Force them to Give Milk

Million: Mill/He/On
Billion   Bill/He/On
Trillion   Thrill/He/On
It is All About Him says   The Code
Lately The Fems are Starting to Have Higher Paying Careers and More Freedom
A Long Time Fight for The Fems with Many Lives Given or Taken Away in the Process   Merci

Mimic: Maim/IC

Mine: MN   2 Fem Sound Letters
M/Motherhood   N/In/Hen/Ann/Virgin   With i/Marriage Act
M/In   The Mother Concept Is In
Mine is Evolution of Number Nine   Mine/Us   Minus
Switch M for D/Pregnant and She Gets a Dime
A Dime is a Very Small Value
Switch M for N/In/Hen/Ann/Virgin and She Gets Nine   At Nine She is then Back to 0 (See # 9 in The Numbers Chapter)

Minimum: MNM   All 3 Fem Sound Letters   Motherhood   to   N/Virgin Waiting for Motherhood   to   M/Motherhood   Again   That is The minimum She can Do
Mine/He/Mum
And Silence to Her says   The Code

Minister: Mine   S/His/Is/Us/Ass/Penis/Hiss/Serpent
T/Fem Cross   Her/R/Ear/Hear/Hair/Err/Heir/Or/Whore/Here/Are/Our/Air/Ire/Ere/Sex
Mine/His/T/Her   The Cross is for Her says the Minister
Mine/Easter
Where Pretty Rabbits Makes The Fems Pregnant with Pretty Colored Eggs to Brighten Her Day of resurrection after being Crossed
Easter: East   R/Her/Are/Whore/Sex
In the East The Fem is Kept Pregnant Veiled and Silenced
Switch M for S/Penis and He Gets Sinister   Because it is Not for Him and his Penis   it is for Her to be Administered by   That Code

Mint: M/Motherhood   In/N/Ann/Donkey/Virgin   T/Fem Cross/Great Curse
Associating M/Motherhood   with   N/Virgin   and   T/Fem Cross/Great Curse   with i/Marriage Act   is Mint in   The Code
It is Meant to Her

Minus: Mine/Us
When M/Motherhood   and   N/Virgin   are in that Order   It Means that Mother would be a Virgin Again through Her Daughter   That is a Big No for   The Code   for Her to Know That so She Gets a Minus

Lise Rochon

The Fem Never Wins in   That Code   It has been that for about 2000 Years   A Lot of History on Her Shoulders

Minute: MNT   3 Fem Sound Letters
From M/Motherhood   to   N/In/Hen/Ann/Virgin   to   T/Fem Cross/Great Curse (See Minute in The Clock Chapter)
Mint and Minute are Close in Sound   it is to Attract The Fem
Mine   You/U   T
My/Nut   Mine/Hot
Minute is a Small Portion of Time
The Time of the Month Relates Only to Her says   The Code

Miracle: Me/Oracle
Me/R/Crawl
When R/Sex Crawls into M/Motherhood it is a Miracle says   The Code   and Answers the Oracle

Mirror: MRR   Sex with the Mother Twice says   The Code
A Mirror for Her
Mare/Mer   Marée in French is Tide
La Mer is the Sea   A Mare is a Horse   Here Come the Whores
Marry/Her   Mary/R   Merry/R
M/Motherhood   Her/R/Ear/Hear/Hair/Err/Heir/Or/Whore/Here/Are/Our/Air/Ire/Ere/Sex
The Mother and The Whore Make a Good and Only Mirror for Her   One or the Other   as Gold
3 Sounds Letters Word   M/Motherhood   R/Her   O/Fem Hole
Admire Her   Add/Mirror   Add/Mire
Mire/Her
Admire: Add/Mire/Her
mire: swampy ground
Mirror is The Cover Word here

Mischievous: Me/She/V/Us
Miss/He/V/Us
Here being Mischievous for The Fems Means is to be V/Fem Sex Active   She will be then a Mother and Miss Anyway says   The Code

The Dam Code The Damn Book

Misconception: Miss/Con/Scept/Eon
She Misses the Scepter
M/Hiss/Concept/Eon
When She Hiss at the Con and Scepter   It is a Misconception says   The Code

Miser: Mice/Her   My/Sir
A Sir that Belong to M/Motherhood is Wrong According to   The Code   so it is Miser to Want to do That

Miserable: Miss/Her/Able
He is Able to Overlook Her Talents
That Makes Her Miserable
She is to Be Left Behind and   Missed   or   Become Maimed
An Example of the Kaleidoscope Vision for Her of   The Code   Here

Misery: M/Sir/He   Me/Sir/He
When M/Motherhood is in Front of a Man/He
She is a Miser says   The Code   Miss/Her/He   When She Misses on Him She is in Misery

Miss: M/Hiss
M/Motherhood   Cannot   Hiss/SSS/S/Is/His/Us/Ass/Penis/Hiss/Serpent   She will Miss
Another Mean Concept in a Good Meaning Word   A Miss is an Unmarried Fem
miss: to fail
The Fem Misses so Much info that She become Maimed   Another Way to Make Her Miss   Then The Fem is a Mam/Maam with 2 AAs/All Men Inside Her to make Her a Mother
The Code   Directs Men into Bygamy/Polygamy
maim: to impair

Missing: MSN
Miss   N/In/Hen/Ann/Virgin   The Young Fem Fall into Anonymity
M/Motherhood   Hiss/S   on   N/In/Hen/Ann/Virgin
As Usual   The Code   Demands that Girls and Boys Get Different Attitudes because of their Sex

Lise Rochon

Boys go Up/Hop   Girl go Down (D/Pregnant   Own)

Mission: Miss/She/On
The Mission is to Miss Her   On and On for an Eon
The Code   Necessitate that All Fems Miss   and   That to Remain a Secret Knowledge   Miss/Eon
The Mission is to Have Her Miss for An Eon
He Ignores Her as Usual Compared to The Boys
A Miss is a Single Fem   A Single Man is a Bachelor
After The Miss Stage She is Then Madame (Mad/Am)   Mame/Maam   Mom   and   Maid/Made

Mistake: M/Motherhood   His/S/Is/Us/Ass/Penis/Hiss/Serpent   Take   Miss/Take   Miss/T/Ache   M/Hiss/T/Ache
It is All about Her and Pain

Mister: Miss/T/Her
Miss   T/Fem Cross   Her/R/Ear/Hear/Hair/Err/Heir/Or/Whore/Here/Are/Our/Air/Ire/Ere/Sex
She Misses an Understanding   Her T/Fem Cross/Great Curse
mister: a man
Mister is a Cover Word here

Misunderstood: Miss/Under/Stood
When a Fem Stands Under   It is Misunderstood
That is the Way to Go says   The Code

Mix: MX   2 Fem Sound Letters
M/Motherhood   X/Fallen Fem Cross
A Perfect Mix for   The Code

Moan: MN   2 Fem Sound Letters
A Feminine or Weak Sound
moan: to lament
Mown
Moan is on The Fems as in Mine
Moaning: MNN   3 Fem Sounds Letters
Mean/In   Man/In   M/Motherhood   In/Letter N/In/Hen/Virgin

The Dam Code The Damn Book

Model: Mode/Hell   Mode/Ill   Mode/Elle   M/Odd/All
The Model says   The Code   for Her is to be Ill   In Hell   or/and   to Ail
Under the Hail   It is All for Elle (She)   etc

Modern: Mode/Urn
M   Odd/Her   N/In/Hen/Ann/Virgin
The Code   is Telling Mothers and Virgins   Their Sex life is Odd   or/
and   She Should Be Back to the Urn (See Urn in The Words Chapter)

Mold: All 4 Fem Letters
M/Motherhood   Old
To Mold is to structure
Women are the Submissive and Yielding Ones says   The Code   Being
Told She is Old in The Process of being Molded is Just Another Way of
Weakening Her
Mold as in Mold in a Bathroom is Very Bad For You

Mole: M/Motherhood   Whole/Hole
M/Motherhood as a Hole   or a   Whole
mole: small mammal living underground   a breakwater   a blemish
Not Much to Look for Mom here   She is a Hole and   a Blemish   and
She is Whole There

Mom: M/Motherhood   O/Fem Hole   M/Motherhood
Mother of Moms
A Chain (She   N/In/Hen/Ann/Virgin) of Events That Brings Her
there   Endlessly
Mom and Moon   All Fems Letters
M is Made With the 2 Inside Collapsed Sticks that Attach Themselves to
The 2 Other Outside Sticks
M is formed with   2 VVs/Fems Sex Active   Reversed
Endless Chain of Motherhood   From Mother to Mother
O/Fem Hole   is being Surrounded by 2 MMs/Motherhood   Make All
Fems Pregnant
And Mum About It (Also She/Shh because Shit   She/It)

Moment: Mom/Aint
Momentum: Mom/Ain't/Home

489

momentum: driving power   force of movement
Powerful Word But Not for Her   She Aint There

Mommy: Mom/He
Switch O/Fem Hole for U/Natural Ovulation and She Gets a Mummy
mummy: a dead body dried and preserved of a human or an animal   a withered shrunken being   a dry shriveled fruit tuber resulting from any of several fungus diseases
The Code Makes it Clear Again here
When Her Fruit is Old She is Dead or Looking Terrible from Funguses/Diseases   No One will Look there

Money: Man/He
A Man Money World
M/Motherhood   O/Fem Hole   N/In/Hen/Ann/Virgin   E/He
When The Virgin Transforms into a Mother
Man/He   Money and Mommy   But She Got None because She in   The Code   is a Mummy
Dead or Inexistent is The Fem in   The Code   as Usual
Mon/He   Mon in French is My in the Masculine Form
Money   Honey   Horny
Penny   Popular Fem Name on TV   Pen/Pan   He
Dime/Dame/Dam/Damn   To Change on a Dime
Nickel   Knick/Nick   All/Ill/Hell/Ail/Elle/Letter L
Add K/Fem Broken Warrior and She Gets a Monkey

Monkey: M/Motherhood and the Key
Monkey Bars: M/Motherhood   Key   Bar
She is Barred from Holding Any Keys   Especially the Motherhood Keys

Monster: Moon/Star
M/Motherhood   N/In/Hen/Ann/Virgin   S/His/His/Us/Ass/Hiss/Serpent/Penis   T/Fem Cross/Great Curse   Her/R/Ear/Hear/Hair/Err/Heir/Or/Whore/Here/Are/Our/Air/Ire/Ere/Sex
Moon   Stay   Her/R/Are/Heir/Or/Whore/Sex
Bad   Weak   or   Poor Words are Fem in   The Code
Here The Moon is Associated with a Monster   And The Fem is a Star because of It

490

The Dam Code The Damn Book

Month: Mount of the Weak/Week   Year/Here   Days/Daze
Mount/Month and Mother are Close
To Mount
The Secret of the Ancients is the Great Curse
Month: M/Motherhood   O/Fem Hole   N/In/Hen/Ann/Virgin   T/Fem Cross/The Curse   H/Societies Secret Grid
All Holes of the Mothers and Virgins are Cursed in Secret
Mount as in to have Sex the Whole Month   Instead of being on a Mating Season   Month/Mount
She Becomes a Mother
The Way   The Code   Emphasizes the Mount/Month is Through a Positive/Normal Definition as in Mount   A Mountain for the Weak of Heart/Art or a   Hill/Ill/All/Elle/Hell/Letter L
Monthly: Month/Lay

Mood: Mood is Entirely Made of Fem Letters
M/Odd   Mode
By Making The Fem Odd She Loses Her Balance and Self Confidence
Moody: Mood/He
Switch D/Pregnant for N/In/Hen/Ann/Virgin and She Gets Moon (Menstrual Cycle)
Moon is All Fems Letters also

Moon: Moon is 4 All Fems Letters   Close to Mom
The Tarot Card "The Moon" from A. Crawley in the Book "The Power of Thoth" is Illusion Deception and Bewilderment for Her
The Moon Represents that for Her on Top of Her Monthly Cycle   Her/Moon as People Call it
The Sun Bring Joy and Warmth and Mirror All Men
The Tarot Card "The Sun" Brings Joy and Warmth and Represents All Men
Sun   SN   S/Serpent and the N/In/Hen/Ann/Virgin
S/In   Sin   San
Moon is close to Man
That She will Be Reminded about All Her Life
Mentor or Mount/Her   Month/Her
That is how   The Code   Works
Coon   Doom   Goon   Loom   Moon   Soon
Words in Oon (2 Fem Holes and a Virgin) are Not so Popular or Powerful

Lise Rochon

Sunny for Him
Moon and Moon Shine (She/In) for Her
Switch N/In/Hen/Virgin for D/Pregnant and She Gets Mood

Moot: Moot is All 4 Fem Letters
moot: little or no practical value   controversial

Mop: M/P
M/Motherhood with Her O/Hole   is in Front of   P/Man Power
That is Bad says   The code   so she is a Mop
Moping: M/O/P   In/N   Adding N/Virgin to Continue

Morality: More/All/He/T
M/Whore/All/He/T
When All Mothers Are Whores with The Fems Curse   it is Called Morality
Says   The Code

More: M/Motherhood   Whore
More of the Whore Mother or the Mother Whore
M/Motherhood and Her/R/Ear/Hear/Hair/Err/Heir/Or/Whore/Here/Are/
Our/Air/Ire/Ere/Sex
Our Mother is that
M/Or   Mother is with Gold   But She is still a Whore
Get More   Or

Morgue: M/Motherhood   Whore/Or   G/Penis Penetration
If Mother and/as a Whore Would be in Front of G the Letter of God
That Would be a Big No from   The Code   so
morgue: a place in which bodies are kept especially the bodies of victims of violence or accidents pending identification or burial   a reference file of old clippings mats books etc in a newspaper office
More   G/Penis Penetration
In French   A Mort (To Death) has Almost the Same Sound as Amour

Morning: Morn/In/G
The G is Silent here as Not existent
Morning: Morn/In
To Mourn   To Start Her Everyday

The Dam Code The Damn Book

Mother: Madder Mat/Her Mate/Her Math/Her Matter Meet/Her M/Odd/Her Mode/Her Mot/Her Mote Her Moth/Her M/Other Mute/Her Mutt/Her mote: a small particle of dust from dust to dust
Mother as Dust
The Code is Cracking because as any Other Code
It Gets to be Used Too Much
People are Starting to figure it Out
M and the Other
Other is Anyone The Motor
Makes No difference This Mother or the Other
La Mer is French for Sea
Related with the Water l'Eau (Letter O/Fem Hole
Back to the Mare/The Fem Horse/Whores for The Fems
The Mother in Law and their Endless Jokes About Her Incompetence
No Matter what and Always Admiring the Father in Law and Never Making Jokes about Him
Mother in Law is a Doomed Term for Her
After their Children are Grown She could Retire with the Husband and be Proud of the Hard Work of Raising Children But The Bad Mother in Law Bad Wraps are Right there Waiting for Her
This is Another Form of Curse to Us Fem
And there are Many of Them in Her life
Every Step of Her Growth in Life is Full
Of that Kind of Pitfalls and Put Down From That Code

Mountain: Mount/In Month/In

Motherfucker: Mate Her Fuck Her
A Motherfucker is a Mean Despicable Person
Her/R/Ear/Hear/Hair/Err/Heir/Or/Whore/Here/Are/Our/Air/Ire/Ere/Sex

Motor: Mate/Her Met/Her M/Hot/Her Mother
The Motor is Her/R/Ear/Hear/Hair/Err/Heir/Or/Whore/Here/Are/Our/Air/Ire/Ere/Sex
Switch M/Motherhood for H/Secret Code Letter and Get Hotter
Switch M for R/Her/Hair/Are/Here/Hear/Ear/Whore/Or/Err/Sex and She Gets Rotor(Rut/Her Root/Her)

Lise Rochon

Move: M/Motherhood   Ov
Mothers Moving into Ovulation
Moo/V   Back to The Cow for Her
Mover: Moo/V/R   Move/Her
Movement: Move/He/Meant

Movie: Move/He
Move/His   Movies   That fun Art is All About Him Says   The Code

Much: M/Motherhood   U/You/Ovulating   C/Young Girl/Open Loins   H/Secret Code Letter
The Code   Pushes Motherhood

Muck: All 4 Fem Letters
M/Motherhood   C/See/Young Girl   U/You/Ovulating   All Heading to be   K/Broken Fem Warrior
All Together without a Masc Letter to Interfere
That would be a Big No from   The Code so
muck: moist farmyard dung   decaying vegetable matter   etc   manure   filth dirt   slime   a state of chaos or sullying remarks
Back to Dung/Shit (She/It) for Her as Usual
This is Where She Lives says   The Code
Switch U for O/Fem Hole and She Gets Mock
She is a Laughable Matter   Not No Worry   it is All Muck

Muffin: Muff/In
muff: slang for fem pubic area
M/Motherhood   Off (Off is Made of 3 Fem Letters)   N/In/Hen/Ann/Virgin
The Mother does Not Become a Virgin Again says   The Code
A Muffin in The Oven is Slang for being Pregnant

Mum: Say Nothing   Be Silent
Mum: M/Motherhood   U/You/Ovulating   M/Motherhood
When 2 MMs are Circling Their U/Uterus   The Code Says No   It is Too Much Power to Her so Be Mum About It

Mumbling: Is How Mom Should Speaks

494

mumbling: to speak in an almost intelligible manner   a low utterance of a sound
Mum   Bling   It is as Precious Jewelry to Mumble for a Fem says   The Code

Murder: Mirror   Dure
dure: hard   severe
Mur/D/Her   Mur is Wall in French
Take Away Her/R/Ear/Hear/Hair/Err/Heir/Or/Whore/Here/Are/Our/Air/Ire/Ere/Sex   and it Sounds as Mother

Muse: M/Motherhood   Use
Her Muse is to Put that Motherhood to Use says   The Code   When Inspired Focus on Motherhood

Music: M/Motherhood   Use   IC
Motherhood to be Used as an Integrated Circuit
Muse/Ic
IC: integrated circuit

Muslim: Mostly/Him

Mute: M/Mom   U/You/Ovulating/Open Loins   T/Fem Cross/Great Curse   E/He
The Fems have been Mostly Kept in a Mute State for 2000 Years and More
No Fems were Allowed to Talk Privately in between them or to Create Alliances with Other Fems
Take E/He Away and She Gets a Mutt

My: Made of 2 Fem Letters
M/Motherhood   Y/Wounded Fem
Motherhood   as   a Wounded Fem Belongs to Her
Myself: My/Seal/F   It is All Sealed from the Fems says   The Code
M/Motherhood   Self
Compare Herself (Heir/Self)   to   Himself (Hymn/Self)

Mystery: Miss/T/Her/He
She Misses Her Own Mystery which is The T/Fem Cross/Great Curse

Lise Rochon

Switch Y for A/All Men and He Gets Mastery (Master/He   Mister/He)
He Also is Master of the Mystery
Mystery   She Misses   and   He is the Master

Mystic: Miss/Stick   Miss/The/Stick   My/Stick
Mystical: Miss/The/Call
IC is an Integrated Circuit   That Inner Wiring
Mystical: Miss/T/Call
Miss/T/He/Call   or   Me/Stick/All
Miss/T/All   All Fems Misses it All

Myth: M/Motherhood   Y/Wounded Fem   T/Fem Cross   H/Silent Secret Society Grid
Switch Y for O/Fem Hole and She Gets a Mot
mot: a witty remark
"Myth is the Search through Ages for the Meaning of Life" Joseph Campbell in "The Rapture"

N n
Intro
Letter N Is the Masc Made Fem Letter for The N/Virgin
All N/Virgins Must Become Mothers   Letter N is Included in Letter M Letter   NMNM
N is Formed with 2 VVs   One is Up The Other is Down
Letter V is V/Sex Active Fem
And V is also in X/Fallen Cross Fem Letter Twice
One is Up   One is Down   from All Angles She is That
NNN is the âne   The Donkey in French
N as In   Come In
N as in An is Commonly Used to points at Small Words   An Apple
I I N M V Y W Have All the Same Shapes Origins
and Those Are All Masc Made Fem Letters   Including the Stick   Because there was a Time Before the Stick was Not the Only Personal Image of Power
But Her Stick Splits in Y/Wounded Fem and Has Completed Sex In V/Sex Active Fem
In L/Sweet Fem Love She has been Defeated and Softens   In K/Wounded Fem Warrior Her Stick is Completely Broken   and   She is Assimilated

in R/Sex as the Circle/Hole To be Transformed in T/Fem Cross/Great Curse   and   Finally in X/Fallen Cross She is Out
Letter n in Semitic Alphabet Means a Large Fish (Fem Symbol) and is Depicted as a Sinuous Snake
n has the Same Shape as a Small h with its Top (Stick) Shorter
Letter n is the Code Root
See Small Cap h and its Relation to the T/Fem Cross and the Sign of Saturn
Words with Letter N   In   An   On   Ann   Hen (The Chick as Her) and Haine
N is the Letter for Fem Names   as Ann Anna

N   n
Nab: N/In/Hen/Ann/Virgin   A/All Men   B/Boy Holding All Fems Breasts
Letter N is in Front of All Men and Boys   A Big No from The Code   so
nab: to arrest   to catch

Nag: Rag   Bag   Nag
Those are Weak Words Starting with The Virgin   A weak Letter in   The Code

Nah: N/In/Hen/Ann/Virgin   A/All Men   H/Secret Code Letter
Easy No from   The Code   All Virgins are Told No   As Usual

Nail: N/Hail
Hail (and all The Rest of Letter L/Sweet Fem Love Light/Oil/Elle/All/Ill/Ail/Hail/Heel/Hell)
to the Virgin
hail: salute   precipitation of ice pellets
N/Hell   Virgin in Hell   N/Elle   Elle is She in French
N/Ail
ail: to feel pain   to be unwell
And The Veil is so Close Where She Fails

Naïve: Beautiful Sound Word
The Word is Looking at You with its 2 Eyes (2 Dots)
naïve: innocent or ignorant as a child
The Nave/Space in a Church Building
The Navel as the BB (See BB)

Naïve Starts with N/Young Girl and has the V/Fem Sex Active to Accentuate It   A Soft Word because it is the N/In/Hen/Ann/Virgin in the Process of Being a V/Fem Sex Active   Is it Another Trap to The Virgin because She is too Young and Naïve to Know Better

Naked: N/In/Hen/Ann/Virgin   A/All Men   K/Broken Fem Warrior   D/Pregnant
When Naked The Virgin is a Fem Broken Warrior   and   Pregnant

Name: NM   2 Fem Sound Letters
Name Is Made After the Virgin and the Mother   As a Connected Pattern
N/In/Hen/Ann/Virgin   A/All Men   M/Motherhood   E/He
A/All Men   All Men Makes N/In/Hen/Virgin into a M/Mother
N to M   Fits a Connected Design   with V/Fem Sex Active and W/All Fems Sex Active
Children Follow Mothers
Switch N/In/Hen/Ann/Virgin for M/Motherhood and She Gets a
Mane   Her
Hair/Her/R/Ear/Hear/Err/Heir/Or/Whore/Here/Are/Our/Air/Ire/Ere/Sex   is Her Name and Her Personality says   The Code

Napkin: Nap/Kin
A Well Known Hygiene Fem Product as Known to Her for Ever   A Napkin
nappe: cloth   tablecloth
A Nappe is Close to the Fems as a Tablecloth   She Works with Every Day
A Nappy is a Sweet Child Sleep
The Sheet of Water that Flows Over a Dam (Ma/Dame) is a Nappe   How Appropriate says   The Code
kin: someone of the same kind

Nasty: Nest/He
Men are Moody at Home   The Code   says He Be Nasty to Him and Her   There has been a Lot of it in the Last 2000 Years
Never is Peace with your Neighbors   or with   Your Love says   The Code   A Nasty Matter (Meet/Her   Mat/Her   Mate/Her   Math/Her   Moth/Her   Imitate/Her   a Mother Cannot be Nasty by the Natural Love that   She/Shh Carries says   The Code)

The Dam Code The Damn Book

Nation: Nay/Neigh   She/Shh   On
Back to the Horses (Whores/R/Her) Whining here for Themselves about a Very Important Word for All   National
nay: a denial or a refusal   *Archaic*   used in dissent denial refusal
so She is Denied as Usual to be Part of   The Nation
As Often 2 Different Meanings Applies to the Same Context Adding Information to the Symbology of the Word
Knit/She/On   Because M/Motherhood   and   N/In/Hen/Ann/Virgin   are Interchangeable
Switch N for M/Motherhood and She Gets a Mate (Mate/She   or   He/On   or   Eon Which Last For Ever)

Nature: Night   Her
The Day (Masc) is for Power and Action   The Night (Fem) is for Sleep   N/ The Virgin   Hate   Her

Naughty: Nut/He   Nut is 3 Fem Letters
naughty: sexual intercourse

Nausea: Nose/He/A
The Nose is an Important Memory and Psychic Intelligence Complex for the Man in   The Code
For Her or the Laymen it Stinks

Nave: Naïve   Navel (See BB In Words)

Need: N/ID
The Virgin as the Instinctual Quest for Pleasure as an ID
N/In/Hen/Ann/Virgin   2 EEs/He   D/Pregnant
The Need of   The Code   is to Have All Virgins Become Mothers as Their Identification
Need: Knit/D   To Create Pregnancy as a Need for Her
Night   The Knight in   The Code   is to Keep The Fems in Darkness

Nefarious: N/F/Heir/Whore/He/Us
2 Fem Letters/Sounds   N/In/Hen/Ann/Virgin   and F/Fem/Fuck   are in Front of Her/R/Ear/Hear/Hair/Err/Heir/Or/Whore/Here/Are/Our/Air/Ire/Ere/Sex

Lise Rochon

Letter R   E/He is After That   With S/Penis
It is Despicable says   The Code
nefarious: despicable   villainous   wicked

Negative: N/In/Hen/Ann/Virgin   Egg   At/Hat   Eve/V/Fem Sex Active
The Virgin Ovulation is Negative and   It in The hat (as a rabbit) and She is
Now V/Fem Sex Active says   The Code
Because Nothing Fem can be Positive in   The Code Language for The
Fems   She is a
Nag/At/Eve   And it is Annoying   Therefore Left Behind in The Mind
of Men
nag: to annoy

Negligence: Nag   L/Sweet Fem Love Light/Oil/Elle/All/Ill/Ail/Hail/Heel/
Hell   Hence
If The Fem Nag it is Her Fault and from Her Own Negligence says   The
Code

Neigh: N/In/Hen/Virgin/Ann/Donkey   A/All/Men
Virgin is with   A/All Men   it is a
neigh: horse cry   to complain   to whine   to cross
To Cross is to go to the Other Side

Nell: A Fem Name
N/In/Hen/Ann/Virgin   That is Ill/L/Sweet Fem Love Light/Oil/Elle/All/Ail/
Hail/Heel/Hell
Kneel   Nil   Weak Words

Nemesis: N/In/Hen/Ann/Virgin   M/Motherhood   Is/S/His/Us/Ass/Penis/
Hiss/Serpent
Note that Nemesis Starts with N/In/Hen/Ann/Virgin Following with M/
Mother and Ends with Is/His/Serpent
A Rare Word   Could have been a Great Assembly of Concepts
But Of Course a Big No from   The Code   so
nemesis: a rival   an opponent whom a person cannot overcome
Nemesis is the Goddess of Divine Retribution and Revenge
Name/His/His   Name/Is/Is   No Fem Here

The Dam Code The Damn Book

Nephew: Knew/Few   New/Few   Nice Delicate Words for Him Compare to Niece (N/Virgin   is On Ice

Net: Knit   N/Ann/Hit
Ann The Virgin is in the Net   It is as a Knitting Piece Tight and Regular   She is The One Being it and Hit

Never: NVR   N/In/Hen/Ann/Virgin   Eve/V/Fem Sex Active Her/R/Ear/ Hear/Hair/Err/Heir/Or/Whore/Here/Are/Our/Air/Ire/Ere/Sex

Her as   N/Virgin   is Alone with   V and   Heir/Or/Whore Her/R/Ear/ Hear/Hair/Err/Here/Are/Our/Air/Ire/Ere/Sex
That Would Be Never says   The Code   Way Too Much Information to Her
There are   2 Almost Silent EEs/He   here for More Precaution Naïve/Her   Nave/Her

New: NU   2 Fem Sounds Letters
Knew
News: N/In/Hen/Ann/Virgin   Use
The News is that the N/Virgin is for Use   By The S/Penis Making it Plural and Giving it More Force

Next: NXT   All 3 Fem Sound Letters
N/In/Hen/Virgin/In/Donkey/Ann/Virgin   Axe/Letter X/Fallen Fem Cross   T/Fem Cross
The Next Virgin Goes to the Cross Under the Axe

Night: N/Height   Knight
Neigh   T/Fem Cross
Knight for Him in the Day and Night
Night for Her Day and Night
neigh: cry of a horse
Horses/Whores   Whinny/Wine/He
Anything Related to Wine is Her Blood Loss in   The Code
Nighty   Ninety (Nine is the Crone or The Female Wisdom Number so She Remains in The Night)
Take T/Fem Cross Away and Get

nigh: *archaic* for near
Switch T for F/Fem/Fuck and She Gets Knifed
The Fems Has been Always Under the Knife Somewhere as a Trapped or Domesticated Animal
The Night is a Powerful Symbol for Fem   And   The Code uses it Plenty
Switch N/In/Hen/Ann/Donkey/Virgin for B/Boy Holding All Fem Breasts and He Gets a Bite
Switch N for C K or Q and She Get a Kite (Fly High Distracted by the Wind   See Nothing)
Switch N for L/Sweet Fem Light and Gets a Light   A Light in The Night is what The Fem Gets
Switch N for M/Motherhood and She Gets Might (a probability)
P cannot be there because it would give Power to Eight/Height as it is Pronounced (see Number 8)
Switch N for Her/R/Ear/Hear/Hair/Err/Heir/Or/Whore/Here/Are/Our/Air/Ire/Ere/Sex   and She Gets a Rite (A Sexual Ritual is What She Gets)
Switch N for S/Is/His/Us/Ass/Penis/Hiss/Serpent
and He Gets a Site/Sight (Easy on Him)
Switch N for T/Fem Cross and She Gets Tight or Tit
V and W Cannot be there it would be Fem Adding Power to Eight an Entirely Fem Number so No Says   The Code

Nightmare: Night/Mare
The Horse (Whores) in the Night
The Night is a Feminine Symbol in   The Code
Mare/Mary   (Mary is Bitter in Italian)
A Bad Dream that Is for Her

Nightshade: a purple flower with a gold center
That Violet (Vile/Viol   He/Hot)
Purple is the Color of God
Viol Means Rape in French   and Rape is Vile
Switch Letter l/Fem Light for N/In/Hen/Ann/Virgin and She Gets The Vine (The Vine is Where the Wine Grapes (Grope) Grows   The Wine is the Symbol for Her Blood Loss   and The Blood Line)

Nil: 2 Fem Sound Letters

N/In/Hen/Ann/Donkey/Virgin   L/Sweet Fem Love Light/Oil/Elle/All/Ill/Ail/Hail/Heel/Hell
Nil: nothing   naught   zero   having no value or existence
So Kneel Nell you are Nil

No: NO   2 Fem Letters
N/In/Hen/Virgin/Ann/Donkey   and   O/Fem Hole   Together (To/Get/Her)
A Very Big No from   The Code   to have 2 Fem Together Without a Masc Letter   So
No   Because
Her O/Fem Hole is Owned by the Stick (See Sheppard Stick in The Words Chapter) says   The Code
(He/Is   His/Is) Yes and See is Close
Non   Nay   Ney   Nah   Nein   Nix   Neg
(active)   Nē   Niet   Nee   Nej   Never   None
Not Much Power at All in Those Fem Words
The No Words Start with N/In/Hen/Virgin in Many Languages
Any   Annie   N/He   Any Time
But The Knowing is Only for the Masc
Switch N/In/Hen/Ann/Virgin for B/Boy Holding All Fem Breasts and
He Gets a Beau (Too Young for The Code (All is Pretty there in   The Code   Boy Childhood)
Switch N for D/Pregnant and She Gets a Different Tone in Do and Get to Do More
Switch N for G/Hymen Perforation and She Gets a Go (of Course says   The Code)
Switch N for H/Secret Code Letter and He Gets a Hoe
Switch N for L/Sweet Fem Love Light/Oil/Elle/All/Ill/Ail/Hail/Heel/Hell and
She Gets a Low   Low Cannot be Written Lo because it would 2 Fems Together Without Mentioning Sex so W/All V/Fem Sex Active   is Added as the Reminder says   The Code
Switch N for P/Man Power and He Gets a Pot (a chamber pot)   P Wants Nothing to do Alone with a Closed O/Fem Hole So He Pees
Switch N for Her/R/Ear/Hear/Hair/Err/Heir/Or/Whore/Here/Are/Our/Air/Ire/Ere/Sex and She Gets Row (Whore/O) (to Row is Hard Work)
Roll (Whore/All) with it says   The Code
Switch N for S/Is/His/Us/Ass/Hiss/Serpent/Penis and He Gets So and Sow

Lise Rochon

Switch N for T/Fem Cross and She Gets a Tow (The Code will Say Yes to Help its Own Goals)
Switch N for V/Fem Sex Active and She Gets a Vow
Make it sound as Fun in   Wow (Wow is When All O/Fem Holes are Opened (in V) and All Fems are Sex Actives from Beginning to End)
Switch N for Z/Sleep on The Code Letter and She Gets All O/Fem Holes Sleeping in Zoo
To Know a Fem in the Bible Sense is to Know Her/R/Ear/Hear/Hair/Err/Heir/Or/Whore/Here/Are/Our/Air/Ire/Ere/Sex
As if you Would Know a Fem just by Putting a Penis in
But   The Code   Says a Big No to Permit Any Knowledge to Any Fem   So No is Her Real Name
To Compare to Yes He/Is/His is Very Important to Understand   The Codes   Roots
Add W/All Fems Sex Active to No and She Gets Now (as in Sex Right Now)
Note that Queer is Mostly Used for being Gay Hiding the Older Meaning   Because
In the Word Queen   If   We Switch N/In/Hen/Virgin for R/Her/Hair/Are/Here/Hear/Ear/Whore/Or/Err/Sex It would give Advantage to Q/Bleeding Fem and You/U/You/Ovulating/Ov
A Big No from   The Code   so
queer: strange or odd from a conventional viewpoint   unusually different   of a questionable nature or character   suspicious   shady   mentally unbalanced or deranged   *Slang   disparaging and offensive* homosexual   Effeminate   unmanly
Queer Makes Queen Bad   A Worthless or a Counterfeit Product (See The Word Queen for More Blood Shed (She/Aid))
Q/Here or Q/Hear

None: 3 Fem Sounds Letters
When N/In/Hen/Virgin/Ann/Donkey   Is   On   it is Called None   Or On for Nothing says   The Code
Switch O/Fem Hole for U/You/Ovulating/OV and She Gets a Nun   Nuns Were persecuted Through Ages   The Fems Cannot be Left Alone says   The Code
Sarcastically Here   The Code   Claim to the Nun that Her Hole is still On/Open for Sex

The Dam Code The Damn Book

Even When She has Declared Herself a N/In/Hen/Virgin For Her God or Jesus
That Mean Nothing (No/Thing) says   The Code   Because The Fem has No Reality Except as an Entity (N/In/Hen/Virgin   2 TTs or All   Are   T/Fem Cross) for Sacrifice (See Letter T in the Letter Chapter)

Nookie: N   OK   He
If N/In/Hen/Ann/Virgin Would Be OK She Would do
nookie: a vulgar term for having sex
N/Hook/He
A N/Virgin Hooks a Man   It is Only for Vulgar Sex
Replace N with R/Whore/Her/Sex and She Gets a Rookie
Switch N for B/Boy Holding All Fem Breasts and He Gets a Bookie
Switch B for C/See/Young Girl and She Gets a Cookie

Noon: NOON   All 4 Fem Letters
All Those Virgins With Their Holes Basking in The Strongest Sun/Son Light of the Day   The Code   is Watching for Her to get Her Moon
Switch N/In/Hen/Virgin for M/Motherhood and She Gets a Moon (Menstrual Cycle)

Normal: No   Her/R/Ear/Hear/Hair/Err/Heir/Or/Whore/Here/Are/Our/Air/Ire/Ere/Sex   Male/Mail
The No Represents Her   Then She is a Whore and The Male is Right there as Sure as a Letter in The Mail
The Code   Says it is All Normal

Not: NOT   3 Fem Letters   N/In/Hen/Ann/Haine/Virgin   O/Fem Hole   T/Fem Cross/Great Curse
NT the Short for Not is Even Stronger   The N/Virgin and T/Fem Great Curse are Together Alone   But There is No Power Here for Her Because it is The Word Not
Also Nut (Stupid)   and   Net
Another Only 2 Fem Letters
No She Must Not know (To Know for Him   A No for Her)
She is a No/Not from the Nut Family (No Matter How Good Nuts are For You)

A Knot Sound   To Tie that Knot/Nut (Tie the Nut) Marriage is the Way to Do it says   The Code   Put a Ring around that Belle/Bell

Nothing: No/Thing for The Fems says   The Code
Know/Thing for the Masc
The Fems are Known as Things in   The Code
"Some Thing" is a Cute (Cut/Clitorectomy) Fem

Notice: No/Tits
No Tits is a Big No From The Code to Her
Note His/Is   Is What The Code Wants   Do Not Notice Her
No/T/S
No T/Fem Cross in Plural would be The End of The Code   So That would be a Big No From The Code
Notice is a Cover Word Here

Notion: No/She/On
The Notion is   No Follows The Fems   No/Shh/Eon
The Notion is She has to Shh and Go On for an Eon   Past and Future
Nut/She/On
The Notion is She is a Nut
The Notion is She is An/Ocean   but it is Only a Notion
notion: vague or imperfect conception   opinion   belief
Switch O/Fem Hole for A/All Men and He Gets a Nation
The Nut as Not and No for The Fems is an Important Sound as Banal as it Sound
The Masc Call Often The Fems a Nut (All 3 Fem Letters)
(See Words Made Entirely of Fem Letters and Get a Feel for it)
nut: a dry fruit consisting of an edible kernel or meat enclosed in a woody or leathery shell   *slang*   the head
Nut the Goddess of the Sky is sometimes shown as a Cow bearing Ra on Her back and the Stars on Her underside
(See Ra and Stars in The Words Chapter)

Notorious: Note   He   Her/R/Ear/Hear/Hair/Err/Heir/Or/Whore/Here/Are/Our/Air/Ire/Ere/Sex   S/Is/His/Us/Ass/Penis/Hiss/Serpent
Note   He has   Her/R/Sex   with S/His/Penis   That Makes Him Notorious says   The Code

The Dam Code The Damn Book

Now: NOW   3 Fem Letters
N/Ow   The N/In/Hen/Ann/Virgin is Hurt in Now
The Bleeding Fem Teenagers Have Very Low Blood Pressure and Many are Anemic
They Suffer from Several Physical Pains and Anxiety from That Huge Blood Loss   No One Talks about it   It is Part of The Great Shame Put on Her from The Great Curse
N/Owe
Girls Always Owe Something   It Keeps Them Under

Nowhere: No/Where   No/Were
In Nowhere   No   Which is The Fems have No Where to Go

Nude: NUD   3 Fem Sound Letters

Number: Numb/Her   (See the Numbers Chapter)

Nun: All 3 Fem Letters
N/In/Hen/Ann/Virgin   U/You/Ovulating   N/Virgin
Perfect Example of Letters Working Together
But No Says The Code a Nun is None
The Nuns are Celibate by Virtue and Oath   The Nuns were Often Under Attack

Nuptial: N/Hop/U/All
Nuptials Should be Faithful But No   The Code   says the Virgin Hops All
N/You/P/T/All
N/In/Hen/Ann/Virgin   U/You/Ovulating   P/Man Power   T/Fem Cross   L/Sweet Fem Love Light/Oil/Elle/All/Ill/Ail/Hail/Heel/Hell   The N/Virgin and Her U/Ovulating Loins Through   P/Man Power   are L/All Aiming at the   T/Fem Cross as   All/Letter L   The Others

Nurse: N/In/Hen/Virgin   Ours
nurse: one that feed with the breast
A Nurse in an Hospital (Why the Name   They do Not Nurse/Give Milk to the Patient   And Why do We Have to be Patient   People Pay a Lot for Medical Help

Doctor (Duck/Her   The Silly Goose is a She) Why the Medical Emblem is a Stick (Male Symbol) Surrounded by a Snake (Masc Symbol for Penis   The Penis Around The Stick
They are Starting Lately in this Century to Accept the Fems as Part of Their Institutions Besides   Her Washing Floors and Emptying Basins since it had Been
Doctor   Dock/Her
Nursing: Nurse   N/In/Hen/Ann/Haine/Virgin

Nut: 3 Fem Letters
N/In/Hen/Ann/Haine/Virgin   U/You/Ovulating   T/Fem Cross
Not   is Also Made of 3 Fem Letters
Nuts are Testicles   because   The Code   Takes Everything from the Fem   Even M/Motherhood is Also Him/M
Switch N/In/Hen/Virgin for M/Motherhood and She Gets a Mutt (A Simpleton)
Note That Mutt is Also All Fems Letters

Nymph: NMF   3 All Fems Sound Letters
When PH (P/Man Power and H/Secret Code Letter Society) Becomes the Letter F   It is in Silence
The Code/Men has Penetrated in Entirely Not Only a Fem World but a Goddess World
nymph: one of the numerous class of lesser deities of mythology conceived of as beautiful maidens inhabiting the sea rivers woods trees mountains meadows etc and frequently mentioned as attending a superior deity   a beautiful or graceful maiden   a maiden   the young of an insect that undergoes incomplete metamorphosis
In   The Code   Reality She Goes from being called a maiden (a title of Spiritual Honor here) serving Godliness until Her/
The   Code   Transformation in a Bleeding Cursed Fem   And it is Viewed from an Insect Size   There is Nothing to See Unless you are a Knower in the Matter (Mate/Her   Mother   etc) says   The Code
Maiden (Made   N/In/Hen/Ann/Virgin) Maid/In   ready to Go   and the most delicious nymphs became nymphomaniacs   How Ugly is   That Code   More Than You Think

The Dam Code The Damn Book

O o
Intro
All the Way from the Phoenician Alphabet 1500 BC   The O Means the Eye
Then there is another Letter Oo with an X/x in its Middle   Its Means the
Wheel (The Wheel of time and the Time of the Month)
O is the O/Fem Hole   Her Loins Letter
O Has No Value Numerically as it is Considered as The Zero   Unless it is
With a Number (Numb/Her) in Front of it
O as a Hole (All Whole) Shape
The Holy/Circle has No Value in Itself
It All Depends on What is in It   Punt Intended
O in the Secret Code is Known as   The Fem Hole   The Chalice   The
Holy Girl   The Holy Grail (Sang Real Not Royal)   A Cup (The Cup
That Leaks in the Grail)   A Vase   The Cup of Jesus with the Wine in it
(Blood)   The Wound   The Uterus Itself etc
O is the Full Size of the Moon and also Represents Pregnancy
O is in the Shape of an Egg   so is Zero
O As in Ov/Ovulation (See Ov/Of in the Words Chapter)
Oeuf in French is an Egg
Her Loss of Blood Is Called Her Moon Cycle
But Has Little to do with the Moon
O Is an Entirely Fem Letter
Almost as the Uu which Serves the Same Purpose
and the C/Young Girl is the Half Moon Cycle
O is Eau in French which is Water
Water is The Eternal Fem Symbol for All Fem
It Follow (FLO) and Flows (FLO) Fall (Fl)   and   Fail (Fl)
FL to be Full is to be Pregnant
F/Fem (FM) or Fuck (FK) Those are all Fem Letter Sounds
All Fem Sounds Letters for all those Weak Concepts
that   Follow   Flow   Fail etc   There is a Lot of that for Her
⊙ Had Sometimes a Dot (the Dowry) in It
Just Another Way of Reinforcing the Same Concept into Her   That She is
a Dot   A Very Small Part of the Real World
A Small Full Moon Circle into Another Larger Empty Circle the O
The Code   says She is Just a Hole   The Whole Language   Secret
Code   is Over It Transforming it   The Code   Never Let go of Letter O
Being Her with All its Mean Components

Lise Rochon

Note that Letter O Now in Any Word is Attached to the Letter E When Next to it   Therefore Never Letting Alone Letter O by Herself
ɸ Sometimes has a Line Crossing It
Reaffirming the Cross between O/Her and the Cross
The Letter T/The Great Fem Curse
Letter O in the Alphabet is an Open Minded Letter
It Can be Easy to Manipulate and Assimilate the O in Different Concepts like Door and Poop
O can be An Element of Surprise
OOH like in Another Pregnancy
O in   The Code   is Known as The Fem Hole   The Cup   The Chalice   and   the Holy Girl (Holy Grail   The Sang /Blood Real Not Royal)
O in   The Code   known as   The Fem Hole   The Cup   The Chalice   the Holy Girl (Holy Grail   The Sang Real Not Royal
In Ancient Hebrew Letter O is the Eye   The Eye of God
O/Fem Hole and D/Pregnant Daughter are Close
When the O/Hole Loins and C/Bleeding Virgin Are D/Pregnant   The I/Male Stick is There
Words with Letter O   Owe   Ho (Prostitute)   Hoe   How   Ow Ooh
Words with Double OOs in it   Poop   Oops   Door

O o
oar: paddle board for rowing
It is Letter R   Her/Ear/Hear/Hair/Err/Heir/Or/Whore/Here/Are/Our/Ere/Air/Ire/Sex

Ocean: All 3 Fem Sounds   O   She   N
O/Fem Hole   She/Shh   In/N/Hen/Ann/Haine/Donkey
(See Fish in The Words Chapter)
Sea is Letter C/See/Young Girl
Sea is All 3 Masculine Letters   The Code   Creating The Sea/C   S/Is/His/Us/Ass/Penis/Hiss/Serpent   E/He   A/All Men Silent Here   But Accentuating the Strength of The Masc Presence
Sea in French is Mer   La Mère   is The Mother
All Water Words are Fem
The See   The Holy See   The/Hole/He/See   D/All/E/C (All/Pregnant Daughters He/See)

The Dam Code The Damn Book

The Secret Society Code Barrier is to Make it Ugly   Few Dare to Look at it and/or Think about It

Odd: 3 Fem Letters Making 2 Fem Sounds Letters
The O/Fem Hole   D/Pregnant
The Double D or the 2 DD s/Pregnants Daughters Implies Plural or All of Them   Along with an O
Pregnancy for Ever for the O/Fem Holes   Is Not what is Making Her Odd
It is   The Code   that Does Hit/It   The Odd One is the One that Does Not Fit (Odd is a Fem Word)
odd: singular different in a strange way   not matching
(Read all 15 Meanings of Odd in Dictionary)
It is Odd How Hard it is to be Odd
Add R/Her/Heir/Whore and She Gets   Odd/Her   Other   Add/Her
Add R/Her and She Gets an Order Whore/D/Her   Herd/Her   Heard/Her   Hurt/Her   etc
Odd Hot and Hat are Close
The Pair (Père is Father in French) and the Odd
The Pair Indicates a Bonding as in the Brotherhood or the Buddies
The Fruit Pear is for Her   The Belly is Large and The Head is Non Existent as in Always Dumb and Pregnant

Of: O/Fem Hole   F/Fem/Fuck
That Word   Of   has Little Meaning by Itself   The Code   Language Uses it as a Connecting Word   She Has No Identity here Either
In   The Code   That Word   Of   is an Important Word   See Fem Letter (See Letter F in The Letters Chapter)
O/Fem Hole is Perforated in V/Fem Sex Active
of: origin   source   cause
Add Another F/Fem/Fuck to Of and She Gets to be Off   From Of Belonging to Something   To Off   To Nothing   When there are More of Her
Turn it Off (T/Urn   The Urn   and   T/Fem Cross)   The Urn has the Same Shape as a Pear

Off: O/Fem Hole   is with   2 FFs/Fem/Fuck
Off is Not Good for Her because Letter F has No Connection to Sex   According to The Code Letter Grid   But

Lise Rochon

F as in Fuck is Used Largely as a Slang Word   It is a Lot for The Fems to Carry   So it Passes Over Her Head says   The Code
Off is Same as Of with More F/Fem/Fuck in it
It is On in Off as being Attached to Something Again Of/Ov   or is   Turned Off from On

Offend: Ov/End
A Big Offence to   The Code   Would Be to End the Ovulation   A Big No says   The Code   so   Off/End
Redundant Meanings here   Off She Is Until the End Offender: Of/End/Her   Off/End/Her   Ov/Vendor   It is All About Undermining/Ending the Power of The Fems

Offensive: Off/N/See/Eve
She Cannot See Herself
Ov/In/Sève (Seve is French for Sap/Semen)
Ov/N/Sieve   She is Off Even if Offensive   She is Off Pronounced with Ov or Of (See Of and Off in Words)

Offer: Of/Her   Off/Her
There is No Offer for Her   She is Off here Also

Office: Off/His   Off/He/Is   Ov/His (His Eggs)
She is Off His Territory
Officer: Off/He/Sire
Here He Got a Promotion to Sir at The Office   She is Still Off hat

Official: Off/She/All   O/Fish/All
Now it is Official She and All Fems are Fishes

Off Shore: Ov/She/Whore
O/Fem Hole   V/Fem Sex Active
All Water Related Words are Fem
The Shore is the Border of a Body of Water
Ov   Shh/She   Her/R/Ear/Hear/Hair/Err/Heir/Or/Whore/Here/Are/Our/Ere/Air/Ire/Sex   She Better Shh about it

Often: OFTN   All 4 Fem Sound Letters

Ov/N   Ov/Ann
Off/N   A/Fin
Ov/Ovulation
T/Fem Cross/Great Curse   N/In/Hen/Virgin/Ann/N/Donkey
Usually a Fairly Loud Letter is Here Not Heard (Herd)
Often   The O/Fem Holes Connect with   T/Fem Cross   and   N/In/Hen/Ann/Haine/Virgin   and Bring Sex Along with   F/Fuck   E/He   is Present but Silent   The Fem is Never Left Alone in   The Code

Oil: L/Sweet Fem Love Light/All/Ail/Hail/Ill/Heel/Hell/Elle/Oil
Holy   Hole/He
Letter L/Sweet Fem Light Knowledge   He/E
The Virgins and the Oil are an Untold Mystery from The Bible
Add T/Fem Cross   She Gets to Toil
Add S/Is/His/Us/Ass/Penis/Hiss/Serpent and He Gets Soil   At the Minute there is Ground (To Plant) the Penis Arrives
Add C/See/ Young Girl and She Gets Coil
coil: to form rings spirals etc   gather or retract in a circular way   a connected series of spirals or rings into which a rope or the as is wound   a single such ring   a noisy disturbance commotion   tumult
She Coils as a Snake and it is Tumult and Disturbance   The Fems in   The Code   can Never do Right   The Right Belongs to The Masc Only says   The Code
It is a C/All for U/All (You/Haul)   It is Annoying   Add a T/Fem Cross and She Gets Anointing (Ann/Hot/Thing)
anoint: to rub or sprinkle or apply an unguent ointment or oily liquid to smear with any liquid
The Virgin and the Oil Dedicated to the Service of That Code God
Note Oil is Part of the Anointing

OK: OK 2 Fem Letters
O/Fem Hole   K/Wounded Fem Warrior
Okay: O/Fem Hole   K/Wounded Fem(Fourth Step)
A/All Men   Y/First Step of Splitting Her Stick (Her I)
Okay has Now Replaced OK in Our Literature
OK Implies that 2 Fems are Together and it Is OK
But No says   The Code   The O/Fem Hole is Now Engaged with K/Broken Fem Warrior into that Lost Battle and it is OK Says   The Code

So Added to OK is the Okay   Adding   A/All Men   and   Y/Wounded Fem   to Such an Important Word in Our Psyche
The First Step is the Y/Wounded Fem Warrior (Oy) The Second Step is the V/Fem Sex Active (Of)   Third is the L/Sweet Fem Light (Hole/All)   The Fourth Step is the K/Broken Fem Warrior (Ok)   Fifth Step is the T/Fem Cross and the Last # Sixth Step is the X/Her Fallen Cross (Her Death) (Ox   The Ox is The Cow)
Y   and   L and   K   and T   and X are All Letters/Symbols of Wounded Fems
Her Sticks Under the Axe (X/Letter is Part of The Wheel)
It Adds for Her Another Step to be OK
hoe and ho: slang for a derogatory term for a woman
A Whore Again by Adding the Letter W/All Fems Sex Active

Old: OLD   All 3 Fem Letters
Hole/Whole   D/Pregnant
Add i/Oiled and Get to Keep The Fems Oiled and Pregnant Until She is Old Hole/D   Whole/D/Pregnant   All/D
O/Fem Hole   L/Sweet Fem Love Light/L/All/Ail/Hail/Ill/Heel/Hell/Elle/ Oil   D/Pregnant
Add H/Secret Code Letter Society and it is on Hold (But Not Over)
Old is a Cornerstone Word in   The Code   Language
Here is a Some Examples
Add B/Boy Holding All Fem Breasts and He Gets Bold
Add C/K/Q and She Gets Cold (Frigid or Sicko)
Add D/T and She Gets Told (To be Pregnant)
Add F/Fem /Fuck and She Gets to Fold Clothes or Fold Her Game in Poker
Add G/Penis Penetration/God Letter and He Gets Gold
Add J/Sheppard Stick and T/Fem Cross and She Gets a Jolt
Add M/Motherhood and She Gets a Mold (Mold is for N/In/Hen/Virgin to become M/Motherhood
Add P/Man Power and He Gets Polled
Add R/Heir/Whore/Err/Her and She Gets Rolled as in Sex and Gone (Rock it and Roll it)
Add S/Penis and He Gets Sold
Add V/and She Gets Volt (It Transforms D/Pregnant Into a T/Fem Cross with a Jolt/Volt)
Add W/All Fems Sex Active and She Gets Wold (Open Country)

The Dam Code The Damn Book

Add X/Fallen Fem Cross and She Gets Sold
Add Z/Sleep On It and She Get Sold for a Second Time (Sleep on it)
The General Message of   Those Code   Words Affiliations
is that The Fems is Cold   She is in a Mold with Her Daughter   She is
Supposed to Fold When She is Told and be in a Wold for Availability
For Him if He is Bold and Hold on to   The Code   He will have Sex with
Many Fem/Dolls and Roll Those Fem Out Jolting Them Selling them and
Sleeping Over it
Here The Work of   The Code   for You

Older: Hole   D/Pregnant   Her
All   D/Pregnant   R/Her/Hair/Are/Here/Hear/Ear/Heir/Whore/Or/Err/Ire/
Ere/Sex
Hold   Her/R
Switch L/Sweet Fem Light for R/Her and She Gets Order (Hoard/
Her   Whore   D/Pregnant   Her)
order: an authoritative direction or instruction command
mandate   proper satisfactory or working condition
The Dictionary has Several Definitions for Order
Orders are also Religious Organizations   As the Free Masons   The
Rosecrucians   are Orders   etc

Olive: OLV   3 Fem Sound Letters
All/Eve   All/V   Hole/He/V
Eve Loins He Opens Making Her a V/Fem Sex Active Then   All/Leave
Olive is a Very Ancient Food (and Word) from the East
I/Love   All/Live
The Olive Branch is a Symbol of Peace
Mont of Olives   Mount/All/Eves

Olympic: Hole/Him/Pick
Greek Mythology has a Lot of   The Code   Symbols
Its Language has Profoundly Influenced All Western Languages We Use
Today

Olympus: Hole/Him/Puss   All/Him/Push
Radical Symbolism here
Add an L to Puss and She Gets a Plus

515

Lise Rochon

Olympus: mythical abode of the Grecians Gods

Om: OM   2 Fem Letters
O/Fem Hole   M/Motherhood
Religious Hindu Mantra
We were All Born from the Universe Regenerating Itself
All of Us Birthed through a Fem
OM the Sound of the Universe is Essentially Fem   It is The Hole as Mother   The Milky Way is Another Example of This Huge Trail Conceptualized by   The Code

Omen: O/Fem Hole   Men
When Her Loins are with Men it is an Omen
Note the Plural Here in Men
omen: phenomenon believed to portend to a future event   prediction
Switch O/Fem Hole with an A/All Men and He gets Amen (A/Man)   Amen is an Important Word Used in Prayer (Pray on Her)

Ominous: O/M/Hen/Us
O/Fems Genitalia   M/Mothers   Hens   with   Us/S/Is/His/Ass/Hiss/Penis/Serpent   That is a Big No from   The Code   for The Fems to be Alone with That Knowledge   so
ominous: threatening   inauspicious
Home   N/Hen/Ann/In/Virgin   E/He   S/Is/His/Us/Ass/Hiss/Serpent/Penis

Omission: O/Fem Hole   Miss   E/He   On
The Fem Hole Misses   and   is Not Included   The Code   says
omission: to leave out

Omit: Home/Hit   See Football/Baseball Rules a Man Sport

On: ON   2 Fem Letters
O/Fem Hole   N/In/Hen/Virgin/In/Haine/Virgin/Donkey
Add E/He and He is Number One   One is Also a Masc Number   It Adds to His Power
Add W/All Fems Sex Active and She Gets Won
Switch O/Hoe/Hole for i/Marriage Act and He Gets In (Literally)
Add an S/is/His/Us/Ass/Hiss/Serpent/Penis and He Gets a Son

The Dam Code The Damn Book

She is On   She is In   She is a Hen

Once: Won/C   On/C
C/See/Young Girl   is On (Won)   Only Once   As She Loses Her Virginity
One/See   On/See   On/Sea
Being on Sea   Bring Her Back to being a Fish
An Ounce is Also Measure of Weight in French

One: Won
Reinforcing   The Code   Concept of the Number 1   Not the IL Letters or the il Letters
Number One is Also a Stick   Check The Letter jJ (Check The Sheppard Stick Ther Letter jJ in The Letter Chapter)

Only: One/Lay   On/Lay   Won/Lay

Ooh: 2 OOs/Fem Holes   and   H/Secret Code Letter
The Code   says it Works   When there are 2 Fem for a Masc   bringing as it often does the Concept of Bigamy and Polygamy
ooh: expression for satisfaction   excitement

Open: Hop/N   Hop/In   Hope/In   Hop/Ann   Hop/Inn   Hope/In   Up/N   Happen
Time to Hop In   N/Hen/Ann/Haine/Virgin
or   V/Fem Sex Active   and She Gets an Oven (A Bun in the Oven   Ov/In   Ovulation is Here)
How Convenient   It is Bound to Happen
Opening: Open/N/In/Hen/Ann/Haine/Virgin   Hop/N/N (Hop All of Them N/In/Hen/Virgins) (See Ops)

Opera: Hop/Her/A   Up/RA   A Sentimental Word   Hop is to Have Sex in Slang

Opium: Hope/He/M
Such a great Word for Hope for Him and Her (as in Motherhood)
Also Unfortunately It Wears the Name of a Highly Addicting Substance for Some   A Sedative   Also Quite an Amazing Pain Killer for it All   It is Under Great Scrutiny in The Unites States Where the Opiates have Killed

517

Lise Rochon

So Many in The Last Few Years Alone   The Greatest Remedy for Cancer Pain   A Great Spirit (So Accessible that Mortals Souls Get Hooked Easily from Their Innate Body and Smoking it Until Reaching It in the Other World (Read The Old History of Opium in China with The British Involved) as in Dead

Too Bad Really for Her   Just as Heroine is a Beautiful Word for a Fem Hero But No   It is Stamped as a Bad Drug Name   No One Uses it   Another Nice Name The Fems have Lost

Opinion: Hop/In/Eon   Hope   He/E   N/Virgin   Eon/He/On
Hopping with N/In/Hen/On/Haine/Virgin for an Eon says   The Code   Hope and Hop for Him to the Virgin for a Very Long Time
Hop   E/He   Ann/In/Hen/Haine/Virgin   He/On
The Masc Hop   N/Ann   the   N/In/Hen/Virgin   for Eon

Opportunity: Hop   Her/R/Ear/Hear/Hair/Err/Heir/Or/Whore/Here/Are/Our/Ere/Air/Ire/Sex   Turn   He/E   T/Fem Cross
Hop/T/Urn/He/T (See Urn in The Words Chapter)
Hop/Her/T/Unity
Hop/Whore/Tune/R/T
The Opportunity here is to Hop Her as an Urn (See Urn In The Words Chapter)
The Code   Tunes Itself

Oppose: Hope/Ose   Hop/Hose
Hope is Always Close or on the Hose
Oser is to Dare in French
Opposing: Hope He is In   Hop He Sing

Option: Hope/She/On
She Has Hopes   But No
Hops She On (Hop is Also Beer   Another Gain for Him)

Opus Dei: Its Symbol is a Cross on Top of an Orb
Orb are Fem and Crosses Too

Oral: Her/R/Ear/Hear/Hair/Err/Heir/Or/Whore/Here/Are/Our/Ere/Air/Ire/Sex   All

The Dam Code The Damn Book

oral: uttered by the mouth   involving the mouth
spoken transmitted by speech
The Code   is Powerful here
Oral Explain that   The Code   is First   Whore/All   Etc
Then Use it Orally With Words
The Mouth Implies Oral/Sex

Orb: Her/R/Ear/Hear/Hair/Err/Heir/Or/Whore/Here/Are/Our/Ere/Air/Ire/
Sex   B/Boy Holding All Breasts of All Fems as   Whore   etc
orb: the eye   to encircle   heavenly bodies   a circle
emblem of royal power   a sphere surmounted by a cross
Secret Hides in the Architecture of the Great Monuments the Ancient
Paintings and Sculptures Often in Plain View
The Breast are the Orbs and the Cross is The Fems Great Curse

Orchard: Whore/She/Hard   Or/She/Heard
Arch/Hard   Where the Apples (Fem Sin) Are
The Code   Says Whores are hard and Can Be Heard in the Orchard (There are Not Many People There to Hear Her)

Ordain: Whore/Den
Quite Appropriate with the Priests Sex Scandals Popping All Over The Place

Order: Whore/D/Her   Horde/Her   Herd/Her   Heard/Her
What Kind of Order Is that   Her being Her/R/Ear/Hear/Hair/Err/Heir/Or/
Whore/Here/Are/Our/Ere/Air/Ire/Sex   A Sick Mind
Ordering: Horde   or   Herd   Her   In   More of The Same

Organ: Whore/Gang   Whore/Gain
The Whore/Her/Heir Gains by having Sex with All Members of the Gang
Sex Organ   or   the Organ as the Musical Instrument with its Many
Pipes (Pipes is Slang for Penisses) Used in Religious Ceremonies and Sport
Events   Both Created by Men

Orgasm: Whore/Her/Heir/Letter R/Are   G/Penis Penetration/God
Letter   Ism
ism: a distinctive doctrine system or practice

Lise Rochon

The Doctrine of the Orgasm here is to have The Fems as a Whore or for Heir through Penis Penetration

Orgy: Whore/Or/Heir   G/Penis Penetration
Here Speaks The Code Clearly About itself

Original: Whore/Her/Heir Letter R   He/E   Gene   All/L/Sweet Fem Love Light/Ail/Ill/Hail/Heel/Hell/Elle/Oil
The Original Sin is No Light Word (See BB in The Words Chapter)

Orator: Whore/Her/Heir/R   Hit/It   Her/Whore/Heir/R
2 Whores/Or/Heirs   with a Hit/It in The Middle   Here is   The Code   Orator From   That Dam Code   Where The Whore or Mother is Also Under a Hit/It
Whore   Hate   Her   The Code   says
Orator is a Cover Word Here

Orb: Whore/Her/Are/Letter R   B/Boy Holding All Breasts Holding All Fems Breasts
orb: a globe bearing a cross
The Fems Lost their Mating Cycles   They Became Whores to Him   And   The Code   Took Advantage of That
The Fems Starting Having Breasts Permanently and Losing Blood Regularly was/Is the Price to pay for The Fems   That was a Long Time Ago
Therefore The Orb Bearing T/Fem Cross or the Great Curse   on the Dome/Breast/Orb Happened

Ordain: Whore/Or/Heir/Her   D/Pregnant   In/N/Hen/Virgin/Ann/Donkey
The Code   Desecrate Real Religion
In a Real Spiritual Religion The Fem and Masc would Practice Love as in Amour (Love) and Ame (The Soul)
But No The Code has put the Soul (the Two of them Under Our Feet   So Our Soul Lives on Dirt
DRT   D/Pregnant   R/Sex   T/Fem Cross
Always the Same Message from   The Dam Code

The Dam Code The Damn Book

Orgy: Whore/Or/Her/Heir G
Her/R/Ear/Hear/Hair/Err/Heir/Or/Whore/Here/Are/Our/Ere/Air/Ire/Sex   G/
Penis Penetration   This is How   The Code   Sees The Fems

Original: Her/R/Ear/Hear/Hair/Err/Heir/Or/Whore/Here/Are/Our/Ere/Air/
Ire/Sex   He/Letter E   Gene   All/Ill/Elle/Hell
From the Beginning of Times   She is the Whore to All
Not the Mother of All says   The Code
Note That The Words Whore and Mother have Almost The Same Letters
Except for W and M Which are The Reverse of Each Other

Ornament: Horn   A/All men   Meant
The Penis is Meant to be A/All Men Ornament
It is   No Shame Here for the Man Compared to The Fem with Her
Constant Alienations

Osiris: O/Sire/Is   Some Strong Word
Osiris: the king and judge of the dead   husband and brother of Isis (Is/Is)
Chagrined I am to see the Name of Isis be put in the Dirt Associated with a
Terrorist Group Name

Other: Adore   Which is an   A/All Men   Door
Odd   Her/R/Ear/Hear/Hair/Err/Heir/Or/Whore/Here/Are/Our/Ere/Air/
Ire/Sex
Add   Her/Whore
Odd/Her   Beating the Odds   Here She Gets Beaten Again
other: additional or further   different in nature or kind   being the
remaining one of two or more
Other is Something in Between   Something that is Not here or does Not
Exist

Ouch: Ouch is 3 Fem Letters that Ends with   H/Secret Code Letter
Society Grid   Not a Good Sign for Her As Usual
O/Fem Hole   She/Shh   How/She   Owe/She
If She Would be Responsible   or   Owner of Herself   or   Her/R/Ear/
Hear/Hair/Err/Heir/Or/Whore/Here/Are/Our/Ere/Air/Ire/Sex
That is a Big No from the Code   So   Ouch to Her

521

Our: Hour   2 RRs/Her/Whore/Or/Heir/Err/Sex   As in All of The Fems
Take U/Uterus Away and Get Or (Which is Gold In French)   or   One or
The Other in English
The Code is Adamant About keeping The Fems as Possession/Object (See
Hour in The Clock Chapter)

Out: Out is Made of 3 Fem Letters
O/Fem Hole   U/You/Ovulating   T/Great Curse/Fem Cross
Hot   How/To
From O/Whole/Hole   to   You/U/You/Ovulating   to   T/Fem Cross
How   The Code   Create The Fems Cross and Gets Out
Outfit: Hot/Fit   The Fem has to Look Hot or Sexy Anyway says

Outlook: Out/Look   Hot/Luck
Look Out
Lots of Enthusiasm and Hope Here Towards The Outside Look for
Her   Such as Fashion   or   The Beauty of Youth

Oval: Ov/All   Ovulate All of Them   L/Sweet Fem Love Light/All/Ail/Ill/
Hail/Heel/Hell/Elle/Oil
Ovulation Time is Not Reliable   A Fem Can be Pregnant
Anytime   During Her Period Also
Oval is in an Egg Shape
Of/All   Off/All   The Code   says Even When Ovulating She is Off
Ovulate All and Be Off

Oval Office   Ov/All   Of/His

Ovation: Ov/Hat/He/On   Ov/A/Shun   Ov/A/She/On
The Hat is The Word for   The Secret in The Secret Art Code Societies

Over: Ov/Her   Of/Her   Off/Her   Hoe/V/Her   O/V/R
Ov/Ovulation   Her/R/Ear/Hear/Hair/Err/Heir/Or/Whore/Here/Are/Our/
Ere/Air/Ire/Sex
Switch O/Fem Hole for E/He and Gets   Ever Eve/R   V/Fem Sex
Active   and   R/Her/Whore/Heir/Sex
In Ever V is Surrounded by   2 EEs/He
O/Fem Hole Starts a Word It Cannot be Good for   The Code so

It is Over Already
There Are about 500 Words Put All Together After the Over Word
It is Over Her Too   Over (Of/Her)   Ov/Her) is Over Used
Overcome: Ov/Her   Come
When Her Ovulation Comes   The Code   is Victorious
overcome: to be victorious

Overbearing: Over/Bear/In   Over/Bear/Ring
It is Over for Her   The Bear is in Her and the Ring (See Ring) is on Her
overbearing: domineering   dictatorial   rude   arrogant

Overlay: Ov   Her/R/Ear/Hear/Hair/Err/Heir/Or/Whore/Here/Are/Our/Ere/Air/Ire/Sex   Lay
The Whore/Or/Heir Ovulates and She is Ready to have Sex
Ov/Her/Lay   She Ovulates and it is Her Lay Time
Over/Lay
overlay: to lay or place one thing over another   to cover
How Convenient says   The Code
over: above in a place or position
Ov/Her   Off/Her/Lay

Overturn: Ov (Egg)   Her/R/Ear/Hear/Hair/Err/Heir/Or/Whore/Here/Are/Our/Ere/Air/Ire/Sex   T/Fem Cross   Urn
The Egg is in Front of R/Her as in Sex   with   T/Fem Cross   That would be a Big No from The Code   so
overturn: to destroy the power of   to defeat

Overwhelm: Ov   Her/R/Ear/Hear/Hair/Err/Heir/Or/Whore/Here/Are/Our/Ere/Air/Ire/Sex   Well/Wheel   M/Motherhood
Mother is Well and Overwhelmed When She Ovulates
The Multiples Faces of   The Code   Makes Her Stay on That Wheel of time
Overwhelming: Ov   Her   Wheel   M/Motherhood   In/N/In/Hen/Virgin/In/Virgin   Here The Virgin is There Too

Ovo: 3 Fem Letters
Ovo is from the beginning   Literally from the Egg

Lise Rochon

When All O/Fem Holes/Loins are V/Fem Sex Opened and having Sex there are Eggs (Pregnancies) Made by those Chicks (Fem)

Ovule: Ov/All   Of/U/All   Off/U/Al
Ovulate   Ov/You/Late
Being Late on Her Period (Pair the Odds) is a Worrying Sign for The Fems
Ovulation: Ov   You   Lay   She/On or Eon
Ov/U/All/She/On
All Fems Discharging Eggs for an Eon
Ov is the Egg in the Making

Ow: O/Fem Hole   W/All Fems Sex Active
All Fems Holes are for Sex says   The Code   or
ow: interjection (used especially as an expression of intense or sudden pain)

Owe: O/Fem Hole is Own   Bottom Line
So No ID Again Here for Her and the Hoe is Close as Usual
It is Ow (Pain) when E/He Goes Missing from Owe   Leaving the 2 Fem Letters in Pain
Add N/In/Hen/Virgin/Ann/Donkey to Ow and She Gets Own
Owe   O/Fem Hole   W/All Fems Sex Active   E/He
He Owns All Fems Holes
She O/Owe That Just Because She has The Loins
She/Owe is Only is Only a Show says   The Code   So It Does Not Exist in Reality

Owl: O/All   Owe/All
Owl: a solemn person

Own: ON   2 Fem Sound Letters
O/Fem Hole   W/All Fems Sex Active   N/Hen/In/Ann/Donkey   Owe/N
Owner: Own/Her   On/Her
O/N/R   O/Fem Hole   N/Ann/N/In/Hen/Virgin/Donkey
Add R/Her/Hair/Are/Here/Hear/Ear/Whore/Or/Err/Sex and She Gets Horn/Her
Honor is the Cover Word Here
As it is an Honor to Her to be Owned

The Dam Code The Damn Book

Oz: Title of a Giant Movie for Adults and Children
O/Fem Hole   and   Z/Sleep on it   would be the Message here from   The Code   to Her

P   p
Intro
Letter P is a Strong Positive Letter in   The Code
P is a Letter of Power   P is Big   It can Over Impose itself being Pompous
Letter P Configuration is a Mix of Masc and Fem Symbols
P is Pi in Greek Astrology The One that Divides itself Endlessly as being The Letter of The Father   The Ruler   The Boss   The Power (Pow/Her   as in to End Her)
In Letter P/Man Power   The Stick/Penis Power is Joined with an Open Circle   Him is Being the Owner of Her Loins/Circle/Dot/Fem Hole Now   The Stick is Carrying it
Letter B has Shed the Mother Breasts in P Adulthood and has Become an Independent Adult in P/Man Power with Another Fem/Circle Attached to Him
The Fem has Sex with Him/P in   R/Sex
Any Circle Letter by Itself Small or Big Cap is Fem in   The Code   She is Now Carried as a Package   As a Bag (Bag Rag Nag Hag) at the End of a Stick (See The Card The Fool in The Tarot Cards)
P/Man Power   B/Boy Holding All Fem Breasts   and   R/Her/Sex   are Related
P and R are a Development of Each Other   When P/Man Power Become the R/Sex Act   His Penis is Out
It Is When She Let Go of Her Last ½ Stick after Being K/Wounded Fem Warrior   The o becomes Part of R After She has been Fighting in K Not to Get There
In Letters bpdqBP   The Masculine Stick in those Letters Holds Different Parts/Directions of Her
In Small b it Shows Letter o Held in the Bottom Part of the Stick and it Touches the Writing Line or the Ground
Letter b (Baby) is the Reflection of Letter d/Pregnant
Small p Holds o from Under the Line/The Subconscious/What is Hidden to Her Not to Him
In Small d the Stick is Holding o from the Front of the Stick as in She is Pregnant   It is a Big Hold

Big B (BB Baby Boy) is Holding Her Opened Breasts Towards Him
In Letter P o is Held at the Top by the Stick
Pope is the Closest with   2 PPs   with   O/Fem Hole   in the Middle   A Pope is a Man Sworn to Chastity
The Code   Hides in Words as Poop and Pope   To Make The General Population Looks Away Fast Especially The Fems from Those   There are Many More   Those Are Big Cover Words   Those are Insulting to People of those Religions
A long Time ago Her Stick/Power was Intact   It is was Her Magic Wand from the Old Legends
Now Her Stick in   The Code   Goes From   I/I   to Y/Why   Then to   V/ Fem Sex Active   Then to   L/Sweet Fem Love Light/All/Ail/Ill/Hail/Heel/Hell/Elle/Oil   Then to K/Wounded Fem Warrior   Then to   t/T/Fem Cross   Ending   in X/Fem Fallen Cross
Our Fem Curse Starts with the Age of Adam and Eve (A/Damn   and   V/Sex Active Fem)
In the Roman Numbers   The Same Code   is Explained With Numbers
She Remains Intact as a Normal Child Until the Age of 3
1 11 111   Then   The Code   Kicks in in 1V (She Starts being Ripped at 4 and by Age 6   The Boy is in Front of Her in V1 (Read More in The Roman Numbers Chapter)
Words in P are Pee   Pay   Pea   Too Nice Words
Words with Double PPs are Poop Pop (Pop the Girl)   Papa   Pope

P   p
Pa: P/Man Power   A/All Men
Papa   the Mental Chain is on from the Repetition of Pa/Pa   Adding Strength to the Concept

Pact: P/Man Power   Act
When a Man Act   No Fem here

Pad: P/Man Power   Add
Pad Embrace Other Definitions as Being   On the Pad   a Fem Humiliation
Key Pad is where you Type the Letters and Symbols of a Code
Pad is a Cover Word here

Paddle: Pad   L/Sweet Fem Love Light/All/Ail/Ill/Hail/Heel/Hell/Elle/Oil
P/Add/All
To Get the Paddle is   To be Beaten With

Pain: PN
P/Man Power   A/All Men   i/Marriage Act   N/In/Hen/Ann/Virgin
All Men   Sex Union   Virgin
Take A/All Men Away and Get a Pin (A Big Loss)
Add S/Penis and Guess what comes Out of that Box Pain/Is   Penis
Take N/In/Hen/Virgin Away and Get Pay

Pair: PR
P/Man Power   Her/R/Ear/Hear/Hair/Err/Heir/Or/Whore/Here/Are/Our/
Ere/Air/Ire/Sex
P/Heir   P/Here   P/Air   PR   Power
No Fem here except for Her as R/Whore/Heir/Her
Père is Father in French
Pairing: Père/In   More Power to Him

Pale: PL   P/Man Power   is Alone with   L/Sweet Fem Light   He is
Uncomfortable
Pale is a cover Word So He gets a P/Ale (Beer)
Pall   P/All   A Pall is a Friend to Him

Pan: PN
P/Man Power   A/All Men   N/In/Hen/Ann/Virgin
pan: a receptacle   a container
Chalice/Uterus Seem Close Enough
Pan is the God of fertility and wilderness
Pan is the Little Messenger of Love
He Carries Bow and Arrows and   Resembles Strangely to Satan the Goat
or the Ram
Add i/Marriage Act and She Gets Pain
Pain   Pain/Is   Penis   PNS

Pang: PNG
pang :   sudden sharp spasm of pain

Lise Rochon

Pain Follows When   P/Man Power   and   N/Hen/Ann/Virgin/In   are Together   With   G/Penis Penetration
Add T/Fem Cross When P/Man Power and T/Fem Cross Meet   Now   They Are (Heir/Whore/Her)   Panting
Pan/T/In   Panty/N
pant: to breathe hard and quickly
As in Having Sex
Add Her/R/Ear/Hear/Hair/Err/Heir/Or/Whore/Here/Are/Our/Ere/Air/Ire/Sex   and She Gets a Panther   Panther is a Sex Fem Symbol   Pant/Her

Pantie: Pant/He
panty: fem underwear
Panties: Pant/Is   Pant/His
Switch N/In/Hen/Virgin for R/Her/Hair/Are/Here/Hear/Ear/Whore/Or/Err/Sex and She Gets a Party (Yes Says The Code a Virgin with Panties and a Man Panting is The Game of The Code)
pansy: a weak effeminate often cowardly man
In The Code Sound World Anything Fem is Disgraced
Panties   Pansies
Pansies: the flower of the violet
Violet is a Fem Name   Violet is the Color of God
When T/Fem Cross become S/Penis   Or   Vice Versa Nothing Make Sense   The Code has it That Way   Her Panties are Not Going to Go for Very Long

Pantyhose: Pant/He/Hose
Hose is Slang for Penis
The Masc in   The Code   is Always There Even in Her Pantyhose
Ose is to Dare in French
Hose/Os/Us
To Hose is to Water (Fem)
Switch N/In/Hen/Ann/Virgin for Her/R/Ear/Hear/Hair/Err/Heir/Or/Whore/Here/Are/Our/Ere/Air/Ire/Sex   and She Gets a Party (Part/He)
Then He Needs to Go   or   Ne Needs to Part with Her
A Patsy is Close by

Papa: 2 PPs/Men Power   2 AAs/All Men
All Masc Letters

Plural Reinforce the Idea of Masc in Ultimate Power

Parable: Père/A/Bowl

Paradise: Pair   A/All Men   Dice
Par/Add/Ice
par: equality in value
Ice: I/See   Eye/See   I/Letter C   I/i Being the Sex Act
The Eye that Sees is on Ice   That Would be Her
Per/A/Dice   It is Always a Throw of Dice When Trying to Seduce a Fem   So She can Believe in Paradise for Herself for a Few Moments

Paramount: Pair/A/Mount
To Mount with a 2 instead of 1
Par/A/Mount   Par/Amount
par: equality in value
To Mount is a Big Word (Mount a Fem   and   Her Time of the Month) in the Language Code Grid   To Mount Two is Way Bigger   Paramount Makes Sure there is Abundance in that Section
paramount: supreme   prominent   above   others in rank or authority
Paramount is an American Film Making Industry   They Make Movies
More Intelligent Fem Heroes are Needed for The Fems in Hollywood Movies

Parent: PRNT
Pair/Aint   Père/Aint   Pair/Hunt   P/Err/Ant
Nothing Positive for The Fems Here or as a Parent
Père is Father in French and here as a Parent it Negates its Own Fatherhood
Note that there is No M/Motherhood or L/Sweet Fem Light in the Word Parent
Parent is to Pair   N/In/Hen/Ann/Virgin   and   T/Fem Cross with Her/R/Ear/Hear/Hair/Err/Heir/Or/Whore/Here/Are/Our/Ere/Air/Ire/Sex Says The Code

Paris: Père/Is   Pair/His
Père is Father in French   Here He Is Making a Pair in Paris   The Dreamy World of the French Language

Lise Rochon

For Example here it Implies 2 with Pair/Père
Is it 2 Fem for 1 Masc   or   More Fantasies
The French are Known for their Frolicking
(See La Putain and Bitch in The Words Chapter)

Part: P/Man Power   Art
Art is the Secret Societies Secret Word in Action to This Day   It All Belong to the Man Power says   The Code
part: to separate
And it Separates Its Knowledge from The Fems

Partner: Part   N/In/Hen/Ann/Virgin/Donkey   Her/R/Ear/Hear/Hair/Err/Heir/Or/Whore/Here/Are/Our/Ere/Air/Ire/Sex
The Code   Separates Itself from The Fems
Par/T/N/R
To Bring to Par 2 Fem Types (Fem Cross   and   N/In/Hen/Ann/Virgin) with   Her/R/Ear/Hear/Hair/Err/Heir/Or/Whore/Here/Are/Our/Ere/Air/Ire/Sex

Pass: P/Ass
pass: making a move to   to move past by
P/Man Power   A/All Men   2 SSs/Is/His/Us/Ass/Hiss/Serpents/Penises
PSSSS   Add a T and it Becomes Psst to Her
The More   S/Is/His/Ass/Us/Hiss/Penis/Serpent
the Better When Making a Pass says   The Code

Passerby: P/Man Power   2SSs/Ass/S/Is/His/Us/Hiss/Penisses/Serpents   Her/R/Ear/Hear/Hair/Err/Heir/Or/Whore/Here/Are/Our/Ere/Air/Ire/Sex   Buy
P/Man Power Gets a Pass to Buy Sex (Her)   As a Passerby

Passion: P/Man Power   Ass/S/Is/His/Us/Hiss/Penis/Serpent   N/In/Hen/Ann/Virgin
P/Man Power is Making a Pass to the N/Virgin with His S/Penis   He Passes   He/On   or   Eon
Passionate: Pass   She   On   Hit/Hate/Hat/Hot/Ate/8
P/Man Power   Ass/S/Is/His/Us/Ass/Hiss/Penis/Serpent   On   It

The Dam Code The Damn Book

The Passion is an important Part/Chapter of the Gospel in the Bible   But in Fact Jesus Death Just Took a Few Words
It is Called a Passion because it Means to Suffer in Greek

Past: PST
P/Male Power   S/Penis   T/Fem Cross/Great Curse
That   Is a Complete Image of Our Past According to   The Code
P/Ass/T   Pass/T   A Piece of Ass   And it is All in The Past   so   Few Care
Passé is Past in French
Passé   Puss   Pussy   Pushy   Bossy   Possy

Pastel: Past/Hell
P/Ass/Tell   Past/Elle   Past/Ill
Past   L/Sweet Fem Love Light/All/Ail/Ill/Hail/Heel/Hell/Elle/Oil
Past/Hill
All this Served in Soft Colors to Her Gulp it All   That The/Her Hell   is in the Past

Pasture: Past/Her
A Pass   To   Her/R/Ear/Hear/Hair/Err/Heir/Or/Whore/Here/Are/Our/Ere/Air/Ire/Sex
The Pastor is Close to the Care of Those Fem Sheeps
Pastoral   Past/Her/All   Past   R/Her/Hair/Are/Here/Hear/Ear/Whore/Or/Err/Sex/All
pastoral: having the simplicity charm serenity or other characteristics generally attributed to rural areas
The Code   makes itself Charming to Get What it Wants
Here Either   She is in the Past   or   She is having a Pass Made to Her

Pattern: Pat/Urn   P/At/Earn
An Urn Has the Shape of a Fem says   The Code
An Urn Keeps Wine (Her Blood Loss Symbol) and Food
Her responsibility
Amphora and Urns have been with Us for at Least 6000 years   All Over Eurasia

Pattern: Pat/Pet/Pit/Put/Pot   Urn

Lise Rochon

The Pattern for The Fems says   The Code   is to Pat and/or be a Pet and Put on that Pot for Dinner
(See Urn Old Fem Symbol in The Words Chapter)

Pauper: Pope/Her
That Could Be a Big Good Word of Power for Her
But it is a Big No from   The Code   so
pauper: a person without any means of support specially   a destitute person who depends on aid from public welfare funds or charity   a very poor person
Poop/Her   Pop/Her   etc
Take U/You/Ovulating Out and Get a Paper   They Write/Rite/Wrote/Road/Rode/etc   The Code   on it
So Innocent of a Word
Paper would be the Cover Word here
Toilet   Toy/Let   Pap/Her   She is Back as Bathroom

Pause: P/Hose
A Pose for His Hose   P as in Peeing
P/Us   Puss as Old Slang for The Fem Sex
Switch P for N/Hen/Ann/Virgin and She Gets a Nose (Watch Out to Her says The Code)

Paw: P/Man Power   A/All Men   W/All Fems Sex Active
The Power (Pow/Her) is in All Men with All V/Fem Sex Active as an Animal Hand Shape
2 Men for a Fem here   She is Under The Paw/Thumb of   The Code   Paws have Claws

Pawn: P/Man Power   Ann/N/Hen/Ann/Donkey/Virgin
pawn: to deposit as security   as to money borrowed   to pledge   stake   risk   especially with a pawnbroker
Pan   Pan/Cakes   P   Ann   C   Ache   Always Hurting The Girl   but   Hiding is   The Code   here Behind Pawn   Which is Her Signature

Pay: P/Hey
hey: to call for attention   greetings

P/Man Power is Calling for Attention
hay: animal food
Pay Attention to   P/Man Power   When He Calls to Pay
Add an Her/R/Ear/Hear/Hair/Err/Heir/Or/Whore/Here/Are/Our/Ere/Air/Ire/
Sex   and She Gets to Prey which is to Pray   That is on Her Knees

Pea: Letter P/Man Power
Pee   Pea/Nut   The Pea (Him) and the Nut (Her)
The Code   can Make Itself Very Little   As a Pea

Peach: P/Man Power   Each
Peach is Slang for a Delicious Fruit
The Bulbous Crack on a Peach Remember Us of The Fems Genitals/
Butt   A Peach Skin
P/Man Power   His/Is   She/Shh
That would Imply She is His and has to Remain Silent

Pearls: Powerless
Pearls are a Great Fem Favorite
Pearl is a Fem Name
P/Man Power   Hurls
Gem   GM   When G/Penis Penetration is With Motherhood   The
Code   Goals are seen

Peddler: Pad   L/Sweet Fem Love Light/All/Ail/Ill/Hail/Heel/Hell/Elle/
Oil   Her/R/Ear/Hear/Hair/Err/Heir/Or/Whore/Here/Are/Our/Ere/Air/
Ire/Sex
Paddle/Her   She Must keep on Paddling to Keep That Ship Going

Pee: The Letter P/Man Power   Pee is All 3 Masc Letters
P/Man Power   2 EEs/He   Twice Amplify the E/Man
There are No Fem Letters in to Pee   The Code   says The Fems do
Not Pee
According to Facts here the Masc Can and Will Pee anywhere He Wants by
a Tree or Not   But The Fems Has to Go and Hide Behind a Bush if She Has
to Pee
Peeing: P/Man Power   2 NNs/In/Hen/Ann/Virgin
Pin

Lise Rochon

The Man Power Owns the Virgin in Peeing says   The Code

Peer: P/Man Power   Here/Letter R/Her/Ear/Hear/Hair/Err/Heir/Or/Whore/Are/Our/Ere/Air/Ire/Sex
There is No Fem Letter in Peer   Except for The Sex Letter R   (The Combat Between the Half Masc and the Half Fem Letter)
The Word Peer Would Not Exist Without Her   Here In Peer
peer: equal worth or quality

Pelvis: Pal   V/Fem Sex Active   His/Is/Letter S/Penis/Serpent
P/Help/His   P/Hell/His
It is All His Says The Code
Say Pelvis and Penis is Next Door

Penis: P/Man Power   E/He   N/In/Hen/Ann/Virgin   i/Marriage Act   S/Is/His/Us/Ass/Hiss/Serpent/Penis   or   Plural
Pen/Is
Pain/Is   Because of Circumcision
Pen Is the Cover Word Here

Penniless: Penis/Less
Penny is a Fem Name and She is Without Money

Pens: Penis   Pain/Is
Men Have Them in Their Hands Many Times a Day   We Write (Rite) with them (Damn)
Anything Sharp or Long in a Tube Form Has been Taken Already by the Masc Language Code
P/In   P/Man Power   Is   In/N/Hen/Virgin/Ann/Donkey
Switch E/He for A/All Men and He Gets Pan (The Infamous God Code Pan
She Cooks with a Pan Every Day
pen: a penitentiary

Penetrate: P/In/He/Trade   Pen/A/Trait   P/N/He/Treat
When He has Penetrated   The Code   Says it is Time for a Change   More of The Rock Them and Roll Them Philosophy

Pensive: Pants/Eve

The Dam Code The Damn Book

Her Pants Makes a Man Pensive
He is Panting When With V/Fem Sex Active
Pensive is a Newer Word
P/Ants/Eve   The Fems are Never Left Alone in Peace   Someone has Ants in Their Pants for Someone

People: Peep/Hole   More of the Same for Her
Pee/Pall (Always are Men Together in Pying Together)
The P/Man   The O/Open Loins   That Creates the Peep/Hole says   The Code
With the Catholic Church Fighting the Old Ways Calling the Fems Pagans All the Way to Find Them in England
The Movie The Mists of Avalon 2001 with Angelica Houston and with Juliana Margulies and Many More is to Get Inspired By   It is the Story Where King Arthur Enters the Story with His Half Sister Morgaine   His Aunt Viviane   His Wife Gwenwyfar and The Lady of the Lake   Him Being the Son of Igraine (A/Grain)   One of The Rare Fem Stories filmed

Père: Père is Father in French
Just as Dead/Dad/Père is Not a Strong Word for its Real Importance in Life
Switch P/Man Power for F/Fem/Fuck and She Gets Fire
Pyr: fire   heat   a variant of pyro
Poor   Pore   Pure   Per   Pair   Peer   Parr (A Young Salmon (See Holy Grail)   Pear   Peur (Fear in French)   Purr   Pare (to cut off ends   to diminish or reduce)   No Interest here for Her   Either it is Small or Scary or Poor
Pierre is Peter Christ Disciple   The Rock

Perceive: Pierce/Eve
To Pierce Eve is a Very Important Piece of   The Code   How to Pierce the O into U   then V   then   W   Another Story to Add for Her Stick Letter I Split into Y V L K T and X
In W The Fems are All the Same   In X The Fems are All Dead
Per/Sieve
per: for each   for every
Pair/Per   See   Eve
The Code   Does Not Allow Eve to See or be Seen so
sieve: to separate or remove

Her Perception has been Removed   The Code   Plan
Père/Pair   See/C/See/Young Girl   Eve/Letter V/Fem Sex Active

Perfect: Père/Fact   Purr/Fact
Père is Father in French   Fatherhood is Perfect   It is a Fact says   The Code
When The Fem Purr/Per/Her (Cat is Fem)   She is Perfect It is a Fact says   The Code   But No   A Pere (Masc) Only can Purr

Perhaps: Père/Per/Purr   Haps
hap: luck   chance   an occurrence
Switch A/All Men for O/Fem Hole and She Gets a Hop (Sex)
With A/All Men He is in His Locked Luck Pun Intended
hap: to cover up   a covering of any kind
The Code is Multi Dimensional and Covers Up for Itself

Perform: Pair/Form
Two Fems for One Masc is the Theme in   The Code
In The Shape of a Père/Form

Period: Pair/He/Odd   Per/Rod   Père/He/Add
odd: strange   bizarre   different
Rod is Slang for Penis
Père is Father in French
Father/He/Odd
The Fems Period is what   The Code   Called the Menstrual (Men/Through/All) Cycle
If the Cycle Would Follow the Moon   The Fems Would All Have it Together   Instead the Fem Follows Unconsciously the Pheromones
The Reality is that the Fem Loses an Incredible Amount of Blood in th Her Lifetime and that Changes Her Life   Want It or Not   It Weakens Her Making Susceptible to Other Weakening Influences
The Fem Do not Develop the Same From Puberty as the Masc Boys do   The Masc Develop Normally in Strength and Density as The All Other Primates
The Fem Develops with a Hormone Imbalance and She does Not Know it   Since then The Fem Started to Lose Blood on a Regular Basis   A Long Time Ago

The Dam Code The Damn Book

Humans Evolution is on a Fast Tract since Then
Not Long Ago The Fems was Not Allowed to Have Friends
Only the Husband and Children to Focus (Fuck/Us) On
Obedience was the Center of Her Attention
In   The Code   The Period Comes After The Sentence
On top of the Small Cap i as in i/Marriage Act is Her and Her Period
It is the Dot at the End of a Sentence
A Sentence is also a Punishment for a Crime
But The .Com of the Internet is the Ultimate Cover Word here   It Is
Another Symbol for When The Period Come or He Comes
Period is the Cover Word Here
We Use it Often When Writing or Dictating as All Is Normal Says The Code

Permission: Per/Miss/He/On
She Misses On as He Goes On
Pair/Mess/He/On   Pire/M/Is/On   Père/Miss/On
Père is Father in French
per: for each   for every   by means of
Pire Means Worst in French

Permit: Pair/Met   Père/Meet   P/Her/Mate

Person: Per/Son   Per/Sun
Every Man is a Sun in   The Code
The Fem is Not Represented Here at All as an Individual
Per is P/Man Power and Her/R/Ear/Hear/Hair/Err/Heir/Or/Whore/Here/Are/
Our/Ere/Air/Ire/Sex

Personal: Per/Son/All   To One and All   All Sons
She is Without a Chance as a Fem
Check Words Starting with or Ending with Son

Pursue: Per   S/Is/His/Ass/Us/Hiss/Penis/Serpent
 You
Père   S/His/Us/Penis   You/U
P/Man Power   Her/R/Ear/Hear/Hair/Err/Heir/Or/Whore/Here/Are/Our/
Ere/Air/Ire/Sex   S/His/Penis   U/Ovulation   Ovulation is the Object of
The Pursuit here

Pervasive: Per   Vase   Eve
As Long as Eve Keep on being the Vase/Chalice for the Loss of Blood
says   The Code   It is
pervasive: spread throughout

Pervert: Per   V/Fem Sex Active   Hurt
per: for each   for every
For Every V/Fem Sex Active is a Fem Hurt in the Hands of a Pervert
says   The Code
Purr/V/Hurt
P (Pee)   Her   V   Hurt
P   Her/whore/Her/Letter R   V   Her   T/Fem Cross
Note here there are 2 Her/R/Ear/Hear/Hair/Err/Heir/Or/Whore/Here/Are/
Our/Ere/Air/Ire/Sex   and 2 EEs/He   in Pervert as in to Enhances its
Meaning
The Code Programming Starts at Birth
We Learn the Language of Our Parents   Our Society
That Language Code that Keeps Us in Misery
Add a T/Fem Cross to Misery it Is Mystery (Miss/T/Ray)
The Holy (Hole/He) Mysteries
Miss/T/Her/He Mist/Her/He   Sweet Word for this Unbearable Burden
Perversity: Per   Verse   Cite   He

Pfft: P/Man Power   to   2 FFs/All Fems/Fuck   Ending in the   T/Fem
Cross   For The Fems it is About Losing All Her Powers
Going Smaller and Emptier to End up with a Curse
Is No big Deal for   The Code so
pfft: dying out or fizzling out

Phallus: Fall/Us   Fell/Us
It is All About Sex In   That Code   Although In a Different Way We Would
Imagine   In a Horrible Way   It is

Phenomenon: FNMN   All 4 Fem Sound Letters
Fen/On/Him/On   F/Hen/Men/On   Fin/On/Homme/On   F/On/Men/
On   F/In/He/On

The Dam Code The Damn Book

Note here that there are 2NNs/Virgin/Hen/Ann Surrounding Motherhood in Phenomenon   With F/Fem/Fuck in Front   As it is a Celebration of Motherhood as a Phenomenon and She Falls for it Again
After He Was In Her   He Moves On says   The Code
fen: low land covered wholly or partially with water   boggy land   a marsh
Not Much for Her to be There
phenomenon: a fact observable   a remarkable person

Phew: Few
phew: used as an exclamation to express disgust   exhaustion surprise impatience relief
A Pew is a Seat in a Church

Phony: FNE
Fun/He   Phone/He   Fan/He
F/Fem/Fuck   is with   N/Hen/Virgin/In/Donkey   and   E/He   it can get Phony Fast
phony: fake

Phrase: Fray/SS   Free/Ass   F/Rays
fray: to frighten   to dispute
The F Rays (If Any) are Meant to Frighten or Dispute   says   The Code
Phrases: F/Fem/Fuck   Raise   S/Is/His/Ass/Us/Hiss/Penis/Serpent
The Fems is Meant to Raise the Penis says   The Code
Frays

Pickle: Pick/All
Pick   L/Sweet Fem Love Light/All/Ail/Ill/Hail/Heel/Hell/Elle/Oil
Pickle is Slang for Penis

Pie: P/Man Power   High/I/Eye
Pi is Where P/Man Power is High
Pi Has a Fem Shape ∞ (The Breast Shape)
It Is the Number Eight (See 8 in The Numbers Chapter) Lying Down   So Small Few Notice it
How Appropriate Says The Code

Lise Rochon

Pi: the 16 Letter in the Greek Alphabet   a consonant transliterated as *p*
(Math) a transcendental number fundamental to mathematics that is the ration of the circumference of a circle to its diameter. Approximate value 3.141 592 symbol Π
Here Again as We all Know The Circle is a Fem Symbol but here The Masc Owns it says   The Code
The Pie Eating is the Cover Word here   So Many Love Pies   It Remind Them of Their Moms   Etc

Pig: Negative Term for a Masc with Bad Manners
P/Man Power   i/Marriage Act   G/Penis Penetration
The Masc Uses Force to Penetrate as a Pig
Pigskin is a Lovely Type of Fabric Used for Ball Gown and Theater   Why Does it have such a Unappealing Name
The Name Dishonor Her Taste

Pill: P/Man Power   L/Sweet Fem Love Light/All/Ail/Ill/Hail/Heel/Hell/Elle/Oil
pill: to rub or plunger
Here is the Masc Education Received from   The Code   in Action   This is what Happens When   P/Man   is with L/Elle
Switch I for U/Uterus and She Gets a Pull (When Sex is Involved She Gets Help)
Switch i for Letter A and He Gets a Pall
Switch I for O/Fem Hole and She Gets a Pole/Poll (Male Sex Organ)

Pillar: Pill/Her
pillar: building support or monument
pill: to rub   to plunger   extortion   something repugnant
The Pillar of   The Code   is to Pill Her

Pillow: Pill/O   To Pill the O
A Pillow is Usually a Comfortable Place   But No Says   The Code   She will be Pilled There Too   And She had/Has
P/Man Power   Ill/Hell/Elle/Ail   O/Fem Hole
And It Happens Through Her O/Fem Hole
Pillow is the Cover Word here

540

The Dam Code The Damn Book

Pimp: P/M/P
M/Motherhood   Surrendered by   2 PPs/Man Powers   The Code   Says it is Just Another Case of Rape

Pin: PN   P/Man Power   In/Letter N/Hen/Ann/Donkey
P/Man Power   is with   N/In/Hen/Virgin
It is a Very Small Event Indeed for The Masc Says   The Code
Walking on Pins   How Many Angels on a Pin

Pink: P/Man Power   Ink
Pink is   The Code   Fem Favorite Color   Why Is that   Pink is the Color of Her Diluted Blood
Same for Purple the Color of Blue   and   Blood Red   Together   Purple is the Color of Grief   Purple is Also The Color of God   Violet   As We are Told in Some Esoteric Schools

Pipe: 2 PPs/Men Powers (as in All or Plural)   One Is With   i/Marriage Act   The Other is with the Other Masc The   E/He
Put that in Your Pipe   That Idea of Homosexuality if it does Not Work with the   i/Marriage Act with the Dot (The Fem) in the First Place   it could Work with E/He Secondary   The Code   says
The Pipe has Always been an Important Instrument for The Masc   Smoking a Pipe for Concluding Business or Contracts or Sharing After Dinner Pleasures
Remember A Pipe is Magical and Always Wants More
Peep   Pee/P
Pipe is an Entirely Masculine Word that Includes i/Marriage Act with The Dot Because it Cannot live Without it (As in The Fem Evidently)

Pyramid: The Pyramid is Where Starts the Letter A Alpha (Also an Ox (See Taurus and Tau) in   The Code
The Eye in the Pyramid Alpha is the Real God Letter J the Stick of the Sheppard (See Sheppard in The Words Chapter) the Eye   the   I/High/Hi   Just as Hello is for Hell   O/Fem Hole

Piss: P/Man Power   2 SSs/Is His/Hiss/His/Serpent/Penis (as in Plural or All of Them)
Switch P for M/Motherhood and She Gets to Miss

541

Lise Rochon

There are No Fem Letter in Piss
What   The Code   Thinks of Peace   It Pisses on it   The Dam Code

Pith: P/It   P/Hit
pith: the core of the matter
The Core of The Matter is   P/Man Power   With i/Marriage Act   and   T/Fem Cross   It is it Hit It

Pity: PT   P/Man Power   T/Fem Cross
P   being Alone with   T   That Puts Him in the Pit   Pit/He   P/It/He   P/Hit/He   He is in the Pit   He Has Pity
There Is/Was No Pity for Her from   The Code
It is Against   The Code   of   T/Fem Cross   being or Wanting the   P/Man Power   Especially in the Shape of Her Menstrual Cycle/The Great Curse
The Center of This Operation Here the Letter T   She has been Dissociating/Disassociated Herself Totally from Him Ages because of The Great Curse

Pivot: P/Man Power   V/Eve/Fem Sex Active   Hot
A Hot Eve/V is of Pivotal Importance for the Masc in   The Code
pivot: a pin or short shaft on which something rotates
pivotal: vital importance
Pivotal: P/Eve/Hot/All
She is being Rotated on a Shaft (Shaft is Slang for Penis in The American Language)   She cannot Avoid it
(See Rota and Tarot in The Words Chapter)

Plan: P/Man Power   Land
Where a Man Lands is The Plan
The Language as   The Secret Code   Augments the Masc
All the Way from   Letters   Symbols   to   Words   and   Phrases
It is in Their Shape   and   in Their Sound   All The Way Through as   The Code   has Organized It

Play: P/Masc Power   L/Sweet Fem Love Light/All/Ail/Ill/Hail/Heel/Hell/Elle/Oil
A/All Men   Y/Wounded Fem

The Dam Code The Damn Book

P/Lay   it is Play for Him
P/Man Power and The Lay (Having Sex)
Then Comes the Hey/Hay   Horses Food to Her
Play as in Pal/A   or   Ball/He   For the B/Boy Holding All Breasts   Because P/Man Power is the Adult of B/Boy Holding All Fem Breasts   He is Learning to Play Ball then He Gets
Playful   P/Lay/Full   Full as in Pregnant   For Her
In Full Switch U/You/Ovulating for O/Fem Hole and She Gets a Fool (Fool is All Fems Letters   Same as Full)
A Player Knows How to Play/Her   To Get Sex   With   Her/R/Ear/Hear/Hair/Err/Heir/Or/Whore/Here/Are/Our/Ere/Air/Ire/Sex
Playful as in P/Lay/Fool   And Yes He can Be
Switch L/Sweet Fem Light for R/Her/Hair/Are/Here/Hear/Ear/Whore/Or/Err/Sex and She Gets Prayer (For Her to Kneel down One More Time for Her Basic Justice Rights)

Playroom: P/Man Power   Lay   Her/R/Ear/Hear/Hair/Err/Heir/Or/Whore/Here/Are/Our/Ere/Air/Ire/Sex   M/Motherhood
A Lay   with   P/Man Power   in a   Room   will Make Her a   M/Mother
Room: RM   R/Her   M/Motherhood
A Room is Not a Place to Sleep for Her says   The Code   It is a Place to Get Pregnant

Please: P/Lease
Say Please and You May get a Lease from P/Man Power
lease: temporary possession
Nothing is Permanent in   That Code   When it Comes to a Comfortable Life
Lise is Fem Name
Pleasing: P/Man Power   Lease   In/Letter N/Hen/Ann/Donkey The Code   Ass it that Way   The Masc is in Charge of The Hen as in Leasing Her To Him and/or Others   Here Pops the Idea of Prostitution or Her having to have a Pimp or a Gigolo/Protector

Pleasure: Play/Sure
P/Man Power   Lay   Sure
When a Fun Lay is a Guaranteed Pleasure to The Masc

Lise Rochon

Here Pleasure is a Positive Word But Only if it is Associated With Sex   And Because there is Her/R/Ear/Hear/Hair/Err/Heir/Or/Whore/Here/Are/Our/Ere/Air/Ire/Sex   it Directs the Experience in that Direction

Plot: P/Man Power   Lot
The Plot here says   The Code   is that The Masc Has it All   A Good Plot in French For Example   Plotte in French is Slang for the Vaginal Area   or   a Fem that has Sex with Many Men   The Fem Never Wins in   That Code

Plow: P/Man Power   Low
Plowed: Plow   D/pregnant
To Plow is to Have Sex In The American Slang
Keep The Fem Low it Makes it Easy to Control Her
Low is L/Sweet Fem Love Light/All/Ail/Ill/Hail/Heel/Hell/Elle/
Oil   Owe   Also   If She is Own or She Owes That Makes Her Low

Pluck: P/Luck
P/Man Power   and   All The Luck He Can Pull
pluck: to pull
Note that Lock and Luck are Entirely Made of Fem Letters

Plural: Pleure/All
Pleurer is to Cry/Sob in French
That Code   is Generating Her Tears for Millenniums
In Plural

Pocket: Poke/It
Any Bag or Orifice is Slang for Her Loins in   That Code
For Example   She is a Slot on the Wall
The Princess and the Pea   What She Worries About is the Very Small While Men Worry about The Real Stuff   Dynasties
Properties   Strategies   Fun   and   Golf

Police: Pole/He/Is
Pole/Hiss
P/Man Power   S/Is/His/Ass/Us/Hiss/Penis/Serpent
No Fem here   Unless She is Part of That Pole

Poem: P/Man Power   O/Fem Hole   M/Motherhood
Pomme is Apple in French (The Bible Apple)
Poet: P/O/Hit   P/O/It   P/O/He/It
The Energy of the Word Changes When the T/Fem Cross was Put There in Poet (Poo/Hit)

Poh: contemptuous exclamation
O/Fem Hole   is with   P/Man Power   and H/The Secret Code   A bad Combination says   The Code   so   It is Disdain

Poison: P/O/See/On
O/Fem Hole sees The   P/Man Power
A Big No from   The Code   It is Called Poison
Poker: Poke/Her
poke: prod   make a hole
The Fems Were/Are Not Welcome at Poker Tables

Pole: P/Man Power   Hole
Switch L/Sweet Fem Light for Her/R/Ear/Hear/Hair/Err/Heir/Or/Whore/Here/Are/Our/Ere/Air/Ire/Sex and She Gets Poor (or a Pour (Alcohol to Deal with that Pole))
Switch L for T/Fem Cross and She Gets a Pot (Start Working)
Switch L for S/Is/His/Ass/Us/Hiss/Penis/Serpent
and He Gets Puss (as in Pussy)
When   P/Man   and   S/Is/His/Ass/Us/Hiss/Penis/Serpent   Meets
Switch P for H/Secret Code Letter and She Gets a O/Fem Hole
Switch P for R/Her/Hair/Are/Here/Hear/Ear/Whore/Or/Err/Sex and She Gets to Roll or get into a Role
Switch P for S/Is/His/Ass/Us/Hiss/Penis/Serpent
and He Gets a Soul (See Sole/Soul in Body Parts)
Switch P for T/Fem Cross and She Gets a Toll (Always Losing   She is)

Politic: Pull   He   T/Fem Cross   IC/Integrated Circuit
Pole   He   Stick
Senator: Sin   Eat/Hate/8/At/Hat   Her/R/Ear/Hear/Hair/Err/Heir/Or/Whore/Here/Are/Our/Ere/Air/Ire/Sex   Wherever the Hat is   The Secret Grid is

Policy: Pole/He/See   Pull/He/See   Pool/He/C
The Masc Sexual Organs Always Win   It is the Policy says   The Code
Poule is a Hen (See N/Hen/In/Ann/Virgin/Donkey) in French   Pole is Slang for a Penis

Ponder: Pawn   D/Pregnant   Her
Pun/D/Her   Pun Intended
Pound   Her/R/Hair/Are/Here/Hear/Ear/Whore/Or/Err/Sex
And Measure it too

Pony: P/Honey
P/Man Power   is with   Honey
Add an Her/R/Ear/Hear/Hair/Err/Heir/Or/Whore/Here/Are/Our/Ere/Air/Ire/Sex   and She Gets Horney

Ponytail: P/Man Power   Honey   Tail
Tail is Slang for Penis or Sex (A Piece of Tail)

Poor: P/Man Power   is with   Her/R/Ear/Hear/Hair/Err/Heir/Or/Whore/Here/Are/Our/Ere/Air/Ire/Sex   It is a Poor Event says   The Code

Here P/Man Power is Separated by 2 OOs/All Fem Holes from Her/R/Ear/Hear/Hair/Err/Heir/Or/Whore/Here/Are/Our/Ere/Air/Ire/Sex   That is a Dangerous Concept to Separate the Masc from Sex says   The Code
Any form of Fem Power is Forbidden by the Language Secret Code   so Make it Poor   Poo   R/Her   Have Sex with Her as with Poop/Excrement
Pour It   P   Whore   Hit
And Power is Close to Power/Pour
Poor is a Power Word   And a Cover Word
Pour: Poor   P/Our   P/Hour
pour: abundant flow
Another Cover Word here in Pour
P and R together   Makes PR

Pop: P/Hop   P/Up
P/Man Power   is   Up and   Hoping
Popping Her (Slang for Sex Act)
pop: to burst open with a sound   to come or go quickly

546

The Dam Code The Damn Book

Switch O/Fem Hole for U/Uterus and She Gets a Pup (Pregnant)
Pop is Slang for Father

Popular: Pop/U/Liar   Pope/U/Liar   P/Hop/U/Lair   Pop/U/Lair
This is a Word Where The Code is at its Best
Using a Perfectly Good Word
And Transforming it in a Sound Barrier to Protect   The Code
So Let s Stay   Look at it and be Strengthen by its Knowledge   It is a
Disturbing Code Word Layer   When
Antagonist Concepts as the Words Pope or Pop or Poop or PeePee
Appears in a Word   Everyone Gets Scared and Run Away and The Code
Lives   The Pope is a Most Important Leader   He is Not to be Deterred
by that

Poop: Poop is a Key Word and Big Cover Word
P/Man Power   2 OOs/Fem Holes   P/Man Power
Man Holds Surrounding All Fems Holes
Because Poop is Feces and the Sound of Pope is Close
It Makes it Difficult to look at
She/It   Shit is Part of Her World in   The Code   Such As   Dodo and Lou
(Words Made Only of Fem Letters)

Pope: P/Man Power   O/Fem Hole   P/Man Power   E/He
Power Over The Fems Holes/Loins   With   2 PPs/Man Power (as in Plural
or All of Them)   Surrounding the O
pope: father origin leader
There Are Strong Stinky Words Around the Word Pope Comparing Pope to
Poop is so Sacrilegious that Most People Turn Away in Shame   And   The
Code   Wins Again Protecting Its Secrets

Popsicle: Pop/He/Suck/All
Cover Word for Children Goodie
Pop: O/Fem Hole   Surrounded by   2 PPs/Men Power (Indicating Plural
or All Men)
Pop   He   Cycle
For Her No Escape From That Cycle says   The Code

Population: Pop/U/Lay/She/On

547

Lise Rochon

Pop Keep on Laying/Lying Down with The Fems   And it Creates Population

Porn: P/Man Power   Horn (Whore/On)
Born   Corn   Dorm   Horn   Morn   Norm   Worn   Poor or Weak Words for Her Again

Poseidon: Ancient God of the Sea
Puss/He/A/Done   Puss/He/Done   Push/He/Done   Pussy/Done   The Pussy is Always Done
puss: a hare   a cat   a woman
Back to be a Rabbit for Her   or   a Cat

Position: Pussy/She/On   Pause/He/She/On
His Choice Pussy or Pause   2 Nice Positions For The Masc
For Her be a Pussy says   The Code

Present: Pre/Scent   The Code is Always Ahead

Preserve: Pre/Serve
The Pre Serve Who Again
pre: before in time rank order or position
All Bases Covered
A Preserve as a Jam is the Cover Word Here (Preserve That Jam That is On Her for 2 Millenniums)

Pus: yellow-white viscid substance found in sores abscesses
In a Word it is So Deterrent No One will Touch it
P/Man Power   with   Us (U/You/Ovulating   and   S/Is/His/Ass/Us/Hiss/ Penis/Serpent   are as One
Sex Creates Juices That Resembles it as a White Substance
Switch U/Uterus for i/Marriage Action and He Gets to Piss   That is a Different Concept for Him Than Her   Everything Goes Down in The Code World
Switch U/Uterus for A/All Men and He Gets a Pass
Here is   The Code   in Action
Possess: Puss/Ass

The Dam Code The Damn Book

Possession: There are 4 SSSS/Is/His/Ass/Us/Hiss/Penis/Serpent in Possession   The Fem was Never Allowed to Own Property   or   have Any Real Political Power
Puss   She/Shh   Eon/He/On
Puss/He/Own for an Eon
He Owns the Pussy that is Already in His Possession
possession: the state or fat of possessing   the state of being possessed   ownership   *Law* actual holding or occupancy   either with or without rights of ownership
Solid Word when   The Code   Talk about The Fems Pussies/He/On Possession is the Position to Hold says   The Code
Pass/S/She/On   And to Pass Over Her Too

Possible: Pussy/Able
Making a Comparison Here Between Impossible and Him/Possible (Which the Opposite of the Possible)
In   The Code   Symbology   Pussy/Able is Always Possible for Pregnancy   M/Motherhood   Pussy/Able
For a Mother if Something is Possible it would be Through Her Loins   Then Motherhood   It is Still a Big No from   The Code   so Impossible

Possibility: Pussy/Bail/He/T   Puss/He/Bill/T
When the Pussy is in the Front   Bill is there to Bail the T/Fem Cross Pussy
Pussy/Ball/Hit/He

Posterity: Puss   T/Fem Cross   Her/R/Ear/Hear/Hair/Err/Heir/Or/ Whore/Here/Are/Our/Ere/Air/Ire/Sex   He/E   T/Fem Cross
2TT s/Fem Crosses (as In Plural or All of Them)
From Her Puss and the T/Fem Cross Will Come an Heir or Sex or Her for Him   The Code Calls it Posterity

Posy: P/Man Power   Hose   He/E
Men Power and His Hose
posy: a flower or a bouquet
Pussy   as a Cat   as a Pussycat (Pussy/Cat)
Pause/He

Again the Fem have No Identity Even When it Comes to a Bouquet of Flowers   Even if it Sounds as a Pussy it is Still an All Masc Sound Letter Word   P/S/He

Pot: A 3 Letter Word Merges as
Butt (Masc)   Cot (Fem)   Dot (Fem) Gut (Masc)   Hot   Nut (Fem)   Lot(Fem)   Mutt (Fem)   Nut (Fem)
The Fems Words Here Are Poor or Weak

Potter: Pot/Her
potter: to move with little energy   to waste time
Here She is Blamed for That Says   The Code

Poupée: French for Doll (Dull) (Dull and Doll are All Fems Letters)
Poop/He   Pop/He   The Code is Hypnotic   He Preps The Fems to Her Only Eventuality

Poverty: P/Man Power   Ov/Ovulation   Her/R/Ear/Hear/Hair/Err/Heir/Or/Whore/Here/Are/Our/Ere/Air/Ire/Sex
Man Power   Ovulation   Sex   and   The Great Curse
If Her Ovulation Her Sex Life and Her Menstrual Cycle
Are Together with P/Man Power Sex Life   That would be too Much Information for Her says   The Code   so No Poverty it Would be

Powerful: Pow/Her/Full
To Pow is to Terminate
Terminate Her Fully   or   Terminate Her in Pregnancy (Full)   It Makes The Masc Powerful   She Gets None of That Power says   The Code

Pragmatic: P/Man Power   Rag   M/Motherhood   Attic/Addict/A/Tic
A Mom on The Rag is The Way to Man Power says   The Code
She Does Not Know about it because She is Either in the Attic (Not on First Floor)   or   She is an   Addict   or   She is being Bothered by a Tic   In Any Way She has No Time to Concentrate on Subjects of The Higher Mind
IC Means Integrated Circuit

Praise: PRS   3 Masc Sounds Letters

P/Man Power   Raise   P/Man Power   Rise   The Power of Man Rise When He is the Prize
Pray/Ace   An Ace is Often a Winning Card
There are No Fem Letters Here Except i/Marriage Act   or   R/Heir/Or/Whore/Sex

Prayer: Prey/Her
Sorry Again I did not create it
Add S/Is/His/Ass/Us/Hiss/Penis/Serpent and He Gets a Sprayer (Spray/Her   as in with Penis))
Take Away Her/R/Ear/Hear/Hair/Err/Heir/Or/Whore/Here/Are/Our/Ere/Air/Ire/Sex   and She Gets Pay/Her
payer: a person who pays   a person named in a bill or note who has to pay the holder
To Give or Pay Anything to a Fem is Strictly Prohibited in   The Code
so   it Makes Sure that Someone/Something is Holding/Her (to Prey on Her)
The Mad Cleverness of   The Code   in Action

Preacher: Preach/Her
P/Man Power   Reach   Her
Through Religion Dogmas He can Reach Her
Pray/Each/Her   Prey/Each/Her
Every One of The Fems Must be Preached and Preyed Upon

Precious: Pre   She/Shh   Us
From Before Comes She as Shh
Her U/Uterus is Connected With S/Penis in Us
pre: prior to   rank   order
precious: a young female toddler
Could be a Rare Nice Term for Her but No says   The Code
Rank and Order (Herd/Her) Comes First Especially here because She is First   A rare Event in   The Code

Predator: Pre/Date/Her
The Code is Violent to The Fems Anytime in Any time in Her Life

Predict: Pre/Dick

Lise Rochon

P/Man Power   Her/R/Ear/Hear/Hair/Err/Heir/Or/Whore/Here/Are/Our/Ere/Air/Ire/Sex   Dick
pre: prior to   rank   order
Predict is the Penis having Rank   as a Prediction Coming From the Past   He is Above Her because of That
DK   D/Pregnant   and   K/Broken Fem Warrior

Predictable: Pre   Dick   Able
From The Past His Penis is Always Able   The Code   says it is Predictable

Preparation: Prep/He/Ration
The Code   Rules to Makes Us Poor

Pressure: Press/Her

Pretty: Prey/T
T/Fem Cross is the Prey
Because She is Raised to Think About Her Shapes (She/Ape) and Forms Take Her/R/Ear/Hear/Hair/Err/Heir/Or/Whore/Here/Are/Our/Ere/Air/Ire/Sex Away and She Gets Petty

Prevail: A Very Troubling Word
Pre/Veil Before the Veil
Prevail: the word prevail means what is going to happen
Prey/Pray
Add S/Penis and He Gets to Spray

Prick: Pray/Prey   Kick
Pay/Rick
Prick is Slang for Penis   All Good for Him says   The Code

Pride: P/Ride
P/Man Power   He Rides on His Pride

Priest: P/Rest
Priestess: Priest/Ass
The Code   in Full Action

The Dam Code The Damn Book

Prince: P/Man Power   Her/R/Ear/Hear/Hair/Err/Heir/Or/Whore/Here/Are/Our/Ere/Air/Ire/Sex   N/In/Hen/Ann/Virgin/Donkey   S/Penis
The Fems is Princess and its Plural is Princesses (Prince/Ass)
Princesses has 3 SSSs/Penisses to make sure She under the Power of His Anyway because of Her Rank
For Fem in Plural Add S/Is/His/Ass/Us/Hiss/Penis/Serpent
   or   Ass   The Fem as a Piece of Ass
Princess Toad Stool in the Fem in the Mario Video Games
The Fems is often Related to Feces in   The Code   Language

Principal: Prince/He/Pal
Prince/He/P/All
A Prince that Give P/Man Power to All Men

Prison: P/Man Power   Re/An Important Musical Tone   Son/Sun
Prisoner: P   Reason   Her/R
If P/Man Power would Try to Reason with Her/R/Ear/Hear/Hair/Err/Heir/Or/Whore/Here/Are/Our/Ere/Air/Ire/Sex   That would be a Big No from   The Code   so   Prison/Her
Praise Him   P/Raise/Him   P/Rise/Him   That would be For Him
Switch N/In/Hen/Ann/Virgin for M/Motherhood and She Gets
Prism: *Optics*   a transparent body often having triangular bases used for dispersing light into a spectrum or for reflecting rays of light
Now She is Almost Invisible   The Secret Code is Highly Intelligent   The Fems are Sometimes Called The Lights in   The Code

Program: Pro/Gram as in to Measure
The Man Wins as the Pro that is   The Code   Program
The Language is Old   There Was No Fem Being Pro Back Then   Mostly Marriage   Motherhood   and being a   Whore   for Her
The Code   Remains

Procedure: Pro/C/Dur
The Pro Sees C/See/Young Girl with Duress   It is The Procedure says   The Code

Profane: Pro/F/In   Pro/Fan
The Pro   Fem/Fuck   N/In/Virgin/Ann/Donkey

553

Pro/Fannie   Fan/He
fanny: the buttocks
pro: in favor
fan: to stir to activity
All in Favor   Stir into Activity   The N/Virgin   into   F/Fem Fuck

Professor: Pro/F/Ass/Her
The Professor is the Pro that Teach The Fems/Fuck about S/Ass/Penis says   The Code
P/Row/Fuss/Her
The Professor Is the One that Keeps The Fems in Rows as They are Fussing Around (See Row in The Words Chapter)

Progressive: Pro/Aggressive
The Pro is Aggressive
Corporations say that   They Used to be All Male   The Fem was/Is Not Allowed to be Aggressive   She would be Called Bossy

Promise: P/Man Power   Her/R/Ear/Hear/Hair/Err/Heir/Or/Whore/Here/Are/Our/Ere/Air/Ire/Sex   O/Fem Hole   Miss
In Promise The Masc Comes First   She Misses Because She is with Heir or a Whore
Pro/Miss
The Pro (an Expert) and Miss (See Miss in The Words Chapter)
pro: in favor of a proposition opinion etc   an argument consideration vote etc for something
Properly: Proper/Lay
Prop/Her/Lay
prop: a stick   a support
With that Stick She will Follow Properly (from Fear of The Stick)

Protocol: Pro/T/Call
The   Call   from the   Pro   is for the Fem as   T/Fem Cross   That is Her life Protocol
pro: in favor of a proposition

Proud: P/Route
To be Proud   is the   Route for   P/Man Power

The Dam Code The Damn Book

The Fems are Not Allowed in   The Code   to be Proud

Provide: Pro   V/Fem Sex Active   Hide
The Pro Hides from Eve/Ovo/Egg When it is Time to Provide says   The Code   and Leave The Fems Deprived
Provider: Provide/Her
The Fems is often the One Being the Provider

Prowl: Prey/All
L/Sweet Fem Love Light/All/Ail/Ill/Hail/Heel/Hell/Elle/Oil
is the Prey
prowl: to rove or go stealthily as in search of pray something to steal   zealously pursuing members of the opposite sex
O/Fem Hole is the Center Letter
Pray/All
For Its Power to go On   The Code   Always Push Some Kind of Religion
P/Man Power   Ray/RA   All

Pry: P/R/Eye   P/R/I   P/R/High   P/Rye
The Letter/Symbol I/Eye/High Relates to   The Code   The Eye in The Pyramid
pry: to look closely or curiously
Add Letter A and He Gets Pray

Pubic: Add L/Sweet Fem Love Light/All/Ail/Ill/Hail/Heel/Hell/Elle/Oil   and She Gets Public
The Message Is Always the Same
All Fems Belong to All but Herself

Pump: P/Man Power   Hump
Switch P/Man Power with The Code Letter H and She Gets Humps
hump: instance of coitus
Switch P/Man Power for M/Motherhood and She Gets the Mumps

Punch: P/Hunch
And Punish is So Close   Just Add an i/Marriage Act

Punish :   P/Man Power   On   Shh/She

555

Lise Rochon

When He is Punishing Her   She Gets the Beat   And She be Silent about It

puppet: small doll held by strings or by a hand into the doll
Metaphorically a Puppet is a Person Whose Actions Are Manipulated by Others
Puppet derivate from French poupette or poupée (Doll) or puppa in Latin   a girl as a doll (Dull)
Pop/It   Pop/Hit
That is   The Code   Marching On Her

Purgatory: Purr/Gate/Whore/He
The Code   says Purgatory is a Place for Her to Purr Once She passes The gate as Her/R/Ear/Hear/Hair/Err/Heir/Or/Whore/Here/Are/Our/Ere/Air/Ire/Sex   Then Meet Him

Purpose: Per   Puss
The Code Purpose is Focused on The Puss
P/Man Power   Her/R/Ear/Hear/Hair/Err/Heir/Or/Whore/Here/Are/Our/Ere/Air/Ire/Sex   P/Man Power   Us/S/is/His/Us/Ass/Hiss/Serpent/Penis
purpose: the reason for which something exists or is done   made   used etc
Switch P for B/Boy Holding All Fem Breasts and He Gets Burp (Too Young for The Code Purpose)

Pursue: Pair/Père   C/See/Young Girl   U/You/Ovulating
P/Man Power   Her/R/Ear/Hear/Hair/Err/Heir/Or/Whore/Here/Are/Our/Ere/Air/Ire/Sex   C/See/Young Girl   U/Uterus/Ovulating/You
The Code Goal Pursue is to make sure the Girl Ovulating   has R/Sex

Push: Puss/He
Push The Bush   Push The Puss
P/Man Power   B/Boy Holding All Fems Breasts   Are Interchangeable in the Secret Code   As Father and Young Son   All is Not Said to the Boys Children to Protect their Innocence   It is Different for The Girls   The Code Uses All That
puss: a hare   affectionate term for a woman   a cat
Take One S/is/His/Us/Ass/Hiss/Serpent/Penis Away and Get Pus

556

pus: substance produced by suppuration
Sex Juices Look as Pus
There Are No Coincidence Here   The Code at Work

Pussy: Puss/He   Push/He
pussy: a female cat   female genitalia
Pus as in Canker
The Astrological The Cancer (Canker) Sign is a Moon Sign and a Weak Word   It is The Sign of Pregnancy and The Loss of Blood for The Fems (Compare to The Moon Sign in The Tarot)
See the Difference Between the Great Respect for the Male Signs Such as The Sun Card and The Moon Card in The Original Tarots and See   See the Total Disrespect Towards Her All the Way into a Hole Literally   Study The Difference Between The Fem Signs

Puzzle: P/Ooze/All
ooze: to flow or exude slowly through small holes
Words Starting with Fem Letters Especially Double as in Ooze Are Rare And to Be Looked at Carefully Especially Where the Letter for Sleep is Right After and The Presence of E/He as Often is Almost Invisible
From Puss to Ooze   It is All/Her

Pyin: Pi/In/N
Pi ∞ is the Number 8 (Pregnancy) Collapsed
When the Secret of Pi is with N/In/Hen/Virgin that would be a Big No from   The Code   so
pyin: an albuminious constituent of pus

Q   q
Intro
Q Is a Masc and a Fem Letter
Q is the Letter for the Menstrual Cycle
The Fem Loss of Blood is The Letter O/Fem Hole/Loins with a Blood Trail Coming Out   The Hole that Leaks
Q is a Cover Letter   Queen Starts with Q
Therefore if a Sovereign Says it Is   All Fem Must Bleed
They Ignore it because the Blood Loss Symbol under the O in Q is Under the Writing Line or Hidden in the Unconscious

Lise Rochon

Few Words Starts with Q
Same for Letters W X Y Z
Q is the Letter that Describes Another Facet of the Great Curse (Curse Word Sound Starts with a Q Sound) Imposed by the Secret Brotherhoods
It is The Great Fall of Mankind after the Garden of Eden Events
The Period Before the Garden Of Eden Starting Age
The One before Adam and Eve Curse
Would have Been an Age When the Fem did Not Bleed
And the World Would have been Different Better
Especially if Kronos/Saturn was Benevolent
Instead of an Impossible Man to Live With
A Grim Reaper with a Scythe in his Hands as in Now
Clitorectomy and Circumcision come to Mind In French (See Saturn in the Astrology Chapter)
Q has the Same Sound as Cul or Ass in French
To Her Insults Pours at All Times from   The Code
Few Words Start with Q
Words with Q are   Cue (A Hint)   Queue   a Tail in French and a Penis in Slang   His Stick is there even in Q/Bleeding Fem

Q   q
Quarry: Queer/He
quarry: an excavation or pit usually open to the air   an abundant supply
There is Plenty of Sex Anyway for Any Man
Q/Bleeding Fem   Her/R/Ear/Hear/Hair/Err/Heir/Or/Whore/Here/Are/Our/Ere/Air/Ire/Sex   He/E   The Bleeding fem is with a Man   Queer Happens

Quarter: Quart/Her
Quarter of an Hour (H/Secret Code Letter   Our)   Quarter of a Year   A Quart of Milk
A Quarter in Money is Little in Value
The 4 Phases of the Moon (See Moon)
Quart
Q/Bleeding Fem   Art
The Code   Hides the Secret Art by Dividing The Fems Ov in 4 Phases (Fey/S) of the Satellite Moon

Queen: Q   In

The Dam Code The Damn Book

Q/Menstrual Cycle   N/In/Hen/Ann/Virgin
The Queue is In
Hide the Secret of   The Code   at its Top of Power   Its Queen
Q/Menstrual Cycle   U/Open Fem/You/Uterus   2 EEs/He (Plural or All of Them)   and   N/In/Hen/Ann/Virgin
The Fem Aspect of Power of Queen is Downgraded to Nothing Again here with 2 Men in The Game   Letter Q Representing Her Bleeding Time Only   You Being her Uterus and   N being a Virgin She Learns about it When it Arrives the First Time   Queen is a Weak Word   It Represents The Immense Blood Loss of The Fems   and   There are Few Words that Start with Q in Our Germanic/Latin Languages
Switch N/In/Hen/Ann/Virgin for Her/R/Ear/Hear/Hair/Err/Heir/Or/Whore/Here/Are/Our/Ere/Air/Ire/Sex and Get Queer
Again No Fem Has Power   Submit is the Ultimate and Only Possibility for Her says   The Code

Query: Q/R/E
Q/Menstrual Blood   Her/R/Ear/Hear/Hair/Err/Heir/Or/Whore/Here/Are/Our/Ere/Air/Ire/Sex   E/He
Queer/He
query: a doubt   a mental inquiry   a mental reservation
When She is Bleeding there is the Question from the Man to Whom with to have Sex   as in with Another Person   In This Case a Man says   The Code   Queer/He
(See Quarry)

Question: Quest/He/On
It is All About Him says   The Code   The Fem was Not Allowed to Ask Questions Because She was Not Allowed to have Answers or Any knowledge

Quick: QK   2 Fem Sound Letters
Q/Menstrual Cycle   K/Broken Warrior Fem

Quiet: Q/Menstrual Cycle   It/Hit
Be Quiet About the Menstrual Cycle
Take Away E/He and He Gets to Quit (as He is Out of it)

Quilt: QLT   3 Fem Sound Letters
quilt: *Obsolete*   a mattress
Take Away L/Sweet Fem Love Light/All/Ail/Ill/Hail/Heel/Hell/Elle/Oil   And She Get to Quit

Quit: Q/Menstrual Cycle   Hit/It
If She Wants to Quit Her Period   She Gets Hit says   The Code   Those are called her Rules

R   r
Intro
Letter R is a Masc and a Fem Letter in   The Code
R is the Letter/Symbol for The Physical Sex Act Itself   It is the I/Masc Stick   with the   O/Fem Hole   and   His Penis Hanging   See The Difference with i/Marriage Act
Letter R   is Her Name as in   Her/R/Ear/Hear/Hair/Err/Heir/Or/Whore/Here/Are/Our/Ere/Air/Ire/Sex   Her as in Sex itself   With Heir   or as a   Whore   with Hair or Not   Hear it   it is Her
The R Sound Represents the Beating of the Drum as in The Sex Act   Rararara   Ra being the Word for a Man Head in the Semitic Alphabet (With an Egyptian Beard)
Ra is   The Egyptian God   The Sun God   There in Ancient Egypt   The Master (Mast/Her) of His World All the Way to the Sun   which is His Son
The Prefix Re Means to Repeat   Then That Sequence can then go on Endlessly   And on a Musical Note   Do Re Mi
After He had Sex in R   His Penis has Retracted   He is P/Man Power   Again
R is The Ass of the Arse   RRS
arse: the buttocks   the anus   a stupid person   sexual intercourse   effrontery
The Ass/Donkey which is Anne/N/Virgin   Again Pops Up Suddenly in the Word is Whores
The Horses   The Horse is a Powerful Sex Symbol for The Fems
Letter Rr in the Alphabet is a Loud Roaring Letter   Because of the Combat to Death Happening There
Words with Letter Our   Whore   Are   Her   Rear   Or (Gold in French)
Words with RR: Roar   Rare   Horror (RR)
R in Plural Would be Only Rs or Arse or Ours or Whores

The Dam Code The Damn Book

Ours is Bear in French (Do Not come Close)

R   r
Ra: The Egyptian King God Sun Ra

Rabbit: Rub/it   Rob/It
The Rabbit Was/Is an Symbol of   Love   Fertility   Vigilance   The Rabbit was One of the Favorite Animals of the Greek Goddess of Love Aphrodite Now The Rabbits are Kept in Small Cages because they have No Voice to Be Able to Complain   Unfortunately
The Code   says Easter (East/Her) Bunny (a Male) Brings Fertility at Easter   Which is 3 Days after Jesus Died   and   that Day   They Say   He came Back to Life
But from this Easter (East/Her   as in   Veil/Day) Day
In The Catholic Religion the Days are Counted to Make the Delivery
On Dec 25TH When that Baby Boy (Heir) is Born Again in The Name of Jesus   Which was Certainly Not born on a 25th of December
That is Why the Easter Date Varies Every Year

Radar: Read   Her/R/Ear/Hear/Hair/Err/Heir/Or/Whore/Here/Are/Our/Ere/Air/Ire/Sex
To be Able to Read Her is to be in The Radar   As All Men Are

Rag: Her/R/Ear/Hear/Hair/Err/Heir/Or/Whore/Here/Are/Our/Ere/Air/Ire/Sex
A/All Men   G/Penis Penetration
Being on the Rag is a Well Known Slang Word for a Menstruating Fem R/Heir/Or/Whore   Egg   Everything is Related to Pregnancies and Poverty says   The Code
Our/Ag
Bag   Dag   Fag   Hag   Lag(L/
Egg)   Nag   Rag   Sag   Tag   Wag   Words in Ag are Poor and Weak   They are a Drag (The/Rag)
Those Words Are Other Forms of Confinement for The Fems Ag/Egg A and G Together Reveals Too Much says   The Code

Rag Doll: a stuffed doll made of cloth   a limp ineffectual person

561

Lise Rochon

Obvious Connection Between a Fem on the Rag and Someone that Cannot Make a Decision by themselves
Says   The Code

Ragtime: a dance that can be only be danced with 2 partners   One Move is Called Yale and The Fems Walks Backward while the Man Advance Forward
Ragged: Rag/D   Rag/ID   Rag/Hid
When a Man can Only Dance with One Fem   It is Called Rag/Time
Ragged   as in   Rugged

Rain: Her/R/Ear/Hear/Hair/Err/Heir/Or/Whore/Here/Are/Our/Ere/Air/Ire/Sex
    N/In/Hen/Virgin/Ann/Donkey
When R/Heir/Or/Whore is In/N   It Rains Her/R/Ear/Hear/Hair/Err/Heir/Or/Whore/Here/Are/Our/Ere/Air/Ire/Sex N/Ann/In
Rain is Water Falling   (Fall/In   F/Fem/Fuck   All/In)   (What/Her)   An Entirely Fem Symbol
The Rain   D/Pregnant   Reign
She Cannot Reign Over Anything says
Still on the Rein of Course says   The Code

Re: R/Sex   E/He   To Lay for Sex Twice for Him   Here She is The R/Whore/Her/Sex   Repeat

rein: any of certain straps or thongs forming part of a harness as a checkrein   to curb   restrain   the controlling or directing power
To Keep that Rain/Fem Water Under Somebody Else Power
Rain Cats and Dogs are 3 Fem Symbols
Rain or Shine   Rain Check   Reine as a Sovereign
R   N/In   She/Shh   K/Broken Fem Warrior
Un Rein is a Kidney in French   Kidneys Filters Water (See Water in The Words Chapter   an Entirely Fem Symbol)
Add an E/He and He Get Reine   Reine is Queen in French
Rein is Reign   A VIP Word
Those are The Code   Rules for The Fems
The Fems go Nowhere in   The Code   but as Slaves

The Dam Code The Damn Book

Add T/Fem Cross and She Gets Train (T/Fem Cross   Rain)
Wagons (Polygamy) are Fem   and   Engine (Only One Driver) is Masc)
   W/All Fems Sex Active for Her/R/Ear/Hear/Hair/Err/Heir/Or/Whore/
Here/Are/Our/Ere/Air/Ire/Sex   and She Gets a   Rag/On   Rag   N/In/
Hen/Ann/Virgin
Switch N for S/Is/His/Ass/Us/Hiss/Penis/Serpent and He Gets a Raise
Switch R for B/Boy Holding All Fems Breasts and He Gets a Ban (Baby Boy is too Young for The Code)
Switch R for C/See/Young Girl and She Gets Cane
Switch R for D/Pregnant and She Gets Dane (Dame   D/In)
Switch R for G/Penis Penetration and He Gets a Gain
Switch R for H/Secret Code Letter and Get Hen/Haine/Ann/Donkey   Back to the Chickens with The Code   Haine is Hatred (A/Thread) in French
Switch R for L/Fem Sweet Love and She Gets a Lain (To Lie in the Past)   Lane (a Narrow Passage)   Laine (Wool in French)   (See Sheep and the Jj/Sheppard Stick in The Words and Letter Chapter) or Lame (See Letters N and M in The Letter Chapter)
Take i/Marriage Act Away and Get Ran (No Sex   No Use Here says The Code)
Switch R for M/Motherhood and Get Main (Main Street   or be Main) or Mane (Horses/Whores) M as in Motherhood
Switch R for P/Man Power and He Gets Pain (Of course)
Switch R for S/Is/His/Ass/Us/Hiss/Penis/Serpent and Gets Sane or Sain (The Sign of the Cross)   Add T/Fem Cross and She Gets a Stain
Switch R for T/Fem Cross and She Gets Tame or Tin (Cheap and Thin)
Switch R for V/Fem Sex Active and She Gets Vain (See Vein/Us   Venus)
Switch R for W/All Sex Fem Active and She Gets Wain (a Carriage) or We   N/In/Hen/Ann/Virgin as in Win   When Sex is Provided The Code Shows Itself a Merciful
Rain is a Big Cover Word for The Code here

Rainbow: Rain/Reine   Bow
The Queen and the Beau   Not   It is a Bow (See BB in The Words Chapter)
When the Queen Bows She Reign says   The Code   This is Where The Code Gets The Fem Stuck   In The Dreams and Daze

Raise: R/Ace

563

A VIP Word for   The Code
Switch R for C/See/Young Girl and She Gets a Case (As an Entrance)
Switch R for D/Pregnant and She Gets Days (Daisy/Dizzy/Daze/He)
Switch R for F/Fem/Fuck and She Gets a Phase (F is Asexual which is Unacceptable in The Code)
Switch R for G/Penis Penetration and Get Gaze
Switch R for H/Secret Code Letter and Get Haze
Switch R for L/Sweet Fem Light and She Gets Lays
Switch R for M/Motherhood and She Gets a Maze
Switch R for V/Fem Sex Active and She Gets a Vase (See Urn in The Words Chapter)
Switch R for W/All V/Fem V/Fem Sex Active and She Gets Ways (When it Comes to Sex the Roads are Open says The Code)

Rally: Her/R/Ear/Hear/Hair/Err/Heir/Or/Whore/Here/Are/Our/Ere/Air/Ire/Sex   All   He
R/Alley   For Her Sex is The Only Rally says   The Code

Ram: RM   R/Am
Her/R/Ear/Hear/Hair/Err/Heir/Or/Whore/Here/Are/Our/Ere/Air/Ire/Sex
ram: male sheep
R/âme   (Âme is Soul in French)
The Goal here is to have Sex with The Fems   It is in Her Soul
In Mythology the Rams Horns were Popular for Leaders and Gods

Random: Ran/Down   Ran/Dumb   Ray/N/Dumb
The King and The Dumb as in Kingdom
Random is Not a Good Way to Live a Secure Life   So it is Left to The Dumb (Her)

Rape: Her/R/Ear/Hear/Hair/Err/Heir/Or/Whore/Here/Are/Our/Ere/Air/Ire/Sex   P/Man Power
R/Her   Ape
Sex with an Ape   A Fem That Is says   The Code
Ape   All/Ill/Hell/Letter L/Sweet Fem Love Light   Apple
The Forbidden Fruit of Garden of Eden
Add W/All Fems Sex Active and She Gets a Wrap
Add E/He and He Gets to Reap

The Dam Code The Damn Book

reap: to cut (wheat rye etc) with a sickle or other implement or a machine as in harvest   to gather or take (a crop   harvest   etc)   to get as a return   recompense   or result
The Code Always Give Rewards and Returns to the Masc
Cut Wheat (Cut When She is Wet)
Sickle: Sick/All
To Reap Profits is a Positive Side of Rape in   The Code
Rape is also the Residue of Grapes After the Juice has been Extracted and is Used as a Filter in Making Vinegar
Vinegar (Vine/Eager) is so Good For You
The Code is so Profound in Our Psyche
Rapist: Rape/Ist
ist: suffix for a person who practices some principles doctrines
And The Reward has to do with Crop (Harvest)
Switch O/Fem Hole for A/All Men and He Gets Crap (Because Men Need The Fems to Function)

Rapper: Wrap   Her   Rape   Her
Sex and Us the Crowds   Making Music
Trying to have Fun   The Code   Sends a Different Message

Rare: RR
Her/R/Ear/Hear/Hair/Err/Heir/Or/Whore/Here/Are/Our/Ere/Air/Ire/
Sex   Twice   A Gathering of Fems is a Rare Thing   Even if   A/All/Men   and   E/He   are There Incognito   Almost Inaudible
Rear is Close By   Look for Your Back
Fucking in The Back is there too as Homosexuality
Rire is to Laugh in French

Rarely: Rare/Lay   Rear/Lay   Rally   Really
Her/R/Ear/Hear/Hair/Err/Heir/Or/Whore/Here/Are/Our/Ere/Air/Ire/
Sex   Lay
Rarely Would be the Word to Use for Lays that are Rare   That is a Big No from   The Code   so it is a Rally
People Love to Have Sex

Rat: The Rat is Known as a Dirty Animal to be Avoided
R/At   R/Hat   Hat and At are Important but Common Secret Words

A/All Men   T/Fem Cross
To At Add Her/R/Ear/Hear/Hair/Err/Heir/Or/Whore/Here/Are/Our/Ere/Air/Ire/Sex   and She Gets Rat
Add W/All Fems Sex Active as a Silent Letter and the H/Secret Code Letter Society Also Silent Letter to Rat and She Gets Wrath   Because The Fems Cannot be There   says   The Code
wrath: fierce anger
As Usual People Stay Away from these Kinds of Words   And   The Code   Secrecy Stays that Way

Rather: Her/R/Ear/Hear/Hair/Err/Heir/Or/Whore/Here/Are/Our/Ere/Air/Ire/Sex   At/Hat   Her/R
Sex and Secrecy are Coming to Her
rather: to a certain extent
Rat/Her

Ravaged: R/V/Egg/D
R/Her/Are/Heir/Hair/Hear/Ear/Whore/Err/Sex   V/Fem Sex Active   and Her Egg/Ovulation   into   D/Daughter Pregnancy
From Sex to Pregnancy   She is Ravaged says   The Code

Ray: Her/R/Ear/Hear/Hair/Err/Heir/Or/Whore/Here/Are/Our/Ere/Air/Ire/Sex   A/All Men   Y/Wounded Fem
Sun Ray   Son/Ray   There is No Sunshine Ray for The fem Men Radiates When they Have Sex and they Decrepit When Not That is Why they Invented a long Time Ago Her Oldest and Only Paying Profession in the World   For Her to have if Not a Mother   The Whore (Or is Gold in French)
Ray is a Man Name

Razor: Rise/Her   Raise/Her
Razor is used for Cutting Roses   Cut the Little Girls Hymen with the Razor as the Barbers do in Islamic Countries   It is Called the Clitorectomy   Rose/Her

Re: Her/R/Ear/Hear/Hair/Err/Heir/Or/Whore/Here/Are/Our/Ere/Air/Ire/Sex   E/He

The Dam Code The Damn Book

The Mother/Or/Whore and The man   She has No Identity She is Just a Program to   Repeat   as a Musical Note
re: to repeat

Reach: R/Each   R/Itch
Sex for Each One Itch says   The Code   Him and Her Silence Shh

Read: RD   2 Fem Sound Letters
Her/R/Ear/Hear/Hair/Err/Heir/Or/Whore/Here/Are/Our/Ere/Air/Ire/Sex   D/Pregnant
Can She Read it   Whore or/and Pregnancy for Her
Red   Road   Rod   Rid
R/Heed
Pay Attention to Sex it Is Red
R/ID
ID is the Unconscious Surge for Pleasure with Boundaries   An ID is also an Identification Card
Reading: Red/In   Rod/In
The Code   Says She has to Read The Signs When Its Red Rod Wants to Get In
Ready: Red/He   Read/He   R/Head/He (a Head is an Erection/Ejaculation)

Real: RL   Her/R/Ear/Hear/Hair/Err/Heir/Or/Whore/Here/Are/Our/Ere/Air/Ire/Sex   All/L/Sweet Fem Love Light/Ail/Ill/Hail/Heel/Hell/Elle/Oil   Sex for All Fems   That is What is Real
R   Hell/Ill/Elle (Elle is She in French)
eel: snake fish   slang for penis
Even in The world of Fishes as Fems   The Code   Infiltrates itself as Men Penisses   Keeping The Guard (G/Penis In   Hard)
reel: a device that turns on axis as a fishing rod reel
Rill/Rile/Roll
Axis: Axe/His   Axe/Is   X/Is   His Axe
An Axis is an Imaginary Line Which an Object Rotates Around (Circle is Fem being in the Shape of an O/Fem Hole)
Much Rotation and Spinning Makes Her Dizzy   Easy (He/See)   Daisy (Days/He)   Lazy (Lays/He)
Axe/In   Eggs/In   Axe is X/Her Fallen Cross

Reality: R/All/T   Real/He/T   R/Heel/All/T/Fem Cross
Sex For All with The Great Curse
Real/T   The Fems Cross is Real   The Code   Says

Really: Real/He   Reel/He
The Eel as in Penis is Present in One Form or Another in   The Code

Reaper: Rape/Her
Reap/Her
reap: to cut with a sickle
The Fem Clitorectomy is the Cut of Her Clitoris with the Sickle (Sick/All)
reaper: a machine for cutting standing grain   a person that reaps   grim reaper

Rear: RR   2RRs/Sex Twice   In the Rear   It Roars Are/Here
Air   Heir   Here   Hair as in Letter R/Her
There are 2 RRs/Her/Ear/Hear/Hair/Err/Heir/Or/Whore/Here/Are/Our/Ere/
Air/Ire/Sex   It Amplifies the Whore and/or Heir Concepts
Rear is a Sexual Term   R is in the Air (R)   Rear is a Big Glass Ceiling Word

Reason: R/Her/Ear/Hear/Hair/Err/Heir/Or/Whore/Here/Are/Our/Ere/Air/
Ire/Sex   He   Son   Sex for the Son
R   Is   On   Rise/On   R/Ease/On   It is The Horizon for The
Son   Powerful Positive Words for The Masc
Sex is Easy and Ongoing   That Is The Logic of the Reason says   The
Code   Lying to its Teeth
If We would Not be So Messed Up Sexually   We could All Have a Happy
Sex Life   Sex is Part of Our Animal Life   Part of Life   But Religions/
Codes Owns Our Sex Life

Rebel: R/He/Bell
R/Sex   with   The Belle (See Bell and Belle in The Words Chapter)
R/He/B/Hell/Ill   Then It Changes   Hell Moves in and Creates Ills to R/Heir/
Or/Whore
She had Sex Which She Is/Was Proud of
Re/Bill says   The Code   so It Always Comes Back to Her

Recall: R/Call

The Dam Code The Damn Book

Her/R/Ear/Hear/Hair/Err/Heir/Or/Whore/Here/Are/Our/Ere/Air/Ire/
Sex   Is   Calling
recall: to bring back from memory

Receive: R/S/V (All Soft Sounds)   R/Sieve
R/Her/Are/Her/Hair/Hear/Ear/Whore/Err/Sex
See/Letter C   Eve/Ovo/Fem Sex Active
sieve: separate the coarse from the fine   the sieve was used in divination
Sève is Tree Sap in French   Especially from The Maple Tree
Receiving: R/S/V/N
Her/R/Ear/Hear/Hair/Err/Heir/Or/Whore/Here/Are/Our/Ere/Air/Ire/Sex   C/
See/Young Girl   V/Ovo/V/Fem Sex Active   N/In/Hen/Ann/Virgin
Vigne is French for Vine in   The Secret Code
(See Chalice in The Words Chapter)

Reckon: Wreck   On/In/Hen/Ann/Virgin/Donkey   Rick/On
The Trick Here says   The Code   is to Wreck Her   Rick (Richard) is On
reckon: to count or calculate as in number or amount
Rock/On   Rochon is My Fam Name

Recognize: Re/Con/Nice   Reckon/Ice
re: prefix for again and again

Reconsider: Re/Con/See/Dur
Always Be Hard on that Con says   The Code

Record: Wreck   Heard
Rack   Her/R/Ear/Hear/Hair/Err/Heir/Or/Whore/Here/Are/Our/Ere/Air/Ire/
Sex   D/Pregnant
The Code   says   Destroy   Her   D/Pregnant   Destroy Her   R/Her/Sex
Keep it on Record   and Make it Heard

Rectum: Wreck/Dumb
The Dumb is The Fems as in Kingdom (The King and The Dumb)
The Fems Is Associated with Feces in   That Code

Red: RD   Her/R/Ear/Hear/Hair/Err/Heir/Or/Whore/Here/Are/Our/Ere/ Air/Ire/Sex   D/Pregnant
As having Her Period   Red Blood as in Losing a Fetus   To be In the Red is a Problem   Red is Past Tense for Read
In Nature When Something Turns Red It is Ready (Red/He Erection) for Something   Red with Anger   Red is a Stimulant Color   Because of That it is Used as a Stop Light at the Traffic Light
Read is a Cover Word here

Redeem: Red   M/Motherhood
Read   M/Motherhood
R/He/Dim
Redeem: to pay off   to recover
P 134 Rudolf Steiner Egyptian Myths and Mysteries
"After the Blood had Flown from the Wounds of the Redeemer"
The Catholics are to be Redeemed by the Blood of the Lamb (Jesus) (See Sheep and Sheppard in The Words Chapter)
The Christ Spirit Descended to the Dead   This is One of the Deepest Most Searched and Respected Mysteries of Mankind   that belong to the Mysteries of Christianity

Reel: Real Her/R/Ear/Hear/Hair/Err/Heir/Or/Whore/Here/Are/Our/Ere/ Air/Ire/Sex   Ill/Elle/Ail/Hell
Reel that Fish In says   The Code (The Fish is Her   See Fish in The Words Chapter)   It is Real
reel: a rotary device attached to a fishing rod at the butt for winding up or letting out the line   a cylinder frame or other device that turns on an axis and is used to wind up or pay out something   frame turning on an axis
rel: a noun suffix having a diminutive or pejorative force

Reins: Reines in Plural (Queens in French)
rein: a leather strap to control the horse
A Simple Word Holding a Lot of   That Code   Knowledge (See Horses/ Whores in The Words Chapter   and   Letter R/Her in The Letter Chapter) Queens are all Tied Up Too   as All the Other Fems

Refer: Reef/Her

The Dam Code The Damn Book

Here She Goes to the Reefs
Is For/Her
refer: to relate   to assign to a class
The Fems Needs to Relate with That Concept (To Be Reefed) That is Her Only Reference says   The Code

Refund: R/Found   Her/Fun/D
R/Her/Are/Her/Hair/Hear/Ear/Whore/Err/Sex   Gets Money for Playing   She Gets D/Pregnant   This is Where She Finds Herself says   The Code

Refusal   Her/R/Ear/Hear/Hair/Err/Heir/Or/Whore/Here/Are/Our/Ere/Air/Ire/Sexv   Fuse/Few (s)   All
Refuse/All That is All Fems as Garbage   Different Levels   Different Meanings   For the Man (My/Ann) and for the Lady (Laid/He)
Refuse Being Garbage   It Fuses All those Her/R/Heir/Or/Whore   Together In That Bin (Been)

Refuse: Her/R/Ear/Hear/Hair/Err/Heir/Or/Whore/Here/Are/Our/Ere/Air/Ire/Sex   Fuse
A Concept that Implies   That No Means Yes
R/Few/Hiss   Few Fem Refuse Penises   R/F/Use   To Fuse with a Fem   It All Means Garbage says   The Code

Regal: R/Egg/All
Sex and Eggs (Ov) for All Fems All The Way From Royalty to the Common Folks
regal: pertaining to a king

Reign: RN   2 Fem Sound Letters
Her/R/Ear/Hear/Hair/Err/Heir/Or/Whore/Here/Are/Our/Ere/Air/Ire/Sex   and   N/In/Hen/Ann/Virgin/Donkey
She Reigns   She is a Queen   Reine is Queen in French   Reina in Spanish   but No She is Not a Queen because   She is Only a Young Virgin   The N/Virgin   and She has to be Restrained as in   The Code   says
rein: to restrain
Only That Code   would Find Ways to Restrain Royalty

Lise Rochon

Rein is Kidney in French   The Kidney is the Seat of the Feelings or Passions according to Webster   also it Filters the Water of the Body

Reindeer: Reine/Dear
reindeer: one of several large deer of the genus *Rangifer*
The Reindeer   Tells us   that Our Dear Reine   does not Exist   Out of the Great Cold Countries Where Santa Claus Exist   I t is So Cold   and   a Fiction World
Back to The Animals to the Fems with the Deer for the Fem

Relationship: Relation/Ship (See Ship in the Words Chapter)
Reel   On   She/Shh   P/Man Power

Religion: Rail/G/Penis Penetration   On/N/Ann/In/Virgin/Donkey
Reel   G   On
reel: a cylinder that turns on an axis
The Endless Movement of   The Code
The Endlessly Turning In Circles Around That/Her Wheel of Time   The Endless Drilling of the Penis Towards   Ahead

Remember: Her/R/Ear/Hear/Hair/Err/Heir/Or/Whore/Here/Are/Our/Ere/Air/Ire/Sex   Member   Member is Slang for Penis   Sex as Her   and   His Penis

Remind: R/Mind   R/M/N/D
Sex from Mother to Virgin with Pregnancy   It is in the Mind
A Reminder says   The Code

Repel: Rip/Rape   Elle/Hell/Ill/Ail   Rape/All
The Code   says Yes to Rape   But Do Not Admit it
repel: to drive or force back   to refuse to accept or admit   reject
Re   P/Man Power   All
re: a tone   in the case of   with reference to   in re   indicating   repetition of an action   recopy   remarry

Replace: R/Place
Place   Her/R/Ear/Hear/Hair/Err/Heir/Or/Whore/Here/Are/Our/Ere/Air/Ire/Sex   and   Replace Her

572

The Dam Code The Damn Book

Repression: Her/R/Ear/Hear/Hair/Err/Heir/Or/Whore/Here/Are/Our/Ere/ Air/Ire/Sex   He/E   Press/   On/In/N Virgin/Ann/Donkey   Press on That Repression on The Virgin to have Sex

Researcher: Her/R/Ear/Hear/Hair/Err/Heir/Or/Whore/Here/Are/Our/Ere/Air/ Ire/Sex   Search   Her
Sex is Looking for   Her/Heir/Or/Whore   It is Re/Searching

Resistance: R/Her/Ear/Hear/Hair/Err/Heir/Or/Whore/Here/Are/Our/Ere/ Air/Ire/Sex   Is/His/S/Penis   Tense/Dense
The Code   Tells How Sex Works here   as in   Force Through the Resistance (as a Rape)
Rise/Hiss/Tents (The Tents were Where The Fems Were Kept in Ancient Times)

Respect: R/Her//Ear/Hear/Hair/Err/Heir/Or/Whore/Here/Are/Our/
Sex   The Heir/Or/Whore is   The Path   To the Pact   for   The Code There is Respect says   The Code

Rest: Her/R/Ear/Hear/Hair/Err/Heir/Or/Whore/Here/Are/Our/Ere/Ire/ Sex   Is/His/Penis   T/Fem Cross
Rest Is When R/Heir/Or/Whore is His as T/Fem Cross/Curse
Arrest: R/Rest   The 2 RRs/Hers/Heirs/Or/Whores Makes Her Guilty Because There Could be an Affiliation of The Fems here   So   No says   The Code   It is Either Put Her at Rest   or   Under Arrest

Restless: Rest/Less   No Rest For Her   R/Is/Less

Retail: Re   Tail
R/Her/Are/Her/Hair/Hear/Ear/Whore/Err/Sex   He   Tell
Wrath   Hell/Elle/L/Sweet Fem Love Light/All/Ail/Ill/Hail/Heel/Oil Rat   Hell/Elle/Hail/L (See Hat and Rat in The Words Chapter)
Even in Retail She Loses

Retarded: Rite/Hard/Head
A Retard would be Someone that Does Not Do or Does Not Understand   The Code   or its Rites which Would be Most of Us   In The

573

Business World They Call Us The Peasants   We are The Ones that Work Every Day for those Corporations for Cheap

Return: R/Her/Ear/Hear/Hair/Err/Heir/Or/Whore/Here/Are/Our/Ere/Air/Ire/Sex   Turn
R/Her/Heir/Or/Whore   Turn   and a   Return
Turn   T/Urn   Return to the Urn (See Urn in The Words Chapter)   An Urn has the Shape of a Pregnant Fem

Reunion Her/R/Ear/Hear/Hair/Err/Heir/Or/Whore/Here/Are/Our/Ere/Air/Ire/Sex   Union says   The Code   A Reunion is an Union with R/Heir/Or/Whore

Reveal: R/Her/Are/Her/Hair/Hear/Ear/Whore/Err/Sex   Veil
The Word Veil is One Of The Most dangerous for The Fems in   The Code   Because When Under That Bedsheet She Has   No Voice   No Image   No Identity
Avoid Veils   A Veil Veils   It Does Not Reveal
R/Her   And the Veiled Woman is to be Revealed   No RVL   R/Eve/Ill
R/Her/Are/Her/Hair/Hear/Ear/Whore/Err/Sex   V/Eve/OV/fem Sex Active   Ill/Elle/Hail/Ail/letter L   Close to That Veil
Revealed: R/Veil/D
Her/R/Ear/Hear/Hair/Err/Heir/Or/Whore/Here/Are/Our/Ere/Air/Ire/Sex   Veils   D/Pregnant   it is a Revelation to Her   Oops Too Late   Pregnant Already
Veil Rhymes with   Hail   Weil   Ail   Hell   Elle   And the Letter L which is The Fem Letter for Sweet Love   Which She has No Chance for

Revelation: R/Veil/A/She/Eon
Her/R/Ear/Hear/Hair/Err/Heir/Or/Whore/Here/Are/Our/Ere/Air/Ire/Sex   Is   Veiled   for an   Eon   It is a Revelation
R/Eve/Lay/She/On
R/Her   V/Eve/Ovo/Ovulation   Lay Together   On Reveal/She/On
The Book of Revelations in The Bible Reveals That Revelation is an Important Word in   The Code   Because It is Used Often in Sermons

The Dam Code The Damn Book

Reverse: R/Eve/Hearse
Her/R/Ear/Hear/Hair/Err/Heir/Or/Whore/Here/Are/Our/Ere/Air/Ire/Sex   V/
Fem Sex Active   Hers
As Long as The Hearse is Hers
And for Her Being in that Hearse   Is Good says   The Code
Hearse: Hers

Revolution: R/Eve/All/V/Eon   R/Veil/O/L/Eon
Anything Against the Veil is Called a Revolution says   The Code

Reward: Re/Ward   R/Word
R/Her/Ear/Hear/Hair/Err/Heir/Or/Whore/Here/Are/Our/Ere/Air/Ire/
Sex   Word/Ward   The Code   Keeps Them Separated   because Most
of it Will go to The Masc   It is a Protected Area
ward: a division   to guard   to protect

Rex: King in Latin
Switch   Her/R/Ear/Hear/Hair/Err/Heir/Or/Whore/Here/Are/Our/Ere/Air/
Ire/Sex and Get Hex
hex: to bewitch   practice witchcraft on   spell charm
Switch R for S/Is/His/Ass/Us/Hiss/Penis/Serpent
and He Gets Sex (How Convenient)
Switch R for N/In/Hen/Virgin and She Gets Next (Rock them and Roll
Them)

Rhythm: Rite/Him   Rite   M/Motherhood
2 HHs/Secret Society Letters   The Rite Here would Be to Make   M/
Motherhood   Happen to   Y/Wounded Fem Through   R/Her/Heir/Or/
Whore/Sex
Rhythm is Related to Music   Another Code to Decipher
Music is Used In Religious Services

Ribbon: Rib/On
A Ribbon is The Most Innocent Word in   That Code   Makes a Bow (Bow
to Who) with it
The Rib   from Adam Body is   On

Rich: R/Itch

Lise Rochon

Her/R/Ear/Hear/Hair/Err/Heir/Or/Whore/Here/Are/Our/Ere/Air/Ire/Sex   Itch   She Wants Sex   It is as Feeling Rich says   The Code

Riddle: Rid/L   Rid/All
riddle: a puzzling question
Is to Get Rid of All/L/Sweet Fem Love Light/Ail/Ill/Hail/Heel/Hell/Elle/Oil
R/Idle   When Sex is Idle Have a   Riddle
idle: not active
Idle is Not a Good Word to Mix with   Her/R/Ear/Hear/Hair/Err/Heir/Or/Whore/Here/Are/Our/Ere/Air/Ire/Sex
riddler: a question   a puzzle
Riddle/Her   Always That Path of Uncertainty for Her With   That Code

Rig: RG   R/Sex   and   G/Hymen Penetration
rig: to install assemble or prepare   to put in proper order

Right: R/Her/Ear/Hear/Hair/Err/Heir/Or/Whore/Here/Are/Our/Ere/Air/Ire/Sex   Height
height: distance upward
Sex Going Up is What is Right
The Right is Masc and the Left (Behind   and   Wrong) is Fem
All Fems is Represented by the Left Side in   The Code
Note That Height Is Close To Hide (Letter D and T are Interchangeable in The Code)
Fight   Night   Bite   Might   Those are Weak Words

Ring: Ring is an Important Word in The Code
R/Her/Ear/Hear/Hair/Err/Heir/Or/Whore/Here/Are/Our/Ere/Air/Ire/Sex   i/Marriage Act   N/In/Hen/Ann/Virgin/Donkey   G/Hymen Perforation
The Ring was Usually Used to Own a Fem in Marriage
The Masc Did Not Have to Wear it
A Ring is Round   The Symbol of Fem for Her Loins and Her Pregnancies
Mary Goes Round
Ring the Bell   Ring that Belle
A Belle is a Beauty in French and Bella in Italian
The Bell has the Shape of the Loins with The Middle Part The Clitoris
There are Several Types of Rings
Boxing Ring   Phone Ring   Criminal Ring   A Bull Ring (See Tau/Taurus)

The Dam Code The Damn Book

Add W/All Fems Sex Active and She Gets Wring as in Taking Water Out of Something (Water is Fem)
To be a Wringer is Hard work
A Ringer is an Expert
Any Word with the Word Ring in it Brings Us to the O/Fem Hole
Switch R for T/Fem Cross or D/Pregnant and She goes from a Ring to a Thing and a Ding
Ring   Wring   Wrung   Wrong
Back in the Ring
Her/R/Ear/Hear/Hair/Err/Heir/Or/Whore/Here/Are/Our/Ere/Air/Ire/Sex   N/In/Hen/Virgin/Ann/Donkey
RN   R/Sex and the N/Virgin
A RN is a Registered Nurse   How Convenient
Switch R for D/Pregnant and She Gets Ding (Small)
Switch R for K/Broken Fem Warrior and She Gets a King
(Here She is Told She Gets a King Says The Code because She Went from R The Fems Fighter to K/Broken Fem Warrior   Her Always Lost battle)
The Place to Hide K/In/N   Keen
Switch R for P/Man Power and He Gets a Ping (it Bounces Right Off)
Switch R for T/Fem Cross and She Gets a Thing (a Fem In American Slang)
Switch R for S/Is/His/Ass/Us/Hiss/Penis/Serpent
and He Gets Sing
Switch R for V/Fem Sex Active and She Gets Vigne
(In French une Vigne is the Vine itself (The Wine/Blood)
Switch R for W/All Fems Sex Active and She Gets Wing (She Gets One Wing because of The Sex Involved   You Still Need Two for it to Work   And That is how   The Code   Works Her

Risk: Her/R/Ear/Hear/Hair/Err/Heir/Or/Whore/Here/Are/Our/Ere/Air/Ire/Sex   S/Is/His/Ass/Us/Hiss/Penis/Serpent
   K/Broken Fem Warrior
He/E   Has   R/Her   with   K/Broken Fem Warrior   it is a Risk or it is with the Wrist
R/Is/C (Hard C)
If R/Her/Whore would be with C/See/Young Girl   It is a Risk Says   The Code

Rite: R/It   Her/R/Ear/Hear/Hair/Err/Heir/Or/Whore/Here/Are/Our/Ere/ Air/Ire/Sex   i/Marriage Act   T/Fem Cross
The Code   Language is the Rite that All of Us Go Through in Our Lives as in   Right/Write/Rite
Switch T/Fem Cross for D/Pregnant and She Gets a Ride (Being Pregnant)
The Rites of Passage (Pass/Age) are Transformations from One Status to Another   Hers is from having Sex being With Heir or a Whore and be Cursed
rite: prescribed form or manner governing the words for a ceremony
The Code   has it All Covered

River: R/V/R
The 2 RRs/R/Her/Are/Her/Hair/Hear/Ear/Whore/Err/Sex (Plural or All of Them) are Surrounding V/Fem Sex Active
As a River Flowing
The R/Her in the Process of becoming a V/Fem Sex Active

Riveting: RVTN
Her/R/Ear/Hear/Hair/Err/Heir/Or/Whore/Here/Are/Our/Ere/Air/Ire/Sex   is in Front of 3 Other Different Types of Fem
The Rivet Comes
R/Eve/Hit/N   R/Eve/T/In   Rivet/In
rivet: a metal pin passing through two or more plates to hold them together
More Holding from   The Code   to The Fems

Road: Red   Rod   Route
Others are
Boulevard: Bull   V   Hard
Avenue: Ov/Of   He/E   New/Knew   Eve   He/E   Knew (In the Bible Sense)
Street: Stray   T/Fem Cross   Stay/Rite Roaming: (Room/In)

Roaming: Room   In/N/Virgin
roam: to ramble   to wander
There is Plenty of Wandering for The Fems if She wants to Provide Room

The Dam Code The Damn Book

Roar: R/O/R   2 RRs/Her/R/Ear/Hear/Hair/Err/Heir/Or/Whore/Here/Are/Our/Ere/Air/Ire/Sex (Plural or All of Them)
Or is Gold in French
The Masc Roars during Sex with 2 Fem or Having Sex in Plural

Robber: Rub   Her/R/Ear/Hear/Hair/Err/Heir/Or/Whore/Here/Are/Our/Ere/Air/Ire/Sex   To Rub Against/Her   Robe/Rub
Rob/Her   To Steal from Her   That Way She Stays Poor
Robe/Her   As Strong as Rubber
robe: loose garment
Get Out/In Fast   Easy for Quick Access to Sex

Rock: ROK   also with   C/Young Girl/See   or   Q/Menstrual Cycle/Time of The Month
R/Her/Ear/Hear/Hair/Err/Heir/Or/Whore/Here/Are/Our/Ere/Air/Ire/Sex   O/Fem Hole   K/Broken Fem Warrior
It is The Rock of Jesus (See Alchemical Word for Stone)
She Wears that Rock on Her Left Finger
Bock/Buck   Cock   Duck   Fuck   Jock (Sheppard) Ock (Smallness)   Guck (Slime or Oozy Dirt)   Cock   Luck/Lock   N/Nock/Nock/Knocked (a Notch)   Muck/Mock   Puck/Pock   Suck   Poor Words for a Fem
Rock is a VIP Word in   The Code
On This Rock I will Build My Church   Said Jesus

Rod: Her/R/Ear/Hear/Hair/Err/Heir/Or/Whore/Here/Are/Our/Ere/Air/Ire/Sex   O/Fem Hole   D/Pregnant
A Rod is an Entirely Masc Symbol Representing a Penis Although it is Made of 2 Fem Letters and R/Sex Act   Add A and That Road Connects All The Fems in   The Code   to That Rod   which Makes Her Pregnant
rod: stick   fishing rod
Erode   Her/Rod   Herod in Bible
The Water Eventually Erodes the Rock but Who has the Time

Rodent: Road/In/T
The Road   is for   N/In/Hen/Ann/Virgin/Donkey   to Arrives at   T/Fem Cross
The Rat is One of the Cover Word in The Code Art

Lise Rochon

R/At   R/Hat
The Art   The Search for the Secret Society Rites
The English Language is One of The Rites   Math is Another   Music Another   Construction Another   Magic Another

Roger: Rogue/Her   Rag/Her   Rage/Her
roger: All right   Ok
The Fems on The Rag is a Good Thing says   The Code
It will Enrage and Rogue Her   Roger to That
rogue: a dishonest knavish person   scoundrel
And She Goes Down again
Rogue: R/Hug   Rag   Back on The Rag for Her

Roman :   R O M N   4 Fem Sound Letters
R/Her/Are/Her/Hair/Hear/Ear/Whore/Err/Sex   Home   N/In/Hen/Virgin/VirgiN/In/Hen/Virgin
The Home For The Fems is to be a R/Whore Through Her O/Fem Hole   M/Motherhood and Her Daughters
Add a C or a S and Get
R   Own   Hence
Roman is a Cover Word here
Because of the Word Romance
The Fems Love Romance   Therefore
Romance: R/Home/Hence

Romantic: Row/Man/T/IC
Men do Not Feel Romance So they Keep on Rowing to get to Her as an Integrated Circuit Created By   The Code   a Long Ago   Also Keep those Fems in Rows

Roof: R/Off   R/Of
Room: Her/R/Ear/Hear/Hair/Err/Heir/Or/Whore/Here/Are/Our/Ere/Air/Ire/Sex   2 OOs/Fem Holes   M/Motherhood
As in Promiscuity or Having Several Sex Partners
Add B/Boy Holding All Fem Breasts and He Gets a Broom
(Too Young for The Code)   Broom is a Slang Word for
Penis   Boom   Doom   Goon   Soon   Toon   Vroom   Wound   Coon   Zoom   are Weak Words for The Fems

The Dam Code The Damn Book

Roommate: Room to Mate

Root: RT
R/Her/Ear/Hear/Hair/Err/Heir/Or/Whore/Here/Are/Our/Ere/Air/Ire/ Sex   with 2 OOs/Fem Holes (as in Plural or All of Them)   and   T/Fem Cross/Fem Great Curse
All O/Fem Loins are Confined Between   R/Her/Heir/Or/Whore   and   T/Fem Cross
The Root is   R/Her/Heir/Or/Whore   with   2 OOs/Fem Holes   and   Her   T/Fem Cross
Switch O for A/All Men and He Gets a Rat   The Code   says No to Roots for Him With Her
Rut   Rot   Ruth   Rat   are Weak Words For The Fems   Rit (e) does Not Exist as a Word   That would be Too Much Information

Rosary: The Rose is the Ultimate Symbol for a Fem (See Rose)
Endlessly Repeating the Same Sentences in Reciting a Rosary   On Our knees as in My Time When I was a Young Girl
Rose: R/Her/Ear/Hear/Hair/Err/Heir/Or/Whore/Here/Are/Our/Ere/Air/Ire/ Sex   O/Fem Hole   S/Is/His/Ass/Us/Hiss/Penis/Serpent   E/Man
Sex for All Men says   The Code
R/Hose   The Hose is a Masc Symbol
To Rose is the Past
Rise Means to Go Up as in Positive   Rose is a Symbol for the Fem Genitalia   A Rose is a Venus Symbol
A Rose is the Symbol for The Brotherhood of the Rosy Cross
The Symbol of the Rosy Cross is a Cross Encircled with a Dot (the Dot is a Small circle) in the Middle
The Rose is the Symbol of the Unfolding Higher Consciousness   The Rose is a Symbol for the Grail   The Rose was Identified with the Wounds of Christ   The Rose is a Most Revered Symbol in Ancient Egypt Sacred to Isis   The Rose is Affiliated with Aphrodite the Goddess of Love   Cybele (Si/Belle as in So Beautiful) the Great Mother Magna Mater Holiday was a Procession with Roses   Hanging a Rose Over a Council Table Meant Everything Must be Kept Secret Sub Rosa   A Rose is the Flower of the Virgin Mary Rosa Mystica   etc
Magnificent Gothic Cathedrals Depicts Roses Windows

Lise Rochon

The Rose in the 12 Century became the Chiefly Symbol of the Re-Emerging Fem as a Fem Principle in Courtly Love
Rosemary and Thyme   Rose/Mary/Time   Rose/Marry/Time   Rose/Merry/Time
Rose is Roads for   The Code

Rosenstein: Rosenberg   or   Any Name Containing the Word Rose
The Jewish People Carry a Lot of Their Secrets in their Names
In America it is Common for Jewish and German to Alter Their Names to Make it Sound More American
Jewish Tradition is Heavy in Esotericism   They Use Tarot Astrology and Symbolism

Roslyn Chapel: Has Thousands of Carved Roses
It is Called a Bible in Stone   Roslyn is Called the Chapel of the Grail   It is Called the Cathedral of Codes   It Stands on the Original Prime Meridian before Greenwich
The Speculation is The Roslyn Links the Merovingian   the Templars   and   the Prieure De Sion
The Saint Clair families Build it in 1466
Prieure de Sion First Grand Master and Master Mind was Sir William St-Clair known as Prodigus 3rd Prince of Orkney
Roslyn Chapel is seen as The Missing Link that Demonstrate the Continuity Between the Knights Templars and the Freemasons

Round: Her/R/Ear/Hear/Hair/Err/Heir/Or/Whore/Here/Are/Our/Ere/Air/Ire/Sex   Hound
hound: bred of hunting dogs   despicable person
And She is back to The Dogs   or   having a Despicable Personality   Sex with a Dog is Having Sex with a Bitch
To Be Round is to be Pregnant

Rounder: Round/Her
Mary Goes Round Again (See Round in The Words Chapter)
rounder: an expert   a game   a tool   a drunk   a dissolute person
All those Definitions are Weakening to The Fems by making Her
a   Cheater   a   Drunk   and an   Expert   at it   says   The Code

The Dam Code The Damn Book

Row: R/Owe   The Fems Are Kept in a Row (See Row in The Words Chapter) and are Owing That Code Ship to make it Move   Not Only are They The Victims of The Code   They are also The Labor Force making it Move
Her/R/Ear/Hear/Hair/Err/Heir/Or/Whore/Here/Are/Our/Ere/Air/Ire/Sex   O/Fem Hole
The R/Heir/Or/Whore   O/Fem Hole   Are The Row says   The Code

Rubber: Rub/Her   Rob/Her   R/Bear/Her
rubber: a prophylactic
Rubber is a Cover Word here

Rubbish: Rub/Is/She   Rob/Is/Shh
Being Rub   Not So Important
To Steal from Her is the Secret   Rob/She
Litter (Let/Her)   Trash (Tear   Shh/She)
Fem are Always Related in   The
Code   as   Inferior   Weak   Sick   Stupid   Animalistic   Ill   Poor   Sinful   Damned Whore   The Fems is a Piece of Garbage or Feces

Rug: Her/R/Ear/Hear/Hair/Err/Heir/Or/Whore/Here/Are/Our/Ere/Air/Ire/Sex   Hug
R/Her/Heir/Or/Whore   G/Penis Penetration
Switch U for A/All Men and He Gets a Rag (So He Goes Away Fast)
Switch U for E/He and He Gets a Reg (Regulation   so He goes Away Fast)
Switch U for i/Marriage Act and She Gets a Rig
rig: to put in proper order for working or use   to fit (a ship mast etc) with the necessary shrouds stays etc   to manipulate fraudulently
(See Ship (She/P and Ocean (O/She/In))
Switch i for O/Fem Hole and She Gets a R.O.G   receipt of goods
Switch R for B/Boy Holding All Fem Breasts and He Gets a Bug (the Boy is too Young to Know about the Rag/Code)
Switch R for C/See/Young Girl and She Gets a Cog
cog: a person who plays a minor part in a large organization activity etc
Switch R for D/Pregnant and She Gets a Dog/Dug or be One/Bitch
Switch R for H/Secret Code Letter and Get Hog

hog: a selfish gluttonous or filthy person   a domesticated swine weighing 120 pounds (54 kilos) or more raised for market   a sheep about one year old that has not been shorn
Shorn   She/Horn   Past for the Word Shear (She/Hear)
She Cannot have a Horn (Power) Because it is in the Past   She Cannot Hear in Present Tense because it is Cut Off
shear: to cut (something)   to strip or deprive   *Chiefly Scot* to reap with a sickle
Sickle   Sick/All   She cannot Hear   The Code   in Action
A Horn is a Phone and an Erection   and   a Musical Instrument to make Us Forget
Her Powers are Cut Off from Her as a Young Child
The Power of Her/R/Ear/Hear/Hair/Err/Heir/Or/Whore/Here/Are/Our/Ere/Air/Ire/Sex   is Cut Off from Her
Then Sheep is Her Name
Switch R for F/Fem/Fuck and She Gets Fog(So She Cannot See that Way)
Switch R for J/Sheppard Stick and Get Jug (The New Fem Big Breasts for Her) The Sheppard says to the Sheep/Her
Bug   Dog   Dug   Rag   Rug   Tog   Tug   Hug   No Power Words for Her in Those Words Related to Rug   Which was Related to the Rag in Older Times   Because The Fems would Sit on a Rug While Bleeding
Switch R for L/Sweet Love and She Gets a Lug (A Woody)
Switch R for M/Motherhood and She Gets a Mug (a Cup) (Oops She Got Mugged)
Switch R for N/In/Hen/Virgin and She Gets a Nog (Only Available between Christmas and New Year Eve)
nog: a beverage made with beaten eggs usually with alcoholic liquor
The   Eggs/Ovo/Eve   are Beaten   The Code   Beat those Eggs   And Nag about it
Add L/Sweet Fem Light and She Gets a Plug   (Socket/Suck/It)
Switch R for P/Man Power and He Gets a Pug
pug: a boxer   to knead clay with water to make it plastic as for brickmaking
It is a Solid Word For The Masc Here
Switch R for T/Fem Cross and She Gets Tug
tug: to pull with force vigor or effort   to move by pulling forcibly   drag   haul
She has No Freedom here Either

The Dam Code The Damn Book

The/Rag/All
Switch R for V/Fem Sex Active and She Gets Vug
vug: a small cavity in a rock or vein often lined with crystals
It is the   Vogue   to be Sex Active for the Fems says   The Code   to be So Small

Ruin: Are/You/In
Her/R/Ear/Hear/Hair/Err/Heir/Or/Whore/Here/Are/Our/Ere/Air/Ire/Sex   U/You/Ovulating   N/In/Hen/Virgin/Ann/Virgin
Heir/Or/Whore   You   Ann   it is All About Ruin to The Fems

Rule: Her/Rule   R/Her/Ear/Hear/Hair/Err/Heir/Or/Whore/Here/Are/Our/Ere/Air/Ire/Sex   U/You/Ovulating   L/Sweet Fem Love Light/All/Ail/Ill/Hail/Heel/Hell/Elle/Oil
The Rule is Sex Bring Love to The Fems says   The Code
Switch O for U/Uterus and She Gets a Roll or To Roll
Rock Them (Dame as in Sex) and Roll (Release) them as in Letting Them Go
Switch U for i/Marriage Act and She Gets Rill
rill: a mall rivulet or brook
A Rally on Rails (2 of them Fems) for the Ruler   Rule/Her
ruler: a strip of wood metal or other material having a straight edge and usually marked off in inches or centimeters used for drawing lines measuring etc
To Rule says   The Code   is to Keep on Measuring and Spying   The Fems
Inch (In/She) Foot (F/Hoot   Hooter   F/Hot) Yard (He/Hard)
yard: *Informal* a large quantity or extent   *Slang* one hundred or usually one thousand dollars

Rumor: Room/Her
A Room for Her is Only a Rumor says   The Code

Run: Her/R/Ear/Hear/Hair/Err/Heir/Or/Whore/Here/Are/Our/Ere/Air/Ire/Sex   N/In/In/On/Ann/Virgin/Donkey
R/Her/Sex   is On for   Ron

Rusty: Her/R/Ear/Hear/Hair/Err/Heir/Or/Whore/Here/Are/Our/Ere/Air/Ire/Sex   Us/S/Is/His/Serpent/Penis   T/Fem Cross
Heir/Or/Whore   S/Penis   T/Fem Cross
Rust/He   Rust is an Old Word for a Dark Red (Dry Blood Color as in Burgundy   The Color of a Dark Red Wine)
Red Always Represents (Her) Blood
Rusty is a Masc Name (Rust/He) because   The Code   Confounds Fems and Mascs Concepts to Confuse Everybody   Especially The Fems

Rut: Route   Root   Rot
rut: the periodically recurring sexual excitement of the deer goat sheep
But   Butt   Gut/Got   Hut Mutt   Nut   Sotte (Stupid in French) are Poor Words
Switch R/Heir/Or/Whore for Hard C/See/Young Girl and She Gets a Cot (Poverty is Around for Her Young or Old

RX: The 2 Letters From the Pharmaceutical/Medical/Pills Prescription World
Her/R/Ear/Hear/Hair/Err/Heir/Or/Whore/Here/Are/Our/Ere/Air/Ire/Sex   X/Fallen Fem Cross   Making an Alliance by Making a Second Cross (X/Death/Fallen Cross) in
Between
Many Words End with Her/R   See in The Text Below
Answer (Ants/Her) Better (Bet/Her) Banner (Ban/Her   Bang/Her) Baker (Bake/Her) Believer (Believe R as Worshipper   Warship/Her) Bidder (Bid/Her) Bigger (Make Her Big (Pregnant) Bag/Her) Binger (Binge/Her) Blinder (Blind/Her) Broker (Broke/Her) Builder (Build/Her   A Code Word) Butcher (Botch/Her) Buyer (Buy/Her   Sell/Her) Calculator (Calculate/Her/R) Cashier (Cash on Her) Chaser (Chase/Her) Cleaner (She Cleans   Clean/R   Keep The Whores Clean   So they do Not Carry Diseases) Copier (Copy R) Detractor (Detract/Her) Destructor (Destruct/Her) Dicker (Dick/Her   a petty bargain) Trader (Trade/Her Ducker (Duck/Her) Dryer (Fry/Her) Falter (Fault/Her) Faster (Fast/Her   Fest/Her) Fertilizer (Fertilize/Her) Further (Fur   T/Her   Lucy/Fur) Harder (Hard/Her) Hitter (Hit/Her) Jailer (Jail/Her) Joker (Laugh Hat/At Her) Kicker (Kick/Her) Killer (Kill/Her) Kidnaper (Take Her Away   Lose/Her) Ladder (Lad/Her   Nothing There for Her) Left (Wrong Side from Mr Right) Locker (Lock/Her) Lover (Love   R/Her/Heir/Or/Whore) Manufacturer

The Dam Code The Damn Book

(Manufacture/Her   Master (Mast/Her) Mixer (Mix/Max/Her) Murder (Bad to Her   Mur are 3 Fems Letters   including Motherhood) No Brain Her (Where is No/Brain/He) Operator (Operate/Her) Order (Herd/Her) Organizer (Organize/Her) Preacher (P/Reach Her/R) Prisoner (Prison/Her) Prosecutor (Prosecute/Her) Provider (Provide/R) Rider (Ride   Her/R) Rocker (Rock/Her From Jesus Terminology I will built My Church on this Rock   To be Stoned to Death) Rounder (Impregnate/Her) Ruler (Rule/Her) Scamper (Scamp R/Her/Heir/Are/Whore/Sex) Seller (Sell/Her) Sewer (Sue/Her) Shutter (Shut/Her   Shh/She) Sicker (Sick/Her) Skewer (Screw/Her   With   R) Spitter (Spit/Her) Splitter (Split/Her) Stalker (Stalk/Her) Stripper (Strip/Her) Stupor (Stupid/Her) Supervisor (Supervise/Her) Temper(Temperature/Her) Terminator (Terminate/Her) Timer (Time Her Time of The Month   She Does   The Fem is Versatile) Transformer (Transform/Her   Men do Not Change) Trainer (Train/Her   A School of Fishes) Trapper (Trap/Her) Traitor (Threat/Her) Truster (Trust/Her Does Not Exist   No Fem There   Trust/He   Only Trustee   2 EE/He (Two or All of Them) with 2 TTs/Fem Crosses   Cannot do Much When Nailed on a Cross) (Thrust/Her) Vibrator (Shake/Her) Washer (She Washes All   The Sins of the World Included) Wastewater (Dirty Water Again for Her) Worker (Work/Her   Whore/K/R) Worshipper (Whore/Ship/Her Warship/Her   See Ship

There is No Worship/He   in That Code   All Worship/Her are Fems   With a S/Penis   at Its End)

Find Some Positive Ones: Cooler (Ops   No Kill/Her) Nicer (N/Ice/R   Ops   No Frigid)

They are Different Energies Between the Suffix Starting in R/Her/Heir/Whore/Sex   and   E/He

Compare here to a Few Words in E/He and See the Difference Between   The Code   Concepts

MASC: Army   Badly   Clumsy   Cocky   Cranky   Crazy   Dirty   Funny   Glossy   Goofy   Greedy   Grumpy   Hairy   Lucky   Messy   Nasty   Prickly   Sadly   Scary   Seedy   Shinny   Study   Sweetie   Men Live in a Different World   Tells   The Code

The Fems Words have an Action Done to Her   as   R/Her/Are/Whore/Sex The Masc Words are More   a   State of Being   and there are   Fewer   than The Fems

S s
Intro
S is the Letter of the Penis Itself
S/Is/His/Ass/Us/Hiss/Penis/Serpent
Serpent and Snake   Both Words Starts with S
SSS is the Sound of Fire in the Sky
S for See   S for Sea (C/Virgin)
All Water (What/Her) Words are Fem Symbols in   That Code
Letter s/S/Penis is Half the Shape of # 8 (Hate/Eat/∞)   Number 8 is Her Pregnancy (See # 8 in The Numbers Chapter)
S is the Sinuous Stick that   Bends   Dances   and   Plays
It Sleeps in Letter ZZZZ Facing the Other Side
Z is The Letter for Sleep on It and Forget it   Z Means   As Above as Below ZZZ
Here is the Zigzag Again in ZZZ   This Time Sideways as it is Crawling as a Snake
S the Snake/Stick is also The Scepter of Gold   Great Power is Associated with It   Popes and Kings have Them   Men Love their Sticks   They are their Weapons and We Need them to Chase Predators and Hunt
It is the Serpent Energy   It is All Masc says   The Code
S Is what Is (S) is His (S)
In The Bible and Other Codes Books
The Snake is with Us Since Genesis First Story/Chapter
And the Great Curse was Generated after Those Events
The Story of A/Damn and Eve/Ov/V/The Now Fem Sex Active as in No More Long Ovulation Cycle Now
When Fem E/He and V Meet   What Can Happen (Hop/In   She was then already Open at all Times to Have Sex No Matter where She was in Her Cycle Time)
"In The beginning was the Word and the Word was with God and the Word was God"
To me that Phrase is the Most Symbolic Phrase in the Book
It Basically says that   Not God   The Language   Constructed God   then People Adored That God
True Religion Lives in the Light of the Heart for Its Deity
It Adopt its Good Principles for Self and Others   says I
As We All Know there Many Secret Codes Through History

The Dam Code The Damn Book

Many New Discoveries of Ancient Codex or New Found Gospels Shedding More Light on Our Ancient Identities
Letter S as Ass also Imply Having Sex in the Ass as Contraception or/and Homosexuality   Man had Sex in the Ass with Animals Too as Goats (Study Satan as the Goat Figure) Donkeys (The N/Âne Ann) and the Horse (Whores)
This is Old Secret Code Put Together in a Rare Way Here
Some Part of that Are Butt Jokes Now
S is the Sign of Money In Front or Behind 1 or 2 Bars $
There is Only One Bar Really
The Bar/War is Against Us the Fem
On All Fronts Since the Beginning of the A/Damn   and   He/V (See Adam and Eve in the Words Chapter)
S is a Plural Letter/Symbol
So Every Time We Add a Plural S on a Word
We Add a Larger Quantity of the Sex/Snake Concept to that Word   A Subtle Concept as Usual
These Concepts Make Their Way into Our Brains Every Time We Use those Letters/Words
S and X are Close in Sounds
It is S/Snake/Penis that Leads   D/Pregnant Daughter   in   T/Fem Cross   and   T in X/Fallen Cross
The Definitive Massive Death/Curse of All Fems
Is a Common View Throughout   The Code
S in the Alphabet Would be a Trail as a Trail in the Sand
S being a Kickass Letter   S is Quiet and Sinuous

Words in S: As   Ass   Hiss   Is   His   Us

S   s
Sac: SAK   SAQ
S/Is/His/Ass/Us/Hiss/Penis/Serpent   is with   K/Broken Fem Warrior   That is the End   K is In the Sack
Her Form has Switched from Letter R to Letter K   With R/Heir/Or/Whore Happening to Her
Sack   Sex/Hack   Sex/Act   Sect
sack: to pillage or loot after capture   plunder   a large bag   dismissal or discharge from a job

Hit the Sack
Add Red to Sack and Get   Sacred   Sac/Red   Red Sac (Her Uterus/U)

Sacred: Sac/Red   the Red Sac is the Rose/Rosicrucian   The Fems
Genitalia   Sacred is Close to Secret
The Secret of the Ancients is the Red Sac Mystery
The Red Rose of the Rosicrucian Symbol
The Red Sack or Bag   Her Loins
Same for the Holy Grail (Hole/He Girl)
The Sang REAL   Not ROYAL Blood as Said in the Da Vinci Code

Sad: S/Is/His/Ass/Us/Hiss/Penis/Serpent   Add
S/Had
When Penis Had It   S/Add
Add i/Marriage Act and it is Said
Switch S for B/Boy Holding All Fem Breasts and He Gets Bad (Too Young for The Code)
Switch S for M/Motherhood and She Gets Mad
Add i/Marriage Act and She Gets to be a Maid
Switch S for H/Secret Code Letter and Get Had (The Same Old Code)
Switch S for L/Sweet Fem Light and She Gets a Lad

Saddle: Sad/All   S/Add/All
saddle: to impose a burden of responsibilities
What s In The Saddle For The Fems is All/Ill/Hell/Hill/Elle

Safe: SF
S/Is/His/Ass/Us/Hiss/Penis/Serpent   F/Fem/Fuck
S/Penis and F/Fuck are Together   It is Safe says   The Code
S/If   Say If You and Me (I Hear a Song)
See the Many Definitions for Safe in Dictionary
Add Her/R/Ear/Hear/Hair/Err/Heir/Or/Whore/Here/Are/Our/Ere/Air/Ire/Sex   to Safe and Get SFR/Safer   Save   R/Her/Heir/Or/Whore   Save/Heir
Safety: SFT
S/Penis   F/Fem/Fuck   T/Fem Cross
The Code   says   S/Penis   is with   F/Fem/Fuck   It Brings Her to T/Fem Cross   It is a Safe Place to Be

The Dam Code The Damn Book

Sage: S/Age   S/His/Penis   Age
The Wise Man that Knows How to Use His Penis

Sailor: Sail/Her   Soil/Her   Sell/Her   Sale/Heir   Soil/Whore
S/Is/His/Ass/Us/Hiss/Penis/Serpent   All
A Girl in Every Port is   The Code   Logo

Saint: SNT
S/Penis   N/In/Hen/Ann/Donkey/Virgin   T/Fem Cross
When Penis is with The Virgin and The Fems Cross   It is Sanctity
Sein is Breast in French   "En Son Sein" (In Her Breast or Her Uterus in French) is Part of the Prayer To Saint Mary
Sang is Blood in English
Sans Means Without or Less in French

Sake: Sac/He   The Sac is the Bag/Chalice/Letter U and O
sake: cause   account   interest   or   benefit   purpose or end   a Japanese alcoholic drink made from fermented rice
Switch C   K   or   Q   for G/Penis Penetration/and He Gets Sag/He (Soggy)   Suck/He   Sock/He

Saloon: Sell/On
A Saloon is Where they Sell Alcohol (All/Cool) and Meet Fem for Money
Salon is Living Room in French   As it is All Normal for   The Code

Salt: S/Is/His/Ass/Us/Hiss/Penis/Serpent   L/Sweet Fem Love Light/All/Ail/Ill/Hail/Heel/Hell/Elle/Oil   T/Fem Cross   Assault   S/Halt Ass/Salt
A Good person would Be Called The Salt of The Earth   Here is a Different Meaning Especially Made by   The Code

Same thing: S/Is/His/Ass/Us/Hiss/Penis/Serpent   Aim/M/Motherhood   Thing/Ding
All Fems the Same says   The Code   She Aims for His Penis and Motherhood

Sanctuary: Sang/Tour/He
Sang is Blood in French   Sang is to Sing in Past Tense)
The Code   Hides in The Most Blessed Religious Words

Sanctus: Sang/T/Us

Sandwich: See   End   Witch (See Witch in The Words Chapter)
A Sandwich by Definition from   The Code   is Made with 2 Pieces of Bread (Bred)   a Symbol for 2 Fems
The Sandwich Islands Represents an Example of   The Code   Sand/Witch   Pélé is a Goddess that the White Man had to Know About When First Arriving in Hawaii a Long Time Ago
Sandwich is a Cover Word here

Sane: S/Is/His/Ass/Us/Hiss/Penis/Serpent   Ann/N/In/Hen/Virgin
The Code   says Ann is with Penis She is Sane The Sin is In S/In

Sarcasm: Sire   K/Broken Fem Warrior   Ism
Ism: a distinctive doctrine theory system or practice

Satan: S/Is/His/Ass/Us/Hiss/Penis/Serpent   A/All Men   T/Fem Cross   N/In/Hen/Ann/Donkey/Virgin
A/All Men Penises   are Followed by the   T/Great Fem Curse   N/In/Hen/Ann/Virgin/Donkey   Sat/Anne
In the Ancient Times they were No Fem Hygiene (High Genes ?) Products   so   Ann Sat On a Rug/Rag When Bleeding (See the Legend of Arthur)
Sat   N/In/Virgin/Donkey
Satin the Soft Fabric is the Cover Word here
Satanic: Sat   N/In/Hen/Virgin/Ann   IC
IC: integrated circuit
When the Christians Denounced Satan
It Meant Basically that it Prohibited Them to go there and See That Kind of Bad Energy
When Ann/N Sit Instead of Working It is Because She is Losing Her Blood
1 D/Day/a Weak/Week a Month Would Be about 4 Days (Dizzy) a Month/Mount   The Length of Time of Her Period   Pair/He/Odd   Here Again is The Concept of Polygamy for The Masc   Her Period Comes After The Sentence   No matter Which One   Here the Sentence is Evil   Eve/Ill   Because it is a Death for Sat/Ann   for The Fems   Satan and Saturn (Sat/Urn   (See Urn in The Words Chapter) Saturn is the Mean God of Bad Times (Time of the Month) Have Close Sounds

sat: the realm of existence populated by people and Gods according to the Vedas mythology
Sat in Sanskrit means literally   Being
Sat in Hinduism is Reality   Satsang   Means True Company

Saturday: Sat/Her/Day
Saturday Afternoon: Sat/Her/Day/After/Noon
The Noon is the Moon in the Day Time   Where She is Represented by the N/In/Hen/Ann/Donkey/Virgin   But She is Too Young or Naïve to Understand   That Her Moon is Coming

Saturn   Sat/Urn
Originally Saturn was Positive
In Ancient Times Saturn was the God of Agriculture the Consort of Ops (Beer) believed to have Ruled the Earth during an Age of Happiness and Virtue
Now is Saturn The God of Endless Hard Times Limitations and Restrictions
Saturn Has Many Moons (Polygamy) and Has a Day Named after Him Saturday   Another Day Of Work
In Alchemy Saturn is the Metal Lead   Which Correspond to the Transubstantiation of Her Blood (Time of the Month)   Saturn is the God of Time in the Symbolic/Alchemical Gold
The Saturn Symbol ♄ is the T/Fem Cross Curse Over the Soul
Saturn is the Reverse of Jupiter the Plentiful
Sat/Urn   In Ancient Greece and Before When The Fems Sat on an Urn/Vase While Bleeding
The Vase is Her Symbol for the Uterus and the Chalice   says   The Code

Save: SV
S/Is/His/Ass/Us/Hiss/Penis/Serpent   V/Fem Sex Active
As Long as V/The Fem has Sex with S/Penis   She is Saved says   The Code
Say/Eve   See/Eve   S/Ave

Savior   Save   He/Her   That could be One of The Reason Why Jesus was Crucified   to save both Him and Her   That was a First   Mary Magdalene was His Beloved

Lise Rochon

Savor is The Cover Word here   Savor is Between People That Love and Savor Each Other

Saved: S/Eve/D
S/Is/His/Ass/Us/Hiss/Penis/Serpent   V/Fem Sex Active   D/Pregnant
She is Saved When Pregnant from Penis says   The Code

Say: S/Hey   S/Hay
S/Is/His/Ass/Us/Hiss/Penis/Serpent   A/All Men   Y/Wounded Fem Warrior
See/A   Something to look for says   The Code
A Very Masc Oriented Word   Who Can Speak Has Power   And Old Say   That is Why   The Code   Keeps The Fems Silenced   Here in Say   Only The Penis Talks

Scamper: Scamp/Her
scamp: rascal   rogue   unscrupulous
Here She Goes Down Again

Scared: Scar/D   S/Care/D
To Scar D/Pregnant is part of   The Code

Scarlet: Scar/Let
scarlet: bright red color   sinful   immoral
Anything Red is Always a Reminder of Blood
The Scarlet Robe Put on Jesus Shoulders by Pilate
Scarlet is a Fem Name
Ecarlate is French Word for Scarlet
Judas Iscariot
Scarlet Has roots in Latin English Arabic French and Greek
"Sins as Scarlet" Isa. 1:18
A word Full of History
For Us Fem Losing Large Amount of Blood on a Regular Basis Certainly Leaves Scarlet Scars

Scary: Scar/He   Scare/He   S/Care/He
His Cares for   S/Is/His/Ass/Us/Hiss/Penis/Serpent
S/Is/His/Ass/Us/Hiss/Penis/Serpent   Care   He/E
Penis taking Care of itself is Scary

The Dam Code The Damn Book

Scat: S/Cat
S/Penis and the Cat
Not a Good Mix   Scat
C/K/Hat
C/See/Young Girl   and   K/Broken Fem Warrior   In the Hat   Seek/Hat   To Seek the Hat for   The Secret Code is a Big No   so Scat

Scene: Sin   Seen   Semen   Sown
The Sin and The Seen are The Same as   The Code   Assimilation for The Fems

Scent: Cent
Sent   Send the Scent as a Perfume on a Letter
Sin   (See/In)   T/Fem Curse
Sin/Tax   Syntax is The Study of the Pattern of Sentences
The Code is in Every Step of the
Language   From   Letters   Words   Sentences   All
Punctuations   and   Symbols
For Example   After a Sentence is a Period   The Period is The Fems Great Curse   It is a Sentence on Her   We are all Cursed According to The Bible Book
Switch E for U/Ovulation and She Gets Cunt

School: Is/S/His/Ass/Us/Hiss/Penis/Serpent   Cool
Learn that the Penis is Cooling   I Always Thought that Myself   Vive la Difference   We do Not Attract Flies with Vinegar

Scissors: CSRS
C/Young Virgin   is in Front of   Her/R/Ear/Hear/Hair/Err/Heir/Or/Whore/Here/Are/Our/Ere/Air/Ire/Sex   and in Between   2 SS/Is/His/Ass/Us/Hiss/Penisses/Serpents
She Is Seized and Get Cut
Seize/Hers   Sees/Hers   Seizures
C/See/Young Girl   is with   S/His/Penis
It Implies Here Her Lost of Virginity with Scissors or a Knife   She is Under the Knife Again as in Clitorectomy
The Cut (C/Hot)   The Cot (C/Hot)   The Dot (D/Hot)

Lise Rochon

The Word Cut in Dictionary.com has a list of 89 Meanings and Usages for Cut
Cut is All 3 Fem Letters
Scissors is Soft Enough to Put to Sleep   SZSrrrSZSrrrSSS
Stay Away from That and you will Not Get Cut
But Not Here   The Fems Will Go Through it (Hit) Anyway as it has been in Our History and the Boys also with The Circumcision
Scissors is a Cover Word here

Scoff: S/Is/His/Ass/Us/Hiss/Penis/Serpent   Cough
S/Penis   Cough
Coughing is also Related to Sex Ejaculation When Men Talk to Each Other in Slang
scoff: to speak derisively mock jeer

Scorpion: Score   P/Man Power   Own/On
The One with the Poisonous Tail

Scorn: S/Is/His/Ass/Us/Hiss/Penis/Serpent   is in Front of Corn so   She Gets a   Scorn
scorn: open or unqualified contempt disdain   an object of derision or contempt
Sound Letter C/See/Young Girl is in Front of a Horn (The Stick of Power)   A Big No from   The Code   so Scorn it is for Her

Secret: Sacred   Sac/Red   Sac/Rite
Seek/Rite
The Secret is About The Red Sac (Her Fem Organs)   Secret is an Important Word in   The Code

Seduction: See   Duck   She/Shh   On/N/Ann/Donkey/Virgin
For The Fems it is Back to the Animals again says   The Code

Semen: See/Men   Sea/Men   C/Men
C/See/Young Girl
The Sea is a Fem Symbol as All Water (What/Her) Related Words
Note in the Dictionary there are No Derogatory Concepts Associated with Semen

The Dam Code The Damn Book

Sentimental: Scent/He/Meant/All
Scent/He/Mental   The Code   Use Concepts as That to Induce Pregnancy

Shack: Shake
To Shack is Slang for Having Illicit Sexual Relations   Shake Her says   The Code
Switch H/Secret Society for N/Virgin and She Gets Snake (She is Not Allowed to Understand)

Shackle: Shake/All
To Shack is to have Sex in American Slang
Add L/Sweet Fem Love and She Gets Shackle   From Shack to Shackles   She Gets Punished for having Sex also
shackle: a ring or other fastening as of iron for securing the wrist ankle etc   anything that serves to prevent freedom of procedure of thought etc
She/Shh   K/Wounded Fem Warrior   All
The Code in Full Force here

Score: S/Core
S/Is/His/Ass/Us/Hiss/Penis/Serpent   C/Young Girl   Her/R/Ear/Hear/Hair/Err/Heir/Or/Whore/Here/Are/Our/Ere/Air/Ire/Sex   S/Penis is Having Sex with a Young Girl   It is Called a Score in American Slang says   The Code

Scorn: S/Is/His/Ass/Us/Hiss/Penis/Serpent   C/See/Young Girl   Horn
Take Away N/In/Hen/Virgin/Donkey and Get a Score (No More a Virgin)

Screw: S/Is/His/Ass/Us/Hiss/Penis/Serpent   Crew
Plural S is Better than Only One   The Crew That Screws
Both Ends are S/His/Penis (Plural or as in All of Them)
Just to make Sure says   The Code
screw: slang for sex   a metal fastener

Scrub: S/Is/His/Ass/Us/Hiss/Penis/Serpent   Rub
Always about The penis says   The Code

Scumbag: Scum   Bag
S/Penis being in Front of 3 Fem Letters   and a Bag   He is The Boss   Another Nasty Fem Definition as Douche Bag is

Sea: S/Is/His/Ass/Us/Hiss/Penis/Serpent   E/He   and a (Silent Here) A/All Men
All Water Words are Fem   but All are 3 Masculine Letters
The/See/Letter C   The Holy See   The Hole/He/See   The Secret Society Code Barrier is to make it So Ugly No One Would Dare to Look at it and/or Think about It

Seal: See/C/Young Girl   L/Sweet Fem Love Light/All/Ail/Ill/Hail/Heel/Hell/Elle/Oil
To See All The Fems is Part of The Seal
The Secret Code Seal Interferes with The Fem Mind   so She Cannot See   The Code   in Action

Search: See/Her/Church
Keep the Faith/Fate Going says   The Code   to The Fems
Sire   She/Shh   Her/R/Ear/Hear/Hair/Err/Heir/Or/Whore/Here/Are/Our/Ere/Air/Ire/Sex   so She Has Sex with Sire

Season: See/Son   See/Sun
Sees/Eon   See/He/Is/On
Boys Being Preferred Over (Ov/Her) Girls
Is our Long Old Story
Seas/He/Is/On
Sea is Fem
C/His/He/On
C is the Young Girl Bleeding Girl No Sex Yet
Seasonal: See/Son/All
It is Seasonal as Seasons Are
The Code Perpetuates Itself that Way

Seat: See/T
If T/Fem Cross/Great Curse Would See Her Own Curse   That Would be a Big No from   The Code
The Seat is Where the Bottom Sits
No One Looks There for that Kind of Analytical Study
The Fems is the Butt of the Joke Still

Second: Sick/On   Sect/On   Sex/On

The Dam Code The Damn Book

Secret: Sacred   Sac/Red   Seek/Rite   Sac/Rite
Note That Secret Includes Rites and The Search for Rites   Which Are Related to The Sac   Sac is Another Slang Word for The Fems Genitals
The Secret of the Ancients is All About The Great Curse
No One Said that the Secret of the Ancients was Nice
The Secret Code of the Language is Only One Aspect of It   May be the Most Important   We are Surrounded Submerged by Its Daily Symbology (See Next Word Sect)

Sect: Sacked   Sex/Act   Set   Secret (Sac/Red)   Sec (One Second)
She is Sacked (See Secret Above) Through The Sex Act   and   Her Monthly Huge Loss of Blood   It Takes Just a Sec to Forget About It

Section: Sect/She/On   Sex/Shh/On   S/Axe/He/On
The Code   Tells Us in Advance How it Was and How it Will Be   Then Translated in Our Own Words and Concepts We Will Tell Ourselves Our Past and Our Future Accorded to That
Sex in Section Comes with (on a Sound Level) Axe (See Letter X/Her Fallen Cross in The Letter Chapter) and with an S/Is/His/Ass/Us/Hiss/Serpent/ Penis   and It Goes On for an Eon   in The Past and in The Future
Extreme Violence at Work from   That Code   When we Talk about an Axe   It has a Powerful Influence on The Unconscious
Since Jesus Time The Christians are Trying to Preach Love Kindness and Consciousness

Seduction: See/Duck/She/On   See/Duck/She/Eon
She Sees Herself as a Duck for an Eon   Back to the Animals For Her
The Silly Goose Term Are for the Young Fems Only   Not for The Boys
See/D/Yuck/She/Eon   See D/Pregnant as Yuck for an Eon   The Code   Cares about Nothing When it Comes to The Fems
Seductive: See/Duck/She/Eve   More of The Same
The Code   says See The Fems as a Duck to Seduce/Her
Seducer: See/Duce/Her
duce: a leader or a dictator
Another Dead End for The Fem

See: Sea   C/See/Young Girl
S/Is/His/Ass/Us/Hiss/Penis/Serpent   He/E

Lise Rochon

He and His Penis Can See
The Great Seal (Sea/See   All) The Holy See (Hole/He   See/Sea)
Several Religious Leaders as We know it have Abused Religion in the Name of God and the Saints
C Come Before D/Pregnant in The Alphabet   The Code   says This Where She Is Heading
Letter C and S Sounds are Close to Each Other

Seen: Sin   Sin/N   See/In   See N/Hen/Ann/In/Haine/Donkey
The Code   Confound here as Often a Cover and a Meaning
Here Sin Is Seen as Seeing N as a Donkey

Seek: See/K   Hard C/See/Young Girl   K/Wounded Fem Warrior
K and C Are The Ones to Look for says   The Code

Seigneur: French Word for God
Hold on to Your Head here
Saigne/Her   Means Literally to Bleed/Her
Senior and Seniora in Spanish

Self: Sell/F
The Fems cannot have an Identity says   The Code   so
Selling The F/Fem/Fuck Makes Her a Slave as Her Nature
self: a person nature

Selfish: Sell/Fish   Self   Shh/She
In   The Code   Fishes are The Fems in The Ocean (O/Fem Hole   She   Ann/N/Donkey)
To be Selfish is to Think about Oneself   The Fems are Taught to Think about Husbands and Children First
There Can be No Selfish in Her   so sell That Fish   it cannot Talk and Complain being a Silent Mouth   So it is an Easy Job says   The Code

Sell: S/Hell   C/Hell   C/Ill (See Ill)
The Weak Skinny Girls Are Always Popular in   The Code   They All Suffer from Anemia Because of The Blood Loss And Often Not Eating Enough or Properly because of Fashion Rules   and Constantly being told they have to be Skinnier or Smaller   The Code   has Remodeled The Fems

The Dam Code The Damn Book

Body   Not One Fem Wants Heavy on the Neck HMelons (They Call Them Jugs in Hollywood) to Hold in the Front of Their Body   And Will Curve their Back and cause Other Permanents Discomforts that Ages Her Faster and Causes Her Endless Pain

Semen: S/Is/His/Ass/Us/Hiss/Penis/Serpent   E/He   M/Motherhood/ Him   E/He   N/In/Hen/Virgin
All Men S/Penisses Semen are with Mothers and Virgin Daughters says   The Code
All Words Related to the Sea (C/See/Young Girl) are Related to
Fem   but   Semen Belongs to Men Exclusively so   it Includes The Fem because His Future cannot be Without Her
C/Sea/Men   C/Seamen   C/See/Men
C/See/Young Girl   Man
Switch M/Motherhood for N/In/Hen/Virgin and She Gets a Sin/Man (Sound as a Song) because She is a Virgin Without Authority on Her Life

Senator: Sin/Hat/Her   Sin/At/Her
Hat or Art are   The Code   Names for Their Secret
The Language Code is Testy on Every Level of Society
That is What Keep it Secret and Closed to a Few
Most Men of Power Never Really Helped The Fems to Get More Power or Money
John and Robert Kennedy were Sensitive to The Poor and The Fems Causes

Senor: Sin   Heir/Or/Whore (See Letter R in The Letter Chapter)
Senior is Man in Spanish   The Code   is in Every Language
La Puta is Part of The Common Daily Language

Sensational: Sin/Say/Shun/All   Sense/A/She/On/All
Sin/Sat/She/On/All
What is Sensational for The Fems says   The Code   is That Sin Shines on All Fems and It Makes Sense That She Sits   As The Fems were forced to Sit on a Rug/Rag When She was Doing Her Monthly Bleeding   The Bleeding Fems were Usually Isolated during that Time from The Mascs

Sensual: Sin   She/Shh   All   Sense   You/U/Uterus   All

Lise Rochon

All Fems are Sinning Silently with Their Uterus and it Makes Sense says   The Code

Sentence: Sin   T/Fem Cross   Hence
hence: from now on
See/N/Tense   From Now On   T/Fem Cross   is To Sin and Be Tense
At the End of a Sentence Come The/Her Period

Sentiment: Sin   T/Fem Cross   Meant   Scent/He/Meant
How a Man Feels Towards a Fem According to   The Code
(He/Mate/Mutt/You/On)   But No   The Code   says it is All About T/ Fems Cross/Curse   To Scarify Her

Serene: A Word with 3 EEEs/He   with   S/Is/His/Ass/Us/Hiss/Penis/ Serpent
Sir   In/N/Hen/Ann/Virgin
A Crowd of E/He/Mascs Are Alone Having R/Sex with N/In/Hen/Virgin   It is Serene says   The Code
The Code   is So Insane It Is Blocked Automatically by Our Deeper Sense of Vulnerability
Serenity: Sire/He/Net/He   And there is a Net   Sir/In/Hat/He   and The Hat (Art) is Protecting it
Serenity is a Rare Form of Virtue
Serenity is a Cover Word here

Series: Sir/He/Is   Seer/He/Is
There Is No Singular or Fem

Serious: Sir/He/Us   Seer/He/Us
All Men are Sires in   The Code   Terms and it is Serious
Sire is a Noble Title   Sirius is a Star   The Code Embellishes Men at All Times

Sermon: Sire/Mon
Mon Means Mine in French   Mon is a Fem Moon Day of The Week Abbreviation   Monday

Serpent: Referred in the Bible as "the old serpent"

Serum: Sir/Home   or   Sire/Homme Which Means Man in French
Serum is a Medical Term for Blood
Some Words are Just Very Strong in   The Code   To Add Weight
See/Rome   Adds

Serve: Sire/V
Sire is an Honor Title for All Men   V/Fem Sex Active
She Serves Him
See   Her/R/Ear/Hear/Hair/Err/Heir/Or/Whore/Here/Are/Our/Ere/Air/Ire/
Sex   V/Fem Sex Active
Seer/V
To See Her Own Sexuality would be a Big No from   The Code   so She is Only Serving Here
seer: a person that has special powers of divination or an observer

Session: C/See/Young Girl   Is/S/His/Penis   On   Sis/He/On
In Session C/See/Young Girl is His for an Eon
Session is a Cover Word Here

Set: Sat   She Sat (in Past)   Sitting is Always Related to the Bleeding Fem   Sat as in Saturday (Saturn Day)
It was The Only Time She Got to Sit   See Seth The Egyptian God

Sever: S/Is/His/Ass/Us/Hiss/Penis/Serpent   Eve   Her/R/Ear/Hear/Hair/Err/Heir/Or/Whore/Here/Are/Our/Ere/Air/Ire/Sex
The Code   says The Masc Has to Separate   Ovo/Eve   from   The R/Heir/Or/Whore   so She would Not Understand   The Code   so
sever: to divide into parts forcibly

Severest: S/Everest   S/Eve/Rest
Mount Everest is a Frigid/Frozen Place   This Is Where   Eve/Rest   says   The Code
Eve/V/Fem Sex Active   will Know No Rest There Either so
severest: harsh   unnecessarily   serious or stem in manner or appearance   grave critical

Sewer: See/Her   Saw/Her   Sow/Her   Sew/Her
C/Young Girl Her/R/Ear/Hear/Hair/Err/Heir/Or/Whore/Here/Are/Our/Ere/Air/Ire/Sex   The Code   Says The Way She Sees Herself is Garbage

sewer: pipe that carries surface water or sewage   in ancient Greek sew is a hymen or thin skin

Wastewater   Waste/Waist   What (We/Hat)   Her/R/Ear/Hear/Hair/Err/Heir/Or/Whore/Here/Are/Our/Ere/Air/Ire/Sex
Here She is Associated with Sewer/Garbage Again   Her Water is Wasted   Being Dirty   And Sower the Seeds
Sewer is a Cover Word here

Sex: CX   2 Fem Sounds Letters
S/Is/His/Ass/Us/Hiss/Penis/Serpent   X/Fallen Fem Cross (See Axe/X Letter in The Letter Chapter)
C/See/Young Girl is Under the X/Axe When it Comes to Sex   says   The Code
SX   S/Is/His/Ass/Us/Hiss/Penis/Serpent   X/Fallen Fem Cross
See/X   Sect
Hit the Sac says   The Code
Switch E for A/All/Men and He Gets a Sax (The Ultimate Sexual Musical Instrument)
Sexual: Sac/You/All   Sect/You/All
All Fems Under The Sect and in The Sac for Sex
Sexy: Sex/He   S/Axe/He   It is All About The Masc says   The Code   There is No Sexshe

Shack: She/Hack   She/Ache   One Way or Another She is Aching   Poor   Hacking   and   Living in a Shack   More of The Same from   The Code   to The Fems

Shackle: Shake/All   She/Ache/All   Shack/All
When a Word Begins with She   It Cannot be Good News for Her so   The Code says   She is On Shackles   and Poor   and   Aching   and   has to Hack for a Living   and She is Living in a Shack

Shade: She/Aid   She/Hide

Shadow: Shade/O
She does Not Know She is Being a Shadow

Keeping Her/R/Ear/Hear/Hair/Err/Heir/Or/Whore/Here/Are/Our/Ere/Air/Ire/
Sex   In the Dark is the Main Idea from   The Code
Being Related to The Moon in the Night Makes Her a
She/Dough (Shadow)
Then She Can be the Pliable Dough   as in   Daughter (Dough/T/
Her)   Ready for Breading (Bread and Blood)

Shaft: She/Shh   F/Fem/Fuck   T/Fem Cross
She   Aft
Switch A/All Men for i/Marriage Act and She Gets a Shift (The Shift after a
Fem has Sex)

Shag: She/Hag
hag: an ugly old vicious woman
shag: to go after   a carpet   slang for intercourse   matted hair or wool
No Power for The Fems Here again says   The Code   She Is Compared
to a   Rug   a   Mattress   a   Vicious Fem   or   Someone to Go After
Leaving Her No Peace

Shake: She/Shh   Ache
The Fem Is Not Allowed to Ache so a Big No from   The Code   She
be   Shh/Silenced
Shaking: She/Shh   Ache   In/N/Virgin/Ann/Donkey   Now N/Virgin is
Implicated so   The Shaking is in Full Action (Shaking being Slang for Sex)
Sheik/He   Lots of Power in a Sheik   Adding to The Masc Power

Shall: She   L/Sweet Fem Love Light/Ill/Hail/Ail/Hell/Elle/Hell/Ill/Ail/Elle/
Hail/Ail   says   The Code   All Fems Should Experience The L/Hell of
being a L/Elle (Fem for She in French)   In The Future too as in Shall

Sham   The Closest Word in   The Code   that Would Say
She   I   Am   That Would be a Big No from   The Code   as She would
Get Too Close to Understanding   The Code   Situation She is In so
sham: something that is not what it purports to be spurious
imitation   fraud   hoax   pretended   counterfeit   feigned   to produce
an imitation of
Absenteeism of Fem would be the Word to Come to Mind here

She/Shh   M/Motherhood   Is Also the Image of The Fem as a
Mom   The Code   Always Expect Pregnancy from The Fem   Nothing
Else to Look Here for Her
Another So Soft of a Sound to Galvanize Something Else on Her

Shame: She/Ame   (âme in French is Soul)   She/Aim
Her Shame has Gone so Deep that True Humility is Gone
Her Soul Name is Shame   Our Soul (Sole) is being Put Under Our Feet
Switch M for N and She Gets a Chain (She   N Letter/Ann/Ane/Hen/In/
Donkey)
If She Would have a Soul   She Would be Afraid of it because it is a
Shameful Place   Still She Aims for it

Shampoo: She/Aim/Poo
This where   Her/Hair/Heir/Or/Whore/R   Is
poo: excrement   to defecate
Ame is Soul in French
P/Man Power is in Front of All OOs/Fem Holes
Pun Intended
Condition/Her   for That after   Shampooing
A Conditioning is a Big Word

Shape: She/Ape
She/Shh   A/All Men   P/Man Power
What Kind of Shape is That   The Shape of a Ape   When She is in The
Front   Nothing is Good for Her says   The Code
Switch A for E/He and He Gets Sheep (He Wins)

Share: She   R/Err/Her/Are/Her/Hair/Hear/Ear/Whore/Sex
When She Shares Herself as a Heir/Or/Whore/Sex   That is Sharing
says   The Code
Switch R/Her for D/Pregnant and She Gets Shade (She is Pregnant Now so
She is gets a Bit of Shade)
Switch R for P/Man Power and He Gets Shape (A Statue   More Man
Power)
Switch R for C Q or K and She Gets Shake (Shackle   Shake/All/L   Not
So Good to Her   She Gets Shaken Anyway   Which Corresponds to
Concussions)

Shatter: She   Hat/Had   Her
Cheddar   Shed/Her
shatter: to beak something into pieces   as in by a blow   to damage as in by breaking or crushing
The Code   Refuses Her to be Part of the   Hat so
Shutters are Called Blinds in The South   Close/Open The
Shutters   Shut/Her   In Plural   as in All of Them/Hers as They are All the Same   Blinds

Shave: She/Have   She/Eve
She/Eve   and   Have   Could Have been a Nice Concept Word for Her   But a Big No from   The Code   so Shave Here is Another Impossible to Reach Positive Concept for Her   Because The Way to be Identified with Something here for Her would be to Shave it Off   And The Fems in General do Not or do it only in Private Places   They do Not Talk about it much   Men Have Complaisance Totally Here   as Usual

She: Shh/Silence
The Fems is Strongly Advised to Keep Quiet says   The Code
Shh Becomes a She Only When Letter   E/He   is Added
S/Is/His/Ass/Us/Hiss/Penis/Serpent   H/Secret Code Curse Letter   E/He
There Are No Fem Letter in She
Shier is to Poop/Shit in French
S/Is/His/Penis   H/Secret Code Letter Society
She/Hay   She/Hey   Shh/She/It   Shh/Hit
She is Thrown at the Bottom of the Sewer as Usual
Replace S with T/Fem Cross and She Gets   The (A No Identity Word)

Shear: She   Hear
shear: to cut (something)   to strip or deprive (usually followed by of)   *Chiefly Scot*   to reap with a sickle
S/Is/His/Ass/Us/Hiss/Penis/Serpent
The Code   Tells When The Fem is in The Here and Now
When it is Time to Get Cut (Cliterectomy) or be Cut Off
Add N/In/Hen/Ann/Virgin/Donkey and She Gets Churn (She/Earn   See Urn)

Sheave: She/Eve   She   V/Fem Sex Active

sheave: to gather   collect or bind into a sheaf or sheaves
Sheaves   She/Eves/V/Fem Sex Active in Plural
Again The Fems are   the Bees   the Fishes   the Chicks   the Cows   and more   The Fems have No Identity of their Her Own and   They All are Kept in a Bundle   Somewhere You can See them says   The Code   They Look All The Same
shive: early 13c   slice of bread
Bread/Bred   There are Many More Other Slices to Breed/Bread from   She/Eve
Sheaf   She/If When in Singular

Shed: She/Had
shed: to pour forth (water or other liquid) as a fountain   to emit and let fall as tears   to resist being penetrated or affected by   to impart or release give up or send forth (light sound fragrance influence etc)
The Answer for The T/Fem Cross is All of the Above
She gives it All and She is in Tears because She Does
Shit (She/It)\
Switch D/Pregnant for T/Fem Cross and She Get Shit (Back to the Feces for Her   It is Her ID Says The Code)
For All This Giving She Gets to Live in a Shed
She/Hide   It Can be Physically or Mentally or Emotionally or Spiritually
shed: a small building or lean-to light construction used for storage shelter
As Usual The Fems has   No Identity   No structure   No Protection   says   The Code
And Here She is Told Through   The Code   She is the Warehouse of All that Giving
Men have No idea the Hell   The Code   gives Us All
All this Around the Shed Word   She/ID as
Her ID   Then She Gets   She/It (Shit)

Sheep: She/Weep
She Weep Because She is Not a Sheep   and   She has a Man with a Stick Controlling Her   The Sheppard
He Shows Her Where He Wants Her   She is Cheap   She is Just an Animal to be Sold says The Code

The Dam Code The Damn Book

And She Better (Batt/Her) be Careful   She/Shh The Sound of the Whip is Also on Her

Sheer: She/Hear
She/Shh   She/Shh
Her/R/Ear/Hear/Hair/Err/Heir/Or/Whore/Here/Are/Our/Ere/Air/Ire/Sex
sheer: transparently   thin   chiffon   voile   unqualified   unmixed
The Secret Language Code Is Hidden in Sounds
She Should Not Hear It
The Veil is Thin and Transparent   But She is Not Equipped (Being Ignorant of it) to Decipher it   and   She Should Not Mingle with It says   The Code   or
shear: to cut   to remove by or as if by cutting or clipping with a sharp instrument
She/Shh   R/Her
The Fems Cannot be an Heir in   The Code (Heiress being the Ass of the Heir) or   Be Here or Hear
Especially She Cannot be She/Her/S   Sure as Sire
Switch R/Her for T/Fem Cross and She Gets Sheet (She/It   Shit)
Cheer   She/R/Her   No Cheers for Her Unless She Plays Mother or Whore   The Fems Never Gets Out of The Boundaries of   That Code

Sheet: She/It   Shit   She/Hit
(Hit the Sac   S/Hack)
That is What is Waiting for The Fems When S/Penis Hack those Fems in Between those 2 Sheets (2 is Always a Sign of Polygamy)   An Endless Reminder for Her that as So Many Other Fem Terms that Identifies Her in The Code   There is Never Only One of Her as Being Special   All Fems are Identical   The Fem is a   Sheep   Cow   Horse   a piece of The School of Fishes   Etc   (See Fish in The Words Chapter)
Bed Sheet   Bad/Shit
When She/Shh is in the Front of a Word   Watch It
A Sheath (She/Hit/It) is a Case for the Blade of a Sword C/Herd (See/Heard)
Note that the Word Sword has the Word Word in it   ("At The Beginning was The Word") With Letter   S/His/Penis   in Front of It
The Penis has a Sheath Called the Foreskin which Naturally Covers it When Non Stimulated Sexually

Lise Rochon

In the Jewish Religion it is Partly Removed at Birth with their Circumcision Religious Ritual Procedure   (Which is Basically Sexual Mutilation) Circumcision Leaves the Penis Permanently Exposed to the Outside   As in when an Erection   Creating Pain and a Dysfunctional Sexuality to Those Men for The Rest of Their Lives   but no One seemed to wake up to be Aware of that Extreme Anomaly until Lately in The Occident
Remember Circumcision is the First of the 5 Conditions to be a Jew   is to be Circumcised   Which Changes Basically Everything in Their Life
A Ritual Done for a Few Thousand Years Already

Shell: She/Hell   She/Elle   She/Letter L   She/Ill   She/Heal   To Heal is One of The Fems Attributes   Always Hidden from Her Under the Accusations of Witchery   Which was Punishable by Death by The State
All Words Related To Water and Their Hidden/Symbolic Meanings are Fem shell: a hard outer layer   a cover
It Takes Those Covers to Keep The Fems Under   The Code   Iron Hands
Shelling: Shell/In/N   Shell/Ann   She/Helen
She/Shh/Hell/In/N   To All Helens   So Sorry
The Code   Hides Also Under the Most Fragile Fem Words (As Their Own Name) and The Smallest in Meaning
A Shelling is a Small Amount of Money in Britain   Pennies for Her   Penny is a Common Fem Name

Sheep: She/Shh   P/Man Power
She is Told Her Real Power Resides into Being a Sheep
Sheppard: Sheep/Herd
She/Shh   P/Man Power   R/Her/Here/Are/Hair/Hear/Ear/Whore/Err/Sex   D/Pregnant   The Code says It (Hit) Clearly
The Sheep (Her) Herd (Her   D/Pregnant as in All of Them) are Pregnant/Or/Whores
Seduction Will Bring Her in That Line of Thought   Making Her Believe Being a Sheep will Save Her from That Unbearable Misery   The Code   Has Imposed On Her for 2000 Years   And She Be Quiet about it
She   Ape   R/Her/Are/Heir/Or/Whore/Sex   D/Pregnant
The Code   Always Maintains Her at an Animal Level of Consciousness   Bitches Fishes Cows Horses (Whores)   and   More
Sheppard is a Ship/Hard   That is a Hard Ship on Her
She/Shh   P/Man Power   R/Her/Heir/Or/Whore/Sex   D/Pregnant

The Dam Code The Damn Book

That Ship Being a Ship Full of Sheeps   of Being a Pregnant/Heir/Or/ Whore is Hard on Her says   The Code   But No it is Part of Her Life Cheap/Shape   R/Her/Are/Heir/Or/Whore/Sex   D/Pregnant   This is How   The Code   Shapes Her for That Job   Poverty and The Powerlessness That Comes with It   The Old Say Barefoot and Pregnant Represents it Clearly here

She/Shh   P/Man Power   Heard
And to Be Silent about it (Hit) as She Hears its Harshness
She Will Not/Has Not Understand/Stood Any of It
Sheep Has 2 EEs/He (Meaning Plural or All of Them) to Add More Force to Him as The Masc Towards Her Because The Sheep is The Fem Attribute/ Identity in   The Code
From Sheep to The Sheppard the 2 EEs in Sheep Transforms Themselves Into Only One E/He in Sheppard   but with 2 PPs/Man Power (as in Plural or All of Them)   Instead which has more Force
The Sheppard Being The Boss of Her Represents The Word of God   Sheppard has 2 PPs/Man Power (Plural or All of Them) from God   It Adds Force to its Godly Power   The Sheppard is Essentially a Man Job says   The Code   That is Why The Fems are Not Allowed to Be Priests (Etc) all The Way to Pope   It is All About The Fems
P/Man Power does Not Reach The Fems Consciousness   Because She has No Power and No Knowledge From Those Concepts
The Sheppard and its Sheeps are VIP Terms in the Roman Catholic Church   It Calls Its Believers Sheeps (Fem) and Tells Its Sheppard to Rules over those Sheeps to Go Along Towards That Religion
It is Explained Many Times in Many Ways in   This Dam Code   Book (Look at Definitions of Cows/Sheeps/Monkeys/Ants/Bees/Etc)
All Different and Great Creations of Our World
But All What Does   The Dam Code   is to Keep Everyone Separating The Real Fem from the Real Masc   By Establishing False Patterns of Human Destruction
The Sheppard is Embodied by   The Code   to do That
The Sheppard Letter J/j (See Letter J in The letter Chapter) in French G Sounds as J and j Sounds as G   No Coincidence here   There are No Coincidences in   That Dam Code

Lise Rochon

So Thread Carefully   I am Just the Messenger Here   I Wrote this Dam Code Book the Way I Discovered it   My Parents were Proud Honest Catholics and Raised Us Children with All The Love They had

Shield: She/Yield
Her Shield is to Yeld   Shh/Yell/D
And She Be Quiet About it   No Yelling
L/Sweet Fem Love Light/All/Ail/Ill/Hail/Heel/Hell/Elle/Oil   D/Pregnant
Here are The Meanings That Comes Along With That Concept for Her to Bear With   Including Pregnancies
No Real Shield for Her here

Shift: She   If/F Letter   T/Fem Cross
The Shift for Her is When She Switches from Fem/Fuck to T/Fem Cross says   The Code

Shinny: Shine/He
The Shine is on The Masc
She/Shh   N/In/Hen/Ann/Donkey   He/E
The Code   is There to Make Sure She Remains in a State of a Silent Virgin Donkey

Ship: She/Shh   P/Man Power
Shh (Commanding Silence)   P/Man Power
Everything Related to Water is Fem
ship: suffix   indicating state or condition   indicating rank office or position   indicating craft or skill
Besides being a Vessel (Vase (See Chalice in The Words Chapter)   Elle/Hell/Ill) on the Water   A Ship Tells a Position in Society
For The Fems the Ship   (She   P/Power) Is Being a Sheep
Switch P/Man Power for T/Fem Cross and She Gets Shit

Shipper: a person who ships goods or makes shipment
In   The Code   The Ship (Sheep) Rides on the Water (What/Her)

Shit: She/It
So Sorry about that One and All Others

612

The Dam Code The Damn Book

In the East People Uses the Left Hand (The Impure Hand) to Wipe their Butt after going to the Bathroom   The Left Hand Being The Fems Hand   Chier (She/Hey) is to Poop in French   Shit is Merde in French   Merde is a Popular Slang Word for Bad Stuff in French   Same as Putain (Whore) is in France
Back to the Feces for Her Again
Switch I for a O/Fem Hole and She Gets Shot
Double the O and She Gets Shoot
Change I for U and She Gets Shut
shithouse: a privy   outhouse

Shitless: She/Shh   It/Hit   Less
The Fems Name is Shit says   The Code   and She It Less
shitless: frightened
The Code   says It makes Her Scared so   She will Not Look at It
She/Eat/Less
Eating Less Makes Her   Weaker   Skinnier   More Vulnerable
The Code   Creates Fashions to Keep Her Thin/Anemic
And Call That a Model (Mode/Hell   Made   Ill/All/Letter L)   (See BB in Words)

Shiver: She/Shh   V/Fem Sex Active   Her/R/Ear/Hear/Hair/Err/Heir/Or/Whore/Here/Are/Our/Ere/Air/Ire/Sex
If She would Dare to Know Her Situation as a Sex Active Heir/Or/Whore   That would be   A Big No from   The Code   so
shiver: to shake or tremble with cold fear excitement etc
Shivering: She/V/Ring   She/V/R/N
The Ring in   The Code   is The Contract for The Fems to Become Forcefully a V/Fem Sex Active
Shh/She   V/Fem Sex Active   Her/R/Ear/Hear/Hair/Err/Heir/Or/Whore/Here/Are/Our/Ere/Air/Ire/Sex
When   She   is in The Front of a Word   Check it Out   That is Not Allowed by   The Code

Shocked: Shh/She   O/Fem Hole   K/Broken Fem Warrior   and   Shush About it   Even If it is Shocking

Shoe: She/Shh   U/You/Ovulating (U/Tear/Us)

She Relates to Sex With Her Shoes   A Silent Code
Shoo
shoo: to request a person to leave
The Code   Leaves The Fems Out   In Ignorance
She/Who   No Identity for   The Fems in   The Code
Shoes: Choose   She/O/S   She/Hose
shh: command to be quiet
The Fems Love Shoes
The Fems Has Been Taught to Learn to Love What on the Different Level Insults Her   For Example Flower/Flaw/Her

Shop: Shh/She   Hop   She/Up
S/Is/His/Ass/Us/Hiss/Penis/Serpent
The Fems Loves to Shop   She Shops   She is Up for a Hop
Hop is Slang for Sex   Hop
hop: bounce   a twinning vine
Hops (Used in Flavoring Beer) are an Example of a Twinning Vine (See Vine in Words The Relationship Between The Vine/Wine and Her Blood Loss in   The Code)   She Can Bounce from That   Beer is Also a Synonym for a Coffin
Add E/He to Hop and He Gets Hope
Switch S for C/See/Young Girl and She Gets Chop
Switch S for P/Man Power and He Gets Pop (Quick Sex in Slang)
Switch S for M/Motherhood and She Gets Mop (Get to Work)
Switch S for T/Fem Cross/Great Curse and She Gets Top (The Top for The Code is Her Blood Loss)

Shore: She   Her/Heir/Or/Whore/Sex
All Names Related to Water are Fem says   The Code
Show/Whore   Show/Or
She   Or/Gold in French   She/Or   Or as In One or Another
Shh/She   R/Her/Heir/Or/Whore/Sex
Another Big Package Here   Words Related to Water and Ocean   or   Their Surroundings Are Heavily Negative in The Code   Symbolism
That is Why it is So Hard for Us The Fems to Look in Those Directions
Sea/See/She

The Dam Code The Damn Book

It is   H/Secret Code Society Letter   that Creates the She (See She/It (Shit)   She/Hot (Shot)
Anything Related to Water Goes that Way in   The Code
See/Sea   The Holy See (The Hole/He/See   The Whole/He/See   The All   He/E   C/See/Young Girl)

Shoot: Shh/She   Hoot
shoot: discharge
Shooter: Shoot/Her   She/Hot/Her
Shot   Her/R/Ear/Hear/Hair/Err/Heir/Or/Whore/Here/Are/Our/Ere/Air/Ire/Sex
It is Hot to Shoot Sex at Her/R/Heir/Or/Whore
Shooting: She/Hoot   In/N/Donkey
hoot: to shout in disapproval
Take One O Away and She Gets Shot (The Code Disapproves for The Fems to be with Other Fems   Division Wins the War)

Shot: Shut   Shout
Shot is a Busy Word In Dictionary.Com   There are More than 68 Usages for the Word Shot
A Shot is a Discharge   A Discharge from   a Man   a Gun   a Bow   Etc
Shot (She/Hot)   Shut (She/Hut)   Shout (She/Out)
When She is Hot   She is in the Shot in The Hut   Then She is Out
Shot Gun: She is Hot Then Gone (Out)   Under The Gun
Switch O for i/Marriage Act and She Gets Shit
Shit is Merde in French   Mère/D   Mère is Mother in French   D/Pregnant   Mothers and the Pregnant Ones are Merde   The Circle Continues From Mom to Daughters
Shit is Mierda in Spanish
Switch T/Fem Cross for E/He and He Gets a Shoe
n Which Means Easy Winner (Win/Her) for Him Shoo In Comes From Horses (Whores) Racing (Only Men Rode Horses in the Far Past)
Shoe   In/N/In/Hen/Donkey/Ann/Virgin Here The Shoe Fits with a Virgin
Switch E/He for D/Pregnant and She Gets Shod (to Provide with a Shoe)   She is pregnant   so She Gets Shoes)
Switch E/He for P/Man Power and He Gets to Shop
Switch E/He for R/Her/Heir/Or/Whore and She Gets Sure or Shore (S/Penis   Whore)

Switch E/He for V/Fem Sex Active and She Gets Shove Switch E/He for W/ All Fems Sex Active and They/She Gets a Show (The Code Agree for Her to have a Show If Sex is Part of It
Add Another O/Fem Hole and She Gets Shoot (As in Shoot All of Them OOs)
When She in Any Word are Starting Letters The Fems Gets Feeble Concepts for Her   It Cannot go Anywhere for Her says   The Code Shot is a Cover Word Here   Shot is Also Being Drunk   Another Weak Concept given to Her

Should: She/She   Hood
She Should be Mum/Mom (Keep Silent) about the Hood
hood: a cover

Shoulder: Should/Her
Shh/She   Hood   Her/R/Ear/Hear/Hair/Err/Heir/Or/Whore/Here/Are/Our/Ere/Air/Ire/Sex   Shh on the Hood about Her Meaning Sex
The Shoulder is an Important Part of the Body for Carrying   Working Hard (as She Should (Her)

Shout: Shh/She   Out
She is Not there To Shout
Silence or Out to Her   One Follows the Other Often

Shove: She   Ov/Ovulation
Shove it   Not Much Good for Her When Ovulating
shove: to move along by force from behind   push   to push roughly or rudely   *Slang Often Vulgar*   to go to hell with
Note that Hell is The Fem Letter L/Sweet Fem Love Light/All/Ail/Ill/Hail/Heel/Hell/Elle/Oil

Show: She   O/Fem Hole   Shh/She   Owe   She/Ho
The Show is Her O/Fem Hole or to
Show the Hole of the Ho
ho: a sexually promiscuous woman   a prostitute   whore   a woman
Note that The Definition of Ho makes No Difference Between a Whore and a Woman
That is Her Show says   The Code

Shower: Show/Her
shower: brief fall of rain   a large quantity or supply
The Code has its Way of Making The Fems All the Same and Available
in Large Quantity as Rain Drops   A Rainfall   Here She Falls (F/Fem/
Fuck   All/Letter L/Sweet Fem Love/Light Again

Shred: Shh/She   Red/Read
The Code   Destroys All Information about Her and the Her Loss of
Blood so
shred: a bit   a scrap   a piece cut off
Shredder: Shh/She Red/Read   Her/R/Ear/Hear/Hair/Err/Heir/Or/Whore/
Here/Are/Our/Ere/Air/Ire/Sex
For The Fems to Be Able to Know/Read Her Real Situation About Her Loss
of Blood in   That Code   Will Not be Permitted therefore it is   Shredded

Shrew: Shh/She   Her/R/Ear/Hear/Hair/Err/Heir/Or/Whore/Here/Are/
Our/Ere/Air/Ire/Sex   U/You/Ovulating
Here Sex for heir or as Whore is in Between She and U/You/Ovulating (Ov)
If Her Sexuality would Belong to Her is a Big No from   The Code   or   for
The Fems to have Sex with Another Fem is a Big No Too so
Shrew: a woman of violent temper and speech
And screw is so Close

Shrine: Shh/She   Reine/Reign
Reine is Queen in French
Shh/Reine   Silence that Queen
shrine: a receptacle for sacred relics
SHRN

Shy: Shh/She   I   Shh/She   High   Shh/She   Eye
The Fem is Rarely Given an Identity in   The Code   Except as a Sex
Object or to Grow into Any Weakness that Will Wound Her
To be Shy is Another Form of Shame Done to The Fems by   The
Code   Here   The Code   Tells Her to See Herself and Feel High About
being Shy
There is No Letter I/Stick (Masc) in Shy   Only the Y/Wounded Fem Behind
the Shh/She   Which Imitates The I
shy: easily frightened away   deficient   retiring

Lise Rochon

Here are Some Words that Appears When Shh/She is taken Away   and Another Letter is Put in Front Instead
Bye (Masc)   Die (Fem)   Guy (Masc)   My (Mother and Y/Wounded Fem)   Pie (∞ See Number 8/Pregnancy)   Rye (Masc and Fem)   Sigh (See/I (Masc)   Tie (Fem)   Why (Fem)
Note The Strengths of the Masc and The Weaknesses of The Fems in Those Words Meanings
Shied: She/Hid   Shh/She/ID
shied: simple past tense and past participle of shy
See Freudian Meaning of ID (Hid   Past Tense of Hide)
That is Her ID (Identification)

Shun: Shh/She   On
shun: to keep away from (a place person object etc) from motives   take pains to avoid
The Fems is On says   The Code   When She Keeps Away From Motives   or   When it Comes to Make Rational Decisions on Her Own

Sick: S/Is/His/Ass/Us/Hiss/Penis/Serpent   IC
C/See/Young Girl   IC/Integrated Circuit
C/See/Young Girl Would Understand Her Bleeding as an Integrated Circuit   Even if it Makes Her Sick
Sick/Seek
She Seeks It Says The Code   As a Man Is Proud to have a Penis
C/I/C   C/I/K   S/I/K   S/I/C
Sick is a Word Where   C   and   K   and   Q   can Have the Same Sound   Although K/Broken Fem Cannot Reverse Itself in a Soft C   Only C Can Reverse into a K
Switch S for D/Pregnant and She Gets a Dick
Switch S for I/Sweet Fem Love and She Gets a Lick
Switch S for M/Motherhood and She Gets a Mic (A Microphone to Tell All about Motherhood)
Switch S for N/Virgin and She Gets a Nick
Switch S for P/Man Power and He Gets to Pick
Switch S for T/Fem Cross and She Gets a Tic (Another Bug)
Switch S for V/Fem Sex Active and She Gets Vic (Victor)
Switch S for W/All Fems Sex Active and She Gets a Wick (A Very Small Thing)

The Dam Code The Damn Book

The Word Sick is a Cover Word to Hide for   The Code   Because No One Wants to Be Sick so They Keep Away from Its Concept
Switch S for K/Broken Fem and She Gets a Kick (Another)

Sickle: Cycle/All
(See Sickle and Cycle in The Words Chapter)

Sieve: CV   2 Fem Sound Letters   See/Eve
From   C/See/Young Girl   To   V/Fem Sex Active
All Eves are Passing Through those Same Little Holes   Again All   Living The Same Simple Experience

Sigh: C/I   CI
C/See/Young Girl   i/Marriage Act   or   I/Male Stick of Power
See/Eye   See/High
Add H/Secret Code Letter Grid and She Gets Shy   She/I   or   She
I   Which is Either Sex   or   The Stick
sigh: to let out one breath audibly as from sorrow weariness or relief
No Fem Is Allowed to See the High/Eye/I in the Pyramid   That Is Only for The Initiates of   That Code
Because it Is All About Her

Sign: Sigh/N
N/In/Hen/Donkey/Ann/Virgin   Sighs   It is a Sign says   The Code
The Sign is For Her to Be Ready to Mate
S/Ass/His/Is/Serpent/Penis   N/Ann/Donkey
Assign: Ass/S/Penis   N/Ann/Donkey/Virgin
Ass   Sign

Silence   See/Lance
A Lance is a Shaft and a Masc Slang for Phallus (Fall/Us   for Her)   See King Arthur Lance in The Holy Grail
See   Letter L/Ill/Sweet Fem Light   N/In/Hen/Virgin/Donkey   C/See/ Young Girl
C/See is Ill   She Sees it   In Silence
That is How Powerful   The Code   Is She has Been Lost in Shame and Been Silenced About Her Fem Blood Loss
S/Ass/His/Is/Serpent/Penis   Ill/L   N/Ann/Virgin   C/See/Young Girl

619

Silencer: Silence/Her
Silence   Her/R/Ear/Hear/Hair/Err/Heir/Or/Whore/Here/Are/Our/Ere/Air/Ire/Sex

Silly: C/See/Young Girl   L/Sweet Fem Love Light/Ill/Hail/Ail/Hell/Elle/Hell/Ill/Ail/Elle/Ill/Hell/Elle   He/E
If The Cursed Fem Loves Him   It is Silly to Him
See/Lay
If She Sees a Lay it is Silly
C/See/Young Girl   Ill   E
If She Sees   He/E   Ill   She Is Silly

Silver: See   L/Ill   V/Fem Sex Active   S/Is/His/Ass/Us/Hiss/Penis/Serpent   C/See/Young Girl/ Letter L/Sweet Fem Love Light/Ill/Hail/Ail/Hell/Elle/Hell/Ill/Ail/Elle   R/Her/Heir/Or/Whore
Soul   V/Fem Sex Active   R/Her
She is Under the Power of   The Code   Her Soul is to Be a V/Fem Sex Active   or   R/Her
Silver is Fem and Gold is Masc   Compare the Prices of Gold   It Averages $1200 Per Ounce   Silver Averages $14. Per Ounce   The Code   is Everywhere
In Alchemy Silver is One of the Base Metals
Sliver: Slave/Her   Slay/Eve/Her
A Sliver is so Small
Take Away L/Sweet Fem Love Light/Ill/Hail/Ail/Hell/Elle and She Gets Sever   Severe (Sieve/Her)   (See   Eve   /Her/R)
Add D/Pregnant and She Gets Severed   Hard to Her is   That Code

Similar: Sim/He/Liar   See/Him/Liar   C/Me/Liar   Sim Means Similar

Simmer: C/See/Young Girl   M/Motherhood   Her/R/Ear/Hear/Hair/Err/Heir/Or/Whore/Here/Are/Our/Ere/Air/Ire/Sex
Simmer: a steady low heat
Want or Not The Fems is Kept in a Latent Sex Drive   Which does Not Happens to Mammals in Nature

Simple: Sim   P/Man Power   All/L
See   M/Motherhood   Pal

The Dam Code The Damn Book

C/See/Young Girl   M/Motherhood   P/Man Power   All
Seen   P   All
Si/M/P/All   Si is Yes in Spanish
The Fems has No Friend   Because to Divide is to Conquer says   The Code
N/In/Hen/Ann/Virgin   M/Motherhood
Sim and Sin are The Same   M and N Are Reversible Letters in   The Code   N being in the Process of Being a Mother   M is Also Him as She has No Identity to Rely On
Simply: Sim/P/Lay
Simply Said   The Lay Finalizes The Definition of Simple

Simulator: Sim/U/Later   See   M/Motherhood   Late   S/Is/His/Ass/Us/Hiss/Penis/Serpent   Sim and Sin are the Outcome of Each Other   Because N/In/Hen/Ann/Virgin will Become M/Motherhood
See The Word Sin in Greek and See the Same   Code   Appearing there too
Concepts are Created according to Sounds in   The Code
Perverse and Wrong Are Affiliated with The Fems
The Old Testament Uses 6 Different Nouns and 3 Verbs to Describe Sin   Note those are Sounds Describing Its Actions

Sin: S/N   S/Ass/His/Is/Serpent/Penis   is with N/In/Hen/Ann/Virgin
S/Is/His/Ass/Us/Hiss/Penis/Serpent   i/Marriage Act   N/In/Hen/Ann/Virgin
S/Penis is in N/Virgin
Note that that i has a Different Meaning When in Capitals
The i/Marriage Act is Fem and Masc   The I/Stick is Masc Only (The Dot/The Fems has been Absorbed After Sex   Only His I/Stick Remains)
S/Penis   I/Stick/Eye in The Pyramid   N/In/Hen/Ann/Virgin
Switch N/In/Hen/Ann/Virgin for M/Motherhood and She Gets Sim/Similar
Switch I for U/You/Ovulating and She Gets Sun (The Sun Shines for Everybody Anyway   No Gain for Her here)
Switch I for O/Fem Hole and She Gets a Son   (Son in French Means His)
Add G/Hymen Penetration to Son and He Gets a Song
Switch I for A/All Men and He Gets San/Saint
(It is a Sane Scene to be Seen says   The Code)
(Seen (S/His/Penis   N/In/Hen/Ann/Virgin)
Those Are Very Light Words for Such an Important Theme as Sin

621

To Sin is Pécher in French   Pécher is also to Fish in French   The Fish is Jesus Logo
Anything Related to Water is Fem

Since: SNC   Sins   Sin/C   Sin/See   C   N/Virgin   C
Sin   S/Is/His/Ass/Us/Hiss/Penis/Serpent
C/See/Young Girl   Is with The Sin   Known as The Great Curse in The Bible
since: from then till now
There a No Breach in   The Code

Sincere: Sin/Sire
Sin   C/See/Young Girl   Her/R/Ear/Hear/Hair/Err/Heir/Or/Whore/Here/Are/Our/Ere/Air/Ire/Sex
Sin/Seer   Scene/See/R
sincere: to act with truth
seer: a person that can see the future   an observer
Sin is in the Past in The Word Since and in the Future with The Word Seer
Sincerely: Sin/See/Her/Lay
Sincerely Makes It Clearer With The Lay to See

Sinew: Sin   You/U/Ovulating
Sin/New   Seen   You/U
sinew: a source of strength and power   a tendon
It is a Source of Power for The Code   To Have That Sin Renewed

Sinful: Full of Sins
The Catholic Church 7 Deadly Sins Are the Human Weaknesses Engendered from   The Code   They Reflects their Effects on All of Us on Every Level   Spiritual   Mental   Emotional   and   Physical   Creating Massive Human Suffering   Pain Killers of Every Kind   People Drink Smoke Escape in Every Way   Buddha Calls Our Civilization The Valley of Tears

Sing: Sin   G/Hymen Penetration
S/Is/His/Ass/Us/Hiss/Penis/Serpent   N/In/Hen/Virgin/Ann/Virgin   G/Hymen Penetration
Singing: Sin   G/Hymen Penetration   N/Ann/Virgin

The Dam Code The Damn Book

A Song for a Sin   A Sin for a Song
The Sex Act is a Song for True Lovers   But No says   The Code It has Manufactured Us that Way for Thousands of Years
The Code   its Ultimate Power Over (Ov/Ovulation   R/Her) the Human Race Through Languages
Switch I for O/Fem Hole and She Gets Song
Switch I for U/You/Ovulating and She Gets Sung
Switch I for A/All Men and He Gets Sang (Sang is Blood in French)
Sing is an Important Word for   The Code   It is a Name (Song) and Verbs   In the Present (Sing) in the Past (Sang) Twice (Sung)   And It Influences Both Sexes
Add E/He to Sing and He Gets a Singe
singe: to burn or slightly scorch (The Code does Not Approves of Any Kindness to a Fem from a Masc)
Singer: Sing   R/Her
Sin   Hymen Penetration   R/Her
That Code   says Sing About   Her/Heir/Or/Whore   in The Name of That God Even if it has Sin in It

Single: Sin/Girl
It is a Sin to be Single says   The Code   for a Fem   All Fems Must be With a Man
A Single Man is a Bachelor   A Single Fem is an Old Maid
Sing/All
Songs Helps a Masc to Get Sex with a Fem as She is Often Hungry for Attention or Love   She Gets None from   The Code   We are Learning That from that Damn Book
S/In/G/All/Ill
S/Is/His/Ass/Us/Hiss/Penis/Serpent   N/In/Hen/Ann/Virgin   G/Hymen Penetration   L/Sweet Fem Love Light/All/Ail/Ill/Hail/Heel/Hell/Elle/Oil
Single   Sync/All   Synchronize All Fems for Sex
Switch S for B/Boy Holding All Fems Breasts and He gets Bingle (Bingo)
Bingle: base hit in baseball slang
Switch S for D/Pregnant and She Gets Dingle
dingle: a deep narrow cleft between hills   shady dell
Switch S for J/Sheppard Stick and He Gets Jingle
Switch S for M/Motherhood and She Gets to Mingle (The Code Agrees with Showing Off Her M/Motherhood)

Switch S for T/Fem Cross and She Gets a Tingle

Singular: Single/Her   See Single Definition Above
Sing/U/Liar
Sin   G/Penis Penetration   U/You/Ovulating   Liar (Layer   Lay/Her)
Singular is a Reinforcement for Her to Sin (Sin/Girl)   Even if The Code Tells Her She is a Liar
singular: unique   extraordinary   remarkable
She is Extraordinary When Sinning

Sinister: Sin Is/S/His/Ass/Us/Hiss/Penis/Serpent
T/Fem Cross   Her/R/Heir/Or/Whore
That Sin is The Fems Cross Given to Her with Sex as a Whore
Sin   S/His/Is/Penis   Tear
Seen   S/His/Is   T/Fem Cross   R/Her/Heir/Or/Whore
That is So Sinister for Her to be Treated as That
sinister: bad   evil   base   wicked   fell   unfortunate
Sinister Belongs to the Tarot Card The Moon According to Aleister Crowley   An Ill Card Especially for Her
Having Your Moon is a Poetic Term for The Fems Blood Loss in   The Code

Sink: Sin   K/Broken Fem   (See Letter K in The Letter Chapter)
Sinking   Sin/King   Once She Has Sunk/Broken He is The King with His Unbroken Stick (i has Been Transformed in a I in Large Caps   His Unbroken Stick)

Sinner: Sin   Her
Seen
Her/R/Ear/Hear/Hair/Err/Heir/Or/Whore/Here/Are/Our/Ere/Air/Ire/Sex
The Code   says She is The Sinner

Sir: SR
S/Is/His/Ass/Us/Hiss/Penis/Serpent
Her/R/Ear/Hear/Hair/Err/Heir/Or/Whore/Here/Are/Our/Ere/Air/Ire/Sex
S/Penis   i/Marriage Act   R/Her/Sex
Add E/He   He Gets Sire   as in to Sire Children
Another Powerful Word for The Masc

The Dam Code The Damn Book

Switch i/Marriage Act for You/U/Ovulating and She Gets Sure   The Code Tells Her to Go Along With That
Sir Was a Term of Honor that Used to be Reserved for Royalty   Now Any Man Any Time Can Call Another Man Sir
Seer (See/Her)

Siren: Sir/In   Sire/In
Another Romantic Way to Attract a Fem to have Sex by Giving Her Power Over a Man Making Her Song an Hypnotic Song
The Siren or Mermaid (Mère/Maid/Made   The Maid Made a Mother   or   The Mother Made a Maid) Has Her Legs Unopened Symbolically as a Virgin
In The Little Mermaid Disney Animation Film it Shows Little Girls and How Great is to Watch Separate or Open Their Legs to Be with Her Prince (Any Dream Man The Fems Loves is a Prince to Her)   The Fems Loves it
The Secret Language Code has Its Way of Recruiting Us Infinitely
A Siren is Entirely a Fem Word   But   The Code   says No
It is a Sir/Sire   N/In/Hen/Virgin/Donkey (A Man Inside a Virgin)
Having Masc Letters in Fem Words is Same as Having a Boy Fishing on the Moon   But it is a Familiar Picture Created by   The Code   Of Course There is No Fem on The Sun/Son
S/I/Reine
S/Is/His/Ass/Us/Hiss/Penis/Serpent   i/Marriage Act   Reign/Reine (Reine is Queen in French)
She Can Be a Queen   The Queen of His Penis and Sex Union   Sirens do Not Exist   So it is Another Dead End for Her
Siren is a Big Popular Cover Word here for the Romantic Fem
Wailing Siren
Wailing/Willing   Sigh   Rein/Reine/Reign/Rain   Arena
(See Rain in The Words Chapter)

Sis: 2 SSs/Is/His/Ass/Us/Hiss/Penisses/Serpent (Plural or All Men)   Surrounding   i/Marriage Act
sis: abbreviation for sister   a suffix that forms nouns from verbs
When there is a Transformation as here   There is Usually a Change
When 2 or Plural or All of Them S/Penisses Surrounds Her and Him in i/Sex Act   It is Very important for   The Code   so it is Hidden Very Well   It is Hidden in the Word Sisters   After All The Sisters (as The Fems

625

Lise Rochon

Community) Know Nothing about   That Code   and   That Code   says All The Fems will have to go Through Sex   Nothing Left to Chance Here

Sissy: Sis/He
See The Sis Definition Above
sissy: a little girl   weak cowardly boy or man
Comparing Masc to Fem in The Code   Anything Fem is Weak Stupid Mad Dirty Down Impure Unloved Non Existent   and The Masc is Always Strong and Right in Every way   says   The Code   Especially When He is Compared to a Fem Aspect
So a Coward (Cow/Herd) or a Weak Man/Boy Steals Here a Fem Name Affiliation to Hide its Weak Behind   and Maintain Its Clean Power   The Dam Code

Sister: Sis   T/Fem Cross   Her/R/Ear/Hear/Hair/Here/Heir/Whore/Or/Err/Are/Our/Ere/Air/Ire/Sex
All Fems are Sisters   All Fems Carry The Same T/Fem Cross says   The Code
Be a Sister   Assist The System (Sees/Stem   Stem is Slang for Penis) Cyst/Her   Another Sick Term for Her from   That Code

Sit: S/Is/His/Ass/Us/Hiss/Penis/Serpent   It/Hit
See/It (Penis)   See/Hit   See/It/Hit
Sitter: See   Hit   Her
See/C   T/Fem Cross   Her/R/Ear/Hear/Hair/Err/Heir/Or/Whore/Here/Are/Our/Ere/Air/Ire/Sex
Add Another S and She is becoming a Sister

Size: SZ   S/Is/His/Ass/Us/Hiss/Penis/Serpent   Z/Sleep on It says   The Code
C/See/Young Girl   Eyes/Highs
S/Is/His/Penis   Eyes/Highs
He sees His Penis as an Eye   It is Mentioned by Heavily Circumcised Men   Penisses are High/Most Precious to All Men
The Fems Think about Size as in Losing More Body Weight
She is Told by   That Code   She is Never Too Small
And She Wonders Why She is Not So Strong   from Losing All This Blood Every Month

The Dam Code The Damn Book

Add E/He and He Gets Seize (A Weak Fem is Easier to Seize (Read the Story About that Slippery Salmon (The Rape of a Young Girl/Grail) in The King Arthur Holy Grail (Holy (Hole/He) Girl/Grail Story)

Sizzle: Seize/All   Size/All   Sis/All
Because of the Double and Rare Combination and Together of   2 ZZs/ Sleep on It Letter (Which Makes it Plural or All of Them)   the Word Sizzle Hides More Something
All Sisters are to be Seized and/or Sized
Sis/All   Implies a Clear/Strong Communication Between All Fems   Which is a Big No from   The Code   so
sizzle: to fry or burn with or as if with a hissing sound   to be very hot   to be very angry harbor deep resentment
How Many Fems have They Burned Alive in the Name of Their Many Religions   They are Still Doing it in India in Some Far Away Villages   When the Husband Dies   They Burn The Wife in The Backyard

Skanky: Skunk/He
S/Is/His/Ass/Us/Hiss/Penis/Serpent   is with   2 KKs/Broken Fem Warriors   a   N/Virgin   and a Y/Wounded Fem
The Code   says it is a Word Key So
Skanky: unattractive   foul smelling   dirty promiscuous
No One Wants to Get Close to That   So   The Code is safe

Skewer: Skew   Her   S/Cue/Her
Skew   Her/R/Her/Hair/Are/Here/Hear/Ear/Whore/Or/Err/Sex
skew: to give an oblique direction   to shape form or cut   to make conform to a specific concept or planned results   slant
Here are Some words related to
skew: alter   bias   contort   mispresent   fake   falsify
The Code Cheats on Her here too
There are No Coincidences in The Code   So
skewer: a pin to keep form of the meat while cooking
It is Torture to Her (Here is a Rhyme Between Torture and To/Her)   It can be a Many Things   Such as Corsets   Tight or Uncomfortable (High Heels) Shoes (So She Cannot Run Away)   Clothing that Attracts Sex   Hair/Makeup/Nails That Takes for Ever to Do and is So Much Loss of Precious Time   Which are Often Expensive to Keep up those Fashions

(?)   So She can be a Model (?)   To Obey that Model She has to Torture Herself into Contorting Her Waist for Example Until She Cannot Breathe Properly or Will Even Pass Out from that
Skewer Defines Men too   That Circumcision Pins the Foreskin Leaving the Penis Exposed for Life Screwing Up His Natural Sexuality at All time   Clitorectomy does to The Fems What Circumcision does to Men
Add R/Her/Err/Heir/Or/Whore to Skew And She Gets Screw/Her (To Screw is Slang for Having Sex)

Skill: S/Is/His/Ass/Us/Hiss/Penis/Serpent   Kill
S/K/L
The Skill to Kill is to   Ill/L/Sweet Fem Love Light/All/Ail/Hail/Heel/Hell/Elle/Oil (The Double LL here Makes it Plural or All of Them)   until Becoming a K/Wounded Fem Warrior

Skip: SKP
S/Is/His/Ass/Us/Hiss/Penis/Serpent   K/Wounded Fem Warrior   P/Man Power
K is in Between a Penis   its Man Power   and   i/The Marriage Union   so She is Eliminated   The Code   says Skip it   S/Kip
kip: the hide of a young
Words Related to Kip are: devastate pillage rob loot ransack berth salvage raid spoil prowl
A Hide to Hide Under for   The Code

Skull: S/Is/His/Ass/Us/Hiss/Penis/Serpent   K/Broken Fem Warrior   You/U/Ovulating   2 LLs/Sweet Fem Love Light/All/Ill/Hell/Elle (Plural or All of The Fems)
S and K Battles   You/U/Ovulating   is Being Kept Silent   The Double L Ends It
Skull: S/C/All
S/Is/His/Ass/Us/Hiss/Penis/Serpent   C/See/Young Girl   All   Skull and Bones   Refer to   The Code

Sky: This/Guy   Is Where the Sun/Son Is (His/S/Penis)
It Goes Along All Together says   The Code

Slain: CLN   3 Fem Sounds Letters

C/See/Young Girl   L/Sweet Fem Love Light/Ill/Hail/Ail/Hell/Elle/Hell/Ill/Ail/
Hail/Elle   N/In/Hen/Virgin/Ann/Virgin
C/See/Young Girl   Lane   Keep C in That Lane
See/C   Eileen/Helen/Elaine (Hell/In)
slain: past participle of slay
slay: to kill by violence   to destroy   to extinguish
The Code   Keeps C Slain
Such Soft Sounds for Such a Carnage

Slam: Slay   M/Motherhood

Slap: S/is/His/Us/Ass/Hiss/Serpent/Penis   Lap
Switch P for B/Boy Holding All Fems Breasts and He Gets a slab
(slab: large piece of stone)   The Philosopher Stone   The Rock is with
the Boy Already   It is on His Laps

Slave: Slay   V/Fem Sex Active
Making Her a Slave Since Eve
S/Lay/V
S/Is/His/Ass/Us/Hiss/Penis/Serpent   Lay   V/Fem Sex Active   She Is On
Call   It is Called Slavery
When S/Is/His/Ass/Us/Hiss/Penis/Serpent   is with L/Sweet Love Light/
Hell/Ill/Ail/Hail/Elle   as V/Fem Sex Active
It is Brutal Says   The Code

Slay: S/Is/His/Ass/Us/Hiss/Penis/Serpent   Lay
S   L/Sweet Fem Love Light/Ill/Hail/Ail/Hell/Elle/Hell/Ill/Ail/Hail/Elle   A/
All Men
S/Penis   is Separated from   A/All Men   by   L/Elle A Big No from   The
Code   so She Gets Slain
slay: to kill by violence
Note the Past Tense of Slay can be Slew Slayed or Slain

Slick: S/Is/His/Ass/Us/Hiss/Penis/Serpent   Licks   When Penis Licks or
Get Licked   It is Slick
slick: smooth and glossy   cleverly devised

Slipper: Shoes that Slips Easily   Also

slipper: to beat or strike with a slipper
Slip/Her   Sleep/Her
Slippery: Slipper   E/He

Slither: Slit/Her
Slut/Her   This One Everyone Knows
May be with a Scythe (See Scythe)

Slot: S/Is/His/Ass/Us/Hiss/Penis/Serpent
is With 3 Fem Letters   (Especially If it Makes the Word Lot) She is An Opening says   The Code
Switch O/Fem Hole for You/U/Ovulating and She Gets to be a Slut (Another Hole)
slut   a prostitute   an immoral woman
Men have been Paying for Sex Since Antiquity (or Longer)
Whys does it have to be an Immoral Service for Something Men Should be Thankful and are Often in a Needy for   Because   The Code   Forbids The Fems to Hold Any Power   Any Money   or   Have Any Self Esteem   Nothing was Left for The Fems Except to be a Wife (No Power for Her Then)   A Mother (As a Wife Only)   or a   Prostitute (Which was Associated with Money but Public Reject in Society)
Switch O/Fem Hole for A/All/Men and He Gets Slat (Buttocks)

Slow: S/Is/His/Ass/Us/Hiss/Penis/Serpent
L/Sweet Fem Love Light/Ill/Hail/Ail/Hell/Elle/Hell/Ill/Elle   Owe/O
Slowly: Slow/Lay

Sludge: Sell/A/Judge
Funny
Sludge is a Good Place for   The Code   to Hide
Cell   Odd (3 Fem Letters Word   See Odd in The Words Chapter)   G/Penis Penetration
She is in a Cell (Prisoner) When G is at Odds
S/is/His/Us/Ass/Hiss/Serpent/Penis   Lodge
S/is/His/Us/Ass/Hiss/Serpent/Penis and Lodging
That Would be a Big No for The Code   Because That Penis Need to Remain in Movement   So

The Dam Code The Damn Book

sludge: mud mire ooze slush   a deposit of ooze at the bottom of a body of water   broken ice as on the sea   sediment deposited during the treatment of sewage
If the Ice/Eyes   Letter i/Marriage Act   I/Eye/High/Hi/Stick/The Eye in the Pyramid would Start Melting for The Fems She would Start Seeing Through   The Code   in Action   A Big No for The Code   so Back to the Sewage and Feces (F/Fem/Fuck   Is) as Usual for The Fems Here are Some More Examples Relating Her to Feces   from   That Code Note The Large Amount of Fem Letters in those Words
Goo   Scum   Gunk   Dung   Muck   Oil   Slime   Crud   Filth   Mucus   Fungus   Dirt   Smut
Letter G/Penis Penetration Starts Goo and Gunk

Slumber: Slam/B/R   Slum/Be/Her
slumber: a state of inactivity   to sleep
Slumber Party: Young Girls type of Party
Where there is No or Little Importance in an Action
It is for The Fems
Slumber is a Word with Double Meaning here
Slum/B/Her
The Boy is Holding All Fems Breasts in a Slum
slum: run down part of town heavily populated inhabited by poor people
Here Goes The Fems Dreams of Slumber Party Dreams

Slut: S/Is/His/Ass/Us/Hiss/Penis/Serpent   Lot
A Lot of Penisses for the Slut
slut: a prostitute   an immoral or dissolute person   a narrow elongated depression
A Narrow Elongated Depression is a Vagina
Slutty: Slut/He
The Code   Owns that Prostitute (Pimp)

Small: S/Is/His/Ass/Us/Hiss/Penis/Serpent
M/Motherhood   All
When S and M are Together it is Small Event
Even Smaller   Small/Her
When it is Small   It Belong to the H/Her/Are/Hear/Heir/Or/Whore

631

Smart: S/M/Art
S/Is/His/Ass/Us/Hiss/Penis/Serpent   M/Motherhood   Art
When S is with M   The Art Comes in to Protect Smart   The Secret Art of the Initiates in   That Code
Smart is   The Code
Smarter   Smart/Her   Smarter than Her

Smear: C/See/Young Girl   Me   R/Her/Are/Hear/Heir/Or/Whore
smear: to spread   to stain   to sully
Nothing Good here for The Fems
S/Mirror
S/Penis and his Reflection
S/Mère
Mère is a Mother in French
S/Is/His/Ass/Us/Hiss/Penis/Serpent   M/Motherhood   Her/R/Ear/Hear/Hair/Err/Heir/Or/Whore/Here/Are/Our/Ere/Air/Ire/Sex
When S is having Sex with M   It is a Smear
Smur or Smir: drizzly rain
Rain is an entirely Fem Symbol   Being Water
Switch Ea (2 Masc Letters) for You/U/You/Ovulating and She would Get a Smur   A Mur is a Wall in French

Smother: S/Mother
S/Is/His/Ass/Us/Hiss/Penis/Serpent   is with   M/Motherhood   It is
smother: to suppress   to extinguish by covering
Smothering: S/Mother/In
When S is With M/Motherhood

Snazzy: extremely attractive or stylish
N/In/Hen/Ann/Virgin   and   S/Is/His/Ass/Us/Hiss/Penis/Serpent   are Together with 2 ZZs/Sleep on It (Plural or All of Them)   It is Snazzy

Snob: S/Is/His/Ass/Us/Hiss/Penis/Serpent   Knob
S is Polishing His Knob

Snoop: S/Is/His/Ass/Us/Hiss/Penis/Serpent   is with N/In/Hen/Virgin/Ann/Virgin and 2 OOs/Fem Holes   so
snoop: to pry

The Dam Code The Damn Book

Snuff: Sin/Off   S/Enough
Here Both Meanings Means Almost the Same
One is   Take the Sex Sin Away   It is Only a Snuff
The Other is   Enough of the S/Is/His/Ass/Us/Hiss/Penis/Serpent
That is Something a Man Want to Snuff from Far
Switch U/You/Ovulating for i/Marriage Act and She Gets a Sniff
Because the Word Sniff has a N and 2 FFs   It Gives Her the Advantage
Being the Ending of the Word   A Big No from The Code   so
sniff: to clear the nose by so doing   to show disdain

So: S/Is/His/Ass/Us/Hiss/Penis/Serpent   is with O/Fem Hole
so: in that manner or fashion
It is a Cemented Concept says   The Code   O/Fem Hole has to be with S/Penis

Sob: S/Is/His/Ass/Us/Hiss/Penis/Serpent   O/Fem Hole   B/Boy Holding All Fems Breasts
If S/Penis would be Separated from the Boy by a O/Fem Hole   That would Be a Big No from   The Code   so
Someone is going to Cry/Sob
SOB   Son of a Bitch

Social: Sexual
The Code   is Always with Us/S/Penis
So   She/Shh   L/Sweet Fem Love Light/Ill/Hail/Ail/Hell/Elle/Hell/Ill/Ail/Elle
When in Public She better Shush about That

Society: So/See/I/T   Sow   C/Young Girl   Err/R   T/Fem Cross
The Only Thing The Fem has to Look for is to be a T/Fem Cross   through R/Sex

Sock: S/Is/His/Ass/Us/Hiss/Penis/Serpent
    O/Fem Hole   C/See/Young Girl   K/Wounded Fem Warrior
Suck   Soaked   Sacked   Because it Ends with Fem Letters   It Makes It Weak Words

Solar: Sol   R/Her/Are/Heir/Or/Whore/Err/Sex
Sol is an Important Musical Note

633

Soil   R   Sole   R   Soul   R
Anything Related to The Sun (Son) is an Entirely Masc Concept   The Fems as R/Heir/Or/Whore/Err/Her has to be there because it is The Life or Centerpiece of   That Code
The Code   Can do Everything to a Fem that Means Nothing to Our Common World   It is Proven by what they do to Fems in the Far East
sol: American Spanish: sun Spanish< Latin Sol   a bronze coin   also called Libra a former gold coin of Peru
The sun is Gold so it is Related to Gold   We are Told Gold is a Nourishing Color   Not the Same for the Moon/Fem Color   The Moon is Grey   A Perfect Color for Her says   The Code   Any one that is Grey has Left the Body   The Weaker The Fem is The Way says   The Code   for Her   Compare the Prices of Gold and Silver
It Takes a Lot of Energy to keep The Fems That Way   Weak/Low
soul: the principle of life   the spiritual part of a human life   The Fems has No soil says   The Code   That is Why   R/Heir/Her/Err/Whore   is There
sole: being the only one   the bottom and lower part of anything   the bottom surface of the foot   a shoe with a sole
Sole is also a Flat Fish to Eat (Delicious) (Not to be Found in Dictionary.com Definitions Yet)
Here the Word Sole Meaning is Flat and Fish (Fem)
A Big No from   The Code   to have a Fem with a Flat Chest   So   We Eat it
In Music There is the Key (See Key in Words) of Sol
The Sun Needs the Soil in Order to Maintain Life   Soil/Her is not a Word   But it is Part of Solar Sound Wise
Take S/Penis Away from Sol/Soul/Sole and She Gets Oil (See Oil in Words) (See The Oil and The Virgins in The Bible Symbolism)
SOL Sole and Soul All have Fem Letters with S/Penis as Its Start   S/Is/As/Has/Ass/Us/His/Hiss/Serpent/Penis   O/Fem Hole   L/Sweet Fem Light
S.O.L: strictly out of luck   shit out (of) luck
The Reason Why this Term S.O.L. Contradicts All Other Sol Words Definitions here of Sol is That The Dots are Entirely Fem in   The Code   (See Dot in The Words Chapter) Dots Separates the Letters of Sol Giving The Dots an Important Position   Not Only Changing its Meaning   It Gives to The Fems Access to   That Code   Just by Being There   There are No Breach in   That Code

The Dam Code The Damn Book

The Sole/Soul is Under the Foots says The Code   The Code   Does Not Want Us To Develop Spiritually   It makes Us Step on That Soul All Day   and We Have Obeyed its Hypnotizing Rules as Laws   Seen or Not   The Arch is Above the Sole/Soul (See Arch and Arc in The Words Chapter) It is the Support for the Body Weight   Same in Architecture (Churches(Ch/Arches) Large Historic Buildings   etc)
Solar (Sole/Are/R) is the Light from the Son (Sun) and We All Share it   But No   In Many Different Ways the Sun/Sun Shines Only for The Masc says The Code

Soldier: Sold/He/Her
Strong Code Word here
Abuse of Fem in the Military was the Best Way to Keep Her Out
As in Many/Most Types of Work
The Code   is Thousands of Year Old
Soul   D/Pregnant   Her/Her/Are/Heir/Or/Whore

Solo: C/See/Young Girl   All/Letter L   2 OOs/Fem Holes (Plural or All of Them)
Divide to Conquer says   The Code   Make The Fems Alone   (See So in The Words Chapter)

Solution: Soul   You/U/Ovulating She/Shh   On
The Solution for The Fems says   The Code   is that Her Loins Remain Available at All Time   On and On   No Ovulation Special Time for Sex as All The Other Mammals   And Shh about it   Because it is in Her Soul

Solve: Soul/Sol/Sole   V/Ov/Eve
Since Eve   On the Soul Level   Under The Sun/Son   As a Flat Chest Fish   She Ovulates
The Code   Solves and Locks Everything from Above Our Heads   From The Past into the Future it Trespasses Unconscious Barriers Inside Us

Some: S/Is/As/Has/Ass/His/Us/Hiss/Serpent/Penis
    is with   M/Motherhood/Him/Home   It is a Non Descriptive Term   That Sums it it

Someone: Some   On/N/Hen/Ann/Virgin

635

Lise Rochon

When Some is a Virgin   She Becomes Someone   Still No Name Here for Her says   The Code

Something: Some   Ding/Thing/Ting   Same/Thing   Sum/Thing
Another Anonymous and General Nebulous Description for Her
As Usual says   The Code   She is a Dinged Thing That Ting   Ring That Ring Around Her Ring Finger   Seals it by Law

Sometime: Sum/Time
Any Word with the Word Time in it (T/Fem Cross   Together with   M/Motherhood) Needs to be Seriously Questioned
Same Time   That Time of the Month Arrives Sometimes and at the Same Time   The T/Fem Cross   is Her Immense Blood Loss

Son: S/Is/As/Has/Ass/His/Us/Hiss/Serpent/Penis
    On/N/Hen/Ann/Virgin
The Penis is On for the Son
The Penis Meets The Virgin   Here Comes a Son/Sun
Switch O/Fem Hole for U/You/Ovulating and She Gets a Sun/Son   The Sun Shines for Everybody   So Not Much Gain for Her here
Switch O/Fem Hole for i/Marriage Act (The Stick/Him and The Dot/Her) and She Gets Sin
Add a Silent G/Penis Penetration and She Gets to Sing (Sexual Sounds)
Switch O for You/U/Ovulating with a Silent G and She Gets a Song (Son/G) in The Present and in The Past in Sung
Songs of Songs   Sons/Ov/Sons says The Old Testament Which is Attached to The Christian Bible
Sons and G/Hymen Perforation are Songs to   The Code

Song: S/Is/As/Has/Ass/His/Us/Hiss/Serpent/Penis On/N/Hen/Ann/Virgin   G/Penis Penetration
The Penis Sings When the Penetration is On

Soon: S/Is/As/Has/Ass/His/Us/Hiss/Serpent/Penis
    2 OOs/Fem Holes (Plural or All of Them) N/In/Hen/Ann/Virgin
All Fems and Virgins to have Sex Asap   A Son Soon

The Dam Code The Damn Book

The Code   says Son/Suns as Soon as Possible   Although Not with the Same Fem as There All implicating All Holes from All Fems Virgins Also   Describing Polygamy
Sooner: Soon   Her/Are/Err/Heir/Or/Whore/Sex
All Fems Busy with Sex

Soot: C/Hut   S/Hut
soot: incomplete combustion of coal
S/Is/As/Has/Ass/His/Us/Hiss/Serpent/Penis   and 2 OOs/Fem Holes (Plural or All of Them)   Ending in   T/Fem Cross
S is With 2 Fems Holes   The Fems Ends in T/Fem Sacrifice (Burning in Hell)
Soot is an Unfinished Process   And it is as Burning in Hell   Till Ashes (Nothing Left for Her here Except Ashes   After Enduring All this Pain   and it Never Ends)

Sorcerer: Sort   See/C/Young Girl   Her/R/Heir/Or/Whore/Sex
Sort (In French un Sort is Bad Fate   or   a Spell Which is a Magical Power that can Controls Your Actions   Sort has T/Fem Cross as a Silent Letter Here
To Spell is Very Closely Related to The Letters of the Alphabet Which This Damn Book Explains in Details   Although Always Incomplete
So   R/Err/Heir/Or/Whore/Her/Sex
C/See/Young Girl   Her
Here in Sorcerer The Whores are in Plural Making All Fems That Way and Seeing Each Other that Way Too as in Sort See Sort
S/Whore/See/Whore
Soar/See/Her   Soar/C/Her
The Code   is Soaring Here with Transforming All Fems in Whores/or with Heirs to The Extend of having Her See it that Way Just as a Spell or un Sort would Do c The Code   Sorts The Fems That Way S/Is/His/Us/Ass/Hiss/ Serpent/Penis   is Working Until Sore with Those
Source/Her   Is a Good Source on How Works That Dam Code
sorcerer: a person who seek control by magic power

Sordid: Sore/He Did

Sore: C/See/Young Girl   or   S/His/Penis   R/Her/Heir/Or/Whore/Sex

Lise Rochon

Switch O/Fem Hole with i/Marriage Act and Get Sire (to Sire Children)
Add U/You/Ovulating
Sour

Sorrow: Sore   O/Fem Hole
Switch O for i/Marriage Act and Get Sire/O
It is All About Sex Sorrows for Her

Sorry: S/Is/As/Has/Ass/His/Us/Hiss/Serpent/Penis
   Whore/Her/Heir/Or/Are/Err/Sex   Her/R/Ear/Hear/Hair/Err/Heir/Or/
Whore/Here/Are/Our/Ere/Air/Ire/Sex   He
Sore/He

Sort: S/Is/As/Has/Ass/His/Us/Hiss/Serpent/Penis   R/Her/Are/Heir/Or/
Whore/Err/Sex   T/Fem Cross
R/Her   and   T/Fem Cross   are with   S/Penis   in the Front   it Needs to be Sorted
sort: to classify to a special group
(See Sort as a Spell in Words)

Soul: S/Is/As/Has/Ass/His/Us/Hiss/Serpent/Penis
    O/Fem Hole   You/U/Ovulating   L/Sweet Fem Light/Ill/Hell/Elle
S   Hole   See/All   See/Hole (See Sole in Body Parts)
soul: principle of life
I Feel Sorry for the Christians and the Honest Bible Believers
Switch S for P/Man Power and He Gets a Pole (Slang for Penis)
Switch S for M/Motherhood and She Gets a Mole (No One Wants to Look at That   says   The Code)
Switch S for N/In/Hen/Ann/Virgin and She Gets Null (Without Value) or a Knoll
knoll: to ring or toll a bell for announce by tolling   the sound of a knell
(See Bell/A Belle to Ring)
knell: the sound made by a bell rung slowly especially for a death or a funeral
Switch E for i/Marriage Act and She Gets to Kneel (See Knee in Body Parts) as usual   She Stays on Her Knees says   The Code

Sound: S/Is/As/Has/Ass/His/Us/Hiss/Serpent/Penis

The Dam Code The Damn Book

Hound
The Code   says The Penis Should be in Constant Attack to The Fems
S is in Front of 4 Fem Letters Which Makes it Vulnerable   So Its Attack is Relentless
hound: to pursue or harass without respite

Source: S/Our/C
S/Penis   Her/R/Ear/Hear/Hair/Err/Heir/Or/Whore/Here/Are/Our/Ere/Air/Ire/Sex
See/C/Young Girl
Sure   C/See/Young Girl   R/Her
Sour/S/He
Here Sour does Not Rhyme with Sour in The Word Source   but   The Spelling is The Same
S/Penis (or the C Sound)   R/Her   C/See/Young Girl
The Code   says Here   Our Ancestors Source   (See Sorcerer) is   S/Penis   R/Sex   and   C/Virgin

Sow: S/Penis   O/Fem Hole
sow: a fem pig   to scatter seeds
S/Penis (Human Penis)   Sows   it Seeds to The Fem Pig
S/Penis   O/Owe
She/Shh   Owes it to Him says   The Code   and She/Shh about it
So   says   The Code   The Aloofness of   The Code   towards Her Pain of Being Treated as a Pig
W/All Fems Sexually Active is Silent   It is Left Out of The Game Even if it is all about Her
Sow is a Cover Word Here

Spank: S/Penis   P/Man Power   Ankh (See Ankh in The Words Chapter)
spank: to strike (a person usually a child) with the open hand   a slipper   especially on the buttocks as a punishment
There is Only One Way to do here   if Not   Get Spank
It is All about The Ankh   Also

Spat: S/Is/As/Has/Ass/His/Us/Hiss/Serpent/Penis
    Pat
spat: a petty quarrel   a light blow   slap   smack

S/Penis   P/Man Power   are Together in the Hat (At)
Hat is a Cover Word here (See Art in The Words Chapter)
The Code   Forgives Easily to Men
Switch A for i/Marriage Act and She Gets Spit (The Code   Hates it When
The Fems Gets Close to the Hat Word   It Has a Heavy Meaning in) so it
Attacks
Switch A for O/Fem Hole and She Gets Spot (a Blood Spot for
Her   or   Something Very Little)

spay: to remove the ovaries and usually the uterus from a female
animal   a tree year old male red dear

Speaker: Speck   Her/R/Ear/Hear/Hair/Err/Heir/Or/Whore/Here/Are/Our/
Ere/Air/Ire/Sex
Something Very Little for Her to Talk About   No One will Respect a Fem
says   The Code

Spear: Spay   Her/R/Heir/Or/Whore/Err/Sex
spay: to remove the ovaries and usually the uterus from a Female
animal   a tree year old male red dear
spear: a long stabbing weapon for thrusting or throwing

Specie: Space/He   S/Pay/See   S/Pay/C
Spay/C   C/Being a Virgin Letter/Young Girl/See
Spice/His   Species

spell: to express words by letters especially correctly   a
word phrase or form of words supposed to have magic
power   charming   incantation   a state of enchantment
any dominating or irresistible influence   fascination
Spell has Several Other Definitions   The More the better says   The
Code   to Confuse the Onlookers
To Spell Words   and   to be Under a Spell Here is No Coincidence   To
Know the Great Spell of   The Great Curse Code   is a Big No from   That
Code   Because Spelling a Word is to be Under the Influence of   The
Code   Spell Itself
Switch P/Man Power for B/Boy Holding All Fems Breasts
And He Gets to See a Bell or a Belle (B/Boy is Too Young for The Code)

The Dam Code The Damn Book

Replace E/He with i/Marriage Act and Get a   Spill
Spine: S/Is/As/Has/Ass/His/Us/Hiss/Serpent/Penis   P/Man Power   N/In/Hen/Ann/Virgin
In the World of Mammals The Male Pees to Attract The Fem   or   to Claim Territory to Other Males
C/See/Young Girl   P/Man Power   In/N/Hen
Take Away E/He and She Gets a Spin   or   S/Penis Gets to Pin Her

Spiral: Spear/All   S/Pair/All   S/Pire/All   S/P/Hare/All
All these Terms   To be Speared   To be Paired   To Be on a Pire (Burn Alive)   To be a Silent Rabbit
Rabbits Hop (Sex) a Lot and Have Lot of Babies   they Have No Voice   Humans Put them in Small Cages
spiral: a plain curve   a helix
Spiral is a Fem Word Because of its Round Shape   The Fems Are Always Doomed in   The Code   Helix   Hell   X/Fallen Fem Cross
S/Is/As/Has/Ass/His/Us/Hiss/Serpent/Penis   P/Man Power   Her/R/Ear/Hear/Hair/Err/Heir/Or/Whore/Here/Are/Our/Ere/Air/Ire/Sex   All/Ill/Elle   All Men Penisses Having Sex with All Fems   That is   The Code   Spiral

Spring: Spray/In   S/P/Ring   Spraying
Summer   Sum/Some   Mer (Mère in French)
Fall   Fem/Fuck   All/L/Sweet Fem Love/Ail/Ill/Hail/Heel/Hell/Elle/Oil
Winter   Went   Her/R   Win/T/Her   As T/Fem Cross She is a Winner says   The Code
Penis Spray in the Spring
Marry in the Summer   Fall (F/All) in the Autumn
Pregnancy in the Winter (Win/T/Her)
To Give Birth in the Spring   To Spring is Also to Jump/Hop (Sex Slang)

Spirit: Spear/It
Holy Spirit: Hole   He   Spear/Spare   It/Hit
The Secret Code   Language Awful   It wants to Make Sure that No Dilettante Dares to Look at   That Code   so   When He Spears   He is Spared by The Holy Spirit

Lise Rochon

Spiritual: Spear/Ritual   Spear/Hit/Through/All   S/Pay/Ritual   Spay/Ritual   Spare/Ritual

Spit: S/P/Hit
Spitter: Spit/Her

Spoil: S/P/Oil   S/Is/His/Us/Ass/Hiss/Serpent/Penis   P/Man Power   Oil/All/Ill
S/Penis and P/Man Power go with the Oil   It Spoils it
Spoiler: Spoil/Her
That Could have been a Nice Word for Her
But No says   The Code so
spoiler: a person that robs or ravages

Sport: S/Penis   P/Man Power   R/Heir/Or/Whore/Err/Sex   T/Fem Cross
S/Penis   and   P/Man Power   Starts The Word with R/Her   Ending in   T/Fem Cross
Take R/Her Away and She Gets a Spot (a spot of Blood   Something Small)

Spread: S/P/Read   Spray/Red
S/Is/As/Has/Ass/His/Us/Hiss/Serpent/Penis   and   P/Man Power   Can Read
He Can Spread Her/R/Ear/Hear/Hair/Err/Heir/Or/Whore/Here/Are/Our/Ere/Air/Ire/Sex
Spreader: Spread/Her (Legs)
spreader: a device for keeping apart 2 objects
That would be the Compass of the Rosicrucian Emblem with   G/Penis Penetration   in its Middle
They Wear that Embroidered Emblem in Front of their Crotch on Their Apron
Few Especially The Fems Dare to Looks there

Square: S/Q/R   S/Queer
S/Is/As/Has/Ass/His/Us/Hiss/Serpent/Penis   Q/Bleeding Fem   Her/R/Ear/Hear/Hair/Err/Heir/Or/Whore/Here/Are/Our/Ere/Air/Ire/Sex   Queer
Square is Part of Sacred Geometry   Study Along

The Dam Code The Damn Book

Stain: Stay/In   A Stay that Stays   In/N/Ann/Hen/Donkey
Stay   Inn/N/Ann   Ann/Stain   Einstein (a Jewish Name)

Standard: Stand/Hard
It is   The Code   Standard   for Her

Star: S/Is/As/Has/Ass/His/Us/Hiss/Serpent/Penis
T/Fem Cross   A/All Men   Her/R/Ear/Hear/Hair/Err/Heir/Or/Whore/Here/
Are/Our/Ere/Air/Ire/Sex
T/Fem Cross   is Surrounded by   S/Penis   and   A/All Men   Ending
with   R/Her   She is Then The Star (Porn Star   Check The Star in The
Keyboard Chapter)
Stay   R/Her   Stare
All Men Penisses are Having Sex with T/Fem Cross and R/Her   The Star
Shape * Represents Her with Her Legs Opened with S/Penis in there
A Star is Bad Luck in Palmistry Because it Represents a Cross with Another
Bar Crossing It   Therefore Doubling it
S/Penis   T/Fem Cross   R/Her/Heir/Or/Whore/Err/Sex
No Chance Here for Her Here Unless The Fem as Whore is Involved
says   The Code
A Star is a Light in the Night Sky and a Famous Person (Per/Son)   Which
Excludes The Fems   Stare at That too
A Star is a Cross Rotating (Rota) on an Axis (X/Is   X/Fallen Fem Cross
is   Axe/Is)
A Circle Around Makes it a Wheel (See Wheel of Time)
There are Multiples Crosses Attached to The Fems
Star is a Multiple of Them   And a Cover Word here
The Star of David has 6 AAAAAAs/A/All Men and 6 Pyramids in it All
Intertwined (See Star)

Start: S/Is/As/Has/Ass/His/Us/Hiss/Serpent/Penis
   T/Fem Cross   Art
Art is the Ancient Name for the Practice of the Secret Society
Rites   Called the Secret Arts
It has the Word Star in it   (See Star Above)
Stay/Art
S/Penis   with   T/Fem Cross (The Great Curse) is One of The Secrets
of   The Secret Code

Lise Rochon

State: Stay/T
The State Rules (Us The State)
The Fems Cross Stays says The State
Stay/Hate   Stay/Ate
Estate   S/Tate   here S/Plural is in front Which is Unusual
State is a Very Important Word   It Implies Lots of Power

Status: Stay/T/Us   State/Us
Note that Status Starts and Ends with 2 SSs/Penisses   Also A/All Men are Surrounded by 2 TTs/Fem Crosses Which is Unusual in   The Code
You/U/Ovulating   is Bordered by   T/Fem Cross   and S/Penis
State   Us   S/Penis   The US is Also United States
Status is a Very Important Word in   That Code

Stay: S/Is/As/Has/Ass/His/Us/Hiss/Serpent/Penis
    T/Fem Cross   A/All Men   Y/Wounded Fem
S with T   A with Y   They are Here to Stay says   The Code
Note that All Letters are Necessary to Create The Word Stay
It Takes All Men Penises to Wound All Wounded Fem to Bring Them to That Tem Cross (Great Curse)
Take A/All Men Away and She Gets a Sty
She Never Gets Out of the Curse of Going Down

Steer: S/Is/As/Has/Ass/His/Us/Hiss/Serpent/Penis   Tear
Stay/Here
The Code   has   S/Penis   and   T/Fem Cross   Together   It is All Powerful and What Follows is a Done Job   Here for Example it is a Tear (Rip) or Tears for Her
steer: to guide the course of something in motion by a rudder helm wheel etc

Stellar: Steal   Her/R/Ear/Hear/Hair/Err/Heir/Or/Whore/Here/Are/Our/Ere/Air/Ire/Sex
Stale/Her
How Can She be Stellar When She is being Staled
Stay   Lay   R/Her   Have Sex and Stay Laid   That is Stellar for Her says   The Code
Stay/Lair

Stay Hidden or in The Mud
S/Is/As/Has/Ass/His/Us/Hiss/Serpent/Penis
Tell   R/Her
Stale/Her
Add i/Marriage Act to Stellar and She Gets Stay/Liar   Stay   Lay   Her

Stick: STIC
S/Is/As/Has/Ass/His/Us/Hiss/Serpent/Penis   with
T/Fem Cross   and   IC/Integrated Circuit
S and T are Together (Stay)   It is a Job Done says   The Code   Here it is
Reinforced Powerfully with IC
S/Penis   and   T/Fem Cross   are an Integrated Circuit With the Sticks (2
Penisses   One with Letter S   The Other with the Meaning of Stick) Penis
and Stick are Redundant
Thus Adding Even More Importance
Note that Stick has Only One Masc Letter The S   The Others T/Fem
Cross   i/Marriage Act   C/See/Young Girl Virgin and K/Broken Fem
Warrior are Fem Almost in Perfect Order to End All Broken
Stay/IC   And The Stick Stays
Take Away ST and replace it with D and She Gets Dick
S/Penis/Dick is so Close to that Stick
Stick to it says   The Code

Sticky: Stick/He   Sticky is an Adhesive   His Penis and His Stick are One
Sticker: Stick   R/Her/Are/Heir/or/Whore/Sex
She is Stuck to that Whore   Or   have an Heir

Stiff: An Erection
S/T/If

Still: S/Is/As/Has/Ass/His/Us/Hiss/Serpent/Penis   T/Fem Cross   L/
Sweet Fem Love Light/Ill/Hail/Ail/Hell/Elle/Hell/Ill/Elle
Stay   Ill/Hell/Elle/Ail/Hail says   The Code   With 2 LL s/L/Elle/Hell/Ill (It is
Either Plural or All of The Fems)
Stay Ill and Be Still About It
Steal it (Her)   It is OK   She is Made of Steel   She can take it

Sting: Stay   N/In/Hen/Ann/Virgin

The Fems Cannot Stay and Get In   That would be a Sting
Add an   Her/R/Ear/Hear/Hair/Err/Heir/Or/Whore/Here/Are/Our/Ere/Air/
Ire/Sex   and She Get a String (Such a Puny Thing)
String and Serene are Close   because   The Code   Eliminates Serene
Switch S/Is/As/Has/Ass/His/Us/Hiss/Serpent/Penis
for P/Man Power and He Gets Spin (Could be a Fortunate Event)

Stir: S/Tear
Stirring that Pot of Tears (Crying) and Tears (Rip)
Stay   R/Her/Hair/Are/Here/Hear/Ear/Heir/Whore/Or/Err/Sex

Stood: Stud
Anything that Stands is a Cool Erect Male
Especially with All those Fems in Line for His/S/Penis   T/Fem Cross   2
OOs/Fem Holes (Plural or All of Them)   and   D/Pregnant   The Circle of
Life for Her says   The Code

Stop: S/Is/As/Has/Ass/His/Us/Hiss/Serpent/Penis   T/Fem Cross   P/Man
Power
Stay Up   Stay Hop   S is at the Top Here
No Communication here for Her   A Stop for Her

Stool: S/Is/His/Penis   Tool
Here S rules Over   2 OOs/Fem Holes   and   L/Sweet Fem Love Light/Ill/
Hail/Ail/Hell/Elle
Stool as a Sex (SX) Tool to Use Against Her   She/It   or   Shit says   The
Code   (See Feces in The Words Chapter)

Story: Store   E/He
Stare at it
Story is The Story for Him to Store
Stay   R/Her/Heir/Or/Whore   He/E
That is Her Story to Store says   The Code
Stow/R/He
stow: to put in place
Stay   Ray A Ray for Him to Stay

Straight: S/T/Rate

S/Penis and T/Fem Cross are Together It is Rated
Stay Rate
rate: to estimate the value or worth
When the Penis is the Rate it is Straight
Take E/He Away and Get a Rat (See Rat in The Words Chapter)

String: Stay/Ring
That Ring Stays
A Ring Made of String is Weak For The Fems What it is to Live on a String/Poverty
string: to arrange in a succession a slender cord
Switch i/Marriage Act for O/Fem Hole and She Gets Strong (She Gets Strong here because She goes from having Sex to be Ready to do it Again)

Structure: Struck/T/Her
In The Past for a Fem to Get a Beating was Called a Domestic Disturbance Not Much Importance
The Code Calls it Part of Its Structure Strike that Cursed Fem

Strut: S/Is/As/Has/Ass/His/Us/Hiss/Serpent/Penis
T/Fem Cross Rot
She is Walking with Him Rotting He is Strutting
strut: to walk with a vain pompous bearing

Student: Stud/Dent
Student: Stud/He/Dent
Study: Stud/He
No Fem Allowed here

Stupid: Stupe/ID
ID in the Unconscious is the Search for Pleasure with Boundaries
Stupe i/Marriage Act D/Pregnant
She is Stupid When Getting Pregnant says The Code
Stupidity: Stupe/P/D/T
Stupe is Short for Stupidit

Stupor: Stupe/Her

stupor: suspension or great diminution of sensibility   mental torpor   apathy
To keep a Fem Stupid Takes a Lot of Work

Suave: SUAV
Soft Sounds are Suave
S/Is/As/Has/Ass/His/Us/Hiss/Serpent/Penis   is with   You/U/Ovulating   of a   V/Fem Sex Active   Getting Close to Have Sex

Subject: S/Is/As/Has/Ass/His/Us/Hiss/Serpent/Penis
Object
Penis has the Complete Attention

Succeeded: Sucks/He/D
With 3 EEEs/He in Succeeded   It is Excessive but   The Code   takes All Precautions to Succeed
Here   S/Is/As/Has/Ass/His/Us/Hiss/Serpent/Penis
is with So Many Fems (2 CCs/Young Girls   1 You/U/Ovulating   and   2 DDs/Pregnants)   It is Successful   All That Sucking
Suck/Seed/D   His Seed has been Sucked in   Sucks/He/Did

Success: Sucks/His
Sucks   S/Is/As/Has/Ass/His/Us/Hiss/Serpent/Penis
The Code   has a Tendency to be Pernicious   Enticing its Members to go Out of Nature Way Where People Fall in Love   or/and   have Sex or do it for Fun   But No says   The Code   It is Forbidden (For   Bid   N/In/Virgin) No Sex Unless People make an Alliance for Life   Such as in Marriage
Suck/Sis
Success   Has 3 SSSs/Penises   One Which Starts the Word   and Has   2 CCs/Young Girls   In It Also
C and U being Fems   Suddenly Transformed into Something Else   Sucking Agents   Sock being the Cover Word here
Successful: Suck/Sex/Full   Being Full being Pregnant   The Way of being Successful for a Man is to Have a Fem Pregnant

Succinct: Suck/In/T
succinct: verbal brevity   concise

The Dam Code The Damn Book

No Talking   and   Time is Succinct While   T/Fem Cross   is Sucking It In   Concise (Con/Size)

Such: S/Penis   Ouch
such: of that particular kind of character

Suck: Sock
Suck   and   Put a Sock on it   Put a Sock (Suck) on before Putting the Shoe (Sex) On   (She/Shh   Hoe/Ho)
hoe: to dig
ho: a whore
Sucker: Suck/Her   Sock/Her   Suck   Her/R/Ear/Hear/Hair/Err/Heir/Or/Whore/Here/Are/Our/Ere/Air/Ire/Sex
sucker: a person easily cheated
Soccer (Suck/Her)

Suds: S/Odd/S
Suds can Only be Plural
2 SSs/His/Us/Ass/Hiss/Serpent/Penises   Mixes with the Odds (The Girls)   It Becomes Sudsy (Suds/He)

Suffer: SFR
S/Penis   is with   F/Fem/Fuck   as   R/Her/Heir/Or/Whore/Err/Sex   There is Suffering
Suffering: Suffer   In/N/Hen/Ann/Virgin
S/U/F/Ring
Add a Ring to it   And See What Happens
Ring All Those Bells (Belles)

Suitor: Soot Her   Sooth/Her
suitor: a man who court a woman   an individual who seek to buy a business
court: a place where justice is administered   an area open to the sky and mostly surrounded by buildings walls etc   to try to win the favors   preference or good will
The Fems have been for Sale for Millenaries   It is All Business for Him   The Code   says a Court is where - Justice (Just Us) Prevail (Pre/Veil   A Court is Surrounded by Walls   as a Prison

Lise Rochon

On The Fems Side it is Presented as Sweet Love   On The Masc Side it is All Business and She has to go Through it   It is The Law

Sultry: Sole/Tree
S/Is/As/Has/Ass/His/Us/Hiss/Serpent/Penis   O/Fem Hole   # 3
The Tree and the Number 3 are Important Words in   The Code   Symbolism
The Pyramid is One Example (See Pyramid in The Words Chapter) The Tree Persons of the Trinity (See #3 in The Number Chapter)   The Tree of Life is also Called The Sephiroth in Hebrew (He/Brew)
Very Few Initiates Get to Look at the Back of that Symbolic Tree With All of its Attributes Where The Fem is All Negative and Suffering and the Masc Side is All Positive and benevolent
sultry: hot with passion
The Code protects itself   Its Men

Summer: Sum/Her   Some   R/Her/Heir/Or/Whore/Err/Sex
The Summer is the Time to Party   Summer is a Fem Name
sum: total
Spring is a Spring   The Call for Mating   Autumn is   Hot/Dumb   Hot/Tom   Winter is Went/Her   Win/D/Her (Pregnant)

Superman: S/Up/R/M/N
S/Is/As/Has/Ass/His/Us/Hiss/Serpent/Penis
is   Hop/Up   having Sex with   M/Motherhood   and   N/Virgin   as   R/Heir/Or/Whore/Her/Err/Sex
Superman   Is The Super Plan for   The Code

Sure: S/Is/As/Has/Ass/His/Us/Hiss/Serpent/Penis   You/U/Ovulating   R/Her/Hair/Are/Here/Hear/Ear/Heir/Whore/Or/Err/Sex
E/He   is Silent Here (Just to Make Sure)
It is Sure That When Penis is With Her Ovulating   There will be a Heir   The Code   Never Mentions with Pride an Heiress (Heir/Ass)   There is No Celebration for a Baby Girl in the Muslim World   In China they Used to Throw Infants Girls Out of Car Windows   So Much That The Fems Population Went Down Then
Add O/Fem Hole to Sure and She Gets Sour
S/Our   S/Penis   with   R/Her/Our/Hour (See Hour in Time Chapter)

The Dam Code The Damn Book

The Penis is a Sure Thing for Her   It is Hers says   The Code   Sour Puss

Surely: Sure/Lay
S/Is/As/Has/Ass/His/Us/Hiss/Serpent/Penis
   You/U/Ovulating   are Starting a Word Finishing in Lay   It is a Sure/Lay
Add O/Fem Hole and She Gets a Sour/Lay   or   a   Sire/Lay   S/R/Lay
What do You Think   Sure   Said Shirley (So Sorry)

Surreal: Sire/Real
The Code   has No Boundaries   Mixing All Realms is Part of its Illusion
S/Is/As/Has/Ass/His/Us/Hiss/Serpent/Penis   R/Her/Hair/Are/Here/Hear/Ear/Heir/Whore/Or/Err/Sex   All/Ill/Hell/Ail/Elle/Letter L   S/Is/Penis   is
with   R/Her/Heir/Or/Whore   He/E   All   Then It Became Serial

Survivor: Sire/Sure   V/Fem Sex Active   R/Her/Hair/Are/Here/Hear/Ear/Heir/Whore/Or/Err/Sex
Sure   Vive   R/Her
Survive/Her
The Word Vive is a Happy Wish for Wellness

Swear: S/Wear
S/Is/As/Has/Ass/His/Us/Hiss/Serpent/Penis   is with   W/All Fem Sex Active   and   R/Her/Hair/Are/Here/Hear/Ear/Heir/Whore/Or/Err/Sex   S/Penis Wears Her   It is The Oath of   The Code
S/Penis   Swears on it   She is in The Sewer says   The Code
swear: to make a solemn declaration
Sway   R/Her
sway: to move or swing to and fro
That is What   The Code   Does

Sweat: S/Wet
S/Is/As/Has/Ass/His/Us/Hiss/Serpent/Penis   Wet
So/Wet
S/Is/As/Has/Ass/His/Us/Hiss/Serpent/Penis
Start a Word with   W/All Fems Sex Active   Ends with T/Fem
Cross   There is a Lot of Sweating (Sweat   Ann/In/Hen/N/Virgin) for Her

Swell: S/Is/As/Has/Ass/His/Us/Hiss/Serpent/Penis

Well/Well
S/Penis   Swells it is Well (All Good) says   The Code
S/Penis is in a Well (A Long Hole in The Ground as a Vagina) it Swells
swell: to rise in waves   to bulge out   to grow in amount degree force
Swell as in a Wave
swell: a wave   especially when long and unbroken or in a series of such waves
S is Well   He has All Fems Sex Active for Him says   The Code

Swine: S/Is/As/Has/Ass/His/Us/Hiss/Serpent/Penis
 is in Front of   Wine (Lost Fem Blood)
The Code   says it is a Swine   No One Wants to Look There
Who Said Men are Pigs   When they Drink a Lot of Wine While One Whine The Other is a Swine
A Strong Cover from   The Code   here to Keep The Fems Away
When the Swine is with the Wine   He is Also with the Bread/Bred   Ready to Breed
Swine is a Strong Cover for   The Code   here
(See Wine in The Words Chapter)

Switch: S/Is/As/Has/Ass/His/ Hiss/Us/Serpent/Penis
   is with the Witch so   He Switches (See Witch in The Words Chapter)   Which is Which
A Different Switch from room   On to Off too

Sword: S/Word
S/Is/As/Has/Ass/His/Us/Hiss/Serpent/Penis   Word
S   Her   D
S/Penis   R/Her   D/Pregnant   Are Under The Sword
Jesus Says I bring a Sword   The Sword Has a T/Fem Cross Shape
The Word   and   The Sword have Complex Symbolisms in The Bible   Research

Syllable: C/See/Young Girl   L/Sweet Fem Love Light/Ill/Hail/Ail/Hell/Elle   Able
Sick or Not 2 LLs/Ills/Elle are All Able to Follow   The Code
Anything Related with   The Word   is a Symbol   or a   Sin/Bowl
Symbols: See/My/Balls   Funny at First Look

The Dam Code The Damn Book

Symbols are The Nests Where   The Code   Hides
Sim Means Similar   All is The Same (A Big Lie) says   The Code
In   The Code   N/Virgin   and   M/Motherhood   are Similar as One (N)
Becomes The Other (M)   Endlessly says   The Code   Seamless (Seem/
Less) Always Minimizing Her   Seem/Less/Lay
M/Motherhood   and   N/Virgin   make The Word Man
Sin is a Prime Ingredient to Keep Humanity (Especially The Fems) Guilty in Many Religions
Sinning   Sin   In/Hen/Ann/Virgin   The Sin is In Her

Sympathy: See/Him/Pat/He   Sin/Path/He
Syn as Synonym is   The Code   Path Here
M and N are an Example They Are Interchangeable and those 2 Fem Letters   M/Motherhood   and   N/Virgin   Creates the Word Man For Him says   The Code
Nothing Creates the Word Woman Except Whoa/Man (Whoa is a Command Used to Stop a Horse (Whore/R/Heir/Whore/Err/Her)   (See Whore as a Horse/Whore In The Words Chapter)
The Complexity of   The Code   Shows Itself in Concepts as those
The Path of the Sin has No Sympathy for The Fems   It is All Hypocrisy Dishonor and Greed Directed to The Fem
It is a Too Small of a Life

Synchronize: Sin/Crone/Eyes
A Powerful Cover Word Here for   The Code
crone: a withered witch as old woman   beldam   woman   hag   ugly
Beldam   A Belle/Dame is in French Literally a Beautiful Woman   Beldam (Belle/Dame) is Defined in the English Language as an Old Woman Especially Ugly
That Code   is Thorough   It Leaves Nothing Positive for Her at All
A Crone Should be a Wise Elder Fem   But No says   The Code
Sin/Crown/Is   That is Her Crown   To Be
Sinful   Ugly   Malicious   Vicious and a Bad Witch
And She Should be Seen That Way says   The Code

Syntax: Sin/Tax
Syn/Sin   T/Fem Cross   Axe/X/Fallen Fem Cross
Sinning makes All Fems as T go Under the Axe (Fallen Cross)

syn: synonymous
The Code   Initiates   Know/No   More
syntax: the study of grammatical sentences

Syrup: Sire/Up   Sire/Hop
A Syrup is Something Soothing When You Need a Lift
But Not For The Fems   Here it is All About Him and His Hopping to Keep Up as Good Syrup   for Him
Add T/Fem Cross and She Gets Stirrups (Yuck)

Swoon: S/Is/As/Has/Ass/His/Us/Hiss/Serpent/Penis   in Front of   W/ All Fems Sex Active   2 OOs/All Fems Holes (As in Plural or Al of Them)   with   N/ Hen/Virgin As in Becoming Virgins again
Here   The Code   Enhances it by Having   W/All Fems Sex Active   and   O/All Fems Holes
That would Make No Sense at   But Not for   The Code   so
swoon: to faint   lose consciousness   to enter a state of hysterical rapture or ecstasy
Here The Fem is Hypnotized Again in becoming Something She is Not   Another Weakness of The Mind Is Imposed to Her that Way
The Code   Fragments Her Consciousness One More Time in a Different Way
T is The Cross that All Fems Carry   T is the Death of Her Natural Dignity   T is The Great Curse Letter Meaning the Menstrual Cycle
The Pattern of the Cross Does Not Appear in Its Large Cap   It Hides in the Nail Shape
Letter T   T is Letter Tau in Ancient Greek   T is the Hebrew Letter Tau or Tav
It is in Shape of a Cross or a Nail
T means Covenant   A Mark   A Sign   Infinity
T Tau Letter in Arabic is somewhat in a Shape of a Breast and so is Nun (None) and Caph (Cow/Calf   Tau is the Symbol of Her Cross   The Egyptian Cross   The Cross Ansata (Latin) The Ankh (Bank   Cank/Her) is in the Shape of a Cross with a Loop as Top
Which the Egyptians Carried as a Portable Cross
They Often Called it The Key of Life   or   Enduring Life
The Old Letter Extinguished Letter Theta (a Double Cross Here) Was in a shape of a Cross in a Circle   or   a Dot in a Circle

T is Tau is for Taurus (Tower/Us)   The Astrological Sign for Prosperity
Personalized by Venus   Goddess of Natural Beauty   Her Astrological
Symbol can be a Masc Symbol Also A Fem Buffalo Bull Has
Horns   Female She is Also Called a Cow There
There Are Over 20 Different Signs of a Cross In the Webster Dictionary
A Sword is in the Shape of a Cross/Crucifix
Jesus Said He Will Bring a Sword
The Crucifix was Invented around the 8th Century   A Vatican Council
Adopted it as Their Church Symbol   Before that it was the Fish The
Symbol of the Catholic Church
The Fish is a Fem Symbol Living in the Water (What/Her)
An All Fem Hebrew Symbol/Letters there is 2 Mem and 2 Nu Letters
(Always 2 Fems)
M/Mom and N/Virgin Live together as Fishes in the Sea as being Part of
Each Other as Letters M and N
Those Old Paintings of Reborn Christians
At the Time Wore a Gold Aura Circle around their Head
When Sanctified
The Circle is the Symbol for All Fem
Here is Another Popular Concept Here   Cross Our T's and Dot your I's
In   The Code   t and f are Hook Connections
The t Hook is at the Bottom of the Letter as in Sex
The f Hook is at the Top as with the Head
Hook/Her   Hook with R/Sex Whore
(Tit or a Head are those Sounds in French)
Th Means an Action (as Birth) a Quality or a condition
Letter t Tau in the Hebrew Letters is called a Nail
The Pyramid is Where Starts The Letter A Alpha   The Eye in the Pyramid
In TTT HHH EEE FFF and LLL Note Only the H can Make the Right Side of
the H/Secret Square Grid
Where the T/Fem Cross Letters/Riddle Live In
For the Normal Man the Cross Grid is a Series of Squares
For   The Secret Code   the Shape of the tT/Cross is the Grid
Fem T/Cross   The Code Logo Story   Goes as Far as Ancient
Egypt   The Egyptian Cross of Life   is a Wrong Name and Statement
Here   and   Right from The Start

Lise Rochon

A Cross Cannot be a Good Thing   Nobody Resuscitates from Being Crossed   Being Crossed is Being Cheated by Life   Being a Helpless Victim
With T/Fem Cross   It Always Ends the Same Way
In   T/The Fems Are Cursed   She is T/The Fem Cross/Great Curse Letter   T/is The Cross and The Nail
But No says   The Code   T is Represented here by the   Plus Sign   +   which is Presented to Us   by a Symbol that has a General Positive Outlook   but is Very Small
When Fusing those 2 Concepts Together
The Code   Tells Us   The Great Curse   is a   Good Thing
It Adds to Her   It is a Plus   The Code   is The One Adding Something   Which is a   Mirage   By Saying that   The Great Curse is a Favorable Event   As being an Addition
The Cross   +   (Fem Sacrifice) is in the Waiting for All Fems
The Fems Letters/Symbols Explains the Destruction of the Real Female Archetype   and its   Reconstruction Into an Artificial One   The Fem Kindness Must Die and be Rebirthed as   in that Grid Demands   as a M/Mother   or a   R/Heir/Or/Whore   As a Dot   (MR is Mister or a Man)   We Are All In   In That Same Game
Letter T in the Alphabet is Often a Losing Letter and a Letter of Grief
Letter T Is the Symbol for   The Cross/Crucifix   Which
Does Not Represents Resurrection but is Death Itself to Bear (The Bear is One of the 4 Biblical Animals) for Her
T is the Cross that All Fems Carry   T is the Death of Her Natural Dignity   T is The Great Curse Letter from the Menstrual Cycle   The Pattern of the Cross Does Not Appear in the Large Cap   It Hides in the Nail Shape T
T is the Letter Tau in Ancient Greek   T is the Hebrew Letter Tau or Tav   It is in Shape of a Cross or a Nail   It is Also Called Nail
Cross and Nail   Same for Jesus
T Means Covenant   A Mark   A Sign   Infinity
T Tau Letter in Arabic is somewhat in a Shape of a Breast   so   is Nun (None)   and   Caph (Cow/Calf)
Tau is the Symbol of Her Cross   The Egyptian Cross   The Cross Ansata (Latin)   The Ankh (Add   B/Boy Holding All Fem Breasts   and Get a Bank) is in the Shape of a Cross with a Loop as Top   as in You Carry it with You All Day   as if The Egyptians Carried it as a Portable Cross

They Often Called it the Key of Life   or   Enduring Life
The Old Extinguished Letter Theta (a Double Cross Here) is The Shape of a Cross Encircled   Making a Circle
Letter T is Tau is for Taurus (Tower/Us) The Astrological Sign for Prosperity Personalized by Venus The Goddess of Natural Beauty   Prosperity   and   The Nourishing of Nature (Which is All)
Her Astrological Symbol can be a Masc Symbol too (as   The Code   says   The Fem Should Never be Left Alone)   It is the Bull with Horns   A Female Buffalo Has Horns   She is Also Called a Cow (Another Symbol for The Fems)
There Are Over 20 Different Signs of a Cross in the Webster Dictionary
A Sword is in the Shape of a Cross/Crucifix
Jesus Said He Will Bring a Sword   The Crucifix was Invented around the 8th Century   A Vatican Council Adopted it as their Church Symbol
For a Long Time The Symbol of the Catholic says The Fish is its Symbol   It is Mute   Not so Smart in Human Term and It Lives under the Water (What/Her)   When Together They are Called Schools
The Old Paintings of Reborn Christians at the Time Wore a Gold Aura Circle around their Head   The Circle is the Symbol for All Fems
t and f are Almost Identical in Shape   t/Fem Great Curse   f/Fem/Fuck In   The Code   t and f are Hooking Connections   The t Hook is at the Bottom of that Letter as in Sex Control
The f Hook is at the Top as in The Mental Control
Hook/Her   Hook with R/Sex/Err/Heir/Or/Whore
T and X are the Crosses Letters and When Superposed They Draw a Circle Around Them in a Wheel Pattern (Letter W will do that Also on That Wheel to Enforce it)
(See The Wheel of Time in The Words Chapter)
The Phoenician Alphabet has Letter Tet (Tit) which Represents the Infamous   th Symbol/Letter   th   Which is so Small No One Pays Attention to it   t/Fem Cross is its Normal Size   Letter h/H being the Letter of the Secret Societies   It Hides so Small there Hooked at the Top Right of t/Cross   The Code   says   th   Means an Action (as birth)   a quality   or a   condition
Symbolically T as it is Symbolized in our Modern Alphabet It is the Top of the Secret Society Grid Shape   She is It
T/Fem Cross Tee is the Mark (The Mark of the Beast) to Aim (M/Motherhood) and it says it Will Be Tea/Time

Such a Good Thing that T   In Adulthood All Fem Are Supposed to be Nailed (to Nail a Fem is to have Sex With Her)
Tea with Crumpets for Her   She Does Not Know What a Crumpet is
Tea is a Big Cover Word here because It has such a Positive/Soothing Image   It is so Good for You
t/Tau in the Hebrew Letter is Called a Nail   Tau has the Shape somewhat of a Pyramid   The Pyramid is Where Starts   A/Alpha   The Eye in the Pyramid   The Base of The Secrecy of   The Code
Letter Tau/Tav Illustrates a Prostrated Fem
In   TTT   HHH   EEE   FFF   and   LLL   Only the Right Side Makes the Right Side of   H/Secret Square Grid   Where T/Fem Cross Letters Riddle is Prisoner of   T/Fem Curse
A Cover Word Here as   Poop and Pope   Lord and Lured   Chapel and Chop/All   Church and She/Hurt
Thee/D/Pregnant   is The Prayer Letter Word   Sorry
Our Real Deities Live Inside Us   Inside Our Love for Them
Not in Words that do Not Support a Decent Meeting
In all the Spheres of Languages Sounds of Higher Intelligence   God Cannot be a Dog in Reverse (See God in The Words Chapter)
For the Normal Man the Cross Grid is a Series of Squares
For   The Secret Code   the Shape of the tT/Cross is the Grid
tee: the mark aimed at various games like curling and   a 3 way joint for pipes and tee
In   The Code   It also Represents Letter t
How Convenient   Here again is Presented the Polygamy Concept   Curls are for Girls
The Word Torture is an Example   2 TTs/All Fems Crosses   2 OOs/All Fem Holes   and R/Heir/Or/Whore/Err/Sex
Put Together Words with Letter T/Tea (Cover Word Here)   To the T (Perfection) Tee
Double TTs Words: Tit   Tot   Tat   Toutou
End of *intro # 1*
Intro # 2
They may be some Repetitions
T Is the Sign of the Cross/Crucifix Which Does Not Represents Resurrection but Is Death Itself
To Bear a Cross Indicates That
T is the Cross that All Fem Carry   T is the Death of Her Natural Dignity

T is The Great Curse Letter for the Menstrual Cycle
The Pattern of the Cross t Does Not Appear in the Large Cap   It Hides in the Nail Shape of Letter T
T is the Letter Tau in Ancient Greek   T is the Hebrew Letter Tau or Tav
It is in Shape of a Cross or a Nail   It is Also Called a Nail
As in Cross and Nail
T Means Covenant   A Mark   A Sign   Infinity
T Tau Letter in Arabic is somewhat in a Shape of a Breast and So is Nun (None) and Caph (Cow/Calf)
The Tau is the Symbol of Her Cross   The Egyptian Cross   The Cross Ansata (Latin) The Ankh (Bank) is in the Shape of a Cross with a Loop as Top
Which the Egyptians Carried as a Portable Cross in Their Daily Activities as Illustrated on The Walls of The Egyptian Pyramids Tombs
They Often Called it the Key of Life   or   Enduring Life
The Old Extinguished Letter Theta (a Double Cross Here for Her) Was in a shape of a Cross in a Circle
The Letter T is Tau is for Taurus (Tower/Us)
It is The Astrological Sign for Prosperity Personalized by The Goddess Venus The Goddess of Natural Beauty
Her Astrological Symbol could be a Masc Symbol
A Bull with Horns   Female and Male Buffalo Have Horns   She is Also Called a Cow There
There Are Over 20 Different Signs of The Cross in the Webster Dictionary
Jesus Said He Will Bring a Sword   A Sword is in a Shape of a Cross/Crucifix
The Crucifix was Invented around the 8th Century   A Vatican Council Adopted it as The Church Symbol
There is also the Fish as the Symbol of the Catholic Church   The Fish is a Fem Symbol Living in the Water
An All Fem Hebrew Symbol/Letters there is 2 Mem and 2 Nu Letters (Always 2 Fem)
M/Mom and N/Virgin Live together as Fish in the Sea as being Part of Each Other   As the Letters M and N
In Greek The Letter M Means Man and N is Noon (4 Fem Letters)
Those Old Paintings of Reborn Christians
At the Time Wore a Gold Aura Circle around their Head When Sanctified
The Circle is the Symbol for All Fems

Here is Another Popular Concept Here
Cross Our T's and Dot your I's
I like to say   You Never Have Been to the Beach (Bitch) Until you Bathe in a River
He Cannot Leave/Live without Her   No Matter What He Call Her   She cannot live without Him Either
t and f are Almost Identical
t/Fem Great Curse   f/Fem/Fuck
In   The Code   the t and f are Hooks Connections
The t Hook is at the Bottom of the Letter as in Sex
The f Hook is at the Top as with Her Head Manipulation
Hook/Her   Hook with R/Her/Sex
T and X are the Crosses Letters   When Superposed They Draw a Circle Around Them in a Wheel Pattern (See The Wheel of Time in The Words Chapter)
The   is a Cross in a Circle (Tit or a Head are those Sounds in French)
The Phoenician Alphabet has the Letter Tet which represents the Infamous th or [th] Symbol/Letter
So Small No One Pays Attention to it
t/Fem Cross is its Normal Size
The Letter h being the Letter of the Secret Societies Hides So Small there Hooked at the Top Right of Letter t/Cross
Th Means an Action (like Birth) a Quality or a condition
Letter T as it is Symbolized in our Modern Alphabet Is the Top of the Secret Society Grid Shape   She is It
T/Fem Cross Tee is the Mark (The Mark of the Beast) to Aim   and it Says it Will Be Tea time   Such a Good Thing that T   In Adulthood All Fem Are Supposed to be Nailed
Tea with Crumpets
Letter t Tau in the Hebrew Alphabet Letters is Called a Nail
Tau has the Shape somewhat of a Pyramid
The Pyramid is Where Starts The Letter A Alpha   The Eye in the Pyramid
In   TTT   HHH   EEE   FFF   and   LLL   Only the H can Make the Right Side of the H/Secret Square Grid   The Others Not
Where the T/Fem Cross Letters/Riddle Lives In
T/Fem Curse is Close to D/Pregnant Daughter Sound
A Cover Word Here Just as Poop and Pope You Get   as Lord and Lured   Chapel and Chop All   Church and She/Hurt

The Dam Code The Damn Book

Thee/D/Pregnant Daughter is The Prayer to God Letter Word
I am Sorry   Our Real Deities Live Inside Us   Inside Our Love for
Them   Not in Words that do Not Support a Decent Meeting
In all the Spheres of Languages Sounds of Higher Intelligence The Word
God Cannot be Dog in Reverse (See God in Words) unless it is Arranged
that Way
For the Normal Man the Cross Grid is a Series of Squares
For   The Secret Code   the Shape of   The/tT/Fem Cross is the Grid

T t
Table: T/Fem Cross   Able
She is Allowed to do Somethings by   The Code   To Serve   Prep Food
Clean Etc
Add S/Is/As/Has/Ass/His/Us/Hiss/Serpent/Penis and He Gets a Stable
stable   a building for the lodging and feeding of horses cattle etc
Nice to Him
(See Horses In The Words Chapter)

Taboo: T/Fem Cross   Boo
T/Fem Cross   A/All Men   Boo
taboo: proscribed by society as improper or unacceptable
So   To/Boo   or   Taboo
Reinforcing the Meaning of   T/Fem Cross   B/Boy Holding All Fems
Breasts   Who
If a B/Boy Holding All Fem Breasts would be in Front of O/All Fem
Holes   That would be Way Too Much for a Child
And He would Lose that Battle   A Big No from   The Code   as Men are
Always Winners there   so
boo: an exclamation of contempt or disapproval
T/Fem Cross   B/Boy Holding All Fem Breasts   Who
The Boy is in Between T and 2 OOs/Fem Holes (Plural or All of Them)   It
is too much Information for Him   So   Who Is Being Asked
Add Another B/Boy Holding All Fem Breasts at the End and He Gets Boob
boob: a stupid person   fool   dunce   *British*   a blunder   mistake   a
female breast
Most People Know What a Boob is Compared to the Other Definitions
Placed Before   The Fems as Usual is Last   and   With Stupid Words in
Front of Her Anatomy

Tact: T/Act
T/Fem Cross   Surrounds   A/All Men   With   C/See/Young Girl   And Another   T/Fem Cross
It Demands an Act of Tact from   The Code   to Keep Hiding Its Secret about The Great Curse   When All of Them T are There   At The Beginning and at The End of a Word

Tactic: T/Fem Cross   Act   IC
IC is an Integrated circuit
The Tactic is   T/Fem Cross/Great Curse   Lives with the Sex Act as Integrated Circuit

Tail: T/Fem Cross/Great Curse   L/Ail/Hail/Hell
Tail is also Slang for Penis
The Code   is Secretive   Because Tail is Basically Fem (The Fems Cross Hurts as Hell   T/Hell)   it Becomes a Tale   Tell the Tale   Follow that Tail   A Piece of Tail   etc

Take: TK   2 Fem Letters
T/Ache
T/Fem Cross   and   K/Broken Fem   are Here Together for the Take   Take a Fem in Sexually or in Marriage
Switch T for B/Boy Holding All Fem Breasts and He Gets Bake
Switch T for C/See/Young Girl or K/Broken Fem or Q/Bleeding Fem and They Get Cake (The Code Agrees with Anything Sexual or Weakening to Her   As Long as She Is Aching)
Switch T for F/Fem/Fuck and She Gets Fake (F is a Letter of More Power than The Weak T   so Her Power is gone Away by being Called a Fake)
Switch T for L/Sweet Fem Love Light/Ill/Hail/Ail/Hell/Elle and She Gets Lick (a Licking is Also a Beating)
Switch T for M/Motherhood and She Gets Make (Making Babies)
Switch T for N/Virgin but We would Get Only Nake as D/Pregnant is Missing to Get Naked to Get Pregnant
Switch T for R/Her/Heir/Or/Err/Whore and She Gets Rake (Rake Those Men)
Switch T for S/Penis and He Gets Sake (Purpose)

The Dam Code The Damn Book

Switch T for W/All Fems Sex Active and She Gets Wake (The Code Does Not Agree with So Many Fems Knowing about That T/Fem Cross Ache   so here She Goes)

Tale: T/Ail   T/Hail   T/Hell
Follow that Tail   It is a Piece of Tail (Sex)
But No says The Code   Trail (Adding R/Her)
The Fems Cross is in Hell and that is The Real Tale

Tally: Tall/He
tally: an account or reckoning   anything which a score or account is kept
The Record says He is Tall   A Good Thing for Him
There is Nothing Positive here for Her   Except in The Cross as in   T/Fem Cross   L/Sweet Fem Love Light/All/Ail/Ill/Hail/Heel/Hell/Elle/Oil   He/E

Tap: Cap (Fem)   Gap (Masc)   Hap (Code)   Hop (Masc)   Lap (Fem)   Map (Fem)   Nap (Fem)
A Wrap (Fem) in a Clap

Tape: T/Ape
Tape that Ape (Her)

Target: T/Fem Cross   R/Her/Are/Err/Heir/Or/Whore   Get   T/R/Get
T/Fem Cross as R/Her is The Target to Get says   The Code

Tariff: When 2 FFs/Fem/Fuck (In Plural or All of Them)   End a Word   It Could be a Win/Power for Her   But No says   The Code
It will Cost F a Tear (Rip) or Tears (Cry)
Tear/If   is Her Tariff
Because   A/All Men   with   R/Her/Hair/Are/Here/Hear/Ear/Heir/Whore/Or/Err/Sex   are Having Sex   i/Marriage Act
T/Fem Cross   is The First Letter of The Word   It is Not Allowed in   The Code   That would be Too Much to Know for a Fem   so   She Forced Out   being Generally a Poor Person (Per/Son)
tariff: bill   cost   charge

663

Tarot: Tarot Starts with a Cross   T/Fem Cross/Great Curse   and Ends with That Same   T/Cross
T/Fem Cross   A/All Men   Her/R/Ear/Hear/Hair/Err/Heir/Or/Whore/Here/Are/Our/Ere/Air/Ire/Sex   O/Fem Hole   T/Fem Cross
Which Means   The Great Curse is for All Fems Holes   says   The Code   Through All/Men   It is All in   R/Our/Whore/Heir/Or/Err   Language
That is How   The Code   Propagated Everywhere
The Tarot as Astrology and Other Divinatory Arts Carry Along Mostly the Old Art Secrets Without Revealing them   Those are Secret Codes   The Jewish Initiates Also Know and Use The Tarot
The 14th Tarot Card is Called The Art   The Alchemy Card
It is the Same Card in the Original Deck Card Known as The Temperance Where a Winged Being Dressed in a White Robe Pours Water from One Chalice (Chalices Transform Blood (Fem Blood) into Wine   Catholics Drink It at Their Church)   To Another Chalice   Which Overflows Over Water   Therefore Contaminating (In a Reverse Way) on a Very Subtle Level The Water (Most Powerful Fem Symbol) with Blood
A Very Silly Card for Her   Such an Empty Action Done by a Celestial Being which on its Robe has a Red Triangle in a Square (See The Pyramid Triangle/Square with and The Eye in it on the US Dollar Bill)
14th Card   The Art Card in the Aleister Crowley Deck Which is Loaded with Symbolism if Closely Carefully Looked at   They Relate to Each Other   It is Just Another Way The Tarot Tells Us the Silly/Stupid Actions   The Code   Make Do The Fems in a Very Subtle Symbolic Way To Keep Her Stupid and NOT Questioning The Meaning of That Immense Loss of Her Blood
The Code   Dares to Start that Word with Men
Menstruation   Men   S/Penis   Through   A/All/Men   Shh/She   On (Menstrual) Men/Through All with   S/Penis   or in Double Plural (S Add Plural Most Times))
Compare to Mercury   The #1 Tarot Card   The Magician   He is The Dealer of the Deck Here   He has All Advantages and Powers in Front of Him to Play With
That is   The Code   in Action   Hypnotizing Us   Giving Us The Illusion That We Can Have All That   Which is a Falsity   That Code   Actually Keeps Us in Ignorance and Gives To Many of Us a Poor Hard Working Life

The Dam Code The Damn Book

The Tarot as a Mean of Divination Started around The Middle of The 17th Century   The Theory was that The Tarot Cards are Keys of the Lost Egyptian Magical Wisdom Originated from Thoth the Egyptian God
In the 19th Century Eliphas Levy (The Occultist) Developed a Correlation Between the Tarot and the Kabbalah (The Hebrew System of Mysticism) The New Belief was that the Tarot Originated in Israel and Contains the Wisdom of the Tree of Life
Many Magical and Esoteric Groups Recognize That The Tarot is Knowledge that is in Every Mystical Path   Which is This Book here   The Dam Code   is About
In United States the Tarot Got Popular and More Readily Available in the 1960 When a Popular Period of Spiritual Exploration Began (When Young People Started to Smoke Pot) Therefore Illuminating The Secret Code Path a Little More
Tarot/Taureau/Taurus/Tau (Fem Sign)
Taurus Is the Sign for The Goddess Venus   She
Created   Agriculture   Prosperity   and   Beauty (The Golden Age Possibly)
The Cow (Taurus) is Forced to Give Her Milk All Year Long Artificially   Then Give Her Body to be Eaten   As in the Ritual of Transubstantiation
A Cow Has Artificial Breasts Just as The Human Fem
(See BB in The Words Chapter) (See Tau)
The Ox is Made of 2 Fem Letters (O/Fem Hole   X/Fallen Fem Cross)   According to Some an Ox is a Castrated Clumsy Stupid Animal Add a F/Fem/Fuck to Ox and She Gets Fox   The Code   is Trapping Her Again

Taste: T/Fem Cross   S/Ass/Is/His/Us/Serpent/Penis   T/Fem Cross
2 TTs/Fem Crosses (as in Plural or All of Them) Surrounds S/Penis   and Both   A/All Men   and   E/He   are Almost Silent   It is a Rare Situation   and it needs to Go Fast as in   T/Haste   There is a Haste for Him to Get Out of that Test

Taunt: T/Haunt
Taunt Starts and Ends with   T/Fem Cross/Great Curse
T is being Haunted by   The Code   as Usual
T/Aunt   T/Hunt   and   Being Hunted

Because the Word Aunt is there (See Aunt in The Words Chapter) It Weakens Her More by being Entirely Fem from its Sound Definition   so taunt: to reproach in a sarcastic insulting matter
Switch T for C/See/Young Girl and She Gets Cunt (See Cunt in The Words Chapter

Tau: Tau Stands for infinity   Tau is the Sign of the Cross
Tau is the Last Hebrew Letter in Their Alphabet   It Means Cross   and   is Represented by Saturn   and   The Concept of Finality   Saturn is that Terrible God Which Represents Time   (That is Until the End of Time   or   The End of That Great Curse)
Tau Represents the Furthest Development in the Physical World
Tau is The 19th Letter of the Greek Alphabet and Means Covenant   a Mark   a Sign
Tou Known as The Mark of The Beast is Tau
The Symbology of the Freemasons/Rosicrucians and Templars Indicate that Tau Represents the One God and Its Tree Attributes
The Tau Cross is Found in the Center of the Rosy Cross
Tau was the Symbol for the Crucifix in Many European and Western Religious Countries
Tau Cross is Letter T in Greek   It is Written as an X
It Clarify More About   T/Fem Cross   and   X/Fallen Fem Cross/Rolling Cross   Explained in This Book
Tau is the Taurus Sign
Taurus: Tau as Cross   Her/R/Ear/Hear/Hair/Err/Heir/Or/Whore/Here/Are/Our/Ere/Air/Ire/Sex   S/Penis
Taurus The Astrological Sign is Represented by Venus   and Her Sense of   Beauty   Fertility   and   Intelligence
The Sign for Venus is a Cross on Top of a Circle Which is The International Sign for All Fems
Taurus   Tower/Us   See The Tarot Card The Tower For More Information about Tau Go to   The Book of Thoth   by Aleister Crowley 1944
As in Thoth or Thought   Think about it

Tax: T/Fem Cross   A/All Men   X/Fallen Fem Cross
A/All Men   are in Between   T   and   X   A Position of Weakness for The   Code

The Dam Code The Damn Book

T/Fem Cross   Is Going Under the   Axe/X for That   X as in Executed   Gone
Gone as an X Husband   Anything X Rated   Etc
Taxes have been with Us Since Biblical Time and Before
Tax is a Bad Word   It Brings Grief
Words Starting with T Cannot be Good Ones   Unless it is Entertaining for   The Code   Such as a Tux   When T   as   You/U/Ovulating   is Open to Be an X   Because of The Glamour (Tux is made of 3 Fem Letters)
Tox (3 Fem Letters Word) as in Toxic   Tox/IC   IC Means Integrated Circuit   She Here Goes Down As Usual in   That Code

Teach: T/Fem Cross/Great Code   Each/She/Shh
In French to Teach is Enseigner (In/N/Ann/Virgin   Saigne   Her/Her/heir/Or/Whore)
God in French is Seigneur (Bleed/Her)   Which Literally   is to   Bleed/Her   As in a Verb and Action
The Code   Says to The Fems That She Bleeds Because God is Telling Her Just as Told in The Bible When God Tells Her About Her Great Curse
How Many Times does a Fem has to Hear "You are Cursed " Before She believes it   Men do Not Say that to Each Other
T/Fem Cross   Goes to   Each/She/Shh   In Silence About That

Teaching: Teach/N   T/Fem Cross   Each/She/Shh   N/In/Hen/Ann/Virgin
The Code   Teaching for T is   Each N/Virgin   is a   T/Fem Cross   and Silence About it

Team: T/Fem Cross/Great Curse   Him/M/Motherhood
It was Almost Impossible to have The Fems Playing Professional Sports for Ages
Because   The Aim (Him   Motherhood) was to Impregnates Her Asap   And Reminds Her She is a Cursed Mother   That is The Concept of The Fems as Team
Switch T for B/Boy Holding All Fem Breasts and He Gets a Beam (Too Young for That Code)
Switch T for H/Secret Code Letter and He Gets Him and She Gets Motherhood

Lise Rochon

Switch M for   Her/R/Ear/Hear/Hair/Err/Heir/Or/Whore/Here/Are/Our/Ere/Air/Ire/Sex   and She Gets Tear (as a Rip   or a Tear as in Crying   Both are Painful to The Fems)

Tear: T/R   T/Fem Cross/Great Curse   is in Front   of   Her/R/Ear/Hear/Hair/Err/Heir/Or/Whore/Here/Are/Our/Ere/Air/Ire/Sex
She Gets Tear as in to Rip   or   Tear as in to Cry
T/Here   T/Fem Cross is Here with Her Tears
T/Fem Cross   R/Her/Heir/Or/Whore/Sex
Tear/Her for The Heir to Come
T/Hear   Tear Comes when She Hear/Ear That She is Cursed as T/Fem Cross
tear: water coming out of eyes
Anything Related to Water Is Fem
Tear is a Cover Word Here

Tease: T/Fem Cross   Ease
She is at Ease   When Teased   Another Laugh to Put on Her

Tee: Letter T
T is The Cornerstone Letter of   The Secret Code
T is The Great Curse Letter (The Immense Fems Blood Loss)
T/Fem Cross   with   2 EEs/He (He/E here is Plural or All of Them Men)
T   an Entirely Fem Letter is Pronounced The Same With a Double E with it
The Fem is Never Left Alone in   The Code
Tee   or   Letter T   Is the Mark Aimed at in Various Games
Letter X/Fallen Fem Cross   is when   T (Still Erected   and She is Still Alive) has Fallen on the Ground in   X/Fallen Cross   and   Gone She is   Fall Asleep on It   Z (See Letter Z in the Letters Chapter)
X/Fallen Fem Cross   has been a Mark or a Signature   Which was Legal on an Official Document for the Illiterates
Switch T for B/Boy Holding All Fem Breasts and He Gets a Bee (All Fems are Working Bees for Their Boys)
Switch T for F/Fem/Fuck and She Gets a Fee (Letter F is too Free for   The Code   so She gets a Fine or a Fee
Switch T for G/Penis Penetration and They Get Gee

668

gee: used as a word of command to a horse or other draft animal to direct it to turn to the right
Gee is 3 Masculine Letters Because it is a Word of Command to Her/R/Heir/Or/Whore/Sex   In The Code   Symbolism She is a Whore in Plural/Horses
Gee is also a Clarified Butter from Cows in India   How Convenient for   The Code   She is Back to be Treated as an Animal (a Horse here   See Horse and R/Hers in The Words and Letters Chapters)
Her/R/Ear/Hear/Hair/Err/Heir/Or/Whore/Here/Are/Our/Ere/Air/Ire/Sex   She is Directed by   The Code   to go in One Direction Only Which is to The Right Side   The Masc Side   as Usual)
Gee is a replacement Swear for The French People
Switch T for M/Motherhood and She Gets a Mee Which Has the Same Pronunciation as Me   Me as a Fem ID is Also a Big No from   The Code   So   She as Mother is Accompanied with 2/EEs/He   Which is Not a Word for   That Code   Because there would be   2 EEs/He   for R/Her   As in having 2 Men or More for Herself and Being in a Polyandrous Relationship   A Big No from   The Code   so Only Men Could Be in the Past   Although Now it is Judged Unpopular by Most Churches   Men in General are Much More Loose about having   Affairs   Concubines   Escorts   Mistresses Etc   Than The Fems
In Some Counties They Just Burn or Stone the Fems in Public for Cheating on Her Husband (Us/Band)   or   having Sex Without being Married   or   when The Husband Dies She is/was then Sacrificed for/with Him in the Fire of The Incineration
Also Mee Would Imply She is in Charge or The Boss of Many Men   Another Big No from   The Code   so   That is Why Some Words Do Not Exist (Food for Thought)
Switch T for N/Hen/In/Ann/Virgin and She Gets Neigh
neigh: the cry of a horse   whinny
Whinny   (Wine/He   See Wine/Blood/Chalice in The Words Chapter)   The Code   has Endless Layers of Lies for The Fems Recreating The Fems as Animals   Horses (Whores) being One of Them
Switch T/Fem Cross for P/Man Power and He Gets to Pee
No Affiliation for Him with T/Fem Cross/Cursed
Men Love to pee   Peeing is Not for The Fem in   That Code   Pee Spells with 3 Masc Letters
A Spell is to Spell Too as One of The Rules of   The Code

Switch T for C K or Q (3 Fem Letters) and She Gets a Key
The Bleeding Fem is the Key to the T/Fem Cross Code
That Code   Also Agrees Here with All Weak Fem Attributes Letters Such as C K Q (All Fems Letters are Weak One Way or Another)
Key has a Different Spelling than with the Double E Presented Above   A Different Spelling   because it is The Key Made for Her   K/Key is the Broken Fem and Y/Why is The Wounded Fem   He/E is Silent but Monitoring as Usual
The Fems Are Never Left Alone in   The Code
Switch T for S/Is/As/Has/Ass/His/Us/Hiss/Serpent/Penis and He Gets to See (The Holy See   The/Hole/He/See   or   Letter C/See/Young Girl/Virgin)
Switch T for W/All Fems Sex Active and She Gets Wee
wee: little   very small   the act or an instance of urinating
Men Pee/P/Man Power   and   Women Wee W/All Fems Sex Active are here again (See We in Words Chapter) Again   No Reward or Respect for All Fems for Having Sex
She Remains as Small as an Ant   With Sex or No Sex   says   The Code
She Gets To Wee   With Many Men There Too
Add H/Secret Code Letter Society to Tee and He Gets Thee (The Respect of a God)
Switch E/He for A/All Men and He Gets Tea
Add R/Her/Heir/Or/Whore to Tee and She Gets a Tree (The Tree of Life)   or   #3 (See # 3 The Breasts in the Number Chapter)
Add R/Her/Heir/Or/Whore at the End of Tea and She Gets Tear (a Rip   or   a   Tear (Cry   2 Bad Choices)

Teen: T/Fem Cross/Great Curse   N/In/Hen/Ann/Virgin
Tin and Thin
Her Bleeding Starts in Early Teen   Which Separates Her from The Male Young Teenagers Immediately   The Boys Insults Coming to Her would do That to Her Also
She Becomes Anemic and All That Which Follows General Weakness She Will be Weak in Sports   Etc
Men do Not Lose their Blood   But They Pay for That Loss/Change in The Next Generation
Alligators Crocodiles etc Since Prehistoric Animals   They Never Lose a Drop of Blood

Teenager: T/Fem Cross   In/Hen/Haine/N/Ann/Virgin   Age/Egg   R/Her/Are/Heir/Or/Whore/Err/Sex
Teen/Age/R
The Code   says the Age for R/Her as Whore or to be Pregnant Starts with Her First Loss of Blood which is about Ten Years Old as it is Done in The Old countries
1 is a Masc Number (The Number of God) for Him   and o/Zero is for The Fems   o is Not Even a Number says   The Code   (Although There would be No Math without o/Zero)
She is Also Called Letter O because   The Code   Sees Her as a Fem Hole Only   Which Brings Her Back to That Hole After Every Time She Ends a Sentence/The Dot   or a   Cycle   1 to 9   Then She is o/Zero Again as in O/Fem Hole

Teeth: Tit
Teeth at the Tit
The Mouth   M/Out   M/Mother is Out   so is   Him/M
See Teeth and Mouth in The Crowley Tarot Hebrew Letters to Study a Greater Mystery

Telephone: Tell/He/Fun   Tail/He/Fun
Not a She in Telephone   Except in Giving Fun to His Tail (Tail is Slang for Penis)

Tell: TL   T/Fem Cross   L/Sweet Fem Love Light/All/Elle/Heel/Hell/Ail/Ill/Hail/Oil
T as the Object of The Great Curse is Kept in Hell by being Ill or Ailing Because of Her Immense Loss of Blood and The Great Shame that has Followed Her in History from That (Think Shaman)
No One Tells Because   The Code   Says She is Just a Piece of Tail (See R/Her/Whore/Or/Heir/Err/Sex in the Letter Chapter)
Tell is a Cover Word here
Teller: T/Fem Cross   L/Sweet Fem Love Light/All/Ail/Ill/Hail/Heel/Hell/Elle/Oil
Same as The Word Tell   Although Teller Adds Another Proof with Sound   with Her/R that Reinforces its Tell Story

Temple: T/Fem Cross   M/Motherhood   P/Man Power   All/L/Sweet Fem Love Light/Ill/Hail/Ail/Hell/Elle
The Cursed Fem as Mother with P as Ill or in Hell
T/Fem Cross is Ample   Ample is Big   Meaning Pregnant
Add T/Fem Cross to Ample and She would Get Tempt/
All   or   Temple   Becoming a Very Important Word in   The Code

Ten: TN   2 Fem Sound Letters   E/He   is Silent/Anonymous   Here T/Fem Cross/Great Curse   In/N/Ann/Hen/Donkey/Virgin
From Losing Her Blood and being Cursed for it at Age Ten   She is a Virgin that is Ready to get Pregnant (From N into Becoming M/Motherhood) says   The Code (See Teen in Words) and Accepting that She is Cursed being a Fem
Tin (Cheap Metal) and Thin (The Weaker/Cheaper the Better for The Fems says   That Code)

Tender: T/Fem Cross   End (ND   From N/Virgin to D/Pregnant)   to   R/Her/Err/Are/Heir/Or/Whore/Sex
When Tender Enough   She is Told of Her End as a Normal Human   She is Now a Cursed   Her/Heir/Or/Whore/Err/Are   That is Looking at Inevitable Pregnancy
Switch D/Pregnant to T/Fem Cross And She Gets Tent/Her   In Ancient Times The Fems were Kept in Tents (Under Surveillance and Isolation) or Locked in Some Ways (Veils are One of Them)   Always Under a Man Eye (The Code Calls it Protection)

Tense: Ten   S/Is/His/Hiss/Serpent/Penis
T/Fem Cross   S/Is/His/As/Has/Ass/Us/Hiss/Serpent/Penis   The Time to have Sex for the Girl is Ten/10 Years Old says   The Code
Tents Arrive for The Fems   Another Symbol of The Veil
tense: stretched tight as a cord fiber etc drawn taut rigid   in a state of mental or nervous strain   high strung taut   characterized by a strain upon the nerves or feelings   a category of verbal inflection that serves chiefly to specify the time of the action or state expressed by the verb   a set of categories or constructions in a particular language   the time as past present or future expressed by such a category
The Code   says The Fems as T/Fem Cross are Always Kept Tense in the   Past Tense   Present Tense   and   Future Tense   And that Verb

The Dam Code The Damn Book

(The Verb (The Power of The Word) Directs The Fems Right (Not Left) into it

Tension: TNCN
T/Fem Cross   N/In/Hen/Ann/Haine/Virgin   See/C/Young Girl/ Virgin   On/Eon
This Word on a Sound Level is All Fem Letters
The Virgin as the Cursed Ovulating Fem is Under Tension for Ever (He/ On   Eon)
Tents/Eon   Tense/Eon   Tents/He/On
Ten/See/On   Ten is The Best Age for The Virgin to have Sex   and   Children says   The Code (See Tent in Words)

Tent: TNT
T/Aint   T/Ant   T/In/T
T/Fem Cross   E/He   N/In/Hen/Ann/Haine/Virgin   T/Fem Cross
For Words that Starts and Ends with   T/Great Curse   Caution is Advised   TNT Letters are Known to be a Powerful Explosive   Do not Touch   The Code   has Ways of Eliminating People that Have Intentions to Research with that Kind of Mental Camouflage
A Tent has the Shape of 2 Open Legs   as a Compass has
The Compass is a VIP Code Symbol   as so Many Marine Instruments
N/In/Hen/Haine/Ann/Virgin   is in Between 2 TTs/Fem Crosses   E/He   is Silenced but Not Absent
There is No choice   The Curse goes On
Being as Small as an Ant and Powerless as an Aunt She has No Power here and She is Also Told She is Not there at All (Aint) so She is Invisible   Silenced   and   Dressed as a Tent
tent: a portable shelter of skins   something that resemble a tent   a tent dress

Tenure: Ten/Your   Ten   You/U/Ovulating   R/Her/Are/Heir/Or/Err/ Whore
Ten is The Age for Sex for The Fems says   The Code   (See Teen)   That is The Position She Holds in Society says   The Code
tenure: the position of holding an office

Terminator: Terminate   Her

terminator: the line dividing the illumined and the unilluminated part of a satellite   planet   especially the moon
Put that in Your Hat (Art without R/Her   A Secret Place   See Art and Hat in The Words Chapter)
The Code   Destroys The Fem Natural Personality in All Ways it Knows
She is Told here that Only One Side of Her being a Moon (Menstrual Cycle/Great Curse) Exists (See Moon in The Words Chapter)   It is the Quarter of a Moon   Because When the Moon is Full She is on Being Pregnant

Terrible: Tear/He/Able
T/Fem Cross   Hear/Her   Able (A/All Men   Ball)
Tear/He/Ball
Terrible Makes Him Able to Tear (Rip) Her   or   Make Her Cry (Tears)
Having a Ball Doing it   All from His Balls says   The Code
Words with T/Fem Cross as the Word Starter with E/He and R/Her Following are Bad News to   The Code   Meaning The Fems would be Able Here/R to Hear   That Code   A Big No from   The Code   so Terrible Happens

Terrifying: Tear   He/E   Fear/For   In/N/Hen/Haine/Ann/Virgin
He Tears   F/Fem   Apart   from   The Young Girl Age

Terror: Tear/Her
T/Fem Cross   2 RRs/Hers/Err/Heirs/Or/Whores/Sex (Makes it Plural or All of Them)   R/Err/Her
Tear/Her   Tear/Whore   T/Err/Her   T/Heir/Her   T/Error
Terror is a Terrible Word   It is a Word for Rape in   That Code   Marking   All Fems   Mothers   or   Whores
There are Actually 3 RRRs/Whores/Or/Heirs/Err in Terror   so it Goes on Endlessly
E/He   is here Silent/Invisible   The Rapist Escapes says   The Code   T/Error   The Code   Reminds She was Erring (Herring   See Fishes in The Words Chapter)   Especially if She got Pregnant (Heir/R) While Not Married During that Rape
How Profoundly Powerful   This Language Code is

Test: TST

The Dam Code The Damn Book

2 TTs/Fem Crosses (Plural or All of Them) Surrounds   His/S/Is/Us/Ass/
Hiss/Serpent/Penis   With   E/He   which is Silent or Invisible
If it Passes The Test   It is in The Text (The Code   Text   See Codex and
Kotex in The Words Chapter)
T/Fem Cross   X/Fallen Fem Cross   T/Fem Cross
From Her being on The Cross to Die on the Cross and Back on The Cross
Endlessly is The Test of   The Code

Testicles: Test/He/Calls   Taste/He/Cul

Text: TXT   3 Fem Letters
T/Fem Cross   X/Fallen Fem Cross   T/Fem Cross
Anything Related to Words or Hidden Knowledge/The Code
Has been Hidden Away from The Fems One Way or Another   It is in the
Text/Word (See Word in The Words Chapter)
Switch X for S/Is/As/Has/Ass/His/Us/Hiss/Serpent/Penis   and He Gets Test

Th: T/Fem Cross/Fem Curse   is With   H/Secret Code Letter
Society   That is Bad for   The Code   so Th Goes in Smaller Size Letters
as indicating a Century (9th) and is Owned by its Addition
T/Fem Cross is Entirely Owned by   The Code
th: a suffix forming nouns of action *(Birth)* denoting quality or
condition   a suffix used in the formation of ordinal numbers

Than: Damned
So Soft Sounds to introduce the Damnation of D/Pregnant   from   N/In/
Hen/Haine/Ann/Virgin   into   M/Motherhood
than: used to introduce the second element of a comparison

That: T/Hat   The/Hat
T/Fem Cross   H/Secret Code Letter Society Letter   At/Hat (See Hat and
Art in Words)
Take Away H and Get Tat
tat: to do   or   make by   tatting
With or Without H   The Code   is in The Doing
It is in The Hat   And It Starts With T/Fem Cross and Ends with T/Fem
Cross   A/All Men Are in It   Knowing or Not

Lise Rochon

The: D/Pregnant   or   T/Fem Cross
T/Fem Cross   H/Secret Code Letter Society   E/He
Add Another E/He and He Gets Thee
thee: the objective case of thou   archaic except in some elevated or ecclesiastical prose
Add   Her/R/Ear/Hear/Hair/Err/Heir/Or/Whore/Here/Are/Our/Ere/Air/Ire/Sex   and She Gets Three and Tree (See Tree and Tree in The Words Chapter)
We are talking about T/Fem Cross or Her Blood Sacrifice
The is a Word that Goes in between 2 Nouns as in to Connect   Pointing a Direction to Something
The/D Has No Identity by itself   As usual Anything Fem has No Significance
The is a VIP Word in   The Code
Back to the Train Engine for The Mascs and Wagons Attached to it for The Fems

Thee: 2 EEs/He (In Plural or All of Them)   Next to   H/Secret Code Letter   Brings a Lot of Power   T/Fem is there in Front
The Code   Applies a Strong Separation   or   is Reserved Only to Initiates
(See The in The Words Chapter) (See Letter D in Letter Chapter)
The Code   has High Fences

Their: The/Heir   D/Heir   T/Heir   There
T/Fem Cross   and   the Heir/R/Her
their: possessor of an action   but not the action itself
D/Pregnant   Possesses Nothing Not Even Her Children   She can Only be a Heir Carrier   or   Err   Or   Whore   The Code   Dares to Do that
In   Her   Hair   Are
Heirs   Here   Hear   Ear   Heir   Or   Whore   Err Letter R/Sex
It is done Over (Ov/Her   Of/Her) There with Letter Her/R/Ear/Hear/Hair/Err/Heir/Or/Whore/Here/Are/Our/Ere/Air/Ire/Sex
There/Their is a Cover Word here

Them: DM   2 Fem Letters
Damn   Dame   Dam   D/Hem   Dim   D/Aim   D/Him   D/Aime
The Theme here is to Damn Them and Aim/Focus (Fuck/Us) on it

676

The Dam Code The Damn Book

Them as in All of The Fems are All in the Same Dim Category   As the Bees/Fishes/Chicken/Cows/Ants etc   The Code   says   Keep Them Together into the
hem: to enclose or confine   the edge border or margin of everything
Aime is to Love in French   Love can be a Trap to Fall in for Her and be Devoured by   The Code   Illusions as a Dam Creates a Wall Between Water and Land
Add E/He and He Gets Theme   Dame/Damn/Them (the Hem) is a Strong Code Cover Word Here

Then: DN   2 Fem Sound Letters
The/Hen   D/Hen   T/Hen   D/In
The Fems are Compared to a Pregnant Domesticated Animal Again   D/Pregnant   N/Virgin   The Endless   Code   Cycle
In the Past Too with Then   T/Fem Cross   is a Hen
She Lays with Him and She Lays Eggs
She is The Cow for the Milk and The Beef for The Meat We Eat (A Piece of Meat She is)
then: at that time

Theory: TRE   T/Fem Cross   R/Her/Hair/Are/Here/Hear/Ear/Heir/Whore/Or/Err/Sex
He/E
D/Her/He   Tear/He   Tore   E   Again says   The Code   God says Tear That is Her (At Any Age)
Theo/R/He
theo: a combining form meaning "God" used in the formation of compound words   Theocrat
Theo is Infiltrated in Regular Ordinary Words/People   The it Brings Them Extra Power from That God Word to Their Voice The Theory here says   The Code   is that T/Fem Cross as R/Her/Whore/Heir/Her/Sex and God are the Same
We are Dealing with   That Code   Madness All Day

Therapy: Tear/Hop/He   Tear/Happy
The Fems Tear is When The Hymen Tear/Perforation Happens   or   Her Tears   or   Any Rip Done to Her Hymen (Hi/Men   High/Men   I/Men (N/Virgin)   It is Plural and Singular   Hi/Man m   Amen

There: Their   D/Pregnant R/Her/Hair/Are/Here/Hear/Ear/Heir/Whore/Or/Err/Sex
The Heir   or   The Whore   The Code   Hides Behind Dear/Deer
There is a Cover Word here

These: DZ   T/Fem Cross   S/Is/His/Hiss/Serpent/Penis
The Fems Crosses Here are in Plural as in These
They are D/Pregnant and Z/Sleeping about it
This (T/His)

Thesis: TSS   T/He/His
T/Fem Cross/Great Curse   S/Is/His/Serpent/Penis
2 SSs/Penis/Serpent (as in Plural or All of Them)
Switch T for F/Fem/Fuck and She Gets Feces
People Look Away from that (Especially Their Nose/Knows) so   The Secret Code is Safe

They: Day   D/Hay   The/Hey
D/Pregnant   Hey/Hay
Hey   Back to The Animals for Her   It is Part of The Fem Day

Thick: T/IC   T/Fem Cross as an Integrated Circuit
A Tic   No One Wants that
Thick also Means Opaque Dense Dull as in Not So Intelligent
Thicker: T/IC/Her
Add R/Her/Hair/Are/Here/Hear/Ear/Heir/Whore/Or/Err/Sex and She Produces an Heir   Or   a   Whore as in Her/R

Thicket: Tic/Hit   Thick/It
The Hit is Always Ticking   Ready or Not for Her
For Millenaries   Divide to Rule says   The Code

Thing: Tin   Ding   Thin
Those are Weak Words
A Thing   or   Something   are Common Slang Words to Address The Fems
Add S/Is/As/Has/Ass/His/Us/Hiss/Serpent/Penis and He Gets a Sting (He is not Supposed to be There as a Masc)

Sting the Thing and Get a Ding

Think: TNK   T/Ink   Thing/K
T/Fem Cross   N/Hen/Ann/Haine/Virgin   K/Broken Fem Warrior
She is Supposed to Think says   The Code   as a Thing (Slang for Fem)
From Virgin to Fem Cross/Great Curse   She is a Broken Fem

Thinking: Thing/King
The King and the Dumb as in Kingdom
Thank/Him for That   as usual   He is The King says   The Code

Third: T/Heard   Turd
Number 3 is a Key Number for All Secret Societies
(See Pyramid   The Eye in the Pyramid   The 3rd Eye)
T/Fem Cross   Herd (See Sheep/Ship in The Words Chapter)
The Code   says She is a Turd (See Feces in The Words Chapter) and for Her to Hear it That way

Thirst: T/Fem Cross/Great Curse   Her/R/Heir/Or/Whore   Stay
Anything with Water is Fem in   The Code   so She is Thirsty for That

This: TS   T/Fem Cross/Great Curse   S/His/Is/Serpent/Penis   The Cross (Her) and The Penis   tsstss   as in a Hissing Serpent   has 4 SSSS s (as in All of Them) and 2 TT s/Fem Crosses Plural or All of Them

Thorn: T/Fem Cross/Great Curse   Horn
No Way that The Fem as T/Fem Cross/Great Curse Could Have a Horn (Slang for Penis)   or a Voice   so She is a Thorn (Best Loved Flowers Roses have Thorns)   She is Torn Anyway
Switch O for U and She Gets a Turn (T/Urn) (See Urn in Words)

Though: Dough
Dough is Slang for Fem (as a Bun in the Oven for Example)
Although: All/Dough   All/L   D/Pregnant

Thousand: Doze   In/N/Virgin   Tau/Send
(See Tau/Taurus in The Words Chapter)

Traction: T/Fem Cross   Rack   Eon
The Rack (Breasts) is On to Her for an Eon

Thrash: T/Fem Cross   Rash
When She is Sick it is Trash   as a Rash

Thread: D/Pregnant   Red
Thread is   Fil   which is Fille (a Girl in French)   Fil is also a Piece of Thread to Sow with
T/Fem Cross   Red   Red is also to Read in The Past Tense
Take Away R/Her/Hair/Are/Here/Hear/Ear/Heir/Whore/Or/Err/Sex and Get The/D Head (Dead)
The Thread of Life   is for Her to See Her Read (Blood Loss)
Pass the Thread (The/Red) through the Needle (Need/All/L Letter)
tread :   to set down the foot or feet in walking step walk   of a male bird   to copulate   to trample or crush under foot

Three: Tree   TRE
T/Fem Cross   R/Her/Heir/Or/Whore/Err/Sex   and   2 EEs/He (In plural or All of Them)
A Tree and a Number with a Long History
That Word Three (3) has the Same Roots from Norse to Latin Greek German Old English Dutch and Sanskrit
That Tree (3) of Life is Old and Vast
Number 3 is Made of 2 Half Circles on Top of Each Other Representing Her Breasts Pointing to the Right Side
It is The Making of Number 8 the Pregnancy Number in Reverse   and/or the 2 OOs/Fem Holes (In Plural or All of Them) for One Masc   Promoting Bigamy/Polygamy for the Mascs
It is Contrary for The Fems to do   Which According to Religion is to Keep that Hole Closed Until Marriage Because if Not She will be Ostracized

Threshold: TRS (Threes or Trees)   Hold
It is a VIP Word for   The Code   it Means an Initiation   Passing The Threshold

Thrill: T/R/Ill   3 Ills/L/Ill/Ail/Hail/All/Elle/Hell (All of Them Fem)

The Dam Code The Damn Book

T/Fem Cross   R/Her/Hair/Are/Here/Hear/Ear/Heir/Whore/Or/Err/Sex and being   L/Ill
The Thrill for   The Code   is to Keep All Fems (3 lIls) on The Great Curse   as   ill   Whores
With Heir or Not She Errs
thrill: wave of emotion

Throne: Throw/N   Thrown
Keep   N/In/Hen/Ann/Virgin   From Any Throne of Power Thrown Away   Throne is Slang for Toilet
Switch T for C/Young Girl   and She Gets Crone
crone: a withered witch as old woman
We have here a **B**ad Interpretation of an Old Fem Sage
The Code   Presents Her (as Usual) as a Dark Entity and Bad for The Girl Sage   She has No Mentor to Look at in The Future

Through: True
To Go Through Her is Truth says   The Code   Be Thorough About It
through: all the way
From the Beginning to the End of Time   Un Trou in French is a Hole (O/ Fem Hole   All/L)

Thrust: T/Fem Cross   Rust
Rust is an Old Word   It is a variation of Color Red   Red is for Blood
thrust: to push forcibly
Open Symbolism for Penis Entering (The Thrusting of Vagina) Vagina Trust is the Cover Word Here

Tiara: TRA   T/Are/A
T/Fem Cross   is a Powerful being a   Her/R/Ear/Hear/Hair/Err/Heir/Or/ Whore/Here/Are/Our/Ere/Air/Ire/Sex   and   A/All Men
The Code   says She Wears a Tiara   Which is Never   or   in Her Dreams   Which are Also Created by   That Code

Tickle: T/IC/L
T/Fem Cross   IC/Integrated Circuit   L/Sweet Fem Love Light/Ill/Hail/Ail/ Hell/Elle
Tick/All   Tick/Thick   L

Time is Ticking for the Dull and Dense Fems which   The Code   Aims for All The Fems
The Code   says because Fem We Cannot Do Anything
T/Ache/All   Nothing here Tickles   It is All Pains for Her
Switch T/Fem Cross for P/All Men and He Gets Pickle
Tickle is a Cover Word here

Tick Tock: T/Fem Cross   Having Sex with the Stick in Tick with   I/Sex Act   and in   Tock (O/Fem Hole/Dot)   Now Alone With   K/Broken Fem Warrior   and   T/Fem Cross
That is the Clock for Us Fems   That Kind of Progression is Important in   That Code

Tidy: Tie/D
D/Pregnant   is All Tied Up with Pregnancy
All is Tidy says   The Code
T/I/D
T/Fem Cross   i/Marriage Act   D/Pregnant
The Fem as   T/Fem Cross   has   i/Sex   and She is   D/Pregnant
It is All Tidy (as a Big Teddy for Her and Him) It Ends Anyway with Y/Wounded Fem
tidy: neat   orderly   trim

Tight: T/Height
The More Tight The Corset the More the Height for The Fem as a T/Fem Cross says   The Code
Height (Hide as a Steal Project)

Tilt: TLT   All 3 Fems Letters
L/Sweet Fem Love Light/Elle/All/Ail/Ill/Hail/Heel/Hell/Oil
is Stuck in Between   2 TTs/Fem Crosses/Great Curse   It Makes Her Tilt
tilt: to slant
T/Fem Cross   Ill   i/Marriage Act   2 LLs/Sweet Fem Love/Ill/Ail/Hell/Elle (Plural or All of Them)
In   That Code   Every Little Detail is to Make Her Tilt or Weak
Then She Fall/Fail (FL   All Fems Letters Also) in Letter F/Fem/Fuck   Then   Then She Dies   in   X/Fallen Fem Cross says   The Code

Timber: T/Fem Cross   M/Motherhood/Aim/Him   B/Be   Her/R Bring   T/Fem Cross   to   M/Him   and Get   R/Her   D/Pregnant   with B/Boy Holding All Fem Breasts   as it is structural for structural uses as in   The Code   Conducts for The Fems
Timber: T/Fem Cross   Be   Her/R/Ear/Hear/Hair/Heir/Whore/Or/Err/ Here/Are/Our/Ere/Air/Ire/Sex
timber: the wood of growing trees suitable for structural uses   personal character or quality
Her Cut (C/Hot) Means Sex to Him
A Woody (Wood/He) is an Man Erection

tee: the mark aimed at various games like curling and   a 3 way joint for pipes and tee also represent Letter t
How Convenient   Here again is Presented the Polygamy Concept
Curls are Girls
Letter T in the Alphabet is Often a Losing Letter and
A Letter of Grief   The Word Torture is an Example
2 TTs/All Fems Crosses (Plural or All of Them)   2 OOs/Fem Holes (Plural or All of Them)   and R/Her/Or/Whore/Err/Sex   All Put Together
Words with Letter T   Tea (Cover Word)   To the T   Tee
Double TTs Words: Tit   Tot   Tat
Letter T INTRO ENDS HERE

Time: TM   2 Fem Sounds Letters
T/Fem Cross/Great Curse   and   M/Motherhood/Him
The Fem is Blamed for The Great Curse   It is Meant in the Word Time says   The Code
Saturn is the God of Time
Saturn Sat/Urn (See Saturn in The Planets Chapter) (See Satan (Sat/Ann) in The Words Chapter)
Ann has to Sit on an Urn while Bleeding Her Blood Every Month for an Average of 5 Days (Daze) a Month (Mount)
T/Fem Cross   i/Marriage Act   in Small Cap (i becomes I/Man Stick in Large Caps)   M/Motherhood   E/He (Silent and Invisible Here as Often)   E/He at the End of the Word Owns the Word
T/Fem Cross   i/Marriage Act   M/Motherhood
Time is a Pivotal Word
It is About Her Time of the Month   The Very Reason of That Curse

One of The Reasons Why Time (Saturn   Sat/Urn) and Clock (See the Clock Chapter) were Invented
Dine   Lime   Mine   Nine   Rhyme   Whine   Vine   Wine
Those Words Above Have Fem Attributes
Beside the Silent E they Spells with All Fems Letters
Switch i/Marriage Act or I/Man Stick for A/All Men and He Gets Tame
Switch T for M/Motherhood and She Gets Mine (How Appropriate)   The Great Curse is therefore Hers
Switch T for R/Her/Hair/Are/Here/Hear/Ear/Heir/Whore/Or/Err/Sex and She Gets Rhyme (Rhyme and legends are a Good Way of Learning The Code for Her)
Switch T for N/In/Hen/Ann/Virgin and She Gets Nine (The Age the Girl is Turning Halfway into Zero (9 then 0) and Start to Grow Sexually) (See Zero in The Number Chapter)
Stone Age: Stay   On   Egg
Calendar: Call/End/Her   Call/Hen/D/Her
Call N/In/Hen/Ann/Virgin   and   Impregnate Her in D/Pregnant
C   All/L/All Fem/Ill/Hail/Ail   N/In/Hen/Ann/Haine/Virgin   D/Pregnant   Her/R/Ear/Hear/Hair/Err/Heir/Or/Whore/Here/Are/Our/Ere/Air/Ire/Sex
Call All Virgins   into Motherhood is   The Code   Agenda All Year Long
Call   N/In/Hen/Ann/Virgin   DR (Have R/Her/Sex as Whore/Or/With Heir and End in D/Pregnant) It Makes Her Feel Important   as a Dr Doctor or as a Doctor would Say
That Calendar Calls says   The Code   is a Call to End Her   Literally
Date   D/Pregnant   Hate/Ate   Something   The Code   Makes Her Eat and She Ate Everyday
Day   is Letter D in French   T/Fem Cross   is The Extension of
D   as   M/Motherhood is The Extension of N/Virgin to be Married and Get Pregnant
Every Day is a T/Crossed Day for The Fems
Date   D/8   # 8 is the Number of   D/Pregnancy   D/Pregnant   is the Extension of   T/Fem Cross   and   Vice Versa   Except She/N can Only Be a Virgin Once   It goes Only in One Direction   N/Virgin   Transforms into   M/Mother   That is it
The Code   Puts   M/Motherhood   First Often as the Only Ending for   N/Virgin   to Hide itself Even More

The Dam Code The Damn Book

A Date is a Sweet Fruit   A Date is a Rendezvous   The Date of the Day   She is in a Daze/Days   Until
Death and Debts Follows and Taxes (T/Axes   X/S) Too because of our Imprisoning   Code   System
The Fem is Blamed for it All says   The Code
Day: They   The   Hey/Hay   Hey and Hay   Horse Food and a   Command
Days/He   Days in a Daze   Daisy   Daze/He   Days/He   Dizzy   Daisy   She Loves Flowers   Till She Gets Dizzy
Day   is (His)   Dais   Déesse is Goddess in French
D/Pregnant   S/Is/As/Has/Ass/His/Us/Hiss/Serpent/Penis
Whole Day is   O/Fem Hole   D/Pregnant   Hey
Switch D for B/Boy Holding All Fems Breasts and He Gets Bay (Too Young for The Code Understanding)
Switch D for F/Fem/Fuck and She Gets a Fay (More Daisies and Dizziness for Her)
Switch D for H/Secret Code Letter and She Gets Hey or Hay (See Hey and Hay in The Words Chapter) Back to The Animals for Her as Usual
Switch D for K/Broken Fem Warrior and She Gets a Quay (See Quay in The Words Chapter   An Important Word for The Code)   So Appropriate says   The Code   Because When a Fish (The Fems) is Out of the Water (What/Her) It Dies
Switch D for L/Sweet Fem Love Light/Ill/Hail/Ail/Hell/Elle   and She Gets Lay (Sex)
Switch D for M/Motherhood and She Gets May (Spring Time is Time to Get Pregnant   She May says   The Code)
Switch D for N/In/Hen/Ann/Virgin and She Gets Neigh
neigh: to utter a cry of a horse
Back to the Animals for Her   (See Horses/Whores in The Words Chapter)
Switch D for P/Man Power and He Gets a Pay
Switch D for Q/Menstrual Cycle and She Gets a Quay
quay: a landing place   especially one of solid masonry constructed along the edge of a body of water   wharf
Woof/Wharf   says   The Code   She is the Dog/Bitch as Usual
The Code   says here that The Fem has Landed or Arrived at Her Destination which is to Bleed   The Great Curse   That She is Out of The Water   Which is an Illusion   Because When a Fish is Out of The Water   it Dies

685

Lise Rochon

It is Quite Rare to Hear from The Masons (My Sons) or Their Work Masonry About a Common Word Such as a Quay   A Very Important Word for   The Code

Switch D for R/Whore/Her/Heir/Err/Sex and She Gets a Ray or a Man Call Ray   The Code   Will Agree with Her as Long as She Stays with the Rules

Switch D for S/Is/His/Penis and He Gets Say   The Code Allows the Mascs Only to Talk (Not The Fems)

Switch D for T and There is Nothing Because D and T (One Becoming The Other) Cannot be Left Alone Together says   The Code

Switch D for W/All Fems Sex Active and She Gets Way (The Code Agrees with All Fems being Sex Active   As Long as There is a Way)

Today: Two/To   D/Pregnant   Hey/Hay

Yesterday: Yes   T/Fem Cross   Her/R   Day

Tomorrow: Two/More/O   Actually No   There are 3 OOOs/Fem Holes (as in All of Them) in Tomorrow

One O/Fem Hole is in the Hiding   Hoarding it for Tomorrow

Monday: Moon/Day

Saturday: Sat/Her/Day   Saturday Afternoon: Sat/Her/Day/After/Noon The Noon is the Symbolic Moon in the Day Time   Where She Represents   2 NN s/Virgins and 2 OOs/Fem Holes (Plural or All of Them) Making Her Aware Already that   The Code   Always Means that There is Always Another Fem   But She is Too Young or/and Naïve to Understand Any of That

Her Moon is Coming Too   Plenty to be Busy in Her Young Head She does Not See Coming

Week: Weak

Month: Mount (as a Horse/Whore/Heir) Time of the Month (See Month in The Words Chapter)

Amount (Pay)

Year: I/Hear   I/Here   You/R/Her/Hair/Are/Here/Hear/Ear/Whore/Heir/Or/Err/Sex

Decade: DKD   3 Fem Letters

D/Pregnant   K/Broken Fem Warrior   D/Pregnant   Again

Always the Same in   The Code   Weak and Pregnant Again She is Add R/Her/Heir/Or/Whore/Sex and She Gets Degrade (The/Grade   The/D   G/Hymen Perforation   Raid

Take Away The Second Pregnancy and She Gets to Decay)

Century: Cent   Her/R/Ear/Hear/Hair/Err/Heir/Or/Whore/Here/Are/Our/Ere/Air/Ire/Sex   A/All Men
Cent/Hurry   A Penny to Her for Sex with All Men as Whore or for Heir Penny is a Popular Fem Name   Penny   Pin/He   Pun/He (Pony)   P/Man Power   Own/On   He/E
Add S/Is/As/Has/Ass/His/Us/Hiss/Serpent/Penis
to Penny and He Gets a Penis   A Penny for Your Thoughts
Millenary: Mill   N/Virgin   R/Her/Hairy
Eon: He/On   As Usual The Fems are Absent from Time   Even if it Carries the Fem Curse All the Way from Saturn The God Of Time

Tip: T/P
T/Fem Cross   is With   P/Man Power
tip: slender or pointed end or extremity   the top summit or apex
The Code   Agrees When a Man is with a Fem as Great/Curse
There are Several Definitions in Dictionary.com for Tip
A Tip is an Extra Gift
P/Man Power is with No Other Fem than T/Fem Cross
At the Top Tip
Tip is a Cover Word here

Tire: Tie/Her
Tie   Her/R/Ear/Hear/Hair/Heir/Or/Whore/Err/Here/Are/Our/Ere/Air/Ire/Sex
Roll Over Her That Way   To Tire Her

Title: Tight/All
She has No Title/No Power in   The Code
(See BB in The Words Chapter)

Tit: Made of 2.5 Fem Letters
2 TTs/Fem Crosses (In Plural or All of Them) with i/Marriage Act in the Middle
T/Hit   T/It
The T/Fem Cross Hits Her Breasts Also

tittle-tattle: Between 6 TTTTTTs/Fem Crosses (All of Them) is Letter i/Marriage Act and A/All/Men

That Would Mean All TTs/Fem Crosses are Surrounding the i/Marriage Act Union and A/All Men with a Title to do so
It is Absolutely an Impossible Situation for   The Code   so
title-tattle: petty gossip or trivial talk

To: 2 Fem Letters   T/Fem Cross   O/Fem Hole
According to Dictionary.com   "There is no real definition for the word "to" because it is a word that primarily just serves as a function   there are 22 uses for the preposition
Here is some of them: toward a contact point or closed position   To as a Direction to Follow   To as in Number Two (as in to Poop) (Dodo is All Fems Letters)
The Code   Often Brings Polygamy or Cheating with Other Fems as a Normal Thing to Do for a Man   Me Too is Another Form or More of the Same Concept
It Amplifies that Go To by Adding Another O/Fem Hole   Making it Plural   or   All of Them
Making All Fems O/Fem Holes and T/Fem Crosses as The Direction to Go
Says   The Code   For The Fems to Accept That a Man Being a Man   He will do That   Naturally   Boys will be Boys says   The Code

Today: Two   D
2 DDs/Pregnants (as in Plural or All of Them)
Having 2 Fem D/Pregnant at the Time is an Everyday Situation for a Man says   The Code
For a Fem having 2 Men in Her Sex Life She would Have Been Stoned to Death Not too long Ago
Too/Day

Together: To/Get/Her
Too   Get   Her/R/Ear/Hear/Hair/Heir/Or/Whore/Err/Here/Are/Our/Ere/Air/Ire/Sex
Two Get   R/Her/Are/Whore
From   The Code   Point of View The Fem and Masc Have a Different Understanding of The Language
together: each other for the other

The Dam Code The Damn Book

Toil: Toil His Made of 3 Fem Letters   and   i/Marriage Act   It is The Code Tool (To/All Fems) To Get Her
toil: hard and continuous work
She Pays the Toll Too for All That as Toil Starts with T/Fem Cross
That is What   The Code   Wants All Fems to Do is   To End in a Toilet (Toil/Hit To/All/It   Toy/Let)

Toilet: Toy/Lit   To/Let   Two/Let
Let: L/Sweet Fem Light   E/He   T/Fem Cross
Her Toy would be a Toilet   or   She is Toy for   That Code   Look it is All Shinny   Toy/Lit
In Reverse the Syllables for Toy/Let is   Let/Her
Lait/Her (Lait is Milk in French) would be a Cover Word here Because it is a Nice Soft Word for All that S H I T (She/It/)   It Comes as a Number Two as Poop)
When 2 PPs/Men Power Holds 2 OOs/Fem Holes (as in Plural or All of Tem) it is as Taking Care of Poop   Again
It Sounds Innocent
So Let Her Be the Toilet says   The Code   or a   Lit/Toy   or   Toy/Let   Toilet Starts with the T/Fem Cross/Great Curse
The Fem in   The Code   is Represented in All Kinds of Connection with Feces   or   Other Bad Concepts Left to Her by   The Code   Such as the Left Hand (Fem Hand) is for Wiping Butt   The Left Hand is Called the Impure Hand
The Code   Hides The Fems Again in a Toilet/Bathroom (Bat/Bate/Butt   Room)   With All this Bate for Poop on Her She Gets To   Ill/Ail/Hail/Elle/Hell
So Sorry for The Fems
Switch T/Fem Cross for S/Is/As/Has/Ass/His/Us/Hiss/Serpent/Penis   and He Gets Soil so   He Immediately Starts Seeding (The Man Seed)
Switch T for B/Boy Holding All Fem Breasts and He Gets a Boil (Too Young for That Code)
Switch T for C or Q or K and She Gets Coil
Take Away T from Toil and He Gets Oil
See Bible Symbology The Oil and The Virgins

Told: T/Hold   T/Old
The T/Fem Cross being on Hold   or   Old

She is What She is Told by   The Code
Any Unmarried Fem After 20 YO was/is Told   she is an Old Maid (The Code Often Dresses Her as a Black Witch with Warts on Her Face   etc
(Note The Double W in The Words Witch and Warts   See Letter W in The Letter Chapter)
He is a Bachelor at Any Age as She becomes an Old maid

Tomb: 3 Fem Letters and a B/Baby
T/Fem Cross   Womb
To   Whom
A Womb is Made of Her Water (What/Her) and Special Nutrients for The Baby   BB (Heirs)   Male Children Only in   The Code
T   Home   un Homme is a Man in French
Switch T for R/Her/Hair/Are/Here/Hear/Ear/Heir/Whore/Or/Err/Sex and She Gets a Room   Whores are Agreed by   The Code
Switch T for D/Pregnant and She Gets Doom (4 Fem Letters)
D/Pregnant   Cannot Look at a Fem Identified as   T/Fem Cross as The Great Curse
(See Dome in The Words Chapter)

Tomorrow: All 8 are Fem Letters
Two   More   3OOO/Fem Holes (Plural or All of Them)
Always More Hope for More Holes Tomorrow says   The Code
There Are 3 OOOs/Fem Holes in Tomorrow (Two/More/O) Even if it says 2 more OO/Fem Holes There is One O in the Hiding/Waiting
T/Fem Cross   O/Fem Hole   M/Motherhood/Him   2 RRs/Hers/Are/Heirs/Or/Whores/Err/Sex   O/Owe
Morrow (More   O/Fem Hole) is the Old Word for Tomorrow   It Used to Mean in the Morning (Morn/In)
Too   M/Him/Motherhood   R/Whore/Heir/Or/Err/Fem Hole
Two/To   M/Motherhood/Him   Heir/Whore/Or/Err/Sex   O/Fem Hole
T/Fem Cross   More   O/Fem Hole
To/Tow   More   O/Fem Hole
Sex is On Tomorrow with Always More Holes from Mothers   as Whores   or   With Heirs   It Ends with W/All Fems Active Which is Here Silent
Because Tomorrow has 3 OOOs/Fem Holes (as in All of Them) in it   Evidently   The Code   Makes Men Polygamists

The Dam Code The Damn Book

Demain is also 2 Hands (2/Mains) for Tomorrow in French   That is the Ultimate Fear for a Man According to   The Code   His Hands Left for His Sex Union

Tone: TNM   3 Fem Sound Letters
T/Fem Cross/Great Curse   On
T/Fem Cross   is On   She is on The Horn if   R/Her/Are/Heir/Or/Whore/Err/Sex   is on it
Switch O/Fem Hole for You/U/Ovulating   It is Time for a Tune   Tune Up   Music

Tonight: To/Night   Two/Knights
The/Night is for The/Knights   The Knights Keep Guard
The Night Stars and The Moon are Fem Symbols (Sin/Bowl)   so   Under Guard The Fem is at All Time   says   That Code

Too: T/Fem Cross   2 OOs/Fem Holes/Loins (Plural or All of Them)
The T/Fem Cross/Great Curse is for All O/Fem Holes
It Is Something To/Too Get Along with (Too as Also)
To indicates a Direction and Too Follows on it
Add K/Broken Fem Warrior and She Gets Took (T/Hook   T/Fem Cross is Hooked in Took   Because She is Broken
A Man Takes a Virgin as His Wife   and   The Code   Makes Her a Hook/Her   Whore/Heir/Or/Err/Sex)
Add a L/Sweet Fem Love Light/Ill/Hail/Ail/Hell/Elle   and   She Gets to be a Tool (4 Fem Fetters)
She Toils   and Pays the Toll (4 Fem Letters) on That Too

Toot: All 4 Fem Letters
2 OOs/Fem Holes (Plural or All of Them) are in between   2 TTs/Fem Cross/Great Curse (Plural or All of Them)
That would be too Much Information from   The Code   to The Fems so Toot Takes it All
toot: lavatory   to blow a horn   affectionate term   drinking spree   cocaine
Switch O/Fem Hole for i/Marriage Act and She Gets Tits
Switch Ending Letter T for L/Sweet Fem Light/Ill/Ail/Elle/Hell and She Gets to be a Tool

Top: T/Fem Cross   O/Fem Hole   P/Man Power
T/Up   T/Hop
T/Fem Cross   is Up and Hopping to Her Top
T/Fem Cross   Starts the Word Top
This could have been a Positive Sign for The Fems in General   But No   T is at the Top Followed by O/Fem Hole and P/Man Power
The Top Priority is that O is with P/Man Power   as   T/Fem Cross/Great Curse   Only
Switch O for I/Marriage Act and She Gets a Tip
Such as to Receive a Piece of Private Information   To Tip Over   To Get a Small Present of Money   A Light Small Blow and More)
Switch O for A/All Men and He Gets a Tap (A Tap on The Hand)

Torah: The Entire Body of Jewish Literature
Known as the Pentateuch
It is the First Five Books of the Old Testament in Genesis "At the Beginning was the Word"   Is Its Most Important Sentence
That Phrase Alone Explains The Ways and Mysteries of   That Code
If You have the Tools to Work/Read That Puzzle
T   Fem Cross/Great Curse
O   Fem Hole
R   Her/Hair/Are/Here/Hear/Ear/Heir/Whore/Or/Err/Sex
A   All Men
H   Secret Code Letter   Always Silent or Almost
To/Ra   The Egyptian Sun God Ra   Tarot (Secret Divination Art) and Rota (See Wheel of Life) are Very Ancient Words
T R A Letters are Together   but in Different Formation
Very Powerful Words here
Torah/Tear/O

Torch: TRCH T/Fem Cross   R/Her/Hair/Are/Here/Hear/Ear/Heir/Whore/Or/Err/Sex   Shh/She/Her
Tore   She/Shh   The Code   says That is Her Light in the Night   To be a Cursed Whore/Or/With Heirs   and Stay Quiet about it
torch: something considered as a source of illumination enlighten guidance etc   *Slang an arsonist*
Arsonist   R/Her/Are/Heir/Or/Whore   Sun/Son   S/Is/His   T/Fem Cross/Great Curse

The Dam Code The Damn Book

The Arsonist Burns it   No Trace for Her here to find Out   How Code   Works
Torches   T/Fem Cross   Whore/Heir/R/Err/Her   She Is
Tear (Rip) (Tears)   Her   and   She/Shh About it from The Past to The Present
Take R/Her Away and She Gets a Touch
The Code   Never Leaves The Fems   It Abuses the Power of the Light (Her) from Its Blaspheming Code Sounds

Torment: T/Fem Cross/Great Curse   R/Heir/Or/Whore/Err/Her   Meant Tower/Meant   Tarot Card #16 The Tower is a Malevolent Card   and   It is All on Her   To/Her/Meant (Torment)
To Her Mint says   The Code   Cheating on Her Again

Torture: TRTR   2 TTs/Fems Curse (as in Plural or All of Them)   and   2 RRs/Whores/Heirs/Her/Sex (as in Plural or All of Them)
The Code   meaning here is Accentuated by The Double Double Sets of Letters   and   in the Same Order
Torture is Essentially a Fem Word Here   Which Implies All Fems are Whores   or   with Heirs   or/and   are Cursed
Understood That Many Men in Real Life are/have been Tortured   The Code   Works on a Different Level of Consciousness with Her   It has its Own Narrow Goals
Tore/T/Her   The Way   The Code   Does it is by Tearing
(Rips   and   Tears) Her Apart in Every Way Possible   and Hypnotizing Men into being Pompous and Often to Despotism from Too Much Power Over The Fems   Such as Commanding Obedience at Marriage Vows That Tradition (Trade/He/On) Stopped in The Nineteen Fifties After Thousand Years of Abuse to Her   On Her Knees She was/Is
The Masc Pays the Price from that too   In a More Distant Way Such as being Tortured by Other Men (No Matter the Reason (Religion   Hunger For Power   Vanity   Jealousy   Money   etc)   All These Erected from Bad Childhood Parenthood (Ignorance) Most of Time   Again Crated by   That Code   Over Time)
Such a Human (You/Man) Imbalance Drives Many Men to Insanity and Extreme Anger   By that Very Madness that   That Code   Creates Endlessly on Us Humanity   To Keep Its Power Hold on Us

Toss: To/Us
T/Fem Cross   O/Fem Hole   and   2 SS s/Is/As/Has/Ass/Us/His/Hiss/
Serpents/Penisses (2-3 Makes it Plural or All of Them)
The Masc is in the Lead by its Number   (See to in The Words Chapter)
Especially That To is Not a Word and has No Meaning by Itself says   The
Code   It Makes it Easier to Toss Her after Done with Her
toss: to throw carelessly   to consume rapidly
toss off: to masturbate in British slang
Dos is Number Two in Spanish
Number 2 Two is Poop in American Slang
Back to the Feces for Her Again

Total: TOTL   4 Fem Sound Letters   A/All Men are Here   But Silent
T/Fem Cross   Surrounds   O/Fem Hole   and it Extends to   All
of Fems   That would be a Lot of Power and Independence to All
Fems   That would be a Big No from   The Code   so   Tut/All
tut tut: an exclamation of mild reprimand   shame or an exclamation of
disdain   contempt
This is How to Make Her Shy (She/I) or Ashamed (She/Aim)
Too/Tall   The Code   has a Hard Look on All Fems   The Fems should be
Small or Anything Weak says   The Code   (Except Her Hair (See R/Her/
Heir/Or/Whore/Err/Sex in the Letter Chapter)

Touch: T/Fem Cross   Ouch
T/Fem Cross/Great Curse   says   The Code   or   Ouch   or   Get
Hurt   Ouch

Touchstone: Touch that Stone   (See Rock in The Words Chapter)

Tough: T/Off
T/Fem Cross/Great Curse   is Not Allowed to be Tough   That would be
Competition for   The Code   Only The Masc Can be so
She is Off   Off is Made of 3 Fem Letters
On is Also Made of 2 Fem Letters   It is All About Her in   The
Code   Especially when Life is Rough

Tournament: Tower/N/Meant
N/In/Hen/Ann/Virgin   is in the Tower

Tow   Her/R/Ear/Hear/Hair/Err/Heir/Or/Whore/Here/Are/Our/Ere/Air/Ire/Sex
The Tarot Card # 16th The Tower is a Malevolent Card
Tournament is Related to Sports   The Fems have been Kept Away from Them
T/Urn/He/Meant
The Fems Must be Kept Away from Sports   Losing their Blood Makes Them Cursed and They Bring Bad Luck (See Urn in The Words Chapter)
T/Fem Cross/Great Curse/Urn   A/All Men   Meant
The Fems is Confined to the   Urn/Earn   He Mean it
Turn/A/Meant
Take Away N/In/Hen/Ann/Virgin   and Get Turn/A/Meat

Towel: Tow   L/Sweet Fem Love Light/Ill/Hail/Ail/Hell/Elle
When She is on The Towel (On The Rag as Men Say)   It is That Time to Toll
Switch L for R/Her/Hair/Are/Here/Hear/Ear/Heir/Whore/Or/Err/Sex and She Gets Tower (Tow/Her   To/Her)
The Tarot Card # 16 The Tower is Malevolent to Her (See The Tower in The Tarot Chapter)
See Tower Below

Tower: T/Fem Cross   and   R/Her/Heir/Or/Whore/Err/Sex
Tau/Her (See Tau in The Words Chapter)   Tau is Cross   Another Illusion from   The Code   for The Fems
Two/O/Her   Tau is The Astrological Sign of Taurus   The Ultimate Fem   She is represented by a Cow   as Usual (Tits for Milk) She has been Transformed into a Milk Provider
To/Her   A Tower is Shaped as an Erect Penis   A Falling Tower is Really Bad News for   The Code   so Here they are in that Card in a Fall Down On The Tower is a Clock (Usually on the Left Tower   Where Often More Symbolism About Her is Hidden)
To/Owe/Her
Towering   Tower/Ring   as in   T/O/R/N (4 Fem Letters Plus)
T/Owe/Her/Ring   The Code   says She is in a Debt Because of that Ring (In a Ring   Men Fight)
That Tower Card Towers Us The Fems

Town: All 4 Fem Letters
T/Own   To/Own
Tau/N/Virgin (See Tau/Taurus in The Words Chapter)
Switch O for i/Marriage Act and She Gets Time (There is Always Time for Sex says   The Code   or is it that Time of The Month)
Switch T for G/Penis Penetration and She Gets Gown
Take W/All Fems Away and She Gets a Tone (See Atonement in Dictionary   a Very Important Word in The Code)
Sacrifice is Ours The Fems with That T/Fem Cross/Great Curse and being Owned
D and T are Interchangeable in   That Code   She Get Down (In Town)

Toxic: T/Ox/IC
T/Fem Cross/Great Curse   O/Fem Hole   X/Fallen Fem Cross   Are Sacrificial Fem Letters   Joined Together By Her Loins Together (To/Get/Her) In such Toxic Way   The Cursed Ox   Which is The Goddess Venus Governing The Taurus Sign Which Represents Fertility of the Land   Beauty   Prosperity   Happiness/Success to All)   Is Accompanied by IC/Integrated Circuit
Enhancing the Fact that those Fem Letters   Are So Badly Oriented in That Kind of Toxicity

Track: T/Fem Cross   Rack
T/Fem Cross and the Rack (Rack is Slang for Breasts)
Estrogen Slows Down The Fems Mental Processes as Shown in Scientific Studies   She is being Influenced That way   It Makes Her Emotional because Naturally She Becomes More Empathic to Communicate with The Baby
More or Too Much Breast Is Related to Too Much Estrogen says Science   Breasts Create Estrogen   The More The Breasts The More the Milk says   The Code
Human Fems and Cows are the Only Mammals that Breasts do Not go Back Inside Her body After Lactating a Baby
track: a wheel rut   a line of travel or motion   parallel lines of rails
Those Tracks are Parallel   Not Touching Often   So Her Understanding Remains Difficult
Tracker: T/Fem Cross   Rack   R/Her/Are/Heir/Or/Whore/Err/Sex

The Dam Code The Damn Book

Tradition: Trade/He/She/On
He Trades The Fems Since an Eon

Train: T/Rein   T/Reign   T/Reine
Take T/Fem Cross/Great Curse Away and She Gets
rein: a leather strap   part of harness   to control   to reign
How Can She Reign When She is on a Harness
Trine
Une Traine is a Royal Cape   or   a Wedding Traine for Her
A Train Can Coil Around Mountains as a Serpent (S/His/Is/Serpent/
Penis   He is The Teacher/Trainer says   The Code)

Trainer: Train/Her   T/Rein/Her
T/Fem Cross   R/Her/Are/Heir/Or/Whore   N/In/Hen/Virgin/Virgin
Through The Rein
rein: a leather strap   part of harness   to control   to reign
She is being Taught that She is a Cursed Whore Since Childhood

Traitor: Threat   R/Her/Are/Heir/Or/Whore
She is Covered in Shame and being Under Threats
Trait/Her
To be a Traitor is a Trait of Her says   The Code
trait: a distinguishing characteristic
Treat/Her
And Treat Her That Way
Switch T/Fem Cross for D/Pregnant and She Gets Trader Trade/Her (for a Young One)

Treason: T/Reason
T/Fem Cross/Great Curse   Meets   Reason
That is a Big No from   The Code   to Her so She is Accused of
Treason   or   T is the Reason for the Treason   as Being Blamed for The
Great Curse   or   T/Fem Cross/Great Curse would be Reasoning
That Would be a Treason says   The Code
Three/Son   Tree/Some   Different Rings here
Tree/Three   S/Is/His/Penis/Serpent   A/All Men   Son
Triangle: The Masonic Emblem with the Eye/I in it
Try/Angle

697

That Will Keep Her Busy as She Waste Precious Time to Evolve in The World

Treasury: Treasure/He
An Important Word for Us Humans   Our Money
treasury: a place where the funds of the government of a corporation or the as are deposited kept and disbursed   a collection or supply of excellent or highly prized writings work of art etc
There is No Space for The Fems in That Treasure/He
It be Called Usury from That Tree/Three Sure   He

Trembling: T/Fem Cross   Rambling
The Idea of T Rambling Would be a Trembling Event to   The Code   so No   She Will Trembles from Fear or Fever   Instead
rambling: to wonder around in a leisurely manner aimless manner   straying from one subject to another

Trial: Try   L/All/Ill/Hell/Elle (See Letter L in the Letter Chapter)
The Hunt for Sex is an Old Reality for All Fems
trial: trying   testing   putting to the proof
Thank Us for The Me Too Movement

Triangle: The Masonic Emblem with the Eye/I in it
Try/Angle   Angle and Angel are Close Together   The Fifth Angle That Never Fits in In The Old Hebrew Tradition   It is still m a Mystery

Trinity: The Mystery of the Holy (Hole/He) Trinity) (Throne   He   T/Fem Cross/Great Curse) Means Basically that Through That Trine Some Men Owns the Throne of Humanity   The 3 Corners of The Pyramid with the Eye in it on the Dollar (Dull/Doll   Her/R/Heir/Or/Whore/Err/Sex   Illustrates it
Transubstantiate Blood to Wine and Wine into Blood   (Her Blood)   and Bread (Bred) into the Body (Her Body) They Call it Breaking The Bread   Breeding by Breaking/Raping   Which in Ancient Times was Common
The Fems had   No Power   No Money   No Identity   (See the Word To in The Words Chapter)

The Dam Code The Damn Book

By Doing That Communion (Transubstantiation) You Will be Forgiven All Your Sins (How Convenient for   That Nasty Code   That Goes on All Day Destroying People (Peep/Hole) Lives)
That is Why it is Stipulated in The Christian Bible that it is an Event that is Real and Alive   And it Is
Passover (Pass/Over) the Jewish Celebration was re Incarnated into That Mystery of Transubstantiation (Pass Over Her)   (Pass   Ov/Ovulation Her/R/Heir/Or/Whore/Err/Sex)   (P/Man Power   Ass/Is/His/Us/Serpent/Penis   Her)   Wild Mammals have an Ovulation Time   and   that is the Only Time The Fem Mammals Allows the Male to Have Sex with Her Pass Over That says   The Code   We have total Ignorance about that   And The Fems are Bleeding a Huge Amount of Blood Every Month in Their Lifetime because of That   For 2 000 or More Years
(Wonder Why Fems are Anemic and Weak at 16th Years Old   Reflect on it   Unfortunately I have No Solution to Fix That Huge Loss of Her Blood It has Happened for Many Millenaries   It has changed the Very Basics Patterns of Evolution
Now Understand Why it was Called Speaking in Tongues of Fire in the Bible   That Secret of Jesus was Heavy   They would have Lost Their Tongues Too if The Illiterates   or   The Code   Naïve Initiates Would have Understood that Message
That Message Too Passed Through from John The Baptist Baptism with Water (What/Her   Water is an Entirely Fem Symbol)   He was Freeing People of Their Sins with Water
The Fems are Used to Forgive All Kind of Men Sins   although   She Pays the Hard Price When Making Tiny Mishaps

Trip: T/Fem Cross/Great Curse   RIP
For The Fems a T/Rip Means Nothing for Her says   The Code   She will be Ripped in Tears   Anyway
RIP   Then She will be Gone   Anyway   The Code   Cares Not About it
Tear/Hip   Tea/Rip   The Sound of Tea Making it Sound Smooth   No Trip is a Cover Word Here

Trophy: Through   F/Fem/Fuck   E/He
E/He   goes through   F/Fem/Fuck   and   He Gets a Trophy says   The Code

Lise Rochon

Troop: True/P
A Good Word for Him says   The Code   A Soldier (Sold/He/Her) Too   To Do What
T/Fem Cross/Great Curse   R/Her/Heir/Or/Whore/Err/Sex   2 OOs/Fem Holes (Making it Plural or All of Them)   P/Man Power
All Cursed Fem Vaginas as for   Heirs   or   Whores   or to   Err   Under the Power of   The Code   as Soldiers/Troup

Trouble: Through   B/Boy Holding All Fem Breasts   L/Ill/Hail/All/Hell/Elle/Aile (Aile is Wing in English)
Boys are Trouble Because   The Code   is Already Influencing Them to be Abusive to All Fems from Early Age as it is Normal from the Sayings of   The Code
Through is a Hole (Un Trou in French) as in a Vagina says in   The Code

True: Through is for Real here   Un Trou in French is a Hole   Anything Hole in   The Code   is a Joke on Her
Anything Round is Fem so   A Hole is Generally Round   No Doubt
true: real   genuine   authentic

Trust: Starts and Ends with   T/Fem Cross/Great Curse
Add H/Secret Code Letter and She Gets
thrust: to push forcibly   shove
That is What a Fem Gets from   That Code
She Trusts   Because She does Not See The Thrust (Rape) Coming

Truth: T/Fem Cross   R/Her/Hair/Are/Here/Hear/Ear/Heir/Whore/Or/Err/Sex   U/You/Ovulating   H/Secret Code Letter
Truth Starts   and Ends   with T/Fem Cross/Great Curse

Try: TRY   3 Fem Sound letters
Try/All   It is The Trial   A Mean Word
Try is a Cover Word

Tuition: Made Entirely of Fem Letters with 2 T/Fem Crosses   U/You/Ovulating   She/Shh   Eon
Her Tuition says   The Code   is to be Cursed with an Open Uterus and having Lots of Sex on Commands from Him for an Eon

tuition: the charge or fee for instruction as a private school or a college or university
See University   Universe/City   Universe/See/T
The Human Destiny is in Seeing T/The Great Fem Curse as Her Universe
The Code   has Assimilated Most of The Symbols that are of Extreme Grandeur to Assimilate Her
See Verse and Universe in The Words Chapter

Tumor: TMR   2 Fem Letters with   R/Her/Sex
T/Fem Cross   and   M/Motherhood/Him   Man are in Front of R/Our/Her/Hair/Are/Here/Hear/Ear/Heir/Whore/Or/Err/Sex
That would be Too Much Information Given to The Fems   A Big No from   The Code   so
tumor: a swollen part   swelling   protuberance   an abnormal growth of tissue   *Archaic*   inflated pride   haughtiness   pompous language   bombast
The Swollen Part here would be The Fems Abnormal Growth of Breasts Compared to what Happens in Natural Mammal Nature
Switch M/Motherhood for N/In/Hen/Haine/Virgin and She Gets Tuner (She is being Tuned here by The Code to be that Tumor) and to Take it with Humor   Just as Her T/Cross and Forget about it and Just be Stupid about Your Life says The Code
Note that Breast Cancer is the Most Common of Those Terrible Tumor Ailments

Tune: TUN   3 Fem Sounds Letters
T/Fem Cross   U/You/Ovulating   N/In/Hen/Ann/Haine/Virgin
Her Tune says   The Code   is to be a Cursed Virgin with Her Uterus Open to Sex Anytime
Switch U for O/Fem Hole and She Gets Tone (There is Only a Tone for Her It is to Stay with that Tune
That Keeps Her in That Tunnel   Tune/Hell   Tune/All

Turd   T/Fem Cross   Heard/Herd
If a Fem would be Heard   or   Hear   or   Learn   that She is a Part of a Herd (See Sheppard in The Words Chapter)
That Is a Big No from   The Code   so
turd: a piece of excrement   a mean   contemptible person

Back to the Feces for Her (She/It   Shit) as Usual
A good Cover for   The Code   No One Wants to Look or Come Close to Turd
Turd is made of 4 Fem Letters   As Usual   She is it
Every Little Thing Counts and Accumulates   It is One of The Rules of   That Code
Letter R   Note That R is a Masc Letter as is Letter I   Both are Masc and Fem

Turn: T/Urn
A Fem Word   3 Fem Letters   and   R/Here/Her/Are/Heir/Or/Whore/Err/Sex
Urn   A Fem Word   with 2 Fem Letters   and   R/Are/Heir/Or/Whore/Err/Sex) Double Meaning as in Fem and Masc
In Antique Greece Urns were Storage for Water Wine Food Ashes Etc
Also that Special Urn that She would Use and Dispose of Her Monthly Blood
The Fems were Isolated in Ancient Time   but   Sat During Their Days of Loss of Blood   Which was Far Less Time and Volume than Now
Turn (T/Fem Cross   Urn)
Clay in the Making of an Urn
Anything That Turns (See Wheel of Time in The Words Chapter (A Wheel can Only Turn) is related to The Fems
Turn that Urn Over into Ovulation (Ov/R   Ovaries) says Saturn (Sat/Urn) the God of Time and Suffering for Us
Time is with Us for Eternity/Eon says Saturn   or   Until the End of Time   Time is an important word in   The Code
The End of the Time of the Month Also From Turn Switch T/Fem Cross to L/Sweet Fem Love Light/Ill/Hail/Ail/Hell/Elle/Ill/Ail/Hail/Hell/Elle   and She Gets Learn (Learn to Turn That Urn)
Take L Away and She Gets Earn   The Code   Lures Her   That She has Benefits in Losing Her Blood   Only Later She Will Realizes The Fems are the Victims of The Longest Curse in History

Turnover: T/Fem Cross   Urn   Ov   Her/R/Her/Are/Heir/Or/Whore/Err/Sex
Turn the Urn to Ov (Ovulation) to That Cursed Fem

The Dam Code The Damn Book

Tush: T/Fem Cross   Hush
Tush is S*lang* for Buttocks   Tushie in Jewish
hush: to make or become silent   to sooth or be soothed
Tush is related to Sex   The Fem That ignores   The Code   is Reminded about being Silent When being Groped   and/or She will Feel Good about it
Tushie   T/Fem Cross   Hush   He   Touch/He
Toucher is to Touch in French
touchy: sensitive to touch
The Code   Hides That Way

Tut: 3 Fem Letters
U/Ovulating are Surrounded by 2 TTs/Fems Crosses (Plural or All of Them)
tut: exclamation of contempt   disdain   shame
Nothing Never Comes Nice for Any Fem says   The Code
Switch U for i/Marriage Act and She Gets Tit
tit   *Archaic*   a girl or a young woman   *Archaic*   a small or poor horse   nag   *Slang* for a female breast   *Slang*   a despicable or an unpleasant person
Back to the Horse for Her/Heir/Or/Whore/Err/Horse/Sex   and on Top   The Code   says She is despicable and Unpleasant and   Poor   or   Too Small
The Fem has No Chance in   The Code
Switch U for O/Fem Hole and She Gets a Tot (Another Child)
tot: a small child
Switch U for A/All Men and He Gets Tat
tat: tatty article or tatty condition   tasteless article
to do or make something by tatting
That is for Him too poor or tasteless   so He is out
tit for tat: retaliation   blow for blow
The Code   Avoids to Mix Men with Meaning affiliation Except When Sex is Involved

Tutor: TTR
2 TTs/Fem Crosses (Plural or All of Them)   and   R/Her/Are/Heir/Or/Whore/Err/Sex
A Tutor Instruct (In/N/Virgin   Struck) The Fems That is What The Fems Learns from a Tutor

703

Lise Rochon

Tutu: 4 Fem Letters   Repeated Twice
2 TTs/Fem Crosses (Plural or All of Them)   2 UUs/Opened Fem Loins (Plural or All of Them)   By Doubling the Same Sound/Letter/Symbol
It Goes On Repeating Itself as a Tune to Learn   TuTuTu as a Bird Song   Which She Loves
tutu is un Toutou a Stuffed Animal in French
tout: to solicit business employment votes or the ads importunately   Taught/You   Tot/You
T/Fem Cross   is with You/U/Ovulation   It is with a
tutu: a short full skirt
She Gets to Danse on Her Toes   To be on your Toes is a Very Uncomfortable Position in Life
The Tutu is a Cover Word Here to Attract Sex to a Fem of Young Age   as the Horse will be in Her Adolescence
A Tutu is a Highly Respected Beloved Aunt in Hawaii

Twist: Starts and Ends with   T/Fem Cross/Great Curse   and has   S/Is/His/Ass/Hiss/Us/Serpent/Penis   in its Middle   with   W/All Fem Sex Active (A Loser)   plus   i/Sex Act
All Cursed Fem are All Sex Active with Penis says   The Code

Type: T/Hype
Her Type as T/Fem Cross/Great Curse   is to Get Excited   so   She will Lose
hype: to excite   to stimulate artificially   a drug addict
Typical: T/Hype/He/Call

U   u
Intro
Letter U is the Open Loins Always Ready for Sex in Her Natural Ovulation Time
It has Almost the Same Shape as Letter V   Although With a Different Meaning
u/U is Also the Same Fem Letter in Big Caps
u in Small Caps has a Stick Holding Her Hole Open
It does Not Need it Anymore in Letter Large Caps U
Same as in Letters m and n which are the Other Side   In Reverse

The Dam Code The Damn Book

As Explained Earlier in the m Chapter   It is the Stick Giving Shape to the ½ Circle

And the I/Stick is with the Fem at All Times That Way   She is Never Left Alone in the World of   The Code

In Large Cap Letter U The Stick is Gone

And U has No Way of Standing by Itself so It Will Keep On Rolling like the Wheel of Time

The One with the Cross in It T/Am

U is the Letter for Uterus and for You/U (Her/R)

U is Vav in Hebrew (2 VVs) and will be Called Later the W/Double U

U is Called Upsilon (a Sum) in Western and Eastern Greek U is In the Shape of a Y or V (Both Fem Sounds)

Letter U is V in Latin

All those Inversions are there to Reinforce the Concept that U is V and vice versa   There is Where The Transition between U and V Happens in   The Code

Same Here you Can Mix W V Y and V

U in the Alphabet is the Other the Recipient   A fairly Passive Letter and Nice to be With

End of U Intro

Ugly: Hug   He   Lay
Uh uh: U/H
You/U/Ovulating   is in front of   H/Secret Code Letter
A Big No from   The Code   Especially When Repeated (As in Plural or All of Them)
Uh uh: interjection   used to indicate disagreement disapproval or dissatisfaction

Ultimate: L/T/Mate
L/Sweet Fem Love Light/Ill/Hail/Ail/Hell/Elle   T/Fem Cross/Great Curse   Mat/Mate
The Ultimate Goal for   The Code   is To Mate with All Cursed Fem   Mat or Not
ultimate: final point

Ultimatum: See ultimate Above
Mate with All Cursed Fem Until they Are All M/Mothers

ultimatum: a final proposal   basic   fundamental

Unable: On/A/Bull
On/N/In/Hen/Virgin   A/All Men   Bull
The Bull Represents Venus The Goddess of Fertility in Nature Prosperity and Harmony   She is Also Represented in the Taurus Sign
Bull/Shit   Bull/She/It   says   The Code

Unavailable: On/A/Veil/Able
On/Available   Available/On
Avail   A/Veil
avail: to be of use or value to   profit   advantage
Therefore   The Code   says a Veil is a Great thing for The Fems   and   it is Available
Very Little is Available for Her in That Code   Unless Sex or abuse is Involved
See Prevail in The Words Chapter for More of the Same

Unbreakable: On/Break/Able
N/In/Hen/In/One/Virgin   Break   Able
The Code   says it/He is Able to Break a Virgin
A Contradiction from the Dictionary Meaning to   The Code   Sound Meaning

Unconscious: On/Cunt/She/Us
On/N/In/Hen/Virgin   Cunt   She/Shh   S/Is/His/Us/Penis
On/Con/She/Us   Same as Above
Con and Cunt have the Same Meaning   They are Slang for Vagina
The Code   Cannot Allow The Fems to be Conscious When it Comes to Know What She is About in   That Dam Code   So Unconscious is Her being   Ignorant about it All
Note That the Word Conscious has the Word Con in it
Conscious   Con/She/Us   She never Get Out of That Maze

Under: NDR   3 Fem Sound Letters
U/Open Fem Hole   N/In/Hen/Ann/Haine/Virgin   D/Pregnant   E/He   R/Her/Hair/Are/Here/Hear/Ear/Heir/Whore/Or/Err/Sex
N as R/Her/Sex is now Pregnant

The Dam Code The Damn Book

Therefore Under Says   The Code
In front of Quiet E/He   and   R/Her/Heir/Whore/Or/Err/Sex
Stay Under Him   with Sex is a Big No Says   The Code   So
Understood   Under/Stood   and She Stands Under as Usual in   The Code

Underdog: Under/Dog
Another Way to Bring Her Down is to Make Her a Loser/Victim
The Underdog is that Bitch   Son of a Bitch
Here Goes The Fems being Compared to an Animal
underdog: a person who is expected to lose in a contest or conflict

Understanding: Same as Understood But in The Present Tense
Here She is a Thing/Ding Too
ding: to cause surface damage   to strike with force   to black mail   to ring or cause to ring esp with tedious repetition   an imitation or representation of the sound of the bell
For The Fems to Understand what She will Have already Understood
She will be Convinced Early in Age by   That Code   by being Dinged or Hit with Force or Blackmailed (which Happens Often)   or   She will be Ring in Marriage   Ring That Bell/Belle
Think about Her Being that Bull (Venus In Taurus) being Enslaved by That Ring in the Nose

Understood: N/On/In/Hen/Ann/Haine/Virgin   D/Pregnant   R/Her/Are/Heir/Or/Whore/Err/Sex   Stood
She as Virgin Stands Pregnant With Heir   or   being a Whore   or to Err says   The Code   Understood
NDR/Under   Stood

Unified: U/You/Ovulating   Nay   Fed
nay: a denial or refusal
neigh: to utter the cry of a horse   whinny   the high pitched of a Horse   *Synonym*   Yell
What   The Code   Tells The Fems is That She is a Horse (Whores/Heirs) and She is Whining as She is Screaming from Pain
Back to the Animals for Her as Usual   and   it is Always Accompanied with Pain for Her

Lise Rochon

Uninvited: NNVTD All 5 Fem Sound Letters
Letter N as On and In are Both Virgins (as Ann and Hen)   V/Fem Sex Active   T/Fem Cross/Great Curse   D/Pregnant
No Fems Are Ever Invited to Anything says   The Code
It has to be Understood in a Time Manner   What is Now was Not there for Thousands of Years

Union: You/U/Ovulating   Neigh/Nay   Eon/On
The Fem as Open Uterus is Totally Rejected   No Union here for Her says   The Code   For an Eon

Unique: U/N/IC   All Fem Letters except for i/Marriage Act
You/U/Ovulating   N/In/Hen/Ann/Virgin   IC/Integrated Circuit
When a Virgin is Ovulating   It can Happen Only One Time in Life says   The Code
A Girl is a Virgin   and   is Not Anymore   It is an Integrated Circuit   She has to Have Sex After That

United: You/Knight/ID   U/Night/Knight   D/Pregnant
U/You/Ovulating   The Knight (Keeps Her in the Night/Dark)   ID/Unconscious Quest for Pleasure
The Code   is United in Keeping The Fems Ovulating   and/or   Pregnant

Universal: Uni/Verse/All
One Story for All Fems
U/You/Ovulating   Nay/Neigh   Verse   All/L/Sweet Fem Love Light/Ill/Hail/Ail/Hell/Elle
There is No Possibility for The Fems to Learn   That Code
See Verse in the Words Chapter

Universe: Uni/Verse   The One Verse
And that One Verse Said   "At the Beginning Was the Word and the Word was with God and The Word was God"
That is   The Code   telling You About   That Code   Sorry About All the Fervent Believers Searching for That God
The Language Code has been Manipulating Us   Since the Beginning of Those Religions   Since The Beginning of Time (Time of The Month it is) which Started after The Golden Age

The Dam Code The Damn Book

University: Uni/Verse/Cite/He   One/Verse/City
The Code   Cites There is Only One Verse ("In The beginning was the Word and The Word Was with God and The Word was God")
The Whole City Knows it   The Whole Universe Knows it says   The Code Jesus Had Broken   That Code   Jesus was Also Called The Word
How Can a Religion Forbids to have Knowledge   That Tree of Knowledge that had Adam and Eve Expulsed Out of That Good Life they had   and   to Be Cursed to Misery   That Knowledge was that Men had Awakened to a Way (by Forcing Her) to have Sex with The Fems Outside of Her Ovulation Time   Different Than the All Other Mammals   She Started to Bleed and be Cursed by Very Frightened Men
The Way We Find Out About Truths and be Able to Resolve Mysteries and Grow Out of Them is True Knowledge
That God Says to stay Away from Knowledge   If We Forbid Ourselves to All knowledge   We would Still Live in Trees
It is That Loss of Blood That Created that Generation Gap that is Still going on Today
And The Fems Are Losing More Blood   Her Cycles (?) are Longer and the Starting Time is Earlier (11 Years Old Compared to 16 year Old a Hundred Years Ago
Menstrual Cycle (Men/Through/All))

Unsuitable: On/Suit/Able
Contrary Meaning Again here   Many Words Starting With Un (One) are Opposite Meaning in   That Code   Its Meaning would have been Too Evident for Her with   U/You/Ovulating   and   N/In/Hen/Haine/Virgin/Ann   in Front of those Words   The Fems would Have Figured Out a Long Time Ago How it Works   The Placement of Letters is Very Important and Evident When You Start to Figure   That Code

Until: Hunt   L/Sweet Fem Love Light/Ill/Hail/Ail/Hell/Elle/All/Ill/Ail/Hail/Hell/Elle
Elle is She in French   Languages Overlaps in   That Code   It Enhances its Cover/Secrecy
The Grid or H/Code is International
One/T/Ill
N/ON/In/Hen/Virgin/Virgin   is   T/Fem Cross   L
Hunt Her   All Fem Cross   Until   She is Ill

Lise Rochon

Hunt L   Hunt All of Them
Hunt Her (N/On/In/Hen/Virgin) Because She is Ill and Weak from Being T/
Fem Cross/Great Curse
Haunt/Ill   She is Hunted as a Ghost
Aunt/Tell   Mothers in Law and Sisters in Law Receives the
Same Bitch Treatment from   That Code   Being Called Big
Mouth   Nosy   Ugly   Old   Etc   Being Hunted in Those Ways Too
One/Till
One Tills   She Works   While the Others are Being Hunted
Until Can Go On for Ever
Until is a Cover Word Here

Untrue: On/Through
One/Through
The # One/The Stick/The I/The God Eye   is The Man/God Number
(Numb/Her   See The Sign (#) for Numbers is in The Shape of a Grid as is
the H/Letter Code (See The Numbers Chapter)

Up: You/U/Ovulating   P/Power Man
You/U/Ovulating   goes with   P/Man Power
Something Goes Up (Go/S/Hop   Goes/Shop)
Add Another O/Fem Hole to Hop (Creating Bigamy) and She Gets a
hoop: a large ring of iron
The Whole (Hole) Code is a Large Ring (See Ring) of Iron (I/Run) Men
Hop/Ann   Having Sex   Up/Hop   and   N/In/Hen/Virgin
Hop/In   Hop/N/In/Hen/Virgin
Up Yours (U/You/Ovulating   and   R/Her/Sex

Upheaval: Up/Eve/All
It Could have Been a Beautiful Concept to Put All Fems Up
But No that does Not Exist for Her in   The Code
upheaval: disruption   disorder   turmoil
Up/Evil
The Code   Says The Fem is Up Because She is Evil
Evil is   Eve that is Ill
Hop/He/Val
When He/His   Up/Hop/Hope   is Down in the Valley
There is an Upheaval   Then

The Dam Code The Damn Book

Up/He/Veil   Back to The Veil for Her

Upset: Hop/Set   Up/Set   Hope/Sat   Hop/Sit
When The Hop/Up or the Hope for the Hop is Sitting   (Sitting is a Nebulous Term for Her Period   In The Past She had to Sit for Days while Bleeding)

Urge: RG
R/Her/Are/Heir/Whore/Or/Err/Sex   G/Penis Penetration
An Impossibility Here says   The Code   Her and the Hymen Penetration so Close to Her Consciousness with Her in Front   so   it is a Fast One   as   in Urgent   No Time to Think

Urgent: Her/G/Hunt
Urgent is   When G/Penis Penetration   Hunts Her to Have Sex with   Her/Sex   as Always in   The Code

Urinal: You/Reine/All
U/You   is Ovulating She is Queen and All   But She is also a Urinal   You Can Pee on Her
You/R/N/All
All   U/You/Ovulating and N/Virgins as Reine/Queen   Go In The Urinal No Power from   The Code   in Any Way to The Fems

Urine: URN   (See Urn in The Words Chapter)
U/You/Ovulating/Ov   R/Are/Her/Hair/Are/Here/Hear/Ear/Heir/Whore/Or/Err/Sex   In/N/Hen/Virgin
U/You is N/In/Hen/Ann/Haine/Virgin
The Code   Makes Him Pee on That
And the Word Urn Popped

Urn: URN   U/Earn
U/You/Ovulating   R/Her/Are/Heir/Whore/Or/Err/Sex   N/In/Hen/Ann/Haine/Virgin
N/Virgin is a Receptacle for Sex as a Whore or for Heirs or to Err (See Urn and Chalice in The Words Chapter)
An Urn is in a Fem Shape as would Desire   The Code   for Her   A Small Hollow Head With a Large Belly (Belle/He) and Large Buttocks

Lise Rochon

An Urn in Antique Greece Was the Receptacle for Food Wine Grains Ashes Etc
Add T/Fem Cross and She Gets Turn
Turn that Urn   the Clay Needs to be Turned to Make an Urn
The Code   says Make Her Dizzy (Daisy   Days/He)
Add B/Boy Holding All Fem Breasts and He Gets Burn (Too Young for The Code)
Add W/All Fems Sex Active and She Gets Worn (All Fem Letters)

US: Phonetically   S is The Most Important Letter in US   The United States of America   as in us (You and Me)
S/Is/His/Us/Ass/Hiss/Serpent/Penis   Rules
He/Is is The Bald US Eagle   No Fem Want to be Bald so
Eagle is Close to The Unfitting Fifth Angle of the Mystery of the Free Masons   The Angle   The Eagle is close by
U/You/Ovulating   S/Is/His/Penis/Serpent
A Perfect Copulating Couple   to Have Her   D/Pregnant   is   The Code   Goal   Making Her Used (USD   ?)
U and C Makes You/See   Letter C has the Same Sound as S in this Case   A Big No From   The Code   so it is US as in Them   The Men

Use: U/See   You/S   You/Z
A Dangerous Word here
If C/See/Young Girl Would See   The Code   That would be a Big No From   The Code   so   U/You/Ovulating   and   Z/Sleep on it
Used: Use/D
D/Pregnant is a Used Object   She is Already from the Past   Sleeping on it   U/Z/D   Usd
When You See D/Pregnant Daughter You See Used

Uterus: You/Tear/Us
U/You/Ovulating   T/Fem Cross/Great Curse   R/Her/Hair/Are/Here/Hear/Ear/Heir/Whore/Or/Err/Sex   /S/Is/His/Ass/Us/Hiss/Serpent/Penis   S Also Implies Plural
Tearing Brings Tears   Losing Her Precious Inner Water (Tears) Along With Losing Her Precious Blood   making her Weaker Every Time
That is The Fems Definition of Uterus says   The Code

The Dam Code The Damn Book

Utter: Hot   R/Her/Are/Heir/Or/Whore/Err/Sex
Then Out/Her
utter: to give audible expression to   speak or pronounce
Utterly   Hot/Her/Lay

V v
Intro
V is a Masc Made Fem Letter   V is the Sex Active Fem Letter
V is   The Secret Code   Plan in Action Since Her Childhood   It is the
Second Degree of Forcing Her into the Great Curse After Her   I/L Fem
Power Stick is Wounded in Y/Wounded Fem   Her Stick is Being Split in Y
Then More Split in V/Sex Active Fem   Then is One Side Down in L/Love
Light/Ill/Hail/Ail/Hell/Elle   The Split Happens Here
K/Fem Wounded Warrior is Next   Her Stick is in 2 Pieces and Re/
Attached to the Man Erected Stick   She then Will Be a T/Fem Cross/Great
Curse   After She has Sex in   R/Her/Heir/Or/Whore   She is Given that
Cross to Bear as a Curse
In V She is at the Stage of V/Fem Sex Active   The V would be the Artificial
Ovulation Letter
OV/Egg with Letter O or the Of common Prefix   There is No Fem Curve
in   V/Eve/Ov   at All   V Is Not O or U or C
Letter V is a Man Made Code Letter to Create a V/Fem Sex Active at Any
Time (Not Only Ovulation Time as Nature Calls it and is now Lost Now for
about 2000 Years Since Adam (A/Damn) and Eve (Ov/Egg) Where E/He
is with V as in Eve   The Fem is Never Left Alone   It Does Not Change
from Child to Adult in the Alphabet/Code   v is V   All Fem must be
Opened   In that Angle
V is Number 5 in Roman Letters (See 5 in The Numbers Chapter)
Then it is W the 2 VVs/All Fems Sex Active
V in Plural Letter W is Called in English a Double U   Which it is Not   It is
a Double VV (W) Not a double U   The Code   System in Action Here
Subtle to Cover up "Le Double VV" as they Call it in French
V Is almost the Same as Letter U But Not the Same
The Perforated O in U is as a Nest
Calling it a Double U is No Coincidence
The Secret Code   is Conveying Her Circles OU (óu Means Where in
French) With the Concept of being Letter V/Fem Sex Active Part of Her
Life Instead of being Letter U   Which is Not the Same

713

V is as the W N and M   The Up Down Up Down   Never a Rest for Her
WVAV have the Same External Shape of the Tent   In Reversed Also   As
it is Shaking It (Shagging It   Name for Sex Act) All the Time Up Down
Except A has 2 feet on the ground and has The Tie in The Middle to
Strengthen it and Unite All Men in it
V is the Check You Check When You Agree on Paper to Something as in
Check that Box
Therefore V/Sex Active Fem is a Positive Thing says   The Code   It is a
Cover Symbol/Concept Too Because of That
Letter V is also the Check Mark as in Accepted/Checked
Then the Good News Again   The Check is in the Mail
The V (the Check) is in the Male   That is   The Code   in Action All
Concepts   For Something Real Ugly   The Plus Sign + as the t/Cross
Symbol is Another
She Dies in X/Fallen Cross or The Fallen tT

V v
Vacuum: V/Fem Sex Active   Hack   M/Motherhood
hack: to cut lice chop or sever (something) with or as with heavy irregular
blows   often followed by up or down   to damage or injure by crude
harsh or insensitive treatment   to reduce or cut ruthlessly trim
The Code is Always Making Fem Enemies of Each Other
Divide to Conquer   Even to Hack a Mother

Vagina: V/Fem Sex Active   Age/Egg   Anna
The Code   No matter The Age   Never Stops to Make Her a Sex Object
Many Fem Names Represent Diverse Aspects of That
Concept   Vivian   Venereal etc   Sorry

Valuable: Val   U/You/Ovulating   Able   Valley/He/Able
Being in a Valley is Good for Her says   The Code   Such as a Valley of
Tears   A Valley Can be a Dangerous Place to be for a Fem
Value: V/All/U
V/Fem Sex Active   All/Ill/Hell/Ail/Elle/Letter L   U/You/Ovulating
Val/You   The Valley is Her Value   which Another False Concept for Her
to Fall In

Vase: V/Fem Sex Active   Ace

The Dam Code The Damn Book

She is an Ace When She Has Sex   Or   When V is With S/Penis   In Plural   She/They Is/Are Receptacles
The Vase is the Symbol (Sin/Bowl) for The Fems Sex Organs since Antiquity   She is the Chalice for the Wine (Her Symbolic Blood in The Code)
Mud (3 Fem Letters) is Vase in French   Mud a Good Place to Hide for   The Code

Vatican: The Symbol of the Vatican Building is a Gold Circle with a Cross on Top
The Circle is an Entirely Fem Symbol   It is Topped with The Fems Cross/Great Curse Symbol

Vault: VLT   3 Fem Sound Letters
V/Fem Sex Active   O/Fem Hole   T/Fem Cross/Great Curse
The Conceptual Relationship of these 3 Fems is Too Close for The Code   So
V/Halt
Stop that Fem   or   She Gets a Volt says   The Code
volt: electrical current of one watt
Revolting   That Code   Even Worst   All the Way to Death
vault: an arched structure   a burial chamber (See Arch in The Words Chapter) There   The Code   is Safe and Well Hidden
Switch V for F/Fem/Fuck and it is Her Fault (Close to FLT   All Fem Letters)
Switch V for C/Young Fem and It Becomes a Cult   A Scary Word for Most   Occult (All Fem Letters)

Vaunt: VNT   3 Fem Letters
vaunt: to brag
Brag About the Rag   Every Fem Knows That Insult

Veil: VL   2 Fem Sounds Letters
V/Fem Sex Active   Is With   L/Sweet Fem Love Light/Ill/Hail/Ail/Hell/Elle
Veil is a Very Bad Word for The Fems   So is Prevail (Pre/Veil)
prevail: to be widespread or current   to succeed to become dominant   to prove superior in strength and power
The Fems are Always a Step Away from that Veil

715

pre: prefix with the meanings "prior to"   "in advance of"   "early"   "forehanded"   "before"
Prevail (Pre/Veil)   She is in the Waiting to Wear that Veil   says   That Code   It is Always There   It Prevails
V   with   L   is Going to Hell/Elle/Ill/L   Wearing that Veil of Secrecy
V/Fem Sex Active   E/He   i/Marriage Act   L/Ill/Hell/Elle
The Modern Fem is Made Friendly with that Veil with as Example the Catholic Wedding Tradition of the Man/Husband Removing that Imaginary White Veil (Which as an Occult Ceremony) from Her Head (Which in fact is Black in The Eastern Countries and Covers Her from Head to Toe Every Day When she to Go Out and   Only if She Goes Out Accompanied by Another Man
In Occident She Gets that Ring instead   Ring That Belle (Ring that Bell) (See Ring in The Words Chapter)
The Father/Man Gives That Fem/Daughter to That Man/Husband (Us/Band) with that Ring
Remember the White Veil of The Girl First Communion (Communion with Another Man as in Jesus here)   and   The Confirmation (of it) a Little Later Which That Confirms The Veil and The Ring) in Our Tender Age of 7 Years Old
She has Never Belong to Herself   In Freedom   Until Now
Change Letters Around of Veil and She Gets Evil (See Evil in the Words Chapter   Eve/Ill   Eve That is ill)   Take Away i/Marriage Act   and   She Find Herself in a Val
Move Around E and He Gets Vile   She Never Gets Out of That Veil
VL   V/Fem Sex Active   is   L/Ill/Hell/Ail/Elle
Add D/Pregnant and She Gets Devil (The Veil)
The Tearing of the Temple Veil after Christ Died   The Lifting of the Veil of Ignorance
Switch L/Ill/Hell/Elle for N/In/Hen/Ann/Virgin and   She Gets Vein/Venus/Vein/Us   The Loss of Her Blood
There were Fem Blood Sacrifices in the Temples of Venus in Our Darkest Human Times
Humans are Going for the Blood   Wars Wars Wars
That Unconscious Hypnotic Claim/Quest   All This Because of The Madness Brought by the Immense Loss of The Fems Blood
Switch V for F/Fem/Fuck and She Gets to Fail (F/Ail)

The Dam Code The Damn Book

Switch V/Fem Sex Active for W/All Fems Sex Active and She Gets to Wail (W/All Fems Sex Active   Letter L/Ail/Ill/Hell/Elle)
wail: a prolonged inarticulate mournful cry as in grief or suffering
V and W are Interchangeable in   The Code   V is a Singular Fem Sex Active and W is All Fems Sex Active   The Code   Calls it a Double U When in Fact it is a Double V   as it is in French   The U is the Normal Ovulation Time   The V is the All The Time Sex Active Fem
Another Example   The Code   Erasing its Tracts   The Natural Ovulation (U) being annihilated (By a Double V) for such a Long time it is all Forgotten Now
W/All   All W/All Fems Sex Active

Vein: VN   2 Fem Sound Letters
V/Fem Sex Active   is with   N/In/Hen/Ann/Virgin
Vin   Vine   V/In   (Wine   Vino)
Vigne in French is the Grape Vine Itself
Grapes (G/Penis Penetration   Rapes) Grow to Make Wine   Wine Represents Her Lost Blood
Veins Carry Blood
The Goddess Venus   Vein/Us   Vain/Us
She is Then Called Vain   Vain is the Cover Word Here as it Presents Her Loss of Blood as Vain

Venereal: Vein   In   Real
Vein   He/E   Real/Rule/Rill/Reel/Rile etc On a Rail
Vein RL
Her/R/Ear/Hear/Hair/Err/Heir/Or/Whore/Here/Are/Our/Ere/Air/Ire/Sex is with   L/Sweet Fem Love Light/Elle/All/Ail/Ill/Hail/Heel/Hell/Oil
venereal: arising from connected with or transmitted through sexual intercourse as an infection   pertaining to conditions so arising   infected with or suffering from a sexually transmitted disease   adapted to the cure of such a disease   of or pertaining to sexual desire or   intercourse   serving or tending to excite sexual desire aphrodisiac   From Free Dictionary.com   In order here the First Four Definitions of Venereal are Pertaining it as a disease
In 5 it is Pertaining to Intercourse   In 6 it is to serve or tend to excite Venereal is a Big Word for   The Code   It is The Sang/Real in the Holy Grail Story Not Royal Blood but Real Blood

Grail   Grill that Girl
G/Vaginal Penetration   L/All/Ill/Ail/Hell/Elle
Vain/He/Real
That Damning Damaged   Code   Speaks and Encourages Vain Behaviors   So Humans will Stay Weak   in   L/Hell/Ill/All   Keeping Humanity Manipulated/Exploited as Little Marionettes They Try Us to Be

Venus: Venus   Vein/Us
Venus: an ancient goddess of gardens and spring identified by Romans with Aphrodite as the Goddess of love and beauty   an exceptionally beautiful woman
Venus is the Closest Planet to the Sun and the Most Brilliant Planet in the Solar System
How Can Beauty of Nature and Plenty Be Called a Disease in the First 4 Definitions   And Being Reduced to Sexual Love as a Servant
We Lost Our Ways to a Perfect World (The Search for Happiness is in The American Constitution)
Venus in Chemistry is Copper (Cup/Her)   (See Cup in The Words Chapter Reduced as in a Breast Size for Her)
The Cops (Punt Intended) are Watching with Their Blue Lights (another Unconscious Fear for Her)
The Painter Botticelli Painted The Birth of Venus
Who is a Fem Favorite for Many Fems   Venus (Vein/Us) is Under Duress by that God   A Black Wings Red Face Man is Blowing Stormy Winds at Her From the Left   A Fem with Blood Red Hair and a Black Cover is Holding Him Legs Opened on His Left Side
Innocent Venus/Virgin is in The Process of Being Covered with the Red Blood Color Blanket with Small Black Stars on it (See Asterisk in The Keyboard Chapter) by a Pregnant Fem that Also has Red Blood Hair That Touches That Red Blanket and The Loins of Venus   The Black Shore (She/Whore) Area is Made of Sharp Points Pointing Towards Venus Body   This Painting is the Story of the Cursed Fem in a Very Artistic Way
Venus was Born of the Sea Says The Legend (See Sea In the Words Chapter) The Sea (See/Holy See) It Keeps The Fems as Fishes Which are Ruled by Neptune Stick (On Sea)   or   That Sheppard Stick (on Earth) That Keeps The Fems in The Sheep (She/P) or The Fish Consciousness)
Vain/Us   V/Fem Sex Active   In/Ann/N/Donkey   S/Us

Planet Venus Rotates Around the Sun/Son (just as a Satellite as The Moon is (Another All Fem Planet Plan/Hit)
The Code   says it is All So Small No Need to Look at it
venial: excusable   trifling   minor   excusable
Venial   Vein   He/E   All   The Fems are being Under the Rule of a Vampire   Code

Vermin: VRMN   4 Fems Sound Letters
V/Fem Sex Active   M/Motherhood/Him   N/In/Hen/Ann/Haine/Virgin
Are Surrounding Her/R/Ear/Hear/Hair/Err/Heir/Or/Whore/Here/Are/Our/Ere/Air/Ire/Sex
That would be Too Much Power   or   Knowledge to The Fems   A Big No from The Code   so
vermin: noxious objectionable or disgusting animals collectively especially those of small size that appear commonly and are difficult to control as flies lice bedbugs cockroaches mice and rats   an objectionable or obnoxious person or such persons collectively
Here She goes again down the Drain

Verse: V/Fem Sex Active   Her/R/Ear/Hear/Hair/Err/Heir/Or/Whore/Here/Are/Our/Ere/Air/Ire/Sex
S/His/Is/Ass/Us/Hiss/Serpent/Penis   or   S (as in Plural or All of Them)
That Verse/Word Says   The Code   is a Fem That has Lost Her Ovulation Cycle and is a Whore With Heir or Not From That   Since Eve   That is Why She is in a Hearse (Her/S   A Tomb/Cerceuil) being Crossed (T) and Gone (X)
V/Hearse
hearse: funeral vehicle
Re/Hearse That
Re/Verse That   Re is in Fact a Prefix that Means Again or Repetition   So We Cannot Reverse a Verse says   That Code   We can Only Rehearse it
Verse is a Very Important Word Because of its Connection To "In the Beginning was the Word and the Word was with God and the Word was God" John1 1
Which is The Most Important Verse/Connection to That God from That Bible   It Relates   The Code   Language with the Language of That God as being One   Then Use That Premise in a Symbiotic Relationship with The Ultimate Power of Our Universe

719

That Code   is Almost Infinite in its Configuration   For Example   Uni/
Verse   Universe
The Code   says   That Only Verse Uni/Verse is as Big as The Universe
uni: consisting of   relating to   or having only
one   unilateral   unisexual
It is for All Sexes Too   Which is a Rare Statement from The Code   Which
Always Separate The Sexes   and   Only Men can be The Representation
of That God/Code
Looking at the Stars and Planets at Night is One of the Few Things
That can Make Us Relate Directly to the Immensity of The Cosmos/
Universe   There is No Sex or Sex Differentiation Up There It is Just a Pure
Immense Grand Endless Silence of Light and Darkness
University (Un/On/One   Verse   City (Cite/He)
Since the Secret Hides in The Words   That Bible has Many Codes and
Dimensions   The Dam Code is Just Another One
The Bible says   A Man Stick to Another   Stick is Slang for a Penis
I am Often Humbled by The Many Dimensions of That Book   Sorry for
Having to being Disrespectful to it
Again I Just Relates My Found Facts

Version: Virgin
V/R/G/N
V/Fem Sex Active   Her/R/Ear/Hear/Hair/Err/Heir/Or/Whore/Here/Are/
Our/Ere/Air/Ire/Sex   G/Penis Penetration   N/In/Haine/Ann/Donkey
Verge/In   A Verge is a Penis in French and a 36 Inches Yard   Dream On
Man   It is Never Big Enough for Some
The Larger the Penis the Larger The Fems Needs to be Inside to Fit
Comfortably with It
Verse   He   On
V/Fem Sex Active   R/Her/Ere/Air/Hair/Are/Here/Hear/Ear/Heir/Whore/Or/
Err/Sex   S/Is/His/Us/Ass/Hiss/Serpent/Penis   Eon/On/N/Own/Hen/Virgin
It Says   Virgins/Version   On for an Eon
The Virgins will be Treated as Whores or   for Heirs by Every Penis
Virgin has 2 iis/Sex Acts (In Plural or All of Them)   in its Meaning with 2
Dots on Top   Also Meaning Bigamy from Childhood
The Verse   is on   for an E/On (See Ann in The Names
Chapter   and Letter N/Ann in The Letter Chapter)   (I have to Apologize
for The Names Chapter)

The Dam Code The Damn Book

"In the beginning was the Word and the Word was with God and the Word was God"
These Hunting 3 Phrases Puzzles The Believers for a Long Time
They should have Written   First   The Name of God in Adoration   Then God Saying
"I am Talking to You Directly Humans With My God Voice Which has Created The Language/Words   Therefore Because I Am God   I Contain the Words/Language That I Want You to Use to be With Me"
If Any of That is Real   Those are Strong Premises
But No
The Traditional Code/Bible Says   That God Started With Words/Language (First Sentence) and as He God Was Being Brought Into The Words/Language (Second Sentence) Then God Was being Assimilated in The Words/Language Code   The Code   Became The Ultimate Cosmic/Universe Deity   God (Third Sentence)
The Universe: The Uni/Verse
There is Only One Verse says   The Code   Read Above The Quotation of John 1.1
All The Way to The Milky Way (Breasts For Ever (Eve/Her) Trillions of Milking Breasts says   The Code
The Code   Creates Breasts on Her All the Way to the Macrocosm   Breast as in B/Boy Holding All Fem Breasts   Rest   The Breast is Where He Rest (R/Est   Est is The East   Where Those Eastern Religions were Born)   R/Are/Her/Sex is with His Rest
D/Pregnant   You/U/Ovulating   N/In/Hen/Ann/Virgin/Donkey   Verse
The Milky Way could Also Look as One Full On Milking Breast   or   No Breasts at All There   Dots of Light
The Tenacity of   The Code   about Breasts is Immense
With All its Planets (Plan   It/Hit in Plural) Content (Con in Tent)   and Many Good Honest Occult Sciences   Such as Tarot and Astrology
That have Tried to Elucidate Those Mysteries as in The Triangle   The Pyramid   That Code   is Always Repeating Itself   Most People Being Unaware for What We are Carrying   for Little Results
Thanks to Modernization People Can Communicate more Freely their Own Truth on the Internet and Get Informed and Stay Connected   A Great Blessing to Humanity it is

Versus: Verse   S/Is/His/Ass/Us/Hiss/Serpent/Penis

Lise Rochon

Verse   Is/Us
versus: as compared to or as one of the two choices   in contrast with
The Code   Verse Word is on Both Sides of The Verse Meanings

Verve: VR   R/Her/Ere/Air/Hair/Are/Here/Hear/Ear/Heir/Whore/Or/Err/
Sex   Is in Between   2 VVs/V/Fem Sex Active   and   2 EE/s/He (Plural or
All of Them)   That is a Lot of people
All Fems as Sex Active as Whores or for Heirs Serve Sex to All Men with
Verve   says   The Sect/Code
verve: enthusiasm or vigor   spirit
Switch R/Her for L/Fem Light and She Gets a Vulve
Switch V   for   S/Is/His/Us/Ass/Hiss/Serpent/Penis and He Gets Served

Very: VRE   V/Ray   V/Hairy   V/Airy
very: to emphasize identity
It Varies According to Definitions
Switch V for F/Fem Fuck and She Gets a Fairy   That is Her Identity here as
a Fem   Fairies are Very Small Frail Beings with Little Power

Vessel: VSL   V/Fem Sex Active   S/Is/As/Has/Ass/His/Us/Hiss/Serpent/
Penis   L/Sweet Fem Love Light/Elle/All/Ail/Ill/Hail/Heel/Hell/Oil   A Vessel
is Also Pregnancy   or   Loins
V   S/Is/Penis   Hell
S in Between V and L (2 Fem Letters)
Anything Water is Fem says   The Code

Vet: VT   2 Fem Sound Letters with a Silent E/He in the Middle
V/Fem Sex Active   in Front of He/E   Ending With   T/Fem Cross
A Big No says   The Code   Too Much Information for Her the V Being the
Word Letter Starter so
vet: to appraise verify or check for accuracy authenticity validity etc
Vet   Wars Veterans is a Cover Word here
It Implies Fighting and Being Hurt   So It does Not Entice People to
Vet   Vetted   VTD 3 Fem Letters Ending in Pregnancy here

Vex: VX
2 Fem Sound Letters that Are Not Often Together

The Dam Code The Damn Book

V/Fem Sex Active Eve   and   X/Fallen Fem Cross   With a Silent   E/
He   The Code is Always There even Silent
They are Not Allowed Together says   The Code
V is Rarely with X in a Word   They are Neighbors Letters   UVWXYZ
W is The Plural or V   It is Unusual in   The Codes   to Creates Fem
Connections The Fems were being Kept Away from Each Other   And
There is More of it   When those 2 Fems Meet   They Fight   That is Why
The Code Puts Them Together Here
vex: to irritate   to annoy   to provoke
So Close to Vortex

Vial: a small container for holding liquids from old French fiol
Viola is Fem Name From Old Provencal French
A Chalice is a Vial
We Agree   No One Love the Vile
We Hunt the Vile   It Is Violent   It Deconstructs
Somehow   The Code   Assembles Certain Words that Leave Behind
Traces Such as   Love   Vile (Evil Letters Scrambled) Live (Evil Letters in
Reverse   sand   Close to Love)   Vial   Viol (Rape)   Life   Fiol   Viola
Musical Instruments   Fuel   Fille (Girl)
Violate   Violable   Violation   Etc
That Vial Named for a Small Container for Holding Liquids could have been
The Receptacle from The Fems Blood Loss
Vial is a Minor Word that is Surprising   It Connects and Reacts Strongly
with Profound Life Words
Switch i/Marriage Act for O/Fem Hole and She Gets Viol (Rape in
French)   Vowels   From V She is Transformed into W)   Ville means City
in French
Vial   Another Soft Sounding   Code   Word that Betrays Her
V being the Head Letter of Vial   The Code   says No to Her To Know
More About Vial   (See Below) Vile it Is
Life is Given with Love From the Universe
When it Is Created it is All to Do and to Learn
There Can be Nothing Wrong with the Words Live or Life or Love
Live in Reverse Cannot Be Evil   and   God Cannot be a Dog in Reverse
We do Not Worship Animals   It is Just Not Magical and Good Enough for
The Humans

Lise Rochon

That Code   says The Fem is Not Supposed to Deserve Any Respect or have Any Power   Being Kept Away from those Alienating Word Games   Where All Fems Go Down

Vice: V/Ice
Eve is Frigid   It is a Vice says   The Code   That is a Cold Place to Be for The Fem
Switch V/Fem Active for N/In/Hen/Ann/Virgin/Donkey and She Gets Nice (Play Too Nice and Lose The Game)
Switch V for M/Motherhood and She Gets Mice (Another Extra Small World for The Fems)
Switch V for D/Pregnant and She Gets a Dice (Not Secure Either)
Switch V for R/Are/Her/Heir/Or/Whore and She Gets Rice(Not Much Food Very basic Only)
Vice as Vice President (Always Second and Carrying The Load to be The Vice)

Vicinity: VCNT   All 4 Fem Sound Letters
V/Fem Sex Active   See/C/Young Girl   Knit   T/Fem Cross
With 3 iii/s/Sex Act/Marriage   Therefore Having 3 Dots above The Word   It is a Close Vicinity for lots of Sex Action
V/Sin/He/T   She is Sin to Him Because of The Great Curse/Fem Cross

Vicious: V/She/Us
V/Fem Sex Active   She/Shh   S/Is/His/Us/Ass/Hiss/Serpent/Penis
Penis is Abusive/Vicious to The Fems and Shh about it
Vice/He/Us (See Vicious)

Victim: Vic/M   M/Motherhood/Him
vic: to look for someone to rob mug etc   to steal   to cheat
V/IC/T/Him
Eve is the Victim because as a Weak Cursed Fem She is Attracted Unconsciously to His Strength for Protection
Evict/Him
Switch M for R/Her/Ear/Hear/Hair/Err/Heir/Or/Whore/Here/Are/Our/Ere/Air/Ire/Sex   and She Gets Victor

View: VU   2 Fem Sound Letters

V/Fem Sex Active   U/You/Ovulating
V and U are Almost Identical   V is an Open Sex Calendar Imposed to Her by   The Code   U is Her Natural Ovulation Time   Coming from Nature   That may Take a While (if) to Come Back into that View and Find a Fem Solution
View   V/All The Time Fem Sex Active   U/Natural Ovulation Time
View here is the Transformation of U into V as in to Blend Both Naturally   That is   The Code   Hypnotic Way to Convince People Unconsciously
Always Men have had   Men Only Club   In One Form or Another   Turkish Bath   Golf Clubs   Poker Games   Sports Games   Etc
Switch V/Fem Sex Active for F/Fem/Fuck and She Gets Few (Very Little as Usual for The Fems   F U is   FU   The F/Fem/Fuck You Abbreviation (See Letter F in The Letter Chapter)
Letter F in   The Code   had No Connection with Sex   or   Sexual Body Parts Involved in   The Curse   F Has the Simple Definition of a Normal Fem (as in Feminine)
It is Only Lately that That F Has been Affiliated with Another Letter The U as in Fuck You
Other Letters R/Her/Whore/Heir/Sex   or   K/Broken Fem Warrior   or   D/Pregnant   or   V/Fem Sex Active Fem   or   W/All Fems Sex Active   are All Affiliated with Sex
Although its F Shape Indicates That She is a Construction of   The Code   (See Letter F in The Letter Chapter)
F in Large Caps is a Part of   The Code   Grid Construction H I T L Are Others Pillars   The Code   Grid is in the Shape of a Screen   Imagine a Screen Door But Huge   We are All in It
The Letter f in Small Caps is in Training to be a T/Fem/Cross   The Top Hook is its Connection to   The Code   and t is The Bottom Hook
You Need to See The Very Little to Understand a Code
F is a Tilting Letter   It is Not Stable   it Falls if Not Connected to Another   E/He is Stable and Independent to Stand by Itself   The F Fits Perfectly in The Secret Square Grid   She Becomes Part of The Structure and Support it   Again She is Never Left Alone in   The Code   On Any Level
The Glass Ceiling is One Proof of That
The Code   Never Ever Approved of Any Fem Independence   as it would Mean the Beginning to Her Real Freedom from it

The Code   Does Not want to Know about The Fems Love   How Wonderful it is to be Loved and to Love   Love is to be Used to Manipulate Her
And that Slavery Never brings Freedom and   The Code   Knows That Already

Vigil: V/Fem Sex Active   Since   Eve/V   G/Vaginal Penetration   L/Sweet Fem Love Light/Elle/All/Ail/Ill/Hail/Heel/Hell/Oil
Which Means All Fems in Hell Have Penetration and Sex   Since Eve (Adam was Cursed Too   A/Damn   a Damn was Formed Between the Fems and The Mac as They Separated The Water from The land   (The Division of La Mer Rouge Comes to Mind and it was Blood Red)
vigil: a watch
The Thing to Watch says   The Code

Vigor: V/Fem Sex Active   Go   R/Her/Heir/Or/Whore/Sex
Vigorous: V   Go   R/Her   Us/S/Is/His/Hiss/Serpent/Penis
V   Go   R/Her/Heir/Or/Whore   With   S/Penis   and   G/Vaginal Penetration   Vigor is the Way to Go Towards That Fem says   The Code

Vile: V/Eve/Fem Sex Active   i/Marriage Act   L/Sweet Fem Love Light/Ill/Hail/Ail/Hell/Elle   and   E/He (Almost Silent here)
Same Constant Theme from   The Code
V/Eve   having   i/Marriage Act   with   L/Sweet Fem Love Light/Ill/Hail/Ail/Hell/Elle   With One Man   As in Bigamy   or   as V being also   L/Sweet Fem Light (a Masc Fantasy)
That would be a Big No from   The Code   so
vile: wretchedly bad   highly offensive   unpleasant   objectionable
V/Ill   Makes it Ville Which Means City in French   a Hiding for   The Code   It is a very Innocent Word   Eve that is Ill is Vile and Evil   She is in Hell
Eve or Elle   (See Evil in The Words Chapter)
The Wheel and the Veil Etc   Wheel   A Will   is Her Testament
A Vial   A Chalice
And Those Fems will be   If Married   Punished   Burnt   or   Sacrificed   from   That Ménage a Trois if She dares
Switch E/He for A/All Men and He Gets a Villa
Villa: Vile/A

The Dam Code The Damn Book

Village: Vile/Age
V/L/Sweet Fem Love Light/Elle/All/Ail/Ill/Hail/Heel/Hell/Oil   Age   Eve that is Ill   for an Age
Village is the Same In English and in French

Villain: VLN   All Fem Sounds Letters
V/Eve/Fem Sex Active   L/Sweet Fem Love Light/Elle/All/Ail/Ill/Hail/Heel/Hell/Oil   N/In/Hen/Ann/Haine/Virgin   V is with Illness and Hell   so   She is Called a Villain   As Usual a Loser She is in   That Code
Vile   N/Virgin
V/Lane   Vile/In
V/Fem Sex Active   L/Ill/Ail   and   N/Virgin   Active Together
We are Close to Words such as Love and Live
But Vile it is   The Secret Code   at Works   Making those 3 Fems Villains
Villain is a Kaleidoscope of Different Definitions   or   Meanings from the Same or Almost the Same Sounds Letters Alone or Together
Close to Violin Which is the Cover for   The Code   Here

Vindicate: VNDCK   All Fems Sound Letters
Vindication: V/Fem Sex Active   N/In/Virgin/Ann/Hen   Dick (Where this is a Dick   There is a Penis)   She   On/Eon
vindication: defense   excuse   justification

Viola: A/Viol is a Rape in French
Violate would be a Diminutive for Rape
V/Fem Sex Active   O/Fem/Hole   L/Ill/All/L   A/All Men
All Fems Sexually Active are to All Men
She is the Vial/Chalice   The Code   says Vile Also
viola: a four-stringed instrument of the violin family slightly larger than the violin
Viola The Fem Name would be the Cover Word here   Along with Music   Voila Accentuates it   and   Viol (Rape in French) Accentuates it

Violation: Vile/O/She/On
Viol is Rape (to Rip) in French   and is a Viola the Musical Instrument
Vial/A/She/On
Fiol is a Vial in French
Vial   to the Chalice   and to The Holy Grail Cup

727

Lise Rochon

When Letter V is in the Front Leading the Word it is Often Bad News from   The Code   to Her

Violent: V/Ill/Hunt   Viol/Hunt   Vile/Hunt
Hunt what is Vile   We Could Say   But No says   The Code It is Really to Search by The Viol (Rape in English)   and   The Vile   to   Hunt V/Sex Fem Active
Viol/Viola is a Bowed Musical Instrument   The Code   is Beyond the Languages Borders
vile: highly offensive   objectionable
Violent: Vile   O/Fem Hole   Lent
Viol as Music is the Cover Word here

Violin: Vile/In
Once You Vile a Virgin She Becomes a Violin says   The Code
Violin is a Cover Word here

Vineyard: Grapevines for Wine
Vineyard has a Sphere of Activity on a High Spiritual Plane
(See Blood   Wine   and   Grapes in The Words Chapter)
To Keep The Fems In Grapes is Easier

Viral: VRL   V/Fem/Sex Active is   The Code   Transformation of   L/ Sweet Fem Light/Ail/Ill/Hell/Elle   into One or Several of Those   R/Her/ Hair/Are/Here/Hear/Ear/Heir/Whore/Or/Err/Ere/Sex   In a Viral Way   It Goes Fast and is Contagious
viral: relating to   or   caused by a virus
A Virus on the Internet is a Cumbersome Break in the Communication Process   That is Important to Us Humans
With Time the Hypnotic Secret of   The Code   Evolves in Small   or   Big Lace Patterns   More Intricate   More Sinuous   Way Too Difficult to Grab on the Go
The Secret Web Code is Extremely Tight
WWW   Is the W/All Fems Sex Active Code International of Conduct Patterns for Her   as W is All Fem Sex Active Repeated 3 Times   Makes No Mistakes
The Code   Add its Hypnotic Control to Itself Constantly

Virgin: VRGN   V/Fem Sex Active   R/Her/Heir/Or/Whore   G/Vaginal Penetration   N/In/Hen/Ann/Virgin
V/Here/Jam   or   V/Heir/Gin   Sounds Fun Many Fems Got Pregnant That Way
A Child is a Responsibility for Life
V/Urge/N   Sex is Calling on The Virgin
V/Fem Sex Active is Urging N/Virgin to Act to have an R/Heir/Or Whore   Verge/In   Verge is Slang for Penis in French
Virgin is   V/Fem Sex Active   i/Marriage Act   G/Hymen Perforation   or   Vaginal Penetration   i/Marriage Act   N/In/Hen/Ann/Haine/Virgin
The Story of   N/Virgin   becoming   V/Fem Sex Active   and Carrying a Boy   Heir/Here/R   Is Told as a Story   that is in Her Hair/Air Already
Therefore Something Sexual has Already Happened in the Letters Forming the Word Virgin
virgin: a female animal that has never copulated   an unfertilized insect   an unmarried girl or woman   a person who had never had sexual intercourse   the Virgin Mary the Mother of Christ
Virgin Goes from a Fem Insect to Virgin Mary   She is Blessed because She Never had Intercourse and was Pregnant   And there is a Penis All the Way Near by
Virgin is for Both Sexes
Except for the Example of the Virgin and the Mother Mary
This is for All The Fems   It is Another Impossible Unattainable Goal   Being Virgins and Still having Sex and Heirs
The Virgin Letters Includes Copulation/G/Vaginal Penetration and a Son/Heir/R/Her/Sex
A Virgin Dressed in White Represents the Pure Lamb
The Lamb (One of Jesus Name in Symbolism) that Has Not Been Slaughtered (Slut/Her   Slot/Her)
That Lamb/Virgin that has Not Seen Yet The Fem Blood   or   The Slaughter (Slot/Her)
slot: a narrow elongated depression   for receiving or admitting something

Virile: VRL   Made of 3 Fem Sound Letters
Virile is a Male Only Attribute

Lise Rochon

Although There is No Masc Letter Except a   Silenced E/He   Having Sex   with   R/Her/Heir/Or/Whore   a   V/Fem Sex Active (Starting The Word) and a   L/Sweet Fem Love Light/Ill/Hail/Ail/Hell/Elle
It is an Anonymous Man having Sex with 3 Fems   Creating The Word Virile
Note That There are   2 iis/Sex Acts   in Virile
Sex With Several Fems as Whores or to have Heirs is Represented Abundantly in   That Code   Words
The Code   is Not Bonded by The Laws of Marriage   As In being Faithful to Your Wife
Take Away E/He in Virile and He Gets a Vrille/Gimlet
gimlet: a small tool for boring holes
Fem Holes are Boring in Virile
V   Are   Ill
Vrille is Slang for Penis   Une Vrille in French is a Drill
Under the Drill The Fems are Going Through that Drill D/Pregnant   R/Her/Sex   L/Ail/Ill/Hell
Drill/Derail   The/Rail/Rule (See Rail in The Words Chapter)
Take   R/Her/Heir/Whore/Or/Err/Sex   Away from Vrille and She Gets Vile (See Chalice and Vial in The Words Chapter)
From Vile She
Gets   Vial   Veil   Vail   Viol   Viola   Vallee   Etc   Always Going Down says   The Code

Vision: V/Fem Sex Active   She/Shh   On
She is Onto Sex and Shh About it   That is   The Code   Vision for Her Vision is Close to Virgin

Visit: V   S   Hit
V/Fem Sex Active   S/Is/His/Ass/Us/Serpent/Penis   Hit
Penis is Visiting with   V/Fem Sex Active
V/Sit   V/Zit
V/Eve   Sit on a Penis
V/See/T   V Cannot Look or Stay Too Long   Because She would Start to See T/Fem Cross as Herself   That would be a Hit for Her   So   No says   The Code   so   A Zit

Visitor: V/Fem Sex Active   See   T/Fem Cross

730

The Dam Code The Damn Book

Her/R/Ear/Hear/Hair/Err/Heir/Or/Whore/Here/Are/Our/Ere/Air/Ire/Sex   V/Sit/Her   Visit/Her
Visitor has a Different Connotation then in Visit   It has The Letter R in it   Implying R/Her/Here/Heir/Or/Whore/Sex
Visiting: Visit   N/In/Ann/Virgin
The Action of Visiting Implies a Real Person so Ann it Is
V/Zit/Her Too

Visual: V/See/U/All
The Code   Sees Everything

Vitriol: VTRL All Fem Letters   V/T/R/All
V/Fem Sex Active   With   i/Marriage Act   With   T/Fem Cross   with   Her/R/Ear/Hear/Hair/Err/Heir/Or/Whore/Here/Are/Our/Ere/Air/Ire/Sex   With   i/Marriage Act   with   O/Fem Hole   With   L/Sweet Fem Love Light/Ill/Hail/Ail/Hell/Elle/Virgin
Vitriol is Mating with 4 Different Cursed Fems
And They Know Nothing About the Others Fems   Because it would become Vitriolic
vitriolic: very caustic   scathing   as criticism

Vixen: VXN   All 3 Fem Sound Letters
V/Fem Sex Active   X/Rolling/Fallen Cross   N/In/Hen/Ann/Virgin
When   V/Fem Sex Active   as   X/Fallen Fem Cross is   N/Ann/In   She is a
vixen: an ill tempered or quarrelsome woman
No Fem Letter or No Fem Word Have Positive Power at All for The Fem and there should be No Communication in Between Them says   The Code
Check Also Shrew (She/Are/You)

Void: V/Fem Sex Active   Odd
Eliminate All Power to Those Fems by making them Odd (See Odd In The Words Chapter)
void: useless   ineffectual   vain
She is to be a Void

Voila: Un Voile is a Veil in French

731

Veil/A   A Veil
voila: used to express success or satisfaction
Voila is a French Word Signifying   It Is Done
See Prevail/Pre/Veil   It is in the Same Vein
Switch L/Sweet Fem Light for N/In/Hen/Ann/Virgin and She Gets Vein (See Venus (Vein/Us) in The Words Chapter)
The Code   Uses Voila as an Accomplished Fact   Putting a Man with a Veil is Viewed as an Accomplished Fact   No Ripple is made in Our Unconscious because it does Not Exist   Only Fems get That as a Must

Volt: V/All/T
Stop Eve with a Volt   To make Her a Fem Cross
vault: an arch structure   to curve   to arch
(See Arch and Arc in The Words Chapter)

Vomit: VOMT   4 Fem Sounds Letters
With i/Marriage Act   The Code   says No to Any Meeting of Only Fems   Especially with Sex   so Vomit it is
Add an Her/R/Ear/Hear/Hair/Err/Heir/Or/Whore/Here/Are/Our/Ere/Air/Ire/Sex and She Gets to Vroom/It

Voracious: V/Fem Sex Active Her/R/Ear/Hear/Hair/Err/Heir/Or/Whore/Here/Are/Our/Ere/Air/Ire/Sex   A/All Men   She/Shh   Us
The Fem as R/Sex (Heirs or Whore) is Eager for More Sex with All Men   Shh it is a Secret says to Her (She)   The Code
voracious: very eager

Vote: V/Oath   V/Oat
V/Sex Fem Active   is in Front of Oat   It is Food a Reward for Her Although   T/Fem Cross/Great Curse   Accompanies Her Here
In Oath   H/Secret Code Letter   is Added to Oat   Bringing Along The Promise Taken by those Initiated to be Silently Faithful of that Promise (Oath) The Vote is Basically an Oath Wrapped in that Basic Food   Which is O/Fem Hole   A/All Men   T/Fem Cross/Great Curse H/Secret Code Letter Which is Every Fem Hole is a Fem Cross   for A/All Men   In Oath it is Under the Watch of   The Code
Sex Always Come Along with The Curse

oath: a solemn appeal to a deity   or some revered person or thing to witness ones determination to speak the truth to keep a promise   etc   an irreverent or blasphemous use of the name of God or anything sacred
oat: slang to have sexual intercourse
Oat is a Cover Word here

Vroom: V/Room
Eve/V/Sex Active is in the Bedroom   The Code   says Yes   Even if There are 2 OOs/Fem Holes (Plural or All of Them)   Implying Again Polygamy
VRM   2 Fems with Sex
vroom: roaring sound

Vowel: Vow is Entirely Made of 3 Fem Letters
as   O/Fem Hole   She Goes from   V/Fem Sex Active   to   W/All Sex Fem Active   That is it   To Vow/All
Vow   L/Sweet Fem Love Light/Elle/All/Ail/Ill/Hail/Heel/Hell/Oil
Numbers (Numb/Her) and Letters (Laid/T/Her   Let/Her) are Created by   The Code   To Own Her   To Manipulate Her into Those Hypnotic Behaviors
The Vow is to Marry a Merry Mary   or   To Vow Her to a God as a Church Sister   She is Still All Possessed by   The Code   With That Ring (See Ring in The Words Chapter)   No Safety here for Her   Nuns Got Invaded and Gang Rape Often in History

W w
Intro
W is a Masc Made Fem Letter
W/All Sexually Active Fems (The Double V Starts with a Single V)
W is All the Fems Sex Active in Plural   W is All V/Fem Sex Active Attached Together   They are All The Same Shape   To Reinforce its Concept
VVVVVWWWW are All Fems   Going Up Down   Up Down   Letter W is Not a Double U   W is a Double V   The Code   Works its Way   and   There are Interchangeable in Some Formats (Fonts) of Writing
It is the Same Concept as Jumping on a Fem Curved Letter   U/ You   Exchanging it With a No Curve Symbol Letter which is The Masc Made Fem Letter V Trying to Make the U (All Fems Ovulating Naturally) in

733

a Double U   Creating a Mental Bridge Between those 2 Different Letters   Concepts that is Commonly Accepted in Our Societies
The Code   Creates a Heir Making Machine   or a   Whore (or to Err) Out of Her/R/Here There Everywhere   Again
W Being the Plural of V   It is a Pattern   Another Concept for Polygamy   The 2 Fems   the V and V Attached Together   w/W contains All Fems from Childhood   having The Same Shape
The Fem Letters Symbols are Always Attached in   The Secret Code   to a Male Symbol One Way or Another
In Greek Letters Letter W/All Fems Sex Active is in Much Rounder Font Shape Letters
It is a Butt seen from Behind (or Large Milking Breasts)
ω ω ω   Designed as a Butt   or   2 Hanging Breasts ω Depending on the Font
Letter Omega   The End Letter is in a Butt Shape
Another Omega Symbol Letter is the Ὠ and Ω
2 Fem Symbols Slightly Different are Referring Again to Polygamy
It Looks as a Fully Rounded Pregnant Belly With 2 Little Hands Holding it In   The Code   Omega Unites the Concept of the Open Circle/Genitals at the Bottom   from the Past into the Future
From Alpha to Omega   is Often Used to Mention From Beginning to End
The Second Letter is Beta as a Beast or a Bête in French   She Meet the Beast in Number 2   The Marriage Number
Alpha Being the Compass of the Freemasons (The One with the G/Hymen Perforation/Vaginal Penetration in it)
Alpha to Omega   A/All Men the Goal   and   Omega ω/The Butt/Breasts
The Targets   All this for That
It Must be a Tight Area to Open in a Fem it Demands All this Hypnotic   Code   Symbology and Negative Forces put on Her to Keep that Part of Her Opened at All Times
There Are More Words Starting with W Now Than Ever
WWW the World Wide Web Is One of the Most Powerful Word in the Words World   It is that Chain of WWW again
More Fem Having Sex   Is it Part of the Chase
As being Put on a Rack   or   Called a Rack (Rack is Breasts in English Slang)

The Dam Code The Damn Book

There are Few Words that Starts with W or Q or X or Y or Z   There are Reasons for That
The Real Fem U would Not Go for That Blind

W   w
Waffle: WFL   All 3 Fem Sound Letters
W/All Fems Sex Active   2 FFs/Fem/Fuck (Plural or All of Them)   L/Sweet Fem Love Light/Ill/Hail/Ail/Hell/Elle
The F Letter would the Most Logical and Free (Except of being Insulted and Undignified in Fuck) Fem in the Group of the Fem Letters Because in   That Code   F has No Affiliation with M/Marriage   D/Pregnancy/Children   R/Her/Sex as Whore   or   for a Heir or to Err   V/Sex Active and W/All Sex Active   or   Fighting for Her Freedom in Y and K   or Being Sick in L/Ill   or   being a T/Fem Cross   or   Dead in X/Fallen Fem Cross
So When 2 F/Fems are Together   with   W/All Sex Fem Active   and L/Sweet Fem Love Light/Ill   It Presents a Possibility of Serious Thinking and Communicating Between Them   That is a Big No from   The Code   so
waffle: to speak or write equivocally
equivocally: in a way that is doubtful in nature or of uncertain significance
Waffle is a Sweet Food
Waffle is a Cover Word Here

Wagon: Wag/On
wag: to move constantly especially in idle or indiscreet chatter   *slang* to play truant
In   The Code   Wagons are Fems   They are Attached Together to One Engine (Masc) There are Usually Several Wagons (Fems   Polygamy)
The Engine (The N/Gene   NGN (2 NNs/Virgins Separated by G/Hymen or Vaginal Perforation/Penetration/Sex)   is Said to be Masc in   That Code
Switch W for B/Boy Holding All Breasts and He Gets a Bag (Too Young for The Code)
Switch W for F/Fem/Fuck and She Gets a Fag (The Fem is Not Aloud in The Code)
Switch W for G/Vaginal Penetration and He Gets a Gag
(The Code   Minimizes to The Masc Everything Related to the Fems)
Switch W for H/Code Letter and Both Get a Hag

735

hag: an old ugly woman especially vicious or malicious one   a witch   or   a sorceress
The Code   Makes it Scary to Her so   No Fem Looks   The Code   Hang High those Magical Fems Calling them Bad Witches and Ridiculing/Humiliating them Endlessly
Switch W for L/Ill/Hell and She Gets to Lag (Stay Behind)
Switch W for M/Motherhood and She Gets Mag (A Fem Name)
mag: to talk   to chatter
Switch W for N/In/Hen/Ann/Virgin and She Gets Nag
No Words here with P/Man Power   The Masc has Nothing to Do with Being a Wag/On (a wagon)
Switch W for R/Her/Whore/Or/Heir/Err/Sex and She Gets a Rag (Her Blood Loss)
Switch W for S/Is/His/Penis and He Gets to Sag
sag: to sink or bend downward by weight or pressure to droop   hang loosely
Penis Cannot be a Wagon says   The Code   The Masc can Only be an Engine (The Boss)
Switch W for T/Fem Cross and She Gets a Tag
The Code   says All Fems are The Same and are All Tagged
Switch W for Z/Sleep On it and All Get a Zig
zig: to move in one or two directions followed in a zig zag course
The Code is All About Fem Control   The Masc is Often Hidden   or   Silent

Wail: WL   2 Fem Sound Letters
We/Ail   We   Ill/All/Hell/L
W/All Fems Sex Active   are with   L/Sweet Fem Light
That Would be a Big No from The Code   So
wail: a prolong mournful cry
Wheel (The Wheel of Time   The Rota (Ta/Ro   The Tarot)
The Word Wheel/Will (The Will is taken Over by The Wheel) has Several Uses Idioms and Definitions (See Wheel in The Words Chapter)
Switch i/Marriage Act   for Another   L/Sweet Fem Light/Ill and She Gets a Wall
Because i/Marriage Act is Gone and Been Replaced with L/Love(That would be a Big No says   The Code   so here is a Wall to Separate Those 2)

Switch W/All Fems Sex Active   for   V/Fem Sex Active and She Gets a Veil (See Veil in The Words Chapter   How Convenient for The Code)
Wailing   Wall/In   Veil/In
The Code   is Always in The Waiting to Veil and isolate The Fems   It Prevails (Pre/veil)

Waist: Waste
When a Fem is Pregnant   She Lose an Aspect of Her
Given   Code   Identity of Her Beauty Criterias   Her Waist
Size   Another Way of Diminishing Her Image
Another Waste of Time for Her   and the Masc Laughs about their Body Fat   While Men Can be as Fat as They Desire

Wait: W/Hate
Hate Towards   W/All Fems Sex Active

Wall: W/All
Have   W/All Fems Sex Active   Separated by a Wall
We   L/Sweet Fem Love Light/Ill/Hail/Ail/Hell/Elle/Heel
All Fems Are Separated from Masc That Way   The Code   is Safe
Wall Paper: We/All/Peep/Her
The Code   House Items Educates about   That Code

Wallet: Wall/It   W/L/Hit   We/All/Hit
W/All Fems Sex Active   and   L/Sweet Fem Love Light/Ill/Hail/Ail/ Elle   are Hit
They Hit the Wall   or   the Wall Hit Them on the Wallet
It is Hard for The Fems because She Never could or Only with Great Difficulty Could Acquire Money   And Often to Lose Her Reputation on The Way
In Old Times a Fem could Only be Independent Monetarily by being a Prostitute/R/Her Whore   Marrying it (having Children)   or   Inheriting it

Wallow: Wall/O   Well/O   W/All/O
Think All Happy   O/Fem Hole   is in Between Walls
As if The Fems could Live as Prisoners and be All Happy to Roll in for Sex (W)   Any Time   The Code says   and   Calls it a Life of Luxury   It is All Smokes and Screens for Her That is

wallow: to roll about or lie in water snow mud or the as   to live in self indulgency luxuriate   to move along clumsily or with difficulty   to surge up or billow forth as smoke or heat
Does Not Look That Great

Walk: WLK   All 3 Fem Sounds Letters
We/All/K   We/L/K
W/All Fems Sex Active   Are   K/Broken Fem Warriors with their Broken L/Hearts
It is as Normal as Walking says   The Code
Walk is a Cover Word here

Wander: Wand/Her
That Could have Been a Powerful Word for The Fems   All Fems Holding Their Own Stick/Wand/Scepter
But No   A Big No from   The Code   so
wander: to ramble without a definite purpose   to go aimlessly   to go ashtray
Here She Goes on her Quest for Power
Switch A/All Men for O/Fem Hole and She Gets to Wonder (Her Head in the clouds   Not Knowing   Questioning)

Want: W/Ant
What a Fem Wants is of Very Small Importance to   The Code
Switch T/Fem Cross for D/Pregnant and She Gets Wand (See Her Wand in Wander Above)
The Only Fem Wand in The Dictionary is for Applying Cosmetics (A Tiny One Indeed)

War: WR   2 Fems Sound Letters
Were (as War in The Past)   W/Are   W/Her
W/All Fems Sex Active   Her/R/Ear/Hear/Hair/Heir/Or/Whore/Err/Here/Are/Our/Ere/Air/Ire/Sex
W   is in Front (or Ruling) of A/All Men   and   R/Her/Heir/Or/Whore/Err/Sex   A Big No from   The Code   so   War it is
Switch A/All Men for O/Fem Hole and Get Wore (as in The Clothing We Wear)

The Dam Code The Damn Book

Add N/Virgin and She Gets Worn (you Cannot Put a N/Virgin with   R/Heir/Or/Whore   and   O/Fem Hole   and   W/All Fem Sex Active   a Virgin will Gets too Worn to Look at it)
Letter A is Almost Useless in the Sound Word War   Except being There Anonymous and Quiet
War as   We were
The Code   In its Wars and Destruction wants to Remind Us   It is Part of Us   in The Past and in The Present

Ward: War   D/Pregnant
ward: a division or district of a city or town as for administrative or political purposes   a division floor or room of a hospital for a particular class or group of patients   any of the separate divisions of a prison   *fortification* an open space within or between the walls of a castle or fortified place   to protect to guard
Switch W for H/Code Letter and It Gets Hard on W/All Fems Active   and   R/Her   and   D/Pregnant   3 Hits with One Rock from   The Code

Warden   War   D/Pregnant   N/In/Hen/Ann/Virgin
The War Against The Fems is on All Levels
All Protection for that   Code   Warden to Keep Virgins Pregnant
Switch A for O/Fem Hole and She Gets Word/In   The Power of The Words is in Her

Warrior: Whore/He/Her
The War Against The Fem Power   and   The Whoring of Her/R Has been the Oldest and Most Adamant One in Our History of being a Prisoner of   That Code   Being Pregnant (Heir/Her) or Married does Not Prevent The Fems from Being Whores in The mind of   The Code

Warm: W/Harm
Letter M/Motherhood and N/Virgin are Interchangeable in   The Code One Grows into the Other   As Seed and Fruit (N/Virgin   into   M/Motherhood)
Switch M/Motherhood for N/Virgin in Waiting to be Pregnant and She Gets Warn (The Very Young Fems are often Warned that They are

739

Cursed   Switch A/All Men for O/Fem Hole and She Gets Worn (All Fem Letters))
Warmer: W/Arm/R
For   The Code   to Mean Something Nice to a Fem is a Big No so   There is a Trap   The Arms are to Harm Each Other
W/All Fems Sex Active   Is Close in Meaning to   R/Her/Heir/Or/Whore/Err   They will Not Get Close Even if it is Warmer

Warn: Wear/N   Where/N   Were/N
To Wear the   N/In/Hen/Ann/Virgin   Is to Have Sex with Her
Worn   In The Past
Switch W for B/Boy Holding All Fem Breasts and He Gets a Barn (Where the Animals (The Fems in The Code   are Cows Horses Sheeps Chickens Ants Bees Etc   See Those Animals in The Words Chapter)
Switch W for D/Pregnant and She Gets Darn (A Weak Complaint)
Switch W for Y/Wounded Fem and She Gets Yarn (Wool from Sheep (See Sheep in the Words Chapter))
Switch N for D/Pregnant and She Gets a Ward (Hospital)
Switch N for F/Fem/Fuck and She Gets a Warf (When The Fish (Her) is Out of The Water It (She) Dies
Switch N for M/Motherhood and She Gets Warm (The Code Tells Her to have Children)
Switch N for T/Fem Cross and She Gets a Wart (The Curse has Happened)

Warning: War   N/In/Hen/Ann/Virgin   Twice (as in Plural or All of Them)   War   to   N   Twice
warning: to give notice of possible arm   to advice to be careful

Warrant: War/Ant   We/Rant   W/Are/Ant
W/All Fems Sex Active   Her/R/Ear/Hear/Hair/Err/Heir/Or/Whore/Here/Are/Our/Ere/Air/Ire/Sex   Ant (See Ant Aunt and Aint in The Words Chapter)
As Small as Ants   W   R/Her/Are   That Warrant is a Warranty
It is a War and   The Code   is Ranting About it
warrant: authorization   sanction   justification
Warranty: War/N/T   War/On/T   War/Ann/T
The Warranty is The War with   N/In/Hen/Ann/Virgin   All The Way to   T/Fem Cross

740

The Dam Code The Damn Book

Chaos is a Place to Hide in   The Code

Was: W/S   W/Ass
W/All Fems Sex Active   and   S/Is/As/Has/Ass/His/Us/Hiss/Serpent/
Penis   of   A/All Men   Together
In the Past   as   Is/His   in The Present

Wash: Was/Shh/She   W/Ash
From Silence to Ashes is   W/All Fems Sex Active   that is How it was in
The Past says   The Code
The Code   says W/All Fems Sex Active   have No Importance   It is a Wash
wash: to remove by the action of water   to free from spiritual defilement or from sin
Wash is a Form of Baptism and a Forgiveness Ritual with Water   Which is an Entirely Fem Symbol
How Convenient for   The Code   All Men Sins are Forgiven and She Gets Silences and Ashes

Waste: Ways/T
The Way to   T/Fem Cross   Is to Waste Her   or Waist Her as in Pregnant
The Fems Waist (See BB in The Words Chapter) is a Waste
Was/T   is in the Past   T/Fem Cross/Great Curse is in the Past   She Was a Waste then and Is Still Now

Watch: W/Hatch
W/All Fems Sex Active   are Hatching (Eggs   See Chicken in The Words Chapter) He Watch
Watchdog   Watch that Dog (Dog/Bitch/Her) says   The Code
The Fem is Never Left Alone   or/and   She is in a Position of Minimal Power   in Any Way

Water: W/All Fems Sex Active   A/All Men   T/Fem Cross/Great Curse   E/He   Her/R/Ear/Hear/Hair/Err/Heir/Or/Whore/Here/Are/Our/Ere/Air/Ire/Sex   With Water The Priests Blesses and Purifies
A Roman Catholic With Water Blesses One Self When Entering a Church and do the Sign of the Cross in Order to Invoke The Grace of Christ   Death on the Cross

741

Lise Rochon

The Jesus Cross Represents the Fem Great Curse says   The Secret of the Secret Societies
Wet/Her   Wheat/Her   What/Her   Wet Her
Waiter: Waitress   Wait/R/Ass
Wait/Her
Another Sub Job for Her
Watering: Water/In   Wet/Her/N   What/Her/In
Ocean: O/Fem Hole or Loins   She/Shh   In/N/Hen/Ann/Virgin
In the Sex Hole She Lives in
Sea in French is Mer   Mère is Mother (Mate/Her)
River (Reef/Her)
Lake: Letter L/Sweet Fem Light/Ill/Ail/Hail/Hell/Elle   Ache   Another Act of Cheating and Manipulating Her Mind from   The Code   It Represents a Lake (A Peaceful Fem Symbol Place is Not a Lack or a Leak)

watershed: line separating waters flowing into different rivers
Switch D/Pregnant for T/Fem Cross (In The Code D Follows on being T   Sound Wise) and She Get Watershit
(Water/She/It/Hit) Not a Word but Another Code Hidden Concept

Wave: WV   2 Fem Sounds Letters
From V/One V/Fem Sex Active to W/All Fems Sex Active
Endless Waves (WV   V/Fem Active   as She Becomes W/All Fems Sex Active says The Code) the Ocean (O/Fem Hole   She Ann) Creating Tides (T/Fem Cross/Great Curse   Hides   The Code   Terminates and Hides Anything about the Great Fem Curse with Insults and Shame Directed to Her for the Last 2000 Years)
Marée (MRA   or   Mary/Merry/Marry   is Tide in French
The V/Fem Sex Active is a Violation of Her Natural Ovulation Rhythms
V and W are as N/Virgin and M/Motherhood   One Becomes The Other   But Not Vice Versa

Way: W/All V/Fem Sex Active   A/All Men
The Way of   The Code   is All Fems Are Sex Active Anytime for All Men
Polygamy and Multiple Partners are Ways for   The Code   Which is for Men   But The Difference is The Fems Will Be Severely Punished (as in Being Burned Alive or Stoned to Death   or   Left in The Desert Alone Where She will Certainly Perish)

The Dam Code The Damn Book

The Man will Receive a Slap on The Hand as Usual   She Being Told It is a Natural Way for a Man   As Men Will Be Men   Extrapolating it into the Future   They Will do it Again

We: W/All Fems Sex Active   E/He
Allied with Him/He/E   W is the Most Marked Letter by   The Code   It is The Letter That Makes Her a R/Are/Whore/Or/Heir/Err/Sex   Even if She Brings a Heir She is Still a Whore says   The Code
W/All Fems Sex Active includes All Other Fems   The F/Fem/Fuck Too
W is in Front of E/He   It is Called   We
W (Called Double U   as in All Fem Natural Ovulation is Transformed Here Discretely in All Fem Sex Active at All Times) Cannot be Alone to Create a Sound Word Letter as Some of the Other Letters do
W Needs E/He to be with to Pronounce Her Letter Name   Reinforcing the Idea that She has to have Sex Anytime says   The Code   Creating The Great Curse/Fem Cross
The Double U Letter W Creates its Own Sound/Meaning
Add Another E and He Gets Wee   A Weak Word (a Cover Word) That Means to Pee (3 Masc Letters)
Oui is Yes In French   Which Reinforces The Concept of We The Code   Uses This Kind of Reinforcement Concept

Weapon: Whip/On   Weep/On
We   Upon
Even if The Fem Never went to war Until Lately   The Word Starts with W/All Fems Sex Active   It is The Oldest War in Our Human History   The Fem being Hunted as an Animal for Sexual Butchery

Weary: WRE
We/Ray   Wear/He   Where/He   Were/He
We   Are/R   He/E
W/All Fems Sex Active is Leader of that Word
That Would Make Him Weak as a Source of Power   It Implies We do Not Know Where He is   or   He is in The Past   or The Fem is Wearing The Masc
A Big No from The Code   so
weary: exertion   strain   fatigue

Lise Rochon

Words Starting with W and Following with Her would be the E/He   Then A/All Men   Then Her/R/Ear/Hear/Hair/Err/Heir/Or/Whore/Here/Are/Our/Ere/Air/Ire/Sex   Ending it in a Y/Wounded Fem (See Letter Y in The Letter Chapter)
Another Big No from   The Code

Weasel: W/Is/All   We/Ease/All
W/All Fems Sex Active   Directs   E/He (Twice)   and   A/All Men   with their   S/Is/As/Has/Ass/Us/His/Hiss/Serpent/Penis   to be with   L/Sweet Fem Love Light/All/Ill/Hail/Ail/Hell/Elle
A Big No from   so
weasel: a conning sneaky person   a small carnivore   an informant

Weather: Wet   Her/R/HereEar/Hear/Hair/Heir/Or/Whore/Err/Are/Our/Ere/Air/Ire/Sex   That is Everyday Weather
Whether is 2 alternatives
It Is Better to have Choices for The Masc When it Comes to Wet/Her
What/R   As in Which   Whore   or   Heir   or   to Err

Weave: WV   2 Fem Sound Letters
We/Eve
W/All Fems Sex Active   are   V/Fem Sex Active   and Vice Versa   Since Eve/Ov/V (as in Vulve   Etc)
The Woven Pattern   We/Oven   Heaven   Women (W/Omen) etc
In the Past Many Fems Weaved   In England in the Beginning of the Twentieth Century the Fems Brains were Kept Busy with Weaving Miles of Lace   Which its Marvels of Beauty and Intricacy can be Seen in Lace Museums in England
weave: to interlace   to compose a connected whole by combining various elements
All Fems Open Sexually from One to All is   The Code   Weaving Pattern (Pat/Urn   See Urn In The Words Chapter)

Wed: Wet
From   W/All Fems Sex Active   to   D/Pregnant   to   T/Fem Cross   That is The Way of   The Code
Add P/Man Power and He Gets Wept

The Dam Code The Damn Book

To Wed is Not a First Priority for a Man   Although it is a Necessary Thing to do in His Life to have Fems for   Chores   Sex   and   Descendants (Heirs/R/Her/Whore/Sex)

Wedding: WDN   3 Fems Sound Letters
Wet/Ding   Way/Ding   Wet   In/N//Hen/Ann/Virgin
ding: to make a ringing sound   minor surface damage
A Thing is Slang for a Fem   The Ring being Its Engagement Symbol (See Ring in The Words Chapter   Ring That Bell (Clitoris/Vagina   Ring That Belle)
We/Thing   We/Ding
Being   Bing   Ding   King   Ping   Ring   Sing   Ting   Vigne   Wing
How do You Get this Thing   T/Fem Cross   N/In/Hen/Ann/Virgin   To make a Cursed Fem Out of a Virgin   By Ringing Her   Even The Largest Bulls Obey to Humans having The Ring Piercing their Nose (The Bull is The Cow or The Tau   The Taurus   The Bull is The Fem Sign Representing Venus Fem Goddess s since Antiquity
Switch W for B/Boy Holding All Breasts and He Gets a
Bed/In   Bedding (Too Young for   The Code   The Code   Always Protects its Heirs   as It Exposes the Girls to All Kinds of Pains Possible)
Wedding is a Word of Many Facets in   The Code   Because of The Ring

Wedge: WDG
W/All V/Fem Sex Active   Pregnant/D   with   G/Hymen Perforation/Penetration
All W/V/Fem Sex Active   are kept in a   V/Fem Sex Active   Formation
As Good as a Piece of Pie (See Pi in The Words Chapter Switch P/Man Power for M/Motherhood and She Gets My)
wedge: a cuneiform character or stroke of this shape   a piece of anything of shape as shape   *Military*   (formerly) a tactical formation generally in the form of a V with the point toward the enemy
V is the Eve Letter   W/All Fems Sex Active   are Born from V/Fem Sex Active   Since Eve
That will Keep W on Edge
If Not for Her a Wedgie is Waiting   (Check Wedgie in The American Slang)
W/All Fem Sex Active   2 EEs/He (Plural or All of Them)

W   is in Front of   2 EEs   It Would Give More Power   and   Possible Polyandry for Her   A Big No says   The Code   so
wee: very small   tiny   minute   to urinate   to mark with urine before copulation
Switch W for P/Man Power and He Pees it Out (Easy)

Weed: We/ID   We/D
W/All Fems Sexually Active   E/He   D/Pregnant
ID is an Identification Card   Weed is   All Fems Sex Active   becoming   D/pregnant   It is Her ID and what Causes Her Unconscious Pleasure   says   The Code
ID: source in the unconscious of instinctive impulses seeking pleasure
Weed Whacker
We/ID   Whack   Her/R/Ear/Hear/Hair/Heir/Or/Whore/Err/Here/Are/Our/Ere/Air/Ire/Sex
Whack Her it is Her ID and She Takes Pleasure from it says   The Code

Ween: WN   2 Fem Sound Letters
She Win
W and N are Surrounding   2 EEs/He (Plural or All of Them)   Putting Those Men in a Weak Position   by Insinuating that   W/All Fems Sex Active   will Win by Being Transformed in a   N/Virgin Position from 2 E/He
We   In/N (as W/We   Are   In/N/Virgin   Win   When)
A Big No from   The Code   so
ween: to think   to suppose   to expect   to intend
wean: to withdraw from a habit
Switch E/He for A/All/Men and He Gets
wane: to decrease in strength
Switch N/In/Hen/Ann/Virgin for   K/Defeated Fem Warrior and She Gets Weak
The Code   is a Maze Where The Fem is Prisoner for Life and Not Knowing about it

Weep: We/P
W/All Fems Sex Active   is in Front of   A/All Men (Double E/he Makes All of Them)   and   P/Man Power   That is a Big No from   The Code   so

The Dam Code The Damn Book

Weep or Get The Whip
W Cannot be Left Alone (Too Much Power for Her) so We Pronounce W as the Double U Sound When Saying W   Therefore Transitioning from   U/ Natural Ovulation   into   V (The Half of W   or a Fem Active Sexually Anytime)
W/All Fems Sex Active   Are the Herd (Heard   Code)   See Sheppard (Sheep/Herd) in The Words Chapter)   Sheeps Cannot be Left by themselves
weeper: mourner   wine that lost its content   a sad story
When She Mourns   Whip/Her
The Wine is The Holy (Hole/He) Blood (Her Blood Loss) and Her Curse
She Mourns Her Lost Blood in Sadness
The Code   has No Care for that   so
We/Pee on it   Adding P/Man Power   The Last Letter of Weep   Creating a Merry Go Round (Pregnant) Effect
weep: to express grief sorrow or any overpowering emotion by shedding tears   shed   cry
Shed is   She   D/Pregnant (She Shed Babies as Easy as That)

Weekdays: Weak/Days (Daisies   See Dizzy in The Words Chapter)
Weekend: Weak/End

Weinstein: Wine/Stein
In   The Code   The Wine is the Fem Blood Loss since The Invention of Communion was Given to Man   it is Same as Blood/Stain
stein: a mug   stein is the amount of beer or other liquid you put in the stein itself
Theoretically the Liquid and the Container are having the Same Name Here   Blood   Uterus (You/Tear Us) as Stein/Stan/Satan/Stain
Stein is a Cup   The Stain and The Cup
The Original Sin Was/Is a Stain
Saint   Holy (Hole/He) Mary did Not Get The Original Sin We Are Told   Because She Remained a Virgin (See Virgin in The Words Chapter)   In the Immaculate Character of the Catholic Church Found on Line   Prof Plinio Corrêra de Oliveira Gives a Lecture or Gives a Wrenching Prayer on Devotion in Asking for a Grace   Having Invincible Devotion to the Catholic Church and Comparing It to the Lady of Good Friday in Her

Lise Rochon

Immaculate Character   With its Priest the Church Lives On that   in the Heart of the People   Identifying itself as Her Purity
I Never Experimented Priests with that Love and Sincerity towards Me as a Catholic Fem Child Growing Up   Priests were Scary Looking in their Tall Black Robes and Never Smiled   With The Immense Sex Abuse on Children Lately Known it is Very Scary for All Those Faithfull
On the Other Hand if the Church is Fem   Why is it The Fems were Never Allowed to Serve as their Priestess (Priest/Ass)
We The Fems are the Center of Attention Here   But in Such a Bad and Big and Secret Way No One Can Look at its Immense Treachery
Fascinating is the Clear Sounds of Jewish Family Names
The Jewish Carried the Word Stein/Stein/Stone in their Names Even in Germany
Stein in German is Rock (Stone)
Rosenstein is   Rose/N/Stein   The Rose and The Stain   Study the Rosecrucian Secret Code
The Roman Catholic Carry the Same Stain/Stone/Rock The Rock of Peter Jesus First Disciple (Perhaps After Mary Magdalena) is to be the First Building Stone for that New Jesus Church
The Alchemical Stone is a Big Item in Symbology

Weird: WRD   3 Fem Sound Letters
Her/R/Ear/Hear/Hair/Err/Heir/Or/Whore/Here/Are/Our/Ere/Air/Ire/Sex   is in Between of   W/All Fems Sex Active   and   D/Pregnant   While   E/He   is Silent
W/Heard   We/Heard   We/Hear/D
If   W/All Fems Sex Active Would Hear (The Language Code)   That They Are All Whores or Pregnants or to Err   That Would be Weird says   The Code   so
The Secret Grid Code Associations then Stays Secret
Ass People Keep Away from the Weird
Weird is a Cover Word here

Welcome: We/Ill/Come   Well/Come   Will/Come   Wheel/Come
For The Fem   The Code   says She is Welcome to Be Ill/Ail/Hell/Hail/Elle/L/Sweet Fem Love   (See Wheel in The Words Chapter)

well: fortunate   happy   properly   in a good or satisfactory
manner   a hole drilled or bored into the earth to obtain water petroleum
natural gas brine or sulfur   a container receptacle or reservoir for a liquid
All is Well says   The Code   When She is being Drained of Something or
Being a Receptacle (Motherhood)
W/Sex Fem Active   Hell
We (The Fems)   are in   Hell/Ill/Ail/Hail/All/Elle/L/Sweet Fem Love
from   That Code
See The Wheel (of Time) in The Words Chapter
The Wheel of Time   The Curse of Time from Saturn
A Wheel is Made of Many Crosses Creating its Shape
The Hole (O/Fem Hole) in the Middle of a Wheel is for the Stick to
Penetrate and Make the Wheel Roll
Well is One of Her Symbols in   The Code
A Well is in a Shape of a Circle
Switch W for B/Boy Holding All Fems Breasts and He Gets a Bell (Too
Young for the Code)
Switch W for C/See/Young Girl and She Gets a Cell   (The Fem Curse is a
Prison for Her)
Switch W for D/Pregnant and She Gets a Dell   (a Dale is a Small Usually
Valley or a Vale where She can get Lost)
Once Pregnant in that Valley She is gone
Switch W for F/Fem/Fuck and She Gets Fell
Switch W for G/Penis Penetration and He Gets a Gel
(Most Men are Immune to Her Hell)
Switch W for H/Secret Code Letter and Get Hell   (The Code Hides Its Hell
in Religion where Hell has being Created to The Fems)
Switch W for J/Sheppard Stick and He Gets a Jell
jell: to congeal   become jelly as in consistency   to become clear
substantial or definite   crystallize
The Jell is the Precursor of Her Jail after The Fems has been with the Stick
and Start to Crystallize from a Child to a Young Bleeding Virgin
Switch W for M/Motherhood and She Gets Mel (The Code   is with
Motherhood for Her)
mel: honey
Switch W for N/In/Hen/Virgin and She Gets Nell (as in Nil
Switch W for P/Man Power and He Gets a Pell (a Good Thing for
Him   another Legacy)

pell: a parchment
Switch W for S/Is/His/Us Has/Ass/Hiss/As/Serpent/Penis and He Gets a Sell (Another Good Thing for Him   Especially if He Gets to Sell a Fem)
Switch W for T/Fem Cross and She Gets a Tell (a Lie)
Switch W for Y/Wounded Fem and She Gets a Yell
The Well is Hell for Her says   The Code

Were: WR
W/All Fems Sex Active   Are in Front of   Her Her/R/Ear/Hear/Hair/Heir/Or/Whore/Err/Here/Are/Our/Ere/Air/Ire/Sex
The 2 EEs/He   (Plural or All of Them) Separating The Fems to Keep Order with The Fem Herd Silently   Preventing Communication Between Fems
If W would be Aware that All Fems are R/Her (Whore/Or/Heir/Err)   They would Never have Accepted That
Were is in the Past   Therefore Gone and Forgotten says   The Code
W/Are   W/Whore   W/Her   W/Wear   Where   W/Err
Letter W Cannot be Alone says   The Code   Therefore
Her Double Name (The Double U) and Double Meaning   U/You/Natural Ovulation   is Transformed into a W/All Fems Sex Active
The Fems Are Kept in Scarring/Scaring Illusions Such as Erring (Being Abandoned) (a Herring is a Fish   See Fish in The Words Chapter)
erring: going astray   in error   wrong
The Code   says Her Hearing (Her/Ring)   is with Her Ear(s) That Her Hair/Heir is What is Most Important
Earring/Ear/N and Hair are Covers for   The Code   to All Fems To Keep its Secrets Anonymous
Add D/Pregnant and She Gets Weird (We/Herd   See Herd and Weird in The Words Chapter)
Switch E/He for A/All Men and He Gets a War (If Nothing Works   Bring More Men)

Wet: WT   2 Fem Sound Letters
W/All Fems Sex Active   T/Fem Cross
With a Silent E/He
With is There to Accentuate the Affiliation
When a Fem is Wet   The Code   Calls it Sexual

The Dam Code The Damn Book

Add P/Man Power and He Gets Wept (In The Past)   (The Code Uses The Past to Undo The Present Also as in Forgetting it) (Men do Not Cry so it is Inactive for Him)
Add S/Is/His/Us Has/Ass/Hiss/As/Serpent/Penis and He Gets Swept (Men do Not Get Wet   so   He is Swept Away from That)
Switch E for i/Marriage Act and She Gets With (Wet with E/He is Close to Witch   Which is Which is All The Fems are All The Same   as Fishes in The Ocean   The Usual Message from   The Code)
Switch E for A/All Men and He Gets What (Men have No Connection with Wet so   What)
Switch T/Fem Cross for D/Pregnant and She Gets Wed (Wedding on Wednesday A Working Day)
Add Another Man E/He and He Gets Weed (A Man do Not Get Wet) Comprehensively with   W/All Fems Sex Active   in Front of   T/Fem Cross   and   E/He   Watching   The War is Lost for The Fem
Wet is a Cover Word Here

Whack: W   Hack
All W/All Fems Sex Active   to be Hacked says   The Code
whack: a strike with a smart resounding blow or blows
hack: to cut notch chop slice chop or sever with or as with heavy irregular blows   followed by up or down

Whale: W/Ail
A Big Fish   All Fishes are Fems (See Fishes in the Words Chapter) to Catch says   The Code   so
Use a Harpoon (Harp/On) (See Harpoon in The Words Chapter)
W/All Fems Sex Active   L/Sweet Fem Love Light/Elle/All/Ail/Ill/Hail/Heel/Hell/Oil   with   A/All Men   in the Middle   and a   Silent E/He
Take Away E/He and She Gets a Wall
Switch W for F/Fem/Fuck and She Gets to Fail or Fall
Switch W for J/Sheppard and She Gets Jail (See Sheppard in The Words Chapter)
Switch W for M/Motherhood/Him and She Gets a Male or it is in The Mail
Switch W for N/Virgin and She Gets a Nail (See Nail and Cross in The Words Chapter)
Switch W for P/Man Power and He Gets Pale (Scary to Catch a Big Animal (a Whale) Then He Put Parts in Pails (Commercialization)

Switch W for R/Are/Heir/Or/Whore/Err/Her and She Gets a Rail (See Rail in The Words Chapter) (She Thinks Life Will Get Easier)
Switch W for S/Is/His/Us Has/Ass/Hiss/As/Serpent/Penis and He Gets to Sail
Switch W for T/Fem cross and She Gets a Tale (a Lie) or a Tail (Scary for Her so She Stays Away   The Code is then Safe)
Switch W for V/Sex Fem Active and She Gets a Veil (Another Step into Her Slavery
Whaling is Not for a Fem (Too Much Information)   The Fem Gets to Ail and Wail (L/Ail/Ill/Hail/Hell/Elle)
Whale is a Cover Word here

Wham: W/Am
W/All Fems Sex Active   Am
All The Fems Get a   Wham
wham: a loud sound produced by a sharp contact or explosion
W/All Fems Sex Active   A/All Men   M/Motherhood/Him
All W as Mothers   or   be with a Man
W/Ham   Ham is Slang for a Fem   Not Much There for Her Except as a Piece of Meat (Pork being Forbidden in Most Eastern Religions)   All are Code Interactions

What: W/Hat   We/At   We/Hat
What   is a Question to Answer to Get More Information
The Code   Real Meaning of What is   W/All Fems Sex Active   In The Hat of   The Secret Code   Societies   as in Hat
We Her/R/Ear/Hear/Hair/Heir/Or/Whore/Err/Here/Are/Our/Ere/Air/Ire/Sex   in the Hat (See Hat and Art in The Words Chapter   Those are Important Words   Heavy Secrets Words in That Code)

Wheat: With
Wheat is a Fem Symbol
Take Away A/All Men and She Gets   Wet   Wed

Wheel: Will   A Will is a Legacy
W/All Fems Sex Active   L/Sweet Fem Love Light/Ill/Ail/Hail/Hill/Heel/Hell/Elle

The Dam Code The Damn Book

The Coded Wheel of Time Code Legacy is All Fems that are Ill   But Still Sex Active   Therefore are   R/Her/Are/Whore/Or/Heir/Err/Sex   or having a Heir Him/M/Motherhood   Etc   Endless Code Manipulations of The Fem Intelligence   Keeping that Hell/Ill/L Going in Her Subconscious for 2 Thousand Years
The Rota (Wheel) and The Tarot (Same Letters) have The Same Information   But The Non Initiate Grasps Only the Superficial Aspects of it
Take Away H/Secret Code Letter and Still Get a Wheel or a Weel (A Well in Scottish   How Convenient for The Code   It is at Will)
Switch Both E/He for A/All Men and He Gets a Wall (Protection)
Switch The 2 EEs/He for i/Marriage Act and She Gets a Will (Legacy   More Will Power for Him)

Wheel Barrel: Will   Bar   All/Ill/Elle/Hell/L/Sweet Fem Love Light W/All Fems Sex Active   and L/Ill/Hell/Elle   are All Barred from The Knowledge of   The Code
As a fem with No Power   A Wheel Barrel Needs to be Pushed to Move

When: WN   2 Fem Sound Letters
W/All Fems Sex Active   are With   N/In/Hen/Ann/Haine/Virgin   it is a Win says   The Code
(See Win in The Words Chapter)
Winnie (Winnie is Both a Fem and a Masc Name)
Win/He is The Masc Part
Winy and Whinny are related in   The Code   by the Wine/Fem Blood Loss
whinny: to utter the characteristic of a horse   neigh
Back to The Horse/Animals for The Fem   (See Horse and Whores/Hers in The Words Chapter)
whine: a long high pitch plaintive cry or moan
Fems are Not to be Taken Seriously says   The Code   They Just Whine
Win   Wine   and   Whine   are Cover Words here

Where: WR   2 Fems Sound Letters
W/All Fems Sex Active   is in Front of   Her/R/Ear/Hear/Hair/Heir/Or/ Whore/Err/Here/Are/Our/Ere/Air/Ire/Sex   along with   2 EEs/He (Plural or All of Them) Which are Very Quiet   and   H/Secret Code Letter
Were Reinforces it as in Something Safe   Where is it   It is in The Past

Lise Rochon

Wear/Her
W/Are   W/Here   W/Hear   W/Err   W   R/Her/Heir/Whore/Or/Err/Sex is in Plural Here with Many Different Fems (W/All Fems Sex Active)
Switch E/He for O/Fem Hole and She Gets Whore (Where are They   Ask the Interested Men)
The Code   is Close to The Fem   She is Wearing (Where/Were/Wear   In/N/Hen/Ann/Virgin) it
Wear and Were and Where are Cover Words in   The Code
wherein: in what or in which   in what way or respect
Whirring   W/Ring
whir: to move fast with a buzzing sound
hurry up   Where is Your Ring
We/Are/In   We/Are/N/Hen/Ann/Virgin   Where/N   Where/In   W/Here/N
Wearing   Wear/In/N   We/Ring

While: Why/L
while: interval of time   in the same time
Meanwhile something else is Happening   Pay No Interest to the Why
Why Why of the Fem being Split in Y from Her I (See Letter Y in The Letter Chapter)

Whim: W/All Fems Sex Active   and   M/Motherhood/Him
All Fems   are with   Letter H/Code Secret Letter   with   i/Marriage   and   M/Motherhood
It is the Full Hidden Goal of   The Code   for All The Fems
whim: capricious notion or desire

Whimper: W   M/Motherhood/Him   Per
Each and All of   W/All Fems Sex Active   Into M/Motherhood
Take Away M/Motherhood and She Gets The Whip (Her/R)   Motherhood (With M/Him is a Must in That Code)   The Whip Surrounds M/Motherhood   She can Only Whimper about it
whimper: to cry with low plaintive broken sounds

Whiny: Win/He   W/In/He   Wine/He   When/He
(See When in The Words Chapter)
Whining is Reserved to Fems and Young Children

The Dam Code The Damn Book

Whip: W/P
W/All Fems Sex Active   in Front of   P/Man Power
The Fem Cannot be On the Same Platform as   P/Man Power so   The Code   says a Big No to that   She Gets the Whip
Another Endless Loss Battle for The Fems
Switch P for T/Fem Cross and She Gets With (Con in Spanish   See Con/Cunt in The Words Chapter)

Whir: W/All Fems Sex Active   Are   Her/R/Ear/Hear/Hair/Heir/Or/Whore/Err/Here/Are/Our/Ere/Air/Ire/Sex
whir: to go fly revolve or otherwise move quickly with a humming or buzzing sound
Whirring   We/Ring   Move That Ring Quickly to Her
We/Are   N/In/Hen/Ann/Virgin   A Big No from   The Code

Whirl: Where   L/Sweet Fem Love Light/Elle/All/Ail/Ill/Hail/Heel/Hell/Oil   is All Dizzy (Days/He   See Days in The Calendar Chapter) From All That Whirl
whirl: to turn around spin or rotate rapidly
She has Little Attention Span or Strength from All that Estrogen Imbalance and Her Loss of Blood (Anemia)
The Code   is Immensely Powerful

Whiz: W/All Fems Sex Active   S/Is/His/Us/Ass/Has/Hiss/As/Serpent/Penis
whiz: to urinate   a wizard   to make a hissing sound
W/His
W/Z   All Fem Sex Active   Sleeping   Z/Sleeping on it   Not Aware

Who: W/All Fems Sex Active   H/Secret Code Letter   O/Fem Hole
Who is a Question   Who is The One Asking
H/Secret   Code   Letter   Stands   in   between   W/All   Fems   Sex Active   and   O/Fem Hole
Her Loins Will Serve to have Sex with   All Men and She Will Become   R/Whore   or have   a Heir   or   Err   That Way All Her Life   No Choice says   The Code
Woo is made of 3 Fem Letters

755

woo: to seek the favor affection or love of especially with a view to marriage
W/All Fems Sex Active   and   2 OOs/Fems Holes (Plural or All of Them) so Woo is   O/All Fem Holes   W/All Fems Sex Active   While She thinks it is All about Marriage/Monogamy
òu is Where in French

Whom: W/Home
Whom is The One Asking
O/Fem Hole   M/Motherhood/Him
Which One of All   VW/Fems Sex Active   Does He Take
OM is The Sound of the Universe
Add P/Man Power to Who and He Gets to
whop: to strike forcibly   to defeat soundly as in a contest to put or pull violently   whip
whopper: something unusually large
Whop/Her
The Code   says strike that Fem   Her/R/Ear/Hear/Hair/Err/Heir/Or/Whore/Here/Are/Our/Ere/Air/Ire/Sex
Look Carefully at the Word Or in Cursive You will See a Prostrated Fem
The Word Gold Means Or in French
Or Also Means One or the Other   Who is Who   or   Which is Witch   Etc   Back to be All Fem being Identical as   The Code   says about Her being   Fishes   or   Horses or   Chickens   Bees   Ants   Wagons   Etc
The Code   has Diminished The Fems to a Receptacle of Insults   and   Curses   and   Plenty of Sperm) She had No Choices in the Past
Now In Our Modern Times It is Different   She Can Chose
The Fems are Not   Whores   or   Hares
Hares (Rabbits) Have a Lot of Babies and are Often Kept in Small Cages Where They Hardly Move   Often in the Dark   Only because they have No Voice to Call for Help and Defend themselves
Add N/In/Hen/Ann/Virgin to Whore and She Gets a Horn (She is Available says The Code)
The Code   Over Time has Attenuated The Fems to Nothing
From Misses to Wall Flowers to Mothers to Whores

The Dam Code The Damn Book

None Can be Successful Because Success Anyway for Her is Just to Suck   Us/S/Serpent   or   Sex/Us
Add D/Pregnant to Whore and She Gets Hoard
hoard: to accumulate for preservation future use   a supply or an accumulation that is hidden or carefully guarded for preservation for future use
Add Another S/Is/His/Us/Ass/Has/Hiss/As/Serpent/Penis
to Whore and She Gets Horror
Whore/Her   Whore/Whore
Horrible: Whore/He/Able   He can do That   Even if it is Horrible
In the Same Word   The Code   Can Jumps Concepts from One Meaning to Another Depending Who is Listening
who: the one or ones belonging to what person or persons
Whop is a Cover Word Here

Whore: Or/Whore   One or the Other as in See Which is Which
Note the Word Whore Involves (In/Vulva) Whore as Gold (Or) and to be (Are/Her/) in its Sound as a Double Mirror (M/Whore   More) Effect in a Rebound of Sounds
Take R Away and She Gets Who   She Never Gets Out   The Code   says She can Only be That

Whose: Who   S/Is/His/Us/Ass/Has/Hiss/As/Serpent/Penis
His Hose is Oozing

Why: The Letter Y
Y is the Letter for the Broken Fem Warrior   Why Why Why   She is Stage One for The Fem Going Down
(See Y in The Letters Chapter)

Wicked: WCKD   All 4 Fem Sound Letters
wicked: morally bad
All W/Fems Sex Active   C/See/Sea/Virgin   K/Broken Fem Warrior   D/Pregnant
wick: a cord or band of loosely twisted or woven fibers   as in a candle cigarette lighter etc   that supplies fuel to a flame
From a Useful Little Wick to Morally Depraved
Wicked is Mostly Associated with a Witch

Lise Rochon

W/Kid   Wick/ID
From That Jump to Weak and Week (See Weak in the Words Chapter   and   Week in The Calendar Chapter)

Wide: W/Hide   We/ID
ID: unconscious instinctive satisfactory search for pleasure modified by the ego before their expression
ID: a mean of identification
W/All Fems Sex Active   are   All the Same and Identified as so
Letter i/Marriage Act   and   D/Pregnant   are Together
The Dot (See Letter i/I in The Letter Chapter and Dot in the Keyboard Chapter) having Sex with the Stick and Being Pregnant
ID has Many Uses   See Dictionary
Add Her/R/Ear/Hear/Hair/Heir/Or/Whore/Err/Here/Are/Our/Ere/Air/Ire/Sex to Wide and She Gets Wider
(Wide/Her   W/All Fems Sex Active   ID   R/Her/Heir/or/Whore/Err/Sex)
All Fem Sex Active being Whores   It is Their ID
wide: having considerable or great extent from side to side   broad
A Broad is a Promiscuous Fem   She is Called a Wide Hole
We/Dough   We/Do   We/Hide
Add O/Fem Hole to Wide and She Gets Widow   Add N/In/Hen/Ann/Virgin to Widow and She Gets a Window
(Window   Win/Dough   Dough is Money   Selling Her Body for Money)

Wife: WF   2 Fem Sound Letters   With   i/Marriage Act   in the middle   and a Silent   E/He
The Code   says W/All Fems are Sex Active   from F/Fem/Fuck   to   V/Single Fem   to   All Wives
A Wife   F/Fem/Fuck   In/N/Ann Plural Switches to   Wives V/Fem Sex Active
W/All Fems Sex Active   and   V/Fem Sex Active   Are in Double Here   In Singular or Plural Both Wife and Wives are All Sex Active   There is No Singular for Wives (Wive) Unless F is there Instead of V with   S/Is/His/Us/Ass/Has/Hiss/As/Serpent/Penis   Ending the Word
No Choice for The Fems as Usual
A Wife in Singular Changes Form   into   Wives in Plural
The Code   Loves Polygamy/Polyandry in Any Form
It Involves Anger Sadness Fighting Revenge and Worst

The Dam Code The Damn Book

The Ultimate Goal of The Code is to Make Everyone Confused and Separated We Then Remain Unaware of That Code and Remain Under its Ultimate Power
Strife Knife Wife
Switch F/Fem/Fuck for T/Fem Cross and She Gets White (Wet We/T Back to Sex and The Fem Cross for Her)

Wild: WLD 3 Fem Sounds Letters
With i/Marriage Act
W/All Fems Sex Active are with L/Sweet Fem Love Light/Elle/All/Ail/Ill/Hail/Heel/Hell/Oil and D/Pregnant
Her Will is to be D/Pregnant The Code says She Thinks it is Wild Another Mirage

Will: WLL 3 Fem Sounds Letters
With i/Marriage Act Uniting W/All Fem Sex Active and L/Sweet Fem Love Light/Elle/All/Ail/Ill/Hail/Heel/Hell/Oil (Plural or All of Them)
W/Ill We/Ill We/Will
W/All Fems Sex Active Ill/Hell/All/Elle
The Will of The Code is to Keep All Fems Sex Active Ill and in Hell It is Her Testament and Her Disposition
will: a faculty of conscious and especially of deliberate action a disposition a testament
The Wheel of Time Created by Saturn is there for That
Wheel The Wheel of Time (With Many Rings Surrounding Saturn (Sat/Urn (See Urn and Ring in The Words Chapter))
A Circle/Cycle/Wheel/Ring That Keeps Rolling Her Backward Forward
A Wheel is Made of Several Crosses Shapes T/Fem Cross/Great Fem Curse Surrounded by a Circle Made of Wood (Cross) or Metal (Met All)

Win: WN
W/All Fem Sexually Active N/In/Hen/Ann/Virgin
All Virgins are Sex Active It is a Win for The Code
Won: W/On
W/All Sexually Active Fem Are On As One

Window: Win The/D/Pregnant O
Win D/Pregnant O/Fem Hole

Lise Rochon

Win the   O/Fem Hole   Here is The Window   A Window of Opportunity (Hop/Her/Tune/He/T) Has Arrived
Window Seal: Win   The   O/Fem Hole   Seal (Secret)

Wine: W/All Fems Sex Active   is with   I/Marriage Act   in the Middle   with   N/In/Hen/Ann/Virgin   and Closing with Silent   E/He All N/Virgins to be V/Fem Sex Active
Wine is the Oldest Symbol for Her Blood Loss
Jesus at the Last Supper   and His Legacy to Drink Wine/Blood and and Eat the Bread (Break The Bread/Body to Breed)
Switch Her/R/Ear/Hear/Hair/Heir/Or/Whore/Err/Here/Are/Our/Ere/Air/Ire/Sex for L/Sweet Fem Love Light/Elle/All/Ail/Hail/Ill/Hell/Heel/Oil in Bread and She Gets to Bleed   The Sheep Bleats (See Sheep in The Words Chapter)
Win   We/In Whine
Take E/He Away from Wine and He Gets Win   WN
(It is a Win When W/All Fems Sex Active and N/In/Hen/Ann/Virgin are Together)
Switch E for G/Vaginal Penetration in Wine and He Gets a Wing (a Wing Cannot Fly Alone) Add S/Penis and He Gets to Swing
How Convenient for   The Code

Wing: Win   G/Penis Penetration Makes it Fly
Wing it

Winner: Win/Her   Wine/Her   Whiner
No Word Win/He for Her
A Weiner is a Sausage and Slang for Penis   Compare Winner to Loser   Loo/Sir   Loose/Her
When a Winner   Win/Her
When a Loser   Sir is at the Loo
loo: a lavatory
Loo is All Fems Letters
Loose/Her   then   Lose/Her
The Code   and its Wirings   There are No Losing for Men in   That Code

Wipe: W/P   We/P

The Dam Code The Damn Book

W/All Fems Sex Active   are in front of   P/Men Power   It is a Big No
from   The Code   so
Wipe that Dirt Off   or   Wipe Your Butt with it
The Whip is Close to Her Here

Wire: W/Ire   W/Hire
On the Wire is All   W/All Fems Sex Active   Angry
ire: anger
Or are/R/Her for Hire as a
wire: metallic conductor
Wiring   Wire   N/In/Virgin   and   W/Are/In
The Wiring of   The Code   is   We/Ring   It is The Wiring

Wisdom: The Wizard (Masc) and The Dumb (Fem)
Same for kingdom   The King and The Dumb

Wish: W/All Fem Sex active   Shh/She
The Code   says The Only Wish for The Fems is to be Sex
Active   and   Shh About it

With: W/T
T/Fem Cross/Great Fem Curse   is with   W/All Fems Sex Active
Oui is Yes in French   Oui/T   The Fem says Yes to That says   The Code
with: accompanied by
Add C/See/Young Girl and She Gets Witch   With/She
Which/Sorceress is a Big No from   The Code
No One is With Her says   The Code   She is Entirely Isolated and
Rejected   No Power   No Money   This Is It
Add E/He and He Gets White (The Code says No to Him being With Her
and Her Being a Witch so He is White/Out of it)
Witches Being Psychic   The Cats Are Associated and Were Also Horribly
Abused in The Past along with The Fems Because Cats are said to Intuitive
Animals
With is a Cover Word Here

Which and Witch are Almost the Same Word   They Associates Easily
Each Other in Our Psyche
A Witch is When T/Fem Cross is Added to Which

761

Then Any (Which is Which) Fem Becomes a Witch (Burning/Torturing Her was Always a Close Possibility)
A Witch is a Witch is a Form of that Concept
Add S/Is/His/Us/Ass/Hiss/As/Serpent/Penis (S as in Plural) to Witch and He Gets to Switch Them (Implying Sex with All Fems)
The Broom/Stick/Penis between The Witch Legs is Iconic and Ironic   They were Really Tortured from That Morbid   Code   Joke for a Couple of Thousand Years
The Difference Between Witches and Men of Great Magical Powers Such as the Magus   the Sage   the Wizard   is No One Talks about their Stick Between their Legs (Witches were Stuck with The Image of Having a Stick/Artificial Penis)
Where/Were/Are/R Our Fems of Great Power
Witches Burned for their Talents   While Many Mages/Magicians were Royalties Counselors   From Histories of Rasputin in Russia (a Poor One) and of Course The Great Merlin   Etc   (Not Much Positive for The Fems   which so Many have What is Called Magical Powers as   Telepathy   Intuition   Premonitions   The Search for Truth   Giving Birth   etc   Those Fems who Dare to do That Were Called Witches and were Destroyed
The Code   Maintains its Hypnotic Stance on Us
It is done that Way to Keep Men Power In and the Fem Out   Since Eve/V and Adam A/Dam(n)
Switch W for F/Fem Fuck and She Gets Fish (See Fish in The Words Chapter)
Take Away W and She Gets an Itch
Switch W for B/Boy Holding All Fem Breasts and She Gets Bitch
Switch W for N/In/Ann/Hen and She Gets a Niche (Something Small)
Switch W for R/Are/Whore/Or/Heir Gets Rich (Rich/Her   Which is Not   Has Never been   except if She Marries it or become a Whore   Anyway She Will Err   The Code   Lies to Her at All Periods (?) of Her Life)

Within: With/N   With/Hen   With/Ann
within: in or into the inner part   inside
W/All Fem Sex Active   N/In/Ann/Virgin
All Virgins to be Sex Active   it is Within Them says   The Code

The Dam Code The Damn Book

Without: With/Out   We/Thought
Without is Made of 5 Fem Letters   H being   The Code   Letter   it
Speaks to Both Sexes   Although The Understanding of The Concept has
2 Different Understandings Depending on The Sex
W/All Sex Fem Active   i/Marriage Act   2 TTs/Fem Crosses/Great Curse
(Plural or All of Them)   H/The Code Letter   O/Fem Hole   U/You/
Ovulating   Ending With a Second T
With/Thought   or   We/Thought   Would be Great for All The
Fems   But No says   The Code   She is Without that   With/Out   Wit/
Out   Out with the Wits for The Fems
Without is a Fem Word with 6 Fem Letters and it Starts with W/All Fems
Sex Active
With/Oat   is The Only Way for Her (See Oats in The Words Chapter   Not
so Good for The Fems to have Hers Spread

Wizard: Magus/Magi
wizard: a man witch or a male who practices or professes to practice
magic or sorcery   obsolete a wise man   super   outstanding
magus: an astrologer   sorcerer or magician of ancient times
There is Great Respect for Men Powers   Even Magical Powers
Compare that to Any Fem Holding Magical Powers (and There are So
Many) She is Called a Witch   They Lost their Properties and Their Lives to
The Pope or The State and Got Tortured too   All Over Europe and in The
World The Most   Smart   Beautiful   Knowledgeable   and   Influencing
were Killed   Often Just to Let Live the Few for Sex and Procreation
The Wizard in the Computer World is a giant Bank of Knowledge
Compare All this Commonly Accepted Men Power to the Powers of
Witches
Exodus 22:18   "Do not allow a sorceress to live"   "Thou should not suffer
a witch to live"
Just Another Harsh Life to The Fems that have Talents in This Area

Woman: Whoa/Woah/Wo/Woe   Man
Woah/Man   Wo/Man   Woe/Man
Whoa and Woah Have the Same meaning
whoa: stop   (used especially to horses)
woah: a command used especially to horses to stop or slow down
Whoa has a Silent A

Lise Rochon

(See Horse and Whores in The Words Chapter)
That is Us The Fems being Commanded as Whores/Horses
wo: archaic spelling of woe
W/All Fems Sex Active   and   O/Fem Hole   is in Front of E/He
woe: grievous distress affliction or trouble   an exclamation of grief   distress   lamentation
ho or hoe: a sexually promiscuous woman   a prostitute   a whore   a woman   habitual offender
Another Way for   The Code   to Stop Her or Separate Her from Men
Add Another O and He Gets to Woos (Plural or All of Them) Bringing in Polygamy)
woo: to seek the favor   the affection or love of especially with a view to marriage   to seek the affection or of someone usually a woman   court
Add Another H/Secret Code Letter and She Gets a Wow   as in W/All Fem Sex Active Fems with O/Holes are Congratulated because of that   but No   W/O is   Means Without

Women: Woah   Men
woah: stop   used especially to horses
Woah is pronounced without the Sounds of   A/All/Men   and   H/Secret Letter
Woo/Men
woo: to seek to persuade   a person   a group etc   as to do something   solicit   importune   to seek the affection or love from someone usually a woman   court
The Fem has No Name for Herself Except as in being Wooed (See Woo in The Words Chapter) by Men   or   by being Stopped (Woah)   or   being Kept in Distress or Affliction (Woe)
W   Omen
The Omen here is   W/All Fems Sex Active   O/Fem Holes   are with Men (Amen   All Men   A/Man)

Won: All 3 Fem Letters
W/All Fems Sex Active   O/Fem Hole   N/In/Hen/Ann/Donkey/Virgin
Virgins with Holes are/Will be All Fems Sexual Active   It is a win
We/On   W/On
Won is Win in the Past   When was the Won   and/or   What did She Won
To/Win   T/Win

The Dam Code The Damn Book

The Fem Won   She became a T/Fem Cross/Great Curse
To/Win   She Got Twins

Wonder: Won   D/Pregnant   R/Her/Are/Heir/Or/Whore/Err/Sex
Create Wonder in a Woman   She Wins   D/Pregnancy
Add U/You/Opened Hole/Natural Ovulation and She Gets Wound/
Her   She Just Fell in a Trap from   The Code

Wonderful   Won/D/Her/Full   Wound/Her/Full
D/Pregnant is Full (Pregnant) that is a Win for   The Code
The Wound and the Womb are from the Same Origin

Wonderland: Won/D/Her/Land
There is One Wonderland for The Fems in   The Code   Pregnancy it
is   She Won That   Wound/Her/Land   is The Way

Woo: All 3 Fem Letters
woo: to seek the favor affection or love with a view to
marriage   especially for a woman
W/All Fems Sex Active   2 OOs/Fem Holes (Plural or All of Them)
The Real Woo for   The Code   is to Have   2 OOs/Fem Holes (Plural or
All of Them from   W/All Fems Sex Active
Switch W for B/Boy Holding All Fems Breasts and He Gets
Boo (Too Young for The Code)
Add D/Pregnant and She Gets Wood (Slang for Male Erection) a Good
Luck Sign for The Mascs   a Natural Substance

Wood: Would   A Good Omen
All 4 Fem Letters
W/All Fems Sex Active   2 OOs/Hole/Loins (Plural or All of Them)   D/
Pregnant
All O/Fem Holes   from   W/All Fem Sex Active   are   D/Pregnant
Woo/D   to Scare   D/Pregnant
Switch D for L/Sweet Fem Love Light/Elle/All/Ail/Hail/Ill/Hell/Heel/Oil   and
She Gets Wool (See Sheep in the Words Chapters)
Switch D for P/Man Power and He Gets to Whop
whop: to strike forcibly   to defeat soundly as in a contest   to pull out
violently

765

Lise Rochon

Contest (Con/Test)
Wood is Lucky says   The Code   (Knock/Touch Wood)   Woody/Wood/He is Slang for Erection

Wool   All 4 Fem Letters
W/All Fems Sex Active   L/Sweet Fem Love Light/Elle/All/Ail/Hail/Ill/Hell/Heel/Oil   Animal (Ann/He/Mal)   Fur (For/Her)   Something Warm and Cozy Because it is   W/All Fems Sex Active   with   2 OOs/All Holes (Plural or All of Them) being L/Ill and in Hell
Wool is The Name for The Sheep Fur   (See Sheep and Sheppard in the Words Chapter) It is a Important Knowledge About How Works   The Code   with The Fems

Woozy: All Fem Letters are Together Ending with Z the Letter for Sleep W/All Fem Sex Active   Guiding   2 OOs/Fem Holes (Plural or All of Them) to   Z/As Above as Below/Sleep on It
That would be a Big No from The Code   so
woozy: stupidly   confused   muddled
That is the Spirit (Spear/Hit   S/Pair/It) of   The Code   She Always Lose

Word: The word Word is a Very Important Word in   The Code
R/Heir/Or/Whore/Err/Her   D/Pregnant   Close to Horde/Herd/Hard/Hoed
W/All Fems   O/Fem Hole   R/Her   D/Pregnant   is The Word   as in
All   O/Fem Holes   Having Sex   and Get   Pregnant
Add L/Ail/Ill/Hell/Elle and Get World
"In the Beginning was the Word and the Word was with God and the Word was God" John1:1
I Try Not to Use the Bible as a Reference in this Book There are Many Codes in the Bible that We Know and Not Know   But This Phrase is a Cornerstone in   The Code   Symbology   It Indicates   That The Language Code Understands the Power of the Word is God
The Bible has a Lot of Levels of Understandings
I do Not know How it Happened but   The Code   Created a Level of Bad Mysteries to Humanity
If the Word is God That Means here that   The Code   Language Created God and Not God Created the Language
In Fact People Created Words and Languages But The Secret Societies Manipulated Them

The Dam Code The Damn Book

No God Came and Gave Us that Language Package for Us the Human Race to Use
The Reflection of Our Words to Our Gods/Goddesses Would be to Use Our Kind Words to Adore the Highest
Scholars in the Time that the Bible was Re-Translated Under Emperor Constantine Knew about the Hidden   Code   in the Everyday Language
The Secret Societies Control the Modern World Through the
Language   The Numbers   The Math Symbols   Music Language   and More
word: a command   a direction   an order   a verbal signal   a password   a watch word
Add S/Is/His/Us/Ass/Has/Hiss/As/Serpent/Penis and He Gets a Sword (The Sword That Jesus was Possibly Talking About)
Add a S at the End of The word Word and He Gets it in Plural (Another Winning Combo for The Man)

Work: WRK   3 Fem Letters Sound Letters
W/All Fems Sex Active   R/Her/Hair/Are/Here/Hear/Ear/Heir/Or/Whore/Err/Ire/Ere/Sex   K/Broken Fem Warrior
It is Her Work says   The Code   to Have All Fems Sex Active as K/Broken Fems
Worker: Work/Her
There is No Workhim in The Language Only Workers as in Work/Her
The Goals of   That Code   Remain The same   Even if Both Sexes are Workers
W/Orc
orc: a mythical monster   an ogre
There is No Mythology in Working for Most of Us
It is a Crude Reality Especially with the Wages of Now
Same for Work for Working: Work   N/In   The N/Virgin is here for Her Work   Her is   WRK   as seen Above in Work

World: 5 Fem Letters
W/All Fems Sex Active   O/Fem Hole   R/Her/Hair/Are/Here/Hear/Ear/Heir/Or/Whore/Err/Ire/Ere/Sex   L/Sweet Fem Knowledge/Love/Ill/Ail/Hail/Hell/Elle   D/Pregnant
We/Old with R
We/Herd/Horde with L

horde: a large group of people
World is Word (See Word in The Words Chapter) with L/Sweet Fem Love Light/Elle/All/Ail/Hail/Ill/Hell/Heel/Oil   in between   R/Err/Heir/Or/Whore/Err/Her   and   D/Pregnancy

Worry: War/He   Whore/He   W/Or/He
The Real War and Worry for   The Code   Here is to Maintain
That   Whore/He   and   Pregnant One as in
Worried: Whore/He/D/Pregnant   War/He/D

Worse: We/Whores
Switch W/All V/Fem Sex Active for H/Secret Code Letter and Get Horse (A Powerful Phallic Symbol) (See Horse and Whores and Heirs and Err/Letter R   in the Words Chapter)
W/All Fems Sex Active are in Front of the Horse/Whores   That is a Big No from   The Code   so
Worse it is for Her   Another Down for Her   as Usual in   The Code

Worship: Worship is a Very Difficult Word   Tread Carefully Reading it
In   The Code   Everything Related to The Water is Fem
As in Whore/Ship
In   The Code   a Whore is an Oar (a Fem Noun) on a Boat at Sea/See/C   An Oar/Whore Propels and Steer a Boat   It is the Only Fem that Survives Above The Water   All Other Fems are Fishes   They Cannot Breathe/Breed Outside Water
The Hook (Hook/Her) is What Brings The Fems Outside the Water on a Ship (Where She will Become a Sheep (She/P) or a Boat (Boot) for the Fisherman (Fish/Her/Man)
The Pope Ring is Called The Ring of The Fisherman   In French it is Called l'Anneau du Pêcheur
In French un Pêcheur is a Person That Sins and is a Fisherman   There is No Fem Word for Fisherman such as Fisherwoman (She Cannot Fish Herself   This is Why There is No Fem Priests or Popes in Our Religions)   Hunter Hunt/Her   goes Right to The Point
It is a Sin Against Consciousness to Treat The Fems as Bates   But No says   The Code   so   Adore   Add/Whore
Or Means Also One or Another   Or/Sheep   The Fem Kept as Whore/Oar/Slave is Gold for   The Code (Or is Gold in French)

The Dam Code The Damn Book

The Whore as Sheep is Now on The Ship   The Sheep is The Fem Kept Under the Stick of The Sheppard (See Sheppard and Sheep in The Words Chapter)
Many Domesticated Animals Represent Different Aspects of The Fems Dominated by   The Code   The Horse is The Whore   Chickens are Chicks as Girls which Keeps Her in Stupidity   The Bees   The Fishes   The Ants   The Donkeys (Ann/N) and Much More depending on The Moment
Worship/Whore Ship is Supposed to be the Religion for The Fems   to be Whores and Sheeps Etc
To Adore (Add/Whore) a Whore is Irrelevant   The Scare Alone Give Shivers (Read about the Temple of Venus a Long time ago where they Used to Kill/Tortured The Fems/Virgins for Money as Offering to Their gods
Switch Letter O/Fem Hole for A/All Men and He Gets
warship: vessel of war
The Code   is Always at War with The Fems to Keep Her Under its Control (Cunt/Roll)   Warships Battle Happen on The Water
worshipper: Worshipper is a Cover Word here
There is No such a Thing as to Worship/Her in   That Code
The Hindu Religion on the Other Side of Our World has Thousands of Goddesses and Gods
There are No Big Organized Religions on Our Side of the Planet (Plan/Hit) that Worship Goddesses
To Transform Men Attributes Such as a God Prince Mayor or Actor To Fem   The Code Adds an S/Is/As/Has/Ass/His/Us/Hiss/Serpent/Penis Such as Prince/Ass (Princess) God/Ass (Goddess) Mayor/Ass (Mayoress)   Actor/Ass (Actress) and Many Others   She is The Laugh of   The Code   as usual
More Emotional Barriers for Her to be Humiliated with as Her Life Advances in   The Code   World

Worst: Whore/See/T
W/All Fems Sex Active   O/Fem Hole   Her/R/Ear/Hear/Hair/Err/Heir/Or/Whore/Here/Are/Our/Ere/Air/Ire/Sex   would see   Her Situation Being   T/Fem Cross   and   Whores/Or/Heirs   That would be a Big No from   The Code   so
Worst it is
Were   S/Is/His   T/Fem Cross

769

Lise Rochon

Worst is in The Past Also to Accentuate its importance

Worth: W/Art
The Fems are the Center of   The Code   Sacred/Secret Arts (H/Secret Code Letter)
Whore/T
It is Worth Gold (Or) to Keep W/All Fems Sex Active as T/Cursed Fem
Her/R/Ear/Hear/Hair/Oar/Err/Heir/Or/Whore/Here/Are/Our/Ere/Air/Ire/Sex
The Code is at War/T Against All Fems
W/Are/T   We are T/Fem Cross
Worth/Wart is The Cover Word Here

Worthy: Worth/He
The Fems Do Not Look at that if Possible   It is a Wart
Were/T   as in the Past to Accentuate its Importance   In The Past too She is a T/Fem Cross   It is Worthy says   The Code

Would: Wood   (See Wood in Chinese Astrology   a Good Omen)
Wood is Slang for Penis Erection   A Good Thing

Wow: 3 Fems Sound Letters
2 WWs/All Fems Sex Active   O/Fem Hole
All Fems Sex Active Twice   and   O/Fem Hole   as In Plural   A Redundant Message   a VIP Term
wow: enthusiastic response
WOW OWE O WOW Infinitely   for Her
All Fem Holes Opened and Having Sex   and   She is Enthusiastic about That says   The Code   Wow

Wrap: W/All Fems Sex Active   Rap
rap: to strike especially with a quick smart or light blow
to utter sharply or vigorously   *Slang*   to talk or discuss especially freely   openly or volubly   chat
a quick smart or light blow   the sound produced by such a blow
to beat the rap   *Slang*   to succeed in evading the penalty for a crime   be acquitted   to take the wrap   *Slang*   *to* take the blame and punishment for a crime committed by another
Rap is Old Important Word

The Dam Code The Damn Book

The Origins of Wrap   from Dictionary.Com   Says in   ORIGIN OF RAP: 1300 1350   akin to Swedish *Rappa*   to beat   drub
Drub is Synonymous of Rap
drub: to beat with a stick   cudgel   flog   thrash   to defeat utterly   as in a contest   to instill with force or repetition   to drum or stamp   a blow as from a stick
Add E/He and He Gets Rape
Rape   is   Bad   Bad   Bad   Religion Religions   So Close to Ape
Rap Sounds as a could have been a Nice Word   But No   says   The Code   Read Again the Definitions of Wrap above   a Violent world it was   Everything goes from Pure Violence   to   Total Forgiveness   to   Conversations   and   Talks   and   Men Being Acquitted   too
It is a Full On Wrap   Especially   Because   W/All Fems Sex Active   are Integrated in that Rap
Rapture Comes to Mind
In the Modern American Language   Rap is Something Happy to Go with   The Code   Often Caches Itself in Contrary Meanings as Our History Evolves   Hiding its Steps as It Goes

Wrath: W/Rat
W/All Fems Sex Active   Rat
The Rat is Present in Many Words   When   Hat   is in It
Wrath is W/All Fems Sex Active   Silenced as being Rats
Were/Hat   Where/At
The Rat is in the Hat with   The Wrath says   The Code
The Hat Lives in the Art   The Secret Arts (See Art in The Words Chapter)
Add B/Boy Holding All Fems Breasts and He/She Gets Brat (Too Young for the Hat and Not Helping Either)
Add F/Fem/Fuck and She Get Frat (She is Excluded from it (F/Rat) as The Fem is Considered a Rat   She will be Excluded from That Knowledge Which Frat Boys are Allowed and have Plenty of Fun about it)
Take Her/R/Ear/Hear/Hair/Heir/Or/Whore/Err/Here/Are/Our/Ere/Air/Ire/ Sex   Away and He/She Gets Fat (That is What happens When a Fem Abandons R/Her/Sex   She gets Fat   a Big Taboo in The Occidental Countries) and Math (A Code Tool) is So Close

Lise Rochon

Wreck: RK
Her/R/Ear/Hear/Hair/Err/Heir/Or/Whore/Here/Are/Our/Ere/Air/Ire/Sex   K/Broken Fem Warrior
The Transformation from K into R Happens here in   Wreck
This is when She (W/All Fem Sex Active) Enters   R/Whore/Or/Heir   After Been   K/Broken Down Fem
wreck: any building structure or thing reduced to a state of ruin
Another Word Starting With a Silenced   W/All/Fems Active   and   She Cannot say a Word about Her being Wrecked by   The Code   She has being Raked by the Old Hood/Hat

Wring: Ring   W/Ring   We/Ring
W/All Fem Sex Active   are Silent   and so is   G/Vagina/Hymen (Hi/Men) Penis Penetration
wring: to twist forcibly   to distress   to extract or to expel by twisting or compression
wringer: a painful difficult or tiring experience   ordeal   usually preceded by *through the*
R/Whore/Or/Heir/Err/Her/Sex   N/In/Hen/Ann/Virgin   R/Her/Are/Whore/Heir/Err/Sex
To Ring Her is a Distressful Situation
Why/Ring   Wear/Ring   It is in the Wiring   as in Connecting Her Wires to Whore/Her   In
Wringer: Ring   Her
whoring: to put to a base or unworthy use   *Obsolete*   *to make a whore of   corrupt   debauch*
The Fems Never get a Chance for Her Imposed Redemption   The Code   Keep on Destroying Her

Writer: Rite/Her
The Secret Code   is The Writing of Their Codes as Religious Rites   Which Includes Her as   R/Her Whore/Or/Heir/Sex   Only

Wrong: One of the last Words of the Dictionary
The Right and the Wrong   The Right and the Left
Here The Fem Stand Again at the Bottom of the Pile
or   at The End of the Line
Wrong   is   Wrung

Wrong Could be a Mantra Word/Sound   If its Meaning was Not Badly Distorted
Wrong Sounds to the Ears as the Sounds of Echoed Fast Drums
Wrong Wrong Wrong   Turns in Circle and Twist Itself in Kaleidoscopic Bell Sounds   Ring that Belle is in The Past   It has Already Happened says   The Code

X x
Intro
X is a Code Made Fem Letter
X is Reserved to The Fems and The Losers
X Shows Her Complete Fall
It is the Letter of the T/Great Curse or Fem Cross in its Last Stage   T/Fem Cross has Fallen   into   X/Fallen Cross   The Code   Grid has Now Succeeded   T is Out   as being Dead/Eliminated   T/Fem Cross is Now The X/Fallen Cross
X is 2 Pyramids One on Top of Each Other   One is Reversed as an Hourglass (See BB in Words)
Looking Down from the Tip Top of a Pyramid it Will Look as a Shape of an X Shape Form
We can Only See 2 Faces When Looking from a Corner
We can Only See 1 Face as we Stand in Front of it
Number 4 is Related to the Sometimes Benevolent Jupiter   or   The Law   When in Fact it is Saturn the Reaper (Rape/Her)   The Code   Man that Rules Over The Fems
The Eye (I/High) of God is in the Pyramid (See a Dollar Bill)
Letter X Is the International Symbol for Closing Something as in a House or a Window Drawing   Being X from a Place   A Movie Being X Rated   etc
There are Few Words that Start with X/Fallen Cross in Reason of its Letter Meaning
In Fact those X Words/Symbols are All Hidden Under All Vowels or Other Letters   The Code   puts a Silent Letter before X as Ex (Expulse   Exert   Exchange Execute   Explore   and Many more)
Ax   Ix   Ox   Ux
In   The Code   The First Letter of a Word Starts its Concept   so Starting a Word with X Would Mean that even as Dead She Would be in Charge of that Word Meaning   Which is Improbable

So Cover Words that would Starts with Another Letter such as with EX or EV   They have   He/E   a Masc Letter in Front of the Fem X or Fem V   as in Showing Her the Way
E/He is Silent as Sound   See Words Starting with Ex or Ox or Ax or Ux Words Starting with Exe or Eve Words are a Barrier to Her as The Code   Encircles Her or is a Close Witness All Around Her   it is Her Always Coming Back to Pregnancies   and   Ovulation at Any Time for The Fems   That is Under The Axe/X
Eggs and X   The Eggs and Her X/Her Fallen Cross
Once Pregnant a Fem has Lost Her Go to Freedom
The Work is Immense for a Mother She has No More Time for Herself and Her Dreams/Goals They Become Almost Impossible to Reach   Especially in Our Past Where She had Very Little Help   Except from Her Family and Sometimes She did/does Not have that
(The Free and the Dumb is His Freedom   So is the Kingdom It is The King and The Dumb   (See Doom/Dome as Fem Breasts in The Words Chapter))
There are No Change Between Small Cap x and Big Cap X She is Doomed from Childhood to Follow that Only Road
The   X/Fallen Fem Cross   is the   T/Fem Cross   that has Failed (fld Sound is 3 Fem Letters) and Fallen (fln Sound is 3 Fem Letters)   Fl (to Fail) and Fn (a Fine) are 2 Losing Words and it is Just Fine to   The Code
Note That X is a Roman Number   Number 10 as in the Complete Sequence from Number 1 to the End of The Keyboard the Zero Which is Her but is Not a Number   She can Only Add says   The Code   Another Example of The Fem Not being a Real Entity
To Put an X is to Put Your Signature to Identify you
Words with X are   Hex (a Spell)   Axe (Death)   Ex (as in Gone and Finished)
End of Intro

X   x
Xoxoxo: X/Fallen Fem Cross   O/Fem Hole
This is When   O/The Fem Hole   has become   X/Fallen Fem Cross in Harmony says   The Code
XOXOXOX are Dead Fem Holes says   The Code   to The Fems but No XOXO   Are Kisses from The People That Love Each Other   Blowing Kisses at Each Other in Letters Writing   and   They Always Return   and   XOXO is a Fun Game for Kids and Big Kids Too

The Dam Code The Damn Book

The Code Games in Action here   Are All Covers for The Perdition of O into X

Y y
Intro
Y y   Is a Masc Made Fem Letter
Y is a Poor Weak Letter   Y is The Wounded Fem (Her Why Why Why Y/Why Why Why is that Loss of Her Blood and that Curse Shame on Her
Y is the First Stage of   The Secret Code Plan   Her Letter I Her Stick of Power (The Masc has The Same Letter as a Start in Life   except Hers is a i (She Carries the Dot   See Dot in The Words Chapter) is Being Split   She will Become the Y/Wounded Fem   The ½ Broken Fem
Y is Her I Fragmentation   All Fems Have to go Through says   The Code
Y/Fem is Her Sexual Heat
Y is the Letter/Symbol in Between Her I on to Be the Letter V/Fem Sex Active   The Spirit of the V is the Letter for Eve   He/V (A/Damn is for The Masc)
W/All Sex Active Fem   are the   Eves/Vs   He/V
Letter Y as in the Wine Glass Shape and the Chalice   The Wine Represents Her Loss of Blood   She Will Whine (Whiner/Wine/Her/Win/Her   Wine/Her Blood Loss Symbol)
That is How they Call it   The Fem Lament   She is Mary (Her Catholic Name is for All Fems as First Name Which Means Bitter)   Bitter in Greek is Amer   so it is in French
Amer in French is Mère/Mother
In Greek Letters the Y is a Triton (the Neptune God Fork that Keep Order (The Code Order) in the Ocean where He is   In Astrology Neptune and his Triton Guards the Pisces Astrological Sign
The Sea is Mem (Letter MM for Mothers)
The Hebrew Letter for the Fish is Nun (NN the Virgins)
Pisceans are Naturally Artistic Sensitive Psychic Gentle and Patient   She has No Need for a Huge Pointy Fork to be Moved Forcefully Around as a Robot in Her Ocean
Then Why
Another Trick of   The Code   here
Pisces is the Last Sign of the Zodiac the # 12 the Number of Achievement/Completion

Lise Rochon

Therefore   The Code   Goal is Attained in the Ocean (O/She/N is an Entirely Fem Symbol)   She is Quiet as a Fish Now
Letter Y is Top Half of Letter X/Fallen Cross Where She Will End After Letter I went Through the Process of the Code Grid
From I to the Y   V   L   K   then   T   then X
Word with Letter Y   Why

Y   y
yank: to pull abruptly
He/Ankh
ankh: a tau cross with a loop at the top   use as symbol of generation   or   enduring life   also called   ansate cross   crux ansata
That Definition/Description is Wrong   Also The Jesus Cross is Not a Sign of Resurrection   He was Nailed on a Cross   No One Survives That and So is She on That   T/Cross Where She will Die in   X/Fallen Cross

Yeah: EA   2 Masc Letters   E/He   A/All Men
In Singular and Plural for The Mascs   It is a Yes says   The Code
There Are No Fems in Power Here on the Sound Level
Yah   (He/Ya) is Slang for Yes (His   He/Is   Iss)
Y/Wounded Fem First Stage Starts the Word Herself   as In Acceptance of the   H/Code
Yea   Ya   Yep

Yield: Yell/D
D/Pregnant   is Yelling While Yielding
Yield is All Fems Letters Except for   E/He   Watching
yield: to give way
Shield   She/Yield   But No   She has No Shield   because She Can Only Yeld

Yell: E/He   L/Sweet Fem Love Light/Elle/Ill/All/Ail/Hail/Hell/Heel/Oil   Starting with   Y/Broken Down Fem Warrior   Which is Silenced Here
He is Associated with Hell   so
yell: to scream with pain
The Code   Hates Compassion (Con/Pass/He/On)

The Dam Code The Damn Book

Yellow: Yell   O/Fem Hole
She Screams All the Time   As Pee Coming Out   All is Normal in   The Code
He   Ill/Hell   Owe
Orange is   R/Heir/Or/Whore   and the   Angel (Ange in French)
Green is   GRN
G/Vaginal Penetration   and   R/Her/Hair/Are/Here/Hear/Ear/Heir/Or/Whore/Err/Sex   for   N/In/Hen/Virgin   is going on a Green Light   Meaning Fem Penetration for All Virgins   for Heirs or as Whores
Purple is a Mix of Red and Blue (as Big as the Sky (All is Blue for The Masc) and the Blood (All in The Red for The Fems)   Purple is Loved by The Roman Catholic Church
Colors are Cover Words in   The Code

Yelp: He/Help
Anything a Man would Do Sweetly such as Helping The Weak is a Big No From   The Code   so
yelp: a quick sharp shrill cry as a dog or fox
She (as   Y/Wounded Fem) Helps   is in 2 Words for the Secrecy of   The Code   Here

Yep: Yes
Y/Wounded Fem First Stage   Starts the Word
S/Is/His/Us/Has/Ass/Hiss/As/Serpent/Penis   is replaced with   P/Man Power
Yep Goes Along with Ya   Yes   Yea   Aye   Ye   All Starts with Y
If   T/Fem Cross/Great Curse   Ends the Word   as in Yet
it is a Big No from   Code   so
Yet   He/Hit   He/It

Yes: Yes is a Masc Word   He/Is
He/E   S/Is/His/Us/Has/Ass/Hiss/As/Serpent/Penis   Y/Wounded Fem   E/He   S/Penis   It is Yes to Break   Y   With   S
Sex   Yes   Success   Yes   (See Success   Suck   His/S/Is/Us/Ass/Serpent/Penis)
Sound as an Orgasm   Great Fun   Yes   He   Is

Lise Rochon

Yes is the Total Symbolic Acceptation of the Eye on Top of the Pyramid and All the Horrific Symbolic History it Brings Along with   The Hidden Language Code
The Small Circle (Cycle)/Dot on Letter i is the Fem
All those are Vital Concepts for the Secret Code   In the Eastern Languages There Are Plenty of Those Dots   Above and Under The Line
i/High/Eye/Sex Act   The Stick
I   Is the Old Syllable for Yes (Aye)
I   is The Man Stick as a Small Boy Stick and Her Dowry (The Dot)
Yea is Same as   Ja   Ya   (See   J/The Sheppard Stick   in the Words Chapter)
It is All Good for Him says   The Code   She has No Chance

Yesterday: Yes   T/Fem Cross/Great Curse   Her/R/Her/Whore/Or/Heir   Day (D/Pregnant)(D/Hey)
The Code   says that Yesterday She Was a Cursed Pregnant or a Whore Compare to Tomorrow (Two/More/O)   Polygamy is Always in the Cards for   The Code
Tomorrow has 3 OOOs/Fem Holes   and   2 RRs/Her/Are/Whore/Or/Heir/Sex   and it Starts with T/Fem Cross/Great Curse
To/Morrow   from The Morning (Morn/In/N/Virgin) She will Suffer Too Tomorrow says   The Code
The Code   is The Saddest Story in the World Knitting the Human Mind

Yet: He/Hit
Always   The Code   Plans a Hit/Violence at Any Moment Towards The Fems
Here   Y/Wounded Fem   is Too Close to   T/Fem Cross   and That would be Too Much Possible Information Coming to The Fems
Y/Wounded Fem/Why   E/He   T/Fem Cross
Y/Wounded Fem   Starts the Word   and   T/Fem Cross/Great Curse   Ends it   and   E/He Unites those 2 Concepts   from Wounded She goes to the Cross
T/Fem Cross/Great Curse   Brings the Time Element (See Time   The Wheel of Time) to Ye
He/It   He/Hit
To Hit on a Fem is to Want Sex from Her

yet: at the present time   up to a particular time   thus far   in spite of that
Switch Y for W/All Fems Sex Active and She Gets Wet
How Convenient for   The Code

Yikes: YKS
Silenced   Y/Wounded Fem   (Why Why Why) and   K/Broken Fem Warrior   are in front of   E/He   and   His/S/Is/Us/Ass/Serpent/Penis
That Would be a Big No from   The Code   as in Too Much Power for Her   so
yike: an argument squabble or fight
yikes: expression of alarm   fear
She cannot Win in   The Code   Especially as a Y

yoo-hoo: There are 4 OOOOs/Fem Holes in this Word
Y/Wounded Fem is the Opening Letter   therefore Calling the Meaning of the Word
With   H/Secret Code Letter in the Middle of those 4 Fems Loins   the 4 Cardinals Points (Compass   Con/Pass   the Rose/Her) Going in Every Direction
Y/Wounded Fem Shows the Way to All Fems Genitalia to Enter into the H/Secret Code Letters Grid
When   Y/Why   Start a Word there is an Acceptation or a Let Go   (See Yes and Yesterday in The Words Chapter)
Yoo Hoo is as Little Wagons Following the Lead of Letter Y/Wounded Fem to the Grid
yoo-hoo: used as an exclamation to get someone attention in calling to another person or the as
When   The Code   Get to Her it is
oho: an exclamation of surprise taunting exultation etc
All Lies and False Tales from   That Code
The Code   Also says that the Veil is Good for Her

Yoyo: Y/Wounded Fem   Twice   with   O/Fem Hole/Uterus/ Loins   Twice
All Wounded Fems Alone with Their Holes
That Cannot be so it is   a Big No from   The Code   so
yoyo: an incompetent person   a spool as toy

Lise Rochon

Words with Repeating Syllables are often Little Rhymes Teaching Secretly   The Code   to Our Subconscious

You: All 3 Fem Letters   The Letter U
Y/Wounded Fem   O/Fem Hole   U/You/Ovulating
You is Her as Another Person   Here Again She is Not Her Own   She is a Receptacle from   The Code
(See Chalice)

Young: You/On   U/On   You/Own
Yong Yong Yong   as a Trampoline Bouncing Sound
Yum Yum says   The Code   M/Motherhood Twice is Around as M and N are Interchangeable in   The Code
Yawn   Yawn Keeps Her Sleepy
Young Yawn and Yum are Cover Words here

Your: UR   You/Are/Her
U/You/Ovulating   Her/R/Ear/Hear/Hair/Heir/Or/Whore/Err/Here/Are/Our/Ere/Air/Ire/Sex
The Sex Object   is Her Uterus (You/Tear/Us)

Yoyo: From   Y/Wounded Fems Twice (Plural or All of Them)   to   2 OOs/Fem Holes (Plural or All of Them)   Up Down   Up Down   They All Go
A Game from   The Code   to Her   There is No Stability for The Fems

Z   z
Intro
Letter Z Means as Above as Below in   The Code
Letter Z is a Rarely Used Letter   But it is an Important Letter
Z is the Last Letter of Our Alphabet
It Indicates that What is Below Will be the Same as it is Above
Letter Z is for Sleep and for Snooze
Z is the Sound of a Saw Cutting into the Wood (Wood is Made from All Fem Letters   Woody Wood/He is a Male Erection) a Known Sleep Inducer Sound which Means to Forget About It All
Z/As Above as Below

The Dam Code The Damn Book

"In the Beginning was the Word   And the Word was with God   And the Word was God"   This is the Turning Point Concept Here When a Deity/God is Described/Created by a Language

Z z
Zero: Z/Sleep on it   E/He   Her/R/Ear/Hear/Hair/Heir/Or/Whore/Err/Here/Are/Our/Ere/Air/Ire/Sex   O/Fem Hole
See/Her/O   See/Her/Owe
C/See/Young Girl   Row
S/Hero   See/Hero   Zorro
Z/Sleep on It   or   Z/As Above as Below
Sir/O
Z/Sleep   R/Her/Sex   O/Fem Hole
Sex is on with Her as a Whore   Sleep on It   It Means Nothing   There is No Math Value in Zero (o is a Fem Symbol)
Any Word Letter or Number in the Shape of a Circle is Fem by Essence says   The Code   The Man Symbols are Sticks
Real Power should Not Only be Represented by/with a Stick
The Code   System is Simple that Way
It Stole Many Fem Symbols and Made them its Own
Zero: Letter Z being Paired with a Hero
She is a Hero When She is the   O/Fem Hole   or   Zero   and   She Sleep on It
zero: the figure or symbol o which in the Arabic notation for numbers stands for the absence of quantity

Zone: Z/Sleep   Own/On   Z/Own
The Code Own Her while She is Sleeping at the Wheel   Pun Intended

Zoo: Z/U   See/U

Zeus: C/See/Young Girl   S/Is/His/Has/Ass/Us/Hiss/As/Serpent/Penis
Seize/Us   Sees/Us   As the Eye on the Dollar Bill

WORDS WITH ONLY FEM LETTERS
Clot (Blood)   Cluck (Chick/In Her/R)   Cocoon (Nest) Cock (Slang for Penis)   Coffin   Common   Con   Coo (To Talk Amorously)   Cook   Coon (an Undignified Person) Coot (Crotchety

Lise Rochon

Old Person)   Cot (Bed)   Cow   Cuckoo (Wood Bird)   Coy (Shy)   Cul   Cunt   Cut   Do Dodo (More Poop on Her)   Dol (unit for measuring pain) Doll   Dong Don t   Dud   Dull   Dung (Poop)   Flood (of Blood or Water Cry)   Flower (Flaw/Her   Flow/R (as a Fish)   Fluid Fog   Food   Fool   Foot   Foul   Follow   Fox   Full (Pregnant)   Doom   Goon   Hot   Hunt   Hoot   How   Hut   Lim   Loco (Crazy in Spanish)   Loll   Loo (Toilet)   Loom Loon (Stupid)   Looter (Loot/Her   Stolen Goods   Pillage) Lot   Lout (Stupid)   Low   Lull   Mock   Miss   Moo (Cow Sound   Her)   Mood (Menstrual Mood)   Mom   Moon (Fem Planet   Blood Loss)   Mud   Mum (Silence)   Mutt (Mix Bred Dog/Bitch)   Nell (Fem Name)   Nil   No   Nod (Accept)   Non (No in French)   Not   Noun (Known)   Now Null (Without Value as in Nil)   Nun   Nut   Odd   Of (to Belong)   Off   Old   Oz   Coucou (Crazy in French)   Out Own   Ov   Wool (See Sheep in The Words Chapter)   To Too   Tool (An Implement)   Toot   Town (T/Own) Tut (Shame)   Tutu (To/Two   in a Tutu)   Void (Empty) Vomit   Two   Woo (To Seek with a View to Marriage)   Wound   Wow   Yuck
Here is Part of   The Code   Zoo (Z/Sleep on Those 2 OOs/Fem Holes) Aside Fem Letters   I Included Here Some of the Strong Words   with   Letter H/Secret Society Code Letter   Which is Entirely Masc being   The Code   itself   H is Often Silent   and/or   Asexual I Also Included Words with Letter i I/Marriage Act   In Big Cap There is No Fem Presence   In Small Caps Only it Includes Her as The Dot on the i Ancients Eastern Writings have them in All Their Writings

           PROPER NAMES   FAMILY NAMES   PRONOMS
The Code   has Embraced Giving Names to Humans that will Identity Themselves   Inside Us
I Apologize in Advance for Any Inconvenience   And I Feel So Sorry for All of Us That Suffers from That for a Very Long Time
Agnes: The Lamb   l'Agneau in French   A Fem Name   The One That Sacrifices Herself   Agnes   Saint   Christian Child Martyr under Diocletian   Feast day
Alex: All   X/Fallen Fem Cross
Alice: All/His
Alma: All/Ma (Mothers)
Amy: Aim/He   Âme/He   Soul is Ame in French

The Dam Code The Damn Book

Ann: N/Ann/In/Hen/Virgin
Annie: Any   NE
Anne-Rose: In/Rose
Agnes: Ann/He/Ass   Agneau is Lamb in French
Baker: B/Boy Holding All Fem Breasts   Ache   Her
Ben: B/In/N   Been In
Betty: Bet/He/E   Beat/He   Batt/He
Brigitte: Bridge It (See Bridge in The Words Chapter)
Carol: Care/All
Darlene: Dear/Line/Laine   Laine is Wool (4 Fems Letters   See Sheep) in French
David: D/Pregnant   Eve/V/Fem Sex Active Since Eve   Hid/id   David is an Ancient Name
All   Fems   Pregnants   From Beginning to End with David   Because   D Starts and Ends the Word David
Diane: Great Fem Name   So Clean and Luminous   But No says The Code   Die/Anne
Two Different Fems Fem here   Diane and Ann   are in That Same Boat
Dick: Richard (Rich/Hard)   (My Brother)
The Code Tarnishes Everything Nice   So   Richard became a Dick   Why   He had Already One
Dickinson: Dick and Son   Dick/N/In/Hen/Virgin/Son   The Way to Go   Kind Of Honest   Too hard   But No R/Whores There
Dixie: A Large Kettle   a mess tin   (Cattle) VIP Name   Dicks/He Dixie is a Fem Name
Doreen: Door/In   D/Whore/N   The/Whore/In
Dear Doreen That is What You Get   Said The Code For having Such a Sweet Name   Adoring
Elizabeth: L/Ail/Hail/All/Elle/Hell/Ill   S/Is/His   A/All Men   Bet/Beat/Bat   All/Is/A/Bet   Elizabeth is a Powerful Name for a Powerful Life   Elisabeth is My Favorite Fem Name   She has/had to Endure   Queen Elisabeth of England Also
Eric: Heir/IC R/Her/Hair/Are/Here/Hear/Ear/Whore/Or/Heir/Err/Sex   IC/Integrated Circuit   Eric is a Roc   A Strong Masc Name   The Fems as Him are   R/Sex   IC   Integrated Circuit   A/All/Men   The Fem is Never Left Alone in   The Code
Fannie: Buttocks   Fan/He   Fan Those Says   The Code

783

Lise Rochon

Felix: Feel/X So So Soft (Fem) for a Masc Name But No says The Code Fail/X Letter X is The Letter of Death Anyways

Fido: FDO 3 Fem Sounds Letters a Popular Male Dog Name Back to The Animals for The Fem (Bitch is One of Her Names)

Google: Internet Related Services Corporation which is 2 GGs/Hymen Penetrations (Plural or All of Them) Surrounding Two or All O/Fem Holes The Code Combo I Goo People of Different Genders Can be Together and Goo Together and it Passes Right Under the Mean Radars of The Code Gogle to All

Helen: Hell/In Helen is a Noble Strong Honest Name Why

Joan: Jo/Ann/N John (Toilet) John and Joan Such Nice Names But No Says The Code A Toilet it is for You

Harry Potter: Hairy/Pot/Her Hair/He/Pot/Her Air/He Pout/Her Are/He/Pot/Her

Hope: Is the Sister of Faith (Hop and Fate)

Jennie: Gene/He

Joel: G Hell/Ill/Elle/All/Letter A Jewel Jell as in Chill

Jim: Gem

Kate: Gate Add S/Penis and Get Skate

Keller: Kill/Her

Kevin: KVN 3 Fem Sounds Letters Cave/N K/Broken Fem Warrior V/Fem Sex Active N/In/Hen/Virgin/In

Lexus: L/Sweet Fem Light X/Fallen Fem Cross Us/S/is/His/Us/Ass/Hiss/Serpent/Penis

Lise: French Name My Birth Name Lies Lice in English

Lulu: Lou (a Toilet All Fems Letters) (Twice as in Plural or All of Them)

Louis and Louise: Loo/ls Lu/Hiss/S All Fems Letters a Toilet

Marah: Another Version of Marie and Mare Marah Means Bitter Waters Marah is a Desert in Saudi Arabia

Mark: M/Arc A Mark (See Arc and Arch) Une Marque in French Signature

Marianne: Marry/In Mary/N Merry/Ann/N Such a Nice Name but The Code Always have Other Intentions

Mary Marry Merry go Round Etc It is to Get Her Married asap as Ann/Donkey As N/Hen/In/Virgin Etc

Marie Therese: Marry/Theirs Mary/T/Rise (She Rises Because She Marries Says The Code The Endless Hook)

Marion: Marry/On

784

Maurice: More/Is/His
Maury: More/He/E
Minnie: Many   Mine/He   So Small
Mulan: Mule N/In/Hen/Virgin   A Mule is a Donkey   And Null is Close as a Twin
Nell: N/Hell/Elle/Ill/Letter L   Nell is Not Known as a Bright Kid/Girl Name
Such a Nice Soft Sound Anyway   But No Says The Code
knell: any mourning sound   the sound made by a bell rung slowly especially for a death or a funeral
Switch E/He for O/Fem Hole and She Gets Knoll
knoll: an archaic or dialect word for knell
kneel: any mournful sounds
Neil: NL 2 Fem Sounds Letters
N/Ill
N/In/Hen/Virgin   L/Ill/Hell/Ail/Hail/Elle
Ophelia: Ophelia is a Dream Name   But No says   The Code   Off/He/Lay/A
Otto: All Fems Letters   a Masc Name   Hot   O/Fem Hole
Paul: P/All/L   P/Man Power   L/Sweet Fem Light   All Pals
Penny: Fem Name   Puny (Insignificant) Amount of Money
Richard: Rich/Hard   Also Known as Dick   Slang for Penis   Such a Nice Name A Name that Works Hard for His Lifestyle
Rick: Wreck (RK) The Battle Between   K/Wounded Fem   With   R/Sex/Her/Heir/Whore/Err/Sex   Until She Loses to R
Roger: Rag/Her   Roger That   The Rag in the Hat (See Art in The Words Chapter)
Ron: Run
Rose-Mary: Two Fems are Better says   The Code   so Call it a Healthy Delicious Cooking Herb   to Make it More Enviable   It Does
A Rose is in   That Spice Word RoseMary (Polygamy) Called in French Romarin   Making it Special   (See Rosecrucian)   Roses are The Fems Sex Symbols Because   An Open Red Rose Looks a Vagina Seen From The Outside
Roxanne: Rocks/In   R/Ox/N/Virgin   Strong is The Virgin   As an Ox
Sarah: SRA   3 Masc Letters (Que Sera Sera   Que Sera Sara)

Here Again a Super Grand Name for a Fem   Disappearing   Why   Why   Sarahs are Strong and Super Nice   But   No Says The Code
Sir/A   You are to Serve   Sire/He
Shannon: She   N/In/Hen/Virgin   is On   Shine/On/Virgin
Sheldon: She/Hell/Done   She/Ill/Done   She/All/Do/On
Sherwood: Share   Wood
The Code   Tendency to make Men Polygamist
Stacey: Stay   C/See/Young Girl   Fem is not suppose to get Old
Stevens: Stay/Even   Stay/V   N/In/Hen/Virgin   Stay   V/Fem Sex Active   N/In/Hen/Virgin
Toby: To/Be
Vivian: 2 VVs makes a W/Fems Sex Active   and   N/Ann/Hen/Donkey/Virgin
Will: Well   Wheel   We/All   W/Ill (W/All Fems Sex Active)
Weinstein: Wine/Stain   A Perfect Example of   The Code
Family Names are Important in   The Code   because   They Remain Over the Time of That Generation itself   which Continues the Message of   The Code
In the Name Weinstein (The Stain of The Menstrual Blood/Wine) here Maintain   That Code   Mentality of Abusing The Fems Young   or   Old to   To Mark Them   Abuse Them   Weaken them   so   The Fems Become/Stay Enslaved
All This is an Unknown War Directed to The Fems for Thousand Years   and   She Knew Nothing about it   Not Even Knowing She was The Taget/Victim of   That Code   That Made Sure   She Kept on Bleeding   Feeding That Curse   T/Fem/Cross/Great Curse

William: Will/He/Aim   Great Noble Name for a Man   Full of Hopes and The Will to Do   M and L Implies Fem Energy All Around Softening it All

The Dam Code The Damn Book

THE ROMAN NUMBERS

I II III IV V VI VII VIII IX X is 1 to 10
L is 50 C is loo D is 500 M is 1000

There are No Coincidences here
In   The Code   The Roman Numbers are All Represented by Fems Letters   Except for The Stick which Until the First 3 Stages Represent Both Sexes   Then After that The Stick will be a Masc Representation Only   as in I (Later will come the P/Father Figure Letter (See P Letter in The P Words Chapter Introduction)
When Scrutinizing its Forms and Shapes these Old Number Symbols from the Roman Numbers Open a More Detailed Vision to Look at   The Code   Because being Older (Old/Her) They are Easier/Simpler to Analyze/Understand
In Occident We Transferred Our Numeric System from The Roman System to the Arabic System
The Comparison with the Arabic Numbers is Done Here
In All The Roman Numbers (Numb/Her   Not   Numb/Him) His Masc Symbol The I/His Stick/The Power of the High (God) will Never Split and it will Never Change (as in Weakening and Destroying Him as it does to The Fem)
The Code   is Specifically Conceived (Con/See/V/D) for Her to Change Her Nature and Make Her Suffer Greatly Until She Has/Had No Power/No Road of Any Kind Over Her Lifetime Except to Follow and Obey The Rules (Commonly Called after the Menstrual Cycle or   The Curse) of   The Code
In This Chapter about the Roman Numbers   The Code   Represents Her in Stages or Steps She will have Go Through in Her Lifetime says   The Rules   of   The Code
In The Roman Numbers The Past is Represented on the Left (a Fem Symbol) of The Roman Number   The Present and Future is Represented by The Number on The Right (The Masc Symbol)
As said in This Damn Book   The Code   Never Leaves The Fem Alone   Except Here When She is in The Earliest Stages of Her Life as in   1/I   2/II   3/III   It is a Powerless Age for Both Sexes
Exceptions   She will be Alone at   V/5/Fem Sex Active All The Time   Where it is the End for Her Natural Evolution in That Numerology   V/5 is the Beginning of the End for Her   Her Next Step is

10/X/Fallen Cross Where She will Meet Her Soon Loss of Blood which is Letter T/Fem Cross which is Not Part of Those Roman Numbers   X/Fallen Cross is The Fallen T/Cross or The Nail

After That   L/50   C/100   D/500   M/1000

The Roman Numbers Uses Only the Number 1/I and the Number 5/V

Number 5 is the End for The Fem at Any Place in   The Code   System Because 6/Six/VI is the Number of 6/Sex and Where She has The Presence of The Masc in Front of Her (as in Under His Authority) This would be Too Much Information for Her says   The Code

Then 7/VII is the Number of His Luck Not Hers   7 is Also The Mystery of The Not Fitting Right Angle   a Secret of The Initiates Only (Masc Only members)

Then 8/VIII is Pregnancy Which She Should Know Nothing About Until it Happens to Her

9/IX is the Crone which She has No Access Generally   in The Past

The Fems would get Killed or die in Earlier Age (as in Giving Birth) Not Knowing/Not being Educated

The Fem can Only go as Far as Her Split V/5   She cannot Trespass The 5 as Numbers from 6 to 9 are Positions of Power for Her   it would Tilt The Balance on The Other Side of Knowledge

In The Roman Numbers There is 1 as in One   Then I/1 as in 10/X/Fallen Cross adding a Zero There is 5 as in # Five   then 5 as in # 50/L/Sweet Fem Loving Light/All/Hail/Ail/Elle/Hell/Ill   Adding a Zero /Her for Multiplication Another 1 in 100/C/See/Young Girl   This Time Adding 2 Zeros/Her as in Bigamy

Another 5 in 500/D/Pregnant

Finally the Last 1 as in 1000/M/Motherhood

So It Jumps from 1 to 5 Only   From Childhood at Stage 5 Letter Vv/Fem Sex Active at All Time will Represent Her from Now On in Her Lifetime   It is Expected to be Wounded being a Fem

After That   The Code   Uses The Pressure of Zero to Make Sure She Has No Incentive No Desire and No Power to Get to a Better Place   She will See Nothing Except Zeros in Her Life and Innumerable Sorrows in Between those Numbers

At Stage # 10 Letter X/Her Fallen Cross Represents Her   as Already Cursed   She will Start Losing Her Blood Soon

At Stage # 50 Letter L/Ill/Elle/Hell/Ail/Hail/Sweet Loving Light   Her Load of Sorrows is Immense (M/Menses)

The Dam Code The Damn Book

At Stage # 100 Letter C/See/Young Girl Represents Her Identity   She is Nothing but a # 1 with Zeros in Front of Her   or   He is #1 with 2 Zeros   Zeros Indicates the Fems so 2 Fems Indicates Bigamy   Another Strike for The Masc

At Stage # 500 Letter D/Pregnant Daughter Represents Her   Again She is Nothing More than Nothing/Zeros even if She is Pregnant   The Code   Reminds Her That at All Times by Adding More Pressure and Weight by Adding More Zeros in Front of Her as The Numbers Advance in Size

At Stage # 1000 Letter M/Motherhood Represents Her

The Code   has Attained its Final Goal   All Fems are D/Pregnant or M/Mothers and She will Carry All The Weight that Those Letters and Zeros Bring Along

She Went from 1 to 10/X/Curse to L/Sweet Fem Love/Ill/Hell/Ail/Hail to D/Pregnant to M/Mother

No Matter which Number   She Carries All The Extra Weight of the Letters Included in The Number and The Sorrows Those Letters Brings with Them from the Previous Stages

She is Alone in   The Code   She will Suffer Great and Greater Suffering Until She Dies (Including the Mother in Law (Cries) Infamy)

For More Information about Those Letters See The Words Chapter for the Meaning of That Letter in the Introduction Chapter of That Letter

The Number 1   is the Letter I (i/Sex Act in Large Cap) It Represents the Power Stick Which is the Male Penis in   The Code (In Reality a Stick is a Raw Natural Power which has No Sexual Connotation   Who Owns it has The Power)   The Stick Represents the Scepter

In Small Cap (Childhood) Letter   i/Sex Union   The Fem is Represented by The Dot   She will Disappear from That Picture and be Integrated in The Male Symbol the I in Adulthood (it is the Same Process in The Change of Her Name to His When She Gets Married)

In   The Code   Letter I is Important   It is Said to be The Power of The High (God) which is Hidden in The Secret of The Pyramid

In The First 3/III Stages of Her Life Her Sticks Remain The Same as The Male Child   She is Unbroken in   I   II   III

In Stage # IV   The Number 4   Letter V/Fem Sex Active Appears   Her I is Now Preparing to be a Split Stick where She Will have to Accept to become # V/5/Fem Sex Active All The Time

Lise Rochon

At Stage IV/4 Her Stick Starts to Be Split from its Top as in Her Head is Starting to be Brain Washed into the Shape of V   Sexual Abuse Starts Often at That Stage

Letter Vv will Remain in the Same Shape All Her Life from Childhood   Far Gone is Her Natural Uu/Letter (Her Natural Ovulation Cycle from a Long Time Ago) which was there before the Age of Eve (Ov/V) and Adam (A/Damn/Dam/Dame/Madame) at Least 2000 Years Ago   In Number 4/IV Her Natural Stick (The I) Accompanies Her Through Her Annihilating Changes Until stage 5/V

In # 4 an Extra Stick is Tying Her Hand/Arm (Harm) to Her Head on the Right Side as in Closing/Eliminating a Natural Passage from Her   Note That without that Extra Stick It would still be Her as a Fem Cross/Great Curse   That Extra Stick is Another Bar/Sorrow   The Code   Imposed to Her   as All the Other Ones that will be Coming in Her Lifetime

In Stage 5/ V is the Letter for V/Fem All the Time Sex Active   Represents Her Life as Almost an Entirely Split Stick   She Continues Her Life with a Handicapped Split Stick/Scepter

5 is   The Code   Right Angle Symbol   It is Above Her Head Over Her Half (Only) Circle (Anything Round or Curved is Fem in The Code) There is No Perfectly Round Circle in   The Code   to Identify Her   Letter O is in a Shape of an Egg (How Convenient for The Code Reminding Her That She is Just a Machine to Make Babies) and the Very Elongated o Represents Nothing Except the Zero (o) that She is says   The Code

In Stage # VI/6   The Letter V/All The Time Fem Sex Active   has the   I/ The Masc Stick/His/Is/Hiss/Serpent/Penis   for the First Time in Front of Her   It is the Sign of   The Code   Power Over Her which will be there for The Rest of Her Life   She is Either Alone with Nothing for Example M is Alone as in Mille/a Thousand is a # I/1 Facing 3 Zeros   A Harem if the Stick is Masc   or   If it is a Fem She is Alone with 3 Zeros   She Always has Sticks/Challenges in Front of Her for Example MXXXVIII   It is All Fem Letters   as All of Them Except the Stick the I

Six is the 666 (Sex Sex Sex) The Mark of The Beast   The Code   Appears as That Force Over Her   It will Continue to Impose itself with More Weight and Number   in   VII   VIII/7   until   IX/9 where She will Meet Another Unbearable Challenge   It is Her   X/Fallen Cross   The Great Curse which Comes with Her imposed   T/Fem Cross/The Great Curse

The Dam Code The Damn Book

In Stage # VII/7   The Code   will Remain Getting Stronger/Heavier on Her   The Amount of Men in Front of Her is Getting More Powerful by its Weight and Number as She Gets More Fragile
Number 7 is His Lucky Number (Not Hers)   It is Also The Angle that does Not Fit in   The Code   That Secret 5th Right Angle   No One Hears about it Anymore
Seven as in Sève/In   Sève is Tree Sap in French   It is from The Tree of Life or/and The Tree of Knowledge
In   The Code   The Tree of Knowledge is The One That Prohibits its Believers to Know from Knowing the Difference Between the Good and the Bad Especially about Sex   The Snake is There   The Snake is Represented by Letter S/His/Is/Hiss/Snake/Penis   The Tree of Knowledge is Our Own Inner Conscience   The Forbidden Fruit is The Apple   The Apple Means Pure Heart and True Love Adam and Eve Get Banished from that Kingdom (the King (Him) and The Dumb (Her)) for Wanting True Conscious Kind Love instead of   That Code   Horror We have Lived by for Generations
In Stage # VIII/8 is the Letter for Her Pregnancy   She has All Men (When There are Repetition of the Same Letter Twice or Three Times it Means Plural or All of Them) in Front Her   Her Power is Now Null (Null is Made of All Fem Letters) or Nil (Nil is 2 Fem Letters plus i/The Marriage/Sex Act)   She is Now Full/Pregnant (in Null Switch N/Virgin for F/Fem and She Gets Full)   Forced Pregnancy has been Common in Our Past and Still is in Many Places
In Stage # IX/9 She will be Falling into Another Level of Suffering   The X/Fallen Cross (The X is the Mark) is Waiting for Her   She is Trying to Integrate the Pain and Suffering from V VI VII and VIII   In IX She is Fragmented and getting Ready to Fall in Completely Powerless in # 10/X/ The Fallen Cross from The T/Fem Great Curse
In Stage # X/10 is the Letter for Her Fallen Cross   Ten as is Thin (Many Girls are Depraving themselves of Food to become Thinner in Weight Adding of the Problem of Losing Lots of Blood Every Month   it is Called Anorexia or Anemia a Common Weakening State but Often Unspoken and Ignored in Women)   and Tin (a Weak and Cheap Material) It is The T/In as in   T/Fem Cross/Great Curse   is in T/In
After X/10 it will be the Same Pattern   The Masc is in Front of Her in   XI   XII   XIII   Until Stage 14/XIV Where the Abuse Continues to Accumulate Until She is at Stage XV/15 Where is the   X/Fallen Cross   and

a Fully   V/Fem Sex Active   That Fragmentation will Continue Under The Pressure of the I/Masc in   XVI   XVII   XVIII   Where She will Crack Again from The Pressure in a Another Weakening Change for Her   the # IXX Where The Crosses Continue to Multiply in She will Continue to Lose More Strength Power in XX   XXI   XXII   XXIII   The Pressure Gets Stronger on Her Until   XXIV   and   XXV   where the Abusing Situation Repeats itself Adding More Pressure to Her as The Pattern Gets Heavier Until She is   XXX/30   Until Another Misery is Added to Her at   XL   Preparing Her for Stage   50/L   Another Transformation is Imposed to Her Again
In Stage # L/50 is the Letter for L/Sweet Fem Love/All/Ill/Elle/Hell/Ail/Hail   Number 5 has Now a Zero in Front of Her Multiplying Her Handicap by 10
Zero/o (Her Symbol) has No Value Unless there is Someone/Something in Front of Her to Give Her a Meaning a Direction
L is Her Hell/Ill Destined to All Fems Even if She is Sweet or Smart Lilith Double LL and a T/Fem Cross was the First Wife of Adam
In Stage # C/100 is the Letter for a Young Girl A Cent or a Penny (a Common Fem Name) Represents Her as the Smallest Amount of Money The Smallest Amount in Value   It is Another Way of   The Code   to Impoverish The Fems   Another Way to Make Her Weak
The Code   Works its Goals those Ways
Eventually it is Her Scent that will make Her a Prey as in Pregnant
The Moon Crescent Represents Letter C
Letter Cc in   The Code   Pictures All Cycles of the Moon   C being the One with the Least Light   The Code   Rules Over Her Ignorance by Keeping Her in The Most Darkness Possible
She Cannot be Pictured by a Black (?) Moon (as in Nothing) as it would be Impossible to See Her at All so   The Code   Chose the Next Smallest Aspect of Her as a Moon Symbol
The Moon Letters Forces All (with the 2 OOs/Fem Holes as in Bigamy) N/Virgins to become M/Mothers   Moon is Made Entirely of Fem Letters Another Obligation from   The Code   The Moon Cycle is to have All Fems to Bleed on a Cycle of 28 Days   When Actually Most Fems Bleed at Different Times (Her Bleeding is Artificial also)
It is   The Code   That Created this Affiliation of the Fem and the Moon   In Fact Scientifically She has No More Affiliation to this Satellite (Something That Follows) than a Masc has
A Masc is Never Represented by a Satellite of Any Kind in The Code

The Dam Code The Damn Book

For The Fems the Choices are Few   it is Heaven (Oven is the Belly Where Babies are) and/or Earth (Hurt)
In Stage # D/500i is the Letter for Pregnancy   It is The Repetition of   50/L/Ill/Hell/Elle   and 5/V/Fem Sex Active   with a Lot More Pressure on Her She has Nothing Else to Look at Except a Bunch of Nothing (The Accumulation of Zeros in Life)   Have a Lot of Sex Even if Ill or in Hell   Get Pregnant or Get Nothing
In Stage # M/1000 is The Letter for Motherhood   She Went through the Mill and came Out as Flour (Flower)
Mil is a Tiny Unit   Mille in French is the Center   The Place to Aim and to Focus for All The Fems
With M/Motherhood The Goal is Attained and the Numbers have No New Letter after That to Represent The Fems in the Roman Numbers

Lise Rochon

THE NUMBERS
D/Pregnant   Numb   Her   S/Serpent/Penis
Cunt   D   Numb   Her   S
Count   the   Numbers (Surveillance)

NUMBERS   FROM 1 to 0
AND
THEIR ASSOCIATED SYMBOLS ON A KEYBOARD

The Way the Symbols and Letters Are Arranged on a Keyboard Fascinated Me as Being Mysteriously Weird Combinations
As Said and Often Repeated in   The Words Chapter   Everything that is Fem in the English Language Symbols/Letter/Numbers is Mostly   Unimportant   or   Transitional   or   Stupid   Something that has No or Little Significance by themselves and Have a   Poor   Weak   Bad   or a   Bimbo   Value   The Fems had No Exit to that Life as Information from All Over The World Proves That The Pattern has been Repetitive   The Silence of The Fems   The Poverty of The Fems   The Forced Pregnancy of The Fems   The General Powerlessness of The Fems   The Total Absence of The Fems in The Religions Gods Books

1   and The Exclamation Point   !
One is Made of 3 Fem Sound Letters   WON
Number 1 is Essentially a Masc Number
Number 1 is Important because it Represents Power
It Represents the I or The Self   It is Also the Number of God   the Power of The High/I/Hi
It Implies Often a Positive Reward to arrive First in a Race   for Example
The # 1 is the Stick or the Penis and it has Its Own Penis at its Top Pointing to the Side as in Showing It   It is On as One
The ! Exclamation Point is the Stick/Penis Pointing or Coming Down Towards Her   The Dot/The Dowry   is The Fem Symbol for Pregnancy   The Dot being Full as in Pregnant
Symbol   !   Is an Exclamation as it is loud   Because   It is the Hidden Sex Command   or   the Sex Call to Her from Him
That is   The Code   Element Surprise here   There is an Immediacy

2   and The At   @
Two/To is Made of 2 Fem Sound Letters
2 is a connection between 2 items as in At
Number 2 is Commonly Perceived as a Relationship Number   or   the Symbol for the Fem Number Being the Second Number   Yes   and More   The # 2 is The Shape of a Half Heart or Half the Shape of a Fem Butt   being Held Down Stable by a Laid Down Stick/Penis
2 says   The Code   is a Connection Between 2 Items (One is Fem   it is the Half Heart or the Half Butt See Letter Omega) The Other is The Laid Down Penis/Stick/I/Letter of God/The High
The   @   is the International Symbol of At   in Our Email Addresses
Its Popular and Inoffensive Symbol Added a Super Protection to The Letter A as in a Super All Armored a/All Men (See A/All Men in the A Introduction of Letter A in The Words Chapter) It Surrounds Letter @   It Makes a Good Hat and Directs Us/S to the   At   A/All Men and T/Fem Cross   as an Entity   Very Subtle is   The Code

3   and The Grid
TRE are The Sounds Letters for # 3
Tree is an Important Word in   The Code   because of   The Tree of Life   and   The Tree of Knowledge   2 Biblical Terms
The Circles   Half   Full   Empty   Represents the Symbols for All Pregnant Fems   or   Her Breasts
3   is The Grid #   It is Letter H   H being   The Code   Grid Letter
Here   The Code   is Represented by   2 HH/s Superposed   It is in Italic as in Fast Forward into Her Future   It is Expending from Past to Future   #######   being Almost Invisible in The Present as That Grid is So Tight and So Fast
Number 3 Represents the 3 Pyramid Corners Seen from a Front Eye Level   One Corner is Not Seen from its Square Structure Foundation   The Eye on the Pyramid   The Secret of the Ancients (The Code) is in it))
3 is the Number 8 Halved   and   Implies Bigamy Because there is Another Reversed Halved 3/Fem Breasts Sealed to Another in # 8
Those 2 3s are Now Facing Each Other in # 8
Number # 8 can be Laid Down Horizontally in the Pi Symbol ∞ Sign or   # 8 can be Standing Up Vertically
8 Represents also 2 Pregnancies

Lise Rochon

Here 2 Dots are Sealed Together in a One Stroke of a Pen   In a Form that Draws a Snake Biting its Tail at the Top Where the Top Circle Loop Closes
The Infinity Sign is The Pi ∞ Sign   Symbol of the Serpent Biting its Tail
8 is also 2 Pairs of Breasts   or   4 Breasts   as in Bigamy
3 Represents All Fems with Very Round and Enlarged Breasts
The Fem in   The World Code   is Pictured as a Domesticated Cow that has Extremely Large Man Made Lactation Glands   as in Tau   A Cow that Represents The Fem in Antiquity
This is How   The Grid Code   Moves Forward
In Reality a Fem is Not That or Not Entirely That   But we are Milk Machines by The Magic of the Universe   and the Milky Way has been Named for Us to Remember That
Italic is the   Hit/All/IC   He/Tall/Lick   or   Hit/it   All/Leak   IC Means Integrated Circuit   The Code   Words
In that # Grid Symbol   The Code   Identifies Itself or its Letters Symbols Expending Fast Forward from the Past into the Future #######
that Way
The # Grid are the Prison Bars/Sticks Where She is Confined in   The Code
(See in The Clock Chapter The 11th Hour)
With its   2 HHs   Standing on Top of Each Other   The Code   Letter Explains its Grid Power in a Different Way as it is The Only   Symbol   or   Letter   or   Number (Except # 8/Pregnancy) That Doubles Itself Upward   Giving it   Higher Position/Higher Vision etc
Pregnancy being The Goal   The Measures to Inforce those have to be Up to That
3   The Word Breast without   R/Her/Sex   Makes the Word Beast   The Mark of the Beast is 666   Sex Sex Sex Because   The Code   is All About Sex
Breast and Beast Words are All Made of Masc Letters Except for the Last One   The T/Fem Cross/Fem Curse   Which is   The Coded   Path for Her and is Her Identity in   The Code as in   Her Goal   and as   Her Achievement   being The Last Letter of The Words Breast and Beast Here

4   and The Dollar Sign $
FR is Made Entirely of Fem Sound Letters
4   is a Long Vertical Bar (Man Stick) with Another Bar Crossing it to Make a Reversed Cross/T/Fem Cross/Great Curse

That Cross Extends a Lien from an Arm Up to the Top of The Cross (Head) Drawing a Right Angle in its Way
4/For   is for the   4/Four   F/Our   also as in the 4 Whores (See The R Introduction in Letter R in The Words Chapter)
F/Fem   O/Hole   R/Her/Sex   All Fem Holes For Sex
It is The Popular Concept of The 4 Wives for 1 Man in the Middle East
Or is Gold in French
Un Four in French is an Oven   Fourrer is Fucking in French Slang
The # 4 is the 4 Corners of the Pyramid
4 is Solid and Strong and has a Square Shape
It Can be Opened Closed or Locked on Any or All of its Faces
Letter T or the nail   being Fem is The Center here   She should Not be there in   The Secret   But Because She is the Reason for That Secret Knowledge as the One Inside that Prison   She has to be there as its Symbol for The Initiates to learn
And She is still Being Blind and Deaf to it/Hit
That Cross has Become the Example of Normality to the Fems
Number 4/Four/For Sound Starts with Letter F/Fem and the Word   Our/Whore/Or
The Sound Heir/R which is Generally Part of The R/Her/Sex is Absent here   its Sound being too Far from Our/R   as in Four/For
That # 4 Makes All Fems All Whores in   That Grid
Switch in The Word Law A/All Men for O/Fem Hole and She Gets Low (The Fem Goes Down Again Here)
4 Has integrated The Cross (Letter T/Her) as a Plus (+) in the Great Law
Take L/Sweet Fem Light Letter Away in the Word Plus and Get Pus   The Fem are Mostly Horrified of that
The Last Letter # 22 the Letter Tau/Taurus/The Cow in Ancient Hebrew is a Cross Sign   or   a Cow Head and it is Called the MARK
That is How Old   That Code   is
In the Middle East in the Villages The Fem/Daughter is Still Called a Sheep by Her Own Father/Husband
The Dollar Symbol $ is Related to Number 4 on the Keyboard
4 is The Number of The Law   It is The # Grid for The Power of   The Code
The Planet Jupiter Rules # 4   Jupiter is Known to be Generous and Represents Money

Jupiter is Represented in The Tarot Card The Wheel of Fortune   What goes Up will go Down (down is made Entirely of Fem Letters) and back again (Note that Up is Made of   U/Ovulating Fem   and   P/Man Power   and that She is in Front of Him being The Start of The Word Up)
The $ Letter S is   S/Is/His/Hiss/Snake/Penis/Stick
For   F/Whore   and   Four   Go Along Well
The Sign of the Cross is Avoided to Men Here by Not Using One   or   the Two Parallel Full Bars on the S   Making it the Money Sign
The S/Penis is an Entirely Guarded Masc Sign   Even More Guarded Behind Those Bars that are Most of The Time on The Dollar Sign   Enough for Everyone to be Able to Identify it that Way
A Dollar is Called a Buck   A Buck is a Male Deer Antelope Hare Rabbit Goat and More
Buck is a Masc Name
The Fem Gets Nothing at All says   The Code   Even if She did Plenty of Work   Thanks to Us All   it is All Changing for The Better

5   and The Per Cent   %
CNQ is Made Entirely of Fem Sound Letters
CNQ as in Synchronicity
5 Is the Middle Number
To Pull Up The Middle Finger is an Insult says the Common Knowledge
In # 5 It is where The Mascs and The Fems Meet in a Capped Fashion as in a Controlled Situation
Over Her Head is The Right Angle of the Masons/My Sons
Number 5 has a Horizontal Top/Cap/Stick/Penis   and   Also a Vertical Protection
2 has the Bottom Horizontal Cap   The Fems are Usually All Surrounded in Symbolism in   The Code
In # 5 Her Circle is Halved (as in Isolating Her)
The Percentage Symbol The   %   Depicts Her as Those So Small   Zero/o/The O/Fem Holes   Separation from the Other Fems by a   Stick/Penis   Represented Here in a Strong Italic Mode as either in Being Erected or Being Down   The Fems Being All Separated from Each Other   Bringing Powerlessness in All Fems
Symbol % is The # 5/Five in The Hiding Where She is So Small Now She has Almost No Value (as Little as King Kong Big Ape is So Big Compared to His Fem Hostage which is The Size of a Small Squirrel)

The Dam Code The Damn Book

Per/Cent does Not Mean Much   How Much is Worth a Cent/Penny   Also The Cent Symbol has a Stick Coming Down Through it as in the $ Sign   It is the Same as is The Pi ∞ Sign   it is The Number 8/Pregnancy Laid Down   so so Small   and it is for Eternity says   The Symbol Sorry for The Lovers of Infinity PI   It is Not as Good as Pie   But You Still can play with it

6   and The Accent Circumflex   ^
CX is Made Entirely of Fem Sound Letters
6 is the Sex Number Unit/Penis Itself   The Snake
Divide 2 by 3 and Get Endless Sixes   666666
Multiplies 2 by 3   and   it is Number 6
The Triple Six   The 666   is the Great Fear of Bible Believers/Readers   It is The Number of the Beast   that Old Goat
The Goat is Represented in the Crowley Tarot (Tear/o) Deck by The Devil Card the # 15   One of the Reason Being Because there was Sex from Man to Goats (or Other Animals) Back then
The Other Reason is Crowley Explaining   The Code   in More Depth than Ever Done   He was Parodied in All Spiritual False Realities and Feared by All   Many Wanted to Know What He Knew   His Tarot Deck is a Study and His Book is   The Book of Thoth (Thought)
Number 6/Six/Sick
Switch S/Penis for D/Pregnant and She Gets Dick (The Code is Impenetrable for the Fems Unless She has The Code)
If She Tries to Imitate the Stick/Penis with Her Fem Letters   The Y and the X   She Gets the Styx   The River of the Dead Styx
6 Happens After the No Number   o/Egg Hole   or   Letter O   Curls into Itself After being Perforated   The Semen is in #   7/Sève/N   and Ready to be Transformed in # 8/Pregnancy after The Sève is in # Seven/7
Number 6/Sex is The Tallest After Number 8/Pregnancy
You Can See that in the Hindu Arabic Numeral System   Six and Eight are Taller than the Others
The Accent Circumflex Adds Importance on Number 6 adding a Form of a Crown Topping The Sex/6

7   and The Ampersand   &
CVN   # 7 is Made Entirely of Fem Letters
7   is   S/Eve/In   Seve/In   S/Penis/Eve/In

Lise Rochon

Sève in French is Sap   Drippings   from The Tree of
Life   or   Knowledge
See   Eve/Ov/Egg   N/Virgin   or   C/See/Young Girl   V/Fem Sex
Active   N/Virgin Daughter are together with Eggs   Since Eve
The Lucky Number/Moment of # 7 is Her Lucky Moment When is She is
Told to be Pregnant in # 8/Pregnancy
sève: the characteristic flavor and body of a wine
The Dictionary says
Switch N/Virgin for R/Heir/Her and She Gets Severed (The Punishing
Nature of The Code Punishes Her Instead of Rewarding Her)
The & Symbol Ampersand was Originally a Mix of the Letters   E/
He   and   T/Fem Cross
It was Being Shaped as an Arrow (a Penis) Piercing a # 8 as in
Pregnancy/# 8

8   and The Asterisk   *
8 is the Number for a Pregnant Fem
It is the   Ate   or the   Hate
8 is The Double Circle on Top of Each Other   Head   and   Pregnancy
8 is Also The Super Development of Her Breasts as a Goal
In the Jewish Kabbalah # 8 and # 9 are Called Unfortunate Numbers   One
being Under the Influence of the Moon and the Other with Saturn
To 89 Someone is to be Banned from the Place
Number Eight and Nine are Both Fem Symbols
8/Pregnancy is the Pi ∞ The Sign of Eternity   it is Laid Down and is Very
Small
In the Ancient World The Old 8 was an Eight in a Shape of a Serpent
In Roman Letters Letter H is Represented by a Square Formed of an
8   The H Grid (#) When Closed at Its Top and Bottom can be in Endless
Numbers   Thousands/Millions of H/Grid/Secret Code Society Letters
Form a Real Grid   As Looking at a Summer Screen Door   or   Just a
Screen
The Letter F/Fem in Cursive is in a Shape of an Elongated 8   Its Bottom
Although is Under The Line
Asterisk   is   S/Snake   T/Fem Cross   and   Risk
The   *   A Mini Star   No   an   Esther/Risk (Est/Her/Risk)
A Star is Something Nice to Look at   or   to Become   it is Somewhat of
a Dream   But No says   The Code

The Dam Code The Damn Book

The Star as in The Asterisk Sign is an Expansion of The Cross   It is made by Adding Tt/Crosses   or an   X Around its Axis (X/Is   See X in The Introduction of The X Letter in The Words Chapter)
The Star is   STR   The   S/Penis/His   T/Fem Cross   R/Sex/Her/Are   She has/had been Crushed Already
A Star in the Hand in Palmistry is a Bad Omen
Everything that is Fem in English Words are Mostly   Bring Suffering   or are   Unimportant   or   Transitional   Words that have No Signification by themselves   or   are Very   Poor   by Themselves   or   are Very Poor in Value as the Penny   A Fem Name   and   the Smallest of The Small Change in Money

9   and The (Opening) Parenthesis   (
9   as in NNs/Double Virgins (a Rare Combination) is Nine as in   None   or   Mine   Either She is Nothing (None)   or   She Belong to Somebody (Mine)
M as N   are Interchangeable from N/Virgin   to   M/Mother in   The Code
The Parenthesis (
In   The Code   it is Her Half Left Breast   Her Other Breast is in the No Number Key the Zero/o   the   )
There are Other Ones   The Square Braces [ ]][and   The Curly Braces {} }{
See Brassiere in French for a Bra in American Language   Too Close to a Brace   Brace Yourself
N/Virgin the 9/Nine is   One of the 2 Parentheses ((Parent/Thesis   Pair and Père Excludes the Fem as M for Mother Here)) Uniting it to the Symbol o by the Most Powerful Alliance   One Breast Cannot be Without the Other Breast on 2 Different Fem Bodies   That is an Unconscious Concepts Transfer
From Number 9/Fem Knowledge to Symbol o where She has No Identity   And After that To Return to Number One/The Beginning   Where Only a Masc Lives Power in   The Code

o/Zero   and The (Closing) Parenthesis   )
Zero   is   O/Fem Hole/Loins
o has No Value by itself/Herself and is Not a Number
Zero has No Name and is Inexistent says   Science

Lise Rochon

Zero Can Only Add to the Value to the Number (s) in Front of Her/It
In   The Code   Because of its Shape   o can Only be a Fem Symbol
So to Stay Behind and Give it All Up is the Message to o
She Is Transformed from this Non Existent Symbol/Number
o   into   Letter O/Fem Hole
Zero is Elongated as in the Shape of an Egg as in Non Pregnant   or   a Virgin
The Fuller Circle of Letter O Indicates Pregnancy
Round (Pregnancy/Full) Numbers are the Ones with the Most Zeroes

Other Numbers Not on the Keyboard

If # 10   T/Cross/In   would have been Her Destiny to See here   She would have seen   The T/Fem Cross is In   As in Accomplished   The Thin Teen made of Tin will Bleed Soon
10 is the Number of The Coupling of The Stick (Masc) and The Hole (Fem)
In # 10 She Becomes the X   The Mark   Symbol in Roman Numbers and the Omega Mark in the Greek Letters   Omega is the End of the Alphabet   It is the Achievement/Completion Letter
In # 11 The Code   is All Passing Over Her Head   The Bars (Bears) have Appeared   and Her Teenagers Years will be Different than The Boys Teenagers
12 is Her Bleeding Start   Years of being Cursed have Begun
The Code has Based Her Fem Cycle on the Totally Structured Stable and Repetitive 28 Lunar Days Cycle
Many Fem Bodies do Not Follow The Artificial Lunar Cycle
But the Code Says NO Your Cycle is Normal Every 28 Days like the Moon Which is an Impossibility because Smaller Mammals Like Dogs the Non Mating Time the Anestrus Cycle is 4 to 5 Months (14 to 16 Weeks) and for an Elephant it can be Up to 5 years of Anestrus
It Makes More Sense that Way
For Horses their Anestrus is the Whole Winter Time
We Have Almost the Same Size Body
It Makes No Sense for Us the Fem to Lose that Flood of Blood 12 Mating Cycles Months per Year and be Immediately in Estrus for the Rest of the Month/Mount

13

The Dam Code The Damn Book

13 is the Tear/Defloration and the Tears of Her Teens
13 is the Thin/Weak/Anemic or the Cheap Tin Material
13 is the First Year of the for 7 Other Years Coming for Her
She will Carry that Bad Luck Number Until the Age of 20 Where She will Start as a Zero Behind the Number 2
Meanwhile the Boy has Choices   being in a Position of Choice

Punctuation and Other Symbols

The Period
The   .   Period Marks The End of a Sentence   It is Made of a Dot   Dots Represents All Fems Only   It Marks Their   Pregnancies   Their Breasts   Their Vaginas
What Comes After a Sentence is The Period (Literally)
The Comma   ,
The Symbol   ,   is the Common Comma
The Come/Ma   Is His Call for Sex
Come/A   A/All Men   Comes Inside Her
The   Come/A   as in Ejaculation of All Men for Procreation or Sexual Pleasure
The Comma Comes Any time Inside The Sentence (Literally)   As a Pause for Sex
The Con/Ma would be the Vagina of a Mother (See Con in the Words Chapter)
The Code   says The Conma and The Period are Part Integral of a Sentence
The Symbol   :   The Colon
In the Symbol   :   This Symbol Commonly Means Equal to
It is When 2 Dots are on Top of Each Other
Not Standing Together Side by Side as Friends or Neighbor
In the Code She is Always Kept Alone and Separated from The Others
In   :   All Dots are Now Pregnant (Repetition of a Symbol or a Letter in a Word or a Sentence Makes it Plural or As in All of Them)   All Dots are Together as One
And that is How the Fem is Identified as a Dot in Our Societies

Lise Rochon

THE PLANETS
☉ ♁ ♀ ☿ ♄ ♆ ☾ ♂ ♃ ♅ ♇
THE PLANNED HITS
AND
THE ZODIAC
♈ ♉ ♊ ♋ ♌ ♍ ♎ ♏ ♐ ♒ ♑ ♓
or
♈♉♊♋♌♍♎♏♐♒♑♓

INTRO
1 SUN ☉
2 EARTH ♁
3 VENUS ♀
4 MERCURY ☿
5 SATURN ♄
6 NEPTUNE ♆
7 MOON ☾
8 MARS ♂
9 NAKED JUPITER ♃
   JUPITER ♃
10 URANUS ♅
11 PLUTO ♇

Intro
Year   Month   Week   Days
THE TWELVE MONTS (Mounts) OF THE YEAR REPRESENTED BY THE 12 ASTROLOGICAL SIGNS IN THE ZODIAC
ARIES ♈
TAURUS ♉
CANCER ♋
GEMINI ♊
LEO ♌♌
VIRGO ♍
LIBRA ♎
SCORPIO ♏
SAGITTARIUS ♐
CAPRICORN ♑
AQUARIUS ♒
PISCES ♓ ♓

Lise Rochon

THE PLANETS
THE PLANNED HITS

Intro

There are Only 2 Fem Named Planets in the Zodiac
for   The Fems   Moon and Venus   The Others are All
Mascs   Sun   Mars   Mercury   Uranus   Jupiter   Saturn   Pluto
The Moon is The Embodiment of Her Bleeding/Curse   and   Venus is
the   Her Abandonment   or/and   Submission to it   As The Model
of Beauty   Beauty being here an Empty   Code   Concept for Her
Because She Will Lose it with Her Pregnancies   and   Her Fast Aging
with Hanging Too Big Breasts that will Bend Her Body and Catch
Her in Tremendous   Pains   Conditions   Illnesses   and   Prevent
Her Life Experience to Focus on Reality even in Old Age   As
She Reaches Maturity She Will   Again   Often Not Be There
Mentally   or   Emotionally   or   Physically   being too Much in
Pain   There are Just Too Many Pains Too Early for The Fems
The 7 Others Male Planets/Planned Hits are All in Position of Power   They
Seem to be Male   But Are in Fact Shadows of   The Code   Power
to Maintain Her (and Him) in That Stupid Humiliation   Blaming   The
Fems   Enslaving them All in That Menstrual Cycle Curse that The Zodiac
Seems to Only Represents   The Code   in so Many Aspects
End of Intro

THE PLANETS
THE/D/Pregnant   PLANNED HITS

SUN   ☉

The Sun Planet Man God (The God Ra) is The Person of Importance
in   The Code
S/Is/His/Hiss/Penis/Snake   and the N/In/Donkey/Hen/Haine/Ann/Virgin
The Sun is the Only Symbol to have a Perfect Round Circle as its
Astrological Emblem (Same in the Alphabet and a Key Board)
The Sun seems to be Just Another Round Symbol in   The Code   as much
as the Fem O Circle and the Zero o   But No   The Fem has Only   o/
Zero/The Nothing Symbol   and   Letter oO/Egg   Both Symbols
Identifying Her   as Eggs Symbols   and Meaning Nothing as in Zero

The Dam Code The Damn Book

Whatever is Round (Pregnancy) is Fem according to Numbers   but No The Sun is The Exception   and   Steals it by Incorporating that Dot (See Dot in The Words Chapter) that Represents Her in His/Her Round Symbol
A Long Time Ago Men Took Powerful Words to Illustrate Himself   He Called Himself The Sun as is His Son   Then He became San as a Saint
San: extremely holy   a saint   sacred is translation for San from Spanish to English
It is All Over The World   San in Japanese is a Suffix for Respect After a Man Title   etc
S/Is/His/Ass/Hiss/Serpent/Penis   A/All Men   N/Hen/In/Virgin
Sun (He Radiates to Her The U/Chalice/Uterus)   Son (He has a Son with O/Fem Hole from The Virgin   The N/Virgin)   Sam (He is a Man with A/All Men with M/Motherhood)   San (He as All Men is Respected as a Saint   with N/Ann/Virgin)   Sum (He Harvests in Motherhood   and   The Chalice/U/Uterus)   Sin (i/Marriage Act (The Dot and the Stick) is Involved   Here come The Sin)
All She Gets is a Symbol of a Moon   the Night Light   and   Planet Venus (Which is in The Night Sky just a Little Bit)
In The Tarot   The Sun (a Perfect Circle   Her Symbol but No it is a Masc   Here we See She has No Control Over Her Herself and Her Pregnancies) Card is Essentially Good News   The Moon Card in Tarot is Essentially Bad News   Her Menstrual is a Flow of Blood Loss   Dogs Barking at Her in The Night is Her Moon Light Fear   Emotions   Romance   Sex   and   Bad News   She Lives with those Concepts   Consciously and Unconsciously
The Sun/Son is the Most Important Planet in Our Solar System and its Name was Appropriated a Long Time Ago excluding the Fems in Books or Symbology There is No Fem on The Sun as there is Plenty of Mascs on The Moon
Sunny as in   Son/He   Sun/He   San/He
The Sun (as The Masc) Along with The Water (What/We Hat (See Hat in The Words Chapter)   Her/R/Sex) both are The Source and Sustainment of Life
but   The Dam Code   has Recreated Symbolically those Elements with Power/Sexual Connotations that They Do Not Have Naturally   The Sky is Not Masc because it Radiates Blue   The Water is Not Fem because it Yields   Mars Energy/Warrior is Not Naturally Violent as the Masc Sex

because it is Spring   Jupiter does Not have to be the Only Sex that is Lucky or Rich   Etc
There is No   Moon/She   or   Moon/He   For Her There is The Looney   We have Luna the New Beautiful to become Soon a Looney as She Ages in   The Code
The Code   Uses Commonly Short Words to Express Itself   they are often the Oldest Words
EARTH   ⊕
Earth is the Center of Importance in Capricorn Virgo and Taurus even if it Does Not Rule there
She (Earth) is The Property of Saturn The Evil Monster When She is in Capricorn   She is The Property of Mercury   the World Changer   The Magician   The Hypnotist   When She is in Virgo/Virgin   She is The Property of Venus   Beauty   Creator of Natural Beauty   When in Taurus/ The Cow/The Provider of   Milk   Beauty   and   Hard Work   The Code   Wants Nothing of That Much Work
Earth is Considered as One of The 4 Elements that Rules the 12 Zodiac Signs   The Problem with That Concept is That Hurt/Earth is Not an Element as the 3 Other Ones   Fire   Air   Water   Earth is a Planet   The One We All Live On   It is The Planet that Contains those 3 Other Elements
RT as in   Planet   Earth/Hurt   is   R/Her/Heir/Or/Whore/Ere/ Sex   with   T/Fem Cross/Great Curse   Here   The Code   is Hiding its Symbols
That Code   is Causing Only Hurt as said Consistently in   This Damn Book
Earth is The Planting Ground in Taurus Virgo Capricorn
Looking at General Sites about Astrology   Planet Earth/Hurt/Her/T is or is Not Part of the   8   or   9   or   10 Planets of The Zodiac   but It has a Symbol ⊕ and it Comes to Life in Astrological Charts in Planting Ground Called Elements   Weird
All The Zodiac Planets have Enigmatic Signs/Symbols
Planet Earth is Represented in the Dictionary as a Circle with a Cross on Top of it
Many Planets have That   T/Fem Cross   Symbol as Part of Their Symbol   Earth is The Starting Point to Many Other Astrological Symbols   which Comprise That Cross in Their Own Symbol   See   Venus ♀   Mercury ☿   Uranus ♅   Neptune ♆   Saturn ♄
A Cross is a Sign of   Condemnation   Death   Reject   etc

The Dam Code The Damn Book

That Cross is Not a Sign of Resurrection in Her Daily Life
More Symbols per Letter Gives More Importance and Expansion to the Symbol/Letter) Concept   For Example
Letter R/Her/Hear/Air/Hair/Heir/Or/Whore/Ire/Ere/Sex is a Long One   Perhaps the Longest Chain of Associated Concepts   They are All Associated to Her/Whore/R/Sex
That R Concept Alone Explains the Rest of the Immensity of   The Code   and   T/Fem Cross/Great Curse   Comes as The Identity Associated with it Creating RT/Earth/Hurt
Heaven is the Oven   Ov/Egg   In/N/Virgin   or   When the Sperm is in   N/Ann/In/Hen/Donkey/Virgin
Heaven is When the Bun is in the Oven   Bun   (Pregnancy   Breed   Bred   Bread   Bed)   All is Well in that Soft Sound Word Even/Oven   Eve is in   So Everybody Sleeps on it   It Sounds as Good as in Honesty   To be Even is Always Nice
Heaven/Oven   and   Earth/Hurt   are Often Together in Common American English Expressions
Hell Which Represents   All Pain of Humanity in   The Catholic Religion   is Again Represented by a Fem Letter The L/Ill/Ail/Hail/Hell/All/Elle/Sweet Fem Light   Another Curse on The Fem Back   As Usual Hell is Towards Her

VENUS   ♀

Venus is The Person of Importance in Taurus and Libra
Vein/Us   Vain/Us   The Venus   Code   Sound Word is Basically Vein/Vain   Us/His/Is/Hiss/Stick/Penis
Being Called Vain She Will Avoid Thinking About Those Concepts
Venus is Represented in   The Code   by   T/Fem Cross   Symbol which has Sitting On Her Head an Empty Circle as in Pregnancy   Big Load   Her Body Shaped in a Ball Standing on Top of a Cross Keeps Her Off Balance at All Times   It is Just Another Impossible Thing to Do for Her
Vein/Vain/Vine (Vine is Where the Grapes are) or as in the Fermented Grape in The Wine (Communion) are)
The Word Vein Represents   The Code   in Action Where it Has Infiltrated in Every Nook and Cranny of Our Language and Our Common and Secret Symbols
The Code   Drops on Her at All Times as He Calls Her Stupid   If She Complains too Much about Her Concerns She Will be Called a Whiner

(Wine/Whine   Her/R/Sex)   That Will Keep Her Even More Away from that Word Which is The Wine/Whine and Her Together
Venus in Our Age Rules in the Taurus Sign   or   The Tau in The Tarot   or Again   the Tau in the Old Hebrew   and in   the Greek Symbolism
She is Called   The Cross   or   The Mark   in Hebrew
She is the Hankh   The Portable Cross of The Egyptian Era   Etc
Tau is a popular Symbol and is Used in Science in Many Ways   Covering Up Unconsciously its Ancient/Original Meaning
She is The Hankh   The Egyptian Portable Cross
It was Meant that Way by The Artists of The Time
Venus is Seen with an Abnormally Small Waist or Present the Illusion of it   and   Too Large Pregnant Breasts Even Not being Pregnant
She is Powerless Because that Small Waist is Crippling Her From the Inside and Her Big Oversized Breasts are Just Really Bad News for Her Especially When She Grows Older as the Breasts Gets Heavier Pushing Down on Her Front Body Creating Stagnation Pain and Weaknesses in Many Places in Her Body
Her Natural Forces and Will Power are Already Weakened by   The Code   Since She is Born   From Multiple Constant Attacks on Her that She is Not Aware of   as being Always Vain   it is in Her Veins
VENUS   ♀   Vein/Us   is The Virgin/Virgo/Goddess
Virgin/Verge/In (The Penis Concept is Inside The Virgin Before The Virgin Knows about it   Being Too Young   and   Too Ignorant)
For Her in   The Code   Venus Rules in The Taurus Astrological Sign   A Symbol of Beauty   Of The Love of Natural Harmony   and   For Her Hard Work (The Cows/Bulls are Attached to a Cart and The Whip is Always Close by   That Cow/Bull has a Ring (See Ring in The Words Chapter) in its Nose (which is One of the Most Sensitive Area of the Body) as She Keeps on Plowing the Soil   and as a Cow Providing Milk   Her So Many Chores Which do Not Pay Much
Venus is said to Brings Harvest by   The Code   She is That Cow/Bull that Plows the Dirt/Soil   Both Words Indicating Something Not good   as The Soil/Dirt is in Fact the Root of Life Her Natural Forces Already Weakened by   The Code   Multiple Constant Attacks on Her since   Ever (Eve/Her)   That She is Not Aware of
Venus Also is Represented in   The Scales   in Astrology   She is Now a Blinded Fem Holding the Books of The Law (?) of Jupiter

Venus in The Virgo Sign Represents the Young Girl as Virgin   The Fem does Not Rule as She should be being The Virgin in Her Own Home/Body   But No says   The Code   Mercury (See Tarot Card # 1 The Magician Ruled by Mercury) that Multiple Facetted Mean Little God/Magician Master of Illusions of All Kinds   Rules Over the Young Virgo Maidens

Planet Venus ♀   is Represented in   The Code   by a Circle (Pregnant)   and a   T/Fem Cross/Great Curse

Venus ♀ has the Same Shape Symbol as Planet Earth ♂ but Upside Down   She is the Atlas Supporting the Earth on Her Fem Shoulders   An Atlas is an Amalgam of Documents   It does Not Say Who Wrote it   or   Created it

The Code   in Action   Has Infiltrated in Every Nook and Cranny Our Languages and Our Common and Secret Symbols

MERCURY   ☿ Mercury is the Person of Importance in Gemini (Day Time) and Virgo (Night Time) Mercury brings its Light in The Day Time in Gemini (The Band of Brothers)   but its Light is Useless in The Night Time as She The Virgin is Sleeping

Mercury Also has The   T/Fem Cross/Great Curse   Symbol Standing Under The Circle and a Crown Made of The Half Circle the Same Size Size of The Circle Under it

Some of these Planets Symbols Keep On Adding or Subtracting Symbols from Each Other Depending on their Meaning or Position   Planet Mercury is an Example of that

Here it is Planet Earth Symbol Inversed   becoming the Venus Symbol   Add a Crown and Transform it in a Man Magician or Not   The Planet Mercury Symbol is the Fem Carrying Her   Tt/Fem Cross   Her Head is Capped with Another Half Circle Above Her Head   it is Called Her 7th Chakra

Mer   Cure   He/E

Mère is Mother in French   La Mer is Sea/Ocean in French   See Matric/Metric and Matrix

Mercury Rules The Tarot Card # 1 The Magician   He is The One That Creates Illusions to Lure People Peep   Hole/Her   Into   The Code   The Code   Creates Beliefs   and   Maintains Pregnancies   and   Those False Hopes for Big False Breasts and Small Waist Injuring Her

811

Permanently and those False Bleeding Cycles That are Never Cured   etc
It is Just Another Cipher that Many do Not See or Suspect
SATURN   ♄
Saturn is the Person of Importance in Capricorn
Saturn also Carries the T/Fem Cross in its Symbol along with   Earth   Venus   Mercury   Uranus   and   Jupiter
Saturn was The First Greek God to Be at the Capital
He was Known as Saturninus Mons (as in Moons)
Sat/Urn   He/E   Us/S/His/Is/Penis/Snake   Mons as in Monsoon When the Water(Her) Pours
Moons (Note the 2 OOs as in Plural or in Polygamy) are So Close to Moms and Numb
M/Motherhood   and   N/Virgin   are Interchangeable in   The Code   as in Being   the Same Concept Developing into the Next Step
Saturn was Originally a Good God before He went Bad   After He Changed His Name to Kronos   or   Adjusting Her Time of the Month When His Mission became to be   The Secret Code   in Action
Saturn is Saturday (Sat/Her/Day) Which was the Old Sabbath (Bat/Day   or   Beating/Sex/Day)
Saturn is The Sat Her of The N/Virgin   The/Day/D/Pregnant   S/Snake   Hat/Code   R/Sex   Urn
Urn/Her   Earn/Her   Urn/Cup/Uterus   was Just Another   Code   Slang Word for the Different Aspects of the Fem in those Ancient Times
Saturn (God of Titans) and His Biggest Moon (A Giant Titan Warrior His Brother Titan) Ignites Together on this Lone Dark Grey Boring Sinful Destructive Planet
Saturn is a Terrible God and that Giant/God Titan is His Moon   Implying Homosexuality
The Secret Band of Thebes were a Group of 150 Male Lovers Warriors that were Picked Up to Form the Elite of the Theban Army in the 4th Century Which Encouraged Homosexuality All The Way Down to Boys
A Titan in Mythology is a God/Man   The Code   Calls this Giant Masc God a Moon   A Moon is Entirely Fem says   The Code   But   No   says   The Code   even if No Man Can be Pregnant   or   Bleed as the Fem Does
That Event Saturn/Sat/Urn is When She Bleeds

The Dam Code The Damn Book

In Ancient Times there was No Fem Hygiene (?) So the Fem Sat on Urns to Gather Her Loss of Blood
There is at Least One Ancient Greek Image that Depicts Several Fem Having Urns Between their Legs
Saturn has 62 Moons as in Different Aspects and Implying Polygamy on a Extremely Large Scale   Some of Saturn Moons are in Different Realms   Probably to Hide Better from Her Encoded/Ignorant Life
Men Chose their Spots of Power Very Carefully
Next to Kronos is Rhea the Mother of the Olympian Gods
Saturn as Kronos Here Carries the Weight of Time (The Fem Curse) to Give it to All Beings   He has No Pity
And because that Cronos (Crown/Us) God/Code is at the Top of the Human Chain with the Ultimate Mother
We are All Attached to the Mother of All Gods and Goddesses
Chronos was Also Identified in Classical Antiquity as The Defeated Saturn by Olympus   He Sent Chronos into Hades/Underworld Called Tartarus (See The Jupiter Chapter)
NEPTUNE ♆
Neptune is The Planet of Importance in Pisces Sign
Neptune Also has a T/Fem Cross Part of its Symbol
Neptune is Represented by a Triton which is] on a T/Great Curse/Fem Cross
Neptune is the God of the Ocean (O/Hole   She/Shh   In/N/Hen/Ann/Virgin   as in the Hole She is In)
She The Fem as The Cross Holds The Triton   but No   The Code   says He Neptune Holds the Triton that has a 3 Points Pointy Fork
He Often Holds a Net (The Grid) to Catch Her as a Fish   Neptune is Not a Friend of Her   He is the Shepherd (See Letter Jj in the Letter Chapter) of the Ocean   Those are Not Sheeps but Fishes   Same   Quiet   Obedient Example Given to the Fems to Follow   etc   The Code   Keeps Her in that Fishnet/Prison Slavery Hell Hole
It is All Changing Now Anyway because Consciousness is Growing Everywhere
Neptune Has   The Repetition of the 3 Arrows Pointing in The Same Direction as a Fork to Eat Something   or   a Fork to Fork Something(in   The Code   a Repetition of Two of The Same is/Can be Plural or All of Them   a Repetition of 3 of The Same is Always All of Them (as said in My Damn Book)

813

Lise Rochon

Mars The War God is Represented by a His 3 Arrows Coming Out/Attached to the   T/Cross/Fem Cross/Great Curse   She has No Chances at All
MOON ☾ ☽   Moon is The Planet (which is a Satellite) of importance is The Cancer Sign
The Moon is a Less Important Symbol even if in the Eyes of Humans and Their Children It/She is Well Known   in Reality this Satellite has Little Influence over The Fem Cycles   Especially the Ones Artificially Constructed by   The Code
The   Code   Logic for Her Blood Loss (Period   Pair   He   Odd)is All Based on The Stable Lunar Natural Cycle

There are 12 Inches in a Foot (Foot is All Fem Letters)
There were 12 Christ Disciples   There are 12 Hours (Ours   Ours is Bear in French) of Daylight and Night Light (D/Pregnant   Light   Delight)
Switch L/Her Light for N/Virgin and from Light She Becomes Night Where   The Code   has Placed Her a Long Time Ago because there is No Light therefore No Growth/Knowledge There   1 Hour is 5 Times # 12
The Word Work is   W/All Fems Sex Active   Accompanied with   R/Her/Heir/Or/Whore/Sex   and   K/Broken Fem Warrior
WRK and WRD   (WRD is All Fem Letter Sounds) WRD as in Weird The Code   Word is Work When Switching D/Pregnant for K/Broken Fem The Code   is Hell
For The Ancients She Represented The Cancer Astrological Sign   The Canker it was Called Pus   it was The Representation of Her Wonderful Precious White Vaginal Juices
Add L/All/Ill/Elle/Fem Love Light and She Gets Plus   Being a Good Sign   but no   It is Another Trap for The Fems
A Crab Keeps the Doors in that Ocean (O/She/In) Where She is in Reality a Fish in a Bowl (a Bowl is Round as in Pregnant   B/Boy Holding All Fem Breasts   is with   L/All/Hole/Fem Love Light
The Master of The House of Cancer (A Moon Sign) A Crab (Scary) Always Keeps Her Doors Locked   so She Stays Inside   as Sheeps in a Field Guarded by Master Dogs (See The Moon Card in The Tarot Rider)
The Crab Illustrates The Secrets Surrounding   The Code
Fishes in a Small Bowl is Accepted by Society Even if it is Cruelty to Animals which is Madness for the Fishes/Fems in   That Code
The Fem here is Represented by the Smallest Crescent Moon Shape
   ☽ ☾   A Sliver Moon as in   Sever   Silver (Her)

The Dam Code The Damn Book

She Will Also Be often an Invisible Moon   Also Called   Black Moon or New Moon   There She is Reborn in The Dark of The Night   Scary/ No Light for Her   Call it Wound Time   It is Where is Hidden Her False Artificial Anestrus
She has No Name while the Other Planets do   Her Name is Only Moon as Millions of Others
In   The Code   there are 4 Phases of Her Moon Representing Her with the Obligatory 4 Different Stages of Having Her Moon/Her Blood Loss   Those 4 Phases of the Moon Represents   Also   The Code   Chosen Different Stages of Her Womanhood as in Her Motherhood Only Path   As in Having Your Moon   As in The Giving Birth Time (Pictured as The Full Moon)   Where that Cycle Returns Eventually to Her Loss of Blood
That Moon Crescent ☾ Represents Her at All Stages of   The Moon   as   Bleeding Time   Ovulation Time   Breast Size   Birth Time   Etc   She is Presented in The Smallest Light so She will Only See Shadows in Her Own Night Which is Scary in Itself
The Moon is Pictured in the Letter Chapter by Letter C/Sea/See/Young Girl   It is The Smallest Part of the Moon   Which She is Not Allowed to Understand   Because if She Would See the World as is as a Young Child   She would Understand that in Some Domains She is More Intelligent than Him as He is More Talented in Other Matters   Nature Had Intended to Form the Complementary Bounds with those 2 Totally Different Entities   The Fem and The Masc   that is Polarizing/Attracting/ Rejecting   Each Other Sexes in a Endless Cosmic Dance which is Not Allowed in that   Dam Code
Also She Would Understand How The   T/Fem Curse   Works Words as Fidelity/True Love are Not Allowed in   The Code   because   The Code   Destroys it to Replace it with   Irony   Sadism   Rejection   Abuse   Solitude   as said in The Tarot Card The Moon
MARS   ♂   The Male Only Symbol that Does Not Contain a T/Fem Cross Mars is The Planet of Importance in the Aries Sign
It is There to Combat Her Without Mercy   That Arrow/Penis is Pointing Out Carrying Out Her as a Dot/Pregnant With Him Everywhere He Goes That is the Only Message   Mars is   M/Motherhood   R/Her/Heir/Or/ Whore/Sex   S/His/Is/Snake/Penis
Mars as in Mercy (Mère/Mom   See/C/Young Girl)

Mars is the International Symbol for The Masc Sex
It is an Arrow Holding on a Circle Adding an Arrow Pointing
North and Giving it Volition Speed and Direction
Sun and Mars Both Have Fire as Their Element says   The Code   That
Sun Carries with Him the   Dot/D/Pregnant Daughter   in its Center
The Sun/Son is the Most Important Planet in Our Solar System for
Creating Life Along With Water (His Perfect Complement)
This Mars Symbol with its Arrow Adds Movement and Speed
That Code   is that Moving Arrow as in   A Moving Penis in Action
That is the Only Message of   The Code   here
NAKED JUPITER ♃
Jupiter is The Planet of Importance in the Sagittarius Sign
The Best   Most Breathtaking   Most Beautiful   Most Impressive in Size
Most Rare   and   Most Natural Gonads Looking   Ever Seen to Me are
Those on The Ancient Statue of Jupiter
All Those Gods Look Extremely Powerful Especially Him Jupiter With   His
Furry   His Very Perfectly Curly Hair Around His Head   and   Around His
Penis
Those Curls Also Means Full On Loaded Penis Power
His Rough Touch is in this Velvet Soft Curly Hairs   But No   The
Code   Objects/Abject to   True Love
"The Man is Tender The Fem is Fire" said this Old American Cowboy Song
Deep Thank You to those Antique Goddesses and Gods that Showed
Themselves as NOT Circumcised or Clitorized and were Immensely
Beautiful
They Saved Us in Immortality on the Olympia Up there Where No Human
was Allowed to Change Nothing of the Past
Therefore those Paintings/Sculptures were Kept Intact as Our Future
World Memories Therefore Holding Our Archetypes Clean
Looking Closer Here at Jupiter Gonads the Whole Genital Area is
Contained in a Pretty Tight Area (Seems Easier to Carry His Equipment
in Ancient Times) His Sac is Extremely Tight and Looking Bright and
Healthy   It is is Not Wrinkled and Hanging   He has Not Descended
Testicles as in having Too Heavy Testicles   or   Because of a Too Thin
Sac   Lots of Men Now have a Genitalia Area that is Overwhelmingly
Large Compared to the Rest of their Body as Circumcision seems to do

The Dam Code The Damn Book

The Jupiter Statue Sac does Not have That Cord Cutting/Separating His Tissues where the Testicles are in Almost in 2 Different Sacs in Many Men Now
Instead Jupiter Testicles are Together Touching at All Times and Tight and are Hot to Look at For a Fem as Me
Circumcision Procedure Could Do That Separation
After the Foreskin is Cut Out it Would Pull Up the Rest of
The Testicles   They are Pressed Bad Back to His Pelvic Area   Creating that Extremely Tight/Painful Cord Cutting in The Masc Sac from that Procedure   Look Around at a Bunch of Naked Men and See for Yourself   we are Creating Mutations on Humans since the Jewish People Invented Circumcision   A Sexual Mutilation with Heavy Consequences over The Lifetime of that Man   Adding To The Fem Clitorectomy (It was Popular in Africa and the Orient) Impoverish the Fems Physical Mental and Emotional Life   Here we are having Two 2 Genital Manipulations/Mutilations on the 2 Sexes
Those Babies with Bad Circumcisions Often Look as they are Extremely Nervous   and   Sensitive to Touch and Often Will Try to Touch Themselves in their Genital Area to the Desperation of their Mothers Which Will Eventually Put on Him Tighter Diapers Tighter Clothing so He does Not Take His Clothes Off and Keep on Pulling On His Small Penis Himself Which Hurts from   That Constriction
When She Changes His Diaper for Example or Washing Him there You Can See the Pain on the Baby Face Immediately and What Will Often Look as a Painful Erection
A Normal Baby Boy Would Not Do that
The Repercussions of that Cursed Sexual Mutilation Ritual are
Large   Those Testicles Are/Were Pressed Bad to His Pelvic Area by that Tight/Painful Middle Cord/Nerve Cutting through the Skin from that Procedure   and   Separating the Testicles that Way
Otherwise that Middle Cord Would have Remained Naturally More Loose
JUPITER   ♃   Jupiter is Zeus in the Roman Mythology and was Called the Son of Saturn Which is an Important Point to Make about   The Code
Jupiter is said to Bring the Wheel of Fortune   It is the One that Goes   Up Down   Up Down as a Wheel Turning
Jupiter is the Planet of the Law (The Tarot Card The Justice is a Blinded Fem Holding Scales   The Scales   being an Astrological Sign   and a Symbol of Justice in The Tarot Representing Him as   Law   and

Its Benevolences   Which Remains to be Seen in the General World Population to This Day Being Held for a Couple of Thousand Years Here   and   Being Under the Grip of   The Secret Code   Having Saturn and His Stupid Greed with Us Instead of Having a Compassionate Intelligent Ruler for Us All   From the Very Top Which Includes Our Religions and Our Myths
Jupiter Being Saturn Son   or   His Reflection in Mythology
Jupiter Expelled Saturn From Olympus Because He Wanted to Create Havoc as Cronos (Being in Charge of Her Monthly Time) The God of Time (Her Time of the Month) Entered in the Roman Mythology as Cronos
chronological: arranged in the order of time
But the Word Time in   The Code   Means Really   TM   T/Fem Cross   and   M/Motherhood   Attached Together as She has No natural Sexual Cycle Any More
Chronos was Also Identified in Classical Antiquity as the Defeated Saturn by Olympus   He Sent Chronos into Hades/Underworld Called Tartarus   Tartarus is a Prison Where the Punishment Fits the Crime
He Was a Prisoner there for a Long Time Until He was Forgiven by Zeus/ Jupiter   He then was Released from Tartarus Along With Other Titans of Gaea Children to Help and Go Kill Uranus
Gaea or Gaya became Mad having so Many of Her Children Thrown in Tartarus by Uranus
That Goddess Gaea Used to   Create Children   by Herself   On Her Own Will   Before this New World was Born After She United with Uranus   Gaea was a Primal Greek Goddess   She was the Mother of Everything   She Governed the Earth Before the Titans Which were Her Children Made with Uranus
Eros/Love God Blessed the Union of Gaea and Uranus After Which Our Universe of Now Came into Form
She Had 18 Children with Uranus
Uranus was Finally Castrated and Killed by Chronos/Saturn With the Help of the Diamonds Scythe (Cite) (See Scythe in the Words Chapter) Made from/by Gaea
It was Gaea that had Asked Chronos and Her Other Children Titans to Kill Her Husband Uranus   Chronos Stepped into that Huge Task (Those Men were Giant Beasts Gods)
There is an Old Painting of that Event by Giorgio Vasari

Called The Mutilation of Uranus by Saturn with
Amazing   Code   Details   Those Men Gods are Unbelievably Strong
Giants   Cronos Enters the Painting Running   Lancing a Long Stick that is
Attached at the End with The Scythe
He is Naked But is Wearing a Large Loose Apron to Protect Him from the
Spilled Blood   Uranus is Falling on His back Only having Time to Show
Surprise before He Was Castrated and Left for Dead Which He Did
Castration   was the Price to Pay for Uranus/ Uranus (Your Anus Letter R/
Sex) in that World
There are Some Fems on the Right Side of the Painting
One Fem is Touching Her Breasts   as in   Making them Grow More   Not
Looking at Nothing   Staring on the Invisible and Not Looking Happy
Looking as an Empty Vessel   She is Ignoring a Man Torment of Being
Castrated Next to Her   She has Probably Seen that Before
The Waist of Those Fem are Larger and Their Arms and Legs are
Larger   Making those Fems Looking More Natural   Stronger   More
Appealing   More Comfortable to Live in their Body as a Dignified Soul
Entering a New Life here on Earth   instead of a Already formulated
Form with a Small waist   big breasts   thin legs   those impossible
Goals Personified with Barbie Doll (Dull) that has Never Stopped to
Reproduce its Concept Since then   Deforming The Fems of Their Natural
Curves   The Mascs are Wearing Beach/Board Shorts   and   T Shirts so
Comfortable   While Her clothing is Imposing Her with Physical Pains
He Saw that When Circumcision Arrived He Would have to Lose a Part of
His Gonads to be Installed in   His/That New Religion   as a Must   Be
First Thing to do at Birth   The Only Ritual Under Death   if Not Obeyed
They Were Always Pursuing the Gentiles (Gentle/Gentil
URANUS   ♅   Uranus is the Planet of importance in Aquarius
Your/Anus
You   Are   N/In/Ann/Virgin   Us/S/Is/His/Hiss/Serpent/Penis
You/U/Uterus/Cup   Are/R/Her/Heir/Or/Whore/Sex   Ann/N/Hen/Donkey/
Virgin   Us/S/His/Is/Serpent/Penis
Planet Uranus   Erroneous as in Wrong   Erroneous   or   as in   U/
Run/Us
Her Fem Cross is Standing on a Very Small Circle Which Keeps Her in a
Gross State of Imbalance

Lise Rochon

That Small Circle is Supporting that Infinite Triple Cross Symbol as its Messenger   They are Facing the Outside and Saying That Cross is Secretly Contained and Protected from Outsiders that Could Lurk in Uranus Also Carries a T/Fem Cross/Great Curse   or   Should say   The Cross Caries The H/Secret Code
Without that Cross it is a Letter H as in The   H/Code Secret Letter Your/Anus   You/U/Uterus/Cup   R/Sex   Ann/N/Virgin   Us/His/S/Penis   as in URN   Us (See Urn in the Words Chapter) or   URNS   or   Your/Anus
PLUTO ♇   Pluto is the Planet of Importance in Scorpio
Pluto does Not have an Esoteric Symbol   therefore it is Exoteric
Pluto is One of Latest Added Planets and Represents Regeneration through Pain and Sacrifice   Which is close to Saturn   Not Much here
It was Found Out that Pluto is Not a Planet but a Male Dog

THE YEAR

Year: Here   He/Here
Month: Mount
Week: Weak
Days: Daze   Daisies
Here Mount the Weak Daisies   Year   Month   Week   Days
Year: U/You/Cup/Vagina/Chalice   and   Hear/Here   or   He/Hear   or   E/He   and   R/Her/Heir/Or/Whore/Sex
The Code   Established Him Having Sex   Anytime   and   Permanently With Her Ignoring Her Natural Mating Cycle   a Very Long Time Ago In the Word Year Switch R/Her/Sex for T/Fem Cross/Great Curse and She Gets Heat (As in a Fem Always in Heat   Always Keep that Fem in Heat the Whole Year Long)
Month: Mount
Take Away N/In/Hen/Ann/Virgin and She Gets Moth (So Small is She in   That Code   Add an Her and She is Under The Hood of Motherhood) Add N and She Gets a Mount

The Dam Code The Damn Book

THE ZODIAC
The 12 MONTHS
Mounts of the Year/He/Hear as
THE 12 ASTROLOGICAL SIGNS
♈♉♊♋♌♍♎♏♐♑♒♓

Intro
The Zodiac Represents   The Coded   Elements That Distributes Its Power Through The Astrological Signs/Symbols
Humans Love Mystery and the The Fantastic   The Code   Knows it   For a Long Time
But here it is Different Story
Under its Veils of Mystery   Mischief   and   Attraction to   The Code   it Presents itself as in a Zoo   Animals in Cages   The Fems are Represented by Many Animals in   The Code   such as   Cows (Taurus   A Bull Tilling The land)   Horses (You Ride on Top of Them   Sexual Mythology   Carl Jung)   Sheeps (Aries   A Male the Ram is in Charge of that War against the Sheeps (She/P))   Chickens (The Chicks as Girls in American Mythology)   Fishes (Pisces   as in Dreams/Cosmic Consciousness/Poetry/Madness)   Ants (Aunts   Hunts)   Bees (Egyptian Mythology)   etc
The Masc is Represented by Forceful Free Animals   a Lion (Leo)   A Male Sheep Ram (Aries)   A Half Beast/Half Man (Sagittarius is Half Horse (Whores/Rs   Her in Plural)   Half Man   etc
The Zodiac is   Zoo   with   D/Pregnant   and to   Hack
hack: to cut notch slice chop
In   The Code   Z is for Sleep   In Zoo there are 2 OOs/Fem Holes (as in Plural or All of Them)   Lots of Sleeping for the   OO/Fem Holes
The Zodiac is Divided into 12 Constellations   Constellation Starts with Cons/Cunts
Cons/Tell/Aeon   or   Con/Stale/She/On   As long as it Goes Down for The Fem says   The Code
Cons/Her/Vaginas   Tell (T/Fem Cross   All/L/Ill/Hell/Elle   A/All Men   She/E   On (O/Fem Hole   and   N/Ann/Virgin   are Attached Together)
Cunts/All/She/On   All She can be
Astrology was Banned by the Roman Church
According to the Bible Rules   No One is Allowed to   Read Signs   Interpret Signs   or   Use Any Form of Symbology

Burn All Witches is an Old Expression from   That Bible
We do Not Burn Witches Anymore
But Common People Respected the
Wizards   Sages   and   Mages   Because they were/are Mascs   While
The Fem Magical Power is Represented by a Witch with Facial Warts
Clothed in Black (Color of Death) with a Pointy Hat (Ridiculing Her) Riding
the Sky on a Broom (a Masc Stick which is the Symbol for being Penetrated
by a Penis here)
The Black Cat with Her is said to be a Sign of Bad Luck
While in Fact the Cat is Just a Symbol of Secure Independence for The Fem
Which   The Code   Will Never Allow Her to have because She Must be
Kept in Basic Unloved Idiocy to Keep Her in that Curse Slavery
And That is Why They   Hated   Burned   Hanged   Destroyed   the
Lovely Cat Along with that Type of Precious Special Fems
ARIES   ♈
In Aries The Person of Importance is Mars The God of Wars
Aries is The First Sign of the Zodiac   It is an Important Sign   It Starts
the Mood and this Mood is   The Usual Code   Mood   The God of War
is Against Her   Mars Rises and Rules in Aries   and   Her Troubles Starts
Here Already
A Sheep is The Symbol for Aries   It is a Male Sheep Called a Ram (See
Sheep   She   P/Man Power   in The Words Chapter)
April is a Fem Month and is a Fem Name   It is The/Her Rain/Reign but No
says   The Code   April is Ruled by The God of War Mars so   Heir/He/
Is   Heiress   Here/Is   R/His   Hear/Hiss   Heir/His   Hair/Ass   Here/
He/Hiss   R/Air/Hair/Ear/Hear/Ere/Ire/Heir/Or/Whore/Ere/Sex   Is/S/
Hiss/Penis/Serpent   R/He/Is   or   R/Her/Sex   E/He   S/Snake/His/Is/
Penis   Here/He   Is/His/S   R/He/Is   R/Her/Sex   Is/S/Snake   It is All
About Hissing Snakes and Sex   and   The Heiress (as in Aries where She
Belong) Just Felt Between the Cracks   To Disappear Anonymously
Also in its Sound Word Aries Indicates Plural or All of Them
The Code   Created that Illusion of Extreme Violence in that # 1
Astrological Sign Coming from that Male Sheep Which is Supposed to be
a Personification of Her but No says   The Code (See Sheep in the Words
Chapter)   Here It Shows the Intensity of   The Code   Wars Against Her
It is Rooted in Our World Reality that the Fem is a Satellite Instead of
a Master Planet   A Moon   A Stupid Invisible Sheep as in Aries   or
a   Milking Cow (Taurus)   or a   Virgin with The Harvest Responsibility

(Virgo)   or a   Blinded Fem (The Scales of Justice)   Etc   Everybody is Accustomed to those Symbols

The Soft Unproblematic Quiet Sheep   will Not Go or Look at Her Home Here (Her Sign) The Aries Sign With a Big Male God that is Unbridled in Constant Violent Wars

She is Out of Her Own House Here and does Not Know it

TAURUS   ♉   The Goddess Venus is the Person of Importance in The Taurus Sign

Naturally in May in Taurus Her Fem Inner Flowers are Opening   It is Spring   But No says   The Code   She is The Animal that does The Hard Work   She Plows

Venus has Not Much Power here   She is in a Shape of a Cow   The Cow being an Animal that is Milked and Imprisoned/Domesticated for a Couple of Thousand Years   Venus has been Reduced to a Milking Machine and a Beast of Burden   She has a Ring in Her Nose that Men uses to Drive Her Around to Labor

The Sound Word for the Word Taurus is Tower/Us

Taurus is The   Tau   R/Her/Sex   S/Us/His/Is/Hiss/Snake/Penis

The Tau is The Cross in The Kabbalah and The Tarot

It is the Destroying Cards # XIII The Death Card and the # XVIII Card The Tower Card

In the Greek Alphabet   She is Tau as the Letter Tt   or   the The/Thee (same sound   The Key of That Code)

The Cross of Tau is in the Shape of a Large Cap Letter H

Letter H Being the Silent Letter of   The Secret Code

The Cross Symbol Meant Execution in Ancient Rome   Christ was Crucified on a Cross   There is Nothing Positive about The Cross/Fem Curse

In the Egyptian Crowley Deck/Dick The Tau is Also Represented by Saturn   Which is More Bad News   for The Fems

Sumer Astrology First Depicted the Fem as a Cross on Top of a Circle

In Real Life here The Taurus Sign is a Very Positive Sign   She Works Hard (The Cow Plows the Ground) and in Virgo She is the Harvest Sign (At Such a Young Age)

Both Signs have Positive Long Term Loving Caring Results

But Virgo is Under the Ruling of Mercury the # 1 The Magus Card   the Manipulator Lurker

The Secret Code   Action is Especially Powerful Here in this # 2 Sign Because it Incorporates the Half Heart of the Number 2 (See # 2 in the Number Chapter)
As in The Aries Sign Where the Peaceful Sheep is Being Invaded and Transformed in a Creator of Wars Causing Pain and Misery for Everybody   Here in Taurus the War is More Subtle   But The Fem is Already Identified as   Tt/Fem Cross/Great Curse (the defeated One) The Tau
GEMINI   ♊♊   The Person of Importance in The Gemini Sign is The God Mercury
June is a Fem Month and is a Fem Name   She is in The Hands of the Gemini Sign (The Brothers) This is When the Band of Brothers Arrives in Town   as She Will be in June in The Cancer Sign of Pregnancy   and/or   be in Her so Called Moon Called in   The Code   Her Menstrual Time
The Gemini Astrological Sign is a Grid and Represents The # 11 in the Numbers and is The Eleventh Hour in the Clock Chapter   Where it is Represented by two # 1 in Roman Numerals (as in Plural or All of Them)
In All Those Tarot Cards there is Always a Smoke Screen in them   # 6 Gemini Sign in the Crowley Tarot Deck is Called   The Lovers   it Look as there is a Marriage there   but No   Gemini is Essentially a Masc Sign Because Originally this Sign Represented   The Code   Initiated (Only Men) Group   Gemini is Originally the Sign of those Twin Brothers Castor and Pollux Holding Each Other in the Crowley/Egyptian Tarot Deck and Some of the Old Decks
The Love Card # 6 with its Multi Layers Shows the Twins which Hands are being Surveilled on by the Eagle and the Lion   2 Beasts of Apocalypse   The Code   Does Not Joke Around
CANCER   ♋ ♋   The Moon is The Center of Interest in The Cancer Sign
The Cancer Sign is Called a Water Sign and a Fem Sign
It Represents Endless Motherhood   and   Her Moon Means The Menstrual Cycle
A Crab is The Logo for Those Fems   It Guards Her Door   So She Never Gets Out   Always Keeps Her Inside   Doors Locked as Sheeps in a Field Guarded by Master Dogs (See The Moon Card in The Tarot Rider)
A Crab is Scary so She Stays
The Crab Also Illustrates   The Secrets   Surrounding   The Code
The Cancer Sign/Symbol is Scary   It is a Canker in a New Word   It is a Scary Mental Image   She Does Not Want That that Illness

The Dam Code The Damn Book

canker: a gangrenous or cancerous sore
In Britain a Canker Rose is Also an Old Name for a White and Pink Wild Flower (The Code   Reproduces itself in Many Ways   in Many Sciences   Herbology/Botany (Boot/Annie)   Anything That is Green   is Also an Important One)
The Code   has Related Her Associated Moon Sign to a Canker   It Gives the Non Initiate an Almost Perfect View of Where That Simple Concept Switch has Created Her as a Wound with Pus in it a Long Time Ago   The Code   Destroys Everything in Her
Where is That Normal Ecstatic Sexual Flow of Love   Associated to The Fem Natural Juices   She is The One with the Rose   Her Honey is in it   That is No Pus   For Lovers Only   In Cancer There seem to be None   Only Fears and Pains
Torrid July Turns into August (a Masc Name) The Sun Emperor When the Sun/Son is at its Fullest   She will be Invisible in The Leo Sign
LEO   ♌♌   The Center of Interest in Leo is The Sun   It Radiates at All Times Over the Leo Sign   The King of the Jungle
August is the Time of the Year that has Always been Represented by a Male Leo/Lion with its Large Mane   He is Carrier of the R/Heir/Hair/Her/Here/Sex
The Leo Sign Reigns in Full Force in August   and   Powers Over The Summer Zenith Light   Summer being a Fem Name
The Sign Following Masc Leo is the Fem Virgo/Virgin Sign
Leo Arrives When She is a Virgin Venus   A Virgin Does Not Know Much and is Extremely Young
The Leo/Lion as   The Code Man   Comes to Her Youth as King   She Will be Fooled from Young Age into that Overwhelming Power
The Leo/Lion Astrological Symbol is a Prostrated Fem (O and R Together written in Cursive) and its Sounds is R   as in the Double RR   Roar
The Word Or is Sound Letter R/Or/Her/Whore/Heir/Are/Here/Hear/Hair/Ire/Ere/Sex
It Represents a Prostrated Fem   Try it Yourself   Write Or in Cursive and Look   You Cannot Avoid it to Draw a Prostrated Fem
The Leo Sign and The Taurus Sign Represents Mythological Beasts from the Old Catholics Religious Texts   Other Ancients Religions   Myths   and   Esoteric Sciences
Not Represented in the Zodiac is the 2 Missing Figures from The 4 Beasts   The Eagle and the One is The Masc Human Face

The Masc Human Face is There to Embody those Powerful Symbols   While the Sun/Son The Lion/Leo Shines on it
VIRGO   ♍ ♍   The Person of Importance in The Virgo Sign is Mercury He Rules in The Tarot Card # 1   He is The Master of illusions   The Illusionist and Magical Villain   The Code   Calls Him a Magician   He is the The Charmer   He is The Starter of That Game
Virgo is a Fem Sign   The Code   Relates to The Fem as a Virgin here September is Virgins Harvest Time
Her Fem Symbol   The Endless Letter M/Motherhood has 2 More Added Bars (Forming a O/Fem Hole with a Cross at its Bottom (A Rare Strange and Different Symbol in itself) Indicates She is Tied Up Now   and   Ready for the Next Step The Sign of the Scorpio
In the Great Great Past People Used to Mate in Autumn
Be Pregnant in Winter and Give Birth in Spring
The Virgo Word Sound is Veer/Go
veer: to change direction
She Changed Because   The Code   Programmed Her a Few Thousand Years Ago
Virgo The Virgin is Responsible for the Work of The Harvest (as in Producing/Providing The Human Food)   How can We Ask a Young Girl to Be Responsible of Such Huge Physical Task as to Provide Food for People Especially When The Fem was Never Allowed to have Power/Money or a Voice in Reality
It Adds to The Mystery Fairy Tale That Hides   the Code   and Keep People in ignorance
Female Slavery Starts Early
LIBRA   ♎   Venus is The Person of Importance in The Libra Sign
She is Beautiful   But She is Blinded with a Blindfold on Top of Her Eyes while She is Holding The Intelligence of Justice   So She Cannot See it   She is Blinded in Her Decisions when it comes to Measuring Justice with The Scales   The Libra Sign Here is The Symbol/Sign for   The Scales (The Law)   It is the Last Greek Letter Omega
She is the Soft Subdued Beauty in the Tarot # 12 The Art Card in the Egyptian/Crowley Deck   She has Several Breasts   She is Ready to Enter Scorpio for Sex Now
SCORPIO   ♏   Mars and Pluto are The Persons of Importance in The Scorpio Sign

It was Originally Mars (The God Of War) He Was Changed Later to the New Comer The More Nebulous Pluto

The Innocent Virgo/Virgin Arrives in the House of Sex and its Mysteries in the Scorpio Sign The Scorpio/Scorpion Sign is a Masc Planet Score/Pion (in French and English) Score P/Man Power On/N/Virgin The Pion is The Weakest Piece on a Chess Board

The Scorpio/Scorpion has His Pointing Sex towards Her Releasing Unknown Dark Fevers of Passion Which will bring the Half Man Half Beast in The Crowning Sagittarius Where She will Lose Herself to Him Only to Fall

Here She as Virgo ♍ has Almost the Same Shape Symbol as Him ♏ Her Sign Shape Symbol is Letter M/Motherhood with a Cross and a O/Fem hole His Scorpio Symbol/Sign is the Same Letter M Except He Has an Arrow/Penis Pointing Out at the End of its Tail ♏

Her Symbol Ends with T/Fem Cross/Great Curse on it His Symbol Ends with His Arrow/Penis/Mars Symbol Pointing Out Where She will be Actually be Having Sex with the Half Beast Half Man Next Door The Sagittarius

SAGITTARIUS ♐ Jupiter is the Person of Importance in Sagittarius Sagittarius is a Masc Sign The Half Beast Half Man is Also Pointing His Arrow/Penis/Mars Symbol as Scorpio and Mars do

Sagittarius is See/Letter C Egg He/E Tower/Us or Sage Hit R/Hairy/Airy S/Snake/Penis

CAPRICORN ♑ Saturn is The Person of Importance in The Astrological Sign Capricorn

Capricorn is a Masc Sign It is The Saturnian Goat from The Code The Goat is Tarot Card # 15 The Devil Card in the Egyptian/Crowley Deck

The Terrible Capricorn Saturnian Sign Will Open its Doors and Bring Her to the Dreamy Aquarian Age Which is Depicted in The Tarot Somewhat in a Ridiculous Way in The # 17 Stupid Card The Star Where as Stupid Can Be She Keeps on Taking Water from Her Left Side/Hand and Pour it Out Next to Her on the Right Side/Right Hand That Hypnotic Gesture will Prepare Her to Live as a Fish as She Arrive in the Next Sign as a Fish (See Fish in the Words Chapter) in the Sign of Pisces The Pisces Symbol is 2 Fishes as in Polygamy or All of Hers

Her Cycle Ends Here She is Now to be Reincarnated in Aries as a Sheep (see Sheep in The Words Chapter) But that Ram is Under the Spell of being The Violent Mars   so   The Code   Story Repeat its Violence on Her

AQUARIUS   ♒   There are 2 Persons of Importance in The Astrological Sign of Aquarius

Uranus (a Very Interesting Planet) Rules the Day Time (which is Masc says   The Code) and Saturn (The Mean God) Rules in The Night Time (Which is Fem   says   The Code)   This is One of The Great Injustices towards The Fems of   The Code   to Differentiate the Fems and The Mascs that Way   Talk about 2 Measures   To One you give Opportunity and Fun (Uranus in Aquarius for The Mascs in The Day Time) and The Other You Give Sorrows for Eons (Saturn in Aquarius for The Fems in The Night Time)

The Aquarius Sign is Simple   After She has Entered That Capricorn Sign   She is Reduced to Nothing   She Floats towards The Pisces where Her Status as Fish is Confirmed

She is Getting Ready Here to Enter The Pisces Sign as the Submitted/Silenced Fish of   The Code

PISCES   ♓   The Person of Importance in The Pisces is Jupiter

One of The Pisces Symbol is in The shape of an H   The Code   Silent Secret Letter

She is Now a Fish in   The Code   Ocean (O/Fem Hole   She/Shh   N/Ann/Donkey

Here as The   O/Fem Hole   She/Shh   N/In/Ann/Virgin She has Entered The World of Silence

She is in a Forced Pair with Another Fem as in a Second Wife

Her Life Cycle is Determined

She Will Not Hear that World Above The Waters (Also Called the Glass Ceiling)

Her World is Ordered from   That Code   She is Totally in   its Power

The Cycle Will Continue   In Aries She will be a Sheep Under The Law of Mars The Warrior God

The Dam Code   has Recreated Symbolically those Elements with Power/Sexual Connotations that They Do Not Have Naturally   The Sky is Not Masc because it Radiates   The Water is Not Fem because it Yields   Mars Energy/Warrior is Not Naturally the Masc Sex   Jupiter does Not have to be the Only Sex that is Lucky or Rich   Etc

SOME BIG NAMES IN OUR CULTURE

The Dam Code The Damn Book

Aladdin: A/All Men   Lad   N/In/Hen/Ann/Virgin/Donkey
Aleve: All   Eve/V/Fem Sex Active
Aleve Sounds are Soothing   There is a Magnetic Call to it
All Relieved because All Fems   are   Sex Active
Ameritrade: A Trading Company
A/Merry/Trade   A/Mary/Trade   A/Marry/Trade
Mary is/was the First Name of All Fems Born Catholic In
Quebec   Baptized/Splashed with Water   Water is an Entirely Fem
Symbol in   The Code   Trading Mary Since The Beginning   in A Good
Merry Light   Says They
ATT: A Phone Company
A/All Men   and   2 TTs/Fem Crosses (Plural or All of Them as in Bigamy
also)   T Travels Over The Phone too
Betty Boop: Sexy Young Girl Showing Her Baby Boobs (Boobs are
Breasts) with Real Big Fun Eyes
Bet/He/Boop   or   Poop   Batt/He/Poop   Bad/He/Pope
A Loving Character to Many Fems
Budweiser: A Beer Company   Bud/Wiser
Bud   Wise   R/Her/Are/Whore/Heir/Sex
Campbell: A Soup Company
A Belle in a Can   Nourishing for All
Caterpillar: An Equipment Construction Manufacturer
Cat/Her/Pill/Her
Cats as Fem Best Friend   They are Independent and Self Centered   And
so Psychic   It is Said
A Caterpillar is Still inside a Cocoon
To Pill a Cat would be Illegal
Men Choose   their Biz Names Carefully   He Chooses One that Makes a
Difference   There is a Pill for Everything
Cutex: A Fem Nail Polish   An Old Rich Business
Cute/X   Cut/X   X/Fem Fallen Cross
To Cut Her as in Clitorectomy   Cute is Mostly Used to Describe Her
The Code   is Always On Alert   Many Fems Love Nail Polish
Dick Tracy: Dick/Trace/He   and/or   He Traces Dicks
A Man Mentor
Dodge: DODG   All 4 Fem Sound Letters
2 DD s/Pregnants   with Her   O/Fem Hole   in the Middle

Lise Rochon

The Word Ends with G/Penis Penetration and E/He As in Doing it Again He Will
dodge: to elude or evade by a sudden shift of position or with strategy
Dumbo: A Favorite Children Disney Character
Dumb O/Fem Hole
Take Away B/Boy Holding All Fems Breasts and Get Dum O/Fem Hole Doom/Beau
Exxon: A Gas and Oil Company Old Oil
X/Sons The X/Her Fallen Cross Twice (Plural or All of Them) and the Son/Sun
XXs/On All X/Fallen Fem Crosses are On and On to Her
The Way the 2 XXs are Put Together in Exxon Reinforces that Concept By Plurality
Eggs/Son
FNGN: A TV Station
F/Fem/Fuck N/In/Hen/Virgin G/Penis Penetration
Add Another N In/Hen/Virgin
Still Going with G/Hymen Penetration
2 NNs/Virgins Penetrated That Day/Time by G
It is as a Carousel of Pregnants Wooden (Wood is Slang for Erection) Horses (Whores) Turning Around Endlessly
The Code Takes Us by the Hand (End) and Control (Cunt/Roll) Us with those Artificial Concepts
(Con and the Cept
Add R and Get Scepter Scepter is The Royal Stick
GM: G/Vaginal Penetration and M/Motherhood
Girls Always Loved Cars Cars Made Many People Happy Still Do It Often Was/Is a Home for Sex Lovers and Hot Stuff
HP: H/Secret Code Letter P/Man Power
Possibly a Secret Pope Here in That Code
Kotex: Sanitary (?) Napkins for The Bleeding Fems
Code/X could be a Name for The Code Operation
The Goal is T/Killing Her After K/Breaking Her In Many Ways and Pieces
It is Attained with X/Fallen Fem Cross
The Crucifixion T/Great Fem Curse is Represented by a Cross/Crux The Letter t or its Nail Letter T Also
Lay's: Sex and Potato Chips Yum (Yum is made of 3 Fem Letters)

830

The Dam Code The Damn Book

L'Oréal: A Hair Tainting Company
Lure/He/All   L/Whore   He   All/Ill/Elle
Alluring is L'Oréal   The R/Heir/Whore is There because of The Or (Or is Gold in French)
Mary Poppins: A Magical Wonderful Nanny Story
But   The Code   says No so
Mary/Pop/N   N/Ann/Virgin/Hen/In   So
See What M Brings
Mary/P/Hop/N   Hop is Slang for Sex
Merry/Pop/N   Pop is to Have Sex   Pop/Her
Merry/P/Hop/N   He Jumps/Hops N and He is Happy About it
Mary/Poop/N/Ing   An Easy Joke for The Boys
MIT   M/Motherhood/Him   I/Self Worth   T/Fem Cross/Great Curse
Switch I from MIT to U/You/Ovulating and She Gets Mute
Switch I for O/Fem Hole and She Gets Mote
mote: a small particle or speck especially of dust   may or might
Matt 7:3-5 "Why do you look at the speck of sawdust in your brother eye and pay no attention to the plank in your own eye
Which Lone Eye is it   Is it The Left or The Right Eye   Probably the Right One   Is it Their Third Eye
Anyway if a Girl Gets a Mote in the MIT Word She is in Heavy troubles   As usual for Her says   The Code
Using The Letters Sound   To Give or Measure its Identity
Here being   M/Motherhood   and   T/Fem Cross
Add Another T and She Gets MTT   She Gets All Cursed and Pregnants
mitt: a mitten   *Slang* a hand
What Can She Do with one Mitten
Switch I for A/All Men and He Gets a Mat   or to Mate
Mate Mattress Matter (Mate/Her) Mother
Palmolive: A Toothpaste Company
P   All   M   O   Live
Palms   All Palms   So Nice   and   All/Holes   Come Alive   Towards   M/Motherhood   to Live   A Very Good Concept   Now How is it done   With a Smile and Clean Teeth
Palmolive Starts with   P/Man Power   The Word is Powerful   And There is a Pal in it
Power/Full   P/Owe/Her/Full   The Power of Him   and The   Full (Pregnant)

Paramount: A Film Industry   Pair/A/Mount   Its Logo Looks as Looking from The Back at 5 Walking Veiled Fems in a Desert   in The Dark Surrounded by Pointy Dark Mountains with Long Shadows
The Top of Scenery is Encircled with a Halo of Stars
Polo: is Pole/O A Man Sport   P/Man Power/Him   and his   Penis Going for the O/Fem Hole is The Sport of His Pole
Princess Toad Stool is The Ultimate Prize or Goal to Reach Her   In the Mario Game
Young Children are Using those Words Ignoring   The Code   in Action
Rolex: A Watch Company   It Works with Clocks (See the Clock Chapter) An Old Science which Measure Time
Roll/X
Roll   X/Fallen/Rolling Cross   Further Far Away from   The Code
First Came The   T/Great Curse/Fem Cross   Then Came The   X/Fallen Cross   Gone
Rock and Roll Them
Time and The Wheel of Time
Rubbermaid: Rub/Rob   R/Her/Are/Whore/Heir/Sex   Maid/Made/Mad   She is Made of Rubber   and   it is All Made from the/a Maid And Mad is Close says   The Code
RX: The Pharma Logo
R   Making a Second   X/Fallen Fem Cross   with the One that Is on Their Logo
From   R/Sex   to   X/Fallen Cross
That Cross is in Between R/Her/Hair/Are/Here/Hear/Ear/Heir/Whore/Or/Err/Sex   and   X/Fallen Fem Cross
RX   Is a Very Important Connection
Tampax: Fem Hygiene (?) Product
Damp   Axe/X
You can Switch   D/Pregnant   for   T/Fem Cross   in The Code   One Brings to The Other   N/Virgin   and   M/Mothers   are the Same Too Interchangeable
Siemens: Semen/See Men with   in Plural
Sony: Son/Sun   He/E
C/See/Young Girl   On/Hon   He/E   Sound/He
In the   Sun/Son   with   N/Virgin   as the   Y/Wounded Fem
TWC: Time Warner Corp   TV
T/Fem Cross   M/Motherhood   C/See/Young Girl

Timex: A Watch Company
Works with Clocks (See Clock in The Words Chapter)
Time/X   To Time   X/Fallen Cross
TNT: 2 TTs/Fems Crosses   Surrounding   N/In/Hen/Ann/Virgin   would Mean Communication Between 3 Fems   as 2 Moms or mature Fems Talking to their Daughter Without Supervision from a Code Masc Letter That would be   A Big No from   The Code   so It Explodes into Dust   TNT

Lise Rochon

THE CLOCK
D/Pregnant under the Cloak (Veil)

The Clock is

12
9   3
6

The Cross Keeps on Rolling as The Wheel Turns Endlessly
Clocks have 4 Corners Numbers   Those are Odd Numbers Including The Sum of 12   1+2: 3
That Top Number is # 3 Which is the Pyramid Number of Walls Seen from One Side   It is The Triangle Top
The Clock   Forces The Shape of The Cross   and   The Wheel of Time Reinforces The Concept as it Turns It Forward Endlessly   The Needles Pushing (Need/All   Need/L   See Letter l/L in The Letter Intro in the Words Chapter) it All Constantly   Keeping it Turning it Around   Into The Future

Clock: C/Virgin   Lock   See/Luck
The Message is   C/See/Young Girl   is Lucky When She is on The Clock   as in Her Monthly Period
He Gets the Luck as in Lucky (Luck   He/E)   She Gets The Lock as in C/Lock The Clock
Take Away L/Fem Light Away and He or She Gets Cock
(Cock is Slang for Penis and is Made of 4 All Fems Letters)
Cluck (Also All Fem Letters) on That   Or/And   Clock on That for All   The Fems
cluck: the sound uttered by a hen when brooding or in calling her chicks
Always Pregnant or Mother that Hen/N/In/Ann/Virgin
Switch K/Fem Broken Warrior to T/Fem Cross and She Gets a Clot (Cloth   Blood Loss   That Will Make Her a Little More Weaker From that)   A Blood Clot can be Dangerous
C/See/Young Girl   and   that Lock/Luck Creates That Clock
Switch K for G/Penis Penetration and She Gets Clog
That Clock is Also the Wheel as in the Wheel of Time
She has Accepted that Wheel/Will from Ignorance and Weakness as   That Code   is So Powerful in its   T/Fem Cross   Goal to All Fems

The Dam Code The Damn Book

Be All Free From that Damn Enslaving   Code
The Chicks (Girls) Clucks (Clocks) on the Clock Under The Cloak Switch
D For B/Boy Holding All Fem Breasts and He Gets a Buck
For C/See/Young Girl and She Gets a Cock
For F/Fem/Fuck and She Gets Fuck
For G/Penis Penetration and She Gets Guck For L/Sweet Fem Light and She Gets Luck
For M/Motherhood and She Gets Muck
For P/Man Power and He Gets Puck (He is Leading The Game)
For R/Her/Hair/Are/Here/Hear/Ear/Heir/Whore/Or/Err/Sex and She Gets Rock (On this Rock I will Build)
For S/Is/His/Us/Ass/Hiss/Serpent/Penis and He Gets to Suck or be Sucked   Yum for The Guys)
For T/Fem Cross and She Gets Tuck (Hey   Girlfriend Being Crossed May Lend you a Hug)   or   a Tock
As a Grandma   So She is Old Already   But No says   The Code   For Y/Wounded Fem   She Gets Yuck
Switch Ck for Th and She Gets Cloth   for Her Loss of Blood A Pro Move here from   The Code
Cloth: C/See/Young Girl   and the Word   Lot (That She Can have a Lot)
Clothing: Cloth/In   C/Lot   N/In/Hen/Ann/Virgin   Cloth/N   (See BB (Belly Button) Letter in The Words Chapter)
The Bottom Quarter   The # 6 AM or PM
Sex/Sex/Sex   or   6 AM/PM   is a the Bottom of The Clock Where the Genitals would be
After Him Being Lucky in # 7/Seve/In   But Not Her   She Enters The Fems Number of   # 8/Pregnancy   which will Lasts Her a Life Time   Then After   She is that Which is That Witch # 9   or   The Older Fem that Carries in Her Head The Egg still to be Made in The Future   or   She is   The Crone   The One that knows More   As She Falls Again Into Zero   Where She is Nothing By Herself Again   Having The Stick in Front of Her in # 10
The Left Quarter   The 9 AM or PM
See # 9 in The Numbers Chapter   It does Not Change from There to Here   and   She Remains Beautiful in So Many Ways   and She is   in The Same Ignorance about Her Destiny

835

10 or 10 O Clock is Next for Her   as # 1/His Stick and Her as the Zero   or   the O/Fem Hole   So Back to Nothing/Zero   or   be a Sex Hole

11 or the 11 PM It is The Darkest Time of the Night for The Fems   or   11 O Clock AM   A Busy Time of The Day

11 as in 11 PM is Where the Barricaded Awake Code Soldiers are Guarding   The Bar Code   with their Two Bars (# 11) and keeping those Fems Away from   The Code   Even in Her Dreams Until Time Enters Completion in # 12 at 12 PM

Only Masc Guards that Entrance

The Fem is Never Left Alone on That Clock/Cluck/Code   or   Any Where There is Always a Symbol Imprisoning Her Somewhere

And Those Are Everywhere so   She Never Gets as Chance to Think by Herself and Compare

The Clock Really Starts at the Top (The Head of the Cross) with   # 1/The Stick   Again Starts   That Code   Game

(See I/Eye/Pyramid Eye)   It is Followed Closely by # 2 to Create the # 12 The Top Quarter   The 12 AM or PM

Then to Start Again in # 1 Where the Stick of the Pyramid Will Be On Her Again To Hurt Her

Twelve is the Teenager One Two   One Two

Twelve to 3 AM is The Time Most Sleep   12PM to 3 Pm Is a Busy Time of the Day for Work

The Right Quarter   The 3 AM or PM

The Next Quarter to the Right is the # 3   1 2 3

Again # 3 is Half of the # 8/Pregnancy

9 6 3 and 12 are the 4 Angles of that Cross   They Blend into Each Other They are Multiple of Each Other Starting with # 1 in # 12 or 12 PM or AM That Clock Needle Moves into a Progression of Numbers   1 3 6 9 12   Until # 12 (Completion)

It is the Way   The Code   Works   It Perpetuates the Secret of its Numbers

The Top of the Clock is the Head of the Cross

That is Why # 12 is the Most Important Number in that Symbology It is Also the Transitional Number before # 13 Hits (Which is Not on the 12 Hour Clock Unless it is a Military Clock)   Where He will Not Be or See Because He will be doing Something Else while She will be Stuck in #

The Dam Code The Damn Book

13 (See # 13 in The Numbers Chapter) where she is Starting to Lose Her Blood and Shame Arrives
After The #1 of 12 is The # 2 of 12   Imagine That Number 2 Mirroring itself   We See a Heart Shape for Her and a Fem Butt Shape for Him   Both on a Plate (The Flat Line Holding that ½ Heart Shape)   That is so Cute   But No says   The Code   (See BB in Words)   That Little Waist just Appeared here   Say No to That (See Corset in BB)
The Clock Vocabulary
Hour: Our/Oar/Whore
Hours: Ours/Oars/Whores
The Oars Carry Small and Large Ships (She/P) on the Water (What/Her)
Oars Deprive Horses Half of their Natural Peripheral Vision
Whores Appears in   The Code   Any Time
Minute: Man/Hit   Mini   T/Fem Cross
M/Motherhood   N/In/Hen/Ann/Virgin   Hit/It
Mine/Hut   Mine/Hot
Second: See/Cunts   Sex/On   Sect/On   Sick/On
Sex/Connes   (Cunt/Con)
Une Conne in French is a Stupid Girl
It does Not Always Imply Sex as in The Fems Organs Con/Conne is Cunt in English (A Very Insulting Word for The Fems Genitals)
Con is an Old Word   Also in French and in Spanish
All with a Slight Difference in Meaning Complementing the Entire Picture
There are Sixty 60 Secs   Sex/Sect/Six   He   or Sex/On   per Minute   and 60 Minutes   Mini/T/Fem Cross   Minutes (My/Nut   Mine/Hot in the Hut) per Hour/Our/Whore/Are/Her/Err/Heir/Letter R/Sex
Sex in   The Code   Relates the Whore as Her
60 is # 6 the Number of Sex/Six   and   Zero/o   Represents Her
Six and Sex are On Around the Clock for The Fems   And that Defines the Word Time
Switch T/Fem Cross for D/Pregnant and She Gets Dime
(Almost a Dame on that Dime)   A Dime a Dozen (Doze   N/In/Hen/Ann/Virgin   Doze/In)
The/Days/Daze/Daisy/Damsel/Dazzling Days/He
Yesterday: Yes   T/Fem Cross   Her/Heir/Or/Whore   D/Day/Pregnant
Yes/Her/Day for T/Fem Cross is   Nice Memories for Her in The Past says   The Code
Tomorrow: Two   More   O

Lise Rochon

Actually it is 3 More OOO s/Fem Holes/Loins
There is Always One O/Fem Hole in the Hiding   May be for Tomorrow
Add N/In/Hen/Virgin and She Gets   To/Two   Morn   O
2 Fems Instead of One Mourning   In The Morning
Day: Is the Letter D in French   D/Pregnant   Hey/Hay
Days: Dais Sounds in French as a Deesse (Day   Is/His)
It is a Goddess in English   But All what She does here in   The Code   is to be a Dizzy Daisy in a Daze on a Dais
Dizzy   Daisy   Daze/He
The Fems Loves those Flowers (Flaw/Her)
Today: T/Fem Cross   O/Fem Hole   Day/D/Pregnant
Today Means to Keep that Fem Cross Hole Pregnant
Daily: D/Pregnant   Lay
That Daily Lay   Keeps Her Pregnant
Month: Mount
Monthly: Mount/Lay   Month/Lay
Year: E/R   He/Here   E/He   Her/R/Heir/Or/Whore
Yearly: He   Hear/Ear   Lay
The Code   is Always Looking for More Lays

THE   SEASONS

Season: See/Sun   See/Son   Sees/On   Seize/On   C/Son   C/C/On
2 CC s/See/Young Girls On   Here again   Bigamy   or   Polygamy   Appears
Seasonal: See/Son/All   See the Sun/Son in All Seasons
Spring: Spring: Spray/In   S/P/Ring   Spraying   S/Is/His/Us/Ass/Hiss/Serpent/Penis   Bring
Spring: leap jump or bound   a bouncing quality   a sudden movement caused by the release of something elastic
The Penis Springs
Summer: Sum   R/Her/Heir/Whore/Or/Err/Sex   Switch M/Motherhood for l/Sweet Fem Light/Ill/All/Hell and He Gets Seller
Fall/Autumn: Hot/Hum/M   She Falls In Autumn
Winter: Went   R/Are/Err/Her/Heir/Or/Whore/Our/Sex   Win/T/Her   As Fem Cross She is a Winner
His Penis (Pain/Is) is Ready in the Spring   She Marry/Merry/Mary in the Summer   She Fall (F/Fem/Fuck   All) in the Autumn/Fall   It is Her Harvest   (Heir   Vest   or   V/East or Vast)

The Dam Code The Damn Book

She is Pregnant in the Winter (Win/T/Her)   The Goal is Attained
Switch i/Sex Act for O/Fem Hole and She Gets Hick
There is No Pity for Her in   The Code   Another Kick (Kick is All Fem Letters)

Lise Rochon

THE 23 CARDS OF THE TAROT

Intro

There is True Magic in Tarot   A Great Mystery Permits Somehow Certain People to Connect to a Different Dimension to Ask Questions about Life through Different Mediums   From Tea Leaves to Chickens Bones to The Tarots Astrology Palm Readings   There are so Many

The Jewish People have been Studying the Tarot for Thousands of Years says Their Kabbalah   Over Time Tarot Cards have Become Receptors to The Occult Sciences in Almost a Magical Way   They have become Instruments of Mediumship   They Surrender Themselves with Prayers and White Light Exalting Their Consciousness into Expansion   It is Serious Here in This Analysis I am at a Level of Research of Ancient Secrecy (The Secret of the Sacred Arts) about The Fascinating Tarot Cards

Tarot Cards are Hermetic Representations of   The Code   Many New Tarot Authors/Creators are Not Part of The Secret of Sects Initiates They Only Tried to Understand its Secrets and Partake it with Symbols Secrecy does Not want to be Known to Many so   Therefore are The Initiates   They have been Carrying its Future   The Code   is what I have been Explaining Through The Damn Book

My Interpretation of Those 2 Tarots has been Constructed from Studying Their Cards Illustrations Construction   and   Not Following The Authors Written Interpretations

Crowley Mentioned in His Book   The Book of Thoth   that The Tarot Cards were Not The Reality of The Matter but Symbols Bringing Us There   Many Students are Trying to Decipher them   Looking at The Finger Pointing to the Moon   or   The Moon Reflection on Water (Moon and Water are Both Fem Symbols)

The Rider Tarot is Older than The Crowley Tarot so its Symbols are More Tangible because They are Simpler and Not as Corrupted or Transformed by The Mentality or The Spiritual Fashions and Religions of The Times Looking at Those Cards Different Interpretations We can Add Information on those Different Researches   As an Example in Several Different Tarots in The Card Death there is a Red (as in Fem Blood Loss) Rose (an Entirely Fem Symbol   Picturing Her Genitals/Vagina since The Rosicrucians/ The Rose Cross)   All Interpretations Depends on His Initiate Degree of Knowledge   and   His (Males Only) Comprehension

The Dam Code The Damn Book

Independently Reading The Official Interpretations of The Rider and The Crowley Tarots Textbooks before Entering My Tarot Cards Interpretations of The Illustrations They Created is Part of This Study
Those Tarot Cards Illustrations Answers Questions also with   Their Chosen Types of Faces Expressions or Genders Faces   Its Card Chosen Forms   Its Chosen Images   Its Chosen Directions   Its Chosen Colors   As an Example All Through the Rider Tarot Cards That Mustard Yellow Color in The Rider Tarot is Present in Many Skies   and   Backgrounds   and   The Sun   and   The Moon (Her Blood Loss   Her Curse/Rejection from   The Code)   The Sun and The Moon are The Most Important Luminaries and The Yellow Skies are their Background   So   The Code   Color of Power is That Yellow That reminds Us of Only a Mustard Color   It is an Innocent Name   Another Way of   The Code To Diffuse Doubts or Questions
The Colors meanings would be   White is Old   Red is Fem Blood/Sacrifice   Yellow is The Code/The Sun/The Masc Law   Blue is an Open Road which is Entirely a Masc Color   Green is Always Growing and Security   Pink is a Fem Color (it is Red Diluted with Water(Her Tears))   Black is Death (Black is Known as The Extension of The Blood Color   Burgundy   into Black)
Crowley has an Immense Sense of Details with Purpose   His Book is a Place to get Lost in   By Confounding The Finger Pointing at The Moon on the Lake   and   The Moon Itself   or   The Finger for the Most Ignorant
An Important Factor in The Crowley Interpretations are The Numerical Values Associated with The Cards   See Page 278 in His Book   The Book of Thoth
For Example   The Emperor Card # 3 with His Numerical Value of 90,900 has The Highest Valued Number   Its Symbol is The Fishhook   The Fem has No Chance here Being   The Code   Fish (See Fish in The Words Chapter)
The Second Highest Numerical Attribution Card is # 16 The Tower Card   It is Called   Pé   and   The Mouth   The God Mars (War) Rules The Fall of The Tower Says   The Crowley Tarot   The Tower has a Super Value of 80,000 for in   The Code   Her Destruction is its Only and Ultimate Goal
It Eats All that Fish   It is Where Everything Falls into Pieces in Her World being The Fish   It has 80,000 Super Value Attribution   A Total of 8

(Pregnancies) with 4 Zeros to Hold Her Down More as in Adding More Weight

The Highest Value Card   The Emperor Has Total Power Over The Empress at 90,000   but He has No Children to Feed   etc   a Huge Less Load

The Third Highest Numerical Attribution Value Card is # 13   It is The Card for Death   Its Value is 50,700   Her Bad Luck Number being 12 is The Number of Completion (The End) It Happens Under The Rule of The Scorpio Sign   It is Called The Fish   (See Fish as Her in The Words Chapter)

Mars Used to Rule in Scorpio being the God of Force (Rape) it has been Put in The Background   It was Changed to Pluto The Unconscious (Weird) as in More Secrecy

The Fourth Highest Numerical Attribution Value Card is # 12 The Hanged Man Card   It is 40,600 in its Attribution Numerical Value   Its Attribute is a Triangle going Down (The Bottom Triangle of The Cross of David)   Its Name Attribution is The Water a Fem Card in The Hiding   She is The Fem being Sacrificed   It Means a Lot   The Hanged Man is Often Called The Jesus Card Being on a Cross

In The Crowley Deck Those Tarot Cards Numerical Value goes from of   The Emperor Card doing The Ruling to   The Card The Tower where She All Fall Down to   The Card Death   through Her Ultimate Sacrifice in   The Hanged Man Card (The Great Fem Curse/The Cross/The Letter T Those are The Highest Cards in Value in The Egyptian Crowley Tarot   They Indicates as a Map What is The Real Goal of The Game of   The Code

The Dam Code The Damn Book

My Interpretations of The Tarot Illustrations

THE FOOL   o
o   The Fool   In The Rider Tarot
The First Card of The Deck here is Really The Fool   Not The Magician
That No Value Card Number The Zero/o   is Also The Letter o/O/Fem Hole
It Represents Her Egg   and   because The Fem is Associated Mentally to
Zero in Shape and Form She as Fem Hole has No Value
In The Rider Tarot The Fool Card is   a Fem   or   a Masc   Impersonation
of a Fem by a Ravine   He/She Seems Not Knowing Anything about
it   or   Is Ignoring it   He/She is Not Looking at it   His/Her Eyes Looking
Towards The Sky   or to   The o above His/Her Head on The Card
His/Her Dress has Fem Symbols on it (Circles and Asterisks) with Red White
and Black Colors (Fem Colors)   The Sky Behind is of an Uninviting Yellow
(?) Under The Light of a White (?) Sun   He/She is Holding Highly Proud a
Full Blown White Opened Flower (Flaw/Her   Flowers are essentially Fem
Symbols)   White is The Lamb (a Fem Symbol)
In His Left Hand He/She is Holding Here a Primitive Representation of
The Fleur de Lys Before it was Stranded with The Band/Bar/The Secret
Code as We Know it Today   (The Québec/Canadian My Home Country
Flag is Made of 4 Fleur de Lys which People Loves Very Much   I am So
Sorry Personally to Present This Analysis which I Know to be True) which
seems to be Responsible for The Menstrual Cycle because of Hormonal
Disturbances which were Conducted/Transmitted by some Men as
Religious Traditions
She/He Looks as Thinking   The Code   Life is a Great Unknown   But
No   See That Yellow in The Card The Moon # 18
In Her/His Right Hand is Holding Only a Small Red Weird Looking Bag
(Menses) Attached at the End of a Black (Fem Curse/Death Color) Stick
(Masc Symbol) which has a Weird Looking Red Piece of Fabric Creating an
Esoteric Bridge Between The Bag and the Top of His/Her Head
The White (Fem/Lamb/Sacrifice Color) Dog (a Fem Symbol/Bitch) Seems
Friendly and Looking Playful here   It could also be going for a Bite   In
The Crowley Deck it is Replaced by a Tiger Biting His Leg   An Important
Difference in The Card Symbolical Meaning   It Could be Indicating the
Fem Revolution/Destruction becoming More Real
She/He seems Ready to Step off The Cliff and Die There   Unless This
Person is Blind (Which is The Fem in   The Code   as for Example in the

Lise Rochon

Tarot and Astrological The Scales Sign or in The Taurus Sign where She (as Goddess Venus) is Transformed into a Domesticated Beast of Burden (an Ox)
When She/He Arrives in Card # 1 She/He will Meet the Mirages of The Code Magician He is Waiting to Lure Her/Him in The Code He will be Disguised as a High Priest (a Sign of Authority) His Old Name Card was The Juggler (a Circus Person) A Juggler is The Holder of The Stick in a Circus He Works That Stick with The Animals/Fems
The Message of This Rider Card is a Masc Impersonating a Fem in a Foolish Way being Foolish by a Ravine That is How The Fem Without being There Arrives in The Tarot as a as a Masc Fem Impersonator Fool

o The Fool In The Crowley Tarot

In The Crowley Tarot The Fool is Encircled in an Egg Shape That Has Symbols Attached to it The Fool with its Open Arms and Legs seems to Float in The Midst of it
Crowley Says The Fool is Aleph the First of 3 Manifestations of The Great Mother Then That Must be a Fem Card With That Weird Masc in Her Egg
The Crowley Egyptian Symbol for The Fool Card is The Pyramid The Tau the Ox/Cow and The Word Plough All Representing The Goddess Venus in The Code
Its Crowley/Egyptian Numerical Value is 1 It is The Lowest Possible She has to be 1 because She is Alive as One which is The Only Mother
There is an Astrological Card for The Tau it is The Taurus where The Ox (Goddess Venus/Tau) is Her Representation
In The Crowley Tarot The o The Fool Card is Now Somewhat of a Male Looking Clown with Horns and has a Sun/Son/Baby Boy on His Genitals He has a Bad Looking Too Skinny Yellowish Face and is Looking as in Under Hypnosis A White Pyramid is Illuminating the Top of His Head giving Him Weird Esoteric Power Dark Blue (Blue is a Positive Color in The Code being The Masc Color) Grapes (Her/Wine/Blood Loss Symbols G/God Letter Rapes) (See Wine and Blood in The Words Chapter) are Standing Effortlessly on His Shoulders as it Would be Growing from as if The Vine/Wine/Fem Blood is Possessed by The Masc Power as He is Harvesting it
A Big Cat is Biting His Left (Fem Animal/Feline) Thigh He is Encircled Almost Entirely with a Luminescent Whitish Symbolic Rope Forming a 2

Eggs (Polygamy) Pattern   Its Surrounds His Heart   The Rope has on it
a Butterfly (Butter   Butt/Her/Fly   Butterfly is an Entirely Fem Symbol)
a Dove (D/Daughter/Donkey/N/Hen/Fem Virgin   Ov/Ovo/Egg   A Fem
Symbol   The White Lamb/Her/Jesus to be Slaughtered   etc)   and   2
Serpents Intertwined which are Attached to The Symbol of a Firebird   as
the Head of the Rope   Meaning The Pattern is Repeated Endlessly as it is
Led by a Firebird (Eternal Rebirth)

Between His Legs a Sun Radiates as in having Full Power in His Sex Life
The Fool has a Big Bag of Money and is Holding Different Powers in
His Hands   being Surrounded with Grapes   and   Wheat   as in Life
Abundance All Coming from The Fems Symbology of   The Code
The Fool seems to be Plunging upon The Reader as   The Code   Does on
Us being There in Power at All Times

The Difference Between the 2 Interpretations of The Fool is that The
Rider Tarot being Older (1909) Represents The Fool More as an Ignorant/
Innocent Person (Fem or Masc) which will Fall in Its Ravine for Sure   In
The Crowley Tarot (1969) it is this Crazy Looking Man with The Light of
God of   The Code   The Triangle is in the Pyramid Shining on Top of
His Head   With Animal Horns and The Light on His Penis He is Looking/
Staring Ahead (at Us The Reader)   He Is Being Bitten by a Big Cat Instead
of having a Friendly Playful White Dog Close by in The Rider Tarot   There
is a Deep Difference in Symbolical Meaning of The Same Card here by
those 2 Tarots   See it as One Card   The Crowley Card Being the Modern
Evolution of The Other (Rider) Card

The Message of This Fool Card in The Crowley Tarot is Powerful   A
Strong Mad Looking Man with Horns (Devil/Goat/The Code) is Hovering
Over The Reader

He is Behind That Fem Egg Shape Designed as a Rope Strung with Sweet/
Attractive Fem Symbols   It is The Deep Hidden Message of   The
Code   It has The Ultimate Power

Number   1   The Magician   I

Intro
E/He/The Code   Masc Stands Alone with Great Power   His Number
is # 1

Tarot Card # 1 is Called The Magician in The Rider Tarot and The Magus
in The Crowley Tarot   A Magus is a Member of a Priestly Caste of

Ancient Persia   and   a Magician is an Entertainer Skilled in Magic   The Difference is in its Origin (The East)
It is an Important Card   It Represents # 1 as in God Wills   Number One being The Number of God in   The Code
The Magician Card is The Illusionist at Work
This Card has Overwhelming Fem Symbols Surrounding The Magician   In His Imposing Priest Robe He Creates and Presents Illusions so She Will Fall and Die as The Endless Prey   To Pray is The Thing to do When being a Prey says   The Code   Religions   So She will Resuscitates Again and Again (The Infinity Symbol on Top of The Magician Head Announces That) in   The Fool Card   The Zero   and Follow (Fall   O/Fem Egg   or   Fellow   Fell/O) in # 1 Card as The Magician Card Bait   She is Thinking She will be The Queen of The World as The Last Card of The Deck Indicates in The Universe Card   When Naked (without Protection) She is Holding The Same Penisses Sticks in Both Hands

                    # 1   The Magician   In The Rider Tarot
Most Important in this Card The Magician has a Large Sign of The Infinity Symbol (an Entirely Fem Symbol (it is The # 8/Pregnancy at Work Being Horizontal)   It is Over His Head Indicating a Mystical Power Certain   and   a Grip on Eternity Certain   says   The Code
The Magician here is Disguised as a High Priest   He is Wearing the Same Colors (Red and White) and Robes Styles   He is Dressed in Fem Colors which is The Colors of Her Sacrifice (Red for Her Blood Loss and White for Her being The Lamb as The Sacrifice Bait for Her Blood Loss)   On His Belt at The Height of the Belly Button (See BB in The Words Chapter) He is Wearing a Belt that Closes in a Snake Head (The Code Animal) Biting its Tail
4 is The Number of The Law (See # 4 in The Number Chapter)   On the Table in Front of Him are for Her Sacrifice The 4 Symbols for the 4 Tarot Suits   The Extra Big Cup/Love/Her/Chalice is Symbolizing The Loss of Her Blood   The Gold Coin is Riches   The Sword is The Cut/The Clitorectomy/The Ban/The Bar in Action/The Mind   The Wand is The Stick/Penis/Authority/War   2 of them are Weapons
His Right Arm (Masc Side) is Pointing Up Holding the White Stick With the Double Penis Heads as Arrows and Lights (See Card The Universe) at Both Ends Towards The Sky/Heavens/Eve/In/S   He is Going Up   His Left Arm (Fem Side) is Pointing/Directing The Index Finger Straight Down to the

Ground   She is Going Down   As Above as Below says   The Code (That is Letter Z/Snooze on it)
At The Top of Him   and   on The Ground Under The Magus are Red (Fem Color) Flowers   White (Fem) Bulb Flowers (Fem) are on the Floor in Front of That Table   Accentuating The Meaning of That Sacrificial Robe Ceremony
The Message of This Card is an Event is About to Happen   It is The Fem Sacrifice Hidden in a Bed of Flowers

1   The Magician   In The Crowley Tarot
This Card is Ruled by The God Mercury says Crowley in The Crowley Tarot   Its Numerical Value is Minimal   it is 2
His Symbol is The House (Beth is a Fem Name as in Elisabeth The Queens)   He Seems to have No Importance   but No The Magician Card is of Grandeur here   Being Almost Naked to The Point of Indecency   He is Wearing the Headdress of a Firebird (Immortality through Endless Rebirthing) which 2 Snakes (Ultimate Masc Symbol and in Plural in   The Code) seems to be Attached to
On His Toes (To be on Your Toes Means Fear or Hiding Something) He is Walking on a Fine Line Painted on that ground   His Feet Seems to be Chained to it   His Arms are Opened   He Shows His Weapons Which are His Supposed Magical Instruments   Those are Close to be The Same as those of The Magician Card in The Rider Tarot   and   More Except Here He is doing an Important Gesture   He is Touching with His Elevated Right (Masc   the Same as in The Other Magician in The Rider Tarot)
Hand and Arm the Same Weird Egyptian Symbol as Illustrated on the Back Cover of The Crowley Book of Thoth Demonstrating that it is an Important Symbolic Piece
An Horizontal Line Closes the Middle Section Not Separating the Midsts of All Many Lines Drawn on This Card   A Strange Strong being is Pointing Fists Towards Him Under That Line
This Magician has No Respectful Stance as a Real Serious Magician Should have here   He Looks as He is Playing/Dancing a Silly Role in that Green Tight with Funny Shoes at a Theater
The Next Card is The High Priestess in The Rider Tarot
She is the High Intelligence of All Fems but The Fem is Kept in an Innocent/Ignorant State to Keep Sex/Procreation Processing Going

The Message of This Magician Card is That He Carries on False Magic and Illusions from   The Code   so   His Power Over The Ignorant Especially The Fems is Immense   He Resembles an Antique Statue of Adonis   The God Who Loved Himself

THE HIGH PRIESTESS   # 2   II
The Priestess   In the Rider Tarot

She is Card # 2 as   Relationships are Often Associated to That Number because The Fem is Never Left Alone in   The Code

In The Rider Tarot What Seems to be in Great Pomp She is Called The High Priestess (Downgraded in The Crowley/Egyptian Tarot to Priestess   (Been a Half/Goddess She is Now The Servant/Priest of a Deity)   She is Sitting on a Poor Looking Throne and is Dressed and Surrounded with Blue Sky and Heavy White Fabric which Indicates Her Fem   Code   Fragility and Purity   She is The Soul of The Impress Card which is The Next Card to Her Which is Under The Power of The Emperor Card which is Next to The Empress Card

The High Priestess has on Her Left and Right Side 2 High Pillars (Pill/Her   in Plural/S/Snake/Penis) Representing The Walls of Her Prison as Depicted in The Gemini Sign which is Same Logo/Symbol as II   and is   The Number 11   and   is on Our Clock (C/Luck/Lock   See Clock Chapter)   The High Priestess Card is The # 2 in the Old Roman Numbers   It is 2 Sticks with a Small Flat Top and a Small Flat Bottom Line which Unites those 2 Numbers Together   Here She is at The Beginning of Her for Ever Bar   and Looks as   The Gemini Astrological Sign   The Brothers   Which Symbol Represents The Alliance of All Men   The Fem has No Chance

The Towers Ends Out at The Top in a Shape We Do Not Recognize Perhaps   a Bulb Flower   or   a Tree Symbol   or   an Ancient Monument   It Looks a Bit Scary   Those 2 Towers Reminds of The Tarot Sign The Moon Card   The Moon Card (an Entirely Fem Card) is Not Good a Card for Anyone   As Everything That is Fem is Negative to Her in The Arts (Ancients Secret Arts) of   The Code

On Her Right Side The Pillar is Black and it is Written Clearly in White on it Letter B) B as in Baby Boy Holding All Fem Breasts (See Letter B in The Letter Chapter)

The Other Pillar on Her Left Side is White and has Letter J in Black (J is The Shephard Letter and His Stick the J/j Guards and Can Beats All or

Any Sheep (She/Shh   P/Man Power   S/Penis as in Plural) (See Letter J/ Sheppard in The Letter Chapter)   As a Forced Sheep to that Sheppard She has No Power But to Follow His Stick   Where She has been Condemned to Silence
There is Clarity of Info about Her Here   The Priestess Has the Very Visible Letter T/t/Fem Cross/Fem Great Curse   In a Crucifix Shape in White and Black in the Middle of Her Chest at The Height of Her Breasts   It Refers as Her Identity
A Small Scroll (S/Penis   C/Daughter   Roll) is on Her Laps (A Close Position to The Body) It is Supposed to Hold Secrets   We Can Read Partially The Word Torah or Possibly Another Word as The Rest of The Word is Covered by Her Veil (See Veil in The Words Chapter)   Knowing That The Tora Contains   The Code   Illusions of Its Mystery   She is Not going Anywhere Except Down
That Too Simple Poor Looking Piece of Fabric Behind Her Creates an Illusion of an Urn/Bottle Shape Where are Strange 7 Looking Pomegranates (Fruit of Her Blood Loss) There are No Riches or Serenity Signs here Around for Her   She is Holding The Symbol of Bleeding Moon on Her Head as a Crown
She is Wearing The Same Heavy White Crown (Not Gold) as in The Crowley Tarot   Her Moon is at The Smallest Crescent (Weakest in Her Light) and Cut in Half   It is Held Solidly on Her Head in The Shape of False Horns (Venus/Ox/Taurus) as in The Crowley Tarot with the Big Circle in The Middle Representing Her as The Dot (See Period in the Keyboard Chapter   and   Letter Ii   and   Letter Jj   and The Dot in The Words Chapter)
The Message of this Card is The Obvious Way the Fem is Manipulated Through   The Code   Illusions by Also Giving Her The Illusions of Science Power and Money
Reading This Card Shows There are None

   # 2   The Priestess   In the Egyptian Crowley Tarot   II
In The Crowley Tarot The (High) Priestess Card is Not Ruled by a Planet or a Deity   It is Ruled by Our Earth (Hurt   Her/T/Fem Cross) Moon (a Small Crescent Moon) Says Crowley   Our Moon is a Earth Satellite without a Name and with No Life on it

The Code   Identifies The Moon Cycles as Her Loss of Blood and Relates it to Pregnancies   Back to the Basics (Procreation   and   The Fem Curse) for Her
Both (High) Priestesses in Both Tarots are Sitting as in Not Doing much   Both do Not Look Bright   Wise   or Happy   In The Crowley Tarot She has Naked Breasts which Makes Her even More Vulnerable   She has Different Kinds of Gentle Pale Blue and Green Colors that Surrounds Her   Softening Her Image   The Blue Surrounding Her Body Starts with The Same Blue Veil and Robe Color From The Rider Card (it is the Same Color Blue as The Sky Behind Her Decorum   Her Throne is in a Shape of a Bottle)   Nothing Has Changed (See Urn in The Words Chapter)
There is a Screen   or   a Fish Net   It is   The Code   Grid of The Walls of Crosses (The Grid is The H Letters   See Letter H in The Letter Chapter) in Front of Her and the Sides of Her   On Her Upper Body it is Strong Swirls and Spiraled Winds as in a Movement   That Grid is Enveloping Her as a Tight Corset with All Kind of Lines/Crosses that are Surrounding All Over Her Entire Body in Different Sizes   Modeling Her   Suffocating Her Creating Pains/Conditions/Illnesses   Difficult to Identify   The Fem is the Victim of The Small Waist Syndrome in Our Modern Societies   The Crosses of Those Grids are Getting Smaller and Tighter All Around Her Waist   More Specifically at the Area of The Belly Button (See BB in The B Words Chapter) Where its Gets to the Tightest/Smallest Crosses Grossly Impairing/Crunching   Pubic Area
That Rope Symbol Ends in Two Large Fish Hooks or Horns
The Priestess is in the Shape of a Double Cross Here   Her Hands are Raised to the Left and Right Top Corners of the Card   as She Would be Holding The Grid Herself   or   is She Attached to it   to Keep that Nest/Grid in Front of Her World
On Top of Her Head is a Crown that is in the Shape of Her Opened Legs   Inside those Legs Sits a Large Dot as in Pregnancies and Her Moon Blood (See Dot in The Words Chapter)
The Priestess is Sitting on Top of a Pyramid that has its Top Missing   Not Surprising   It Represents Her as Its Secret The Big Knowledge is at its Top   and   It is All About Her
In Front of The Net at the Bottom of The Card are an Assembly of Unimportant Symbols Designated to Represent Her   An Open Flower (Flaw/Her   a Fem Symbol) a Dromadere

(They Carry Obey and Go with Little Water (Love is Water Water is a Fem Symbol)) The Camel is The Symbol of That Card in the Egyptian/Crowley Tarot but is a Dromadere Pictured Instead Garnishing The Front of The Net There are Other Minor Symbols as a Flower Resembling the Hair of The Hermit Card and Other Vague Geometrical Symbols She is Behind That Veil /Grid and Seems to have No Access to that Either

The Message of The High Priestess Card is Weakness Her Crowley Numerical Value is a 3 which is Very Small She Lost Her Name of High Priestess from The Rider Tarot becoming The Priestess Only here She is Receptive Fragile and Without Real Knowledge it Weakens Her The Scroll of Knowledge is Not With Her at All Now as it is in The Rider Tarot Because of That it Eliminated The Real Understanding of Her Soul/ Life Source (She Lost Her Way) It is Almost the Same as in The Tarot Card The Scales (Justice Just/Us) Where Her Eyes are Blinded from being Covered by a Blinder (Blind/Her)

The Name Priestess is a Mirage to Her Except for Her Intuitive Mind Which is Often Unknown to Her

The Code has Owned Her from The Magician Tricks Through and The Power of The Emperor Card as in All Men Owning All Types of Fems as History Proves it

THE EMPRESS # 3 III

3 The Empress In The Rider Tarot

The Empress Card is Another Weak Fem Card (as All Fem Tarot Cards Are One Way or The Other in The Code) In Numerology with the # 3 We Enter the Public (Pubic) Area

Under a yellow Sky The Empress is Sitting Outside (Her palace?) in a Strange Looking Environment with in Her Background Skinny Black as in Burned Trees and a Small Water Source Pouring Next to Her A Green Tree seems to Want to Hide That Bad Landscape Behind Her She is Wearing an Ugly White Dress Looking as a Child Nightgown It Indicates Poverty and Non Realization The Dress White Background (Innocence Virginity The Sheep Innocent Ignorant Stupid Being Also the Sacrificial Lamb as Jesus Represented) and The Color Black/Death (Another Fem Symbol) Surrounds Those Look alike Roses on Her Tunique Those

are Red (Blood Loss) Spots on it   Her Slippers seems also Blood Red (We Can Only See One of Them and Little of it   a Sign of Weakness also)
She is Wearing a Crown of Stars (See Asterisk in the Keyboard Chapter   and   Star in The Words Chapter) in The Shape of a Pyramid (See Pyramid in The Words Chapter) Her Scepter Looks as a Child Toy   and   is Almost Colorless and Powerless as it is in The Same Color as The Sky Behind Her   Which Color does Not Exist for a Sky but Represent   The Code
There is Very Little Blue on The Card A Small Blue River and a Waterfall Flowing   Which are Made of a Few Stripes of Blue   but are Separated with Black Stripes the Same Size and Length as the Blue Ones (Indicating Obstacles   and   Dark Times)
In the Next Card The # 4 Card The Emperor is Wearing that Same Blue on His Metallic Armor Under His Top Garment
This Empress is Sitting on a Blood Color Red Chair (On Black) which Holds Several Shades of Red Cushions (The Fems in Ancient Times Used to Sit on Rags When Bleeding)
She is Wearing the Colors of   The Code   In that Loose Long Dress which Resembles a Nightgown (for Easy Sex to Him   and   to Hide the Marks on Her Body When He Beats Her)   Her Throne Looks as a Poor Makeshift of a Bed into a Chair with Cushions   It is Part of That Poor Landscape Around Her
Next and Under Her Chair is a Big Pale Purple Heart (Pale Purple is a Very Weak Color) Looking as a Valentine Day Chocolate Box (A Purple Heart is a Medal given by The American Military to Injured Soldiers in Wars) with The Fem Cross Attached to a Circle on it   It is Planet Earth (In The Code it Means Hurt) Which Reversed is Planet Venus/Pure Love (Vein/Us in   The Code   it is)
The Small Looking Cement Floor Around Her Where Her Throne Sits is Pale Grey (a Weak Color for the Fem)   On it is The Heart Shape which is Almost The Color on The Ground (A Heart should Not be on a Floor)   The Blood Red (Her Blood Loss) Fabric She Sits On Surrounds That Heart to Accentuate its Meaning
In Front of Her The Empress has Uncut Long Yellow Grass as Yellow Bars which Look Pointy   Not a Good Sign   Those are The Same Weird Yellow Color as in That Sky and Her Baby Toy Scepter
There are No Flowers (Rewards) on This Fem Card for Her

The Message of This Card is it is a Weak   and   Silly Looking Fem Card as Most Other Fem Cards are in   The Code   except here we are Talking as The Highest Rank (A Queen/Empress) in The Life of a Fem   and   is Worth Pregnancies Only

#3   The Empress   In the Egyptian/Crowley Tarot
This is Another Weak Card for The Fems   This is The Card of Her Lost Powers   Crowley Says Venus Rules this Card   and   that Her Crowley Symbol is a Door and Her Planet is Earth (as in All of The Fems)
His Empress Card has No Mouth (as a Fem is Not Allowed to Speak) and She is Almost Totally Turned Towards The Right (Masc Side) Side   She is Facing The Emperor in the Next Card # 4 (A Powerful Number for The Masc   The Number of God Law   The Pyramid)
The Empress is Seen Only from the Right Side   Presenting Herself with The Same Type of a Foreign Looking Flower than in The High Priestess Card to The Emperor in The Next Card Where He is Looking at Her Exclusively and Intensively   He Seems Prepared   and   Angry   He has a Hard Man Looks
The Empress Card has Moon Crescents Symbols and Other Soft Permeable Symbols in Front of Her Inside 2 Translucid Circles
She is Dressed in   a Simple Vibrant Pink Top   and a   Gentle Green Bottom   Colors of Appeasement to The Fems   Meaning/Indicating Her Openness to Him/The Emperor   Her Legs Seems to be Immense in that Fabric and Her Feet Abnormal in Size and Shape (The fem in   The Code is Often Represented in a Weird Way   One Way or Another
The Empress Number Card is # 3 The Number of The General Population   and   Children   It is a Weak Number for Her as an Individual because She is a Sovereign
The Empress is Wearing Almost the Same Crown as in # 2 Card The High Priestess   But it has Now an Old Roman Red Maltese Cross (Which Indicates Victory of   The Code) on Top Instead of in The Emperor Card Where He is Holding it in His Hand   That Full Blue (Hope for All Mascs) Circle (Contrary of The One in The Emperor Card in Full Burgundy (Dry Blood Color/Fem Curse Which He Holds in His Left (Her) Hand) in a Sign of Power Over Her   Hers being on Top of Her Head so She Cannot See it   That Symbol Indicates She is Venus as it is the Planetary Symbol there   and   it is The Symbol of The Planet Earth/Hurt/Her/T/Fem Cross/ Great Curse   in Reverse   The Code   is Now Inside Her

Her Arms Position is in a Shape of an Egg   or   Opened as in   Holding a Baby   or as in   Holding Her Stomach or in Pregnancy   The Emperor has Also The Same Design of an Egg Pattern from His Shoulders All The Way to His Arms and Hands Where Venus/Maltese Cross and The Scepter are being Held

The Scepter She is Holding is a Fully Opened Flower (A Weak Scepter is a Flower)   by Her Heart   It Means Full Receptivity from Her to Him

Her Thighs and Legs are Weird Looking being Way too Big   They Seems to be Wrapped in a Pair of Heavy Sky Pants   Her Feet are Not Recognizable

At Her Ankles Levels Stands a Man Armor   It is the Same Armor as on The Emperor Card Meaning those are His Armors

On The Bottom Left of The Card is a Pink Swan which is a Sweet Dream Animal to The Fems   It is Sitting on a Nest Full of Golden Looking Eggs Shells and New Born Chicks   Another False Bait for Her from   The Code   to get Pregnant

The Empress is Surrounded in Blue (Hope   a Masc Color) Color All the Way to The Upper of The Card as in Another Veil on Her

She has a Moon in Front of Her Face But it is Under Her Eyes as in Not Seeing it   This Moon is in a Dark Grey Color (Color of Death) to illustrate it as Full   its Very Narrow Quarter is in White (Both are Symbols of Innocence)

The Blue Algaes   A Water/Ocean/O/She/In   Product are in Front and back of Her   Meaning She is Under The Water   Therefore in a Position of Weakness as in being The Fish (Which would Explain the Largess of Her Legs as in Almost a Fish Form) (See Fish in The Words Chapter)

She has Another Same Moon in Her Low Back Touching Her Behind Identifying with Her

Those 2 Moons are Full and in a Quarter (which represents the 2 Forms of her   Pregnancy and The Virgin) in the Same Time as seen Before in the Rider Deck The Moon Card # 19

The Top Half of The Picture Shows that She has been Inserted in an Egg Form Almost a Dome Here up

At The Bottom of The Card are 2 Fleur de Lys   The Fleur de Lys is The Emblem of Many Flags and an Important Symbol in   The Code   It Represents Her Genitals Tied up from the Inside of Her Body by the Bad Belly Button that All Fems Get in   That Code   Just as The Circumcision is Imposed to All Boys in The Jewish Religions and in All Hospitals until a Few Years Ago   Now a Parent Signature is needed to have Your Son Penis being Cut off 9Sexual Mutilation) of His Foreskin which is a Principal Agent of Pleasure in Sex for a Man   It is as Barbarian as in Cutting Off The Clitoris on a Fem   That is Called Clitorectomy and is/was Used all The Way Far in Africa

The Message of The Empress # 3 Card is She is Weak and Obedient   She is The Intermediary Between the High Priestess (The Daughter) and Her as The Mother (The Empress) which The Card Encourages to get Pregnant Belonging to Him She is Entirely at His Mercy   He is in The Next Card   The Emperor # 4

End of Empress

THE EMPEROR   # 4   IV

4   The Emperor   In The Rider Tarot

4 is a Power Number   The Law   The Code   The Pyramid/Jupiter/The Secrets Arts   are Represented in That Number (See # 4 in The Numbers Chapter)

He is an Entirely Looking Male Figure Contrary to Many Other Ambivalent Cards   He has a Long White Beard as in Old Respected Grandfather Knowledge   He Wears a Gold Crown which has a Zero (Her) Symbol on The Forehead   He is Dressed in The Colors of a Blood Sacrifice   He is The High Priest of The Fem Loss of Blood   He Sits on a Grey (a Color of Great Masc Stability/Strength) Throne which Only Decorations are The Ram Horns which Represents The Aries   It is the First Astrological Sign   It is Mars/War Directed towards Her which Rules The Sign of The Emperor which we find also in The Crowley Tarot Deck   His Gold Scepter has a Cross (See Letter T/The Fem Cross in The Words Chapter) Representing His Power Over Her (The Empress Holds Only The Top Part on Her Scepter   and   it is Above Her Head   His is Planted on His Throne Solidly   In His Left Hand is a Round Piece of Gold Symbolizing His Riches and The World which He Owns in His Hand   He Surrounds Himself with Gold   The Empress Sits on Cushions Outside   She is Dressed in a Nightgown with a Child Toy in Her Hands   A Situation Where the Fem has Tiny Power

The Message of The Emperor Card is That The Life Meanings Empress Card and those of The Emperor Card are Immensely Different   All is Power and Goodness for That King and All is Incertitude and Weaknesses for That Queen   All is Accentuated with The Differences of Ages   The Very Old Power Man and The Very Young Helpless Girl/Wife/Mother

#4   The Emperor   In The Egyptian/Crowley Tarot
In The Crowley Deck The Emperor is a Strong Masc Card   His Numerical value is 90 900   He is said to Represent The Aries Sign where Mars The War/Terror God Reigns   and   The Sun being Exalted in Aries Gives The Emperor radiating/Ultimate Power   His Symbol is a Fishhook (She Has No Chance here being The Fish)   The Emperor Rules with Full Barbaric Power in Spite of His Nice Clothing
The Emperor would be The Most Important Card in That Tarot The Crowley Egyptian Tarot because of its Immense Numerical Value of 90 900 (Making a Total of 9 again   Plus Many Zeros (Fem) After to Accentuate its Greatness)
Number 9 is the Number of the Mature Fem in My Book (See # 9 in The Numbers Chapter)
That Emperor Card # 4 is in Burgundy and Gold   Only
Therefore Dry Red/Blood on Gold are the Colors of The Emperor to Her   That is All What He Shows to Her
Here The Emperor Gaze is Concentrated on The Empress in Card # 3   His Head is Turned Entirely to the Left Side (Her Side)   He is Looking Straight at Her Eyes   She is The Center of His Attention   His Message is Clear
In The Background Between His Eyes and Her Eyes is a Huge Pair of Horns   Those are from a Ram   The Ram Rules Aries Which Rules The Emperor Card (instead of a Goat   Being Almost The Same Looking Horns and Face as The Goat in   The Code   Which is its Power Animal)
The Emperor Body and The Empress Body are Facing Forward but Their Faces are Looking at Each Other Directly   He has Different Fem Symbols around Him   The Sacrificial Lamb   The Fleur de Lys   The Planet/Goddess Venus
The Male Symbols around Him are The Rams with the Extra Large Big Horns (There are Rams in The Rider Tarot Also)   The Scepter (Stick/Penis) He is Holding
in His Left Hand is a Sculpture of The Symbol of Planet Venus   t is a Full (as in Pregnant) Red (Her Blood Loss) Circle/Dot with a Maltese (Victory) Cross on Top of it   That is Planet Venus in Astrology and Tarot   Her Cross Symbol Attached to a Circle is The Great Curse/Fem Cross   It is The Earth/Her/T/Hurt Symbol Upside Down

The Cross is The Most Important Symbol in   The Code   It is Represented by Letter T/Fem Cross/Great Curse   Which is The Pillar of   The Grid   and Blends in the Grid with The H/Code Letter   The Crossed Leg of The Emperor on His Knee Draws a T Letter
In His Right Hand He Holds The Symbol of His Success   His Scepter   It Resembles a Large Stick/Penis Ending with the Face and Horns of The Ram (Mars in Aries   Wins the Battle Over Her The Sheep/The Fems) Probably at Both Ends   Although We do Not have Access to See That Other End of That Stick/Scepter
Both Hands and Arms All Along with the Shoulders Form an Ensemble Resembling an Egg (Fem Symbol of Fertility)   It is Enhanced in The Design in The Card Shapes   From The Sculpture of Venus in a State of Sacrifice in His Left Hand   to   The Power of The Ram Horns (Which is same as a Goat Horns) Scepter in His Right Hand
On Both Sides of His Hips Touching Him are 2 Star Symbols in a Circle (Lots of Crosses in them) (See Star/Asterisk in The Keyboard Chapter)
At His Feet on the Right Side is The Sacrificial Lamb (Jesus Sacrifice which is The Fem Sacrifice in My Book   Another Entirely Fem Symbol (The Sheep/Her Blood Loss) with its Banner (Ban/Her)
On the Left of the Emperor is almost The Same Armor that Stands by Her Leg in The Empress Card   Indicating that it is His Armor   Therefore He has The Ultimate God Power   His Card Number # 4 (The Number of the Law) Seems to be a Primitive Representation of The Fleur de Lys   There are 2 Fleur de Lys Close by
The Code   has been Always Ahead of Her
The Emperor with The Most Numerical Value of 90 900 is Far Away Above of The Other Cards in The Deck   He Has Absolute Power   It is Amazing Compared to The Empress Card with a Numerical Value of 4   The Card # 2 The High Priestess Her Value is 3   Another Huge Discrepancy   And The Card # 1 The Magus (Being a Tool Man) has a Value of 2 Creating Another Big Discrepancy   making Him Practically a Fool which is # 0 Card with a Numerical value of 1
The # 5 Card The Hierophant (Which is Dressed as a Pope) is The Next Card   it has a Value of 4   That is How Big The Emperor is
The Fishhook is His Image in The Crowley/Egyptian Deck   and   The Last Card of The Crowley Tarot has a Fishhook Coming Out of The Eye of The Pyramid (See Pyramid in The Words Chapter) Along with Another   Code   Symbol which is The Serpent

The Message of The Emperor Card is That He is The Total King of Her No Matter Her Title   All His Attention is Directed to Her as She Represents here The Pregnant Fem   He has Her Life in His hands   It is Also Represented in the Venus Sculpture in His Hand which Symbolizes The Fem Carrying The Cross of Sacrifice   Same as The Symbol of Planet Earth The Symbol Repeats the Same Message Upside Down   It is The Same Message in Both Tarots   The Rams/War are Ruling

THE   HIEROPHANT   # 5   V

#5   The Hierophant   In The Rider Tarot
See # 5 in The Number Chapter   He is Dressed as a High Catholic Figure   a Bishop   or   a Pope   He has 3 Crosses (Fem Crosses/Great Curse) on His Outfit   He Commands Great Respect   He is Dressed on a Blood Red (Her Blood Loss) Color Outfit   His Scepter is Made of a Triple Cross as The 3 Crosses on His Outfit and the 3 Layers on His Gold Headdress   The Keys (Representing The Secrets in The Hierophant Work) of The Church are at His Feet   They also Creates an X as Her Fallen Cross/T
The Hierophant Sits on a Grey Throne Confounding with the Grey Wall behind   Solid as Cement
The Message of The Hierophant Card Shows The Richness of The Ultimate Religious Power Symbols of The Fem Sacrifice

#5   The Hierophant   In the Egyptian/Crowley Tarot
The Card # 5 is The Hierophant (See # 5 in The Number Chapter)   The Hierophant Card Follows The Empress Card and The Emperor Card as in a Consecration of That Union   That Happens After The High Priestess has Fallen in The Hands of The Magician   In The Ancient Greece an Hierophant was Known to be The Holder of The Secrets of   The Code   He was Called The Interpreter of The Secret Mysteries and Arcane Principles   Crowley Calls it The Taurus Card which is Ruled by The Goddess Venus Which is Under The Ultimate Man   Code   Power
arcane: known or understood by very
few   mysterious   secret   obscure   esoteric
The Tarot is Made of Arcanes   Arcanas Major and Minor
The Hierophant is The Initiator   Those Secret Mysteries are Called The Eleusinian (as in Illusions) Mysteries   That is The Story (Repeated Over Centuries and Millenaries) of The Goddess Demeter (The/Meter   as in

to Measure Time (Menstruations) The/Mother) that Looses Her Daughter Persephone (as in The One That Pierced The Phone (as in Being Psychic)) to Death which was Imposed by Hades   He is The God of The Underworld Known as Hell   (Hide   S/His) He Lied to Her and Manipulated Her into Give Him All Her Jewelry and Precious Stones that Covered Her Body and Gave Her Magical Protection Wealth and Her Beauty   She Gave Her Riches to Him One Piece at The time   In Confidence/Innocence She Gave Him All He Asked Which was Everything to be Given to Him   When She was Totally Naked He Killed Her   That is Part of The Eleusinian Mysteries Clarified for You   (That would be Called Conjugal Violence in Our Days)   To Finish That Story after Her Death Her Mother Found Seeds which She Planted at The Place Her Daughter had Disappeared for Ever and Corn was Created That Day for The First Time
In   The Code   No Fem Never Held Positions of Power
According to Crowley in The Ancients Tarot Decks That Card Was Called The Nail   Nine (a Fem Number) Nails Are on Top of That Card and Pointing Towards That Hierophant Head   which is Already Surrounded by a Flower with 4 Petals (Fem Symbol) making the shape of a Cross)   Nails Indicates No Choice but to Follow   Nails and Cross (Jesus Sacrifice) are Part of Each Other in   The Code   Symbolism
The Hierophant is Surrounded by 3 Different Beasts Scary Masks and a Human Face Mask   The Hierophant Himself seems to Wear a Face Mask   as if This Card would be an Illusion at The Theater   The Hierophant has No Opened Eyes Which Indicates More Hiding   The Code   is All about Hiding   and   Lying
Card # 5 is Mostly in Red/Her Blood Loss   The Beast that is Wrapped Around the Large Hierophant Lower Body Hips is a Huge Bull (Her as in Venus from The Taurus Sign)   The Second Beast The One on Top of the Bull is an Elephant (Phallic/Him) Half Wrapped Around The Hierophant Chest in the Same Way as the Bull is   Those 2 Animals are Real   They are Not Wearing Masks   Wondering Who is in Charge in This Card Starting at the Top Right (Masc Side) Corner of The Hierophant Head There is a Human Gold Mask (Empty Eyes) or a Petrified Face   It is Hiding Something   At the Top Left Corner is a Head Mask of an Eagle in Flight   That Animal is Coming Down Facing the Hierophant   At the Bottom Left (Fem Side) of the Card is a Bull (Her/Venus) Skeleton Face Mask   At the Right Bottom Corner is a Scared Looking Beast Mask With

Horns   That Tongue is Out Showing in an Open Scared Kind of a Tortured Mouth   Those are Scary Symbols to Surround a Pope/Hierophant
The Number/Letter for the Pope/Hierophant is The V/Open Sex from Her to Him   It is The Roman Numerical # V/Her Split Stick of Power/Consciousness/Knowledge Being Split or Being Opened by   The Dam Code   (See V in The Roman Numeral Chapter)
The Whole Card is Covered with Different Transparent Pyramids   some with Unfinished Design   a Half Finished Cross of David is Also There Up to the Hierophant Head where it Stops at the Bottom of His Auric White Crown which is Also in the Pyramid Sign   This Pyramid is Pointing Up   That One is Enveloping His Crown and His Head as in Secrecy
The Head of The Egyptian Priestess is Where His Gonads Stands
The Next Card being The Union of The Lovers   From The Empress and The Emperor The Hierophant is there to Sanctify/Legalize Their Sex Union The Message from The Hierophant Card with All This Ancient Symbology is here to Illustrate   The Code   History in The Daylight   Because so Few Understand   The Code   there is No Fear Here to Expose All the Splendor of Its Power

THE   LOVERS   # 6   VI

Intro
6 is The Number for Sex   On a Clock # 6 is situated where The Genitals would be
The Original Meaning of The Lovers Card Has Changed a Long Time Ago   The Old Code   Version Was Called The Brothers   It was The Gemini (Genuine) Card with 2 Men in it   It was Castor and Pollux The "Heavenly Twins" in the Constellation of Gemini (in a Mythology Dictionary See The Story of Castor and Pollux)   The Crowley Deck Illustration is More in That vein   The Rider Deck Allows/Bless The Sex Union as in Adam and Eve Sex Sin/Curse
Number 6 Represents Sex   Triple 666 is What We have been Told
                #6   The Lovers   In the Rider Tarot
In The Lovers Card a Masc and a Fem are Naked
A Large Fem Looking as a Celestial Being is Appearing from a Blue Background Sky on a Grey (Bad News/Weather) Cloud (as in from Magic) as in Blessing Their Union from The High   The Celestial Being Has Large Blood Red Color on Black Wings and is Wearing a Purple Robe (Purple is

The Dam Code The Damn Book

The Color of Sacrifice   It is The Mix of Blue/Masc Color   and   Red/Her Blood Loss)
Both of Them have a Tree (The Tree of Life) behind Them
Her Tree is The Apple   There is Wrapped Around it a Long Snake (Penis Symbol) Coming at Her
This Card does Not Represent The Real Gemini Twins Boys   Only   The Code   Hypnotizing Message
In The Crowley Deck   The Picture is Clearer

    # 6   The Lovers   In the Crowley/Egyptian Tarot
The Lovers Card was Known in The Past as The Brothers Card
Crowley says   The God Mercury Rules in Gemini   Which is a Masculine Sign
No Matter The Illusion of Marriage Between That Couple Here
The Lovers Gives a More Complicated Picture Explanation in The Crowley Deck
Considering The God Mercury Rules in The Juggler/The Magician   He has All Powers Given to All Men as Gemini (Gem/He/Nigh   Nigh is Fem as in No) Stipules   It is All Men United   and   All Fems Have to be Married and be Possessed by Marriage Blood
It has been for a Couple of Thousand Years
Here is the Union Between The Masc and The Fem   Their Garments are a Cape of Ermine (Very Expensive/Rare   Representing a Royal Event) Indicating The Importance of that Act in   The Code   The Groom Garment is Gold (as in Radiating The Sun/Leo/Aries of Leadership)   Hers is Red (The Color of The Great Curse) as in She will Belong by The Blood (Her Blood Loss)   His Crown is Gold   Hers is Grey on Black   Her Crown is The Same as in The Empress and The Priestess Cards   It is made of Her Planetary Sign (Venus) Indicating the Sacrifice of Her Blood Loss)
The Code   All Men Bonding/Union is Showed here as Young Boys Castor/White is Holding a Bouquet of Flowers (Indicating All Fems are Cut Flowers (Roses Indicates The Fem Genitals) which is are Short Lived Weak Symbols for that Important Object of Power) and Pollux/Black is Holding a Big Stick as (Implying All Men Power from Youth)   Castor is in Front of the Groom (Which could be a Fem as it has No Real Face Recognition)   He is Extending His Arm Holding High The Fem Gold Cup/Chalice/Uterus (With a Dove on it Plunging Down to The Ground) in Front of Her Genitals as in Offering it   and/or in   She Will be Drinking it (as in The Sacrament of Communion)

Pollux is on The Bride Side Extending His Arm Towards the Groom Genitals Holding a Lance Along with The Groom
At the Bottom of the Stick is an Egg Wrapped in a Snake   It is The Orphic Egg   Those are The Ultimate Symbols of Her and Him as Defined in   The Code   Wikipedia Associates it to Lucifer The Being That Brings The Light (of The Cosmos)   The Symbol for Pharma is Close to that Symbol   Those Symbols are Worth More Study
There is a Blinded Cupidon (That Mean Little Man) Ready to Shoot   Blindly as in Obeying a Force   He Will Hypnotizes Her and Him to Fall in Love
The 4 Corners of The Lovers Card from the Top Right   It is a Naked Fem on The Right that Looks Apprehensive with a Strange Looking Stomach as She would be Handicapped or Weak   There is Another Fem on The Top Left Side   This One Also Looks Impaired and Seems to Have a Too Small Waist and also Looks Weak
From the Top Corners Fems Seems to be Flowing Grey on Black Lines that Descends All The Way to Touching a Pink Cape that is Wrapping them Coming from Above where a Veiled God or a Priest or a Priestess with their Blessing Hands are   There is No Head Showing/Identifying to Those Large Important Hands   His/Her Habits are Pink/Mauve which is a Fem Color
White Castor (Cast/Her) Represents the Fem   He is Holding Flowers   Black Pollux (Poll/X) Represents The Masc He is Holding a Big Stick   There is No Hope for The Fems here At All Times
The Tail of The Lion is Strange Looking   The Lion has a Tail with Hooks on it (Unnatural   Mean   Scary) Describing The Pure Raw Predator Nature of the Lion   That Lion Here is a Reconstruction as Everything Else in   The Code   He is Sitting on the Opened Phoenix Red Wings   A Position of High Esoteric Power   The Phoenix Wings Spans All the Way to Pollux With The Snake and Egg   (Steak and Eggs is So Close   The Code   is So Good at That Kind of Sinuosity that Connects Different Concepts to Create Unconscious Soothing Associations) in the Middle   The Eagle is Sitting on The Other Wing   Both are Having a Fake Smile
The Eagle and the Lion are Symbolically Related
in   Religion   and   State Symbols   But Their Message here is Bleak
The Attribution for The Lovers Card # 6 is the Sword as in to Cut (Clitorectomy) or Defend against Her The Enemy

The Astrological Sign of Gemini   Which is Another 2 Vertical Bars from   The Code   See Also The Eleventh Hour in The Clock Chapter   They have Almost The Same Symbol   Being Hermetic Only Men are Allowed in Both
The Lovers Card Numerical Value is 7/Lucky (Luck/He   as Usual   it is in   The Code   Lock)
The Message of The Lovers Card is   An Important Change of Message Through Different Symbols as if Nothing Happened Between The Times of The Rider Card and The Crowley Interpretation
In The Rider Tarot The Lovers Card Seems Just an Acknowledgment of The Benediction from Above (The Code)   In The Crowley Tarot That Card Shows that Union as an   All Organized Set with its Rules and Obligations for Her   Such as Obedience Under The Power of the Stick if One can Read Its Symbols

#7   THE CHARIOT   VII

Intro
Number 7 is a Masc Number and it Indicates Good Luck   Al though Many Disapprove of of its validity
Comparing Both Cards   Both of them are Protected from Above as Their Chariots/Carts have a Protective Top   Both of Them are being Carried to Destination without Reins   and   are Not Moving   Both have Funny Looking Sphinxes (Symbol for Secrecy) in Front of The Chariot   They do not Seems to be Attached to The Chariot   Both Chariots Drivers have No Reins to Drive Their Beasts Towards a Destination   The Crowley Deck has 4 Weird Looking Sphinxes as The Rider Deck has only 2   but Both Decks have One Sphinx With Breasts Which are Not Explained in Their Books Explaining that Card   Crowley says it Represents The Holy Grail   Bringing Us Back to to The Fem Loss of Blood (The Bleeding Lance and The Cup)   Both Cards Carts Have Big Wheels Which Represents The Wheel of Time   In Both Cards The Chariots are Resting on Safe Grounds   The Rider Chariot is on Green Grass   and   The Crowley Chariot is on a Gold Stone Road   In The Crowley Deck The Driver does Not have a Stick/Scepter but He Has a Crab on His Helmet as its Symbol   The Crab Symbol is from the Cancer Sign which Rules That Card   He is Already Fully Armed to Combat The Fems to Keep Them Aligned with   The Code

#7   The Chariot   In The Rider Tarot

In The Chariot Card Background are Several Castles (Cast   All/Ill/Elle/Hell/Letter L) Roofs Blood Red Color Pointy Pics   There is No Rest for The Fem Endless Slavery   The Chariot is The Same Color as Those Grey Sad Looking Castles Towers and Walls   Therefore Representing The Power There as in Belonging to it   The Chariot Stands Immobile on The Grass on The other Side of a Body of Water (Which Separates the Fems from the Secrets of   The Code as in The Castle (Cast/All/Ill/Elle)   He is a Special Messenger   He Wears Moons and Stars (Fem Symbols   The Same Stars as on Her Crown in The Empress Card # 3) as Ornaments   On His Head is a Large Star (or Her Multiple Crosses   See Star is Made of Crosses in The Asterisk Symbol in The Keyboard Chapter)   The Driver Seems there to be Admired   The 2 Sphinxes (The Code is Pulling Through The Sphinxes The Secret of   The Code   The Chariot) are Resting   For That Special Occasion They are Replacing The Normal 2 Horses (See Letter R/Her as in Horses/Heirs/Whores) Carriage

His Uniform is The Same Blue Sky (A Yes Color for The Masc) as The Symbol for The Eagle   Symbol of The Ultimate Law and Power Over People   Its Wings are in Front of His Chariot   The Wheels (The Wheel is the Wheel of Time is an Important Symbol in   The Code) and Sky   In the Front of His Chariot is a Unusual Form for Her Red Cross   The Red Symbolic Cross (Her Curse Symbol) is Made with a Red Wood Piece in The Shape of a Nail in the Center of a Round Piece of Wood (As in The Mechanism of an Old Wooden Wheel (See The Wheel of Time) Indicating   All Fems to Sex and Pregnancy

The Driver is Holding a Scepter (same Stick as in The Magician Card) in His Right Hand

He has a White Square on His Chest as The High Priestess Card has a Cross on Her Chest (a Cross/Crucifix Makes a Square/Rectangle Shape When Surrounded   as in Mission Accomplished)   A Square is Essentially a Masc Symbol   It is The Symbol of The Law/Pyramid   Its # 4 a Most Power Number in   The Code   Geometry (See The Cross with a Hand being Held to The Head)

#7   The Chariot   in the Crowley/Egyptian Tarot

Crowley says The Cancer Sign Rules The Chariot Bringing The Fem Moon Along

The Dam Code The Damn Book

Jupiter is Exalted here so there is an Element of Luck or Protection for The Card   The Top of The Chariot is Blue as in a Sign of Protection from Above   In The Rider Deck the Driver is Also Protected from Above with its Top made of the Same Stars as in Her Crown in The Empress Card
The Chariot Card is   The Code   Anonymous Soldier Man in Full Armor with a Gold Crab on His Head   It is the Same Crab that Lives in the Water in The Cancer Sign Card   It is The Crab of The Moon Card   He holds The Same Duties as The Sheppard to The Sheeps   The Fems are The Fishes of The Ocean (as Explained Many Times and in Many Forms in My Book   The Damn Book   The God Neptune with His 3 Picks Surveils the Fishes The Crab Bites (Cancer is a Deadly Disease) to Death
The Sitting Gold (The Color of Ultimate Power   as in   The Sun in Leo   or   Mars in Aries) Armored Man is Holding on Top of His Genitals what Seems to Be a Round Disk Sculpture   which is The Red Dot/Stain   of The Holy (Hole/He) of The Graal/Girl   That Dot is Huge here   The Fem as Dot here is Encircled/Hidden with Other Blue Security Shades Circles All The Way into a Purple (Color of Her Sacrifice) Circle as its Last Layer   She has No Chance All the Way   One Hides   The Other Sacrifices
The Wheels of The Chariot are Huge and are Red Blood Color   The Wheel is an Important   Code   Symbol (See The Wheel of Fortune in The Words Chapter   and The Card)
In Front of The Chariot are 4 (# 4 The Number of The Law in   The Code) Grotesque Figures Remembering Ancient Mythological Figures that would be have Disfigured and Transformed in Many Ways
One Looks as a Little Horsie for Children (Although it is Black)   The Rider Tarot has Also a Black Sphinx (Although He is less Altered)   The Second One has Human Legs and Human Feet with a Strange Body on Top with a Strange Animalistic Face   The Third One has the Feet of a Chicken and an Almost Normal Human Head   The 4th One is Fem and has Horse (Whores) Hoofs Feet and has a Dog Head Hiding in a Heavy Wig Hair Cut   She has Naked Breasts to Keep Her in Shame   So Horse Feet   Dog Head   and   Mythical Rounded (Pregnant) Naked Breasts in the Middle of its Flying Horse Torso is a Weird Spectacle   as if   The Code   was Trying to Creates Humans Hybrids
The 2 Sphinxes have Survived in The Crowley Deck from The Rider Deck but they have been Metamorphosed and are Surrounded with Parts of Powerful Weird Looking Mythological Religious Animals

They All Have Wings   Making them Somewhat Unreal   Those 4 Animals and The Chariot are Standing on a Gold Road Meaning Being Great Importance
The Message of The Chariot Card is that He is The Carrier or Messenger of Victory and Power of   The Code   That has Succeeded in Establishing Her Blood Loss as a Secret Treasure to Protect for The Control of All (See Hell/Elle/Letter L)

THE STRENGTH   # 8   VIII

Intro
That Card is an Entirely Fem Card   and   is a Losing Card (See # 8 or/and VIII in The Numbers Chapter)
From The Rider Deck (as Strength) to The Crowley/Egyptian Deck (as Adjustment) Those Two Cards are Her Evident Transformations from One Era to Another   and She is Still Under   The Code   Domination

8   The Strength   In the Rider Tarot
She is Seen in a White Peasant Dress with a Red Flowery Apron   She is Trying to Close a Lion Big Open Mouth with its Big Furious Tongue Out at Her Bare Hands (In Ancient Mythologies Pulling Out The Tongue had Special Powers) Is That Courage or Madness
In The Card The Strength She has a Soft Fem Face that Looks Patient and in Charge Although She is Trying to Keep Closed the Mouth of a Lion which is The King of All says The Astrological Sign Leo where The Sun and Mars in Aries Reign Together from Perpetual Wars with the Help of Saturn At that Point in   The Code   (She is Probably a Mother) She has Lost Most Powers   That is Why She Has Only Her Bare Hands to Defend Herself Against a Lion which is The Endless Male Sex Call which Keeps Her Endlessly Forcefully Pregnant
The Flowers on Her Dress Almost Blends in with the Lion Mane   They Blend Especially with The Red Flowers All Over The # 1 Card The Magus   Another Factor of Recognition of The Connection Between The # 1 Card and The # 8 is That The Sky behind them in Both Cards is Yellow   Which Seems to be The Color of   The Code   in That Rider Tarot   Also # 8 and # 1 Share All The Same Other Colors   The Blue (The Color of Success)   Mountains Should Inspire Hope   But No She Would Not Survive the Icy Heights   The Code   Hides in False Blessings/Gifts   Since the First Card

The Dam Code The Damn Book

1 Card with That Luring Magician (Which Only Blue Spot is The Sword to Cut Her/U/You Out)
The Most Important Thing in That Card is that The Fem has The Infinity Symbol Above Her Head   The Magician Card # 1 has the Same Symbol Above His Head   Hers is Tilted on One Side it Follows Her Everywhere   The Flowers on Top of Her Head Look as Primitive Fleur de Lys (See Fleur de Lys in the Words Chapter) which is an Important Symbol in   The CodeIn My Book The Infinity Symbol Represents # 8/Pregnant which is The Number of This Card (See # 8 in the Number Chapter) From Her Size She could have Possibly have Given Birth (There is No Clear Birth Card   or   Pregnant Fem Card in The Trumps Cards) The Way She is Dressed   and   Her Age
The Scene Being on Green Ground She in   The Code   Fertile Territory The Message of This Card is Means Endless Pregnancies in   The Code   This is is an Entirely Fem Card   Therefore She is in a Weakest Spot   which it is   as No One Can Win with Bare Hands Against a Lion Mouth   Therefore Her Days/Minutes are Counted   Another Weak Card for Her
End of Strength in The Rider   Called Adjustment in Crowley

      # 8   The Adjustment   In the Egyptian/Crowley Tarot
In The # 8 Card of the Egyptian/Crowley Analysis Tarot Book Her Jewish Letter Name is Called Lamed (Lame/D/Pregnant   She Receives No Chances in Life)   That is How She Gets   a
Loser   Poor   Boring   Miserable   Ugly   Dishonest   and   of Course Pregnant   etc in   The Code   It is a Real Bad Losing Curve for The Fem   She had to Adjust to That Too   The Long Sharp Sword in Between Her Legs Indicates The Importance of The Phallus   Especially that Crowley said The Card Adjustment was The Card # 11 now Called Lust (Another Proof that   The Code   is The Control of The Fem Sexuality) Crowley Says That The Ruling Sign of The Adjustment Card is Ruled by The Libra Sign Which is Ruled by Venus   Saturn is Exalted here (of Course   for Sex)
In The Crowley Deck She is Also Called The Cow/Ox/Tau/Venus (Vein/Us) as in a Goddess Reduced to Really Hard Work and So Below Her Capacities   The Ox Plows   Brings   Reproduces   That is All

In The Crowley Tarot Book Attributions (P 278) She is Called Not an Ox but an Ox Prod   Here again She has No Chance   A Goad is Anything that Pricks and Wounds
goad: a stick with a pointed or electrically charged end for driving cattle oxen etc prod
in   The Code   Goad is Close to Goal   Goal is an Honest Word   But Letter L/All/Elle/Hell/Ill is All Fem   and   Makes The Goal of   The Code   The Goad   It is Finishing with Letter D as in Letter D/Pregnant/ The Donkey (See Letter D In The Letter Chapter) being what Happens to Her after The Goad as in Sex Act)   Goad is being Close to   Code   The Goat is Also Close See Goat in The Words Chapter
An Ox is a Big Animal   Hard to Transform to your Will   But with a Prod/Goad it is All Possible   The Code   Makes Her   a Sheep   or   a Horse/Whores/Rs   or   an Ox   or   a Cow   or   Fishes   or   Bees   or   Ants   Etc   She is All of them and More in   The Code   Including the Bitch Dog   and   the Independent Cat   Etc   Her Crowley Lamed Numerical Value is 30   Which in the Journalistic World Means the End of an Article   It Means Also The Death of a Journalist   Not a Happy Ending for Her on Top of being Under a Prod

In Card # 8 The Crowley Tarot Changes The Names Cards from The Strength to The Adjustment   Although Specifying that it Replaces it with The Justice Card # 11 (Lust) So She Goes To Fighting as in The Strength Card to Finish in The Adjustment Card Meaning She is Now Under the Law of   The Code   Which is The Scales Card   Her Vision is Blocked and so is Her Comprehension   She Has Adjusted to the Situation of the Old Rider Deck Where She was Someone Else then (Then She was Trying to Fight The Lion)

In Her Crowley Card Image here She is Enclosed in Blue and Green Symbols Mostly Circles Looking as Balloons (A Shallow Symbol says   The Code) See Dot in The Words Chapter) Surrounding Her

She is Holding The Heavy Scales Chains as High as Her 7th Chakra which are Held with a Heavy Duty Holding System Which is Hanged to Something Outside The Picture of The Card

On Her Shoulders is a Mantel Made of Pointy Sharp Edges That Ends in The Scales   She is Blinded to All that   Her Eyes being Covered With a Mask that Gives Her Only a Slivered Vision of Reality   Her Mask is in the Same Dark Blue and Dark Green Colors   Everything on Top of Her Head

Blends in those 2 Colors with a Touch of White   The Code   Says it is All Good   No Red Here
In The Scales Card on The Left Side is Hidden Letter A in Large Cap and it Relates to that Greek Alpha the First Letter of Their Alphabet   In the Left Scale is the Last Greek Letter Omega Relating and Amplifying that Way The Arabic Numbers with Those Greek Letters   From Alpha to Omega is an Old Expression to Says All Territory has Been Covered/A Thorough Job/etc   Yes   The Code   says here Again it is All Hidden There in The Ancient Greek   Roman   Jewish   Letters   Numbers   Etc it Suffices to Understand Their Symbols to Follow on Their Story
The Too Long Sword She is Holding in Front of Her Reaches from the Ground Up to the Height of Her Upper Chest   She is Looking Straight at it Bending Her Head Towards it   Her Legs are Slightly Bended Also Outwardly   That Sword Handle is in a Shape of an Angry Looking Animal Face with a Pointy Beak
That Sword Points to the Ground She Stands on   Which There is None Being on a Ball   She has Tiny Feet in a Impossible Ballerina Pointing Toes Position   The Sword Seems Longer Than Her Feet   Therefore it is from The Sword Point that the Diamond Shape is Drawn All The Way to The Scales Than Closing Up at Her Her 7th Chakra   She is Surrounded by It
Her Body Looks as She has been Pregnant   She has Large Full Hips but here Too t Her Waist is Too Small as in being Entangled   Any Form of Corset is   The Code   for Her
The Same Pattern of The Accepting Green and Blue Color Balloons/Dots   At the Bottom of The Card Those Circles Looking as Balloons (Very Fragile Things) are being Held Together by 4 (The Code Number   The Law) Solid Bars With Long Pointy Lines Which Extends to the Top of Her Head Holding or Touching More of Those Balloons in The Same Pattern   A Strange Spectacle for Such an Important Serious Card   As She Would be Held By Balloons
She Sees None of that   She is Being Focused on the Top of Her Legs on That Ball/Penis Handle at the Top of That Long Sword
The Message of This Card Most Important is Her Falsely Imposed Blindness   She is Also Standing on Points   She has No Power of Decision   Very Little Equilibrium   and   No Comprehension in Spite of the Powerful Allure of The Card   and its Important Meaning   Therefore it is Another Weak Card for The Fems   being Sustained by Balloons Full of Air   No Power here   Especially that Crowley says it Replaces The

Card Lust # 11 (Called Justice in the Rider Deck   as in There are No More Justice/Just/Us Which Seems to be The Core of   The Code   in Tarot   End of The Strength/Adjustment/Lust

THE HERMIT   #   9   IX
9   The Hermit   In The Rider Tarot

The Hermit Seems a Simple Card that Does Not Say Much   It Hides   The Hermit Represents The Acceptation of The Silence and Solitude of the Initiates of   The Code

But Number 9 in itself is an Entirely Fem Number   It Follows # 8 which is The Symbol for Pregnancy   # 9 is The Crone   The Wisdom After The Reproductive Years   That will Fall into Zero in The Next Number   Which is Not a Number   She Falls Down to Nothing   Until Her Rebirth in #1 at Birth   No Power here Either

What She Meet in This Card is   This Old Code   The Hermit is Cloaked in Dark Grey   He is Wearing a Hood   He Seems Looking Down Towards the Ground in Front of Him   but No His Eyes are Closed   He is Not Communicating   His White Beard is Hiding His Mouth   He is Not Talking   He is Showing/Presenting The Only Light from His Lantern   Its Light in a Shape of a Star (See Star and Asterisk in The Keyboard Chapter)   An Important Symbol in   The Code   The Star is The Message and Its Carrier from   The Code   Presented to The Fems (# 9)   A Star is in The Shape of Multiple Crosses Superposed   This is What is Coming to Her

His Stick has that Same Yellow (Hail/O/Hole   Yell/All/O   He/Hell/O) Color Which is the Same Color as the Light from That Lantern   It is Also the Same Yellow Color of The Moon and the Strange Looking Yellow Dog in The # 18 The Death Card (a Fem Card) in the Rider Deck   and

His Stick is as Tall as the Top of His Head as He was Defeated by The Stick from   The Code   and its Journey   His Long Straight Yellow Stick is Parallel to Another Long Grey Stick Created by The Folds of His Tunic (as it is Now Part of Him)   His Cloak is a Sad Grey with Small Horizontal Black Bars as in   The Code Bars   His Back Side Robe All The Way from His Shoulders to His Feet is Perfectly Parallel to the Sticks and Horizontal to The Bars Lines

The Background of The Card is Not a Night Time Sky as One could Imagine   It is Made of a Very Cold Blue/Greyish Color   The Landscape is So Barren   He seems to Stand on Snow or Above it All   There are Few

The Dam Code The Damn Book

Colors in This Card   All Attention is on The Yellow Light and The Yellow Stick   Those are Meant to make it Obey to The Stick   The Card # 1 The Magician was Called The Stick Holder

The Message of This Card is That Comparing Both # IX in The Rider and The Crowley   we see that Both Hermits are facing Towards The Left Side (Fem Side)   Both are Bended from The Weight   Both are Not Looking at That Light they Carry   and   seems Not to be Using it

Instead of The Gold Stick of Power in The Rider Deck   There are a 3 Headed Non Aggressive Dogs by His Leg

End of The Hermit Card

9   The Hermit   In the Crowley/Egyptian Tarot

Crowley Says The Astrological Sign Virgo (as Goddess Venus The Virgin and The Whore) Rules The Hermit Sign   She is Again Alone in   The Code

Here Again The Hermit is The Carrier of The Light   He seems Blinded by it in The Rider Deck and is Simply Carrying it in The Crowley Deck   Both of Them Seems Not to Use Their Lantern to Light their Path/Road

He Now Has No Stick as in The Rider deck   He has Mythical Dogs With Him   This Hermit Now Carries Her Red/Blood Loss Shades   From Darker Burgundy Color to Paler Shades of Red as His Robe   We Cannot See His Face but He Seems to be Looking at a Snake Surrounding an Egg

The Orphic Egg   A Popular Symbol in   The Code   The Old Greek Mythology says The Orphic Egg is of Cosmic Knowledge and Is a Sign of Victory   It is a Serpent as The Masc Penis Strangling/Operating The Power of The Fem Fertility which is Here Represented by The Egg

The Hermit is Old Curved Down and Faded   same as in The Hermit from The Rider Deck   Both Seems Detached

Several Different Patterns Hiding in the Light Rays Meet in the Middle of That Lantern   Where a Sun is Pictured

That Sun is the Same Asterisk Symbol or Her Multiple Crosses Symbols (See Asterisk Symbol in The Keyboard Chapter)

The Design here of the Lantern Rays and The Hand Form a Fem Body Shape   Her Light Emerging from The Lantern Sun

We See Only the Left/The Receiving Fem Side Arm of the Hermit   Surrounding Him are Corns   or   Wheat/Wet/With/ What   Sticks   Wheat is a Symbol for Reproduction and so is Corn   Crowley Mixes Them Up

In the Crowley/Egyptian   the Numerical Hermit is Valued at 10   Not a Lot   But The Zero has O Value
The Letter Yod is the Foundation of All the Other Letters in the Hebrew Alphabet   Which is Mainly Combinations of its Small Sign in Various Ways   It Represents Fertility and the Sign of the Virgo/Virgin Together   Crowley says Yod is the Phallus then it is a Hand (Almost Funny) then it is Logos   or   The Virgin (to Aim at Something Nicer)
The Logos Meaning is the Divine Word or the Rational Principle that Govern the Universe (Which is to Aim at The Virgin Here)   Have We attained The Summit of the Mountain to Observe that
The Message of This Card is The Virgin and Fertility   They are Attached Here in   The Code   by an Old Man/Hermit that Says Nothing   and   Keeps on Blinding Her with Sex
End of The Hermit Card

THE WHEEL OF FORTUNE   # 10   X

Intro
10 is One of the Most Powerful Card in The Deck   This is When She is Pregnant or Ready to be as Indicated in The Zero/o/Oo   She is Now Behind the Power Stick of # 1 (Man or God) and She is Attached to it   If She Separates from it She becomes Again a Zero   If Not Behind a Number Symbol O has No Value
10 is a Complicated Card
From Roman Numerals She is Letter Xx   It is Her as The Standing Cross/ Letter Tt that has Now Fallen Completely in # 10/# X   She Dies there as the Pregnant or Ready to be says   The Code
That Event is Called   The Wheel of Fortune   It Goes Up Down Up Down as in Her Other Symbols in   The Code   and Brings Her Destruction that Way (Any/Way)   The Code   is the Same Everywhere
Note Here That The Symbols Attached to The Wheel has No Fun or Happiness Showing as Possibilities   The Body of a Red Mutant   a Serpent   and a Sphinx with Breasts   Going Up or Down   is of No Good Augur   But the Illusion Remains

10   The Wheel of Fortune   In the Rider Tarot

This Wheel of Fortune Card has 8 (Pregnancy) Spikes (Compared to a regular Clock which has 12   So it Ends there in 8/Pregnancy for The Fems

The Dam Code The Damn Book

The Top Spike/Needle is Towards Letter T/Fem Cross/Great Curse in Large Cap and is Conducted by Mercury (See its Symbol on the Line) to the Bottom that has a Reversed R/Her/Heir/Or/Whore/Sex in Large Cap   It is in The Astrological Sign of Aquarius (Lets remember That The Sign of Aquarius (The Aquarium) is Before the Pisces Sign where The Fishes (The Fems) Lives says   The Code   # 2 Spike Symbol is in a Strange Shape that Connects to its Other Side with L/Her/Sweet Fem Light/Ill/Elle/Hail/All in Large Cap Letter L is the Secret of the Fifth Angle Which is The Unfitting Angle of The Masons   # 3 Spike is Letter A with a High Bar as in Greater Secrecy   and   in the Shape of a Pointed Arrow Coming from Letter O/Fem Hole in Large Cap on The Other Side   The Hey is Letter A (See Letter A in The Words Chapter   and   the So Called Horse Call   The Hey   or   the Hay/Horse Food/Whores   # 4 Spike is the Hebrew Letter The hé Again and it Ends at the Other End in the # 7 Spike Letter as the Same Letter hé (The Star Card   The Most Useless Card (See The Star Card))

Those Spikes are Contained in 2 Circles that are Within Each Other   Also There is a Center One That makes a Star or an Asterisk (See Asterisk in the Keyboard Symbols Chapter) Pattern as in Multiple Crosses/Fem Cross/ Great Curse

On the Right of the Wheel is a ½ Looking Human Naked All Red Blood Color Strange Looking Creature with Long Pointy Doggy Ears and Mouth with Eyes that are Looking towards The Reader   Almost Upside Down That Creature Back seems Glued to That Wheel from its Torso All the Way to its Feet   It Seems to be an Important Symbol as The Crowley Tarot Puts Also Around The Wheel Strange Figures Along with a Pharaoh/ Sphinx Close by   It Seems to Indicate the Mutations Engendered by The Immense Loss of Blood of The Fems   Which would be in That Case a Mutation Between the 2 Sexes (as Seen Today with the lgbtq) and Animals as Its face Shows   Close to the Bottom of His Feet (a Sensitive Area of the Body) is the Long Thin Yellow (Code Color) Snake/Penis/Hiss/His/Is which is one of The Emblem of   The Code   That Serpent Arrives from the Back (A Blind Spot for That Red Creature) and is Pointing its Tongue Full Out Straight to Attack its Foot Bottom   The Red Creature does Not See that Coming   But it is There and It Will Attack   The Name of The Card is The Wheel of Fortune   That Weird Red being could Represents the Menstrual Cycle Time as on That Clock Representation which is The Rota/Tarot/The Fem Cycle

On Top of the Wheel/Rota/Tarot is a Blue Sky Weird Looking Comfortably Installed Sphinx/Pharaoh as if That Wheel was Not Turning at All   It Blends Seamlessly in the Same Color as the Blue Sky Immensity behind Him/Her as being Part of the Absolute Reality of Immortality of The Universe being   The Code   Message of that Sphinx/Pharaoh   That Sphinx has Breasts and His/Her Face Looks Strangely as a Queer   His Ong Tail comes through in Between its Legs Looking as an Extra Long Penis   That Pharaoh Seems to be a Hermaphrodite   The Pharaoh is Wearing as Scepter a Long Sword   That Sword Handle is in the Shape of a Erected Circumcised Penis and is Held Above His Genital Area   The Sword Tip is Almost Touching The Wing and The Face of the Mythical Eagle which is Carrying the Book of   The Code   with Nothing Written in   and it is in Front of a Dark Grey Cloud (Bad Augur   or   Awaited Pour/Rain/Tears) There are 4/The Law Number Dark Grey Corners Clouds that are Carrying Secretly Literally   The Code   with a Mythical Animal   or   a Human (as a Mythical Being)   All 4 Have Wings and are on its Own Grey Cloud

Around that Wheel (We/Ill/L) it is on Letter hé   It is The Most Important Letter it is Called The Mother Letter says Crowley/Jewish Alphabet   The Code   is All Constructed (Con/Struck/D/Pregnant Daughter) on The Fems since its Beginning and is Focused on How to   Enslave   Steal   Sap   Hurt   that Energy of Her Feminity and Her Fecundity

In the Top Right The Mythical Eagle Seems in Flight Trying to Hold Still to Hold The Book with the White Pages   and   Keep it Open (All 4 Books are Opened) He is Not Reading it (Nothing is Never Written About   The Code) Its Top Wing is Touching The Card # which is Xx/Fem Death Letter/# 10/Fem Fallen Cross/Her Great Curse (See Letter X in The Letter/Words Chapter)

The Eagle Face is Close to the End Point of That Sword   Its Beak is Almost Touching it   The Being on the Cloud on The Left Side is Looking at The Eagle Not His Book   He is Not Reading that Open Book Sitting on His Laps because There is Nothing Written in it   He is Sitting so Comfortably that He has His Foot on a Cloud as it would be an Ottoman   Going to the Bottom Left Grey Cloud The Bull (Ox/Goddess Venus) is Lying Down Quietly on The Grey Cloud Paying Attention to The Strange Mythical Lion in Front of Him also Sitting on a Grey Cloud   He is also Holding the Same Looking Book with Nothing Written in it   On the Bottom Right

The Dam Code The Damn Book

Grey Cloud a Weird Looking Mythical Lion Seems Fascinated Looking at that White Pages Book   Its Only Tail is Straight Up   Those 4 Figures are Very Important Symbols in Mythologies and Religions as The 4 Faces of That God Even if They Look All a Little Strange   They Surround That Wheel   The Code   Called That Wheel The Rota/The Tarot which Tries to Explain How   The Code   Works with Its Symbols and The Passing of Its Messages

    # 10   The Wheel of Fortune   In the Crowley/Egyptian Tarot Crowley says   The Wheel of Fortune is an Entirely Masc Card   The God Jupiter Rules in The Wheel of Fortune Card   Its Numerical Value is Great   20 500 (See Page 278 in Crowley Book of Thoth) It is The 4th in Value in That Chart
In My Book # 10/# X/x (as in from Her Childhood) is The Number of Ultimate Sacrifice as Her Death being Imminent in Letter T/Great Curse/Fem Cross/The Nail is Now Confirmed Dead in Letter X/Fallen Cross (See Letter X in The Letter Chapter)
At The Top of the Wheel is a Comfortably Laid Sphinx (as if That Wheel does Not Spin)   The Sphinx Meaning the Silence of   The Secret Code   He Has Breasts Also The same as in The Rider Tarot
On a Regular Clock The Sphinx is Standing on its Top Where is # 12 o Clock   # 12 Means The Plan is Completed (See # 12 in The Numbers Chapter)   A Strange Reptile Form Looking Creature is Smiling Looking at You   It is Holding a Pharaoh Curved Stick in His Left Hand and the Cross of Life in His Right   His Head is on the Wheel at the 6 o Clock Time   666/Sex Sex Sex/The Mark   on   The Code   Clock It Represents The Genital Area
Everything Means Something in   The Code   Know The Meaning of Those Symbols and Follow The Trail
The Whole Background of The Card is Pale or Dark Purple which seems to Roll Around towards the Right   Note There is an Almost Transparent Top Triangle Inside The Wheel
Color Purple Represents The Fem Sacrifice because it is the Male Blue Positive Color Mixed with Her Negative Red Blood Loss Color   Those were Designed by   The Code
The Wheel of Fortune as Fallen Cross Xx and in # 10 is a Very Metrically Crafted Card Prepared to Kill   Another Terrible Card for The Fems

In the Back of that Wheel of Time are   8 (Pregnancy)   Very Long Orange Lightning Rods going through a Purple Whirl   Those Arrows Starts or Arrives at the Top of The Eyes of The Sphinx in a Straight Horizontal Row   Above it   as in a Different Higher level   The Sky is Blue   and   the Large Yellow Pointy Stars/Asterisks/Multiple Crosses are Connected to a Much Larger Star with Crosses in them that Stands Giant in the Middle of That Sky   Above that thin Blue Sky is The same purple sign of The Curse that is the Sky color   The Top Big Star is Connected Upwards to Something Higher

The Message of This Card is the Same as in The Rider Tarot Card   Mutations are Happening Around that Wheel of Time Under The Influence of The Stars/Asterisks from Above as The Unseen Above Our Eyes   In a Straight Line

End of Wheel of Fortune

LUST   OR   JUSTICE   # 11   XI

Intro

11   Justice   In The Rider Tarot

#11 is The number of the Bar/Ban (See the Clock Chapter at 11 o clock) Contrary to the The Common Belief if We Look Closer at this Card It is Not The Face of a Fem but a Fair Young Man   He is Holding The Scales of Justice and He is Not Blindfolded   In Their Drawings The Rider Tarot has no problem to Identify the Sexes or Other Specific Details on Its Cards (for Example the Fem Face of The Card Strength # 8 is a Soft Fem Face so is Card # 3 The Empress and Card # 2 the High Priestess)   He Wears The Crown of a King   It is The Usual King Crown of 3 Pillars/Towers/Bars on Top of His Head with a Visible Square (which is The Number of the Esoteric Pyramid (Entirely Made of Men))   It is The Man Law Number (Jupiter The All Powerful Rules 4 (See # 4 in The Number Chapter)   It is   The Code   Temple as in A/All Men (See the Pyramid Letter in The Letter Chapter)   And this Card is Called Justice

His Left Hand is Holding The Scales of Justice/Just/Us   But Here He is Not Blind as The General Verdict on Justice say is Blind (?) and Most Esoteric Symbols Said When a Fem was Holding Them   He Wears a Green (Color of Life and Prosperity and Continuity) Cape Over His Large Blood Red Robe (Her Blood Loss)   His White Shoe makes Him Innocent   We Imagine Him Sitting on a Throne   But No   He is Sitting on a Plain Small Grey Looking Cement Bench   Indicating He is in an Humble Position   It

Indicates That He is an Obedient Servant to   The Code   System   It is The Same Grey as the 2 High Pillars (Pill/Her in Plural Pillars are Penises Symbols (Circumcised or Not)) on Both Sides of Him   Gray being The Color of The Law   It is The Symbol of The Obligatory Consequences from   The Code

The Dark Pink Drape (a Fem Color and a Veil) that is Hanged in the Back of Him is a Symbol of Secrecy   Its Border Stands Parallel to The King Fully Erected Blue Sword (Representing Only the Mascs)   The Pink Drape is Attached to the 2 Grey Columns   In That Poor Looking Background is also that Weird Yellow Color which is a Very Important Color in   The Code   It is The Same Color as That Crown which Indicates His Ultimate Power   The Scales (Another Symbol of Ultimate Power   The Law)   and   The Sword Yellow Handle is to Decide and Enforce it   That Same Yellow Background Acts as 3 Discrete Borders on That Card   The Bottom is Grey as its Foundation   That Yellow Background It is an Important Part of The Card   It is The Limit Established by   The Code The Usual All Smoke and Screens of   The Code   Symbolism

The Message from This Card is its Implacable Outcome   Every Angle is Perfect   It Goes from the Sun Color to The Fem Pink to The Blood Red Costume of The Holder of the Sword and the Scales in His hands by The green Suggest over his Cloak that He has All Powers given by   The Code End of Justice in the Rider Deck

11   Lust   in The Egyptian/Crowley Tarot

An Amazing Transformation has Happened here which could be Called Almost Alchemical   The Justice Card has been Corrupted   It is Now Called The Lust Card

Strange Enough It has Already been through a Transformation from the Usual Representation of the Esoteric/Occult Justice as a Fem   In The Rider Tarot The Justice Card is a Man   Here in the Crowley Tarot It has Transformed into a Full on Fem again which Seems to be in Full on Lust this Time   She has only Eyes for that Cup Looking as a Chalice which could be the Offering of Her Blood   So Powerful that it Creates a Depression in The Horizon   She has 2 Full Naked Large Breasts and is Sitting Totally Naked on a Mythical Lion with Many Heads in a Weird Looking Painful Position which Looks Essentially Sexual   She is Pulling The Reins on that Mythical Lion that has 6 Different Heads of Possibly Different Sexes   The One at the Top is Looking Straight at that Irradiating Cup of Blood She is

Holding Which could be The Holy Graal   It is a Beast that Looks Sad and Shows Anxiety and Fear   The Second Head on the Left is a Weird Little Round Face   He is Looking at The Cup also   The Head Under these 2 Heads is a Large Monarch (Ruler) Looking Head   It is in a Shape of a Triangle   The Little Dots (See Dot in The Words Chapter) that Form His Crown Indicates that He is Under The Power of   The Code   His Eyes are Closed in Secrecy and Ignorance   He is Wearing a Beard   and   a Long Moustache Which are Other Symbols for Secrecy   The Leash She is Holding Ends in a Round Red Blood Color Dot (as in Pregnant) with The Same Design in it as The Decorations on the Earthy Stone Wall behind Her Where The Action seems   Under The Ground   That Red Dot is Touching the King Head at His Temple   The Temple is Where the Pyramid/The Code Rules from   A Sad Looking Man Who Looks as He has Given Up and Has Capitulated is Under the King Head which is Already Surrounded and has 2 Heads Above His   The Sad Man Head seems Compressed by those Enormous Heads Around Him   That Sad Man Neck is Being Held in a Tight Collar as a Clown Collar   That is the Mane (Man/He) of that Mythological Lion and it Expands into being the Thighs of the Lion All the Way to the Bottom at The Lion Feet Where the Nails have been Painted in the Same Color Red of Her Uterus (You/Tear/Us) and Leash in this Too Bright Color (?) Another Sign Here of The Ambiguity of Sexes in   The Code   For Example in The Wheel of Fortune Card the Red Being Around the Wheel is Also a Red Mutation   There is an Old Man Being Caught on the Leash   He seems Smiling   The Code   Do Not Joke about its Secrets   So She is Being Kept in Pain so She Cannot Focus   She is Holding All those Men Heads because   The Code   Says She must be Having Sex with All of Them because She is a R/Our/Heir/Her/Hour/Whore and this is what they Do (See Letter R in The Letter Chapter   Ours is a Bear in French   What seems to be a Blood Red (Color of Sex Also) Leash Coming at Them is Her Vagina That has Expended Largely   It is that Loop She is Holding in Her Extended Towards The Back Left Arm   That Arm Extend Towards the Bottom as in Going Down (See in The Magician Card) In Her Right Hand She is Holding Her Uterus/Cup   That Cup is Full of Blood and is Overflowing in a Straight Small Point Towards the 10 Bars that Are Pointing at Her as Rays (# 10 is a Card of Completion for The Fems where 0 Stands Behind the # 1 in The Arabic Numbers)   The Rays are in an Attractive Warm Yellow Color   Its Background is Pale Green   See those Comforting Colors

The Dam Code The Damn Book

Surrounding those 10 Rays is a ½ Circle Made from Small Red Flowers in a Shape of a Pretty Necklace   Encircling the Red Flowers is Another Small Gold Circle   In the Small Red Flowers are Tiny Symbols or Letters   Surrounding that Pretty Green are Several Brown Snakes Tails Looking as They are Running Away from the center   Others Resembling Elephant Trumps to Ribbons   Serpents Without a Head is a Major Contrast in Occult Sciences   The Gold/Pink Horizon Line that Runs Across The Card is Separating Her and Her Illusion (The Samsara) to See Above that Gold Line Where is the Overflowing Blood Cup that Seems to be an Offering to the Above   or/and   a Gift from The Above (The Code) or/and   a Sacrifice   That Gold Line Separates them from the Bottom of the Picture Where That Full Cup is Her/Fem Holding it on a Lion(a Mythical Animal from Many Religions) Keeping too Busy and Weak as She Knows Nothing of   The Code   and Has No Time to Understand it   Her Head does Not Show Her Face because She Represents All Fems   She is Looking Up in a Twisted Weakening Posture at this Lion Tail End Which is Most Strange With its Biting Head   It is Standing on a Long Giraffe Neck Shape   It is a Small Looking Fearful and Anxious Head Staring Straight at the Cup of Blood and Not Seeing it Because He sees Only The Gold Bag Holding the Cup
The Message of This Card is in Pure Symbolism   The Fem is Holding The Graal   It is feeding The Snakes above the Gold Line   On That Lion She is Sitting Next to a Bunch of Men that are Represented by That King of The Jungle   and   She is Naked on it   She has No Chance but to Obey   She does as She Bends Down Backward   Ready for Sex Anytime for The Last 2 Thousand Years

THE HANGED MAN   # 12   XII
12   The Hanged Man   In The Rider Tarot
12 is The Number of Completion (See 12 in The Clock Chapter)
The Hanged Man is a Puzzling and Terrible Card
12 is The Card of Achievement   Here Being Death   Which Comes Next in The # 13 (Bad Luck Number) The Death Card
Looking at The # 12 Card Upside Down   There is a Man That Seems Suspended from a Tree (Tree of Life) which is in The Shape of a   T/Her Cross/Great Curse/Death   in   X/Fallen Cross   (See Letter T/Fem Cross and X in The Letter Chapter) by a Yellow Tiny Rope   The Man Seems Willing to be There as in Invoking Symbolically Something   His Left

Leg folded Behind the Right One may Indicate the Fem Broken Power behind the Right One but No in The Crowley Tarot He has His Right Leg Folded in Front Not Behind the Other   He has His Arms behind His back Creating a Cross   He is Immobile on That Cross   He Looks Radiating   There are No Other Visible Ties   The Code   Keeps that One Highly Symbolic   That Small Tying Cord is the Same Yellow as in The Moon Color Card (and its Others Manifestations in That Rider Deck)   it is The Same Yellow as His Hair Which are Blending in the Same Yellow Aura Around His Head   Wow Another Saint   His Head Aura is Surrounded by All Those Bars   The Code   Isolation War Sticks   The Color of The Thighs Covering His Legs is the Same Red Color Starting with the Red Flowers on The # 3 The Empress Card Dress which will Represents Her Blood Loss All Through That Tarot

His Torso is Covered with a Blue Tunic (a Color Indicating an Open Road) (Again Full of Bars as in Other Cards   and   Others Not at All) that does Not Follow Gravity   Making this Card Symbolically Upside Down   For a Young Man He has a Small Waist which is Surrounded by a Thin Red Belt Contouring It Representing the Fem Blood Loss Saying it is Normal and is All Good Because it is on a Solid Grey Background

His Yellow Shoes are in the Same Color as the Aura Around His Head and his Air   Meaning   The Code   Means it   He is Tied/Suspended Up to That Cross by Only His Right Foot Which Extend to the Top of The T by a Same Yellow Tie   From His Shoes to His Head and The Top Tie   In that Yellow   That Color Yellow is the Color of # 18 The Moon Card   Making that Man a Symbolic Fem as   The Code   Projection   From Head to Toe He is that Yellow that Moon Color as in Her

The Top Tree/The Tree of Life Pillar of the T Letter Shows Green Leaves Still Growing from that Wood Cross Log Meaning The Code is Old Still Alive and Growing

The Back of the Card is Plain Grey Not to Attract Attention   Grey Being a Color of Death   or   a Rock Color

"On this Rock I will Build My Church"   The Rock Being the Philosophers Stone of the Ancients   He Was Pierre or Peter His First Disciple   The Name Pierre Means Peter is English   and   a Pierre is also a Rock in French

End of Hanged Man in the Rider Tarot

12   The Hanged Man   In the Crowley/Egyptian Tarot

In Numerology Number 12 is The Number of Completion   or   a Form of Achievement

In The Crowley Book of Egyptians The Hanged Man Card Hebrew Name is Called Mem   Its Attribution is Water (an Entirely Fem Symbol)   The Double M Meaning Motherhood Twice   With an E/He in the Middle   Meaning There is a Man Separating Those 2 Fems with Children Endlessly (The Usual for Her)

Its Numerical Value is 40 600   It is Almost as a Wanted Poster   She is # 1 here with the 4 and 6 Added Together

Once She is Caught as in The Hanged Man Card She is Worth a Lot   Just as a Source of Water She is

The Hanging Start at The Top Where The Number of The Card   The # 12 is Where The Ankh (See Ankh in The Words Chapter (also a Man Name) Seems to be Birthed from the Outside of the Card (Mystery) to the Inside in The Midst of a Great Gran Sun Center   It Guides Us to The Egyptian Code   Here the Masc is Tied from The Ankle to the Reversed Ankh Compared to the Masc in The Rider Tarot which is Loosely Attached to T/Fem Cross Around His Ankle   The Cross and The Ankh are the Same Symbol for The Message of The Hanged Man Card

That Ankh   and   a Curled Snake Passing Through the Hank Ring Only Once   That Tie to the Hankh and Cross is as Thin as His Yellow Tie is on That Cross on The Rider Card   The   Serpent/Penis/Ss/Hiss/Is/ His   Seems in the Hiding   It is The Lien to the Hanged Man and that Cross   There is Another Larger Snake on Top of His Head as being Part of His 7th Chakra   It is All Curled Up in a Half Circle (a Fem Symbol) in a Black (Secrecy) Background

The Man Elongated Arms Form an Almost Artificial Looking Triangle Meeting in a Bottom Apex at the Bottom of His Chest   The Letter V/Fem Sex Active is Also Obvious and Pointing Towards The Obvious BB (See BB in The Words Chapter) and The Genitals (Small and Circumcised here) (As Age Happens Circumcised Penis are Long Thin Limp   or   All Tied Up to The Top Creating a Strange Eye Effect   with Falling Testicles in a Thin Transparent Sac   It Get Worst Over Generations of doing it   Look at The Greek Statues for a Better Looking Healthier Gonad Uncircumcised)

Why Both Hanged Men from The Rider and The Crowley Tarots are Both Upside Down and   with One Crossed Leg and One Leg that Seems Free   Is it to Create a Pattern

Looking at the Card When Inverted   At the Bottom Portion of The Card It Shows That Up Standing Hankh Still Hooked from Nowhere   or   The Unknown as No One Knows The Root of Ankh because it Roots is at the Border of The Card   It Stands in a Comforting Pale Green Background with a Touch of Yellow as in The Middle of a Soft Radiating Sun   Around it are 2 Circles within Each Other (Polygamy) to Accentuate its Importance   and   There are Sun Rays/Bars (See Bar in The Words Chapter) Sprouting/Piercing from the Center of the 2 Inner Circles Where The Hank/Cross Bottom Part Meets Radiating Sun Rays from Its Root Also (Sun   and   The Code   Secrets are Part of The Same Symbols)   The Middle Smaller Circle is in a Soft Pink with a Touch of Blue in it Making it Slightly Purple Color   Purple is the Mix of Blue/Masc and Red/Her Blood Loss from   The Code   Code   Seems So Soothing

The Rays are Touching the 2 Pale Blue and Green Grid Above Where The Body of the Hanged Man is

The Center Grid of The Card is a Square with More Blue in it as in Hiding and the Other Grid the Larger One has More Yellow as in More Softness in the Light in it

It Keeps Humanity Crossed Which is Specifically Targeting the Bottom Parts of His Body

This So Sad Man with Designer Tears has His Left/Fem Side Leg Seeming Shorter   It is Nailed on That Invisible Cross (Representing The Fem Cross) but with 3 Nails that Forms a Perfect Triangle Shape with The Ankh   Not   with   His Right Foot which is Nailed on His Left Side   His Foot and 2 Arms are Encircled with the Same Pale Blue   Although They Are Encircled as in to Give Them an Even More Powerful Stance

The Code   Associates Both Events as the Same

He has His Hands Opened as in Being Opened to that Sacrifice

The Message of This Card is The Grid (See Grid in The Words Chapter) Rules Here Again   It is All Over in The Background   That Cross He is Nailed On is The Invisible Cross   The Endless Slavery from The Cross of Life The Fem Bleeding   The Man is Attached to The Hank by The Serpent (S/His/Is/Hiss/Snake/Penis) at The Top and Another is at The Other End of His Body

And The Most Powerful Planet The Sun Gives its Sweet Light to All That   The Sun is an Entirely Masc Symbol   and   It Rules Leo   The Lion is its Impersonation   it is Most Ancient knowledge

End of The Hanged Man

The Dam Code The Damn Book

DEATH   # 13   X111
13   Death   In The Rider Tarot

First Lets Remind Us that The Number 13 Internationally is Known to be a Bad Number   Why
The Code   Invented those to Keep the Fems Out of Any Power   Even in Numbers   So it is Death That Awaits Her (for The Most Advanced here 3 111 with an X (Fallen Fem Cross) in Front of its 3 III would Mean an Army for the Fems as One   so No   Not Allowed in   The Code   Therefore # XIV is Back on Her to Put Her Down with Another Fracture   Another V from Her I   See Card # I4 Where She is Acting as a Winged being   Looking Mindless as a Young Child Pouring Water from One Vase into Another   Not Knowing/Ignoring that those are Chalices   and that Those Carry Blood Only   He has His Feet in The Water   and   a Firing Target on His Forehead (Which is Also a Fem Symbol (a Dot in a Circle   The Breast   Etc))
The Card # 13 The Death Card has a Skeleton Dressed in a Black Horseman or Horsewoman Armor and Mounting a White (Her as Innocent Fem   and   the Real Moon Color   and   The Code Color for being Ancient) Horse (Whores/Heirs/Her/Hair/R/Sex etc)
She/He is Holding The Black and White Banner (Ban/Her)
The Emblem on it Looks as 5 Bees are Engulfed in All 5 Flower Shape Petals   Both are Fem Symbols
His/Her Right Hand is Holding the Double Black Reins (Reine is Queen in French   See Horse/Hers Accessories in The Words Chapter) which Has Tiny Crossed Bones and Other Symbols of Death on One   The Other Tells The Horse (Hers/Heirs/R/Sex) What to Do
His Saddle is The Color of Blood with Water (Blood and Water are Powerful Fem Symbols) in it   or   a Soft Pink (a Fem Color)
The Tail on His Hat Armor is Blood Red (Her Blood Loss)
It Looks as it has Splashed on The Face of a Pope   and   the Dying   and   the Dead   That are Around Him Mostly Covered in Blood on The Ground Close to The Horses Hoofs
The White Horse(Whores/Heirs/Hers/Sex) has Blood Red Eyes   A Sign That is a Ghost from   The Code   Also It is The Same Color as The Hat Tail from its Rider
A Dead Man is Wearing a Pale Blue on White Garment   That Would Represents a Good Honest Man Loving Colors   or   a King   Next to Him a Little Boy Dressed in The Same Blue Seems Waiting to be

Slaughtered   The Little Girl/Fem/Innocence/Virginity in White Looks as Dying   The Pope All Dressed in Yellow (Moon and Dog Color in This Tarot) is Standing in Front of The Horse with His Hands Together   A Sign of Obedience and Pledging

His Pointy Hat is Also Yellow and Touches the Same Yellow Sun Rays (The is Moon Never Shown Radiating That Strong Rays) in Between The 2 Towers in The Landscape That Reminds of The Cards The Tower Where it All Falls Down for Her   and   in The Card The Moon The Two Towers are There   and   There is Fear as Dogs (Fems) are Barking in Fact at a Radiating Sun Disguised as a Sliver of Moon (She is Too Young to Know Anything)   Grey is More Real Bad News Looking at Card # XIX The Sun Instead of being White or Gold as The Card The Sun would Merit to Fully Admire/Adore The White Boy with Gold Hair Full of Red Flowers on a White Horse   But No It is a Grey Horse   and   the Next Card # 20 Being the Judgement (a Scary Card Which Shows The Trumpet that Brings Again the Red Cross/The Endless Cross of Humanity will Announce That The Red Cross Curse will Continue Despite Their Begging/Prayer for Liberation) Shows the Dead Coming Out of The Ground in The Same Dead Grey

        # 13   Death   In the Crowley/Egyptian Deck If Anyone Still had Hope in Either   Life   Salvation   or   Redemption   from the Hanged Man in # 12   it Dies here in # 13 The Death Card   (# 12 in The Rider Tarot is Where the Hanged Man Looks Alive and Radiating   He is Looking Directly in Front of Him Wearing Clean and Pretty Colors Garments   in The Crowley a Sad Hanged Man with Tears Looks more as a Crucified Man hanging from a Hankh)   The Result is Definitive When He Arrives in # 13   The Very Bad Luck # 13 (See in the Numbers Chapter)   The Grim Reaper (Rape/Ripe/Rip   Her) is a Black Skeleton in Full Mad Fast Action Killing Anything in its Web   The Reaper seems Holding a Web that Looks as a Fishnet (See Fishnet in the Words Chapter) but it is The Eagle (Egg   All/L   See L in The Letter Chapter) in The Left Corner Top that Throws The Threads of that Huge Operation   The Eagle is One of The 4 Most Important Animals in the Mystical Esoteric Tradition   The Code   In Front of The Skeleton is a Strange Human Form that Seems to being Engulfed in a Spiral   His Next Victim   It Seems to Close Under The Sweeping Motion of the Scythe (See Scythe in The Words Chapter)   In Front of The Skeleton are 8 or 9 Circles

The Dam Code The Damn Book

which Seems to Contain the Same Self Transforming Spirals Cocoon Forms in Different Stages
From the Egyptian/Crowley Deck the # 13 is Letter Nun (None as a Nun   as Nuns Have No Sex)   The Thick of The Web Seems to Start from Where The Skeleton Reaper Gonads were   and   Looking Close The Directions and Positions of His Hands and Arms Show That it is Trying to Get Rid of that Web with its Scythe by Cutting it Close to its Skeleton   His Left (Fem) Thigh is Attached to That Web with Many Threads   and its Skeleton Skull is Covered with what could be a Iron Mask Used for Torture in Older Times   The Nun Letter is Represented by the Fish (Her) and its Value is 50,700   Quite a High Value   for a Dead Virgin/Nun/None   Virgo is Assigned to Her in The Cowley Book P 278   When There is a Cross/Fem Curse on The Virgo Sign (as in Dead   The Virgo and the Scorpio are Both M Symbol as in Mother so be a Mother or/and be Dead) which makes it The Scorpio Sign   Scorpio is Sex and Death
The Hermit Sign Carries The Scorpio Sign there   Hermits Do Not have Sex
The Message of This Card is   The Code   Destroys   One Way or Another   The Card is Puzzling in its Design   and   Message   None is Good   The Sun Radiates on a Grid that has a Masc Nailed Upside Down on an Invisible Cross There are a Snake on Top of Him   and   a Snake at His Feet   He is Attached/Hooked to All that with an Ankh   The Ancient Egyptian Life Symbol   Its been a Long Time
The End of Death # 13

            TEMPERANCE   or   ART   # 14   XIV
            # 14   Temperance   In the Rider Deck
Number XIV is a Number in Between 2 Sacrifices for The Fems
The Word Temperance Proposes a Lot of Equilibrium   But No Not here   Everything is in a Form of   Disequilibrium or   Impossibilities
We are Now in The Card After The Death Card   The World is Different   We are Now in The LaLa Land   Here She/He is Now Wearing a Celestial Being   or   an Angel Garment   She/He has a Foot in Shallow Calm Blue Water (That Water (Her Tears) That Thins Her Blood into More Blood Loss Manifesting   The Transformation   or   the Transubstantiation   or   The Communion   or   Mutations (See The Wheel of Fortune Card   in My Book) in Their Religious Rituals   The Being is Holding The 2 Cups/Chalices doing The Magic of That

Transubstantiation   It has Blue Water from The Water in It what Seems in Endless Reserve Under His/Her Feet
Water is Transparent Not Blue   (Blue is a Masc Color Only)   but Transubstantiation Means the Changing of One Substance into Another
Her/His Right Foot in The that Water is Supporting Her/His Whole Body   Her/His Left Foot is Barely Touching the Ground
The Same Skin Color is That Dirt Road that is Going or Coming Through Green Hills and Blue Mountains   The Sun is Crowning Over that Dirt Road with an Empty Crown Made of Dots (See Dot in The Words Chapter)
On Her/His Forehead is a Headband with a Yellow Circle (Circle is Fem) with That Dot (Pregnancy) in the Middle   A Headband as this One Symbolically Means a Belonging
Her/His Simple Tunic is White as the Lamb/Christ/The Fems to be Slaughtered   It has a Skin Color Pyramid Design at The Height of The Heart (Chakra)   The Pyramid is in a Square   Making The Pyramid/ The Code   the Blazon of its Owner   Now He/She Belong to   The Code   Not Only from The Headband also from The Core of His/Her being   The Heart   The Colors of the Inside of that Pyramid are The Same as His/Her Skin Color   as a Hole in The Fabric could   There are Few Cards That has The Humans have a Skin that Has that Double Color of Beige and Red   The Devil Card # 15 is One of Them
There are 3 Beings with Wings   They have This Mixed of Red/Black/White Colors   Red as Always in Secrets Arts such as The Rosecrucians/Rose Cross Indicates The Fems Blood Loss/Cross being The T Letter (See T in The Letter Chapter) as in The T/Tree From Where The Hanged Man is Hanging Close by The Most Scary One is # 20 The Judgement Where That being with Red Wings and a Empty Look Brings the Bad News to Those Humans Looking as Zombies (That Gray is the Lack of Blood)   Its Loud Message is They will have to Live with that Red Cross (Which is Made of a Red and White Color Grid (See Grid in The Words Chapter)   They are Standing on a Sea of Water/Tears Having Nothing   Number 3 Being with Red Wings is Card # 6 The Lovers (a card being blessed By a Huge Radiating Sun and a Wing Being   In The Crowley Tarot   Those Cards are Almost Identical in The Card The Devil # 15 but There The Humans are Chained to The Devil Ring (See Ring in The Words Chapter)
That Card Temperance is a Programming being Blessed
Those Red Wings are Immense   They Give The Impression of   Calm Power   Security   and   Serenity   But No   Red

and Black are Not Good Colors for Peace   and   Those Wings
Look   Artificial   Stuffed   and   Disheveled   The Artists that Design
Tarot Cards are Precise   If They Leave White Spaces   or   if The Work
Looks Sloppy as in Those Red Wings There are No Coincidence
There are Jewish Symbols/Letters Above that Square with the Pyramid
in it on That White Tunic   The Card The Star # 17 Represents About the
Same   and   Resembles The Moon which is The the Next Card   The
Moon is Most Important Fem Symbol in   The Code   It is The Same
Resemblance with the Same Cards Numbers in The Crowley Tarot
The Message of This Card is it is an Illusion from a Slave Messenger (The
Wings)   That Card is a Form of Hallucination Sent to Her/Him to Keep
Them Numb After The Cross/Death Card has Happened   Those Chalices
(2 Fems/Vase/Uterus   Polygamy) are Exchanging Pure water Which
Symbolizes Their Essence   The Sky is as Grey as The Begging Zombies
in Card 20   In The Crowley Tarot Art has become This Card Name and it
is a Mutation or Transubstantiation   Alchemy means also the transfer of
liquids   and it is a Widespread Word in Old times

   # 14   Art (as Temperance)   In The Crowley/Egyptian Tarot
The Card Art is Where Her Alchemy (All/Ill/Letter L   K/Broken Fem (See
Letter K in The Letter Chapter)   M/Motherhood   and   E/He (The Fem
is Never Left Alone in   The Code) Happens in That Very Important Word
Alchemy Where He/E is With 3 Types of Fems   The L K M) Happens
Art is Another Terrifying and Complex Card
Here The Fem Now has 7 Breasts which have The Same Colors as Her
2 Incomplete Faces (One Part is So White it Looks Sick and The Other
So Gray it Looks Sick)   Face and Body are All Split in Those 2 Colors to
Demonstrate that Its Châtiment is for All Fems   and   The Fem Role is
Only Breasts to Feed and as The Cauldron is in Front of Her and She is
Doing the Concoction to Feed those 2 Ugly Scary Mutations of the Eastern
Religions Most Important Beasts   The Lion (Sun Rules in Leo) and The
Eagle which is The Power from Above   It is the Second Ruler in Scorpio/
Sex/Death)   Those 2 Animals are Represented on Other Cards as   The
Hierophant # 5 (In Masks with No One Behind)   The Lovers # 6 (as in
Smiling to The Situation Looking at The Sex Union)   The Sun # 19 (as
Radiating as The Lion on Country Flags Standing Up Roaring in Power
Its/His Fiery Tail Up)   and   The Last Card   The Universe # 21 (The 4
Corners are Full ` with Those Faces Blowing Air/Life in a Same Blue

Background   They Seems to All Have Lost Focus in Their Looks   They Seems Hypnotized   The Human Face is Looking Straight at You with a Big happy Smile   The Code   was Created by Men)
The 7 Breasts are Packed in an Egg Shape Showed on Her Chest as if it would be Naked The Top of That Egg is Not Showing   A Pale Rainbow Color Cape Meets in The Middle   There is a Pointed Arrow in The Middle of the Front of That Shawl   That Shawl goes all The Way to The Cauldron   and   The Arrow seems to be There to Indicate the Direction of The Energy as in from The Cauldron to The Top of Her Shoulders
Her Green Dress has   Code   Symbols on as Curses/Symbols Hanging on Her
The Code   Creates Wars Against Her on Every Plane of Consciousness
There is Another Long Incantation (Which Seems to be in Latin) of The   Secret Code   Written Around Her in Big Tall Tight Letters in the Shape of a Larger Egg (An Egg Always Represents Pregnancies   and/or   The Loss of Her Blood) Behind Her
The Words Over Her Head Encircled in the 2 Thin Sliver Moons that are Crossing Each Other   are the Word Rectif on The Right Side   Rectif is a Strange Sound Word between Erect and Stiff which is in a Permanent Erected Penis with the Word If (as Almost in) in it   On the Left Side is Written Cando or Camdo   Cando or Camdo are Almost the Same Sounds (Nn is the Virgin Letter   Mm is the Motherhood Letter)
The Message Here is She as a Fem is a Mother After being a Virgin   With Erected Penis (The Rectif Word)
The Word Occult is in the Lower Part of that Belt Surrounding Her   She Cannot See it   It is Behind Her in The Past in which She could Not be Educated in
Those 4/The Law/Pyramid Parts are Separated with 2 Super Thin White/Her Moons Crossing Each Other Right Above the Height of Her Third Eye Blocking it (Few Fems Think they are Psychic) Forming a Cross/Curse/X/Fem Death Fem on Top of Her Head/Crown Chakra
That Cross also Hides the 2 Tops of a Simple Crown on Her Head   That Crown is Gold on Her Left Side of the Head and is White/Silver on the Right Side   That Crown is Made of Pointy Waves   2 Gold Ones and 1 White/Silver One
She has a Blue Arm on the Right Side   and   a White Arm on the Left Side   Do Not Let Know Your Left Hand Know what Your Right Hand Does

The Dam Code The Damn Book

She is Wearing a Tiara   or   a Coronet (Part of the Horse Hoof (See Horse in The Words Chapter))   or   a Bishop Mitre
Her Heads and Bodies Sides are Confusing to Recognize   Her Left Head Hair Color is Blue and Her Arm is White   The Right Side of Her Face is White   and Her Arms are Blue   The Belt of Curses Encircles Her Aura and so is the Cape She is Wearing
This Orange Cape Extend All the Way From Her Orange Cape to the Orange Magic Cauldron Where the Orange is Transformed in Electrifying Orange/Red Rods/Penisses/Sticks Which She Pours the White Wine/Tears from the Blue Cup/Uterus/Chalice   The Blue Droplets Transforms into Red (Blood) Ones
The New Mixture is Different   The Alchemy is Happening here in that Transformation in That Card Called Art Which is   The Secret Code   Name of the Ancients   as in The Ancients Secret Arts
The Cauldron is Where a Strange Mean and Mutant Looking Eagle and a Looking Mutant Mad Lion are Sitting as if they are Starving   They are Animals Sanding/Burning on Flames Themselves
The Lion is Blue as in Masc and the Eagle is Red as in Her Blood Loss (One is Bleeding and the Other Crying)
The Message is as seen in Her Face She has Now Accepted that Horrible Life of Nourishing Mutants Beasts with Her 7 Breasts (Endless Milk) and Her Cauldron (Food)   7 Breasts are Unknown in any Normal Mammals   Another Way for Her To Suffer and be Weak Annihilated from any Force or Power
End of Art/Temperance

THE DEVIL   # 15   XV
15   The Devil   In The Rider Tarot

In a Grey and Black Background it is Already a Sinister Environment   The Wings of that Beast are Bat Wings   That Half Goat has The Paws of a Bird of Prey to Catch it All   The Fem and the Masc are Chained to a Mysterious Box Under That Beast on a Big Ring (it could be a Door) (See Ring in The Words Chapter) With Heavy Chains   His/Its Horns Starts where the 3rd Eyes is
Looking Upside Down on The Card See the Star of David above its Head   Its Right Hand is Up and Painted with a Cross Sign (See Cross in The Words Chapter)   Both Fem and Masc have Horns Showing The Influence of That Half Beast on Humanity

The Message of That Card is That The Devil is Totally in Power of Humans and Their Reproductive System   The Fem has Grapes (See Wine and Grapes in The Words Chapter) coming out of a False tail Barely Touching it   The Masc has the Sexual Fire Coming Out of its Tail   It Seems to be Fed by the Devil Wand of Fire Behind Him Powering Huge Fires of Sex   That Very Message is Synthetized in The Same Card in The Crowley Tarot where The Card is Concentrated on a Huge Penis and Testicles Reproducing itself with the Goat (Devil) in Charge

#15   The Devil   In the Crowley/Egyptian Tarot
In a Soft Background of Pale Pink/Girly Color and Pale Grey   The Code   is in Disguise
The Huge Fully Erected Penis has a Goat in Front Standing on its Testicles   It has an Open 3rd Eye Seeing it All   The Horns are so Long that They go Over the Picture Borders Indicating Secrecy from   The Code
A Firebird Wings which Contains the Red Dot (See Dot in The Words Chapter   Her as Her Blood Loss) Stands on a Long Stick that Reaches the Border of The Card Indicating Secrecy   Those Blue Wings (Remembering of The Egyptian Symbol) are at the Height of its Sexual Gonads
Under those Wings are 2 Snakes (One of The Code Animal) Pointing Away from Each Other as in Surveilling it All
That Old Ugly Grey Goat Stands on Nothing as in Floating in the Air (R/Heir/Sex) Touching the Testicles Indicating its Prey
Inside The Testicles are Swimming Human Forms   In One Testicle are Moving Hard Fems   One with Too Large Breasts Representing   The Code   Ultimate Goals Along With Her Fem Loss of Blood   She is Touching One of the Black   Bars/The Code   a Symbol That Means to Stop   as Her 3 Other Fems Too   They are Fighting to Break The Envelope Around Them   The Other Side Testicle Represents The Mascs   They are Fighting to Get Out   One of Them is Also Looking as a Mutant   They Seems to be Holding Together a Fight
That Ugly Goat wants to Look Festive to Attract the Girls so it Put Itself a Twisted Smile   and   a Lay (Necklace   to Lay is to have Sex) of Blue (Masc Color) Flowers/Pearls is on of One Only of His Huge Horn
Around the Penis at the Top is a Soft Blue Fluorescent Light Aura that is Blessing Penetration from Above (If It Goes Beyond The Borders of The Card its Essence is in Secrecy)

The Name of this Card is A'ain (so Close to Ann/Letter N/Donkey/The Virgin) and its Letter Looks as a Y
She is Ann or the Donkey   or   the Whore/Horse/R   or   the Dog/Bitch   or   the Hurt Cat   and so Many Other Animals
In the Egyptian Crowley Deck The Devil is a Value of 70 Where The Lucky Number # 7 is with The Zero/The Fems which is a No Value Number and The Capricorn Sign the Most Harsh Sign for All Fems Reigns Here
The Message of This Card is The Goat and Sex Belong Together   If The Goat (Capricorn/Saturn/Bad God) would Not have been There it would be Only Mascs Genitals   The Goat as in The Devil (The/D/Daughter/Donkey   Eve/Letter V/All Fems Sex Active   Ill/Letter L/Hell/All) Saturn The Awful God of Time (Menstrual Cycle) Rules The Card

THE TOWER   # 16   XVI
16   The Tower   In The Rider Tarot

The Card is Entirely Dark and so is in The Crowley Card   There is No Hope here   In a Black Background with Clouds The Tower Card Tower Which had a Gold Crown has Lost it (Same as The Man (Which Looks as a Fem) with The Blue Dress Falling from The Tower) He/She is Looking at Us The Lightening Coming from an Unknown Source Stroke That Tower   Almost The Same is That Tower that can be Found Again in The Moon Card (In Double here as in All Fems)   In The Moon Card She/They have Only One Eye as in Under a Veil with One Window   In The Tower Card She has 3 Eyes (2 Eyes   and   a Third Above)   That is Why She and He are being Destroyed All The Way Up to Any Gold Crown   The 2 People Falling from the Tower Represents All Parts of The Population   From The One that has a Crown (Power) to the Other that is Indigent   No One is Spared   The Spits of Fire are The Same in The Moon Card Under The Sun/Son which Hides inside The Full Moon Shape   Spitting Heat Down to the Dogs (Bitches/Fem Animals)
The Striking Light Coming from Above (Unknown Design   Secrecy from The Code) that Destroys the Tower is in the Shape of Letter W/All Fem Sex Active and with Card Upside Down in the Shape of an M as in Motherhood The Message in Both Tarots is Clearly The Same   There is That Fall (The Image of The Fall is Important in The Jewish/Catholic Writings) and It Is The End
Perhaps The Most Important Aspect of This Card Resides in That Tower Base/Roots   Those Long Bars that Looks as Straight Up Ice Mountains

seems Blending in as being Part of it   But Those are The Bars (See Bar in The Words Chapter) from   The Code   Its Roots

16   The Tower   In The Egyptian/Crowley Tarot

The Fire is Coming from Below in That Tower Card
Looking at it Sideways The Mouth Throwing Fire with Big Teeth Looks as a Potted Plant
The Eye from Above from   The Code   Radiates in Every Direction as Seen Here
Those Flames coming from the Bottom are Penetrating Towards the Door of The Inside of That Hardly Recognizable Tower   Its Entrance is Made of The Grid/H/Secret Code Letter Pattern (Which is Made of T (See Letter T/ Fem Sacrifice in The Letter Chapter)   There are Many Symbols Around The Tower   They do Not seem Important as They are being Stricken by The Light of That Immense Eye (See Eye/I/High/Pyramid in the Words Chapter)   A Dove Flying Away   a Broken Down/Mutated Reptile   and Many Geometrical Symbols   The Eye is Burning it All
The Message of The Card is The same as in the Rider Tarot All is Black on Red   No Good News here   All is Hell From That Card Also

THE STAR   # 17   XVII

Intro
The Star is an Entirely Fem Card (See The Asterisk in The Keyboard Chapter)   Its Main Symbol is Also Entirely Fem
She has Submitted to the Sacrifice Made in The Card # XIV Art in The Crowley Deck   It is Called The Temperance Card in The # XIV in the Rider Tarot because of Her Adjustment to This Constant Disturbance   She has Now Reincarnated in The Star Card   Where in The Rider Deck the Angel with the Heavy Red Wings Pours Water from One Cup to Another Stupidly   and   a Fem with Her 6 Breasts seems to do a Magical Concoction for 2 Looking Despaired Mythical Animals in The Crowley Deck   They Called it Art as in The Ancients Arts (Secret Arts) in Action

17   The Star   In The Rider Tarot

She has Now Developed Full Artificially Large Breasts   and   Her Hair is the Same Yellow Color as the Biggest (8/Pregnancy) Branches Star   The Same Color as The Moon/Hidden Card   Surrounding that Big Moon are 7/

Luck Other Smaller White(Her Moons) with 8 Branches   Pregnancies are Within Pregnancies
(Pregnant/Sees   and   P/Power   Rag   N/Daughter/Virgin/ Donkey   Sees/C)
The Fem Face Looks Pretty Although Not Entirely Fem (A Common Sight in   The Code)   She Seems Happily Doing Something that makes No Sense   Acting as a Very Young Child at the Beach   Unconsciously She is Saying that Her Breasts are Endlessly Pouring Out The Love/Water (What/Her) as Both Jars are Pouring Out Water
Behind Her on Top of a Hill (Ill/Elle/All/L) is a Poor Looking Tree of Life (Code) Holding a Weird Too Large Bird (See Bird in Mythology) at its Top   Its Looking Towards Her   She has Her Right Leg Floating on Water
The Message of This Card is The Same Message as in The Crowley Tarot The Star which is in the same Situation on a Planetary Level   Her Hair/R/Sex/Her/Here is so Long it Touches The Ground which seems to be made of Crystals This Card is Another Card that Rules the Hypnotized Fem   She is Under The Empire of The Stars as There are 7 of Them Plus The Big One   A Total of Eight as in Pregnancies   Lost in The Endless Valley of Tears as She Loses Her Time Spilling and Spoiling Water All Naked

17   The Star   In The Egyptian/Crowley Tarot

That Star Card has Evolved into being a More Modern/New Age in its Esoteric Design Although it is The Same Message   The Fem is Still Pouring from Both Hands That Water that is Now Red (Her Blood Loss)   and   Planet Earth is in The Same Color as in Accentuating The Importance of That Symbolic Act   The Whole Earth (Hurt   Her/T/Fem Cross) is That
Her Breasts are Here Hidden and Replaced by Their Symbol The Cups   As in Those Huge Cups Which have become that Large Compare to a Chalice or a Wine Cup
The Blood Red Flows Pouring from Her Both Cups (Breasts) is in a Spiral Shape that Starts with a Blue Tiny Perfectly Shaped Star Which She is Looking at with Her Faceless Face   That Spiral is Not Fluid   It Seems to be Made of Glass   or   is Crystallized   or   is Frozen (Frigidity) and its Color Starts in Pale Shades Beige/Comforting that Contrast with the Burgundy (Dark Blood) Color Giving it its Shape
She is Standing in a Precarious Position as On Air Above the Blue Crystals Barely Touching at the Bottom of Her Feet

Her Too White Skinny Naked Body with Frail Arms (No Good for Her Working Hard) with Endless Strong Mythological Long Hair (The Girls/Curls   Loves   Hair/Her/R/Whore/Sex) Seems Melted into the Shape of Poetic Flowing Water   She has a Little Foot   and   a Foot That Seems to be Infirm

Her Blue Purple and Pink (a Fantasy as so Many Including being a Virgin Giving Birth) Hair (Heir/R/Whore/Her/Sex) as Long as Her Body (An Impossibility) Disappears into the Blue (a Go Color) Crystals with Strokes of Red Blood Stains in Them   The Code   Throws at Her Heavy Duty Symbolism   Always

The Color of that Flow Blends into a Darker Pink   Pink (Fem Color) is the Color of the Rosicrucians (The Open Rose being the Flower that Describes the Fem Genitalia)   The Rosicrucian Order is also Called "The Ancient Mystic Order Rosae Crucis"   or   The Order of the Crucified Rose

Any More Doubt about   The Code   Ends Here   Keep on Rereading

Look at This Card as in a Young Children Book   It is Pale Yellow/Soothing on Pale Blue and Pink (To be Bourgogne as in a Good Vine and a Good Color) The Star has 7 Points with Pale Pink and Blue   Both are Baby ColorsThat Yellow Star (See Star as The Asterisk Symbol in The Keyboard Chapter and in The Words Chapter) Creates The Largest Rays in The Card   Every Point Radiates so is from The Tiny Star from the The Upper Cup (That Seems to be Feeding from it)   Every Point Radiates Energy that Creates The Spiral That Will Spiral and Spill All The Way to The Ground Below   Through Her in a Straight Jet (The Only One) to Her Genitals and Stomach Area and Stop There   Until It Comes Out of The Left Cup

Those Star Rays Envelops Her Entire Cosmic World Here

As She Keeps On Pouring All this Shade of Red Blood Color From Her   It Should Weaken Her   and Does   The Fem Constantly Loosing Blood for So Many Generations would Thin the Race Blood   and   Push/Transform the Humans in a Mutational State   a Generation at the Time   The Most Ancients Mammals Do Not Lose a Drop in a Century and Have Remain The Same   or   Almost

The Bottom Cup has a Longer Neck   In Reverse It is also a Large Nail Penetrating that Cup that has a Large Hole Bottom   The Bottom of The Cup is in a Shape of an Egg (See Egg in The Words Chapter)   if That Egg would be a Spotlight it would Put Light on Her Pale Butt Shoulders Arms and Neck

The Dam Code The Damn Book

With The Card Viewed Sideways The Star Generating that Spiral on The Earth (Hurt) has been placed on Her 7th Chakra   an Amazing Flow from Cosmic to Physic/Physical from   The Code   and done Artfully by Crowley   She is a Prisoner of   The Curse   from Any and All Angles of Life
She is Keeping the Top Hole Cup Tightly Closed with the Nail in it with Her Hand Pressing on its Bottom
In the Bottom Cup She is Pressing on the Neck to Keep it Opened   That Way She is Being Blind to that Knowledge at the Top and Opened for Sex at the Bottom in the Same Time   Weird
In the Crowley/Egyptian Tarot The Star Card is Called a Window   As Fluid as This Card Seems She is in the Hands of Aries says Crowley   A Mean Boss
Her Numerical Value is 15 a Very Low Value   Because   it is a Card for a Fem   A Crumb She is   Her Name is Hé   She is Hey   or   Food for Horses/Whores/R/Us   Hey is its Command   Follow the Hair/R/Her/Heir Which is in Excessive Amount Here
The Message of This Card is Silliness   But The Waste of Blood is an Immense (M/Mense) Waste   Transformed into a Planetary Event such as Bleeding for All Fems and Creating that Way Humane Mutations Every Generation   The Generation Gap
End of The Star Card

THE MOON   # 18   XVIII
#18   The Moon   In The Rider Tarot

In Numerology The Number 18   Indicates   The Code   with The # 1 (The Stick   See The Number 1 in The Number Chapter)   It is in Front of Her as She is The # 8/Pregnancy (See Number 8 in The Number Chapter) It is a Very Difficult Thing to Beat the # 8 from   The Code
Looking on Different Texts Forms # 8 is often a Bigger Number than the # 1   As in The Big 8   Being a Mother She is a Difficult Adversary to Beat   The Code   Knows it
2 Ugly Looking Scared and Miserable Dogs (as in All Bitches   See Bitches and Dogs in The Words Chapter) are Barking at that Full Artificial Moon   It is Not a Moon But a Sun in The Hiding as in Representing the Light of   The Code   She (The Moon (Noon   See Noon in The Words Chapter (All Fem Letters)) is Actually Barking at Herself   Being Both of Them in   The Code   Symbols   Therefore She is Weakening Herself by

Herself   That Moon Card is in a Thin Crescent with No Face   The Second One has The Scolding Mean Profile Inside it   It is Looking Down Radiating Only at those Bitches   The Dog on the Right/Masc does Not Look as a Real Normal Happy Dog   His Bad Color is in the Same Weird Yellow Color as that Moon Above (A Real Moon is White   A Sun is Yellow)   It is Also the Same Color as that Long Narrow in The Shape of a Serpent Path/Road Bringing to High Unfriendly Mountains which Seems to go Nowhere Behind The Barking Frightened Dogs a Scorpion (Sex/Death/Un conscious Astrological Sign) is Coming Out of a Small Blue Part of a Body of Water with Small Waves (We/W/All Fems Sex Active   V/Eve/Ovo) Ready to Attack or Push Forwards on The Yellow Path in Those Mountains which Blends into the Same Color Rare Blue Sky   That is an Ugly Blue

That Sun/Moon is Shining Strong and Pouring Drops (Same Drops as in The Tower Card (in The Middle of The Night) of Something in the Middle of that Sunny Day Without Clouds

The 2 Dogs are Barking to a Moon that is Full Therefore Pregnant   That Moon/Sun has a Scolding Down Right Profile in it Looking Condescending at the Dogs/The Bitches/Her

The Yellow Dog does Not Look as a Real Dog   It Looks Weird as There is Fear All Over it   it is Also in the Same Weird Yellow Color as This Yellow Moon (Our Moon is White) is and in Other Rider Cards such as The Hanged Man Card   etc

Those 2 Grey High Boulders (The Code   is Called   The Greys) on Both Sides of The Endless Yellow Path in The Desert Have Only 1 Breathing Hole at the Top   They Represents the Same Towers in the Card # 16   The Whole Picture is Scary Especially with the 2 Tall Cement Walls Towers (the Bars   Around Her) with One Window/Hole at its Top Indicating that Her Body is Fully Encapsulated in that Cement (The Veil)   The Only Hole is at the Height of Her 3rd Eye   and   It is Hollow

The Moon Planet has Dark Meaning in Other Divinatory Sciences

The Message from This Card is Clear   The Moon (The Assigned Code Name for Her Identity) is a Territory with No Hospitality   Those 2 Towers with One Window Only Represent Desperation   All is an Endless Battle   and   Road of Endless Punishment in Many Aspects   The Begging of The Judgement Card will Not Help their Well being or Salvation as They Call it

18   The Moon   In The Crowley/Egyptian Tarot

The Dam Code The Damn Book

The Moon is an Entirely Fem Card says   The Code
Crowley says that The 18th Card Represents The Pisces
(See Pisces in The Astrological Chapter   it is The Sign of
All Fems as Fishes are Attached Together by the Waist (See BB in The
Words Chapter) All are the Same   Living in Water (The Glass Ceiling) as
in The Emotions   Mute and Deaf to Human Sound   and   almost Blind
from what is Happening on Earth The Fems are being Kept in a Different
World than The Mascs Which are Represented with Multiples Facets   for
Example   Mars/Aries/War/Action   Sun/Leo/Radiating   Saturn/
Capricorn/Mean/Punishing   Mercury/Gemini/Intelligence   Jupiter/
Justice/Sagittarius/Half Man Half Beast   Rules   and   He Rules
Over All Fems in The Pisces also (A Great Masc/God That Keeps All Fems
as Fishes   and   Justice Blind)
That Moon Card is Sinister to Look at   It Seems The Bad Yellow Moon/
Sun   and   The Bad Mutant Dogs/Bitches from The Rider Tarot have
been Assimilated into a Fortress of Darkness which seems to go through
a Long Valley in Between Mountains which have become the Towers
Guardians   The Labyrinth is in Between Her Legs   Her Moon Passage
has been Opened Artificially   The V Passage is in a Shape of Letter V/
Fem Sex Active (See V in The Letter Chapter Compared to the U/Normal
Uterus)
The Towers here Black (Before Grey) are Hiding as in been
Assimilated   Guardians are There with Weapons and Mean Looking
Animals   It is Serious
The Other Side of The Horizontal Long Black/Death Thin Line Separates
The Card Into 2 Different Worlds   The Conscious and Unconscious
Upside Down The Card Shows The (Monster) Contoured Legs of The
Beetle/Scarab Holding the Egg which is to be Dropped in that Beige/
Pink Soothing and Quiet Color and Birth Canal Shape that Enters from
Behind Her into the Next Part of The Card on the Other Side of the Black
Line of The Unconscious in a Funnel Shape that Will Land that Egg in a
Crescent Moon Basket which is at the Bottom (On Top when the Card is
Down   When Fertile)
Under that Beige Pink Moon Shape is a Pale and Dark Grey as in   The
Code   Background   That Top Grey Background Starts The Card When
Turned Back Up
Starting the Reading from the Top   The Top is Card is Grey   A Bad Sign

That Beige Passage is Still there   It has Changed Significations   The Red Droplets Now Represents Her Loss of Blood   So The Card Upside Down Represents Her Loss of Blood and Upside Up it Represents Her 12 Times a Year Ovulation Times which is Highly Abnormal Compared to Other Mammals The Same Size
The Thin Moon here is Now Upside Down   A Bad Sign
Her Blue Legs have Round Knees that Go Around the Black/Death Towers (See in the Moon Card the 2 Towers) that Are Shaped as the Towers of a Castle (Cast/All)   Only One Window Per Tower Here Again
2 Egyptian Soldiers are Holding the Crosses of Life (See Ankh in The Words Chapter)   They are Holding Long Sticks with the Egyptian Bird Head on it Being Used to Fork Her   Those Are Holding Her Legs Opened Permanently
With The Card Upside Down   Under the Black Line which Represents the Unconscious are what Seems to be 2 Hands Holding/Offering the Egg inside a Huge Sun Shape which the Color is Pouring down into the in Between of Her Legs on The Other Side of The Black Line   We can see a Fem Body with Arms Up to the Neck with No Fem Face here as Usual   Any Way to Veil Her says   The Code
Crowley says Her Attribution is the Back of the Head (Ancient Brain)   and   Her Numeral Value is 100   which is Low
The Sad Message of This Card is The Same as in The Rider Tarot   The Fem is Forced into This Unbearable Unconscious Pattern of Destiny

THE SUN   # 19   XIX

Intro
XIX Card is One of the Happiest Card in the Deck   It is The Fem Entity Prisoner in Between 2 XX s (X/Fem Death/Fallen Cross   See X in The Letter Chapter)   Not Good for Her At All

#19   The Sun   In the Rider Tarot   XIX

Clearly Related in   The Code   The Sun is the Son   Entirely   Therefore That Card is a Masc Card
There is a Background of Sunflowers (Son/Flaw/Her) as in Sun Flowers   as if a Masc an could be a Flower   When a Flower means The Fem Genital Organs   Again   The Code   has Stolen Every Fem Natural Identity
In the Arabic Numbers The # 19 is When She as # 9 Reaches Her Mature Years   It is then The Time when She is Sent Back Down   In # 9 Her Cycle

of Bleeding and Childbearing being Finished   She Will Return All the Way to # 1 (Being a Zero in Between) Where the Basic Suffering of Hell/Elle/Letter L on Earth from   The Code   Will Start for Her Again   The Masc Numbers Stop at # 7   So The Masc do Not go Through # 8 and # 9 being Both Fem Numbers

The Card # XIX Card Numbers are 2 Fallen Crosses   The Fallen T/Fem Cross Curse Letter becomes Letter X/Fallen Cross   Which are Keeping Here Her Real and Only Stick of Power The # 1   It is Prisoner in Between Those 2 XXs   Her # 1/I is in Between those 2 Walls of Death Therefore The Positive Forces of The Sun Do Not Attain Her Broken Power   Surrounded by Pain   Being too Much in Pain/Weak/being Crucified as The Sign of The Cross Indicates   From the Point of View of the Secret/Hidden Symbolic of The Roman Numbers The Fem is Now Imprisoned in   The Code   XIX is The Same Upside Down A Last Combat for The Fems before Entering # XX   it Never Ends for the Fems There is Always   Another Cross Another Wound   Until it is All Over as in The X/Fallen Cross   In The Numbers comes Next the # XXX   Number 30 is an Old Known Term in the Journalistic World Meaning The End/Death)

The Weird Yellow Color Sun is Immense and so is the Full Moon Man Face Painted on It   and   The Sunflowers   and   The Boy Hair   are The same Color Indicating   The Code   Affiliation   That Yellow Color of the Sun is the Same Color as the Painted Moon   and   that Yellow Mutated Dog   and   The Moon/Sun in the Rider Card # 18 The Moon   When a Face is in the Shape of a Mask it Usually Hides Something   Hiding Your Face can be a Sign of   Guilt   Shame   Sadness   Secrecy

Here it is Only Hypocrisy   The Sun/Son Sleepy Eyes are Looking Right at You   The Man has a Confident Peaceful Face

A Thick Black (Death   See The Death card as an Example) Circle Shapes the Sun Form Which is a Really Bad Sign for Her   It is the Typical Treatment Done to the Fems by   The Code   The Sun Rays have   Curved/Fem   and   Straight/Masc   Bars around (to be Round is to be Pregnant) it (The Sun/Son Radiates Power on All for the Best/Mascs   and   for The Worst/Fems as in Whores with a T/Fem Cross (See Whores in The R/Letter Chapter   and   t/T/Fem Cross in The Words Chapter)

The Boy Left Arm is Touching a Long Floating Red Blood Color Banner (Ban Her   B/Baby Boy Holding All Fem Breasts   B/N/R as in the B/Baby   the N/Virgin   and   R/Her/Sex)   It Starts Floating from the

Bottom Edge of The Card Meaning The Origin/Base of that Banner is Unknown to The Reader of the Card Picture going Upwards into the Sky Touching the Sun/Son Rays (Ray being a Masc Name)   The Red Velour/Velvet (an Attractive Fabric) Banner Holder Stick is being Held by The Young Child That does Not Know What He is doing   The Child Left (Fem Side) Leg is Invisible The Child is Not Directing The Horse (Whores/Hers/Ours/Oars/Letter R/Heir/Here)   There are No Reins and No Saddle Needed for Him Because the Horse/Her/Whores is so Tamed it can Carry that Child Boy Well with Much Dignity and Yet Gets None   An Absurdity   But   That Horse is Not Happy   The Looks in Its Eyes is Kind of Funny   It Seems to Represents a Deep Silent Long Time Frustration The Code   Grey Wall is behind the Boy and His Horse as if The Sunflowers are Growing in   The Code   Wall   Which is a Reality in   The Code   World

There is a Strange Looking Red Snake coming Out of the Boy Hair   The Snake is a   Code   Animal since the beginning of Times   The Serpent and Adam (a/Dam) and Eve/Ovo (See Letter V in The Words Chapter) The Message # XIX is it is a Happy Card in   The Code   Because it Shows The Masc has Won Here   The Card Shows Falsely to the World that Happiness and Kindness have Arrived While Hiding All this Hell/Ill/Elle/Letter L/All that is The fem hell   See the Moon Card as in One in a Multiple Example Where The Fem is being Diminished to its Minimum Life as in Always Falling/Failing Etc

            # 19   The Sun   In The Egyptian/Crowley Tarot
The Sun here has its Natural Color
The # 19 Sun is Even Bigger here a   It is Almost as Big a The Card   Its Largest Rays are Orange Yellow Beige and White   It is The Slow Reverse Graduation to the Red Blood Color which seems done in a Such Peaceful Way
There is a Green Mount Behind the 2 Little Naked Mythological Dancing Girls or Boys or a Mix of The Twos   Because They have Wings it Indicates The Superficiality of That Message
They are Looking/Longing at that Gold and Orange Big Ring that Encircles the Top of that Mount That Same Ring in Smaller Encircle the Sun/Him The 12 Signs of the Zodiac are Around them and The Sun   One Sun Bar in Between The Signs   Each Ray Separates one from The Other   They Do

The Dam Code The Damn Book

Not See Much of Each Other as Known Divide/Separate People to Rule Them Easier Keeping The Secret Unconsciously
The Message of This Card Enhances The Tarot Sun Power in The Rider Deck Here it is Adoration of The Sun in Happiness The Astrological Signs Surrounding The Sun Card Say that All Around The Zodiac is in Accord with That Lie The Aura of The Sun is in The Shape of an Egg/Ovo/Letter V The Son is in The Egg

THE JUDGMENT # 20 XX
20 In The Rider Tarot
or
THE AEON In The Crowley Tarot
20 The Judgment In The Rider Tarot

The Double XX represents Death Twice There is No Hope Here
This Card Symbolizes The Judgement Day or the Last Judgement This Card has a Long Religious History It is an Event Many People Fear Greatly
It is the Moment of Truth When People have been Feeling as they Were Dead (the Color Grey Indicates the Color of Death and The Code Color) or Possessed by Something that Controls them Here The Greys are Praying Imploring to Be Saved by that Big Celestial Being Angel that Brings Unfortunately The Code Bad News of The Red Cross Banner The Endless Pains of Losing Their Blood and being Endlessly Weak Small and Dying Young
That Banner is an Exact Copy of The Emblem of the Rosicrucian (Rosicrucian or the Secret Pink Cross) They Wear it on The Front and The Back on Their White Tunics
That Red Cross is Attached to the Gold Trumpet (Male Organ) He is Blowing
The Messenger is Not Looking at the Greys Standing on Grey and Black Boxes on Top of a Blue/Soothing Body of Water The Messenger is Looking Ahead as in Being Unfocused or Hypnotized or Under a Spell
He is Wearing the Same Heavy Burgundy Red Orange Purple Wings as in The Card # 6 The Lovers When She is Being Married According to The Code Rules in The Garden of Eden where The Snake is Behind Her Neck Ready to Poison Her and Let Her Die Which is the Story of The Code in Our History

The Heavy Wings are Also Present with the White Being Wings from Card # XIV The Temperance   The Card I Call the Hypnotized Fem Card (Her Head Aura is in the Shape of a Fish (F/Fem   Shh/She)
The Messenger is Standing on Grey Clouds/Bad Weather in a Perfect Blue/Soothing Background Day
The Message is Clear   More Bad News are Coming Up
The Grey People in the Grey Boxes Also Have
The Same Yellow Color Hair as The Hanged Man Card Hair   and   The Messenger Hair (Hare/Heir/Her/R/Whore/Sex) is the Same Weird Yellow Color as in The Moon Card # XVI that Little Mutated Dog   and   The Moon Itself too   A Bad Sign for All
That Yellow is the Background Sky for the Card The Fool # 0   and the Magician # 1 (When He Lures the Fem with Illusions)
The Colors are as Important in The Rider Tarot than in The Crowley Deck
The message of This Card is That There is No Hope for The Humans because of   The Code   Ancient Plans
End of The Judgement

         # 20   The Aeon   In The Crowley/Egyptian Tarot   XX
It is Called The Judgment Card in The Rider Tarot   The Name of the Card Changes as if Mr Crowley would have Mutated a Concept to Another as in Adding Information Bits   Which is The Case here
That Card is Called The Aeon (He/On   as in the Letter E/He   and   On) as He is Moving Forward During an Eon   or   For an Eon
That Well Taken Care Fat Little Big Still Baby Boy Knows Nothing of   The Code   He Shows that by Putting His Right Index (Commanding Finger) in His Mouth as He Knows Nothing   His Body is Transparent and We can See a Sitting Egyptian God with that Same Soldier Stick that is Shown in The Crowley Tarot Deck The Moon (A Bad Sign) Card # 18   In that Transparency That Little Boy has   Snakes/Sticks/Penisses/Snakes/Letter S/The Code Animal/666   Around His Head   and   the Top of the Stick is Touching the Snakes as There is a Relation
That Little Boy is Enveloped in Different Layers and Different Colors Protection   He Seems Still in The Womb   The First One in the Dark Soothing Blue are 2 Strong Long Arms with Silver (Fem Moon/Sliver) Bracelets that Almost Look as the Omega Sign/Symbol in Greek

In the Left Side Part of the Blue Arms are Hidden Snake Forms   The Whole Picture is Surrounded by Soft Colors of Burnt Orange and Apple Green
The Wings of the Phoenix are Crossing in a Large Red Dot   It is the Same Red Dot on the Mouth of the Little Boy above the Egyptian Sitting God there
That Little Boy is Standing in a Egg Form or a Fish Depending on The Angle   The Soft Blue and Other Warm Colors Illuminates The Card as in Protection
In the Crowley/Egyptian Deck that Cherub Card Value is 300 (Which Follows the # 200 of the Sun/Masc Card # 19 and the # 100 Card of The Moon/Her Fem Blood # 18)
They United in the Aeon with that Boy Child
That Union Arrives in Card # 21 The Ending Card The Universe Where She will Step in that in that Same Pregnant Oval/Egg Circle Where She Will Then Return to The Fool Card and Get Lured by the Magician # 1 One More Time
Crowley says The Aeon is the Letter Shin (She/In   Shh/She   N/Virgin/Donkey/In) the Word Sin with The H/Code Letter in it   The Hebrew Shin Symbol has 3 (Polygamy) Flowers/Flaw/Her   in Plural)   or   3 Flames (Tied Together at the Base (It Starts Young)   Its Symbol is The Pyramid Where the Secret is   and   The Fleur De Lys
The Message of this Card is Concordant with the Rider Card as in The Same Message Is Accepted on an Deeper Unconscious Level

THE WORLD   # 21   XXI
21   The World   In The Rider Tarot

That World Card is Simple and Easy to Understand as All   The Code   Action has Already Happened
Here in a Blue Soothing Background is the Naked with Full Breasts Fem Being Supported by the 4 (Number of The Pyramid) Cherubs Who Hides in Grey (The Code Color) Clouds
The Cow/Ox/Taurus/Tau/The Cross/Letter T/Fem Curse Used to be First in the Old Texts   In the Newer Texts She is Not there at All Not Even as as the She Has Been Replaced by a Boy Child
That is How   The Code   Works Constantly Imitating the Old Texts but Making Some Subtle Differences Along to Adapt   That Hides Him/The

Masc More Behind All Kind of Powers and Diminishes Her/The Fem to Nothing Again
There is a Green/Go Color Egg Shape Enveloping Her
It Has a Blood Red Bow in a Shape of an X/The Axe/The Fallen Cross/All Fem Curse Closing it at the Top Above Her Head and Bottom Also   She Does Not See it   (See Letters X and T in The Words Chapter)
She is Holding the 2 Sticks of   The Code   Polygamy World   They represents Penisses at both Ends
There is a Banner Around Her Body that seems to be Her Long Hair (a Fem favorite) in the Same Time
That Banner Goes All the Way to Under Her Feet and Separate Her Folded Left Foot from Her Right One as in Isolating the Knowledge from the Right Foot Which is the One Apparently Touching the Ground
But there is No Ground here She is Levitating to Her Next Card Returning to The Fool Card as # 0 in that Perfect Soothing Blue Sky That will paly with the Magician and be fooled by its Illusions
The 4 Usual Beasts are Hiding in Grey Clouds as in The Judgement Card (The No Hope Card)   The Faces of those Animals are Again Looking Different from Reality   It is Not a Mistake or a Lack of Drawing Skill   Looking at The Perfectly Tender of The Fem Face and Body in The Middle of The Egg Showing The Perfection of The Drawing   The Lion Looks Queer   The Taurus Looks too Human   The Eagle Looks Disheveled   The Human Shows only The Right Side of His Face   The Fem Side/The Left is Absent
The Message of The Card is the Same as in The Crowley Tarot   The Fem is Entirely Connected With Both Hands and Body with S/Snake/Hiss/His/Penis/The Serpent/Stick which is The Root of   The Code   She is under The Sticks

THE UNIVERSE   # 21   XXI

21   The Universe   In The Egyptian/Crowley Tarot
This Card is Another Illusion for Her   She Looks as She is the Queen of the Universe has said   The Code   which is a Fem Great Envy of what Seems Real Power   She Has in Fact Lost All Her Powers in This Card   She is Trying to Hold that Huge Snake which is Around Her   She is Standing on Its Head But There is No Victory here   What She is Holding Instead is The Compass (See Compass/Cunt Pass/Con Pass in The Words Chapter) of the Secret Societies with Her Right Hand and The Snake in the Other

Together   That Compass is Connected to the Eye (The Eye on Top of the Pyramid) Above Her That is Beaming from its Gold Center   A Gold Beam that Blows into Shape The Snake
The 4 Cherubs are Pumping/Blowing Green Air (Hair/Her/Heir) Towards The Outside in an Almost Violent Way as if they are Ready to Attack   They are Protecting that Big Secret Coming Out of That Big   Code   Eye That is Exposed Here
The Egg Circling Around Her is Made of a Soothing Blue but is Showing in the Open the Eye of   The Code
The 4 Beasts(Masks) Blocking Her Accesses in the 4 Corners are Exposing   The Dark Grey Code

Conclusion
For Health Reasons   The Tarot Chapter is Unfinished   I Included it as I Included All The Others Chapters   To Prove More of What I am Explaining At The Beginning The Idea was to Prove   The Code   is in The Language (Words/Letters)   The Other Chapters Created Themselves Over Time from That Core (Words/Letters)   There is Another Chapter Called Phrases which Needs too Much work to be Published as is
Lise Rochon

CPSIA information can be obtained
at www.ICGtesting.com
Printed in the USA
LVHW050815300623
751126LV00002B/19